D1192828

Greek Melic Poets

By

Herbert Weir Smyth

Biblo and Tannen

New York

1963

BIBLO and TANNEN
BOOKSELLERS and PUBLISHERS, Inc.
63 Fourth Avenue New York 3, N. Y.

Library of Congress Catalog Card Number: 63-10769

Printed in U.S.A. by
NOBLE OFFSET PRINTERS, INC.
NEW YORK 3, N. Y.

PREFACE.

It is usually the fate of the maker of an anthology to please none of the judicious because each is convinced that his taste is superior to that of the editor. The possibility of escaping this fate on the part of the author of the present volume, which aims at collecting those fragments of the song-writers of Greece that have a distinctly human interest, is all too great: an untoward chance has bequeathed to us such a meagre portion of the wealth of Greek song that the task of selection is comparatively easy. The triumphal odes of Pindar have indeed been handed down fairly complete and are elsewhere accessible. Only in the case of Bacchylides, who has now almost passed from his position as a fragmentary poet, is the material over abundant for the purpose of an anthology. If I have not included all that is best in him, it is because a few of his finer odes are mutilated in parts beyond all hope of certain restoration. Of the rest of the song-poetry of Greece only broken columns and ruined architraves remain to attest the beauty of the unshattered edifice.

Though I have refrained from inserting in the text much that is of importance to the student of mythology, metre, and language—indeed the briefest fragments acquire a value incommensurate with their size when all we possess is so little—, I have not hesitated in the commentary to draw upon the whole extant body of Greek lyric in the hope of making the work as comprehensive as possible within the limits of a single volume. The notes aim largely at illustrating the poets from each other, and especially with reference to Pindar and Bacchylides. I have also endeavoured to show at least in part the debt of all the melic poets to Homer. Theokritos has been often cited and still more frequently Horace. The parallel passages from ancient and from modern writers embrace much that is less the result of conscious imitation than of happy coincidence, the natural expression of the language of poetry in all ages; and their inclusion is partially intended to stimulate the student to notice for himself traces of the kinship between the poets of different climes and periods. Marked as is the individuality of the Greek lyrists, the economy of their vocabulary is largely conservative; and purely verbal parallels have not been disregarded when they point to the dependence of the later upon the earlier artist.

Since the aim of the present edition is interpretative rather than critical, the textual apparatus has been made as brief as possible. The text is based upon an examination of all the MS. evidence, but the fact that, apart from Bacch. i.-x. and a few minor selections, the fragments in this volume are preserved, and that often in a very corrupt form because of their metrical and dialectal difficulties, in the MSS. of more than eighty different authors, grammarians, scholiasts, geographers, and the like, will, I trust, justify the complexion of the critical apparatus. The decision to restrict this part of the work was reached only with great unwillingness, but a conspectus of the various readings, to say nothing of the innumerable conjectures, would, I believe, have only served to embarrass the younger student for whom the book is primarily designed. Bergk's *Poetae*

Lyrici Graeci remains the indispensable guide to all thorough-going study of the text; but it is to be hoped that the new edition of the second and third volumes by Prof. Crusius, to whom the investigation of Greek lyric is already so greatly indebted, will remove the many defects that still disfigure Bergk's monumental work.

Except as regards the Aiolic forms, accents, and breathings, for which Attic has been substituted hundreds of times in the MSS., marks of apostrophe, itacistic spellings, and the like, I have adopted no reading which involves a departure from the MSS. without a statement to that effect; and I have often included in the critical apparatus some of the more marked of the above-mentioned matters that the student might gain some acquaintance with the textual problems at issue. The citation of readings unaccompanied by the name of a MS. indicates that the readings in question are found in all or in the best MSS.; specific mention is usually made of one or more MSS. only when they contain the best traditional reading. The names of the authors of emendations will be found in Bergk, except in the case of such as have appeared since the publication of his last edition (1882). These are duly recorded either in the margin or in the notes. In dealing with fragments often of the briefest compass it has not been found advisable to relegate all the critical notes to the marginal commentary.

The *Bibliography* makes mention of the chief books that have been used in the preparation of the text and notes. From these I have drawn freely. Of those that have been of most assistance I may mention the anthology of Michelangeli, which is especially valuable as regards the history of the text, Reitzenstein's *Epigram und Skolion*, and the articles by Crusius in Wissowa's edition of Pauly's *Real-Encyclopädie.*

I owe much to Jebb's Sophocles and to the editions of Pindar's epinikian odes, and I am especially indebted to the work on Pindar and Greek syntax by the distinguished scholar whose name I am privileged to associate with this book.

The commentary on Bacchylides was begun shortly after the appearance of Kenyon's edition, and no small part of the notes has, in consequence, been anticipated by the later editors. Blass' text reached me after my work was well under way, the edition of Jurenka, the French and Italian translations of Desrousseaux and Festa respectively came into my hands after the printing had begun. The commentary has profited much from the contributions to the text and interpretation of the newly discovered poems that have appeared in the twelfth volume of the *Classical Review* and in other journals. To the authors of these articles I desire to make here acknowledgment of an indebtedness that has not been stated at every point in the notes. The difficulty of apportioning the credit of priority with regard to the emendations of the text of Bacchylides is great, and in following the order of the articles in the *Classical Review* I have adopted what seemed the only feasible plan.

As has been well said by Schroeder, the prospective editor of Bergk's Pindar, the study of Greek metre is at present in a state of anarchy; and I am not certain that an attempt to grapple with the various theories put forward since the time of Westphal and J. H. H. Schmidt has tended to improve the book. In the case of poetry that is largely fragmentary uncertainty is the result of the best attempt. As regards Bacchylides I have contented myself with presenting the scansion of the lines as they stand in the papyrus, and in the main according to the doctrine of Westphal, which still holds its ground among a large body of metrical scholars; and in general I have preferred, in a book of this character, to follow a conservative course rather than adopt the theories of Weil, who leans to the revival of the antispast, of Wilamowitz, or of Blass, which are still undeveloped in detail.

The collection embraces, apart from the folk-songs, which are of uncertain date in many cases, only such poems as are the product of the classical period. As many will be glad to read the *Anakreonteia* in conjunction with the genuine poems of Anakreon, I have added a selection in the Appendix, which contains also the skolia attributed to the Sages, the paian of Isyllos, and several of the lyrics that have lately been discovered in the course of the excavations at Delphi by the French School. While the sheets were passing through the press I was able to find a place for the new poem of Sappho, though it has not been successfully restored, and for the fragment attributed to Alkman.

My sincere thanks are due to Dr. Mortimer Lamson Earle, whose assistance has been of the greatest service both in the interpretation and emendation of several passages and in the reading of the proofs.

American School of Classical Studies,
Athens, *Nov.* 27/15, 1899.

To

BASIL LANNEAU GILDERSLEEVE

CONTENTS.

PAGE

Introduction, - - - - - - - - xvii
Hymn, - - - - - - - . - - xxvii
Prosodion, - - - - - - - xxxiii
Paian, - - - - - - - - xxxvi
Dithyramb, - - - - - - - - xliii
Nome, - - - - - - - - - lviii
Adonidion, - - - - - - - lxviii
Iobacchos, - - - - - - - - lxix
Hyporcheme, - - - - - - - - lxix
Enkomion, - - - - - - - - lxxv
Epinikion, - - - - - - - - lxxx
Skolion, - - - - - - - - - xcv
Erotikon, - - - - - - - - cvii
Hymenaios, - - - - - - - - cxii
Epithalamium, - - - - - - - cxii
Threnos, - - - - - - - - cxx
Epikedeion, - - - - - - - - cxx
Partheneion, - - - - - - - cxxviii
Daphnephorikon, - - - - - - cxxxii
Oschophorikon, - - - - - - cxxxiii
Votive Songs, - - - - - - cxxxiv
Bibliography, - - - - - - - cxxxv
Abbreviations, - - - - - - - cxliii

	Text. PAGE	*Notes.* PAGE
EUMELOS,	1	163
TERPANDER,	1	164
ALKMAN,	2	170
ARION,	15	205
ALKAIOS,	16	210
SAPPHO,	24	226
ERINNA,	36	254
STESICHOROS,	36	254
IBYKOS,	41	268
PYTHERMOS,	44	280
ANAKREON,	45	280
LASOS,	53	299
TELESILLA,	53	301
SIMONIDES,	53	301
TIMOKREON,	66	332
KORINNA,	68	337
LAMPROKLES,	70	340
PRATINAS,	70	341
PHRYNICHOS,	72	345
DIAGORAS,	73	345
KYDIAS,	73	347
PRAXILLA,	73	347
PINDAR,	74	349
BACCHYLIDES,	90	381
MELANIPPIDES,	132	453
ARIPHRON,	133	456
LIKYMNIOS,	134	458
ION,	135	459
EURIPIDES,	136	460
PHILOXENOS,	136	460
TIMOTHEOS,	137	462
TELESTES,	139	465
LYKOPHRONIDES,	141	467
ARISTOTLE,	142	468
MELIC ADESPOTA,	143	472
SKOLIA,	148	474

	Text. PAGE	*Notes.* PAGE
Hybrias,	153	487
Folk-Songs,	154	488
Appendix—		
Skolia attributed to the Sages,		515
Anakreonteia,		516
Delphic Paian to Dionysos,		524
Paian of Aristonoos,		527
Paian of Isyllos of Epidauros,		528
Hymn to Apollo (i.),		529
Hymn to Apollo (ii.),		532
Greek Index,		539
Index of Subjects,		553

INTRODUCTION.

For that broad department of poetry coordinate with the epic and the drama which we call lyric, the Greeks had no comprehensive name. To the writers of the Alexandrian age,[1] who introduced and gave currency to the expression, lyric meant primarily what the name imports—poetry sung to the accompaniment of the lyre. By an inexact but natural extension of the range of the word, lyric came to include all verse sung to music without prejudice to the supremacy of the lyre,

[1] λυρικός appears for the first time in the *Ars Gramm.* (p. 6. l. 10 Uhlig) of Dionysios Thrax, the pupil of Aristarchos, who speaks of λυρικὴ ποίησις. Plut. *de liberis educ.* 13 B has λυρικὴ τέχνη; the later introduction to the pseudo-Anakreontic collection (2 B, 2), λυρικὴ μοῦσα. Cicero *Orat.* 55. 183 uses the Greek λυρικοί (cf. Plut. *Numa* 4), and his contemporary Didymos Chalkenteros wrote a treatise περὶ λυρικῶν ποιητῶν that was a storehouse of information to later students of literature. A tractate of no importance in Boissonade's *Anecdota* has the title περὶ λυρικῶν (cf. Schmidt *Didymi Frag.* 395). Clem. Alex. (about 200 A.D.) quotes from Bacch. as a λυρικός (*Strom.* 5. 731). The title of the work by Euphorion (born 276 B.C.)—περὶ μελοποιῶν—is in agreement with the usage of the classical period and of later inscriptions. Plato sometimes (*Phaidr.* 243 A, *Gorg.* 449 D) uses μουσική, μουσικός where the modern equivalent is 'lyric.' Horace, Ovid, Quintilian and other Roman writers use *lyricus* to denote the melic poet. λυρικός appears under the name Anakreon in *C. I. Sic. et Ital.* 1132; and in a late inscr. from Egypt (*C. I. G.* 4716 add. *d* 44).

which was the first instrument employed in the history of Greek poetry. Besides the numerous other stringed instruments used by the Greek poets to accompany their songs, the flute was adopted in the instrumentation of many lyrical poems, such as the processionals, dirges, paians, partheneia, and some of the hyporchemes; and both flute and lyre were employed by Pindar in giving an instrumental setting to several of his triumphal odes. More appropriate therefore than lyric, as an exact and comprehensive designation of all poetry that was sung to a musical accompaniment, is melic, the term in vogue among the Greeks of the classic age.

Melos consists of three elements—words, melody, and rhythm.[1] In the meaning 'song,' μέλος is later than Homer,[2] in whom the word denotes a 'member'; and melic poetry is, in fact, so called not because of any connection with μέλπω,[3] but because it is divided into members.[4] Just as ποιεῖν embraces the creative activity of poet and of musical composer, so μέλος comprehends the text and the melody, both of which are divided into members.[5] The term melic was not

---

[1] Plato *Rep.* 398 D τὸ μέλος ἐκ τριῶν ἐστὶ συγκείμενον, λόγου τε καὶ ἁρμονίας καὶ ῥυθμοῦ, cf. Arist. Quint. 1. 6 χρὴ γὰρ καὶ μελῳδίαν θεωρεῖσθαι καὶ ῥυθμὸν καὶ λέξιν, ὅπως ἂν τὸ τέλειον τῆς ᾠδῆς ἀπεργάζηται.

[2] *Hymn* 19. 16, Archil. 77, Alkm. i.

[3] Euripides' alliteration μολπὰν μελέων (*Alk.* 454) possibly points to the poet's belief in the etymological connection of the words.

[4] Mar. Vict. 184. 8 (cf. 54. 13) hints at this explanation: *sicut et corporis nostri partes Graece μέλη appellantur.* *Glied* and *Lied* (L. and. S.) is a specious parallel.

[5] μέλος is cognate with Skt. *marman* 'joint.' The reason for the musical connotation of the word is not perfectly clear. Allen, *Harvard Stud. in Class. Philol.* 4. 207, suggested that it came into use from the singing-school (cf. Plato *Protag.* 325 E ff.) and with special reference to the phrases (members)

extended to cover elegiac, iambic, and even epic, poetry because the musical accompaniment was not so vital a feature of these forms of poetical composition (so long as they were still sung, either in part or entire) as it was in the case of melic verse, which was marked by flexibility of rhythm and melody. It is in the strophe of choral poetry, where the members are not uniform as in the epic hexameter, which preceded melic, that we may best observe the arrangement of the words in members (κατὰ μέλη) which mark the movement of the air in its several phrases.[1] It is, however, questionable whether μέλος was first used with special reference to the strophe. The nome, when provided with a text, was composed in hexameters, and it is included under μέλος. We may therefore assume that the name melic is due, not to the articulations of the strophe, but to the complete musical setting which was the essential feature of the numerous species of verse that fall under this class.

The general name for 'song' is ᾆσμα. In so far as the words of a poem have been set to music from beginning to end the poem is a μέλος.[2] ᾠδή, on the other hand, in its strictest application is a poem that is sung merely, and is therefore the specific name for a folk-song, which is only then called μέλος when it has been adapted and transformed by the artist who sets it to music. Sometimes ᾠδή appears to designate lyric as opposed to other species of poetry, and thus to usurp the place of μέλος; but only when

---

of the four-line stanza. So in Sanskrit, *pāda*, 'foot,' denotes a line of a tetracolic stanza and 'verse.' Cf. πούς and κῶλον. In the meaning 'tune,' μέλος occurs as early as Alkman (vi.). Cf. γλῶσσα καὶ μέλος Eur. *Alk.* 357.

[1] In his *carmina divides* Horace (1. 15. 15) has possibly preserved a trace of this conception.

[2] A single, definite poem is called μέλος in Hdt. 5. 95, ᾆσμα Plato *Protag.* 339 B.

no stress is laid upon the fact of musical composition. Our use of 'ode' in speaking of a poem of Sappho or Pindar is derived from the employment of ᾠδή to signify a single, definite poem.

CANON OF THE MELIC POETS.

The Alexandrian scholars included in their Canon the following nine melic poets[1]: Alkman, Alkaios, Sappho, Stesichoros, Ibykos, Anakreon, Simonides, Pindar, and Bacchylides. This number was increased by the addition of the name of Korinna; so that, whereas Quint. 10. 1. 61 says *novem lyricorum longe Pindarus princeps*, Petron. *Satir.* 2 has *Pindarus novemque lyrici.* The existence of a more exclusive list has been wrongly concluded from Statius *Silv.* 5. 3. 94 *quosque orbe sub omni ardua septena numerat sapientia fama.*

MONODIC AND CHORAL MELIC.

From one point of view Greek melic may be regarded as sacred or profane. Almost all of the lyrics of the Greeks arose in connection with the cult of the gods, and in course of time, as the artistic instinct was developed, were to a greater or less degree divorced from their primitive ritualistic function. More clearly marked, however, is the division, in the literary period, into monodic (to which some scholars would restrict the term melic) and choral song.[2] Originally almost all melic poetry was led by

---

[1] See *An. Par.* 4. 196, Usener *Dion. Halic. de imit.* 130.

[2] Plato in the *Laws* 700 B ignores this method of division when he classifies melic poetry according to contents (εἴδη) and form (σχήματα). If the εἴδη are hymns, threnoi, paians, etc., and the σχήματα are aulodic and kitharoedic, the nome would be both an εἶδος and a σχῆμα. In *Pol.* 8. 7 Aristotle records a division into ethical (ἠθικά) melodies, melodies of

a single voice, while the chorus sang only the refrain; and certain kinds became entirely choral at different times and places. According to the instrumentation, melic was of two species: kitharoedic, when the words were accompanied by the notes of a stringed instrument, and aulodic, when the flute, or rather the clarinet, was employed. The two forms of musical accompaniment were occasionally combined. The instrumentation (κροῦσις) was subordinate to the text in the best melic period. Between the music, rhythms, and musical modes of monodic and of choral song there is no thoroughgoing distinction. Choral song was in unison except when an interval of an octave was the result of the participation of men and boys or women in the same chorus. This is the only form of modern 'harmony' that ancient Greek choral music has to show.

Monodic melic, or that which is sung by a single voice, is represented in the earliest stage of Greek song by the nome; and this form remained monodic until the end of the fifth century. The chief representatives of the monody are the Aiolians and the Ionic Anakreon. Its stanzas were repeated without interruption and were of brief compass, usually consisting of four or five simple verses, often arranged in regular succession (κατὰ στίχον); the metre was generally some form of logaoedic. The sphere of the monody is the sphere of emotion—the deepest feelings of the individual, his joy and sorrow, hate and friendship; or his trifling moods are equally the subject of this song that exists for itself alone because it is the outpouring of the heart and unprompted by the requirements of a ritual. Its wealth of emotion, unimpaired by the accidents

---

action (πρακτικά), and passionate melodies (ἐνθουσιαστικά). These correspond to Aristoxenos' ἡσυχαστική, συσταλτική, and διασταλτικὴ μελοποιΐα, and to Aristeides' νομικός, τραγικός, and διθυραμβικὸς τρόπος.

of time and place, makes it for us the most enduring of the relics of Greek song; whereas we find it difficult to represent the occasions that gave birth to the choral ode, which, because of its intimate association with the religious faith and cult of the Greeks, is stamped with the distinctive qualities of the ancient world.

Choral melic is in large measure public in character and epideictic. It is devoted to the worship of the gods and heroes, and is therefore a solemn expression of the united voice of the state. It is not confined to the narrow spirit of a canton, but has an international catholicity though the poets are mainly aristocrats. Though choral melic is public in mood, it is none the less an expression of the individual poet, and it is ill-advised to define choral poetry as objective in contrast to the subjective monody. In the pre-Attic age the chorus is only the mouthpiece of the poet, whether it chants a hymn, a threnody, a paian, or a triumphal ode. Not only does the poet show a consciousness of the public: he is conscious of himself and of his art. But in the fifth century at Athens, where he composes for the musical festivals in charge of the sovereign people, he surrenders something of his former freedom of expression because he is the representative of the whole state.

In the union of song, music, and dance (ᾠδὴ τελεία) the ancients discovered the perfection of melic, and those poems were most esteemed which required the cooperation of all three arts. The poet himself was not merely the artificer of the words: he was a master of musical composition and skilled in arranging the evolutions of the dance, so that the union of the arts which was present to his imagination as a poet took audible and visible effect under his direction as chorodidaskalos. Almost all choral melic was accompanied by the dance proper or by marching, which gave plastic life to the words of the poet and distinctness to the phases of the rhythm. There were three kinds of lyric dance: the pyrrhic, which was warlike and rapid, the grave and solemn gymnopaidic, and the sportive hyporchematic. The Dorian choruses were usually quadrangular, arranged in ranks (ζυγά) according to breadth and in files (στοῖχοι) according to depth. The rhythms of choral melic were varied, and each poem had a different metre. The arrangement was now monostrophic, now in groups of triads, consisting of strophe, antistrophe, and epode, now in free rhythms without grouping. The equilibrium of the grouping by triads gave precision and severe beauty with mobility and grace. The ampler and more intricate strophes and epodes were a work of the most complicated art and often required the services of guilds of trained singers. The choruses were composed of men and boys, and occasionally of girls, as in the marriage songs and in connection with the worship of the gods.

If we call the first of the two divisions *Aiolian*, it is without prejudice to the fact that the Lesbian epithalamia were choral and that the Aiolians chanted in chorus the praises of the gods at their religious festivals. On the other hand much that is *Dorian* is purely personal and needed no orchestic accompaniment. The Greeks did not separate private from public life as do the moderns; hence much that is regarded by us as proper only to the sphere of the individual finds an outlet in the choral ode, which is an expression of the common sentiment of the state. Most of the choric poets were not Dorians, but the Dorian stamp is upon all choral poetry in its language, rhythm, and metre.

SUBDIVISIONS OF MELIC POETRY.

The writers of the classical period made no attempt to classify all the various forms of their melic poetry.

Pindar alludes, in Frag. 139, to paians, dithyrambs, threnoi, the Linos-song, hymeneals, and the ialemos. In a passage[1] that does not aim at exhaustiveness Plato mentions hymns, threnodies, paians, dithyrambs, and nomes. Hymns to the gods, enkomia in honour of good men and women, and hymeneal songs[2] alone find a place in the Platonic ideal state that safeguards its citizens from the demoralizing influence produced by the fictions of the poets, who mix evil with good. When Aristotle[3] distinguishes lyric from epic and dramatic poetry, he employs the term dithyrambic, though he also alludes to the nome, mainly because the dithyramb and the nome were the chief representatives of melic in his day. His treatise περὶ ποιητῶν is lost, as are the various works by the Peripatetics that bore the same title or dealt with the history of music, the musical contests, etc.

It was not till the great library at Alexandria was established that any external necessity was felt to group exactly all the great mass of melic poetry then extant but now almost completely lost. An Apollonios of Alexandria, for example, gained his name ὁ εἰδογράφος from his activity as a classifier, especially of the poems of Pindar. While the undermentioned three-fold division may be anterior to the founding of Ptolemy's library, its elaboration is certainly the result of the labours of the editors and scholars of Alexandria, who for the first time made complete editions of the works of Alkman, Alkaios, Sappho, Pindar, and other lyric poets, which they arranged either according to contents or according to metre.

The only approximately exact divisions of Greek

---

[1] *Laws* 700 B.

[2] *Laws* 802 A, *Rep.* 459 E, 607 A; hyporchemes *Ion* 534 C.

[3] *Poetics* 1447 a 15, b 25.

melic that have come down to us were made in Alexandria and have been transmitted, through the medium of Didymos' περὶ λυρικῶν ποιητῶν, to Proklos, who in his *Chrestomathy*[1] arranges the various forms of melic under the following three heads.[2]

1. TO THE GODS.

Hymn (ὕμνος).	Nome (νόμος).
Prosodion (προσόδιον).	Adonidion (ἀδωνίδιον).
Paian (παιάν).	Iobacchos (ἰόβακχος).
Dithyramb (διθύραμβος).	Hyporcheme (ὑπόρχημα).

2. TO MEN.

Enkomion (ἐγκώμιον).	Hymenaios (ὑμέναιος).
Epinikion (ἐπινίκιον).	[Sillos (σίλλος).][3]
Skolion (σκόλιον).	Threnos (θρῆνος).
Erotic song (ἐρωτικόν).	Epikedeion (ἐπικήδειον).
Epithalamium (ἐπιθαλάμιον).	

3. TO GODS AND MEN.

Partheneion (παρθενεῖον).	Oschophorikon (ὠσχοφορικόν or ὀσχοφορικόν).
Daphnephorikon (δαφνηφορικόν).	Votive songs (εὐκτικά).

---

[1] Westphal's *Metr. Gr.* 1. 243. Cf. Menand. *Rhet. Gr.* 9. 127 ff. Brief definitions of many of the species appear in an anonymous writer (*An. Ox.* 4. 313).

[2] Cf. Theokr. 16. 1 αἰεὶ τοῦτο Διὸς κούραις μέλει, αἰὲν ἀοιδοῖς, | ὑμνεῖν ἀθανάτους, ὑμνεῖν ἀγαθῶν κλέα ἀνδρῶν, Hor. *ars poet.* 83 ff.: *Musa dedit fidibus divos puerosque deorum | et pugilem victorem et equum certamine primum | et iuvenum curas et libera vina referre.*

[3] Silloi was the name for lampoons after the time of Timon of Phleius (280 B.C.), who attacked the philosophers. The title was in course of time given to the lampoons of Xenophanes, who lived in the sixth century, but the sillos is not a melic poem.

To the above three classes Proklos adds a further division embracing songs on 'casual occurrences' (*προσπίπτουσαι περιστάσεις*), which, he says, are not species of melic, though the poets themselves undertook their composition. They are: *πραγματικά, ἐμπορικά, ἀποστολικά* (cf. Athen. 14. 631 D), *γνωμολογικά, γεωργικά, ἐπισταλτικά*. These names probably represent an attempt at classifying certain poems which resisted enrolment among the various divisions of the orthodox system of the early Alexandrians. If, as seems probable, such poems as Alkm. x., Alk. xvi., Sa. xli., and, possibly, some of the folk-songs are in point, Proklos, or his source, is inconsistent in calling this class pseudo-melic. *κλεψίαμβοι*, mentioned by Hesych. as a form of melic composition, derive their name merely from the stringed instrument called the *κλεψίαμβος*.

This method of classification is defective from several points of view. The sharp differentiation between the divine and the human element is not visible, for example, in the skolia, or even in the epinikion because of its pervasive religious tone. It lacks historical perspective, since the forms of melic were continually changing their character : the human side was continually gaining ground at the expense of the divine. It exaggerates the difference between poems of similar form and content, differences that were often evanescent to the ancients.[1] It is largely dependent upon the use of words, that were, for the most part, not employed in the lyric age in a technical sense ; and it leaves us uncertain as to the designation of many of the poems of Alkaios, Sappho, Anakreon, and other poets (*e.g.* Pindar's 11th *Nemean*). Still, it is the only relatively complete system of arrangement that was made by the ancient scholars who had access to the entire body of Greek song ; and as such it may form the basis of a sketch of the different species that appear in this volume.

---

[1] For example Pind. x. ; so with the paian and hyporcheme

HYMN.

The word ὕμνος is derived from a root that appears in Lat. *suere*, Eng. 'sew,' and means strictly that which is sewed or joined together.[1] In Sanskrit we find the connected word *syūman*, 'bond,' 'strap,' and in a passage of the Rig Veda (1. 113. 17) the 'sacrificial singer' is said to 'sound forth his songs in continuous (*syūmanā*) strain'; the words of his song are, as it were, stitched together so as to form one piece. So in θ 429 (cf. *Hymn* 3. 451) ἀοιδῆς ὕμνος is a 'joining of song,' and by a like figure Hesiod (Frag. 227) speaks of himself and Homer as ἐν νεαροῖς ὕμνοις ῥάψαντες ἀοιδήν. Between ὕμνος and ῥαψῳδία the difference is primarily only of degree, and μέλος 'articulated song' is not far removed.

Originally then a 'hymn' was any song whether secular or sacred, and is so used in Homer, to whom the story of Odysseus' part in Troy's taking is a 'hymn.' The songs in praise of the gods precede the 'hymn' to the men and women of old, says an *Homeric Hymn* (1. 160). It is only by holding to the early meaning of the word that we are justified in putting in the same class with the lyric poems the so-called *Homeric Hymns.* Unlike the latter the lyric hymns were never used as preludes[2] to epic recitals, nor do they aim at a purely secular or poetic effect. Only that modern point of view which emphasizes the presence of religious feeling could regard the *Homeric Hymns* as a source of lyric song. The post-classical

---

[1] ὕμνος is neither 'web' of song, as if from ὑφαίνω (despite ὑφάνας ὕμνον Bacch. ii. 9); nor merely 'melody,' as Reimann takes it to mean, equating the word with νόμος. Cf. Philodemos *de mus.*, Frag. 10.

[2] Alkaios' hymn to Apollo is called a prooimion by Paus. 10. 8. 4, probably because it recalled the style of the old prooimia, as the *Homeric Hymns* were called at an early date (Thuk. 3. 104).

hymns of a devotional character, such as those of Mesomedes, Proklos, and the *Orphica*, were not melic in sentiment and are the product of philosophical and theosophical speculation. They afford little information with regard to their predecessors of the lyric class.

In course of time the range of the hymn was gradually restricted, so that, in distinction from the epic hymns, a lyric hymn came to mean a simple religious song containing a prayer and in praise of any divinity,[1] marked by no special form, and not limited to any special occasion of worship. As a form of lyric poetry, ὕμνος resists precise definition because it lacks the specific attributes that distinguished certain other forms of lyrical composition which were differentiated from it.[2] The paian, for example, differs from the hymn in the character of the invocation, the hyporcheme is accompanied by a special

---

[1] Plato *Laws* 700 B καί τι ἦν εἶδος ᾠδῆς εὐχαὶ πρὸς τοὺς θεούς, ὄνομα δὲ ὕμνοι ἐπεκαλοῦντο. In Arist. *Poetics* 1448 b 27 ὕμνοι, as a type of early poetry, are set off against ἐγκώμια—the divine and the human—, and both are regarded as stages in the development of the poetic art.

[2] In its generic sense ὕμνος was used till a late period of almost any lyric effusion. Proklos p. 244 says in fact that all the forms of melic are merely specialized hymns (ὡς εἴδη πρὸς γένος). ὕμνος προσοδίου (the gen. of definition: not προσόδιον ὕμνου) is a processional hymn, ὕμνος παιᾶνος a paian (cf. Alk. 2; the paian of Aristonoos (Appendix) is called a 'hymn'); ὕμνος ἐγκωμίου (ἐπικώμιος ὕμνος) is used when a man, not a god, is the object of praise. So too with the dithyramb. Anakr. 171 used ὕμνος of a threnody (ὕμνων . . . ᾠδὰν ἐπικήδειον Eur. *Troad.* 512), Pind. *Ol.* 2. 1, *Nem.* 3. 11, of an epinikion (ἐπινίκιον appears for the first time as a substantive in Bacch. 2. 13). Even the folk-songs were called hymns whether connected (as v.) or unconnected (as i., iii.) with a religious cult. Plato *Rep.* 468 D speaks of ὕμνοι addressed to men, and Proklos says ἐκάλουν δὲ καθόλου πάντα τὰ εἰς τοὺς ὑπερέχοντας (ὑπηρέτας MS.) γραφόμενα ὕμνους. This generic use is to be sharply distinguished from the special sense of the word; as in the *Laws* 700 D Plato says that threnoi and hymns were

form of dance, and the nome is dissimilar to it because of the nature of its musical setting. In course of time as the paian, the dithyramb, and the other forms of religious song were developed by art, the hymn was restricted more particularly to the worship of the divinities other than Apollo and Dionysos. Zeus is the god to whom most hymns were addressed; after him come those gods in whose ritual there was no specialized form of cult-song (Aphrodite, Hermes), or whose cult was celebrated under special circumstances and conditions (Hera). One of the reasons why the hymn outlasted many other forms of melic is the absence of a characteristic colour, which, while it gave to the other kinds of song their individuality, charm, and vogue, ensured their speedy decline under conditions of society which no longer prompted their composition.

The only distinguishing marks of the hymn are that it was sung (1) to the accompaniment of the lyre, and (2) by a stationary chorus grouped about the altar of the god.[1] So long as the hymn remained

---

confounded by the degenerate poets of the time. (Here threnoi and hymns are used as examples of what is diametrically opposed.) We are often uncertain whether *ὕμνος* is to be taken in the wider or the narrower sense.

[1] In Proklos' definition (p. 244): *ὁ δὲ κυρίως ὕμνος πρὸς κιθάραν ᾔδετο ἑστώτων*, it is uncertain whether *ἑστώτων* is to be taken literally or in a freer sense (cf. *στάσιμον*) which would allow stately evolutions on the part of the chorus during the singing of the strophe and antistrophe. When Athen. 15. 631 D says that some hymns were accompanied by dancing, he is probably using the word hymn in its wider meaning, which includes prosodia, paians, etc. In the time of Kallimachos, however, it is certain that an ancient hymn of Olen, which was sung every evening by boys, was accompanied by orchestic movements on the part of girls. It is possible that, while in the earliest period the chorus may not have shifted its position, later on, and especially during the predominance of choral lyric, some stately movement was occasionally permitted.

a strictly religious song it must have played a chief part in the festivals of the gods, and have been sung either immediately before or after the sacrifice.

While most hymns gave expression to public devotion, some were intended to be sung by a single voice. In the most ancient and pre-lyric times, if we are to believe Pausanias (10. 7. 2), there were contests between individuals in the singing of hymns, and prizes were awarded to Chrysothemis, Philammon and others. In the lyric period the hymns of Terpander, Alkaios, Sappho, and Anakreon were all monodic. When the hymn was choral the chorus usually consisted of men, sometimes of women. In early times there may have been guilds of singers as there were professional or official hymnographers in the post-classical period.[1]

The character of the hymn varied with time, cult, and locality. The Thebans loved to sing of Herakles; the Spartans, of Kastor and Polydeukes. Though the Dorians produced few hymn-writers, the cultivation of the hymn was peculiarly suited to their deep religious sense. Without becoming absolutely secular at any period, even among the Aiolians and Ionians, who gave it an erotic or even sympotic character, the hymn tended to degenerate into a mere embellishment of the festival, gaining indeed in finish, delicacy, and grace, but ceasing to be the outpouring of a fervent piety. In abandoning its choral form among the Aiolians, the hymn lost its affinity with the ritual of the cult; though Sappho and Anakreon retain the invocation. On the other hand in the Dorian colonies of the west the choral hymn was secularized by Stesichoros, who made the heroes the chief theme

---

[1] *C. I. G.* 2715 (time of Tiberius) says that the Karian city of Stratonikeia commissioned the city-clerk to compose a hymn in honour of Hekate. A certain Ptolemaios wrote *περὶ τῶν κατὰ πόλεις τοὺς ὕμνους ποιησάντων.*

instead of the gods. Ibykos went a step further in composing erotic hymns in honour of Ganymede and Endymion. Thus the way was prepared for the enkomion and triumphal song, which substituted outright the praise of contemporary men for the worship of the gods and demi-gods. It is noteworthy that the secularization of the hymn in widely distant parts of Greece is conterminous with the period of its highest artistic excellence. The old religious hymn suffered eclipse, but it did not die out completely.

The remnants of the choral hymn are too scant to permit any attempt at defining its contents. Probably it dealt, not with any chance circumstance in the history of the god, but with the story of his birth, his marriage, or his death, and with the sanctuaries consecrated to his worship which he loved to honour by his residence. A certain archaic, epic, and objective tone was inevitable in conjunction with the prayer, and in like manner, though to a less degree than in the more ancient liturgies, such as were composed by Olen, Musaios, Pamphos, and Orpheus, the old-time hieratic character was preserved by the invocation of the god with epithets that compelled his favour and ensured the efficacy of the petition. So, on the other hand, the powers that made for evil were subdued and their maleficent activity chained (δεσμεύειν) by a comprehensive register of their attributes.

The wealth of material at the command of the poet affected the hymnodic style at the time of Pindar, who feigns embarrassment (ἀπορία) in the selection of the appropriate myth (Pind. i., cf. Mel. Adesp. 84). Usually the hymn was tranquil in tone, plain in style, simple, and free from excessive ornament. In early times the metre was probably the dactylic hexameter, but later any measure appropriate to the theme was employed. The normal form of composition consisted of strophe, antistrophe, and epode. The mode was generally the solemn Dorian, but we know that Stesichoros used the Phrygian, and Lasos the Aiolian. Of the famous melic poets almost all, from Alkman to Timotheos, are reported to have composed hymns.

So varied in character is the hymnal ode that the mint-marks of subdivision are elusory. The rhetorician Menander[1] sought to establish two species, but it is uncertain whether he is not using 'hymn' in the collective sense.

1. Kletic or invocatory hymns, which summon the god to leave his present abiding-place. It was a favourite device of the poets to describe the rivers, meadows, shrines, and dancing-places where the god might be tarrying and whence he was expected to come at the call of his petitioner. So common was this feature that it degenerated into a mannerism, which is imitated by Aristophanes in *Nubes* 270 ff. In case a prayer followed upon the invocation, the element of description was abridged. Examples of kletic hymns are Alkm. 21 Κύπρον ἱμερτὰν λιποῖσα καὶ Πάφον περιρρυτάν (of Aphrodite), Alk. ii., Sa. i., v., 6 ἤ σε Κύπρος καὶ Πάφος ἢ Πάνορμος (*scil.* ἔχει, of Aphr.), Aristoph. *Ranae* 875 ff., *Lysistr.* 1296 ff., (Aisch. *Eum.* 287 ff.). Echoes in Theokr. 1. 123, 15. 100, Kallim. 1. 4, Catull. 36, Hor. 1. 30. 2., cf. A 38.

2. The valedictory (ἀποπεμπτικοί) hymns dealt with the supposed or actual absence of the god and contained a prayer for his return. The country, city, and people which he is quitting, the place of his future sojourn—any spot that fancy could paint as the domicile of the god—became the object of a description even more elaborate than that of the kletic class. Bacchylides is reported to have excelled in the composition of valedictory hymns.

---

[1] *Rhet. Gr.* 9. 135 ff.

PROSODION.

Prosodia (προσόδια *scil.* ᾄσματα; also called προσοδιακοί) were chorals of supplication or thanksgiving, sung to the music of the flute in solemn processions to the temples or altars of the gods. Their character varied somewhat with the god whose sanctuary was visited or to whom offerings were made. Sometimes the festival was in honour of a god whose cult was native; sometimes a festal chorus or θεωρία was sent abroad to a famous shrine, and the prosodion was sung when the representatives of the state reached their destination, as in the case of the Messenian embassy to the Delian Apollo (Eumelos). The prosodia were often petitionary (Plato *Laws* 796 c).

The prosodia naturally formed the introductory part of the festival—while the approach was made to the temple or while the sacred offerings were brought to the altar. After the prosodion came a hyporchematic song, and this was followed by the hymn proper. ἐξόδια or ἀποτρεπτικά seem to have attended the departure from the shrine of the god. Apollo and Artemis claimed most of the prosodia proper, which were particularly cultivated at Delphi and at Delos; but other gods were honoured with processionals, as for example, Dionysos.[1] As the processional song is only a species of hymn, so there are various species of prosodia, *e.g.* the partheneia and daphnephorika. We hear of prosodia as ciresionai at the Pyanepsia, at the Eleusinia, Thesmophoria, Heraia, Haloa, etc. Sometimes the prosodion was akin to the paian, and we have prosodiac paians, *e.g.* in Pindar Frag. vi., though according to Proklos this was a misuse of words. παιάν is here the wider, προσόδιον the narrower, term. If Σ 567 ff.

---

[1] Schol. Hephaist. 134.

is a prosodion, X 391 is closely akin to a prosodiac paian, perhaps nearer to the prosodion than to the paian. It is noteworthy that Homer does not allude to the ancient form of the simple prosodion.

Prosodia and embateria may have been accompanied originally by the music of the lyre.[1] It was the flute, however, that was regarded as the proper instrument for processions whether these were attended by songs or not. In a Delphic inscription (Wescher-Foucart no. 45) an αὐλητής is especially provided for the prosodia; flute players are seen in the frieze of the Parthenon that represents the Panathenaic procession; and a flute player accompanied the boy who carried the laurel bough from Tempe to Delphi. (A vase (no. 1686) in the Berlin Museum represents a procession with lyrists as well as flute players.) The story that Klonas, the aulode, was the 'inventor' of prosodia (and the prosodiac metre) shows merely that there was a close connection in early times between aulodic and this form of melic. Some think that it was Klonas who first employed the flute instead of the lyre to accompany the prosodia.

The movements of the chorus were solemn, stately, and in harmony with the contents of their songs and the Dorian mode to which they were sung. Of the metre in the earliest period we have no accurate information—but it is probable that the dactylic hexameter, measured by dipodies, was in common use; and a reminiscence of this early form may be seen in the closing hexameters of the *Frogs*. When the influence of the epos was on the decline, lyric poetry employed the 'prosodiac' rhythm to increase the liveliness of the movement. Westphal thinks that –́ ⏑ ⏑ –́ ⏑ ⏑ –́ ⏑ ⏑ was the original

[1] Cf. Athen. 4. 139 E on the Lakonian prosodia at the Hyakinthia; Pollux 4. 64.

form, and that ⏑ ⏑ ⁞ –́ ⏑ ⏑ –́ ⏑ ⏑ –́ ∧ was substituted for the dactylic tripody at a time when flute music became prominent—perhaps in the time of Klonas. The anapaestic parodes of the scenic poets are descendants of the old prosodia. Pindar used dactylo-epitrites and logaoedics, and Bacchylides employed the latter metre both alone and mixed with cretics.

Eumelos of Korinth was the author of the first prosodion of which we have record. It was intended to be sung at Delos, and this seat of the Apolline cult remained the chief place for the presentation of this form of melic. Next in point of time is Klonas the founder of aulodic. The prosodia of Pindar, in two books, and of Bacchylides were famous. Pronomos of Thebes, the teacher of Alkibiades, is said to have composed a prosodion to be rendered at Delos by the Chalkidians, but unless we suppose that there was no text, it is probable that he merely set to music the words of another.[1] His fame rested solely on his ability as a musical virtuoso (he could play the three modes—the Dorian, Lydian, and Phrygian—on one set of flutes). The return of Demetrios to Athens (FOLK-SONGS xxvii.) was hailed with ithyphallic songs and prosodiac choruses, and the song in honour of a god was profaned to suit the degeneracy of the times. At the festival of the Soteria, at Delphi, between 275 and 255 B.C., prosodia were sung that were the compositions of Alexinos, Xenon, and Dexinikos (Wescher-Foucart *Inscr. de Delphes* 5. 13). Kleochares of Athens, who probably lived in the third century, was honoured by the Delphians on account of a processional (*B.C.H.* 18. 71), and Weil thinks the choral in cretics (see APPENDIX) that was sung at Delphi is

---

[1] ᾆσμα αὐλεῖν may refer to a poem set to music, or to the music alone (ψιλὴ αὔλησις).

a prosodion. We hear of an Amphikles (*B.C.H.* 10. 36, 13. 245) at Delos. Two late inscriptions (*C. I. Sept.* 1760, 1773) record the continuance of prosodia in Boiotia till very late times. The musical games, at least in the late period, were opened by processional songs sung by the whole body of the artists, priests, etc., as they entered the scene of the contest.

PAIAN.

The paian, which derives its name from the burden *ἰὴ παιάν*,[1] was one of the most ancient of the Greek lyrics. In its earliest form it is intimately connected with the worship of Apollo, the patron god of music and song, the sender and averter of calamity. In ascribing its introduction to Apollo himself, tradition made the paian as old as the cult of the god. When

---

[1] In like manner the Linos-song, the hymenaios, and possibly the dithyramb received their names from the refrain (*ἐφύμνιον*). *παιήων* in Homer, Archil. 76. Dor. *παιάν*, Ionic — Attic *παιών* contain a different suffix. *παιών* is not generic, or *παιάν* specific (cf. schol. Plato *Symp.* 177 A: *παιῶνας: ᾠδὰς ἐπὶ εὐτυχίᾳ καὶ νίκῃ, παιᾶνας: ὕμνους εἰς Ἀπόλλωνα ἐπὶ καταπαύσει λοιμοῦ*). The etymology is unknown. Baunack's *ἴ' ἐπ' αἰᾶνα* 'come for healing' is incredible; Fick suggests a connection with *ἔμπαιος*, 'skilled' in healing. *Φοῖβος* is himself the 'healer.' It is possible to regard Apollo's victory over the Python as a triumph over pestilence and to see in the paian a prayer for deliverance to the god who has power to heal all distress. Against this, however, is the fact that, despite Π 528, where Apollo performs the office of a physician, he is distinct from *Παιήων* in Homer and Hesiod. *Ἰηπαιήων* is used of Apollo in *Hymn* 2. 94, but with reference to the god of Delphi. Possibly the paian was originally a song of triumph which was identified with the prayer to relieve pain or distress when Apollo came to be regarded as the god of medicine (Asklepios was his son) and *Παιάν* and *Παιών* were held to be equivalents. The exclamation *ἰή* was connected by the ancients with *ἵημι*: cf. Kallim. 2. 103 *ἰὴ ἰὴ παιῆον, ἵει βέλος.* See on Timoth. viii.

Apollo had slain the python, with lyre in hand he led the Cretans to his sanctuary at Delphi (*Hymn* 2. 336 ff.).

> οἱ δὲ ῥήσσοντες ἕποντο
> Κρῆτες πρὸς Πυθὼ καὶ ἰηπαιήον' ἄειδον,
> οἷοί τε Κρητῶν παιήονες, οἷσί τε Μοῦσα
> ἐν στήθεσσιν ἔθηκε θεὰ μελίγηρυν ἀοιδήν.

Homer narrates (A 472 ff.) how the Achaians before Troy sang the paian to propitiate Apollo after the expiatory sacrifice which cleansed them from pollution.

The localities in which the paian was first cultivated—in Crete, at Sparta in conjunction with the festivals of the Hyakinthia and Gymnopaidia, at Delphi and in Delos—are all Dorian and closely connected with the cult of Apollo; and the association with the Apolline ritual remained a common feature of the paian throughout the classical age. On occasions of public danger or calamity, and especially when the state was afflicted by plague, the paian was sung in solemn chorus to express the devotion of the people to the god and to implore his succour as ἀλεξίκακος.[1] When the divinity who occasioned the distress stayed the pestilence or the assault of the enemy, paians of thanksgiving were raised in his honour.[2] With Apollo, his sister Artemis[3] was associated as a protecting divinity: Ἔντι μὲν χρυσαλακάτου τεκέων Λατοῦς ἀοιδαὶ ὥριαι παιανίδες (Pind. Frag. 139).

As early as Homer the paian appears as a triumphal

---

[1] Cf. Soph. *O. T.* 5, 186. Vernal paians were supposed to have a remedial effect in cases of madness (Aristox. Frag. 36). Even in the presence of danger the paian might be full of confidence (Aisch. *Sept.* 268).

[2] Cf. Theogn. 779, Aristoph. *Vesp.* 869 ff.

[3] Cf. Eur. *I. T.* 1404, *I. A.* 1469.

hymn that is totally disconnected from the cult of Apollo. In X 391 after Achilles has slain Hektor, who was the favourite of the god, he bids the Achaians raise the paian as they march to the ships (the prosodiac paian). In course of time other gods[1] were hymned with paians, and the refrain was often employed as an accompaniment of any exciting event or when any enterprise was crowned with success.

In times of political and moral degeneracy the paian was addressed to conquerors and princes. Lysander was thus honoured as if he had been a god (FOLK-SONGS xxvi.). Aratos saluted Antigonos with a paian, and that prince and Demetrios Poliorketes were flattered in the same manner by the Athenians. Alexinos composed a paian in honour of Krateros; the Rhodians celebrated Ptolemy I., the Korinthians Agemon, while the Chalkidians still chanted Titus Flaminius in the time of Plutarch. Even this debased form of the paian contained the sacred refrain. Aristotle was charged with impiety because his detractors regarded his ode in honour of Hermeias as a paian.

It is as a song of thanksgiving and praise—a ὕμνος εὐχαριστήριος—that the paian is best attested in

---

[1] We hear of paians to Zeus (Xen. *Anab.* 3. 2. 9; cf. Hesych. *s. v.* Ζεὺς παιάν); Poseidon (Xen. *Hell.* 4. 7. 4; during an earthquake); Dionysos (in the Appendix); Asklepios (by Sophokles; in a late period paians to Ask. were sung annually; Makedonian paian, carm. pop. 47; cf. *C. I. A.* 3. 171 with appendices; Athen. 6. 250 C); Hygieia (Ariphron); the Nymphs in conjunction with Apollo (cf. *I. G. A.* 379); the Fates (? Mel. Adesp. xiii.); Serapis (by Demetr. Poliork.); Peace (Bacchylides). Not only Apollo and Asklepios are called Παιάν, but also Helios (*Orph. Hymn* 8. 12), Pan (*ib.* 11. 11), and Herakles (Stat. *Theb.* 4. 157) who is also an ἀλεξίκακος. Athena is called παιωνία as a goddess of healing. Servius on Verg. *Aen.* 10. 738 erroneously says *unde Pindarus opus suum, quod et hominum et (quod omnium?) deorum continet laudes, paeanes vocavit.*

ancient literature. It was pre-eminently a song of joy.[1] 'Thetis ceases to mourn for Achilles when she hears the sound ἰὴ παιῆον (Kallim. 2. 21), and Niobe, turned to stone, no longer weeps.' Apollo enjoined that the paian should be sung in the springtime at Delphi, and it was regularly chanted there at the expiatory festival in the first month of spring, after the distress of winter had passed. In the three winter months it gave place to the dithyramb.

This joyous character of the paian appears in its two semi-religious forms, the sympotic, and the martial paian. Both may be regarded as descendants of the Apolline paian, although all immediate connection with the god has disappeared.

The sympotic, banquet paian, or choral "grace," is first attested in Alkman (xxviii.), but the custom is referred to the heroic age in Aisch. *Agam.* 246. It was much in vogue among the Dorians, who transferred to their common meals in time of peace the customs of their camp-life. At Athens after the libations were made, the paian with the refrain was sung by all the guests in chorus as an introduction to the symposium proper. Usually it was not accompanied by music: an inspiring tune expressed the animated feelings of the guests. The song was addressed either to all the gods or to the one to whom the feast was consecrated. In case a libation was made to the Muses during the symposium, the paian to Apollo Musagetes was sung, and in general whenever libations were made on the mixing of a fresh bowl the paian was repeated. The close of

---

[1] Such locutions as π. 'Ερινύων Aisch. *Agam.* 645, π. τοῦ θανόντος *Choeph.* 151, π. τῷ κάτωθεν ἀσπόνδῳ θεῷ Eur. *Alk.* 424 are shown to be oxymora by Aisch. *Sept.* 869, Eur. *I. T.* 185, *Troad.* 126. As Death is the ἰατρὸς κακῶν, Aisch. Frag. 255 and Eur. *Hippol.* 1373 are justified in using the expression Θάνατος Παιάν.

the banquet was attended by a libation and a paian. The ratification of peace was often celebrated by a banquet with the attendant libations and paians (Xen. *Hellen.* 7. 4. 36); and Arrian (7. 11) reports that the paian was sung in chorus by nine thousand Makedonians and Persians. The frequent confusion between skolia and paian was occasioned by the custom of singing the former after the latter (cf. Antiphanes 4). The use of the cup and the myrtle branch in singing the paian helped the confusion.

The martial paian, which was sung before a battle on land or sea, and after victory, was alike an incitement to valour and a song of repose after the struggle. At Sparta it was in high esteem: the king himself sounded the march-paian (ἐμβατήριος παιάν), and the troops took up the strain as they advanced against the enemy. At Athens the paian was raised when the fleet set sail. On the battle-field it followed the prayer and preceded the war-cry to Enyalios, and during a military or naval engagement it was often sung on the occasion of each fresh attack. The paian in X 391 is essentially of the martial type. Polyneikes boasts in anticipation of his success that he will sing a ἁλώσιμος παιάν over Thebes (Aisch. *Sept.* 635). After the victory at Aigospotamoi, Lysander ordered the paian to be sung as the fleet sailed away to Lampsakos.

In the earliest period the paian may have been a monody interrupted at irregular intervals by the cries of the people. Gradually the burden[1] (παιανικὸν ἐπίρρημα) of the chorus was given a definite place during the singing of the ἐξάρχων or leader, and at last the paian became choral throughout, the chorus

[1] The ancients disputed whether the refrain could be absent from the paian proper. Cf. Athen. 15. 696 B. Ariphron's ode to Hygieia lacks the ἐπίφθεγμα, and so Aristotle's ode to Virtue, though it was held by his detractors to be a paian.

taking the place of the ἐξάρχων, as was not infrequent.[1] As in the case of the dithyramb, the difference between the primitive and the artistic paian consists in the substitution of the activity of the chorus for that of the soloist. The choruses were usually composed of men, sometimes of boys, as at Delphi; at Delos the paian might be sung by girls (Eur. *H. F.* 689). The musical accompaniment, which is apparently later than the *Iliad*, was furnished by the lyre (the instrument of Apollo), or by the flute,[2] which was better suited to regulate the singing of a large chorus and hence was employed in the battle-paian and sometimes at banquets; or by lyre and flute together.[3] The number of the chorus was not fixed: Bacch. ix. was probably sung by fourteen. The mode was the Dorian, which was best suited for male choruses. The composition was well-ordered and free from excess, but apparently high poetic excellence was not essential to its success. Gravity and dignity rather than uncontrolled exultation were appropriate to its style; the delivery was quiet and devoid of passion, but a certain element of liveliness must have marked the Cretan paians because of their use of the paionic measure. The presentation was sometimes accompanied by dancing, which was akin to the stately ἐμμέλεια of tragedy. The Mantineans danced when under arms on an occasion reported by Xen. *Anab.* 6. 1. 11. Intermediate between the prosodion and the paian is the processional paian, of which we have examples in X 391, Pindar Frag. vi., and Isyllos. Various metres were employed. The old Cretan paians by Thaletas were written in paions, which

---

[1] Suidas has Τρῶες παιᾶνας ἐξάρχοντες. Cf. Theogn. 779 παιᾶσιν χορῶν.

[2] Archil. 76, Eur. *Troad.* 126, schol. Pind. *Pyth.* 12. 45, Plut. *Vita Lys.* 11.

[3] συναυλία. Cf. Theogn. 761.

took their name from their use in the paian, and were a good measure for orchestic movement. Simonides (26 B) retains this ancient use. The old Ionic paian was in hexameters (cf. Soph. *O. T.* 151 ff.). In a fragment (76) in trochaic tetrameters Archilochos says that he himself led the 'Lesbian paian.' Later on, logaoedics and dactylo-epitrites were common. Isyllos of Epidauros wrote in ionics.

The paian was taken over in part by the tragic poets as an ornament of the drama, and was cultivated to the latest times. Thaletas saved Sparta by his paians, which are now lost, as are those by his scholars Xenodamos and Xenokritos. We have a fragment by Alkman, who composed an entire book. Of the paian (probably sympotic in character) by Tynnichos of Chalkis, Plato said that it was the most beautiful song in existence, and that its author was justified in calling it an 'invention of the Muses.' Other poets who wrote paians are: Dionysodotos, one of the early poets of Sparta, Stesichoros, Diagoras, Kydias, Simonides, Pindar, Bacchylides, Ariphron, Likymnios, Sophokles (Bergk 2. 245 ff.; cf. *Trach.* 205, if not a hyporcheme: it is to be noted that the passage is an ἀπολελυμένον μέλος), Timotheos, Aristonoos of Korinth (400 B.C.?), Dionysios the Younger, Aristotle (?), Alexinos (about 325), Philodamos of Skarpheia, Hermippos of Kyzikos (about 300), Hermokles, Isyllos of Epidauros (about 280), Diophantos of Sphettos (249), Kleochares of Athens (3rd cent.), Isodemos of Troizen, Makedonios, the Pythagoreans, the Italiots, etc. Inscriptions have preserved paians by unknown authors, *e.g. C. I. A.* 3. 171, with appendices, *Revue. Arch.* 13. 70. Semos of Delos wrote a book περὶ παιάνων.

DITHYRAMB.

1. **PRIMITIVE DITHYRAMB.**
Represented by ARCHILOCHOS and ARION.

2. **OLD DITHYRAMB** (from about 550 to about 475).
LASOS of Hermione: instituted a dithyrambic agon under Peisistratos at the Dionysia. His authorship of the *Centaurs* is uncertain. HYPODIKOS of Chalkis: victorious in 508, on the first occasion of the appearance at Athens of a male chorus, probably at some other festival than the Dionysia. SIMONIDES: *Memnon, Europa, Danaë* (?). PRATINAS of Phleius (about 500): *Dysmainai* or *Karyatides*. APOLLODOROS, AGATHOKLES, teachers of PINDAR. LAMPROKLES of Athens. PHRYNICHOS, the rival of Aischylos. TYNNICHOS of Chalkis. KEDEIDES (his grandson appears as a dithyrambic διδάσκαλος, *Athen. Mittheil.* 8. 34). Kekeides is possibly the same person (Schol. Aristoph. *Nubes* 981).

3. **MIDDLE DITHYRAMB** (from about 475 to about 400).
MELANIPPIDES, founder of the new style: *Marsyas, Persephone, Danaids, Narkissos, Oineus*. BACCHYLIDES: *Antenoridai, Herakles, Theseus, Idas, Io, Philoktetes* (?). DIAGORAS of Melos. KYDIAS. PRAXILLA of Sikyon: *Adonis, Achilles*. PHRYNIS of Mytilene, the teacher of Timotheos, and a ruinous innovator according to the comic poets. ION of Chios, the tragic poet: described the burning of Antigone and Ismene by Laodamas, Eteokles' son. KINESIAS of Athens: *Asklepios*. ARIPHRON of Sikyon. LIKYMNIOS of Chios. NIKOSTRATOS (*C. I. A.* 1. 336). HIERONYMOS (?). PANTAKLES (*C. I. A.* 1. 337). ARCHESTRATOS (*C. I. G.* 211).

4. **NEW DITHYRAMB** (from about 400).
PHILOXENOS of Kythera (435-380): *Kyklops* or *Galateia, Hymenaios, Mysoi, Komastes, Persai, Syros* (or *Satyros*). TIMOTHEOS of Miletos: *Kyklops, Elpenor, Nautilos, Sons of Phineus, Birth-pangs of Semele*, etc. TELESTES of Selinus (first victory 402/1): *Argo, Asklepios*. POLYEIDOS: *Atlas*. PAIDEAS (*B. C. H.* 6. 521; shortly after 400). KREXOS instituted *parakataloge* in the dithyramb. STESICHOROS the second (victorious 370). ARISTARCHOS (*C. I. G.* 1. 226 *b*; 400-385). LYKOPHRONIDES. PHILOPHRON (Pittakis 'Εφ. ἀρχ. no. 2792). PAMPHILOS (*C. I. G.* 223; 366/5). EUKLES (Dittenb. *Syll.* 411; 365/4). LYSIADES of Athens (Ross *Arch. Aufs.*, 2. 479, no. 2; 352/1). ANTIGENES (after 350). EPIKUROS of Sikyon (Dittenb. *Syll.* 414; 344/3). CHARILAOS of Lokris (*l.l.* 416; 328/7). KARKIDAMOS Sotios (*l.l.* 423; 320/19). PANTALEON of Sikyon (Rangabé *Ant. Hell.* 986; 320/19).

Nikokles of Tarentum (before 300), a famous kitharoede, victor at the Lenaia with a dithyramb. Kleomenes of Rhegion: *Meleager*. Hellanikos of Argos. Eraton of Arkadia, etc. Demosthenes Thrax wrote περὶ διθυραμβοποιῶν.

The cult of Dionysos, which is one of the latest developments of early Greek religion, gave birth to an orgiastic song that became the source not only of tragedy, but also of a form of melic that eclipsed all other lyric poetry in popularity.

The worship of the god of wine was an importation from Thrace or Phrygia,[1] the languages of which countries were closely allied and of Indo-European stock; and together with the cult of the god came the obscure word δῑθύραμβος, which seems to have been originally an epithet of the divinity in whose honour the dithyramb was sung at the gatherings of the country-folk.

Of the various etymologies[2] of the word that have

---

[1] Arist. *Pol.* 8. 7 says the dithyramb is Phrygian. It is with the Phrygian songs in praise of the Great Mother that Pindar compares the dithyramb (Frag. 79 B). Cf. Telest. ii.

[2] (1) From λῦθι ῥάμμα, the cry of Zeus on bearing the child Dionysos from out his thigh; so Pind. Frag. 85, who equates λυθίραμβος with διθύραμβος. (2) Eur. *Bacch.* 526 ἴθι, Διθύραμβ', ἐμὰν ἄρσενα τάνδε βᾶθι νηδύν· ἀναφαίνω σε τόδ', ὦ Βάκχιε, Θήβαις ὀνομάζειν. This points to a fanciful derivation either from δὶς θύρας βαίνειν (impossible because of the quantity) or from Διὸς θύρας βαίνειν. The god was twice-born (διμήτωρ, δισσότοκος): once from Semele, again from Zeus' thigh. (See Kuhn *Herabkunft d. Feuers* p. 147.) Cf. Plato *Laws* 700 B: Διονύσου γένεσις διθύραμβος λεγόμενος. (3) From the bringing to Zeus of the θρῖον or leaf-enveloped heart or body of the god; so Donaldson *New Cratylus* § 319. (4) From τιτυρίαμβος (τίτυρος = σάτυρος 'goat'); so Schmidt *Diatribe*, p. 181. (5) From Διὸς θρίαμβος = θόρυβος, the appearance of Zeus with thunder and lightning being the generative storm of the springtime; so Hartung *Philol.* 1. 398. (6) = διθρίαμβος, double three-step; τρίαμβος = *tripudium*; so Schoemann *Alterth.*[3] 2. 494. (7) = διθέραμβος 'skin-chant' (ἀμβο- = ὀμφή); so Fennell on Pind. Frag. 79.

been proposed, only one has any semblance of probability. According to this, *διθύραμβος* is connected with *θρίαμβος*, an equivalent of *θύραμβος*. The meaning of *θρίαμβος* is indeed unknown, but the word was used as an epithet of the god,[1] and may be compared with *triumpe* in the Arval Song.[2] The interjection then, as in the case of *παιάν*, *οἰτόλινος*, *ἰόβακχος*, gave birth to an appellative with the meaning 'song' or 'dance' in honour of Bacchos.[3] The initial member of the compound (*δῑ-* from *δι-*) may denote either a *θύραμβος* in praise of a god, or one that is beautiful.[4]

The first mention of the dithyramb is made by the Parian and Thasian poet Archilochos. The islands were the first station of the Dionysiac song as it passed over to the mainland. Naxos was the home of the dithyramb according to Pindar, though that poet also attributes the honour of the invention to Korinth, the seat of the culture of the northern Peloponnese, and to Thebes. Korinth points to Lesbos, whence Arion is reported to have come at the invitation of Periander, under whose patronage the dithyramb and the satyr play were developed; and at Thebes, the city of Semele, the dithyramb was afterwards in high vogue.

From Archilochos 77

> Ὡς Διωνύσοι' ἄνακτος καλὸν ἐξάρξαι μέλος
> οἶδα διθύραμβον, οἴνῳ συγκεραυνωθεὶς φρένας

---

[1] Ἴακχε θρίαμβε (*e conj.*) Mel. Adesp. 109. Pratinas i. 16 has θριαμβοδιθύραμβε of Dionysos. Cf. Βακχέβακχος.

[2] *triumphus* points to an original *τρίαμφος. The φ of Διθύραμφος, on a vase, *Ant. Denkm.* 3. 125, may be due to assimilation.

[3] θρίαμβος· Διονυσιακὸς ὕμνος Hesych. Cf. Kratinos 36 τοὺς καλοὺς θριάμβους ἀναρύτουσα. ἴθυμβος, also a Dionysiac song, is probably Thracian.

[4] Wilamowitz would defend the latter meaning by Διὸς ἐγκέφαλος, Διὸς βάλανος. Less appropriate are his formally more perfect comparisons Δῑπόλια, Δῑσωτήριον.

we may infer that the earliest form of the dithyramb was a monody—the song of the reveller at the κῶμος, when he is smitten in his soul by wine's thunder—attended perhaps, if we insist on the meaning of ἐξάρξαι, by a refrain on the part of the other revellers.

The development of the dithyramb into a choral song is associated with the name of Arion. A kitharoede of Methymna in Lesbos, he is said to have been the inventor of the τραγικὸς τρόπος, to have been the first to institute the cyclic chorus, and to have introduced satyrs speaking in verse. The exact significance of each of these innovations is obscure. Arion himself is a mythical personage; and the relation of the dithyramb as improved by him to the dithyramb of a century later, to the satyr play, and to its development in tragedy, is involved in controversy at every step. We are here concerned only with the history of the dithyramb as a lyric production apart from tragedy, but it may be said that the lyric species actually known to us at the time of Pindar must have differed in some measure from the form of the dithyramb that gave birth to the satyr play and tragedy. Neither the satyr play nor tragedy is a development of the Pindaric dithyramb, otherwise the latter would have been absorbed; but the satyr play and the Pindaric dithyramb are descendants of a mimetic form of the archaic dithyramb that is possibly to be associated with the name of Arion.

The subject of the dithyramb was primarily Dionysos, and in the early period, at least till the time of Pindar, the birth and life of the god remained the chief theme. The history of Dionysos is the romance of the Greek pantheon. Born of hapless Semele amid the lightning of his omnipotent father; the husband of Ariadne, who was set among the stars; whose cult was introduced only after continuous struggle; the god whose death was bewailed with the extinction of vegetation, and whose return to life with the spring was welcomed with cries of exultation,—his career abounded in situations that evoked the passionate sympathy of his worshippers. His cult was, too, the source of merriment, licence, and revelry: the satyric as well as the tragic drama lay dormant in the primitive Bacchic song.

The centrifugal tendency that appears in all Greek melic that is restricted at the outset to the service of one divinity soon made itself felt in the dithyramb. Early in the sixth century, Adrastos, the idol of the Dorian aristocracy, is reported to have usurped the place of Dionysos in the dithyramb of the Sikyonians.[1] From the early part of the fifth century the tendency to have recourse to themes alien to the cult of the god is clearly marked, though the pre-eminence of the dithyramb at Athens made Dionysos virtually the patron-god of choral poetry. The cycle of Dionysiac myth may indeed show traces more or less faint of a connection between the god and the legends of Meleager (Bacch. ii.), Achilles (Praxilla i.), Endymion (Likymn. iii.), etc., but the fact remains that the overwhelming majority of the titles given on p. xliii. shows that the artistic tendency rapidly effected an almost complete divorcement of the theme from the narrower Dionysiac sphere. The dithyramb became in fact a special form of the lyric setting of heroic subjects embodying a succession of incidents.[2] Philoxenos even introduced a purely

---

[1] Hdt. 5. 67. The Sikyonians may have worshipped Dionysos as Adrastos, the 'Invincible,' and Kleisthenes' opposition to the mortal of the same name may have prompted his edict, which demanded the restoration of the common name of the god.

[2] ἡρωικῶν ὑποθέσεων πράγματα ἐχουσῶν Herakl. Pont. in Plut. *de mus.* 10, who states that the paians of Xenokritos were regarded as dithyrambs by some. Xenokr. certainly did not write dithyrambs.

erotic *motif*. It was not merely at the Dionysia, the festival sacred to Dionysos, that dithyrambs were produced at Athens; they were also brought before the public at the Thargelia in honour of Apollo. Though the mythological and legendary range was unrestricted, the Bacchic exaltation and fervour, the heirlooms of the primitive orgiastic song, remained as characteristic qualities of the dithyrambic style.

In the primitive dithyramb the rôle of the leader (ἐξάρχων) was all-important. He led the song, while the chorus, which performed a mimetic dance, fell in at appropriate intervals. Gradually a form was developed in which a choral alternated with the song of the leader, who impersonated the god; and an echo of this amoebean type would seem to be the *Theseus* of Bacchylides, except that the leader there plays a secular rôle. For the lyric metres of the leader primitive tragedy substituted trochaics and iambics: primitive tragedy, according to Aristotle, was developed from the 'leaders of the dithyramb' and was at first mere improvisation. It is uncertain whether the part of the leader was afterwards taken by the poet or by the koryphaios, and whether there was any fixed relation between the leader and the flute player. In the *Skylla* of Timotheos we know that the aulete took the rôle of Skylla, while the koryphaios impersonated Odysseus[1]—a relation that recalls the early form of tragedy in which there was a single actor, who discoursed with the koryphaios representing the chorus.

It has been generally held that from the time of Arion until that of Philoxenos, who introduced solos, the dithyramb was choral throughout. But as early as the *Theseus* of Bacchylides we have a balanced lyric dialogue between a single actor and

---

[1] Cf. Aristoph. *Plut.* 290 ff.

either the chorus or the koryphaios; and the innovation ascribed to Philoxenos may refer to *arias* that were sung at irregular intervals.

The dithyrambic dance, in which numerous figures were employed, was called the *tyrbasia*,[1] and was lively and enthusiastic, often wild and extravagant. Kinesias made use of the pyrrich dance.

The number of the chorus is first reported as fifty by Simonides in 476 (Frag. 147). This probably holds true from the sixth century until after 300, when the number was much reduced.[2] When the dithyramb came under Peloponnesian influence after 600 the choreutai represented satyrs who wore goat-skins,[3] and by their unbridled and tumultuous actions represented the attendants of the wine-god. Later on, and at Athens before 500, the chorus was composed either of silens (though they received the Peloponnesian name of satyrs) or of personages appropriate to the theme.

---

[1] *Tyrbe* is the name of a festival of Dionysos in Argos. Metag. 7 says the chorus pranced about like horses.

[2] Athen. 5. 199 A reports a chorus of sixty; Hyginus 273, one of seven.

[3] τραγικοὶ χοροί at Sikyon under Kleisthenes (Hdt. 5. 67). In Aisch. Frag. 207 τράγος is used of a satyr. In Doric σάτυρος = 'goat.' The τραγικὸς τρόπος of the Arionic dithyramb refers simply to the goat-chorus. Various other explanations have been put forward on the assumption that the style was 'tragic': (1) because the combination of song by the chorus and verses spoken by the satyrs was an anticipation of tragedy; (2) because of its lofty diction and theme; (3) because of the expansion of the dithyramb by the inclusion of heroic myths; (4) by contrast with the calm νομικὸς τρόπος. We hear of a chorus of goats at Sikyon shortly after 600 (Hdt. 5. 64). Why the goat, the creature of Pan, was selected to typify the attendant of Dionysos, has not been satisfactorily explained. On an early Attic monument (*Athen. Mitth.* 11. 78) the train of Dionysos is made up of wild creatures (in goat-skins) that resemble horses. This recalls the *Centaurs*, a dithyramb ascribed to Lasos.

The choruses of the Attic period were composed of men or of boys, and received the name *cyclic*[1] from the fact that their dances were performed in a measured circle about the altar of Dionysos in a round orchestra. A division into two semi-choruses of twenty-four each, with a leader for each, would seem to have been made at times; but the evidence is lacking on this point.

Each of the ten tribes of Attica provided a choregos and a chorus of fifty for the Greater Dionysia, at which there were two contests, that between the five choruses of boys preceding that between the choruses of men. In the fifth century each of the ten choruses was allotted a poet, whose work had been admitted by the archon for presentation. When Athens became democratic, the guilds of singers that had been employed by the aristocrats, such as the Peisistratidai, were displaced (for the first time in 508) by the civic choruses, which thus bore their part in rendering the state a service, as did the rich choregos, who fulfilled his larger obligations by furnishing the splendid equipments and defraying the expense of the performance.[2] But as the demand on the technical skill of the performers increased with the growing intricacy of the musical element which kept pace with the elaboration of the instruments, recourse was had by the choregi of the fourth century to professional singers, flute players (who were not Athenians), and dancers. At Athens

---

[1] Cf. Xen. *Oikon.* 8. 20 κυκλ. χορὸς . . . καὶ τὸ μέσον αὐτοῦ καλὸν καὶ καθαρόν. See Kallim. 4. 312 ff. The name *cyclic* is often regarded as denoting a circular chorus in contradistinction to the Spartan and tragic chorus, which was rectangular. Hartung maintained that *cyclic* refers to the regular alteration and repetition in appropriate order of strophe, antistrophe, and epode in the older dithyramb.

[2] Andokides, Lysias, Plato, and Demosthenes were choregi of cyclic choruses.

the control by the state of the musical festivals so enhanced the vogue of the dithyramb that it became a rival of the drama for popular applause. Under the influence of the drama it developed its native mimetic quality and in turn influenced tragedy, particularly the Euripidean form of the art. The fashion of giving titles to dithyrambs that came in after 400 is derived from tragedy. In the third century the same 'Dionysiac artists' played tragedies and comedies, as well as dithyrambs.

The Attic choregic inscriptions of the fifth century mention the successful tribe or tribes, the composition of the chorus (*ἀνδρῶν, παίδων*), the choregos of the victorious tribe, and the name of the poet, who was the chorus-master.[1] In the fourth century the name of the flutist and of the archon is added, and from about 300 the name of the flute player takes precedence over that of the poet. In this period the success of a piece became entirely dependent upon the flutist, and the choregi vied with each other to obtain the best. In the time of Demosthenes the old dithyrambs were often represented either with the old or with new music (*διασκευαί*); in either case the function of the didaskalos had lost its pre-eminence,[2] and though the name was retained, he sank to the position of assistant to the choregos.[3] Some

---

[1] *διδάσκαλος, χοροδιδάσκαλος, κυκλιοδιδάσκαλος.*

[2] The statement in Plut. *de mus.* 30 that the poet was paid by the flutist after the time of Melanippides would seem to hold true only in exceptional cases in the fifth century. The older poets protested against the growing importance of the flute, for which they were themselves responsible. Cf. Melan. ii. Melan. introduced a kithara with twelve strings.

[3] The difference of the several periods may be illustrated as follows. (1) Fifth century: *Οἰνηΐς ἐνίκα παίδων, Εὐμένης Μελετεῶνος ἐχορήγει, Νικόστρατος ἐδίδασκε* (*C. I. A.* 1. 336). (2) 365/4 B.C.: *Αἴσιος Μνησιβούλου Σφήττιος χορηγῶν ἐνίκα Ἀκαμαντίδι Πανδιονίδι παίδων, Εὐκλῆς ἐδίδασκε, Εὐδαμίσκος ηὔλει, Χίων*

of the most famous auletes of the time—Pronomos, Antigenidas, Timotheos (not the poet), Kraton—were willing to furnish the accompaniment for cyclic choruses.

The dithyramb was usually presented in the spring when Dionysos had awakened from his sleep during the winter months. At Delphi, however, according to Plutarch,[1] the dithyramb was sung for three months from the beginning of winter, while the paian was heard for the rest of the year; and some scholars [2] have expended much ingenuity in seeking to discover traces of a winter dithyramb of a lugubrious character in contrast to the joyous song of the springtime. Of this former species there exist, however, no well marked remains; nor is there any satisfactory evidence of a 'tragic' dithyramb or of 'tragic dramas' or 'lyric dramas' as forms of the dithyramb.[3]

In Attica dithyrambs were performed at the festival of the Greater or City Dionysia that was instituted by Peisistratos (at the full moon of Elaphebolion, March 28—April 2), and were here given before the tragedies and comedies; at the Lesser Dionysia (Dec. 19-22); at the Greater Panathenaia (Aug. 13) from 446 on; at the Thargelia founded by Peisistratos (May 25); and at the Lenaia (Jan. 28-31) towards the end of the fourth century.[4] The chief festivals

---

ἦρχεν (Dittenb. *Syll.* 411). (3) 335/4 B.C.: Λυσικράτης Λυσιθείδου Κικυννεὺς ἐχορήγει, Ἀκαμαντὶς παίδων ἐνίκα, Θέων ηὔλει, Λυσιάδης Ἀθηναῖος ἐδίδασκε, Εὐαίνετος ἦρχε (*l.l.* 415). The koryphaios often took the place of the didaskalos. Lucian *de salt.* speaks of κυκλικοὶ αὐληταί, not of the poet.

[1] *De E Delph.* § 9 C.

[2] Especially Schmidt *Diatr.* 205 ff., who thought that the hibernal dithyramb was produced at the Lenaia; Lübbert *de Pind. carm. dramaticis tragicisque.*

[3] See the Introduction to Pindar.

[4] Performances of dithyrambs at the Hephaisteia and Prometheia are not proved.

in question were the Greater Dionysia and the Thargelia, and at both the dithyramb was rendered in the same way, though at the latter celebration the setting was less splendid.[1] The performances were given in the market-place, the Dionysiac theatre, and the Odeion (finished shortly before 444), in a measure the opera house of Athens; for here the musical contests took place during the Panathenaia. To the victor in the older period an ox[2] was given, to the second best an amphora, to the third a goat. In the fifth century and later the usual prize was a tripod.[3] Every city of note had its musical contests, and the great festivals were in effect 'historical concerts' since they embraced the presentation, not only of dithyrambs, but also of rhapsodies, hymns, tragedies and comedies.

Prior to the fifth century the dithyramb seems to have been composed in triads. A momentous change in its structure was effected (in all probability) by Melanippides, who cast off the shackles of the arrangement of the older style and made the rhythms absolutely free (ἀπολελυμένα). The repetition of the same melody seemed to savour of rigidity, of monotony,

---

[1] It is uncertain whether two tribes had only one choregos at the Thargelia. Each tribe had its own choregos at the Dionysia.

[2] Hence βοηλάτας διθύραμβος Pind. *Ol.* 13. 25.

[3] The tripods won by the successful tribes were publicly dedicated by the choregi. Those gained at the Greater Dionysia were deposited in the sanctuary of Dionysos, while the Pythion was the receptacle for the prizes gained at the Thargelia. It is from the inscriptions on these tripods that we get our chief knowledge of the victories of the cyclic choruses at Athens. In the case of scenic representations (tragedies and comedies) the state kept an official record, but the names of the poets and musicians were not inscribed in the public and official records of the dithyrambic contests. The institution of the choregia was succeeded by that of the agonothetai at the end of the fourth century.

and it was contrary to nature. In place of the fixed grouping of the older dithyramb, *ἀναβολαί*[1] were now employed. These were musical preludes,[2] which were performed during the intermission of the singing; and by them the different divisions of the piece were marked off as effectively as by the recurrence of the melody in the older style. The innovation of Melanippides, which was not adopted at once (Bacchylides still retained the older structure), ultimately led to the complete supremacy of the musical accompaniment over the text, a supremacy already menaced in the time of Pratinas. The deterioration of the poetic quality of the dithyramb is due in large measure to the fact that, since many of the older forms of melic, such as the prosodion, partheneion and hyporcheme, were no longer written, and the other kinds, such as the hymn, paian and enkomion, were supplanted in popularity, all poetical genius of the highest order was called into requisition by the drama. During the fifth century the poet composed his own texts, but he gradually became more and more a musician. With the abandonment of the strophical structure, the melodies forsook their ancient simplicity and severity and became highly complicated and difficult because of their frequent trills and runs.[3] From the time of Philoxenos the choral songs were varied by the introduction of monodies, which were *bravura* airs that no chorus could render with success. The mimetic element also increased in importance. The Middle Dithyramb is practically a species of melodrama or operetta.

One flutist, occasionally more, rendered the 'preludes' and accompanied the singing throughout, and

---

[1] Cf. Arist. *Probl.* 19. 15, *Rhet.* 3. 9.

[2] Others regard the *ἀναβολαί* as (1) changes in the melody, or (2) long, loosely-jointed monodies.

[3] *μυρμηκιαί.* The *συβαρισμὸς αὐλητῶν* is also castigated.

sometimes, especially in the fourth century, when the dance was tumultuous, the lyre supported the flute.[1] The mode best suited to the flute was the Phrygian or the milder Hypophrygian (the relaxed Ionian), the passionate and vehement character of which gave expression to the orgiastic frenzy of the Bacchic style. Of Philoxenos the story is told that he attempted to compose a dithyramb in the solemn Dorian[2] mode but unconsciously fell back into the Phrygian. Dionysios of Halikarnassos (*de comp. verb.* 19) says that in the New Dithyramb all bounds were overstepped. It "combined all moods, inventing one," like Browning's Cleon: the Dorian, Phrygian, and Lydian were used in the same song, the chromatic, enharmonic and diatonic genera were shifted, and great licence taken with the *tempo.* Colorature was a common feature: Philoxenos' *Kyklops* represented the bleating of Polyphemos' flock. The singing of the chorus was in unison, in Aristotles' time probably an octave higher than the accompaniment.

As regards the rhythms employed, it is noteworthy that, in the first mention of the dithyramb, Archilochos uses the trochaic tetrameter, the measure which was adopted in the dialogue parts of the earliest tragedy. The use of hexameters before Archilochos can scarcely be inferred from the character of the *Hymn to Dionysos*, but this measure was

---

[1] On the flute (κύκλιοι αὐλοί) see Pind. iv. 20, [Sim.] 148. In the Alexandrian age kitharoedes, such as Nikokles, were dithyrambists, but it is singular that Arion was a kitharoede. The personified Dithyramb holds a kithara (*Alte Denkm.* 3. 130).

[2] Lamprokles may have used this mode: at least Dion. Halik. says the older dithyramb was well-ordered (τεταγμένος). When Arist. *Pol.* 8. 7 says that the Dorian mode was not compatible with the ethos of the dithyramb, he is referring to contemporary style.

certainly employed by Praxilla and Lamproklcs (cf. Aristoph. *Nubes* 967). Of Arion's metre we know nothing. Dactylo-epitrites were occasionally used by Pindar and other poets, but the accentuated dithyrambic style demanded measures full of excitement, with concurrent ictuses (cretics, bacchics, choriambics) and frequent resolutions and syncopations. In the old, middle and new periods the freedom of shifting rhythms was a marked feature.

Of the dithyramb prior to his time Pindar (Frag. 79) says that it was long-drawn (σχοινοτένεια) and full of the sound of *san*, the Doric sibilant corresponding to the Ionic *sigma*. Lasos, his older contemporary, had affected an entire avoidance of the sibilant, a rough sound[1] which may have suited the rude goat-chorus of the archaic period. Pindar's own dithyrambs are full of manly vigour and free from the artificiality of Lasos which he castigates. They partake, however, of the boldness germane to the dithyrambic mood:

seu per audaces nova dithyrambos
verba devolvit numerisque fertur
lege solutis (Hor. 4. 2. 10).

These 'new words' are the compounds,[2] which were employed with even greater freedom by the successors of Pindar, who luxuriated in a jungle of

---

[1] Aristoxenos (Athen. 11. 467 A) held that both *san* and *sigma* were cacophonous in singing and out of harmony with the music of the flute. *San* may have differed from *sigma* as Eng. *sh* from *s*, or as Germ. *sch* from *s*.

[2] χρησιμωτάτη ἡ διπλῆ λέξις διθυραμβοποιοῖς Arist. *Rhet.* 3. 3. 3. These διπλ. λέξεις were used first by Antheas of Lindos (ὃς πάντα τὸν βίον ἐδιονυσίαζεν). He was a contemporary of Kleobulos of Lindos, one of the Seven Sages. The statement in Proklos that 'simple words' were used in the dithyramb belongs in the description of the nome and has been misplaced. As examples of these words "full of sound and fury," Demetr. *de eloc.* 91 gives θεοτεράτους πλάνας, ἄστρων δορύπορον στρατόν.

ornamental epithets and colour effects. Our knowledge of the New Dithyramb, which was largely the creation of poets not of Attic stock, is derived in the main from the vituperative criticism of its opponents. The diction was turgid, a mere parade of words; abandoned to a fury for innovation, and given over to every licence of metaphor. The periods were disjointed (the λέξις εἰρομένη) and polymetochic: the heaping of participles added pomp and rapidity. The impetuosity of the thought was unimpeded, and the sudden transitions were effected by the rush and swirl of the song. Against the turbulence and protervity of the dithyramb, the adherents of the reactionary old school, the comic poets,[1] Plato,[2] who is himself reported to have composed dithyrambs, and Aristoxenos,[3] the master of musical theory, protested, but in vain. The very condition of the continued existence of melic in the Attic period was the accentuation of the musical element; and the loss of almost all the enormous mass of dithyrambic poetry is due not merely to the fact that it was not worth preserving as poetry, but also to the fact that the scores were not handed down. The dithyramb was meretricious art and appealed to the taste of the groundlings, but it was sovereign. It virtually displaced all other forms of melic except the nome, which it corrupted, as it had corrupted the paian; and when the splendour of the drama suffered eclipse, the dithyramb, the sister of tragedy,

---

[1] Comp. *e.g.* Pherekrates 145, Aristoph. *Nubes* 333, 970, *Pax* 830, *Aves* 1385, Anaxand. 6. 41, 22, Theopomp. 3, Antiph. 112, 207. The contrary note is rare (Antiph. 209).

[2] *Laws* 700 D: (ποιηταὶ) βακχεύοντες καὶ μᾶλλον τοῦ δέοντος κατεχόμενοι ὑφ' ἡδονῆς, κεραννύντες δὲ θρήνους τε ὕμνοις καὶ παιῶνας διθυράμβοις. On the other side, cf. Arist. *Metaph.* 10. 3. The dithyramb found a defender in Xenophon.

[3] In Plut. *de mus.* 31.

remained supreme. Both Plato[1] and Aristotle[2] were forced to use "dithyrambic" as a generic term for "lyric" in contrast to epic and dramatic poetry. When the dithyramb died, Greek melic was paralysed. A return to the unartificial lyric of the classical age was no longer possible.

NOME.

The oldest certain[3] example of *νόμος* used with reference to song and music occurs in Alkm. xxv.: *οἶδα δ' ὀρνίχων νόμως παντῶν.* By the time of Pindar this usage is extended and developed.[4] So far as we can trace back the history of the term in its earliest signification, *νόμος* means 'air,' 'tune,' 'strain,' without connoting the presence of words; and the earliest nomes were probably simple melodies for the lyre or

---

[1] *Apol.* 22 B, *Rep.* 394 C. In the latter passage Plato says that the dithyramb furnishes the most abundant examples of the 'simple recital of the poet in his own person' in contrast to epic and the imitative drama. While there may have been a good deal of narrative in the choral songs, it cannot be disputed that the dithyramb, at least in the time of Philoxenos and Timotheos, was highly mimetic; as indeed is expressly attested by Arist. *Probl.* 19. 15. Costumes were used appropriate to the situation and the actors even rode on horseback. The *Kyklops* of Philoxenos was called a 'drama.' It is an error to assume that Plato deduced his theory of the mimetic character of all poetry from the dithyramb.

[2] *Poet.* § 1.

[3] The genuineness of *νόμος ᾠδῆς* *Hymn* 1. 20, usually emended to *νόμοι ἀοιδῆς*, is suspected. If an interpolation, it is very old. Some scholars venture to find here a distinct reference to the nome and to regard this *Hymn* as the model followed by Terpander in his arrangement of the parts of the kitharoedic nome. The change to *νομοί* (cf. Υ 249, Hes. *W. D.* 403) is not called for.

[4] Cf. *Ol.* 1. 101 *ἱππείῳ νόμῳ*, *Nem.* 5. 25, *Pyth.* 12. 23, Frag. 178, Telest. iii.

flute. While it is impossible to divorce νόμος in this meaning from νόμος 'custom,' 'law,'[1] it is uncertain whether the musical term is merely a specialized meaning of the latter signification—with which we might compare τρόπος, οἴμη, Germ. *Weise*, Eng. and French *air*—or whether it reverts directly to the root that underlies νόμος 'law,' *i.e.* as νόμος 'law' is that which is apportioned (νέμεται) to each man according to his station, so the nome is distributed into several distinct parts.[2] Before the time of Terpander, the first of the kitharoedic poets concerning whom we have relatively accurate knowledge, the nome was marked off into divisions:[3] so that it is probably the quasi-legal character of its form and the rigour of its construction that gave rise to the peculiar name. Nome and law alike were distinguished by a prescribed and well defined character.[4] The adoption of

---

[1] This use is at least as old as Hesiod. In the dispute on the etymology of εὐνομίη ρ 487, Aristarchos pronounced in favour of the derivation from εὖ νέμεσθαι on the ground that νόμος was unknown to Homer.

[2] Cf. Pollux 4. 66 μέρη νόμου . . . κατανείμαντος (of Terpander).

[3] These are thought to have been four in number—ἀρχά, μεταρχά, ὀμφαλός, σφραγίς. There is evidence of a three-fold arrangement which, whatever the technical names, resolves itself into prologue (invocation), middle (myth), and epilogue (prayer and farewell). Philammon is mentioned as a predecessor of Terpander.

[4] Suidas says νόμος . . . ἁρμονίαν ἔχων τακτὴν (that is, the mode did not shift) καὶ ῥυθμὸν ὡρισμένον, and Plutarch states that the nome received its name because the artist had to preserve τὴν οἰκείαν τάσιν. The main point of the latter remark is clear, whatever τάσις may denote. Monro *Music* p. 26 takes it to mean 'key.' But Plut. implies that all the *ancient* nomes were characterized by the same τάσις, and it is unlikely that all the old nomes were sung to the same key. Perhaps he uses the word with reference to the later elaboration of the lyre and the increase in the number of its tones. The irregular character of the nomes of the classical period may have been the cause of the emphasis laid by the ancients on the connection with νόμος 'law.'

the word νόμος to designate melody or song would have been appropriate only at a time when musical regularity was exceptional, that is, in the period anterior to the fully developed artistic lyric.

Apart from the specific application of the term to designate a concrete instrumental or vocal melody, nome was also used in a generic sense of the normal, classic form of music.

So Plato *Laws* 700 B. Plato's attention was naturally attracted to the nome in the Νόμοι (cf. 722 D, 799 E), where he touches upon the coincidence of the expressions, though his remarks help little in explaining the points of contact. Aristotle (*Probl.* 19. 28) mentions the fanciful theory that νόμος was transferred to the first nomian poem because in the early period, before a knowledge of letters, the laws were sung. The moderns propound various explanations from the connection of 'nome' with 'law.' Westphal held that it was the stable quality of its language in contrast to that of ordinary speech; Croiset refers the designation to the fact that the nome had an appointed place in the ritual; Bernhardy and Volkman found the point of contact in the contents of the nome: in his invocation to the gods the poet gave expression only to those sentiments that were rooted in the moral consciousness and hallowed by the unwritten traditions of the people—sentiments that might thus claim for themselves a normal value as authoritative as the enactments of the lawgiver.

Nomes are of four kinds and may be divided into two classes, both of which were agonistic:

1. The purely instrumental type: the kitharistic and the auletic nome.

The kitharistic nome was never very popular. It came into vogue after the kitharoedic and probably after the auletic; and was given a place in the Delphic festival only in the eighth Pythiad. At the Panathenaia it was subordinate to the kitharoedic and there were only three prizes, while there were five for the kitharoedes. A famous kitharist was Stratonikos, who lived in the early part of the fourth century.

Olympos, the mythical representative of all ancient music, is reported to have been the author of the auletic nome and the composer of melodies that moved the enthusiastic admiration of Plato. The auletic contest at Delphi dates from the first Pythiad, in which Sakadas was victor. The most celebrated auletic nomes were the *Polykephalos* and the *Pythian*; others were the *Harmateios*, *Epikedeios*.

2. The nomes provided with words: the kitharoedic and the aulodic nome.

The kitharoedic nome was in high vogue from the earliest to the latest times. Its first appearance in literature is connected with the name of Terpander, whose supremacy lasted for two centuries. His nomes appear to have been of two kinds: (1) those that contained a melic prooimion, followed by a portion of Homer, and ending in a melic epilogue, (2) those of which all the parts were composed by the melic poet himself. The names of the latter have been preserved and are given in the introduction to the fragments of Terpander. Next in order to Terpander is Arion, who is called a kitharoede. The scene in which he attires himself in all his splendour, holding in his hand the instrument of the god, before he plunges from the pirates' ship, recalls the public appearance of the kitharoedes at the musical contests as it is depicted in the later works of art. The kitharoedic agon at Athens is attested many years before its inauguration by Perikles at the Panathenaia, where the victor received a golden crown. Kitharoedes contended at the Spartan Karneia, the Delphic Pythia, at the Nemea, Isthmia, etc. 'Pythian' kitharoedic nomes were common.

The aulodic nome, which was inspired by the triumphs of Terpander, required the services of two persons, the singer and the flute player (often called the Pythian aulete because of the celebrity of the

Pythian nome), whose role was inferior to that of the poet singer. As in the auletic nome, the double flute was used. The invention of the aulodic nome is generally attributed to Klonas of Tegea, who lived shortly after the time of Terpander. Ardalos of Troizen, a predecessor of Klonas, is also credited with the invention. Early in the sixth century, upon the reorganization of the Pythian games, the managers of the Delphic festival admitted the aulodic nome to a place in the programme; but after a single trial, in which Echembrotos was victor, it was excluded on the ground that its lugubrious character was ill suited to the joyous festival of Apollo (cf. Stes. xii.). Plutarch says the best nomes of this class were Ἀπόθετος, Ἔλεγος, Κωμάρχιος, Σχοινίων, Κηπίων, Τενέδιος and Τριμελής. The aulodic nome reappears occasionally in later times—for example at a Panathenaic contest in the first part of the fourth century (*C. I. A.* 2. 2. 965), and in Boiotia as late as Sulla; but it was completely overshadowed by the popularity of the kitharoedic and auletic forms. κιθαρῳδός is in fact often the equivalent of 'nomic poet.'

In the early period the nome was sung by a single[1]

---

[1] The choral character of the nome before Timotheos is controverted. The text of Proklos 244 says that in the archaic period, while the chorus was singing the nome, Chrysothemis the Cretan stood up and sang the nome alone; and from his time on the song remained an agonistic monody. The passage has been interpreted in the light of the statement (l.l. 245) that the nome was an off-shoot of the paian, and that it was the latter that the chorus was singing on the occasion of Chrysothemis' innovation. Sakadas, in the early part of the sixth century, is said to have trained a chorus to sing his τριμερὴς νόμος, which was divided into three strophes, each of which was composed in a different mode (Plut. *mus.* 8). Hiller *R. M.* 31. 76 thought S. merely adapted the 'three-part' aulodic nome of Klonas to choral delivery. Reimann defends the existence of a choral nome against Guhrauer, Walther, and

artist, who was both poet and composer. Often he was the priest as in Vedic times. The instrument was generally the kithara, but Terpander is said to have provided the kitharoedic nome with a flute accompaniment (*αὐλοὶ κιθαριστήριοι*), which may have had a special function in connection with the ritual; but the use of both instruments does not represent the beginnings of a polyphonic instrumental accompaniment. The early nome appears to have been one continuous poem, and the music accompanied the words from beginning to end. As there was no dance, there was no division into strophes and antistrophes: the division into parts was a compensation for the absence of the antistrophic arrangement. Various musical modes were used: Dorian, Phrygian, Ionian, Aiolian, and Lydian. The last was usual in the later period.

From Terpander to the beginning of the fifth century the chief rhythm was the dactylic hexameter, which was best suited to the accompaniment of the kithara; but the solemn 'greater spondees,' orthian iambics, and semanto-trochees (cf. on Terp. i.) were also used. The orthian nome was pitched high; cf. Aisch. *Agam.* 1153. (Galen reports that a nomic singer once burst a blood-vessel.) The aulodic nome was usually composed in elegiac distiches, but may also have contained prosodiacs. The transition from one melody or rhythm to another within the separate parts was forbidden, but the metres may have varied with the parts. This is controverted, but at least we may argue from an auletic nome of Olympos in which a trochaic followed on a paionic movement

---

others, adducing as evidence *e.g.* the *Κωμάρχιος* nome of Klonas, Aisch. *Choeph.* 822, Plato *Laws* 700 D. Cf. Dippe *Wochenschr. f. kl. Phil.* 1888, 1018 ff. At any rate the choral nome was exceptional until the time of Timotheos. The agonistic nome was essentially monodic (cf. Arist. *Probl.* 19. 15).

that some variation was permitted in the vocal nome. The nomes of Terpander may have begun with the long-drawn 'greater spondees,' orthian iambics or semanto-trochees, which were followed by the hexameter in the central part where the myth was narrated in detail. In the 'three-part' auletic nome of Sakadas the Dorian mode was used in the beginning, then the Phrygian, and the conclusion was made with the Lydian. The early nome was solemn and stately, adapted to calm the mood of the worshipper. In its noble simplicity and dignity it resembled our old sacred music. The *tempo* was slow. The diametrical opposite of the nome was the enthusiastic dithyramb, at least in the early period. In some particulars the nome resembled the paian, of which, according to some ancient writers, it was a development.

Before the time of Terpander the nome was simple in structure though the parts were clearly marked. Terpander enriched its architectonic by adding three parts, so that a musical theme was carried through the entire seven divisions in a systematic form.

The parts of the Terpandreian nome are thus given by Pollux 4. 66: 1. ἀρχά, 2. μεταρχά, 3. κατατροπά, 4. μετακατατροπά, 5. ὀμφαλός, 6. σφραγίς, 7. ἐπίλογος. Terpander is thought to have added 2, 4, and 7. Bergk did not succeed in excusing the apparent irregularity in the position of the ὀμφαλός on the ground that the movement of all good poetry is more rapid as the end draws near. Other scholars would change the order, so as to bring the ὀμφαλός in the middle (Westphal, Lübbert, Christ). It is more likely that the 'beginning' and the 'after-beginning,' the 'transition' and the 'after-transition' formed only two groups (Crusius). This would give us five main parts, as in the Pythian (auletic) nome of Sakadas. Each part corresponded in some way to a ceremony connected with the cult. Westphal's rearrangement (προοίμιον, ἀρχά, κατατροπά, ὀμφαλός, μετακατατροπά, σφραγίς, ἐξόδιον) is too radical. The use of Doric forms in the names evidences a high antiquity; as does the designation ὀμφαλός, which was certainly derived from the cult of Apollo at Delphi (ὀμφ. ἐριβρόμου χθονός). The 'navel' was epic in tone and contained the main theme. A favourite subject of the myth in the Apolline nomes was the Slaying of the Dragon, the battle of light with darkness that was to be waged by Siegfried and is found in the legends of all Indo-European peoples. The famous auletic nome of Sakadas dealt with the same subject and treated of Apollo's search for the dragon, the challenge to combat, the death-agony, the prayer after the victory, etc. Other kitharoedic nomes told of the deeds of other gods and of heroes. The epilogue, whose presence shows that there was no antistrophic arrangement, may have contained the χαῖρε ἄναξ of the singer. The 'seal,' another quaint and archaic name, is supposed to have contained either a gnome that compressed the substance of the myth into a wise reflection (Bergk), or various matters that were more or less personal (Crusius), or a prayer (v. Jan), as in the σφραγίς of the church language of Modern Greece. It may have been sung in an elevated pitch.

According to Westphal *Proleg. zu Aeschylos* 69 the Terpandreian form of composition was the τεθμός followed by Pindar in his epinikia. An examination of this mooted question does not concern us here, but it may be noted that, beyond all doubt, Pindar did not adhere strictly to this scheme either in his less ornate or in his greatest odes, *e.g. Ol.* 2, *Pyth.* 1, 2. It is very rare that the divisions, when they do exist, agree with the strophic arrangement (*Ol.* 13). It is not imperative that Pindar should have adopted all the seven divisions —all the seven parts of the parabasis of comedy are rarely found—, but clear-cut introductory formulas or transitions do not occur with sufficient regularity or frequency to persuade most scholars of the dependence of Pindar upon Terpander.

A seven-fold division of Bacch. ii. is not imperative. From the rest of the melic poets we derive no information on the subject. The seven strophes of Sappho's passionate ode to Aphrodite have actually been regarded as a ἑπτάλογχος στόλος. Not only Pindar and Sappho, if we are to listen to the critics, but also the *Homeric Hymn* to Apollo (not to speak of the dirge in the last book of the *Iliad*), Solon 13, Theognis, Aischylos (whose dramas are reported to have been influenced by the nomic form) in the *Persai* 65 ff., 633, 852, and, with prelude and postlude, 922. Later on, Theokritos 16, 17, 22, 26, Kallimachos 2, 5, 7, Catullus 64, 68 B, Tibullus 2, 5, Propertius 5, 6. Apart from the correctness of the theory that the Terpandreian norm influenced the construction of Alexandrian literature, it is quite probable that the *Hymn to Demeter* by Kallimachos has preserved the best example of the character of the ancient kitharoedic nome. Alexandrian literature returned with partiality to the pre-Attic type. Aisch. *Agam.* 1072 ff. has been regarded as an example of the spirit of the old nome.

The great choral poets of the sixth century did not cultivate the nome, which in consequence suffered a temporary decline. Choral poetry was the fashion in the Dorian school, and the extraordinary popularity of the Pythian (auletic) nome militated against the old-time vogue of the kitharoedic form. Besides, Pindar and Simonides were not musical virtuosos. The nome was the only form of vocal solo adopted in the musical festivals of the fifth century, and its revival followed as a result of the inauguration of a new style of music. The price of its renewed life was the transformation of its ancient simplicity.

This transformation was the work of Phrynis, who flourished in the early part of the fifth century. Adopting some of the musical innovations of Lasos, Phrynis mixed the modes, and employed the freer lyric forms in conjunction with the hexameter. His innovation was the result of the substitution of a kithara with nine strings for the traditional heptachord. Provided thus with an instrument of greater range, Phrynis instituted coloratura singing and 'twisted and turned the voice like a top.' Phrynis' scholar, Timotheos, the detestation of the old Athens, the darling of the new, introduced his changes gradually, but under him the nome received the classic form that it maintained until the Empire. Though he still used the hexameter, he also employed the freer metres (*τὰ ἀπολελυμένα*), but the most radical change of all was that he made the nome choral (*νόμος ἄνομος*).[1] We may indeed suppose that the solo remained an integral part, as the nome was the main form of solo concert; in fact we hear that

[1] This is disputed: Guhrauer 326.

the celebrated kitharoede Pylades sang alone during the entrance of the Persians in the *Persai* of Timotheos. The new nome was in many respects akin to an oratorio. The antistrophic form was not adopted, since it was unable to give the flexibility that was regarded as imperative. Nome and dithyramb now grew more and more alike in language and tone. Transition (μεταβολή) from one mode to another was frequent. 'Outraging music with his twelve strings,' Timotheos painted a storm at sea, infused dramatic life, and endowed the kitharoedic nome with the passion that was native to the orgiastic flute. The virtues of κιθαρῳδία and αὐλῳδία were now confused (Plato *Laws* 700 D). Eur. *Or.* 1369 ff. is an example of the tone of the later nome. The music was soft, sweet, and tender. It was pathos rather than ethos that was depicted. While the nome approached the dithyramb in temper, the νομικὸς τρόπος was not completely surrendered. Its style remained less excited; different musical instruments were employed, and the nome may have retained more of the epic quality.

The subjects of nomic poetry were the majesty and benevolence of the gods and prayers for the prosperity of the worshippers. Of the gods Apollo stands in the forefront (cf. Pind. *Nem.* 5. 24 φόρμιγγ' Ἀπόλλων ἑπτάγλωσσον χρυσέῳ πλάκτρῳ διώκων ἁγεῖτο παντοίων νόμων), and it was in conjunction with the worship of Apollo that the nome was developed. We hear, however, of nomes in honour of Zeus, Athene, Ares, and the Dioskuroi. Like the other forms of lyric it was gradually secularized, as, for example, in the *Persai* of Timotheos; and parodies were composed by Telenikos and Argas.

Of the extent of the nome we are not accurately informed; those of Timotheos would seem on an average to have been slightly shorter than the shortest books of the *Iliad* or *Odyssey.* Timotheos attained immense popularity, and his successor Kleon 'won more crowns than any other mortal.' But after their time the purely instrumental auletic form was preferred.

ADONIDIA.

Adonis-songs were sung by women, whose grief at the death of Adonis symbolized the transitoriness of the loveliness of nature. Primarily they were an importation, by way of Kypros, from Phoinikia (*adonai* 'lord'; cf. Jerem. 22. 18 "They shall not lament for him, saying, Ah lord! or Ah his glory!"). In Syria and Phoinikia they appear as songs of lament to the music of the flute. The Ἀδωνίδια were celebrated in midsummer at Athens, where there was a special festival for women, at Sikyon, at Alexandria, Byblos, Antioch, and many other places till a late period. At Athens, Adonis was represented by the figure of a wooden doll, which the women laid out for interment on the roofs of the houses. The celebration moved the scorn of the comic poets (Kratin. 15, of the poet Gnesippos: ὃν οὐκ ἂν ἠξίουν ἐγὼ | ἐμοὶ διδάσκειν οὐδ' ἂν εἰς Ἀδώνια). The Ἀδωνιάζουσαι of Theokritos (idyl 15) depicts the rejoicing of the women at Adonis' return from Acheron, after his sojourn there for a year, and his reunion with Aphrodite, and alludes to their sorrow at his enforced departure. The Adonis-lays of the people have been completely lost, since at an early period the poets treated the same theme: Sa. xxiii., ὦ τὸν Ἄδωνιν Frag. 63, 108 (whence the Adonic verse), the *Adonis* of Praxilla, which was perhaps the source of the famous ἐπιτάφιος Ἀδώνιδος of Bion, which was intended for the second day of the Adonis festival at Alexandria under Ptolemy Philadelphos. Cf. Aristoph. *Lysistr.* 393, 396. The bucolic poets were especially fond of the legend.

IOBACCHOS.

The iobacchoi, which take their name from the initial exclamation[1] ἰὸ Βάκχε,[2] were originally sung at the sacrifices and festivals of the god Dionysos (ἰοβάκχεια). Though they were different from the dithyramb, of their contents we know little, since only a few isolated lines have been preserved. Proklos says that they were 'soaked in the insolence of Dionysos.' Their introduction into literature seems to have been due to Archilochos, who may have been influenced by Thrakian folk-songs. The metrical form was a syncopated (asynartetic) iambic tetrameter (or iamb. dim. acatal. + troch. dim. catal.): Δήμητρος ἁγνῆς καὶ κόρης τὴν πανήγυριν σέβων (Archil. 120). The trochee, we are told, was first used in the festivals of Dionysos and Demeter. The iobacchic measure appears in Eupol. 356, Mel. Adesp. 51, and in Aristoph. *Aves* 1755, which Westphal regards as an example of the joyous tone of the thiasos. Pindar is reported to have composed βακχικά, which are not to be regarded as iobacchoi.[3]

HYPORCHEME.

The name ὑπόρχημα 'dance-song,' which occurs for the first time in Plato *Ion* 534 C, is not adapted to distinguish the hyporcheme from the other forms of choral melic that were accompanied by orchestic evolution. The structure of the word, however, indicates that there was a closer engagement between the

[1] See Bentley on Hor. *Sat.* 1. 3. 7 *Io Bacche.*

[2] ἰό varies with ἰώ as ἰέ with ἰή.

[3] Lübbert *de Pind. carm. dram. trag.* 13 thought the βακχικά were songs for Dionysiac πομπαί. Probably the name is a late interpolation.

dance and the theme than was usual in other choral songs.[1] Though our knowledge of ancient dancing is too fragmentary for us to distinguish accurately between the orchestic mimic that characterized the hyporcheme and that of the dithyramb, it is clear that, to the later writers at least, such as Plutarch,[2] the hyporcheme appeared to form the link connecting the sister arts of poetry and dancing. It bodied forth in words what was pourtrayed by the sympathetic rhythm and the pantomimic dance. When stress is laid upon a lively mimetic and scenic representation of the words, the text tends to become a mere accessory; and such seems to have been the character of the hyporcheme at Sparta in the earliest period. A passage in Athenaios (628 D) informs us that the name

---

[1] *ὑπό* in composition here, as often, denotes that the action in question is performed under another's influence or as an accompaniment to another action. To interpret *ὑπορχ.* simply as a dance that accompanied music ignores its distinctive quality. Strictly speaking, the hyporcheme is a dance accompanying another dance, as is described below; but in the absence of the words *ὕπᾳσμα, ὑπῳδή* it was early transferred to songs that were accompanied by the dance. Proklos 246 says *ὑπόρχημα τὸ μετ' ὀρχήσεως ᾀδόμενον μέλος ἐλέγετο· καὶ γὰρ οἱ παλαιοὶ τὴν* **ὑπό** *ἀντὶ τῆς* **μετά** *πολλάκις ἐλάμβανον.* So, quoting Archil. 123 (*ᾄδων ὑπ' αὐλητῆρος*), the schol. on Σ 492 and Aristoph. *Aves* 1426 say *ὑπό=μετά* (cf. Eur. *I. A.* 1036 ff.). So we have *ὑπαείδω*, Kallim. 4. 304, 'sing to the accompaniment' (of the dance), *ὑπ' αὐλὸν ᾄδοντες* Plut. *de aud.* 7, *αὐλήσει χρῆσθαι καὶ κιθαρίσει πλὴν ὅσον ὑπὸ ὄρχησίν τε καὶ ᾠδήν* Plato *Laws* 669 E, *ὑπὸ τὴν ᾠδὴν κρούειν*, the technical expression of instrumental accompaniment. *ὑπορχεῖσθαι* occurs first in Aisch. *Choeph.* 1025, where the metaphorical use bespeaks the antiquity of the word. Hes. *Shield* 282 has *παίζοντες ὑπ' ὀρχηθμῷ καὶ ἀοιδῇ*. Besides *ὑπό*, the foll. prepositions are used of musical accompaniment: *εἰς, ἐν, κατά, περί, πρός.*

[2] *Quaest. Symp.* 9. 15. 2 (748 B) *ὀρχηστικῇ δὲ καὶ ποιητικῇ κοινωνία πᾶσα καὶ μέθεξις ἀλλήλων ἐστί, καὶ μάλιστα μιμούμεναι περὶ τὸ ὑπορχημάτων γένος ἐνεργὸν ἀμφότεραι τὴν διὰ τῶν σχημάτων καὶ τῶν ὀνομάτων μίμησιν ἀποτελοῦσι.*

originated from the custom observed by the early poets, who arranged dances for freeborn men and made use of orchestic figures only as emblems of what was sung, 'always preserving the principles of nobleness and manliness in them.'

The hyporcheme was called Cretan (Sim. x.) because it was native to Crete, whence Thaletas introduced it into Sparta in the middle of the seventh century. Crete was the chief seat of the artistic dance, and it was there in connection with the cult of Zeus and particularly of Apollo that the graphic and vivacious hyporchematic dance was invented and practised by persons of noble birth. In part akin to the paian, which was also sacred to Apollo and from which it may not have been differentiated in the early period, the hyporchematic song gave expression to foreboding or to joy; but it was unlike that more solemn and religious chant in its rapid and fiery melodies and rhythms. The paian's province was, originally at least, the severer aspect of the cult of Apollo; whereas the hyporcheme celebrated the more joyous character of the god (ὀρχήστ' ἀγλαΐας ἀνάσσων Pind. Frag. 148). Plutarch says that by the rhythm alone he could distinguish a hyporcheme from a paian. In the paian the dance was subordinate because it was performed by the singers, more stately, and devoid of pantomime; and the singing was simpler. The musical modes of the hyporcheme were probably the Phrygian and the Dorian.

A hyporcheme is, as we have seen, both a song and a dance. To the sportive hyporchematic dance, one of the three technical divisions of melic orchestic and in a measure akin to the kordax of comedy, most of the hyporchematic poems were sung; but at times they were attended by the pyrrhic,[1] a dance of Cretan

[1] Athen. 630 E, schol. Pind. *Pyth.* 2. 127.

origin and similar to the hyporchematic but more akin to the sikinnis of the satyr play. There were at least two different modes of presentation:

1. One person played and sang, while the rest danced. This is the 'hyporchematic manner' which the ancients recognized in θ 262, where the minstrel Demodokos with the phorminx takes his position in the centre, while around him are grouped the youths δαήμονες ὀρχηθμοῖο. This form of the hyporcheme was not common in later times, though Kallim. 2 offers some analogies to it.

2. The usual form, described by Lucian *de salt.* 16 as existing in Delos in his own day, may be of high antiquity.[1] One or more musicians played, a selected number of the best dancers gave full plastic expression to the theme,[2] while the larger body, which sang, accompanied the music with a sedate orchestic movement. It is in connection with this form that ὑπόρχημα and ὑπορχεῖσθαι acquired their purely technical signification. The presence of the first body, consisting only of dancers and officiating in conjunction with the chorus, distinguishes the hyporcheme from all other forms of melic. The dance was performed about the altar during the sacrifice of the victims.

---

[1] Cf. *Hymn* 2. 10 ff. In Σ 593 ff. (a Cretan scene) one played and sang, a 'chorus' of youths and maidens danced, while in the centre there were two tumblers. In Heliod. *Eth.* 3. 2 the chorus is divided into two groups, one of which sang while the other danced. Livy 7. 2 describes the innovation of Livius Andronicus where pantomime accompanied the music. The *geranos* or crane-dance, which was instituted by Theseus in Delos on his return from Crete and still witnessed by Plutarch, may have been of the hyporchematic type. Its turnings and windings imitated the hero's escape from the mazes of the labyrinth. The dancers were arranged in files with leaders at each of the two wings.

[2] Cf. Athen. 15 D . . . ἐστὶν ἡ τοιαύτη ὄρχησις μίμησις τῶν ὑπὸ τῆς λέξεως ἑρμηνευομένων πραγμάτων, and Arist. *Poet.* 1. 6.

The chorus was composed of men or boys or women, or of both sexes. In the Homeric age the kithara was the only instrument employed, but with the advent of the second musical epoch at Sparta, which was inaugurated by Thaletas, the flute became the preferred instrument. Simonides mentions a Molossian species of flute that he seems to have adopted. In the time of Pratinas the flute arrogated to itself a prominence that threatened the position of the poet. Sometimes both flute and kithara were heard in conjunction (συναυλία). The hyporcheme is properly consecrated to Apollo, but as early as the beginning of the fifth century it was adapted by Pratinas (i.) to the expanding cult of Dionysos; Bacchylides (23) celebrated the Athena of Iton in Boiotia. That the theme was not confined to strictly religious subjects is clear from the remains of the two books of Pindar, who alludes to the unrest of the time during the Persian invasion (xii.) and to the deeds of Herakles (111). He even substitutes the hyporcheme for the epinikion or enkomion when he sings the praise of Hieron, and gives a vivid and detailed picture of the consternation at Thebes during an eclipse (x.). Pindar's hyporchemes were so famous, or his mode of presentation so novel, that he was even called the 'inventor' of the species. The fragments show some heterogeneousness of subject (105, 106) and considerable amplitude of detail (x.).

Much of the wealth of melic poetry passed over to the drama, and the hyporcheme in particular, it is currently believed, was impressed into the service of tragedy as a dramatic device for relieving the monotony resulting from the regular recurrence of the stasima, which were necessarily of a certain amplitude and accompanied by the solemn ἐμμέλεια dance. In contrast to the repose that was afforded by the stasimon, there was sometimes occasion for an expression of sudden and exuberant joy or hope, and here Sophokles is thought to have had recourse to the hyporcheme. Most of the songs in question[1] are brief and occur immediately before the catastrophe though without any presentiment of its outcome on the part of the chorus, thus vitiating by a species of dramatic irony the continuity of the plot, but relieving the intense strain of the situation. The tragic form of the hyporcheme suggests the modern ballet.

Some of the cretic odes of comedy (*e.g.* Aristoph. *Lysistr.* 1247 ff.; cf. *Thesmoph.* 953 ff., *Ekkles.* 1166 ff.) and of the lost satyr plays may have reproduced the spirit and form of the hyporcheme, which, with the development of the drama, practically ceased to exist as a separate form. Bacchylides is the last poet known to have composed a hyporcheme.

The native metre was the excited cretic with its swifter paionic forms; the fourth paion (⏑⏑⏑—) was in fact called the 'hyporchematic' or 'cretic' foot.[2] Bacchylides still uses cretics (23) and so too Simonides (x.), but the latter poet, like Pindar, preferred the light and nimble logaoedics. The

---

[1] *O. T.* 1086-1109, *Antig.* 1115-1154, *Aias* 693-718 (to Pan and Apollo), *Trach.* 205-224, 633-662. Some scholars would even add *Phil.* 507-518. *Trach.* 205 ff. recalls the paian rather than the hyporcheme. Muff (*Chor. Tech. d. Soph.* 38) thought that the second of the above described forms of presentation was adopted by tragedy. No ancient writer classes any one of these passages as a hyporcheme, though Tzetz. *Trag. Poes.* mentions the hyporchematikon as a part of tragedy. Sophokles is the only tragic poet who makes use of this form of choral; and there is no evidence from the lyric age that the hyporcheme was used in the manner outlined above.

[2] In commenting on the prose rhythms of the orator, Dion. Halik. (*de adm. vi dic. Dem.* 43) says that Demosthenes occasionally had recourse to those of the hyporchematic type, which, he adds, deserve censure equally with the Ionic and effeminate rhythms.

hyporchemes of tragedy are all entirely logaoedic, or logaoedic and trochaic, and have only strophe and antistrophe. Pindar's famous hyporcheme (x.) belongs to the free (ἀπολελυμένον) class, as does Soph. *Trach.* 205 ff. When singers and dancers have separate functions, a song that is free from antistrophic balance would not prove too difficult. The hyporcheme approached the style of the dithyramb when the latter lost its antistrophic structure; both emphasized the mimetic element; and the decline of the hyporcheme was hastened by the popularity of the dithyramb.

Thaletas, the founder of Spartan choral orchestic music, composed the first texts, and with him the hyporcheme became famous in Dorian lands. Xenodamos of Kythera and Xenokritos of Epizephyrian Lokris belonged to his school, which made a specialty of paians and hyporchemes. But the genius of the hyporcheme reached its highest excellence with Simonides, who, according to Plutarch, actually outdid himself (αὑτὸς αὑτοῦ κράτιστος) in an art in which he was conscious of his own superiority. So vivid was its imitative character that Plutarch felt himself compelled to reject Simonides' famous comparison of poetry with painting, and call the dance silent poetry, poetry a speaking dance.

ENKOMION.

The enkomion,[1] one of the latest developments of the melic art, is, in its strictest sense, the song that was sung at the revel (ἐν κώμῳ),[2] the boisterous

---

[1] ἐγκώμιον μέλος, ἐγκώμιος ὕμνος. ἐπικώμιος ὕμνος Pind. *Nem.* 8. 50.

[2] κῶμος denotes either the revel or the band of revellers which sallied forth upon the conclusion of the festivities to

termination of the banquet. Originally it may have been in honour of the giver of the banquet in celebration of some happy event.[1] The restriction as to character and place soon disappeared and the word came to denote a laudatory poem of a dignified character in honour of men, as opposed to the hymn which was consecrated to the gods.[2] As 'hymn' is used in a wider sense to embrace almost any form of melic (including the enkomion), so enkomion is in turn a generic expression, though of a narrower range, and includes also the triumphal ode, which was often sung at the komos,[3] and even the threnos or panegyric of the dead. Every komos offered an opportunity for a song of praise. The epinikion was called forth by a definite and splendid external occasion that demanded corresponding magnificence of treatment on the part of the poet, who was in a measure under bonds to the victor; the enkomion on the other hand was not invariably prompted by a like external event, and was, therefore, a rarer and more intimate expression of the poet's homage; though in most cases, we may surmise, it was not unaccompanied by a douceur. If the

---

escort a guest to his home or to serenade a mistress of one of the guests. In a loftier sense it is a company of friends who escort a victor to a temple or to the banqueting hall.

[1] Cf. Aristoph. *Nubes* 1205 ἐπ' εὐτυχίαισιν ᾀστέον μοὐγκώμιον.

[2] Cf. Plato *Rep.* 607 A ὕμνους θεοῖς καὶ ἐγκώμια τοῖς ἀγαθοῖς, a distinction that is not discredited by *Laws* 802 A. In *Symp.* 177 A enkomion is used sportively in reference to Eros, but in 'Εφ. ἀρχ. 1869, p. 347, no. 412, l. 13, we find mention of an ἐγκώμιον εἰς 'Απόλλωνα of Tamynai. This use is late and untechnical. Arrian *Anab.* 4. 3 and *Et. Gud.* 540. 42 expressly distinguish ὕμνοι εἰς τοὺς θεούς, ἔπαινοι (ἐγκώμια) εἰς ἀνθρώπους.

[3] Cf. Pind. *Ol.* 13. 29 (an ode called an enkomion by Chamaileon), 2. 47, 10. 77, *Pyth.* 10. 53, Bacch. v. 12; Aristoph. *Nubes* 1356.

enkomion differed on the one hand from the more formal and public epinikion,[1] it differed in turn from the more private skolion by the greater stateliness of its theme.

In its limited and specific application the enkomion denotes a panegyric of living personages illustrious for their station or deeds[2]—kings,[3] princes, warriors, victors at the national games, magistrates, and, in the latest times, the emperors of Rome. Its performance at a komos seems not to have been obligatory, and the tone was more solemn than in the original type of 'revel-song.'

The enkomion was the creation of Simonides, though its beginnings antedate his time. Aristotle in fact says in one passage (*Poetics* 4) that enkomia and hymns formed one part of all earlier poetry; in another (*Rhet.* 1. 9. 38), that the first enkomion was composed for Hippolochos, of whom we know nothing

---

[1] The distinction between epinikion and enkomion is not made by the poets themselves and often eludes definition; both words are in fact actually used of the same poem (the ode to Alkibiades by Euripides). We are not certain when enkomion is used in the generic sense and when it is strictly employed. See on Sim. i. Suidas calls the *Helen* of Stesichoros an enkomion, but he evidently has in mind the speeches of Gorgias and Isokrates. From Proklos' statement with regard to the epinikion—that its delivery followed closely upon the victory—we might conclude that, in his (lost) article on the enkomion, the grammarian made the latter independent in respect of the time of production. But the statement does not hold true of the epinikion. Songs that were the product of native talent were often sung in honour of a victor at his native place; cf. Pind. *Ol.* 10. 14, 11. 19, 13. 22, *Nem.* 4. 89, 7. 9, Frag. 1. 6, etc.

[2] Aristotle (*Rhet.* 1. 9. 38, *Eth.* 1. 12. 6) distinguishes *ἐγκώμιον* from *ἔπαινος*. The former deals with *τὰ ἔργα*, results of actions; the latter with the *μέγεθος ἀρετῆς*, the virtuous character of the actions in themselves. In the unphilosophical use *ἐγκώμιον* is often equated with *ἔπαινος*.

[3] Cf. Hor. 4. 2. 13 (of Pindar): *seu deos regesve canit* etc.

else, though the name points to Thessaly. Polymnastos is said to have written a laudation of Thales (Thaletas?) for the Lakedaimonians; but a distinct and separate poem in praise of a living poet as early as the first half of the seventh century is not to be credited. The use by Alkaios (Frag. 94) and Anakreon (Frag. 70) of the enkomologic metre (⏖ ⏑ ⏑ ⏖ ⏑ ⏑ ⏖ ⏓ ⏖ ⏑ ⏖ ⏓) is untrustworthy evidence of the existence of a monodic 'revel-song.' Eurylochos of Larissa, the leader in the Sacred War, after he had conquered Krissa and renewed the Pythian games, was saluted by the maidens of Delphi with a choral song that Bergk regarded as an example of the primitive enkomion.[1]

But the innovation of Simonides depends not so much on these isolated antecedents as on the gradual transformation that had come over the spirit of choral poetry. In the time of Alkman the partheneion was in part devoted to the laudation of demigods and of mortals. Stesichoros dispossessed the gods of their exclusive control of the hymn proper, and the chorals of Ibykos in praise of the beautiful youths of the court of Polykrates gave the final impetus to Simonides, who in the epinikion, as in the enkomion, produced a form of choral melic whose main purpose was the glorification of the human, though not to the abasement of the divine— a secular hymn that recognized the privilege of men who had reached the summit of human splendour or renown to share in the poetry that had heretofore been consecrated to the gods or heroes. The time was auspicious. With the passing away, in the latter part of the sixth century, of the tyrannies in central Greece and in the islands, private persons came into positions of wealth and importance that stimu-

[1] The poem is called an *ἰήϊος* by Euphorion.

lated a rivalry with the art-loving princes who had been displaced; and wherever tyrannies maintained their strength, as in Thessaly, or attained to new splendour, as in Sicily, the panegyric ode was in high favour. The increasing fame of the great games likewise focussed the attention of the entire Greek world upon men who had proved by the severity of their physical and moral training that they were entitled to claim a share of the poet's praise.

Our knowledge concerning the manner of presenting an enkomion is inadequate. The band of singers sometimes sang and danced during the banquet; or their revelry was transferred to the streets, where they paraded with torches and merry-making. The more formal enkomion was probably sung and danced by a body of trained singers during or after the banquet. Information is lacking as to the musical modes that were employed, but it is probable that the Dorian was preferred, while the Lydian may also have been adopted. The extant fragments are composed in dactylo-epitrites, which took over the enkomologikon, and in logaoedics. There is no evidence to support Crusius' contention that the enkomia of Pindar, as well as those of the Hellenistic period (Theokr. 17), followed the seven-fold division of the Terpandreian nome.

Only the poets of the universal melic are authors of enkomia. Simonides is the first to be credited with the composition of the new form of melic, but, of the poems in question, the eulogy on the heroes of Thermopylai might with better right be called a threnody, were it not the poet's intention to praise their heroism rather than bewail their death. The poem on Skopas (ii.) partakes rather of the nature of an enkomion than of a skolion. Simonides may have composed an enkomion in honour of Xenokrates of Agrigentum. From Pindar's single book we have fragment xiv. to Alexander of Makedon, nos. 118, 119 to Theron of Agrigentum; Bergk regarded xv. as belonging to this class, and Fennell does the like with the 11th *Nemean.* Diagoras eulogized Arianthes and Nikodoros, Ion wrote in praise of Skythiades; and Euripides' panegyric of Alkibiades is cited both as an enkomion and as an epinikion. Timotheos closes the list of classical writers of enkomia. In the Alexandrian age Theokritos (17) sings of Ptolemy. Late Boiotian inscriptions occasionally refer to composers of panegyrics, who regularly took part in the musical contests: thus we find an ἐγκ. εἰς Μούσας *C. I. G. S.* 1773. 13 (second century A.D.), ἐγκ. ἐπικόν, which is not identical with a rhapsody, *ib.* 416. 9, ἐγκ. λογικόν 419. 11 (ἐγκ. καταλογάδην 418. 2), all of the first century B.C. An ἐγκωμιογράφος appears at the festival of Aphrodisias *C. I. G.* 2759 (about 200 A.D.), an ἐγκωμιογράφος εἰς τὸν Αὐτοκράτορα *C. I. G. S.* 1773. 11. An ἐγκώμιον to Apollo has already been mentioned.

EPINIKION.

For the almost total wreck of the earlier forms of choral song we are indemnified by the survival of that species which the judgment of the ancients pronounced to be the best. The extant body of triumphal songs in honour of the victors at the national agonistic festivals exceeds in bulk the rest of the remains of Greek melic. The splendour of the contests and the renown that was accorded to the successful competitors inspired the epinikion; and this, the latest creation of the melic art, though of brief duration—its life scarcely compassed more than a century—, so captivated succeeding generations that it was preserved, at least in large part, as the most splendid product of the lyric age; while the more intimate expressions of the varied personal and national lyric life gradually lost their hold on the popular fancy. The epinikia of Pindar and Bacchylides owe their preservation to their intrinsic merit, though the music of the former was highly esteemed. The other forms of choral song were either too narrow in their range and too local in their cults[1] to awaken the sympathy of the Greeks of the Alexandrian age, who had ceased to cling to the traditional faith; or, as in the case of the dithyramb and the nome, whose success depended on the virtue of their music, neglect was the result of the loss of the melodies. To us, however, the epinikion is at best so distinctively Hellenic, so distinctly the emanation of a particular era and occasion, that it fails to win that spontaneous appreciation which, under the impulse of a common humanity, we accord to many other forms of Greek song.

A detailed examination of the epinikion from the point of view of its opulent style and of its complicated structure, is beyond the scope of this volume, which, in excluding Pindar, excludes the most individual type. As the commentaries on that poet and the histories of Greek literature, which contain an ampler description of the epinikion than of the other classes of melic, are easily accessible, the following account aims at presenting only the chief facts and such points of approach as will serve as an introduction to the study of Bacchylides.

THE GAMES.

The four great national games were religious festivals (ἀγῶνες ἱεροι).

---

[1] Cf. Eust. *Proleg. to Pind.* (οἱ ἐπινίκιοι) περιάγονται μάλιστα διὰ τὸ ἀνθρωπικώτεροι εἶναι καὶ ὀλιγόμυθοι καὶ μηδὲ πάνυ ἔχειν ἀσαφῶς κατά γε τὰ ἄλλα.

1. The Olympic games, in honour of Zeus, were celebrated after 776 in uninterrupted succession. Herakles was their mythical, Oxylos their prehistoric, founder. Iphitos of Elis, about a century before the first Olympiad, restored them and made them pentaeteric. The contest took place in the Altis at Elis, near the Alpheios, at the foot of the hill of Kronos, and close to the tomb of Pelops. They were held in July (or August), when the moon was full, and (after 472) lasted for five days. The contests were equestrian and gymnic, in all twelve kinds up to 408. From the seventh Olympiad on the prize was a crown of wild olive, which was adjudged by the Hellanodikai. The victor might erect a statue of himself at Olympia.

2. The Pythia, in honour of Apollo, date in their renewed form from 582 (or 586) and were held in the middle of August every four years, in the third year of each Olympiad. The contests were musical, gymnic, and equestrian; the prize, a laurel crown; the judges, the Amphiktyons. The musical contest was held at Delphi; the others, in the neighbouring plain of Krissa.

3. The Nemea, in honour of Zeus, were held in July at the time of the new moon, in the second and fourth year of each Olympiad. They are said to have been originally funeral games founded by the seven leaders of the expedition against Thebes; and were renewed in 573. In the classical period the contests were chiefly gymnic, but the race with the four-horse chariot was admitted. The prize was a crown of fresh celery; the umpires, who wore dark-coloured robes, the Kleonaians, and later the Argives.

4. The Isthmia, in honour of Poseidon, took place in April near the gates of Korinth, every second and fourth Olympiad. According to one account they were instituted to commemorate the drowning of

Melikertes, and the prize, in the earliest period, was a wreath of pine leaves. The other tradition makes Theseus, Poseidon's son, their founder. Their re-establishment in 580 gave them a national significance. The contests were gymnic and equestrian: the prize, in the classical period, a crown of dry celery; in the first century B.C., a wreath of pine. The judges were originally the chiefs of the Amphiktyonic league, later the Korinthians.

Besides these national games there were local contests in almost every canton of Greece, for many of which the poets wrote prize odes, *e.g.* the Petraia in Thessaly, the Heraia in Argos, the Pythia at Sikyon, the Iolaeia at Thebes.

FORMS OF CONTEST.

Of the three kinds of contest only those forms are mentioned below which occurred in the lyric age.[1] The dates are those of the introduction of the contests at Olympia, which set the standard for the other festivals. Each of the contests is celebrated by one or more poems of Pindar or Bacchylides. All the victors at a festival were not honoured by odes.

1. *Equestrian.*

With the four-horse chariot (ἅρματι, ἵππων τελείων δρόμῳ, τεθρίππῳ, or simply ἵπποις: 680). Racing with the mule-car (ἀπήνῃ) was introduced in 500 but abolished in 444. With the single running-horse (κέλητι: 648).

2. *Gymnic.*

1. Running.

---

[1] The following were instituted after the lyric period: with the two-horse chariot (συνωρίδι ἵππων τελείων: 408), with the four-foal chariot (πώλων ἅρματι: 384), with the two-foal chariot (264), with the single running-foal (256), boys' pankration (200).

Stadion: a race of about 200 yards (192.27 metres) at Olympia, where there was a stadion for men (776) and a stadion for boys (632).

Diaulos: twice the stadion; for men or boys (724).

Dolichos: twelve times the stadion (720).

Running in armour (ὁπλιτῶν δρόμος: 520).

2. Wrestling: for men (708), for boys (632).

3. Boxing: for men (688), for boys (616).

4. Pankration: wrestling and boxing combined (648). At the Nemea for boys also.

5. Pentathlon: leaping, running, throwing the discus, hurling the javelin, wrestling (708).

3. *Musical.*

The musical contests consisted of singing to the accompaniment either of the kithara or of the flute, and in playing the kithara or the flute. In the lyric age they were held only at Delphi. At the Nemea they were introduced in the third century B.C., and they are attested at the Isthmia in the time of Nero. At Olympia they were unknown.

Triumphal song had cheered the victor long before the increasing celebrity of the games in the first quarter of the sixth century prompted the rivalry of statuary and poet to perpetuate his fame. The 'Strain of Archilochos,' the "Conquering Hero" of the Greeks,

Τήνελλα καλλίνικε
χαῖρ' ἄναξ Ἡράκλεες,
αὐτός τε καὶ Ἰόλαος αἰχμητὰ δύο,

that was still sung in the time of the great choral poets, had celebrated the victor in the early Olympiads. But the epinikion[1] proper, the bloom of the

[1] ἐπινίκιον *scil.* μέλος, ᾆσμα. The word is first used in this sense, as a substantive, by Bacch. (2. 13). Pind. has only the adj.: ἐπινικίοισιν ἀοιδαῖς *Nem.* 4. 78; ἐπινίκιος ὕμνος Diod. 5. 29. The form ἐπίνικος is used for ἐπινίκιον in post-classical times. Pind. usually refers to his triumphal odes as ὕμνοι.

lyric age, is the creation of Simonides, whose only predecessors were the local bards who had chanted the exploits of the native athletes.[1]

The occasions for singing the song of victory were numerous. At Olympia on the evening of the day when the name of the victor was proclaimed by the herald before the throng assembled from every quarter of the Greek world, his friends led him in triumph to a temple, where he offered thanks to the gods for his happy fortune, and a revel (κῶμος) closed the day. On this occasion either the hallowed song of Archilochos was sung, or the poet, if he was present in person, improvised a brief ode.[2] But as the victor had not only won undying fame for himself but covered his native city with honour, his return home became the chief occasion of celebrating a success achieved after many months of incessant training which had resulted in that harmonious development of mind and body so prized by his countrymen. He was received with every mark of honour. Plutarch reports that a breach was made in the walls to allow his triumphal entry; at Sparta the Olympian victor might take his station next the king on the battle-field; in Solon's time he received a prize in money; his image might be stamped upon the coins of his native city; and a Roman triumph conferred no greater honour upon a consul than did the simpler ceremonies that fell to the portion of an Olympian victor. As his success had been gained at

---

[1] Timokritos and Euphanes are local poets mentioned by Pindar. Cf. *Nem.* 4. 13, 89, 6. 30. The 'epinikion' of Archilochos was properly a hymn in honour of Herakles after his contest with Augeas, and the thrice-repeated refrain τήνελλα καλλίνικε was taken over by the poet from the language of the people. From Hesychios we learn that the τετράκωμος was an 'epinikion attended by dancing in honour of Herakles.'

[2] Pind. *Ol.* 8, 11, Pyth. 6, 7, Bacch. 4 may be examples in point.

a festival sacred to the gods, so the celebration was a religious act. A joyous band accompanied him to the temple of the patron deity of the city or to that of the divinity especially worshipped by his family, and here he offered sacrifice and dedicated the crown received from the judges. On this occasion the epinikion was sung in marching; or the song was reserved for the evening banquet, when a chorus of the victor's townsmen, if they were his guests, took their places at the door of the court. Sometimes the celebration took place in a temple or in the prytaneion. The triumph of a prince was often celebrated by odes composed by different poets. At the anniversary of the victory the original ode was revived or a new one written for the occasion; and at festivals devoted to the worship of the native heroes and at family festivals the epinikion was in place. The triumphal ode was not merely a tribute to the person of the victor; it appealed to national or civic pride: if it glorified the exploits of the victor and of his family, its theme was also the gods, the heroes, the religious cult, the political and mythological traditions dear to the community. Sometimes the poet, who had also composed the music and arranged the dance, lent his presence to the celebration; sometimes he entrusted his ode to the care of a trained chorus-master: but in either case the words, though sung by a chorus, were the expression of his own personality, and the body of singers and dancers only his interpreters. The chorus was often composed of the victor's townsmen or friends who were musical amateurs and offered their services voluntarily.

Almost all the extant odes deal with victors in the equestrian or gymnic contests; only one (Pind. *Pyth.* 12) celebrates a musical triumph. The equestrian victors were princes and aristocrats, who coveted not only the popularity that justified the expense of equipping the chariots and of breeding such racers as Pherenikos, but also the assurance of present and posthumous fame that was conferred by the song of the poet. With their lordly patrons, Hieron of Syracuse, Theron of Agrigentum, Arkesilaos of Kyrene, the poets associated on terms of friendship from which servility was absent. If they usually received pay for their art—examples of odes composed out of friendship are not lacking—, their thrift did not follow upon fawning. Charges of avarice were brought against Simonides and Pindar, and the latter poet speaks with regret of the time when the muse was not to be bought with gold. But the spirit of the time condoned the departure from the ancient fashion, and it is possible that the reproach brought against the ἀργυρωθεῖσαι ἀοιδαί, as Pindar calls them, was provoked as much by the size of the douceur as by hostility to the fact that the poet did not lend his services without thought of compensation. The workman was conscious of his lofty prerogative as a poet; his end was truth, praise of the noble, condemnation of the base. Success and merit were not convertible terms. If Simonides, Pindar, and Bacchylides withdraw their gaze from the dark spots in the career of kings and princes, they did what panegyrists have done in all climes and ages. But the contrary note is not unheard—greatness begets danger and envy, earthly splendour is a thing of a day, and lordly station an opportunity for good.

The festivals at which the epinikia were sung were modelled on the religious celebrations which permitted the praise of men after the laudation of the gods. While the subject of the triumphal ode is taken from the human sphere, the scene of the victory was fraught with religious associations; the games were themselves sacred to the gods, and had been established by their sons, and victory itself was due to divine favour. The epinikion accentuates the divine no less than the human, so that an unknown poet (Melic Adesp. 85) can say of his ode ὕμνον ὧν | κλύετε· πέμπω δέ νιν | . . . | Ἀπόλλωνι μὲν θεῶν, | ἄταρ ἀνδρῶν Ἐχεκράτει κ.τ.λ.; cf. Theokr. 17. 1 ff. Pindar often seems to allude to the fact that his theme is the praise of some god and that the mention of the victor is an addition.

With a subject limited in its range by the character of the occasion that inspired it, the epinikion shows a marvellous variety in theme, in style, and in rhythm. Always the same, it is continually different; unity is created out of diversity.

The permanent elements in the longer and typical odes are three in number: 1. The personal or enkomiastic. 2. The gnomic. 3. The mythological.

From the earliest period poetry had been the vehicle of sententious wisdom. The mythological element was the fibre of the religious hymns, of the secular *Homeric Hymns*, in fact of almost all the old choral lyric. With the praise of the gods had been associated in the ancient hymns the celebration of 'the men and women of old' (*Hymn* 1. 160). The characteristic feature of the epinikion as a distinct species of melic is the grafting of the personal element, in the form it assumed in the sixth century, upon the other two.[1] The problem before the poet was to weld into an harmonious whole the new, worldly aspect of his art and the inherited religious poetry that lay at his command: to idealize, to transmute the ephemeral into the eternal.

The personal or enkomiastic portion, which is in place at the beginning and the end, is the frame in

[1] Bergk inverts the point at issue when he alludes to the question whether Simonides was the first to *insert* the myth in the epinikion.

which the poet sets his theme. It defines the particular situation and gives the realities of the ode. At the outset we learn the name of the victor and his character, his family, the triumphs won before either by himself or by his ancestors, the city that has been rendered illustrious by the exploit of its son, the scene of his dexterity, strength, and good fortune—"Olympia, the fairest place in Greece," Delphi, the seat of the voice of God. The trainer, the charioteer, the victorious horse have also their share of praise. But the glory of the victor must not be tarnished by reference to the defeat of his rivals,[1] and the suppression of undue laudation safeguards him against Nemesis. Though Simonides and Bacchylides dilate upon the scene and the character of the struggle more than Pindar, who hastens to paint the heroic prototype of the victor, nevertheless the circumstances of the victory, even in Bacchylides, rarely encroach upon the province of the myth. On the other hand Bacchylides is more sparing than Pindar in allusions to contemporary events. At times the description of victor and victory is so slight that we are tempted to believe that the ode was constructed on a stereotyped plan and that the personal part was added with only the necessary links to connect it with the myth. This is, however, far from the truth, at least in Pindar; and large as was freedom granted the the poet in the selection of a myth, each ode has its individual colouring.

The gnomic or reflective element is indeed common to every form of choral song, but it is peculiarly apposite in the triumphal ode. Its accentuation there is, historically considered, the result of the

---

[1] Simonides once (Frag. 13) violates this canon of good taste by a punning allusion to the name of a defeated antagonist; nor is the same poet free from the charge of undue glorification (iv.).

influence of the elegy; for the epinikion represents the union of the Dorian choral ode with the spirit and tone of the Ionian elegy. The gnomic element pervades the entire poem: it may appear at the outset, it traverses the main body of the ode, it is heard in the final prayer. But the poet has no systematic doctrine or theory to profess; he preaches by parenthesis. His counsel to the victor echoes the lyrical *motif* that dominates the myth. Struggle the law of success; ἀρετά not won without toil and expense; the uncertainty of the future; the limits set to human achievement; man's imperfections; the confusion of good and evil; the virtue of moderation; the penalty of the infraction of the divine law; success from God, to whom the glory must be given:—these are the echoes of the wisdom of the Prophet of Delphi that sound continually in the ears of the victor who has attained the height of human felicity and renown. The joy of the Greeks is tempered by a note of responsibility and sadness.

The myth occupies the central part of the ode. It is the main body, the anatomy of the entire poem. Few odes lack it altogether, some have two myths. The lustre of the victory is invested with an added splendour that is derived from the past glories of the race. The myth idealizes the struggle of the victor; the heroes from whom he is sprung lend their confederate sympathies to enhance the renown of his success. In the clear ether to which the song is elevated we behold only the moral intensity of the struggle, not the dust and turmoil of the palaestra. The victorious athlete, who may have been a person otherwise uninteresting enough, is apparelled with a new light when he becomes the representative of his race, of his ancestors, and of the hereditary saints of the popular faith. The freedom in the selection of a myth was almost unlimited; the whole treasure-house of the past was at the command of the poet, provided only the myth he selected had some connection, be it never so remote, with the subject of his panegyric. It might be the career of some member of the family of the victor; it might deal with the traditions of the founding of his native city by the favour of the gods. Most of the extant odes are in fact composed for victors from the colonies—Sicily, Magna Graecia, Kyrene, and Rhodes. Or again it might deal with scene of the triumph, the creation of the games, the deeds of their founders. Complete parallelism between the victor and the mythical prototype was not sought for. In Bacchylides the myth is at times almost independent of the victor. Variation too was imperative; one-fourth of Pindar's epinikia are in honour of inhabitants of the little island of Aigina, whose tutelary hero was Aias. Though the myth contains the chief beauties of the poem, it was not inserted, at least in the early stage, as a mere embellishment. Its purpose was ideal. The victor was to be encouraged by the story of heroic effort; or warned by the recital of reverses consequent upon the departure from the moral law. If the career of the victor or of a member of his line has been disfigured by sin, the poet does not hesitate to indicate his knowledge of the transgression by a salutary reference. The myth forms the objective portion of the poem; it has an epic quality, but it avoids the epic fulness by throwing into relief only those details that enhance the artistic effect.

The apprehension of the essential unity in a work like the epinikion, complicated structurally, and diverse in contents, is no light task. The theme is lyric, is musical. There are odes in which it is not difficult to grasp the ground-note; but this is often interrupted, varied, or even concealed by the numberless artifices at the disposal of the poet. Fortunately for us, perhaps, the epinikion possesses a charm that is not entirely dependent on the elucidation of the central lyric note, which in the case of Pindar has provoked the most divergent theories; a fact that should warn us of its subtle and elusive quality. Sometimes it resists logical analysis, it is an abstraction—the glory of music and song bodying forth the life of man, the imperativeness of self-restraint, the battle between right and wrong, the inevitableness of moral necessity. In Bacchylides the problem is simpler; there are few, if any, interlacing motives and the conscious effort to dominate the whole poem by a musical unity of theme is less marked than in Pindar.

Structurally the epinikion falls into three main divisions: the personal portion at the beginning, the myth in the centre, while the conclusion returns to the victor and often contains a prayer. Transitions are effected in various ways: the myth is introduced by an apophthegmatic utterance, sometimes by a relative pronoun, or καί; sometimes there is no link. At the termination of the myth the poet hastens to the close.

Reference has already been made on p. lxv. to the supposed presence of a seven-fold division on the lines of the nome of Terpander. Mezger's theory of the recurrent word in exactly the same place in the verse of different strophes, antistrophes, and epodes, would have us believe that these responsions are the clews to guide us through the labyrinthian mazes of the theme. Occasionally the recurrence is as indisputable and as effective as it is in the choruses of tragedy. It recalls the repetition of *stelle* in the concluding lines of the divisions of the *Divina Commedia.* But in the extent claimed for his discovery by the German scholar and more especially in its enlargement by Mr. Bury, who is haunted by verbal echoes of large import even though they occur independently of the metrical responsion, the theory tends to degenerate into a subtlety foreign to the plastic genius of choral song. The repetition of the significant idea is often independent of the metre; and the tautometric responsions (to use Dr. Fennell's phrase) are frequently of the most trivial character and deal with mere sound, as I have shown in the notes on Bacchylides.

As regards the arrangement of the rhythmical and musical parts, the presence or absence of the epode constitutes the mark of a two-fold division. (1) The grouping by triads—strophe and antistrophe, followed by an epode in a different melody. This arrangement gives unity and balance and is almost universally adopted. One triad is often given to the beginning, one to the end, while the interior triads are claimed by the myth. (2) Monostrophes (Pindar *Ol.* 14, *Pyth.* 6, 12, *Nem.* 2, 4, 9, *Isthm.* 8, Bacch. iii., 4); that is, the strophes succeed each other in unbroken succession as in the Aiolic monody.

The absence of the epode in a considerable number of epinikia has been accounted for on the ground that the odes in question were processionals. The point is not settled, and odes containing epodes were also sung by a komos in marching (*Ol.* 8, 13). Overlapping between the different strophes or between the different parts of the triad is not uncommon, and stands in striking contrast to the rigorous division of the choral songs of tragedy. Possibly the interval between the groups was marked by the manner of the instrumentation.[1]

Not less varied than the style, which shifts from solemnity to melancholy or joy, are the rhythms. From the epico-lyric hymns of Stesichoros the epinikian poets derived the calm and stately cadences

---

[1] The contrary opinion is set forth by Vogt *de metris Pind.* in the *Dissert. Argent.* 4. 71, and in *Philol. Anz.* 13. 663.

of the dactylo-epitrite; the gay and lively logaoedics have an Aiolic colouring; while the rarer and impetuous paionics are ultimately of Cretan origin. With a single possible exception (*Isthm.* 3 and 4, which are in honour of the same victor), the metre of every ode is individual. The musical modes were the solemn Dorian, the varied Aiolian, and the tender Lydian. Variation between the modes within the limits of a single ode was probably not permitted. The dactylo-epitritic measures have an affinity for the Dorian mode, the logaoedic for the Aiolian and Lydian, and the paionic for the Aiolian.

Simonides used a stringed instrument of many chords (Theokr. 16. 45), but whether his kithara contained more strings than the heptachord is uncertain. Pindar, who alludes to the musical accompaniment more frequently than any other poet, was an innovator, and his music was highly esteemed in later times. The common form of accompaniment seems to have been a combination of wind and stringed instruments.[1] Sometimes several kitharas were employed, but it is not probable that more than one flute took part in the accompaniment.

Whether the whole chorus (the number is unknown) sang all the parts of the triad is uncertain. Boehmer contends that strophes were sung by semichoruses, and that only the epodes were rendered by the whole body of singers. Possibly the koryphaios sang a part of the introductory strophe. Some odes were sung as processionals, but whether all the others had orchestic accompaniment is not clear as the circumstances of the banquet are not well known.

---

[1] Pindar expressly refers to the συναυλία in many places. We are not certain that the mention of one class of instruments in a given ode excludes the participation of the other class. Since the flute was double, αὐλοί may mean no more than αὐλός. See Graf *de vet. re musica* 40.

In the ancient editions the epinikia of Simonides were arranged according to the class of the contest, a method of division that in Pindar is subordinate to the classification according to the festival. The victories with the four-horse chariot were placed first. The four books of Pindar's epinikia represent only a part of that poet's triumphal odes, and the *Isthmia* are manifestly incomplete. Bacchylides is the last of the professional writers of epinikia; and Euripides' poem on Alkibiades' victory in 420 is the latest epinikion on record. The words ἐπινίκιον and ἐπινίκια that occur in late Boiotian inscriptions[1] refer to the victories won in the musical festivals that were popular in the first century B.C.

SKOLION.

The convivial songs known as skolia take their name from σκολιός 'curved.' In many ancient books the oxytone accent is given to the substantive, but the correct accentuation is σκόλιον, which is thus differentiated from the adjective (σκολιὸν μέλος). Cf. ὠχρός ὦχρος, γλαυκός Γλαῦκος. The ancients found great difficulty in accounting for the name, which has an antique flavour; as is clear from the following statement of divergent opinions:—

A. σκολιόν = ἐπικαμπές (curved).

a. Because of the position of the singers. The oblique order was explained in two different ways:—

1. Only the proficient sang (Dikaiarchos, Artemon, Plutarch, Schol. Aristoph. *Vespae* 1222, 1239).

---

[1] Cf. *C. I. G. S.* 1. 416. 31, 542. 10, 543. 6, 1761. 11, 1762. 14, 2727. 29, 2728. 4, 3196, 37, 3197, 50. See G. Hermann *Opusc.* 7. 237.

2. All sang, but the order was oblique because of the arrangement of the couches at marriage festivals (Aristoxenos, Phyllis).
b. Because of the character of the melody, *i.e.*
3. The melody was 'curved' (Eustathios, Schol. Aristoph. *Ranae* 1302).

B. σκολιόν = δύσκολον (difficult).

a. Because the singing was difficult (Plutarch, Schol. *Vespae* 1222, who have two views, Hesychios).
1. Only the proficient took part.
b. Because the singing was easy. (A *lucus a non lucendo.*)
2. κατ' ἀντίφρασιν (Suidas, Tzetzes).
3. The guests were so tipsy that what was easy became difficult (Orion, Proklos).

The indefensible explanation of the skolion as a difficult song goes back to Didymos, who is, however, not to be made responsible for the absurdities of his successors, though the fact that he put forward several etymologies of the word shows that he was dissatisfied with the current theories about its application. Some modern scholars still accept that ancient explanation which refers the name to the irregular, zigzag order in which the songs were sung. It must be confessed that this would be a highly singular method of naming a species of lyric song, especially in view of the fact that, as will be shown later on, the name skolion was restricted by the author of this explanation to a class of convivial songs that was sung only by the guests skilled in music, a class that did not come into existence before the fifth century. This ancient explanation derives no support from the supposed analogy of 'cyclic' songs, which were the special province of the dithyrambic chorus.

While it is impossible to reach a perfectly satisfactory explanation of this much disputed word, it is clear that σκολιός must be opposed to ὀρθός, ὄρθιος, or εὐθύς (cf. skol. xiv.). Following the suggestion of

Eustathios, which is doubtless a mere guess, since Aristoxenos, the master of musical theory, expressly denied any connection with a *σκολιός* melody, Engelbrecht has put forward an explanation which opposes the skolion to the dactylic hexameter, the *ὄρθιος* verse (*ὄρθιον, ἑξαμερὲς τετόρων καὶ εἴκοσι μέτρων*): Before the time of Terpander, the reputed inventor of skolia, hexametric dactylic poetry was sung with only a brief musical prelude. By his adoption of the lyre with an octave interval, Terpander was enabled to accompany throughout the words of the non-hexametric nomes (the long drawn-out rhythms of Frag. i.-iii.). The rising and falling of the notes of the lyre as they accompanied the words of the singer, Engelbrecht regards as a kind of 'obliquity' (*σκολιότης*), and the skolion, as it were, a species of 'winding bout.' This is not clear. Engelbrecht is forced to assume that the name skolion was originally appropriate to all melic poetry, and that at first all melic poetry on the profane side was convivial, while hymns, hymeneal songs, in fact all poetry of a sacred character, was composed in hexameters. Later on, he argues, when this division between sacred and profane poetry broke down, and hymns etc. became 'melic,' the name skolion, though restricted in its use, was still retained to express the most ancient form of melic poetry. Be this as it may, Engelbrecht's explanation is vicious, because the Greeks did not employ a technical term to denote two totally different things. *σκόλιον* cannot denote the opposition between complete and partial musical accompaniment and at the same time the opposition between melic and hexametric dactylic measures. Hexameters had complete musical accompaniment as early as Terpander. Nor is there any need to restrict the 'straight' rhythms to dactylic hexameters. 'Straight rhythms' are those that are made up of feet of one kind, whether dactyls, trochees, etc. 'Crooked' rhythms are those that are bent out of the straight line because of the insertion of a foot that is different from the rest, that is, they are logaoedic rhythms; and, as a matter of fact, almost all the skolia are composed in logaoedics. (For the method of naming we may compare δόχμιος and καμπή.) Logaoedic verse is exceedingly old, certainly older than Alkman, in whose poems it first appears. Terpander, the 'inventor' of the skolion, did not invent it: he merely gave the logaoedics of the skolia a complete musical accompaniment. Like logaoedics, convivial poetry is as old as the oldest Greek civilization. The gods on Olympos sang at their banquets.

The above explanation, which was suggested by Hiller in Bursian's *Jahresbericht*, 1883, p. 23, is not to be impugned because of a supposed metrical foot called the σκολιός (⏑ — ⏑), a name that recurs in σπονδειοσκόλιος (— — ⏑ — ⏑), σκολιοχόρειος (⏑ — ⏑ ⏑ ⏑ ⏑) etc. The *amphibrevis* does not occur in the skolia, nor were poems written in such a measure. Melic Adesp. 109: Ἴακχε θρίαμβε, σὺ τῶνδε χοραγέ, if not a grammatical figment, is a dact. tetrap. with anacrusis. It is certain that the foot called σκολιός by the late grammarians was derived (absurdly enough, as is shown by Ilgen p. cxxii.) from the σκόλιον poem, and not *vice versa*. The title of the treatise of Tyrannion—περὶ σκολιοῦ μέτρου—written at the command of Caligula, has a suspicious look.

Numerous other explanations have been put forward in recent times. Some scholars believe that the liberties and irregularities allowed in improvisation justified the name (Ottfried Müller); others that the word σκόλιον conveys in itself (cf. σκέλος) the idea of motion, which in this case was zigzag (Hanssen); others think that the obscurity and *double entendre* occurring in passing a song unexpectedly to the succeeding singer account for the 'obliquity' of the poems in question.

The scholiast on Plato *Gorgias* 451 E has preserved statements of the two chief sources of information in regard to the banquet songs: Dikaiarchos and Aristoxenos, in whose time the custom of singing such songs had not died out. Both were scholars of Aristotle, who was himself the author of a skolion. In an extract from Artemon, Athen. 15. 694 A has set forth the explanation of Dikaiarchos; and a part of a passage in Plutarch *Quaest. Sympos.* 1. 1. 5 = 615 B, goes back to the same source. The scholiast on Aristoph. *Nubes* 1364 is also drawn from Dikaiarchos. All other authors are secondary in importance, and their testimony is not to be considered unless supported by that of Attic comedy. The description of Dikaiarchos refers to the usage of the fifth century, but in his time the three classes that he distinguishes were confused; and we have no evidence descriptive of convivial songs older than the fifth century. Much of the obscurity that attaches to the skolia is due to the fact that they underwent a series of more or less gradual changes. The skolia of Alkaios differed from those of Terpander, and the choral skolia of Pindar were quite different from the monodic skolia of Alkaios. It is in fact impossible to discover any one predominating characteristic that marks all convivial songs.

From the above sources we learn that there were three classes of banquet songs.

1. *Songs sung by all the guests in unison.*

These songs were the paians. The paian was sung after the δεῖπνον and as an introduction to the wine. When the guests had dined, three libations were offered (1 to Zeus and Hera, 2 to the Heroes, 3 to Zeus Soter). After the third libation was ended, the symposion began, the entire company uniting in singing the paian. Cf. Plato *Sympos.* 176 A, Xenoph. *Sympos.* 2. The earliest reference in melic poetry to the sympotic paian, which is, however, as old as Homer (A 472), occurs in Alkman xxviii. The choral song was the formal introduction to the special kinds of songs that followed. By the time of the comic poet Antiphanes (85 K.) it would seem that the paian had lost its proper place. The confusion was the easier since the myrtle branch (see below) played a part in the singing of the paian.

2. *Songs sung by all the guests, but separately, not in unison.*

As a substitute for the lyre, and as its representative, a branch of myrtle or of laurel (αἴσακος) was used. This, as well as the loving-cup (ᾠδός), was passed from guest to guest. According to Plutarch, who has followed some unknown source, the myrtle was passed from one couch to another in the following manner: the first singer on the first couch passed it to the first on the second couch, the latter to the first on the third; whereupon the second on the first couch handed it to the second on the second, and so on. This explanation must have been unknown to Aristoxenos, whose own explanation—that the songs were called σκόλια because of the oblique position of the couches at marriage festivals—though far-fetched, presupposes a regular order of succession in the songs (παρὰ μέρος ἐξῆς). The passage in Plutarch is not an attempt to set up a different explanation from that of Aristoxenos, but is an endeavour to account for the name σκόλιον as applied to the second class, whereas its use and the ancient explanation of its meaning are properly restricted to the third class. The manner of procession in the singing described by Plutarch is not borne out by Aristoph. *Vespae* 1217 ff. If it is correct, it holds good of a later period.

A picture of the skolia πρὸς μυρρίνην that is coloured by the situation occurs in *Vespae* 1217 ff., where we have a modern scene that would suit the times (422 B.C.). Here there is no mention of the paian or of the songs of the 'proficient.' Incidentally it may be mentioned that Aristophanes has sketched a scene in which the law μὴ ᾆσαι ἐπὶ τὰ κακίονα is violated (Hypereides 2. 33 Kenyon, Demosth. *Falsa Leg.* 280). The beginner of a skolion has the right to call at will upon any guest to take up his verse, no matter where the latter is seated. When the verse of the first singer has been capped, the duty of beginning a new song falls to the guest who is next to the first singer. He in turn may call upon any one to answer his song, and so the right of starting a theme proceeds in regular order of succession. In actual practice one and the same guest did not always take up the theme as Philokleon does. The continuation could be either in the same or in a different metre, and strict adherence to the theme was not obligatory. The first singer might, if he preferred, sing an entire strophe to its end and then pass the myrtle to the next in regular order; or he might sing only a portion, and call upon any one he wished to complete the passage.

The simpler songs, such as those of the Aiolic lyric, of Anakreon, and of the short elegy, were gradually restricted to the second class, because of the introduction of the Dorian odes at the end of the sixth and beginning of the fifth century. The improvisations probably fall under the second class. The influence of the Ionians upon the 'Attic' skolia, which is to be ascribed to the popularity enjoyed by Anakreon in Athens, is seen in the fact that of the entire number thirteen are composed in the metre first employed for the purpose by Pythermos of Teos. This metre he may have derived from the Aiolians; and the skolion occupied a place among this people, who were its chief early cultivators, that is comparable to the position of the elegy among the Ionians.

The title παροίνια 'songs over the wine cup' is given by Ilgen to the songs of this class. Pollux 4. 53, and perhaps 6. 108, it is true, differentiates σκόλια and παροίνια, but it is open to doubt whether παροίνιον is a special kind of banquet song. Unless the ancients use σκόλιον in a general sense, it follows from certain passages that they did not apply the name παροίνια in the use given to it by Ilgen. Thus Hesychios defines σκόλιον by παροίνιος ᾠδή, the schol. on Aristoph. *Vespae* 1231, referring to 'Admetos' (no. xv.), calls it a skolion, but on 1232 calls it a παροίνιον. Proklos (246 w) says that the skolion was sometimes called παροίνιον. We do not know what special name, if any, was given by Dikaiarchos to the poems of the second class. We conclude that the skolion was merely a species of παροίνιον.

3. *Songs sung only by the proficient* (συνετοί).

These followed after the 'round-the-table' songs had been concluded, and were the skolia proper according to Dikaiarchos, who avoided using the word σκόλιον of the first two classes. Other authors were not so precise; and by the time of Dikaiarchos the word had already begun to be used of the second division. Originally there was no essential difference between class 2 and class 3, but either the technical difficulties that arose in singing certain songs to the lyre, or an agreement that confined certain kinds of songs to certain proficient singers, gave birth to the third class of sympotic poetry. As early as the time of Themistokles it was possible for a guest to refuse the lyre when passed to him (*Them. . . . cum in epulis recusaret lyram, est habitus indoctior*: Cic. *Tusc.* 1. 4). The songs of the third class were especially those of the Dorian lyric. About the beginning of the Peloponnesian War selections from tragedy and comedy were substituted for passages from Alkman, Stesichoros, Pindar, and Simonides. The order of singing in this class was from left to right, but the guests did not all sing in turn.

There was, however, no hard and fast line, at least in the early period, between the poets whose verses were made the subject of sympotic singing. While Alkaios and Anakreon were tolerably easy to sing, it is possible that some of the guests felt them too difficult; hence their songs come under the second or under the third class. In the later period, when enigmas and various puzzles were proposed at the end of the symposium, it may have become more and more difficult to get together an entire company which could sing even Alkaios and Anakreon.

The three-fold division that has been outlined above may have existed in the Attic banquets of the fifth century; but that the term skolion was restricted in an earlier period to the third class as described by Dikaiarchos may well be doubted. The word seems to be used in a general sense on its first occurrence in literature (Pindar, Frag. 122. 11). Actual references in early literature to skolia are exceedingly rare (Timokreon iv. in Aristoph. *Acharn.* 532; the praise of health (no. vi.) in Plato *Gorgias* 451 E) and imply no specific application of the term.

Reitzenstein has shown that the 'Attic' skolia mentioned by Athen. 15. 693 F formed a collection—a sort of Commersbuch—that was made in Athens after the Persian Wars (shortly before 450) and in fact by persons belonging to the aristocracy. The title 'Ἀττικὰ σκόλια came into existence later. This book of songs was perhaps used by Aristotle ('Αθην. πολ. 19, 20). The order in which the poems are given by Athenaios is that of the fifth century, and shows marks of a regular progression in pairs. So in the collection of elegies under the name of Theognis we often find balanced distichs which point to a sympotic origin or use. Mure *Gr. Lit.* 2. 105 has worked out with an over-refinement of ingenuity a system of interconnexion between the pairs of skolia.

The character of these 'Attic' skolia, which were sung by all the guests, is quite different from that of the elaborate poems called skolia that were written by Alkaios, Pindar, Timokreon, and Aristotle. Their prevailing characteristic is, in simple form, to reproduce or twist the thought of some famous poem, to amplify some well-known sententious utterance, or to picture some scene from a popular story. Sometimes they are almost like hymns, only shorter (i.-iv.). They may deal therefore with subjects that are serious, perhaps even sorrowful (πενθήρη μέλη), or they are sportive. The scoffing quality is as old as the *Hymn to Hermes* 56 (ἥβηταὶ θαλίῃσι παραίβολα κερτομέουσι). Their language is simple even to boldness. They are all the result of improvisation, at least originally; and hence may fairly be classed with the folk-lyric.[1]

All convivial songs were of course not improvisations such as we find in the 'Attic' skolia. Poems of politics, poems of war and of love were sung at banquets, but they may not have been written with a sympotic purpose; whereas, on the other hand, many of the great lyric poets composed songs that were intended to grace the banquet. Both are termed skolia. All convivial songs may in truth be called skolia, and it is impossible to distinguish accurately between those that were improvised and those that were not. There is little doubt that almost all of Alkaios' poems were sung at symposia, whether we class them, with Bergk, as στασιωτικά, παροίνια, or ἐρωτικά; in fact a frequent ancient method of 'publishing' a new poem was to produce it at a banquet. But the other poets are not like Alkaios, who is said to have regarded every season and every circumstance as an invitation to drink. Songs in praise of wine and feasting, and to a less degree love songs (especially in Athens at the close of the fifth century) may often be preempted as skolia proper. Beyond this the sign-marks are obscure; and in the case of a Dorian poet like Alkman, praise of the bowl and of good cheer may not have been permitted at banquets, though he lived at a time when the rigour of the system of Lykurgos had been much relaxed. Sappho's poems were sung at banquets, and on one occasion, it is related, the guests put down their cups from very shame when they heard her verses. Solon is said, on hearing one of Sappho's

---

[1] Cf. Tiersot, *Histoire de la chanson populaire en France*, p. 253, for improvisations of the people, where each one of the company in turn sings a verse.

songs at a banquet, to have asked that it might be taught him *ἵνα μαθὼν αὐτὸ ἀποθάνω*. But women did not write skolia as such. The ascription to Sappho of skol. xv. is due to a confusion between the actual skolia and the poetry that might be sung at a symposion; and the reputation of Praxilla as a writer of banquet songs has been freed from reproach by the recent investigations of Reitzenstein. The assumption of a poetess Kleitagora (*Vespae* 1243) is a mistake. In Κλειταγόρας (μέλος) ᾄδειν the genitive is objective.

Of the Aiolians, Terpander and Alkaios wrote banquet songs; of the Ionians, Pythermos, Anakreon, Battalos (?), Simonides, Bacchylides, but not Archilochos; of the Dorians, Alkman (cf. x., xxvi. ff.), Hybrias, Timokreon, Pindar; of the Attics, Kallistratos, Meletos, the accuser of Sokrates, Aristotle. Stesichoros may have written table paians. The *συμποτικοὶ νόμοι* attributed to Aristotle, Xenophanes, etc. were merely regulations of the banquet festivities.

As we have seen, it is not merely the 'skolia' of the lyric poets that were sung at the symposia; verses from epinikia, partheneia, and other species of lyric, even selections from the poems of Homer, could be utilized as convivial songs. There was practically no limit to the choice of the singer. The symposium was a school for strengthening an Athenian gentleman's acquaintance with the masterpieces of Greek song; and the knowledge of choral poetry was furthered in Attic society till after the middle of the fifth century by the custom of sympotic singing. Gradually tragedy and comedy—notably the lyric portions—usurped the place of esteem formerly occupied by the lyric poets. Aischylos was a favourite, and later on Euripides, whose *fin du siècle* themes delighted the younger generation and horrified the gentlemen of the old school (cf. Aristoph. *Nubes* 1353 ff.). Erotic poems became more and more popular at the end of the fifth century. The older comedy contributed its share to the entertainment, but in general it was too severely political to lend itself to the needs of a later generation. About 350 the 'Attic' skolia became old-fashioned. It was the later comedy that yielded the greatest number of passages packed with good advice and wise sayings to help a man along in life. Books of selections for sympotic singing came into existence with choice ῥήσεις; and the earliest anthologies may have grown up in a society whose chief social delight consisted in the banquet graced by song.

We know little of the musical modes employed. The Ionian is mentioned and was probably introduced by Pythermos of Teos. That different modes were employed is clear from the various forms of logaoedics in the 'Attic' collection. Until the time of Pindar and Timokreon the skolia were monodic, and they were usually sung by a single voice in the fifth century. Fragment xv. of Pindar has been arranged in strophe, antistrophe, and epode, but some scholars adopt the monostrophic form, which may be regarded as excluding the participation of a chorus. Bacchylides is, I think, wrongly supposed to have followed the example of Pindar in making the skolion choral, and of herein approximating it to the enkomion. In the 'Attic' skolia four-line strophes are common, as are also those of two lines. The flute seems to have been used as well as the lyre: Κλειταγόρας ᾄδειν, ὅταν Ἀδμήτου μέλος αὐλῇ (Kratinos 236). The exact distinction between the use of the lyre and of the branch of myrtle cannot be discovered. A song from Simonides is to be accompanied by the lyre, but Strepsiades gives his son the myrtle branch when he requests him to recite a ῥῆσις from Aischylos

(Aristoph. *Nubes* 1355, 1364). The myrtle is in place in the second, the lyre in the third class. Even when the paian was sung, the myrtle branch may have been used. Cf. *Frag. comic. incert.* (1203 K) ὑμνεῖ δ' αἰσχρῶς κλῶνα πρὸς καλὸν δάφνης | ὁ Φοῖβος (*i.e.* the paian) οὐ προσῳδά.

The metres employed in the 'Attic' skolia are, with one exception (no. xii.), logaoedics of various forms. Nearly one half consist of tetrastichic groups that recall the Aiolic strophe, though varying from it in several details, *e.g.* absence of ⏑ ⏑ in the basis. Verses 1, 2 are phalaecea, which have the cyclic dactyl one place nearer the beginning than the Sapphic hendecasyllables. The basis is generally — >, occasionally — ⏑, once ⏑ — and once ⏑ ⏑ —. The phalaecea may be written as hexapodies ending ⏊ ⏑ ⌞ ⏓ ∧. Verse 3 contains anacr. + two catalectic dipodies, sometimes with diaeresis after the first. After the easily moving hendecasyllables these dipodies give an animated effect, which is kept up to the end. Verse 4 is made up of two catalectic tripodies, each of the form that is found in the Alkaic strophe (τῶν ἀνέμων στάσιν); and without diaeresis after the first, except in ii., where we have elision. Verse 4 is usually connected with v. 3 by synaphea (v. is an exception). The whole strophe has the form *a a b c d d*; *b* + *c dd* making a short triad.

The use of the stately dactylo-epitrites by Pindar is probably due to the fact that his skolia were intended to be sung at sacred feasts. Bacchylides employs the same measure in xvii, and trochees in xviii. On Timokreon see p. 335.

EROTIKON.

'Love,' says Euripides, 'makes a poet even of the man who has no music in him':

πoιητὴν δ' ἄρα
Ἔρως διδάσκει, κἂν ἄμουσος ᾖ τὸ πρίν.

But the unlettered love song has been well-nigh displaced by the artistic compositions of the great lyric poets, who, from the earliest to the latest period, owned their allegiance to the power of Aphrodite. The temperament as well as the religion of the Greeks fostered the artistic love song. The introduction of boy-love from Lydia in the sixth century, though debasing to the national character as a whole, was capable of spiritualization; and the perversity of the sexual affinities of the Greeks does not impair for us the charm of many of their songs in praise of youthful beauty. Love songs to women[1] are relatively rare: the Dorians cultivated chiefly the erotic ode to boys, the Aiolian songs fall rather under the head of hymenaia and epithalamia; while the seclusion of their sex in Ionia and Attica withdrew virtuous women, at least, from the province of love poetry. The modern spirit of romantic attachment towards women rarely appears before the comedy of the fourth century.

Under the ancient system of classification, the ἐρωτικόν is apportioned to the human sphere alone, but here, as in other forms of melic, the profane does not exclude the divine; the gods may be invoked to vouchsafe accomplishment to a lover's prayers. Sappho's appeal to Aphrodite (i.) and Pindar's ode to Theoxenos (xv.) are alike representatives of the love song, though the former is a hymn, the latter a skolion. The range of the love song is as extensive as its popularity. It rises to the loftiness of a prayer to the Queen of Love and to the passionate laudation in idealized form of the *eromenos*, and descends to the serenade of an amorosa. The choral was adopted by

---

[1] παρθενεῖα were erroneously interpreted as songs addressed to maidens (schol. Aristoph. *Aves* 919).

the Dorians, the monody by the Aiolians, and by the Ionians when they did not employ the elegiac form.

Alkman is called the founder of erotic song, but before him Archilochos had given it a place in artistic literature. Some of the love poetry of the Parian poet was not classed as lyric by the ancients because it was composed in iambics or trochaics; but his passionate epodes in shifting metres are the legitimate antecedents of the more complicated odes of his successors. Alkman's love poems may have constituted a separate book. A misinterpretation of the spirit of his partheneia occasioned the report that he was given to amorous pursuits, a report that rests on that worst of witnesses, Chamaileon. A slightly older contemporary of Alkman, and like him a resident of Sparta, was Polymnastos, who transformed the aulodic nome by the introduction of erotic motives under the influence of the love elegy of his townsman Mimnermos of Kolophon.

The intensity and passion of the Aiolians made them the masters of the poetry of love. The island of Lesbos was the home of the chief forms of love song, the serenade, the epithalamium, and the hymenaios. Though the Aiolians are charged by the later Greeks with amorous indulgences and 'every species of relaxation,' their love poetry is infinitely higher in tone than the erotic that was current in Athens in the time of Perikles. Alkaios' stormy nature made him a votary of love. In his fragments we find the first mention of the serenade (κῶμος) and of boy-favourites (46 Menon, 58 Lykos). Both Alkaios and Sappho caught the tone of the folk-song. In Sappho even the hymn is made tributary to the theme of love, and all her verse is essentially erotic.

The conjunction of love and satire that we observe in Anakreon, who succeeded the Aiolians, may be a reversion to the style of Archilochos, whose love of Neobule was mingled with hatred of her father when he rejected the poet's suit. Lokris, too, was a land of poetry (Pind. *Ol.* 11. 19, *Pyth.* 2. 19), and the sensuous temperament of its people, akin in some degree to the Aiolians, fostered the cultivation of a voluptuous artistic lyric, the echoes of which survive only in the poems of Nossis. Possibly the recently discovered Alexandrian erotic fragment, which is essentially a lyric mime, reproduces the spirit of the Lokrian love song (cf. FOLK-SONGS xxi.). There was a pathetic Lokrian mode, which, though said to be the invention of Philoxenos, was known in the time of Pindar and Simonides, but soon fell into contempt.

The innovation effected by Stesichoros in the choral hymn consisted in part in the introduction of tales of love taken from the ancient legends, as in the *Europeia* and *Helena*, or of stories of unhappy love that were derived from the life of the common people and inspired his *Kalyka* and *Rhadina*. The tale of the beautiful Daphnis he also derived from his Sicilian home. His songs in praise of boy-loves are no longer extant.

The amatory element in the hymns of Stesichoros did not lead him to abandon the epic objectivity of his style. His successor Ibykos, however, gave expression to a genuine or a simulated fervour that recalls the Aiolian monody. His love odes in celebration of beautiful youths were choral, and to the stateliness of that form of presentation he added the fire of the individual lyric. Ganymede and Tithonos served him as mythical prototypes. His παιδικοὶ ὕμνοι[1] set the form for the future. Whether the youths for whom he expressed his passion were victors in beauty-contests, as Welcker thought, or whether they were

[1] Cf. Pind. *Isthm.* 2. 1 ff.

conquerors in any form of contest is entirely uncertain; perhaps they were merely pages at the courts of the tyrants.

The erotic songs of Bacchylides deal with boys and the demi-monde. A fragment (54 K., 25 B.) of a παιδικὸς ὕμνος—

Ἦ καλὸς Θεόκριτος· "οὐ μόνος ἀνθρώπων ἐρᾷς"
(Said fair Theokritos: thou art not the only man in love)—

is interesting from the fact that the refrain (ἐπιφθεγματικόν) was delivered by the chorus after the strophe had been sung by a single voice, and, like the burden that we find in Theokritos, Vergil, and in modern song, is closely connected in sense with what precedes; whereas the usual refrain (ἐφύμνιον) has no such intimate connection. Another fragment of the same poet, and not choral, describes an hetaira or dancer: 'When from the cup, raising aloft her white arm, she makes the cast (at the kottabos) for the beaux about her.'

In the fifth century love songs of the debased sort were popular with the *jeunesse dorée* of imperial Athens. The songs of Anakreon and of Polymnastos (the notorious Πολυμνήστεια)[1] were in high favour. The wanton serenades and adulterous lyrics of the Attic period are entirely lost, and the names of their composers[2] are known only through the attacks of the comic poets. Erotic myths were popular in the later dithyrambs.

---

[1] Cf. Aristoph. *Eq.* 1287, Kratin. 305. In his note on the second passage Kock is in error in separating this Polymnastos from the older poet of that name.

[2] Gnesippos, son of Kleomachos, the παιγνιαγράφος; Meletos, the writer of dithyrambs and tragedies, and the accuser of Sokrates; Kleomenes of Rhegion, also a dithyrambic poet, perhaps a contemporary of Philoxenos; Oionichos of Miletos; and Lamynthios of the same city, who was in love with the

In some cases the Dorian mood was employed, but the Aiolian and Lydian were preferred. At Athens, Lydian instruments were used, *e.g.* the ἰαμβύκη and τρίγωνον (Baumeister fig. 391).

MARRIAGE SONGS.

(Hymenaios, Epithalamium.)

A concise description of the ceremonies at an ancient Greek wedding will help us to represent the occasions on which marriage songs were sung. On the wedding day, which was usually in the winter month Gamelion and near the time of the full moon, the bridegroom (νυμφίος; γαμβρός in Sappho), attended by his parents, appeared towards evening at the house of the bride. The ceremony was a religious rite. The father offered sacrifices (the προγάμια or προτέλεια) to the gods of marriage—Zeus Teleios, Hera Teleia, Artemis, Aphrodite Urania, Peitho, and, at Athens, the Erinyes—in the presence of all the guests. Then followed the banquet (θοίνη γαμική), at which cakes of sesame (πλακοῦς γαμικός) were eaten. Ladies were sometimes present, though they ate at separate tables, and with them sat the bride closely veiled. After the meal had been concluded with libations and wishes for the prosperity of the newly wedded pair, the bride was conducted to her new home in a chariot, with her husband seated on one side, and on the other the best man

---

Lyde who inspired Antimachos. See Chionides (Philonides?) 4, Kratin. 15, 97, 256, Eupol. 139, Epikr. 4, Athen. 13. 597 A. Charixena, who is called an erotic poetess, may have been an hetaira, like Nossis. Battalos of Ephesos was the maker of voluptuous lays. These writers and many others were probably treated at length by Klearchos in his Ἐρωτικά.

(*παρανύμφιος* or *πάροχος*). Flowers were thrown into the vehicle, and a throng of friends, relatives, and servants followed with torches, singing to the accompaniment of kitharas and flutes, and indulging in folk-songs and broad jests. Behind the chariot walked the mother of the bride carrying torches lighted at the parental hearth and intended to kindle the household fire at the new home, a symbol of the continuity of the family life. When the procession reached the house of the bridegroom, which was richly decorated with flowers, his mother received him and his bride with lighted torches and scattered *καταχύσματα* as a sign of future plenty, and the bride ate a quince, the symbol of fecundity. Sometimes the banquet took place at the house of the husband after the arrival of the wedding procession. Not until the bride entered the bridal chamber (*θάλαμος*, *νυμφών*) did she unveil herself before her husband. The door was locked and guarded by a friend of the bridegroom (*θυρωρός*).

Nuptial songs were sung on three occasions in connection with these ceremonies: at the wedding banquet, during the procession, and before the bridal chamber. Apart from the little used *γαμήλιος*, *ὑμέναιος* is the generic term that covers all three parts of the ceremony and includes the specific epithalamium, which was circumscribed in time and place.[1] This extension of the word *ὑμέναιος* and the lack of explicit statements in ancient writers make it difficult to distinguish with precision the banquet song, the

---

[1] Cf. Pind. *Pyth.* 3. 17 ff. *ὑμεναίων, ἅλικες | οἷα παρθένοι φιλέοισιν ἑταῖραι | ἑσπερίαις ὑποκουρίζεσθ' ἀοιδαῖς*, Apoll. Rhod. 4. 1160. Theokr. calls his Epithalamium of Helen (18) a *ὑμέναιος*. In Soph. *Antig.* 813 *οὔθ' ὑμεναίων . . . οὔτ' ἐπινύμφειος . . . ὕμνος*, the first expression denotes the processional, the second the epithalamium. For *ἐπιθαλάμιον* (*scil. μέλος* or *ᾆσμα*) the masc. form (*scil. ὕμνος*) is sometimes used, and sometimes the femin. (*scil. ᾠδή*). In Latin, epithalamium is sometimes used in the generic sense.

processional, and the epithalamium. Some scholars, without good reason, give the name ἁρμάτειον μέλος to the song sung during the procession.[1]

Concerning the banquet hymeneal we have no definite information.[2] Sappho xviii. is a mythological allusion to the custom of wishing prosperity to the bridegroom on this occasion. Catullus 62 (*surgere iam tempus, iam pinguis linquere mensas*, l. 3) was sung when the banquet took place in the house of the bridegroom before the arrival of the bride.

The hymeneal that accompanied the wedding procession is attested as early as Homer in his famous description of the shield of Achilles, Σ 491 ff.:

> ἐν τῇ μέν ῥα γάμοι τ' ἔσαν εἰλαπίναι τε,
> νύμφας δ' ἐκ θαλάμων δαΐδων ὕπο λαμπομενάων
> ἠγίνεον ἀνὰ ἄστυ, πολὺς δ' ὑμέναιος ὀρώρειν,
> κοῦροι δ' ὀρχηστῆρες ἐδίνεον, ἐν δ' ἄρα τοῖσιν
> αὐλοὶ φόρμιγγές τε βοὴν ἔχον· αἱ δὲ γυναῖκες
> ἱστάμεναι θαύμαζον ἐπὶ προθύροισιν ἑκάστη.

This is the only reference to the hymeneal in Homer, though the poet elsewhere has occasion to mention or describe a marriage (δ 1 ff., ζ 28). It is noteworthy that he nowhere alludes to the religious element in the celebration of the rite. Hesiod, *Shield* 272 ff., imitates and expands the Homeric description:

> τοὶ δ' ἄνδρες ἐν ἀγλαΐαις τε χοροῖς τε
> τέρψιν ἔχον· τοὶ μὲν γὰρ ἐυσσώτρου ἐπ' ἀπήνης
> ἦγοντ' ἀνδρὶ γυναῖκα, πολὺς δ' ὑμέναιος ὀρώρει·
> τῆλε δ' ἀπ' αἰθομένων δαΐδων σέλας εἰλύφαζε
> χερσὶν ἔνι δμωῶν· ταὶ δ' ἀγλαΐῃ τεθαλυῖαι
> πρόσθ' ἔκιον· τῇσιν δὲ χοροὶ παίζοντες ἕποντο.

---

[1] Cf. Eur. *Or.* 1385 and schol.

[2] Cf. Plut. *Quaest. Symp.* 4. 3. 2 ἡ δὲ γαμήλιος τράπεζα κατήγορον ἔχει τὸν ὑμέναιον μέγα βοῶντα. Alkm. xxvi. may describe a wedding feast.

Neither these passages nor later sources give us any definite knowledge about the character of the processional hymeneal.

Concerning the epithalamium, however, our information is more satisfactory thanks to the fragments of Sappho and to the imitation by Catullus (62), which follows the Greek type. The epithalamium was the most important of the bridal songs but, though of great antiquity, is probably not so ancient as the march song. (It is difficult to follow Croiset, who is inclined to regard it as the creation of a relatively late age and not popular in origin like the other forms.) Though it was invariably sung before the door or below the window of the bridal chamber, the manner of delivery seems to have varied considerably. The chorus consisted either of girls alone,[1] or of girls and youths who danced and sang responsively. At times there was an alternation of the chorus with a single voice: the bride herself is represented by Sappho as taking part (*αἰπάρθενος ἔσσομαι* 96, *ἦρ' ἔτι παρθενίας ἐπιβάλλομαι* 102), and some of the songs were dramatic in tone.

In the amoebean song the maiden friends of the bride laud her beauty, protest against the cruelty that separates her from her mother, chant the blessedness of the virgin state, heap reproaches on the bridegroom, or hold him up to ridicule, make fun of the porter who will not allow them to enter the thalamos,[2] and indulge in playful allusions to the new life of the bride. On the other hand, the band of youths defend and congratulate their fortunate com-

[1] Pind. *Pyth.* 3. 17 ff., Aisch. *Prom.* 556, Eur. *I. T.* 366, Catull. 61. Theokr. 18 is represented as sung by twelve Spartan girls, friends of Helen.

[2] Demetr. *de eloc.* 117 says that the style of these reproaches in Sappho admitted words so prosaic as to make them seem unsuited to a chorus and the lyre.

rade, deprecate the condition of the "unprofitable virgin," and give expression to all manner of jests and jibes. Himerios, who had access to the entire book of Sappho's epithalamia, gives (1. 4) a florid description of the reception of the bride and the following ceremonies, but we get a better picture of the Greek original from the exquisite verses of Catullus.

Besides the epithalamium sung in the evening (the κατακοιμητικόν, lulling song), there was also the waking song (διεγερτικόν or ὄρθριον), which was rendered by a chorus of maidens and youths, or of maidens alone. Cf. Aisch. Frag. 43.

> κἄπειτα δ' εἶσι λαμπρὸν ἡλίου φάος,
> ἕως ἐγείρω πρευμενεῖς τοὺς νυμφίους
> . . . . . . σὺν κόροις τε καὶ κόραις

and Theokr. 18. 56

> νεύμεθα κἄμμες ἐς ὄρθρον, ἐπεί κα πρᾶτος ἀοιδὸς
> ἐξ εὐνᾶς κελαδήσῃ ἀνασχὼν εὔτριχα δειράν.

The refrain doubtless occurred in all three forms of the wedding song.[1] It is uncertain whether the

---

[1] Ὑμὴν ὦ Ὑμέναιε, probably the usual form, does not occur before Theokr. (18. 58). We find Ὑμὴν Ὑμέναι' ὦ Aristoph. *Pax* 1332, Ὑμὴν ὦ Ὑμέναι' ὦ *Aves* 1743, Ὑμὴν ὦ Ὑμέναι' ἄναξ Eur. *Troad.* 314, Ὑμὴν ὦ Ὑμέναι' Ὑμήν *ib.* 331, Ὑμὴν Ὑμήν Frag. 781. 14, where the choral may not be an hymenaios, but, as Mahaffy suggests, an ode to Aphrodite. With Ὑμὴν Ὑμέναιος *Anth. Pal.* 7. 407, cf. ὑμὴν ὑμέναιον ἀείδων Oppian *Kyn.* 1. 341 (as ἰὴ παιῆον ἀκούσῃ Kallim. 2. 21). Catullus has *O Hymenaee Hymen, O Hymen Hymenaee.* The υ of Ὑμήν, which form occurs only in the stereotyped formula, is long except in Eur. *Troad.* 331; that of ὑμέναιος, Ὑμέναιος is always short. In Latin the *y* of *Hymen* is anceps. The etymology of the word is disputed. Some refer it to Skt. *syūman* 'band,' 'strap,' 'chain,' making Hymenaios the god of the marriage bond (so Osthoff *Morph. Unters.* 4. 139); others derive it from √*sū* 'create,' 'bear' (cf. υἱός). Fick suggests, without explanation, the division ὑμέ—ναιος.

name of the god gave rise to the appellative or whether it was derived from the burden. In the former case the Homeric use of the appellative would be later than that of Sappho, who is the first to mention the proper name, which she employs as a mesymnion between the lines (xxxiii.). The parentage of the god, who is, according to the older legends, the child of Apollo and of one of the Muses (Kalliope, Terpsichore, Kleio, Urania),[1] also argues for the presumption that the god is merely a personification of the marriage hymn; and examples are not wanting of the creation of mythical personalities from obscure ἐπιφωνήματα (so Ialemos, Linos). On the other hand the relatively early use of the name in a stereotyped refrain might seem to make for the conclusion that Ὑμέναιος was originally a divine person (Sauer in Roscher's *Lexikon* 1. 2802). The song took its name from the burden as in the case of the paian. In Attika and Argos, where lawful marriage was first established, Hymenaios became the subject of many legends at a later period. In Attika the story was current that he rescued a band of maidens who had been seized by pirates; and he was also represented as a beautiful youth who disappeared on his wedding day.[2]

The introduction of a mythological element gave a certain divine attestation to the present happiness: the transference of a human institution to the divine sphere, the picture of the marriage festivals of the gods and the heroes, such as Kadmos and Harmonia, Peleus and Thetis, or Menelaos and Helen, dignified the marriage of commonplace people.[3]

---

[1] The tradition that makes Hymenaios the child of Dionysos and Aphrodite is late.

[2] Cf. Pind. Frag. 139. 6.

[3] Zeus and Hera's bridal is introduced in Aristophanes' travesty, *Aves* 1741.

The joy of the festival was not unvaried by a note of sadness. Proklos tells us, though the statement probably holds true only of the later Attic songs, that the nuptial song contained expressions of longing for the youth Hymenaios, who had vanished never to return.

The delivery of the processional song and of the epithalamium was attended by dancing. The instrumental accompaniment of the processional was provided by the flute and the phorminx in the Homeric age. The flute was the usual instrument, but the pektis and syrinx were also employed; in accompanying the epithalamium the kithara was used.[1] The Lydian mode was preferred both because it was better adapted to the range of youthful voices of either sex, and because of its tender character. Sappho may have used also the Aiolian and the Mixolydian.

Apart from the hexameter, a number of shorter verses were employed—logaoedic tripodies (with anacrusus, = prosodiacs *Aves* 1731 ff.), tetrapodies, choriambics, etc.

The artistic hymeneal was merely an elaboration of the folk-song, and throughout its history stood in close connection with the latter. Homer, who first mentions the hymenaios, is in fact called a composer of epithalamia, and Hesiod was the author of the Epithalamium of Peleus and Thetis, a subject touched upon by Pindar (*Nem.* 5. 22 ff.) and taken over by the fictitious Thessalian poet Agamestor and by Catullus (63). Cf. Hes. Frag. 71: τρὶς μάκαρ Αἰακίδη καὶ τετράκις, ὄλβιε Πηλεῦ, κ.τ.λ. In the lyric age

[1] Cf. Eur. *I. T.* 367 (flute), *H. F.* 11 (λωτός). Since πάμφωνος is used by Pind. only of the flute, παμφώνων ὑμεναίων *Pyth.* 3. 17 will refer to the flute accompaniment. Kithara, flute, and syrinx, Eur. *I. A.* 1036; kithara, Dion. Halik. *Ars Rhet.* 4. 1.

only Dorians and Aiolians participated in the composition of the hymeneal. At Sparta, where the primitive custom of carrying off the bride by force survived in part, marriage songs were composed by the state-poet Alkman, and probably in hexameters. Leonidas in *Anth. Pal.* 7. 19 says

τὸν χαρίεντ' Ἀλκμᾶνα, τὸν ὑμνητῆρ' ὑμεναίων
κύκνον, τὸν Μουσῶν ἄξια μελψάμενον.

That the hymeneals of Alkman should have attracted the attention of a poet of the Alexandrian period as the most excellent of his lyrics, is a surprising testimony to their fame. But in the lyric period Sappho reigned supreme. Her bridal hymns surpassed those of all the earlier and later poets, and were famous throughout all antiquity. The exquisite *Epithalamium of Helen* that is included in the collection of the idyls of Theokritos and is almost certainly the work of that poet, is modelled only in part on Sappho. The absence of a marked lyric element points to its indebtedness to the *Epithalamium of Helen* by Sappho's younger contemporary Stesichoros.

Bacchylides represented the hymeneal as sung by Spartan girls at the wedding of Idas and Marpessa. The poem is either a dithyramb or an hymeneal.[1]

Σπάρτᾳ ποτ' ἐν [εὐρυχόρῳ]
ξανθαὶ Λακεδα[ιμονίων]
τοιόνδε μέλος κ[όραι ᾆδον,]
ὅτ' ἄγετο καλλιπά[ρᾳον]
κόραν θρασυκάρ[διος Ἴδας]
Μάρπησσαν ἰο[πλόκαμον,]
φυγὼν θανάτου [τέλος, ὡς πόρε δίφρον]
ἀναξίαλος Ποσι[δᾶν]
ἵππους τέ οἱ ἰσαν[έμους· ὁ γὰρ ἐλθὼν]
Πλευρῶν' ἐς εὐκτ[ιμέναν]
χρυσάσπιδος υἱὸ[ν Ἄρηος] . . .

[1] Ken. 20. The restorations are by Kenyon, Jebb, Wilamowitz, and Platt.

The epithalamium was less suited to the conventional social conditions of Athens than to the freer life of Lesbos. At the end of the *Birds*, Aristophanes gives us an hymeneal on the marriage of Peisthetairos and Basileia, which, in the arrangement of the verses and the anaphora, reproduces in part the Aiolian type. This burlesque is the oldest complete hymeneal song extant. In the *Troades* of Euripides (308 ff.) Kassandra sings a wild hymeneal in frenzied imagination of marriage with Agamemnon. Of the dithyramb entitled *Hymenaios* by Philoxenos only the opening verse is preserved (Γάμε, θεῶν λαμπρότατε), which was sung by the poet as an unbidden guest at a wedding banquet at Ephesos. A dithyrambic *Hymenaios* by Telestes and a comedy of this name by Araros, the son of Aristophanes, are also reported. Eratosthenes may have composed a poem in distiches entitled *Epithalamion*. Of the two poems by Catullus, one (61), in honour of Junia and Mallius, is Roman rather than Greek, though there are touches that suggest a recollection of the Hellenic models that inspire the other ode (62) throughout. Calvus and Ticida are quoted as authors of epithalamia, but Philodemos, the contemporary of Cicero, reports (*de mus.* 5) that in his time the art of composing this form of lyric had almost entirely disappeared.

DIRGES.

(Threnos, Epikedeion.)

Like the nuptial ode, hymn, paian, and hyporcheme, the funeral lament had its roots in the folksong. Linos and Ialemos are numbered among the primitive minstrels no less than Hymenaios. In the two passages in which Homer pictures at greater length the ritual of the dirge, the poet has preserved a reminiscence of an established usage which antedates the last books of the *Iliad* and *Odyssey*. The description of the lament over the body of Hektor (Ω 720 ff.) is difficult to follow in detail and is no doubt more or less an idealization of the primitive folk-song unincumbered by the rude ὀλολυγμός that characterized the actual scene. At the laying-out of the hero the 'leaders of the dirge' take their places by the bier and sing their dolorous songs, while the women wail antiphonically—a distribution of parts that recalls the kommatic threnoi of tragedy. In addition to the songs of the hired threnodes, which were probably of a fixed type, and the responsive lamentations of the chorus, solos are sung by Andromache, Hekabe, and Helen, and the whole body of mourners wails in accord. In the *Odyssey* (ω 60 ff.) the nine Muses sing in turn over the corpse of Achilles, while Thetis, the Nereids, and the Achaians join in the refrain. Pindar (*Isthm.* 8. 64) speaks of the πολύφαμος θρῆνος on this occasion.[1]

Apart from the games that were celebrated in honour of a dead hero, the funeral ceremonies of the Homeric age were retained by the power of religious conservatism far down into the classical period. After the body of the deceased had been anointed, it was clothed in white linen and crowned with flowers. On the second day there ensued the solemn laying-out (πρόθεσις) on a couch that was covered with branches. The corpse was placed in the vestibule with the feet turned towards the door. The ceremony was witnessed by the relations of the deceased and by the friends that were invited to participate in the rite; and this company, together with the women of the family and the maid-servants

[1] Cf. also Σ 51, 314.

who were stationed about the corpse, raised the song of lament. Sometimes in the later period singers of either sex were specially engaged for the occasion.[1] The singing was responsive: first the men, then the women;[2] while the refrain was wailed by the entire company. The carrying-out (*ἐκφορά*) of the body in the early morning, the men preceding, the women following, the bier, was also an opportunity for renewing the formal lamentation.[3]

Other occasions of singing the threnos may have been the days—the third and the ninth—sacred to the cult of the dead, and on which offerings were made at the grave; and at the banquet (*περίδειπνον*) which was set out after the house of death had been purified. At Athens offerings were again made and another funeral meal prepared on the thirtieth day after the burial. The threnoi were preserved in the family of the deceased and repeated from year to year as an anniversary office at the *νεκύσια*.

Besides threnos, the general term for 'dirge,' there were current various other analogous words, between which it is impossible to draw sharp distinctions. Some of the laments in question were rarely if ever sanctioned as formal divisions of the lyric art. The *ὀλοφυρμός*, *ὀδυρμός*, and *οἶκτος*, for example, are less to be regarded as separate species of the threnody than as names for the 'keening' of the mourners whose purpose was to excite the feelings and arouse

---

[1] *θρήνων σοφιστής*; Καρῖναι (*θρηνῳδαὶ μουσικαί*).

[2] Cf. Eur. *Andr.* 93 ff. *ἐμπέφυκε γὰρ | γυναιξὶ τέρψις τῶν παρεστώτων κακῶν | ἀνὰ στόμ' ἀεὶ καὶ διὰ γλώσσης ἔχειν.*

[3] In Keos lamentation was proscribed on this occasion, and men were forbidden to observe any period of mourning. Cf. *I. G. A.* 395 A and on Bacchyl. p. 382. At Sparta too lamentation was restricted. At Athens excessive indulgence in the outward signs of grief must have been common in Plato's time (*Laws* 800 D). The philosopher also complains (*ib.* 700 B, D) that the poets of his day confounded dirges with hymns.

compassion. When they did assume a literary form, they were generally absorbed by the elegy.[1] The ἰάλεμος (ἰήλεμος), which takes its name from the cry ἰά (ἰή), was an extravagant improvised lament and probably, in its origin, of an Oriental type.[2] That the funeral lament was early cultivated under this name is clear from the fact that Ialemos appears in Pindar as a distinct personality, the son of Apollo and Kalliope. At a later period ἰάλεμος was used as an equivalent of threnos (cf. Theokr. 15. 98). Some part of these various forms of funeral lyric may have influenced the style of the tragic laments, particularly the κομμοί.

The classical age did not attempt to distinguish between the several species of the threnody. In Alexandrian and Roman times, however, scholars were at a loss to distinguish between the threnos and the epikedeion,[3] one of the species of melic that is enumerated by Proklos, and which did not, I believe, gain any currency before the Alexandrian period. There is general agreement that both threnos and epikedeion contained a laudation of the deceased person. The dirge is in fact only a form of the enkomion, and its eulogistic character in the lyric age is probably due to the influence of Simonides. The epikedeion seems to have been the song at the laying-out, while the threnos was not circumscribed in time, that is, it might be sung before the burial, after the burial, and at the anniversaries.

---

[1] Homer is said to have bewailed his blindness in an ὀλοφυρμός.

[2] Aisch. *Choeph.* 424; cf. also *Suppl.* 115, Eur. *H. F.* 109, *Suppl.* 281, Lucian *Pseudol.* 24 (ἰαλέμων ποιηταί). ἰήϊος was also used for θρῆνος, Soph. Frag. 575, Ion 12.

[3] ἐπικήδειος ᾠδή Eur. *Troad.* 514, Plato *Laws* 800 E. The substantive ἐπικήδειον (*scil.* μέλος or ᾆσμα) is late. There is constant variation between -ειον and -ιον.

The foregoing distinction is that adopted by Proklos 247, *Et. Mag.* 454. 50, *Et. Gud.* 200. 30 (from Didymos?), Servius on Verg. *Ecl.* 5. 14, Eust. *Od.* 1673. 48, and in part by Tryphon p. 80 (ἐπικήδιον . . . τὸ ἐπὶ τῷ κήδει· θρῆνος δὲ τὸ ἐν ᾠδῇ). If it is applied strictly to the passage in Homer, the threnoi over the bodies of Hektor and Achilles are properly epikedeia. Some of the ancients ignored the epikedeia entirely, while others defined them as laudations of the dead accompanied by a moderate expression of grief. Aristokles of Rhodes, a grammarian of the latter part of the first century B.C., regarded both the threnos and the epikedeion as unrestricted in the time of delivery. Cf. Francke *Callinus* 125 ff., Bapp in *Leipz. Stud.* 8. 134 ff. The extant fragments that bear the name epikedeia are few in number and all point to the elegiac form. The tone is also that of the elegy and the poems are commemorative rather than expressions of immediate and personal grief; though Parthenios (in the first century B.C.), in addition to epikedeia addressed to other persons, composed one on the death of his wife. Hesiod's 'epikedeion' to Batrachos is a figment. Epikedeia by Melanippides are not to be inferred from Plut. *de mus.* 15. Plutarch uses the word more than any other writer, and in his vocabulary epikedeion means nothing more than epigram. He reports an epikedeion by Euripides on the Athenians who fell at Syracuse (*Nic.* 17), another on the loss of some Spartans (*Pelop.* 1), and one on Pindar (1020 A).

The connection between the dirge and the elegy was of ancient date. During the earlier part of the lyric period the latter attained the greater importance because of its more intimate association with the epic. It was not till the extension of the Dorian choral lyric throughout Greece in the sixth century that the melic dirge came into prominence, and even in that and the following period the threnos was rivalled in importance by the elegy. The more private character of the funeral lament withdrew it from publicity, though I venture to believe that the threnos emphasized the merits of the deceased as much as it gave expression to a grief that would be sacred to his kinsmen; while the threnetic elegy, though not excluding the element of laudation, was not sung at funerals, and was intended, at least in the time of

Simonides, to serve as a funereal epitaph. Still the difference was mainly one of form and delivery rather than of contents. Elegos was used in Attic as an equivalent of threnos.

The artistic threnos was a choral song unattended by the responsive lamentations and monodies that formed a part of the Homeric lament. When it was designed to contribute to the splendour of the funeral of a prince, the spectacle produced by a large chorus clad in black must have been magnificent. A stately dance augmented the solemnity of the occasion. The balanced grouping in strophe, antistrophe, and (possibly) epode, gave an effect of calmness and dignity. The Greek sense of proportion and moderation in the expression of grief debarred all recourse to the excited forms of the ἀπολελυμένον μέλος; nor did any poet ever adopt the passionate rhythms of the dochmiac class.

The flute was invariably[1] used to accompany the words, which were sung either in a low or in a high key. The flute was originally employed solely to give expression to lament, and auletic dirges (νόμοι θρηνητικοί, ἐπικήδειοι—on the Python, ἐπιτύμβιοι) were common at an early period.

The mode was the plaintive Lydian (*querulus Lydius modus*), which, according to Plato, awakened the θρηνῳδές καὶ φιλοπενθές temper of the spirit. The philsopher also mentions the pathetic Mixolydian and Syntonolydian (*i.e.* the Hyperlydian) as suited to the character of the threnos. Perhaps Pindar[2] also used the Dorian, which was common in the laments of tragedy.

---

[1] αὐλὸς ἐπικήδειος Suid. *s.v.* ἔλεγος. The expression is designedly free in Aisch. *Agam.* 990 ἄνευ λύρας ὑμνῳδεῖ θρῆνον Ἐρινύος.

[2] *Ol.* 14, *Nem.* 4 contain references to death and are both Lydian.

With respect to the metres adopted in the early threnodies, it is probable that the use of hexameters by Euripides in *Androm.* 103 ff. represents an archaic established usage that gradually gave way to the elegiac distich. The melic threnodies of Pindar are composed in dactylo-epitrites, those of Simonides in the more pliant logaoedics. Ionics were also suited to the spirit of the threnos.[1]

For the wild expression of passionate lament that was natural to a more primitive state of society, there was substituted in the lyric age an ennobling and purifying song that released the mourner from too close an engagement with his grief. The story of the sufferings even of the demi-gods and of the other heroes of the popular faith might assuage the sorrow of the afflicted and direct their thoughts into other channels. The lyric age had, however, apart from the clarified doctrines of the Orphic and Pythagorean sects and of the Eleusinian mysteries, of which Pindar is the interpreter, but little consolation to offer to the living as to the welfare of their dead.[2] Stesichoros even says that all lament is vain. In the popular belief of the lyric age the only real life consisted in the union of soul and body; the only bond that connected the dead with the living was the pious memory of the departed; the only reward of virtue and noble deeds, the poet's praise, whose faint echoes might reach the dull ear of death. The heroes might be translated to heaven, or retain in Hades a semblance of their power on earth, but for the common man the life beyond the grave knew nothing of happiness. Even for the heroes of Thermopylai

---

[1] Cf. Schol. Aisch. *Prom.* 128, and *Pers.* 694 ff., 700 ff., Wilamowitz regards as ionics lines 948 ff. in the latter play, and also the lament over Alkestis and the prayers of the seven Argive mothers.

[2] Cf. Rohde *Psyche* 490 ff.

Simonides cannot picture an eternal life of future blessedness. Immortality is only on this side the νυκτὸς θάλαμος. Scarcely any lyric poet touches upon the cult of departed spirits. But with all the lamentation over the pain of life, its brief span, its toil and trouble, the inevitable end, that dominates the tone of the Greek lyric outside of Pindar, there still remained the conviction that the good and the evil of life was to be borne with tranquility and with a stout heart. The lugubriousness of the Ionian lyric is, furthermore, a traditionary poetical feature rather than the deliberate expression of a theory of life.

Whether or not Simonides had a predecessor in Stesichoros,[1] it is certain that the Keian poet first developed the artistic form of the threnos by assimilating it to the genius of the Doric style. With all his tenderness and power to speak to the heart, Simonides' view of life is filled with gloom; the only comfort that he vouchsafes to the bereaved is that all are bondmen to the common master Death. The pessimism of the sophist unites in him with the pessimism of the Ionian lyrist. Perhaps it was in a dirge that he set forth the paradoxical doctrine that the soul does not desert the body; it is the body that quits the soul at death. With him the threnody attained its perfection. The pathos of his songs gave them a celebrity that ensured his fame even in Roman times (*Ceae neniae, maestius lacrimis Simonideis*). He was commissioned to compose threnoi on Skopas, prince of Krannon, who together with his retainers was overwhelmed by the falling of his palace, Antiochos, an Aleuad of Larissa, and Lysimachos of Eretria. The lines on Danae, if a portion of a dirge, proves the poet's unique mastery of this form of choral song; but it is more probable that the fragment is from a dithyramb.

---

[1] Letters of Phalaris 21; cf. Aristeid. 1. 127.

Pindar alone did not attempt to offer consolation or awaken commiseration by lamentation over the wretchedness of existence. Rolling back the curtain that hides the life beyond he consoles the stricken with a picture of the progress of the soul through the aeons and of the joys of paradise. Pindar alone grasped the full meaning of the relation of death to life. The soul is to him immortal because divine, and its destiny is endless felicity or endless pain. After death, men receive the just awards of virtue or of impiousness. Rising above the transitoriness of life he contemplates with sublimity and calmness the purgation of the spirits of just men until they are released from all taint of evil. An entire book of his threnodies is reported, but Hippokrates of Athens, the brother of Kleisthenes, is the only person known to us as the subject of a funereal ode. Probably his dirges were intended exclusively for the anniversary festivals. The second *Isthmian* was called a threnos by some of the ancients because the poem was sent to the son of the dead victor.

Timotheos is credited with a θρῆνος τοῦ Ὀδυσσέως. See Gomperz *Mitteil. aus Papyrus Rainer*, 1. 84-88.

The threnos is often mentioned by the tragic poets, some of whose choral songs recall the tone of the lyric dirge.[1]

PARTHENEION.

We now pass to that class of melic poetry which embraces choral songs containing both a sacred and a

[1] Cf. Aisch. *Agam.* 991, 1322, *Choeph.* 335, Soph. *O. K.* 1751, 1778 (after the passing of Oidipus), Eur. *Andr.* 103, *Suppl.* 88 and foregoing, *Elektr.* 112, *Helen* 166, *Rhes.* 976 and often in Eur.

secular element. The partheneion,[1] or virginal song, includes the following division of the daphnephorikon, but excludes the hymn and the epithalamium, though both were occasionally sung by girls alone.

The cultivation of virginal choruses was restricted to Dorian countries. At Athens and in Ionian lands the public sentiment that enjoined seclusion upon women would have regarded their official appearance as members of a civic chorus in the musical and religious festivals as a violation of social convention and decorum. It was different at Sparta. In Lakedaimon maidens not only witnessed the gymnastic exercises of the other sex; they themselves participated in contests of running[2] and throwing the quoit and spear in the presence of men. They were trained in the arts of singing and dancing,[3] and bore a conspicuous part in the musical contests. They were regarded as members of the state; their patriotism and heroism was not less marked than that of the men; and the homage accorded them was as much a tribute to their grace and beauty—the women of Lakedaimon were celebrated for their loveliness—as an acknowledgment of their position as the future mothers of a race of warriors. Though Spartan

---

[1] The accent varies between παρθενεῖον (cf. παρθενήϊος and παρθενεύω; ἀνδρεῖος, γυναικεῖος) and παρθένειον (*scil.* μέλος or ᾆσμα). The distinction set up by some of the ancients (cf. schol. Aristoph. *Aves* 919) between παρθένεια, songs sung by virgins, and παρθενεῖα, songs sung in honour of virgins, is ill-founded. The forms παρθένιον (perhaps an hypokoristic formation) and παρθένιος (*scil.* ᾠδή) also occur. Nothing can be made of the statement in Athen. 14. 631 D that the partheneia are ἀποστολικοί. The definition might possibly suit the daphnephorika.

[2] Cf. Theokr. 18. 39. The name of these races was Endriones. Some modern critics find in Alkm. iv. 58 ff. a reference to the running-races.

[3] Some of the Spartan dances for girls were the ὅρμος, βίβασις, the Karyatid dance.

women took part in the festivals of Dionysos, it was the festivals in honour of Hera, Artemis, and Apollo that afforded the girls of Sparta the chief opportunities to render homage to the gods. In Epizephyrian Lokris the freedom allowed to women made it not unseemly for them to sing hymns of thanksgiving because of the success of Hieron's arms (Pind. *Pyth.* 2. 19). At Delphi a chorus of maidens saluted Eurylochos, the leader in the Sacred War.

At Delos too girls took part in the state service of Apollo by singing hyporchemes. The partheneion was, however, radically different from that species of lively mimetic song and dance. In many respects it recalls the prosodion, and processional songs sung by a chorus of girls in approaching the altars of the gods are in fact entitled to the name partheneia. But the virginal song was not always employed in solemn pomps like the prosodion, nor was its contents identical with that stately song of devotional entreaty. Together with the worship of the gods, which found expression in myths significant of their power, in legends of the demi-gods consecrated by the local cult, or in tales of the heroes and heroines of the epic, there was an element devoted to the secular side of life. The grave severity of the religious service was relieved and the spirit of the song accommodated to the character of the chorus. The girls who chant the praises of the gods or heroes become themselves the recipients of the homage of the poet. The contents of the song was thus of a heterogeneous character: the objective religious element was strangely blended with a highly personal lyric.

The song was always attended by the dance, though it is uncertain whether at times a supernumerary body of dancers did not perform their part while the chorus ceased its own orchestic evolutions. Some of the dance-figures must have been of a highly original character if the title Kolymbosai (the divers) given to one of Alkman's compositions refers to the manner of dancing. The music was furnished by the flute,[1] though the kithara was possibly also employed. The mode was the Dorian, which must have relaxed something of its stateliness to suit the gentler form of the chorus. Recourse may have also been had to the softer Lydian. Some of the partheneia may have been sung at night.

With Alkman, its creator, the virginal song attained the summit of its excellence. Of the extant fragments that represent all that is preserved of at least one book, only one has been handed down in a fairly complete condition, and it is our chief source of information regarding the style and mode of presentation in the archaic period. This poem (iv.) is distinguished by a highly dramatic element: in v. the chorus addresses the poet—a privilege not accorded to it by Pindar—, or the latter speaks in his own person to the whole body of singers or singles out individual members as the recipients of his gallantry and tenderness. The chorus alludes to the leaders of their band, whose personal attractions they celebrate with winsome artlessness.

Whether his successors in the cultivation of the partheneion adopted with equal grace Alkman's exquisite felicity in combining the human with the divine portion of the virginal ode, is unknown. After Alkman there is a gap[2] until we come to Simonides, whose Frag. xxxii. is the only bit that recalls the 'graceful Alkman.' Pindar composed no less than three books, two of which were probably intended for the usual cult, while a third, which bears the strange title *κεχωρισμένα παρθενείων*, may have dealt with

---

[1] *παρθένιοι αὐλοί* Pollux 4. 81.

[2] I see no reason for placing Alkaios among the writers of partheneia (Boeckh).

extraordinary occasions. Many scholars think that the daphnephorika were here included.[1] Some of the partheneia of the Theban poet were in honour of Apollo, the leader of the Muses, others were dedicated to Pan, *σεμνᾶν Χαρίτων μέλημα τερπνόν* (Frag. 95), the god that was especially honoured in the family of the poet. Of the style of Pindar's partheneia we learn almost nothing from the extant remains, but Dionysios gives us the interesting information that, though the virginal odes preserved the nobility and gravity of the austere and archaic diction characteristic of Pindar, they were essentially different from all the other works of the poet. Bacchylides is reported to have written partheneia, but nothing has survived. Possibly the fragment of Telesilla and Korinna iv. may be added to the scanty list.[2] Christ would compare, as an example of the spirit of the partheneion, the Doric song at the end of Aristophanes' *Lysistrata.* The *Carmen Saeculare* of Horace is a partheneion only in the fact that it was sung by girls; and the like will hold true of the virginal song composed by Livius Andronicus after the appearance of a portent at Rome.

The metres of the partheneia are logaoedics, dactylic hexameters and shorter dactylic verses, anapaests, etc.

DAPHNEPHORIKON.

This form of the virginal ode was sung in connection with the Apolline festival of the Laurel-branch in Boiotia and at Delphi. The Boiotian ceremony

---

[1] Bergk placed here the odes to Pan and even the eleventh *Nemean.*

[2] Blass would add Mel. Adesp. 139 because of *τὸ δὲ παρθένος ἄεισ' ἀγλαὸν μέλος παρθενήϊας ὀπὸς εὐηράτω στόματι πέραναν.* Bergk took the fragment to be part of an epinikion.

was of immemorial antiquity and was even referred to the time of the first settlement of the land by the Aiolians who left their home at Arne and took possession of Thebes; and Herakles himself is said to have been the daphnephoros of Apollo. It was celebrated every ninth year by a procession to the temple of Apollo Ismenios. The priest, who was chosen for a year, at least in the time of Pausanias (9. 10. 4), was a noble youth of beautiful form, both of whose parents were alive. As daphnephoros, bearing the holy bough and wearing a crown of gold, he led the procession, though his nearest kinsman walked in front of him carrying a staff of olive-wood covered with laurel and decorated with globes and garlands symbolical of the sun, moon, stars and the days of the year. Behind the priest came a band of maidens bearing boughs and singing chorals.[1] At Delphi the daphnephoros was saluted by choirs of girls on his return from Tempe, whence he brought a bough of sacred laurel every nine years. The festival of the daphnephoria was also held in Thessaly (*S. G. D.-I.* 372) and at Athens, but there is no record of partheneia in connection with the ritual in either place. No fragments exist of the daphnephorika of Pindar, whose son once held the office of laurel-bearer. Whether Alkman or Konniar composed songs for the festival is uncertain. In Boiotia there were also songs called tripodephorika.

OSCHOPHORIKON.

Nothing remains of this form of prosodiac melic, which was sung at the Attic vintage festival of the *ὠσχοφόρια* (from *ὤσχη*, a vine branch full of grapes).

---

[1] The ceremony is described at length in Proklos 247 (translated in Smith's *Dict. Antiq.* 1. 597).

The chorus proceeded from the temple of Dionysos at Athens to the shrine of Athena Skiras at Phaleron. The elaborate ritual is described by Plut. *Thes.* 23, Proklos 249 (Smith *Dict. Antiq.* 2. 303). The dancing was peculiar and resembled that which was usual in the Bacchic cult.

VOTIVE SONGS (EUKTIKA).

Under this title, which is probably later than the Alexandrian age,[1] are included petitions addressed to the gods for the bestowal of some favour either upon the poet or upon a friend. In all probability they lauded the beneficence of the gods and described the worthiness of their petitioner. None of the Greek lyrics is ascribed to this class by the ancient writers, but it is possible that they would have included under this designation such poems as Sa. i., xlii., Anakr. ii., many of the so-called kletic hymns (p. xxxii.), and the *κατευχαί* of Simonides.

---

[1] It appears in Pollux 4. 53, Proklos, *Anth. Pal.* 1. 118. Menand. (*Rh. Gr.* 3. 333 Sp.) speaks of εὐκτικοὶ ὕμνοι.

SELECTED BIBLIOGRAPHY.

ALKAIOS.

MATTHIAE: *Alcaei Mytilenaei reliquiae*, Lips. 1827. AHRENS: in his *De Graecae linguae dialectis* 1. 241 ff., Gottingae 1839. FICK: *Die Sprachform der lesbischen Lyrik* in *Bezz. Beitr.* 17 (1891) 182 ff. HOFFMANN: *Die griechischen Dialekte* 2. 165 ff., Gött. 1893. WELCKER: *Alkäos* in his *Kl. Schr.* 1. 126 ff., Bonn 1844. KOCK: *Alkäos und Sappho*, Berl. 1862.

ALKMAN.

WELCKER: *Fragmenta Alcmanis lyrici*, Gissae 1815; cf. *Kl. Schr.* 4. 37 ff. NIGGEMEYER: *De Alcmane poeta laconico*, Monasterii 1869. BENSELER: *Quaest. Alcmanicarum pars* i., Eisenach 1872. CLEMM: *De fragmento quodam Alcm. comm.*, Gissae 1876. INGRAHAM: *De Alcmanis dialecto*, Novi Ebor. 1877. SPIESS: *De Alcmanis poetae dialecto* in *Curtius' Studien* 10 (1877) 331 ff. Leipz. SCHUBERT: *Miscellen zum Dialekte Alkmans*, Wien 1879. SITZLER: see under EUMELOS.

ANAKREON.

BERGK: *Anacreontis carminum reliq.*, Lips. 1834. ZURETTI: *Anacreonte ed Anacreontee*, Torino 1889. WELCKER: *Anakreon* (1835) in his *Kl. Schr.* 1. 251 ff. STARK: *Quaest. Anacreonticarum libri duo*, Lips. 1846. FICK: *Die Sprachform der altionischen Lyrik* in *Bezz. Beitr.* 13 (1888) 208 ff. WEBER: *Anacreontea*, Gott. 1895.

ANTIQUITIES, ART, ARCHAEOLOGY.

BIESE: *Die Entwickelung des Naturgefühls bei den Griechen*, Kiel 1882-84. BAUMEISTER: *Denkmäler des klass. Altertums*, 3 vols., München und Leipzig 1885-88. BAUMSTARK: *Der Pessimismus in der griech. Lyrik.*, Heidelb. 1898. BRUCHMANN: *Epitheta deorum*, Lips. 1893. DEVENTER: *Zu den griech. Lyrikern. Natur und Naturgefühl bei denselben*, Gleiwitz 1887. GRASBERGER: *Erziehung und Unterricht im klass. Alterthum*, 3 vols., Würzburg 1864-81. GUHL and KONER: *The Life of the Greeks and Romans*, transl. from the 3rd Germ. ed., Lond. VON JAN: *Die musischen Festspiele in Griechenland* in the *Verhandl. der 39sten. Philol.-Versamml.*, Leipz. 1888, p. 71 ff.

MÜLLER—WIESELER: *Denkmäler der alten Kunst*, 3rd ed., Gött. 1877. PANOFKA: *Bilder antiken Lebens*, Berl. 1843. PRELLER: *Griech. Mythologie*, 4th ed. by Robert, Berl. 1894. REISCH: *De musicis Graecorum certaminibus*, Vindob. 1885. ROSCHER: *Ausführl. Lexikon d. griech. u. röm. Mythologie*, Leipz. 1884 ff. *Wiener Vorlegeblätter für archäol. Uebungen*, Wien 1889 ff.

ARION.

WELCKER: *Der Delphin des Arion* (1833), etc., in his *Kl. Schr.* 1. 89 ff. LEHRS: in his *Popul. Aufsätze* 197 ff., Leipz. 1856.

BACCHYLIDES.

NEUE: *Bacchylidis Cei fragmenta*, Berol. 1822. KENYON: *The Poems of Bacchylides*, Lond. 1897. BLASS: *Bacchylidis carmina cum fragmentis*, Lips. 1898. JURENKA: *Die neugefundenen Lieder des Bakchylides*, Wien 1898. DESROUSSEAUX: *Les Poèmes de Bacchylide de Céos traduits du grec*, Paris 1898. FESTA: *Le odi e i frammenti di Bacchilide, testo greco, traduzione e note*, Firenze 1898. CHRIST: in *Sitz.-Ber. der Bayer. Akad.* 1898, p. 3 ff., 597. CRUSIUS: in *Philol.* 57 (1898) 150 ff. FRACCAROLI: in *Rivista di Filol.* 26 (1898) 70 ff. DELLA GIOVANNA: in *Rivista di Filol.* 16 (1888) 465 ff. HENSE: in *R. M.* 53 (1898) 318 ff. LIPSIUS: in *Neue Jahrb.* 1 (1898) 225 ff. LUDWICH: in *Verzeichn. d. Vorles. zu Königsberg*, Somm. Sem. 1898. MICHELANGELI: *Della vita di Bacchilide*, Messina 1897. *Dopo il B. pubblicato dal Museo Britannico* in *Rivista di storia antica*, 3 (1898) no. 1. RAMBALDI: *Bacchilide di Ceo ed i suoi tempi*, Torino 1888. ROBERT: in *Hermes* 33 (1898) 130 ff. SCHROEDER: in *Berl. Philol. Wochensch.* 1898, nos. 11 and 28. SMITH: in *J. H. S.* 18 (1898) 267 ff. WEIL: in *Journal des Savants*, 1898, 43 ff., 174 ff. WILAMOWITZ: *Bakchylides*, Berlin 1898; *Gött. Gel. Anz.* 1898, 125 ff. ZURETTI: in *Rivista di Filol.* 26 (1898) 134 ff. Also articles in the *Athenæum* for Dec. 1897, Jan., Feb., 1898, and *Class. Rev.* 12. by Nairn, Platt, Ellis, W. Headlam, Housman, Pearson, Richards, F. W. Thomas, Tyrrell, Jebb, van Herwerden, Farnell, Earle, Walker, Goligher.

DIAGORAS.

MOUNIER: *De Diagora Melio*, Rotterd. 1838. MÜNCHENBERG: *De Diagora Melio*, Hal. Sax. 1877.

DITHYRAMB.

LUETCKE: *De Graecorum dithyrambis et poetis dithyrambicis*, Berol. 1829. M. SCHMIDT: *Diatribe in dithyrambum poetarumque dithyrambicorum reliquias*, Berol. 1845. HARTUNG: *Ueber den Dithyrambus* in *Philol.* 1 (1846) 397 ff. SCHEIBEL: *De dithyramborum Graecorum argumentis*, Liegnitz 1862. WILAMOWITZ: in *Euripides' Herakles*[1], pp. 63, 78, Berl. 1889.

EDITIONS.

(I.) BERGK: *Poetae Lyrici Graeci*, 3 vols., 4th ed., Lips. 1878-1882; vol. 3: *Poetae Melici.* (II.) *Selections* (1) *with explanatory notes.* JACOBS: *Anthologia Graeca*, 13 vols., Lips. 1794-1804. MEHLHORN: *Anthologia Lyrica*, Lips. 1827. SCHNEIDEWIN: *Delectus poetarum elegiacorum, iambicorum, melicorum reliquiae*, Gott. 1838. See also his *Beiträge zur Kritik der Poetae Lyrici Graeci*, Gött. 1844. HARTUNG: *Die griechischen Lyriker*, vols. 5 and 6, Leipz. 1855-57. STOLL: *Anthologie griechischer Lyriker*, 2 vols.; vol. 2, 5th ed., Halle 1883 (for schools). MICHELANGELI: *Frammenti della Melica Greca da Terpandro a Bacchilide*, five parts, Bologna 1889-1897. INAMA: *Antologia dei Lirici*, Milano 1891 (for schools). FARNELL: *Greek Lyric Poetry*, Lond. 1891. BIESE: *Griechische Lyriker*, 2 vols., Leipz. 1891-92 (for schools). MORGAN: *Brief notes on Elegiac, Iambic, and Lyric Poets*, Cambridge, Mass. 1895. BUCHHOLZ: *Anthologie aus den Lyrikern der Griechen*, 2 vols., vol. 2, *Die melischen u. choregischen Dichter*, 4th ed. by Sitzler, Leipz. 1898. This is the best of the school editions. BROOKS: *Greek Lyric Poets*, selected and translated, Lond. 1896. *Selections* (2) *with textual notes.* BRUNCK: *Analecta veterum poetarum Graecorum*, 3 vols., Argentorati 1776. GAISFORD: *Poetae minores graeci*, 5 vols., vol. 3, Sappho, Alcaeus, Stesichorus, Lips. 1823. STADTMUELLER: *Eclogae poetarum Graecorum*, Lips. 1883. POMTOW: *Poetae lyrici graeci minores*, Lips. 1885. HILLER: *Anthologia Lyrica*, the 4th ed. (1890) of Bergk's *Anthol. Lyr.*; new. ed. by Crusius, Lips. 1897.

EPINIKIA.

KRAUSE: ΕΛΛΗΝΙΚΑ *oder Institute, Sitten und Bräuche des alten Hellas*: part i. in two vols.: *Die Gymnastik und Agonistik der Hellenen*, Leipz. 1841; part ii. vol. 2 *Die Pythien, Nemeen und Isthmien*, Leipz. 1841. Also *Olympia oder Darstellung der grossen olympischen Spiele*, Wien 1838. BOETTICHER: *Olympia, das Fest und seine Stätte*, Berl. 1883.

EPITHALAMIUM AND HYMENAIOS.

SIEBDRAT: *De carminibus veterum nuptialibus* in his *Theocr. Epithalamium*, Lips. 1796. SOUCHAY; in *Mémoires de l'acad. des inscript.*, 9. 305 ff. SCHMIDT: *De hymenaeo et Talasio dis veterum nuptialibus*, Kiliae 1886. KOERBER: *De Graecorum hymenaeis et epithalamiis*, Vratislav. 1877. HARTUNG: *Hymenäus (Brautlied)* in *Philol.* 3 (1848) 238 ff.

ERINNA.

RICHTER: *Sappho und Erinna*, Quedlinb. and Leipz. 1833. MALZOW: *De Erinnae Lesbiae vita et reliquiis*, Petrop. 1836. WELCKER: *De Erinna et Corinna poetriis* in his *Kl. Sch.* 2. 145. SUSEMIHL: *Geschichte der griech. Litteratur in d. Alexandrinerzeit*, 2. 527, Leipz. 1891.

EUMELOS.

SITZLER: *Die Lyriker Eumelus, Terpander und Alkman in ihrem Verhältnis zu Homer*, Karlsruhe 1886.

FOLK-SONGS.

ZELL: in his *Ferienschriften*, Freiburg 1826. KOESTER: *De cantilenis popularibus veterum Graecorum*, Berol. 1831. RITSCHL: *Ode (Volkslied) der Griechen* (1830) in his *Opusc.* 1. 245 ff. SCHNEIDEWIN: review of Koester in *Schulzeitung*, 1832, p. 926. WELCKER: *Ueber den Linos* (1830) in his *Kl. Schr.* 1. 8 ff.; *Ueber den Ursprung des Hirtenlieds*, ib. 1. 402 ff. BENOIST: *Des chants populaires dans la Grèce antique*, Nancy 1857. CERRATO: *I canti popolari della Grecia antica* in *Rivista di Filol.* 13 (1884-85) 193 ff., 289 ff.

HYMENAIOS.

See under EPITHALAMIUM.

HYPORCHEME.

WALTHER: *Comment. de Graecorum hyporchematis pars prior*, Bochum 1874.

IBYKOS.

SCHNEIDEWIN: *Ibyci Rhegini carminum reliquiae*, Gott. 1833. WELCKER: *Die Kraniche des Ibykos* (1833) in his *Kl. Schr.* 1. 89 ff.; *Ibykos* (1834) in his *Kl. Schr.* 1. 220 ff. G. HERMANN: in *Jahn's Jahrb.* 8 (1833) 371 ff.

ION.

KOEPKE: *De Ionis Chii poetae vita et fragmentis*, Berol. 1836. ALLEGRE: *De Ione Chio*, Parisiis 1890.

KORINNA.

BOECKH: in *C. I. G.* 1. 720. AHRENS: in his *De Graecae linguae dialectis* 1. 277. WELCKER: see under ERINNA.

LANGUAGE, DIALECTS,[1] ETC.

(I.) KRÜGER: *Griechische Sprachlehre*, 5th ed., Leipz. 1875-79. BRUGMANN: *Griechische Grammatik*, 2nd ed. (1888), in the 2nd vol. of the *Handbücher d. klass. Altertums-wissenschaft*, München. *Grundriss d. vergl. Gramm. d. indogerm. Sprachen*, 4 vols., Strassburg (2nd ed. of vol. 1, 1897). Syntax by Delbrück, 1897. KÜHNER: *Ausführliche Grammatik der griech. Sprache*, 3rd ed.; Morphology, vols. 1. 2. by Blass (1890-92); Syntax, vol. 1. by Gerth (1898), Leipzig. MEYER: *Griechische Grammatik*, 3rd ed.

---

[1] See also under the several authors.

Leipz. 1896. (II.) AHRENS: *De Graecae linguae dialectis*: vol. 1, Aiolic, vol. 2, Doric, Gott. 1839-43. *Ueber die Mischung der Dialecte in der griech. Lyrik* (*Verhandl. der Gött. Phil.-versamml.* 1852). MEISTER: *Die griech. Dialekte*; vol. 1, Aiolic, Boiotian, Thessalian (1882), vol. 2, Eleian, Arkadian (1889), Göttingen. HOFFMANN: *Die griech. Dialekte*, vol. 2, Aiolic, Thessalian (1893), vol. 3, Ionic (1898), Gött. SMYTH: *The Ionic dialect*, Oxf. 1894. FÜHRER: *De dialecto Boeotica*, Gött. 1876; *Die Sprache und die Entwickelung der griech. Lyrik*, Münster 1885. SCHAUMBERG: *Quaestiones de dialecto Simonidis Cei, Bacchylidis, Ibyci*, Celle 1878. MUCKE: *De dialectis Stesichori, Ibyci, Simonidis, Bacchylidis aliorumque poetarum choricorum cum Pindarica comparatis*, Lips. 1879. HOLSTEN: *De Stesichori et Ibyci dialecto et copia verborum*, Gryphisw. 1884. FICK: *Die Sprachform der altionischen und altattischen Lyrik* (Anakreon) in *Bezz. Beitr.* 13 (1888) 173 ff.; *Die Sprachform der lesbischen Lyrik* in *Bezz. Beitr.* 17 (1891) 177 ff. MONRO: *Grammar of the Homeric Dialect*, 2nd ed., Oxf. 1891. SCHULZE: *Quaestiones Epicae*, Gueterslohae 1892. CAUER: *Delectus inscriptionum Graecarum propter dialectum memorabilium*, 2nd ed., Lips. 1893. GERSTENHAUER: *De Alcaei et Sapphonis copia vocabulorum* in *Dissert. Philol. Halenses*, vol. 12, Hal. Sax. 1894. (III.) BIEBER: *De duali numero apud Epicos, Lyricos, Atticos*, 1864. WILPERT: *De schemate Pindarico et Alcmanico*, Vratisl. 1878. STURM: *Geschichtliche Entwickelung der Constructionen mit πρίν*, 3rd part of Schanz' *Beiträge zur histor. Syntax d. griech. Sprache*, Würzburg 1882. BIRKLEIN: *Entwickelung des substantivierten Infinitivs*, 7th part of Schanz' *Beiträge*, Würzburg 1888. DOERWALD: *De duali numero in dial. aeol. et dor.*, Rost. 1881. SCHAUB: *De usu conjunctivi et optativi in enuntiatis lyricorum Graecorum secundariis*, Liestal 1889. MOMMSEN: *Griech. Präpositionen*, Berl. 1895. (IV.) HENSE: *Poetische Personification in griech. Dichtungen*, Halle 1868.

LASOS.

SCHNEIDEWIN: *De Laso Hermionensi* in *Ind. lect. hib.*, Göttingen 1842.

LITERATURE.

MÜLLER: *History of the Literature of Ancient Greece*, Lond. 1840. MURE: *Critical History of the Language and Literature of Antient Greece*, 5 vols., Lond. 1850-57, vol. 3 deals with Melic. BODE: *Geschichte der hellenischen Dichtkunst*, 3 vols., Leipz. 1838-39; vol. 2 *Gesch. d. lyrischen Dichtkunst.* WALTHER: *De Graecae poesis melicae generibus*, Hal. Sax. 1866. MÖLLERS: *De origine poesis melicae apud Graecos*, Monasterii 1869. BERNHARDY: *Grundriss der griechischen Litteratur*, 2 vols.; vol. 2, part i. 3rd ed. (Halle 1877) deals with Melic. BERGK: *Griechische Literaturgeschichte*, 4 vols., Berl. 1872-87; vol. 2 deals with Melic. FLACH: *Geschichte der griechischen Lyrik*, Tübing. 1884. SITTL: *Geschichte der griechischen Literatur*, 3 vols., München 1884-1887. NAGEOTTE: *Histoire de la poésie lyrique grecque*, 2 vols., Paris 1888-89.

CROISET: *Histoire de la littérature grecque*, vol. 1, Paris 1887, vol. 2 (Lyrisme), 2nd ed., 1898. CRUSIUS: Articles on Alkaios, Alkman, Anakreon, and Bacchylides in Pauly-Wissowa's *Real-Encyclopädie*, Stuttgart 1894 ff. CHRIST: *Geschichte der Griechischen Litteratur*, 3rd ed., München 1898. LOHAN: *Poesis melicae generum nominibus quae vis subiecta sit a classicis scriptoribus Graecis*, pars i. (paian, hymn), Lauban 1898.

MELANIPPIDES.

EMPERIUS: in *Zeitschr. für Alterthumswissenschaft*, 1835, p. 8 ff. SCHEIBEL: *De Melanippide Melio, partic.* i. ii., Guben 1848, 1853.

METRE.

GRASER: *De stropha Alcaica*, Madgeburgi 1865. SCHMIDT: *Die Eurhythmie in den Chorgesängen der Griechen*, Leipz. 1868; *Die antike Compositionslehre*, 1869; *Griechische Metrik*, 1872; *Rhythmic and Metric*, transl. by White, Boston 1878. VELKE: *De metrorum polyschematistorum natura*, Gott. 1877. CHRIST: *Metrik der Griechen und Römer*, 2nd ed., Leipz. 1879. ZAMBALDI: *Metrica Greca e Latina*, Torino 1882. GLEDITSCH: *Metrik der Griechen u. Römer*, in *Handbuch d. klass. Altertums-wissenschaft*, vol. 1. 491 ff., Nördlingen 1885. ROSSBACH AND WESTPHAL: *Theorie der musischen Künste der Hellenen*, vol. 1, *Griech. Rhythmik* by Westph., Leipz. 1885, vol. 2, *Griech. Harmonik u. Melopoeie* by Westph., 1886, vol. 3. 1, *Allgem. Theorie d. griech. Metrik* by Westph. and Gleditsch, 1887, 3. 2, *Griech. Metrik*, 3rd ed. by Rossb., 1889. LUTHMER: *De choriambo et ionico a minore diiambi loco positis*, Argent. 1884. WILAMOWITZ-MOELLENDORFF: *Ioniker bei den Lyrikern* in *Isyllos von Epidauros*, 9th part of *Philolog. Untersuch.* ed. by Kiessling and W.-M., Berl. 1886. USENER: *Altgriechischer Versbau*, Bonn 1887. BUTZER: *Der Ionicus a maiore*, Frankfurt a. M. 1889. KALKNER: *Symbolae ad historiam versuum logaoedicorum*, Marpurgi 1892. JUSATZ: *De irrationalitate studia rhythmica*, Lips. 1893. LAMER: *De choriambicis Graecorum poetarum versibus*, Lips. 1896. GRAF: *De Graecorum veterum re musica quaest. capita duo*, Marburg 1889. SMYTH: *Mute and liquid in Greek melic poetry*, in the *Trans. Amer. Phil. Assoc.* 28 (1897) 111 ff., 29 (1898) 86 ff.

NOME.

WALTHER: See under LITERATURE. GUHRAUER: *Der Pythische Nomos* in *Jahrb.* 8 suppl. vol., p. 311 ff., Leipz. 1876; cf. *Jahrb.* 121 (1880) 689 ff.; *Zur Geschichte der Aulodik bei den Griechen*, Waldenburg 1879. REIMANN: *Studien zur griech. Musik-Geschichte: A. Der* Νόμος, Ratibor 1882. CRUSIUS: See under STESICHOROS. DIPPE: in *Wochenschr. f. klass. Philol.* 5 (1888) Nos. 33 ff.

PAIAN.

SCHWALBE: *Ueber die Bedeutung des Päan als Gesang des apollinischen Cultus*, Marburg 1847.

PHILOXENOS.

WYTTENBACH: *Diatribe de Philoxenis* in his *Opusc.* 1. 294 ff., Leyden 1821. BERGLEIN: *De Philoxeno Cytherio dithyramborum poeta*, Gott. 1843. BIPPART: *Philoxeni, Timothei, Telestis dithyr. reliquiae*, Lips. 1843. KLINGENDER: *De Philoxeno Cytherio*, Marburgi 1845.

PINDAR (*Fragments*).

BOECKH: *Pindari opera*, vol. 2. 1, 553 ff., Lips. 1821. DISSEN: *Pindari opera*, vol. 2. 603 ff., Gothae et Erfordiae 1830. BERGK: *Poetae Lyrici Graeci*, 1. 367 ff., 4th ed., Lips. 1878. SEYMOUR: *Selected Odes of Pindar*, 208 ff., Boston 1882. FENNELL: *Pindar*, 2. 196 ff., Cambridge 1883. CHRIST: *Pindari carmina*, 380 ff., Lips. 1896; *Beiträge zum Dialekte Pindars* in *Sitz.-Ber. d. Bayer. Akad.*, München 1891, 25 ff. PETER: *De dialecto Pindari*, Hal. Sax. 1866. LIND: *De dialecto Pindarica*, Lundae 1893.

PRAXILLA.

NEUE: *De Praxillae Sicyoniae reliquiis comment.*, in *Ind. Schol.*, Dorpati 1844.

PROSODIA.

REIMANN: *Studien zur griech. Musik-Geschichte: B. Die Prosodien*, Glatz 1885; *Disputat. de prosodiorum similiumque apud Graecos carminum natura nuper editae additamentum*, Gleiwitz 1886.

SAPPHO.

VOLGER: *Sapphus Lesbiae carmina et fragmenta*, Lips. 1810. NEUE: *Sapphonis Mytilenaeae fragmenta*, Berol. 1827. WOLF: *Sapphus poetriae Lesbiae fragmenta*, Hamburgi 1833. AHRENS: in his *De Graecae linguae dialectis* 1. 256 ff., Gott. 1839. HOFFMANN: in his *Die griech. Dialekte* 2. 133 ff., Gött. 1893. WHARTON: *Sappho: Memoir, Text, Selected Renderings* and *Literal Translations*, 2nd ed., Lond. 1887. Contains a good bibliography. WELCKER: *Sappho von einem herrschenden Vorurtheil befreyt* (1816) in his *Kl. Schr.* 2. 80 ff.; *Ueber die beiden Oden der Sappho* (1856), *ib.* 4. 68 ff. KOCK: see under ALKAIOS. SCHÖNE: *Untersuchungen über d. Leben der Sappho* in the *Symb. philol. Bonn.*, Leipz. 1864-67. RIEDEL: *Der gegenwärtige Stand der Sapphofrage*, Ilgau 1881. COMPARETTI: *Saffo e Faone* in the *Nuova Antologia*, 2nd ser., vol. 1. 253 ff., Firenze 1876; *Saffo nelle antiche rappresentanze vascolari* in *Mus. ital.*, 2 (1888) 40 ff. LUNAK: *Quaestiones Sapphicae*, Kazaniae 1888. CIPOLLINI: *Saffo*, Milano 1889.

SIMONIDES.

SCHNEIDEWIN: *Simonidis Cei carminum reliquae*, Brunsvigae 1835. CESATI: *Simonide di Ceo*, Casale 1882.

SKOLIA.

ILGEN: ΣΚΟΛΙΑ *hoc est carmina convivalia*, Jenae 1798. HALLSTRÖM: *De scoliis Graecorum comment. academ.*, Londini Gothorum 1827. GRIM: *Prolusio scholastica de scoliis Graecorum*, Dordraci 1839. KOESTER: *Comment. de scoliis*, fasc. 1, Flensburg 1846; see under FOLK-SONGS. A. F. RIBBECK: *Ueber die Tafelgesänge der Griechen*, Berl. 1848. RUNCK: *De scoliorum origine et usu*, Berol. 1876. ENGELBRECHT: *De scoliorum poesi*, Vindob. 1882. REITZENSTEIN: *Epigramm und Skolion*, Giessen 1893. WILAMOWITZ-MOELLENDORFF: *Die attische Skoliensammlung* in *Aristotles und Athen*, 2. 316 ff., Berl. 1893.

STESICHOROS.

KLEINE: *Stesichori Himerensis fragmenta*, Berol. 1828. WELCKER: *Stesichorus* (1829) in *Kl. Schr.* 1. 148 ff. BERNAGE: *De Stesichoro lyrico*, Lutet. Paris. 1880. SEELIGER: *Die Ueberlieferung der griech. Heldensage bei Stes.* 1, Meissen 1886. CRUSIUS: *Stesichoros und die epodische Komposition in der griechischen Lyrik* in the *Commentat. philologae* in honour of O. Ribbeck, Leipz. 1888.

TELESILLA.

NEUE: *De Telesillae Argivae reliquiis comment.*, Dorpati 1843.

TELESTES

See under PHILOXENOS.

TERPANDER.

LOEWE: *De Terpandri Lesbii aetate comment.*, Halis 1869. SITZLER: see under EUMELOS.

TIMOKREON.

BOECKH: *De Timocreonte Rhodio* (1833) in his *Kl. Schr.* 4. 375, Leipz. 1874. G. HERMANN: in his *Opusc.* 5. 198, Lips. 1834. AHRENS: in his *De Graecae linguae dialectis*, 2. 477 ff.; *R. M.*, 2 (1843) 457 ff. ENGER: *De Timocreontis Rhodii carmine a Plutarcho servato*, Posen 1866.

TIMOTHEOS.

See under PHILOXENOS.

ABBREVIATIONS.

A. J. P. = American Journal of Philology.
B. C. H. = Bulletin de Correspondance Hellénique.
Carm. pop. = Carmina popularia in Bergk's *Lyrici*.
Cauer = Cauer's Delectus inscriptionum Graecarum propter dialectum memorabilium.
C. I. A. = Corpus Inscriptionum Atticarum.
C. I. G. = Corpus Inscriptionum Graecarum.
C. R. = Classical Review.
Hymn = Homeric Hymn.
I. G. A. = Inscriptiones Graecae antiquissimae.
Jahrb. = Jahrbücher für classische Philologie.
J. H. S. = Journal of Hellenic Studies.
Kaibel = Kaibel's Epigrammata Graeca ex lapidibus conlecta.
L. and S. = Liddell and Scott's Greek Lexicon.
Mnem. = Mnemosyne.
Mus. ital. = Museo italiano.
Penthim. = Penthemimeral or penthemimeres.
Philol. = Philologus.
R. M. = Rheinisches Museum.
S. G. D.-I. = Sammlung der griechischen Dialekt-Inschriften.

The melic fragments not included in the text but referred to in the notes, and the fragments of the elegiac and iambic writers, are cited in Arabic numerals following the order of Bergk. The fragments with Roman numerals are those of the text. Pindar is cited from Bergk, the scenic poets from Dindorf, the tragic fragments from Nauck, the comic fragments from Kock. The fragments of Bacchylides follow Kenyon's numbering; and Arabic numerals are used in citing from omitted portions of odes that have been included in this edition. Hephaistion is cited by the pages of Westphal.

< > indicates words omitted by the writer of a MS.

[ ] indicates omitted letters or words which were probably found in the MS. or MSS.

In the text of Alkman iv. and of Bacchylides i.-x., the brackets are used to denote only those lacunae of the papyrus which are of some length or open to doubt. In the case of the latter poet, all emendations not specially referred to other sources are due to Kenyon.

GREEK MELIC POETS.

EUMELOS.

ΠΡΟΣΟΔΙΟΝ ΕΙΣ ΔΗΛΟΝ.

–́ ⏑ ⏑ –́ –   –́ ⏑ ⏑ –́ ⏑ ⏑ –́ ⏑ ⏑ –́ ⏓
–́ ⏑ ⏑ –́ ⏑ ⏑ –́ ⏑ ⏑ –́ ⏑ ⏑ –́ ⏓

Τῷ γὰρ Ἰθωμάτᾳ καταθύμιος ἔπλετο Μῶσα
ἁ καθαρὰ καὶ ἐλεύθερα σάμβαλ' ἔχωσα.

TERPANDER.

I. (1).[1] ΕΙΣ ΔΙΑ.

– – – – – –
– – – – – –
– – – – –
– – – – – – –

Ζεῦ πάντων ἀρχά,
πάντων ἁγήτωρ,
Ζεῦ, σοὶ πέμπω
ταύταν ὕμνων ἀρχάν.

II. (2). ΕΙΣ ΑΠΟΛΛΩΝΑ.

Ἀμφί μοι αὖτε ἄναχθ' ἑκαταβόλον ἄειδ', ὦ φρήν.

Eumelos—1. Μῶσα Führer: μοῖσα. 2. ἔχωσα Hiller: ἔχουσα.
Terpander—I. 3. πέμπω (σπένδω Bergk).
II. ἑκατηβόλον. ἄειδ' ὦ: ἀοιδέτω Suid. A; ἀειδέτω Suid. B.

[1] The numerals in parentheses give the order of the Fragments in Bergk.

III. (3). ΕΙΣ ΑΠΟΛΛΩΝΑ ΚΑΙ ΜΟΥΣΑΣ.

– – – – – – –
– – – –
– – – – –
– – – –

Σπένδωμεν ταῖς Μνάμας
παισὶν Μώσαις
καὶ τῷ Μωσάρχῳ
Λατῶς υἱεῖ.

IV. (4). ΕΙΣ ΔΙΟΣΚΟΥΡΟΥΣ.

– – – – – – – – – – – – – – ⏓

Ὦ Ζηνὸς καὶ Λήδας κάλλιστοι σωτῆρες.

[V. (5).] THE SEVEN-STRINGED PHORMINX.

Σοὶ δ' ἡμεῖς τετράγηρυν ἀποστέρξαντες ἀοιδήν
ἑπτατόνῳ φόρμιγγι νέους κελαδήσομεν ὕμνους.

VI. (6). SPARTA.

Ἔνθ' αἰχμά τε νέων θάλλει καὶ μῶσα λίγεια
καὶ δίκα εὐρυάγυια, καλῶν ἐπιτάρροθος ἔργων.

ALKMAN.

I. (1). EXORDIUM OF A PARTHENEION.

–́ ⏑ ⏑ –́ ⏑ ⏑ –́ ⏑ ⏑ –́ ⏑ ⏑
–́ ⏑ ⏑ –́ ⏑ ⏑ ≚ ⋀
⏑ ⁞ –́ ⏑ –́ ⏑ –́ ⏑ –́ ⏑ –́ ⏒

TERPANDER—III. 1. *μνάμαις.* 2. *μούσαις.* 3. *μουσάρχῳ.* 4. Λατοῦς AC; Λητοῦς SC.

Μῶσ' ἄγε, Μῶσα λίγεια πολυμμελὲς
αἰενάοιδε μέλος
νεοχμὸν ἄρχε παρθένοις ἀείδην.

II. (9). THE DIOSKUROI.

> ⁞ –́ ⏑ –́ > –́ ⏑ –́ > –́ ⏑ –́ ⏑ –́ ⏑ –́ ∧
> ⁞ –́ ⏑ –́ > –́ ⏑ . . .

Κάστωρ τε πώλων ὠκέων δματῆρες, ἱππόται σοφοί,
καὶ Πωλυδεύκης κυδρός

III. (16). A MAIDEN'S OFFERING TO HERA.

–́ ⏑ –́ ⏑ –́ ⏑ –́ ⏑
–́ ⏑ –́ > –́ ⏑ –́ ⏑
–́ ⏑ –́ ⏑ –́ ⏓

Καὶ τὶν εὔχομαι φέροισα
τόνδ' ἑλιχρύσω πυλε͜ῶνα
κήρατῶ κυπαίρω.

IV. (23). PARTHENEION.

–́ ⏑ –́ ⏒ –́ ⏑ –́ ∧
⏒ ⁞ –́ ⏑ ⏑ –́ ⏑ ⊔́ –́ ∧
–́ ⏑ ⏑ –́ ⏒ –́ ⏑ –́ ∧
⏒ ⁞ –́ ⏑ ⏑ –́ ⏑ ⊔́ –́ ∧

5–8 = 1–4.

–́ ⏑ –́ ⏒ –́ ⏑ –́ ⏒ –́ ⏑ –́ ⏑ ⏓
10 –́ ⏑ –́ ⏒ –́ ⏑ –́ ⏒ –́ ⏑ –́ ⏓
–́ ⏑ –́ ⏒ –́ ⏑ –́ ⏑

ALKMAN—I. 2. αἰὲν ἄειδε Plan. Schol. An. 3. νεωχμόν Plan. Par. 2916, cf. Erotian 262; παρσένοις . αιειδεν Prisc.; καὶ ἄειδε Plan.

II. 1. δαμάντορες A; ταχέων δμητῆρες Schol. κ 513; ἐλατῆρες *ib.*; ἐλατῆρε Eust. 1667. 34. 2. Πολυδεύκης.

III. 2. πυλεω A. 3. ακηράτων A. κυπερω A.

– ⏑ – ≥ – ⏑ – ⏓
– ⏕ – ⏑ ⏑ – ⏑ ⏑ – ⏑ ⏑
{ – ⏕ – ⏑ ⏑ – ⏑ – ⏓ or
{ – ⏕ – ⏑ ⏑ – ⏑ ⏑ – ∧

(*Seven verses missing.*)

[τὸν ἔκτανε] Πωλυδεύκης. στρ. α′ P. I.
[οἶον οὐ] Λύκαιθον ἐν καμῶσιν ἀλέγω,
[ἀλλ'] 'Εναρσφόρον τε καὶ Σέβρον ποδώκη,
[Βωκόλο]ν τε τὸν βιατάν,
5 [Ἱπποθῶ]ν τε τὸν κορυστάν,
Εὐτείχη τε, Ϝάνακτά τ' Ἀρήϊον,
[Ἄκμον]ά τ' ἔξοχον ἡμιθίων.

[καὶ στρατῶ] τὸν ἀγρέταν στρ β′.
[Σκαῖον] μέγαν Εὔρυτόν τε,
10 [Ἄρεος ἂν] πώρω κλόνον
[Ἄλκωνά] τε τὼς ἀρίστως
[ἄνδρας οὐ] παρήσομες.
[κράτησε γ]ὰρ Αἶσα παντῶν
[καὶ Πόρος,] γεραιτάτοι
15 [θιῶν· ἀλλ' ἀπ]έδιλος ἀλκά.
[μήτις ἀνθ]ρώπων ἐς ὠρανὸν ποτήσθω,
[μηδὲ πει]ρήτω γαμῆν τὰν Ἀφροδίταν,
[Κυπρίαν] ἄνασσαν, ἤ τιν'
[ἠυειδ]ῆ παίδα Πόρκω
20 [εἰναλίω. Χά]ριτες δὲ Διὸς δόμον
[εἰσβαίνου]σιν ἐρογλεφάροι.

ALKMAN—IV. 2. Λύκαισον. καμοῦσιν. 7. ἡμισίων. 8. ἀγρόταν. 18. τινα scriptio plena. 19. ἠυειδῆ Crusius.

(*Twelve verses mutilated.*) ἄλαστα δὲ
35 ἔργα πάθον κακὰ μησαμένοι. P. II.

ἔστι τις θιῶν τίσις· στρ. δ'.
ὁ δ' ὄλβιος, ὅστις εὔφρων
ἁμέραν [δι]απλέκει
ἄκλαυστος. ἐγὼν δ' ἀείδω
40 Ἀγιδῶς τὸ φῶς· ὁρῶ
Ϝ' ὥτ' ἅλιον, ὅνπερ ἇμιν
Ἀγιδὼ μαρτύρεται
φαίνην· ἐμὲ δ' οὔτ' ἐπαινῆν
οὔτε μωμήσθαι νιν ἁ κλεννὰ χοραγὸς
45 οὐδ' ἁμῶς ἐῇ· δοκεῖ γὰρ ἤμεν αὔτα
ἐκπρεπὴς τώς, ὥπερ αἴ τις
ἐν βοτοῖς στάσειεν ἵππον
παγὸν ἀεθλοφόρον καναχάποδα
τῶν ὑποπετριδίων ὀνείρων.

50 ἦ οὐχ ὁρῇς; ὁ μὲν κέλης στρ. ε'.
Ἐνετικός· ἁ δὲ χαίτα
τᾶς ἐμᾶς ἀνεψιᾶς
Ἁγησιχόρας ἐπανθεῖ
χρυσὸς ὣς ἀκήρατος·
55 τό τ' ἀργύριον πρόσωπον —
διαφάδαν τί τοι λέγω;
Ἁγησιχόρα μὲν αὔτα.
ἁ δὲ δευτέρα πεδ' Ἀγιδὼν τὸ Ϝεῖδος
ἵππος Εἰβήνῳ Κολαξαῖος δραμείται.
60 ταὶ Πελειάδες γὰρ ἇμιν

IV. 35. πάσον. 41. ρ'. ὤιτε corr. to ὦτε. 43. φαίνεν. 44. μωμέσθαι. 45. δοκέει. 46. ὤιπερ. 51. ἐνέτικός.

'Ορθίᾳ φᾶρος φεροίσαις
νύκτα δι' ἀμβροσίαν ἅτε σήριον
ἄστρον ἀυειρομέναι μάχονται.

οὔτε γάρ τι πορφύρας — στρ. ζ'.
65 τόσσος κόρος ὥστ' ἀμύναι,
οὔτε ποικίλος δράκων
παγχρύσιος, οὐδὲ μίτρα
Λυδία, νεανίδων
ἰανογλεφάρων ἄγαλμα, — P. III.
70 οὐδὲ ταὶ Ναννῶς κόμαι,
ἀλλ' οὐδ' Ἀρέτα θιειδής,
οὐδὲ Θυλακίς τε καὶ Κλεησιθήρα,
οὐδ' ἐς Αἰνησιμβρότας ἐνθοίσα φασεῖς·
"Ἀσταφίς τέ μοι γένοιτο
75 καὶ ποτιγλέποι Φιλύλλα
Δαμαρέτα τ' ἐρατά τε Ϝιανθεμίς" —
ἀλλ' Ἁγησιχόρα με τηρεῖ.

οὐ γὰρ ἁ καλλίσφυρος — στρ. η'.
Ἁγησιχόρα πάρ' αὐτεῖ,
80 Ἀγιδοῖ δ' ἴκταρ μένει,
θωστήριά τ' ἅμ' ἐπαινεῖ;
ἀλλὰ τᾶν εὐχάς, θιοί,
δέξασθε· [δι' ἅ]ν γὰρ ἄνα
καὶ τέλος χοροστάτις.
85 εἴποιμί κ', "ἐγὼν μὲν αὐτὰ
παρθένος μάταν ἀπὸ θράνω λέλακα
γλαύξ — ἐγὼν δὲ τᾷ μὲν Ἀώτι μαλίστᾳ

ALKMAN—IV. 61. ὀρθρίαι corr. to ὀρθίαι. 71. σιειδής. 72. Συλακίς. Κλεησισήρα. 76. Ἰανθεμίς. 82. σιοί. 86. παρσένος.

ἁνδάνην ἐρῶ· πόνων γὰρ
ἇμιν ἰάτωρ ἔγεντο —,
90 ἐξ Ἁγησιχόρας δὲ νεάνιδες
[εἰρ]ήνας ἐρατᾶς ἐπέβαν."

τῷ τε γὰρ σηραφόρῳ — στρ. θ'.
αὐτῶς ἔ[αδεν] μέγ' [— ⏓]
τῷ κυβερνάτᾳ δὲ χρὴ
95 κὴν νᾷ μάλ' [ἀΐεν] ὦκα.
ἁ δὲ τᾶν Σηρηνίδων
ἀοιδοτέρα μὲν [οὐχί],
θιαὶ γάρ, ἀντὶ δ' ἕνδεκα
παίδων δεκ[ὰς οἷ' ἀεί]δει.
100 φθέγγεται δ' [ἄρ'] ὥτ' ἐπὶ Ξάνθω ῥοαῖσι
κύκνος· ἁ δ' ἐπιμέρῳ ξανθᾷ κομίσκᾳ

(*Four verses missing.*)

V. (24). A DEFENCE OF THE POET.

> ⁝ –́ ⏑ –́ ⏑ –́ ⏑ –́ ⏑
–́ ⏑ –́ ⏑ –́ ⏑ ⏑ –́ ⏑
–́ ⏑ –́ ⏑ –́ ⏑ –́ ∧
> ⁝ –́ ⏑ ⏑ –́ ⏑ –́ ⏑ –́ ⏒
–́ ⏑ –́ ⏑ –́ ⏑ –́ ⏒

Οὐκ ἦς ἀνὴρ ἀγροῖκος οὐδὲ
σκαιὸς οὐδὲ *παρὰ σοφοῖσιν
οὐδὲ Θεσσαλὸς γένος
οὐδ' Ἐρυσιχαῖος οὐδὲ ποιμήν,
ἀλλὰ Σαρδίων ἀπ' ἀκρᾶν.

IV. 98. σιαί.
V. 1. ἦς Chr.; εἶς St. B. 4. ἐρυσίχαιος Schol. Apoll. Rhod. 4. 972.

VI. (25). ICH SINGE WIE DER VOGEL SINGT.

⏑ ¦ –́⏑⏑ –́⏑⏑ –́ –́∧
–́⏑ –́> –́⏑ –́∧
–́⏑⏑ –́⏑⏑ –́⏑⏑ –́∧

Ἔπη τάδε καὶ μέλος Ἀλκμὰν
εὗρε, γεγλωσσαμένον
κακκαβίδων στόμα συνθέμενος.

VII. (26). IN OLD AGE.

Οὔ μ' ἔτι, παρθενικαὶ μελιγάρυες ἱμερόφωνοι,
γυῖα φέρην δύναται· βάλε δὴ βάλε κηρύλος εἴην,
ὅστ' ἐπὶ κύματος ἄνθος ἅμ' ἀλκυόνεσσι ποτῆται
νηδεὲς ἦτορ ἔχων, ἁλιπόρφυρος εἴαρος ὄρνις.

VIII. (28). NAUSIKAA'S PLAYMATES.

– ¦ –́ – –́⏑⏑ –́⏑⏑ –́∧
– ¦ –́⏑⏑ –́⏑⏑ –́⏑⏑ –́∧

Λῦσαν δ' ἄπρακτα νεάνιδες, ὥστ'
ὄρνεις ἱέρακος ὑπερπταμένω.

IX. (29). NAUSIKAA'S PRAYER.

–́⏑⏑ –́⏑⏑ –́⏑⏑ –́–

Ζεῦ πάτερ, αἰ γὰρ ἐμὸς πόσις εἴη.

ALKMAN—VI. ἐπῆγε δέ A. 2. τε γλωσσαμένον A. 3. ὄνομα A.
VII. 1. ἱερόφωνοι. 2. φέρειν. 4. νηλεές Antig.; ἀδεές Phot. 348. 22.
VIII. ὑπερπταμένωι A.

X. (33). A GIFT.

–́ ⏕ –́ ⏕ –́ ⏑ ⏑ –́ ⏕

Καί ποκά τοι δώσω τρίποδος κύτος,
ᾧ κ' ἔνι ⟨σιτί' ἀολ⟩λέ' ἀγείρῃς·
ἀλλ' ἔτι νῦν γ' ἄπυρος, τάχα δὲ πλέος
ἔτνεος, οἷον ὁ παμφάγος Ἀλκμὰν
5 ἠράσθη χλιερὸν πεδὰ τὰς τροπάς·
οὔ τι γὰρ ἠὺ τετυγμένον ἔσθει,
ἀλλὰ τὰ κοινὰ γάρ, ὥσπερ ὁ δᾶμος,

ζατεύει.

XI. (34). A BACCHANTE.

–́ ⏑ ⏑ –́ ⏕ –́ ⏑ ⏑ –́ ⏕

Πολλάκι δ' ἐν κορυφαῖς ὀρέων, ὅκα
θεοῖσι ϝάδῃ πολύφανος ἑορτά,
χρύσιον ἄγγος ἔχοισα μέγαν σκύφον,
οἷά τε ποιμένες ἄνδρες ἔχουσιν,
5 χερσὶ λεόντεον ἐν γάλα θεῖσα,
τυρὸν ἐτύρησας μέγαν ἄτρυφον
ἀργύφεόν τε

XII. (35). LYRE AND SWORD.

> | –́ ⏑ –́ ⏑ –́ ⏑ ⌊–́ –́ ⏑ ⏑ –́ ⏑ ⏑ ⌊–́ –́ ∧

Ἕρπει γὰρ ἄντα τῶ σιδάρω τὸ καλῶς κιθαρίσδην.

X. 2. ὠκένιλεα Γειρης A. σιτί' Crusius; ἀολλέ' Jurenka. 5. χαιερον παιδα A. 6. ἠύ: οὐ. τετυμμένον A. 7. καινά A.

XI. 2. θεοῖς ἄδῃ A. 3. χρύσεον A. 5. ἐπαλαθεισα A. 7. ἀργειοφεονται A; ἀργειοφόνται BP; ἀργύφεόν τε VL.

XII. τῷ σιδάρῳ. κιθαρίσδειν.

XIII. (36). LOVE.

⏑ ⁞ –́ ⏑ –́ ≥ –́ ⏑ –́ ⏑ –́ ⏓

Ἔρως με δαὖτε Κύπριδος Ϝέκατι
γλυκὺς κατείβων καρδίαν ἰαίνει.

XIV. (37). MEGALOSTRATA.

–́ ⏑ –́ > –́ 〈⏑ –́ 〉> –́ ⏑ –́ ⏑
> ⁞ –́ ⏑ –́ ⏑ –́ ⏑ –́ ∧
–́ > –́ ⏑ ⏑ –́ ⏑ –́ ∧

Τοῦτο Ϝαδειᾶν 〈ἐμὶν〉 Μωσᾶν ἔδειξεν
δῶρον μάκαιρα παρθένων
ἁ ξανθὰ Μεγαλοστράτα.

XV. (38). EROS.

–́ ⏑ ⏑ – –́ ⏑ ⏑ – –́ ⏑ ⏑ – –́ ⏑ ⏑ – –́ ⏑ ⏑ – –́ – ∧

Ἀφροδίτα μὲν οὐκ ἔστι, μάργος δ' Ἔρως οἷα παῖς παίσδει
ἄκρ' ἐπ' ἄνθη καβαίνων, ἃ μή μοι θίγῃς, τῶ κυπαιρίσκω.

XVI. (40). PARIS.

Δύσπαρις, αἰνόπαρις, κακὸν Ἑλλάδι βωτιανείρᾳ.

XVII. (41). KIRKE.

Καί ποκ' Ὀδυσσῆος ταλασίφρονος ὤϜαθ' ἑταίρων
Κίρκα ἐπαλείψασα

ALKMAN—XIII. δ' αὖτε A. ἕκατι A.
XIV. 1. αδειαν μοῦσαν A. 2. μακαίρᾳ παρθένῳ PVL.
XV. ἄνθη M. 2. τῶ κυπαιρίσκω A ; κιπαρίσσω Apost.
XVI. βωτιανείρῃ.
XVII. ποτ'. ὦτά θ'. ἑτάρων. Κίρκη.

XVIII. (45). INVOCATION OF KALLIOPE.

Μῶσ' ἄγε, Καλλιόπα, θύγατερ Διός,
ἄρχ' ἐρατῶν ἐπέων, ἐπὶ δ' ἵμερον
ὕμνῳ καὶ χαρίεντα τίθει χορόν.

XIX. (48). DEW.

Οἷα Διὸς θυγάτηρ
ἔρσα τρέφει καὶ Σελάνας
δίας.

XX. (58). MOUNT RHIPA.

Ῥίπας ὄρος ἀνθέον ὕλᾳ
νυκτὸς μελαίνας στέρνον.

XXI. (60). NATURE'S SLEEP.

XVIII. 2. ἱερόν Plan. 3. ὕμνῳ Heph.; ὕμνον Plan., Schol. Hermog. p. 400.
XX. Ῥιπὰς. ἔνθεον ὕλαι. στέρνων (στέρνον Tricl.).

Εὕδουσιν δ' ὀρέων κορυφαί τε καὶ φάραγγες,
πρώϝονές τε καὶ χαράδραι,
φῦλά θ' ἑρπετὰ τόσσα τρέφει μέλαινα γαῖα,
θῆρές τ' ὀρεσκῷοι καὶ γένος μελισσᾶν
5 καὶ κνώδαλ' ἐν βένθεσι πορφυρίας ἁλός·
εὕδουσιν δ' οἰωνῶν
φῦλα τανυπτερύγων.

XXII. (62). TYCHE.

–⏑⏑ –⏑ –> –⏑ –⏓
–⏑ –> –⏑⏑ – . . .

⟨Τύχα⟩
Εὐνομίας ⟨τε⟩ καὶ Πειθῶς ἀδελφὰ
καὶ Προμαθείας θυγάτηρ.

XXIII. (63). THE BEGINNING OF LEARNING.

–⏑ –⏑ –⏑⏑ –⏓

Πεῖρά τοι μαθήσιος ἀρχά.

XXIV. (66). PRAISE OF THE POET.

⏑ ⁞ –⏑ –⏑ –⏑ –∧
–⏑ –⏑⏑ –> –⏑ –⏑

Ὅσαι δὲ παῖδες ἁμέων
ἐντί, τὸν κιθαριστὰν αἰνέοντι.

ALKMAN—XXI. 1. φάλαγγες. 2. πρωτονέστε. 3. θ' ὅσα. 4. μελισσῶν. 5. πορφυρῆς. 6. οἰωνῶν.
XXII. ἀδελφή. Προμηθείας.
XXIV. παῖδες.

XXV. (67). THE NOTES OF THE BIRDS.

–́ ⏑ –́ ⏑ –́ ⏑ –́ ∧
–́ — . . .

Οἶδα δ' ὀρνίχων νόμως
παντῶν.

XXVI. (74 B). A BANQUET.

1–3 ⏒ ¦ –́ ⏑ –́ ⏒ –́ ⏑ –́ ⏑ –́ ⏓
4 ⏑ ¦ –́ ⏑ –́ ⏑ –́ ⏑

Κλῖναι μὲν ἑπτὰ καὶ τόσαι τράπεσδαι
μακωνίδων ἄρτων ἐπιστέφοισαι
λίνω τε σασάμω τε κὴν πελίχναις
παίδεσσι χρυσοκόλλα.

XXVII. (76). "FOUR SEASONS FILL THE MEASURE OF THE YEAR."

⏑ ¦ –́ ⏑ –́ ⏒ –́ ⏑ –́ ∧

Ὥρας δ' ἔθηκε τρεῖς, θέρος
καὶ χεῖμα χὠπώραν τρίταν
καὶ τέτρατον τὸ Ϝῆρ, ὅκα
θάλλει μέν, ἐσθίεν δ' ἄδαν
οὐκ ἔστιν.

XXV. δι' A. πάντων.
XXVI. 2. ἐπιστέφοισαι A; ἐπιστεφεῖς σελίνῳ CE. 3. λίνῳ. σασάμῳ. 4. πέδεσσι.
XXVII. 1. ἔσηκε. 2. χειμάχωι· παραν A. 3. τοηροκας ἀλλ' εἰ μὲν A. 4. ἐσθειεν A.

XXVIII. (22). A BANQUET PAIAN.

– ⁞ –́ ⏑ ⏑ –́ ⏑ ⏑ –́ ⏓
–́ – –́ ⏑ ⏑ –́ ⏑ ⏑ –́ ⏑ ⏑ –́ – –́ ⏑ ⏑ –́ –

Φοίναις δὲ καὶ ἐν θιάσοισιν
ἀνδρείων παρὰ δαιτυμόνεσσι πρέπει παιᾶνα κατάρχην.

XXIX. (85 A). APOLLO AND THE MUSES.

⏑ ⏑ ⁞ –́ – ⏑ ⏑ –́ – ⏑ ⏑ –́ – ⏑ ⏑ –́ – ⊼

Ἕκατον μὲν Διὸς υἱὸν τάδε Μῶσαι κροκόπεπλοι

XXX. (86). A PRAYER TO APOLLO.

⏑ ⁞ –́ ⏑ –́ ⏑ –́ ∧
⏑ ⁞ ⏑́⏑ > –́ > –́ ⏑ –́ ∧ (?)

Ἅδοι Διὸς δόμῳ
ὁ χορὸς ἁμὸς καὶ τοί, Ϝάναξ.

XXXI. (87). TANTALOS.

⏑ ⁞ –́ ⏑ –́ ⏑ –́ ⏑
⏑́ˣ⏑ –́ ⏑ ⏑ –́ ⏑ ⏑ ⊔́ –́ ⏑ ⏑ –́ ⏓
⏑ ⁞ –́ ⏑ ⊔́ –́ ⏑ ⏑ –́ ⏑

Ἀνὴρ δ' ἐν ἀσμένοισιν
ἀλιτήριος ἧστ' ἐπὶ θάκω κατὰ πέτρας,
ὁρέων μὲν οὐδέν, δοκέων δέ.

XXXII. THE MAIDENS OF DEMETER.

Ἤνθομεν ἐς μεγάλας Δαμάτερος ἐννέ' ἐάσσαι
παίσαι παρθενικαί, παίσαι καλὰ ἔμματ' ἐχοίσαι·
καλὰ μὲν ἔμματ' ἐχοίσαι ἀριπρεπέας δὲ καὶ ὅρμ[ως]
πριστῶ ἐξ ἐλέφαντος ἰδῆν ποτεοικότας α[ἴγλᾳ].

ALKMAN—XXVIII. *φοίνες* B. *θοίναις* n. *ἀνδρίων* BC, etc.
XXX. *γ' ἄναξ.*
XXXI. 2. *θάκας.*

[ARION.]

Ὕψιστε θεῶν,
πόντιε χρυσοτρίαινε Πόσειδον,
γαιάοχ', ἐγκύμον' ⟨ἀν'⟩ ἅλμαν·
βράγχιοι περὶ δὲ σὲ πλωτοὶ
5 θῆρες χορεύουσι κύκλῳ,
κούφοισι ποδῶν ῥίμμασιν
ἐλάφρ' ἀναπαλλόμενοι, σιμοί,
φριξαύχενες, ὠκύδρομοι σκύλακες, φιλόμουσοι
δελφῖνες, ἔναλα θρέμματα
10 κουρᾶν Νηρεΐδων θεᾶν,
ἃς ἐγείνατ' Ἀμφιτρίτα·

ARION—3. χαιήοχ' ἐγκυμονάλμαν a; γαιήοχε κυμονάρχα b; γαιηόχε ἐγκύμου ἀλμάς Tzetz. 4. βράγχια Tz.; -οις Herm. 5. χορεύουσ' ἐν MS. except bv. 6. ῥιπάσμασι Tz.

οἵ μ' εἰς Πέλοπος γᾶν ἐπὶ Ταιναρίαν ἀκτὰν
ἐπορεύσατε πλαζόμενον Σικελῷ ἐνὶ πόντῳ,
κυρτοῖσι νώτοις ὀχέοντες,
15 ἄλοκα Νηρεΐας πλακὸς
τέμνοντες, ἀστιβῆ πόρον, φῶτες δόλιοι
ὥς μ' ἀφ' ἁλιπλόου γλαφυρᾶς νεὼς
εἰς οἶδμ' ἁλιπόρφυρον λίμνας ἔριψαν.

ALKAIOS.

I. (5). ΕΙΣ ΕΡΜΗΝ.

1–3 –́⏑ –́⏒ –́⏑⏑ –́⏑ –́⏓
4 –́⏑⏑ –́⏓

Χαῖρε Κυλλάνας ὁ μέδεις, σὲ γάρ μοι
θῦμος ὔμνην, τὸν κορύφαισ' ἐν ἄγναις
Μαῖα γέννατο Κρονίδᾳ μίγεισα
παμβασίληϊ.

II. (9). ΕΙΣ ΑΘΗΝΑΝ.

⏒ ⁞ –́⏑ –́⏒ –́⏑⏑ –́⏑ –́∧
⏒ ⁞ –́⏑ –́⏒ –́⏑⏑ –́⏑ –́∧
⏒ ⁞ –́⏑ –́⏒ –́⏑ –́⏓
–́⏑⏑ –́⏑⏑ –́⏑ –́⏓

Ϝάνασσ' Ἀθανάα πολε⟨μάδοκος⟩,
ἄ ποι Κορωνείας ἐπιδεύαο
ναύω πάροιθεν ἀμφὶ ⟨βώμῳ⟩
Κωραλίω ποτάμω παρ' ὄχθαις.

ARION—14. *χορεύοντες.* 17. *ἀλιπλοῦ* a; *-πλούου* b. 18. *ῥίψαν.*

ALKAIOS—I. 1. *ὅ* A; *ὁ* S; *ὅς* Fl. 2. *ὑμνεῖν . κορυφαῖσιν ἀγναῖς* U; *κορυφᾶσιν αὐγαῖς* KS. 3. *γέννα τῷ . κρόνιδα* U. *μαιεία* KS; *μεγίστα* U.

II. 1. *ἄσσ' ἀθάνα ἀπολε.* 2. *ἀπὸ κοιρωνίας . ἐπιδεων αυω* A; *ἐπιδέων αὔω* C.

III. (13 B). EROS.

δεινότατον θέων
⟨τὸν⟩ γέννατ' εὐπέδιλλος Ἶρις
χρυσοκόμᾳ Ζεφύρῳ μίγεισα.

IV. (18). THE SHIP OF STATE.

Ἀσυνέτημι τῶν ἀνέμων στάσιν·
τὸ μὲν γὰρ ἔνθεν κῦμα κυλίνδεται,
τὸ δ' ἔνθεν· ἄμμες δ' ὂν τὸ μέσσον
νᾶϊ φορήμεθα σὺν μελαίνᾳ,
5 χείμωνι μοχθεῦντες μεγάλῳ μάλα·
περ μὲν γὰρ ἄντλος ἰστοπέδαν ἔχει,
λαῖφος δὲ πὰν ζάδηλον ἤδη
καὶ λάκιδες μεγάλαι κατ' αὖτο·
χόλαισι δ' ἄγκυλαι.

V. (19).

Τὸ δ' αὖτε κῦμα τῶν προτέρων ὄνω
στείχει, παρέξει δ' ἄμμι πόνον πόλυν
ἄντλην, ἐπεί κε νᾶος ἔμβᾳ

VI. (20). NUNC EST BIBENDUM.

Νῦν χρῆ μεθύσθην καί τινα πρὸς βίαν
πώνην, ἐπειδὴ κάτθανε Μύρσιλος.

III. 2. *γείνατο . εὐπέδιλος.* 3. *μιχθεῖσα.*

IV. 1. *ἀσυνέτην νή* AB; *συνίημι* Cocond.; *ἀσυνετῆ ἐκt* Oxon. *ἀσυνέτημι* Theod. *Can.* iv. 83. 3. 3. *ἂν* AB. *μέσον* AB. 6. *περὰ* AB. 9. *ἄγκυραι* AB.

V. 1. *τὸ δ' αὖτε* Oxon.; *τόδ' εὖτε* AB. *τω προτέρω νέμω* AB; *νόμω* Oxon. 2. *στίχει* AB. 3. *καὶ* AB. *ἐμβαίνει* AB.

VI. 1. *μεθύσκειν* A. 2. *πονεῖν* A.

VII. (30). DEATH IN BATTLE.

τὸ γὰρ
Ἄρευι κατθάνην κάλον.

VIII. (27). THE TERROR OF THE FOE.

Ἔπταζον ὤστ' ὄρνιθες ὦκυν
αἴετον ἐξαπίνας φάνεντα.

IX. (34). "WHEN ICICLES HANG BY THE WALL."

Ὕει μὲν ὁ Ζεῦς, ἐκ δ' ὀράνω μέγας
χείμων, πεπάγαισιν δ' ὐδάτων ῥόαι.
. . . .
. . . .
κάββαλλε τὸν χείμων', ἐπὶ μὲν τίθεις
πῦρ, ἐν δὲ κέρναις οἶνον ἀφειδέως
5 μέλιχρον, αὔταρ ἀμφὶ κόρσᾳ
μάλθακον ἀμφι⟨βάλων⟩ γνόφαλλον

X. (35). DISSIPAT EUHIUS CURAS EDACIS.

Οὐ χρῆ κάκοισι θῦμον ἐπιτρέπην·
προκόψομεν γὰρ οὖδεν ἀσάμενοι,
ὦ Βύκχι, φάρμακον δ' ἄριστον
οἶνον ἐνεικαμένοις μεθύσθην.

XI. (53). WINE THE WINDOW OF THE SOUL.

Οἶνος γὰρ ἀνθρώποισι δίοπτρον — ⏓

ALKAIOS—VII. καταθανεῖν.
VIII. ἐξαπτήνας.
IX. 1. ὠρανῶ AC. 2. πεπάγασιν A. 3. κάββαλε AC. 4. κέρναις Meister: κίρναις A.
X. μῦθον A. ἐπιτρέπειν A.
XI. ἀνθρώποισι Fick: -οις.

XII. (55). SHAME QUELLS MY SPEECH.

Θέλω τι ϝείπην, ἀλλά με κωλύει
αἴδως.

XIII. (55). TO SAPPHO.

⏑ ⁞ –́ ⏑ –́ > –́ ⏑ ⏑ –́ ⏑ –́ ⏓

Ἰόπλοκ' ἄγνα μελλιχόμειδε Σάπφοι

XIV. (36). GARLANDS AND MYRRH.

Ἀλλ' ἀνήτω μὲν περὶ ταῖς δέραισι
περθέτω πλέκταις ὐποθύμιδάς τις,
καδ δὲ χευάτω μύρον ἆδυ κατ τῶ
    στήθεος ἄμμι.

XV. (23). "WHAT CONSTITUTES A STATE?"

–́ ⏒ –́ ⏑ ⏑ ⊔́ –́ ⏑ ⏑ –́ ⏑ –́ ∧

Ἄνδρες γὰρ πόλιος πύργος ἀρεύιοι.

XVI. (33). ΠΡΟΣ ΑΝΤΙΜΕΝΙΔΑΝ.

Ἦλθες ἐκ περάτων γᾶς ἐλεφαντίναν
λάβαν τῶ ξίφεος χρυσοδέταν ἔχων,
⟨ἐπειδὴ⟩ μέγαν ἆθλον Βαβυλωνίοις
συμμάχεις τέλεσας, ῥύσαό τ' ἐκ πόνων,

XII. τ' εἰπῆν A.
XIV. 1. ἀννήτω A. δέραις A. 2. πλεκτὰς ὑποθυμιάδας A. καδδ' ἐχεύσατο A; καδδεχεύατο E.
XV. πόλεως. ἀρεύιος Schol. *Pers.* 347. πύργοι ἀρήϊοι Schol. *O.T.* 56.

5 κτέννais ἄνδρα μαχαίταν βασιληΐων
παλαίσταν ἀπυλείποντα μόναν ἴαν
παχέων ἀπὺ πέμπων.

XVII. (82). THE LAST MOVE.

νῦν δ' οὗτος ἐπικρέτει
κιννήσαις τὸν ἀπ' ἴρας πυκίνως λίθον.

XVIII. (37 A). PITTAKOS.

τὸν κακοπάτριδα
Πίττακον πόλιος τᾶς ἀχόλω καὶ βαρυδαίμονος
ἐστάσαντο τύραννον μέγ' ἐπαίνεντες ἀόλλεες.

XIX. (39). SUMMER.

Τέγγε πλεύμονα Ϝοίνῳ· τὸ γὰρ ἄστρον περιτέλλεται,
ἀ δ' ὤρα χαλέπα, πάντα δὲ δίψαισ' ὐπὰ καύματος.
ἄχει δ' ἐκ πετάλων Ϝάδεα τέττιξ, πτερύγων δ' ὔπα
κακχέει λιγύραν ⟨πύκνον⟩ ἀοίδαν, ⟨σέλας⟩ ὄπποτα
5 φλόγιον κατὰ γᾶν πεπτάμενον ⟨πάντα⟩ καταυάνῃ.
ἄνθει καὶ σκόλυμος· νῦν δὲ γύναικες μιαρώταται,
λέπτοι δ' ἄνδρες, ἐπεὶ ⟨καὶ⟩ κεφάλαν καὶ γόνα Σείριος
ἄζει.

ALKAIOS—XVI. 5. βασιλήων. 6. μόνον ἀνίαν.

XVII. ἐπικρέκει. κιννήσαις Fick: κινήσας. τὸν πείρας πυκινόν.

XVIII. πόλεως. ἐπαινέοντες.

XIX. 1. πλεύμονας Pl., Athen. AC; πνεύμονα Gel. οἴνῳ. 2. ὑπό A. 3. Ϝάδεα: τάδε ἂν. 4. ὅτι ποτ' ἂν R. 5. καθέταν ἐπιπτάμενον καταυδείη R; θέος ὅπ. φλόγμον πρὸς κ. ἱστάμενος θῇ καματώδεα Emper; φλόγισμον κατὰ γᾶν πεπτ. θῇ καμ. Hiller; φλογίαν (=φλόγα) ἐπὶ γᾶν π. Gerstenhauer. σέλας Crusius. 6. ἀνθεῖ δὲ καὶ AB; μιαρ. γυν. AB. 7. δέ τοι AB. κεφαλὴν AB.

XX. (41). A REVEL IN THE GLOAMING.

Πίνωμεν· τί τὰ λύχν' ὀμμένομεν; δάκτυλος ἀμέρα.
καδ δ' ἄερρε κυλίχναις μεγάλαις, αὔιτα, ποικίλαις·
οἶνον γὰρ Σεμέλας καὶ Δίος υἶος λαθικάδεα
ἀνθρώποισιν ἔδωκ'· ἔγχεε κέρναις ἔνα καὶ δύο
5 πλέαις κακ κεφάλας· ἀ δ' ἀτέρα τὰν ἀτέραν κύλιξ
ὠθήτω.

XXI. (42). IN OLD AGE.

Κατ τᾶς πόλλα παθοίσας κεφάλας κακχεάτω μύρον
καὶ κατ τῶ πολίω στήθεος.

XXII. (44). THE VINE ABOVE ALL.

Μῆδεν ἄλλο φυτεύσῃς πρότερον δένδριον ἀμπέλω.

XXIII. (83). CONTUMELIAM SI DICIS AUDIES.

Αἴ κ' εἴπῃς τὰ θέλεις, ⟨αὐτὸς⟩ ἀκούσαις ⟨κε⟩ τά κ' οὐ
[θέλοις.

XXIV. (15). THE POET'S ARMOURY.

– ⏒ – ⏑⏑ – ⏑ ⌞– – ⏒ – ⏑⏑ – ⏑ – ⏒ – ⏑ – ∧

Μαρμαίρει δὲ μέγας δόμος χάλκῳ· παῖσα δ' Ἄρῃ κεκό-
σμηται στέγα
λάμπραισιν κυνίαισι, κατ τᾶν λεῦκοι κατύπερθεν
ἴππιοι λόφοι

XX. τὸν λύχνον ἀμμένομεν A. 2. ἄειρε A; αιτα ποικιλα and ποικιλλις A. 4. κιρναις and κερνα A. 5. ἑτέραν A.
XXII. δένδρον AC.
XXIII. εἴκ' εἴποις. οὐ θέλεις.
XXIV. A has 1. πᾶσα. στέγη. 2. λαμπραῖσι. καθύπερθεν.

νεύοισιν, κεφάλαισιν ἄνδρων ἀγάλματα· χάλκιαι δὲ
πασσάλοις
κρύπτοισιν περικείμεναι λάμπραι κνάμιδες, ἄρκος
ἰσχύρω βέλευς,
5 θώρακές τε νέω λίνω κούιλαί τε κατ' ἄσπιδες βεβλή-
μεναι·
παρ δὲ Χαλκίδικαι σπάθαι, παρ δὲ ζώμματα πόλλα καὶ
κυπάσσιδες·
τῶν οὐκ ἔστι λάθεσθ', ἐπειδὴ πρώτιστ' ὑπὰ Ϝέργον
ἔσταμεν τόδε.

XXV. (49). MONEY MAKES THE MAN.

Ὦς γὰρ δή ποτ' Ἀριστόδαμόν φαισ' οὐκ ἀπάλαμνον ἐν
Σπάρτᾳ λόγον
εἴπην· "χρήματ' ἄνηρ·" πένιχρος δ' οὔδεις πέλετ' ἔσλος
οὐδὲ τίμιος.

XXVI. (48 A). AIAS.

⏓ –⏑⏑ ⊔ –⏑⏑ ⊔ –⏑⏑ ⊔ –⏑⏑ –⏑ ⏓∧

Κρονίδα βασίληος γένος Αἴαν, τὸν ἄριστον πεδ' Ἀχίλλεα.

XXVII. (62). TO A BEAUTIFUL GIRL.

> ⋮ –⏑ ⊔ –> –⏑⏑ –⏑ –∧

Κόλπῳ σ' ἐδέξαντ' ἄγναι Χάριτες, Κρόκοι.

Alkaios—XXIV. 3. νεύουσιν. πασάλοις. 5. θόρρακες. νεωι. κοιλαι. 6. ζώματα. κυππαττιδες. 7. πρώτισθ' ὑπὸ ἔργον.
XXV. 1. Ἀριστόδημόν φασιν. 2. εἰπεῖν.
XXVI. παῖδ'.
XXVII. Κρόνῳ.

XXVIII. (45). DRINK, FOR SPRING HAS COME!

Ἦρος ἀνθεμόεντος ἐπάιον ἐρχομένοιο.

ἐν δὲ κέρνατε τῶ μελιάδεος ὄττι τάχιστα
κράτηρα.

XXIX. (92). POVERTY AND HELPLESSNESS.

Ἀργάλιον πενία κάκον ἄσχετον, ἃ μέγα δάμναι
λᾶον ἀμαχανίᾳ σὺν ἀδελφίᾳ.

XXX. (25). PITTAKOS.

Ὤνηρ οὗτος ὀ μαιόμενος τὸ μέγα κρέτος
ὀντρέψει τάχα τὰν πόλιν· ἀ δ' ἔχεται ῤόπας.

XXXI. (93). THE ROCK OF TANTALOS.

Κεῖσθαι περ κεφάλας μέγας, ὦ Αἰσιμίδα, λίθος

XXXII. (57). IN VINO VERITAS.

Οἶνος, ὦ φίλε παῖ, καὶ ἀλάθεα.

XXVIII. κέρνατε Meister: κιρνᾶτε A.
XXIX. ἀργαλέον. δάμνησι. ἀμηχανίᾳ. ἀδελφεᾷ.
XXX. κράτος RV. ἀνατρέψεις RV.
XXXI. παρ A.
XXXII. ἀλήθεια.

XXXIII. (59). "BUT LEFT THE THORN WI' ME."

⏑⏑ ¦ –́ – ⏑⏑   –́ – ⏑ ⏑   –́ – ⏑⏑   –́ ⏓ ⊼

Ἔμε δείλαν, ἔμε παίσαν κακοτάτων πεδέχοισαν.

XXXIV. (56). SERENADE.

> ¦ –́ ⏑   –́ >   –́ ⏑   –́ >   –́ ⏑   –́ ⏑   –́ ⏑   –́ ∧

Δέξαι με κωμάζοντα, δέξαι, λίσσομαί σε, λίσσομαι.

SAPPHO.

I. (1). TO APHRODITE.

1–3   –́ ⏑   –́ ⏒   –́ ⏑ ⏑   –́ ⏑   –́ ⏓
4   –́ ⏑ ⏑   –́ ⏓

Ποικιλόθρον', ἀθάνατ' Ἀφρόδιτα,
παῖ Δίος, δολόπλοκε, λίσσομαί σε,
μή μ' ἄσαισι μηδ' ὀνίαισι δάμνα,
πότνια, θῦμον·
5 ἀλλὰ τυῖδ' ἔλθ', αἴ ποτα κἀτέρωτα
τᾶς ἔμας αὔδως ἀίοισα πήλυι
ἔκλυες, πάτρος δὲ δόμον λίποισα
χρύσιον ἦλθες
ἄρμ' ὐπαζεύξαισα· κάλοι δέ σ' ἆγον
10 ὤκεες στροῦθοι περὶ γᾶς μελαίνας
πύκνα δίννεντες πτέρ' ἀπ' ὠράνω αἴθερος διὰ μέσσω.

Alkaios—XXXIII. πᾶσαν A.

Sappho—I. 1. *v.l.* ποικιλόφρον M. Ἀφροδίτα DMAU. 6. αὐδῶς P; αὐδὰς DM. πόλυ P; πηλοὶ L. 8. χρύσειον P. 9. ὑπασδεύξαισα L; ὑποζεύξασα P. 11. δινῆντες P; διννηντε V (a copy of L); δινεῦντες DM. ωρανω θερος L; αἰθέρος M.

αἶψα δ' ἐξίκοντο· τὺ δ', ὦ μάκαιρα,
μειδιάσαισ' ἀθανάτῳ προσώπῳ,
15 ἤρε', ὄττι δηὖτε πέπονθα κὤττι
δηὖτε κάλημι,
κὤττι ἔμῳ μάλιστα θέλω γένεσθαι
μαινόλᾳ θύμῳ· "τίνα δηὖτε Πείθω
μαῖς ἄγην ἐς σὰν φιλότατα, τίς σ', ὦ
20 Ψάπφ', ἀδικήει;
καὶ γὰρ αἰ φεύγει, ταχέως διώξει,
αἰ δὲ δῶρα μὴ δέκετ', ἀλλὰ δώσει,
αἰ δὲ μὴ φίλει, ταχέως φιλήσει
κωὐκ ἐθέλοισα."
25 ἔλθε μοι καὶ νῦν, χαλέπαν δὲ λῦσον
ἐκ μερίμναν, ὄσσα δέ μοι τέλεσσαι
θῦμος ἰμμέρρει, τέλεσον· σὺ δ' αὔτα
σύμμαχος ἔσσο.

II. (2). IN THE PRESENCE OF THE BELOVED.

Φαίνεταί μοι κῆνος ἴσος θέοισιν
ἔμμεν' ὤνηρ, ὄστις ἐνάντιός τοι
ἰζάνει καὶ πλάσιον ἆδυ φωνείσας ὐπακούει
5 καὶ γελαίσας ἰμμέροεν, τό μοι μὰν
καρδίαν ἐν στήθεσιν ἐπτόασεν·

---

15. δ' ἦυ τὸ P. κὤτι DM. 17. κωτεμω L; κὄττι ἐμῷ C. 18. τινα δηυτε πειθω και σαγήν εσσαν L; τιναδ' ἐυτεπείθωμαι σαγηνέσσαν P. 20. ἀδικήη *Et. Mag.* 485. 41. 21. ἤ L; εἰ other MSS. 24. κωῢκ ἐθέλουσα L. 27. ἰμμέρρει Fick: ἳμέρει P.
II. P has 3. πλησίον. φων-σαῖσ. 5. ἰμερόεν. μὴ ἐμὰν.

ὤς σε γὰρ ϜΊδω, βροχέως με φώνας
οὖδεν ἔτ' εἴκει·
ἀλλὰ καμ μὲν γλῶσσα Ϝέαγε, λέπτον δ'
10 αὔτικα χρῷ πῦρ ὐπαδεδρόμακεν,
ὀππάτεσσι δ' οὖδεν ὄρημ', ἐπιρρόμ-
βεισι δ' ἄκουαι·
ἀ δέ μ' ἴδρως κακχέεται, τρόμος δὲ
παῖσαν ἄγρει, χλωροτέρα δὲ ποίας
15 ἔμμι, τεθνάκην δ' ὀλίγω 'πιδεύην
φαίνομαι ἄλλα.

III. (3). INTER IGNES LUNA MINORES.

Ἄστερες μὲν ἀμφὶ κάλαν σελάνναν
ἂψ ἀπυκρύπτοισι φάεννον εἶδος,
ὄπποτα πλήθοισα μάλιστα λάμπῃ
γᾶν ⟨ἐπὶ παῖσαν.⟩

IV. (4). A GROTTO.

ἀμφὶ δ' ὔδωρ
⟨ὔψοθεν⟩ ψῦχρον κελάδει δι' ὄσδων
μαλίνων, αἰθυσσομένων δὲ φύλλων
κῶμα καταρρεῖ.

V. (5). INVOCATION TO KYPRIS.

ἔλθε, Κύπρι,
χρυσίαισιν ἐν κυλίκεσσιν ἄβρως

SAPPHO—II. 7. ὠσ γὰρ σἴδω. 9. κἂν . ἔαγε. 10. χρῶ. 11. ὀππάτεσι . ὀρῆιμὴ. 13. ἐκαδε μ' ἰδρῶσ ψυχρὸσ κ'ακχέεται. 15. πιδεύσην. 16. ἀλλὰ παντόλμα τον ἐπεὶ καὶ πένητα οὐ θαυμάζεις.
III. σελάναν . ἀποκρύπτουσι φαεινόν . ὀπότ' ἄν.
V. 2. χρυσείαισιν A. αβροῖς A.

συμμεμείγμενον θαλίαισι νέκταρ
οἰνοχόεισα.

VI. (11). SAPPHO'S GIRL FRIENDS.

τάδε νῦν ἐταίραις
ταῖς ἔμαισι τέρπνα κάλως ἀείσω.

VII. (16). THE DISMAY OF THE BIRDS.

Ταῖσιν ⟨αὖ⟩ ψαῦκρος μὲν ἔγεντο θῦμος,
παρ δ' ἴεισι τὰ πτέρα.

VIII. (28). THE HONEST THOUGHT FEARS NOT.

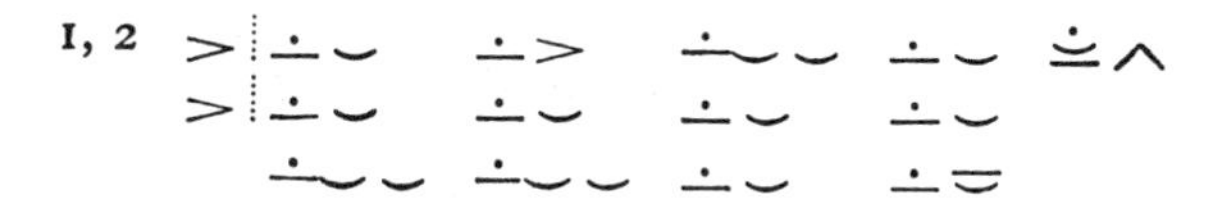

Αἰ δ' ἦχες ἔσλων ἴμμερον ἢ κάλων,
καὶ μή τι ϝείπην γλῶσσ' ἐκύκα κάκον,
αἴδως κέ σ' οὐ κ⟨ατ⟩ῆχεν ὄππατ',
ἀλλ' ἔλεγες περὶ τῶ δικαίω.

IX. (29). THE BRIDE.

> ¦ –́ ⏑ –́ > –́ ⏑ ⏑ –́ ⏑ ⏓́ ∧

στᾶθι κἄντα, φίλος,
καὶ τὰν ἐπ' ὄσσοισ' ὀμπέτασον χάριν.

---

3. συνμεμιγ-. Sm. 4. οἰνοχοοῦσα A.
VI. ἐμαῖς A.
VII. ψυχρὸς . ἐγένετο.
VIII. 1. ἐς ἐσθλῶν ἵμερον A. 2. τειπῆν γλῶσσαι κυκᾶι A.
3. κέν σε οὐκ εἶχεν A. ὄμματ' A. Neue δέ κέν σ' οὐκ εἶχεν.
Ahrens κε νῦν σ' οὐκ ἦχεν.
IX. ἀμπέτασον A.

X. (32). NON OMNIS MORIAR.

⏒ > — ⏑ ⏑ — ⏑ ⏑ — ⏑ ⏑ — ⏑ ⏓

Μνάσεσθαί τινά φαμι καὶ ὕστερον ἀμμέων.

XI. (33). ATTHIS.

Ἠράμαν μὲν ἔγω σέθεν, Ἄτθι, πάλαι πότα.

XII. (34). ATTHIS.

Σμίκρα μοι πάϊς ἔμμεν' ἐφαίνεο κἄχαρις.

XIII. (42). LOVE THE STORM WIND.

Ἔρος δ' ἐτίναξ' ἔμαις
φρένας ὠς ἄνεμος κατ' ὄρος δρύσιν ἐμπέσων.

XIV. (101). BEAUTY AND GOODNESS.

Ὀ μὲν γὰρ κάλος, ὄσσον ἴδην, πέλεται <κάλος>,
ὀ δὲ κἄγαθος αὔτικα καὶ κάλος ἔσσεται.

XV. (39). THE ANGEL OF THE SPRING.

Ἦρος ἄγγελος ἰμμερόφωνος ἀήδων.

SAPPHO—X. μνάσασθαι.

XI. ἄτϊ C. πόκα.

XII. ἔμμεναι. φαίνεο.

XIII. Ἔρως ἐτίναξε τάς.

XIV. 1. ὅσον ἰδεῖν. κάλος suppl. Herm., ἄγαθος Bergk. μόνον Hiller. 2. ἔσται.

XV. ἰμμερ- Fick: ἱμερ-.

XVI. (40). LOVE'S ASSAULT.

⏓ ⏓ – ⏑ ⏑ – ⏑ ⏑ – ⏑ ⏓

Ἔρος δαὖτέ μ' ὀ λυσιμέλης δόνει,
γλυκύπικρον ἀμάχανον ὄρπετον.

XVII. (41). ATTHIS.

Ἄτθι, σοὶ δ' ἔμεθεν μὲν ἀπήχθετο
φροντίσδην, ἐπὶ δ' Ἀνδρομέδαν πότῃ.

XVIII. (51). A WEDDING FESTIVAL.

1–3 > ⋮ – ⏑ ⏑ ⊔ – > – ⏑ ⏑ – ⏓
4 > ⋮ – ⏑ ⏑ ⊔ – ⏑ ⏑ – ⏑ – ⏑

Κῆ δ' ἀμβροσίας μὲν κράτηρ ἐκέκρατο,
Ἔρμας δ' ἔλεν ὄλπιν θέοισ' οἰνοχόησαι.
κῆνοι δ' ἄρα πάντες καρχήσιά ⟨τ'⟩ ἦχον
κἄλειβον· ἀράσαντο δὲ πάμπαν ἔσλα
5 τῷ γάμβρῳ.

XIX. (52). DESERTED.

⏒ ⋮ – ⏑ ⏑ – ⏑ – ⏓

Δέδυκε μὲν ἀ σελάννα
καὶ Πληΐαδες, μέσαι δὲ
νύκτες, παρὰ δ' ἔρχετ' ὤρα,
ἔγω δὲ μόνα κατεύδω.

XVIII. 2. δὲ ἐλών ACE. 3. ἔχον A. 4. καὶ ἔλειβον A.
XIX. καθεύδω.

XX. (53). PERVIGILIUM.

Πλήρης μὲν ἐφαίνετ᾽ ἀ σελάννα·
αἰ δ᾽ ὡς περὶ βῶμον ἐστάθησαν

XXI. (54). CRETAN DANCES.

Κρῆσσαί νύ ποτ᾽ ὧδ᾽ ἐμμελέως πόδεσσιν
ὤρχεῦντ᾽ ἀπάλοισ᾽ ἀμφ᾽ ἐρόεντα βῶμον
πόας τέρεν ἄνθος μάλακον μάτεισαι.

XXII. (60). AN INVOCATION.

Δεῦτέ νυν, ἄβραι Χάριτες, καλλίκομοί τε Μοῖσαι.

XXIII. (62). ADONIS IS DEAD.

Κατθναίσκει, Κυθέρη᾽, ἄβρος Ἄδωνις, τί κε θεῖμεν;
"καττύπτεσθε, κόραι, καὶ κατερείκεσθε χίτωνας."

XXIV. (68). NEGLECT OF THE MUSES.

Κατθάνοισα δὲ κείσεαι οὐδέ ποτα μναμοσύνα σέθεν
ἔσσετ᾽ οὐδ᾽ ἔρος ⟨εἰς⟩ ὕστερον· οὐ γὰρ πεδέχεις Ϝρόδων
τῶν ἐκ Πιερίας· ἀλλ᾽ ἀφάνης κὴν Ἀίδα δόμοις
φοιτάσεις πεδ᾽ ἀμαύρων νεκύων ἐκπεποταμένα.

SAPPHO—XX. σελάνα.

XXII. νῦν AC.

XXIII. 1. καταθνάσκει. Κυθέρει᾽ v.l. PM. 2. κατερύκεσθε AP.

XXIV. 1. οὐδέποκα Stob. κ. πότα κωὐ μ. σ. Bergk. 2. οὐδέποκ᾽ ὕστερον Stob. οὔτε τότ᾽ οὔτ᾽ ὕστερον Herm., Bergk. ἔρος Crusius. Ϝρόδων Fick: βρόδων. 3. κεὶν. Ἀΐδαο A. 4. παῖδ᾽.

XXV. (69). A GIFTED SCHOLAR.

Οὐδ' ἴαν δοκίμοιμι προσίδοισαν φάος ἀλίω
ἔσσεσθαι σοφίαν πάρθενον εἰς οὔδενά πω χρόνον
τοιαύταν.

XXVI. (70). ANDROMEDA.

τίς δ' ἀγροίωτίς ⟨τοι⟩ ἐπεμμένα
σπόλαν . . . θέλγει νόον . . . .
οὐκ ἐπισταμένα τὰ Ϝράκε' ἕλκην ἐπὶ τῶν σφύρων;

XXVII. (72). SAPPHO'S TEMPERAMENT.

ἀλλά τις οὐκ ἔμμι παλιγκότων
ὄργαν, ἀλλ' ἀβάκην τὰν φρέν' ἔχω . . .

XXVIII. (75). "AGE AND YOUTH CANNOT LIVE TOGETHER."

–× ⏑ –⏑⏑ –⏓
⏑⏑ –⏑⏑ –⏑ ⏓∧
–> –⏑⏑ –⏑ –∧
–⏑ –⏑⏑ –⏑ –∧

Ἀλλ' ἔων φίλος ἄμμιν
λέχος ἄρνυσο νεώτερον·
οὐ γὰρ τλάσομ' ἔγω συνοί-
κην ἔοισα γεραιτέρα.

XXVI. 1. ἀγροιῶτις C; ἀγροιώτατον E; ἀγροιωτειν Max. 2. στολήν. 3. βράκεα CE. ἕλκειν C.

XXVII. 1. ἔμμιν. 2. ὀργάνων. παμφρενα.

XXVIII. 1. ἀμῖν. 3. ξυνοικεῖν 4. ἔσσα S; οὖσα AB.

XXIX. (78). THE GODS LOVE FLOWERS.

Σὺ δὲ στεφάνοις, ὦ Δίκα, πέρθεσθ' ἐράταις φόβαισιν,
ὄρπακας ἀνήτοιο συνέρραισ' ἀπάλαισι χέρσιν·
εὐάνθεα ⟨μὲν⟩ γὰρ πέλεται καὶ χάριτος μακαίραν
μᾶλλον προτέρην· ἀστεφανώτοισι δ' ἀπυστρέφονται.

XXX. (80). WEALTH WITHOUT VIRTUE.

'Ο πλοῦτος ἄνευ ⟨τᾶς⟩ ἀρέτας οὐκ ἀσίνης πάροικος.

XXXI. (85). SAPPHO'S CHILD.

Ἔστι μοι κάλα πάις, χρυσίοισιν ἀνθέμοισιν
ἐμφέρην ἔχοισα μόρφαν, Κλεῦις ἀγαπάτα,
ἀντὶ τᾶς ἔγω οὐδὲ Λυδίαν παῖσαν οὐδ' ἐράνναν

XXXII. (90). I CANNOT MIND MY WHEEL.

1, 3
2, 4

Γλύκεια μᾶτερ, οὔτοι
δύναμαι κρέκην τὸν ἴστον,
πόθῳ δάμεισα παῖδος
Ϝραδίναν δι' Ἀφροδίταν.

Sappho—XXIX. 1. ωδικα A. παρθεσθ A. 2. αννητωι A. ἀπαλλαγιση A. 3. χάριτες μάκαιρα A.

XXXI. 1. χρυσέοισιν. 2. ἐμφερῆ. Κλεΐς. 3. πᾶσαν.

XXXII. 1. γλυκῆα AP. 4. Ϝραδίναν Fick: βραδίναν.

ΕΠΙΘΑΛΑΜΙΑ.

XXXIII. (91). THE BRIDEGROOM.

5

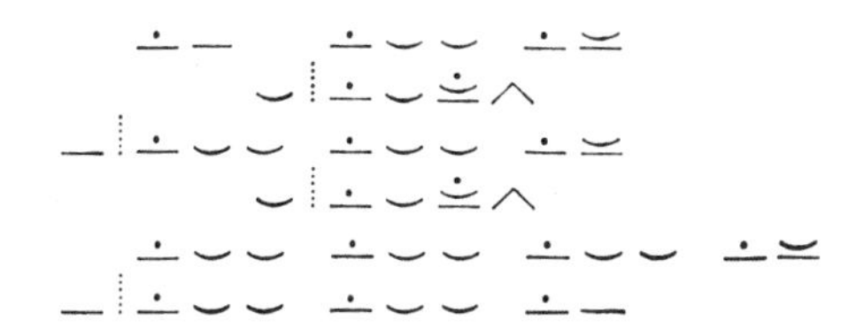

Ὕψοι δὴ τὸ μέλαθρον
— Ὑμήναον —
ἀέρρετε τέκτονες ἄνδρες·
— Ὑμήναον. —
5 γάμβρος ἐσέρχεται ἴσσος Ἄρευι,
ἄνδρος μεγάλω πόλυ μείζων.

XXXIV. (93). "FOR LOVE IS CROWNED WITH THE PRIME."

Οἶον τὸ γλυκύμαλον ἐρεύθεται ἄκρῳ ἐπ' ὄσδῳ,
ἄκρον ἐπ' ἀκροτάτῳ, λελάθοντο δὲ μαλοδρόπηες,
οὐ μὰν ἐκλελάθοντ', ἀλλ' οὐκ ἐδύναντ' ἐπίκεσθαι.

XXXV. (94). THE UNPROFITABLE VIRGIN.

Οἴαν τὰν ὐάκινθον ἐν ὄρρεσι ποίμενες ἄνδρες
πόσσι καταστείβοισι, χάμαι δέ τε πόρφυρον ἄνθος

XXXIII. 3. ἀείρετε C. 5. εἰσέρχεται ἴσος Dem. R; ἔρχεται ἴσος Heph. 6. μεγάλου πολλῷ Dem. R.
XXXIV. 3. ἐφικέσθαι.
XXXV. 1. τήν. οὔρεσι. 2. καταστείβουσι.

XXXVI. (95). VESPER.

Ϝέσπερε, πάντα φέρων, ὄσα φαίνολις ἐσκέδασ' αὔως,
φέρεις οἶν, φέρες αἶγα, φέρεις ἄπυ μάτερι παῖδα.

XXXVII. (98). THE DOORTENDER.

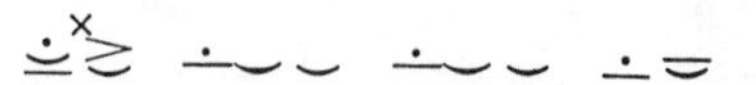

Θυρώρῳ πόδες ἐπτορόγυιοι,
τὰ δὲ σάμβαλα πεντεβόεια,
πίσυγγοι δὲ δέκ' ἐξεπόνασαν.

XXXVIII. (99). THE BRIDAL DAY.

⏑́⏑⏑ ⏑́⏑ ⏑́⏑

Ὄλβιε γάμβρε, σοὶ μὲν
δὴ γάμος, ὡς ἄραο,
ἐκτετέλεστ', ἔχῃς δὲ
πάρθενον, ἂν ἄραο.

XXXIX. (104). THE BRIDEGROOM.

Τίῳ σ', ὦ φίλε γάμβρε, κάλως ἐικάσδω;
ὄρπακι Ϝραδίνῳ σε μάλιστ' ἐικάσδω.

SAPPHO—XXXVI. 1. *φέσπερε* Et. Gud. 2. *φέρεις οἶον φέρεις, οἶνον φέρεις, αἶγα φέρεις ἄποιον μητέρι π.* Vetus Et. Mag.; *φέρεις οἶνον, φέρεις αἶγα, φέρεις ματέρι π.* Dem.

XXXVII. 1. *θυρωρῷ* A. *ἐπταθορρόγυιοι* ACP; *ἐπταθόργυιοι* M. 2. *πεντεβόηα* ACP; *πενταβόεια* M.

XXXIX. *τίω* . *βραδίνῳ*.

XL. (109). VIRGINITY.

–́ ⏑ ⏑ ⌞–́ –́ ⏑ ⏑ ⌞–́ –́ ⏑ ⏑ –́ ⏑ –́ ⏓
–́ ⏑ ⏑ ⌞–́ –́ ⏑ ⏑ ⌞–́ –́ > –́ ⏑ ⏑ –́ ⏓

A. Παρθενία, παρθενία, ποῖ με λίποισ' ἀποίχῃ;
B. Οὔκετι εἴξω, ⟨οὔκετι εἴξω⟩ πρός σ', οὔκετι εἴξω.

XLI. (136). TEARS AND THE MUSE.

–́ ⨯ ≥ –́ ⏑ ⏑ ⌞–́ –́ ⏑ ⏑ –́ ⏑ –́ ∧

Οὐ γὰρ οἰκίᾳ ἐν μοισοπόλῳ θέμις
θρῆνον ἔμμεναι· οὐκ ἄμμι πρέπει τάδε.

XLII. TO HER BROTHER CHARAXOS.

[Κύπρι καὶ] Νηρήϊδες, ἀβλάβη[ν μοι]
[τὸν κασί]γνητον δότε τυῖδ' ἴκεσθαι,
[κὤσσα ϝ]ῷ θύμῳ κε θέλῃ γένεσθαι
[ταῦτα τε]λέσθην,

5 [ὄσσα δὲ πρ]όσθ', ἄμβροτε, πάντα λῦσα[ι,]
[ὠς φίλοισ]ι ϝοῖσι χάραν γένεσθαι,
[κὠνίαν ἔ]χθροισι· γένοιτο δ' ἄμμι
[μήποτα μ]ήδεις.

[τὰν κασιγ]νήταν δὲ θέλοι πόησθαι
10 [ἔμμορον] τίμας· [ὀν]ίαν δὲ λύγραν
[ἐκλάθοιτ',] ὄτοισι [πάρ]οιθ' ἀχεύων
[κἄμον ἐδά]μνα

XL. 1. λιποῦσα οἴχῃ. 2. οὐκ ἔτι ἥξω πρός σε, οὐκ ἔτι ἥξω.

XLI. 1. οὐ γ. θέμις ἐν μουσοπόλων οἰκίᾳ; μοισοπόλω Schneid. 2. εἶναι.

XLII. 1. Κ. καί Earle. μοι Wilam. 2. τόν Wilam. τυΐδ. 5. λῦσαι Wilam. 9. τὰν Wilam. 10. ἔμμορον Wilam.

[κῆρ, ὀνείδισ]μ' εἰσαΐων, τό κ' ἐν χρῷ
[κέρρον ἦλ]λ' ἐπ' ἀγ[λαΐ]ᾳ πολίταν,
15 [καὶ βρόχυ ζ]άλειπ[ον ὀ]νῆκε δαῦτ' οὖ-
[δεν διὰ μά]κρω.
(*Four mutilated verses.*)

ERINNA.

ΗΛΑΚΑΤΗ.

I. (2). GRAY HAIRS.

Παυρολόγοι πολιαί, ταὶ γήραος ἄνθεα θνατοῖς.

II. (3). SILENCE IN HADES.

Τουτόθεν εἰς Ἀίδαν κενεὰ διανήχεται ἀχώ,
σιγᾷ δ' ἐν νεκύεσσι· τὸ δὲ σκότος ὄσσε κατέρρει.

STESICHOROS.

ΓΗΡΥΟΝΗΙΣ.

I. (5). THE TARTESSOS.

⏑ ⏑ –́ ⏑ ⏑ –́ – –́ ⏑ ⏑ –́ –
–́ – –́ ⏑ ⏑ –́ ⏑ ⏑ –́ ⏑ ⏑ –́ ⏑ ⏑ –́ ⏑ ⏑ –́ –
–́ – –́ ⏑ ⏑ –́ . . .

σχεδὸν ἀντιπέρας κλεινᾶς Ἐρυθείας,
Ταρτησσοῦ ποταμοῦ παρὰ παγὰς ἀπείρονας ἀργυρο-
ἐν κευθμῶνι πέτρας [ρίζους,

Sappho—XLII. 15. οὖδεν Smyth.
Erinna—I. πολιοὶ τὰς γήρας.
II. τοῦτό κεν.
Stesichoros—I. Ἐρυθίας. κευθμώνων.

II. (7). HERAKLES AND PHOLOS.

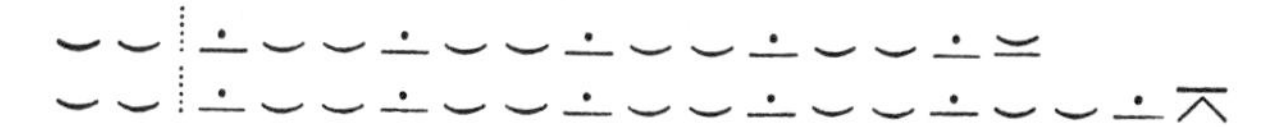

Σκύφιον δὲ λαβὼν δέπας ἔμμετρον ὡς τριλάγυνον
πί' ἐπισχόμενος, τό ῥά οἱ παρέθηκε Φόλος κεράσας.

III. (8). HELIOS' CUP.

–́⏑⏑ –́⏑⏑ –́⏑⏑ –́⏑⏑ –́⏑⏑ –́⏓
–́⏑⏑ –́⏑⏑ –́⏑⏑ –́⏑⏑ –́–
⏑⏑ ⋮ –́⏑⏑ –́⏑⏑ –́⏑⏑ –́⏑⏑ –́–
⏑⏑ ⋮ –́⏑⏑ –́⏑⏑ –́⏑⏑ –́⏑⏑ –́⏑⏑ –́⊼
5 ⏑⏑ ⋮ –́⏑⏑ –́– –́⏑⏑ –́⏑ ⏓́⊼
–́⏑⏑ –́⏑⏑

Ἀέλιος δ' Ὑπεριονίδας δέπας ἐσκατέβαινεν
χρύσεον, ὄφρα δι' Ὠκεανοῖο περάσας
ἀφίκοιθ' ἱερᾶς ποτὶ βένθεα νυκτὸς ἐρεμνᾶς
ποτὶ ματέρα κουριδίαν τ' ἄλοχον πάιδάς τε φίλους·
5 ὁ δ' ἐς ἄλσος ἔβα δάφναισι κατάσκιον
ποσσὶ πάις Διός.

ΙΛΙΟΥ ΠΕΡΣΙΣ.
IV. (18). EPEIOS.

– ⋮ –́⏑⏑ –́⏑⏑ –́– –́⏑⏑ –́⏑⏑ –́– –́⏑⏑ –́⏓

Ὤικτιρε γὰρ αὐτὸν ὕδωρ αἰεὶ φορέοντα Διὸς κούρα
βασιλεῦσιν.

II. πί' E; πῖ' A.
III. 1. ἅλιος A. 3. ἀφίκηθ' A. 4. παῖδας A. 6. παῖς A.
IV. ᾤκτιρε Smyth: ᾤκτειρε A. ἀεί A.

ΕΛΕΝΑ.

V. (26). APHRODITE'S WRATH.

Οὕνεκα Τυνδάρεως
ῥέζων ποτὲ πᾶσι θεοῖς μούνας λάθετ' ἠπιοδώρω
Κύπριδος· κείνα δὲ Τυνδάρεω κόραις
χολωσαμένα διγάμους τε καὶ τριγάμους τίθησιν
5 καὶ λιπεσάνορας.

VI. (29). THE WEDDING OF HELEN AND MENELAOS.

Πολλὰ μὲν Κυδώνια μᾶλα ποτερρίπτευν ποτὶ δίφρον
πολλὰ δὲ μύρσινα φύλλα [ἄνακτι,
καὶ ῥοδίνους στεφάνους ἴων τε κορωνίδας οὔλας.

VII. (32). THE PALINODE.

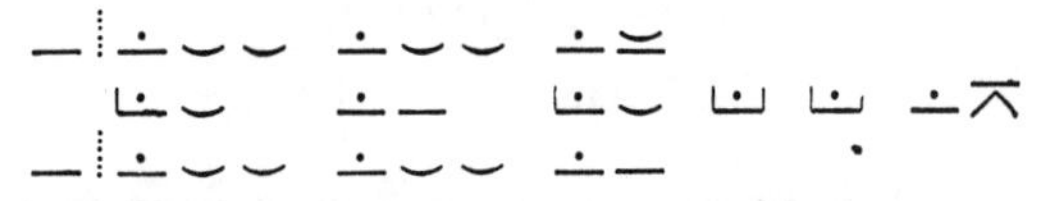

Οὐκ ἔστ' ἔτυμος λόγος οὗτος·
οὐδ' ἔβας ἐν ναυσὶν εὐσέλμοις,
οὐδ' ἵκεο πέργαμα Τροίας.

Stesichoros—V. 2. ποτέ from οὔνεκά ποτε, l. 1, ABM. μόνας A; μιᾶς BMI. ἠπιοδώρου. 4. χολωσαμένη.
VI. 1. ποτερρίπτουν APL. 2. μύρσεινα A; μύρρινα PLV.
VII. νηυσίν.

ΟΡΕΣΤΕΙΑ.

VIII. (35). THE MUSE'S THEME.

–́⏑⏑ –́⏑⏑ –́> –́⏑⏑ –́⏑⏑ –́⊼
– ⁞ –́⏑⏑ –́⏑⏑ –́– ⌊–́⏑ –́– –́⏑⏑
[–́⏑⏑ –́⊼

Μοῦσα, σὺ μὲν πολέμους ἀπωσαμένα μετ' ἐμεῦ
κλείουσα θεῶν τε γάμους ἀνδρῶν τε δαῖτας καὶ
θαλίας μακάρων.

IX. (36). THE SWALLOW.

. . . ⏑⏑ ⌊–́⏑ ⊔ –́⏑⏑ ⌊–́⏑ –́–

Ὅταν ἦρος ὥρᾳ κελαδῇ χελιδών.

X. (37). SONGS FOR THE SPRING.

–́⏑⏑ –́⏑⏑ –́– –́⏑⏑ –́⏑⏑ –́⊼
– ⁞ –́⏑⏑ –́⏑⏑ –́– ⌊–́⏑ –́–
–́⏑⏑ –́⏑⏑ –́ . . .

Τοιάδε χρὴ Χαρίτων δαμώματα καλλικόμων
ὑμνεῖν Φρύγιον μέλος ἐξευρόντας ἁβρῶς
ἦρος ἐπερχομένου.

XI. (42). KLYTAIMNESTRA'S DREAM.

–́⏑⏑–́⏑⏑ –́⏑⏑–́> –́⏑⏑–́⏑⏑–́⏓
–́⏑⏑–́⏑⏑ ⊔ –́⏑⏑–́⏑⏑–́⊼

Τᾷ δὲ δράκων ἐδόκησε μολεῖν κάρα βεβροτωμένος
ἄκρον·
ἐκ δ' ἄρα τοῦ βασιλεὺς Πλεισθενίδας ἐφάνη.

X. ἐξευρόντα.

ΡΑΔΙΝΑ.

XII. (44). INVOCATION TO THE MUSE.

Ἄγε Μοῦσα λίγει', ἄρξον ἀοιδᾶς ἐρατωνύμου
Σαμίων περὶ παίδων ἐρατᾷ φθεγγομένα λύρᾳ.

ΕΞ ΑΔΗΛΩΝ ΕΙΔΩΝ.

XIII. (50). APOLLO AND HADES.

μάλα τοι *μάλιστα
παιγμοσύνας ⟨τε⟩ φιλεῖ μολπάς τ' Ἀπόλλων·
κάδεα δὲ στοναχάς τ' Ἀίδας ἔλαχεν.

XIV. (51). FOR THE DEAD NO TEARS.

Ἀτελέστατα γὰρ καὶ ἀμάχανα τοὺς θανόντας
κλαίειν.

XV. (52). NO REGARD FOR THE DEAD.

Θανόντος ἀνδρὸς πᾶσ' ἀπόλλυται ποτ' ἀνθρώπων χάρις.

STESICHOROS—XII. λιγεῖα. ἐρατῶν ὕμνους.
XIII. 3. κήδεά τε.
XIV. ἀμήχανα.
XV. ὄλλυτ' ἀνθρ. vulg.; πᾶσα πολιά ποτ' ἀνθρ. Vind.

IBYKOS.

I. (1). SPRING-TIDE AND LOVE.

1-3 ‒́⏑⏑ ‒́⏑⏑ ‒́⏑ ‒́∧
‒́⏑⏑ ‒́⏑⏑ ‒́> ‒́⏑⏑
5, 6 ‒́⏑⏑ ‒́⏑⏑ ‒́⏑⏑ ‒́⏑⏑
‒́⏑⏑ ‒́⏑⏑ ‒́⏑ ⌊‒́ ‒́⏑⏑ ‒́⏑⏑
[‒́⏑ ‒́∧
‒́⏑⏑ ‒́⏑⏑ ‒́⏑ ⌊‒́ ‒́⏑⏑ ‒́⏑⏑
[‒́⏑⏑ ‒́⏑⏑ ‒́⏑⏑ ‒́⏑⏑ ‒́⏓
‒́⏑⏑ ‒́⏑⏑ ‒́⏑ ‒́⏓

Ἦρι μὲν αἵ τε Κυδώνιαι *στρ.*
μαλίδες ἀρδόμεναι ῥοᾶν
ἐκ ποταμῶν, ἵνα παρθένων
κᾶπος ἀκήρατος, αἵ τ' οἰνανθίδες
5 αὐξόμεναι σκιεροῖσιν ὑφ' ἕρνεσιν
οἰναρέοις θαλέθοισιν· ἐμοὶ δ' ἔρος
οὐδεμίαν κατάκοιτος ὥραν, ἅθ' ὑπὸ στεροπᾶς φλέγων
Θρη†ίκιος Βορέας, ἀίσσων παρὰ Κύπριδος ἀζαλέαις μα-
νίαισιν ἐρεμνὸς ἀθαμβὴς
ἐγκρατέως πεδόθεν τινάσσει

10 ἁμετέρας φρένας. *ἀντ.*

II. (2). LOVE IN OLD AGE.

⏑⏑ ⁞ ‒́⏑⏑ ‒́⏑⏑ ‒́⏑⏑ ‒́⏑⏑ ‒́⏑⏑ ‒́⏑⏑
‒ ⁞ ‒́⏑⏑ ‒́⏑⏑ ‒́⏑⏑ ‒́⏑ [‒́⏑⏑ ‒́∧
‒́⏑⏑ ⌊‒́⏑ ⌊‒́⏑ ‒́‒

Ibykos—I. 2. μολίδες A. ῥοάν A. 4. κῆπος A. οἰνανθίδος A. 7. κατάκητος. κατάκηλος Kaibel. ἅθ': τε A. 8. Θρηίκοις A. ἀθάμβησεν κραταιῶς A. 9. παῖδ' ὅθεν φυλάσσει A; τινάσσει Naeke; σαλάσσει Schoemann. 10. ἡμετέρας.

— ¦ –́ ⏑ ⏑ –́ ⏑ ⏑ –́ ⏑ ⏑ –́ ⏓ ⊼
–́ ⏑ ⏑ –́ ⏑ ⏑ –́ ⏑ ⏑ –́ ⏑ ⏑ –́ ⏑ ⏑ –́ —
⏑ ⏑ ¦ –́ ⏑ ⏑ –́ ⏑ ⏑ –́ ⏑ ⏑ –́ ⏑ ⏑ –́ ⊼

Ἔρος αὖτέ με κυανέοισιν ὑπὸ βλεφάροις τακέρ᾽ ὄμ-
κηλήμασι παντοδαποῖς ἐς ἄπειρα [μασι δερκόμενος
δίκτυα Κύπριδός ⟨με⟩ βάλλει·
ἦ μὰν τρομέω νιν ἐπερχόμενον,
5 ὥστε φερέζυγος ἵππος ἀεθλοφόρος ποτὶ γήραι
ἀέκων σὺν ὄχεσφι θοοῖς ἐς ἅμιλλαν ἔβα.

III. (3). THE RADIANCE OF THE STARS.

⏑ ⏑ ¦ –́ — –́ ⏑ ⏑ –́ ⏑ ⏑ ⊔ –́ ⏑ ⏑ –́ ⏑ ⏑ –́ ⏓

Φλεγέθων, ᾇπερ διὰ νύκτα μακρὰν σείρια παμφανόωντα

IV. (4).

–́ — –́ ⏑ ⏑ –́ ⏑ ⏑ –́ ⏑ ⏑ –́ ⏑ ⏑ –́ ⏑ ⏑

Αἰεί μ᾽, ὦ φίλε θυμέ, τανύπτερος ὡς ὄκα πορφυρίς

V. (5). EURYALOS.

–́ ⏑ ⏑ –́ — –́ ⏑ ⏑ –́ ⏑ ⏑

–́ ⏑ ⏑ –́ ⏑ ⏑ –́ ⏑ ⏑ –́ ⏑ ⏑
–́ ⏑ ⏑ –́ ⏑ ⏑ –́ — –́ ⏑ ⏑ –́ ⏑ ⏑ –́ ⏑ ⏑ –́ ⏓

Εὐρύαλε, γλαυκέων Χαρίτων θάλος,

καλλικόμων μελέδημα, σὲ μὲν Κύπρις
ἅ τ᾽ ἀγανοβλέφαρος Πειθὼ ῥοδέοισιν ἐν ἄνθεσι θρέψαν.

IBYKOS—II. 2. εἰς. 6. ἀσκῶν.
III. ᾇπερ διὰ: ἅπερ τὰ.
IV. θυμέ: ούμε A.

VI. (6). FLORAL OFFERINGS.

Μύρτα τε καὶ ἴα καὶ ἑλίχρυσος
μᾶλά τε καὶ ῥόδα καὶ τέρεινα δάφνα

VII. (7). THE DAWN.

Τᾶμος ἄυπνος κλυτὸς ὄρθρος ἐγείρῃσιν ἀηδόνας.

VIII. (9). KASSANDRA.

Γλαυκώπιδα Κασσάνδραν,
ἐρασιπλόκαμον κούραν Πριάμου φᾶμις ἔχῃσι βροτῶν.

IX. (16). THE MOLIONES.

Τούς τε λευκίππους κόρους
τέκνα Μολιόνας κτάνον,
ἅλικας ἰσοπάλους, ἑνιγυίους,
ἀμφοτέρους γεγαῶτας ἐν ὠέῳ
5 ἀργυρέῳ.

VI. τέρινα δαφηα, A.
VIII. κόρην A; κόραν CD. πριάμου AB; πριάμοιο CD. ἔχησι.
IX. 1. κούρους. 3. ἰσοκεφάλους. ἑνιγύους.

X. (22). ORTYGIA'S DIKE.

παρὰ χέρσον
λίθινον ἔκλεκτον παλάμαισι βροτῶν·
πρόσθεν νιν πεδ' ἀναριτᾶν
ἰχθύες ὠμοφάγοι νέμοντο.

XI. (24). THE VOX POPULI NOT THE VOX DEI.

Δέδοικα, μή τι παρ θεοῖς
ἀμβλακὼν τιμὰν πρὸς ἀνθρώπων ἀμείψω.

XII. (27). NO MEDICINE FOR DEATH.

Οὐκ ἔστιν ἀποφθιμένοις ζωᾶς ἔτι φάρμακον εὑρεῖν.

PYTHERMOS.

Οὐδὲν ἦν ἄρα τἆλλα πλὴν ὁ χρυσός.

Ibykos—X. 2. *τὸν παλάμαις.* 3. *πρόσθε . παῖδα νήριτον.*
XI. 1. *παρά* Plato, Plut., Suidas; *περί* Suidas, s.v. *Ἰβυκ. ῥησ.* 2. v.l. *ἀμπλακών.*

ANAKREON.

I. (1). ΕΙΣ ΑΡΤΕΜΙΝ.

-́ > -́ ⏑ ⏑ -́ ⏑ -́ ∧
-́ > -́ ⏑ ⏑ -́ ⏑ -́ ∧
-́ > -́ ⏑ ⏑ -́ -́ ∧

Γουνοῦμαί σ', ἐλαφηβόλε,
ξανθὴ παῖ Διός, ἀγρίων
δέσποιν' Ἄρτεμι θηρῶν·
ἥ κου νῦν ἐπὶ Ληθαίου
5 δίνῃσι θρασυκαρδίων
ἀνδρῶν ἐσκατορᾷς πόλιν
χαίρουσ'· οὐ γὰρ ἀνημέρους
ποιμαίνεις πολιήτας.

II. (2). ΕΙΣ ΔΙΟΝΥΣΟΝ

Ὦ 'ναξ, ᾧ δαμάλης Ἔρως
καὶ Νύμφαι κυανώπιδες
πορφυρῇ τ' Ἀφροδίτη
συμπαίζουσιν, ἐπιστρέφεαι δ'
5 ὑψηλῶν κορυφὰς ὀρέων,
γουνοῦμαί σε· σὺ δ' εὐμενὴς
ἔλθ' ἡμῖν, κεχαρισμένης δ'
εὐχωλῆς ἐπακούειν.
Κλευβούλῳ δ' ἀγαθὸς γενεῦ
10 σύμβουλος· τὸν ἐμὸν δ' ἔρωτ',
ὦ Δεύνυσε, δέχεσθαι.

ANAKREON—II. 3. *πορφυρέη.* 5. *ὑψηλὰς ὀρέων κορυφάς* BVMW.

III. (3). KLEUBULOS.

Κλευβούλου μὲν ἔγωγ' ἐρέω,
Κλευβούλῳ δ' ἐπιμαίνομαι,
  Κλεύβουλον δὲ διοσκέω.

IV. (4). LOVE UNHEEDED.

Ὦ παῖ παρθένιον βλέπων,
δίζημαί σε, σὺ δ' οὐ κοεῖς,
οὐκ εἰδώς, ὅτι τῆς ἐμῆς
  ψυχῆς ἡνιοχεύεις.

V. (7). A STORM.

Μεὶς μὲν δὴ Ποσιδηϊὼν
ἕστηκεν, νεφέλαι δ' ὕδει
⟨βρίθονται⟩, βαρὺ δ' ἄγριοι
  χειμῶνες παταγεῦσιν.

VI. (8). MODERATION IN DESIRE.

Ἔγωγ' οὔτ' ἂν Ἀμαλθείης
βουλοίμην κέρας οὔτ' ἔτεα
πεντήκοντά τε κἀκατὸν
  Ταρτησσοῦ βασιλεῦσαι.

VII. (14). A LESBIAN LOVE.

Σφαίρῃ δηὖτέ με πορφυρῇ
βάλλων χρυσοκόμης Ἔρως

ANAKREON—III. 1. ἐρῶ. 3. διοσκνέω CD.
IV. 2. οὐ καιεις A ; οὐκ ἀΐεις E.
VI. 1. ἐγώ τ' ἂν οὔτ'. Ἀμαλθίης. 2. οὔτε τὰ. 3. καὶ ἑκατόν.
VII. 1. δεῦτε A. πορφυρενι A.

νῆνι ποικιλοσαμβάλῳ
συμπαίζειν προκαλεῖται·
5 ἡ δ', ἐστὶν γὰρ ἀπ' εὐκτίτου
Λέσβου, τὴν μὲν ἐμὴν κόμην,
λευκὴ γάρ, καταμέμφεται,
πρὸς δ' ἄλλην τινὰ χάσκει.

VIII. (17). WEIN WEIB UND GESANG.

–> –⏑⏑ –⏑ ⊔ –> –⏑⏑ ⊔ ⏓∧

Ἠρίστησα μὲν ἰτρίου λεπτοῦ μικρὸν ἀποκλάς,
οἴνου δ' ἐξέπιον κάδον, νῦν δ' ἁβρῶς ἐρόεσσαν
ψάλλω πηκτίδα τῇ φίλῃ κωμάζων παιδ' ἁβρῇ.

IX. (19). THE LEUKADIAN CLIFF.

–> –⏑⏑ –⏑ ⏓∧
–> –⏑⏑ ⊔ –⏑⏑ ⊔ –⏑⏑ –⏑ –⏑

Ἀρθεὶς δηὖτ' ἀπὸ Λευκάδος
πέτρης ἐς πολιὸν κῦμα κολυμβῶ μεθύων ἔρωτι.

X. (20). THE DELIGHTS OF YOUTH.

τίς ἐρασμίην
τρέψας θυμὸν ἐς ἥβην τερένων ἡμιόπων ὑπ' αὐλῶν
ὀρχεῖται;

XI. (21). ARTEMON.

1,2,8,10 –⏑⏑ ⊔ –⏑⏑ ⊔ ≥– ⏑– ≥– ⏑⏓
4, 5, 7 –⏑⏑ ⊔ –⏑⏑ ⊔ –⏑⏑ –⏑ –⏑ –∧
3,6,9,12 ≥ – ⏑–≥ – ⏑–

VII. 3. ποικίλος λαμβάνω A. 4. ἀπευκτικοῦ A.
VIII. 3. παιδί.
X. θρέψας. ἐσέβην τέρεν ὡς ἡμίοπον.

Πρὶν μὲν ἔχων βερβέριον, καλύμματ' ἐσφηκωμένα,
καὶ ξυλίνους ἀστραγάλους ἐν ὠσὶ καὶ ψιλὸν περὶ
πλευρῇσι ⟨δέρριον⟩ βοός,
νεόπλυτον εἴλυμα κακῆς ἀσπίδος, ἀρτοπώλισιν
5 κἀθελοπόρνοισιν ὁμιλέων ὁ πονηρὸς Ἀρτέμων,
κίβδηλον εὑρίσκων βίον,
πολλὰ μὲν ἐν δουρὶ δεθεὶς αὐχένα, πολλὰ δ' ἐν τροχῷ,
πολλὰ δὲ νῶτον σκυτίνῃ μάστιγι θωμιχθείς, κόμην
πώγωνά τ' ἐκτετιλμένος·
10 νῦν δ' ἐπιβαίνει σατινέων χρύσεα φορέων καθέρματα,
πάις Κύκης, καὶ σκιαδίσκην ἐλεφαντίνην φορεῖ
γυναιξὶν αὔτως ⟨ἐμφερής⟩.

XII. (24, 25). EROS FLIES FROM THE AGED.

Ἀναπέτομαι δὴ πρὸς Ὄλυμπον πτερύγεσσι κούφαις
διὰ τὸν Ἔρωτ'· οὐ γὰρ ἐμοὶ ⟨παῖς⟩ ἐθέλει συνηβᾶν.

(Ἔρως) ὅς μ' ἐσιδὼν γένειον
ὑποπόλιον χρυσοφαέννων πτερύγων ἀήταις
παραπέτεται.

XIII. (28). RELICTA NON BENE PARMULA.

Ἀσπίδα ῥίψας ποταμοῦ καλλιρόου παρ' ὄχθας.

ANAKREON—XI. 5. καὶ ἐθ. AE. ὁ πονηρὸς ὁ A. 7. τιθεὶς A. 8. δ' ἐν ὤτω σκυτίνω A. 10. φαρέων A. 11. παῖς A. 13. αὔτως.
XII. 2. θέλει. 4. ἀετοῖς.
XIII. ριψες B. ποταμὸν A. ιλλιροου with κα superscr. over ιλ A. παρ' ὄχθας : τροχοὰς AB.

XIV. (41). MEGISTES.

⏑ ⏑ ⁞ ‒́ ‒ ⏑ ⏑ ‒́ ‒ ⏑́ ⏑ ‒́ ‒ ⏑ ⏑ ‒́ ‒ ⩘

⟨Ὁ⟩ Μεγίστης δ' ὁ φιλόφρων δέκα δὴ μῆνες ἐπεί τε
στεφανοῦταί τε λύγῳ καὶ τρύγα πίνει μελιηδέα.

XV. (42). THE PROPER MIXTURE.

Καθαρῇ δ' ἐν κελέβῃ πέντε ⟨τε⟩ καὶ τρεῖς ἀναχείσθω.

XVI. (43). OLD AGE AND DEATH.

1, 2, 4, 5 ⏑ ⏑ ⁞ ‒́ ⏑ ‒ ⏑ ‒́ ‒ ⏑ ⏑ ‒́ ⏑ ‒ ⏑ ‒́ ‒ ⩘
3, 6 ⏑ ⏑ ⁞ ‒́ ‒ ⏑ ⏑ ‒́ ‒ ⏑ ⏑ ‒́ ⏑ ‒ ⏑ ‒́ ‒ ⩘

Πολιοὶ μὲν ἡμὶν ἤδη κρόταφοι κάρη τε λευκόν,
χαρίεσσα δ' οὐκέτ' ἥβη πάρα, γηραλέοι δ' ὀδόντες.
γλυκεροῦ δ' οὐκέτι πολλὸς βιότου χρόνος λέλειπται·
διὰ ταῦτ' ἀνασταλύζω θαμὰ Τάρταρον δεδοικώς.
5 Ἀίδεω γάρ ἐστι δεινὸς μυχός, ἀργαλῇ δ' ἐς αὐτὸν
κάθοδος· καὶ γὰρ ἑτοῖμον καταβάντι μὴ ἀναβῆναι.

XVII. (45). THE POET'S CHARM.

Ἐμὲ γὰρ λόγων ⟨μελέων τ'⟩ εἵνεκα παῖδες ἂν φιλοῖεν·
χαρίεντα μὲν γὰρ ᾄδω, χαρίεντα δ' οἶδα λέξαι.

XVIII. (46). THE DICE OF EROS.

‒́ ⏑ ⏑ ‒́ ⏑ ‒́ ⏑ ⌞‒́ ‒́ ⏑ ⏑ ‒́ ⏑ ‒́ ⏑ ‒́ ⏓

Ἀστραγάλαι δ' Ἔρωτός εἰσιν μανίαι τε καὶ κυδοιμοί.

XVI. 1. ἡμῖν. 2. οὐκ ἔθ'. 6. ἕτοιμον.
XVIII. εἰσι. κυδοίμοιο.

XIX. (47). EROS THE SMITH.

⏑ ⏑ ¦ ⏗ — ⏑ ⏑ ⏗̆ ⏑ ⏗ ⏑ — ⏑ ⏗ — ⌅

Μεγάλῳ δηὖτέ μ' Ἔρως ἔκοψεν ὥστε χαλκεὺς
πελέκει, χειμερίῃ δ' ἔλουσεν ἐν χαράδρῃ.

XX. (50). DEATH FREES FROM PAIN.

Ἀπό μοι θανεῖν γένοιτ'· οὐ γὰρ ἂν ἄλλη
λύσις ἐκ πόνων γένοιτ' οὐδαμὰ τῶνδε.

XXI. (51). THE DESERTED FAWN.

Ἀγανῶς οἷά τε νεβρὸν νεοθηλέα
γαλαθηνόν, ὅστ' ἐν ὕλῃ κεροέσσης
ἀπολειφθεὶς ὑπὸ μητρὸς ἐπτοήθη

XXII. (54). THE FESTIVAL OF DIONYSOS.

Ἐπὶ δ' ὀφρύσιν σελίνων στεφανίσκους
θέμενοι θάλειαν ὁρτὴν ἀγάγωμεν
Διονύσῳ.

XXIII. (62). EROS THE BOXER.

Φέρ' ὕδωρ, φέρ' οἶνον, ὦ παῖ,
φέρε ⟨δ'⟩ ἀνθεμοῦντας ἡμὶν
στεφάνους, ἔνεικον, ὡς δὴ
πρὸς Ἔρωτα πυκταλίζω.

ANAKREON—XXI. 3. ὑπολ- v.l. ἀπό v.l.
XXII. ἑορτήν, perhaps with synizesis.
XXIII. 2. ἀνθεμεῦντας ἡμῖν. 3. δή Orion; μή Athen. CE.

XXIV. (63). SOBRIETY IN THE REVEL.

Ἄγε δή, φέρ' ἡμίν, ὦ παῖ,
κελέβην, ὅκως ἄμυστιν
προπίω, τὰ μὲν δέκ' ἐγχέας
ὕδατος, τὰ πέντε δ' οἴνου
5 κυάθους, ὡς ἀνυβρίστως
ἀνὰ δηὖτε βασσαρήσω.

ἄγε δεῦτε μηκέτ' οὕτω
πατάγῳ τε κἀλαλητῷ
Σκυθικὴν πόσιν παρ' οἴνῳ
10 μελετῶμεν, ἀλλὰ καλοῖς
ὑποπίνοντες ἐν ὕμνοις
. . . .

XXV. (65). EROS THE SOVEREIGN.

⟨Τὸν⟩ Ἔρωτα τὸν γὰρ ἁβρὸν
μέλομαι βρύοντα μίτραις
πολυανθέμοισ' ἀείδειν·
ὅδε γὰρ θεῶν δυνάστης,
ὅδε καὶ βροτοὺς δαμάζει.

XXVI. (74). THE POET'S TEMPERAMENT.

⏑⏑ ⏑⏑ > ⏑ —

ἐγὼ δὲ μισέω
πάντας, ὅσοι χθονίους ἔχουσι ῥυσμοὺς
καὶ χαλεπούς· μεμάθηκά σ', ὦ Μεγίστη,
τῶν ἀβακιζομένων.

XXIV. 1. ἡμῖν. 5. ἂν ὑβριστιῶσανα A. 6. δευτε A. 7. δηυτε μηκέθ' A.
XXV. 2. μέλπομαι.
XXVI. 2. ὅσοι: οἵ. ῥυθμούς. 3. μεμαθήκασιν, ὡς μεγίστη: perhaps δ' ὦ.

XXVII. (75). A COY MAIDEN.

´– ⏑ ´– ≥ ´– ⏑ ´– ≥ ´– ⏑ ´– ≥ ´– ⏑ ´– ⏓
´– ⏑ ´– ≥ ´– ⏑ ´– ≥ ´– ⏑ ´– ⏑ ´– ⏑ ´– ∧

Πῶλε Θρῃκίη, τί δή με λοξὸν ὄμμασιν βλέπουσα
νηλεῶς φεύγεις, δοκεῖς δέ μ' οὐδὲν εἰδέναι σοφόν;

ἴσθι τοι, καλῶς μὲν ἄν τοι τὸν χαλινὸν ἐμβάλοιμι,
ἡνίας δ' ἔχων στρέφοιμί ⟨σ'⟩ ἀμφὶ τέρματα δρόμου.

5 νῦν δὲ λειμῶνάς τε βόσκεαι κοῦφά τε σκιρτῶσα παίζεις·
δεξιὸν γὰρ ἱπποσείρην οὐκ ἔχεις ἐπεμβάτην.

XXVIII. (76). AN OLD MAN'S LOVE.

Κλῦθί μευ γέροντος, εὐέθειρα χρυσόπεπλε κούρη.

XXIX. (86). THE EFFEMINATE MAN.

> ⁝ ´⏑⏑ ⏑ ´– > ´– ⏑ ´– ⏑ ´– ⏑ ´– ⏑ ´– ⏑ ´⏓ ∧

Καὶ θάλαμος, ἐν τῷ κεῖνος οὐκ ἔγημεν, ἀλλ' ἐγήματο.

XXX. (89). LOVE UNDER CONTROL.

⏑ ⁝ ´– ⏑ ´– ⏑ ´– ⏑ ´– ∧
> ⁝ ´– ⏑ ´– > ´– ⏑ ´– ∧

Ἐρέω τε δηὖτε κοὐκ ἐρέω
καὶ μαίνομαι κοὐ μαίνομαι.

ANAKREON—XXVII. 2. δοκέεις. 6. ἱπποπείρην. οὐχ ἕξεις.
XXVIII. v.l. εὐέθειρε Schol. κούρα.
XXIX. ᾧ.
XXX. ἐρῶ.

LASOS.

ΥΜΝΟΣ ΕΙΣ ΤΗΝ ΕΡΜΙΟΝΙ ΔΗΜΗΤΡΑ.

Δάματρα μέλπω κόραν τε Κλυμένοι' ἄλοχον
Μελίβοιαν ὕμνων ἀναγνέων
Αἰολίδ' ἅμα βαρύβρομον ἁρμονίαν.

TELESILLA.

Ἅδ' Ἄρτεμις, ὦ κόραι,
φεύγοισα τὸν Ἀλφεόν.

SIMONIDES.

ΕΓΚΩΜΙΑ.

I. (4). ΕΙΣ ΤΟΥΣ ΕΝ ΘΕΡΜΟΠΥΛΑΙΣ ΘΑΝΟΝΤΑΣ.

Τῶν ἐν Θερμοπύλαισι θανόντων
εὐκλεὴς μὲν ἁ τύχα, καλὸς δ' ὁ πότμος,

Lasos—2. ὕμνον ἀναγνῶν A. 3. ἅμα Wilam.: ἀνά.

βωμὸς δ' ὁ τάφος, πρὸ γόων δὲ μνᾶστις, ὁ δ' οἶκτος
ἐντάφιον δὲ τοιοῦτον οὔτ' εὐρὼς [ἔπαινος·
5 οὔθ' ὁ πανδαμάτωρ ἀμαυρώσει χρόνος.
ἀνδρῶν ἀγαθῶν ὅδε σακὸς οἰκέταν εὐδοξίαν
Ἑλλάδος εἵλετο· μαρτυρεῖ δὲ καὶ Λεωνίδας
ὁ Σπάρτας βασιλεύς, ἀρετᾶς μέγαν λελοιπὼς
κόσμον ἀέναόν τε κλέος.

II. (5). ΣΚΟΠΑΙ ΤΩΙ ΚΡΕΟΝΤΟΣ ΘΕΣΣΑΛΩΙ.

Ἄνδρ' ἀγαθὸν μὲν ἀλαθέως γενέσθαι χαλεπόν, στρ. α'.
χερσίν τε καὶ ποσὶ καὶ νόῳ τετράγωνον, ἄνευ
ψόγου τετυγμένον.

(*Five verses missing*).

οὐδέ μοι ἐμμελέως τὸ Πιττάκειον νέμεται, στρ. β'
καίτοι σοφοῦ παρὰ φωτὸς εἰρημένον· χαλεπὸν
φάτ' ἐσθλὸν ἔμμεναι.
5 θεὸς ἂν μόνος τοῦτ' ἔχοι γέρας· ἄνδρα δ' οὐκ ἔστι
μὴ οὐ κακὸν ἔμμεναι,
ὃν ἀμάχανος συμφορὰ καθέλῃ.
πράξας γὰρ εὖ πᾶς ἀνὴρ ἀγαθός,

SIMONIDES—I. 3. προγόνων . οἶτος. 6. ὁ δὲ σηκὸς οἰκετᾶν.
7. εἵλατο.
II. 6. ὃν ἄν. 7. πράξας μὲν γάρ.

κακὸς δ', εἰ κακῶς ⟨τι·⟩
καὶ τὸ πλεῖστον ἄριστοι, τοὺς θεοὶ φιλέωντι.

10 τοὔνεκεν οὔποτ' ἐγὼ τὸ μὴ γενέσθαι δυνατὸν   στρ. γ'.
διζήμενος κενεὰν ἐς ἄπρακτον ἐλπίδα μοῖραν
αἰῶνος βαλέω,
πανάμωμον ἄνθρωπον, εὐρυέδεος ὅσοι καρπὸν
αἰνύμεθα χθονός·
ἐπί τ' ὔμμιν εὑρὼν ἀπαγγελέω.
πάντας δ' ἐπαίνημι καὶ φιλέω,
15 ἑκὼν ὅστις ἕρδῃ
μηδὲν αἰσχρόν· ἀνάγκᾳ δ' οὐδὲ θεοὶ μάχονται.

. . . . στρ. δ'.
. . . . ἐξαρκεῖ γ' ἐμοί,
ὃς ἂν ᾖ κακὸς μηδ' ἄγαν ἀπάλαμνος, εἰδώς γ'
ὀνασίπολιν δίκαν,
ὑγιὴς ἀνήρ· οὐδὲ μή μιν ἐγὼ
20 μωμήσομαι· τῶν γὰρ ἀλιθίων
ἀπείρων γενέθλα.
πάντα τοι καλά, τοῖσί τ' αἰσχρὰ μὴ μέμεικται.

ΕΠΙΝΙΚΟΙ.

III. (7). VICTORIOUS MULES.

–́ ⏑ ⏑ –́ ⏑ ⏑ –́ > ⌊́ ⏑ –́ –

Χαίρετ' ἀελλοπόδων θύγατρες ἵππων.

II. 9. ἐπὶ πλεῖστον δὲ καί. 13. ἔπειθ' ὑμῖν. 16. ἀνάγκῃ. 18. ὃς μὴ κακὸς ᾖ. γε ὀνήσει πόλιν. 19. οὐ μὴν ἐγώ. 20. ἠλιθίων. 21. γένεθλα. 22. μέμικται Smyth.

IV. (8). ΓΛΑΥΚΩΙ ΚΑΡΥΣΤΙΩΙ ΠΥΚΤΗΙ.

–́ ⏑ –́⏑⏑ – ⊔́ ⏑ –́ ⊼
–́ ⏑ –́ – –́ ⏑ ⏑ –́ ⏑ ⏑ –́ –
–́ ⏑ ⏑ –́ ⏑ ⏑ –́ – ⊔́ ⏑ ⏓́ ∧

οὐδὲ Πολυδεύκεος βία
χεῖρας ἀντείναιτ' ἂν ἐναντίον αὐτῷ,
οὐδὲ σιδάρεον Ἀλκμάνας τέκος.

V. (10). ΑΣΤΥΛΩΙ ΚΡΟΤΩΝΙΑΤΗΙ.

⊔́ ⊔́ ⊔́ ⏑ ⊔́ ⏑ –́ ⏑
⏑ ⏑ ⁞ ⊔́ ⏑ –́ – –́ ⏑ ⏑ –́ ⏑ ⏑ –́ ⏑ ⏑ –́ ⏑ ⏑ –́ –
⏑ ⏑ ⁞ –́ ⏑ ⏑ –́ ⏑ ⏑ –́ ⊼

Τίς δὴ τῶν ⟨γε⟩ νῦν τοσάσδε
πετάλοισι μύρτων ἢ στεφάνοισι ῥόδων ἀνεδήσατο νίκας
ἐν ἀγῶνι περικτιόνων;

VI. (12). HALCYON DAYS.

–́ ⏑ ⏑ ⊔́ –́ ⏑ ⏑ –́ ⏑ ⏑ –́ ⏑ ⏑ –́ –
– ⁞ –́ ⏑ ⏑ –́ ⏑ ⏑ ⊔́ ⏑ ⏓́ ⊼
–́ ⏑ ⏑ –́ ⏑ ⏑ ⊔́ –́ ⏑ ⏑ –́ ⏑ ⏑ –́ ⏑ ⏑ –́ ⊼
–́ – –́ ⏑ ⏑ ⊔́ ⊔́ ⏑ –́ ⊼
–́ ⏑ ⏑ –́ . . .

Ὡς ὁπόταν χειμέριον κατὰ μῆνα πινύσκῃ
Ζεὺς ἄματα τέσσαρα καὶ δέκα,
λαθάνεμόν τέ μιν ὥραν καλέουσιν ἐπιχθόνιοι
ἱρὰν παιδοτρόφον ποικίλας
ἀλκυόνος.

SIMONIDES—IV. ἐναντίας.
V. τοσάδε vulg.; τόσας δή Flor.

VII. (18). THE PELEIADES.

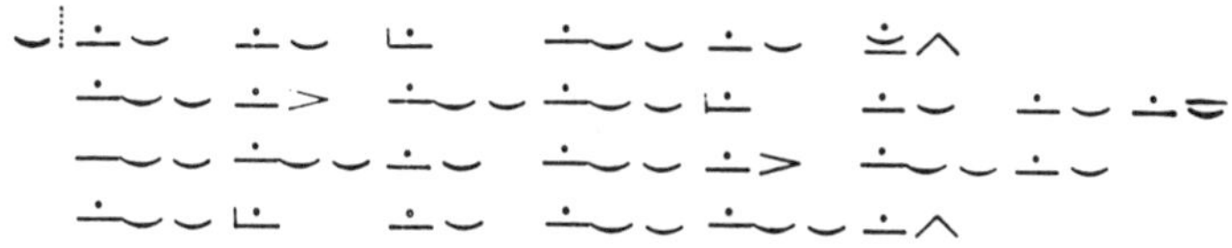

Δίδωτι δ' εὖχος Ἑρμᾶς ἐναγώνιος,
Μαιάδος οὐρείας ἑλικοβλεφάρου παῖς· ἔτικτε δ' Ἄτλας
ἑπτὰ ἰοπλοκάμων φιλᾶν θυγατρῶν τάν γ' ἔξοχον εἶδος,
ταὶ καλέονται Πελειάδες οὐράνιαι.

ΥΠΟΡΧΗΜΑΤΑ.

VIII. (29). A WINDING BOUT.

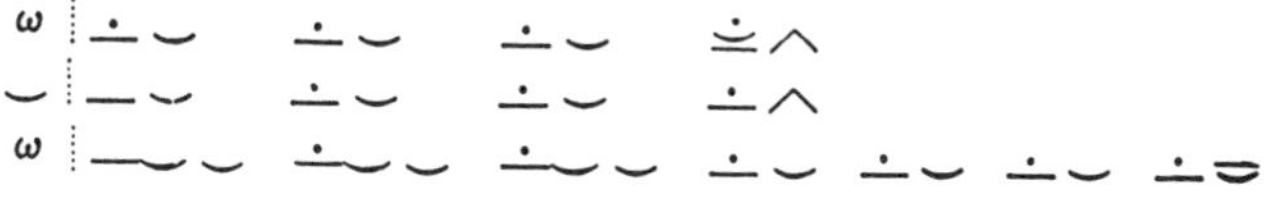

Ἀπέλαστον ἵππον ἢ κύνα
Ἀμυκλαίαν ἀγωνίῳ
ἐλελιζόμενος ποδὶ μίμεο, καμπύλον μέλος διώκων.

IX. (30). THE CHASE.

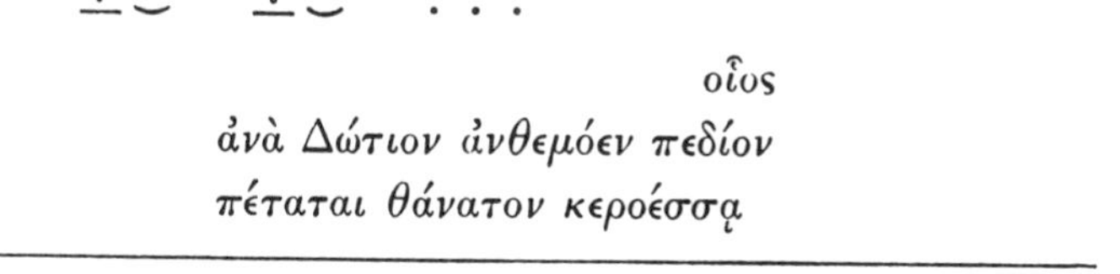

οἷος
ἀνὰ Δώτιον ἀνθεμόεν πεδίον
πέταται θάνατον κεροέσσᾳ

VII. 1. δευτεσερμας A. εὖχος Jacobs. 3. ἔπιτα A. φίλαν θυγαγέρων A. 4. ἀγικαλ-. A.
IX. 2. τε πεδίον. 3. κεράσασα.

εὑρέμεν ματεύων ἐλάφῳ·
5 τὰν δ' ἐπ' αὐχένι στρέφοισαν ἕτειρ' ὃν κάρα
πάντ' ἐπ' οἶμον.

X. (31). THE CRETAN STRAIN.

–́ ⏑ –́ ⏑ – –́ ⏑ – –́ ⏑ – –́ ⏑ ⏓
–́ ⏑ –́ ⏑ ⏑ –́ ⏑ ⏑ –́ ⏑ –́ ⏑ –́ ⏑ –́ ⏑

*ὅπα δὲ γαρῦσαι
σύν τ' ἐλαφρὸν ὄρχημ' ἀοιδᾷ ποδῶν μιγνύμεν
Κρῆτά μιν καλέουσι τρόπον, τὸ δ' ὄργανον Μολοσσόν.

ΘΡΗΝΟΙ.

XI. (32). ΕΙΣ ΣΚΟΠΑΔΑΣ.

> ⁞ –́ ⏑ ⏑ ⊔́ – ⏑ ⏑ ⊔́ –́ ⏑ ⏑ –́ ⏑ ⏑ –́ ⏑ ⏓́ ∧
> ⁞ –́ ⏑ ⏑ ⊔́ –́ ⏑ ⏑ ⊔́ –́ ⏑ ⏑ –́ ⏑ –́ ∧
> ⁞ –́ ⏑ ⏑ –́ ⏑ ⏑ –́ ⏑ ⏑ ⊔́ ⊔́ –́ ∧
⊔́ ⊔́ –́ ⏑ –́ ⏑ ⏑ . . .

Ἄνθρωπος ἐὼν μήποτε φάσῃς ὅ τι γίνεται αὔριον,
μηδ' ἄνδρα ἰδὼν ὄλβιον, ὅσσον χρόνον ἔσσεται·
ὠκεῖα γὰρ οὐδὲ τανυπτερύγου μυίας
οὕτως ἁ μετάστασις.

XII. (36). THE LIFE OF THE DEMI-GODS.

–́ ⏑ ⏑ –́ ⏑ ⏑ ⊔́ –́ ⏑ ⏑ –́ ⏑
> ⁞ –́ ⏑ ⊔́ –́ ⏑ ⏑ ⊔́ –́ ⏑ –́ ⏑ ⏑ –́ ∧
–́ ⏑ ⏑ ⊔́ –́ ⏑ ⏑ –́ ⏑ –́ > –́ ⏑ ⏓́ ∧
> ⁞ –́ ⏑ –́ > –́ ⏑ ⏑ ⊔́ ⊔́ ⏓́ ∧

SIMONIDES—IX. 4. μανύων. 5. στέφοιαν ἕτερον κάρα. 6. πάντα ἕτοιμον.
X. ὅταν δὲ γηρῶσαι νῦν ἐλαφρὸν ὄρχημα οἶδα.
XI. 1. φήσῃς.

Οὐδὲ γὰρ οἳ πρότερόν ποτ' ἐπέλοντο,
θεῶν δ' ἐξ ἀνάκτων ἐγένονθ' υἷες ἡμίθεοι,
ἄπονον οὐδ' ἄφθιτον οὐδ' ἀκίνδυνον βίον
ἐς γῆρας ἐξίκοντο τελέσσαντες.

XIII. (37). DANAE AND PERSEUS.

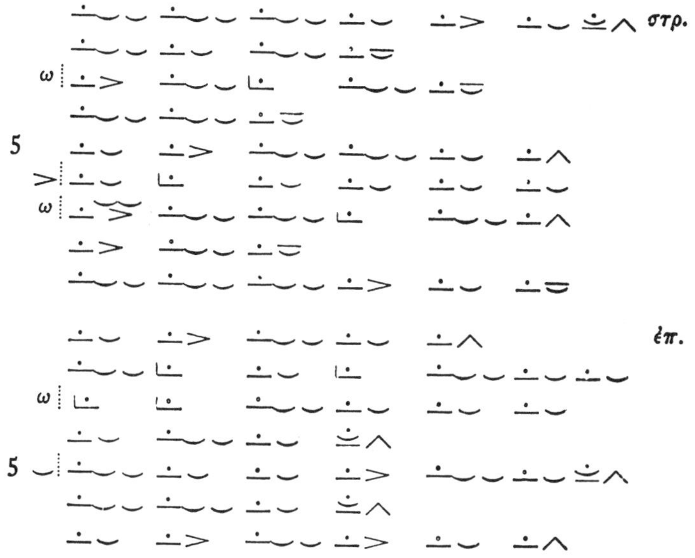

στρ.

ἐπ.

῞Οτε λάρνακι δαιδαλέᾳ ἄνεμος τέτμε πνέων
κινηθεῖσά τε λίμνα,
δείματι ἤριπεν οὐκ ἀδιάντοισιν παρειαῖς

ἀμφί τε Περσέϊ βάλλε φίλαν χέρ', εἶπέν τ'· "ὦ
5 οἷον ἔχω πόνον· σὺ δ' ἀωτεῖς· [τέκος, ἀντ.

XII. τελέσαντες.

XIII. 1. ἐν δαιδαλαίᾳ. τε μὴν πνέων. 2. δέ. 3. δείματι ἔριπεν οὔτ' ἀδίαν τοῖσι. 5. οὐ δ' ἀυταῖς Reg.; σὺ δ' αὖτε εἰς Athen.

γαλαθηνῷ δ' ἤθεϊ κνώσσεις ἐν ἀτερπεῖ
δούρατι χαλκεογόμφῳ,
νυκτιλαμπεῖ κυανέῳ τε δνόφῳ ταθείς·
ἅλμαν δ' ὕπερθεν τεᾶν κομᾶν βαθεῖαν
10 παριόντος κύματος οὐκ ἀλέγεις, οὐδ' ἀνέμων
φθόγγον, πορφυρέαισιν
κείμενος ἐν χλανίσι⟨ν, προσέχων καλὸν⟩ πρόσωπον.

εἰ δέ τοι δεινὸν τό γε δεινὸν ἦν, ἐπ.
καί κεν ἐμῶν ῥημάτων λεπτὸν ὑπεῖχες οὖας.
15 κέλομαι εὗδε βρέφος, εὑδέτω δὲ πόντος,
εὑδέτω ⟨δ'⟩ ἄμετρον κακόν·
μεταιβολία δέ τις φανείη, Ζεῦ πάτερ, ἐκ σέο.
ὅττι δὲ θαρσαλέον ἔπος
εὔχομαι καὶ νόσφι δίκας, σύγγνωθί μοι."

XIV. (38). DEATH THE END OF ALL THINGS.

–́ ⏑ –́ ⏑ ⏑ –́ > –́ > –́ ⏑ ⏑ –́ ⏑
–́ ⏑ ⏑ –́ ⏑ ⏑ –́ ⏑ ⏑ –́ ⏑

Πάντα γὰρ μίαν ἱκνεῖται δασπλῆτα Χάρυβδιν,
αἱ μεγάλαι τ' ἀρεταὶ καὶ ὁ πλοῦτος.

XV. (39). "MAN'S FEEBLE RACE, WHAT ILLS AWAIT?"

–́ > –́ ⏑ ⏑ –́ > –́ ⏑ –́ > –́ ⏑ ⏑ –́ ⏑
> ⁞ –́ ⏑ ⏑ ⌞́ –́ ⏑ ⏑ –́ ⏑ ⏑ –́ ∧ [–́ ∧
⏑⏑ ⁞ –́ ⏑ ⏑ –́ ⏑ –́ ⏑ ⏑ –́ ⏑ ⏑ –́ ∧

SIMONIDES—XIII. 6. ἐγαλαθηνωδεῖ θεικνοώσσεις. 7. χ. δέ. 8. ταθεὶς: τὰ δ' εἰς. 9. ἅλμαν: αὐλέαν. τεὰν κόμαν. 10. περιόντος. ἀνέμον. 11. πορφυρέα. 12. χλανίσι πρόσωπον. 13. ἦν: ἢ. 14. κεκεν. λεπτῶν. 17. μαιβουλία. 18. ὅτι δή. 19. εὔχομαι κνόφι.

Ἀνθρώπων ὀλίγον μὲν κάρτος, ἄπρακτοι δὲ μεληδόνες,
αἰῶνι δὲ παύρῳ πόνος ἀμφὶ πόνῳ·
ὁ δ' ἄφυκτος ὁμῶς ἐπικρέμαται θάνατος·
κείνου γὰρ ἴσον λάχον μέρος οἵ τ' ἀγαθοὶ
5 ὅστις τε κακός.

ΕΞ ΑΔΗΛΩΝ ΕΙΔΩΝ.

XVI. (40). ORPHEUS.

τοῦ καὶ ἀπειρέσιοι
πωτῶντ' ὄρνιθες ὑπὲρ κεφαλᾶς, ἀνὰ δ' ἰχθύες ὀρθοὶ
κυανέου 'ξ ὕδατος ἅλλοντο καλᾷ σὺν ἀοιδᾷ.

XVII. (41). ORPHEUS.

Οὐδὲ γὰρ ἐννοσίφυλλος ἀήτα τότ' ὦρτ' ἀνέμων,
ἅτις κατεκώλυε κιδναμένα μελιαδέα γᾶρυν
ἀραρεῖν ἀκοαῖσι βροτῶν.

XVIII. (42). MAN BEGUILED BY THE GODS.

Ῥεῖα θεοὶ κλέπτουσιν ἀνθρώπων νόον.

XVI. 3. ἐξ.
XVII. 1. ἀήτη. 2. σκιδναμένα.

XIX. (46). THE MUSE'S HARVEST.

Ἁ Μοῖσα γὰρ οὐκ ἀπόρως γεύει τὸ παρὸν μόνον,
ἀλλ' ἐπέρχεται
πάντα θεριζομένα· μή μοι καταπαύετ', ἐπείπερ ἄρξατο
τερπνοτάτων μελέων ὁ καλλιβόας πολύχορδος αὐλός.

XX. (52). ARCHEMOROS.

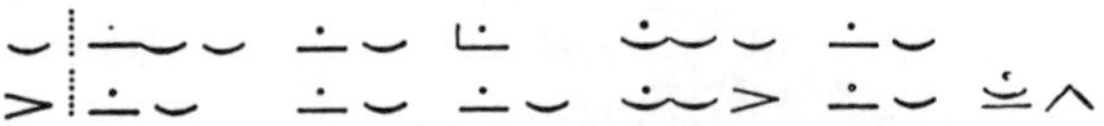

⟨Εὐρυδίκας⟩
ἰοστεφάνου γλυκεῖαν ἐδάκρυσαν
ψυχὰν ἀποπνέοντα γαλαθηνὸν τέκος

XXI. (53). MELEAGER.

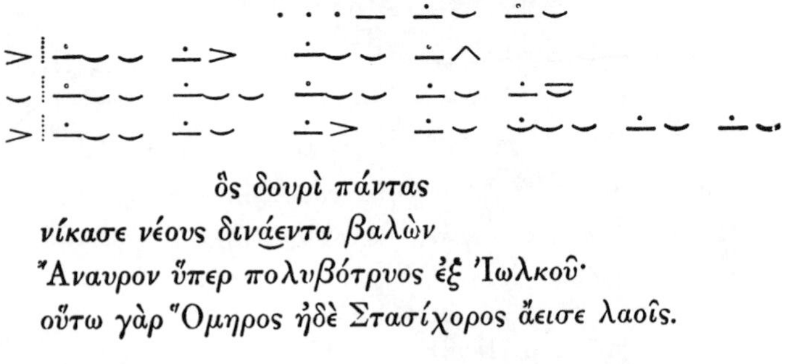

ὃς δουρὶ πάντας
νίκασε νέους δινάεντα βαλὼν
Ἄναυρον ὕπερ πολυβότρυος ἐξ Ἰωλκοῦ·
οὕτω γὰρ Ὅμηρος ἠδὲ Στασίχορος ἄεισε λαοῖς.

XXII. (57). AGAINST KLEOBULOS.

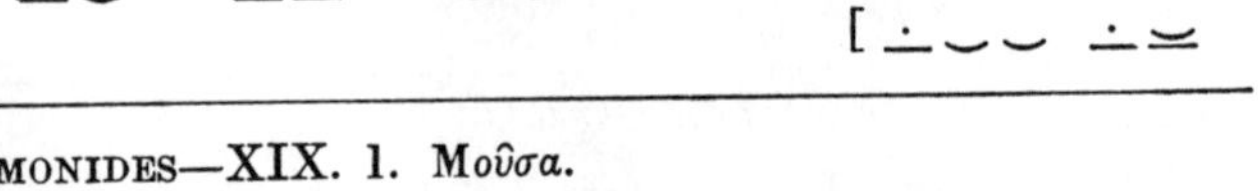

SIMONIDES—XIX. 1. Μοῦσα.
XXI. 2. νικᾶις ενεους A.

```
 –̇⏑⏑  –̇⏑⏑  –̇>   –̇⏑⏑  –⏑⏑  –̇⊼
 –̇⏑⏑  –̇⏑⏑  –̇–   –̇⏑⏑  –̇–
 ⏗̇⏑   –̇–   ⏗̇⏑   –̇–   –̇⏑⏑  –̇⏑⏑
                [⏗̇   ⏗̇   –̇⊼
5 ⏑¦–̇⏑⏑ –̇⏑⏑  –̇–   ⏗̇⏑   –̇⏓
 –̇⏑⏑  –̇⏑⏑  –̇–   ⏗̇⏑   –̇–   ⏗̇⏑
                [–̇>   ⏗̇   –̇∧
```

Τίς κεν αἰνήσειε νόῳ πίσυνος Λίνδου ναέταν Κλεό-
ἀενάοις ποταμοῖσιν ἄνθεσί τ' εἰαρινοῖς [βουλον
ἀελίου τε φλογὶ χρυσέας τε σελάνας
καὶ θαλασσαίαισι δίναις ἀντί⟨α⟩ θέντα μένος στάλας;
5 ἅπαντα γάρ ἐστι θεῶν ἥσσω· λίθον δὲ
καὶ βρότεοι παλάμαι θραύοντι· μωροῦ φωτὸς ἅδε βουλά.

XXIII. (58). VIRTUE.

```
   –̇⏑   –̇⏑  ⏓∧
   –̇⏑⏑  –̇>  –̇⏑   –̇⏑   –̇⏑⏑  –̇⏓
 >¦–̇⏑   –̇>  –̇⏑   –̇⏑   –̇⏑   –̇∧
   –̇⏑   –̇   –̇⏑⏑  –̇>   –̇⏑   –̇⏑
5 >¦–̇⏑⏑  –̇⏑  –̇⏓
   –̇⏑   –̇⏑  –̇⏑   ⏗̇    –̇⏑   –̇⏑
   –̇>   –̇ . . .
```

Ἔστι τις λόγος
τὰν Ἀρετὰν ναίειν δυσαμβάτοις ἐπὶ πέτραις·
ἁγνὰν δέ μιν θεὰν χῶρον ἁγνὸν ἀμφέπειν.
οὐδὲ πάντων βλεφάροις θνατῶν ἔσοπτος,
5 ᾧ μὴ δακέθυμος ἱδρὼς
ἔνδοθεν μόλῃ, ἵκηταί τ' ἐς ἄκρον
ἀνδρείας.

XXII. 1. νῷ. 2. ποταμοῖς. 3. χρυσᾶς. 4. ἀντιθέντα στήλας. 6. βρότειοι.

XXIII. 3. νῦν δέ μιν θυάν. 6. ἵκητ' ἐς.

XXIV. (60). THE DEAD IN LIFE.

– ⁞ ⏑́ ⏑ –́ – –́ ⏑ ⏑ –́ – –́ ⏑ ⏑ –́ ⏑ –́ –

Ὤνθρωπε, κεῖσαι ζῶν ἔτι μᾶλλον τῶν ὑπὸ γᾶς ἐκείνων.

XXV. (61). VIRTUE IS OF HEAVEN.

–́ ⏑ ⏑ –́ ⏑ –́ ∧
ω ⁞ –́ ⏑ ⏑ –́ ⏑ ⏑ –́ ⏑ –́ ∧
⏑́⏑ ⏑ ⏑́ –́ ⏑ ⏑ –́ > –́ ⏑
–́ ⏑ –́ ⏑ –́ > –́ ∧

Οὔτις ἄνευ θεῶν
ἀρετὰν λάβεν, οὐ πόλις, οὐ βροτός.
θεὸς ὁ πάμμητις· ἀπήμαντον δὲ
οὐδέν ἐστιν ἐν θνατοῖς.

XXVI. (62). RES HUMANAE INSTABILES.

. . . –́ > –́ ⏑ –́ ∧
⏑ ⁞ ⏑́⏑ ⏑ –́ ⏑ –́ > –́ ⏑ ⏑ –́ ⏑ ⏑ –́ ∧
–́ ⏑ ⏑ –́ > –́ ⏑ – . . .

οὐκ ἔστιν κακὸν
ἀνεπιδόκητον ἀνθρώποις, ὀλίγῳ δὲ χρόνῳ
πάντα μεταρρίπτει θεός.

XXVII. (65). MORS ET FUGACEM PERSEQUITUR VIRUM.

⏑ ⁞ –́ ⏑ ⏑ –́ ⏑ ⏑ –́ – ⏑́⏑ > –́ ⏑

Ὁ δ' αὖ θάνατος κίχε καὶ τὸν φυγόμαχον.

SIMONIDES—XXIV. γῆς.
XXV. 4. αὐτοῖς.

XXVIII. (66). SILENCE.

Ἔστι καὶ σιγᾶς ἀκίνδυνον γέρας.

XXIX. (69). WHAT'S DONE IS DONE.

Τὸ γὰρ γεγενημένον οὐκέτ' ἄρεκτον ἔσται.

XXX. (70). HEALTH.

Οὐδὲ καλᾶς σοφίας ἐστὶν χάρις,
εἰ μή τις ἔχει σεμνὰν ὑγίειαν.

XXXI. (71). PLEASURE.

Τίς γὰρ ἁδονᾶς ἄτερ
θνατῶν βίος ποθεινὸς ἢ ποία τυραννίς;
τᾶς δ' ἄτερ οὐδὲ θεῶν ζαλωτὸς αἰών.

XXXII. (72). ROSY LIPS.

πορφυρέου
ἀπὸ στόματος ἱεῖσα φωνὰν παρθένος.

XXXI. 2. θνητῶν. 3. ζηλωτός.

XXXIII. (73). THE NIGHTINGALE.

Εὖτ' ἀηδόνες πολυκώτιλοι,
χλωραύχενες, εἰαριναί

XXXIV. (74). THE HARBINGER OF SPRING.

Ἄγγελε κλυτὰ ἔαρος ἁδυόδμου,
κυανέα χελιδοῖ

XXXV. (75). WINE AND POETRY.

ἐξελέγχει ⟨δ'⟩ ὁ νέος
οἶνος οὐ τὸ πέρυσι δῶρον ἀμπέλου· ὁ δὲ μῦθος
ὅδε κενεόφρων.

XXXVI. (76). APPEARANCES AND TRUTH.

Τὸ δοκεῖν καὶ τὰν ἀλάθειαν βιᾶται.

TIMOKREON.

I. (1). THEMISTOKLES.

στρ.

—¦ ⏗⏑⏑ ⏗⏑⏑ ⏗— ⌊⏗⏑ ⏗— ⌊⏗⏑ —— *ἐπ.*
⏗⏑⏑ ⏗⏑⏑ ⏗— ⌊⏗⏑ ⏗> ⏗⏑⏑ ⏗—
⏗⏑⏑ ⏗⏑⏑ ⏗⩘
—¦ ⌊⏗⏑ ⏗— ⌊⏗⏑ ⌊⏗⌋ ⌊⏗⏑ ⏗— ⌊⏗⏑ ⏗—

Ἀλλ' εἰ τύγε Παυσανίαν ἢ καὶ τύγε Ξάνθιππον
αἰνεῖς *στρ.*
ἢ τύγε Λευτυχίδαν, ἐγὼ δ' Ἀριστείδαν ἐπαινέω
ἄνδρ' ἱερᾶν ἀπ' Ἀθανᾶν
ἐλθεῖν ἕνα λῷστον, ἐπεὶ Θεμιστοκλῆ' ἤχθαρε Λατώ,

5 ψεύσταν, ἄδικον, προδόταν, ὃς Τιμοκρέοντα ξεῖνον
ἐόντα *ἀντ.*
ἀργυρίοισι κυβαλικοῖσι πεισθεὶς οὐ κατᾶγεν
ἐς πατρίδ' Ἰάλυσον·
λαβὼν δὲ τρί' ἀργυρίου τάλαντ' ἔβα πλέων εἰς ὄλεθρον,

τοὺς μὲν κατάγων ἀδίκως, τοὺς δ' ἐκδιώκων, τοὺς
δὲ καίνων, *ἐπ.*
10 ἀργυρίων ὑπόπλεος· Ἰσθμοῖ δ' ἐπανδόκευε γελοίως
ψυχρὰ κρέα παρέχων·
οἱ δ' ἤσθιον κηὔχοντο μὴ ὥραν Θεμιστοκλέος γενέσθαι.

II. (2).

⌊⏗⏑ ⏗> ⌊⏗⏑ ⏗⩘
⏗⏑⏑ ⏗— ⌊⏗⏑ ⏗⩘
⌊⏗⏑ ⏗— ⏗⏑ ⏗⏓

Μοῦσα, τοῦδε τοῦ μέλεος
κλέος ἀν' Ἕλλανας τίθει,
ὡς ἐοικὸς καὶ δίκαιον.

TIMOKREON—I. 4. Θεμιστοκλῆα vulg., -κλέα δ' Fa. 6. σκυβαλικοῖσι vulg.; βαλικοῖσι i; κυμβαλικοῖσι Fa., c. superscr. 7. εἰς. 10. ὑπόπλειος Fa. 12. ὥραν Θεμιστοκλέους.

III. (3).

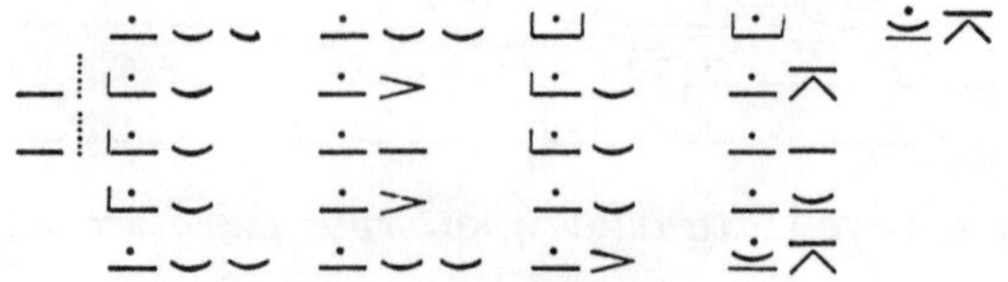

Οὐκ ἄρα Τιμοκρέων μοῦνος
Μήδοισιν ὁρκιατόμει,
ἀλλ' ἐντὶ κἆλλοι δὴ πονηροί·
οὐκ ἐγὼ μόνα κόλουρις·
5 ἐντὶ καὶ ἄλλαι ἀλώπεκες.

IV. (8). PLUTOS.

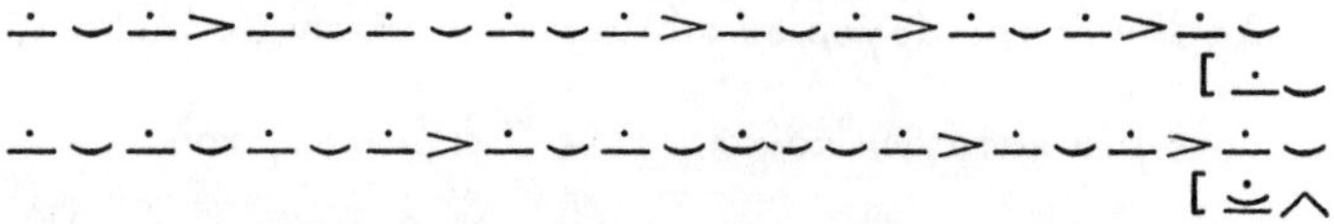

Ὤφελέν σ', ὦ τυφλὲ Πλοῦτε, μήτε γῇ μήτ' ἐν θαλάσσῃ
μήτ' ἐν ἠπείρῳ φανῆμεν,
ἀλλὰ Τάρταρόν τε ναίειν κἀχέροντα· διὰ σὲ γὰρ πάντ'
⟨ἔστ'⟩ ἐν ἀνθρώποις κακά.

KORINNA.

I. (2). ORION.

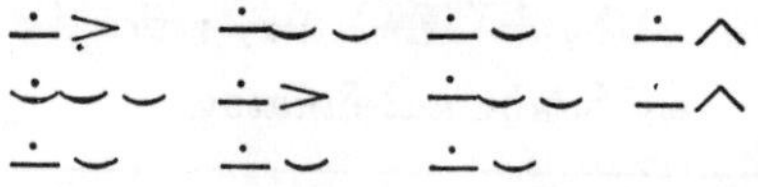

TIMOKREON—III. 2. ὅρκια τέμοι vulg.
IV. 1. ἐν γῇ. φανήμεναι.

Νίκασ' ὃ μεγαλοσθένης
Ὠαρίων, χώραν τ' ἀφ' ἑῶς
πᾶσαν ὠνύμανεν.

II. (9). AWAKE, KORINNA!

Ἦ διανεκῶς εὕδεις; οὐ μὰν πάρος ἦσθα, Κόριννα, . . .

III. (10). HER THEME.

⏑ ⁞ –́ > –́ > –́ ⏑ ⏑ –́ ⋀
> ⁞ –́ ⏑ –́ ⟨⏑ –́ ⏓>

Ἰώνη δ' ἡρώων ἀρετὰς
χἠρωάδων ⟨ἀείδω⟩

IV. (20). SONG AT TANAGRA.

–́ ⏑ ⏑ –́ ⏑ –́ ⏑ ⏑ –́ ⋀

Καλὰ γεροῖ' ἀεισομένα
Ταναγρίδεσσι λευκοπέπλοις·
μέγα δ' ἐμὰ γέγαθε πόλις
λιγυροκωτίλαις ἐνόπαις.

V. (21). MYRTIS' CONTEST WITH PINDAR.

. . . –́ ⏑ –́ ⏑
–́ ⏑ ⏑ ⌞–́ –́ ⏑ ⏑ –́ ⏑
–́ ⏑ ⏑ ⌞–́ –́ ⏑ –́ ⋀
–́ ⏑ –́ ⏑ ⏑ –́ ⋀

μέμφομαι δὲ
καὶ λιγυρὰν Μυρτίδ' ἰώνγα,
ὅτι βανὰ φῦσ' ἔβα
Πινδάροι ποτ' ἔριν.

KORINNA—I. 2. ἀπ' ἑοῦς. 3. ὤνυμανεν Michelangeli: ὠνούμηνεν.
III. 1. ἴωνει ηδ'. χειρωαδων.
IV. 1. γέροια εἰσομένα. 3. ἐμή. 4. λιγουροκωτίλης ἐνοπῆς.
V. 2. λιγουράν. 3. φοῦσ'. 4. Πινδαρίοιο.

VI. (23). THESPIA.

Θέσπια καλλιγένεθλε, φιλόξενε, μωσοφίλητε.

LAMPROKLES.

ΕΙΣ ΑΘΗΝΑΝ.

–́ ⏑ ⏑   –́ ⏑ ⏑   –́ –   –́ ⏑ ⏑   –́ ⏑ ⏑   –́ ⏓
⏑ ⋮ –́ –   –́ ⏑ ⏑   –́ ⏑ ⏑   –́ –
–́ ⏑ ⏑   –́ ⏑ ⏑   –́ ⏑ ⏑   –́ ⏓

Παλλάδα περσέπολιν, δεινὰν θεὸν ἐγρεκύδοιμον,
ποτικλήζω πολεμαδόκον, ἁγνὰν
παῖδα Διὸς μεγάλου δαμάσιππον

PRATINAS.

I. (1). AGAINST THE ENCROACHMENT OF THE FLUTE ACCOMPANIMENT.

⏑ ⏑ ⋮ ⏑́ ⏑ ⏑ ⏑   ⏑́ ⏑ ⏑ ⏑   ⏑́ ⏑ –   ⏑́ ⏑ ⩘
⏑ ⏑ ⋮ ⏑́ ⏑ ⏑ ⏑   ⏑́ ⏑ ⏑ ⏑   –́ ⏑ ⏑   ⏑́ ⏑ ⏑ ⏑   ⏑́ ⏑ ⏑ ⏑
[–́ ⩘
⏑ ⏑ ⋮ ⏑́ ⏑ ⏑ ⏑   ⏑́ ⏑ ⏑ ⏑   –́ ⏑ ⏑   –́ ⏑ ⏑   –́ ⏑ ⏑
⏑ ⏑ ⋮ ⏑́ ⏑ ⏑ ⏑   –́ ⏑ ⏑   –́ ⏑ ⏑   –́ ⩘   [–́ ⩘
5   –́ ⏑ ⏑   –́ ⏑ ⏑   –́ ⏑   –́ ⏑   –́ ⏑   –́ ⏑
[⏓́ ∧
–́ ⏑   ⊔́   –́ ⏑   ⊔́   –́ ⏑   –́ ⏑
[–́ ⏑ ⏑   –́ ⏑ ⏑ ⊔́   ⏓́ ∧
–́ ⏑   –́ ⏑   –́ ⏑   ⊔́   –́ ⏑   –́ ⏑
[–́ ⏑   –́ ∧
> ⋮ –́ ⏑   –́ ⏑   –́ ⏑   –́ ⏑   –́ ⏑ ⏑   –́ ⏑ ⏑
[–́ ⏑   –́ ⏑   ⊔́   –́ ∧

KORINNA—VI. μουσοφίλητε.
LAMPROKLES—1. περσέπτολιν v. l. 2. ποτικλητ̈ζω.

10

15

Τίς ὁ θόρυβος ὅδε; τί τάδε τὰ χορεύματα;
τίς ὕβρις ἔμολεν ἐπὶ Διονυσιάδα πολυπάταγα θυμέλαν;
ἐμὸς ἐμὸς ὁ Βρόμιος· ἐμὲ δεῖ κελαδεῖν, ἐμὲ δεῖ παταγεῖν
ἀν' ὄρεα σύμενον μετὰ Ναϊάδων
5 οἷά τε κύκνον ἄγοντα ποικιλόπτερον μέλος.
τὰν ἀοιδὰν κατέστασε Πιερὶς βασίλειαν· ὁ δ' αὐλὸς
ὕστερον χορευέτω· καὶ γάρ ἐσθ' ὑπηρέτας.
κώμῳ μόνον θυραμάχοις τε πυγμαχίαισι νέων θέλει
ἔμμεναι στρατηλάτας. [παροίνων
10 παῖε τὸν φρυνίου
ποικίλου πνοὰν ἔχοντα·
φλέγε τὸν ὀλεσισιαλοκάλαμον,
λαλοβαρυόπα παραμελορυθμοβάταν θ',
ὑπα⟨ί⟩ τρυπάνῳ δέμας πεπλασμένον.
15 ἤν ἰδού· ἅδε σοι δεξιὰ
καὶ ποδὸς διαρριφά, θριαμβοδιθύραμβε·
κισσόχαιτ' ἄναξ, ἄκουε τὰν ἐμὰν Δώριον χορείαν.

PRATINAS—I. 4. *σύμενον* B; *θύμενον* AC. Ναΐδων. 6. *κατεστας ἐπιερεις βασιλεια* A. 8. *κωμῶν* A; *κώμων μόνων* E. *θεαεὶ πάροινον* A. 10. *φρυναίω.* 11. *προανέχοντα* A. 12. *ὀλοσιαλοκάλαμον* A. 13. λαλοβαρυοπαραμελορυθμοβαταν *θυπα* A; λαλοβαρυπαραμ-. E. 16. *πόλος* A.

II. (5). THE AIOLIAN MODE.

Μήτε σύντονον δίωκε, μήτε τὰν ἀνειμέναν Ἰαστὶ μοῦσαν,
ἀλλὰ τὰν μέσαν νεῶν ἄρουραν αἰόλιζε τῷ μέλει.

πρέπει τοι πᾶσιν ἀοιδολαβράκταις Αἰολὶς ἁρμονία.

PHRYNICHOS.

I. (1). ΕΙΣ ΑΘΗΝΑΝ.

Παλλάδα περσέπολιν κλῄζω, πολεμαδόκον, ἁγνάν,
παῖδα Διὸς μεγάλου, δάμνιππον αἰεὶ παρθένον.

II. (2). "THE PURPLE LIGHT OF LOVE."

Λάμπει δ' ἐπὶ πορφυρέαις παρῇσι φῶς ἔρωτος.

PRATINAS—II. 1. ιασιτὶν οὖσαν AE. 3. ἀοιδὰ λαβρακταις.
PRYNICHOS—I. 2. δαμνοπῶλον ἄϊστον.
II. παρηίσιν A; παρειαῖσι E.

DIAGORAS.

I. (1). ΕΙΣ ΑΡΙΑΝΘΗΝ ΑΡΓΕΙΟΝ.

Θεός, θεὸς πρὸ παντὸς ἔργου βροτείου
νωμᾷ φρέν' ὑπερτάταν,
αὐτοδαὴς δ' ἀρετὰ βραχὺν οἶμον ἕρπει.

II. (2). ΕΙΣ ΝΙΚΟΔΩΡΟΝ ΜΑΝΤΙΝΕΑ.

Κατὰ δαίμονα καὶ τύχαν
τὰ πάντα βροτοῖσιν ἐκτελεῖται.

KYDIAS.

Εὐλαβεῦ δὲ μὴ κατέναντα λέοντος
νεβρὸς ἐλθὼν μοῖραν αἱρεῖσθαι κρεῶν.

PRAXILLA.

I. (1). ΑΧΙΛΛΕΥΣ.

Ἀλλὰ τεὸν οὔποτε θυμὸν ἐνὶ στήθεσσιν ἔπειθον.

Diagoras—II. 2. ἐκ τελε . . θαι (τελεῖται Sext. Emp.).

II. (2). ΑΔΩΝΙΣ.

Κάλλιστον μὲν ἐγὼ λείπω φάος ἠελίοιο,
δεύτερον ἄστρα φαεινὰ σεληναίης τε πρόσωπον
ἠδὲ καὶ ὡραίους σικύους καὶ μῆλα καὶ ὄγχνας.

III. (5).

–́ ⏑ ⏑ –́ ⏑ ⏑ –́ ⏑ ⏑ –́ ⏑ –́ ⏓

Ὦ διὰ τῶν θυρίδων καλὸν ἐμβλέποισα,
παρθένε τὰν κεφαλάν, τὰ δ' ἔνερθε νύμφα.

PINDAR.

ΥΜΝΟΙ.

I. (29, 30). ΥΜΝΟΣ ΘΗΒΑΙΟΙΣ.

— ⋮ ⌊́ ⏑ –́ — –́ ⏑ ⏑ –́ ⏑ ⏑ –́ ⋀
— ⋮ ⌊́ ⏑ –́ — –́ ⏑ ⏑ –́ ⏑ ⏑ –́ —
— ⋮ –́ ⏑ ⏑ –́ ⏑ ⏑ –́ —
⌊́ ⏑ –́ — –́ ⏑ ⏑ –́ ⏑ ⏑ –́ ⋀
5 — ⋮ ⌊́ ⏑ –́ — –́ ⏑ ⏑ –́ ⏑ ⏑ –́ ⏓
⌊́ ⏑ –́ — –́ ⏑ ⏑ –́ ⏑ ⏑ –́ — –́ ⏑ ⏑
[–́ ⏑ ⏑ –́ —

Ἰσμηνὸν ἢ χρυσαλάκατον Μελίαν, στρ.
ἢ Κάδμον, ἢ σπαρτῶν ἱερὸν γένος ἀνδρῶν,
ἢ τὰν κυανάμπυκα Θήβαν,
ἢ τὸ πάντολμον σθένος Ἡρακλέος,
5 ἢ τὰν Διωνύσου πολυγαθέα τιμάν,
ἢ γάμον λευκωλένου Ἁρμονίας ὑμνήσομεν[–́ ⏑ ⏑ –́ —;]

* * *

πρῶτον μὲν εὔβουλον Θέμιν οὐρανίαν στρ.
χρυσέαισιν ἵπποις Ὠκεανοῦ παρὰ παγᾶν

PRAXILLA—II. 3. ὄχνους.
PINDAR—I. 8. ἵπποισιν. πάγον.

Μοῖραι ποτὶ κλίμακα σεμνὰν
10 ἆγον Οὐλύμπου λιπαρὰν καθ' ὁδόν,
σωτῆρος ἀρχαίαν ἄλοχον Διὸς ἔμμεν.
ἁ δὲ τὰς χρυσάμπυκας ἀγλαοκάρπους τίκτεν ἀλαθέας Ὥρας.

II. (42). THE ADVICE OF AMPHIARAOS.

–́ ⏑ ⏑ –́ – ∟́ ⏑ –́ – –́ ⏑ ⏑ –́ ⋀
∟́ ⏑ –́ – –́ ⏑ ⏑ –́ ⏑ ⏑ –́ ⋀
⏓ ⁞ ∟́ ⏑ –́ – ∟́ ⏑ –́ – ∟́ ⏑ –́ – ∟́ ⏑ [–́ –
–́ ⏑ ⏑ –́ ⏑ ⏑ –́ – –́ ⏑ ⏑ –́ ⏑ ⏑ –́ –
5 ∟́ ⏑ –́ – ∟́ ⏑ –́ – ∟́ ⏑ –́ ⏓

Ἀλλοτρίοισιν μὴ προφαίνειν, τίς φέρεται
μόχθος ἄμμιν. τοῦτό γέ τοι ἐρέω·
καλῶν μὲν ὦν μοῖράν τε τερπνῶν ἐς μέσον χρὴ παντὶ λαῷ
δεικνύναι· εἰ δέ τις ἀνθρώποισι θεόσδοτος ἄτα
5 προστύχῃ, ταύταν σκότει κρύπτειν ἔοικεν.

ΠΑΙΑΝ.

III. (61). "THERE IS NO SEARCHING OF HIS UNDERSTANDING."

⏑ ⁞ –́ ⏑ –́ ⏑ ⏑ ∟́ –́ ⏑ –́ ⏑ ⏑ ⏓́ ⋀
⏑ ⁞ –́ ⏑ ⏑ –́ ⏑ –́ ⏑ –́ ⋀
–́ ⏑ –́ ⏑ –́ ⏑ ⏑ –́ > –́ ⏑ ⏑ –́ > –́ ⏑ ⏑
–́ ⏑ ⏑ ∟́ –́ ⏑ ⏑ –́ ⏑ ⏑ –́ ⋀

Τί δ' ἔλπεαι σοφίαν ἔμμεν, ᾇ <τ'> ὀλίγον
ἀνὴρ ὑπὲρ ἀνδρὸς ἰσχύει;
οὐ γὰρ ἔσθ' ὅπως τὰ θεῶν βουλεύματ' ἐρευνάσει βροτέᾳ φρενί, θνατᾶς δ' ἀπὸ ματρὸς ἔφυ.

I. 10. Ὀλύμπου. 11. ἔμμεναι. 12. ἀλαθέας Ὥρας: ἀγαθὰ σωτῆρας.
II. 2. ἄμιν. 4. ἀνθρώποις ἀθεόσδοτος ἄτη. 5. σκόπει.
III. 1. εἶναι. 2. ἐρευνᾶσαι Clem. Eust.

ΔΙΘΥΡΑΜΒΟΙ.

IV. (75). FOR ATHENS.

Ἴδετ' ἐν χορόν, Ὀλύμπιοι,
ἐπί τε κλυτὰν πέμπετε χάριν, θεοί,
πολύβατον οἵτ' ἄστεος
ὀμφαλὸν θυόεντα
5 ἐν ταῖς ἱεραῖς Ἀθάναις
οἰχνεῖτε πανδαίδαλόν τ' εὐκλέ' ἀγοράν.
ἰοδέτων λάχετε στεφάνων
τᾶν Ϝεαριδρόπων λοιβᾶν·
Διόθεν τέ με σὺν ἀγλαΐᾳ

PINDAR—IV. 8. τε ἀρι- FE ; τ' ἐαρι- P. λοιβάν PM.

10 ἴδετε πορευθέντ' ἀοιδᾶν.
δεῦτ' ἐπὶ κισσοδέταν θεόν,
τὸν Βρόμιον Ἐριβόαν τε βροτοὶ καλέομεν.
γόνον ὑπάτων μὲν πατέρων μελπέμεν
γυναικῶν τε Καδμειᾶν ἔμολον·
15 ἐναργέα τελέων σάματ' οὐ λανθάνει,
φοινικοεάνων ὁπότ' οἰχθέντος Ὡρᾶν θαλάμου
εὔοδμον ἐπάγῃσιν ἔαρ φυτὰ νεκτάρεα.
τότε βάλλεται, τότ' ἐπ' ἀμβρόταν χθόν' ἐραταὶ
ἴων φόβαι, ῥόδα τε κόμαισι μείγνυται,
20 ἀχεῖ τ' ὀμφαὶ μελέων σὺν αὐλοῖς,
ἀχεῖ τε Σεμέλαν ἑλικάμπυκα χοροί.

V. (76). ATHENS.

> ⁞ −́⏑⏑ −́⏑⏑ −́⏑⏑ −́⏑⏑ −́⏑ −́∧
> ⁞ −́⏑⏑ −́≥ −́⏑⏑ −́⏓
−́⏑⏑ −́⏑⏑ −́ −́∧

Ὦ ταὶ λιπαραὶ καὶ ἰοστέφανοι καὶ ἀοίδιμοι
Ἑλλάδος ἔρεισμα, κλειναὶ Ἀθᾶναι,
δαιμόνιον πτολίεθρον.

ΠΡΟΣΟΔΙΑ.

VI. (87, 88). ΕΙΣ ΔΗΛΟΝ.

— ⁞ −́⏑ −́− −́⏑⏑ −́⏑⏑ −́⏒
— ⁞ −́⏑ −́− −́⏑⏑ −́⏑⏑ −́⏓
— ⁞ −́⏑⏑ −́⏑⏑ −́− −́⏑ −́− −́⏑⏑
[−́⏑⏑ −́⏒

IV. 10. ἀοιδάν FM. 11. δεύτερον ἐπὶ τόν κισσοδόταν P. 12. Βρόμιον τόν P. 13. μέλπομεν F. 15. ἐν ἄλγεα F; νέμεα or νεμέω μάντιν P; τεμέων τε μάντιν P. 16. φοίνικος ἑανῶν P. οἰχθόντες ὧραν θάλαμοι F. 17. εὐόαμον ἐπάγοισιν F; ἐπαίωσιν P. 19. μίγνυται. 20. ἀχεῖ τε ὀμφᾶι F; οἰχνεῖτ' ὀμφαῖς P. 21. οἰχνεῖτε PF.

– ⁞ ⏗⏑ –́– –́⏑⏑ –́⏑⏑ –́–
[⏗⏑ –́– –́⏑⏑ –́⏑⏑ –́⏓
5 –́⏑⏑ –́⏑⏑ –́–
– ⁞ ⏗⏑ –́– –́⏑⏑ –́⏑̄
⏗⏑ –́– ⏗⏑ –́– –́⏑⏑ –́⏑⏑
[–́–
–́⏑⏑ –́⏑⏑ –́– –́⏑⏑ –́⏑⏑ –́⏓

Χαῖρ', ὦ θεοδμάτα, λιπαροπλοκάμου — στρ.
παίδεσσι Λατοῦς ἱμεροέστατον ἔρνος,
πόντου θύγατερ, χθονὸς εὐρείας ἀκίνητον τέρας,
ἅντε βροτοὶ
Δᾶλον κικλήσκοισιν, μάκαρες δ' ἐν Ὀλύμπῳ
τηλέφαντον κυανέας χθονὸς ἄστρον.

(*Six lines missing.*)

5 ἦν γὰρ τὸ πάροιθε φορητὰ κυμάτεσσιν παντοδαπῶν ⟨τ'⟩ ἀνέμων — ἀντ.
ῥιπαῖσιν· ἀλλ' ἁ Κοιογενὴς ὁπότ' ὠδίνεσσι
θύοισ' ἀγχιτόκοις ἐπέβαινεν,
δὴ τότε τέσσαρες ὀρθαὶ
πρέμνων ἀπώρουσαν χθονίων
ἂν δ' ἐπικράνοις σχέθον πέτραν ἀδαμαντοπέδιλοι
10 κίονες· ἔνθα τεκοῖσ' εὐδαίμον' ἐπόψατο γένναν.

VII. (89). ΕΙΣ ΑΦΑΙΑΝ.

⏑ ⁞ –́⏑⏑ –́⏑⏑ –́> –́⏑⏑ –́⏑⏑ –́⏓
⏗⏑ –́– ⏗⏑ –́– ⏗⏑ –́– –́⏑⏑
[–́⏑⏑ –́–

Τί κάλλιον ἀρχομένοισιν ἢ καταπαυομένοισιν,
ἢ βαθύζωνόν τε Λατὼ καὶ θοᾶν ἵππων ἐλάτειραν ἀεῖσαι;

PINDAR—VI. 2. παιδός. 3. θυγάτηρ. 4. τηλέφατον.
6. καιογενής. ὠδίνεσι. ἐπεβαίνειν.

VIII. (90). ΕΙΣ ΔΕΛΦΟΥΣ.

πρὸς Ὀλυμπίου Διός σε,
χρυσέα κλυτόμαντι Πυθοῖ,
λίσσομαι, Χαρίτεσσί τε καὶ σὺν Ἀφροδίτᾳ
ἐν ζαθέῳ με δέξαι θρόνῳ
5 ἀοίδιμον Πιερίδων προφάταν.

ΥΠΟΡΧΗΜΑΤΑ.

IX. (106). ΙΕΡΩΝΙ ΣΥΡΑΚΟΣΙΩΙ.

Ἀπὸ Ταϋγέτοιο μὲν Λάκαιναν
ἐπὶ θηρσὶ κύνα τρέφειν πυκινώτατον ἑρπετόν·
Σκύριαι δ' ἐς ἄμελξιν γλάγεος
αἶγες ἐξοχώταται·
5 ὅπλα δ' ἀπ' Ἄργεος· ἅρμα Θηβαῖον· ἀλλ' ἀπὸ τᾶς
Σικελίας ὄχημα δαιδάλεον ματεύειν. [ἀγλαοκάρπου

VIII. 3. ᾄσομαι ΓΘ. χάριτες. 4. χρόνῳ. 5. Πιερίων vulgo.
IX. 2. τρέφειν Eust.; τρέχειν Ath. 3. γλάγους Eust.; γάλακτος Ath. 5. ἀλλ' Schol. *Pax* 73. τῆς.

X. (107). ΕΙΣ ΗΛΙΟΝ ΕΚΛΕΙΠΟΝΤΑ.

Ἀκτὶς Ἀελίου, τί πολύσκοπε μήσεαι, ὦ μᾶτερ ὀμμάτων;
ἄστρον ὑπέρτατον ἐν ἀμέρᾳ κλεπτόμενον,
ἔθηκας ἀμάχανον ἰσχὺν
πτανὸν ἀνδράσι καὶ σοφίας ὁδόν·
5 ἐπίσκοτον ἀτραπὸν ἐσσυμένα
ἐλαύνεις τι νεώτερον ἢ πάρος;
ἀλλά σε πρὸς Διὸς ἵππους ζαθόας ἱκετεύω
ἀπήμον᾽ ἐς οἶμόν τινα τράποις Θήβαις,
ὦ πότνια, πάγκοινον τέρας.

PINDAR—X. 1. ἐμῆς θεῶ μ᾽ ἄτερ. 5. ἐσσαμένα. 7. ἵππος θαθοάς. 8. ὄλβον . τρόποιο.

10 πολέμου δ' εἰ σᾶμα φέρεις τινός,
ἢ καρποῦ φθίσιν, ἢ νιφετοῦ σθένος
ὑπέρφατον, ἢ στάσιν οὐλομέναν,
ἢ πόντου κενέωσιν ἀμ πέδον,
ἢ παγετὸν χθονός, ἢ νότιον θέρος
15 ὕδατι ζακότῳ διερόν,
ἢ γαῖαν κατακλύσαισα θήσεις
ἀνδρῶν νέον ἐξ ἀρχᾶς γένος,
ὀλοφύρομαι οὐδέν, ὅτι πάντων μέτα πείσομαι.

XI. (108). SUCCESS IS OF GOD.

⏑ ⁞ –⏑ ∟ –⏑ –⏓
⏑ ⁞ –⏑ ∟ –⏑ ∟ –⏑ –⏑ ∟ ⏖⏑ –⏑
⏑ ⁞ ∟ –⏑ –⏑⏑ ⏓∧ [–∧

Θεοῦ δὲ δείξαντος ἀρχάν,
ἕκαστον ἐν πρᾶγος εὐθεῖα δὴ κέλευθος ἀρετὰν ἑλεῖν,
τελευταί τε καλλίονες.

XII. (109). CONCORD IN THE STATE.

⏖× –⏑ ∟ –⏑ –⏑ –⏑ –∧
⏖× –⏑ –⏑⏑ –⏑⏑ –⏑⏑ –⏑ ∟ –⏑
⏖⏑ –⏑⏑ ∟ ⏖⏑ ⏖⏑ –∧ [⏓∧
⏖× –⏑ ∟ ⏓∧
5 –> –⏑⏑ ⏓∧

Τὸ κοινόν τις ἀστῶν ἐν εὐδίᾳ τιθεὶς
ἐρευνασάτω μεγαλάνορος Ἁσυχίας τὸ φαιδρὸν φάος,
στάσιν ἀπὸ πραπίδων ἐπίκοτον ἀνελών,
πενίας δότειραν,
5 ἐχθρὰν κουροτρόφον.

X. 10. πολέμου δὶς ἅμα. 12. οὐλομένην. 13. ἀλλὰ πέδον. 15. ἱερόν. 16. κατακλύσασα θήσει. 17. ἀρχῆς. 18. ὀλοφ . . . δέν.
XII. 2. Ἡσυχίας.

XIII. (110). "HE JESTS AT SCARS WHO NEVER FELT A WOUND."

Γλυκὺ δ' ἀπείροισι πόλεμος· πεπειραμένων δέ τις
ταρβεῖ προσιόντα νιν καρδίᾳ περισσῶς.

ΕΓΚΩΜΙΟΝ.

XIV. (121). ΑΛΕΞΑΝΔΡΩΙ ΑΜΥΝΤΑ.

πρέπει δ' ἐσλοῖσιν ὑμνεῖσθαι . . .
. . . καλλίσταις ἀοιδαῖς
τοῦτο γὰρ ἀθανάτοις τιμαῖς ποτιψαύει μόνον·
ῥηθὲν ⟨σθένει⟩, θνᾴσκει δὲ σιγαθὲν καλὸν ἔργον.

ΣΚΟΛΙΟΝ.

XV. (123). ΘΕΟΞΕΝΩΙ ΤΕΝΕΔΙΩΙ.

στρ.

ἐπ.

PINDAR—XIII. πόλεμος ἀπείροισιν Stob.
XIV. 1. ὄλοισιν. 3. τιμαῖσι. 4. δὲ σιγαθέν : δ' ἐπιταθέν.

Χρῆν μὲν κατὰ καιρὸν ἐρώτων δρέπεσθαι, θυμέ, σὺν
ἁλικίᾳ· στρ.
τὰς δὲ Θεοξένου ἀκτῖνας προσώπου μαρμαριζοίσας
ὃς μὴ πόθῳ κυμαίνεται, ἐξ ἀδάμαντος [δρακεὶς
ἢ σιδάρου κεχάλκευται μέλαιναν καρδίαν

5 ψυχρᾷ φλογί, πρὸς δ' Ἀφροδίτας ἀτιμασθεὶς ἑλικοβλεφάρου, ἀντ.
ἢ περὶ χρήμασι μοχθίζει βιαίως, ἢ γυναικείῳ θράσει
*ψυχρὰν φορεῖται πᾶσαν ὁδὸν θεραπεύων.
ἀλλ' ἐγὼ θεᾶς ἕκατι, κηρὸς ὣς δαχθεὶς ἕλᾳ

ἱρᾶν μελισσᾶν, τάκομαι, εὖτ' ἂν ἴδω παιδὸς νεόγυιον
ἐς ἥβαν ἐπ.
10 ἐν δ' ἄρα καὶ Τενέδῳ Πειθώ τ' ἴαινεν
καὶ Χάρις υἱὸν Ἀγησίλα.

ΘΡΗΝΟΙ.

XVI. (129). THE ELYSIUM IN HADES.

⌊ – ⏑ – – – ⏑ ⏑ – ⏑ ⏑ – – – ⏑ ⏑
[– ⏑ ⏑ – ⏑
– ⁞ – ⏑ ⏑ – ⏑ ⏑ – – – ⏑ ⏑ – ⏑ ⏑ – –
– ⏑ ⏑ – ⏑ ⏑ – – ⌊ – ⏑ – – ⌊ – ⏑
[– ⏑
– ⁞ ⌊ – ⏑ – – – ⏑ ⏑ – > ⌊ – ⏑ – –
5 ⌊ – ⏑ – – ⌊ – ⏑ – – – ⏑ ⏑ – ⏑ ⏑
[– – ⌊ – ⏑ – > – ⏑ – ⏑
– ⁞ – ⏑ ⏑ – ⏑ ⏑ – – ⌊ – ⏑ – ⏑
– ⁞ – ⏑ ⏑ – – – ⏑ ⏑ – ⏑ ⏑ – – – ⏑ ⏑
[– ⏑ ⏑ – –

XV. 1. μέν : με. ἡλικίᾳ. 7. φορεῖτε. 8. θεᾶς δ' ἕκατι : δεκατιτας A. ἕλᾳ ἱρᾶν : ἐλεηρὰν. 9. τήκομαι. 10. ἴαινεν : ἔναιεν. 11. Ἀγησιλάου.

Τοῖσι λάμπει μὲν μένος ἀελίου τὰν ἐνθάδε νύκτα
κάτω, στρ.
φοινικορόδοις τ' ἐνὶ λειμώνεσσι προάστιον αὐτῶν
καὶ λιβάνῳ σκιαρὸν καὶ χρυσέοις καρποῖς βεβριθός.
καὶ τοὶ μὲν ἵπποις γυμνασίοις ⟨τε⟩, τοὶ δὲ πεσσοῖς,
5 τοὶ δὲ φορμίγγεσσι τέρπονται, παρὰ δέ σφισιν
[εὐανθὴς ἅπας τέθαλεν ὄλβος·
ὀδμὰ δ' ἐρατὸν κατὰ χῶρον κίδναται
αἰεὶ θύα μειγνύντων πυρὶ τηλεφανεῖ παντοῖα θεῶν ἐπὶ
[βωμοῖς.
* * *
ἔνθεν τὸν ἄπειρον ἐρεύγονται σκότον ἀντ.
βληχροὶ δνοφερᾶς νυκτὸς ποταμοί.

XVII. (131). THE SOUL.

⌞–⏑ –> ⌞–⏑ –– –⏑⏑ –⏑⏑
[–– ⌞–⏑ ––
–¦ ⌞–⏑ –– –⏑⏑ –⏑⏑ –> ⌞–⏑
[–⏔
–¦ –⏑⏑ –⏑⏑ ⌞⌟ ⌞–⏑ –– –⏑⏑
[–⏑⏑ –⏔
⌞–⏑ –– ⌞–⏑ –– –⏑⏑ –⏑⏑
[–– ⌞–⏑ –– ⌞–⏑ ––
5 –¦ ⌞–⏑ ⌞⌟ ⌞–⏑ –– –⏑⏑ –⏑⏑
[–⏔

Ὀλβίᾳ δ' ἅπαντες αἴσᾳ λυσίπονον ⟨μετανίσσονται⟩
[τελευτάν.
καὶ σῶμα μὲν πάντων ἕπεται θανάτῳ περισθενεῖ,
ζωὸν δ' ἔτι λείπεται αἰῶνος εἴδωλον· τὸ γάρ ἐστι μόνον
ἐκ θεῶν· εὕδει δὲ πρασσόντων μελέων, ἀτὰρ εὑδόντεσσιν
[ἐν πολλοῖς ὀνείροις
5 δείκνυσι τερπνῶν ἐφέρποισαν χαλεπῶν τε κρίσιν.

PINDAR—XVI. 2. ἐν . προάστειον. 3. χρυσοκάρποισι βέβριθε. 5. τέθηλεν. 6. ἐρατῶν. 7. ἀεὶ θύματα μιγ-.
XVII. 5. ἐφέρπουσαν.

XVIII. (133). JUST MEN MADE PERFECT.

Οἷσι δὲ Φερσεφόνα ποινὰν παλαιοῦ πένθεος
δέξεται, ἐς τὸν ὕπερθεν ἅλιον κείνων ἐνάτῳ ἔτεϊ
ἀνδιδοῖ ψυχὰς πάλιν·
ἐκ τᾶν βασιλῆες ἀγαυοὶ καὶ σθένει κραιπνοὶ σοφίᾳ τε
[μέγιστοι
5 ἄνδρες αὔξοντ'· ἐς δὲ τὸν λοιπὸν χρόνον ἥρωες ἁγνοὶ
[πρὸς ἀνθρώπων καλεῦνται.

XIX. (137). THE ELEUSINIAN MYSTERIES.

Ὄλβιος ὅστις ἰδὼν κεῖν' εἶσ' ὑπὸ χθόν'· οἶδε μὲν βίου
οἶδεν δὲ διόσδοτον ἀρχάν. [τελευτάν,

ΕΞ ΑΔΗΛΩΝ ΕΙΔΩΝ.

XX. (141). THE GIFTS OF GOD.

Θεὸς ὁ τὰ πάντα τεύχων βροτοῖς
καὶ χάριν ἀοιδᾷ φυτεύει.

XVIII. 1. οἷσι γὰρ ἄν. 3. ψυχάν.
XIX. ἐκεῖνα κοινὰ εἰς.
XX. φοιτεύει.

XXI. (142). AN ECLIPSE.

Θεῷ δὲ δυνατὸν ἐκ μελαίνας
νυκτὸς ἀμίαντον ὄρσαι φάος,
κελαινεφέϊ δὲ σκότει καλύψαι
καθαρὸν ἁμέρας σέλας.

XXII. (143). THE GODS' FELICITY.

Κεῖνοι γάρ τ' ἄνοσοι καὶ ἀγήραοι
πόνων τ' ἄπειροι, βαρυβόαν
πορθμὸν πεφευγότες Ἀχέροντος.

XXIII. (155). A POET'S PRAYER.

τί δ' ἔρδων φίλος
σοί τε, καρτερόβροντα Κρονίδα, φίλος δὲ Μοίσαις,
Εὐθυμίᾳ τε μέλων εἴην·
τοῦτ' αἴτημί σε.

XXIV. (159). TIME THE SAVIOUR OF THE JUST.

Ἀνδρῶν δικαίων χρόνος σωτὴρ ἄριστος.

PINDAR—XXI. κελαινεφέει.

XXV. (169). SOVEREIGN LAW.

Νόμος ὁ πάντων βασιλεὺς
θνατῶν τε καὶ ἀθανάτων
ἄγει δικαιῶν τὸ βιαιότατον
ὑπερτάτᾳ χειρί· τεκμαίρομαι
5 ἔργοισιν Ἡρακλέος· ἐπεὶ Γηρυόνα βόας
Κυκλωπίων ἐπὶ προθύρων Εὐρυσθέος
ἀναιτήτας τε καὶ ἀπριάτας ἔλασεν.

XXVI. (194). A SONG FOR THEBES.

Κεκρότηται χρυσέα κρηπὶς ἱεραῖσιν ἀοιδαῖς·
εἶα τειχίζωμεν ἤδη ποικίλων
κόσμον αὐδάεντα λόγων·
⟨ὃς⟩ καὶ πολυκλεῖταν περ ἐοῖσαν ὅμως Θήβαν ἔτι μᾶλ-
5 καὶ κατ' ἀνθρώπων ἀγυιάς. [λον ἐπασκήσει θεῶν

XXV. 7. ἀναιρεῖται.
XXVI. 2. ποικίλον.

XXVII. (199). SPARTA.

Ἔνθα βουλαὶ γερόντων καὶ νέων ἀνδρῶν ἀριστεύοισιν
καὶ χοροὶ καὶ Μοῖσα καὶ Ἀγλαΐα. [αἰχμαί,

XXVIII. (205). A PRAYER TO TRUTH.

Ἀρχὰ μεγάλας ἀρετᾶς, ὤνασσ' Ἀλάθεια, μὴ πταίσῃς ἐμὰν
σύνθεσιν τραχεῖ ποτὶ ψεύδει.

XXIX. (214). HOPE.

Γλυκεῖά Ϝοι καρδίαν
ἀτάλλοισα γηροτρόφος συναορεῖ
ἐλπίς, ἃ μάλιστα θνατῶν πολύστροφον
γνώμαν κυβερνᾷ.

XXX. (218). WINE THAT MAKETH GLAD THE HEART OF MAN.

PINDAR—XXVII. ἀριστεύουσι. Μοῦσαι.
XXVIII. 2. ποτέ.
XXIX. 1. οἱ. 2. ξυναορεῖ.

⏗⏑ –– –⏑⏑ –⏑⏑ –– ⏗⏑ –⏓
5 . . . ⏑–– –⏑⏑ –⏑⏑ –– ⏗⏑ –⏓

Ἀνίκ' ἀνθρώπων καματώδεες οἴχονται μέριμναι
στηθέων ἔξω, πελάγει δ' ἐν πολυχρύσοιο πλούτου
πάντες ἴσᾳ νέομεν ψευδῆ πρὸς ἀκτάν·
ὃς μὲν ἀχρήμων, ἀφνεὸς τότε, τοὶ δ' αὖ πλουτέοντες . . .
5 . . . ἀέξονται φρένας ἀμπελίνοις τόξοις δαμέντες.

XXXI. (221). CHACUN A SON GOUT.

⏑ ¦ –⏑⏑ ⏘ ⏗⏑ –– ⏗⏑ ––
–– –⏑⏑ –– ⏗⏑ –– –⏑⏑ –⏑⏑
⏗⏑ –> –⏑⏑ –⏑⏑ ⏓∧ [–∧
–⏑⏑ ⏘ ⏗⏑ –– – . . .

Ἀελλοπόδων μέν τιν' εὐφραίνοισιν ἵππων
τιμαὶ καὶ στέφανοι, τοὺς δ' ἐν πολυχρύσοις θαλάμοις
τέρπεται δὲ καί τις ἐπ' οἶδμ' ἅλιον [βιοτά·
ναΐ θοᾷ σῶς διαστείβων.

XXXII. (222). GOLD.

. . . ⏑– ⏗⏑ –⏓
⏗⏑ –– ⏗⏑ ⏘ ⏘ –∧
⏗⏑ ⏘ –⏑⏑ –⏑⏑ –– –⏑⏑ –∧

Διὸς παῖς ὁ χρυσός·
κεῖνον οὐ σὴς οὐδὲ κὶς δάπτει,
δάμναται ⟨δὲ⟩ βροτέαν φρένα κάρτιστον κτεάνων.

XXX. 2. ἔξωθεν . πολυχρύσου. 3. ἴσα. 4. ἀφνειός.
XXXI. 1. εὐφραίνουσιν.
XXXII. 3. κράτιστον φρενῶν.

BACCHYLIDES.

ΕΠΙΝΙΚΟΙ.

I. (3).[1] ΙΕΡΩΝΙ ΣΥΡΑΚΟΣΙΩΙ ΙΠΠΟΙΣ ΟΛΥΜΠΙΑ.

⏒ ⁝ –⏑ –⏖⏒ –⏖⏑ –⏑ –⏓ στρ.
⏒ ⁝ –⏑⏑ –⏑⏑ –⏑ –⏓ (or –⏑⏑ –∧)
⏒ ⁝ –⏑⏑ –⏑⏑ –⏑ –⏑
–⏑ –⏒ –⏑⏑ –⏑ –⏓

⏒ ⁝ –⏑⏑ –⏑⏑ –– ἐπ.
–⏑ –⏒ –⏑ –∧
–⏑ –⏒ –⏑ –∧
> ⁝ –⏑ –⏖> –⏑ ⏖∧
5 ⏖⏑ –⏒ –⏑ –⏒ –⏑ –∧
–⏑ –⏒ –⏑ ⏖∧

Ἀριστοκάρπου Σικελίας κρέουσαν — στρ. α΄.
Δάματρα ἰοστέφανόν τε κούραν
ὕμνει, γλυκύδωρε Κλειοῖ, θοάς τ' Ὀ-
λυμπιοδρόμους Ἱέρωνος ἵππους.

5 [σεύον]το γὰρ σὺν ὑπερόχῳ τε Νίκᾳ — ἀντ. α΄.
[σὺν Ἀγ]λαΐᾳ τε παρ' εὐρυδίναν
[Ἀλφεόν, τόθι Δ]εινομένεος ἔθηκαν
ὄλβιον [γόνον στεφάνω]ν κυρῆσαι.

θρόησε δὲ λ[αὸς ἀπείρων·] — ἐπ. α΄.
10 "ὦ τρισευδαίμ[ων ἀνήρ,]
ὃς παρὰ Ζηνὸς λαχὼν
πλείσταρχον Ἑλλάνων γέρας
οἶδε πυργωθέντα πλοῦτον μὴ μελαμφαρέϊ κρύπτειν σκότῳ."

BACCHYLIDES—I. 6. σύν Palmer. 7. τόθι Palmer. 9. ἀπείρων Blass.

[1] The numerals in parentheses give the order of the Fragments in Kenyon.

15 βρύει μὲν ἱερὰ βουθύτοις ἑορταῖς, στρ. β'.
βρύουσι φιλοξενίας ἀγυιαί·
λάμπει δ' ὑπὸ μαρμαρυγαῖς ὁ χρυσὸς
ὑψιδαιδάλτων τριπόδων σταθέντων

πάροιθε ναοῦ, τόθι μέγιστον ἄλσος ἀντ. β'.
20 Φοίβου παρὰ Κασταλίας ῥεέθροις
Δελφοὶ διέπουσι. θεόν, θ[εό]ν τις
ἀγλαϊζέτω, ὁ γὰρ ἄριστος ὄλβων.

ἐπεί ποτε καὶ δαμασίππου ἐπ. β'.
Λυδίας ἀρχαγέταν,
25 εὖτε τὰν πεπ[ρωμέναν]
Ζηνὸς τελε[ιοῦσαι κρί]σιν
Σάρδιες Περσᾶ[ν ἐπορθεῦντο στρ]ατῷ,
Κροῖσον ὁ χρυσά[ρματος]

φύλαξ' Ἀπόλλων. [ὁ δ' ἐς ἄ]ελπτον ἆμαρ στρ. γ'.
30 μολὼν πολυδ[άκρυον] οὐκ ἔμελλε
μίμνειν ἔτι δ[ουλοσύ]ναν, πυρὰν δὲ
χαλκοτειχέος π[ροπάροι]θεν αὐ[λᾶς]

να[ήσ]ατ', ἔνθα σὺ[ν ἀλόχῳ] τε κεδνᾷ ἀντ. γ'.
σύν τ' εὐπλοκάμοις ἐπέβαιν' ἄλα[στον]
35 θυγατράσι δυρομέναις· χέρας δ' ἐς
αἰπὺν αἰθέρα σφετέρας ἀείρας

[γέγω]νεν· "ὑπέρβιε δαῖμον, ἐπ. γ'.
ποῦ θεῶν ἐστιν χάρις;

I. 21. *θεόν, θεόν* Palmer. 22. *ἀγλαϊζέτω, ὁ* Bl.: *ἀγλαϊζέθω*. 25. *πεπρωμέναν* Palm. 26. *κρίσιν* Platt. 27. Π. *ἐπορθεῦντο* Housm. 29. So Jebb. 30. *μολών* Jebb; *μόλ' ὤν·* Bl. 31. *δουλ.* Jebb. 33. *ναήσατ'* Bl. 37. *ὑπέρβιε* Bl.

ποῦ δὲ Λατοίδας ἄναξ;

(*Five corrupt verses.*)

45 ἀεικελίως γυναῖκες
ἐξ ἐϋκτίτων μεγάρων ἄγονται·

τὰ πρόσθε δ' ἐχθρὰ φίλα· θανεῖν γλύκιστον." ἀντ. δ'.
τόσ' εἶπε, καὶ ἁβροβάταν κέλευσεν
ἅπτειν ξύλινον δόμον. ἔ[κλαγ]ον δὲ
50 παρθένοι, φίλας τ' ἀνὰ ματρὶ χεῖρας

ἔβαλλον· ὁ γὰρ προφανὴς θνα- ἐπ. δ'.
τοῖσιν ἔχθιστος φόνων·
ἀλλ' ἐπεὶ δεινοῦ πυρὸς
λαμπρὸν διάϊ[σσεν μέ]νος,
55 Ζεὺς ἐπιστάσα[ς μελαγκευ]θὲς νέφος
σβέννυεν ξανθὰ[ν φλόγα].

ἄπιστον οὐδέν, ὅ τι θ[εῶν μέ]ριμνα στρ. ϵ'.
τεύχει· τότε Δαλογενὴς Ἀπόλλων
φέρων ἐς Ὑπερβορέους γέροντα
60 σὺν τανυσφύροις κατένασσε κούραις

δι' εὐσέβειαν, ὅτι μέ[γιστα θ]νατῶν ἀντ. ϵ'.
ἐς ἀγαθέαν ⟨ἀν⟩έπεμψε Πυθώ.
ὅσοι ⟨γε⟩ μὲν Ἑλλάδ' ἔχουσιν, οὔτι[ς],
ὦ μεγαίνητε Ἱέρων, θελήσει

65 [φάμ]εν σέο πλείονα χρυσὸν ἐπ. ϵ'.
[Λοξί]ᾳ πέμψαι βροτῶν.

(*Nine corrupt verses.*)

BACCHYLIDES—I. 47. ἐχθρά Palm. 56. φλόγα Palm. 60. τανυσφύροις Smyth: τανισφύροις. 62. ἀνέπεμψε Housm. 63. γε Bl. 65. φάμεν Thomas. σέο Palm. 66. Λοξίᾳ Bl. βροτῶν Nairn: βροτῷ.

76 ὁ δ' ἄναξ ['Απόλλων]
[τοιόνδ' ἔπ]ος εἶπε Φέρη[τος υἷι·]
"θνατὸν εὖντα χρὴ διδύμους ἀέξειν

γνώμας, ὅτι τ' αὔριον ὄψεαι — ἐπ. ζ'.
80 μοῦνον ἁλίου φάος
χὤτι πεντήκοντ' ἔτεα
ζωὰν βαθύπλουτον τελεῖς."
ὅσια δρῶν εὔφραινε θυμόν· τοῦτο γὰρ
κερδέων ὑπέρτατον.

85 φρονέοντι συνετὰ γαρύω· βαθὺς μὲν — στρ. η'.
αἰθὴρ ἀμίαντος· ὕδωρ δὲ πόντου
οὐ σάπεται· εὐφροσύνα δ' ὁ χρυσός·
ἀνδρὶ δ' οὐ θέμις, πολιὸν π[αρ]έντα

γῆρας, θάλειαν αὖτις ἀγκομίσσαι — ἀντ. η'.
90 ἥβαν. ἀρετᾶ[ς γε μ]ὲν οὐ μινύθει
βροτῶν ἅμα σ[ώμα]τι φέγγος, ἀλλὰ
Μοῦσά νιν τρ[έφει]. Ἱέρων, σὺ δ' ὄλβου

κάλλιστ' ἐπεδ[είξ]αο θνατοῖς — ἐπ. η'.
ἄνθεα· πράξα[ντι] δ' εὖ
95 οὐ φέρει κόσμον σιω-
πά· σὺν δ' ἀλαθείᾳ βαλὼν
καὶ μελιγλώσσου τις ὑμνήσει χάριν
Κηΐας ἀηδόνος.

I. 77. *τοιόνδ' ἔπος* Wilam. *υἷι* Platt. 88. *παρέντα* Jebb.
91. *σώματι* Ingram. 96. *βαλών* Platt.

II. (5). TO HIERON.

στρ.

```
   – ┆ –⏑⏑  –⏑⏑  –⊼
       ∟⏑   ––   ∟⏑  –⏓
   – ┆ –⏑⏑  –⏑⏑  –⊼
   – ┆ –⏑⏑  –⏑⏑  –≥  ∟⏑  ⏓⊼
5      –⏑⏑  –⏑⏑  –⊼
   – ┆ –⏑⏑  –⏑⏑  ⏓⊼
       ∟⏑   ––   ∟⏑  ––
       ∟⏑   –≥   ∟⏑  ⏓⊼
   – ┆ –⏑⏑  –⏑⏑  ––  ∟⏑  ––
10     –⏑⏑  –⏑⏑  ⏓⊼
   – ┆ –⏑⏑  –⏑⏑  –⊼ (or ––)
       ∟⏑   ––   ∟⏑  ⏓⊼
   – ┆ –⏑⏑  –⏑⏑  ––
       –⏑⏑  –⏑⏑  ⏓⊼ (or –⏓)
15     ∟⏑   ––   ∟⏑  ⏓⊼
```

ἐπ.

```
   – ┆ –⏑⏑  ⊔    ∟⏓⏑(?) ––  ∟⏑  –⏓
       –⏑⏑  –⏑⏑  ⏓⊼
   – ┆ –⏑⏑  –⏑⏑  –≥  ∟⏑  ––
       ∟⏑   ––   ∟⏑  ––
5      –⏑⏑  –⏑⏑  –⊼
   – ┆ ∟⏑   ––   ∟⏑  –≥  –⏑  ⏓⊼
   – ┆ –⏑⏑  –⏑⏑  –⏓
       ∟⏑   –≥   ∟⏑  –⏓
       –⏑⏑  –⏑⏑  –⊼
10     ∟⏑   ––   ∟⏑  –≥  ∟⏑  –⏓
```

Εὔμοιρε Συρακοσίων στρ. α'.
  ἱπποδινήτων στραταγέ,
γνώσῃ μὲν ἰοστεφάνων
  Μοισᾶν γλυκύδωρον ἄγαλμα, τῶν γε νῦν
5 αἴ τις ἐπιχθονίων,
  ὀρθῶς· φρένα δ' εὐθύδικ[ο]ν
ἀτρέμ' ἀμπαύσας μεριμνᾶν
  δεῦρ' ἄθρησον ⟨σὺν⟩ νόῳ·

ἢ σὺν Χαρίτεσσι βαθυζώνοις ὑφάνας
10 ὕμνον ἀπὸ ζαθέας
νάσου ξένος ὑμετέραν πέμ-
πει κλεεννὰν ἐς πόλιν,
χρυσάμπυκος Οὐρανίας κλει-
νὸς θεράπων· ἐθέλει δὲ
15 γᾶρυν ἐκ στηθέων χέων

αἰνεῖν Ἱέρωνα. βαθὺν — ἀντ. α'.
δ' αἰθέρα ξουθαῖσι τάμνων
ὑψοῦ πτερύγεσσι ταχεί-
αις αἰετός, εὐρυάνακτος ἄγγελος
20 Ζηνὸς ἐρισφαράγου,
θαρσεῖ κρατερᾷ πίσυνος
ἰσχύϊ, πτάσσοντι δ' ὄρνι-
χες λιγύφθογγοι φόβῳ·
οὔ νιν κορυφαὶ μεγάλας ἴσχουσι γαίας,
25 οὐδ' ἁλὸς ἀκαμάτας
δυσπαίπαλα κύματα· νωμᾶ-
ται δ' ἐν ἀτρύτῳ χάει
λεπτότριχα σὺν Ζεφύρου πνοιαῖσιν ἔθειραν, ἀρίγνω-
30 τος μετ' ἀνθρώποις ἰδεῖν.

τὼς νῦν καὶ ⟨ἐ⟩μοὶ μυρία παντᾷ κέλευθος — ἐπ. α'.
ὑμετέραν ἀρετὰν
ὑμνεῖν, κυανοπλοκάμου θ' ἕκατι Νίκας
χαλκεοστέρνου τ' Ἄρηος,
35 Δεινομένευς ἀγέρω-

BACCHYLIDES—II. 9. ἢ Platt: η. 28. πνοιαῖσιν Platt: πνοαῖσιν. 31. ἐμοί Bl. 33. ὑμνεῖν Palm.: υμνεῖ.

χοι παῖδες· εὖ ἔρδων δὲ μὴ κάμοι θεός.
ξανθότριχα μὲν Φερένικον
'Αλφεὸν παρ' εὐρυδίναν
πῶλον ἀελλοδρόμαν
40 εἶδε νικάσαντα χρυσόπαχυς 'Αώς,

Πυθῶνί τ' ἐν ἀγαθέᾳ· στρ. β'.
γᾷ δ' ἐπισκήπτων πιφαύσκω·
οὔ πώ νιν ὑπὸ προτέρων
ἵππων ἐν ἀγῶνι κατέχρανεν κόνις
45 πρὸς τέλος ὀρνύμενον·
ῥιπᾷ γὰρ ἴσος Βορέα
ὃν κυβερνήταν φυλάσσων
ἵεται νεόκροτον
νίκαν 'Ιέρωνι φιλοξείνῳ τιτύσκων.
50 ὄλβιος ᾧτινι θεὸς
μοῖράν τε καλῶν ἔπορεν
σύν τ' ἐπιζήλῳ τύχᾳ
ἀφνεὸν βιοτὰν διάγειν· οὐ
γάρ τις ἐπιχθονίων
55 πάντα γ' εὐδαίμων ἔφυ.

[καὶ μάν π]οτ' ἐρειψιπύλαν ἀντ. β'.
[παῖδ' ἀνίκ]ατον λέγουσιν
[δῦναι Διὸς] ἀργικεραύ-
νου δώματα Φερσεφόνας τανυσφύρου
60 καρχαρόδοντα κύν' ἄ-
ξοντ' ἐς φάος ἐξ 'Αίδα,
υἱὸν ἀπλάτοι' 'Εχίδνας·

BACCHYLIDES—II. 49. φιλοξείνῳ K: φιλοξένῳ. 53. ἀφνεόν K: αφνειον. 58. δῦναι Palm. 59. τανυσφύρου Sm.: τανι-.

ἔνθα δυστάνων βροτῶν
ψυχὰς ἐδάη παρὰ Κωκυτοῦ ῥεέθροις,
65 οἷά τε φύλλ' ἄνεμος
Ἴδας ἀνὰ μηλοβότους
πρῶνας ἀργηστὰς δονεῖ.
ταῖσιν δὲ μετέπρεπεν εἴδωλον θρασυμέμνονος ἐγ-
70 χεσπάλου Πορθανίδα·

τὸν δ' ὡς ἴδεν Ἀλκμήνιος θαυμαστὸς ἥρως ἐπ. β'.
τεύχεσι λαμπόμενον,
νευρὰν ἐπέβασε λιγυκλαγγῆ κορώνας,
χαλκεόκρανον δ' ἔπειτ' ἐξ-
75 είλετο ἰὸν ἀνα-
πτύξας φαρέτρας πῶμα· τῷ δ' ἐναντία
ψυχὰ προφάνη Μελεάγρου
καί νιν εὖ εἰδὼς προσεῖπεν·
"υἱὲ Διὸς μεγάλου,
80 στᾶθί τ' ἐν χώρᾳ, γελανώσας τε θυμόν

μὴ ταὔσιον προΐει στρ. γ'.
τραχὺν ἐκ χειρῶν ὀιστὸν
ψυχαῖσιν ἔπι φθιμένων·
οὔ τοι δέος." ὣς φάτο· θάμβησεν δ' ἄναξ
85 Ἀμφιτρυωνιάδας,
εἶπέν τε· "τίς ἀθανάτων
ἢ βροτῶν τοιοῦτον ἔρνος
θρέψεν ἐν ποίᾳ χθονί;
τίς δ' ἔκτανεν; ἦ τάχα καλλίζωνος Ἥρα
90 κεῖνον ἐφ' ἁμετέρᾳ

II. 71. Ἀλκμήνιος K : αλκμηιος. 78. προσεῖπεν K : προσεειπεν.

πέμψει κεφαλᾷ· τὰ δέ που
Παλλάδι ξανθᾷ μέλει."
τὸν δὲ προσέφα Μελέαγρος
δακρυόεις· "χαλεπὸν
95 θεῶν παρατρέψαι νόον

ἄνδρεσσιν ἐπιχθονίοις. ἀντ γ'.
καὶ γὰρ ἂν πλάξιππος Οἰνεὺς
παῦσεν καλυκοστεφάνου
σεμνᾶς χόλον Ἀρτέμιδος λευκωλένου
100 λισσόμενος πολέων
τ' αἰγῶν θυσίαισι πατὴρ
καὶ βοῶν φοινικονώτων·
ἀλλ' ἀνίκατον θεὰ
ἔσχεν χόλον, εὐρυβίαν δ' ἔσσευε κούρα
105 κάπρον ἀναιδομάχαν
ἐς καλλίχορον Καλυδῶ-
ν', ἔνθα πλημύρων σθένει
ὄρχους ἐπέκειρεν ὀδόντι,
σφάζε τε μῆλα, βροτῶν
110 θ' ὅστις εἰσάνταν μόλοι.

τῷ δὲ στυγερὰν δῆριν Ἑλλάνων ἄριστοι ἐπ. γ'.
στασάμεθ' ἐνδυκέως
ἓξ ἄματα συνεχέως· ἐπεὶ δὲ δαίμων
κάρτος Αἰτωλοῖς ὄρεξεν,
115 θάπτομεν οὓς κατέπεφ-
νεν σῦς ἐριβρύχας ἐπαΐσσων βίᾳ,
Ἀ[γκ]αῖον ἐμῶν τ' Ἀγέλαον

BACCHYLIDES—II. 106. ἐς Palm.: ὅς. 110. εἰσάνταν Bl.: εἴσαντ' ἂν K. 115. οὓς K: τούς. κατέπεφνεν K: -φνε. 117. Ἀγέλαον K: αγγελον.

φ[έρτ]ατον κεδνῶν ἀδελφεῶν,
[ὃν τέ]κεν ἐν μεγάροις
120 [πατρὸ]ς Ἀλθαία περικλειτοῖσιν Οἰνέος.

[τῶν δ' ὤ]λεσε μοῖρ' ὀλοὰ — στρ. δ'.
[πλέονα]ς· οὐ γάρ πω δαΐφρων
[παῦσεν] χόλον ἀγροτέρα
Λατοῦς θυγάτηρ· περὶ δ' αἴθωνος δορᾶς
125 μαρνάμεθ' ἐνδυκέως
Κουρῆσι μενεπτολέμοις.
ἔνθ' ἐγὼ πολλοῖς σὺν ἄλλοις
Ἴφικλον κατέκτανον
ἐσθλόν τ' Ἀφάρητα, θοοὺς μάτρωας· οὐ γὰρ
130 καρτερόθυμος Ἄρης
κρίνει φίλον ἐν πολέμῳ·
τυφλὰ δ' ἐκ χειρῶν βέλη
ψυχαῖς ἔπι δυσμενέων φοι-
τᾷ θάνατόν τε φέρει
135 τοῖσιν ἂν δαίμων θέλῃ.

ταῦτ' οὐκ ἐπιλεξαμένα — ἀντ. δ'.
Θεστίου κούρα δαΐφρων
ματηρ κακόποτμος ἐμοὶ
βούλευσεν ὄλεθρον ἀταρβακτος γυνά·
140 καῖέ τε δαιδαλέας
ἐκ λάρνακος ὠκύμορον
φιτρὸν ἐγκλαύσασα, τὸν δὴ
μοῖρ' ἐπέκλωσεν τότε
ζωᾶς ὅρον ἁμετέρας ἔμμεν. τύχον μὲν

II. 119. ὃν Wilam. 121. τῶν Jebb. 122. πλέονας Housm. 137. κούρα K : κορα.

145 Δαϊπύλου Κλύμενον
παῖδ' ἄλκιμον ἐξεναρί-
ζων ἀμώμητον δέμας,
πύργων προπάροιθε κιχήσας·
τοὶ δὲ πρὸς εὐτικμέναν
150 φεῦγον ἀρχαίαν πόλιν

Πλευρῶνα· μίνυνθα δέ μοι ψυχὰ γλυκεῖα· ἐπ. δ'.
γνῶν δ' ὀλιγοσθενέων,
αἰαῖ· πύματον δὲ πνέων δάκρυσα τλ[άμων,]
ἀγλαὰν ἥβαν προλείπων."
155 φασὶν ἀδεισιβόαν
'Αμφιτρύωνος παῖδα μοῦνον δὴ τότε
τέγξαι βλέφαρον, ταλαπενθέος
πότμον οἰκτίροντα φωτός·
καί νιν ἀμειβόμενος
160 τοῖ' ἔφα· "θνατοῖσι μὴ φῦναι φέριστον,

μηδ' ἀελίου προσιδεῖν στρ. ε'.
φέγγος· ἀλλ' οὐ γάρ τίς ἐστιν
πρᾶξις τάδε μυρομένοις,
χρὴ κεῖνο λέγειν ὅ τι καὶ μέλλει τελεῖν.
165 ἦρά τις ἐν μεγάροις
Οἰνῆος ἀρηϊφίλου
ἐστὶν ἀδμήτα θυγατρῶν
σοὶ φυὰν ἀλιγκία;
τάν κεν λιπαρὰν ἐθέλων θείμαν ἄκοιτιν."
170 τὸν δὲ μενεπτολέμου

BACCHYLIDES—II. 146. ἐξεναρίζων Bl.: ἐξαναρίζων. 154. προλείπων K: προλιπων. 158. οἰκτίροντα Bl.: οικτέιροντα. 160. τοῖ' Housm.: τοιδ' with ι deleted. 161. μηδ' Richards (Stob.): μητ'. 165. ἦρα Bl.: ἦ ῥα K. 169. ἐθέλων K: θελων.

ψυχὰ προσέφα Μελεά-
γρου· "λίπον χλωραύχενα
ἐν δώμασι Δαϊάνειραν,
νῆϊν ἔτι χρυσέας
175 Κύπριδος θελξιμβρότου."

λευκώλενε Καλλιόπα, ἀντ. ε΄.
στᾶσον εὐποίητον ἅρμα
αὐτοῦ, Δία τε Κρονίδαν
ὕμνησον Ὀλύμπιον ἀρχαγὸν θεῶν,
180 τόν τ' ἀκαμαντορόαν
Ἀλφεόν, Πέλοπός τε βίαν
καὶ Πίσαν, ἔνθ' ὁ κλεεννὸς
ποσσὶ νικάσας δρόμῳ
[ἦλθ]εν Φερένικος ⟨ἐς⟩ εὐπύργους Συρακούσ-
185 σας Ἱέρωνι φέρων
[εὐδ]αιμονίας πέταλον.
χρὴ δ' ἀλαθείας χάριν
αἰνεῖν, φθόνον ἀμφοτέραισιν
χερσὶν ἀπωσάμενον,
190 εἴ τις εὖ πράσσοι βροτῶν.

Βοιωτὸς ἀνὴρ τάνδε φών[ησέ ποτ' ὀμφὰν] ἐπ. ε΄.
Ἡσίοδος πρόπολος
Μουσᾶν, ὃν ⟨ἂν⟩ ἀθάνατοι τι[μῶσι, κείνῳ]
καὶ βροτῶν φήμαν ἕπ[εσθαι.]
195 πείθομαι εὐμαρέως
εὐκλέα κελεύθου γλῶσσαν ο[ὐκ ἐκτὸς προεὶς]

II. 184. emend. by Housm. 187. ἀλαθείας Bl.: αληθειας. 191. τάνδε Housm. φώνησε Bl. ποτ' ὀμφάν Housm. 193. ἂν Bl. τιμῶσι κείνῳ Wilam. 194. ἕπεσθαι Bl. 196. οὐκ ἐκτός Bl. προείς Juren.

πέμπειν Ἱέρωνι· τόθεν γὰρ
  πυθμένες θάλλουσιν ἐσθλ[ῶν,]
  τοὺς ὁ μεγιστοπάτωρ
200 Ζεὺς ἀκινήτους ἐν εἰρήν[ᾳ φυλάσσοι.]

III. (6). ΛΑΧΩΝΙ ΚΕΙΩΙ ΣΤΑΔΙΕΙ ΟΛΥΜΠΙΑ.

⏑ ⁞ –⏑ –⏑ ⌞ ⏓∧
ω ⁞ –⏑ –⏑ ⌞ ⏓∧
  –⏑⏑ ⌞ –⏑⏑ –⏑ ⌞ –∧
⏑ ⁞ –⏑⏑ –⏑
5 –⏑ –⏑ –⏑ ⏓∧
⏑ ⁞ ⌞ –⏑⏑ –⏑ –∧
  –⏑ –⏑⏑ –⏑ –⏓
ω ⁞ –⏑ ⌞ –∧

Λάχων Διὸς μεγίστου *στρ. α΄.*
λάχε φέρτατον πόδεσσι
κῦδος ἐπ᾽ Ἀλφεοῦ προχοαῖσ[ι νικῶν.]
δι᾽ ὅσσα πάροιθεν
5 ἀμπελοτρόφον Κέον
ἄεισάν ποτ᾽ Ὀλυμπίᾳ
  πύξ τε καὶ στάδιον κρατεῦ[σαν]
στεφάνοις ἐθείρας

νεανίαι βρύοντες. *στρ. β΄.*
10 σὲ δὲ νῦν ἀναξιμόλπου
Οὐρανίας ὕμνος ἕκατι νίκ[ας,]
Ἀριστομένειον
  ὦ ποδάνεμον τέκος,

BACCHYLIDES—II. 198. ἐσθλῶν Juren. 200. φυλάσσοι Platt.
III. 3. Ἀλφεοῦ K: αλφειου. νικῶν Blass.

γεραίρει προδόμοις ἀοι-
15 δαῖς, ὅτι στάδιον κρατήσας
Κέον εὐκλέϊξας.

IV. (9). ΑΥΤΟΜΗΔΕΙ ΦΛ[Ε]ΙΑΣΙΩΙ ΠΕΝΤΑΘΛΩΙ ΝΕΜΕΑ.

στρ.

ἐπ.

Δόξαν, ὦ χρυσαλάκατοι Χάριτες, στρ. α'.
πεισίμβροτον δοίητ', ἐπεὶ
Μουσᾶν ἑλικοβλεφάρων θεῖος προφ[άτ]ας
εὔτυκος Φλειοῦντά τε καὶ Νεμεαίου
5 Ζηνὸς εὐθαλὲς πέδον
ὑμνεῖν, ὅθι μηλοδαΐκταν
θρέψεν ἁ λευκώλενος
Ἥρα περικλειτῶν ἀέθλων
πρῶτον Ἡρακλεῖ βαρύφθογγον λέοντα.

IV. 1. ἐπεὶ Wilam.: ἔπει K. 3. ἑλικοβλεφάρων Wilam.: τε ἰοβλ-. 6. ὅθι K: οτι.

10 κεῖ[θι φοι]νικάσπιδες ἡμίθεοι — ἀντ. α'.
πρ[ώτιστο]ν Ἀργείων κριτοὶ
ἄθλησαν ἐπ' Ἀρχεμόρῳ, τὸν ξανθοδερκὴς
πέφν' ἀωτεύοντα δράκων ὑπέροπλος,
σᾶμα μέλλοντος φόνου.
15 ὦ μοῖρα πολυκρατές· οὔ νιν
πεῖθ' Ὀϊκλείδας πάλιν
στείχειν ἐς εὐάνδρους ἀγ[υιάς.]
ἐλπὶς ἀνθρώπων ὑφαιρ[εῖται πρόνοιαν.]

ἃ καὶ τότ' Ἄδραστον Ταλ[αϊονίδαν] — ἐπ. α'.
20 πέμπεν ἐς Θήβας Πολυνείκεϊ πλα[ξίππῳ πέλας.]
κείνων ἀπ' εὐδόξων ἀγώνων
ἐν Νεμέᾳ κλεινοὶ βροτῶν
οἳ τριέτει στεφάνῳ
ξανθὰν ἐρέψωνται κόμαν.
25 Αὐτομήδει νῦν γε νικά-
σαντί νιν δαίμων ἔδωκεν.

πενταέθλοισιν γὰρ ἐνέπρεπεν ὡς — στρ. β'.
ἄστρων διακρινεῖ φάει
νυκτὸς διχομήνιδος εὐφεγγὴς σελάνα·
30 τοῖος Ἑλλάνων δι' ἀ[πείρ]ονα κύκλον
φαῖνε θαυμαστὸν δέμας,
δισκὸν τροχοειδέα ῥίπτων,
καὶ μελαμφύλλου κλάδον
ἀκτέας ἐς αἰπεινὰν προπέμπων
35 αἰθέρ' ἐκ χειρὸς βοὰν ὤτρυνε λαῶν,

BACCHYLIDES—IV. 10. φοινικάσπιδες Bl. 13. ἀωτεύοντα Neil: ασαγένοντα. 18. ὑφαιρεῖται Bl. πρόνοιαν Christ. 28. διακρινεῖ φάει Bl.: διακρίνει φάη. 32. ῥίπτων Housm.: ριπτῶν.

ἢ τελευταίας ἀμάρυγμα πάλας· ἀντ. β′.
τοιῷ[δ' ὑπερθύ]μῳ σ[θένε]ι
γυια[λκέα σώ]ματα [πρὸς γ]αίᾳ πελάσσ[ας]
ἵκετ' ['Ασωπὸ]ν παρὰ πορφυροδίναν,
40 τοῦ κ[λέος π]ᾶσαν χθόνα
ἦλθε[ν καὶ] ἐπ' ἔσχατα Νείλου·
ταί τ' ἐπ' [εὐν]αεῖ πόρῳ
οἰκεῦσι Θερμώδοντος, ἐγχέων
ἵστορες κοῦραι διωξίππ[οι' Ἄ]ρηος,

45 σῶν, ὦ πολυζήλωτε ἄναξ ποταμῶν, ἐπ. β′.
ἐγγόνων γεύσαντο καὶ ὑψιπύλου Τροίας ἕδος.
στείχει δι' εὐρείας κελεύθου
μυρία παντᾷ φάτις
σᾶς γενεᾶς λιπαρο-
50 ζώνων θυγατρῶν, ἃς θεοὶ
σὺν τύχαις ᾤκισσαν ἀρχα-
γοὺς ἀπορθήτων ἀγυιᾶν.
(*Fifty-two corrupt verses.*)

V. (11). ΑΛΕΞΙΔΑΜΩΙ ΜΕΤΑΠΟΝΤΙΝΩΙ ΠΑΙΔΙ ΠΑΛΑΙΣΤΗΙ ΠΥΘΙΑ.

— ⁞ –́ ⏑ ⏑ –́ ⏑ ⏑ –́ ⏓ στρ.
∟ ⏑ –́ — ∟ ⏑ –́ ⏓
— ⁞ –́ ⏑ ⏑ –́ ⏑ ⏑ –́ ⏕
∟ ⏑ –́ ≥ ∟ ⏑ –́ ⏓
5 –́ ⏑ ⏑ –́ ⏑ ⏑ –́ ⏕
— ⁞ –́ ⏑ ⏑ –́ ⏑ ⏑ –́ ⏕
∟ ⏑ –́ — –́ ⏑ ⏑ –́ ∧

IV. 38. πελάσσας K: πελασσω with ω corrected to α. 39. 'Ασωπόν Bl. 42. εὐναεῖ Jebb. 44. κοῦραι K: κοραι. 45. πολυζήλωτε Platt: πολυζήλωτ'. 46. ἐγγόνων Weil: ἔγγονοι.

— ⁞ —⏑⏑ —⏑⏑ ≚⊼
— ⁞ —⏑⏑ —⏑⏑ —≥ ⌞⏑ —⏓
10 — ⁞ —⏑⏑ —⏑⏑ —⊼
— ⁞ —⏑⏑ —⏑⏑ —⊼
— ⁞ —⏑⏑ —⏑⏑ —≥ ⌞⏑ —⏓
— ⁞ —⏑⏑ —⏑⏑ ——
⌞⏑ —— ⌞⏑ —⏓

— ⁞ —⏑⏑ —⏑⏑ —⊼ ἐπ.
— ⁞ —⏑⏑ —⏑⏑ —> ⌞⏑ ——
—⏑⏑ —⏑⏑ —⊼
— ⁞ —⏑⏑ —⏑⏑ —⊼
5 ⌞⏑ —— ⌞⏑ —⏓
— ⁞ —⏑⏑ —⏑⏑ —⊼
— ⁞ ⌞⏑ —— ⌞⏑ ≚⊼
— ⁞ —⏑⏑ —⏑⏑ —≥ ⌞⏑ —⊼
— ⁞ —⏑⏑ —⏑⏑ —⊼
10 — ⁞ —⏑⏑ —⏑⏑ ≚⊼
⌞⏑ —— ⌞⏑ —— —⏑ —⏓
—⏑⏑ —⏑⏑ —⊼
— ⁞ —⏑⏑ —⏑⏑ —⊼
⌞⏑ —— ⌞⏑ —⏓

Νίκα γλυκύδωρε, [μεγίσταν] στρ. α'.
σοὶ πατ[ὴρ τιμὰν ὄπασσεν]
ὑψίζυγ[ος Οὐρανιδᾶν·]
ἐν πολυχρύσῳ δ' Ὀλύμπῳ
5 Ζηνὶ παρισταμένα
κρίνεις τέλος ἀθανάτοι-
σίν τε καὶ θνατοῖς ἀρετᾶς.
ἔλλαθι, [βαθυ]πλοκάμου
κούρα [Στυγὸς ὀρ]θοδίκου· σέθεν δ' ἕκατι

Bacchylides — V. 1. μεγίσταν Hense. 2. τιμάν Platt. ὄπασσεν Juren. 3. Οὐρ. Juren. 8. βαθυπλοκάμου Jebb. 9. Στυγός Fennell.

10 καὶ νῦν Μεταπόντιον εὐ-
γυίων [κατέχ]ουσι νέων
κῶμοί τε καὶ εὐφροσύναι θεότιμον ἄστυ·
ὑμνεῦσι δὲ Πυθιόνικον
παῖδα θαητὸν Φαΐσκου.

15 ἵλεῴ νιν ὁ Δαλογενὴς υἱ- ἀντ. α'.
ὸς βαθυζώνοιο Λατοῦς
δέκτο βλεφάρῳ· πολέες
δ' ἀμφ' Ἀλεξίδαμον ἀνθέων
ἐν πεδίῳ στέφανοι
20 Κίρρας ἔπεσον κρατερᾶς
ἦρα παννίκοιο πάλας·
οὐκ εἶδέ νιν ἀέλιος
κείνῳ γε σὺν ἅματι πρὸς γαίᾳ πεσόντα.
φάσω δὲ καὶ ἐν ζαθέοις
25 ἁγνοῦ Πέλοπος δαπέδοις
Ἀλφεὸν παρὰ καλλιρόαν, δίκας κέλευθον
εἰ μή τις ἀπέτραπεν ὀρθᾶς,
παγξένῳ χαίταν ἐλαίᾳ

γλαυκᾷ στεφανωσάμενον ἐπ. α'.
30 πορτιτρόφ[ον ἂν πεδίον πάτραν] θ' ἱκέσθαι.
[οὔ τι δολοφροσύνα]
παῖδ' ἐν χθονὶ καλλιχόρῳ
ποικίλαις τέχναις πέλασσεν,
ἀλλ' ἢ θεὸς αἴτιος, ἢ
35 γνῶμαι πολύπλαγκτοι βροτῶν

V. 11. κατέχουσι Nairn. 21. παννίκοιο K : παννίκοι. 30. So Bl. 31. So Festa. 35. πολύπλαγκτοι K : -γκοι.

[ἄ]μερσαν ὑπέρτατον ἐκ χειρῶν γέρας.
νῦν δ' Ἄρτεμις ἀγροτέρα
χρυσαλάκατος λιπαρὰν
[ἡμέ]ρα τοξόκλυτος νίκαν ἔδωκε.
40 [τᾷ] ποτ' Ἀβαντιάδας
βωμὸν κατένασσε πολύλ-
λιστον εὔπεπλοί τε κοῦραι·

τὰς ἐξ ἐρατῶν ἐφόβησε — στρ. β'.
παγκρατὴς Ἥρα μελάθρων
45 Προίτου, παραπλῆγι φρένας
καρτερᾷ ζεύξασ' ἀνάγκᾳ.
παρθενίᾳ γὰρ ἔτι
ψυχᾷ κίον ἐς τέμενος
πορφυροζώνοιο θεᾶς·
50 φάσκον δὲ πολὺ σφέτερον
πλούτῳ προφέρειν πατέρα ξανθᾶς παρέδρου
σεμνοῦ Διὸς εὐρυβίᾳ.
ταῖσιν δὲ χολωσαμένα
στήθεσσι παλίντροπον ἔμβαλεν νόημα·
55 φεῦγον δ' ὄρος ἐς τανύφυλλον,
σμερδαλέαν φωνὰν ἱεῖσαι,

Τιρύνθιον ἄστυ λιποῦσαι — ἀντ. β'.
καὶ θεοδμάτους ἀγυιάς.
ἤδη γὰρ ἔτος δέκατον
60 θεοφιλὲς λιπόντες Ἄργος
ναῖον ἀδεισιβόαι

BACCHYLIDES—V. 36. ἄμερσαν Palmer. 39. ἡμέρα Bl., after Purser's ἁμέρα. 54. So κ: στηθεσιν and εμβαλε νομμα. 55. τανύφυλλον Sm.: τανυ-.

χαλκάσπιδες ἡμίθεοι
σὺν πολυζήλῳ βασιλεῖ.
νεῖκος γὰρ ἀμαιμάκετον
65 βληχρᾶς ἀνέπαλτο κασιγνήτοις ἀπ᾽ ἀρχᾶς
Προίτῳ τε καὶ Ἀκρισίῳ·
λαούς τε διχοστασίαις
ἤρειπον ἀμετροδίκοις μάχαις τε λυγραῖς.
λίσσοντο δὲ παῖδας Ἄβαντος
70 γᾶν πολύκριθον λαχόντας

Τίρυνθα τὸν ὁπλότερον — ἐπ. β′
κτίζειν, πρὶν ἐς ἀργαλέαν πεσεῖν ἀνάγκαν·
Ζεύς τ᾽ ἔθελεν Κρονίδας,
τιμῶν Δαναοῦ γενεὰν
75 καὶ διωξίπποιο Λυγκέος,
παῦσαι στυγερῶν ἀχέων.
τεῖχος δὲ Κύκλωπες κάμον
ἐλθόντες ὑπερφίαλοι κλεινᾷ πόλει
κάλλιστον, ἵν᾽ ἀντίθεοι
80 ναῖον κλυτὸν ἱππόβοτον
Ἄργος ἥρωες περικλειτοὶ λιπόντες.
ἔνθεν ἀπεσσύμεναι
Προίτου κυανοπλόκαμοι
φεῦγον ἄδματοι θύγατρες.

85 τὸν δ᾽ εἷλεν ἄχος κραδίαν, ξεί- — στρ. γ′.
να τέ νιν πλᾶξεν μέριμνα·
δοίαξε δὲ φάσγανον ἄμ-
φακες ἐν στέρνοισι πᾶξαι.
ἀλλά νιν αἰχμοφόροι

V. 68. ἤρειπον K : ἤριπον. 79. κάλλιστον, Housm.: κάλλιστον K.

90 μύθοισί τε μειλιχίοις
καὶ βίᾳ χειρῶν κατέχον.
τρεισκαίδεκα μὲν τελέους
μῆνας κατὰ δάσκιον ἠλύκταζον ὕλαν
φεῦγόν τε κατ' Ἀρκαδίαν
95 μηλοτρόφον· ἀλλ' ὅτε δὴ
Λοῦσον ποτὶ καλλιρόαν πατὴρ ἵκανεν,
ἔνθεν χρόα νιψάμενος φοι-
νικοκ[ραδέμνοι]ο Λατοῦς

κίκλῃ[σκε θύγατρα] βοῶπιν, ἀντ. γ'.
100 χεῖρας ἀντείνων πρὸς αὐγὰς
ἱππώκεος ἀελίου
"τέκνα δυστάνοιο λύσσας
πάρφρονος ἐξαγαγεῖν·
θύσω δέ τοι εἴκοσι βοῦς
105 ἄζυγας φοινικότριχας."
τοῦ δ' ἔκλυ' ἀριστοπάτρα
θηροσκόπος εὐχομένου· πιθοῦσα δ' Ἥραν
παῦσεν καλυκοστεφάνους
κούρας μανιᾶν ἀθέων·
110 ταὶ δ' αὐτίκα οἱ τέμενος βωμόν τε τεῦχον,
χραῖνόν τέ μιν αἵματι μήλων
καὶ χοροὺς ἵσταν γυναικῶν.

ἔνθεν καὶ ἀρηϊφίλοις ἐπ. γ'.
ἄνδρεσσιν ⟨ἐς⟩ ἱπποτρόφον πόλιν⟨δ'⟩ Ἀχαιοῖς

BACCHYLIDES—V. 92. τρεισ- Bl.: τρισ-. 93. ἠλύκταζον K: ἠλυκταξον. 94. κατ' Ἀρκ. Palm.: κατακαρδῖαν. 110. ταί Bl.: γαι. 114. ἐς Jebb. δ' add. Ludwich; χώραν Wilam.; ποίαν Housm.

115 ἔσπεο· σὺν δὲ τύχᾳ
ναίεις Μεταπόντιον, ὦ
χρυσέα δέσποινα λαῶν·
ἄλσος τέ τοι ἱμερόεν
Κάσαν παρ' εὔυδρον, πρόγο-
120 νοι ἔσσαν ἐμοί, Πριάμοι' ἐπεὶ χρόνῳ
βουλαῖσι θεῶν μακάρων
πέρσαν πόλιν εὐκτιμέναν
χαλκοθωράκων μετ' Ἀτρειδᾶν. δικαίας
ὅστις ἔχει φρένας, εὑ-
125 ρήσει σὺν ἅπαντι χρόνῳ
μυρίας ἀλκὰς Ἀχαιῶν.

VI. (13). FROM AN ODE TO PYTHEAS OF AIGINA.

— ⁝ –́ ⏑ ⏑ –́ ⏑ ⏑ –́ ⊼
⏓ ⁝ ⌞–́ ⏑ –́ ⏓ *στρ.*
–́ ⏓⏓ (or –́ ⏓ ?) –́ ⏑ ⏑ –́ ⏓
⌞–́ ⏑ –́ ≥ ⌞–́ ⏑ –́ ⏓
5 — ⁝ –́ ⏑ ⏑ –́ ⏑ ⏑ –́ ⏓
⌞–́ ⏑ –́ — ⌞–́ ⏑ ⏓́ ⊼
— ⁝ –́ ⏑ ⏑ –́ ⏑ ⏑ –́ ⊼
⏓ ⁝ ⌞–́ ⏑ –́ —
–́ ⏑ ⏑ –́ ⏑ ⏑ –́ ⏓
10 –́ ⏑ ⏑ –́ ⏑ ⏑ –́ ⏓
–́ ⏑ ⏑ –́ ⏑ ⏑ –́ ⊼
— ⁝ ⌞–́ ⏑ –́ ≥ ⌞–́ ⏑ –́ ⏓

— ⁝ –́ ⏑ ⏑ –́ ⏑ ⏑ –́ ≥ ⌞–́ ⏑ –́ ⊼ *ἐπ.*
— ⁝ –́ ⏑ ⏑ –́ ⏑ ⏑ –́ ⊼
⏑ ⁝ ⌞–́ ⏑ –́ —
⌞–́ ⏑ –́ — –́ ⏑ ⏑ –́ ⏑ ⏑ –́ ⊼

V. 120. *ἔσσαν ἐμοί* Palm.: *ἐσσάμενοι*; *προγόνων ἐσσαμένων* Wilam.; *προᾶγον* Richards; *πρὸ γουνοῖ' ἔσσαν ἔμεν* Platt; *θέσαν οἱ σοὶ πρόγονοι Πρ.* Reinach.

5 — ⋮ –́ ⏑ –́ – ⏑–́ ⏑ –́ ⏓
— ⋮ –́ ⏑ ⏑ –́ ⏑ ⏑ –́ ⏓
⏑–́ ⏑ –́ ⏓ ⏑–́ ⏑ –́ ⏓ –́ ⏑ –́ ⏓
–́ ⏑ ⏑ –́ ⏑ ⏑ –́ ⏓
⏑–́ ⏑ –́ ⏓ ⏑–́ ⏑ –́ ⏓

. . . .

Αἴαντα σακεσφόρον ἥ[ρω,]
ὅστ' ἐπὶ πρύμνᾳ σταθεὶς
 ἔσχεν θρασυκάρδιον [ὁρ-]
 μαίνοντα ν[ᾶας]
5 θεσπεσίῳ π[υρὶ καῦσαι] 75
Ἕκτορα χαλ[κοκορυστά]ν,
ὁππότε Π[ηλεΐδας]
 [τρ]α[χεῖ]α[ν] [Ἀργείοισι μ]ᾶνιν

ὠρίνατ[ο, Δαρδανίδας] ἀντ. γ'.
10 τ' ἔλυσεν ἄ[τας·] 80
οἳ πρὶν μὲν [θεότιμο]ν
Ἰλίου θαητὸν ἄστυ
[οὐ] λεῖπον, ἀτυζόμενοι [δὲ]
[πτ]ᾶσσον ὀξεῖαν μάχαν,
15 εὖτ' ἐν πεδίῳ κλονέων 85
 μαίνοιτ' Ἀχιλλεὺς
λαοφόνον δόρυ σείων.
ἀλλ' ὅτε δὴ πολέμοιο
λῆξεν ἰοστεφάνου
20 Νηρῆδος ἀτρόμητο[ς υἱός,] 90

BACCHYLIDES—VI. 5. καῦσαι Bl. 6. χαλκ. Bl. 7. ὁππότε K: ὁπότε. 8. So Bl. 9. ὠρίνατο Bl.: ωρέινατο. Δαρδανίδας Desrouss. 10. ἄτας Desrouss. 11. θεότιμον Sm. 13. οὐ Bl. 14. πτᾶσσον Platt.

ὥστ' ἐν κυανανθέϊ θ[ύων ναυβάτας] ἐπ. γ'.
πόντ[ῳ Βορ]έας ὑπὸ κύ-
μασιν δαΐζει
νυκτὸς ἀντάσας ἀναπ[επτομένας·]
25 λῆξεν δὲ σὺν φαεσιμ[βρότῳ] 95
'Αοῖ, στόρεσεν δέ τε πό[ντον]
οὐρία· νότου δὲ κόλπ[ωσαν πνοαῖς]
ἱστίον ἁρπαλέως τ' ἄ-
ελπτον ἐξίκοντο χ[έρσον·]

30 ὣς Τρῶες, ἐπ[εὶ] κλύον αἰ- στρ. δ'. 100
χματὰν 'Αχιλλέα
μίμνοντ' ἐν κλισίῃσιν
εἵνεκεν ξανθᾶς γυναικός,
Βρισηΐδος ἱμερογυίου,
35 θεοῖσιν ἄντειναν χέρας 105
φοιβὰν ἐσιδόντες ὑπαὶ
χειμῶνος αἴγλαν.
πασσυδίᾳ δὲ λιπόντες
τείχεα Λαομέδοντος
40 ἐς πεδίον κρατερὰν 110
ἄιξαν ὑσμίναν φέροντες.

ὦρσάν τε φόβον Δαναοῖς· ἀντ. δ'.
ὤτρυνε δ' Ἄρης
εὐεγχής, Λυκίων τε
45 Λοξίας ἄναξ 'Απόλλων· 115
ἷξόν τ' ἐπὶ θῖνα θαλάσσας·

VI. 21. *θύων* Bl. *ναυβάτας* Crusius; *ναῦν θοάν* Bl. 24. *ἀναπ.* Cr.; *ἀντάσασαν ἀπεχθομένας* Bl. 27. *οὐρία* K: *ουριαι.* *κόλπωσαν πνοαῖς* Bl. 35. *θεοῖσιν* Bl. 36. *φοιβάν* Bl.: *φοίβαν* K. 38. *πασσυδίᾳ* K: *πασσυδιας.* 46. *θῖνα* K: *θεινα.*

ναυσὶ δ' εὐπρύμνοις παραὶ
μάρναντ', ἐναριζομένων
[δ' ἔρ]ευθε φωτῶν
50 [αἵμα]τι γαῖα μέλαινα 120
[῾Εκτορ]έας ὑπὸ χειρός—
(*Twenty mutilated verses.*)
οὐ γὰρ ἀλα[μπέσ]ι νυ[κτὸς] 142
πασιφανὴς 'Αρετὰ
κρυφθεῖσ' ἀμαυρο[ῦται δνόφοισιν,]

55 ἀλλ' ἔμπεδον ἀκ[αμάτᾳ] ἀντ. ε'. 145
βρύουσα δόξᾳ
στρωφᾶται κατὰ γᾶν [τε]
καὶ πολυπλάγκταν θ[άλασσαν.]
καὶ μὰν φερεκυδέα ν[ᾶσον]
60 Αἰακοῦ τιμᾷ, σὺν Εὐ- 150
κλείᾳ δὲ φιλοστεφ[άνῳ]
πόλιν κυβερνᾷ,
Εὐνομία τε σαόφρων,
[ἃ] θαλίας τε λέλογχεν
65 ἄστεά τ' εὐσεβέων 155
ἀνδρῶν ἐν εἰρήνᾳ φυλάσσει·

νίκαν τ' ἐρικ[υδέα] μέλπετ', ὦ νέοι, ἐπ. ε'.
Πυθέα μελέτ[αν τε] βροτω-
φελέα Μενάνδρου,
70 τὰν ἐπ' 'Αλφειοῦ τε ῥο[αῖς θ]αμὰ δὴ 160
τίμασεν ἁ χρυσάρματος

BACCHYLIDES—VI. 47. παραί Platt: παρά. 49. ἔρευθε Palmer. 53. 'Αρετά Wilam., cf. 60, 63. 54. δνόφοισιν Tyrrell. 55. ἀκαμάτᾳ Platt. 70. θαμά Nairn.

σεμνὰ μεγάθυμος Ἀθάνα,
μυρίων τ' ἤδη μίτραισιν ἀνέρων
ἐστεφάνωσεν ἐθείρας
75 ἐν Πανελλάνων ἀέθλοις. 165

εἰ μή τινα θερσιεπὴς στρ. ζ'.
φθόνος βιᾶται,
αἰνείτω σοφὸν ἄνδρα
σὺν δίκᾳ. βροτῶν δὲ μῶμος
80 πάντεσσι μέν ἐστιν ἐπ' ἔργοις· 170
ἁ δ' ἀλαθεία φιλεῖ
νικᾶν, ὅ τε πανδαμάτωρ
χρόνος τὸ καλῶς
ἐργμένον αἰὲν ἀ[έξει.]

(*Twenty-four mutilated verses.*)

VII. (14.) ΚΛΕΟΠΤΟΛΕΜΩΙ ΘΕΣΣΑΛΩΙ ΙΠΠΟΙΣ ΠΕΤΡΑΙΑ.

⏑́ ⏑ –́ – –́ ⏑ ⏑ –́ ⏑ ⏑ –́ ⏕ στρ.
– ⁞ ⏑́ ⏑ –́ ⏓
⏑́ ⏑ –́ – ⏑́ ⏑ –́ –
[⏑́] ⏑ –́ – ⏑́ ⏑ –́ ⏓
5 [– ⁞ –́] ⏑ ⏑ –́ ⏑ ⏑ –́ –
[⏑́] ⏑ –́ – ⏑́ ⏑ –́ –
[⏑́] ⏑ –́ – ⏑́ ⏑ –́ ⏕

[– ⁞ –́] ⏑ ⏑ –́ ⏑ ⏑ –́ ⏕ ἐπ.
[– ⁞] –́ ⏑ ⏑ –́ ⏑ ⏑ –́ –
[⏑́ ⏑] –́ – –́ ⏑ ⏑ –́ ⏕
–́ ⏑ –́ – –́ ⏑ ⏑ –́ ⏑ ⏑ –́ [⏓]
–́ ⏑ ⏑ –́ ⏑ ⏑ –́ ⏕

VI. 76. θερσι[ε]πής Bl.: θερσ[οε]πής K.

— ⁞ ⏗ ⏑ ⏗— ⏗⏑ ⏗—
⏗ ⏑⏑⏗⏑⏑⏗—
⏗ ⏑ ⏗— ⏗⏑ [⏗≥ ⏗⏑ ⏗⏓]

Εὖ μὲν εἱμάρθαι παρὰ δαί[μονος ἀν-] στρ. α'.
θρώποις ἄριστον·
συμφορὰ δ' ἐσθλόν ⟨τ'⟩ ἀμαλδύ-
[νει β]αρύτλατος μολοῦσα,
5 [καὶ κλειν]ὸν [ἴδ'] ὑψιφανῆ τε[ύ-]
[χει κ]ατορθωθεῖσα· τιμὰν
[δ' ἄλ]λος ἀλλοίαν ἔχει·

μυρί]αι δ' ἀνδρῶν ἀρεταί, μία δ' ε[ὐ-] ἀντ. α'.
[δαίμω]ν πρόκειται,
10 [ὃς τὸ] παρ χειρὸς κυβερνᾷ
[σὺν δι]καίαισι φρένεσσιν.
[οὔτ' ἂ]ν βαρυπενθέσιν ἁρμό
[ζοι μ]άχαις φόρμιγγος ὀμφὰ
[καὶ λι]γυκλαγγεῖς χοροί,

15 [οὔτ' ἐ]ν θαλίαις καναχὰ ἐπ. α'.
[χαλκ]όκτυπος, ἀλλ' ἐφ' ἑκάστῳ
[καιρὸς] ἀνδρῶν ἔργματι κάλ-
λιστος· εὖ ἔρδοντα δὲ καὶ θεὸς ὀ[ρθοῖ.]
Κλε͜οπτολέμῳ δὲ χάριν
20 νῦν χρὴ Ποσειδᾶνός τε Πετρ[αί-]

BACCHYLIDES—VII. 1. *δαίμονος* Platt, etc. 3. *τ'* Jebb. 5. *καὶ κλεινόν* Jebb. *ἴδ'* Housm.: *ἤδη* with *καί* superscr. *τεύχει* Platt. 8. *εὐδαίμων* Jebb. 10. *τό* Headlam, Pearson. 11. *σύν* Pearson. 12. *οὔτ' ἄν* and *ἁρμάζοι* Platt. 13. *μάχαις* Jebb. 15. *οὔτ'* Platt. 17. *καιρός* Jebb. 20. *Ποσειδᾶνος* Wilam.: *Ποσιδ-*.

ου τέμενος κελαδῆσαι
Πυρρίχου τ' εὔδοξον ἱππόν[ικον υἱόν.]
(*The rest is mutilated or wanting.*)

ΔΙΘΥΡΑΜΒΟΙ.

VIII. (15.) ΑΝΤΗΝΟΡΙΔΑΙ [Η ΕΛΕΝΗ]Σ ΑΠΑΙΤΗΣΙΣ.

— ⋮ –́ ⏑ ⏑   –́ ⏑ ⏑   –́ ⊼   στρ.
— ⋮ –́ ⏑ ⏑   –́ ⏑ ⏑   –́ ≥   ⌊–́ ⏑   –́ ⊼
⏓ ⋮ ⌊–́ ⏑   –́ —   –́ ⏑ ⏑   –́ ⏑ ⏑   –́ ⊼
— ⋮ ⌊–́ ⏑   –́ —   ⌊–́ ⏑   –́ ⊼
5   ⌊–́ ⏑   –́ —   ⌊–́ ⏑   –́ —   ⌊–́ ⏑   –́ —
–́ ⏑ ⏑   –́ ⏑ ⏑   –́ —   –́ ⏑ ⏑   –́ ⏑ ⏑   –́ ⊼
⌊–́ ⏑   –́ —   ⌊–́ ⏑   –́ —   ⌊–́ ⏑   –́ ⏓

— ⋮ ⌊–́ ⏑   –́ —   –́ ⏑ ⏑   –́ ⏑ ⏑   –́ ⊼   ἐπ.
— ⋮ ⌊–́ ⏑   –́ —   ⌊–́ ⏑   –́ —
⌊–́ ⏑   –́ —   –́ ⏑ ⏑   –́ ⏑ ⏑   –́ ⊼
— ⋮ –́ ⏑ ⏑   –́ ⏑ ⏑   –́ ⏓
5   ⌊–́ ⏑   –́ —   ⌊–́ ⏑   –́ ⊼
— ⋮ –́ ⏑ ⏑   –́ ⏑ ⏑   –́ ⊼
— ⋮ ⌊–́ ⏑   –́ —   ⌊–́ ⏑   –́ ⏓

(*Thirty-six lines mutilated or wanting.*)

Πατὴρ δ' εὔβουλος ἥρως
πάντα σάμαινεν Πριάμῳ βασιλεῖ
παίδεσσί τε μῦθον 'Αχαιῶν.
ἔνθα κάρυκες δι' εὐ-   40
5   ρεῖαν πόλιν ὀρνύμενοι
Τρώων ἀόλλιζον φάλαγγας

δεξίστρατον εἰς ἀγοράν.   στρ. γ'.
πάντᾳ δὲ διέδραμεν αὐδάεις λόγος·

VII. 22. ἱππ. υἱόν Blass.
VIII. Title Η: Reinach.

θεοῖς δ' ἀνίσχοντες χέρας ἀθανάτοις 45
10 εὔχοντο παύσασθαι δυᾶν.
Μοῦσα, τίς πρῶτος λόγων ἆρχεν δικαίων;
Πλεισθενίδας Μενέλαος γάρυϊ θελξιεπεῖ
φθέγξατ', εὐπέπλοισι κοινώσας Χάρισσιν·

"ὦ Τρῶες ἀρηΐφιλοι, ἀντ. γ'. 50
15 Ζεὺς ὑψιμέδων, ὃς ἅπαντα δέρκεται,
οὐκ αἴτιος θνατοῖς μεγάλων ἀχέων,
ἀλλ' ἐν μέσῳ κεῖται κιχεῖν
πᾶσιν ἀνθρώποις Δίκαν ἰθεῖαν, ἁγνᾶς
Εὐνομίας ἀκόλουθον καὶ πινυτᾶς Θέμιτος· 55
20 ὀλβίων παῖδές νιν αἱρεῦνται σύνοικον.

ἁ δ' αἰόλοι[ς ψε]ύδεσσι καὶ ἀφροσύναις ἐπ. γ'.
ἐξαισίοις θάλλουσ' ἀθαμβὴς
Ὕβρις, ἃ πλ[οῦτον] δύναμίν τε θοῶς
ἀλλότριον ὤπασεν, αὖτις 60
25 δ' ἐς βαθὺν πέμπει φθόρον,
[κεί]να καὶ ὑπερφιάλους
[Γᾶς] παῖδας ὤλεσσεν Γίγαντας."

IX. (17.) ΗΙΘΕΟΙ [Η] ΘΗΣΕΥΣ.

στρ.

5

Bacchylides—VIII. 11. λόγων ἆρχεν Purser: ἆρχεν λόγων. 18. ἀνθρώποισι Δίκαν ὁσίαν ἁγνάν Clem. 19. Θέμιδος Clem. 20. παῖδες ὦ νιν εὑρόντες Clem. 21. αἰόλοις ψεύδεσσι Palmer. 23. ἅ Jebb. πλοῦτον Palm. 27. ὤλεσσεν κ: ωλεσεν.
IX. Title Η: Blass.

⏑ – ⏑   ∸ ⏔ ⏑   ∸ –
⏑   ∸ ⏑ –   ∸⏑⏑ ⏑ –   ∸⏑⏑ ⏑ –
⏓ ⁞ ∸ ⏑ –   ∸ ⏑ ⏑⏑   [∸ ⊼
∸ ⏑ –⏑   ∸ ⏑ –
10 – ⁞ ∸⏑⏑ – ⏑   ∸ ⏑
–⏑   ∸ ⏑ ⏑ –   ∸⏑⏑ –
⏒ (?)   ∸ ⏑ –⏑   ∸ ⏑ –
⏑ ⁞ ∸ ⏓ ⏒   ∸ ⏑ –
⏑   ∸ ⏑ ⏖   ⏖ ⏑ ⏒
15 ∸ – ⏑   ∸ – ⏑   ⏓ ⊼
∸ ⏑ ⏑⏑   ∸ ⏑ –   ∸
⏑ ⏑ (?)
⏑ –⏑   ∸ ⏑ ⏓
⏓ ⁞ ∸ ⏑ –⏑   ∸ ⏑ –⏑   ∸
– ⏑   ∸⏑⏑ – ⏑   ∸ ⏓ ∧
20 ⏓ ⁞ ∸ ⏑ ⏑⏑   ⏖ ⏑ –   ∸ ⊼
⏑ ⁞ ⏖ – ⏑   ∸⏑⏑ –
⏑   ∸ ⏑ –   ∸ ⏑ –
∸ ⏑ –⏑   ∸⏑⏑ – ⏑   ∸ – ⏑   ∸ ⊼

⏑ ⁞ ∸ ⏑ ⏑⏑   ∸ ⏑ –   ∸   ἐπ.
⏑ –⏑   ∸ ⏑ –
∸ ⏑ ⏑⏑   ∸ ⏑ –
∸ ⏑ ⏑⏑–⏑ (?)   ∸ ⏑ –   ∸ ⏑ –⏑   ∸ ⏑ ⊼
5 ⏑ ⁞ ∸ ⏑ ⏑⏑   ∸ ⏑ –
∸ ⏑ –   ∸ ⏑ ⏑⏑   ∸ ⏑ –
∸ ⏑ ⏑⏑   ∸ ⏑ –   ∸ ⏑ –   ∸ ⊼
– ⁞ ∸ ⏑ –   ∸ ⏑ –   ∸ ⏑ ⏓
∸ ⏑ –⏑   ∸ ⏑ –⏑   ∸ ⊼
10 ⏑ ⁞ ∸⏑⏑ – ⏑   ∸ ⏑ –
∸ ⏑ –   ∸ ⏑ –
⏑   ∸ ⏑ –   ∸ ⏑ –   ∸ – ⏑   ∸
⏑ –⏑   ∸ – ⏑   ∸
– ⏑   ∸ ⏑ –⏑   ∸ ⊼
15 ∸ ⏑ –⏑   ∸
⏑ –⏑   ∸ ⏑ ⏒   ⏖ – ⏑   ∸ ⊼
⏑ ⁞ ∸ ⏑ –   ∸ ⏑ ⏔   ∸ ⏑ –
∸ ⏑ ⏔   ∸ ⏑ –⏑   ∸
⏑ ⏑⏑   ∸ – ∧
20 ⏑ ⁞ ∸ ⏑ –   ∸ ⏑ –   ∸ ⏑ –

Κυανόπρῳρα μὲν ναῦς, μενέκτυπον — στρ. α'.
Θησέα δὶς ἑπτά τ' ἀγλαοὺς ἄγουσα
κούρους 'Ιαόνων,
Κρητικὸν τάμνε πέλαγος·
5 τηλαυγέϊ γὰρ ἐν φάρεϊ
Βορήϊαι πίτνον αὖραι
κλυτᾶς ἕκατι π[ο]λεμαίγιδος 'Αθάνας.
κνίσεν τε Μίνωϊ κέαρ
ἱμεράμπυκος θεᾶς
10 Κύπριδος [αἰν]ὰ δῶρα·
χεῖρα δ' οὐκέτι παρθενικᾶς
ἄτερθ' ἐράτυεν, θίγεν
δὲ λευκᾶν παρηΐδων·
βόα[σέ τ' 'Ερ]ίβοια χαλκο-
15 θώρακα Πανδίονος
ἔκγ[ον]ον· ἴδεν δὲ Θησεύς,
μέλαν δ' ὑπ' ὀφρύων
δί[ν]α[σ]εν ὄμμα, καρδίαν τέ οἱ
σχέτλιον ἄμυξεν ἄλγος,
20 εἶρέν τε· "Διὸς υἱὲ φερτάτου,
ὅσιον οὐκέτι τεᾶν
ἔσω κυβερνᾷς φρενῶν
θ[υμόν·] ἴσχε μεγαλοῦχον, ἥρως, βίαν.

ὅ τι μὲν ἐκ θεῶν μοῖρα παγκρατὴς — ἀντ. α'.
25 ἄμμι κατένευσε καὶ Δίκας ῥέπει τά-
λαντον, πεπρωμέναν
αἶσαν ἐκπλήσομεν, ὅταν

BACCHYLIDES—IX. 4. τάμνε K : τάμνεν. 8. Μίνωϊ K : Μινω. 16. ἔκγονον Palmer. 17. μεῖλαν? cf. Ω 79, [Plut.] *Vita Hom.* 1075 B.

ἔλθῃ· σὺ δὲ βαρεῖαν κάτε-
χε μῆτιν. εἰ καί σε κεδνὰ
30 τέκεν λέχει Διὸς ὑπὸ κρόταφον Ἴδας
μιγεῖσα Φοίνικος ἐρα-
τώνυμος κόρα βροτῶν
φέρτατον, ἀλλὰ κἀμὲ
Πιτθέος θυγάτηρ ἀφνεοῦ
35 πλαθεῖσα ποντίῳ τέκεν
Ποσειδᾶνι, χρύσεόν
τέ οἱ δόσαν ἰόπλοκοι
κάλυμμα Νηρηΐδες.
τῶ σε, πολέμαρχε Κνωσσίων,
40 κέλομαι πολύστονον
ἐρύκεν ὕβριν· οὐ γὰρ ἂν θέλοι-
μ' ἀμβρότου ἐραννὸν Ἀοῦς
ἰδεῖν φάος, ἐπεί τιν' ἠθέων
σὺ δαμάσειας ἀέκον-
45 τα· πρόσθε χειρῶν βίαν
δείξομεν· τὰ δ' ἐπιόντα δαίμων κρινεῖ.'

τ[όσ' εἶ]πεν ἀρέταιχμος ἥρως· *ἐπ. α'.*
τάφον δὲ ναυβάται
[κούρου] ὑπεράφανον
50 θάρσος· Ἁλίου τε γαμβρῷ χολῶ[σατ' ἦτορ,]
ὕφαινέ τε ποταινίαν
μῆτιν, εἶπέν τε· "μεγαλοσθενὲς
Ζεῦ πάτερ, ἄκουσον· εἴπερ μ[ε κούρ]α
Φοίνισσα λευκώλενος σοὶ τέκ[ε,]
55 νῦν πρόπεμπ' ἀπ' οὐρανοῦ θ[οὰν]

IX. 39. τῶ Platt: τῷ K. 42. ἀμβρότου Wilam.: ἀμβρότοι'. 49. κούρου Juren. 53. με κούρα Bl. 55. θοάν Palm.

πυριέθειραν ἀστραπὰν
σᾶμ' ἀρίγνωτον· εἰ
δὲ καὶ σὲ Τροζηνία σεισίχθονι
φύτευσεν Αἴθρα Ποσει-
60 δᾶνι, τόνδε χρύσεον
χειρὸς ἀγλαόν,
δικὼν θράσει σῶμα πατρὸς ἐς δόμους,
ἔνεγκε κόσμον βαθείας ἁλός.
εἴσεαι δ' αἴ κ' ἐμᾶς κλύῃ
65 Κρόνιος εὐχᾶς
ἀναξιβρόντας ὁ πάντω[ν μεδέω]ν."

κλύε δ' ἄμεμπτον εὐχὰν μεγασθενὴς — στρ. β'.
Ζεύς, ὑπέροχόν τε Μίνῳ φύτευσε
τιμὰν φίλῳ θέλων
70 παιδὶ πανδερκέα θέμεν,
ἄστραψέ θ'· ὁ δὲ θυμάρμενον
ἰδὼν τέρας χέρα πέτασσε
κλυτὰν ἐς αἰθέρα μενεπτόλεμος ἥρως,
εἶρέν τε· "Θησεῦ, ⟨σὺ⟩ τάδε
75 μὲν βλέπεις σαφῆ Διὸς
δῶρα· σὺ δ' ὄρνυ' ἐς βα-
ρύβρομον πέλαγος· Κρονίδας
δέ τοι πατὴρ ἄναξ τελεῖ
Ποσειδὰν ὑπέρτατον
80 κλέος χθόνα κατ' ἠύδενδρον."
ὣς εἶπε· τῷ δ' οὐ πάλιν

BACCHYLIDES—IX. 58. Τροζηνία Bl.: Τροιζ-. 66. ἀναξιβρόντας K: -βρεντας. 67. ἄμεμπτον Bl.: αμεπτον. 72. χέρα Richards: χειρας. 74. σύ Jebb. 80. ἠύδενδρον K: ευδενδρον.

θυμὸς ἀνεκάμπτετ', ἀλλ' εὐ-
  παγῶν ἐπ' ἰκρίων
σταθεὶς ὄρουσε, πόντιόν τέ νιν
85 δέξατο θελημὸν ἄλσος.
τᾶ[ξ]εν δὲ Διὸς υἱὸς ἔνδοθεν
κέαρ, κέλευσέ τε κατ' οὖ-
  ρον ἴσχεν εὐδαίδαλον
νᾶα·—μοῖρα δ' ἑτέραν ἐπόρσυν' ὁδόν·—

90 ἵετο δ' ὠκύπομπον δόρυ· σόει — ἀντ. β'.
νιν Βορεὰς ἐξόπιν πνέουσ' ἄητα·
  τρέσσαν δ' Ἀθαναίων
ἠθέων ⟨πᾶν⟩ γένος, ἐπεὶ
ἥρως θόρεν πόντονδε, κα-
95 τὰ λειρίων τ' ὀμμάτων δά-
  κρυ χέον, βαρεῖαν ἐπιδέγμενοι ἀνάγκαν·
φέρον δὲ δελφῖνες ἁλι-
  ναιέται μέγαν θοῶς
Θησέα πατρὸς ἱππί-
100 ου δόμον, μέγαρόν τε θεῶν
μόλεν· τόθι κλυτὰς ἰδὼν
ἔδεισε Νηρῆος ὀλ-
  βίου κόρας. ἀπὸ γὰρ ἀγλα-
  ῶν λάμπε γυίων σέλας
105 ὦτε πυρός, ἀμφὶ χαίταις
  δὲ χρυσεόπλοκοι

IX. 82. *εὐπαγῶν* Christ: *εὔπακτων*. 88. *ἴσχεν* K: *ἴσχειν*. 91. *νιν* Ellis, etc.: *νειν*. *ἐξόπιν* K: *ἐξόπιθεν*. *ἄητα* Housm.: *αήτᾱ*. 93. *πᾶν* K. 95. *δά|κρυ* Jebb: *δακρυ*. 97. *ἁλι-* Palmer: *ἐνᾰλι-*. 100. *μεγ. τε θ. μόλεν* Wilam., Housm.: *ἔμολέν τε θ. μέγαρον*. 102. *Νηρῆος* K: *Νηρέος*. 105. *ὦτε* Bl.: *ωιτε* (?).

δίνηντο ταινίαι· χορῷ δὲ τέρ-
πον κέαρ ὑγροῖσι ποσσίν·
εἶδέν τε πατρὸς ἄλοχον φίλαν
110 σεμνὰν βοῶπιν ἐρατοῖ-
σιν Ἀμφιτρίταν δόμοις·
ἅ νιν ἀμφέβαλεν *ἀϊόνα πορφυρέαν,

κόμαισί τ' ἐπέθηκεν οὔλαις ἐπ. β'.
ἀμεμφέα πλόκον,
115 τόν ποτέ οἱ ἐν γάμῳ
δῶκε δόλιος Ἀφροδίτα ῥόδοις ἐρεμνόν.
ἄπιστον ὅ τι δαίμονες
θέωσιν οὐδὲν φρενοάραις βροτοῖς.
νᾶα παρὰ λεπτόπρυμνον φάνη· φεῦ,
120 οἵαισιν ἐν φροντίσι Κνώσιον
ἔσχασεν στραταγέταν, ἐπεὶ
μόλ' ἀδίαντος ἐξ ἁλὸς
θαῦμα πάντεσσι· λάμ-
πε δ' ἀμφὶ γυίοις θεῶν δῶρ', ἀγλαό-
125 θρονοί τε κοῦραι σὺν εὐθυμίᾳ νεοκτίτῳ
ὠλόλυξαν, ἔ-
κλαγεν δὲ πόντος· ἠΐθεοι δ' ἐγγύθεν
νέοι παιάνιξαν ἐρατᾷ ὀπί.
130 Δάλιε, χοροῖσι Κηΐων
φρένα ἰανθεὶς
ὄπαζε θεόπομπον ἐσθλῶν τύχαν.

BACCHYLIDES—IX. 107. δίνηντο Bl.: δινῆντο. 108. ὑγροῖσι ποσσίν K: υγροισιν εν ποσιν. 112. ἀμφέβαλεν K: -βαλλεν. 118. θέωσιν Crus.: θέλωσιν. 124. γυίοις K: γυοις. ἀγλαο- K: αγλο-.

X. (18). ΘΗΣΕΥΣ.

ΧΟΡ. ΑΘ. Βασιλεῦ τᾶν ἱερᾶν Ἀθανᾶν, *στρ. α'.*

τῶν ἁβροβίων ἄναξ Ἰώνων,

τί νέον ἔκλαγε χαλκοκώδων

σάλπιγξ πολεμηΐαν ἀοιδάν;

5 ἦ τις ἁμετέρας χθονὸς

δυσμενὴς ὅρι' ἀμφιβάλλει

στραταγέτας ἀνήρ;

ἢ λῃσταὶ κακομάχανοι

ποιμένων ἀέκατι μήλων

10 σεύοντ' ἀγέλας βίᾳ;

ἢ τί τοι κραδίαν ἀμύσσει;

φθέγγευ· δοκέω γὰρ εἴ τινι βροτῶν

ἀλκίμων ἐπικουρίαν

καὶ τὶν ἔμμεναι νέων,

15 ὦ Πανδίονος υἱὲ καὶ Κρεούσας.

X. 9. ἀέκατι Palm.: δ' εκατι. 12. φθέγγευ Bl.: φθεγγου.

ΑΙΓ. [Νέ]ον ἦλθεν δολιχὰν ἀμείψας στρ. β'.
κᾶρυξ ποσὶν Ἰσθμίαν κέλευθον·
ἄφατα δ' ἔργα λέγει κραταιοῦ
φωτός· τὸν ὑπέρβιόν τ' ἔπεφνεν
20 Σίνιν, ὃς ἰσχύϊ φέρτατος
θνατῶν ἦν, Κρονίδα Λυταίου
σεισίχθονος τέκος·
σῦν τ' ἀνδροκτόνον ἐν νάπαις
Κρεμμυῶνος, ἀτάσθαλόν τε
25 Σκίρωνα κατέκτανεν·
τάν τε Κερκυόνος παλαίστραν
ἔσχεν, Πολυπήμονός τε καρτερὰν
σφῦραν ἐξέβαλεν Προκό-
πτας, ἀρείονος τυχὼν
30 φωτός. ταῦτα δέδοιχ' ὅπᾳ τελεῖται.

ΧΟΡ. ΑΘ. Τίνα δ' ἔμμεν πόθεν ἄνδρα τοῦτον στρ. γ'.
λέγει, τίνα τε στολὰν ἔχοντα;
πότερα σὺν πολεμηΐοις ὅ-
πλοισι στρατιὰν ἄγοντα πολλάν;
35 ἢ μοῦνον σὺν ὀπάοσιν
στείχειν ἔμπορον οἷ' ἀλάταν
ἐπ' ἀλλοδαμίαν,
ἰσχυρόν τε καὶ ἄλκιμον
ὧδε καὶ θρασύν, ὅσ⟨τε⟩ τούτων
40 ἀνδρῶν κρατερὸν σθένος

Bacchylides—X. 16. νέον Palm. ἦλθεν K : ηλθε. 24. Κρεμμυῶνος K : Κρεμυῶνος. 28. ἐξέβαλεν K : εξεβαλλεν. 35. σὺν ὀπάοσιν Weil : συνοπλοισιν. 36. στείχειν K : στιχειν. 39. ὅστε Palm. 40. κρατερόν K : καρτερον.

ἔσχεν; ἦ θεὸς αὐτὸν ὁρμᾷ,
  δίκας ἀδίκοισιν ὄφρα μήσεται·
οὐ γὰρ ῥᾴδιον αἰὲν ἔρ-
  δοντα μὴ 'ντυχεῖν κακῷ.
45 πάντ' ἐν τῷ δολιχῷ χρόνῳ τελεῖται.

ΑΙΓ. Δύο οἱ φῶτε μόνους ἁμαρτεῖν στρ. δ'.
  λέγει, περὶ φαιδίμοισι δ' ὤμοις
ξίφος ἔχειν [ἐλεφαντόκωπον,]
  ξεστοὺς δὲ δύ' ἐν χέρεσσ' ἄκοντας
50 κηὔτυκτον κυνέαν Λάκαιναν κρατὸς πέρι πυρσοχαίτου,
  στέρνοις τε πορφύρεον
χιτῶν' ἄμφι, καὶ οὔλιον
Θεσσαλὰν χλαμύδ'· ὀμμάτων δὲ
55 στίλβειν ἄπο Λαμνίαν
φοίνισσαν φλόγα· παῖδα δ' ἔμμεν
  πρώθηβον, Ἀρηΐων δ' ἀθυρμάτων
μεμνᾶσθαι πολέμου τε καὶ
  χαλκεοκτύπου μάχας·
60 δίζησθαι δὲ φιλαγλάους Ἀθάνας.

XI. (K. 44, B. 7). KORINTH.

–́ ◡ ◡ –́ ◡ ◡ –́ – |–́ ◡ –́ – |–́ ◡ –́ ⊼

Ὦ Πέλοπος λιπαρᾶς νάσου θεόδματοι πύλαι.

X. 48. ἐλ. Desrouss. 51. πέρι Jebb: ὑπέρ. 52. στερ. τε πορφ. | χιτῶν' ἄμφι Wilam., Platt: χιτ. πορφ. | στερ. τ' ἄμφι. 56. ἔμμεν K: εμεν.

ΥΜΝΟΣ.

XII. (K. 45, B. 11). GRIEF THAT LIES TOO DEEP FOR TEARS.

– ¦ –́ ⏑ ⏑ –́ ⏑ ⏑ ≚ ⋀
⌊́ ⏑ –́ – –́ ⏑ ⏑ –́ ⏑ ⏑ –́ – ⌊́ ⏑ –́ –

Αἰαῖ τέκος ἁμέτερον,
μεῖζον ἢ πενθεῖν ἐφάνη κακόν, ἀφθέγκτοισιν ἶσον.

ΠΑΙΑΝΕΣ.

XIII. (K. 46, B. 13). PEACE.

– ¦ ⌊́ ⏑ –́ – ⌊́ ⏑ –́ – –́ ⏑ ⏑ ≚ ⋀
–́ – ⌊́ ⏑ –́ – ⌊́ ⏑ –́ – ⌊́ ⏑ ≚ ⋀
–́ ⏑ ⏑ –́ ⏑ ⏑ –́ – ⌊́ ⏑ –́ – ⌊́ ⏑ –́ ⋀
– ¦ –́ ⏑ ⏑ –́ ⏑ ⏑ –́ > ⌊́ ⏑ –́ –
5 –́ ⏑ ⏑ –́ ⏑ ⏑ –́ – ⌊́ ⏑ –́ – ⌊́ ⏑ –́ ⋀
–́ ⏑ ⏑ –́ ⏑ ⏑ –́ – ⌊́ ⏑ –́ –
⏑ ⏑ ¦ –́ – ⌊́ ⏑ –́ –
– ¦ ⌊́ ⏑ –́ – ⌊́ ⏑ –́ – –́ ⏑ ⏑ –́ ⏑ ⏑ –́ –
⌊́ ⏑ –́ – ⌊́ ⏑ –́ – ⌊́ ⏑ ≚ ⋀
10 ⌊́ ⏑ –́ – ⌊́ ⏑ –́ – –́ ⏑ ⏑ –́ ⏑ ⏑ –́ ⋀
⌊́ ⏑ –́ – ⌊́ ⏑ –́ ⋀
–́ ⏑ ⏑ –́ ⏑ ⏑ –́ – ⌊́ ⏑ –́ – ⌊́ ⏑ –́ –
[⌊́ ⏑ –́ –

Τίκτει δέ τε θνατοῖσιν εἰρήνα μεγάλα,
πλοῦτον καὶ μελιγλώσσων ἀοιδᾶν ἄνθεα,
δαιδαλέων τ' ἐπὶ βωμῶν θεοῖσιν αἴθεσθαι βοῶν
ξανθᾷ φλογὶ μῆρα τανυτρίχων τε μήλων,
5 γυμνασίων τε νέοις αὐλῶν τε καὶ κώμων μέλειν·
ἐν δὲ σιδαροδέτοις πόρπαξιν αἰθᾶν
ἀραχνᾶν ἱστοὶ πέλονται·

BACCHYLIDES—XIII. 1. εἰρήνη. 2. ἀοιδῶν. 3. ἔθεσθε. 4. μῆρα ταν.: μηρῦταν εὐτρίχων A (μηρίταν Vind. Ars.). 6. αἴθαν.

ἔγχεά τε λογχωτὰ ξίφεά τ' ἀμφάκεα δάμναται εὐρώς·
χαλκεᾶν δ' οὐκ ἔστι σαλπίγγων κτύπος·
10 οὐδὲ συλᾶται μελίφρων ὕπνος ἀπὸ βλεφάρων,
ἁμὸν ὃς θάλπει κέαρ.
συμποσίων δ' ἐρατῶν βρίθοντ' ἀγυιαί, παιδικοί θ'
[ὕμνοι φλέγονται.

XIV. (K. 47, B. 14). SAPIENS ALIUS AB ALIO.

‒⏑⏑ ‒⏑⏑ ‒⏑ ‒‒ ‒⏑⏑ ‒⏑⏑ ‒∧
‒⏑ ‒‒ ‒⏑ ‒> ‒⏑⏑ ‒⏑ ‒∧
‒‒ ‒ . . .

Ἕτερος ἐξ ἑτέρου σοφὸς τό τε πάλαι τό τε νῦν.
οὐδὲ γὰρ ῥᾷστον ἀρρήτων ἐπέων πύλας
ἐξευρεῖν.

ΠΡΟΣΟΔΙΟΝ.

XV. (K. 48, B. 19). HAPPINESS IN TRANQUILLITY.

‒⏑ ‒⏑ ‒⏑ ‒⏑ ‒⏑ ‒⏑⏑ ‒⏑ ‒∧
‒⏑ ‒⏑⏑ ‒⏑ ‒> ‒⏑⏑ ‒⏑⏑ ‒⏑ ‒∧
‒⏑ ‒‒ ‒⏑⏑ ‒⏑⏑ ‒⏑ ‒∧
‒⏑⏑ ‒‒ ‒⏑ ‒‒ ‒⏑ ‒> ‒⏑ ‒∧
‒⏑⏑ ‒⏑ ‒‒ ‒⏑⏑ ‒⏑⏑ ‒⏑ ‒∧

Εἷς ὅρος, μία βροτοῖσιν ἐστὶν εὐτυχίας ὁδός,
θυμὸν εἴ τις ἔχων ἀπενθῆ διατελεῖν δύναται βίον·
ὃς δὲ μυρία μὲν ἀμφιπολεῖ φρενί,
τὸ δὲ παρ' ἆμάρ τε καὶ νύκτα μελλόντων χάριν
5 ἑὸν ἰάπτεται κέαρ, ἄκαρπον ἔχει πόνον.

XIII. 9. χαλκεᾶν: -έων Stob.; -έαν Plut. 11. ἁμὸν: ἆμος (ἇμος Vind.).

XV. 2. διατ. δυνατ. βίον Bergk: δυνατ. διατ. βίον. 3. ὃς: οἷς. 4. παρ' . . . νύκτα: παρόμαρτε νύκτα. 5. ἑὸν ἰάπτεται: αονι ἅπτεται.

ΥΠΟΡΧΗΜΑ.

XVI. (K. 51, K. 22). THE TOUCHSTONE OF VIRTUE.

–́ ⏑ –́ > –́ ⏑ ⌊–́ –́ ⏑ –́ ∧
–́ ⏑ ⌊–́ –́ ⏑ ⏑ –́ ⏑ ⏑ –́ ⏑ –́ ⏑ –́ ⏑ –́ ⏑ ⏑ ⌊–́ –́ ⏑

Λυδία μὲν γὰρ λίθος μανύει
χρυσόν, ἀνδρῶν δ' ἀρετὰν σοφία τε παγκρατής τ'
[ἐλέγχει ἀλάθεια.

ΣΚΟΛΙΑ.

XVII. (K. 56, B. 27). DIONYSIAC CASTLES IN THE AIR.

– ⁞ –́ ⏑ ⏑ –́ ⏑ ⏑ –́ ≥ ⌊–́ ⏑ –́ –
–́ ⏑ ⏑ –́ ⏑ ⏑ –́ ≥ ⌊–́ ⏑ –́ ⏓
–́ ⏑ ⏑ –́ ⏑ ⏑ –́ – ⌊–́ ⏑ –́ ⏓
⌊–́ ⏑ –́ – ⌊–́ ⏑ –́ – ⌊–́ ⏑ –́ ∧

γλυκεῖ' ἀνάγκα
σευομενᾶν κυλίκων θάλπῃσι θυμόν,
Κύπριδος ⟨δ'⟩ ἐλπὶς διαιθύσσει φρένας

ἀμμειγνυμένα Διονυσίοισι δώροις. στρ. β'.
5 ἀνδράσι δ' ὑψοτάτω πέμπει μερίμνας·
αὐτίχ' ὁ μὲν πόλεων κράδεμνα λύει,
πᾶσι δ' ἀνθρώποις μοναρχήσειν δοκεῖ·

χρυσῷ δ' ἐλέφαντί τε μαρμαίρουσιν οἶκοι, στρ. γ'.
πυροφόροι δὲ κατ' αἰγλάεντα ⟨πόντον⟩
10 νᾶες ἄγουσιν ἀπ' Αἰγύπτου μέγιστον
πλοῦτον· ὣς πίνοντος ὁρμαίνει κέαρ.

BACCHYLIDES—XVII. 2. σευομένα C. θάλπησι. 3. Κυπρ. ἐλπὶς δ' αἰθύσσει (δ' ἐνθύσσει E) CE. 4. ἀμμειγ. Blass: ἀναμιγν. CE. 6. αὐτίχ' ὁ: αὐτάς C; αὐτή E. κρήδεμνον. 9. αἰγλήεντα. 10. νῆες. ἀπ': ἐπ' CE.

XVIII. (K. 57, B. 28). THE FESTIVAL OF THE DIOSKUROI.

–⏑ –⏑ –⏑ –⏑ –⏑ –⏑ –⏑ –⏑ –⏑ –⏑
[–⏑ –⏑ –⏑ –∧
–⏑ –⏑ –⏑ –⏑ –⏑ –⏑ –⏑ –⏑ –⏑ –⏑

Οὐ βοῶν πάρεστι σώματ' οὔτε χρυσὸς οὔτε πορφύρεοι
τάπητες, ἀλλὰ θυμὸς εὐμενὴς
Μοῦσά τε γλυκεῖα καὶ Βοιωτίοισιν ἐν σκύφοισιν
οἶνος ἡδύς.

ΕΞ ΑΔΗΛΩΝ ΕΙΔΩΝ.

XIX. (K. 62, B. 36). FATE.

θνατοῖσι δ' οὐκ αὐθαίρετοι
οὔτ' ὄλβος οὔτ' ἄγναμπτος Ἄρης οὔτε πάμφθερσις [στάσις,
ἀλλ' ἐπιχρίμπτει νέφος ἄλλοτ' ἐπ' ἄλλαν
γαῖαν ἁ πάνδωρος αἶσα.

XX. (K. 66, B. 40). HEKATE.

Ἑκάτα
δᾳδοφόρε Νυκτὸς ⟨ὦ⟩ μελανοκόλπου θύγατερ.

XIX. 1. θνητοῖς. 2. ἄκαμπτος. 4. γᾶν.
XX. ὦ Weil. μεγαλοκόλπου.

MELANIPPIDES.

I. (1). ΔΑΝΑΙΔΕΣ.

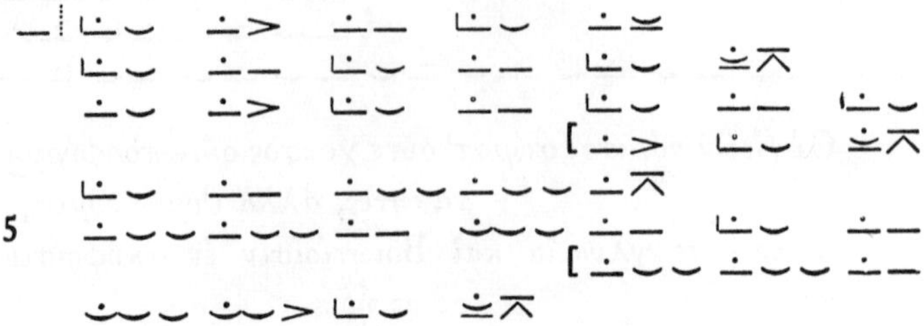

Οὐ παρθένων φόρευν μορφᾶεν εἶδος,
οὐδὲ τὰν αὐδὰν γυναικείαν ἔχον,
ἀλλ' ἐν ἁρμάτεσσι διφρούχοις ἐγυμνάζοντ' ἀν' εὔδι'
πολλάκις θήραις φρένα τερπόμεναι, [ἄλσεα
5 ⟨πολλάκι δ'⟩ ἱερόδακρυν λίβανον εὐώδεις τε φοίνικας
τέρενα Σύρια σπέρματα. [κασίαν τε ματεῦσαι,

II. (2). ΜΑΡΣΥΑΣ.

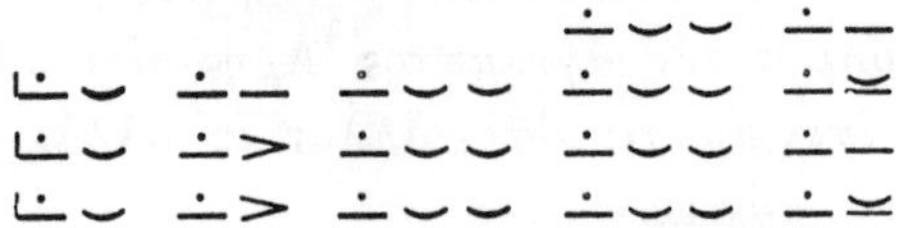

ἁ μὲν Ἀθάνα
τὤργαν' ἔρριψέν θ' ἱερᾶς ἀπὸ χειρός,
εἶπέ τ'· "ἔρρετ' αἴσχεα, σώματι λύμα,
οὔ με ⟨τᾷ⟩δ' ἐγὼ κακότατι δίδωμι."

Melanippides — I. 1. *παρθένων* : *ἀνθρώπων* A. *μορφὰν ἐνεῖδος* A. 2. *αὐδάν* : *αὐτάν* A. *γυναικίαν* A. 3. *ἀν' . . . ἄλσεα* : *ἀνευηλιάσδεα* A. 4. *θῆρες* A. 5. *πολλάκι δ'* Hiller. *ἱερόδακρυ* A. *πατεῦσαι* AB. 6. *Συρίας τέρματα* A.

II. 1. *αθάνατα ὄργανα* A. 2. *ἔρριψέ τε* A. 4. *οὔ με τᾷδ'* : *ἐμὲ δ'*.

III (4). WINE'S MADNESS.

Πάντες δ' ἀπεστύγεον ὕδωρ,
τὸ πρὶν ἐόντες ἀΐδριες οἴνου,
τάχα δὴ τάχα τοὶ μὲν οὖν ἀπωλλύοντο,
τοὶ δὲ παράπληκτον χέον ὀμφάν.

IV. (6). A PRAYER.

κλῦθί μοι, ὦ πάτερ,
θαῦμα βροτῶν, τᾶς ἀειζώου
ψυχᾶς μεδέων.

V. (7). LOVE THE SOWER.

Γλυκὺ γὰρ θέρος ἀνδρὸς ὑποσπείρων πραπίδεσσι
[πόθου.

ARIPHRON.

ΕΙΣ ΥΓΙΕΙΑΝ.

V. πραπίδων πόθῳ.

—¦ –⏑⏑ –⏑⏑ –– –⏑⏑ –⏑⏑ ––
[⌊⏑ –∧
5 –⏑⏑ –⏑⏑ –– ⌊⏑ –– –⏑
[⏓∧
⌊⏑ –– –⏑⏑ –– ⌊⏑ –>
[⌊⏑ ⌊⌋ –⏑ –⏑ ––
⏑⏑¦ –⏑⏑ –⏑⏑ –⏓
⏑¦ ⌊⏑ –> –– –⏑⏑ –⏑⏑ ⏓∧
⏑¦ ⌊⏑ –> ⌊⏑ –– ⌊⏑ –∧

Ὑγίεια, πρεσβίστα μακάρων, μετὰ σεῦ ναίοιμι τὸ
[λειπόμενον
βιοτᾶς, σὺ δέ μοι πρόφρων σύνοικος εἴης·
εἰ γάρ τις ἢ πλούτου χάρις ἢ τεκέων
⟨ἢ⟩ τᾶς ἰσοδαίμονος ἀνθρώποις βασιληΐδος ἀρχᾶς ἢ
5 οὓς κρυφίοις Ἀφροδίτας ἕρκεσιν θηρεύομεν, [πόθων,
ἢ εἴ τις ἄλλα θεόθεν ἀνθρώποισι τέρψις ἢ πόνων
μετὰ σεῖο, μάκαιρ' Ὑγίεια, [ἀμπνοὰ πέφανται,
τέθαλε πάντα καὶ λάμπει Χαρίτων ὄαρος.
σέθεν δὲ χωρὶς οὔτις εὐδαίμων ⟨ἔφυ.⟩

LIKYMNIOS.

I. (4). ΕΙΣ ΥΓΙΕΙΑΝ.

⏑⏑ –⏑⏑ –⏑ –– ⌊⏑
—¦ ⌊⏑ –– –⏑⏑ –⏑⏑ –– [–∧
–⏑⏑ –⏑⏑ –⏓
⌊⏑ –– –⏑⏑ –⏑⏑ –∧
5 —¦ –⏑⏑ –⏑⏑ –– –⏑⏑ –⏑⏑ ––
⏑¦ ⌊⏑ –> ⌊⏑ –– ⌊⏑ –∧

ARIPHRON—4. ἢ from Likymn. 5. ἄρκυσιν Athen.; ελκεσι inscr. 8. ὄαρος or ὄαροι Athen. A; ὄαρ E; ὄαρι epit. Hoeschl. 9. ἔφυ from Likymn.

λιπαρόμματε μᾶτερ ὑψίστα, θρόνων
σεμνῶν Ἀπόλλωνος βασίλεια ποθεινά,
πραϋγέλως Ὑγίεια·

* * * * * *

Τίς γὰρ ⟨ἢ⟩ πλούτου χάρις ἢ τεκέων,
5 ἢ τᾶς ἰσοδαίμονος ἀνθρώποις βασιληΐδος ἀρχᾶς;
σέθεν δὲ χωρὶς οὔτις εὐδαίμων ἔφυ.

II. (1). ACHERON.

Μυρίαις παγαῖς δακρύων ἀχέων τε βρύει.

III. (3). HYPNOS.

Ὕπνος δὲ χαίρων ὀμμάτων αὐγαῖς ἀναπεπταμένοις
ὄσσοις ἐκοίμιζε κοῦρον.

ION.

ΔΙΘΥΡΑΜΒΟΙ.

I. (9). WINE.

ἄδαμνον
παῖδα ταυρωπόν, νέον οὐ νέον, ἥδιστον πρόπολον
βαρυγδούπων ἐρώτων, οἶνον ἀερσίνοον,
ἀνθρώπων πρύτανιν.

Likymnios—I. 3. ὑγεία. 4. τοκήων. 5. ἀνθρώπου.
Ion—I. 1. ἄδαμον. 3. ἀερσίπνοον.

II. (10). LUCIFER.

Ἀοῖον ἀεροφοίταν ἀστέρα
μείνωμεν ἀελίου λευκοπτέρυγα πρόδρομον.

EURIPIDES.

EPINIKION TO ALKIBIADES (B. 3).

Σὲ δ' ἀείσομαι, ὦ Κλεινίου παῖ·
καλὸν ἁ νίκα· ⟨τὸ⟩ κάλλιστον ⟨δ'⟩ ὃ μηδεὶς ἄλλος
[Ἑλλάνων ⟨ἔλαχες⟩,
ἅρματι πρῶτα δραμεῖν καὶ δεύτερα καὶ τρίτα⟨τα⟩,
βῆναί τ' ἀπονητὶ Διὸς στεφθέντ' ἐλαίᾳ
5 κάρυκι βοᾶν παραδοῦναι.

PHILOXENOS.

GALATEIA (B. 8).

ION—II. 1. ἠεροφοῖταν. 2. μείνωμεν Ven. Ald.; μῆνα μέν Rav. Suid.

EURIPIDES—4. Διός: δίς.

ὯΩ καλλιπρόσωπε
χρυσοβόστρυχε Γαλάτεια,
χαριτόφωνε, θάλος ἐρώτων.

TIMOTHEOS.

I. (1). ΕΙΣ ΑΡΤΕΜΙΝ.

–⏑⏑ –⏑⏑ –⏑⏑ –⏑⏑

Μαινάδα, θυιάδα, φοιβάδα, λυσσάδα.

II. (4). ΚΥΚΛΩΨ.

> | –⏑ ⏖ –⏑ ⏖ –⏑ –⏑ –⏒
⏑⏑⏑ –⏑ –⏑ –⏑ –⏑
–⏑ –⏑ ⏑⏑⏑ ⏑⏑⏑ –⏑
–⏑ –⏑ –⏑ –⏑ ⏑⏑⏑ –⏑ –⏒

Ἔγχευε δ' ἓν μὲν δέπας κίσσινον μελαίνας
σταγόνος ἀμβρότας ἀφρῷ βρυάζον·
εἴκοσιν δὲ μέτρ' ἀνέχευ', ἀνέμισγε δ'
αἷμα Βακχίου νεορρύτοις δακρύοισι Νυμφᾶν.

ΠΕΡΣΑΙ.

III. (8).

–⏑⏑ –⏑⏑ –– –⏑⏑ –⏑⏑ –⏓

Κλεινὸν ἐλευθερίας τεύχων μέγαν Ἑλλάδι κόσμον.

IV. (9).

⏑ | –> –⏑ ⏖ ⏑⏑⏑ ⏖ ⏑⏑⏑ –∧

Σέβεσθ' αἰδῶ σύνεργον ἀρετᾶς δοριμάχου.

Philoxenos—2. χρυσεοβόστρυχε. 3. κάλλος AE.
Timotheos—II. 1. ἔχευεν δ' A. 3. εἴκοσι. ἀνέχευαν ἔμισγε διαμα A ; ἐνέχευεν, ἀνέμισγε δ' ἅμα E. 4. νύμφαν.
IV. δουρυμάχου.

V. (10).

Ἄρης τύραννος· χρυσὸν δ' Ἑλλὰς οὐ δέδοικε.

VI. (11). "TIMOTHEOS WINS!"

Μακάριος ἦσθα, Τιμόθεε, κᾶρυξ ὅτ' εἶπεν·
" νικᾷ Τιμόθεος Μιλήσιος
τὸν Κάμωνος τὸν ἰωνοκάμπταν."

VII. (12). NEW SONGS THE BEST.

Οὐκ ἀείδω τὰ παλαιά,
καὶ τὰ καινὰ γὰρ ἅμα κρείσσω·
νέος ὁ Ζεὺς βασιλεύει,
τὸ πάλαι δ' ἦν Κρόνος ἄρχων·
5 ἀπίτω Μοῦσα παλαιά.

VIII. (13). APOLLO HELIOS.

TIMOTHEUS—VI. 1. ὅτε κῆρυξ. 2. Τ. ὁ. 3. Κάμβωνος. VII. 2. So Hiller; τὰ γὰρ ἅμα A; καινὰ γὰρ *epit.* 4. παλαιόν.

Σύ τ', ὦ τὸν ἀεὶ πόλον οὐράνιον
ἀκτῖσι λαμπραῖς Ἅλιε βάλλων,
πέμψον ἑκαβόλον ἐχθροῖσιν βέλος
σᾶς ἀπὸ νευρᾶς, ὦ ἰὲ Παιάν.

TELESTES.

I. (1). ATHENA AND THE FLUTE.

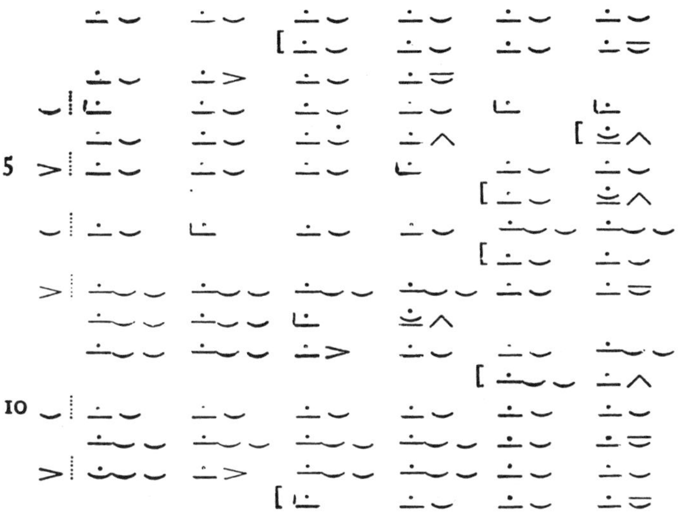

Ὃν σοφὸν σοφὰν λαβοῦσαν οὐκ ἐπέλπομαι νόῳ
ὀργάνων δίαν Ἀθάναν [*δρυμοῖς ὀρείοις*
δυσόφθαλμον αἶσχος ἐκφοβηθεῖσαν
αὖθις ἐκ χερῶν βαλεῖν,
5 *νυμφαγενεῖ χοροκτύπῳ φηρὶ Μαρσύᾳ κλέος.*
τί γάρ νιν εὐηράτοιο κάλλεος ὀξὺς ἔρως ἔτειρεν,

VIII. 2. *λαμπραῖς ἀκτῖσι ἥλιε.* 3. *ἐχθροῖσιν* Farnell : *ἐχθροῖσι.*
TELESTES—I. 1. *ὄριοις.* 2. *ὄργανον.* 5. *χειροκτύπῳ.*

ἃ παρθενίαν ἄγαμον καὶ ἄπαιδ' ἀπένειμε Κλωθώ;
ἀλλὰ μάταν ἀχόρευτος
ἅδε ματαιολόγων φάμα προσέπταθ' Ἑλλάδα μουσο-
10 σοφᾶς ἐπίφθονον βροτοῖς τέχνας ὄνειδος. [πόλων,
* * * * * *
ἃν συνεριθοτάταν Βρομίῳ παρέδωκε σεμνᾶς
δαίμονος ἀερθὲν πνεῦμ' αἰολοπτερύγων σὺν ἀγλαᾶν
[ὠκύτατι χειρῶν.

II. (2) THE LYDIAN AND THE DORIAN MODE.

–́ ⏑ ⏑ –́ ⏑ ⏑ –́ – –́ ⏑ ⏑ –́ ⏑ ⏑ –́ ⏓
–́ ⏑ ⏑ –́ ⏑ ⏑ –́ ⏓
–́ ⏑ ⏑ –́ ⏑ ⏑ –́ – –́ ⏑ ⏑ –́ ⏑ ⏑ –́ –
– ⏑ ⏑ –́ ⏑ ⏑ –́ – –́ ⏑ ⏑ –́ ⏑ ⏑ –́ ⊼

Ἢ Φρύγα καλλιπνόων αὐλῶν ἱερῶν βασιλῆα,
Λυδὸν ὃς ἥρμοσε πρῶτος
Δωρίδος ἀντίπαλον μούσας νόμον αἰόλον ὀμφᾷ,
πνεύματος εὔπτερον αὔραν ἀμφιπλέκων καλάμοις.

III. (5). THE INTRODUCTION OF THE PHRYGIAN MODE.

– ⁞ ⌞́ ⏑ –́ – ⌞́ ⏑ –́ – ⌞́ ⏑ –́ –
⏑ ⏑ ⁞ –́ – ⏑ ⏑ –́ – ⏑ ⏑ –́ – ⊼
⏑́ ⏑ ⏑ –́ – ⌞́ ⏑ ⏓́ ⊼
– ⁞ ⌞́ ⏑ –́ – ⌞́ ⏑ –́ – ⌞́ ⏑ ⏓́ ⊼
5 –́ ⏑ ⏑ –́ ⏑ . . .

TELESTES—I. 7. ἃ : αιγὰρ A. ἀγανὸν A. 8. ἀναχορευτος AE.
9. φημα A pr. m. 11. συμεριθοταταν A.
II. 2. Λυδὸν ὃς A : αὔδονος. ηροσε A. 3. μούσης νομοαίολον ὀρφναί.

Πρῶτοι παρὰ κρατῆρας Ἑλλάνων ἐν αὐλοῖς
συνοπαδοὶ Πέλοπος ματρὸς ὀρείας
Φρύγιον ἄεισαν νόμον·
τοὶ δ' ὀξυφώνοις πηκτίδων ψαλμοῖς κρέκον
5 Λύδιον ὕμνον.

LYKOPHRONIDES.

I. (1). TRUE BEAUTY IS SEEMLY.

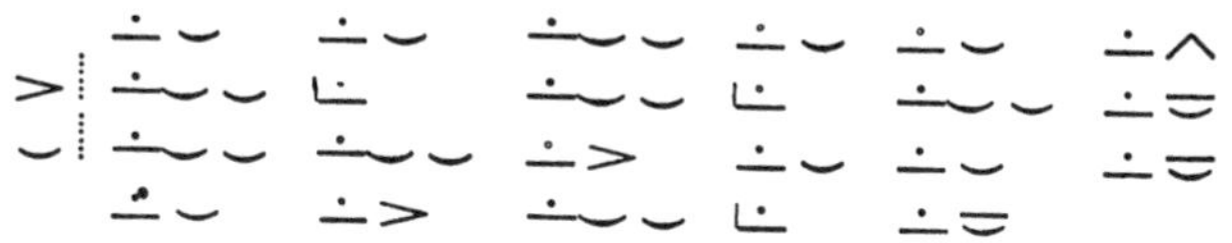

Οὔτε παιδὸς ἄρρενος οὔτε παρθένων
τῶν χρυσοφόρων οὔτε γυναικῶν βαθυκόλπων
καλὸν τὸ πρόσωπον, ἐὰν μὴ κόσμιον πεφύκῃ.
ἡ γὰρ αἰδὼς ἄνθος ἐπισπείρει.

II. (2). A LOVE OFFERING.

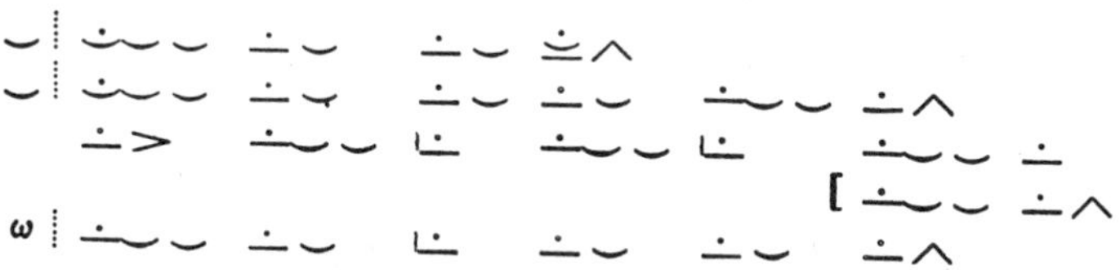

Τόδ' ἀνατίθημί σοι ῥόδον
καλὸν ἀνάθημα καὶ πέδιλα καὶ κυνέαν
καὶ τὰν θηροφόνον λογχίδ', ἐπεί μοι νόος ἄλλᾳ κέχυται
ἐπὶ τὰν Χάρισιν φίλαν παῖδα καὶ καλάν.

III. 1. Ἑλλήνων.
Lykophronides—I. 2. οὐδέ. 3. ἐὰν μή: ἀλλὰ A. πεφύκῃ: πεφύκει A.
II. 2. ἀνάθημα: νόημα A. 3. τήν A. ἄλλαι. 4. Χάρισι.

ARISTOTLE.

ΑΡΕΤΑ (B. 6).

⏑ ⏑ ⁞ –́ ⏑ ⏑ –́ ⏑ ⏑ ⌞́ ⏑ –́ –
– ⁞ ⌞́ ⏑ –́ – ⌞́ ⏑ –́ ⋀
–́ ⏑ ⏑ –́ ⏑ ⏑ –́ –
⌞́ ⏑ –́ – –́ ⏑ ⏑ –́ ⏑ ⏑ –́ ⏓
5 ⌞́ ⏑ –́ – –́ ⏑ ⏑ –́ ⏑ ⏑ –́ ⏓
–́ ⏑ ⏑ –́ ⏑ ⏑ –́ –
–́ ⏑ ⏑ –́ ⏑ ⏑ –́ – ⌞́ ⏑ –́ –
–́ ⏑ ⏑ –́ ⏑ ⏑ –́ – ⌞́ ⏑ –́ –
–́ ⏑ ⏑ –́ ⏑ ⏑ –́ ⏑ ⏑ –́ – ⌞́ ⏑ –́ –
10 ⌞́ ⏑ ⌴́ ⌞́ ⏑ –́ –
⌞́ ⏑ –́ – –́ ⏑ ⏑ ⏓́ ⋀
–́ ⏑ ⏑ –́ ⏑ ⏑ –́ – –́ ⏑ ⏑ –́ ⏑ ⏑ ⌴́
[⌴́ ⏓́ ⋀
–́ ⏑ ⏑ –́ ⏑ ⏑ –́ – –́ ⏑ ⏑ –́ ⏑ ⏑ –́ ⏑ ⏑
[–́ ⏑ ⏑ –́ – ⌞́ ⏑ –́ –
–́ ⏑ ⏑ –́ ⏑ ⏑ –́ – –́ ⏑ ⏑ –́ ⏑ ⏑ –́ –
[⌞́ ⏑ –́ –
15 –́ ⏑ ⏑ –́ ⏑ ⏑ –́ > –́ ⏑ ⏑ –́ ⏑ ⏑ –́ –
[–́ ⏑ ⏑ –́ ⏑ ⏑ ⌞́ ⏑ –́ –

Ἀρετά, πολύμοχθε γένει βροτείῳ,
θήραμα κάλλιστον βίῳ,
σᾶς πέρι, παρθένε, μορφᾶς
καὶ θανεῖν ζηλωτὸς ἐν Ἑλλάδι πότμος
5 καὶ πόνους τλῆναι μαλεροὺς ἀκάμαντας·
τοῖον ἐπὶ φρένα βάλλεις
καρπὸν ἐς ἀθάνατον χρυσοῦ τε κρείσσω
καὶ γονέων μαλακαυγήτοιό θ᾽ ὕπνου·
σεῦ δ᾽ ἕνεχ᾽ οὑκ Διὸς Ἡρακλέης Λήδας τε κοῦροι
10 πόλλ᾽ ἀνέτλασαν ἔργοις

ARISTOTLE—7. εἰς. 9. ἕνεχ᾽ ὁ E; ἕνεκ᾽ ἐκ Diog.

σὰν ἀγρεύοντες δύναμιν.
σοῖς δὲ πόθοις Ἀχιλεὺς Αἴας τ' Ἀίδαο δόμους ἦλθον·
σᾶς δ' ἕνεκεν φιλίου μορφᾶς καὶ Ἀταρνέος ἔντροφος
[ἀελίου χήρωσεν αὐγᾶς·
τοιγὰρ ἀοίδιμος ἔργοις, ἀθάνατόν τέ μιν αὐδήσουσι
[Μοῦσαι
15 Μναμοσύνας θύγατρες, Διὸς ξενίου σέβας αὔξουσαι
[φιλίας τε γέρας βεβαίου.

MELIC ADESPOTA.

I. (86 B.). THE GIFT OF SONG IS NOT FOR ALL.

–⏑ –⏑ –⏑ –> –⏑ –⏑ –⏑ –⏓
–⏑⏑ –⏑⏑ – . . .

Οὐ γὰρ ἐν μέσοισι κεῖται δῶρα δυσμάχητα Μοισᾶν
τὠπιτυχόντι φέρειν.

II. (87). A POET'S OATH.

– ¦ –⏑ ⊔ –⏑⏑ –⏑⏑ –– –⏑ ––
–⏑ –– –⏑⏑ –⏑⏑ ⊔ ⊔ –⋀

Ναὶ τὰν Ὄλυμπον καταδερκομέναν σκαπτοῦχον Ἥραν,
ἔστι μοι πιστὸν ταμιεῖον ἐπὶ γλώσσας.

III. (89). PEACE.

–⏑ –– ⊔ –⋀
–⏑⏑ –⏑⏑ – ⋀

Ὦ γλυκεῖ' εἰρήνα,
πλουτοδότειρα βροτοῖς.

---

12. Ἀχιλλεύς AE. 13. ἀταρτανεος A; ἀταρνέως E. 14. αὔξουσαι Wilam.: αὐξήσουσι.
Mel. Adesp.—III. εἰρήνη.

IV. (92). HADES.

Νυκτὸς αἰδνᾶς ἀεργηλοῖό θ' ὕπνου κοίρανος.

V. (96). DEATH THE END OF SONG.

Ἔπειτα κείσεται βαθυδένδρῳ
ἐν χθονὶ συμποσίων τε καὶ λυρᾶν ἄμοιρος
ἰαχᾶς τε παντερπέος αὐλῶν.

VI. (98). NIOBE.

θαλέθοντι βίῳ
βλάσταις τε τέκνων βριθομένα γλυκερὸν
φάος ὁρῶσα

VII. (99). MEN'S CARES ARE DIVERSE.

ἄλλον τρόπον
ἄλλων ἐγείρει φροντὶς ἀνθρώπων.

VIII. (101). HEKABE.

Mel. Adesp.—VII. τρόπος.

χαροπὰν κύνα· χάλκεον δέ οἱ
γναθμῶν ἐκ πολιᾶν φθεγγομένας ὑπάκουε μὲν Ἴδα
Τένεδός τε περιρρύτα
Θρηΐκιοί τε φιλάνεμοι γύαι.

IX. (104 A). THE EARTH IS GARLANDED.

— ¦ ⏗ ⏑ ⏗ — ⏗ ⏑ ⏑ ⏗ ⏑ ⏑ ⏗ ∧

Ποικίλλεται μὲν γαῖα πολυστέφανος.

X. (104 B). VIRTUE RATHER THAN UNJUST GAIN.

— ¦ ⏗ ⏑ ⏑ ⏗ ⏑ ⏑ ⏗ — ⏗ ⏑ ⏑ ⏗ ⏑ ⏑ ⊔ ⏗ ⏑ ⏗ ∧

Οὐ μήποτε τὰν ἀρετὰν ἀλλάξομαι ἀντ' ἀδίκου κέρδεος.

XI. (138). CONCORD.

— ¦ ⏗ ⏑ ⏗ > ⏗ ⏑ ⏑ ⏗ ⏑ ⏑ ⏗ — ⏗ ⏑ ⏗ —
[⏗ ⏑ ⏑ ⏗ ⏑ ⏑ ⏗ ∧
— ¦ ⏗ ⏑ ⏗ — ⏗ ⏑ ⏗ — ⏗ ⏑ ⏑ ⏗ ⏑ ⏑ ⏗ —
[⏗ ⏑ ⏗ —
⏗ ⏑ ⏗ — ⏗ ⏑ ⏑ ⏗ ⏑ ⏑ ⏗ — ⏗ ⏑ ⏗ —
[⏗ ⏑ ⏗ ∧
⏗ ⏑ ⏑ ⏗ — ⏗ ⏑ ⏗ — ⏗ ⏑ ⏗ ⏓

Οὐ χρυσὸς ἀγλαὸς σπανιώτατος ἐν θνατῶν δυσελπίστῳ
[βίῳ, οὐδ' ἀδάμας
οὐδ' ἀργύρου κλῖναι πρὸς ἄνθρωπον δοκιμαζόμεν' ἀσ-
[τράπτει πρὸς ὄψεις,
οὐδὲ γαίας εὐρυπέδου γόνιμοι βρίθοντες αὐτάρκεις γύαι,
ὡς ἀγαθῶν ἀνδρῶν ὁμοφράδμων νόησις.

VIII. 2. ὑπακουέμεν. 3. περιρρυτά. 4. φιλάνεμοι Hermann, γύαι Wilam.: φιλίην ἔμοιγε.
X. οὐ μήν ποτ' ἂν ἀρ. ἀλλάξωμαι. κέρδους.

XII. (139). TYCHE.

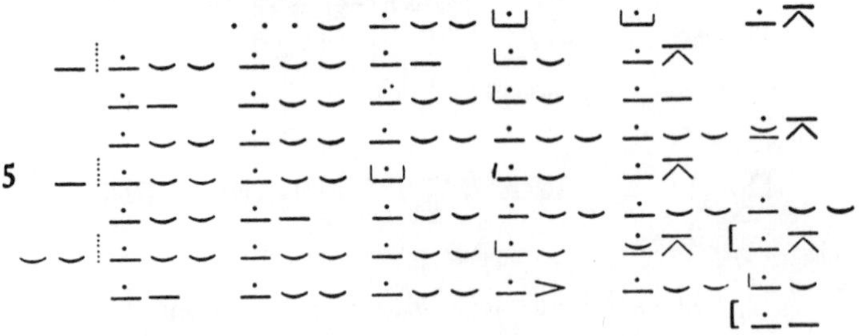

```
            . . . ⏑  –̇ ⏑ ⏑ ⏑ ⊔̇      ⊔̇       –̇ ⊼
     – | –̇ ⏑ ⏑  –̇ ⏑ ⏑  –̇ –   ⊔̇ ⏑    –̇ ⊼
         –̇ –    –̇ ⏑ ⏑  –̇ ⏑ ⏑ ⊔̇ ⏑    –̇ –
         –̇ ⏑ ⏑  –̇ ⏑ ⏑  –̇ ⏑ ⏑  –̇ ⏑ ⏑  –̇ ⏑ ⏑  ⏓̇ ⊼
5    – | –̇ ⏑ ⏑  –̇ ⏑ ⏑  ⊔̇      ⊔̇ ⏑    –̇ ⊼
         –̇ ⏑ ⏑  –̇ –       –̇ ⏑ ⏑  –̇ ⏑ ⏑  –̇ ⏑ ⏑  –̇ ⏑ ⏑
   ⏑ ⏑ | –̇ ⏑ ⏑  –̇ ⏑ ⏑  –̇ ⏑ ⏑ ⊔̇ ⏑    ⏓̇ ⊼  [ –̇ ⊼
         –̇ –    –̇ ⏑ ⏑  –̇ ⏑ ⏑  –̇ >    –̇ ⏑ ⏑ ⊔̇ ⏑
                                                [ –̇ –
```

Τύχα, μερόπων ἀρχὰ
καὶ τέρμα· τὺ καὶ σοφίας θακεῖς ἕδρας,
καὶ τιμὰν βροτέοις ἐπέθηκας ἔργοις·
καὶ τὺ καλὸν πλέον ἢ κακὸν ἐκ σέθεν, ἅ τε χάρις
5 λάμπει περὶ σὰν πτέρυγα χρυσέαν·
καὶ τὸ τεᾷ πλάστιγγι δοθὲν μακαριστότατον τελέθει·
τὺ δ' ἀμαχανίας πόρον εἶδες ἐν ἄλγεσιν,
καὶ λαμπρὸν φάος ἄγαγες ἐν σκότῳ, προφερεστάτα θεῶν.

XIII. (140). PRAYER TO THE FATES.

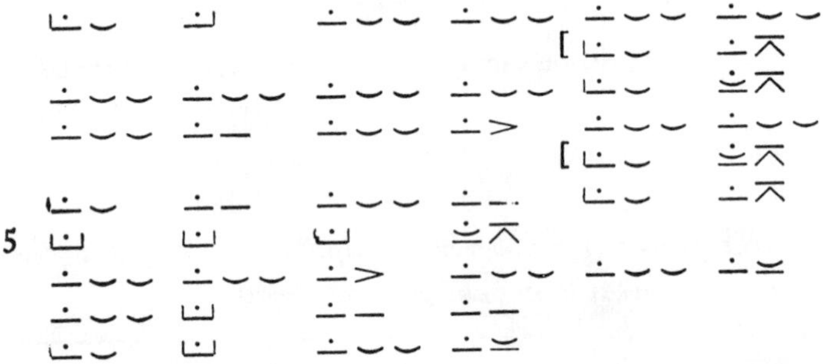

```
     ⊔̇ ⏑    ⊔̇      –̇ ⏑ ⏑  –̇ ⏑ ⏑  –̇ ⏑ ⏑  –̇ ⏑ ⏑
                                [ ⊔̇ ⏑    –̇ ⊼
     –̇ ⏑ ⏑  –̇ ⏑ ⏑  –̇ ⏑ ⏑  –̇ ⏑ ⏑  ⊔̇ ⏑    ⏓̇ ⊼
     –̇ ⏑ ⏑  –̇ –    –̇ ⏑ ⏑  –̇ >    –̇ ⏑ ⏑  –̇ ⏑ ⏑
                                [ ⊔̇ ⏑    ⏓̇ ⊼
     ⊔̇ ⏑    –̇ –    –̇ ⏑ ⏑  –̇ –    ⊔̇ ⏑    –̇ ⊼
5    ⊔̇      ⊔̇      ⊔̇      ⏓̇ ⊼
     –̇ ⏑ ⏑  –̇ ⏑ ⏑  –̇ >    –̇ ⏑ ⏑  –̇ ⏑ ⏑  –̇ ⏓
     –̇ ⏑ ⏑  ⊔̇      –̇ –    –̇ –
     ⊔̇ ⏑    ⊔̇      –̇ ⏑ ⏑  –̇ ⏓
```

MEL. ADESP.—XII. 2. τ. τύ: τέρματι. θακεῖς ἕδρας: ἄκος δρᾷς.

–́ ◡ ◡ –́ ◡ ◡ –́ > ⌞–́ ◡ ⌞–́⌟ ⌞–́ ◡
[–́ ⩞
10 –́ ◡ ◡ –́ ◡ ◡ –́ – ⌞–́ ◡ –́ > ⌞–́ ◡
–́ ◡ ◡ –́ . . . [◡́◡ > –́ ◡ ◡ –́ ⏓

Κλῦτε Μοῖραι, Διὸς αἵτε παρὰ θρόνον ἀγχοτάτω θεῶν
ἑζόμεναι περιώσι' ἄφυκτά τε μήδεα
παντοδαπῶν βουλᾶν ἀδαμαντίναισιν ὑφαίνετε κερκίσιν,
Αἶσα ⟨καὶ⟩ Κλωθὼ Λάχεσίς τ', εὐώλενοι
5 κοῦραι Νυκτός,
εὐχομένων ἐπακούσατ', οὐράνιαι χθόνιαί τε
δαίμονες ὦ πανδείμαντοι·
πέμπετ' ὔμμιν ῥοδόκολπον
Εὐνομίαν λιπαροθρόνους τ' ἀδελφάς, Δίκαν
10 καὶ στεφανηφόρον Εἰρήναν· πόλιν τε τάνδε βαρυφρόνων
συντυχιᾶν. [λελάθοιτε

XIV. IMMORTAL SONGS FOR THE GODS.

–́ – –́ ◡ ◡ –́ – –́ ◡ ◡ –́ ◡ ◡ –́ > ⌞–́ ◡ –́ –

Ὑμνέωμες μάκαρας, Μοῦσαι Διὸς ἔκγονοι, ἀφθίτοις ἀοιδαῖς.

XV. ZEUS.

⌞–́ ◡ –́ – –́ ◡ ◡ –́ ◡ ◡ –́ ◡ ◡ –́ –

Ζεὺς ὁ καὶ ζωᾶς θανάτοιό τε πείρατα νωμῶν.

XVI. HADES.

–́ ◡ ◡ –́ ◡ ◡ –́ ◡ ◡ –́ ◡ ◡ –́ ◡ ◡

⟨Ἀίδας⟩
⟨ὃς⟩ μόνος οὐ δέχεται γλυκερᾶς μέρος ἐλπίδος.

XV. ζωῆς καὶ θανάτου: corr. Hense.
XVI. So Crusius.

SKOLIA.

ΣΚΟΛΙΑ ΑΤΤΙΚΑ (I.–XXIV.).

I. (2). TO ATHENA.

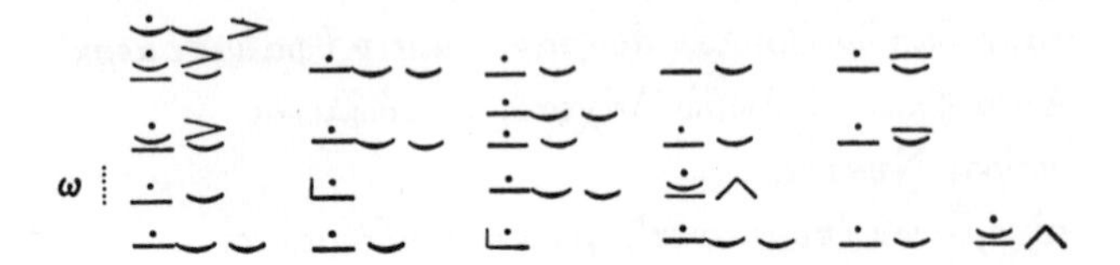

Παλλὰς Τριτογένει', ἄνασσ' Ἀθάνα,
ὄρθου τήνδε πόλιν τε καὶ πολίτας
ἄτερ ἀλγέων καὶ στάσεων
καὶ θανάτων ἀώρων, σύ τε καὶ πατήρ.

II. (3). TO DEMETER AND PERSEPHONE.

Πλούτου μητέρ', Ὀλυμπίαν ἀείδω
Δήμητρα στεφανηφόροις ἐν ὥραις,
σέ τε, παῖ Διὸς Φερσεφόνη·
χαίρετον, εὖ δὲ τάνδ' ἀμφέπετον πόλιν.

III. (4). TO APOLLO AND ARTEMIS.

Ἐν Δήλῳ ποτ' ἔτικτε τέκνα Λατώ,
Φοῖβον χρυσοκόμαν, ἄνακτ' Ἀπόλλω,
ἐλαφηβόλον τ' ἀγροτέραν
Ἄρτεμιν, ἃ γυναικῶν μέγ' ἔχει κράτος.

SKOLIA—I. 1. Ἀθάνα conj. Bergk: Ἀθηνᾶ. 3. τε και.
II. 4. ἀμφετον A.
III. 2. ἀπόλλων' A.

IV. (5). TO PAN.

Ὦ Πάν, Ἀρκαδίας μεδέων κλεεννᾶς,
ὀρχηστά, Βρομίαις ὀπαδὲ Νύμφαις,
γελάσειας, ὦ Πάν, ἐπ' ἐμαῖς
εὔφροσι ταῖσδ' ἀοιδαῖς κεχαρημένος.

V. (7). THE WINDOW OF THE SOUL.

Εἴθ' ἐξῆν, ὁποῖός τις ἦν ἕκαστος,
τὸ στῆθος διελόντ', ἔπειτα τὸν νοῦν
ἐσιδόντα, κλῄσαντα πάλιν,
ἄνδρα φίλον νομίζειν ἀδόλῳ φρενί.

VI. (8). THE SCALE OF BLESSINGS.

Ὑγιαίνειν μὲν ἄριστον ἀνδρὶ θνατῷ,
δεύτερον δὲ φυὰν καλὸν γενέσθαι,
τὸ τρίτον δὲ πλουτεῖν ἀδόλως,
καὶ τὸ τέταρτον ἡβᾶν μετὰ τῶν φίλων.

HARMODIOS AND ARISTOGEITON.

VII. (9).

Ἐν μύρτου κλαδὶ τὸ ξίφος φορήσω,
ὥσπερ Ἁρμόδιος καὶ Ἀριστογείτων,
ὅτε τὸν τύραννον κτανέτην
ἰσονόμους τ' Ἀθήνας ἐποιησάτην.

VIII. (10).

Φίλταθ' Ἁρμόδι', οὔ τί που τέθνηκας,
νήσοις δ' ἐν μακάρων σέ φασιν εἶναι,

IV. 1. ἴω AE. 3. γελασίαισΐω A. 4. εὔφροσι Wilam.: εὐφροσύναις AE.

V. 3. εἰσιδόντα A: ἰδόντα E. κλῄσαντα Sm.: κλείσαντα.

ἵνα περ ποδώκης ʼΑχιλεύς,
Τυδεΐδην τέ φασιν ἐσθλὸν Διομήδεα.

IX. (11).

ʼΕν μύρτου κλαδὶ τὸ ξίφος φορήσω,
ὥσπερ ʽΑρμόδιος καὶ ʼΑριστογείτων,
ὅτʼ ʼΑθηναίης ἐν θυσίαισʼ
ἄνδρα τύραννον ῞Ιππαρχον ἐκαινέτην.

X. (12).

Αἰεὶ σφῷν κλέος ἔσσεται κατʼ αἶαν,
φίλταθʼ ʽΑρμόδιος καὶ ʼΑριστογείτων,
ὅτι τὸν τύραννον κτανέτην
ἰσονόμους τʼ ʼΑθήνας ἐποιησάτην.

XI. (14). LEIPSYDRION.

Αἰαῖ, Λειψύδριον προδωσέταιρον,
οἵους ἄνδρας ἀπώλεσας, μάχεσθαι
ἀγαθούς τε καὶ εὐπατρίδας,
οἳ τότʼ ἔδειξαν οἵων πατέρων ἔσαν.

XII. (27). TO KEDON.

–́ – –́ – –́ ⏑ ⏑ –́ ⏑ ⏑ –́ ⏑ ⏑ –́ –
–́ – –́ ⏑ ⏑ ⊔ –́ ⏑ ⏑ –́ ⏑ ⏑ –́ ⏖

῎Εγχει καὶ Κήδωνι, διάκονε, μηδʼ ἐπιλήθου,
εἰ χρὴ τοῖς ἀγαθοῖς ἀνδράσιν οἰνοχοεῖν.

Skolia—VIII. 3. αχιλλεύς AE.
X. 3. ʽΑρμόδιε. ʼΑριστόγειτον.

XIII. (15). ADVICE TO THE MARINER.

⟨Ὡραῖον⟩ ἐκ γῆς χρὴ κατίδην πλόον,
εἴ τις δύναιτο καὶ παλάμην ἔχοι·
  ἐπεὶ δέ κ' ἐν πόντῳ γένηται,
  τῷ παρεόντι τρέχειν ἀνάγκη.

XIV. (16). THE CRAB AND THE SERPENT.

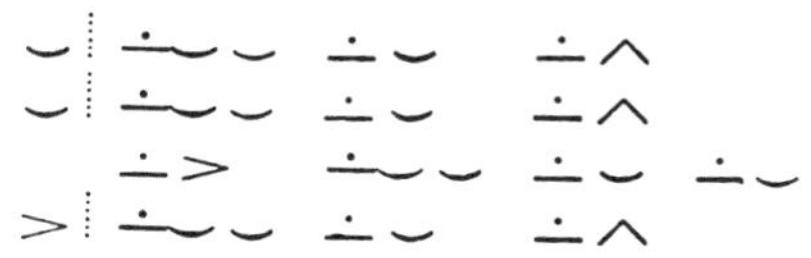

Ὁ καρκίνος ὦδ' ἔφα
χαλᾷ τὸν ὄφιν λαβών·
"εὐθὺν χρὴ τὸν ἑταῖρον ἔμμεν
καὶ μὴ σκολιὰ φρονεῖν."

XV. (21). ADMETOS.

Ἀδμήτου λόγον, ὦ 'ταῖρε, μαθὼν τοὺς ἀγαθοὺς φίλει,
τῶν δειλῶν δ' ἀπέχου, γνοὺς ὅτι δειλοῖς ὀλίγα χάρις.

XVI. (22). THE IDEAL COMRADE.

Σύν μοι πῖνε, συνήβα, συνέρα, συστεφανηφόρει,
σύν μοι μαινομένῳ μαίνεο, σὺν σώφρονι σωφρόνει.

XIII. 1. ὡραῖον Stadtmüller.
XIV. 3. ἐν μὲν A; ἔμεν E.
XVI. 2. σωφρονήσω σωφρονι A; συσσωφρόνει σώφρονι E.

XVII. (23). TRUST NOT THE UNSEEN.

Ὑπὸ παντὶ λίθῳ σκορπίος, ὦ 'ταῖρ', ὑποδύεται·
φράζευ, μή σε βάλῃ· τῷ δ' ἀφανεῖ πᾶς ἕπεται δόλος.

XVIII. (24). POSSESSION AND DESIRE.

Ἁ ὗς τὰν βάλανον τὰν μὲν ἔχει, τὰν δ' ἔραται λαβεῖν·
κἀγὼ παῖδα καλὴν τὴν μὲν ἔχω, τὴν δ' ἔραμαι λαβεῖν.

XIX. (26). FIDELITY.

Ὅστις ἄνδρα φίλον μὴ προδίδωσιν, μεγάλαν ἔχει
τιμὰν ἔν τε βροτοῖς ἔν τε θεοῖσιν κατ' ἐμὸν νόον.

XX. (17). AIAS.

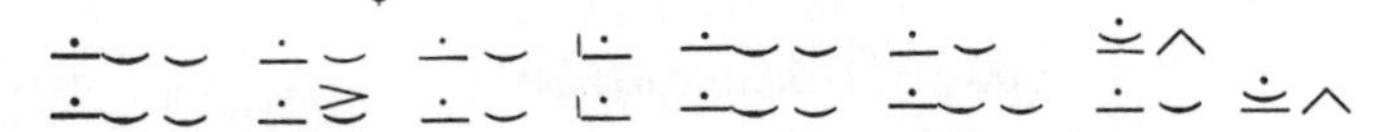

Παῖ Τελαμῶνος Αἶαν αἰχμητά, λέγουσί σε
ἐς Τροΐαν ἄριστον ἐλθεῖν Δαναῶν μετ' Ἀχιλλέα.

XXI. (18).

Τὸν Τελαμῶνα πρῶτον, Αἴαντα δὲ δεύτερον
ἐς Τροΐαν λέγουσιν ἐλθεῖν Δαναῶν καὶ Ἀχιλλέα.

XXII. (19). A WISH.

Εἴθε λύρα καλὰ γενοίμαν ἐλεφαντίνα,
καί με καλοὶ παῖδες φοροῖεν Διόνυσον ἐς χορόν.

SKOLIA—XX. μετ' Ἀχ. Eust.; καὶ Ἀχ. AE.
XXII. 1. καλή. 2. φέροιεν Athen. A: φορέοιεν Dion cod. Par. Gr. 1773.

XXIII. (20). A WISH.

Εἴθ' ἄπυρον καλὸν γενοίμην μέγα χρυσίον,
καί με καλὴ γυνὴ φοροίη καθαρὸν θεμένη νόον.

XXIV. (30). AN EPICUREAN.

–́ > –́ ⏑ ⊔́ –́ ⏑ –́ –́ ⏑ –́ ⏑ –́ ∧
–́ ⏑ –́ ⏑ –́⏑⏑ –́ ⏑ –́ ⏓

Οὐ χρὴ πόλλ' ἔχειν θνητὸν ἄνθρωπον, ἀλλ' ἐρᾶν
καὶ κατεσθίειν· σὺ δὲ κάρτα φείδῃ.

HYBRIAS.

XXV. (28).

–́ ⏑ –́ > –́ ⏑ –́⏑⏑ –́ ⏑ ⏔́ ∧
–́⏑⏑ –́ > –́ ⏑ –́ ⏑ –́ ⏑ –́ ⏓
> –́⏑⏑ –́ > –́ ⏑ –́ ⏓
> –́ ⏑ –́ ⏑ –́ ⏑ –́⏑⏑ –́ ⏑ –́ ∧
5 { –́ > –́ ⏑ –́⏑⏑ –́ ⏑ –́ ⏓
{ – ⏑ –́⏑⏑ – ⏑ – ⏑ – ⏑

Ἔστι μοι πλοῦτος μέγας δόρυ καὶ ξίφος *στρ. α'.*
καὶ τὸ καλὸν λαισήϊον, πρόβλημα χρωτός·
τούτῳ γὰρ ἀρῶ, τούτῳ θερίζω,
τούτῳ πατέω τὸν ἁδὺν οἶνον ἀπ' ἀμπέλω·
5 τούτῳ δεσπότας μνοΐας κέκλημαι.

τοὶ δὲ μὴ τολμῶντ' ἔχειν δόρυ καὶ ξίφος *στρ. β'.*
καὶ τὸ καλὸν λαισήϊον, πρόβλημα χρωτός,
πάντες γόνυ πεπτηῶτες ἀμὸν
⟨πάντες χαμαί με προς⟩κυνέονθ' ἅτε δεσπόταν
10 καὶ μέγαν βασιλῆα φωνέοντες.

XXV. 6. τολμῶντες AE. 8. ἀμὸν Hiller: ἐμόν. 9. πάντες Stadtmüller. χαμαί με προσκ. Sitzler: κυνέοντι δεσπόταν. 10. βασιλέα AE.

FOLK-SONGS.

I. (1). SONG OF THE SHEAF.

–́ ⏑ –́ ⏑ –́⏑⏑ –́ ⏑ –́ ⏑ ⊔́ –́ ∧

Πλεῖστον οὖλον οὖλον ἵει, ἴουλον ἵει.

[II. (2). LINOS.]

Ὦ Λίνε ⟨πᾶσι⟩ θεοῖσιν
τετιμένε, σοὶ γὰρ ἔδωκαν
πρώτῳ μέλος ἀνθρώποισιν
φωναῖς λιγυραῖς ἀεῖσαι·
5 Φοῖβος δὲ κότῳ σ' ἀναιρεῖ,
Μοῦσαι δέ σε θρηνέουσιν.

III. (4). ΕΙΣ ΑΦΡΟΔΙΤΗΝ.

⏑ ⁞ –́⏑⏑ –́ ⏑ –́ ⏑
–́⏑⏑ –́ ⏑ –́ ⏓

Ἀνάβαλ' ἄνω τὸ γῆρας,
ὦ καλὰ Ἀφροδίτα.

IV. (5). ΕΙΣ ΔΙΟΝΥΣΟΝ.

⏑ – ⏑ ⏑ ⏑
⏑ ⏑ ⁞ –́ ⏑ ⏑ –́ – –́ ⏑ ⏑ ⊻́

Καλεῖτε θεόν.
"Σεμελήϊ' Ἴακχε πλουτοδότα."

V. (6). ΕΙΣ ΔΙΟΝΥΣΟΝ.

Ἐλθεῖν, ἥρω Διόνυσε,
Ἀλεῖον ἐς ναὸν

FOLK-SONGS—II. Schol. Ven. B, Σ 570: *θεοῖς τετιμημένε σοὶ γὰρ πρώτῳ μ. ἔδ. ἀθάνατοι ἀνθρώποισι.* 5. *δέ σε κότῳ.* The text is Bergk's.

V. 2. Ἀλεῖον : ἄλιον.

ἁγνὸν σὺν Χαρίτεσσιν,
ἐς ναόν,
5 τῷ βοέῳ ποδὶ θύων.
ἄξιε ταῦρε,
ἄξιε ταῦρε.

VI. (7). ITHYPHALLIC SONG.

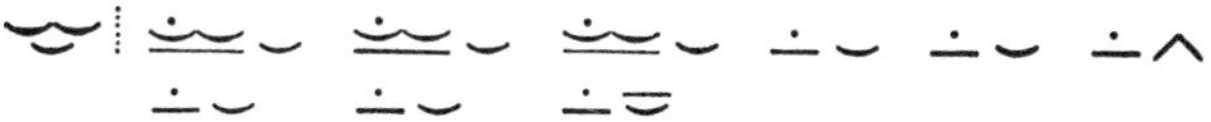

⟨Ἀνάγετε πάντες,⟩ ἀνάγετ', εὐρυχωρίαν
τῷ θεῷ ποιεῖτε·
ἐθέλει γὰρ ὁ θεὸς ὀρθὸς ἐσφυδωμένος
διὰ μέσου βαδίζειν.

VII. (8). SONG OF THE PHALLOPHOROI.

Σοί, Βάκχε, τάνδε μοῦσαν ἀγλαΐζομεν
ἁπλοῦν ῥυθμὸν χέοντες αἰόλῳ μέλει,
καινάν, ἀπαρθένευτον, οὔτι ταῖς πάρος
κεχρημέναν ᾠδαῖσιν, ἀλλ' ἀκήρατον
5 κατάρχομεν τὸν ὕμνον.

VIII. (11). RITUAL OF THE LIBATION.

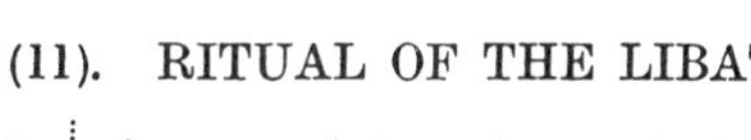

Τίς τῇδε; "πολλοὶ κἀγαθοί."
ἐκκέχυται· κάλει θεόν.

VI. 2. ποιεῖτε τῷ θεῷ. 3. ἐσφυρωμένος.
VII. 3. καὶ μάν. 4. κεχρημενηαν A.

IX. (12). HELIOS APOLLO.

> ⁞ ⏑́⏑ ⏑ —́ > ⏑́⏑ ⏑ —́ > — ⏑ —́ ∧

Ἥλιος Ἀπόλλων, ὁ δέ γ' Ἀπόλλων ἥλιος.

X. (14). THE HERALD'S PROCLAMATION.

— ⁞ —́ ⏑ ⏑⏑ —́ — —́ ⏑ ⏑ —́

Ἄρχει μὲν ἀγὼν τῶν καλλίστων
ἄθλων ταμίας, καιρὸς δὲ καλεῖ
μηκέτι μέλλειν.

XI. (16).

Λήγει μὲν ἀγὼν τῶν καλλίστων
ἄθλων ταμίας, καιρὸς δὲ καλεῖ
μηκέτι μέλλειν.

XII. (17). DANCE SONG.

> ⁞ —́ ⏑ —́ > —́ ⏑ —́ ∧
⏑ ⁞ ⏑́⏑ ⏑ —́ > —́ ⏑ —́ ∧

Πόρρω γάρ, ὦ παῖδες, πόδα
μετάβατε καὶ κωμάξατε
βέλτιον.

XIII. (18). SPARTAN CHORAL.

> ⁞ —́ ⏑ —́ ⏑ —́ ⏑ —́ ⏑ —́ ⏑ —́ ∧

Ἁμές ποκ' ἦμες ἄλκιμοι νεανίαι.
Ἁμὲς δέ γ' ἠμές· αἰ δὲ λῇς, αὐγάσδεο.
Ἁμὲς δέ γ' ἐσσόμεσθα πολλῷ κάρρονες.

Folk-Songs—XII. κωμάσατε.
XIII. 1. ἅμες, so 2, 3; vulgo ἅμμες. 2. ἡμές: εἰμές. 3. πολλῶν κρείσσονες.

XIV. (19). FLOWER SONG.

> – ⏑ – ⏑⏑ > – ⏑ – ⏑⏑ > – ⏑ – ⏑⏑ ⏑ – – ∧
⏑ – ⏑ – ⏑⏑ ⏑ – ⏑ – ⏑⏑ ⏑ – ⏑ – ⏑⏑ ⏑ – – ∧

Ποῦ μοι τὰ ῥόδα, ποῦ μοι τὰ ἴα, ποῦ μοι τὰ καλὰ σέλινα;
"Ταδὶ τὰ ῥόδα, ταδὶ τὰ ἴα, ταδὶ τὰ καλὰ σέλινα."

XV. (20). BLINDMAN'S BUFF.

– ⁞ – – – – – – ⊼

Χαλκῆν μυῖαν θηράσω.
Θηράσεις, ἀλλ' οὐ λήψει.

XVI. (21). TORTOISE.

≥ ⁞ – ⏑ ⏑⏑ – > ⏑⏑ – ⏑ – ≥ – ⏑ – ∧

A. Χέλει χελώνη, τί ποιεῖς ἐν τῷ μέσῳ;
B. "Μαρύομ' ἔρια καὶ κρόκαν Μιλησίαν."
A. Ὁ δ' ἔκγονός σου τι ποιῶν ἀπώλετο;
B. "Λευκᾶν ἀφ' ἵππων εἰς θάλασσαν ἅλατο."

XVII. (22 A). PHILELIAS.

– ⏑ – ⏑ – ⏑ – ∧

Ἔξεχ', ὦ φίλ' Ἥλιε.

XVIII. (23). SONG OF THE BOTTIAIAN GIRLS.

⏑ ⁞ – ⏑ – ⏑ – ⏓

Ἴωμεν εἰς Ἀθήνας.

XIV. 2. ποῦ μοι ταδί τὰ ῥόδα.
XVI. 1. ποιεῖς, and ποιῶν 3. 2. ἔρια μαρύομαι. κρόκην.

XIX. (24). PASTORAL SONG.

≥ ⋮ –́⏑⏑ –́⏑ –́⏓

Μακραὶ δρύες, ὦ Μενάλκα.

XX. (26). NURSERY SONG.

–́⏑⏑– –́–⏑⏑ –́–⏑⏑ –́–⏑̄
–́⏑⏑– –́⏑–– –́⏑–⏑ –́–⏓∧

Στρίγγ᾽ ἀποπομπεῖν νυκτιβόαν, στρίγγ᾽ ἀπὸ λαῶν,
ὄρνιν ἀνωνυμίαν ὠκυπόρους ἐπὶ νῆας.

XXI. (27). LOKRIAN LOVE SONG.

–́⏑–– –́⏑–– –́⏑––
– ⋮ –́⏑–– –́⏑––
–́⏑ ⊔ –́⏑⏑–– –́––⏑– –́⏑–⏑̄
–́⏑–– –́⏑ ⊔ –́–⏑⏑⏑ –́⏑⏑–

Ὦ τί πάσχεις; μὴ προδῷς ἄμμ᾽, ἱκετεύω·
πρὶν καὶ μολὲν κεῖνον, ἀνίστω·
μὴ κακὸν μέγα ποιήσῃ σ⟨ε⟩ κἀμὲ τὰν δειλάκραν·
ἁμέρα καὶ δή· τὸ φῶς δι‿ὰ τᾶς θυρίδος οὐκ ἐσορῇς;

XXII. (41). RHODIAN SWALLOW SONG.

– ⋮ –́⏑⏑ –́–
⏑⏑ ⋮ –́⏑⏑ –́⏓
– ⋮ –́⏑⏑ –́–
⏑⏑ ⋮ –́⏑⏑ –́–
5 ⏑⏑ ⋮ –́⏑⏑ –́⏓
• ⏑⏑ ⋮ –́⏑⏑ –́–
– ⋮ –́⏑⏑ –́–
– ⋮ –́⏑⏑ –́⏓

FOLK-SONGS—XX. συρριντα πομπειεν νυκτικομαν στριντατολαον ορνιν ανωνυμιον ω. ε. ν.

XXI. 2. μολεν CE : μολιν AB. 3. ποιήσῃς καί με A. 4. ἤδη A.

— ¦ ∸ ⏑ ⏑   ∸ ⏓
10 — ¦ ∸ ⏑ ⏑   ∸ —
∸ ⏑ ⏑   ∸ —
∸ ⏑   ∸ >   ∸ ⏑   ∸⏑ ⏑   ∸ ⏑   ∸ ⏑   ∸ ⏑
13-16 ≥ ¦ ∸ ⏑   ∸ ≥   ∸ ⏑   ∸ ≥   ∸ ⏑   ≚ ∧ [≚ ∧
17 ∸ ⏑ ⏑   ∸ ⏓
⏑ ⏑ ¦ ∸ ⏑ ⏑   ∸ ⏓
19-20 ≥ ¦ ∸ ⏑   ∸ ⏑   ∸ ⏑   ∸ ⏑   ∸ ⏑   ≚ ∧

Ἦλθ', ἦλθε χελιδών,
καλὰς ὥρας ἄγουσα
καλοὺς ἐνιαυτούς,
ἐπὶ γαστέρα λευκά,
5 ἐπὶ νῶτα μέλαινα.
παλάθαν σὺ προκύκλει
ἐκ πίονος οἴκου
οἴνου τε δέπαστρον
τυροῦ τε κάνυστρον.
10 καὶ πύρνα χελιδὼν
καὶ λεκιθίταν
οὐκ ἀπωθεῖται. πότερ' ἀπίωμες ἢ λαβώμεθα;
εἰ μέν τι δώσεις· εἰ δὲ μή, οὐκ ἐάσομες·
ἢ τὰν θύραν φέρωμες ἢ θοὐπέρθυρον
15 ἢ τὰν γυναῖκα τὰν ἔσω καθημέναν·
μικρὰ μέν ἐστι, ῥᾳδίως μιν οἴσομες.
ἂν δὲ φέρῃς τι,
μέγα δή τι φέροιο.
ἄνοιγ', ἄνοιγε τὰν θύραν χελιδόνι·
20 οὐ γὰρ γέροντές ἐσμεν, ἀλλὰ παιδία.

XXII. 3. καὶ καλούς AC. 6. π. οὐ προκυκλεῖς AC. 10. πυρῶν αχελιδὼν A: πυρῶν ἁ χελ. B. 14. φέρομες C. τὸ ὑπερθ. AC. 16. οἴσομεν. 17. δέ: δή. 18. φέροις AC.

XXIII. (42). SONG OF THE SICILIAN SHEPHERDS.

–̇ >   –̇ ⏑ ⏑   –̇ ⏑   –̇ ∧
–̇ >   –̇ ⏑ ⏑   –̇ ⏑
–̇ ⏑ ⏑   –̇ ⏑ ⏑   –̇ ⏑   –̇ ∧
–̇ ⏑ ⏑   –̇ ⏑ ⏑   –̇ ⏓

Δέξαι τὰν ἀγαθὰν τύχαν,
δέξαι τὰν ὑγίειαν,
ἃν φέρομες παρὰ τῆς θεοῦ,
ἃν ἐκαλέσσατο τήνα.

XXIV. (43). LESBIAN MILL-STONE SONG.

⏑ — ⏑ ⏑ ⏑ —
— ⁝ –̇ — ⏑ ⏑   –̇ — ⊼
⏑ ⏑ ⁝ ⌴̇   ⏑ ⏑   –̇ — ⏑ ⏑   –̇ — ⊼

Ἄλει μύλα ἄλει·
καὶ γὰρ Πιττακὸς ἄλει,
μεγάλας Μιτυλάνας βασιλεύων.

XXV. (44). CHALKIDIAN LOVE SONG.

— ⁝ –̇ ⏑ ⏑   –̇ ⏑ ⏑   –̇ >   –̇ ⏑ ⏑   –̇ ⏑ ⏑   –̇ —
⌴̇ ⏑   –̇ —   –̇ ⏑ ⏑   –̇ ⏑ ⏑   –̇ —
⌴̇ ⏑   –̇ —   –̇ ⏑ ⏑   –̇ ⏑ ⏑   –̇ >   –̇ ⏑ ⏑
[–̇ ⏑ ⏑   –̇ —   –̇ ⏑ ⏑   ⏒̇ ⊼

Ὦ παῖδες, ὅσοι Χαρίτων τε καὶ πατέρων λάχετ'
μὴ φθονεῖθ' ὥρας ἀγαθοῖσιν ὁμιλεῖν· [ἐσθλῶν,
σὺν γὰρ ἀνδρείᾳ καὶ ὁ λυσιμελὴς ἔρως ἐπὶ Χαλκιδέων
θάλλει πόλεσιν.

XXVI. (45). PAIAN TO LYSANDER.

≥ ⁝ –̇ ⏖   –̇ ⏑ ⏑   ⌴̇   ⊼
–̇ —   –̇ —

Folk-Songs—XXIV. 1. ἀλεῖ vulgo.
XXV. 1. ὅσοι : οἱ. ἐλάχετε. 2. ὁμιλίαν.

Τὸν Ἑλλάδος ἀγαθέας
στραταγὸν ἀπ' εὐρυχόρου
Σπάρτας ὑμνήσομεν, ὢ
ἰὴ Παιάν.

XXVII. (46). ITHYPHALLIC SONG TO DEMETRIOS POLIORKETES.

. . . .

ὡς οἱ μέγιστοι τῶν θεῶν καὶ φίλτατοι
τῇ πόλει πάρεισιν.
ἐνταῦθα ⟨γὰρ Δήμητρα καὶ⟩ Δημήτριον
ἅμα παρῆχ' ὁ καιρός.
5 χἡ μὲν τὰ σεμνὰ τῆς Κόρης μυστήρια
ἔρχεθ' ἵνα ποιήσῃ,
ὁ δ' ἱλαρός, ὥσπερ τὸν θεὸν δεῖ, καὶ καλὸς
καὶ γελῶν πάρεστιν.
σεμνόν τι φαίνεθ', οἱ φίλοι πάντες κύκλῳ,
10 ἐν μέσοισι δ' αὐτός·
ὅμοιον, ὥσπερ οἱ φίλοι μὲν ἀστέρες,
ἥλιος δ' ἐκεῖνος.
ὦ τοῦ κρατίστου παῖ Ποσειδῶνος θεοῦ
χαῖρε κἀφροδίτης·
15 ἄλλοι μὲν ἢ μακρὰν γὰρ ἀπέχουσιν θεοί,
ἢ οὐκ ἔχουσιν ὦτα,
ἢ οὐκ εἰσίν, ἢ οὐ προσέχουσιν ἡμῖν οὐδὲ ἕν,

XXVII. 3. Δημήτριος A. 4. παρῆχ' Richards: παρῆν A. 7. καλὸς καί. 9. σεμνὸν ὅθι A. 11. ὅμοιος.

σὲ δὲ παρόνθ' ὁρῶμεν,
οὐ ξύλινον οὐδὲ λίθινον, ἀλλ' ἀληθινόν·
20 εὐχόμεσθα δή σοι.
πρῶτον μὲν εἰρήνην ποίησον, φίλτατε·
κύριος γὰρ εἶ σύ.
τὴν δ' οὐχὶ Θηβῶν, ἀλλ' ὅλης τῆς Ἑλλάδος
Σφίγγα περικρατοῦσαν,
25 Αἰτωλὸς ὅστις ἐπὶ πέτρας καθήμενος,
ὥσπερ ἡ παλαιά,
τὰ σώμαθ' ἡμῶν πάντ' ἀναρπάσας φέρει,
κοὐκ ἔχω μάχεσθαι·
Αἰτωλικὸν γὰρ ἁρπάσαι τὰ τῶν πέλας,
30 νῦν δὲ καὶ τὰ πόρρω·
μάλιστα μὲν δὴ κόλασον αὐτός· εἰ δὲ μή,
Οἰδίπουν τιν' εὑρέ,
τὴν Σφίγγα ταύτην ὅστις ἢ κατακρημνιεῖ
ἢ σπίλον ποιήσει.

RIDDLES (ΓΡΙΦΟΙ).

XXVIII. (29).

Ἐν φανερᾷ γενόμαν, πάτραν δέ μου ἁλμυρὸν ὕδωρ
ἀμφὶς ἔχει· μάτηρ δ' ἔστ' ἀριθμοῖο πάις.

XXIX. (32).

Τί ταὐτόν ⟨ἐστιν⟩ οὐδαμοῦ καὶ πανταχοῦ;

XXX. (35).

Γαστὴρ ὅλον τὸ σῶμα, πανταχῇ βλέπων
ὀφθαλμός, ἕρπον τοῖς ὀδοῦσι θηρίον.

Folk-Songs—XXVII. 24. περιπατοῦσαν AC. 26. πάλαι AC.
31. σχόλασον. 34. σπεινον A; πεινῆν C.

NOTES.

EUMELOS.

EUMELOS of Korinth, a Bacchiad, must have been one of the famous poets of Peloponnese to have received the commission to write a prosodion for the Messenians. He is said to have founded Syracuse together with Archias in 734 B.C. Pausanias 5. 19. 10 suggests, improbably enough, that he may have been the author of the inscriptions on the chest of Kypselos. Eumelos is reported to have composed an historical epic Κορινθιακά, and other epics entitled Βουγονία, Εὐρωπία, Τιτανομαχία, Νόστοι. Probably all early Korinthian poetry was attributed to him. Schoeffer *de Deli insulae rebus*, p. 8, refers the verses of the prosodion to the fifth century.

Paus. 4. 33. 2: cf. 4. 4. 1, 5. 19. 10. This prosodion, the oldest extant cult song known to the Greeks, and older than the *Homeric Hymn* to Apollo, was sent to the musical festival at Delos on the occasion of the first participation by the Messenians in the famous agon held there in honour of Apollo. The presence of Messenians at a national Ionic festival (cf. Thuk. 3. 104) may point to hostile relations with the Spartans in the time of the Messenian king Phintas, whose reign fell before the first Messenian war (743-724; Busolt *Gr. Gesch.* 1. 151). In connection with the prosodion of Eumelos the fact may be recalled that Kallimachos' *Hymn to Delos* was written for a sacred embassy sent by Ptolemy.

1. Ἰθωμάτᾳ: sing. as *δέξο, Fάναξ Κρονίδα, καλὸν ἄγαλμα ἰλήFῳ θυμῷ τῷ Λακεδαιμονίῳ I.G.A.* 75 (unless we read *τοῖλ Λακεδαιμονίοι<s>*). **ἔπλετο**: 'became.' In sending an embassy to Delos the Messenians recognize the cult of another god besides the Zeus of Ithome, in whose honour the musical festival and agon called Ἰθωμαῖα was celebrated every year. The 'Muse' is the Muse of Delos, of Apollo (Ἀπολλωνίς?). **καταθύμιος**: *significat* (*apud Hom.*) *i.q.* ἐνθύμιος, κατὰ ψυχήν, *non, inquit* (*Aristarchus*), *quod apud nos, sc.* ἀρεστός (as here and Theogn. 617); Lehrs *de Arist. studiis Hom.* 146. Cf. Ψ 548 φίλος ἔπλετο θυμῷ.

2. A dactylic pentapody after an hexapody is found in Stes. iii. Since Paus. speaks of ἔπη, we might expect two hexapodies, though nothing is really known about the metre of the early prosodia. Bergk read καθαρὰ⟨ν κίθαριν⟩, as if the poet were attacking the flute, which was then, he maintained, chiefly played by foreigners, slaves, and barbarians. But, apart from the unusual expression—which is not well supported by [Sim.] 148. 8 πνεῦμα χέων καθαροῖς ἐν αὐλοῖς, or by Kallim. 2. 12 σιωπηλὴν κίθαριν—aulodic was at least not common till Klonas, long after Eumelos. Reimann thinks καθ. κίθαριν refers to the Aiolian mode which was κιθαρῳδικωτάτη. This is improbable. Sitzler suggests κραδίαν. **ἐλεύθερα**: may refer to the liberties of Messenia, which were even then in danger. So ἐλευθ. κρητήρ Z 528, of the freeing of Troy. **σάμβαλ'**: Aiolic (Sa. xxxvii.) and Ionic (Anakr. vii.). **Μῶσα**: under the influence of the usage current in the later choral lyric the Aiolic Μοῖσα was wrongly substituted for the Doric form, perhaps after the restoration of Messenia by Epaminondas when interest in its native poetry was revived. ἔχουσα was incorrectly transcribed from ΕΧΟΣΑ. Note the end rime, which is uncertain in Homer; cf. the leonine rime in B 484 ἔσπετε νῦν μοι, Μοῦσαι, Ὀλύμπια δώματ' ἔχουσαι.

TERPANDER.

TERPANDER was born in the island of Lesbos, one of the homes of epic and cyclic poetry. It was to the Lesbian shore that the head of the mythical singer Orpheus was borne after it had been cast into the waters of the Hebros. Terpander led the life of a wandering flute-player and rhapsode until he took up his residence in Sparta, whither he was summoned on the advice of the Delphic oracle to heal the internal disorders of the state that seem to have succeeded the conclusion of the first Messenian war. The importation of genius into Lakedaimon is consistently connected by tradition with the existence of civil feud or some other internal distress. Terpander, Thaletas,

Alkman, and Tyrtaios are said to have become Spartans from a like cause. Though there were ancient skeptics as to this sequence of plague and poet, the evidence points at once to a distrust of its own powers to placate the offended gods on the part of the Spartan state and to the efficacy of over-sea prophecy and poetry. In later times the strife of adjacent cities was often settled by the arbitrament of a stranger; and Rome called upon Livius Andronicus to help the state by means of song. Terpander is said to have flourished under Midas II. (738-695 ?), but the only certain date in his history is 676, when the poet, already advanced in years, instituted a musical and poetical agon in conjunction with the Karneian festival of Apollo, and was proclaimed victor in the contest. The period of the poet's activity in Greece may be regarded as the first quarter of the seventh century.

Terpander was the founder of the first musical epoch (*κατάστασις*) in Sparta. His successor, the founder of the second epoch, was Thaletas, who introduced the paian, hyporcheme, pyrriche, inaugurated the festival of the gymnopaidia, and established the choral lyric. Terpander cultivated the kitharoedic nome, which he enriched and enlarged, so that it received a sevenfold arrangement, traces of which certain scholars seek to discover in Sappho, Pindar, Solon, Aischylos, Kallimachos, and even in the Latin poets. He modified the existing lyre of seven strings by putting the highest note (*νήτη*) in place of the third from the last (*τρίτη*), so that his scale was *e*, *f*, *g*, *a*, *b*, –, *d*, *e*, that is, an octave with the omission of one note in the scale. The lyre adopted by him remained the chief stringed instrument till the fifth century. As Olympos, his predecessor, is the founder of instrumental music because of his invention of the flute with seven stops, so Terpander may be called the founder of ancient vocal music, because the lyre is better suited than the flute to accompany the human voice. Olympos introduced the Phrygian and Lydian modes into Greece. Terpander adapted the famous old Dorian mode to the lyre, introduced the Aiolian mode, which was always regarded as best suited to the lyre, and created the Boiotian mode. He set to music the poems of Homer, probably the *Hymns*, and used the nomes as preludes to the recitations of longer poems at the musical contests. He enfranchized the lyre in a Dorian state, gave the nome a place in the festivals where the secular prooimia of the rhapsodes had been exclusively sung, fixed the melodies and arranged the instrumental accompaniment; in short, founded the Spartan school of kitharoeds. So great was his influence that the school created by him lasted till the time of Phrynis, who lived in the Persian wars. Sappho (92) alludes to him in the line, *πέρροχος ὡς ὅτ' ἄοιδος ὁ Λέσβιος ἀλλοδάποισιν*, and the proverb, *μετὰ Λέσβιον ᾠδόν*, referred to the custom at the Karneia of calling upon the disciples of Terpander before all the other contestants. The titles of his nomes are: Αἰόλιος, Βοιώτιος, names derived from the modes employed, the *ὄρθιος* to Apollo (Frag. ii.), perhaps identical with the *ὀξύς*, the *τροχαῖος*, a designation that does not imply the use of *τροχαῖοι σημαντοί*, the *τετραοίδιος*, of obscure meaning, the Τερπάνδρειος, and the Καπίων, which is taken from the name of a pupil. Terpander also wrote skolia to the accompaniment of the flute and in spondaic rhythms.

I. Clem. Alex. *Strom.* 6. 784 (Arsen. *Viol.* 261, Apostol. 3. 29 c): quoted to illustrate the solemnity of the Dorian mode. The simple style and the rhythm give a liturgical tone to the poem which is well adapted to illustrate this stately mode.

1. ἀρχά: of the various possible explanations I prefer the following. Though the whole poem is in honour of Zeus, the special mention of his name at the outset is the proper 'beginning.' The naming of Zeus is the *ἀρχά*. Cf. Alkm. 2 *ἐγώνγα δ' ἀείσομαι | ἐκ Διὸς ἀρχομένα*, Pind. *Nem.* 2. 1 *ὅθεν περ καὶ Ὁμηρίδαι | ῥαπτῶν ἐπέων τὰ πόλλ' ἀοιδοὶ | ἄρχονται, Διὸς ἐκ προοιμίου*, *Nem.* 1. 8 *ἀρχαὶ δὲ βέβληνται θεῶν*, 'the foundations of the song have been laid in the mention of the gods,' 5. 25 *αἱ δὲ πρώτιστον μὲν ὕμνησαν Διὸς ἀρχόμεναι σεμνὰν Θέτιν*, Hes. *Theogon.* 47 *Ζῆνα . . . ἀρχόμεναί θ' ὑμνεῦσι θεαὶ λήγουσαί τ' ἀοιδῆς*, the proverbial *ἐκ Διὸς ἀρχώμεσθα καὶ ἐς Δία λήγετε* Theokr. 17. 1, Aratos *Phain.* 1, *ab Jove principium* Verg. *Ecl.* 3. 60, Calpurn. *Ecl.* 4. 82.

Less acceptable explanations are: (1) The poem is the 'orthian' nome of Terpander, and *ἀρχά* is the technical designation of the first main division. This strains the meaning, and, besides, the metre of the orthian nome of Terpander was in all probability the dact. hex. (2) *ἀρχά* denotes the *σπονδή*, and the whole poem is a *σπονδεῖον*. So Immisch *R. M.* 44. 559. Solemn songs were, it is true, sung at the beginning of the symposium at which libations were offered to Olympian Zeus, etc. (Ion 2. 6 ἐκ Διὸς ἀρχόμενοι πίνωμεν). But ὕμνων in v. 4 must then be interpreted as a reference to the succession of libations (and songs) which were made on the appearance of each fresh bowl. (3) In a cosmogonic sense. But the theory that Zeus was the 'beginning of all things' was not developed till a late period, and then chiefly among the Stoics. Zeus became the pantheistic All in All, the A and Ω of all things ("First hymn they the Father | Of all things:—and then | The rest of immortals."—M. Arnold). Cf. Proklos on Plato *Timaios* 2. 95. 49 Ζεὺς κεφαλή, Ζεὺς μέσσα, Διὸς δ' ἐκ πάντα τέτυκται, *Orphic Hymn* 20. 5 Δία παγγενέτην. This explanation is not to be defended by (Ζεὺς) πατὴρ ἀνδρῶν τε θεῶν τε A 544 (Hes. *Theogon.* 47), or Aisch. Frag. 70. Pind. xxviii. is in no wise parallel.

2. ἁγήτωρ: cf. B 669 *ὅς τε θεοῖσι καὶ ἀνθρώποισι ἀνάσσει*. In Sparta *Ζεὺς ἁγήτωρ* was the leader of the troops in battle.

3. πέμπω: is appropriate in the case of offerings to divinities. Cf. Theogn. 777, and Aisch. *Pers.* 939, *Sept.* 443, Eur. *I.T.* 171, *Anth. Pal.* 5. 17. 1, a Dodonaian inscr. (*R. M.* 39. 197) *Ζεῦ Δωδώνης μεδέων τόδε σοὶ δῶρον πέμπω*, Eur. Frag. 640 *δαπάνας ὅταν θανοῦσι πέμπωσιν κενάς*. So the gods *πέμπουσι χάριν* Pind. iv. 2. For the solemn repetition cf. Pind. *Isthm.* 5. 52 *Ζεὺς τά τε καὶ τὰ νέμει, | Ζεὺς ὁ πάντων κύριος*, and *Pyth.* 2. 49.

4. ὕμνων: the first mention, outside of Homer, of this class of lyric poetry.

Metre: the fragment has been arranged in two, three, and four lines. The metre has been regarded as consisting of paroemiacs (Ritschl, Bernhardy), as molossi (O. Müller), as orthian iambics (Caesar), and as *τροχαῖοι σημαντοί* and *σπονδεῖοι διπλοῖ* (Rossbach, Bergk). Lengthened spondees (⏗ ⏗) can be arranged rhythmically, *e.g.* ⏗ ⏗ ⏗ ⏗ ⏗ ⏗ = 𝅗𝅥 𝅗𝅥 𝅗𝅥 | 𝅗𝅥 𝅗𝅥 𝅗𝅥 (metrically two molossi), and classed with the rhythms of the *γένος διπλάσιον*, because in the lengthened molossus ⏗ ⏗ may be taken as the thesis, ⏗ as the arsis (when the twelve-time foot ⏗ ⏗ ⏗ is a *τροχαῖος σημαντός*); or ⏗ as the arsis, ⏗ ⏗ as the thesis (orthian iambic). Each ⏗ ⏗ ⏗ is a colon by itself. But the identification of the poem with the *νόμος τροχαῖος* of Terpander is entirely uncertain. The name of this nome may be derived from the melody, not from the rhythm. *ὄρθιοι ἴαμβοι* and *ὄρθιοι νόμοι* are not equivalent. *ὄρθιος*, as applied to metre, means (1) that the thesis and arsis are alike—either longs or shorts, (2) that the same foot recurs in the same form, as in pure iambics and in pure dactylic hexameters. When used of melody, *ὄρθιος* means 'high-pitched.' The same term does not necessarily include metre and melody. See Graf *R. M.* 43. 515. We may have here a pure spondaic rhythm.

II. Schol. Aristoph. *Nubes* 595, from the prooimia of Terpander, Suidas *s.v.* ἀμφιανακτίζειν.

This form of prelude was so stereotyped in the dithyramb that ἀμφιανακτίζειν became an equivalent for προοιμιάζεσθαι, and the poets using it were called ἀμφιάνακτες. Parallels with ἄναξ, apart from *Nubes* 595 (ἀμφί μοι αὖτε Φοῖβ' ἄναξ), are wanting, but we find ἀνεβάλλετο καλὸν ἀείδειν | ἀμφ' Ἄρεος φιλότητος θ 266, a line which, though perhaps later than Terpander, shows the antiquity of the phrase. ἀμφί with accus. is frequent in preludes in the *Hom. Hymns*: 7. 1, 19. 1, 22. 1, 33. 1 (cf. 3. 57), Mel. Adesp. 30 A, Eur. *Troad.* 511. **μοι** is a part of this formula when the verb is not in the first person. The enclitic form after a preposition, as in Aisch. *Choeph.* 220; so περί μου, ὑπέρ μου in the scenic poets. **ἑκαταβόλον**: Fεκαβόλον as Fάνακτα? Read Fεκηβόλος in P 333. But also in A 21, X 302 conjecture is necessary to preserve the F of Fεκηβόλος. **ἀειδ' ὦ φρήν**: so Crusius; ἄειδε φρήν, Hiller, a verse ending like ἠῶθι πρό, βέβριθε χθών. For **φρήν** = ἐγώ, cf. carm. pop. 3. Hermann's ᾀδέτω φρήν introduces a contraction of αFει that is unwarranted in this period. Bergk made ἀειδέτω φρήν (iamb. penthim.) the beginning of v. 2. Against this is the statement of [Plutarch] *de musica* 4, that the prooimia of Terpander consisted of dact. hexameters. The 'orthian' nome of Terpander, from which Suidas quotes this prooimion, can scarcely have received this name, as Bergk thought, because it contained iambics which originally were called ὄρθιοι. See on I. If the iambics are correct, then 'prooimion' is loosely used by the schol. on Aristoph. *Nubes* 595, and means merely the beginning of a nome, not one of the poems in hexameters which were usually called prooimia. The relation of the prooimia to the nomes is involved in much obscurity. Perhaps νόμος is a generic, προοίμιον a specific, expression. The latter may have been used of the nome when it was an ouverture to a rhapsodic recitation, a sacrifice, or a festival (Crusius).

III. Keil *Anal. Gramm.* 6. 6: the name spondee is derived from the rhythm employed in songs sung at the libations; cf. παρὰ σπονδῇσιν ἀείδειν Kallim 1. 1. Attributed to Terpander.

1. Μνάμα: a short form for Μνημοσύνη, whose daughters were the Muses (Hes. *Theogon.* 54, 915).

3. Μωσάρχῳ: for the common Μουσαγέτης. **Λατῶς**: Doric. Λατοῦς *v.l.* is the form used by the choral and dramatic poets in lyrics (Eur. *Ion* 128, *Hippol.* 65).—Metre: the spondees are often arranged as orthian iambics or semanto-trochees.

See on I. A certain case of prolonged spondees is *Ion* 126-8 ὦ Παιάν, ὦ Παιάν, | εὐαίων εὐαίων | εἴης ὦ Λατοῦς παῖ, where it is to be noted that all the syllables are long by nature.

IV. Dion. Hal. *de comp. verb.* 17: quoted as examples of molossi. Attributed to Terpander. (Trag. Adesp. 139). *Hymn* 17. 3 calls the Dioskuroi sons of Zeus and Leda, whereas Homer makes Tyndareus the father of both. The Vedic *Açvins*, the prototypes of the Dioskuroi, are also 'Saviours.'—Metre: often arranged as orthian iambics or semanto-trochees.

[V.] Strabo 13. 618, Clem. Alex. *Strom.* 6. 814, Eukleides *Introd. Harmon.* in *An. Par.* 1. 56. 10: quoted to show that Terpander first used the heptachord in place of the tetrachord lyre. The ancients doubted the authenticity of the fragment. It is the production of a late writer who wished to make the poet give documentary evidence of the musical invention currently attached to his name. The heptachord Lydian pektis was certainly pre-Terpandreian. Cf. Arist. *Probl.* 19. 32.

1. τετράγηρυν: refers to the four tones of the old lyre of the epic ἀοιδοί and the poets of nomes, and not, as Bergk thought, to the old nome of four parts. Cf. μελίγηρυν ἀοιδήν *Hymn* 2. 341; τετρα-, as in τετράκυκλον Ω 324 (late).

2. ἑπτατόνῳ: cf. ἑπτακτύπου φόρμιγγος Pind. *Pyth.* 2. 70, φ. ἑπτάγλωσσον *Nem.* 5. 24, ἑπτὰ δὲ συμφώνους ὀίων ἐτανύσσατο χορδάς *Hymn* 3. 51, where the invention is attributed to Hermes, κέλαδον ἑπτατόνου λύρας Eur. *I. T.* 1129. The heptachord lyre held its ground till the fifth century. The restoration of exclusively Doric or Aiolic forms is needless, as the fragment may have been composed in the late mixed dialect.—Metre: dact.-hexam.

VI. Plut. *Vita. Lycurg.* 21 (also Arrian *Tact.* 44. 3): quoted, together with Alkm. xii., Pind. xxvii. (cf. *Ol.* 13. 22), to prove that the Lakedaimonians were both μουσικώτατοι and πολεμικώτατοι. Sokrates Eleg. 3 refers to the Spartans: οἳ δὲ χοροῖς κάλλιστα θεοὺς τιμῶσιν ἄριστοι | ἐν πολέμῳ, and Aristotle *Pol.* 8. 5 says that the Spartans knew at least how to appreciate music. Cf. Müller *Dorians* 2. 329 ff. It is uncertain whether the fragment is a part of the poem by which Terpander quelled the disorders of the Spartan state. Some think it is from a prooimion.

1. αἰχμά: strictly 'spear-point,' whence 'martial spirit' here, and Pind. *Isthm.* 5. 33 Κάστορος δ' αἰχμὰ Πολυδεύκεός τ' ἐπ' Εὐρώτα ῥεέθροις, *Nem.* 10. 13 θρέψε δ' αἰχμὰν Ἀμφιτρύωνος, 'impulse' (γυναικὸς αἰχμᾷ Aisch. *Agam.* 483, γυναικείαν αἰχμάν *Choeph.* 630). αἰχμή is often derived from ἀίσσω, as θυμός from θύω, but we should then have ἀιχμή or ᾆχμα. αἰχμὰ νέων = αἰχμηταὶ νέοι. Cf. Alkm. iv. 70. **θάλλει**: in Hom. and Hes. only the perfect is used in this sense (Εἰρήνην τεθαλυῖαν Hes. *Theogon.* 902). The present appears in Semonides 7. 85, FOLK-SONGS xxv., Pind. *Pyth.* 7. 19 etc. Cf. *Much Ado* 5. 1. 76 "His May of youth and bloom of lustihood."

λίγεια: 'shrill,' 'clear-toned,' 'sweet-voiced,' since the Greeks loved a high pitch, as did the Lydians (Telestes iii.), to whose music they were much indebted. So the 'shrill pibroch' is sweet to the Scotch. λιγύς of the phorminx I 186 etc.; of the muse ω 62, *Hymn* 14. 2 etc., Alkm. i. 7, Stes. xii. 45, Mel. Adesp. 33 A, Theokr. 22. 221; of the note of the nightingale Theogn. 939, Aisch. *Agam.* 1146, Theokr. 12. 6 (cf. ὀξύφωνος Soph. *Trach.* 963); λίγειαν 'Ορφείην κεφαλήν Phanokles, p. 141. So with λιγυρός Pind. *Ol.* 6. 82; Myrtis is called λιγυρά by Korinna v. So καπυρὸν στόμα Theokr. 7. 37. ὄρθιος is often used of the high pitch, and so κλυτός (see on Sim. xxxiv.). Cf. Lehrs *Quaest. epicae* 169. In Attic, λιγύς and ἐλαχύς retract their accent in the feminine, but here, Alkm. i., Stes. xii., Mel. Adesp. 33 A, there are traces of λιγεῖα. L. and S. say λιγέᾱ is Doric (?).

2. εὐρυάγυια: a variation on εὐρυόδεια, which Homer uses with χθών. Cf. *Hymn* 5. 16. Cf. Arat. *Phain.* 105 Δίκη . . . ἀγειρομένη δὲ γέροντας | ἠέ που εἰν ἀγορῇ ἢ εὐρυχόρῳ ἐν ἀγυιῇ, and the name Εὐρυδίκη. εὐθυάγυια might be defended by Solon 4. 37, Pind. *Pyth.* 4. 153.

ἐπιτάρροθος: in Hom. always of a helping god, and so carm. pop. 47. 7. In Mel. Adesp. 33 A (τάρροθε, Μῶσα λίγεια), we have a clip-form of ἐπιταρ., just as πλόμενος is used for περιπλόμ., ἦϊον for παρήϊον.

ἔργων: Wilamowitz thinks the fragment is spurious because the word does not show *F*. But there are eighteen such places in Homer, some of which are difficult to cure, *e.g.* Δ 470, Λ 703, Ρ 279.—Metre: dact.-hexam.

ALKMAN.

ALKMAN, the chief cultivator, if not the creator, of early choral poetry, and the first representative of the fully developed melic style, was a Sardian by birth, as he tells us in Frag. v. A Lydian birthplace does not, however, disprove Hellenic extraction. Like the name of his father

(Damas, or Titaros), his name is Greek. He calls himself Ἀλκμάων and Ἀλκμάν, a name connected with ἄλκιμος, as are Ἀλκμήνωρ, Ἀλκμήνη, Ἵππαλκμος. The statement νῦν δέ μοι Ἀλκμὰν οὔνομα that is put into his mouth by a poet in the *Anth. Pal.* (7. 709) at least implies the existence of a tradition that the poet once bore a Lydian name, though this may be the result of a false inference. It is possible that his father was an Aiolian who lived in Sardis as a metic. At least it is difficult to see how a barbarian could have so completely identified himself with Spartan institutions and Spartan speech as did the stranger who was afterwards to be known as 'the Lakedaimonian poet.' Despite the explicit statement in Frag. v., the Pergamene scholars held that he was a Lakonian from Messoa. Doubtless some passage in the poet gave rise to this tradition. As Crusius suggests, ΜΕΣΣΟΑΤΑΣ, and ΜΕΣΣΟΓΙΤΑΣ an inhabitant of Mt. Messōgis in Lydia, may have caused the confusion. That he was a Lakedaimonian by birth is improbable, since all the early great poets who lived in Sparta were aliens: Terpander from Lesbos, Thaletas from Crete, Polymnastos from Kolophon, and Tyrtaios (probably) from Miletos. The similarity between his father's name, Titaros, and Teutaros, the slave of Amphitryon, may have given rise to the story that the poet was of servile origin, or actually a slave who was manumitted when his master discovered the marks of his genius. (In some places in Greece Lydians stood in the relation of *perioikoi* to the Dorians.) The cultivation of poetry was generally restricted to the aristocracy in the melic period, but, as in the case of the tradition which made a schoolmaster of Tyrtaios, there is evidence of a tendency on the part of Lakedaimon to depreciate the social position of the artists whom she invited to her territory. If Alkman was in truth a slave he may have been made a prisoner of war in one of the forays of the Kimmerians (Kallinos 1), and sold over-sea to the Spartan Agesidas.

The only date that is handed down concerning the poet is connected with the seventh year of the Lydian king Ardys. According to Africanus, this fell in 657, which is probably nearer the truth than Apollodoros' 672, since that chronologer regularly puts the dates farther back than other scholars. Eusebios' 612 represents an attempt to synchronize Alkman with Stesichoros.[1]

Alkman is certainly later than the second musical period at Sparta which was founded by Thaletas. His official position as teacher of the state choruses, his command over the cantonal speech, his acquaintance with the specifically Lakonian myths, and his reproduction of Lakonian manners, show that the poet must have passed much of his life in Sparta. He died at an advanced age, and was buried between the shrines of the Hippokoontidai, whose death he sung, and the *heroon* of Herakles, near the district called Sebrion (Paus. 3. 15. 2).

Alkman's life fell in a period of material prosperity and artistic development in the Spartan state. The old-time severity of the institutions of Lykurgos had been somewhat relaxed. The plastic arts flourished. The Σκιάς was built. Still, notwithstanding these traces of sympathy with the arts on the part of the state, and the partial fusion between seriousness and playfulness that gave a more secular tone to life—both the results of the second musical epoch, of which Alkman was the heir—these causes are not sufficient to account for the character of his art. There is a non-Dorian touch. He is an Aiolian in his tenderness, buoyancy, imagination, grace (ὁ χαρίεις Ἀλκμάν), love of beauty; and he has more of Ionic suppleness than Dorian vigour. His love of the pleasures of life, his quick sensibilities, are not Dorian, though his humour is not alien to his new home.

There were six books of Alkman's poems current in Hellenistic times: partheneia, hymns, hyporchemes, paians (both intended for the gymnopaidia), erotika, and hymenaia. Some of his poems suggest the skolia. The deities he celebrated in the partheneia and hymns—Zeus, Hera, Artemis, Aphrodite—were those held in special honour in the Spartan cult. If the nome had been displaced by his immediate predecessors, he gave to the partheneion a perfection that was never equalled even by the great poets of the sixth and fifth centuries. The universal character of the later choral lyric rendered it

---

[1] Rohde *R. M.* 33. 199. In the Greek biographies γέγονε usually denotes the ἀκμή. This is regarded as forty years after birth; and a similar period is supposed to elapse between the ἀκμή of a teacher and the ἀκμή of a pupil. So with Alkman and Arion.

ill-suited to the display of the fine personal qualities, the delicate reverence and even romantic gallantry towards women that distinguish the first cultivator of this class of melic composition. By a pardonable error, which ignores the predecessors whom he eclipsed, the poet was in fact called the founder of erotic song. But his passion does not consume the heart like that of his Aiolic successors.

No choral poet of Greece loves to speak of himself so much as does Alkman. No choral poet has such winsome ingenuousness in giving us his confidence; but he is proudly conscious of his position as a poet who has learned from nature the secret of his art. He is the most amiable of the Greek singers. If he does not compass the loftier range of the idealistic poets, he has the serenity of the humbler sphere wherein he was a master. His feeling for nature is almost modern.

Technical originality is displayed by Alkman only in his use of metre. The lyric hexameter he, indeed, employs, and with fine effect; but the preference of Terpander for the hexameter has yielded in him to a love of shorter dactylic verses, notably the tetrameter, in which spondees rarely find a place. Through the influence of Archilochos, and possibly of folk-song, the splendour of the epic verse has at last suffered eclipse. Alkman often uses pure trochaic and iambic metres of various forms, and also employs these measures in conjunction with dactyls, following herein the innovation of Archilochos. His anapaests he probably derived from the melodies of the people. His cretics show the influence of Thaletas; while ionics, the first examples of which appear in his fragments, are due to his predecessor, Polymnastos. His logaoedics show various forms that are simple and graceful.

In the arrangement of his verses Alkman makes use both of systems, consisting of the same measures repeated (such as dactylic tetrapodies, iambic dimeters, and catalectic trimeters), and of strophes. The latter are usually of simple structure, consisting of three or four verses, and are monostrophic in arrangement (dactylic and trochaic lines). The long logaoedic partheneion stands midway between the systems and the elaborate odes of Stesichoros and Pindar. Alkman probably instituted the tripartite division of strophe, antistrophe, and epode, which is usually referred to Stesichoros.

Alkman was placed first in the Canon of the melic poets established by the Alexandrian grammarians. He was still sung at Athens in the time of Perikles. The bucolic poets regarded him as a predecessor. Pausanias testifies that he was read in the second century A.D., and that the local Lakonian idiom, which was then accounted harsh, did not destroy the sweetness of his muse. His dialect consists mainly of the severe Lakonian of the day, with a touch of Aiolism and several Homericisms. In his choice of vocabulary he was largely influenced by Homer, from whom he drew the story of Nausikaa. He is also indebted to Hesiod and the cyclic epics.

I. Max. Plan. (*Rhet. Gr.* 5. 510), Priscian 2. 425, *Et. Mag.* 589. 47. From a partheneion of the first book, and probably addressed to Zeus Lykaios.

1. πολυμμελές owes its *μμ* to the analogy of *φιλομμειδής*, *ἐυμμελίης*, where *μμ* is from *σμ*.

2. αἰενάοιδε: as *αἰένυπνος* Soph. *O. K.* 1578.

3. νεοχμόν: love of new songs is as old as song itself. Cf. "I will sing a new song unto thee" *Ps.* 144. 9, "And they sung a new song" *Rev.* 5. 9; *τὴν γὰρ ἀοιδὴν μᾶλλον ἐπικλείουσ' ἄνθρωποι | ἥ τις ἀκουόντεσσι νεωτάτη ἀμφιπέληται α* 352, *'Αργὼ πᾶσι μέλουσα μ* 70, [Terp.] v., Pind. *Ol.* 3. 4, 9. 48, Sim. xxxv., Bacch. 19. 9, Eur. *Troad.* 512, Timoth. viii., *ἐν τοῖς μουσικοῖς τὰ νέα εὐδοκιμεῖ* Xen. *Kyrop.* 1. 6. 38. So in Plutarch's time (*de lect. poet.* 11). La Bruyère complained that all had been said, but still the world must have novelty. **ἄρχε**: as Pind. *Nem.* 3. 10 *ἄρχε δ', οὐρανοῦ πολυνεφέλα κρέοντι θύγατερ, | δόκιμον ὕμνον.* *ἄρχε* after *Μῶσ' ἄγε*, as in xviii. The imperative after *ἄγε*, as *γ* 475.—Metre: a complete strophe, consisting of a dactylic tetrap., a dactylic penthim., and a catal. iamb. trim. Rossbach unnecessarily writes vv. 1 and 2 in one line (of two cola); and classes the fragment under the hyporchematic dactylo-trochaics. His comparison of the epodes of Archilochos will not hold. In two bits from the same poem (*καὶ ναὸς ἀγνὸς εὐπύργω Θεράπνας* 4; *χερσόνδε κωφὸν ἐν φύκεσσι πιτνεῖ* 6) we have — — in the fourth foot of the iambic measure, a usage adopted also by Simonides (1). Cf. Usener 109. Regarded as trochaics with anacrusis, the last dipody of v. 3 is ⏗ ⏑ ⏓.

II. Herodian περὶ σχημάτων 61 (*Rhet. Gr.* 8. 606) etc.: quoted to illustrate the σχῆμα Ἀλκμανικόν. This poetical figure allows by anticipation a plural (or dual) noun or verb to intervene between the subjects in the singular. It occurs in E 774 ἧχι ῥοὰς Σιμόεις συμβάλλετον ἠδὲ Σκάμανδρος, Υ 138, κ 513; Pind. *Pyth.* 4. 178 πέμπε δ' Ἑρμᾶς . . . διδύμους υἱοὺς . . . |τὸν μὲν Ἐχίονα, κεχλάδοντας ἥβᾳ, τὸν δ' Ἔρυτον, where, however, a plural precedes; Eur. *I. A.* 195. See Valckenaer on Lesbonax, p. 79. The figure may have been especially frequent in Lakonian. The Dioskuroi are called ἐπιβήτορες ἵππων, λευκώλενοι, εὔιπποι etc. Two MSS. have ἱππότα σοφώ, but the dual is rarer in Doric than in Attic. **Πωλυδεύκης**: for Πολυ-; see on iv. 1.—Metre: iambic tetrameter. The fragment may consist of three iambic dimeters and be connected with v.

III. Athen. 15. 681 A. In 678 A we read πυλεών· οὕτως ἐκαλεῖτο ὁ στέφανος, ὃν τῇ Ἥρᾳ περιτιθέασιν οἱ Λάκωνες. Hence this partheneion is probably in honour of Hera. Pollux 5. 96 classes the πυλεῶνες among the κεφαλῆς κοσμήματα. κύπαιρος, attested as Alkmanic by Eust. *Od.* 1648. 7, is borrowed from Hebrew *kōfer*, a fact that may explain the variation with κύπειρος. We have, however, Cret. ὄναιρον = ὄνειρον.—Metre: trochaic. The tripody concludes the strophe.

IV. This partheneion, the oldest example of Greek choral composition in strophes, is written on a papyrus, perhaps of the first century A.D., that was discovered in 1855 by Mariette in a tomb near the second pyramid of Sakkarah. It was first published by Egger in 1863. For the earlier discussions of the fragment, see Bergk[4] (No. 23). The chief contributions to the subject since Bergk (1880) have been made by Sitzler *Philol. Rundschau* 1883, p. 934; Blass *R. M.* 40; Piccolomini *Studi de filol. greca* 1; Diels *Hermes* 31; Jurenka *Wiener Stud.* 17, *Serta Harteliana*, p. 36, *Sitz.-ber. d. Wien. Akad.* 135, *Philol.* 56; Wilamowitz *Hermes* 32. The poem consisted of 140 verses in ten strophes, of which the first two and part of the third are missing. In many places the fragment is exceedingly obscure, and no one of the possible interpretations of the last three strophes is convincing. Most of the lacunae in vv. 1-21 have been filled out by Blass.

The first five strophes (to v. 36)—the portion of the partheneion reserved for the gods and the myth—dealt mainly with the death of Hippokoon and his sons, a story that to the Spartan poet assumed an importance comparable to the tale of Pelops' line and the house of Labdakos in tragedy. According to the legend (schol. Clem. Alex. 4. 107), Herakles slew them because they had killed his friend Oionos. In the extant part of the poem, however, Herakles is not mentioned in connection with the Hippokoontidai, though from v. 31 we may infer that he appeared as an instrument of divine vengeance in connection with the overthrow of the Giants. In v. 1 Polydeukes is mentioned as one of the combatants. Now in a local Spartan legend the Dioskuroi would naturally appear in their capacity as σωτῆρες (cf. Pind. *Nem.* 10. 54); but, apart from this, and the possibility that they may have come to the rescue after Herakles was wounded, there is evidence of the existence of a feud between the Tyndaridai and the Hippokoontidai. Plutarch tells us that Tyndareus was fearful of the brutality of Enarsphoros (v. 3) when Helen was a child; and it is reported that the Dioskuroi were rivals of the Hippokoontidai, the enmity of the fathers having descended to the sons. Hippokoon was the elder (half?) brother of Tyndareus. After the death of his father, he expelled Tyndareus, who was not restored to his kingdom until the death of his persecutor and his sons at the hands of Herakles. A relief depicting the battle may be found in *Arch. Zeit.* 1861, p. 169. The crime of the Hippokoontidai was ὕβρις, which provoked the τίσις θιῶν (36).

The number of the sons of Hippokoon is variously reported. Apollodoros 3. 10. 5 enumerates twelve, all of whom were slain. Diodoros 4. 33. 6 says that there were twenty (a number that suits the family of Kepheus, the ally of Herakles), but that only the father and ten sons fell. Variations in the myth show that the local legend conflicted with that current outside of Sparta.

To what deity was the poem addressed? We have no evidence to show that the partheneion is the same as the hymn in honour of the Dioskuroi (Frag. ii.), and the poet may well have written more than one ode to Sparta's tutelary chieftains, the twin sons of Zeus and Tyndareus. The only other suggestion is that we have a song addressed to Artemis. If the reading Ὀρθίᾳ in v. 61 is correct, this interpretation is supported by the fact that the worship of Artemis Orthia was well known in ancient Sparta. Choruses of girls participated in her festival, and Helen as a child (Plut. *Theseus* 31) danced in her temple. That the poet should pass over in silence the scourging of the ephebi connected with the rites of Artemis Orthia is natural enough; nor is it surprising that the myth dealt with a story unconnected with her cult. Hymns to the gods may sing the praises of men and women (*Hymn* 1. 160 μνησάμεναι ἀνδρῶν τε παλαιῶν ἠδὲ γυναικῶν | ὕμνον ἀείδουσιν, Kor. iii.). Perhaps

Helen was mentioned in the strophes that have been lost at the beginning. Diels thinks the poem was intended to placate the wrath of Artemis against Lakedaimon.

The partheneion was probably sung at night (Frag. xi., xxi.). Cf. Sa. xix., Eur. *Herakl.* 781 ὀλολύγματα παννυχίοις ὑπὸ παρθένων ἰαχεῖ ποδῶν κρότοισιν, *C. I. A.* 2. 163 τοὺς δὲ ἱεροποιοὺς τοὺς διοικοῦντας τὰ Παναθήναια τὰ κατ' ἐνιαυτὸν ποιεῖν τὴν παννυχίδα ὡς καλλίστην τῇ θεῷ καὶ τὴν πομπὴν πέμπειν ἅμα ἡλίῳ ἀνίοντι. With 40 ff. cf. Eur. *I. A.* 157.

1. Πωλυδεύκης: (cf. ii.) with Doric metrical lengthening of Πολυ- (Sim. iv.). Cf. the Ionic Πουλυδάμας, πουλυβότειρα in Homer, the Aiolic Πολ(λ)υανάκτιδα Sa. 86 (with metrical 'sharpening' of the liquid). Sometimes the metrical licence is not graphically expressed, as in ἦ κε μέγ' οἰμώξειε ὁ Πελοπίδης 'Αγαμέμνων Hdt. 7. 159. Cf. 'Ενετικός (⏑ — ⏑ ⏑) in l. 51. Brugmann derives Doric πωλ- from πολϝ-, but has no better example than πώλυπος (Epicharm. 33, Sem. 29). The derivation of πολύπους from πολύ + πούς may be a folk's etymology, and *pōlypus*, Hor. *Epod.* 12. 5, is scarcely taken from a Doric source.

2. οἶον οὐ: an emphatic inversion, as μίαν οὐκ = οὐδεμίαν Hdt. 8. 119 (cf. Xen. *Anab.* 5. 6. 12); followed by ἀλλά for ἀλλὰ καί. So Soph. *Phil.* 555 οὐ μόνον (which some read here) βουλεύματα | ἀλλ' ἔργα. Either the scholiast found in his sources Λύκαιθος called a son of Derites, a relative of Hippokoon, or he failed to recognize the Hippokoontid under the clip-name Λύκων or Λυκάν (Apollod.). Some read οὐκ ἐγών, as if L. escaped. Diodoros says, in fact, that only ten out of the twenty sons fell, whereas Apollod. reports that all twelve lost their lives. The poet mentions only ten sons, and from v. 13 we infer that all were killed. Which legend he adopted as to the number of the sons we do not know. **καμῶσιν**: as in Homer, hence not = *defuncti* (L. and S.), which would require the perfect, but 'those who have succumbed to the toil of life.' The ἀνὴρ κεκμηώς can refresh his powers, οἱ καμόντες have their powers exhausted in death. The Attic is not the Homeric usage, as L. and S. think. **ἀλέγω**: 'count,' here the positive use, as Pind. *Ol.* 2. 86 Πηλεύς τε καὶ Κάδμος ἐν τοῖσιν ἀλέγονται. In the epic poets, ἀλέγω, generally with οὐ, means 'heed,' and so Sim. xiii. 10. The negative adheres in Οὐκαλέγων.

3. The recapitulation of the fallen is in the epic style; so in the passage, Aisch. *Pers.* 957 ff., which frequently suggests this fragment. Cf. ll. 70 ff. **'Εναρσφόρος** = ὅς τὰ ἔναρα φέρει. ἐναρσ- is the weak form of ἐναρεσ-, parallel to ἐναρο-;

for the variation between stems in -ς and in -ο, cf. *σαφής*, *σάφα*. Alkm. used *ρς* in *μάκαρς* 10, *Περίηρς* 149. **Σέβρον**: he is called *Τέβρος* by Apollod.

5. Ἱπποθῶν: from **θοάω*=*θοάζω*. The name appears on a vase, *C. I. G.* 7434 *b*. Cf. *Δειθῶν*.

6. Quoted in *An. Ox.* 1. 159. 2, as *Εὐτείχη τ' ἄνακτα 'Αρήϊον*. **'Αρήϊος** is not elsewhere reported as a Hippokoontid, but the name occurs of one of the Argonauts, and of a Kentaur. *'Αρήϊτος* was a Hippokoontid according to Pherekydes. Tradition may have varied. **ἄναξ** precedes the noun, as in Ο 453, Ψ 588. The adj. generally follows in this poem.

7. "Ακμονα: cf. Ovid *Metam.* 14. 484. *"Αλκμονα* (Christ) is unknown. *Δορκέα* would suit if syllaba anceps were possible at the end of v. 6.

8. ἀγρέταν: *ἀγρόταν* (papyrus) is confused with *ἀγρέταν* also in Aisch. *Pers.* 1002 (*ἀγρέται στρατοῦ*). *ἀγρέταν· ἡγεμόνα*, Hesych. Cf. Hdt. 7. 5 *στρατιῆς ἄγερσις*. *ἀγρότας* Eur. *Or.* 1270, is from *ἀγρός*. The papyrus' reading is not to be defended by *'Αγρότα*, *'Αγρότις*, *'Αγροτέρα*.

10. "Αρεος: ⏑⏑⏑ not —⏑ with synizesis; *ἀρχόν* Jurenka. **πώρω**: *ὁ πῶρος*=*belli tumultus*. **κλόνον**: cf. Ε 167 *ἄν τε μάχην καὶ ἀνὰ κλόνον*.

13 ff. Destiny and Device conquer all. Against their power strength avails nothing. *'Αλκά* does not possess the sandals of Hermes and Athene that are automatous and annihilate space.

14. Πόρος: the father of Eros. Cf. Plato *Symp.* 203 B.

16. Cf. ρ 565 *τῶν ὕβρις τε βίη τε σιδήρεον οὐρανὸν ἵκει*.

17. Cf. Pind. *Pyth.* 2. 34 *Διὸς ἄκοιτιν ἐπειρᾶτο*, 4. 90 *Τιτυὸν βέλος 'Αρτέμιδος . . . ὄφρα τις τᾶν ἐν δυνατῷ φιλοτάτων ἐπιψαύειν ἔραται*, Aisch. *Prom.* 894 ff. *μήποτέ μ', ὦ πότνιαι Μοῖραι, λεχέων Διὸς εὐνάτειραν ἴδοισθε πέλουσαν· | μηδὲ πλαθείην γαμέτᾳ τινὶ τῶν ἐξ οὐρανοῦ*.

19. Hesych. *s.v.* *Νηρεύς* has *θαλάσσιος δαίμων. 'Αλκμὰν καὶ Πόρκον ὀνομάζει*. Cf. α 72. Is there a reference to the marriage of Thetis and Peleus?

21. ἰογλεφάροι: *γλέφαρον*, Doric for *βλ.*, as *γλέπω* in l. 75 for *βλέπω*.

23–34 contained a further example of insolence and its punishment; v. 31 (*μαρμάρῳ μυλάκρῳ*) may point to Herakles' participation in the battle of the Giants. Cf. Pind. *Nem.* 1. 67, Strabo 10. 488.

35. After the myth, the moral. Cf. Pind. *Nem.* 10. 64 *καὶ μέγα Fέργον ἐμήσαντ' ὠκέως | καὶ πάθον δεινὸν παλαμαῖσι* 'Αφαρητίδαι Διός (in reference to the combat with the Tyndaridai); Soph. *O. K.* 537 *ἔπαθον ἄλαστ' ἔχειν.*

36. The *envoy* of the first part of the partheneion is carried over asyndetically to the second half of the poem. It links the obligatory myth to the secular portion of the poem which allowed freer play to the individuality of the poet. **τίσις**: cf. *α* 40.

37. εὔφρων: cf. Sem. 7. 99 *οὐ γάρ κοτ' εὔφρων* ('in peace and quiet') *ἡμέρην διέρχεται | ἅπασαν.* The tranquillity of the *ἀκίνδυνος βίος* (Eur. *I. A.* 17) is contrasted with the life of the great that is assailed by *ὕβρις.* For the sentiment cf. Pind. *Pyth.* 11. 50, Aisch. *Eum.* 313, Soph. *Antig.* 582, Eur. *H. F.* 504. Instead of the contest of Kastor and Polydeukes with Hippokoon's sons, the friendly rivalry of the Spartan maidens. Rather the quiet radiance of Agido's beauty than the splendour of the sun of the impious that sets in blood. Cf. Hor. 2. 12.

38. διαπλέκει: Hdt. 5. 92. 6 *διαπλεξάμενος τὸν βίον*, cf. Plato *Laws* 7. 806 A. *διαπλέκειν* is used absolutely in Aristoph. *Aves* 753. For the figure cf. Shakespeare's "The web of life is of mingled yarn."

39. ἄκλαυστος: 'tearless,' like *ἄκλαυτος δ* 494. *ἄκλαυστος* is found in Soph. *El.* 912. Hermann's distinction between *κλαυστός* (*lacrimandus*) and *κλαυτός* (*defletus, lacrimabilis*) will not hold. The difference is primarily chronological, the *σ*-forms being later. Cf. *ἄγνωτος* and *ἄγνωστος*: Jebb on Soph. *O. T.* 361, Bishop *A. J. P.* 13. 174, Hayley on Eur. *Alk.* 173. Perhaps we should read the earlier form here.

The abrupt transition recalls *Hymn* 1. 169, where the *κοῦραι* are addressed. So in Hor. 4. 6. 29, a poem that has an Alkmanic flavour, the poet turns to the chorus after the mythological introduction. After a wise saw Pindar frequently shifts to the personal sphere.

40. φῶς: of a person, *ρ* 41 *Τηλέμαχε, γλυκερὸν φάος.*

41. F(ε) = *ἕ*, for *ῥ'* of the papyrus (Jurenka, Diels). *ῥά* follows only monosyllables. *ρ* is confused with *F* in *τρέ· σέ* and *δεδροικώς*, Hesych. The old reading *ὁρῶρ'* (with Doric accent?) can be defended only if *ὥτε* is consecutive, like *ὥστε* (65), 'the light of Ag. has risen, so that the sun shines for us.'

For the comparison of Agido to the sun, cf. Theokr. 18. 26 *πότνι' ἅτ' ἀντέλλουσα καλὸν διέφανε πρόσωπον | 'Αὼς ἢ ἅτε λευκὸν ἔαρ χειμῶνος ἀέντος· | ὧδε καὶ ἁ χρυσέα 'Ελένα διαφαίνετ' ἐν ἁμῖν*, Xen. *Symp.* 1. 9 *ὥσπερ ὅταν φέγγος τι ἐν νυκτὶ φανῇ* . . .

οὕτω καὶ τότε τοῦ Αὐτολύκου τὸ κάλλος κ.τ.λ., Q. Catulus in Cic. *de nat. deor.* 1. 28. 79; Shakesp. "It is the morn and Juliet is the sun." Cf. *φάος* Eur. *Hek.* 841. See on Sa. iii. **ἆμιν**: after *φαίνην*, cf. Aristoph. *Nubes* 586.

42. μαρτύρεται: Agido invokes the rays of the sun to witness the truth—whether she or Hagesichora, the *χοραγός* (44), is more beautiful. Cf. *ἥλιον μαρτυρόμεσθα* Eur. *H. F.* 858, and Wilamowitz *ad loc.* Some take the passage to mean that since Agido is the sun, she is herself the proof that the sun really shines; and compare Sim. i. 7, Pind. *Isthm.* 5. 48.

43. φαινΕν: for *φαίνην*, either the shorter, Doric form of the inf., or a relic of the old alphabet that expressed both *ε* and *η* by E; cf. *μωμΕσθαι* in 44. On the meaning see Sa. xx.

44. There is no thought of actual blame. *μ.* is added simply to round out the expression; cf. K 249 *μήτ' ἄρ με μάλ' αἴνεε μήτε τι νείκει.* **νιν**: Agido. **κλεννά**: the Aiolic form. There seems no good reason for Diels' comparison of Cretan *κλῃνός*, 'beloved,' which would make Agido the *ἐράστρια*, Hagesichora the *ἐρωμένη*. The expression is too technical, and does not harmonize with *χοραγός*. **χοραγός** in Sparta *ὁ καθηγούμενος τοῦ χοροῦ* (the later *κορυφαῖος*), not *ὁ μισθούμενος τὸν χορόν*. Cf. Athen. xiv. 633 A. Hagesichora as *χορ.* is playfully said not to permit the chorus to praise her rival in beauty. Agido is indeed the more beautiful, but the poet lingers over the charms of Hagesichora. The rivalry between the two is the key-note of the secular portion of the poem.

45. οὐδ' ἁμῶς: *ne tantillum quidem.* Hom. has *ἀμόθεν*. With the neg. cf. *οὐδ' ἠβαιόν* N 106.

46. ὥπερ αἰ: the first occurrence of this formula; Soph. *O. K.* 776 *ὥσπερ τις εἰ.*

47. The comparison accords with ancient taste, and is not unknown in modern literature. *ἀγέλα* was a technical expression in Sparta: *Λάκαινα παρθένων ἀγέλα* Pind. Frag. 112, *ἅτε πῶλοι ταὶ κόραι . . . ἀμπάλλοντι . . ., ταὶ δὲ κόμαι* (cf. l. 51) *σείονθ' . . . ἁγῆται δ' ἁ Λήδας παῖς ἁγνὰ χοραγὸς* (cf. l. 44) *εὐπρεπής* (cf. l. 46) Aristoph. *Lysistr.* 1308; so *βοῦς* Pind. *Pyth.* 4. 142; *πῶλος* Anakr. xxvii.; in Sparta *πῶλος* was the name of the priestess of Demeter and Kora. Cf. also Theokr. 18. 30 *ἅρματι Θεσσαλὸς ἵππος, | ὧδε καὶ ἁ ῥοδόχρως Ἑλένα Λακεδαίμονι κόσμος.* The comparison in Alkman is an adaptation of B 480 *ἠύτε βοῦς ἀγέληφι μέγ' ἔξοχος ἔπλετο πάντων | ταῦρος· ὁ γάρ τε βόεσσι μεταπρέπει ἀγρομένῃσιν· | τοῖον ἄρ' Ἀτρεΐδην θῆκε Ζεὺς . . . | ἐκπρεπέ' ἐν πολλοῖσι.* Cf. also Z 506, X 22, Ibyk. ii., *Daniel Deronda*, chap. 3 (of Gwendolen), "Imagine a young race-horse in the paddock among untrimmed ponies and patient hacks." *στάσειεν ἐν* as Ω 350. The *βοτά* (l. 47) are horses, not cattle.

48. Cf. I 123 *ἵππους πηγοὺς ἀθλοφόρους*, Ibyk. ii. 5 *ἵππος ἀεθλοφόρος*, Λ 699. **καναχάποδα**: cf. Xen. *de re eques.* 1. 3, *καναχήποδες ἵπποι* Hes. *Certamen* 316. 22; *καναχὴ ἡμιόνοιιν* ζ 82; *quadrupedante putrem sonitu quatit ungula campum* Verg. *Aen.* 8. 596.

49. 'A horse such as one sees in winged dreams.' The gen. is descriptive. Cf. *εἴκελον . . . ὀνείρῳ ἔπτατο* λ 207, *πτεροῖς ὀπαδοῖς ὕπνου κελεύθοις* Aisch. *Agam.* 426, Theokr. 9. 16, Apoll. Rhod. 2. 306. **ὑποπετρ.** contains the strong, *πτερόν* the weak form of the root. Cf. *πέτ-ε-σθαι* with *πτ-έ-σθαι*. The ground-form **petrā* yields O.H.G. *fedara*, A.S. *fether*. Cf. *penna* from **petsna*. The assumption of a **πτετρον* whence **πετρον* and *πτερόν* (as *ἔκπαγλος* and *ἔκπλαγος* <**ἔκπλαγλος*, *φάτρα* and *φατρία*> *φράτρα*, *φρατρία*) is to be abandoned. So also the suggestion that there was a **πετερον*, **ὑποπετεριδ.*—either original or secondary, whence *ὑποπετριδ.* by syncope. Such secondary forms as Ἐρεμῆς = Ἑρμῆς, *ἀράχοντος* = *ἄρχοντος*, occur only in the case of liquids. *ὑποπετρ.* is not from *ὑποπτερ.* by metathesis. The usual form is *ὑπόπτερος* in the lyric poets (Mimn. 12. 7) and elsewhere.

50. **ἦ οὐχ**: synizesis as E 349. **ὁρῇς**: the emphatic use of *ὁράω* (*οὐχ ὁρᾷς* O 555, ρ 545, Kallim. 2. 4) to attract attention to an object grows in the Attic period.

51. **Ἐνετικός**: the pre-eminence of the horse with which Hagesichora is compared is summed up in this word. Cf. B 852 *ἐξ Ἐνετῶν, ὅθεν ἡμιόνων γένος ἀγροτεράων*. These Enetoi from Paphlagonia were later called *Veneti*, and regarded as the ancestors of the dwellers on the Adriatic (Strabo 5. 212). Cf. Mel. Adesp. 43 B (probably Alkmanic) *Ἐνετίδας πώλως στεφαναφόρως*, Eur. *Hippol.* 231 (see Hadley *ad loc.*), 1131. **χαίτα**: strictly the mane. Cf. *ἵππος χαιτέεσσα* Sem. 7. 57, one of the types of womankind.

52. **ἀνεψιᾶς**: the members of the chorus may have been related—a *θίασος* of kindred. Cf. Hesych. *κάσιοι· οἱ ἐκ τῆς αὐτῆς ἀγέλης ἀδελφοί τε καὶ ἀνεψιοί. καὶ ἐπὶ θηλειῶν οὕτως ἔλεγον Λάκωνες.* Cf. Ahrens *Philol.* 27. 611. Hagesichora is not Alkman's cousin.

53. **Ἁγησιχόρα** should have the asper. Cf. Spartan Ἁγηΐστρατος. That she is *χοραγός* is a chance equivalence of name and function, but the name points to an office that had been held by members of her family. **ἐπανθεῖ**: cf. *Hymn* 1.

135 *χρυσῷ δ' ἄρα Δῆλος ἅπασα | ἤνθησε*, and the imitation in Kallim. 4. 263 *χρύσειον δ' ἐκόμησε γενέθλιον ἔρνος ἐλαίης.*

54. ὡς (*ὥτ'*?): placed as in λ 413 *κτείνοντο σύες ὡς ἀργιόδοντες.*

55. A silver face crowned by golden hair. Cf. ζ 232, Verg. *Aen.* 1. 592. Homer conjoins the fairest of metals, ψ 159; cf. Hes. *Shield* 224; Goethe *Den Silberbach in goldne Ströme fliessen.* See Bury on Pind. *Isthm.* 2. 7. **ἀργύριον** = Attic *ἀργυροῦν.*

57. αὔτα: cf. Pind. *Ol.* 4. 26 *οὗτος ἐγὼ ταχύτατι.*

58. ἁ δέ, 'and she'; *δέ* is continuative, and not opposed to *μέν*. *μέν* in 57, as in *ἐγὼ μὲν οἶμαι.* Cf. *μέν . . . δέ* 50, 51, where the clauses are formally opposed, though the ideas are akin. Cf. Hes. *Theogon.* 656, Hdt. 7. 9. **πεδ'**: cf. Alk. xxvi., Skol. xxi.; *δεύτερον μετ' ἐκεῖνον* Hdt. 1. 31.

59. The race is a contest in beauty. The animated style avoids the adverb of comparison (*ὥτε*). **Εἰβήνῳ**: perhaps itacistic spelling for *'Ιβήνῳ*. The *'Ιβηνοί* (with Ionic *η* in a proper name) were a Lydian people who may have bred race-horses. (Lydian chariots, Pind. Frag. 206; *δαμασίππου Λυδίας* Bacch. i. 23.) The dative depends on *δραμεῖται.* So the dative is used after *μάχομαι, ἀγωνίζομαι, ἐρίζω* (Bacch. 1. 30). **Κολαξαῖος**: Kolaxaïs was an ancient king of Skythia (Hdt. 4. 5 and 7), a land that was famous for its fleet horses. The parallel suits the stranger poet. The emphasis on the beauty and the speed of the horse has a non-Lakonian ring, though the escort of the Spartan kings was composed of "*ἱππῆς.*" They served on foot, but the name is old.

Εἰβήνῳ was formerly connected with *ἐβῆνοι*, a breed of dogs crossed with the fox, and the passage interpreted as if the K. horse kept pace with the hound. Pollux 5. 41 speaks of *πάριπποι*, Cretan dogs that kept exact pace with horses. For Κολαξαῖος, Blass formerly read *κόλαξ ἀές* (*κ.* = *ἀκόλουθος, θεράπων*).

60 ff. The difficulties in this passage are mainly occasioned by two words: (1) **ὀρθρίαι**: the papyrus has a line drawn through the second *ρ*, and the scholiast has *ὀρθιαι.* Interpretations vary between *ὀρθρίαι*, 'early'; *'Ορθρίᾳ*, 'the goddess of the morning,' supposed to be Artemis; and *'Ορθίᾳ*, Artemis Orthia. (2) **φᾶρος**: so the papyrus, *φαρος* the schol. *ἄροτρον* is superscribed in both, and the schol. reports that a certain Sosiphanes took the word to mean 'plough.' Herodian 2. 942. 13 referring to Alkman, reports *τὸ φάρος* = *ἱμάτιον* and *ἄροτρον.* The word is perhaps Semitic (Lewy, *Fremdwörter*, 82), whence the variation in the quantity. We know nothing of an offering of a robe to Artemis (a peplos is offered to Athene, Z 271). On a coin from Leontinoi (*Brit. Mus. Cat.*

Coins Sicily 93) we find a plough and a head of Artemis, who is also a goddess of agriculture. In the imperial period boys offered sickles to Artemis Orthia which they had won in musical contests (*Athen. Mitth.* 22. 334). That *φάρος*= 'plough' follows from *φαροῦν· ἀροτριᾶν* Hesych. The confusion between *πελειάδες*, 'doves' (so the schol.) and 'Pleiads' is probably intentional and sportive. Cf. Sim. vii. and Lamprokl. 2 *αἵτε ποταναῖς* | *ὁμώνυμοι πελειάσιν αἰθέρι νεῖσθε*. *poussinière* is analogous. Doves cannot strictly be compared with the *σήριον ἄστρον*. They are usually the emblem of timidity. The comparison with the Pleiads was the more fitting as one of them (Taygeta) was the mother of Lakedaimon and Eurotas. Since in Sparta choruses of maidens took their names from goddesses or heroines, Diels thinks that Πελ. is the name of two rival choruses.

I adopt the following explanation of this much-vexed passage. As Hagesichora is only less fair than Agido in the *μάχῃ κάλλους*, so the chorus of the Pleiads is only less beautiful than our chorus in a like contest (*μάχονται*). Our chorus needs the support of the loveliness of the rivals, since the Pleiads, rising like a gleaming star through the divine night, contest the prize of beauty with us as we bear the plough, our offering to Artemis Orthia. Like the maidens, the Pleiads form a chorus (*Pleiadum chorus* Hor. 4.14. 21, Prop. 4. 5. 36).

In this explanation there are two difficulties: (1) Ὀρθίᾳ: Elsewhere in the papyrus the late Lakonian spelling *σ* for *θ* (except when initial, after *ν*, *σ*, and before *λ*) has been adopted—though in l. 72 Συλακίς has *θ* superscribed. The corrector who deleted the *ρ* may have passed over the *θ*, or Ὀρθία may have retained its *θ*. We find both Βωρθέα and Βωρσέα in late Lak. inscr. (The *F* of *ὀρθFός is scarcely to be taken into account.) (2) The Pleiads are compared with *σήριον ἄστρον*. In reality, as Aratos *Phain.* 263 says, the Pleiads are *ὀλίγαι καὶ ἀφεγγέες*, Alkyon, their chief star, being only of the third magnitude. Nevertheless as a *group* they are called by Athen. 11. 490 C *τὸ ἐνδοξότατον τῶν ἀπλῶν ἄστρων*. Prop. *l. l.* speaks of their *spissus ignis*. Sa. xix. is to be added to the passages in Athen. 11. § 79 ff. which show that their importance for agriculture is the cause of their importance in poetry.

Two other explanations may be mentioned: (1) Retaining ὀρθρίαι: 'For the Pleiads of the spring time, it seems to us (ἅμιν ethical dative), as they rise, like a beaming star through the ambrosial night, contend (in beauty) with those of the autumn (those that bear the plough).' So Blass. The rivalry between the two girls is now symbolized by the contest of the Pleiads. The point of comparison here, as in 58, is the equality, actual or approximate, of their charms. The Pleiads of spring and autumn are distinguished in Hes. *W. D.* 383 Πληϊάδων Ἀτλαγενέων ἐπιτελλομενάων | ἄρχεσθ' ἀμητοῦ, ἀρότοιο δὲ δυσομενάων. In an ancient period of astronomy that set the nomenclature, the Pleiads of the vernal equinox rose in the morning with the sun. Cf. schol. Arat. *Phain.* 264 ὑπὸ τὸν ὄρθρον γὰρ ἀνατέλλουσι σὺν ἡλίῳ ὄντι ἐν τῷ Ταύρῳ (the ἑῴα ἀνατολή: ἀνειρομέναι = ἐπιτελλόμεναι). The Pleiads that appear in the evening, the 'setting' Pleiads, are those that bring the plough of autumn. The setting of the Pleiads is, however, not a characteristic mark of autumn, nor is their rising in the morning particularly bright. Against this interpretation is the order of the words, especially the dislocation of φεροίσαις and ἅμιν, and the position of ὀρθρίαι. The absence of the article with φεροίσαις might be paralleled by Aisch. *Pers.* 245, Eur. *I. T.* 1301, Aristoph. *Vesp.* 755 etc. (2) Reading 'Ορθρίᾳ: the 'goddess of the morning.' So Jurenka. The epithet is elsewhere unknown, and the identification—and that in the seventh century—of Artemis with a goddess of light who is not the Moon is very improbable. Even the identification with the Moon is relatively late (Timoth. 2). The epithets φωσφόρος and σελασφόρος, even if they refer to the Moon-Artemis, need not be ancient.

62. νύκτα δι' ἀμβροσίαν: cf. K 41. The words belong to the comparison, and are not necessarily connected with the time at which the partheneion was sung. Cf. Pind. *Ol.* 1. 1 χρυσὸς αἰθόμενον πῦρ ἅτε διαπρέπει νυκτί κ.τ.λ. **ἅτε**: as adv. first here, then Ibyk. i. 7. **σήριον ἄστρον**: cf. Σείριος ἀστήρ (Hes. *W. D.* 417). διαφέρει ἀστὴρ καὶ ἄστρον· ἀστὴρ γὰρ μονοειδής, ἄστρον δὲ τὸ ἐκ πολλῶν ἀστέρων συγκείμενον (schol. *Ol.* 1. 6) does not, I think, hold here. Since Ibyk. iii. uses σείρια of all the stars, it is uncertain whether Alkman means Sirius, but this is more probable than to take the words, in a complexive sense, of the Pleiad group. Despite the astronomical blunder Sirius is connected with the Pleiads in Eur. *I. A.* 7 Σείριος ἐγγὺς τῆς ἑπταπόρου | Πλειάδος ᾄσσων ἔτι μεσσήρης. Comparison of persons with stars, Z 401, Λ 62, X 26, Eur. *Hippol.* 1122, Soph. *El.* 66.

63. ἀνειρομέναι: the *F* of ἀFείρω would seem to be vocalized after the Aiolic fashion, but not, as in that dialect, when α*F* stands under the ictus. The shortening of αυ<α*F* is so singular that it is probable that υ is a mistake for *F*. In Pind. *Pyth.* 2. 28 read ἀFάταν for αὐάταν (⏑ ⏑ —). In Alkman, Frag. 79, δάFιον is a mistake for δαύιον. On a late Lakon. inscr. *C. I. G.* 1466, we have Λαυαγήτα for ΛāF-. αἴρῃ of the rising of stars, Soph. *Phil.* 1331, where Jebb says there seems to be no other classical instance of the intransitive use.

64 ff. Neither ornaments nor companions avail us. Hagesichora is our defence. **πορφύρας**: *Laconicae purpurae*, Hor. 2. 18. 7.

65. κόρος: *scil.* ἀμῖν ἐστι. **ἀμύναι**: 'defend'; a schol. on E 266 says that Aristophanes, the grammarian, regarded ἀμύνασθαι (*sic*) in this passage as = ἀμείψασθαι. Cf. Pind. *Pyth.* 6. 54, where ἀμείβεται is 'surpasseth.' Blass tr. 'aid,' Bergk 'change,' 'we haven't such an abundance as will allow a change' (χλαῖνα ἀμοιβάς ξ 521, ἐπημοιβοὶ χιτῶνες ξ 513). But ἐσθῆτα ἀμύνειν is not Greek.

67. μίτρα: Eur. *Hek.* 924 πλόκαμον ἀναδέτοις μίτραισιν ἐρρυθμιζόμαν. Cf. Hdt. 1. 195.

68. Λυδία: Λ. μίτραν πεποικιλμέναν Pind. *Nem.* 8. 15, *Lydia mitra* Prop. 4. 17. 30, *Maeonia m.* Verg. *Aen.* 4. 217. For Lydian work, cf. Δ 142, Sa. 19.

69. ἰανογλεφάρων = ἑανοβλ. Cf. Hesych. ἰανοκρήδεμνος and ἰανόκροκα· λεπτά. In Homer ἑανός is used of that which is fine and delicate. Here = μαλακός. Cf. Ibyk. v. ἀγανοβλέφαρος Πειθώ. **ἄγαλμα**: cf. Alk. xxiv. 3.

70. Ναννῶς κόμαι = N. εὔκομος, as Κάστορος αἰχμά = Κάστωρ αἰχματάς Pind. *Isthm.* 5. 33. Cf. Ἀγιδῶς τὸ φῶς l. 40. Supply in the following, ἀμῖν ἐστι ὥστ' ἀμύναι. Diels thinks the girls here mentioned belong to a semi-chorus.

71. θιειδής = θεοειδής, the Spartan instead of the epic form.

72. Κλεησιθήρα: cf. Κλεήσιππος Mel. Adesp. 45, from *κλεϝέω. With Κλεισιθήρα, Lykoph. *Alex.* 1222, cf. Κλεισιππίδας *S. G. D.-I.* 3549. 264.

73. Ainesimbrota is less probably the mother of the four girls than their teacher in music. She may have had a μοισπόλος οἰκία, like Sappho (xli.). **ἐνθοῖσα** = ἐλθοῦσα, a hybrid, with Aiolic οι and the Doric paroxytone.

77. τηρεῖ = φυλάσσει; cf. *Hymn* 5. 142, Pind. *Pyth.* 2. 88.

80. ἴκταρ: with the dat. as ἄγχι in Hom. and Pind., πέλας in Pind. and trag. (rare). So πλησίον and ἐγγύς with gen. and dat.; cf. *prope ad* and *prope ab.* Hagesichora does not withdraw from Ag. despite the rivalry. In 79 αὐτεῖ = αὐτοῦ.

81. θωστήρια: -τηρια often occurs in the names of festivals (οἰνιστήρια, προχαριστήρια, ὑστήρια). This festival is either a celebration in honour of the gods or a festal gathering of the 'club' such as was formed by the Spartan ladies of good society (αἱ καλαὶ κἀγαθαὶ γυναῖκες). **τ'**: is not roughened before the asper; so often in Doric and other dialects. **ἄμ'** = ἡμέτερα.

82. ἀλλά: the precative use with sudden transition is typical; cf. *Hymn* 5. 491, 20. 8. Diels includes Helen under the θιοί; cf. Theokr. 18.

83. ἄνα = ἄνυσις. The initial ᾱ is unusual, but α is anceps in ἄνειν (ἀνϝ-).

84. *δι' ἂν . . . χοροστάτις* (*ἐστί*), Wilam. Cf. *διὰ τὼς θεὼς τώσδε νικῶντι τοὶ Σελινώντιοι* Roberts *Epigr.* 1. 117.

86. An ironical allusion to an unknown proverb, *γλαῦξ ἀπὸ θράνω λέληκε.* There may be a reference to Hes. *W. D.* 746 *μηδὲ δόμον ποιῶν ἀνεπίξεστον καταλείπειν | μή τοι ἐφεζομένη κρώζῃ λακέρυζα κορώνη.* **θράνω**: beam of the ceiling. **λέλακα**: in Homer often of animals; in tragedy of rapid or confused speech. The passage recalls indirectly Hor. 4. 6. 41 *nupta iam dices "ego dis amicum—reddidi carmen."*

87. **δέ**: continuative. **'Αώτι**: 'Αῶτις is probably identical with Artemis Orthia. (Alkman is reported to have used many peculiar epithets of Artemis.) Cf. Artemis *Προσηῴα.* Perhaps connected with *ἀώς* = *ἠώς.* For the form of the name, cf. *Καρυᾶτις, Δερεᾶτις.* **μαλίστᾳ** = *μάλιστα,* formed like the adv. in -*ᾳ* (*πάντᾳ, ὅπᾳ, ἁμᾷ*).

88. **ἐρῶ** = *ἐπιθυμῶ,* as Archil. 25. **πόνων**: I can see no reference to the distress occasioned by the second Messenian war (Jurenka, Diels). Rather the anxiety as to success in the musical contest.

89. **ἰάτωρ**: fem. as *'Ερινύες λωβητῆρες, τύχη σώτηρ.* **ἔγεντο**: so Hesiod, Sappho, Pind.

91. **εἰρήνας** = *ἡσυχίας* opposed to the *πόνοι,* the struggle for supremacy between the two maidens. **ἐπέβαν**: 'entered on'; *ἐπιβαίνειν ἐυφροσύνης ψ* 52, *εὐσεβίας* Soph. *O. K.* 189, *δόξης Phil.* 1463.

92. The 'trace-horse' is Hages., who assists in the singing. Since the schol. states that there were two semi-choruses, one of 11, the other of 10 members (cf. 98), Diels suggests that Agido, who on his view is the *κορυφαῖος,* now decides to take part in the contest in order to help the weaker semi-chorus; the second being formed of Hages., the *σηραφόρος,* and 9 others. There are, however, only 10 girls mentioned, and the schol. may have erred.

93. **αὔτως**: = *αὔτως* Anakr. xi. 12. *ἔαδεν μέγ' ἄγχην* Diels: *ἔαδ' ἁμὲ δέρρην* Jurenka: *ἕπεται μέγ' ἅρμα* (= *ζυγός*) Crusius.

95. A reference to the playful dissension among the members of the chorus that is alluded to in 43. **νᾷ**: Doric, so also Sophokles (*R. M.* 47. 406. 22). **ἀίεν**: with the dative as *ἀκούω, π* 515.

99. **οἷα**: exclamatory; Bacch. ix. 120.

Metre: logaoedic. In 1-8 each two verses form a pair, the log. complementing the trochees. Since the final syllable is long in 4 and 8, except in v. 95, I assume syncope in the log. and make all the verses tetrapodies. 9-10 are acat. troch.

trim., an unusual form of verse. Christ would divide into a dipody and a pentapody (— ⏑ — ⏑ — ⏑ ⏗ — ∧). We find, however, in v. 2 the penultimate resolved. 11-14: Christ would make an octapody of 11-12. 13-14 form a single period united by synaphea. The alternative trochaics at the end bring the strophe to a graceful conclusion after the preceding dactyls. The variation at the close may be apportioned between the ten strophes as follows: —⏑ ⏑ — ∧ (1), 3-5, 9; — ⏑ — ⏓ (2), 6-8, (10). It is a coincidence merely that in the strophes ending —⏑ ⏑ — ∧ the penult is accented. Hiatus appears in 45, 56, 65 etc. There is no synaphea except in 13, as there is none in Archilochos. The distribution of the verses is uncertain (Diels finds two semi-choruses); nor do we know how far solos were admitted. Vv. 43, 77 do not necessarily imply a single voice. Blass' examination of the papyrus has shown that the paragraphs of the scholiast, which were supposed to divide the 14-line stanza into two groups (1-8, 9-14), are in reality only marks of punctuation. Nevertheless we can scarcely imagine that as early as Alkman single strophes exceeded in length the longest strophes of Pindar. If, however, the arrangement 8+6 holds, it is that κατὰ περικοπὴν ἀνομοιομερῆ (α, β, α′, β′). I cannot follow Christ in dividing 8+2+4, since we should then have an actual strophe of 14 verses. Since 5-8 repeat 1-4, we have practically strophe and antistrophe, and, if this is the case, 9-14 may fairly be called an epode, which invariably ends with a full stop, though elsewhere (x. xi.), Alkman may foreshadow the Pindaric overlapping. Even in the developed choral lyric the epode may be longer than the strophe (Pind. *Ol.* 7, *Nem.* 8).

On this assumption, it may be argued that Alkman foreshadowed, if he did not actually invent, the 'triad of Stesichoros,' which is usually referred to strophe, antistrophe, and epode. If this is correct, Stesichoros merely followed the τεθμός of Alkman, though he so perfected or popularized the triadic arrangement that its invention was attached to his name. The 'invention' of the antistrophe is actually ascribed to Alkman (though it may be Semitic as well as Hellenic), but the theory that the choral epode was added by Stesichoros depends entirely upon the interpretation of the proverb, οὐδὲ τὰ τρία τῶν Στησιχόρου γινώσκεις.

In the *Comment. Ribbeckianae*, p. 1 ff., Crusius has shown that, whereas some of the late Greeks referred this to the 'triad,' the unanimous modern view dates back only to 1777, when it was hesitatingly put forward by Van Lennep. Crusius would omit τά (it is omitted in Zenob. Ath. 1. 23), and translate 'You do not know even three (verses) of Stes.' (cf. Aristoph. *Nubes* 1365, τῶν Αἰσχύλου λέξαι τί μοι), three being a typical number in proverbs. If τά be kept, it may refer to three famous verses (the palinode, Frag. vii.). Crusius' argument is not entirely convincing. Of course, even if we suppose that Stes. was not the inventor of the triad, its invention might still be attributed to him. Nothing is more common with these 'inventions.' (Because of their innovations, Plut. *Mus.* 12 brings Alkman and Stes. into conjunction.) It may be remarked, however, that the *τριχορία* of the Spartans favours a Spartan origin of the triadic arrangement.

V. Steph. Byz., *s.v.* Ἐρυσίχη, Chrysipp. περὶ ἀποφατικῶν 21, Strabo 10. 460. The fragment is taken from the beginning of the second partheneion. The chorus vindicate the poet from the charge of rusticity and obscurity of origin. It seems that the poet had found detractors in his new Spartan home, and that the chauvinistic Lakonians, with their native hostility to immigrants, had taunted him with outlandish manners and foreign extraction. There is a proud ring about l. 5 that does not bespeak a servile origin. To the poet, Sardis is the type of culture and civilization. Homer knew of snowy Tmolos, and if his Hyde is Sardis, Sardis may have been old in song as well as πολύχρυσοι. With the fragment, cf. the words of the girl in Philetas 4 οὔ μέ τις ὀρέων ἀποφώλιος ἀγροιώτης | αἱρήσει κλήθρην, αἱρόμενος μακέλην, | ἀλλ' ἐπέων εἰδὼς κόσμον καὶ πολλὰ μογήσας, | μύθων παντοίων οἶμον ἐπιστάμενος.

1. ἦς: ἐσσ' may be correct (ΕΣ), as perhaps in Φ 150 where we have the later Ionic εἶς. ἐσσί is Doric (Epicharm., Korkyraian and Sicilian inscr.).

ἀγροῖκος: the accent is uncertain (Chandler 388). Ammonios says ἄγροικος = ὁ σκαιὸς τοὺς τρόπους (in Aristotle's *Ethics*, the man who cannot see a joke), ἀγροῖκος = ὁ ἐν τῷ ἀγρῷ κατοικῶν. Aristoph. *Nubes* 655 ἀγρεῖος εἶ καὶ σκαιός, does not disprove the first meaning here, and Amm. was writing of the Common dialect. Theophr. defines ἀγροικία as 'ignorance offending against propriety.' If Doric varied as did Attic, we should have Old Doric ἀγροῖκος, New Doric ἄγροικος; cf. ἑτοῖμος and ἕτοιμος, ἐρῆμος, and ὁμοῖος, which is reported as Doric. The word shows the only example in Alkm. of a medial mute and liquid failing to make position.

2. σκαιός: σκαιότης (*gaucherie*), according to the Stoic Chrysippos, is due to ignorance of the art of well-disposed and pleasing intercourse between man and man. So *ineptus* in Cic. *de orat.* 2. 4; connected with ἀγριότης Plato *Rep.* 411 E; τὸ σκαιὸν εἶναι πρῶτ' ἀμουσίαν ἔχει Eur. Frag. 1033. **οὐκ . . . οὐδέ**: note οὐ followed by several clauses with οὐδέ, and contrast οὐ . . . οὔτε Z 450, δ 566, a construction allowed in Attic as an imitation of epic usage. **οὐδὲ παρὰ σοφοῖσιν** is difficult, and can be retained only if οὐδέ = *ne quidem*, thus breaking the sequence of the negatives. οὐδὲ μὲν (γὰρ) οὐδέ B 703, E 22, θ 32 is not parallel. A sentence of the form οὐ . . . οὐδέ . . . ἀλλά (θ 246), when expanded, as in Isokr. *Areop.* 48, 51, would not easily admit the intrusion of the adverbial negative. Hence 'nor unskilled even in the judgment of those wise in song' (σοφός as Solon 13. 52, Sa. 69, Pind. *Pyth.* 3. 113 etc.; παρά as Soph. *Aias* 620) is open to objection. σοφοῖσιν certainly does not refer to the chorus as 'clever critics,' though an allusion to the criticism of fellow-artists would not be impossible (Sa. 92). σκαιός is often opposed to σοφός (Soph. Frag. 704, 835, Eur. *El.* 972, Frag. 290, 657), but is properly contrasted with δεξιός; cf. Theokr. Epigr. 19. 5 ἐπιδέξιος | ἔπεά τε ποιεῖν πρὸς λύραν τε ἀείδειν. Conjectures: παρ' ἀσόφοισιν (Welcker), *scil.* born or bred among those unskilled in song (ἄσοφοι Pind. *Ol.* 3. 45); παράσοφος (Jacobs), πανάσοφος (Hiller) do not occur. Less likely are παράκοπος, παράφορος. Michelangeli deletes the troublesome οὐδέ. Perhaps an adj. has dropped out before παρά.

3. The Thessalians were notorious for deceit and gluttony; Θετταλῶν σόφισμα was proverbial; cf. Eur. *Phoin.* 1407, Aristoph. *Vespae* 1271, Frag. 492, Antiph. 276, Ephippos 1, Hermippos 41, Athen. 10. 418 B.

4. The hamlet 'Ερυσίχη in Akarnania is regarded as the type of a rustic district. Aristeides 2. 508, says that Alkman was so fond of mentioning out-of-the-way peoples, that the luckless schoolmasters had to enquire where on earth they were situated. ἐρυσίχαιος would be a determinative compound, 'dragging a shepherd's staff' (χαῖος), *i.e.* a βουκόλος or αἰπόλος.—Metre: trochaic dimeters. Blass connects No. v. with ii., and arranges the verses as iambic dimeters.

VI. Athen. 9. 390 A: the discovery of music is due to the imitation of the notes of the birds. Cf. Plutarch *de sollert. animal.* 20 καὶ τῶν λιγυρῶν, κύκνου καὶ ἀηδόνος, ἐν ᾠδῇ κατὰ μίμησιν, Lucr. 5. 1379 ff. *at liquidas avium voces imitarier ore | ante fuit multo quam levia carmina cantu | concelebrare homines possent aurisque iuvare.* So in the Chinese fable of the king and the nightingale. "Even as the linnet sings, so I, he said" (Watson); Alkm. xxv. Cf. Aisch. *Suppl.* 58 ff., Aristoph. *Aves* 749 (on the songs of Phrynichos).

1. ἔπη καὶ μέλος: 'verses and tune'; cf. μέλεα καὶ ἐλέγους Echembrotos, Theokr. 19. 5 quoted on v., βοὰν αὐλῶν ἐπέων τε θέσιν Pind. *Ol.* 3. 8. Usually μέλος includes the text.

2. εὗρε: the particularizing middle is unnecessary. **γεγλωσσαμένον**: 'note-giving'; from γλωσσάω found only here. The singing partridge is rarely referred to. Some partridges κακκαβίζουσι, others τιττυβίζουσι. ἐπὶ περδίκων κακκαβάζειν, ἐπὶ γλαυκῶν κικκαβάζειν Zenodotos *On the Sounds of Animals*; cf. *Studi ital. di filol. class.* 1. 89. Stat. *Silv.* 2. 4. 20 says *quaeque refert iungens iterata vocabula perdix.* With κακκάβη, κακκαβίς, names of the πέρδιξ, cf. Skt. *kukkubha.*

3. συνθέμενος: cf. ὄπα σύνθετο υ 92.—Metre: logaoedic dactyls enclosing a catal. troch. dimeter. Reading ἐπῆγε δέ Rossbach thinks we have the end of a dactylic verse.

VII. Antig. Caryst. *Hist. Mirab.* 27. The male halcyons, which are called κηρύλοι, when enfeebled by age are carried by their mates. Cf. also Aelian *H. N.* 7. 17, Plut. *de sollert. animal.* 35. A partheneion of the poet's old age, when he was no longer able to join in the choruses of the Spartan maidens. Cf. Ibyk. ii. Croiset says of the poet: *jusque dans la vieillesse, il trouvait des images aimables pour traduire ce sentiment vague d'amour qui n'est plus qu'une sorte de galanterie poétique, mais sincère et sans fadeur.*

1. οὔ μ' ἔτι=οὐκέτι με, the emphatic position, as in οὐ πάμπαν ἔτι N 7. **παρθενικαί**: substantive, as Bacch. ix. 11, Theokr. 18. 2 (of Spartan girls). See on Praxilla ii. **μελιγάρυες**: of hymns, Pind. *Ol.* 11. 4 etc. The adj. is restricted to the utterances of the poet or the singer. **ἱμερόφωνοι**: of the Graces, Theokr. 28. 7; of the nightingale, Sa. xv.

2. βάλε: from a weak form of the root of βούλομαι <βολ-νομαι. The α is due to the fact that the accent was originally oxytone (βαλέ). ἄβαλε, *i.e.* ἆ βάλε, is also Modern Greek: ἄβαλε ἔσφαξεν μίτυλόν τέ σε ἄιδ' ἴαψε, *utinam iugulasset mutilumque te in Orcum misisset.* **κηρύλος**: in Aristoph. *Aves* 300 Sporgilos, the barber, is an ἄνθρωπος ὄρνις, hence he is called κειρύλος, the 'razor-bird,' as if from κείρω. Hesych. has κεῖρις· ὄρνεον, ἱέραξ, οἱ δὲ ἀλκυόνα. The etymology of κηρύλος (with η also Archil. 141) is unknown. Some identify the word with κῆυξ (Ceyx and Alcyone, Ovid *Metam.* 11. 410). See Thompson's *Greek Birds s.v.* κηρύλος. Cf. Soph. Frag. 435 γενοίμαν αἰετὸς ὑψιπέτας, | ὡς ἀμποταθείην ὑπὲρ ἀτρυγέτου | γλαυκᾶς ἐπ' οἶδμα λίμνας.

3. ὅστ': as in Homer, *e.g.* E 545 with the generic particle τε that emphasizes the "permanent element in facts" (Monro *H. G.* § 266). **ἄνθος**: cf. Aisch. *Agam.* 659 ὁρῶμεν ἀνθοῦν πέλαγος, *Anth. Pal.* 5. 206. 4 ἁλὸς ἄνθεσι, *à fleur d'eau, a fior d'acqua.* **ἅμα**: here the Homeric usage as in Pindar in at least three passages (*Ol.* 9. 70, *Nem.* 9. 52, Frag. 74). Elsewhere in the lyric poets ἅμα occurs only in Bacch. i. 91. **ἀλκυόνεσσι**: the identification with the kingfisher is uncertain. The form with the asper is due to the mistaken connection with ἅλς: note Lat. *alcedo.* Cf. Sim. vi. The passage is imitated in Aristoph. *Aves* 250 ὧντ' ἐπὶ πόντιον οἶδμα θαλάσσης | φῦλα μετ' ἀλκυόνεσσι ποτῆται (so Cobet for ποτᾶται).

4. νηδεές (Boissonade) 'fearless,' though unattested, is appropriate. νηλεές Antig. (from νηλεὲς ἦτορ ἔχων Hes. *Theogon.* 456), ἀδεές Phot. 348. 22, *i.e.* ἀδϝεές; Bergk νηλεγές =ἄνοικτον here 'unlamenting.' L. and S. take νηλεγές as= late ἀνηλεγές 'reckless'; rather 'untroubled,' 'tranquil.' **ἔχων**: this (epic) use in the minor melic poets occurs also in Alk. xvi. 2, Anakr. 32. **ἁλιπ. εἴαρος ὄρνις**: in apposition with ὅς; cf. H 187, Plato *Apol.* 41 A. **ἁλιπόρφυρος**: as Ibyk. 8 (Herm., Schneid., λαθιπορφυρίδες, Bergk); τανύπτερος πορφυρίς Ibyk. iv., and in 8 ἀλκυόνες τανυσίπτεροι. Homer has φάρεα ἁλιπόρφυρα ν 108; cf. Anakr. 138. Tennyson wrote "the sea-blue bird of March," though he afterwards altered the epithet (*Nature Notes* 1. 93, 2. 173); Carducci *cerilo purpureo nunzio di primavera.* Thompson *Greek Birds s.v.* thinks ἁλιπ. implies more than a colour epithet, and compares ἁλιάετος. But cf. ἁλίβαπτος, a purple bird (Alkm. 126, Alk. 122). **εἴαρος**: by epic lengthening. Schulze *Quaest. epicae* 212 reads εἴερος 'quick' (ταχέες οἰωνοί ξ 133) a meaning found in Quint. Smyr. 13. 207 ἀμπαύσει καὶ τῇδε θοὸν πτερὸν ἱερὸς ὄρνις. Cf. ἱερὸς ἰχθύς. **ὄρνις**: but ὀρνίχων 67 which is certainly Doric. Metre: tetrastichic strophe, consisting of lyric hexameters arranged κατὰ στίχον. The feet are invariably light dactyls, the last syllable always long. There are three cases of penthemimeral, three of bucolic, and one of the trochaic caesura. The poem was sung by a single voice accompanied by the flute (or lyre?), and perhaps accompanied by the evolutions of the chorus. The use of hexameters recalls Alkman's predecessor Terpander.

VIII. Athen. 9. 373 E. From the story of Odysseus; cf. ζ 138 τρέσσαν δ' ἄλλυδις ἄλλη, of the attendants of Nausikaa at the sight of the shipwrecked hero. **λῦσαν** may be retained, as we are ignorant of what preceded (perhaps τὸν χορόν); Bergk δῦσαν though we expect ἔδυν; Kaibel ἄυσαν; Sitzler νεῦσαν. Cf. χ 302, Alk. viii., Sa. vii., Archil. 106 πτώσσουσαν ὥστε πέρδικα, Soph. *Aias* 168 παταγοῦσιν ἅτε πτηνῶν ἀγέλαι· | μέγαν αἰγυπιὸν δ' ὑποδείσαντες | τάχ' ἂν . . . | πτήξειαν. For **ὥστε** we expect ὥτε.—Metre: dact. tetrap. with anacrusis=anap. dim. (without caesura). Rossbach writes in one line.

IX. Schol. ζ 244: αἰ γὰρ ἐμοὶ τοιόσδε πόσις κεκλημένος εἴη, the prayer of Nausikaa. Cf. Pind. *Pyth.* 9. 99.—Metre: dact. tetram.

X. Athen. 10. 416 C: Alkman calls himself an ἀδηφάγος. Cf. Aelian *V. H.* 1. 27. The poet seems here to defend himself against a charge of daintiness, though the Sparta of the seventh century was not inevitably the Sparta of black broth. The γαστρὸς ἀνάγκη is a theme for song, and Alkman shows that he was a connoisseur in wines (117). In 74 B–76 there is a flavour of gastronomy. The poem recalls a skolion sung by a single voice rather than a choral song; but the division of the six books of the poet does not warrant our placing the skolia in book iii. No. xxvii. has a better claim to be classed as a skolion, and it was placed in book v. Perhaps the arrangement of the books was metrical. This fragment may fall under the class of ἀποστολικά, like Theokr. 28, but the recipient of the present is not necessarily a woman (as Welcker thought).

1. τοί: τίν in iii. **δώσω**: not the Doric δωσίω. **κύτος**: the vessel of the tripod, called γάστρη Σ 348. Cf. Eur. *Suppl.* 1202 ἔγγραψον ὅρκους τρίποδος ἐν κοίλῳ κύτει, *Kykl.* 399 λέβητος ἐς κύτος χαλκήλατον, and *I. A.* 1052 κρατήρων γυάλοις. Tyrt. 11. 24 has ἀσπίδος γαστρί. Welcker *R. M.* 10. 409 = *Kl. Schr.* 4. 63 regarded τρ. κύτος as a 'caldron on a tripod,' the κύτος being detachable. Others take it to be 'a three-footed caldron.' We have no examples of these tripods from an early period. See Guhl and Koner *Life of the Greeks* 154. We may take the words together as a humorous expression for 'a capacious tripod.' Cf. *dolium ventruosum.* So δράκοντος φόβος = δράκων φοβερός, χρυσὸν ἐπῶν, βάθος ὕλας = *silva alta*, συὸς χρῆμα (in prose), Ναννῶς κόμαι, iv. 70. Cf. Kühner-Gerth 2 § 402 *d.*

2. Welcker read ᾧ κ' (= καί) ἔνι λεῖα (!) τριήρης (a cup used as a ladle); Bergk ᾧ κ' ἐνὶ παισὶν ἐπαίκλι' ἀγείραις; Meineke ᾧ κ' ἐν (Schubert κεν) ἐδέσματα πόλλ' ἐναγείρῃς; Clemm ᾧ τί καν ἰλάως ἐναγείρῃς. Anastrophe (ἔνι) is not Doric according to *An. Ox.* 1. 171.

3. ἄπυρον λέβητα, λευκὸν ἔτ' αὔτως Ψ 267, shows that the τρίποδος κύτος is one not yet touched by the fire (opposed to ἐμπυριβήτης, ἀμφίπυρος), and not a mere ornamental gift. ἄπυροι τρίποδες, as presents, I 122.

4. παμφάγος is interpreted as ἀδηφάγος by Athen., as πολυβορώτατος by Aelian. Perhaps it was a nickname of the poet. It is hard to draw the line between 'gluttonous' and 'omnivorous.' Herakles is παμφάγος (*Orphic Hymn* 12. 6). On the other hand, in contradistinction to ζῳοφάγα and καρποφάγα, Arist. *Pol.* 1. 3. 3 has παμφάγα as a technical division (so crow, raven, bear); and Pliny *H. N.* 5. 30. 35

differentiates *agriophagi*, *pamphagi*, and *anthropophagi*. The scientific use of *παμφ.* is scarcely as old as Alkman, though l. 7 indicates a willingness on the part of the poet to eat all kinds of food (=*πάντα φαγών*).

5. **ἠράσθη** with accus., as *ἱμείρω*, Soph. *O. T.* 59, *ἔλδομαι* E 481, *α* 409. So *θιγγάνω* Frag. xv. The form does not recur till Hdt., Aisch. Meineke's *ἔσθειν οὔτι*, in 6, destroys the rhythm; Sitzler has *ἦρ ἔσθει*, 'through the spring,' as if the gnomic aorist could not be followed or preceded by the present. Cf. Tyrt. 12. 20, Solon 13. 74, Soph. *Aias* 674, *El.* 26. See Goodwin *M. T.* 155. **πεδὰ τᾶς τροπᾶς**: 'after the (winter) solstice,' not 'after the autumnal equinox'; cf. *μετὰ τροπᾶς ἠελίοιο* Hes. *W. D.* 564. For **χλιερόν** we might expect *χλιαρόν*.

6. **ἠύ**: elsewhere Alkm. has *εὖ*. Perhaps we should read *οὔτε*, and suppose the loss of a line after 6. This would help the metre, but *τετυγμ.* requires an adv. Cf. *εὔτυκτα* of *κρέα*, Hdt. 1. 119, and *τετύκοντο δαῖτα* A 467. For the hiatus, cf. Aristoph. *Pax* 116; Soph. *Phil.* 1205 (change of speakers).

7. **ἀλλά . . . γάρ** gives at once the opposition and the reason for the opposition. In English we wait for the causal clause. When there is an ellipsis, *γάρ* may be translated 'in fact'; when there is none, it is='since.' **κοινά**: cf. Hes. *W. D.* 723 *μηδὲ πολυξείνου δαιτὸς δυσπέμφελος εἶναι | ἐκ κοινοῦ*.

8. **ζατεύει**=*ζατεῖ*. Note the pairs (from *ε-ι̯ω* and *ευ-ι̯ω*): *ἀχέω, ἀχεύω*; *οἰνοχοέω, -εύω*; *τυρέω* (xi. 6), *-εύω*. A new strophe begins with *ζατεύει*.

Metre: dact. tetram, the odd verses ending — ⏑ ⏑, the even verses — —. (After l. 6, we might expect a line with a dactylic ending, though the next fragment does not observe the sequence of — ⏑ ⏑ and — —) The rule that no independent verse should end with a light dactyl is therefore preserved. The fragment might be arranged in three dactylic octapodies, with l. 7, a tetrapody, as an epodikon.

XI. Athen. 11. 498 F. A Bacchante at the festival of Dionysos. The nocturnal festival of the Mainads, held, for example, at Delphi in the month *Δᾳδοφόρος*, was intended to awaken the child Dionysos, who had been slumbering during the winter. Nocturnal festivals in honour of the god of wine are reported by Pausanias from various parts of Peloponnese. The same author (3. 20. 4) speaks of a place not far from Taygetos where the cult of the god was restricted to Spartan women. Cf. 3. 13. 5 (*αἱ Διονυσιάδες*), and 19. 6, 22. 2, Aristoph. *Lysistr.* 1309, Aelian *V. H.* 3. 42. Welcker

R. M. 10. 255 erred in regarding the fragment as a description of an offering made by Spartan women to Artemis and the Nymphs; likewise Hartung, who proposed to refer the festival to the Nymphs and Artemis Καρυᾶτις (Paus. 3. 10. 8).

1. πολλάκι: with ἐτύρησας. On π. with the aorist (A 396) see Goodwin *M. T.* 156. **ὀρέων**: probably Taygetos. Cf. Verg. *Georg.* 2. 487 *virginibus bacchata Lacaenis Taygeta*, on which verse Philargyr. notes that the Bacchantes were called δύσμαιναι by the Spartans.

2. πολύφανος: only here; 'with many torches' (φᾶνοί). Torches in connection with the worship of Διόνυσος Νυκτερινός Soph. *Antig.* 1125, Eur. *Phoin.* 226, *Ion* 716, 1125, *Bacch.* 307.

πολύφανος is not Doric for -φωνος, and the contracted θεαρός, πρᾶτος etc., are not to the point. φαηνός would become φηνός in Doric (cf. Hesych. φηνόν· λαμπρόν); hence πολύφανος ἑορτά is not to be defended by θυσίαισι φαενναῖς Pind. *Isthm.* 5. 30, though the form of the adj. might be paralleled by Hom. πολύπικρος. Bergk adopted Fiorillo's πολύφαμος. This suits the ἀγορά (β 150).

3. χρύσιον: the divine sphere demands a metal worthy of the god. The σκύφος (Guhl and Koner 152) was used only by rustics and the poor (Asklepiades in Athen.), as by Eumaios ξ 112, Theokr. 1. 143. The Centaur Pholos offered a σκύφιον δέπας to Herakles (Stes. ii.). In reference to a god, σκύφος τοῦ θεοῦ Achaios 33 N. A σκύφος was one of the attributes of Dionysos. ὁ σκύφος here as Sophron 48, Eur. *Kykl.* 256, Anakr. 82; τὸ σκύφος Epicharm. 61, Eur. *Kykl.* 390. Pindar has both genders.

4. 'A golden pail—one of the sort that.' The logical antecedent is a part. gen. Cf. ε 422 κῆτος . . . οἷά τε πολλὰ τρέφει Ἀφροδίτη, ξ 62 κτῆσιν . . . οἷά τε ᾧ οἰκῆϊ ἄναξ ἔδωκε. Note οἷον in x. 4. The neut. pl. is generic; cf. ν 60, 410. **τε** of permanent characteristic. **ποιμένες ἄνδρες** has an epic flavour (αἰπόλος ἀνήρ Δ 275). Cf. Sa. xxxv., Sem. 20. 2. **ἔχουσιν** (ἔχοισιν ?).

5. ἐν γάλα θεῖσα (Herm. ἒν, but Doric disliked anastrophe) comes nearest to the MS. ἐπαλαθεισα (Π for ΓΓ, *i.e.* ἐγ γάλα). Bergk has θήσαο, but even if we excuse the omission of the augment (γαλ' ἐθήσαο ?), or the open vowels (Spiess θῆσα), as epic reminiscences, the asyndeton is harsh. Hiller supposed a lacuna after θήσαο. Schubert conj. (Aiolic) θαῖσα (θεῖσα ?), but *θάω is 'suckle.' Cf. γάλα θῆσθαι δ 89, and so Emper read here, making the inf. depend on ἔχοισα. With λεόντεον γάλα, cf. αἴγειον τυρόν Λ 639. Aristeides, 1. 49, substituting the god for his devotee, says that 'a Lakonian poet' attributed to Dionysos the power to milk lions. The error in the allusion is the more excusable when we remember that the god is often made to bear the torch or devour raw flesh, which are properly functions of the Mainads. The Mainads suckle the lion's whelps in the mountain wilds (Eur. *Bacch.* 699) or lay hands on them (*Orest.* 1493). If the earth is only scratched by the maddened worshippers of the god, milk flows forth (*Bacch.* 142), and the springs yield them milk (Plato *Ion* 534 A). Reading λεόντειον σπαλαθεῖσα or παλαθεῖσα, Welcker thought a cheese shaped like a lion or ornamented with the figure of a lion was offered to Artemis (πότνια θηρῶν; cf. Theokr. 2. 67). 'Animal-cakes' (*e.g.* cow, stag) were no doubt offered to the gods, but both the verbs are figments.

6. τυρὸν ἐτύρησας: as βουλὴν βουλεύειν, νικᾶν νίκην. **ἄτρυφον** =ἄθρυπτον (cf. ἄρτον τετράτρυφον Hes. *W. D.* 442) rather than 'very delicate,' or 'not delicate,' 'rustic.' Hesych. has ἄτροφος (Welck. ἄτρυφος) τυρὸς ὁ πησσάμενος ὑπὸ Λακώνων. Cheeses were offered to the gods in Crete (Athen. 14. 658 D). Cf. κηροῖο μέγαν τροχὸν μ 173, τυρόεντα μέγαν λευκοῖο γάλακτος Theokr. 1. 58. An ancient grammarian (*R. M.* 10. 256, *Philol.* 10. 350) cites ἀργύφαν and ἀργϊφόντα from this line, whence Welcker conj. ἀργιφόνταν, 'shining,' 'white,' a strange use because of the intransitive sense of the second member. A reference to Ἀργεϊφόντης is hopelessly obscure. ἀργύφεόν τε (Musurus and Casaub.) at least makes sense.

Metre: dact. tetram. We might arrange in octapodies, taking v. 5 as a clausula and v. 6 as the beginning of a new strophe. Those who read ἀργιφόνταν in v. 6 find a dipody and a logaoedic tetrap. (cf. Eur. *Herakl.* 615, all dactyls), the rhythm being retarded at the close. The — — at the end of 2, 4, and 6 (ἀργιφόνταν) would divide the strophe into three periods.

XII. Plut. *Vita Lycurgi* 21, *de fort. Alex.* 2, quoted from ὁ Λακωνικὸς ποιητής, together with Terp. vi., Pind. xxvii. Before battle the Spartan king sacrificed to the Muses, and sang the first notes of the ἐμβατήριος παιάν (cf. Tyrtaios 15). As they advanced to battle the Spartans sang the 'Strain of Castor.' Sparta as a heroine has a lyre in her hand (Paus. 3. 18. 8). *Kampf ohne Sang hat keinen Klang* (Henry the Lion). Cf. Archil. 1 εἰμὶ δ' ἐγὼ θεράπων μὲν Ἐνυαλίοιο ἄνακτος | καὶ Μουσέων ἐρατὸν δῶρον ἐπιστάμενος. Like the next three fragments, this bit is possibly from a partheneion. **ἕρπει ἄντα**, 'rivals.' Cf. Φ 331 ἄντα σέθεν γάρ | Ξάνθον . . . μάχῃ ἠΐσκομεν εἶναι, Υ 75 θεοὶ ἄντα θεῶν ἴσαν. **ἕρπει** is colourless, as often in tragedy (ἕρπεθ' ὡς τάχιστα Soph. *O. K.* 1643). **σιδάρῳ**: with ἄντα the dat. would be out of place. Cf. π 294 αὐτὸς γὰρ ἐφέλκεται ἄνδρα σίδηρος. **τό**: the articular inf. appears only three times in the melic poets before Pindar, in whom it occurs nine times. Here, Alk. vii., Sim. xxxvi., the nom. If the poet is replying to objectors, the artic. inf. has its early opprobrious force : 'this minstrelsy that you claim is scorned in Sparta.' In the elegy the only sure instances are Kleobulina 2, Sim. 100, Ion 1. 10 (gen.), Kritias 2. 26 (accus.), Krates 16. Theogn. 256, 288 are uncertain.—Metre: logaoedic (asynartete).

XIII. Athen. 13. 600 F, from Archytas, on the authority of Chamaileon, to show that Alkm. was the first writer of amatory songs. With this frag. cf. Hor. 4. 1.

1. **Ἔρως** as xv. Most editors have Ἔρος (Sa. xiii.) against the MSS. **δαὖτε** often of a renewed assault of love. The tone is that of the folk-song, which loves fixed formulas. Cf. Sa. xvi., 55, 84 ; Anakr. vii., ix., xix., 61, 68, 91 ; *αὖτε* Ibyk. ii. Cf. Alk. v. Homer has *δὴ αὖτε* with synizesis, *ι* 311, 344. *δεῦτε* Sa. xxii. and Anakr. xxiv. 7. Weber *Anacreontea* 41 needlessly demands the form *δεῦτε* everywhere. Cf. Buttmann *Lexil.* 2. 231. **ϝέκατι** : cf. Archil. 84, Pind. xv. 8 of Aphrodite. See Blaydes on Aristoph. *Lysistr.* 306.

2. **κατείβων** : Hes. *Theogon.* 910 *τῶν καὶ ἀπὸ βλεφάρων ἔρος εἴβετο δερκομενάων.* **ἰαίνει** : Pind. *Pyth.* 1. 11 *ἰαίνει καρδίαν*, *ο* 379 *θυμὸν ἰαίνει.* Alkm. wrote a kletic hymn to Aphrodite (*Κύπρον ἱμερτὰν λιποῖσα καὶ Πάφον περιρρυτάν*, Frag. 21). This poem recalls the personal Aiolian lyric. Dance accompaniment is improbable.—Metre : iamb. trim. catal.

XIV. Athen. 14. 600 F, who says that Megalostrata was a poetess of whom Alkman was enamoured. Probably this statement is due to Athenaios' source, the scandal-loving Chamaileon. Megalostrata may have been the leader of one of Alkman's choruses. **ϝαδειᾶν** : cf. *Μοῦσαι ἡδυεπεῖς Hymn* 32. 2. **δεῖξε** : as *Hymn* 5. 474 *δεῖξε . . . δρημοσύνην.* The gift was doubtless a poem : Hes. *Theogon.* 93 *οἵά τε Μουσάων ἱερὴ δόσις ἀνθρώποισιν.* **μάκαιρα παρθένων** as *τάλαινα παρθένων*, *φίλα γυναικῶν*, *sancte deorum.* One MS. has *μακαίρᾳ παρθένῳ*, *i.e.* Artemis or Athena.—Metre : logaoedic.

XV. Hephaist. 76, Apostol. 4. 62. 2. The connection of the lines is obscure. Perhaps the fragment is from an epithalamium, or is a remnant of a love song, in which a girl compares herself to a cyperus. Cf. Sa. xxxiv. Schubert, not very clearly, thinks that Aphrodite represents Beauty, while Eros is Grace, and that the girl to whom the poem is addressed was graceful rather than beautiful. The verses have an Anakreontic flavour.

1. **παίσδει** (with Aiolic *σδ*), *ludit*, of "amorous play" (*Par. Lost*).

2. Υ 227 (cf. Hes. Frag. 221) ἄκρον ἐπ' ἀνθερίκων καρπὸν θέον οὐδὲ κατέκλων, Verg. *Aen.* 7. 808 *illa* (*Camilla*) *vel intactae segetis per summa volaret* | *gramina*, Plato *Symp.* 196 B οὗ δ' ἂν εὐανθής τε καὶ εὐώδης τόπος ᾖ, ἐνταῦθα καὶ ἵζει καὶ μένει (ὁ Ἔρως). **καβαίνων**<καββ-. This verb does not prove Eros to have been winged. The only early testimony to the conception as Πτέρως is the verse in Plato *Phaidr.* 252 C, which may be Plato's invention. The oldest monuments of art (end of sixth century), do, however, represent Eros with wings. **θίγῃς**: the oldest occurrence of this use of the subj. in a relative clause. The jussive infin. in relative clauses is common, *e.g.* Aisch. *Prom.* 712. **μή μοι**: in deprecation, *e.g.* μή μοι θίγγανε Eur. Frag. 924 (cf. Frags. 16, 22), and often with ellipsis; sometimes in scorn, especially when followed by σύ. The accus. with θιγγάνω is very unusual: Archil. 71 χεῖρα (χειρὶ?) Νεοβούλης θιγεῖν, Soph. *Antig.* 546 μηδ' ἃ μὴ 'θιγες | ποιοῦ σεαυτῆς is explained by Jebb (who says there is no case of θ. with the accus. in classical Greek) as a rare instance of attraction for ταῦτα ὧν. Others take 'θιγες as = ἐποίησας. Pindar is fond of the (personal) dative of approach with θιγγάνω. Note that in *Antig.* 546 and here we have the accus. of a neuter pronoun. Cf. the accus. with ἠράσθη, x. 4. **κυπαιρίσκω**: probably the *cyperus esculentus.* Cf. Fragment iii.—Metre: the cretics are divided by the caesura into a tetrameter and a dimeter (catal.), and seem to be used κατὰ στίχον. We might make four verses of the fragment. The use of cretics in Alkman shows the influence of his predecessor the Cretan Thaletas.

XVI. Schol. Γ 39 (Δύσπαρι, εἶδος ἄριστε). Cf. δυσελένας Eur. *Or.* 1388; αἰνόπαρις *Hek.* 944; Π. αἰνόλεκτρος Aisch. *Agam.* 714; Π. αἰνόγαμος Eur. *Hel.* 1120. In Z 282 Paris is a μέγα πῆμα Τρωσί.—Metre: dact. hexam.

XVII. Schol. Π 236. Cf. μ 47 ἐπὶ δ' οὔατ' ἀλεῖψαι ἑταίρων | κηρὸν δεψήσας μελιηδέα, μή τις ἀκούσῃ | τῶν ἄλλων, and μ 173. **ἐπᾱλείψασα**: by epic lengthening before the liquid. Metre: dact. hexam.

XVIII. Hephaist. 40, Max. Plan. 5. 510, Arsen. *Viol.* 360, Apostol. 11. 94. 4. Kalliope is the chief Muse according to Hesiod (*Theogon.* 79), who is supposed to have invented the names of the Muses. On the François vase, which follows Hesiod, K. carries the syrinx, and has not therefore become the Muse of heroic song. Homer has merely Μοῦσαι Διὸς αἰγιόχοιο θυγατέρες, but *Hymn* 31. 1 Διὸς τέκος Μοῦσα ἄρχεο | Καλλιόπη. In 59 Alkm. has Μῶσα, Διὸς θύγατερ ὠρανίαφι λίγ' ἀείσομαι (with a misuse of -φι). For the invocation cf. Stes.

xii., 35, 45 δεῦρ' ἄγε Καλλιόπεια λίγεια, Alkm. i. Reading ὕμνῳ, we have tmesis and zeugma: ἐπιτίθη δὲ ἵμερον ὕμνῳ καὶ χαρίεντα τίθη χορόν (cf. A 509 ἐπὶ Τρώεσσι τίθει κράτος). This is better than ἐφίμερον δὲ τίθη ὕμνον; cf. Theogn. 993 ἐφίμερον ὕμνον ἀείδειν. Cf. edd. on Pind. *Pyth.* 1. 40. χάρις is that which ἅπαντα τεύχει τὰ μείλιχα θνατοῖς *Ol.* 1. 30; Teichmüller *Aristot. Forsch.* 2. 315 shows that in Pindar χάρις is the cause of joy, and participates in all that is divine and complete. Alkman was called ὁ χαρίεις. Hephaist. reports that Alkm. composed whole strophes in this metre (dact. tetram.), and Max. Plan. says the strophe consisted of three isometric dactylic cola. There is no allusion to an epode, which we might expect. The dactyls form systems ἐξ ὁμοίων. Syllaba anceps is excluded.

XIX. Plut. *Symp.* 3. 10. 3 etc., explaining Διός = ἀέρος. The air sheds most dew, he says, when the moon is full, the time of the festival of Selene. Cf. Macrob. *Sat.* 7. 16. 31; Natalis *Com. Myth.* 3. 255 referring to Alkman, says *quidam tradiderunt Lunam fuisse uxorem Aeris, e quo Rorem filium conceperit ac genuerit.* See also Cic. *N. D.* 2. 50. **οἷα**: the plants nourished by the dew.—Metre: (1) dact. penthim.; (2) tetrap., apparently logaoedic.

XX. Schol. Soph. *O. K.* 1248 (*αἱ, scil.* ἄται, δ' ἐννυχιᾶν ἀπὸ Ῥιπᾶν). The Ῥῖπαι were fabulous mountains in the extreme north, beyond farthest Skythia, whence proceed the blasts (ῥιπαί) of Boreas. The Hyperboreans, the people of light, of Apollo, lived beyond the Ῥῖπαι according to Hellanikos. Eur. *Or.* 176 locates the home of Night in the gloom of Erebos. Night is generally thought of as situated in the uttermost West. **ἀνθέον**: cf. Archil. 21 ὕλης ἀγρίης ἐπιστεφής of Thasos. For the figure cf. *Venus and Adonis* 143 "The morning, from whose silver breast the sun ariseth in his majesty"; Bacch. xx.—Metre: logaoedic (cf. 31 τῷ δὲ γυνὰ ταμία σφεᾶς ἔειξε χώρας).

XXI. Apoll. Soph. *Lex. Hom. s.v.* κνώδαλον, which, he says, is properly used only of marine creatures, whales and the like, though Homer once uses the word of any wild animal: οὐ μὲν γάρ τι φύγεσκε βαθείης βένθεσιν ὕλης | κνώδαλον ρ 316; cf. schol. *ad loc.*, Eustath., and schol. Nikand. *Ther.* 760. Hesiod did not restrict the word to sea monsters: κνώδαλ', ὅσ' ἤπειρος πολλὰ τρέφει ἠδὲ θάλασσα (*Theogon.* 582). The poem describes the sleep of inanimate and animate nature in "midnight's solemn trance," not the sleep of winter. The lines may form a part of a partheneion sung at midnight.

The silence of night is a favourite subject with ancient as with modern poets. Cf. Eur. *Ion* 1150 ff., *I. A.* 9 οὔκουν φθόγγος γ' οὔτ' ὀρνίθων | οὔτε θαλάσσης· σιγαὶ δ' ἀνέμων | τόνδε κατ' Εὔριπον ἔχουσιν, Theokr. 2. 38 ἠνίδε, σιγῇ μὲν πόντος, σιγῶντι δ' ἀῆται, where the poet contrasts man with nature, Apoll. Rhod. 3. 744 ff., Orph. *Argon.* 1007 κοιμήσας δ' ὄγε φῦλα πανημερίων ἀνθρώπων | καὶ ζαμενεῖς ἀνέμων πνοιὰς καὶ κύματα πόντου | πηγάς τ' ἀενάων ὑδάτων ποταμῶν τε ῥέεθρα | θῆράς τ' οἰωνούς τε τά τε ζώει τε καὶ ἕρπει | εὐνάζων ἤμειψεν ὑπὸ χρυσέαις πτερύγεσσιν. We may also compare Dionysios' *Hymn to Helios* εὐφαμείτω πᾶς αἰθήρ, | γῆ καὶ πόντος καὶ πνοιαί, | οὔρεα, τέμπεα σιγάτω, | ἦχοι φθόγγοι τ' ὀρνίθων. So in Latin, Verg. *Aen.* 4. 522 ff.: *nox erat, et placidum carpebant fessa soporem | corpora per terras, silvaeque et saeva quierant | aequora, cum medio volvuntur sidera lapsu, | cum tacet omnis ager, pecudes pictaeque volucres, | quaeque lacus late liquidos, quaeque aspera dumis | rura tenent, somno positae sub nocte silenti | lenibant curas et corda oblita laborum;* 6. 26: *nox erat, et terras animalia fessa per omnis | alituum pecudumque genus sopor altus habebat; Ecl.* 9. 57; Ovid *Metam.* 7. 184: *per muta silentia noctis | . . . homines volucresque ferasque | solverat alta quies . . . | immotaeque silent frondes, silet humidus aër.* Tasso *Jerusal. Deliv.* 2. 96 (Wiffen): "'Tis eve; 'tis night; a holy quiet broods | O'er the mute world—wind, waters are at peace, | The beasts lie couched amid unstirring woods, | The fishes slumber in the sounds and seas; | No twittering bird sings farewell from the trees, | Hushed is the dragon's cry, the lion's roar; | Beneath her glooms a glad oblivion frees | The heart from care, its weary labours o'er, | Carrying divine repose and sweetness to its care"; also 8. 57; Ariosto, *Orl. Fur.* 8. 79; *Par. Lost* 4. 598. Cf. Wordsworth's *Song at the Feast of Brougham Castle:* "The silence that is in the starry sky, | The sleep that is among the lonely hills." We may add Goethe's *Ueber allen Gipfeln:* "Beyond all heights | Is peace. | In the tops of the trees | Stirreth no breeze; | Silent the birds in the woods. | Thou hast but to wait, | Soon shalt thou, too, know rest" (Schütz-Wilson in *Academy*, 1891, No. 987).

Detailed descriptions of nature are infrequent in classical Greek poetry, and when they occur, subserve an ulterior purpose. Their rarity is far from proving insensibility to the charm of nature on the part of the Greeks, and it is only our modern conception that makes them seem to lack the "lyric soul." Nor does the poverty of their vocabulary in words for colour stamp the Greeks as lacking in the colour sense. In their lyrics, nature is often represented as moulding the mood of man (cf. *e.g.* Alk. ix., xix., xxviii., Ibyk. i.). But in this fragment Alkman does not mark the contrast between nature and man. (On this subject see Kittlitz *Naturbilder aus der griech. Lyrik.*)

Personification of natural objects often extends to sleep: E. 524 ὄφρ' εὕδῃσι μένος Βορέαο, Sim. xiii. 16 εὑδέτω δὲ πόντος, εὑδέτω δ' ἄμετρον κακόν, where see note, Aisch. *Agam.* 565. εὕδω in the figurative sense is more usually said of things than of men (Jebb on Soph. *O. K.* 306). With this conjunction of the animals of the land, sea, and air, cf. *Hymn* 4. 4 καί τ' ἐδαμάσσατο φῦλα καταθνητῶν ἀνθρώπων, | οἰωνούς τε διιπέτεας καὶ θηρία πάντα, | ἠμὲν ὅσ' ἤπειρος πολλὰ τρέφει ἠδ' ὅσα πόντος. Taken piecemeal, the fragment is largely a cento of epic words and phrases, and displays, as a whole, the Homeric amplitude.

1. εὕδουσιν: the epic form may stand, though we might expect εὕδοισιν. A Doric εὕδοντιν is impossible. **ὀρέων κορυφαί**: cf. M 282 ὑψηλῶν ὀρέων κορυφὰς καὶ πρώονας ἄκρους, *Hymn* 5. 38 ὀρέων κορυφαὶ καὶ βένθεα πόντου, Alkm. xi. 1. Note in 1-5 τε καί, τε καί + τε, τε – καί + καί; and cf. τε – καί + τε δ 111; τε + τε – καί γ 429; τε – καί + καί δ 341; τε – καί unites complements, like or unlike. **φάραγγες**: cf. Aisch. *Prom.* 142.

2. πρώϝονες: Baunack in Curtius' *Stud.* 10. 132. T was often mistaken for *F*, *e.g.* τείπην Sa. viii. 2, τάδεα (= ἠδέα) Alk. xix. 3.

3. τόσσα: for ὅσσα, as τόσσος for ὅσσος, Pind. *Nem.* 4. 5, Kallim. *Apoll.* 94, though in both places τόσος precedes. The MSS. have here θ' ὅσα. Some omit the τε, others read ἑρπέθ' ὁπόσσα; Bergk φύλλα θ' ἑρπετά θ' ὅσσα, thus introducing a conception which, though graceful (cf. Shakesp. "The marigold that goes to bed wi' the sun"; Byron, "The woods drooped darkly as inclined to rest"), is here inappropriate. The repetition of φῦλα in l. 7 accords with the repetition of εὕδουσιν. θῆρες here bisects the ἑρπετὰ καὶ πετεινά of Hdt. 1. 140; cf. Theokr. 15. 118. δ 417 ὅσσ' ἐπὶ γαῖαν | ἑρπετὰ γίγνονται, P 447, *Anth. Pal.* 14. 64. The poets are fond of the three-fold division, *e.g.* *Hymn* 6. 4, 30. 3, Hes. *W. D.* 277, Emped. 106. So θῆρας, ἑρπετά, πετεηνά *B. C. H.* 2. 401. **τρέφει**: Λ 741 ὅσᾱ τρέφει εὐρεῖα χθών, E 52, Eur. Frag. 484. 5, Eur. *Hippol.* 1277. For the weak position here cf. ε 422, ν 410, Alkm. xix. Apart from ἀγροῖκος in v., *positio debilis* occurs in Alkman only between words (47., xxvi.). **μέλαινα**: of the earth, O 715, λ 587, Archil. 56. 2, Sem. 1. 14.

4. ὀρεσκῷοι: cf. φηρσὶν ὀρεσκῴοισι (the Centaurs) A 268; θῆρ' ὀρειβάτην Soph. *Phil.* 955. **γένος**: γ. βοῶν *Hymn* 3. 309; γ. ἵππων Mimn. 17; γ. ἰχθύων Soph. Frag. 855. 9; ἔθνεα μελισσάων B 87; ἔθνη θηρῶν Soph. *Phil.* 1147.

5. βένθεσι: cf. ἐν βένθεσσιν ἁλός A 358. **πορφυρίας**: the Doric form for πορφυρέας. πορφ. of the sea ν 85 etc., [Arion] 18, Sim. 51, Sem. 1. 16, Theog. 1035; "The seas that mourn in flowing purple," Omar.

6. εὕδουσιν, with neuter pl. (*constr. ad sensum*); so with ἔθνεα B 87 (Krüg. 2. 63, 2. 1).

7. φῦλα: of birds, as Soph. *Antig.* 343; φῦλα πτεροφόρα, Aristoph. *Aves* 1757; of flies, T 30; φῦλα πόντου Eur. Frag. 27. **τανυπτερύγων**: the stereotyped epithet, though the activity denoted by the adj. has ceased, as in Z 108, οὐρανὸς ἀστερόεις, by daylight; ε 65 ὄρνιθες τανυσίπτεροι εὐνάζοντο; the 'swift sea-cleaving ships' are stationary, Soph.

Aias 710. Cf. οἰωνοῖσι τανυπτερύγεσσι M 237; Ibyk. iv., Sim. xi.

Metre: The arrangement of the logaoedics shows that metre still in its beginnings, though more highly developed than in Frag. iv., because of the less rigid arrangement of the cola. The fragment presents, however, some noteworthy metrical forms. (1) The caesura after ὀρέων divides thesis and arsis, a phenomenon that is common in true dactyls, and here perhaps borrowed from them, though noteworthy in a cyclic dactyl, where —◡ forms the thesis. The cyclic dactyl is regularly dismembered in the *Sapphicus minor* as employed by Horace (—|◡◡ and —◡|◡). (4) Troch. hexapody with anacr. The tripody before the caesura has the form — ◡ — > ⌊ (unless ὀρεσκῷοι has a short penult), which occurs in tragedy, but is singular in early lyric. (5) Log. hexap. with anacr. Cf. the pentapody called Alkmanic: ◡ ⁞ — ◡ ⌊ —◡◡ —◡ ⏓. Writing βένθεσσι and πορφυρίας we have a troch. trim. catal. (6) Pherecratic with — > as a basis. ὀϊωνῶν gives greater rapidity to the rhythm than the MS. οἰωνῶν. Cf. Usener 103. The dialect is generally epic in the MSS. I have adopted Doric μελισσᾶν and πορφυρίας. Perhaps τράφει should be read. Wilamowitz *Comment. grammat.* 1879, p. 4, has attempted unsuccessfully to restore the Doric forms throughout. The style lacks the originality of the other poems of Alkman.

XXII. Plut. *de fort. Rom.* 4. Forethought is the mother of Reverence (Pind. *Ol.* 7. 44), whose daughter is Moderation (*C. I. A.* 2. 2339), while Excuse is the child of Afterthought (Pind. *Pyth.* 5. 27). Tyche is here allied, through Eunomia, to the Hours, who are the daughters of Themis. Cf. Adesp. xii., xiii. Sappho called Peitho the daughter of Aphrodite. Alkman, who is fond of such genealogies (cf. xix.), made the Muses the children of Heaven and Earth. Plutos is the child of Tyche according to Paus. 9. 16. Cf. Alk. iii., xxix., Krates 2 (Εὐτελίη, ἔγγονε Σωφροσύνης).—Metre: logaoedic.

XXIII. Schol. Pind. *Isthm.* 1. 56. **τοι** as in ἀρχὴ δέ τοι ἥμισυ παντός, the sententious τοι. Cf. Theogn. 571 δόξα μὲν ἀνθρώποισι κακὸν μέγα, πεῖρα δ' ἄριστον, for the expression, Pind. xxviii.—Metre: logaoedic.

XXIV. Apoll. *de pron.* 121 A. The chorus praise the poet for his skill in playing the kithara. Bergk and Croiset think κιθαριστάς is the old expression for κιθαρῳδός, a term which was adopted relatively late. In classical times κιθαρῳδός is practically = 'lyric poet.' The first kitharist in the strict sense of the word was Aristonikos of Argos, a contemporary of Archilochos. Since the partheneia were sung to the accompaniment of the flute, some other choral song, perhaps a hymn, seems to be referred to. In Pind. *Nem.* 11. 7 λύρα is used with reference to a hymn. Stesichoros was not the first to accompany a chorus with the lyre. In Sparta a choral poet was called χοραγός = the Athenian διδάσκαλος.—Metre: logaoedic.

XXV. Athen. 9. 374 D. This is the oldest example of the use of νόμος with the meaning 'tune.' Cf. ἱεροὺς νόμους μελέων Aristoph. *Aves* 745. The poet learned his art from the birds (Frag. vi.). The birds, who carry the messages of the gods to the prophets who understand their language, were called by the Persians the interpreters of heaven.—Metre: logaoedic.

XXVI. Athen. 3. 110 F.

2. ἐπιστέφοισαι is used in the sense of ἐπιστεφόμεναι. Perhaps ἐπιστεφεῖσαι (Kaibel) is correct. The ancients used the poppy and sesame so much that Petron. *Satir.* 1 says: *audiunt . . . mellitos verborum globulos et omnia dicta factaque quasi papavere et sesamo sparsa.* **3. λίνω** depends on ἐπιστεφ. **4. παίδεσσι**: MS. πέδεσσι, which is scarcely Aiolic for μέτεστι, though ἔσσι = *est* or *sunt* occurs in a late Aiolic inscription. Bergk conj. πέδεστι = μέτεστι. Welcker thought the poet refers to a marriage feast.—Metre: catal. iamb. trim.; a catal. dim. concludes the strophe.

XXVII. Athen. 10. 416 D (cf. No. x.). This is the first distinct mention of four seasons. Homer and Hesiod know of only three: ἔαρος ὥρη (cf. Stes. ix.), θέρεος ὥρη, χείματος ὥρη. ὀπώρα is technically the period from the end of July (from the rising of Sirius) to the rising of Arcturus in September, and thus includes the hottest part of the year. It is the fruit season; cf. Pind. *Nem.* 5. 6 τέρειναν μάτερ' οἰνάνθας ὀπώραν (Alkm. 75 calls honey 'waxen fruit,' κηρίνα ὀπώρα). Eur. Frag. 990, allots only two months each to ἔαρ and ὀπώρα, four each to θέρος and χειμών. Hippokrates gives as the names of the four seasons χειμών, ἦρ, θέρος, φθινόπωρον (the last name occurs first in Hdt.). The sevenfold division of the year is late. See *Dict. of Antiq.* 1. 233, where the present passage is overlooked.

1. ἔθηκε: the subject (Ζεύς) probably occurred in the preceding line. **τρεῖς**: we expect τρῆς, or τρῖς (accus. as nom.).

2. χὠπώραν: the Doric crasis would be χἀπώραν. ὀπ-ώρα is the 'late season' or 'late summer' (μέρος θέρους τὸ τελευταῖον Eustath.); cf. ὄπ-ισθε, ὀψέ. The asper is vouched for by Ὀπωρίς on a Lakonian inscription (Cauer 6), ὀπίσθιον, Attic, *B. C. H.* 12. 284. ὀπάρα is a *vox nihili.*

3. τέτρατον: perhaps Doric as well as epic. Pind. has both *τέτρατος* and *τέταρτος*. Note the chiastic order.

4. θάλλει: impersonal as *ὕει, βροντᾷ, ἐχείμαζε*. The poem, like x., xxvi., does not seem to be choral. Perhaps it may belong to the class called *κλεψίαμβοι*, and attributed to Alkman; if so, the song may have been interrupted by recitation accompanied by the notes of the *κλεψίαμβος*.—Metre: iambic dimeter.

XXVIII. Strabo 10. 482.

1. φοίναις: Aiolic; cf. *θοίνης δὲ καὶ εἰλαπίνῃσι* Theogn. 239. The short form of the dat. pl. appears also in iv. 47. 61. **ἐν**: for the position, cf. Pind. *Nem.* 10. 38 *Χαρίτεσσί τε καὶ σὺν Τυνδαρίδαις*, where Dissen remarks *hoc artificio poetico nova vis et alacritas secundo membro conciliatur*. Cf. *Pyth.* 1. 14, 2. 59, *Isthm.* 1. 29, and Soph. *O. T.* 734. The comic poets use this construction only in choral parts, or when the language is lyrical. In *ἢ ἁλὸς ἢ ἐπὶ γῆς μ* 27, *ἁλὸς* is prob. local gen.

2. ἀνδρείων: the old name for the *συσσίτια*, or common meals; cf. Müller *Dorians* 2. 294, Schoemann *Antiq.* 269, 306. The Cretans retained the name *ἀνδρεῖα*, which was afterwards abandoned by the Spartans. In Sparta these banquets were also called *φειδίτια*, perhaps a jocose name, or *φιλίτια*. **δαιτυμόνεσσι**: cf. *μετ' ἀνδράσι δ. χ* 12. **πρέπει**: so used Aisch. Frag. 355. **παιᾶνα**: Philochoros (Athen. 14. 630 F) says that it was the custom among the Spartans *ἂν δειπνοποιήσωνται καὶ παιωνίσωσιν, ᾄδειν καθ' ἕνα τὰ Τυρταίου*. **κατάρχην**: as FOLK-SONGS vii. (accus.), Eur. *H. F.* 750, 891; cf. *ἐξάρχων παιήονα* Archil. 76. This is the earliest mention of a sympotic paian in post-Homeric poetry.—Metre: dactylic. Since a paroemiac with short anacrusis does not occur in the old *κατὰ δάκτυλον εἶδος*, I do not make a third verse of *πρέπει κ.τ.λ.* Cf. Ibyk. v. 3.

XXIX. Hephaist. 38; fragment of a song to Apollo, perhaps a hyporcheme. First extant specimen of ionics in Greek poetry. Alkman also employed anaklasis in ionics (83).

XXX. Apoll. *de pron.* 365 A: quoted for the orthotone *τοί*. Probably from a hymn to Apollo. **ἅδοι** as Pind. *Ol.* 3.1, *Pyth.* 1. 29. **δόμῳ**: *νόῳ*?—Metre: uncertain.

XXXI. Schol. Pind. *Ol.* 1. 60 (97), quoting Archil. 53 *μηδ' ὁ Ταντάλου λίθος | τῆσδ' ὑπὲρ νήσου κρεμάσθω*, Alk. xxxi. Homer, who places Tantalos in Hades (λ 582), mentions only the tortures of hunger and thirst, though the overhanging rock is a necessary ingredient of the original myth, which is adopted by the lyric and tragic poets. Poetic fancy and an ethical purpose transferred, as early as the Νέκυια of Homer, the tortures of Tantalos, Sisyphos, etc., to the nether world. The earliest form of the legend appears in Athen. 7. 281 B (from the Cyclic 'Return of the Atreidai'), according to which Tantalos, who lived in heaven with the gods, had a rock suspended over his head by Zeus, who had pledged himself in advance to grant any request that his son might make; but who was filled with wrath when Tantalos petitioned that his appetites be gratified, and that he live in the same manner as the gods. This scene is laid in heaven, and the suspended rock not merely robs the *conviva deorum* of his power to enjoy the divine nectar and ambrosia, but is an added torture because of his immortality (μετὰ τριῶν τέταρτον πόνον Pind. *Ol.* 1. 60). Pindar does not certainly localize Tantalos in Hades. Cf. Comparetti *Philol.* 32. 230. On the view that Alkman keeps to the original story, ἐν ἀσμένοισιν of the MSS. is 'among the blissful,' 'the well pleased gods.' The rock of terror was explained by Welcker *R. M.* 10. 242 as merely the creation of the distressed mind of the living sufferer. For such phantasms, cf. those of Io, Orestes (Aisch. *Choeph.* 1051), Pentheus (Eur. *Bacch.* 918, Verg. *Aen.* 4. 469). Hecker's ἁρμένοισιν is taken to mean either 'the bound' captives, or 'in bonds,' and transfers the scene to the nether world, thus making the poet follow Homer rather than the Cyclic epic. The rock is then a reality, and all the more awful because invisible. I doubt whether ἁρμένοισιν can have either of the above meanings. It should mean 'amid pleasures,' 'good cheer'; cf. Hes. *W. D.* 407, *Shield* 84, Theogn. 275, and such expressions as ἀγαθὰ πάντα, ἄφθονα πάντα. Hecker supplied πᾶσιν before ἐν (Pind. *Nem.* 3. 58 ἐν ἁρμένοισι πᾶσι; cf. schol.).

2. θάκω: the MS. θάκα = θᾶκος might be defended by the pair σκοπός σκοπή, etc. Welcker took κάτα (*sic*) with ἧστο. Hermann wrote θάκοις κάτω. ἧστο presupposes motion, so there is no difficulty about the κατά. There is no need to take it with ὀρέων, or to regard πέτρας οὐδέν as = οὐδεμίαν πέτραν.

3. Eust. *Od.* 1701. 23 has ὀρέοντι and δοκέοντι, whence Bergk δοκέοντι δ' (ἐοικώς).—Metre: uncertain, probably logaoedic.

XXXII. *Oxyrhynchus Papyri* 1. No. viii. Attributed to Alkman by Blass. From a partheneion. It is possible that the poem is a happy imitation of Alkman's manner by some Alexandrian.

1. ἤνθομεν: cf. ἐνθοῖσα iv. 73. The ending -μεν is either epic or Aiolic, and seems to be used, as the editors remark, in order to avoid the sigmatism of -μες ἐς. In iv. 12 παρήσομες. **μεγάλας**: this epithet of Dem. does not recur until Kallim. 6. 121 μεγάλα θεὸς εὐρυάνασσα; μεγαλαῖσι θεαῖσι of mother and daughter, *Anth. Pal.* app. epigr. 1. 59. 3 (Cougny). **ἐάσσαι** = ἐοῦσαι. Dor. ἔασσα <* ἐσ̥ητ̯ια reappears in Philolaos and the Pseudo-pythagoreans. In Messen. and Argive we find ἔασα, in Cretan ἴαττα. In 64 Alkm. has παρέντων.

2. παρθενικαί: see on vii. 1. Cf. η 20 παρθενικῇ . . . κάλπιν ἐχούσῃ.

3. κᾱλά: for the variation with κᾰλά, l. 2, see Folk-Songs i. In xii. Alkm. has κᾰλῶς. **ὅρμως**: not ὅρμους, as the editors write.

4. πριστῶ ἐλέφαντος: cf. σ 196 λευκοτέρην δ' ἄρα μιν (Penelope) θῆκε πριστοῦ ἐλέφαντος, τ 563 πρ. ἐλεφ. of one of the dream-gates, θ 404 κολεὸν νεοπρίστου ἐλέφαντος. **αἴγλᾳ** (Blass) is paleographically uncertain. Blass suggests that the next verse began λευκοτάτας χιόνος.—Metre: dact.-hexameter. Whether the Frag. is connected with vii. is uncertain.

ARION.

The only early account of Arion's rescue that is extant is Herodotos 1. 24, where it is introduced as an anecdote, based on Korinthian and Lesbian sources, in connection with the mention of Periander (625-585). Most of the later recounters of the tale—*e.g.* Hyginus 194, Dio Chrys. 37, p. 455, Plutarch *Sept. Sap. Conv.* 18, Fronto 262—and the numerous writers who allude to it, depend ultimately on Herodotos, though some may have derived the legend from some Hellenistic poet. The story was greatly embellished in later times, Plutarch, for example, throwing moonlight on the scene, and making the story subserve his reverence for nature and his piety. The fragment is cited by Aelian *Hist. An.* 12. 45 to show the dolphin's love of music.

Herodotos says that at Tainaron there was a bronze statuette of Arion, a man riding on a dolphin. Aelian gives the epigram on the votive offering: ἀθανάτων πομπαῖσιν Ἀρίονα Κύκλονος υἱόν, | ἐκ Σικελοῦ πελάγους σῶσεν ὄχημα τόδε. This inscription may have been added after the time of Herodotos. That the legend wandered from Sparta to her colony, Thera, was concluded from an epigram found there (Kaibel 1086), but now shown to be worthless evidence (*Athen. Mittheilungen* 21. 253). Neither the inscription nor the figure of Arion on coins of Methymna is proof of the existence of a poet of this name.

The legend of Arion's romantic rescue is due to a misinterpretation of the figure at Tainaron. The statuette was either that of a god or of some hero originally identical with the god, but in course of time individualized and dissociated from him. The rider has been identified with the Korinthian Melikertes-Palaimon (cf. *Ant. Denkm. d. Arch. Inst.* 1. 7. 26, *Inscr. Sicil. et Ital.* 2519 C); or with Taras, the son of Poseidon, who rode from Tainaron to Tarentum on a dolphin's back. Studniczka, *Kyrene* 181, has, however, shown that the rider was not Taras, but Phalanthos, who, at first a form of Poseidon, gradually became an historical person connected with the emigration of the *partheniai.* Hartung thought the rider was Orpheus. Most probably it was either Poseidon or Apollo, with whose cults the dolphin is intimately associated. In Lakonia there was a goddess Ἀριοντία (*I. G. A.* 79), in whose honour horse-races were established. Mr. Paton (*Class. Rev.* 4. 134) thinks that she corresponds to Demeter Erinys of Thelpusa, the mother of the mythical horse Arion, whose father was Poseidon. Now both horse and dolphin are symbolical manifestations of the god of waters, and it is noteworthy that the only places mentioned in the story of Arion—Methymna on the island of Lesbos and Korinth of the double sea, the birthplace of the poet, and the place where he is said to have practised the dithyramb—are the seats of legends of grateful dolphins.

It is, in fact, probable that the poet Arion is one and the same with the mythical horse, the manifestation of Poseidon. Exactly how the invention of the cyclic chorus and of the τραγικὸς τρόπος came to be attributed to him we cannot say; doubtless Lesbian legends are here at work, just as they created Phaon, the mythical lover of Sappho. It may be noticed that, apart from the steed of Adrastos (Ψ 346, Hes. *Shield* 120), the name Arion occurs nowhere in early literature. It is possible to derive it from ἀρι-Ϝτων, 'very swift' (Maass *Ind. Forsch.* 1. 166), though Fick-Bechtel (*Personennamen* 433) propose to connect it and the Arkadian form Ἐρίων (coin of Thelpusa *S. G. D.-I.* 1253) with Ἐρινύς, *rivalis.* Κυκλεύς and Κύκλων, the names of the father of the supposed poet, are inventions made to account for the belief that his son first set up the κύκλιος χορός, an institution which is involved in obscurity, though it is supposed that a circular chorus of fifty members took the place of the older rectangular arrangement in ranks and files. Some suppose that Arion first made the dithyramb choral, it having been monodic up to his time, and that the τραγικὸς τρόπος, which he invented, alludes to the 'fashion' of satyrs, who, clothed as goats, spoke in verse, thus forming the beginning of the 'tragic' drama. Others think the 'goat-fashion' is the pathetic fashion in contradistinction to that of the nome; others refer it to the introduction of the tales of heroes. Many theories, little certainty. Despite the statement in Herodotos that Arion was the founder of the dithyramb, some Hellenistic critics seem to have doubted his existence, and given that honour to Lasos, Pindar's teacher. Most of the statements in Suidas may be an expansion of Herodotos' account, or based on some book on the Korinthian festivals. Arion is strangely enough called the scholar of Alkman.

The authenticity of the poem was first disputed by Van der Hardt in 1723. Hermann regarded it as an example of *ornatus qui varietate et venustate constat.* Welcker (*Kl. Schr.* 1. 89 ff.) was inclined to regard it as old, if not by Arion himself. But considerations of style, metre, and dialect show that it must be later than the lyric age. It cannot be a forgery by an author of the quality of Aelian, as Lehrs supposed (*Popul. Aufsätze* 204), nor indeed the composition of a nomic writer of an early period (Boeckh *Berl. Acad.* 1836. 74), but is rather the production of an Athenian dithyrambic poet of the last period of Euripides, or later. The style, despite its partial smoothness, recalls the fulsomeness, the veneer, of the later dithyramb; the metre is ornate, with its many resolutions, syncopated feet, and anacruses, and shows its late authorship by its frequent instances of *positio debilis.* The dialect is Attic diluted with Doric, a mixture that became common in the fifth century. Rossbach conjectures that the poem is either the work of a scholar of the dithyrambic poet Phrynis, or of the master himself. Aelian quoted the poem in good faith, but originally it was put into the mouth of Arion, without intent to deceive, in order to serve as an exaltation of the power of music, a theme that was popular with the later dithyrambic poets, to judge from the *Argo* of Telestes, a fragment of which is akin to the hymn of Arion in the frequency of anacruses. Just so Kallimachos made Simonides himself tell of his miraculous rescue by the Dioskuroi; and so the story of Sappho's leap from the Leukadian cliff and of her love for Phaon arose from her mention of this resort of hapless lovers and her story of the ferryman of Aphrodite.

The poem falls into two parts: (1) 1-11, invocation of Poseidon, around whom the dolphins dance; and (2) 12-18, the rescue of the poet. The mention of the dolphins is withheld till v. 9, *θῆρες* standing in epexegetical apposition. Throughout we have a series of pictures produced by ornamental and 'characteristic' epithets. The poet is prodigal in his use of colours.

---

2. χρυσοτρίαινε may be defended by *χρυσηλάκατος*, *χρυσοκέφαλος*. Hermann and Bergk read *-τρίαινα* from a nom. in *-ης*, with which cf. *χρυσοχαίτης*, *χρυσομίτρης*, *χρυσοκόμης* (*χρυσεοκόμα* Sim. 26 B; Alk. iii. *χρυσοκόμας*). Alk. xiii. has *μελλιχόμειδε*, though we have *φιλομμειδής*; in Anakr. xxviii. there is warrant for *εὐέθειρε* and *εὐέθειρα*; Sim. xxvii. has *φυγόμαχος*; Sa. xxii. *καλλίκομος*. Pindar's Ὀρσοτρίαινα, Ἀγλαοτρίαιναν, Εὐτρίαιναν, are sometimes explained as Boiotisms (-ᾰ for -ης). Aristoph. *Equit.* 559 *ὦ χρυσοτρίαιν᾽, ὦ | δελφίνων μεδέων* (where the schol. has *χρυσοτρίαινα*), is not necessarily either a parody or an imitation of this poem. Cf. M. 27 Ἐννοσίγαιος, *ἔχων χείρεσσι τρίαιναν*. **Πόσειδον**: the Attic form.

3. γαιάοχος is the 'earth mover' (*γαίης κινητήρ*), as *ἐννοσίγαιος*, *ἐνοσίχθων*, *ἐλασίχθων*. Cf. Lakon. *γαιάϜοχος*, Pamphyl. *Ϝεχέτω*, *veho*. -(*Ϝ*)*οχος* was later confused with -(*σ*)*οχος* (in *πολιάοχος*, *ῥαβδοῦχος* etc.), and Artemis is called *γαιάοχος*, Soph. *O. T.* 160. **ἀν᾽** is due to Hermann, who connected *ἐγκ. ἀν᾽ ἅλμαν* with the following.

4. βράγχιοι: if correct, is a neologism. Hermann read *βραγχίοις περὶ δή*; Buchholz *περί σέ γε*; Sitzler *ἐν κύμασι πάλμυ βρυχίοις*. Cf. N 27 *βῆ δ᾽ ἐλάαν* (Ποσ.) *ἐπὶ κῦμα· ἄταλλε δὲ κήτε᾽ ὑπ᾽ αὐτοῦ | πάντοθεν ἐκ κευθμῶν, οὐδ᾽ ἠγνοίησεν ἄνακτα.*

5. θῆρες: a bold innovation on established usage, which restricted the word to 'beasts,' a generic term (Schmidt *Synom.* 2. 432 is wrong). Cf. Archil. 74. 7 μηδ' ὅταν δελφῖσι θῆρες ἀνταμείψωνται νομόν. The dolphin was a fish to the ancients. **χορεύουσι**: χορὸς ἰχθύων Soph. Frag. 695 and *Anakreont.* 55. 27; 55. 24 δελφῖσι χορευταῖς. **κύκλῳ**: cf. Thuk. 2. 84 περιέπλεον κύκλῳ.

6. A fanciful variation on κούφοισιν ποσίν Pind. *Ol.* 13. 114. Schneider says *pedes affinxit poeta delphinis quia saltare facit*; cf. καλλίχοροι δελφ. Eur. *Hel.* 1454. Pindar's use is bolder (ἐλαχυπτερύγων *Pyth.* 4. 17).

7. ἀναπαλλόμενοι: cf. ἀναπάλλεται ἰχθύς Ψ 692.

8. On the speed of the dolphin cf. Pind. *Nem.* 6. 64 δελφῖνί κεν τάχος δι' ἅλμας | ἴσον εἴποιμι, Frag. 234 παρὰ ναῦν δ' ἰθύει τάχιστα δελφίς, Pliny *H. N.* 9. 8 *velocissimum omnium animalium, non solum marinorum, est delphinus, ocrior volucre, acrior telo.* **σκύλακες**: cf. Eur. *Hippol.* 1277 σκ. πελαγίων. **φιλόμουσοι**: Pind. Frag. 235 τὸν (δελφ.) μὲν . . . αὐλῶν ἐκίνησ' ἐρατὸν μέλος, Eur. *El.* 435 ὁ φίλαυλος δελφίς.

9. ἔναλα: cf. Aristoph. *Thesmoph.* 325 Νηρέος εἰναλίου τε κόραι.

13. Σικελὸς πόντος, first in Euripides. Lucian *Dial. Mar.* 8, doubtless following Lesbian tradition, puts the scene in the Aigaian Sea. Cf. Spenser *F. Q.* 4. 11. 23 "And even yet the Dolphin, which him bore | Through the Agaean seas from Pirates vew, | Stood still by him astonisht at his lore."

15. ἄλοκα: cf. Mel. Adesp. 88 'Αφροδίτης ἄλοκα (conj.) τέμνων καὶ Χαρίτων ἀνάμεστος. The form ἄλοξ does not occur before the fifth century. The details of the following scene are too precise to admit of Welcker's symbolical interpretation; nor can it be regarded as pure embellishment due to imitation of a previous mention in literature of the thankful dolphin.

18. Perhaps the dithyrambic poet was capable of writing ἁλιπόρφυρον (only here of the sea). ἁλι- may have crept in from 17; Bergk πορφυροῦν; Reiske ἁλιπορφύρου. Cf. ἅλς πορφυρέη Π 391, Sim. 51, Sem. 1. 16, Eur. Frag. 882, Theogn. 1035 πορφυρέης λίμνης, Soph. Frag. 435 γλαυκᾶς ἐπ' οἶδμα λίμνας. Note Attic νεώς in 17.

Metre: The fragment is astrophic, a fact that agrees with its composition by a late dithyrambic writer. The metre is either degenerate free logaoedic or degenerate dactylo-epitritic with frequent — ⏑ ∟ and — ⏑ ⏑ ∟ or — ⏑ ⏑ — ∧. The epitrite is not found except at the end, where it may be a ditrochee.

ALKAIOS.

THE close of the seventh century witnessed a change in the established order of things in Lesbos that has left a profound impression upon the poetry of Alkaios. The tide of democracy was sweeping in upon the princely Penthelidai, who traced their descent from Orestes, and upon the other noble houses whose power had been sanctioned by centuries of prescription. For eight years Alkaios and the other aristocrats struggled against the demagogue Melanchros, who had utilized the popular uprising to make himself tyrant. Had their party possessed sufficient power they would not have suffered the even more detested rule of Myrsilos, which followed upon the murder of Melanchros (612 ?) at the hands of Pittakos and Antimenidas, the poet's brother. Though Myrsilos himself was finally slain, other tyrants rose in his stead. We have no certain landmarks by which to date the events of this period of faction and unrest. We do not even know when the contest was waged with the Athenians for the possession of Sigeion, in which Alkaios lost his shield. The account in Hdt. 5. 94, which places this event after 560, is confused, and should not have misled Beloch into making Alkaios a contemporary of Anakreon (cf. Töpfer *Philol.* 49, Crusius *Philol.* 55); though it must be confessed that it is surprising enough to hear of Athens warring in the Troad at the end of the seventh century, the period to which the struggle is usually referred. Alkaios himself, perhaps not unmindful of a similar confession on the part of Archilochos (6), sang of his loss, and bade the herald report that, though he was safe, his shield had been hung up as a trophy by the victors in the temple of Athene at Sigeion. We may well believe that a remembrance of the disaster that had befallen the two Greek poets, whom he was to make his models, must have softened the bitterness of flight to the young tribune at Philippi (Hor. 2. 7).

It may have been in 595 that Alkaios was exiled, together with Antimenidas, Sappho, and other members of the aristocratic faction. No doubt Alkaios, too, had lusted after power (οὐδ' αὐτὸς καθαρεύων τῶν τοιούτων νεωτερισμῶν, Strabo 13. 617). The poet wandered about in

Thrace, and voyaged as far as Egypt, but even in exile did not cease to foment attempts to effect a return by force of arms. To counteract these schemes, Pittakos, once the adherent of the aristocrats and the champion of the Lesbians against the Athenians, was (in 590 ?) appointed dictator (αἰσυμνήτης: Alkaios calls him 'tyrant') to defend the constitution. Under his rule tranquillity was restored to the island, and the poet, weary of incessant contest, was content, after fifteen years of exile, to accept the offer of clemency on the part of the sage, who thus put into execution his doctrine that pardon was better than punishment (συγγνώμη τιμωρίας κρείσσων).

Akenside's lines on Alkaios reflect the spirit of the liberty-loving Englishman or of the Roman republican, not the narrowness of the fierce champion of the Lesbian oligarchs:

> With louder impulse and a threatening hand
> The Lesbian patriot smites the sounding chords;
> Ye wretches, ye perfidious train,
> Ye cursed of gods and free-born men,
> Ye murderers of the laws;
> Though now ye glory in your lust,
> Though now ye tread the feeble neck in dust,
> Yet time and righteous Jove will judge your dreadful cause.

Alkaios was not an apostle of liberty, though he possessed the art of painting partisanship in the colours of patriotism. The poetry of his contemporary Solon shows us at once the statesman and the patriot. Alkaios' creed was 'down with all tyranny—except that of my own party!' His poetry is full of the storm and stress of the time. He sings the *dura navis, dura fugae mala, dura belli* (Hor. 2. 13). He lives in the present, and projects himself into his every utterance. He fights with the lyre as with the sword. The passion that Archilochos had vented in personal rancour, Alkaios transfers to the larger canvas of politics and war. For the first time in its history the pure Melic of the Greeks looses the bonds which bound it to a mythological past, and becomes the warm and spontaneous expression of the heart. By birth a Lesbian, Alkaios displays the Aiolic temperament, which is seen at its fullest in the noble,—high-spirited, proud of his order, frank, generous and free, fearless and open-handed as the Stuart cavalier, joyous and resolute even in disaster, delighting in love and wine. With his fondness for magnificence there is a dash of pretence and pompousness. His sensuousness is tempered by a high-minded enthusiasm.

Of his style, Dionysios of Halikarnassos, who read him when his poems were not mere fragments, says that it was distinguished by its magnificence (μεγαλοπρεπές), by its brevity, by its combination of grace and force (δεινότης), and that his figures were remarkable for their clearness (*de vet. script. cens.* 2. 8 ; cf. Quint. 10. 1. 63). When the veil of the metre has been removed there remains, he says, a rhetorical quality that savours of the orator. To us Alkaios suffers by the unjust but inevitable comparison with Sappho. Though a vigorous and a graceful poet his fame is largely a reflection of that of his great countrywoman. He is always genuine, often vivacious and tender ; he possesses a fine feeling for nature, and a love of detailed pictures. He speaks a direct language, and his figures are not richly coloured. He is fond of sententious sayings. In the imaginative quality he is deficient, nor can he lay claim to high originality ; though hatred of Pittakos hammers out for him such startling compounds as σαράπους, χειροπόδης, ζοφοδορπίδας.

His dialect—which Dionysios characteristically says impaired the appreciation of his beauties—was the native idiom of his time with (possibly) a touch of epic form. Both Alkaios and Sappho show conscious adaptation of epic phraseology. The light and elastic logaoedics were peculiarly suited to the lively Aiolic temperament. With the name of Alkaios is associated the four-line strophe that he employs in such perfection, and which Horace transformed by the admission of diaeresis. The Alkaic stanza, whether invented by the poet or not—Crusius seeks to discover its first traces in Alkman (cf. iv.)—is a marvellous combination of fire, grace, and variety, welded together in perfect unity.

Alkaios also employed the softer 'Sapphic' stanza. His choriambics (Asclepiads), which constitute a large part of his verse, are full of restless energy and a certain stateliness. Besides these he wrote in Aiolic dactyls with the free, undetermined first foot, in ionics, and in iambics. The latter recall Archilochos, with whom he has much in common.

The Alexandrians divided his poems into at least ten books, probably arranged according to the elusive criterion of the predominant note. To the composition of hymns Alkaios' genius was apparently ill-suited. At least those we have are mere silhouettes. Himerios summarizes the paian to Apollo, which described how at the birth of the god Zeus gave him a lyre and a chariot drawn by swans to bear him to Delphi to proclaim his ordinances of justice and right to the Hellenes. But the god hastened to the Hyperboreans, where he tarried for a year until the songs of entreaty uttered by the Delphians prevailed upon him. Then he came in the fulness of summer; the nightingale, the swallow, and the cicada sang for joy, and Kastalia poured forth her silver streams.

The political songs (*στασιωτικά*) are passionate and defiant like the *sirventes* of Bertran de Born. His love songs were so generally devoted to the praise of boys that Quintilian laments that he did not devote his muse to higher themes. The traditionary story of Alkaios' passion for Sappho fails to stand the test of criticism, as we shall see on Sa. viii. The skolia overlap the other divisions. All Alkaios' poetry, except the hymns, is virtually sympotic.

Alkaios enjoyed great popularity in Athens in the fifth century. His songs graced the banquets of Athenian gentlemen, and Aristophanes knew him well. The Alexandrians edited his works and wrote commentaries on them. Theokritos imitated him (28, 29), but his greatest admirer was Horace.

I. Hephaist. 44: quoted with the remark that it is doubtful whether Sappho or Alkaios invented the 'Sapphic' strophe. Vv. 3-4 are from Choirob. on Hephaist. (*R. M.* 36. 464). The hymn mentioned the theft of the kine of Apollo, which is referred to by Horace in the ode (1. 10) that is based on Alkaios.

1. μέδεις: the ancients disputed whether *μέδεις* was the part. from *μέδημι* (so Apoll. Dysk.), or 2nd pers. of *μέδω* (so Apion). On the one hand (1) we have Ἑρμῆν . . . Κυλλήνης *μεδέοντα* *Hymn* 3. 2, 18. 2, and the various other passages in L. and S. (where read *Eq.* for *Ib.*), to which may be added Bacch. ix. 66; Melanip. iv.; skol. iv.; *μεδέουσα* Smyth *Ionic Dial.* p. 69. On the other hand (2), *ὃς μέδεις* Soph. *Antig.* 1119, Frag. 342. In Alk. 48 B, Bergk read Ἀχίλλευ, *ὃ μέδεις* (ὃς μεδέεις, MSS.). The dispute cannot be decided. Classen *Beobacht. z. hom. Sprachgebr.* 46, remarks that μέδεις in Sophokles is an arbitrary (Homeric) archaism because the verbs in actual, though poetical, usage were μέδομαι (Hom. μ. πολέμοιο, μ. νόστοιο) and μήδομαι. μεδέων is a real, μέδων, even in Homer, a crystallized participle, like γέρων, κρείων, θεράπων.

2. Cf. carm. pop. 3 Ἄρτεμι, σοί μέ τι φρὴν . . . | ὕμνον ὑφαινέμεναι, Ovid *Metam.* 1. 1 *fert animus dicere.* **ἄγναις**: αὔγαις, *v.l.*, 'on the gleaming peak,' is indefensible. Hermes was born ἄντρου ἔσω παλισκίου. Bergk read αὔταις, which is = *in solis montibus* according to Schulze *Q. E.* 251; Fick κορύφας ἄκτᾳ; Sitzler ἄντρῳ or ἰώγᾳ; Kock αἴπαις.

4. Cf. *Hymn* 18. 3 ὃν τέκε Μαῖα . . . Διὸς ἐν φιλότητι μιγεῖσα, Verg. *Aen.* 8. 139 *Mercurius, quem candida Maia | Cyllenae gelido conceptum vertice fundit.*—Metre: the 'Sapphic' strophe (three Lesser Asclepiads + Adonic): 5.5.5. + 2. ἐπῳδικόν.

II. Strabo 9. 411.

1. **Ἀθανάα**: so Ἀθανάας Theokr. 28. 1 (Aiolic). ἄνασσ' Ἀθάνα Eur. *I. T.* 1475, skol. i., etc. The hymns of the lyric poets and of the Orphic collection begin with an invocation in the vocative, herein differing from the *Homeric Hymns.* A relative pronoun often follows the vocative clause, as here, Pind. iv. 3, Aristoph. *Eq.* 551. **πολεμάδοκος** of Athena, Kaibel 1035. 4, *Anth. Pal.* 9. 59. 3.

2. **ποι**: as κου Anakr. i. 4. **ἐπιδεύαο**, Fick; cf. Hesych. ἐπιδεῦσαι· ἐπιστρέψαι; ἐπίδε(υ)ον· ἐπίστρεψον. Κύπριοι. Cf. ἐπιστρέφεαι Anakr. ii. 4. Bergk read ἐπὶ πίσεων.

3. Homer always places πάροιθεν before the genitive.

4. **Κωραλίω**: cf. Kallim. 5. 63 ἢ 'πὶ Κορωνείας, ἵνα οἱ τεθυωμένον ἄλσος | καὶ βωμοὶ ποταμῷ κεῖντ' ἐπὶ Κουραλίῳ. Here was celebrated the festival of the Παμβοιώτια in honour of Athene Itonia at the end of the month Alalkomenios. **ποτάμω παρ' ὄχθαις**: cf. ποταμοῖο παρ' ὄχθας Δ 487; for the order of the words, cf. Pind. *Pyth.* 4. 46, *Isthm.* 5. 42; and see Mommsen *Griech. Präp.* excurs. 6.—Metre: Alkaic strophe = two Alkaic hendecasyllabli, an Alkaic enneasyllabus, and an Alkaic decasyllabus (I. 5.5. II. 4.4.).

III. Plut. *Amator.* 20. Perhaps from a hymn to Eros. As a cosmogonic god, Eros was called the child of Chaos (Hesiod, Ibykos), of Night and Day, of Erebos and Night, of Heaven and Earth, of Chronos, etc. As the god whose power commands gods and men alike (Anakr. xxv.), he is generally called the child of Aphrodite. Sappho (132) made him the son of Uranos and Aphrodite or Earth, in 74 the servant of Aphrodite; Simonides (43), the son of Aphrodite and Ares; Olen called him a son of Eileithyia; Euripides, the child of Zeus. In Apuleius, Zephyros is a servant of Eros. His genealogy as given in Alkaios characterizes his stormy, impetuous nature (cf. Sa. xiii., Ibyk. i., Anakr. xix.). The connection of Zephyros with Iris, the sister of the Harpies, is old.

IV. Herakleid. *Alleg. Homer.* 5. An allegory of the distress of the Mytilenaians under the tyrant Myrsilos.

The comparison of the state to a ship is frequent in Greek poetry. (Schol. Aristoph. *Vesp.* 29 ἀεὶ οἱ ποιηταὶ τὰς πόλεις πλοίοις παραβάλλουσι.) Cf. Pind. *Pyth.* 1. 86, 4. 274; Theogn. 671-680 οὕνεκα νῦν φερόμεσθα καθ' ἱστία λευκὰ βαλόντες | Μηλίου ἐκ πόντου νύκτα διὰ δνοφερήν· | ἀντλεῖν δ' οὐκ ἐθέλουσιν· ὑπερβάλλει δὲ θάλασσα | ἀμφοτέρων τοίχων κ.τ.λ.; Aisch. *Septem* 2, 62, 758-765 κακῶν δ' ὥσπερ θάλασσα κῦμ' ἄγει· | τὸ μὲν πίτνον, ἄλλο δ' ἀείρει | τρίχαλον, ὃ καὶ περὶ πρύμναν πόλεως καχλάζει κ.τ.λ.; 795 πόλις δ' ἐν εὐδίᾳ . . . ἄντλον οὐκ ἐδέξατο, 1077; Soph. *O. T.* 22 πόλις γάρ . . . ἄγαν ἤδη σαλεύει, 101; *Antig.* 163; Eur. *Rhes.* 248; Plato *Rep.* 6. 4; Cic. *pro Sestio* 20, § 46; Hor. 1. 14 *o navis, referent in mare te novi* | *fluctus*, etc. (cf. Quint. 8. 6. 44.).

1. ἀσυνέτημι: we may double the *ν* under the ictus; cf. *συννεχές* M 26 (*Ven. A.*). Survival of the original sibilant of *σετος (*(σ)ί(σ)ημι) is not probable. Cf. *σὺν ὀλίγῳ* (— ⏑ ⏑ —) Theokr. 28. 25; *ἐνόχλης* (— ⏑ —) 29. 36, both Aiolic idyls. Aristoph. of Byz. wrote *ἐνιμμεγάροισιν* β 94. See La Roche *Hom. Textkr.* 354, 391. **στάσιν**: cf. Aisch. *Prom.* 1085 *σκιρτᾷ δ' ἀνέμων* | *πνεύματα πάντων εἰς ἄλληλα* | *στάσιν ἀντίπνουν ἀποδεικνύμενα.*

2. κῦμα κυλ., Λ 307.

4. σύν personifies. The 'black bark' is their companion in distress; Soph. *Phil.* 1022 *ζῶ σὺν κακοῖς πολλοῖς τάλας.* In the minor melic poets this (epic) use of *σύν* occurs also in Alk. xxix., Ibyk. ii. 6, FOLK-SONGS v.

6. περ: see on Sa. i. 10. Theogn. 673, quoted above, has *ὑπερβάλλει.* The ship is *ὑπέραντλος.*

7. Cf. *ι* 70, *μ* 410. **λαῖφος**, as *Hymn* 2. 228 (un-Homeric use). **ζάδηλον**: either 'transparent,' 'full of holes,' or better, 'utterly destroyed' (*δηλέομαι*). *δῆλος*, 'visible,' from **δε-ηλος*, **δη-ελος*, or **δειαλος* (cf. *δέαμαι*); not from **δειελος*, whence *δέελος* K 466, because this form would have become *δεῖλος* in Ionic and Aiolic. Horace has *non tibi sunt integra lintea.*

9. When the ship is labouring in the open sea, anchors (and these Greek anchors) are not in place, even in an allegory. Hence for *ἄγκυραι* (cf. Kiessling on Hor. i. 14. 6), Unger read *ἄγκοιναι*, ropes for making the yards fast to the mast. Michelangeli's ἄγκυλαι is nearer the MSS.; *ansae quae mediam antemnam in malo continent* (Thesaurus), the *ansa* being here the end of a rope so tied as to make a sort of ring. Compare the storm described in O 381, 624, Theokr. 22. 10-18; also Archil. 54.

V. Herakleid. *l.l.* Probably from the same poem as iv.

1. τὸ δ' αὖτε: Cf. Alkm. xiii. If we read 'νέμω = ἀνέμω, the gen. follows κῦμα, as in κύματα παντοίων ἀνέμων B 396. The sense is, however, inferior to that of the text (Bergk).

2. Note the parechesis; cf. πόνος πόνῳ πόνον φέρει Soph. *Aias* 866; πόνου πολλοῦ πλέῳ 1112; πῆμα πήματος πλέον Eur. *Hek.* 1168; Sa. 38; Aristoph. *Nubes* 1049; *Ran.* 829; Aisch. *Prom.* 98; *Agam.* 63. (Alliteration with π often denotes anger or vexation.)

3. ἔμβᾳ: Bergk suggested ἐμβᾶ νῆ(ατα), the 'hold,' for ἐμβαίνει. Others ἐμβαί|νῃ. νᾶος depends on an omitted word, or ἐμβαίνω may take the partitive gen., either directly or by analogy to ἐπιβαίνω.

VI. Athen. 10. 430 C: Alkaios is ready to drink at all seasons. "Who drinks well, loves the commonwealth." **πρὸς βίαν**: not *violentius*, but *invitum, coactum*, as Soph. Frag. 669; Aristoph. *Acharn.* 73 (π. βίαν πίνειν). So πρὸς ὀργήν, πρ. καιρόν, πρ. ἡδονήν. πρὸς βίαν is rarely used of force other than physical. **τινα**: subj. of μεθύσθην. **πώνω** and πίνω (xx. 1) are both Aiolic: χαῖρε καὶ πῶ τάνδε Alk. 54 A; δεῦρο σύμπωθι 54 B. Cf. πέπωκα, πῶμα, *pōculum*; Skt. *pāti*, 'drinks.' An anonymous critic in Porto's work *ad Lyric. Frag.* 1598 conj. καὶ χθόνα π. βίαν παίειν, as if Hor. 1. 37. 1 *nunc est bibendum, nunc pede libero | pulsanda tellus* were derived from this fragment of Alkaios. But Horace may have had in mind another line of his Greek exemplar. The tautology is not intolerable.

VII. Choirob. *Epim.* 1. 210. For the rare articular inf. see on Alkm. xii. Cf. Tyrt. 1. 1 τεθνάμεναι γὰρ καλὸν ἐπὶ προμάχοισι πεσόντα, Hor. 3. 2. 13 *dulce et decorum est pro patria mori.*

VIII. Herodian 2. 929. 15. Cf. Alkm. viii. **ἔπταζον**: πτάζω = πτήσσω, of the cowering of birds, Eur. *H. F.* 974, *Kykl.* 408; Aristoph. *Vesp.* 1490. Cf. Soph. *Aias* 171.

IX. Athen. 10. 430 A. Imitated by Hor. 1. 9 *vides ut alta stet nive candidum | Soracte, nec iam sustineant onus | silvae laborantes, geluque | flumina constiterint acuto? | dissolve frigus, ligna super foco | large reponens, atque benignius | deprome quadrimum Sabina, | o Thaliarche, merum diota;*

also *Epod.* 13 *horrida tempestas caelum contraxit et imbres* | *nivesque deducunt Iovem.* Campion's *Winter Nights*: "Now winter nights enlarge | The number of their hours; | And clouds their storms discharge | Upon the airy towers. | Let now the chimneys blaze | And cups o'erflow with wine."

1. ὔει Ζεῦς; cf. *ξ* 457. The phrase contains a survival of the original meaning of Ζεύς, *i.e.* sky, heaven.

2. Cf. *χειμὼν πολύς δ* 566; *πολὺς δ' ἐξ οὐρανοῦ ὄμβρος* Theokr. 22. 14. With *χείμων* there is an ellipsis of the predicate (*γίγνεται, ἔστι*, or perhaps *ἄησι*. Cf. *ὑόμενος καὶ ἀήμενος ζ* 131). **πεπάγαισιν**: the MS. *πεπάγασι* can be defended if Aiolic has -ᾰσι = Dor. -ᾰτι in the perfect (borrowed from the present of reduplicating verbs). Homer has *πεφύκᾰσι*, Xenophanes *πεφήνᾰσιν*.

3. Cf. the scene in Theokr. 7. 66 ff. **κάββαλλε**: perhaps the expression is derived from the palaestra. Cf. *stravere ventos.* **ἐπί**: tmesis as Alkm. xviii.; cf. Alk. xiv. 3, xx. 2, xxviii. 2; Sa. vii., xix. 3.

4. κέρναις (with tmesis = *ἐγκιρνάς*) = *κιρνάς π* 14. An Aiolic inscr. has the inf. *κέρναν*.

5. αὔτάρ: the accent in Aiolic is uncertain, as is that of *οὐδέν*. In Homer the ictus always falls on the initial syllable. *αὐτάρ* is parallel to *μέν* in Π 732 etc.

6. *ἀμφι⟨τίθεις⟩* or *-τίθει* would suit as well as *-βάλων*. **γνόφαλλον**: a cushion filled with wool. Pliny *H. N.* 27. 10 has a derived meaning: *gnaphalion . . . cuius foliis albis mollibusque pro tomento utuntur.*

X. Athen. 10. 430 B. Probably from the same poem as ix.

2. προκόψομεν: *proficiemus*, strictly of the preparation by the pioneer of the path for an army. Cf. Eur. *Alk.* 1079 *τί δ' ἂν προκόπτοις, εἰ θέλεις ἀεὶ στένειν*; *Hek.* 961 *ἀλλὰ ταῦτα μὲν τί δεῖ | θρηνεῖν προκόπτοντ' οὐδὲν εἰς πρόσθεν κακῶν*; 'making no progress forwards in evils.' **ἀσάμενοι**: from *ἄσᾱμαι*. Theogn. 657 *μηδὲν ἄγαν χαλεποῖσιν ἀσῶ φρένα.*

3. Βύκχι is said to be Aiolic for Βάκχι, as *βύθις* for *βάθις*. But *α* does not become *υ* in this dialect. The *υ* of *σύρξ, πέσσυρες* is not derived from *α*. **φάρμακον**: cf. Sim. 14 *πῖνε, πῖν' ἐπὶ συμφοραῖς.*

4. ἐνεικαμένοις (scil. *ἄμμε*). Aiolic inscr. have *ἤνικαν, ἐσένικαι* probably with *ῐ*. The Aiolic may also be the Homeric-Ionic form (*ἐνεῖκαι*). The middle = 'have brought in'; so *ἐγχεώμεθα*, 'have poured in,' Xen. *Symp.* 2. 26; *ηὐλοῦντο*, 'had the flute played,' *Kyrop.* 4. 5. 7. So *ἐδιδάξατο*, 'had taught.'

XI. Tzetz. *Lycophr.* 212. Cf. Frag. xxxii., Theogn. 500 ἀνδρὸς δ' οἶνος ἔδειξε νόον, Aisch. Frag. 393 κάτοπτρον εἴδους χαλκός ἐστ', οἶνος δὲ νοῦ, Hor. 1. 18. 16 *arcanique fides prodiga, perlucidior vitro.* The Greeks had a proverb οἶνος οὐκ ἔχει πηδάλια. To Plato indulgence in wine is a test of self-command, and a measure of the facility with which men are tempted to extravagance (*Laws* 649, 671 ff.). We read ἀνθρώποισι, as we expect the full form in Aiolic, and suppose a loss of — ⏖ at the end.—Metre: as xiii.

XII. Arist. *Rhet.* 1. 9. Bergk placed this fragment with No. xiii. See on Sa. viii., with which it probably belongs.

XIII. Hephaist. 45. **ϝιόπλοκ'** 'dark-tressed,' as ἰόπλοκοι Νηρηΐδες Bacch. ix. 37; cf. *Anth. Pal.* 9. 542. 10. Hesych. has ἰόπλοκος (MSS. ἰοπλόκος), ἰόπεπλος ἀπὸ τοῦ χρώματος, *i.e.* πλόκος = πλόκαμος. In Pind. *Ol.* 6. 30, Bergk conj. Ϝιόπλοκον Εὐάδναν for ἰοπλόκαμον, ἰοβόστρυχον of the MSS.; and in *Isthm.* 6. 23 Ϝιοπλόκοισι Μοίσαις for ἰοπλοκάμοισι. Cf. ἰοπλοκάμων θυγατρῶν Sim. vii.; ἰοπλοκάμων Μοισᾶν Pind. *Pyth.* 1. 1, as Mel. Adesp. 53 (Sappho ?), where Ϝιοπλόκων suits the metre better. The Greek violet (ἴον μέλαν) was darker than ours. λευκόϊα are probably pansies. Ruskin thinks that ἴον in Homer was the blue or purple iris. ἰόπλοκ' might mean 'violet-weaving' (with recessive accent for ἰοπλόκ'). **μελλιχόμειδε**: the nom. is given by Hesych. as μειλιχομείδης (cf. φιλομμειδής), whence Blomfield conj. μελλιχόμειδα here. Cf. on Arion 2.—Metre: the Sapphic pentapody with the masculine anacrusis.

XIV. Athen. 15. 674 C (vv. 1, 2), 687 D (vv. 3, 4). Cf. xxi. The Aiolic writing of the multiform ἄνηθον is ἄνητον (Sa. xxix.). Acro on Hor. 4. 11. 3 *vel quia Alcaeus frequenter se dicit apio coronari.* Crowns of dill were often used (Theokr. 7. 63, 15. 119; Verg. *Ecl.* 2. 48). Cf. Sa. 46 κἀπάλαις ὑποθύμιδας | πλέκταις ἀμφ' ἀπάλᾳ δέρᾳ, Xenophan. 1. 2; Plut. *Symp.* 3. 1. 3; Anakr. 9 στήθεα χρισάμενος μύρῳ.—Metre: Sapphic strophe.

XV. Schol. Aisch. *Pers.* 347 (ἀνδρῶν γὰρ ὄντων ἕρκος ἐστὶν ἀσφαλές). From Aristeid. 1. 791, 821, 2. 273, we infer that the preceding thought was that of Sir William Jones' *What Constitutes a State.* A later age made Lykurgos the author of the saying (Plut. *Vita* 19). Plato may be referring to Alkaios (*Laws* 778 D). For the sentiment, cf. Soph. *O. T.* 56; Hdt. 8. 61; Thuk. 7. 77; Dio Cass. 66. 6; and Pind. *Pyth.* 5. 56; Theogn. 233. **πύργος**: so used λ 556 τοῖος γάρ σφιν π. ἀπώλεο, Soph. *O. T.* 1201, Eur. *Med.* 389, *Alk.* 311.

With π. ἀρεύιος cf. τεῖχος ἄρειον Δ 407. Another saying of Alkaios' was, 'Emblems on shields inflict no wounds.'—Metre: Lesser Asclepiad.

XVI. Hephaist. 34, Liban. 1. 406 (vv. 1, 2), the remainder in a paraphrase, Strabo 13. 617, whose words have to be rearranged and Aiolized. Antimenidas, the brother of Alkaios, was one of the leaders of the oligarchical faction in Mytilene who had been driven into exile. He entered the service of Nebuchadnezzar, king of Babylon (604-561 B.C.), and may have performed the deed of valour here recounted in Syria or in Egypt in the war against Hophra. Some think he may have been present at the capture of Jerusalem (586). The employment of Greek mercenaries was as old as Adramalech, son of Sanherib; and later, under the reign of Psammetichos, they were engaged in Egypt. The chronology of the period is uncertain, but it is improbable that Antimenidas served in 604 in the war against Egypt. The brothers seem to have returned in 580, when Pittakos recalled the exiles and laid down his office. Cf. *R. M.* 33. 215.

1. Imitated in Thuk. 1. 69. 5 τὸν Μῆδον αὐτοὶ ἴσμεν ἐκ περάτων γῆς . . . ἐλθόντα. Hom. has πείρατα γαίης Θ 478. In 85 Alk. has περράτων.

2. **χρυσοδέταν**: the compound adj. has only here the more poetical fem. ending.

3. **Βαβυλωνίοις**: -οις for -οισι at the verse-end; cf. i. 2.

5. **μαχαίταν**: from the desiderative μαχαίω or μάχαιμι; μαχητής is from the stem of μαχή-σω.

6. **παλαίσταν**: Ionic also has the αι form. Cf. Τροιζήν, Τροζήν; Γεραιστός, Γεραστός. **ἀπυλείποντα**, as Hes. *W. D.* 696 μήτε τριηκόντων ἐτέων μάλα πόλλ' ἀπολείπων. 'Lacking but a single hand's breadth of five royal ells,' *i.e.* about 8 ft. 4 ins. Hdt. 1. 178 says the royal ell exceeded the common (Attic?) ell by 3 δάκτυλοι. As the ell consisted of 6 παλαισταί=24 δάκτυλοι, the relation of the ells was as 24 : 27, or as 21 : 24. If we reckon the Persian ell as 528 mill. (Oppert says 525-530), and the Attic at 462 mill., the ratio is 24 : 21. The passage in Hdt. 7. 117, in reference to Artachaies (ἀπὸ πέντε πηχέων βασιληΐων ἀπέλειπε τέσσερας δακτύλους), would seem to be borrowed from Alkaios, with a slight change. A statue of Herakles (schol. Pind. *Isthm.* 3. 87) was four δάκτυλοι shorter than the πελώριος ἀνήρ who was slain. The common stature for giants was five cubits (Skylax 54, Apoll. Tyan. 2. 4).

7. **πέμπων**: the Aiolians inflected 5, 10, 40, 50, 90.—Metre: Lesser Asclepiads in stichic arrangement.

XVII. Eust. *Od.* 1397. 32, *Il.* 633. 61. A political song, doubtless referring to Pittakos. In the Greek game of draughts (*πεττεία*), the stone on the *ἱερὰ γραμμή*, or middle line of the five, was moved only as a last resort. Hence *κινεῖν τὸν ἀφ' ἱερᾶς* = 'try one's last chance.' Cf. Sophron 98 *κινησῶ δ' ἤδη τὸν ἀφ' ἰαρᾶς*, Theokr. 6. 18 *καὶ τὸν ἀπὸ γραμμᾶς κινεῖ λίθον*, and Smith's *Dict. of Antiq.*, s.v. *Latrunculi*; Becker's *Charicles* 352. Note the pregnant use of *ἀπύ*. Bergk read *πύματον* for *πύκινον*, Crusius *πυκινῶς*. Metre: as xv.

XVIII. Arist. *Pol.* 3. 9. 5; cf. Plut. *Erot.* 18. **κακοπάτριδα** may be either (1) 'of a low-born father'—Pittakos is reported to have been the son of a Thrakian father and a Lesbian mother—or (2) 'the ruin of his country.' The first explanation is preferable. *κακός* = *δυσγενής* (δ 64). That *κακόπατρις* = *κακοπατρίδης* (Blass would read *κακοπατρίδαν*) is clear from Theogn. 193, the only other occurrence of the word. In Attic, -*πατρίδης* was the ending (cf. *εὐπατρίδης*). *κακόπατρις* is both masc. and fem., as *ἄναλκις*, *φιλόπατρις*, *φιλόπολις* etc. **ἀχόλω** means 'chicken-hearted' (cf. B 241) and should be retained. Bergk *ζαχόλω*, 'wrathful,' and later, *διχόλω* (cf. *δίχολοι γνῶμαι*); Fick *ἀβόλω* = *ἀβούλου* (cf. Soph. *O. K.* 940 *πόλις ἄβουλος*). **ἐστάσαντο**: this is the earliest instance of *ἵστασθαι* for *αἱρεῖσθαι*. **ἐπαίνεντες**: *ἐπαινέοντες*, if correct, would be the only case in Aiolic of a verb in -*εω* showing synizesis. Elsewhere *εο* is either open (*ποτέονται* 43) or contracted to *ευ* (if *μοχθεῦντες* iv. 5, and not *μόχθεντες*, is correct), or disappears, -*εω* being inflected like a -*μι* verb.—Metre: Greater Asclepiad.

XIX. V. 1. Athen. 1. 22 E, X 430 B, Proklos on Hes. *W. D.* 584, Gell. 17. 11. 1, Macrob. *Sat.* 7. 15. 13, Plut. *Symp.* 7. 1. 1, Eust. *Il.* 890. 47, *Od.* 1612. 14. V. 2. Athen., Prokl. V. 3. Partly in Prokl., partly in Demetr. *de eloc.* 142. Vv. 4, 5. Demetr. V. 6, 7. Prokl. With a few variations that show a nice attention to detail, the fragment is a lyric setting of Hes. *W. D.* 582 ff.: *Ἦμος δὲ σκόλυμός τ' ἀνθεῖ καὶ ἠχέτα τέττιξ | δενδρέῳ ἐφεζόμενος λιγυρὴν κατεχεύετ' ἀοιδὴν | πυκνὸν ὑπὸ πτερύγων, θέρεος καματώδεος ὥρῃ, | τῆμος πιόταταί τ' αἶγες καὶ οἶνος ἄριστος, | μαχλόταται δὲ γυναῖκες, ἀφαυρότατοι δέ τε ἄνδρες | εἰσίν, ἐπεὶ κεφαλὴν καὶ γούνατα Σείριος ἄζει, | αὐαλέος δέ τε χρὼς ὑπὸ καύματος· ἀλλὰ τότ' ἤδη | εἴη πετραίη τε σκίη καὶ βίβλινος οἶνος κ.τ.λ.* Hesiod is imitated also in xxiii.

1. **πλεύμων** is the older form (*pulmo*, Skt. *kloman*); *πνεύμων* is due to folk's etymology, which connected the word with *πνέω*. The best MSS. of Attic writers often have the *πν*- form, though *πλεύμων* is well attested. In Plutarch, *l.l.*, the physician Nikias says that it is not surprising that a poet

was guilty of an error in physiology that was committed even by the philosopher Plato. The reading πνεύμονας is due to ignorance of the *F*. **ἄστρον**, Sirius, though some take it of the sun (so Unger *Philol.* 44. 648). Cf. Theogn. 1040 ἄστρου καὶ κυνὸς ἀρχομένου, *i.e.* ὁ ἀστρῷος κύων. On ἄστρον)(ἀστήρ see on Alkm. iv. 63; Pind. *Ol.* 1. 6 uses ἄστρον of the sun κατ' ἐξοχήν; so *sidus*, Tibull. 2. 1. 47; cf. Hor. 3. 29. 18 *iam Procyon furit*, which rose July 15, eleven days before Sirius. **περιτέλλεται**: *in orbem redit et sic denuo oriri et apparere incipit* (Iani).

2. **δίψαισι**: the plural emphasizes the diffusion of the heat. Cf. Hor. 4. 12. 13 *adduxere sitim tempora.*

4. **κακχέει**: cf. τ 521 χέει πολυηχέα φωνήν. **λιγύραν**: in Sparta the cicada was called λιγαντάρ. On its music see Γ 151, Aristoph. *Pax* 1159, Theokr. 1. 148, 16. 94; and cf. *Anakreont.* xxv. It began to sing at the end of June (Arist. περὶ ζῴων 5. 17. 2, 24. 2). The modern names are τσίτσικος and τσιτσίδα from the note τσι-τσι. **σέλας**: cf. Hes. *Theogon.* 867 τήκετο γαῖα σέλαι πυρὸς αἰθομένοιο.

5. **πεπτάμενον**: cf. P 371 πέπτατο δ' αὐγὴ ἠελίου ὀξεῖα. πεπτ. excludes the reading καθέταν 'perpendicularly.' **καταυάνῃ**: -ανω and -αινω interchange; cf. κυδάνω, γρυπάνω, ἀζάνω, μελάνω.

7. Cf. Σείριος ἀζαλέος Hes. *Shield* 153. Archil. 61 has Σ. καταυανεῖ, where Σ. is said to = ἥλιος.—Metre: as xviii.

XX. Athen. 10. 430 D, 11. 481 A.

1. **λύχνα**: ὁ λύχνος perhaps τ 37; τὸ λύχνον Hipponax 125. The neuter plural is the common form. Cf. *vivae lucernae* Hor. 3. 21. 23. It is περὶ λύχνων ἁφάς (Hdt. 7. 215), but the poet is unwilling to lose time. **δάκτυλος**: Heron Μετρικά 308 says the δακτ. is the smallest of all measures, and is also called the unit; cf. Arist. *Metaph.* 13. 1. 7. Cf. Mimn. 2. 3 πήχυιον ἐπὶ χρόνον. Sir Charles Newton (*Halicarnassus*) reported that the Greek sailors of to-day measure the distance of the sun from the horizon by the finger's breadth. The passage is imitated in *Anth. Pal.* 12. 50 πίνωμεν Βάκχου ζωρὸν πόμα· δάκτυλος ἀώς. | ἢ πάλι κοιμιστὰν λύχνον ἰδεῖν μένομεν; but the concluding thought (τὴν μακρὰν νύκτ' ἀναπαυσόμεθα) should not have been interpreted into Alkaios (Schweighäuser *punctum est quod vivimus*). Cf. Hor. 1. 1. 20 *partem solido demere de die*; 2. 7. 6 *morantem saepe diem mero | fregi.*

2. **καδ δ' ἄερρε** = *deprome* Hor. 1. 9. 7. **αἴτα** 'beloved.' In Sparta (Alkm. 125 αἴτα, of maidens), in Thessaly (Theokr. 12. 14), and in Lesbos αἴτας = Attic καλός *i.e.* ἐρώμενος, Cretan *κληνός*. Theokr. has *ἀΐτας*. For the Aiolic *ῐ*, cf. *κνάμῑδες* xxiv. 4; note also *σατῐνη* Anakr. xi. 10, *ἄτῐτος* and *ἄτῑτος*. *ἀΐτης* is derived from *α* copul. + *Fίτης* < *Fίεμαι*, Lat. *in-vitus*; not from *ἀΐω*, which would have produced *ἀΐστης*. Is the *ῐ* due to the influence of *ἵεμαι*, which received the initial short vowel of *ἵημι*? **ποικίλαις**: cf. Verg. *Aen.* 9. 263 *aspera signis pocula.*

3. λαθικάδεα: cf. *οἶνον ἀμύντορα δυσφροσυνᾶν* Sim. 86, *βότρυος ἕλικα παυσίπονον* Aristoph. *Ranae* 1321, *oblivioso Massico* Hor. 2. 7. 21, *vinoque novos compesce dolores* Tibull. 1. 2. 1.

4. ἕνα καὶ δύο: since the proportion of water is usually mentioned first, most scholars understand *ἕνα* as *ἕνα ὕδατος κύαθον*; but others, mindful of Alkaios' fondness for wine, supply *οἴνου κύαθον*. One of water to two of wine was a proportion for a toper, and Anakr. xxiv., enjoining sobriety, calls for ten of water to five of wine; the mixture of 5 : 3 in Anakr. xv. is, according to Athen., *ζωρότερον* than 1 : 2 in Alk. Hence in the latter poet we have ⅔, in Anakr. ⅝ water. Athen. 10, § 21 ff., discusses the various proportions at length. Half and half (*ἴσον ἴσῳ*, Aristoph. *Plutos* 1132) was a mixture that might produce madness (Athen. 2. 36 B), but was recommended by Hippokrates (*Aphorism.* 7. 56) in cases of chill, etc. 3 : 1 is praised by Hes. *W. D.* 596, Pollux 6. 18; 3 : 2 in Aristoph. *Equit.* 1187. Mention is also made of 4 : 1 and 4 : 2 in the comic writers. Ameipsias makes Dionysos praise 5 : 2. The wine in *ι* 209 was so strong as to require 20 : 1. The Greeks generally preserved their *σωφροσύνη* in drinking. Alexis (Frag. 9) says *τοῦτ' ἔσθ', ὁρᾷς, Ἑλληνικὸς | πότος, μετρίοισι χρωμένους ποτηρίοις | λαλεῖν τι καὶ ληρεῖν πρὸς αὑτοὺς ἡδέως.* *οἶνος* in general means 'wine and water.' Cf. Theogn. 477 ff.; Plut. *Symp.* 3. 9; *de San.* 19; Clem. Alex. *Paedag.* 2. 2; Amm. Marc. 27. 363. Toasts (*ἐπιχύσεις*) were often pledged in unmixed wine (Aristoph. *Vespae* 525; Theokr. 2. 152). Pure wine (*ἄκρατος*) produced paralysis according to the poet in Athen. 2. 36 B. On *Symposia* see Becker *Charicles* 333-347, and *Dict. Antiq. s.v.*

5. *πλήαις* may be better than **πλέαις.** From *πλῆος* comes Ionic *πλέως*. **κακ κεφάλας**: 'full to overflowing,' *plenas usque ad summum.* Cf. Theokr. 8. 87 *αἶγα, | ἅτις ὑπὲρ κεφαλᾶς αἰεὶ τὸν ἀμολγέα πληροῖ.* *ἔγχεε πλέαις κ. κεφ.* = *ἐπιστέφου ποτοῖο.*

6. ὠθήτω: the thought is different in *οἴνῳ τὸν οἶνον ἐξελαύνειν*, Antiphan. 300.—Metre: as xviii.

XXI. From Plut. *Symp.* 3. 1. 3. Cf. xiv. *πολλὰ παθών* is epic. Cf. *ω* 417 *χεύατο κακ κεφαλῆς πολιῆς.* Plut. has (*κελεύων*) *καταχέαι.*—Metre: as xviii.

XXII. Athen. 10. 430 C. Imitated by Hor. 1. 18. 1 *nullam, Vare, sacra vite prius severis arborem.* Note that Horace does not, like Alkaios, end a colon in the middle of a word. **δένδριον**: in Theokr. 29. 12, *δενδρίῳ* may be a product of grammatical theory. If *δένδρεον* is from *δένδρεFον* the *ε* would not pass into *ι*.—Metre: as xviii.

XXIII. Proklos on Hes. *W. D.* 721 (εἰ δὲ κακὸν εἴποις (*v.l.* εἴπῃς), τάχα κ' αὐτὸς μεῖζον ἀκούσαις). Cf. Υ 250 ὁπποῖόν κ' εἴπῃσθα ἔπος, τοῖόν κ' ἐπακούσαις, Eur. *Alk.* 704 εἰ δ' ἡμᾶς κακῶς | ἐρεῖς, ἀκούσῃ πολλὰ κοὐ ψευδῆ κακά, Liban. 2. 84 δρῶντες ἅττα ἐθέλουσι πάσχειν δύναιντ' ἂν ἅττα ἂν οὐκ ἐθέλοιεν, Plaut. *Pseud.* 1156 *contumeliam si dicis audies*, Caecil. 24 *audibis male, si male dicis mihi*, Ter. *Andr.* 920 *si mihi perget quae volt dicere, ea quae non volt audiet.* For the form of the condition, cf. Goodwin *M. T.* 505. **θέλοις**, by assimilation, *ib.* 558, as Mimn. 1. 2. Perhaps we should read *αἰ* Ϝείπῃς or Ϝείποις, to save the Ϝ.—Metre: as xviii.

XXIV. Athen. 14. 627 A: Alkaios, for a poet most devoted to the muses, showed himself overfond of war. Hor. 2. 13. 26 *et te sonantem plenius aureo* | *Alcaee, plectro dura navis,* | *dura fugae mala, dura belli.* | *utrumque* (Sappho and Alc.) *sacro digna silentio* | *mirantur umbrae dicere; sed magis* | *pugnas et exactos tyrannos* | *densum umeris bibit aure volgus*; 4. 9. 7 *Alcaei minaces camenae.* Alkaios' warlike spirit appears in vii., viii., 22, 28, 29, 31. The last line shows that the poem is more than mere "military millinery," though the Lesbian noble, with his aristocratic pride and his Aiolian fondness for display, is far removed from the Dorian, who would have scorned to describe his "arms hung up for monuments." There is a bit of the swaggerer about Alkaios. Bergk inaptly calls the poem a 'fiery summons' to combat. Contrast the impassioned appeals of Tyrtaios and Kallinos. Cf. Longfellow: "This is the Arsenal. From floor to ceiling | Like a huge organ, rise the burnished arms."

1. μαρμαίρει: cf. Ν 801 χαλκῷ μαρμαίροντες (Τρῶες). **Ἄρῃ**: 'in honour of Ares,' not 'by Ares.' Cf. Pind. *Ol.* 6. 68 πατρὶ | ἑορτάν τε κτίσῃ, Xen. *Hell.* 4. 3. 21 ἐκέλευσε στεφανοῦσθαι πάντας τῷ θεῷ, Eur. *Hippol.* 1425 κόραι κόμας κεροῦνταί σοι, Theokr. 7. 3 τᾷ Δηοῖ ἔτευχε Θαλύσια. In vii. we have the form Ἄρευι.

2. The passage is a reminiscence of Λ 41 κρατὶ δ' ἐπ' ἀμφίφαλον (λαμπρόν) κυνέην θέτο τετραφάληρον | ἵππουριν· δεινὸν δὲ λόφος καθύπερθεν ἔνευεν. Cf. Ο 537 ἵππειον λόφον.

3. Cf. Eur. *Andr.* 1123 κρεμαστὰ τεύχη πασσάλων καθαρπάσας. Captured arms were generally suspended on the walls of temples (Aisch. *Agam.* 579; Eur. *Bacch.* 1214, *Herakl.* 695; Hor. 3. 26. 3).

4. κνάμιδες = Ion. κνημῖδες. **ἄρκος**· ἄρκεσμα, βοήθεια, Hesych. Cf. ἤρκεσε θώρηξ Ο 529. Casaubon read ἕρκος (ἕρκος βελέων Ε 316, ἕρκος ἀκόντων Δ 137). ἄρκος is not a dialectal form of ἕρκος. In Frag. 67 Alk. has τῶν χαλίνων ἄρκος. **ἰσχύρω**: cf. κρατερὸν βέλος Ε 104.

5. Cf. λινοθώρηξ B 529. **κούιλαι**=κοϝ-ιλαι (*cav*-us), with ϝ vocalized. The other lines are against reading κόϝιλαι with ⏑ ⏑ in the basis. κοίλος, in Mimn. 12. 6, is a 'distracted' form like ὀμοίιος. Crusius' comparison of such forms as βωμοιοῖσιν=βωμοῖσιν, hymn to Apollo (i.) with musical notes, is not cogent.

6. Chalkis in Euboia was famous for its work in metals. Chalkidian swords are alluded to in Aisch. Frag. 356, αὐτόθακτον Εὐβοικὸν ξίφος. ποτήρια Χαλκιδικά were esteemed (*C.I.A.* 1. 149, Aristoph. *Eq.* 237). Stephanos of Byz. says the σπάθαι are here called Chalkidian διὰ τὸ χαλκουργεῖα πρῶτον ἐν αὐτοῖς (Χαλκιδεῦσι) ὀφθῆναι. **κυπάσσιδες**: ὁ κύπασσις λίνου πεποίητο, σμικρὸς χιτωνίσκος, ἄχρι μέσου μηροῦ, Pollux 7. 60. The ττ of the MSS. represents Ͳ (*sampi*; cf. Rob. *Epigr.* 1. p. 177).

7. ϝέργον Ἄρηος Λ 734. The 'work' of war may be an attack upon the Athenians, who were contending with the Lesbians for the possession of Sigeion in the Troad. More probably the allusion is to the war waged by the aristocratical party against one of the tyrants, Melanchros or Myrsilos. Cf. *Anth. Pal.* 9. 184 καὶ ξίφος Ἀλκαίοιο, τὸ πολλάκις αἷμα τυράννων | ἔσπεισεν, πάτρης θέσμια ῥυόμενον.—Metre: each of the two glyconic cola has a free basis — ⏑ or — >. The first colon ends with a syncopated foot, as in the asynartetes of Archilochos. At the end of the second colon the irrational long marks the *ritardando* before the catalectic trochaic clausula begins. The Greater Alkaic verse was not restricted to warlike songs. It is also sympotic (50, 51).

XXV. Schol. Pind. *Isthm.* 2. 11 (νῦν δ' ἐφίητι (Terpsichore) τὸ τὠργείου φυλάξαι | ῥῆμ' ἀλαθείας ὁδῶν ἄγχιστα βαῖνον, | χρήματα χρήματ' ἀνήρ, ὃς φᾶ κτεάνων θάμα λειφθεὶς καὶ φίλων). Also Diog. Laert. 1. 31. Aristodamos was regarded as one of the Seven Sages. The fragment, whether or not written during Alkaios' exile, expresses the noble's contempt for the rich commoner who, in the course of the sixth century, subverted the power of the aristocracy. For the sentiment cf. Frag. xxix., Hes. *W. D.* 686 χρήματα γὰρ ψυχὴ πέλεται δειλοῖσι βροτοῖσι, Theogn. 181, 697, 699 πλήθει δ' ἀνθρώπων ἀρετὴ μία γίνεται ἥδε, | πλουτεῖν· τῶν δ' ἄλλων οὐδὲν ἄρ' ἦν ὄφελος, 929 εἰ μὲν γὰρ πλουτεῖς, πολλοὶ φίλοι, ἢν δὲ πένηαι, | παῦροι, κοὐκέθ' ὁμῶς αὐτὸς ἀνὴρ ἀγαθός, Pythermos, Pind. *Pyth.* 3. 54, Plato *Rep.* 408 B, Hor. 3. 24. 42, *Sat.* 2. 5. 8, *Epist.* 1. 1. 52, Juv. 3. 164. Michelangelo said 'Men are more than money.' **ἀπάλαμνον**: Theogn. 481 μυθεῖται δ' ἀπάλαμνα. Quotation more or less direct, and usually of gnomic utterances, appears in Hesiod (from the Cyclic poets); in Solon 20 (Mimnermos);

Theogn. 17, 425; in Sim. (see on xxii.); in Polymnastos; in Pind. (*Pyth.* 3. 81, 4. 277, 9. 94; *Nem.* 9. 6; Frag. 216); Bacchyl. ii. 192. Cf. Aisch. *Prom.* 887; Soph. *Antig.* 623.—Metre: as xxiv.

XXVI. Hephaist. 35. **Αἴαν**: accus. from a stem Αἰᾱ-. Alkm. 68 apparently has a nom. Αἶας. Alkaios rarely touches upon the Epic. Unless Aiolic inflected proper nouns in -ευς differently from appellatives, **Ἀχίλλεα** is an Homericism. For the position of Aias, cf. B 768 ff.; Pind. *Nem.* 7. 27; Soph. *Aias*, 1341; Skol. xx.—Metre: basis + three choriambs + a pherecratic (Ἀλκαϊκόν).

XXVII. Hephaist. 34. Cf. Theokr. 17. 36 *τᾷ μὲν* (Berenike) *Κύπρον ἔχοισα Διώνας πότνια κούρα | κόλπον ἐς εὐώδη ῥαδινὰς ἐσεμάξατο χεῖρας.* Stat. *Sil.* 2. 7. 36 *humum per ipsam | primo murmure dulce vagientem | blando Calliope sinu recepit.* *ῥοδόκολπον* Εὐνομίαν Mel. Adesp. xiii. **Κρόκοι**: cf. Κρόκος, a man's name, *B. C. H.* 11. 249. 2. Bergk's Κρίνοι should be Κρίννοι.—Metre: logaoedic hexapody.

XXVIII. Athen. 10. 430 B. Cf. Pind. iv. 16. **ἐρχομένοιο**: the ending -οιο only here in Lesbian poetry. It may be old Aiolic as well as Epic. *ἦρος ἐπερχομένου* Stes. x.; Theogn. 777; *ἦρι ἐπερχ.*, Aristoph. *Nubes* 311.—Metre: five Aiolic dactyls with basis.

XXIX. Stob. 96. 17. Cf. xxv., Tyrt. 10. 8 *χρησμοσύνῃ τ' εἴκων καὶ στυγερῇ πενίῃ*, Theogn. 384 *πενίην μητέρ' ἀμηχανίης*, Hdt. 8. 111 *καὶ θεοὺς δύο ἀχρήστους οὐκ ἐκλείπειν σφέων τὴν νῆσον, ἀλλ' αἰεὶ φιλοχωρεῖν, Πενίην τε καὶ Ἀμηχανίην*, Bacch. 1. 33 *πενία ἀμάχανος.* For the personification, see on Alkm. xxii.—Metre: prob. dact. hexam. Since no — — occurs, the dactyls may be cyclic.

XXX. Aristoph. *Vespae* 1234, schol. *ad loc.* and *ad Thesmoph.* 162. A partisan attack on Pittakos, who had been appointed aisymnetes. **ἔχεται ῥόπας** (gen.): 'its fate hangs in the wavering balance' (*ἐπὶ σμικρᾶς ῥοπῆς*). **μέγα κρέτος**: Λ 753.—Metre: basis + four Aiolic dactyls.

XXXI. Schol. Pind. *Ol.* 1. 60 (97). See on Alkm. xxxi. Anton. Liberal. *Metam.* 36 *Τάνταλον δέ, ἐπεὶ τὸν ὅρκον ἐψεύσατο, κατέβαλε καὶ ἐπῃώρει αὐτῷ ὑπὲρ κεφαλῆς τὸν Σίπυλον.* The *λίθος Ταντάλου* early became proverbial, even in medicine (Hippokr. *de morbis* 2, 482 F). Cf. Pind. *Isthm.* 8. 11. **περ**: see on Sa. 1. 10.—Metre: as xxx., with which this fragment is to be connected.

XXXII. Schol. Plat. *Symp.* 217 E. Cf. xi. Imitated by Theokr. 29. 1 *οἶνος, ὦ φίλε παῖ, λέγεται καὶ ἀλάθεα· | κἄμμε* χρὴ μεθύοντας ἀλαθέας ἔμμεναι. Cf. Hor. *Sat.* 1. 4. 89 *condita cum verax aperit praecordia Liber.* If ἀλάθεα = ἀλάθεια, -εσια has become -εα in Aiolic, a phenomenon that is otherwise unattested, unless μάομαι < μασιομαι is analogous. Hoffmann suggests that ἀλάθεα is neuter plural (Homer ἀληθέα εἰπεῖν, ἀγορεύειν).—Metre: three Aiolic dactyls with basis.

XXXIII. Hephaist. 38. The fragment recalls the tone of the folk-song; cf. Sa. xxxii. Traces of 'objective' lyric in Alkaios are very rare. Imitated by Hor. 3. 12 *miserarum est neque amori dare ludum neque dulci*, the only occasion on which the Roman poet used ionics. The Romans were not fond of this measure, either because it proved too difficult or because it did not yield an agreeable result. The poem was composed in strophes consisting of ten feet, without hiatus or syllaba anceps. Some would arrange in 2 tetram. + 1 dim., others 2 dim. + 3 trim., and still others 2 trim. + 1 tetram. But essentially the whole strophe was one long verse. Cf. Bentley on Hor. 3. 12. From the same poem we have the fragments: ἔπετον Κυπρογενήας παλάμαισιν (60) and τερένας ἄνθος ὀπώρας (61).

XXXIV. Hephaist. 18. A serenade (κῶμος, cf Aristoph. *Ekkles.* 960). Flach thinks the poem is addressed to Sappho. There is nothing to prove this. Hermesianax, who says (47) Λέσβιος Ἀλκαῖος δὲ πόσους ἀνεδείξατο κώμους | Σαπφοῦς φορμίζων ἱμερόεντα γάμον, was just the person to twist the fragment out of its original application. λίσσομαι is followed by δέξαι in Pind. viii., and also by the imperative, as in Pind. *Ol.* 12. 1, *Pyth.* 1. 71. The anaphora recalls folk-song. See on Sa. xxxvi., and cf. Hor. 4. 1. 2 *precor precor.*—Metre: iambic tetrameter.

SAPPHO.

'Sappho,' said Strabo, writing in the age of Augustus, 'is a marvel; in all history you will find no woman who can challenge comparison with her even in the slightest degree.' Of her life we know virtually nothing. She was a contemporary of Alkaios—whether older or younger is uncertain—and she was born at Eresos in Lesbos of noble parents, Skamandronymos and Kleïs. Local forms of her name are Psapha and Psapho. One of her brothers, Larichos, held the high office of cup-bearer in the prytaneion at Mytilene. Her husband's name is unknown; her daughter bore the name of the poetess' mother. She lived at Mytilene until she was exiled together with Alkaios and other members of the oligarchical faction. Whether she returned to Lesbos, like Alkaios, or died in exile, perhaps in Sicily, cannot be discovered. Romance and contumely fill out the picture. Romance makes her seek refuge from the pangs of despised love by the death-leap from the Leukadian cliff—

> Where yonder cliff rears high its crest in air,
> White glittering o'er the distant wave,
> There Sappho, headlong, in a briny grave
> Entombed with frantic plunge her grief and her despair.

The story of Sappho's death, like that of her love for Phaon, to which it is merely a pendant, resolves itself into the thin air of legend. Phaon is a creation of the popular fancy, like Glaukos, the sea-god. The ferryman of Aphrodite, he receives from the goddess the gift of a beauty that no woman can resist, but is condemned to remain for ever insensible to passion. If Sappho, whose poetry with all its art is at times akin to the folk-song, did but recount the tale of Phaon, *Dichtung*, ever mightier than *Wahrheit* to the Greeks, would associate her, the poetess of love, with him, the object of fruitless love. The Leukadian rock typifies the last act of hopeless passion. Stesichoros, Sappho's contemporary, sang of the nymph Kalyke, who sought death from the cliff because of unrequited love, but Anakreon (ix.) shows that the leap had become a mere figure for the intoxication of love. Originally associated with expiatory sacrifices, the "far projected rock of woe" had at an early time become fixed in popular fancy as the resort of unhappy lovers. Aphrodite supplants Apollo.

Contumely made of Sappho a courtesan. The writers of the middle and the new comedy, misled in part by equivocal expressions (see Frag. vi.), but still more because they were unable to comprehend the free and rich life of noble Aiolian women whose honour was unimpeached, and because they confounded the 'emancipation' of women with licence and the noble simplicity of love with the effrontery of the vile, succeeded in fixing upon her a character that pervades all succeeding classical literature. They it is who are ultimately responsible for Chamaileon the scandal-monger, who set down as sober truth the scurrility of gossip which was fostered by the aspersions of the comic stage. If their vilification defiled the Alexandrian sources from which Ovid drew the materials for his *Epistle*, this partial excuse for Roman *brutalité* will not palliate the misconceptions of Louys' *Bilitis* at the present day. At least six writers of comedy produced a *Sappho*, not to speak of Plato's and Antiphanes' *Phaon* and Menander's *Leukadia*. The problem fascinated these students of manners, of love and intrigue: the poetess of love—what could she be but another Aspasia from across the sea? Athenian women of breeding must follow Perikles' advice (Thuk. 2. 45). Alkaios was called her lover; so too Archilochos, though he died long before the birth of Sappho; so too the freezing beggar Hipponax, and the gay trifler Anakreon, who were children when Sappho was past her prime.

But some of the Greeks, the race in whom morality merges its outlines with the beautiful, were forced to disengage from the fictitious Sappho the poetess who had been called the 'pure' by Alkaios, whose image had been stamped on their coins by her fellow-citizens (a like honour was accorded to Stesichoros, but also, it must be confessed, to Anakreon), and whose house (the μοισόπολος οἰκία of Frag. xli.) was the home of girls who came from far and wide to acquire proficiency in music and song.

The only authentic source of a true conception of Sappho's position is the fragments of her poetry, βαιὰ μέν, ἀλλὰ ῥόδα. She gave instruction that would qualify her pupils to appear in festivals sacred to the gods, for, apart from the partheneia, there was no lack of occasions when women's song was esteemed in Greece (cf. Pind. *Pyth.* 2. 19). It is the relation in which Sappho stood to her pupils that determined the character of her verse. Her pupils were more than mere scholars in music, poetry, the graces of mind and heart; they were bound to her by an affection in which the older felt for the younger a love that is almost masculine in its nature. The Spartan clubs or coteries of women, with their ἀῖται ('beloved,' Alkm. 125), are not so exact or instructive a parallel as the relation between Sokrates and his band of devoted youths (Max. Tyr. 24). Sappho followed with her songs the life of her girl friends until the day of parting came, when she composed their bridal ode.

If the appreciation, by the same sex, of the beauty of man or woman demands the highest degree of purely artistic sensibility, Sappho's passion for her pupils is in one sense the key-note of her artistic nature. We may reject as ill-attested the statement that she herself was 'small and dark,' and therefore not beautiful according to Greek ideas; certain it is, however, that Aiolis was the land of fair women, and that contests of beauty (καλλιστεῖα) were held in the temple of Hera in Lesbos. Love of the beautiful in nature or in man easily assumes in a poet, and that a woman, the form of passion. The vividness, the tumultuousness of Sappho, her perfect sincerity, renders her for ever to us an aesthetical, a psychological enigma. To interpret her, we need more than the master-key of the poet: we need the trembling sensitiveness of the Aiolian. Sappho stands alone in the ancient and the modern world for the utter naturalness with which her passion finds graceful and dignified expression. To the sincerity and immediateness of her verbal economy there is no hesitation; as there is no departure from a taste that admits of no grossness or profanation. Her speech is 'mingled with fire,' as Plutarch says, but her utterance never loses its grandeur, sweetness, and delicacy. 'I love delicacy,' she says, 'and for me love has the sun's splendour and beauty.' Narrower in her range than Alkaios, her insight is deeper. The ardour of Alkaios for war, and adventure, and the revel, she concentrates upon a single theme.

> All thoughts, all passions, all delights,
> Whatever stirs this mortal frame,
> All are but ministers of Love,
> And feed his sacred flame.

The centre and periphery of her existence is love. No note of patriotism: Aphrodite alone dwells in Olympos. If Sappho suffers from excess of love, it is because her gift is from the gods, who couple joy with pain. Sappho is thoroughly womanly withal. She is not above jealousy of her rivals, Andromeda and Gorgo. She scorns those who have no share in the roses of Pieria.

Sappho's style is a combination of extremes. She couples intensity with grace, vehemence with sweetness; she is distinguished alike by simplicity and elegance, passion and sobriety, lucidity and depth. She has the opulence of the Aiolian, though she is not overfond of metaphor. Her expression is vigorous, often rapid, but it always preserves its melody. Her very adjectives, one might say with Turgenieff, are a guide to her life: she is no less a worshipper of the beauty of the external world than of human loveliness. Sappho's verse-technique is of extraordinary variety, and displays sensitiveness alike to form and sound. Possibly she uses more metres than any other poet. She introduced the Mixo-lydian mood, which was adapted for lament, and perhaps employed in the Adonis-songs. By universal consent she was regarded as the greatest love-poet of Greece. She bore the title of 'The Poetess,' as Homer was 'The Poet,' and Plato called her the 'Tenth Muse.' We hear of nine books of her poems, which were probably arranged according to the metres. Her dialect is the pure Aiolic of Lesbos. In many places she adopts Homeric words and phrases.

I. Dion. Hal. *de comp. verb.* 23: cited as an example of the smooth style, which was adopted also by Hesiod, Anakreon, Simonides, Euripides, and Isokrates. The melody and grace of Sappho's poem arise, Dionysios says, from the connection of the words and verses, and from the smoothness of the composition. In this ode Sappho implores Aphrodite to aid her in winning the love of a woman who had requited her affection with coldness.

1. ποικιλόθρον': found only here. Pindar uses *εὔθρονος* of Aphr., *Isthm.* 2. 5 (a more stately but less individual epithet than *ποικ.*), of Kleio, the Horai at Delphi (cf. Jebb *J. H. S.* 3. 1. 117), the daughters of Kadmos (the only mortals that have thrones), and *ἀγλαόθρονος, ὁμόθρονος, χρυσόθρονος* (Homer); *λιπαρόθρονος* Adesp. xiii. 9, of Justice and Peace. Cf. Aisch. *Eum.* 806. The Greek does not personify like the modern ("The seat, where love is throned," *Twelfth Night*). It is possible that the epithet *ποικ.* is derived from a sculptured work. Though Welcker urged that a throne inlaid with precious metals presupposes too advanced a stage of art for the early sixth century at Mytilene, it is to be remembered that as early of Homer we hear of stained and coloured ivory, and facing slabs of marble in various colours. On the chest of Kypselos gold, ivory, and cedar were used. Pausanias mentions a *seated* Morpho at Sparta, and the statue by Kanachos (3. 15. 10; 2. 10. 5). See Müller-Wieseler *Denkm. alt. Kunst* 2. pl. 24, Nos. 257, 258 A; Klein *Griech. Vasen* p. 136, No. 2. Wustemann (*R. M.* 23. 238) comparing θρόνα ποικίλα X 441, regarded 'Αφρ. ποικ. as 'Αφρ. ῎Ανθεια. The form ποικιλόφρον' is not Aiolic for -θρον'; nor is Swinburne's "Thou of divers-coloured mind" in place here. **'Αφρόδιτᾰ**: with Aiolic shortening.

2. δολόπλοκε: first used by Sa. Cf. Mel. Adesp. 129 δολοπλόκας Κυπρογενέος; Theogn. 1386; Aphr. is δολόμητις Sim. 43; δολιόφρων Eur. *I. A.* 1301; δόλιος Bacch. ix. 116. **λίσσομαι** takes, besides the accus. of the person supplicated, the content of the supplication in the direct form (as here) or in the direct form (inf. etc.). The content of the supplication may be represented by a pronoun (β 210).

3. ὀνίαισι: ἀνιάω of the pain of love, Theokr. 2. 23; ῎Ερως ἀνιηρέ 2. 55. **δάμνα**: cf. Hes. *Theogon.* 122 (῎Ερος) δάμναται ἐν στήθεσσι νόον. δάμνα is from δάμνᾱμι.

4. θῦμον after με: the σχῆμα καθ' ὅλον καὶ μέρος as in μ' ἔρως φρένας ἀμφεκάλυψεν Γ 442; cf. Sa. viii. 3.

5. τυῖδ' ἔλθ'=δεῦρ' ἔλθ' Aristoph. *Eq.* 559. So εἴ ποτε . . . ἔλθετε καὶ νῦν Soph. *O. T.* 165 (cf. below, l. 25). In such prayers οὕτως suits the apodosis; here ἀλλά, because of l. 3.

6. αἴοισα: aorist in form as ἔκλυες (cf. ζ 185). Both verbs may be aoristic in sense here. Hes. *W. D.* 9 has κλῦθι ἰδὼν αἴων τε, cf. ω 48 ἦλθε . . . ἀγγελίης ἀίουσα with Λ 603 ἀκούσας ἔκμολεν. ἀίω is used of immediate, physical hearing (cf. Alk. xxviii.), whereas κλύω implies intent, obedience to the call: δ 505 τοῦ . . . ἔκλυεν αὐδήσαντος. Cf. ὑπακούω ii. 4. So εὐχομένων ἐπακούσατε Mel. Adesp. xiii.; Anakr. ii. 5. Cf. Pind. *Isthm.* 6. 42 ὁ δ' . . . αὔδασε . . . εἴ ποτ' ἐμᾶν, ὦ Ζεῦ πάτερ, | θυμῷ θέλων ἀρᾶν ἄκουσας, | νῦν σε, νῦν εὐχαῖς ὑπὸ θεσπεσίαις | λίσσομαι. Aisch. *Eum.* 297 κλύει καὶ πρόσωθεν ὢν θεός.

8. χρύσιον might go with ἄρμ' (χρυσάνιος 'Αφρ., Soph. *O. K.* 692), but the Adonic belongs to the third colon. In Sa. Frag. 84 δεῦρο δηῦτε Μοῖσαι, χρύσιον λίποισαι, the adj. seems to be used as here. Cf. *Orphic Hymn* 40. 14 δρακοντείοισιν ὑποζεύξασα χαλινοῖς (of Demeter).

9. ἆγον: the imperfect marks the process that culminates in ἐξίκοντο. The imperfect of ἄγω is often preferred to the aorist (cf. Thuk., Xen.).

10. ὤκεες: *ὠκύς*, *celer*, generally of inherent, as *θοός*, *velox*, of actual speed. But cf. Mimn. 12. 9. Contrasted with *ταχύς*, *ὠκύς* has the goal in view. **στροῦθοι**: many animals and birds that have numerous offspring are sacred to Aphrodite. Cf. Hor. 3. 28. 14 *quae Cnidon | fulgentisque tenet Cycladas, et Paphium | iunctis visit oloribus*, and 4. 1. 10. **περί**: the poetical gen. with *περί*, 'over,' is almost extinct: ε 68 *ἡ δ' αὐτοῦ τετάνυστο περὶ σπείους γλαφυροῖο | ἡμερὶς ἡβώωσα*, ε 130 *τὸν μὲν ἐγὼν ἐσάωσα περὶ τρόπιος βεβαῶτα*. With Alk. xxxi. *κεῖσθαι περ κεφάλας*, contrast Archil. *ὑπέρ* (53), also in reference to the rock of Tantalos. Eur. *Troad.* 816 is doubtful. Monro, *H. G.* § 188, 2, thinks the gen. may be akin to the partitive gen. of place.

The idea 'over,' 'above' appears in *περίειμι*, *περιγίγνομαι*, *περὶ πάντων* δ 231, in *πέρροχος* Sa. 92=*ὑπείροχος* in Hom. Cf. Alk. iv. 6, xxiv. 4. In the allied Thessalian dialect *περ*=*ὑπέρ* in *ὀνέθεικε περ τοῖ παιδός* (*ἀνέθηκε περὶ τοῦ π.*) *S. G. D-I.* 346, *περ γᾶς τᾶσδε ἀριστεύων* Roberts, *Epigr.* 1. 237. (*ἀμύνομαι περί* Thuk. 2. 39. 2.) In the orators *περί* and *ὑπέρ* often interchange, but the syntactical substitution does not reproduce a common original form. Skt. *upári* is=*ὑπέρ*; *pári*=*περί* is not to be derived from *upári*.

μελαίνας: see on Alkm. xxi. 3. After the Hom. epithet we have an Homeric reminiscence (*ἐπιδινηθέντε τιναξάσθην πτερὰ πυκνά* β 151).

11. πύκνα πτέρα: Λ 454, Ψ 879, *densis alis* Verg. *Georg.* 1. 382. **δίννεντες**: from **δῖνϝημι*=Attic *δινέω*. **ὠράνω αἴθερος**: a bold case of synizesis. Hoffmann writes *ὠρανῶιθερος*. Cf. Τ 351 *οὐρανοῦ . . . δι' αἰθέρος*. Pindar has the masc. *αἰθήρ* in two Dorian, the Hom. femin. in two Aiolian odes.

13. *αἶψα δ' ἵκοντο* Σ 532; cf. Ζ 514 *ταχέες δὲ πόδες φέρον. αἶψα δ' ἔπειτα | . . . ἔτετμεν*. *ἐξ* of the attainment of the goal.

14. *φιλομμειδὴς* 'Αφρ. Γ 424, *ἡδὺ γελοιήσασα φιλομ.* 'Αφρ. *Hymn* 4. 49, *ἐφιμερτῷ δὲ προσώπῳ αἰεὶ μειδιάει Hymn* 10. 2, *Erycina ridens* Hor. 1. 2. 33.

15. Cf. Theokr. 1. 77 *ἦνθ' Ἑρμῆς πράτιστος ἀπ' ὤρεος, εἶπε δέ· Δάφνι, | τίς τυ κατατρύχει, τίνος, ὠγαθέ, τόσσον ἐρᾶσαι;* **δηὖτε**: see on Alkm. xiii.

17. κὤττι: *ι* is pronounced as *y* with the foll. vowel. See on Anakr. viii.

18–19. Πείθω | *λαῖς ἄγην ἐς σάν* Seidler (*μαῖς* Bergk), *πείθω- | μαι σ'* (*σοι*) *ἄγην* Blass. The active *μάω* does not occur elsewhere (*μάομαι* Sa. 23, *μαιόμενος* Alk. xxx.). Blass' *σ*(*οι*) is harsh since *σάν* follows. The word-breaking in *πείθω-μαι*, though elsewhere unknown in the second pentapody, might be defended by the elision in Catullus 11. 22, Hor. 2. 2. 18, 16. 34, 4. 2. 22. On Peitho, see Ibyk. v.

20. Ψάπφ' may stand either for Ψάπφοι (so 59, Σάπφοι Alk. xiii.), or for Ψάπφα; cf. Γύριννα = Γυρίννω. On coins of Mytilene we find Σαπφώ, Σαφφώ, Ψαπφώ, in Cretan Φσαφώ, etc. The word is a certain case of the otherwise disputed change of ψ and σ (ψάμαθος, Ἀμαθῷ, ἄμαθος). πσαπφώ lost its π by dissimilation because of πφ. For the use of her own name, cf. Catull. 51. 13.

21. With exquisite delicacy Sappho puts into the mouth of the Queen of Love the wishes of her own heart. Love's pain is known without the telling. Cf. Theokr. 6. 17 καὶ φεύγει φιλέοντα καὶ οὐ φιλέοντα διώκει, 11. 75 τί τὸν φεύγοντα διώκεις; Hiller thought there was a proverb νήπιος ὃς φιλέοντα φυγὼν φεύγοντα διώκει. Cf. Kallim. epigr. 33. 5, Hor. *Sat.* 1. 2. 108, Ter. *Eun.* 4. 7. 43, "They flie from me, that sometime did me seek," Wyatt.

22. With the repetition of αἰ and ταχέως, cf. that of *otium* in Hor. 2. 16, Catull. 51. **ἀλλά** (Goodwin *M. T.* 512) emphasizes more vigorously than δέ the opposition of the apodosis to the protasis. So A 82, Θ 154, Soph. Frag. 854 εἰ σῶμα δοῦλον, ἀλλ' ὁ νοῦς ἐλεύθερος, Deinarch. 2. 15 εἰ μὴ πάντα, ἀλλὰ πολλά γε ἴστε; cf. *si—at certe.*

23. The φιλήματα follow the φιλότας. φιλέω has replaced the Hom. κύσω.

24. Blomfield's ἐθέλοισαν was strenuously defended by Welcker, *R. M.* 11. 266, who held that the subject of φιλήσει was a man. No MS. whose readings were known before 1892 settled the dispute. Now Piccolomini's *VL* show ἐθέλουσα (*Hermes* 27).

27. ἰμμέρρει = ἱμείρει, from *ἴσμερ-ιω. **τέλεσον**: metrical convenience dictates the choice of the σ or the σσ form. τέλεσσαι is Epic and Aiolic.

28. σύμμαχος: cf. Ovid *Am.* 1. 9. 1 *militat omnis amans, et habet sua castra Cupido.*—Metre: logaoedic (three Lesser Sapphics and an Adonic).

II. Longinos *de sublim.* 10: the sublime appears in the selection of the most striking circumstances and in the power of combining them into one animate whole. After citing the ode, Long. says: 'Are you not astonished how at the same time her soul, body, ears, tongue, sight, colour, all vanish and disappear as completely as if they were not her own? She experiences contradictory sensations—at one and the same moment she freezes, burns, raves, reasons; so that it is not a single passion that is here set forth, but a congress of passions.' The ode is a pathological picture of the tumultuous passion experienced by Sappho in the presence of a woman she loves (τῆς ἐρωμένης ἐπιφανείσης Plut. *Amator.* 18, p. 763 A). It is not an expression of jealousy. It remains to this day the undying type of the passion of love that consumes the body. Sappho never describes woman's beauty: she shows only its effect as Homer shows the effect of Helen's loveliness.

The poem was translated by Catullus (51) with additions, omissions, and other modifications. The fourth stanza is original with the Latin poet.

Ille mi par esse deo videtur, | *ille, si fas est, superare divos,* | *qui sedens adversus identidem te* | *spectat et audit* | *dulce ridentem, misero quod omnis* | *eripit sensus mihi: nam simul te,* | *Lesbia, adspexi, nihil est super mi* | —⏑⏑ —⏓ | *lingua sed torpet, tenuis sub artus* | *flamma demanat, sonitu suopte* | *tintinant aures, gemina teguntur* | *lumina nocte.*

Imitations are frequent: Theokr. 2. 106 ff. πᾶσα μὲν ἐψύχθην χιόνος πλέον, ἐν δὲ μετώπῳ | ἱδρώς μευ κοχύδεσκεν ἶσον νοτίαισιν ἐέρσαις, | οὐδέ τι φωνᾶσαι δυνάμαν, οὐδ' ὅσσον ἐν ὕπνῳ | κνυζεῦνται φωνεῦντα φίλαν ποτὶ ματέρα τέκνα· | ἀλλ' ἐπάγην δαγῦδι καλὸν χρόα πάντοθεν ἶσα. So Apoll. Rhod. *Argon.* 3. 962 ff. ἐκ δ' ἄρα οἱ κραδίη στηθέων πέσεν, ὄμματα δ' αὔτως | ἤχλυσαν· θερμὸν δὲ παρηΐδας εἷλεν ἔρευθος. | γούνατα δ' οὔτ' ὀπίσω οὔτε προπάροιθεν ἀεῖραι | ἔσθενεν, ἀλλ' ὑπένερθε πάγη πόδας. Lucr. 3. 152 ff. transferred to fear the symptoms of love (cf. ἔφριξ' ἔρωτι Soph. *Aias* 693): *verum ubi vementi magis est commota metu mens,* | *consentire animam totam per membra videmus* | *sudoresque ita palloremque existere toto* | *corpore et infringi linguam vocemque aboriri,* | *caligare oculos, sonere auris, succidere artus.* Cf. also Valerius Aedituus in Gellius 19. 9, Racine, 'Phèdre' 1. 3, *Je le vis, je rougis, je palis à sa vue;* | *Un trouble s'éleva dans mon âme éperdue;* | *Mes yeux ne voyaient plus, je ne pouvais parler,* | *Je sentis tout mon corps et transir et brûler.* Euripides would seem to have had the ode in mind when he describes the passion of Phaidra in the *Hippolytos.* In his *Life of Demetrios* 38, Plutarch borrows from Sappho the description of Antiochos' love for Stratonike (cf. Lucian *Syria dea* 17). In words that recall Sappho's sensations at the sight of human beauty, Plato in the *Phaidros* 251 A describes the effect of divine beauty upon him who has been recently initiated and has thus become the spectator of the glories of the other world: πρῶτον μὲν ἔφριξε . . . ἰδόντα δὲ αὐτόν, οἷον ἐκ τῆς φρίκης, μεταβολή τε καὶ ἱδρὼς καὶ θερμότης ἀήθης λαμβάνει. We may also compare, though the intent and situation are radically different, a passage (§ 13) in the temptation of Buddha by the *Dhītaro* (daughters): 'For if with this temptation they draw near an ascetic or Brahmin whose heart is not free from desire, then his heart will break, or madness and frenzy will seize upon him, or, as a green reed that has been cut dries up, is parched, withers away, so will he dry up, become parched, and wither away.' The Modern Greek poet Soutsos in his Βάσανος has imitated this ode of Sappho.

1. ἴσος θέοισιν: cf. Eur. *El.* 67 ἐγώ σ' ἴσον θεοῖσιν ἡγοῦμαι φίλον, *Hek.* 356; *sum deus* Plaut. *Curc.* 167.

2. ὄττις: the demonstrative antecedent κῆνος is shown to be indefinite by the use of ὄστις, which, itself generic and qualitative ('such an one as'), does not need the support of the generic subjunctive; Goodwin *M. T.* 534. Cf. *quisquis* with indic. κῆνος is therefore not a rival of Sappho, but a creation of her fancy, perhaps the man who may win her lovely scholar. Cf. Eur. *Hippol.* 943 τόνδ', ὄστις κ.τ.λ., *talis vir qui.* The reference is often to a definite antecedent with causal force. ὄστις defines or explains (see Herm. pref. to Soph. *O. T.*). κεῖνος . . . ὄστις as οὗτος . . . ὄστις β 124 (=τοιοῦτος οἷος), Eur. *Alk.* 76, 620. Cf. ὅς followed by ὄστις Anakr. 94. Homer has after κεῖνος ὅς the generic indic. (ξ 156) or the generic subj. (I 312). The generic condition has the ordinary form (without κεν) in Sa. 12 ὄττινας γὰρ εὖ θέω, κῆνοί με σίννονται.

Aiolic has not here, like Ionic in places, displaced the simple by the compound relative: Hdt. 6. 47 τὴν νῆσον ταύτην, ἥτις, Bechtel *Ion. Inschr.* 240. 43 γῆν, ἥτις ἦν Κακρᾶδος, Thuk. 6. 3 βωμόν, ὅστις νῦν ἔξω τῆς πόλεώς ἐστι, which is due to an Ionic model, Antiochos of Syracuse. Cf. the displacement in ἐξ ὅτου for ἐξ οὗ, and ὁπότε for ὅτε in Pindar.

3. φωνείσας: from φώνημι.

4. Cf. *dulce ridentem Lalagen amabo,* | *dulce loquentem* Hor. 1. 22. 23, εὔλαλον Ἡλιοδώραν *Anth. Pal.* 5. 155, εὐδαίμων ὁ βλέπων σε· τρισόλβιος ὄστις ἀκούει· | ἡμίθεος δ' ὁ φιλῶν. ἀθάνατος δ' ὁ γαμῶν *ib.* 5. 94. **ὐπακούει**: *attente et cum silentio audit* (Weiske). So ἐπακούσω Theokr. 11. 78; cf. Lucian *Amor.* 46 ἀλλ' ἐμοὶ μὲν βίος εἴη διηνεκὴς οὗτος, ἀπαντικρὺ τοῦ φίλου καθέζεσθαι, καὶ πλησίον ἡδὺ λαλοῦντος ἀκούειν, *ib.* 53.

5. Cf. δακρυόεν γελάσασα Z 484. With γελαίσας supply αἰσθάνεται from ὑπακούει. Cf. ι 167, Aisch. *Prom.* 21. The zeugma is different in Catull. **τό**: *i.e.* τὸ ἡδὺ φωνεῖν καὶ ἱμερόεν γελᾶν. Ahrens conj. τὸ δὴ 'μαν.

6. καρδίαν ἐν. στήθεσι: so κραδίη ἐν στήθεσσιν δ 548. **ἐπτόασεν**: gnomic aorist. Cf. χ 298 φρένες ἐπτοίηθεν, Eur. *I. A.* 587 ἔρωτι ἐπτοάθης, Apoll. Rhod. 1. 1232 τῆς δὲ φρένας ἐπτοίησεν Κύπρις. Also of fear, Aisch. *Prom.* 856. Mimn. 5. 2 has πτοιῶμαι δ' ἐσορῶν ἄνθος ὁμηλικίης. Robortello conj. στήθεσ' ἐπεπτόασεν. Dion. Hal. praises the euphony of

Sappho's style in its treatment of vowels and consonants. It will be noted that each word in this line ends with *ν*.

7. Of the numerous conjectures, that of Ahrens requires only a slight change, and is here adopted. Hermann, Seidler, Blass *ὡς γὰρ εἰσίδω*. Bergk's *εὔιδον* is incorrect. **βροχέως**: *συντόμως*. *Αἰολεῖς* Hesych., from this passage. Some take the adverb with *Fίδω*, others with the last clause. Love, like Fancy, is "engender'd in the eyes, with gazing fed"; *amor, ut lacrima, ab oculis oritur, in pectus cadit*, Publ. Syrus 40. Fick suggests *βρόχεος* 'throat' (gen. of source) and Westphal supplied in Catull. v. 8 *gutture vocis* (cf. *vox faucibus haesit*). *βρόχος* is unattested in this meaning, but might be inferred from *δ* 222, *μ* 240. **ὡς** with subj. = *ὅταν* is rare; cf. Hdt. 1. 132, 4. 172 (without *ἄν*).—**8**. **εἴκει** (Dor. Phok. *εἴκω*): *ἰκ-νέομαι* shows the weak form of the root. The radical in *ἥκω* is different.

9. **Fέαγε**: whether Sa. said *FέFαγε* is uncertain. Cf. *torpebat vox spiritusque* Livy i. 25. Note the elision at the verse-end.

11. Cf. Archil. 103 *τοῖος γὰρ φιλότητος ἔρως ὑπὸ καρδίην ἐλυσθεὶς | πολλὴν κατ' ἀχλὺν ὀμμάτων ἔχευεν | κλέψας ἐκ στηθέων ἁπαλὰς φρένας*, Ernst Schulze *Aber wenn du nah gekommen | Kann ich doch dich nimmer sehn, | Weil vor Freud' und Schmerz und Zagen | Mir die Augen übergehn.* **ἐπιρρόμβεισι**: only here. Hesych. has *ῥόμβος· ψόφος, ἦχος*. Hence not *vertigine aures rotantur!* (Neue). Cf. *Anth. Pal.* 5. 212, *αἰεί μοι δύνει μὲν ἐν οὔασιν ἦχος Ἔρωτος*. Ringing in the ears was generally regarded as a sign to a lover that his absent mistress was thinking of him (Ellis on Catull. 51. 11). Bergk conj. *ἐπιβρόμεισι*, because of Apoll. Rhod. 4. 908 *ἐπιβρομέωνται ἀκουαί*. Others *ἐπιβομβεῦσιν* (*ἐβόμβει τὰ ὦτα* Lucian, *Dial. Meretr.* 9. 2).

13. **ἀ δέ μ' ἴδρως**: *ἰδρώς* is said to be fem. in Aiolic (*Anecd. Ox.* 1. 208. 13), and the statement is probably derived from this passage. Bergk's *μίδρως* is impossible as *F* (**σFιδρως sudor*) does not become *μ*. If *μ'* is correct, cf. *μ(οι)* Z 165, Sa. i. 20, and Mimn. 5. 1 *αὐτίκα μοι κατὰ μὲν χροιὴν ῥέει ἄσπετος ἰδρώς*. If *ἰδρώς* retained its *F*, *μ'* may be a stop-gap. The article is singular from the Attic point of view. Ahrens' *καδ δέ μ'* is objectionable because of *κακχέεται*. Cf. Prop. 3. 22. 12.

14. **παῖσαν** = *ὅλην*; cf. Theokr. 2. 106. . **ἄγρει**: *ἀγρέω* is Aiolic and Ionic (Archil. 4. 3); cf. *ἐφαγγρένθειν* (= *ἐφαιροῦνται*) in Thessalian. It is not a by-form of *αἱρέω* but derived from *ἄγρα*. **χλωροτέρα**: cf. Longos *Pastor.* 1. 17 *χλωρότερον τὸ πρόσωπον ἦν πόας θερινῆς*, so K 376 *χλωρὸς ὑπαὶ δείους*. Cf. the use of *ξηρός*. George Eliot has "withered paleness."

15. ἐπιδεύην = ἐπιδεύεσθαι, only here. Herm. conj. ἐπιδεύης. Longinos says παρ' ὀλίγον τέθνηκεν. The phrase is μικροῦ δέω, not ὀλίγου δέω.

16. ἄλλα: ἄλλος from *ἄλιος = ἠλός O 128. ἠλεὲ φρένας β 243 is a fuller form. In Ψ 698 for ἄλλο φρονέοντα Fick writes ἆλλο. The words that follow in Longinos: παντόλματον ἐπεὶ καὶ πένητα (before οὐ θαυμάζεις) have been taken by some as Sappho's, though no satisfactory sense has ever been extracted from them. Probably they are a part of Longinos' statement. Hersel *Philol.* 133. 535 emends to πᾶν τὸ ᾀσμάτιον ἐπεῖπον ἵνα καὶ σὺ θαυμάζοις, Müller *Berl. Phil. Wochenschr.* 1890, p. 1066 πᾶν ⟨τὸ⟩ ποιημάτιον ἔπειτα καὶ ⟨τὴν⟩ ποιήτριαν, Bergk suggested ἐπεῖπον· εἶτα οὐ θαυμάζεις.

III. Eust. *Il.* 729. 20, Cramer *Anecd. Par.* 3. 233. 31.—**1.** Cf. Θ 555 ὡς δ' ὅτ' ἐν οὐρανῷ ἄστρα φαεινὴν ἀμφὶ σελήνην | φαίνετ' ἀριπρεπέα, X 28, 317, Pind. *Isthm.* 4. 24 'Αωσφόρος θαητὸς ὣς ἄστροις ἐν ἄλλοις, Milton *Lycidas* 168, Petron. 89 *iam plena Phoebe candidum extulerat iubar | minora ducens astra radianti face.*—**2. ἄψ** (Bergk αἶψ') may stand if we picture the moon obscured for a moment by fleeting clouds.—**3. πλήθοισα**: Σ 484 σελήνην πλήθουσαν. For μάλιστα Ahrens suggested κάλιστα.—**4.** Neue supplied ἐπὶ παῖσαν from Θ 1 ἠὼς μὲν κροκόπεπλος ἐκίδνατο πᾶσαν ἐπ' αἶαν (cf. Eur. *Ion* 83 ἥλιος ἤδη λάμπει κατὰ γῆν, | ἄστρα δὲ φεύγει πῦρ τόδ' ἀπ' αἰθέρος). This suits the usual intransitive use of λάμπω. The object of the transitive verb must have an inherent radiance of its own. If μέν in l. 1 indicates a comparison of the moon with some Lesbian beauty, the parallel in Hor. 1. 12. 45 is the more apposite: *micat inter omnes | Iulium sidus velut inter ignes | luna minores.* So Hes. Frag. 83. 4 Θηρώ τ' εὐειδῆ, ἰκέλην φάεσσι σελήνης, Wotton *Elizabeth of Bohemia*, "You meaner beauties of the night, | Which poorly satisfy our eyes | More by your number than your light, | You common people of the skies, | What are you, when the Moon shall rise?" Milton's "At whose sight all the stars | Hide their diminished heads." See on Alkm. iv. 41 and cf. Bacch. iv. 29. Sappho called the moon ἀργυρία in this poem (Julian *Epist.* 19).

IV. Hermog. περὶ ἰδεῶν 2. 4 (*Rhet. Gr.* 3. 315 Walz).—**1.** Neue deleted ὕδωρ as a gloss and took ψῦχρον κελ. = ψυχρὸς κέλαδος. Sa. seems to have in mind ρ 209 κατὰ δὲ ψυχρὸν ῥέεν ὕδωρ | ὑψόθεν ἐκ πέτρης.—**2. ὔψοθεν** is suggested by Theokr. 1. 8 καταλείβεται ὑψόθεν ὕδωρ, cf. v. 33 ψυχρὸν ὕδωρ τουτεῖ καταλείβεται. ἠρέμα might be supplied from Lucian *Philop.* 3 τό τε ὕδωρ ἠρ. κελαρύζον τὰς ψυχὰς καταθέλξειε. **κελάδει** of water Σ 576.—**4. καταρρεῖ**: κατά for κατ is objectionable since in no poem that is certainly Sapphic do we find the full form of the prep. (xix., xxxv. are doubtful). The suspicious contraction in *ῥέω* Gerstenhauer thinks is borrowed from Ionic. It occurs in Erin. ii. Ahrens began a pentapody with *κῶμα καρρέει. κατάγρει* (Bergk, Meister) demands an object. Hom. has *κῶμα κάλυψεν σ* 201. Bergk thought Sappho was describing the garden of the nymphs, a subject that Demetrios *de eloc.* 132 says was a favourite with her. See on Ibyk. i. and cf. Theokr. 7. 136 *τὸ δ' ἐγγύθεν ἱερὸν ὕδωρ* | *Νυμφᾶν ἐξ ἄντροιο κατειβόμενον κελάρυζε.* With the fragment, cf. [Plato] 25: *ὑψίκομον παρὰ τάνδε καθίζεο φωνήεσσαν* | *φρίσσουσαν πυκνοῖς κῶνον ὑπὸ ζεφύροις,* | *καί σοι καχλάζουσιν ἐμοῖς παρὰ νάμασι σύριγξ* | *θελγομένῳ στάξει κῶμα κατὰ βλεφάρων,* Soph. *Phil.* 18 *ἐν θέρει δ' ὕπνον* | *δι' ἀμφιτρῆτος αὐλίου πέμπει πνοή,* Propert. 5. 4. 4 *multaque nativis obstrepit arbor aquis,* Hor. *Epod.* 2. 27 *fontesque lymphis obstrepunt manantibus,* | *somnos quod invitet leves,* Verg. *Georg.* 2. 470 *mollesque sub arbore somni.*

V. Athen. 11. 463 E. A kletic hymn with which Frag. 6: *ἤ σε Κύπρος καὶ Πάφος ἢ Πάνορμος* (cf. Alkm. 21 *Κύπρον ἱμερτὰν λιποῖσα καὶ Πάφον περιρρύταν,* Hor. 1. 19. 10, 30. 2), seems to be connected. As Hebe pours out nectar to the gods (*νέκταρ ἐοινοχόει· τοὶ δὲ χρυσέοις δεπάεσσιν* | *δειδέχατ' ἀλλήλους* Δ 3), so Kypris is invited to leave her favourite abodes and come to pour out love's nectar. The song of the poet is *νέκταρ χυτόν,* Pind. *Ol.* 7. 7; cf. *ὕμνους οἰνοχοεῖν* Dionys. Chal. 4. 1. Bergk thought there was a reference here to Larichos, Sappho's brother, who was cup-bearer in Mytilene. This would be out of place. **θαλίαισι**: 'joy' (Volger 'flowers'); Ahrens conj. *θαλέεσσι.* Since the nectar is figurative, *συμμεμείγμενον* recalls *εὐθαλεῖ συνέμειξε τύχᾳ* Pind. *Pyth.* 9. 72. Cf. *οἴκτῳ συγκεκραμένην* Soph. *Aias* 895. After v. 4 Athen. adds *τούτοις τοῖς ἑταίροις ἐμοῖς τε καὶ σοῖς,* whence Kaibel extracts the verse *ταῖσδε ταῖσ' ἔμαισι κάλαισ' ἑταίραις.*

VI. Athen. 13. 751 D: quoted to show that freeborn women and maidens call their associates and friends *ἑταῖραι.* Cf. Frag. 31 *Λάτω καὶ Νιόβα μάλα μὲν φίλαι ἦσαν ἕταιραι.* To avoid the short dat. form Hoffmann reads *ἔμαις* (accus.) *τέρποντα.* See on Alk. xvi. 3.

VII. Schol. Pind. *Pyth.* 1. 6 (*εὕδει δ' ἀνὰ σκάπτῳ Διὸς αἰετός, ὠκεῖαν πτέρυγ' ἀμφοτέρωθεν χαλάξαις*). Fear produces the same result in the case of doves that music does in the case of Pindar's eagle. Cf. Ψ 879 *σὺν δὲ πτερὰ πυκνὰ λίασθεν·* | *ὠκὺς δ' ἐκ μελέων θυμὸς πτάτο.* **ψαῦκρος**: 'swift' (Fick); terror made them eager to fly but paralysed their wings.

VIII. Arist. *Rhet.* 1. 9. 20 (1367 A 7): 'for shameful things we are ashamed of when we say them, do, or intend to do them' ὥσπερ καὶ Σαπφὼ πεποίηκεν εἰπόντος τοῦ Ἀλκαίου: "θέλω τι Ϝείπην, ἀλλά με κωλύει αἴδως (No. xii.) αἰ δ' ἦχες" etc.

This passage has been interpreted in various ways: (1) The line quoted from Alkaios is part of an Alkaic stanza: θέλω τι Ϝείπην, ἀλλά με κωλύει | αἴδως and occurred in an amoebean poem by Sappho. Stephanos, a Byzantine commentator on Aristotle (*An. Par.* 1. 266. 25), says 'whether Alkaios was in love with some maiden, or whether it was some one else, at any rate Sappho composed a dialogue in which the lover says to the object of his love θέλω τι' etc. Anna Comnena (born 1083) says, as if quoting from memory, that the words ἀλλά . . . αἴδως are Sappho's (*Alex.* 15. 486). From Aristotle we cannot, it is true, infer, either that Alkaios was not one of the *dramatis personae* in Sappho's dialogue or that θέλω τι etc. is not a genuine expression of the poet's passion. But it is difficult to see how Stephanos' explanation can be derived from Aristotle unless there existed some tradition in its favour. I believe therefore that θέλω τι etc. is by Sappho. Cf. Comparetti *Saffo e Faone* 266, *Mus. ital. di antichità class.* 2. 40, ff. Horace's lyrical idyl in dialogue form (3. 9) may be founded on Aiolic models. (2) The text of Aristotle is corrupt, and εἰπόντος τοῦ Ἀλκαίου should be omitted. This procedure assumes the falsity of the current tradition about the love of Alkaios for Sappho, and aims at making Aristotle's words square with the truth. It is objectionable because it may have suited the critic's immediate purpose to acquiesce in the gossip of the day, or in older tradition. Furthermore, the Alkaios mentioned may be the Alkaios of Sappho's dialogue, which Aristotle possessed entire. Comparetti deletes Ἀλκαίου, and reads του. Cf. Weil *Bull. des Humanistes*, 1894, 2. p. 25. (3) The poet Alkaios, whom tradition regarded as Sappho's lover, actually expresses his passion for his Lesbian countrywoman. This was the view of Bergk, who regarded the line θέλω τι etc. as an example of Sappho's logaoedic pentapody with an anacrusis, and associated with it a line preserved by Hephaistion (ἰόπλοκ' ἄγνα μελλιχόμειδε Σάπφοι No. xiii.). Though two cyclic dactyls do not occur in conjunction in the remains of the Sapphic stanza, Bergk preferred to scan κωλύει αἴδως as —◡ ◡— ⏑ if we cannot accept a bold synizesis between the words, which might be defended by i. 11, xxiv. 1. The exchange of metrical gallantry, Sappho using the Alkaic stanza, Alkaios the Lesser Sapphic with a masculine anacrusis, strikes one as artificial under the circumstances. Though the 'bard of revolutions' may have cherished a passion for "The small dark body's Lesbian loveliness | That held the fire eternal," probability makes for the view that the story of this passion is the work of the scandal-mongers, who called Archilochos, Hipponax, and Anakreon (14, cf. [Sa.] 26) Sappho's lovers. Welcker (*Kl. Schr.* 4. 75, cf. 1. 111) was inclined to think that the line θέλω τι etc. may have been fabricated and added to ἰόπλοκ' etc. in order to connect Sappho's poem. The words of Sappho, he thought, were a bit of Sappho's teaching for the benefit of her pupils.

Sappho xxviii. has been supposed to be an answer to Alkaios, whose proposal of marriage she declined on the score of difference in years. Two works of art have been thought to prove the correctness of the tradition of Alkaios' love. 1. A vase from Agrigentum of the fifth century, now in Munich, representing Alkaios with bowed head addressing Sappho (Baumeister *Denkm.* No. 1607). 2. An archaic terra-cotta relief from Melos, now in the British Museum

(Overbeck *Plastik*³, 1. 163). Overbeck refused to believe that the anecdotes about literary personages were reproduced on works of art in early times (the relief dates 540–500 B.C.), and thought that we have here one of the *genre* scenes which appear on the reliefs of Melos together with mythological subjects. The names are not given as on the Munich vase. Welcker and Jahn regarded the figures as those of Sappho and Alkaios. Comparetti (*Saffo nelle antiche rappresentanze vascolari* in *Museo italiano* 2. 40-80) concludes that the representations on vase and relief are those of the Lesbian singers as poets, not as lovers, and that Alkaios is pictured as offering his respect and admiration to his Lesbian compatriot as the lofty ideal of poetry.

3. The eye is the seat of shame, as it is the seat of fear (Soph. *Aias* 140) and security (Pind. *Pyth.* 2. 20). Cf. *Hymn* 5. 214 (from Sa.?), Aisch. *Prom.* 134 θεμερῶπιν αἰδῶ, Theogn. 85, Eur. Frag. 457, Aristoph. *Vespae* 447, Eur. *I. A.* [1090], Theokr. 17. 69. He cannot gaze ὀρθαῖς κόραις, *lumine recto*. Cf. Eur. *Hek.* 970-972.—**4**. If τῷ δικαίῳ is too harsh, I prefer δικαίως either 'straight-forwardly' or from δικαίωμι ('δικαίως) 'about that which thou deemest fitting.'—Metre: Alkaic strophe.

IX. Athen. 13. 564 D. Theokr. 18. 37 ὡς Ἑλένα, τᾶς πάντες ἐπ' ὄμμασιν ἵμεροί ἐντι is perhaps a recollection of this fragment, which is not to be restored with certainty. There is no need to take ἐπί after the verb (the *terminus* of a definite purpose). V. 2 is an Alkaic hendecasyllable. As the fourth verse of the strophe Kaibel suggests στᾶθι καὶ ἄντα φίλος φίλᾳ μοι.

X. Dio Chrys. *Or.* 37. Cf. μ 212 καί που τῶνδε μνήσεσθαι ὀίω. For the sentiment cf. Mel. Adesp. 53 (Sappho?), ἔγω φᾶμι ἰοπλοκάμων Μοῖσαν εὖ λαχεῖν, Swinburne, 'Anactoria,' "I Sappho shall be one . . . with all high things for ever." Alkm. 118, speaks of his fame reaching to foreign peoples. Cf. θ 580, Pindar xiv., Theogn. 251, Theokr. 7. 93, 12. 11, Verg. *Ecl.* 10. 33, Hor. 1. 1. 29, 2. 20, 3. 30. 6 *non omnis moriar*, Ovid *Am.* 1. 15. 41 *ergo etiam cum me supremus adederit ignis,* | *vivam, parsque mei multa superstes erit*, *Metam.* 15. 875 *parte tamen meliore mei super alta perennis* | *astra ferar, nomenque erit indelebile nostrum . . . perque omnia saecula fama,* | *si quid habent veri vatum praesagia, vivam.* Cf. Shakespeare's *Sonnets* 54, 63, 81, 107, Dante's 'sacred' poem *al quale han posto mano e cielo e terra*, Johnson's remark to Goldsmith in the Poet's Corner in Westminster

Abbey, *forsitan et nostrum nomen miscebitur istis*, Manzoni's song in 'Cinque Maggio' *che forse non morrà*, Keats: "I think I shall be among the English poets after my death."—Metre: four dactyls (if ἀμμέων is not a dissyllable) with — — as basis.

XI. Hephaist. 25. "I loved thee—Atthis, of old time, once—long since in old time overpast," Swinburne, 'On the Cliffs.' Cf. xv.—Metre: as x.

XII. Plut. *Erot.* 5, schol. Pind. *Pyth.* 2. 42, Max. Tyr. 24. 9. Plut. says **ἄχαρις** = ἡ οὔπω γάμων ἔχουσα ὥραν. Composed after Atthis had deserted Sappho for Andromeda. Terent. Maur. 2154 says *cordi quando fuisse sibi canit Atthida | parvam, florea virginitas sua cum foret.* Cf. Theokr. 5. 35-37, Goethe *Röm. Elegieen* 8.—Metre: as x.

XIII. Max. Tyr. 24. 9. Cf. ε 368 ὡς δ' ἄνεμος . . . θημῶνα τινάξῃ. Love is a storm-wind, Ibyk. i. 8.—Metre: as x. with ⏑ ⏑ as basis.

XIV. Galen *Protrept.* 8. If the fragment belongs among the Epithalamia, it may be that an ill-favoured bridegroom points the moral.—**1. ὅσσον ἴδην**: *visu tenus*; cf. ὅσον δοκεῖν Soph. *O. T.* 1191, ὅσον ἀποζῆν Thuk. 1. 2, ὅσον γενέσθαι Xen. *Anab.* 4. 8. 12; Goodwin *M. T.* 759. The phrase = καθ' ὅσον ἰδεῖν ἐστι.—**2. καί** with both ἄγαθος and κάλος because the ideas stand in mutual relation. So Z 476 δότε δὴ καὶ τόνδε γενέσθαι | παῖδ' ἐμόν, ὡς καὶ ἐγώ περ, ἀριπρεπέα Τρώεσσιν, Plato *Euthyphro* 6 A νῦν οὖν εἰ καὶ σοὶ ταῦτα ξυνδοκεῖ . . . ἀνάγκη δὴ . . . καὶ ἡμῖν ξυγχωρεῖν. Sappho's words are equivalent to ὃς δὲ καὶ ἀγαθός ἐστιν, ἐκεῖνος καὶ καλὸς ἔσται. Perhaps Theogn. 933-4 is by Solon: παύροις ἀνθρώπων ἀρετὴ καὶ κάλλος ὀπηδεῖ· | ὄλβιος, ὃς τούτων ἀμφοτέρων ἔλαχεν. "How near to good is what is fair!", Ben Jonson. Wealth follows beauty in the scale of blessings in skol. vi.—Metre: as x. with ⏑ ⏓ in the basis.

XV. Schol. Soph. *El.* 149: the nightingale is called Διὸς ἄγγελος because it is the harbinger of spring. Cf. τ 518 ὡς δ' ὅτε Πανδαρέου κούρη χλωρηῒς ἀηδών | καλὸν ἀείδῃσιν ἔαρος νέον ἱσταμένοιο κ.τ.λ., Aristoph. *Aves* 682 ἀλλ', ὦ καλλιβόαν κρέκουσ' | αὐλὸν φθέγμασιν ἠρινοῖς after the apostrophe to the nightingale, Sim. xxxiii., Ben Jonson, 'The Sad Shepherd,' "The dear good angel of the Spring | The nightingale." The swallow, also the harbinger of spring (Stes. ix., FOLK-SONGS xxii.), often has the same epithets as the nightingale.—Metre: as x. with — ⏑ as basis.

XVI. Hephaist. 40. Attributed to Sappho.—**1.** **δαῦτε**: see on Alkm. xiii. **λυσιμέλης** of πόθος Archil. 85, of ἔρως Hes. *Theogon.* 911, FOLK-SONGS xxv. **δόνει**: ἔρως με δονεῖ Aristoph. *Ekkles.* 954, νόον ἔρωτι δονεύμενος Mosch. 5. 5, δονέουσι μέριμναι Bacch. 1. 41.—**2.** **γλυκύπικρον**: cf. Theogn. 1353 πικρὸς καὶ γλυκύς ἐστι καὶ ἁρπαλέος καὶ ἀπηνής, | ὄφρα τέλειος ἔῃ νέοισιν ἔρως κ.τ.λ., γλ. Ἔρως *Anth. Pal.* 5. 134, γλυκύδακρυς *ib.* 12. 167, πικρὸς Ερως Plato; (*dea*) *quae dulcem curis miscet amaritiem* Catull. 68. 18, *dulcium | mater saeva Cupidinum* Hor. 4. 1. 4; "Surely most bitter of all sweet things thou art, | And sweetest thou of all things bitter, love," Swinburne, 'Bothwell,' 1.1, *O Lieb wie bist Du bitter, O Lieb wie bist Du süss*, Scheffel. Sa. called Eros ἀλγεσίδωρος. The comparison of love with a nettle is common, *e.g.* Bacch. ix. 8. **ὄρπετον**: perhaps Aiol. for the weak form *ἀρπετόν. Attic ἑρπετόν may be due to folk-etymology from ἕρπω, or the initial α was assimilated to the ε. It is uncertain whether Sa. used the word in the etymological sense or whether it meant any animal (δ 418, σ 130, Pind. ix. 2, Soph. *Phil.* 1207). Sem. 13 used it of the beetle. Ahrens took it as 'rapacious beast' whether from ἁρπάζω (cf. ἅρπυν· ἔρωτα. Αἰολεῖς, Hesych.) or from ἕρπω. Niket. Eug. *Dros. et Char.* 2. 217 has Ἔρως ὁ πικρός, ὁ δρακοντώδης γόνος.—Metre: basis ⏑ ⏓ + three dactyls.

XVII. Hephaist. 25. Andromeda, Sappho's rival, is mentioned in 58: ἔχει μὲν Ἀνδρ. κάλαν ἀμοίβαν, and referred to in xxvi. Max. Tyr. 24. 8 shows that the frag. is Sapphic. —Metre: as xvi. (basis — ⏓).

XVIII. Athen. 10. 425 C (2. 39 A)=vv. 1-2; 11. 475 A, Macrob. *Sat.* 5. 21. 6=vv. 3-5. From an epithalamium with a mythological subject. Ahrens referred the scene to the marriage of Herakles and Hebe, others, with greater probability, to the bridal of Peleus and Thetis, the ideal marriage, which had already been celebrated by Hesiod. Cf. Pind. *Pyth.* 3. 88. On the François Vase (Baumeister *Denkm.* No. 1883) the procession of the gods at this wedding is depicted with Hermes in a car. See van Herwerden, *Mnem.* 14. 54. The Muse celebrates the θεῶν γάμοι, Stes. viii. —**1.** **κῆ**: an instrumental with locative function, = ἐ-κεῖ. Though Sa. v. uses νέκταρ, she here makes ἀμβροσία the drink of the gods. This use is post-epic. Alkm. 100 has νέκταρ ἔδμεναι. Cf. γ 390 κρητῆρα κέρασσεν | οἴνου.—**2.** **Ἔρμας** or Ἐρμᾶς (the accent is uncertain): Hermes is the cup-bearer, as he is the general servitor, of the gods. In Lucian *Dial. deor.* 24. 1, he complains to Maia of his task of preparing their symposia. His duty here is that of the heralds in Homer (so

Ἰδαῖος Γ 248, cf. 269). Cf. *Arch. Zeit.* 38. 9. Tümpel, *Philolog.* 49. 717, regards Hermes as the Hermes-Kadmos of the cult of the Kabeiroi (Roscher 2356). **θέοισ᾽** preserves the full ending, but violates the *F* of *οἰνοχόησαι*. *θέοις* would preserve the *F*.—**3. καρχήσια**: see Guhl and Koner 153, Panofka pl. viii. 9.—Metre: logaoedic (anacr. + choriambic + pherecratic). V. 4 with first pherecratic (hyperthesis), may indicate the close of the strophe. Wilamowitz *Isyllos* 127 find ionics here.

XIX. Hephaist. 37. Attributed to Sappho. Perhaps it is a genuine bit of folk-song. Cf. the old Scottish ballad "Yestreen I made my bed fu' brade, | The night I'll make it narrow, | For a' the livelong winter's night | I'll lie twin'd of my marrow"; the German song ending *Des Abends wenn ich schlafen geh, | So find ich mein Bettchen alleine*, and Mörike, '*Die Verlassene*': *Früh, wenn die Hähne kräh'n | Eh' die Sternlein verschwinden*, etc.—**2. Πληΐαδες**: see on Alkm. iv. 60. Cf. *Anth. Pal.* 5. 189 (of a scorned lover) *νὺξ μακρὴ καὶ χεῖμα, μέσην δ' ἐπὶ Πλειάδα δύνει*.—**3. νύκτες**: *horae nocturnae*; cf. *ἐκ νυκτῶν* μ 286, Theogn. 460, *ἆμαρ ἢ νύκτες* Pind. *Pyth.* 4. 256 (*ἆμάρ τε καὶ νύκτα* Bacch. xv.), *μεσέων νυκτῶν κἠμέρης* Anan. 5. 9. *μέσαι νύκτες* without the article is regular, *e.g.* Hdt. 4. 181. We find *μέσον νυκτῶν* Xen. *Kyrop.* 5. 3. 52. *νὺξ μέσση* first in *Ilias parva* 11, *νύκτα μέσην* Hdt. 8. 9. The sing. varies with the pl. according to the conception: *πρόσω τῆς νυκτός* Hdt. 9. 44, *πόρρω τῶν νυκτῶν* Plato *Protag.* 310 D. **παρά**: see on iv.—**4.** Cf. Aristoph. *Ekkles.* 912 *αἰαῖ, τί ποτε πείσομαι, | οὐχ ἥκει μοὐταῖρος· μόνη δ' αὐτοῦ λείπομαι*, Theokr. 20. 45 *μούνη δ' ἀνὰ νύκτα καθεύδοις*, Bion 2. 28 *αὐτὰρ ἐγὼ μούνα, μούνα δὲ σὺ νύμφα καθεύδεις*, Grenfell *Erot. Frag.* 1. 22 *μονοκοιτήσω*, Ovid *Her.* 1. 7, Hor. 3. 7. 6, Prop. 1. 12. 13.—Metre: logaoedic. Christ thinks the strophe consists of tetrapodies (⏓ ⋮ –́⏑ ⏑ –́⏑ ⊥́ –́∧), the absence of a clausula being accounted for by the spondaic close of the cola. The ancients regarded the metre as ionic a maiore with the first syllable anceps.

XX. Hephaist. 36: an example of brachycatalectic ionic trimeter (*Praxilleum*) – – ⏑ ⏑ | – ⏑ – ⏑ | – ⏓. Some modern scholars accept this scansion, others (*e.g.* Schmidt, Rossbach) regard the metre as logaoedic (hypercat. first glyconic with anacrusis) > ⋮ –́⏑ ⏑ –́⏑ –́⏑ –́⏑. Distinguish *φαίνω* 'shine' (*σελάνα, φαῖνε καλόν* Theokr. 2. 11) from *φαίνομαι* 'rise' (*ἄστρα φαεινὴν ἀμφὶ σελήνην | φαίνετ'* Θ 556). I see no hint of magical rites here (Volger, Schneidewin). The mention of the full moon suggests a wedding, Pind. *Isthm.* 8. 47, Eur. *I. A.* 717. Blass joins the following fragment as part of a strophe of different metrical value but belonging to the same poem. For hymns sung at night, see on Alkm. iv.

XXI. Hephaist. 36 (vv. 1-2), 37 (v. 3). Attributed to Sappho. The verses are quoted as acatal. ionic a maiore trimeters and they are so regarded by Wilamowitz: ⏓ — ⏑ ⏑ | — ⏓ ⏒ ⏑ | — ⏑ — ⏒. Others think they consist of anacr. + choriamb. monom. + first pherecratic: ⏒ ⁞ ⏗ ⏑ ⏑ ⏗ | ⏗ ⏑ ⏑ ⏗ ⏑ ⏗ ⏒. Rossbach compares Anakr. 33 *οὐδ' ἀργυρέη κώκοτε ἔλαμπε πειθώ*, where the open *εη* is wrong. On Cretan dances, see on Sim. x.—**1.** **ἐμμελέως** 'in time.' Cf. Anakr. 40, 122 (*πηκτίδων ἐμμελεστέρα*), Sim. ii. 3. The *ἐμμέλεια* was a solemn dance.—**2.** **ὤρχεῦντ'**: if correct, Aiolic had also open verbs as well as those in *-μι* (*ὤρχηντ'* ?).—**3.** **πόας**, but *ποίας* ii. 14. Cf. *τέρεν' ἄνθεα ποίης* ι 449, *τερένας ἄνθος ὀπώρας* Alk. 61; *ὠρχεῦντ' ἐν μαλακᾷ ποίᾳ* Theokr. 6. 45. **μάτεισαι**: van Herwerden, *Mnem.* 14. 54, wants *πάτεισαι* unnecessarily. *ματέω* is etymologically distinct from *πατέω*, and connected with *emineo.*

XXII. Hephaist. 31. Another form of invocation in Frag. 65 *Ϝροδοπάχεες ἄγναι Χάριτες, δεῦτε Δίος κόραι.* Pindar invokes the Graces in *Ol.* 14. Cf. Anakr. 69 *καλλίκομοι κοῦραι Διὸς ὠρχήσαντ' ἐλαφρῶς.*—Metre: Greater Sapphics. Greek choriambics permit, as Latin choriambics do not, the juxtaposition of stressed long syllables in the same word. In Horace each choriambic closes with a final long syllable. In Horace's only ode in Greater Sapphics (i. 8), we have ⏗ ⏑ ⏗ > for ⏗ ⏑ ⏑ ⏗; and some would read *νῦν* here, thus finding an exact Greek original for the Latin form. An initial choriambic in Aiolic poetry is rare. Note the regular caesura after the second choriambic. Some make ⏗ ⏑ ⏑ ⏗ ⏑ ⏗ ⏗ ∧ of the final pherecratic.

XXIII. Hephaist. 34. For the cult of Adonis, and based on a folk-song. Cf. *Anth. Pal.* 7. 407. 7 (of Sappho), *ἢ Κινύρεω νέον ἔρνος ὀδυρομένη, Ἀφροδίτῃ | σύνθρηνος.* The lines are Sappho's without doubt, since Paus. 9. 29. 8 says that she sang of Adonis. **Κυθέρηα** (so Mel. Adesp. 71) is = *-ηια*, as *Κυπρογένηα* = *-ηια*; probably analogues of stems in *-ης*, *-ες.* —**2.** Cf. *κόπτεσθ' Ἄδωνιν* Aristoph. *Lysistr.* 396; *τά τε ἐσθῆτος . . . εἶχον, ταῦτα κατηρείκοντο* Hdt. 3. 66. Mel. Adesp. 79 A of Adonis: *κάπρος ἡνίχ' ὁ μαινόλης | ὀδόντι σκυλακοκτόνῳ | Κύπριδος θάλος ὤλεσεν.*—Metre: logaoedic. Instead of the ending (⏗ ⏑ ⏑ ⏗ ⏑ ⏗ ∧) of the Greater Asclepiad, we have the Adonic (cf. *ὦ τὸν Ἄδωνιν* Sa. 63).

XXIV. Stob. *Flor.* 4. 12, Plut. *Praec. coniug.* 48, *Symp.* 3. 1. 2. Addressed to a rich but uncultivated woman. Cf. ὅστις νέος ὢν Μουσῶν ἀμελεῖ, | τόν τε παρελθόντ' ἀπόλωλε χρόνον | καὶ τὸν μέλλοντα τέθνηκε Eur. Frag. 927 N[1].—**1. κείσεαι**: cf. Sim. xxiv., Soph. *Antig.* 73. **μναμοσύνα**: Dr. Verrall (*J. H. S.* 1. 260) contends that substantives in -συνη are used either by the Ionian poets or in imitation of Ionic models. It is difficult to prove this for Sappho, who has also ἀβροσύνα in 79.—**2.** Hoffmann ἔσσ. οὐδ' ὄνυμ' εἰς ὕστερον. Garlands of roses were sacred to the Muses.—**3. Πιερίας**: here Orpheus was born and here was the home of the Muses. Cf. *Anth. Pal.* 6. 14 of Sa., ἃς μέτα Πειθώ | ἔπλεκ' ἀείζωον Πιερίδων στέφανον. **κῆν**: from κ(αί)+ἐν, the ε of which is lengthened. κῆμέ occurs on an old Aiolic inscr. Elsewhere in Aiolic καί+ε=κᾱ- by contraction. δόμῳ Fick (δομοφοίτασις one MS.) to avoid the short form of the dative. Cf. Theokr. 16. 29 Μουσάων δὲ μάλιστα τίειν ἱεροὺς ὑποφήτας, | ὄφρα καὶ εἰν 'Αΐδαο κεκρυμμένος ἐσθλὸς ἀκούσῃς. The contemner of the Muses is punished as a soul stained with guilt: cf. Plato *Phaidon* 81 C, Pind. Frag. 132. Hades often means to the poet deprivation of the enjoyment of song: Theokr. 1. 62 τὰν γὰρ ἀοιδάν | οὔτι πᾳ εἰς 'Αΐδαν γε τὸν ἐκλελάθοντα φυλαξεῖς, *Anth. Pal.* 7. 420 οὐκ ᾠδάς, οὐ χορὸν οἶδ' 'Αχέρων, Mel. Adesp. v.—**4. πεδ'**: though etymologically different from μετά, πεδά has the same use. In older poetry when followed by the genitive, the genitive is plural. (Pind., Ibyk. x., skol. vi.; and so in Prat. i. 4, Philox. 2. 30, Bacchyl. v. 123.) For μετά with the sing. see on Ariphron. Pind. uses μετά also of things, a usage that in the minor lyric poets occurs only in Philox. 2. 30. Sappho does not use σύν (Alk. iv.). **ἀμαύρων**: cf. εἴδωλον ἀμαυρόν δ 824. **ἐκπεποταμένα**: cf. λ 222. —Metre: Greater Asclepiads, perhaps to be arranged in distichs.

XXV. Chrysipp. περὶ ἀποφατικῶν 13. Doubtless from the same poem as the foregoing. The remark may apply to Sappho herself or to a pupil.—**1. δοκίμοιμι**: Ahrens δοκίμωμι. **φάος ἀλίω**: cf. υ 207 ζώει καὶ ὁρᾷ φάος ἠελίοιο, etc.—**2. σοφίαν**: skill in song; accus. explanatory of τοιαύταν.—Metre: Greater Asclepiads.

XXVI. Athen. 1. 21 C, Eust. *Od.* 1916. 49, Max. Tyr. 24. 9. Sappho's friend Andromeda has become her rival.—**1. ἀγροίωτις**: Hiller ἀγροϊῶτις like the supposed Aiolic ὄϊδα. **ἐπεμμένα** = ἐφειμένα.—**3. ϝράκεα**: rather 'rags' than 'fine clothes' (βράκος· ἱμάτιον πολυτελές).—Metre: probably Greater Asclepiads.

XXVII. *Et. Mag.* 2. 43.—**1.** **τις**: cf. Theokr. 7. 38 ἐγὼ δέ τις οὐ ταχυπειθής.—**2.** **ὄργαν**: gen. pl. **ἀβάκην**: ἀβακής = ἡσύχιος, πρᾶος, εὐήθης; 'placid' rather than 'innocent.' Cf. Anakr. xxvi., Archil. 33 βάβαξ = λάλος, Hippon. 53 ἐμβαβάξαντες = ἐμβοήσαντες.—Metre: Greater Asclepiads.

XXVIII. Stob. *Flor.* 71. 4, Apostol. 2. 52 d. There is little warrant for the suggestion that Sappho is here declining a proposal of marriage from Alkaios. The verses might be arranged as two Greater Asclepiads, if (1) ἄρνυσο is correct and to be defended as an optative like δαινῦτο Ω 665, and (2) συνϜοΐκην can be explained as ὄϊδα Alk. 145, a strange Aiolic diaeresis. Hoffmann writes ἄρνυσσο (*sic*) imperat. **γεραιτέρα** as δικαίτατα on an Aiol. inscr.—Metre: pherecratics and glyconics.

XXIX. Athen. 15. 674 E.—**1.** **δέ** in the thesis is very rare in lyric. **Δίκα** is perhaps a clip-name for Μνασιδίκα, a pupil of Sappho. Cp. Frag. 76 εὐμορφοτέρα Μν. τᾶς ἀπάλας Γυρίννως. **πέρθεσθ'**, with αι elided as in ii. 2; inf. for imper. Cf. on Anakr. ii. 8.—**2.** **ἀνήτοιο**: crowns of dill, Alk. xiv.—**3.** Corrupt. Bergk read εὐάνθεσιν ἐκ γὰρ πέλεται καὶ χάριτος μακαιρᾶν | μᾶλλον προτέρην 'for to those who are adorned with fair flowers it is given to stand first even in the favour of the goddesses,' taking ἐκ πέλεται as ἐκπέλει Soph. *Antig.* 478. Blass' reading is nearer the MSS.: εὐανθεΐα . . . καὶ χάρις ἐς μάκαιρας 'the adornment of flowers is even grace to stand first in the esteem of the gods.' But εὐανθεΐα does not occur, and even εὐανθία is very late and rare. I follow Seidler in reading μέν, and take πέλεται as γίνεται in Theogn. 474 οὐ πάσας νύκτας γ. ἁβρὰ παθεῖν. **χάριτος** depends on the adj. πρότερος in προτέρην; cf. τέλειος τῆς ἀρετῆς 'perfect in virtue.' —**4.** For **προτέρην** some read προσόρην (πελ. προσ. = πέφυκε προσορᾶν). **ἀστεφανώτοισι**: dat. of interest with ἀπυστρ. This construction is often more sympathetic, more tender than the usual genitive.—Metre: logaoedic. The metre recalls Alk. xx. except that we have an anacrusis instead of a basis, and a complete tripody at the end. Wilamowitz finds here a catal. ionic tetram.

XXX. Schol. Pind. *Ol.* 2. 53 (ὁ μὰν πλοῦτος ἀρεταῖς δεδαιδαλμένος φέρει τῶν τε καὶ τῶν | καιρόν). For the sentiment, cf. πλοῦτόν τε καὶ χάριν ἄγων | γνησίαις ἐπ' ἀρεταῖς *Ol.* 2. 11, ὁ πλοῦτος εὐρυσθενής, | ὅταν τις ἀρετᾷ κεκραμένον καθαρᾷ | βροτήσιος ἀνὴρ πότμου παραδόντος αὐτὸν ἀνάγῃ | πολύφιλον ἑπέταν *Pyth.* 5. 1; Alk. xxv., ἀνδρὸς φίλου δὲ χρυσὸς ἀμαθίας μέτα | ἄχρηστος, εἰ μὴ κἀρετὴν ἔχων τύχοι Eur. Frag. 163; οὔτ' ἀρετῆς ἄτερ ὄλβος ἐπίσταται ἄνδρας ἀέξειν, | οὔτ' ἀρετὴ ἀφένοιο Kallim. 1. 95.

πάροικος perhaps = *παρροικος <*παρϜοικος. σύνοικος is commoner in the lyric poets than πάροικος, *e.g.* Bacch. viii. 20. Ariphr.; Oppian, *Hal.* 2. 681, has σύνοικος of Justice.—Metre: as xxix.

XXXI. Hephaist. 54. Attributed to Sappho. If the statement of the ancients that Sappho's mother bore the name Κλέϊς or Κλῆϊς is not an inference from this fragment, it is possible that we have here a reference to the poetess' daughter, and not an allusion to one of Sappho's girl friends, or a fragment of an epithalamium. In xli. Sappho addresses her daughter, and Ovid *Epist. to Phaon* 70 speaks of her *filia parva.*—**2.** **Κλεῦις** is Κλέϊς with Ϝ vocalized. Cf. Κλειώ from ΚλεϜιώ. The verb *κλεϜέω appears in Κλεησιθήρα Alkm. iv. 72. Κλεῦας is also a clip-name (*S. G. D.-I.* 1317, Thessaly). **ἀγαπάτα**: cf. Ἑκτορίδην ἀγαπητόν Z 401, ἄγαπατός Pind. Frag. 193 (of himself as a child). The initial ā is from ἁ (the article) + ἀγ-.—**3.** Hermann deleted ἀντί and read ἄπαισαν. Λέσβος ἐραννά Moschos 3. 90 suggests that Λέσβον followed. Supply some such phrase as κεν θέλοιμ' ἄμευσαι, and cf. Hor. 2. 13. 22.

Hephaist. measured the lines thus:

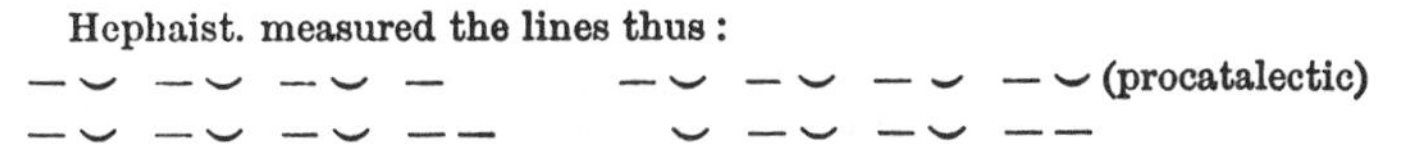

Κλέϊς ἀγαπάτα cannot have stood in his text. Ahrens read Κλέϊς μόν' ἀγ., Bergk Κλῆϊς, others Κλέηϊς. Christ (*Metrik der Griech.* 519) would make the first colon vary: 1-2 = — ◡ — ◡ — ◡ ⌞; 3 = — ◡ — ◡ — ◡ — ◡ ⌞. Probably the metre of all three lines was alike, viz. trochaic tetrap. + ithyphallicus, the whole a so-called brachycatalectic tetrameter. The irrational long appears only in the tetrapody. The ithypallicus may have the value of a tetrapody (⊥ ◡ ⊥ ◡ ⌞ ⊥ ∧). Rossbach proposes a different setting of the poem.

XXXII. Hephaist. 35. An instance of the adoption by the Aiolic poets of the spirit and language of the folk-song. Such songs are common in English: "O mother, put the wheel away, | I cannot spin to-night; oh, mother take the wheel away and put it out of sight"; Landor's 'Margaret' "I cannot mind my wheel"; and in German: *Dos soulld a Maedle speinne,* | *Dos Radle woulld ni gien;* Rückert *Ach süsse Mutter, ich kann nicht spinnen,* | *Ich kann nicht bleiben im Stübchen drinnen,* | *Ich muss hinaus;* Hor. 3. 12. 4 *tibi qualum Cythereae puer ales, tibi telas,* etc. Some think the allusion is to Erinna, the author of the Ἠλακάτη.—**3.** **δάμεισα**: μ' . . . δάμναται πόθος Archil. 85, ὑποδμηθεῖσα διὰ χρυσέην Ἀφροδίτην Hes. *Theogon.* 962, cf. Anakr. xxv. 5.—Metre: 1, 3 catalectic, 2, 4 acatalectic ionic dimeters of the free form.

Note that Horace used ionics only in the poem cited above, and that Alkaios employed the same metre in a poem (xxxiii) on a love-sick girl. Others regard the verses as brachycatalectic trochaic dimeters with anacrusis (⏑⏑ ⋮ ∸ ⏑ ∸ ⏑ ⌞∸ ∸ ∧). The arrangement as iambo-trochaics: ⏑ ∸ ⏑ ∸ ⏑ ∸ ⌞∸ | ∸ ⏑ ∸ ⏑ ∸ ⏑ ∸ ⏑ is not correct. The verses are often written as two lines.

XXXIII. Hephaist. 72: the *μεσύμνιον* is the refrain after a verse, the *ἐφύμνιον* the refrain after a strophe. v. 6 is added in Demetr. *de eloc.* 148. Sappho preserves here the traditional form of the popular epithalamium.—**1.** **ὔψοι**: cf. *ὑψόσ' ἀείρας* K 465. **μέλαθρον**: the lintel (*ὑπέρθυρον*), Hesych.; or the roof-tree may be meant (cf. "her head hat the roof-tree o' the house," Ballad of 'King Henry,' Child 1. 148). The situation is different in Catull. 61. 76: *claustra pandite ianuae,* | *virgo adest.* **Ὑμήναον**: Aiolic for *Ὑμέναιον*; accus. of exclamation representing *ἔσπερ'* or *μέλπετ' Ὑμήναον* (Sa. 107).—**3.** **τέκτονες ἄνδρες** recalls the epic phrase *ποιμένες ἄνδρες*, Alkm. xi., Sa. xxxv.—**5.** **γάμβρος** = *νυμφίος* Sa. xviii., Pind. *Ol.* 7. 4. Servius on Verg. *Georg.* 1. 31: *generum vero pro marito multi accipiunt iuxta Sappho.* **ἴσσος Ἄρευι**: cf. *ἶσος Ἄρει βίαν* Aisch. Frag. 74, *Ἄρευος στρατιωτέροις* Alk. 29.—**6.** Demetr. notes the grace of the change by which the 'impossible hyperbole' of v. 5 is corrected.—Metre: 1, 3, 6 are dactylic tripodies with or without anacrusis. Some omit the verb to make 5 correspond to 1, as 3 to 6, and to rescue the *Ϝ* of *ἴσσος*. Usener 97 reads *ὔψι* and *ἔρχεται*, believing that the poem illustrates the ancient rhythm regulated by beats and not by quantity alone. Many scholars, *e.g.* Bentley, Schneidewin, Westphal, regard the metre as dactylic hexameter interrupted by the *μεσύμνιον*. The refrain is an iambic monometer, which was often used in exclamations, cf. *e.g.* *ἰὴ ἰή, ἰὼ ἰώ, ἰὼ ξένοι, ἰὴ Παιάν*. After v. 5 the refrain may have dropped out.

XXXIV. Schol. Hermog. *περὶ ἰδεῶν* (*Rhet. Gr.* 7. 883 Walz). The fragment is referred to by Longos *Pastor.* 3. 33, Himerios 1. 16. Sung by a chorus of maidens. In the Hymeneal of Catullus the friends of the bride compare her to a flower (62. 39 ff.): *ut flos in saeptis secretus nascitur hortis,* | *ignotus pecori, nullo convulsus aratro* | . . . | *multi illum pueri, multae optavere puellae;* | *idem cum tenui carptus defloruit ungui,* | *nulli illum pueri, nullae optavere puellae.*—**1.** Cf. Plato epigr. 32 *πορφυρέοις μήλοισιν ἐοικότα παῖδα Κυθήρης*, Theokr. 7. 117 *ὦ μάλοισιν Ἔρωτες ἐρευθομένοισιν ὁμοῖοι*, 26. 1 *μαλοπάραυος Ἀγαύα*, Kaibel 243. 12 *ἐρεύθεται ἄνθεα μήλων*,

Longos 1. 24 Δάφνις εἴκασε μήλῳ τὸ πρόσωπον αὐτῆς (Χλόης) ὅτι λευκὸν καὶ ἐνερευθὲς ἦν, Tibull. 3. 4. 33 *et cum contexunt amarantis alba puellae | lilia et autumno candida mala rubent*, Ovid *Metam.* 3. 483 *non aliter quam poma solent, quae candida parte, | parte rubent*, 4. 330 *sed et erubuisse decebat. | hic color aprica pendentibus arbore pomis | aut ebori tincto est, aut sub candore rubenti.* **ἄκρῳ**: the boughs were out of reach as those in μ 435 (ἀπήωροι δ' ἔσαν ὄζοι). Cf. Theokr. 15. 112 παρ μὲν ὀπώρα κεῖται, ὅσα δρυὸς ἄκρα φέροντι.—**3.** "Forgot it not, nay! but got it not, for they could not get it till now" (Rossetti). The correction in οὐ μάν is *naïvement spirituelle* (Croiset). Cf. Δ 127 οὐδὲ σέθεν θεοὶ μάκαρες λελάθοντο.—Metre: dact. hexam. with only two heavy dactyls. Cf. Alkm. vii.

XXXV. Demetr. *de eloc.* 106. Attributed to Sappho. The chorus of youths depicts, in reply to the maidens, the despised condition of the unwedded girl—the "unprofitable virgin" of Jonson's 'Barriers' which translates Catullus 62. 49 ff.: *ut vidua in nudo vitis quae nascitur arvo | nunquam se extollit, nunquam mitem educat uvam, | . . . hanc nulli agricolae, nulli accoluere iuvenci.* The amoebean character of the song is clear from the parallelism of thought and language. Still, many doubt the authenticity of the fragment. The dialectal forms have to be restored throughout. οὔρεσι, if original, is an epic reminiscence, as in Pind. *Pyth.* 6. 21. The full form κατά is less suspicious because it occurs in hexameters (see on iv.).—**1. ὐάκινθον**: fem., masc. in Homer.—**2. πόσσι**: but πόδεσσιν xxi. Cf. however χέρσιν xxix. **καταστείβω** here and Soph. *O. K.* 467 κατέστειψας πέδον (retained by Jebb). Tmesis is generally denied in *Hymn* 19. 4 αἵ τε κατ' αἰγίλιπος πέτρης στείβουσι κάρηνα. The epic **δέ τε** (B 456, Hes. *Theogon.* 40) only here and Bacch. vi. 26, xiii. 1 in melic. The (generic) τε is not a conjunction and does not affect the meaning of the conjunction δέ. So with μέν τε, καί τε etc., Monro *H. G.* § 266. **πόρφυρον** for πορφύριον is derived from *πορφυρρον <-ιον, as ἄργυρα on an Aiolic inscription and ἀργύρροι (gen.) in Thessalian, from ἀργύριον. In Sa. 44 πόρφυρα may be correct. Sa. 64 has πορφυρίαν. Bergk's χάμαι δ' ἐπιπορφῦρει is metrically impossible. The hyacinth is purple according to Meleager *Anth. Pal.* 5. 147 (ὑάκινθον πορφυρέην); cf. Verg. *Ecl.* 3. 63 *suave rubens hyac.* Catullus' *defloruit* fills out the thought; Bergk κάππεσεν. Cf. Theokr. 7. 121 τό τοι καλὸν ἄνθος ἀππορρεῖ.—Metre: dact. hexameter.

XXXVI. v. 1 *Et. Mag.* 174. 43 etc., v. 2 *Et. Flor.* 129 Miller (*Vetus Et. Mag.*), Demetr. *de eloc.* 141.—Catullus' address to Hesperus 62. 20 ff. may be based on this passage, though his attitude is different and his touch is rougher. The concluding thought in Sappho was no doubt that Vesper brings the bride home to her husband. The lines were probably sung by a chorus of youths. From Himerios 1. 20 we may get the Sapphic line Ϝέσπερός σ' ἔκοισαν ἄγοι δόμονδε. Sappho called Ϝέσπερος 'the fairest of all stars' (Himer. 13. 9), and so Catullus: *Hespere, qui caelo lucet iucundior ignis?*— **1**. φαινολὶς ἠώς *Hymn* 5. 51 perhaps borrowed from Sappho.— **2**. For the sake of the metre, Bergk wrote φέρες, a form that is nowhere attested as Aiolic, though it appears in the related dialect of Kypros (ἔρπες).—ες is never necessary in Theokritos, though it appears in the MSS. and is reported by the grammarians. **ἄπυ** (anastrophe as ἐκρίθην ἄπο Theokr. 8. 74) 'back,' as ἀποισῶ οἴκαδις Aristoph. *Acharn.* 779. **φέρεις ἄπυ**: *restituis* not *eripis* as some take it, referring to Catullus line 21: *Hespere—qui natam possis complexu avellere matris.* Sappho is fond of anaphora in her epithalamia (xxxiv., xxxviii., xxxix., xl., 103, 105, 109). So Theokr. 18. 49-53, Catullus 62. 59-64. Dionysios of Halikarnassos called anaphora an artificial and Gorgianic figure. But it is native to all emphatic poetry, to prose as well as to inartistic speech. Cf. FOLK-SONGS xxiii., Alk. xxxiv.—Metre: v. 1 dact. hexam. Bergk regarded the line as consisting of Aiolic dactyls with — ⏑ ⏑ as the basis for the ordinary ⏒ ⏓. No such basis occurs in the other Aiolic dactyls, though a dactylic basis has been assumed in FOLK-SONGS xxiii. If the fragment belongs with xxxiv., xxxv. we expect lyric hexameters; which would not admit φέρεις in v. 2. It must be confessed however that we do not know much about the Lesbian use of the lyric hexameter and Aiolic dactyls. Many transpose the words of v. 2, *e.g.* Koechly, who read οἶν σὺ φέρεις τε καὶ αἶγα φέρεις καὶ μάτερι παῖδα (Demetr. omits ἄπυ).

XXXVII. Hephaist. 41; Demetr. *de eloc.* 167 says that the prosaic words manifest the sarcasm of the chorus. **1**. **θυρώρῳ**: Pollux 3. 42 καλεῖταί τις τῶν νυμφίου φίλων καὶ θυρωρός, ὁ ταῖς θύραις ἐφεστηκὼς καὶ εἴργων τὰς γυναῖκας βοηθεῖν τῇ νύμφῃ, Hesych. θυρωρός· ὁ παρανύμφιος, ὁ τὴν θύραν τοῦ θαλάμου κλείων. Cf. Anakr. 52 σινάμωροι πολεμίζουσι θυρωρῷ. **ἐπτορόγυιοι**: cf. ὀρόγυιαν (conj.) Pind. *Pyth.* 4. 228, ἑκατοντορόγυιον Aristoph. *Aves* 1131. The original inflection was *ὀρέγυια (ὀρέγω), gen. ὀργυιᾶς, whence ὄργυια. A gen. *ὀρεγυίας, formed to *ὀρέγυια, became *ὀρογυίας by assimilation. The nom. ὀρόγυια was then extracted from *ὀρογυίας.—**2**. **σάμβαλα**: cf. Eumelos.—**3**. **ἐξεπόνασαν**: from πονάω a by-form of πονέω. —Metre: logaoedic tripody with basis.

XXXVIII. Hephaist. 57. Most editors write in two lines, but cf. the schol., where for πέντε read τέσσαρα. So Anakr. 15, 16 are best written as pherecratics.—**1.** **ὄλβιος** was regularly used in hymeneals: Hes. Frag. 71 τρὶς μάκαρ Αἰακίδη καὶ τέτρακις, ὄλβιε Πηλεῦ, Theokr. 18. 16 ὄλβ. γάμβρ'. ὀλβίζω is to congratulate the newly wedded (Eur. *Helen* 640). Other forms of address are χαιρέτω ὁ γάμβρος Sa. 103, χαῖρε, νύμφα, χαῖρε, τίμιε γάμβρε, πόλλα 105, χαίροις, ὦ νύμφα, χαίροις εὐπένθερε γαμβρέ Theokr. 18. 49; *bene vivete* Catull. 61. 233, *vivete felices* Tibull. 3. 5. 31.—**2.** **ἄρᾱο** = ἠρῶ, from ἀρᾰεσο if from ἀράομαι; from ἄρᾱσο if from ἄρᾱμαι.—**3.** **ἐκτετέλεστ'**: τελέειν γάμον Kallim. 1. 14. **ἔχης** is a doubtful form.—Metre: pherecratics.

XXXIX. Hephaist. 24. Attributed to Sappho.—**1.** **τίῳ** = τίνι; cf. τίοισιν 168. **ἐικάσδω** = ϝεϝικάζω, not ἐ-ϝικάζω with prothetic ε. Cf. ζ 152 ἄγχιστα ἐίσκω. In v. 1 ἐικάσδω is subj. **ὄρπακι** in comparison as ἔρνος in Hom.; cf. Σ 56 ὁ δ' ἀνέδραμεν ἔρνεϊ ἶσος. Nausikaa is compared to a φοίνικος νέον ἔρνος ζ 163. See Bacch. ii. 87.—Metre: dactylic tetrapody with basis.

XL. Demetr. *de eloc.* 140. A dialogue between a bride (νύμφα) and her virginity. Demetrios remarks on the beauty of the repetition (ἀναδίπλωσις). Cf. Alk. xxxiv. and on Sa. xxxvi. All attempts at restoring v. 2 are unconvincing. We are not even certain that the metre of v. 2 corresponded to that of v. 1, *i.e.* two choriambs and a first pherecratic, as in Sa. xxii. The second παρθενία, though due to an ancient correction, is probably right. Neue read, and Usener 98 defends, ποῖ με λίποισ' οἴχῃ as a short verse of 3½ beats. If the verse is quantitative, the ending ⏑́⏑ ⏑ ⌊́ ⌊́ –́ ∧ is objectionable. Bergk's προτί in v. 2 (οὔκετι, νύμφα, προτὶ σ' ἴξω, προτὶ σ' οὔκετ' ἴξω) is against the dialect, as is ποτί. εἴκω may have ϝ: Skt. *viçáti* 'come.' But in ii. 8 we have ἔτ' εἴκει, perhaps from a different root (Arkad. ἰκόντα, not ϝικόντα). I have adopted Hiller's reading which gives a second instead of a first pherecratic by hyperthesis (– > –⏑⏑ ⏑ –́ ⏓). Cf. xviii. 4. Cf. the closing line in 'O waly, waly.'

XLI. Max. Tyr. 24. 9: ἀνθάπτεται (Σωκράτης) τῇ Ξανθίππῃ ὀδυρομένῃ, ὅτι ἀπέθνησκεν, ἡ δὲ (Σαπφὼ) τῇ θυγατρί. The poem is usually regarded as the message of Sappho on her death-bed to Kleïs; but Lunak thinks the reference is to the death of Kleïs' father. It was probably in the same poem that Sappho said: 'To die is bitter; and so the gods deem. For they had suffered death themselves, had death been sweet.'

Bergk suggested that this is the poem concerning which Stob. 29. 58 tells the following story about Solon: *παρὰ πότον τοῦ ἀδελφιδοῦ αὐτοῦ μέλος τι Σαπφοῦς ᾄσαντος, ἥσθη τῷ μέλει καὶ προσέταξε τῷ μειρακίῳ διδάξαι αὐτόν· ἐρωτήσαντος δέ τινος διὰ ποίαν αἰτίαν τοῦτο ἐσπούδασεν, ὁ δὲ ἔφη, ἵνα μαθὼν αὐτὸ ἀποθάνω.* Cf. Theokr. 9. 32 *ἐμὶν* (*φίλα*) *δέ τε* Μοῖσα *καὶ ᾠδά.* | *τᾶς μοι πᾶς εἴη πλεῖος δόμος.* For the thought, cf. Stes. xiii.—Metre: basis + choriamb + pherecratic.

XLII. *Oxyrhyncus Papyri*, 1. No. viii. (third century A.D.). Attributed to Sappho. The poem represents an attempt of the poetess to effect a reconciliation with her erring brother Charaxos. Hdt. 2. 135 is the first writer to refer to the infatuation of Charaxos, who appears to have been younger than Sappho, for the famous courtesan Rhodopis, whose real name Doricha was alone used by the poetess. Charaxos voyaged to Naukratis as a trader in the wines of Lesbos, and here he ransomed the girl for a great sum from her master Xanthos who had brought her to Egypt. She was a Thrakian by birth and had been the fellow-slave of Aesop. Suidas *s.v.* *Αἴσωπος* and *'Ιάδμων* reports that Charaxos had children by her. The disgraceful connection moved the indignation of Sappho whose reproaches in turn provoked the enmity of Charaxos. Hdt. says *Χάραξος δὲ ὡς λυσάμενος 'Ροδῶπιν ἀπενόστησε ἐς Μυτιλήνην, ἐν μέλεϊ Σαπφὼ πολλὰ κατεκερτόμησέ μιν* though here *μιν* may refer to Rh., who, according to Athen. 596 B, was attacked by Sappho because she had been the cause of her brother's extravagance. In the *Epistle of Sappho to Phaon* (vv. 63 ff.) Ovid says *arsit inops frater victus meretricis amore,* | *mixtaque cum turpi damna pudore tulit.* | *factus inops agili peragit freta caerula remo,* | *quasque male amisit, nunc male quaerit opes.* | *me quoque, quod monui bene multa fideliter, odit.*

The poem contains an appeal for Charaxos' return from Egypt and an expression of the hope that the memory of the past differences between brother and sister may be blotted out. Sappho's sensitiveness to the voice of public reproach occasioned by her brother's ill-fame is morally inconceivable had she herself not been innocent of the turpitude with which she was charged by the Athenian writers of comedy. The text is mainly that of Blass, though his restorations leave much that is obscure.

1. Κύπρι: Aphr. as *Εὔπλοια*, *Γαληναία*, has power over the sea (Hor. 3. 1). She is often associated with the Nereids in works of art. **Νηρήϊδες**: this is perhaps the earliest prayer to the daughters of Nereus. Cf. Soph. *Phil.* 1470 *Νύμφαις ἁλίαισιν ἐπευξάμενοι* | *νόστου σωτῆρας ἱκέσθαι*, Eur. *Hel.* 1585, Aristoph. *Thesm.* 325. Lesbos was one of the seats of the cult of the Nereids. The early conception of the Greeks did not confine their activity to an idyllic life of tranquillity but gave them actual power over the waves. So Hes. *Theogon.* 252 ff., in his catalogue of the Nereids, says *Κυμοδόκη θ', ἣ κύματ' ἐν ἠεροειδέϊ πόντῳ | πνοιάς τε ζαχρηῶν ἀνέμων σὺν* Κυματολήγῃ | *ῥεῖα πρηΰνει.* Other names evidencing the same beneficent activity are Σαώ, Γαλήνη, Εὐλιμένη, Φέρουσα, Αλιμήδη, Ποντοπόρεια, Εὐπόμπη.—**2. τυῖδ'** : as i. 5.—**3.** Cf. i. 26.—**5.** Aphrodite is implored to blot out utterly the memory of the former dissension between Sappho and her brother. Aphrodite is not merely the divine agent of love and passion: she it is who cements the affection of kindred.—**6. ὡς** : the earliest case of the consecutive use. **ϝοῖσι** : *ϝός* 'his' appears also in Alk. 50. Charaxos, not *χάραν* and *ὀνίαν* as we might expect, is the subject of *γένεσθαι.* **χάραν** *κ.τ.λ.* cf. ζ 184 *πόλλ' ἄλγεα δυσμενέεσσι,* | *χάρματα δ' εὐμενέτῃσι,* Livy 3. 72 *hoc socios audire, hoc hostes, quo cum dolore hos, quo cum gaudio illos.* This is the earliest instance of the concrete use of *χαρά.* Cf. *χάρμα φίλοις* Theogn. 692, *χάρμα φίλοις ἑτάροισι* P 636.—**7. κὠνίαν** : *ὀνία* is used like *πῆμα* Γ 50, *πένθος* Soph. *Aias* 615 (*φίλοις π.*).—**8. μήδεις** : the predicate is *ἔχθρος.*—**10** ff. A satisfactory sense cannot be extracted from these lines: and may he utterly forget the sore distress (gen. pl.) at which he grieved aforetime and (by which) he broke my heart, hearing the reproach which stung him to the quick and often overpowered him amid the festal merriment of the citizens—the reproach which ceased awhile but came back all too soon.—**11. ὄτοισι** : to avoid the harsh constr. Blass takes *ὄτοισι* as fem. referring to *ὀνίαν.* Grenfell and Hunt note that such a usage appears only in Eur. *I. T.* 1071 *μητρὸς πατρός τε καὶ τέκνων, ὅτῳ κυρεῖ,* a verse that is considered spurious by most editors for this and other reasons. **ἀχεύων** : cf. *φίλοισι ἄχος* Soph. *O. T.* 1355.—**12. ἐδάμνα** : cf. i. 4.—**13. ἐν χρῷ** : cf. Hdt. 4. 175 *κείροντες ἐν χροΐ,* Soph. *Aias* 786 *ξυρεῖ ἐν χρῷ.*—**14. ἦλλ'** : from *ἔλλω* (=*εἴλω*)· *κατέχειν* Hesych. The bitterness of self-reproach would be augmented at the public festivals and particularly at those in which the members of a family participated. Cf. Soph. *O. T.* 1489 *ποίας γὰρ ἀστῶν ἥξετ' εἰς ὁμιλίας,* | *ποίας δ' ἑορτάς, ἔνθεν οὐ κεκλαυμέναι* | *πρὸς οἶκον ἵξεσθ' ἀντὶ τῆς θεωρίας*; with Jebb's note, *El.* 982. For *κε* with the imperf. indic. see Goodwin *M. T.* 162.—**15. βρόχυ** and **ὀνῆκε** : Blass *βράχυ* and *ἀνῆκε.* **δαῦτ'** : see on Anakr. xxiv. 6.—Metre: Sapphic strophe.

ERINNA.

ERINNA is called by Suidas a scholar of Sappho, while Eusebios places her in the middle of the fourth century. Another tradition reports that Naukydes (*floruit* 400) made a statue of her. If all the epigrams current under her name are genuine, she cannot well have been a contemporary of Sappho. The remains of the Ἠλακάτη, a poem of 300 hexameters 'worthy of Homer' which she composed while working at the wheel 'from fear of her mother' are too scant to warrant any conclusion as to her date. Erinna was probably a native of the island of Telos near Rhodes and wrote in Doric. Her death at the age of nineteen may have served to increase the esteem in which her poetry was held. She is said to have been inferior to Sappho in the composition of songs, but to have excelled her in hexameters (*Anth. Pal.* 9. 190).

I. Stob. *Flor.* 115. 13. *πολιοκρόταφον γῆρας* Bacch. 42 (B 3) is *γῆρας λευκόν* Soph. *Aias* 625 (*λευκανθὲς κάρα O. T.* 742).—Metre: dact. hexam.

II. Stob. *Flor.* 118. 4. Cf. Pind. *Ol.* 14. 20 *μελαντειχέα νῦν δόμον | Φερσεφόνας ἔλθ', Ἀχοῖ.* **τουτόθεν** Michelangeli (*τουτόθε* Theokr. 4. 10), *τούτω κῆς* Meineke. **σκότος**: neuter in Doric (Sophron 80). **κατέρρει**: cp. Sa. iv. Intransitive verbs when compounded with a preposition may become transitive. So *καταπολεμέω, κατακράζω; τὴν ἀτραπὸν κατερρύην* Aristoph. Frag. 143. Bergk suggested *καταγρεῖ* as Sa. 43 *πάννυχος ἄσφι κατάγρει* (*ὕπνος*).—Metre: dact. hexam.

STESICHOROS.

IT is the peculiar distinction of a distant Greek colony to have been the home of the poet who created a new era in the history of choral song. Stesichoros of Sicily transformed the existing choral lyric; and from his influence none of his successors ever emancipated himself. In 648 Himera was founded by Ionian Chalkidians from Zankle together with Dorians from Syracuse. The father of

Stesichoros, if not one of the founders of the city, was certainly one of its early settlers, and seems to have removed thither from Metauros in Epizephyrian Lokris. It is a proof that we are getting on surer chronological ground to find that Stesichoros is the first personage in Greek literary history of whom the birth-year and the death-year are recorded; though it is curious that 632-556 are reported by Dionysios of Halikarnassos: 632 is just forty years—a generation according to the counting of the biographers—after one dating of Alkman, of whom Stesichoros was regarded as the successor; and 556 is the year of the birth of Simonides. Still, these dates are approximately correct.

The poet owes his name, properly Στασίχορος (Sim. xxi.), to his occupation as 'marshal of the chorus.' Originally called Teisias—a name that reappears in Sicily in connection with the early history of rhetoric—, his name was changed ὅτι πρῶτος κιθαρῳδίας χορὸν ἔστησε, though the addition of πρῶτος in Suidas is at variance with truth. This substitution of names is not unexampled; Plato and Theophrastos are familiar examples; and Terpander may conceal a name less indicative of the minstrel's calling. With his Lokrian blood Stesichoros may have inherited a taste for music and song (Pind. *Ol.* 11. 15) which we find already in the Lokrian Xenokritos. Tradition indeed connected his family with Hesiod, who died in Naupaktos in Ozolian Lokris, but there are no special marks of affinity between his poetry and that of the didactic, *bourgeois* author of the *Works and Days* and *Theogony*.

With the mother-wit of the Dorians, Stesichoros warned his fellow-citizens against the schemes of Phalaris by reciting the fable of the horse that took man as a master in order to revenge himself on the stag. His advice went unheeded and he was compelled to escape to Katana where he is said to have died. Here he was buried by the 'Stesichorean gate' and here was his octagonal tomb with its eight columns which bore the name πάντα ὀκτώ; whence a throw of two aces and two trays at dice was called the Στησιχόρειος ἀριθμός. Cicero saw a statue of the poet at Himera, and his image was stamped on the coins of that city,—the extant specimens date after 241 B.C.

(Baumeister, fig. 1795). Whether Stesichoros visited Greece is uncertain, but his fame was soon widespread. Simonides (xxi.) speaks of him as of a classic, using his evidence to corroborate that of Homer. For the story of his temporary blindness see on Frag. v., vii.

The poems of Stesichoros were comprised in twenty-six books, of which the hymns formed the chief portion. The titles recall those of the epic rhapsodies and embrace a wide field of mythological interest. The Ἆθλα ἐπὶ Πελίᾳ described the funeral games held by Akastos in honour of his father. The Γηρυονηΐς, Κέρβερος, and Κύκνος dealt with the adventures of Herakles, the Σκύλλα (an Italo-Sicilian tale) either with Odysseus or with Herakles, the Συοθῆραι recounted the story of the Kalydonian boar-hunt, the Εὐρώπεια told of the rape of Europa by Zeus, the Ἐριφύλα narrated the death of Amphiaraos and the murder of Eriphyla by Alkmaion. From the epic cycle we have the Ἰλίου πέρσις, Ἑλένα, Παλινῳδία, Νόστοι, Ὀρέστεια (two books). Furthermore he wrote of the Argonautic expedition, of Aktaion, etc.

These hymns were at once a revival and a transformation of the old religious chants. Terpander, Archilochos, and Alkman had composed hymns, but under the hand of Stesichoros this form of lyric, though still closely connected with the public worship, was somewhat secularized. Instead of the gods and demi-gods, or the local worthies who appear in Alkman and later on in Pindar, it was the great heroes of the Panhellenic faith, who were worshipped with peculiar sanctity in connection with the foundation of the western colonies (Arist. περὶ θαυμ. ἀκουσ. 106-110), that formed the inspiration of Stesichoros' poetry. The contents were epic, the setting melic. We have in fact a species of hymnodic epic that was sung by a chorus to the sound of the kithara. In these musical epopees, though the poet relied for his story on Homer, Hesiod, and the Cyclic lays, he often departed from his models. Stesichoros is in fact the first of the poets to exercise the prerogative of the lyric artist with reference to the myths. While he usually has faith in the tales of mythology, he lacks the sincerity of a devout religious feeling to accord to them his passive acceptance. He boldly transforms the accredited myth when it is ill-suited to his feeling, but his spirit of innovation is not always governed by the religious awe that masters Pindar. At times he is even a rationalist. He refuses to attribute to Helen the disasters of the Trojan war; Aktaion's death is occasioned by the deer-skin thrown upon his shoulders by Artemis whose dogs tore him in pieces (the *motif* in the metope of Selinus); Iphigeneia is made the daughter of Theseus and Helen; Astyanax dies a natural death. Stesichoros was the first to describe Athena leaping full-armed from the head of Zeus.

Some of his paians were famous as late as the time of the younger Dionysios. But, apart from the hymns, it was the folk-tale in which the genius of the poet found freest expression. As a Lokrian he was naturally attracted to tales of love—one writer says that the poet himself was οὐ μετρίως ἐρωτικός—, and even in the more sacred hymns devoted to the public cult the great heroines of the past occupy a conspicuous place. It is an extraordinary achievement to have enfranchized in Greek literature the impersonal love-poem, an achievement that makes Stesichoros the forerunner of the Greek Romance (Rohde *Der griech. Roman* 29). From the oral legends of the people he drew the tales of unhappy love for his Ῥαδινά, and Καλύκα, the latter poem taking its name from the girl who threw herself from the Leukadian cliff. If the poet carried the myths of the East to the Western Greeks, Sicily in return gave him the story of Daphnis, who was blinded because of his unfaithfulness. It is however an error to assume that, because he was 'the first to write bucolic songs,' as Aelian states, he was a bucolic poet and the founder of an art that was possible only at a period when the world turned to the pastoral to find an enjoyment in nature from which it was debarred in life. The classification of these songs drawn from the folk-story is problematical; but they may represent the more human side of the hymn, the sphere of which was otherwise heroic.

Stesichoros represents a period of the development of choral song intermediate between Alkman and Pindar. From the former he is separated by the grandeur of his themes, his solemnity (*graves camenae* Hor. 4. 9. 9), and epic stateliness; to the latter he is akin both in the mechanism of his verse and in its content. Pindar's art is in fact conditioned by that of his predecessor. Of this poet who has left so great a name, who was worthy to be read by kings according to the saying of Alexander, who has profoundly influenced both tragedy and art, we possess scarcely more than fifty lines. Longinos called him Ὁμηρικώτατος, and Antipater said that the soul of Homer had passed into him. Even in the scanty fragments we may recognize something of the calm elevation, the suppression of the personal element, of the epic, and of that wealth of epithets which Quintilian says he applied to the prejudice of his art, but which Hermogenes regarded as the source of the sweetness (ἡδύ) of his style. As an inventor of striking compounds Stesichoros is the precursor of Pindar, though he lacked the latter's splendour and lyric fire. The Roman critic in a famous passage (10. 1. 62) says *Stesichorum quam sit ingenio validus, materiae quoque ostendunt, maxima bella et clarissimos canentem duces et epici carminis onera lyra sustinentem. Reddit enim personis in agendo simul loquendoque debitam dignitatem ac, si tenuisset modum, videtur aemulari proximus Homerum potuisse, sed redundat atque effunditur, quod, ut est reprehendendum, ita copiae vitium est.* He had not in fact mastered the art of transforming the epic into the lyric that in part made Pindar *novem lyricorum longe princeps.* Still he had grasped the lyric ideal: he rendered preeminent, not the deeds of the heroes, but their character, their feelings. Dionysios of Halikarnassos (*script. vet. cens.* 2. 7) refers to his μεγαλοπρέπεια τῶν κατὰ τὰς ὑποθέσεις πραγμάτων, ἐν οἷς τὰ ἤθη καὶ τὰ ἀξιώματα τῶν προσώπων τετήρηκεν. The same writer (*de comp. verb.* 24) classes Stesichoros with Alkaios, Sophokles, Herodotos, and Demosthenes as an example of the style intermediate between the 'grand' and the 'plain.'

Stesichoros created a High-Doric dialect by combining epic with Doric, a fusion that is not to be ascribed to the influence of his bilingual home (Thuk. 6. 5). With a few exceptions, *e.g.* πέποσχα = πέπονθα, his Doric forms are such as may have occurred in the choral poetry previous to his time; and his vocabulary contains nothing that is specifically Doric. The Ionicisms show no evidence of local colour. It is evident that the broad sweep of his themes could not have appealed to a wide commonalty of interest had his dialect been narrow in its sympathies. The ᾱ's are both Doric and Aiolic, and the epic ει and ου of κλεινᾶς, κλαίειν, Μοῦσα, κούρα were also known to certain Doric states. Aiolisms he seems not to have employed.

The elaborate structure of his odes was peculiarly adapted to the lyric development of the myth and compensated for his comparative poverty of metrical resource. All his poetry was epodic, that is, arranged in strophes, antistrophes, and epodes; whereas Alkman had made only a rude beginning with the triad (see on Alkm. iv.). The example of Stesichoros determined the future of choral poetry. Pindar recurs to the simpler structure only occasionally, and all later modifications of the Stesichorean norm are merely modifications of detail. We must however be on our guard against the assumption that the three-fold division was accompanied by the movement of the dance. Though choral, Stesichoros' hymns, if they preserved the ancient form, were not followed by the evolutions of the dance. στροφή etc. does not refer primarily to orchestic movement, but to the circuit of words and musical notes which form a period. The metres used by Stesichoros are: (1) Pure dactylic lines, sometimes with anacrusis (anapaests). We find variations on the hexameter, the long, swelling octameter, etc. (2) Epitrites in connection with dactyls. The epitritic trimeter ⏗́ ◡ –́ – ⏗́ ◡ –́ – ⏗́ ◡ –́ – was called Στησιχόρειον. (3) Logaoedics in the love-songs. Stesichoros used the Dorian mode and occasionally the Phrygian.

Stesichoros' popularity at Athens is attested by the parodies and by the fact that his poems were often sung at the symposia. Sokrates desired to learn one of his songs when in prison before his execution. Tragedy and art were profoundly influenced by his treatment of the myths. The paintings by Polygnotos in the Λέσχη at Delphi followed the Ἰλίου πέρσις. Cf. Robert *Bild und Lied* 170.

I.-III. The *Geryoneïs* recounted the story of the tenth labour of Herakles. The hero was commanded by Eurystheus to fetch the cattle of Geryoneus or Geryon, a monster with three bodies, six hands, six feet, and winged, who was the offspring of Chrysaor (the brother of Pegasos) and the Okeanid Kallirhoe. The name (cf. γηρύων) points to a personification of the giant power of the storm. The herd of Geryoneus was watched by Eurytion and the dog Orthros, the brother of Kerberos, on the island of Erytheia. There were three acts in the story: Herakles' journey to the west, the capture, and the return. In the early tradition Erytheia was an island in Okeanos, to which Herakles proceeded in the cup of the sun. Later, when the island off Gades was fixed upon as the scene of his exploit, in consequence of the establishment there of the worship of the Phoinikian Melkart with whom Herakles was identified, the hero reached his goal by a march through Libya. After setting up the pillars that bore his name he arrived at Erytheia. Here, according to tradition, Eurytion was born, though it is more likely that Strabo, like Skylax, has confused the herdsman with the master of the herd. Cf. Eur. *H. F.* 423. After the victory, which brought death to Geryoneus, Eurytion, and Orthros, Herakles put the oxen into the cup of the sun, disembarked them on the mainland, and returned the cup to Helios (cf. Frag. iii.). Driving his oxen before him, the hero proceeded homeward, meeting with adventures in Iberia, Gaul, Liguria, Italy, Sicily etc. Frag. ii. describes an event that happened in Arkadia.

Geryoneus is mentioned in Hes. *Theogon.* 287 ff., 979 ff., and the story of this labour of Herakles was treated by Pindar (Frags. xxv. and 81). Stesichoros may have been influenced by Peisandros of Rhodes (about 645 B.C.) who in his epic *Herakleia* first fixed the number of the labours of his hero, and gave him the club (as Melkart?) and the lion's skin. Representations of the combat with Geryoneus are frequent. Cf. *J. H. S.* 5. 176, Roscher 1. 1630, 2203, Baumeister, *s. v. Herakles.*

I. Strabo 3. 148.—**1. ἀντιπέρας**: an accus. pl. used adverbially; cf. μάτας = μάτην 47. πέρα (subst.) is a land lying opposite, across a body of water. (Aisch. *Agam.* 190 Χαλκίδος πέραν ἔχων.) πέρα (prep.) = 'to some point beyond,' *ultra*, πέραν (prep.) = 'on the other side of,' *trans*, less usually = 'to the other side of,' *trans*; as an adv. 'on the other side,' less usually 'to the other side.' See Jebb on Soph. *O. K.* 885. **κλεινᾶς**: of places, Hom. uses κλειτός and κλυτός; κλεινὴ νῆσος Solon 19. 3. **Ἐρυθείας**: Erytheia was also a name of one of the Hesperides. The name denotes the land touched by the ruddy beams of the setting sun. The eastern equivalent is the Ἐρυθρὰ θάλασσα of the Aithiopians. The island was located in various ways.

Strabo says that the ancients called Gadeira and the neighbouring islands by the name Ἐρύθεια. Pliny states that at the mouth of the Baetis there were two islands, that nearer to the continent being called Erytheia.—**2. Ταρτησσοῦ**: the ancient name of the Baetis (Guadalquivir). **παγάς**: the Doric ending occurs as early as Hesiod. Wilamowitz (*Hermes* 14. 169) wrongly objects to the form in a Chalkidian poet and arranges thus: *σχεδὸν ἀ. κ.* Ἐρ. | Ταρτ. *π. παρὰ παγάς* | *ἀπ. κ.τ.λ.* Because he thought Eurytion (Geryoneus?) was born opposite Gades and at the same time 'hard by the *sources* of the Tartessos,' Bergk transposed thus: Ταρτ. *ποτ. σχεδὸν ἀντ. κλ.* Ἐρυθ. | *ἐν κευθ. πέτρας παρὰ παγὰς ἀπ. ἀργ.*, that is, he was born near the Tartessos (not far from its mouth), opposite Gades, and close to the silver mines. For *παγάς* in this sense, compared Aisch. *Pers.* 238 *ἀργύρου πηγή*. But Strabo says that the mines were in mount Kastlon, the source of the Tartessos. If **παγὰς ἀργυρορ.** cannot mean 'streams deep-rooted in silver ore,' and must refer to 'springs,' *ἀντιπέρας* may either cover all the intervening space, or (less probably) Stes. may have regarded the source as not far from the coast. If Aristotle believed that the Tartessos and the Ister rose in the Pyrenees, Stes. may be pardoned for such an error. Perhaps we should read *ἀργυροριζου*. The Epitome of Strabo 3. 25 says *εἰσὶ περὶ τὰς ὄχθας αὐτοῦ* (the river) *μέταλλα ἄλλα τε καὶ ἄργυρος πλεῖστος*. The Phoinikian traders found such an abundance of silver there that they made all their utensils and even their anchors of this metal (Arist. *περὶ θαυμ. ἀκουσμ.* 135). With *ἀργυροριζους*, cf. *γηγενέταν ἄργυρον* Timoth. 14.—**3.** Cf. *πέτρης ἐς κευθμῶνα Hymn* 3. 229.—Metre: dact. heptameter.

II. Athen. 11. 499 A, E. Herakles visits the Centaur Pholos in Pholoe, a rough mountain between Arkadia and Elis. Here he is entertained with wine that Dionysos had given Pholos in preparation for his coming. The rest of the Centaurs are attracted by the perfume of the noble wine and fall upon the hero, who rescues himself with difficulty. Epicharmos wrote a Ἡρακλῆς *παρὰ Φόλῳ*, and there was a proverb *νοῦς οὐ παρὰ Κενταύροισι* that originated with Peisandros. The contest is represented on the frieze of Assos (*Papers of the Amer. School* 1881), and on an archaic Korinthian bowl (*J. H. S.* 1. 1). See Roscher 1. 2193, 2. 1040. The contest with the Centaurs is generally told in conjunction with the hunt of the Erymanthian boar, but Athen. says that the fragment is from the *Geryoneïs*. Either Stes. combined in part the two stories or, as Sitzler suggests, this fragment formed an episode.

1. σκύφιον (Guhl and Koner p. 152) only here as an adj. = *σκυφοειδές* (Athen.). With *δέπας* it means a 'capacious beaker,' holding over two gallons. The *σκύφος* was generally used by rustics (see on Alkm. xi.). It often appears as an attribute of Herakles, Roscher 1. 2914. **ὡς** *fere* (post-Hom., first here). Cf. *ἐπί*, *εἰς* of measurement. **τριλάγυνον**: cf. Anakr. 32 *τρικύαθον κελέβην*. Cf. Juv. 12. 44 *urnae cratera capacem et dignum sitiente Pholo.*—**2. ἐπισχόμενος** 'putting to his lips,' not 'in one draught'; cf. Plato *Phaidon* 117 C *ἐπισχόμενος ἐξέπιε* (see Stallbaum), Lucian *Tox.* 37 *ἐπισχόμενοι πίωμεν*, Apoll. Rhod. 1. 472 *ἦ καὶ ἐπισχόμενος πλεῖον δέπας ἀμφοτέρῃσιν | πῖνε χαλίκρητον λαρὸν μέθυ.* The scene is pictured in Gerhard's *Auserl. Vasen* 119, 120 3, 5, *Arch. Zeit.* 1865, pl. 201, 1. Cf. Roscher 1. 2194. **ῥά οἱ**: hiatus as in Hom. **παρέθηκε**: *apposuit;* cf. *Il.* I 90 *παρὰ δέ σφι τίθει μενοεικέα δαῖτα.* Theokr. 7. 149 *ἆρά γέ πᾳ τοιόνδε Φόλῳ κατὰ λάινον ἄντρον | κρατῆρ' Ἡρακλῆϊ γέρων ἐστήσατο Χείρων*;—Metre: dact. pent. + catal. hexam. (with anacr.). Bergk read *σκύπφειον* and *πῖνεν* making v. 1 dact. hexam., 2 catal. heptam.

III. Athen. 11. 469 E, 781 A; cf. Eust. *Od.* 1632. 23. The myth of the cup of Helios was invented to account for the rising of the sun in the east after it had set in the west (the *τροπαὶ ἠελίοιο* ο 404). Together with his steeds Helios embarks upon his golden vessel and courses from Erytheia over Okeanos to his place of rising (*ἀνατολαί*), where his palace is situated. In the Veda and in Germanic and Lettic myths the sun appears in the form of a golden cup. Okeanos represents the sky. We find Herakles in the cup of Helios on a vase in Roscher 1. 2204, where his presence has been explained as due to the fact that he is the Oriental sun-god. It is improbable that the cup was originally his attribute and later transferred to Helios.

1. Stes., like most of the later poets, probably follows the Hesiodic tradition that Helios is the son of the Titan Hyperion (*Theogon.* 371-374, cf. 1011), a view that is the result of interpreting *Ὑπεριονίδης* as a patronymic. Originally Hyperion was not the father but a by-name of Helios. In Homer Hyperion is Helios (α 8, 24). In *Ἠέλιος Ὑπεριονίδης* μ 176 the latter word is not a patronymic, but an equivalent of *Ὑπερίων*. Cf. *Ἡρακλείδης* = *Ἡρακλῆς*. *Ὑπερίων* is a quasi-patronymic. The suffix *-ῑων* is the same as that found in comparatives, and probably denotes mere connection (cf. *Οὐρανίωνες caelicolae*). Cf. Max Müller *Essays* 2. 410. **δέπας**: the story of the cup of the Sun was probably derived by Stes. from Peisandros' *Herakleia*. The *δέπας* appears also in a corrupt fragment of Aisch. (69) ἔνθ' ἐπὶ δυσμαῖς ἴσου | πατρὸς Ἡφαιστοτευχὲς | δέπας, ἐν τῷ διαβάλλει | πολὺν οἰδματόεντα ⟨πόντου⟩ | φέρει δρόμου πόρον συθεὶς | μελανίππου προφυγὼν | ἱερᾶς νυκτὸς ἀμολγόν, in Frag. 74 ὠκεανὸν περάσας ἐν δέπᾳ χρυσηλάτῳ, in Antimach. 4 . . . τότε δὴ χρυσέῳ ἐν δέπαϊ | Ἠέλιον πόμπευεν ἀγακλυμένη Ἐρύθεια, and in Pherekydes (Athen. 11. 470 c). In Mimn. 12 it is a winged, golden bed that transports Helios from the land of the Hesperides to that of the Aithiopians.—**2.** **ὄφρα** has an archaic flavour, though it still the chief final conjunction in the choral lyric of the sixth century. After Pindar it died out almost entirely.—**3.** The sequence calls for the optative. So usually in Homer and in the lyric poets, except in Pind. *Pyth.* 4. 92, Hippon. 19. 4 (universal application), Pind. *Ol.* 7. 16 (after κατέβαν= perfect), Bacch. 72=49 (no reference to the present). **ἱερᾶς**: Hom. ἱερὸν ἦμαρ, ἱερὸν κνέφας; cf. ἱερᾶς νυκτός in Aisch. quoted above. **ἐρεμνός**: of νύξ, λ 606. Fennell remarks that in Pindar when two adj. agree with one subst. and are not connected by a conjunction or separated by a pause, one is generally a constant epithet, the other descriptive. Cf. ii. 2. Perhaps the double epithets are hinted at in the criticism of Quint. **βένθεα**: in Hom. of the sea and the forest, not of night.—**4.** **ματέρα**: the Night; Soph. *Trach.* 94. **κουριδίαν ἄλοχον**: epic, Tyrt. 10. 6.—**5.** **ὁ δ'**: explained by πάις Διός, the epic use. **ἄλσος**: perhaps that of the Hyperboreans, which one Doric legend located in the far west. Herakles is said to have penetrated to this 'ancient garden of Phoibos.'—**6.** **ποσσί**: the Greek loves to add to a verb of motion the instrum. dat. of the part of the body in motion. So ρ 27 ποσὶ προβιβάς, Σ 599 θρέξασκον πόδεσσι, Theocr. 8. 47 βαίνει ποσίν, 7. 153 ποσσὶ χορεῦσαι, *Hymn* 5. 57 ἴδον ὀφθαλμοῖσιν, ὄμμασι δερκόμενος Ibyk. ii. 1, ὄμμασιν βλέπουσα Anakr. xxvii.; cf. τίναξε χερσίν Pind. *Ol.* 9. 30. (In βαίνω πόδα Eur. *El.* 94 the verb is transitive.) So often when opposition is implied or expressed. There is no need to interpret with Schneidewin *quo egregie ob oculos ponitur gravis H. incessus.* The meaning is simply that the hero proceeded on foot after returning the cup to Helios.—Metre: it is uncertain whether the strophe is complete. 1. dact. hexap. 2. dact. pentap. Some make ⏑⏑ ⏓ ⏔ of the last foot. 3. anacr. and dact. pentap.=anap. hexap. catal. 4. anacr. and hexam. catal. The words πάιδας to Διός have been arranged in a dozen different ways.

IV. Athen. 10. 456 F, Eust. *Od.* 1323. 57. From the Ἰλίου πέρσις, which was the main source of the *Tabula Iliaca* in the Capitoline Museum in Rome. The first mention of

Aeneas' flight to Italy, wherein the poet was doubtless influenced by the Italic tradition, occurred in this poem (see however Seeliger *Die Ueberl. der gr. Heldensage bei Stes.* p. 34). Athen. says that in the temple of Apollo at Karthaia in Keos there was a representation of Epeios drawing water for the Atreidai. Simonides (173) wrote an enigmatical distich on an ass called Epeios because it performed a task like that of the builder of the Trojan Horse (θ 493). The 'daughter of Zeus' is Athena, who is represented together with Epeios on a vase in Roscher 1. 1279. Farnell quotes *Tempest* 3. 1. 11: "My sweet mistress | Weeps when she sees me work." **ᾤκτιρε**: 'felt pity' (*ἐλεεῖν* 'have pity'). *οἰκτίρω*, not *οἰκτείρω*, is the proper form.—Metre: dact. octameter.

V. Schol. Eur. *Or.* 249 (*ἐπίσημον ἔτεκε Τυνδάρεως ἐς τὸν ψόγον | γένος θυγατέρων δυσκλεές τ' ἀν' Ἑλλάδα*). From the exordium of the *Ἑλένα*. Stes. follows Hesiod (Frag. 164), who first attributed to Aphrodite the 'evil fame' of the daughters of Tyndareus. Cf. λ 436. It was the vituperation of Helen in this poem that moved her wrath and led to the blinding of the blasphemous poet. The story is told by Plato *Phaidros* 244 A, Isokr. *Hel. enkom.* 64, and alluded to in innumerable later writers. In the *Ἰλίου πέρσις* Stes. bore witness to the beauty of Helen: when the vengeful Achaians were preparing to stone her, they dropped their missiles in astonishment at her beauty. Bergk (*Gr. Lit. gesch.* 2. 290) suggests, as an explanation of the story of the blinding of the poet and the restoration of his sight, that Stes. dreamed that Helen threatened him with blindness, and composed the *Recantation* after waking with pain in his eyes. An Icelandic scald Thormod dedicated the same poem to two maidens, one of whom appeared to him in a dream and threatened him with the loss of sight unless he made public amends for the insult. Awaking with smarting eyes he paid penance and was cured.—**2**. **ἠπιοδώρω**: of Hekabe Z 251; *δῶρ' Ἀφρ.* Γ 54. Aphr. is the neglected fairy of the fairy-tale.—**3**. **Τυνδάρεω**: *-ου* λ 298, *Πηνελέωο* Ξ 489.—**4**. *χολωσαμένη* (MSS.), after *κείνα*, would not be the usage of Pindar, who Doricizes. **διγάμους**: an allusion to the adultery of Klytaimnestra and Timandra. **τριγάμους**: Helen was the bride of Theseus, Menelaos, and Paris. Hesiod does not include Theseus. Helen is called *πολυάνωρ* Aisch. *Agam.* 62, *τριάνωρ* Lykophr. *Alex.* 851.—Metre: dact.-epitrite.

VI. Athen. 3. 81 D.—**1**. **Κυδώνια μᾶλα**: see on Ibyk. i. 1. **ποτερρίπτευν**: the compound may be defended by *ἀνερρίπτουν* ν 78. That *ῥιπτέω*=*iacto*, *ῥίπτω*=*iacio* is not proven. The ceremony of *φυλλοβολία* was common on other occasions: Pind. *Pyth.* 9. 123 *πολλὰ μὲν κεῖνοι δίκον | φύλλ' ἔπι καὶ στεφάνους*, iv. 18, Eur. *Hek.* 574.—**3. κορωνίδας**: *Et. Mag.* *κορωνίς· εἶδος στεφάνης πεπλεγμένης ἐξ ἴου.* Perhaps this singular usage is Chalkidian; but it is less likely that the word is borrowed from *corona* than that the Latin word is a loan. Sim. 174 has *χορωνός.* Though Κορωνίς, the beloved of Apollo, had her name from her beauty (*τὸ κάλλος ἐπεκλήθη*: Isyllos), she may be the 'crow' not the 'garland.'—Metre: dact.-epitrite.

VII. Plato *Phaidros* 243 A: for those who have sinned in their treatment of the myths, there is an ancient purification, unknown indeed to Homer, but recognized by Stes., who, blinded because of his slander of Helen (probably in the *Ἰλίου πέρσις*), discovered the cause since he was a poet, for he forthwith wrote *οὐκ ἔστ' κ.τ.λ.* and received his sight immediately thereafter. These three verses of the Palinode, the most famous perhaps in all Greek poetry, are quoted by a host of later writers, and passed into a proverb. The thought that preceded v. 1 was: 'They say that thou wast seized with love of Paris and carried off to Troy.' Plato *Rep.* 586 C says that, according to Stes., it was Helen's semblance for which, in ignorance of the truth, the Greeks and Trojans contended. Whether this bold innovation on tradition was borrowed from Hesiod (cf. schol. Lykophr. 822) or original with the poet cannot be discovered. At any rate Stes. received the credit of it; and it is a characteristic of his genius to break with tradition. The poet seems to have implored the assistance of Helen's brothers: cf. Hor. *Epod.* 17. 42 *infamis Helenae Castor offensus vicem | fraterque magni Castoris, victi prece, | ademta vati reddidere lumina.* Hdt. 2. 112 relates that Proteus retained Helen in Egypt but dismissed Paris, who returned to Troy without his stolen bride and the treasure. In his *Helen*, Euripides recounts that she was carried off by the command of Zeus and that she abode in Egypt until Menelaos, returning with the *εἴδωλον*, discovers her and both escape to Greece. Euripides endeavoured to outdo his predecessors in transforming the post-Homeric version. The story was amplified at a later period: Paus. 3. 19. 13 makes Helen, who is living with Achilles in the island of Leuke, send a message to Stes. telling him that his loss of sight is due to her anger; and Konon *Narr.* 18 says that the message enjoined the poet to write the Palinode if he would regain his sight. In *Od.* 1. 16 Horace follows the example of Stes. —**2.** Cf. *ἔβαν κοίλῃς ἐνὶ νηυσὶν* α 211. Some retain the epic *νηυσὶν* here.—**3.** The terminal accus. with *ἱκνέομαι* is less noteworthy than that with ἐλθεῖν. ἱκνέομαι has practically become transitive ('reach'). **πέργαμα**: the plur. is first used by Stes. of an acropolis in general, here defined by Τροίας. In Homer ἡ Πέργαμος is the citadel of Troy. Pindar recurs to the Homeric usage, *Ol.* 8. 42, while Soph. *Phil.* 353 has τἀπὶ Τροίᾳ πέργαμα.—Metre: dact.-epitrite. Reading εὐσέλμοισιν Rossbach makes one verse of ll. 2 and 3.

VIII. Schol. Aristoph. *Pax* 775 (Μοῦσα, σὺ μὲν πολέμους ἀπωσαμένη μετ' ἐμοῦ | τοῦ φίλου χόρευσον | κλείουσα κ.τ.λ. σοὶ γὰρ τάδ' ἐξ ἀρχῆς μέλει) says these verses are a πλοκή (παραπλοκή?) or 'intertwining' of the words of Stes., as in the case of Frag. ix., x. It is uncertain how much belongs to the lyric, how much to the comic poet; some think the entire passage is taken from Stes. (Klein, Schneid.). The *Oresteia*, from which we have three fragments, was based either on the cyclic epic or on Xanthos. It embraced two of the twenty-six books of the poet.—**1.** **Μοῦσα**: we might expect Μοῖσα (Pind.) or Μῶσα.—**2.** **κλείουσα**, here and *Hymn* 32. 19, does not follow the usage of Homer, in whose text κλεέω is always possible.—Metre: dact.-epitrite.

IX. Schol. Aristoph. *Pax* 800 (ὅταν ἠρινὰ μὲν φωνῇ χελιδὼν | ἡδομένη κελαδῇ). On the swallow, see FOLK-SONGS xxii. **κελαδῇ**: -έῃ Mucke, on the ground that the choral poets do not contract outright.—Metre: dact.-epitrite.

X. Schol. Aristoph. *Pax* 797 (τοιάδε . . . καλλικόμων | τὸν σοφὸν ποιητὴν | ὑμνεῖν). **Χαρίτων**: cf. Pind. *Ol.* 9. 27 Χαρίτων νέμομαι κᾶπον· | κεῖναι γὰρ ὤπασαν τὰ τερπνά. **δαμώματα**: hymns composed for public delivery by choruses of men and youths at the festivals in the western colonies (δημοσίᾳ ᾀδόμενα). Hesychios thought the word meant a song of jollity, a meaning that suits Pind. *Isthm.* 8. 8 παυσάμενοι δ' ἀπράκτων κακῶν | γλυκύ τι δαμωσόμεθα. I do not agree with Bury who thinks our fragment is a song of joy sung by the members of the δᾶμος on the return of spring. **ἁβρῶς** is chiefly Ionic (cf. Anakr. viii., xxv.) but also used by Sappho *e.g.* xxii. **ἦρος ἐπερχ**: Alk. xxviii. Though the measures are dactylo-epitrite, the musical mode was the Phrygian, not the Dorian as we might expect. So the mode of Pind. *Nem.* 8 was Lydian, and several odes of the same poet, though Dorian in rhythm, show a mixture of the Dorian and the Lydian 'harmony.'

XI. Plut. *de sera numin. vind.* 10. The serpent in the ominous dream of Klytaimnestra was Orestes according to the legend followed by the tragic poets: Aisch. *Choeph.* 527

τεκεῖν δράκοντ' ἔδοξεν, Eur. *Or.* 479, 1424 μητροφόντης δράκων. Some (*e.g.* Seeliger p. 19) think that Πλ. here means Orestes, the descendant of Pleisthenes, just as Agam. is called Πελοπίδης and Ταντaλίδης. It is however generally supposed that Stes. substituted Agam. for his son. One version of the genealogy of the Pelopidai made Pl. the father of Agam. To reconcile this with the Homeric statement, the story was invented that Pl. died young, leaving his two sons to the care of his father Atreus; whence Agam. and Men. were called Atreidai. In Aisch. *Agam.* 1569 they are called Πλεισθενίδαι. Robert *Bild u. Lied* 171 suggests that in the further narration of the dream of Kl., the serpent Orestes, who drew blood instead of milk from his mother's breast, was the result of the union of the serpent Agam. and Kl. The account of the dream in Aischylos and Sophokles (*El.* 417) was therefore, on this view, derived from Stes., the second part of the dream being selected for dramatic purposes. The serpent with bloody crest indicates the wounds inflicted upon the head of Agam. (σχίζουσι κάρα φονίῳ πελέκει Soph. *El.* 99).—Metre: v. 1 dact. tetrap. + trip. v. 2 two dact. trip. catal. with the form of an elegiac hexam. (unusual). v. 1 might be written in two lines. Bergk wrote ἐδόκησεν to get an epitrite.

XII. Strabo 8. 347: Rhadina sailed with the west wind from Samos to Korinth, the tyrant of which city she wedded. Her brother and her cousin Leontichos sailed to Delphi at the same time. Leont. being in love with Rh. started thence for Korinth. On his arrival he was put to death by the tyrant together with Rhadina. We have in this story one of the elements out of which the Greek romance arose. Strabo thinks it is Samos in Triphylia that is meant, while Paus. 7. 5. 13 maintains that it is the Ionic island, and states that (on the road to the temple of Hera) there was a monument to Rhadina and Leontichos, at which unfortunate lovers offered their prayers.—**1.** Cf. Alkm. i. **λίγει'**: see on Terp. vi. **ἐρατωνύμου**; as Bacch. ix. 31. Bergk suggested 'Ερατοῖ, νόμους. Alkm. xviii. has ἐρατῶν ἐπέων.—Metre: logaoedics, which are rarely used by Stes., are felicitously chosen as the vehicle of a love story.

XIII. Plut. *de E apud Delph.* 21: quoted to show the antagonism between Apollo and Pluto. Bergk suggested that Stes. may have participated in the Delphic poetical contests that were newly organized during his life-time.—**1.** To take μάλα with φιλεῖ and μάλιστα (MSS.; possibly a dittography of μάλα τοι) with παιγμ. is harsh. Can μάλα τοι μάλιστα mean 'certainly above all things'? Bergk read μελιστᾶν, from μελιστάς (= μελικτάς Theokr. 4. 30) probably ||

κιθαριστάς Alkm. xxiv., since flute contests at Delphi were abandoned soon after their introduction. For the thought cf. Sa. xli., Plato *Laws* 947 B (when the chief priest of Apollo is buried there are no dirges), Aisch. *Sept.* 868, Frag. 161, Soph. *O.T.* 30, *O.K.* 1221, Eur. *El.* 142, *I.T.* 184, Kallim. 2. 20. Lyric poetry was less austere in the sixth century than in the time of Terpander.—Metre: dact.-epitrite.

XIV. Stob. *Flor.* 124. 15. **ἀτελέστατα**: apart from the verbals in -τέα, the neut. pl. of adj. used as a predicate appears in early poetry in Z 56, five times in Pind., once in Theognis (C.F. Smith *Trans. Am. Phil. Assoc.* 25. 73). For the sentiment cf. Sem. 2 τοῦ μὲν θανόντος οὐκ ἂν ἐνθυμοίμεθα, | εἴ τι φρονοῖμεν, πλεῖον ἡμέρης μιῆς, Archil. 9.—Metre: dact.-epitrite (or possibly logaoedics).

XV. Stob. *Flor.* 126. 5, Apostol. 8. 83 D. Cf. Archil. 63 οὔ τις αἰδοῖος μετ' ἀστῶν κἀναρίθμιος θανὼν | γίγνεται· χάριν δὲ μᾶλλον τοῦ ζοοῦ διώκομεν | οἱ ζοοί· κάκιστα δ' αὐτῷ τῷ θανόντι γίγνεται, Soph. *Aias* 1266 τοῦ θανόντος ὡς ταχεῖά τις βροτοῖς | χάρις διαρρεῖ. "The evil that men do lives after them, | The good is oft interred with their bones." For the elision in **ποτ'**, cf. Pind. *Ol.* 7. 90; ποτθέμεν Epicharm., ποτ τάν Aristoph.—Metre: dact.-epitrite. Some find here a troch. tetram. catal. (without caesura).

IBYKOS.

IONIAN and Dorian civilizations with their divergent ideals came together in the city in which the poet Ibykos was born. Rhegion in Bruttium was founded by Chalkidians from Ionic Euboia with whom were associated many Dorian fugitives from Messene. Thuk. 6. 43, 79 calls the inhabitants Chalkidians, but under the rule of Anaxilas (500-470) the city was Doric rather than Ionic. Whether the poet was of Ionic or Doric stock, or whether he was of mixed blood, is uncertain; in any event he must have been familiar with both Ionic and Doric, since both dialects were spoken in his birthplace. Early inscriptions of Rhegion show a non-Ionic element.

The meaning of his name is unknown. Some of the ancients connected it with ἴβυκος a screaming bird; a derivation which has doubtful support from such bird-names as Αἴγιθος, Ἔποψ, Κύψελος. Until he settled in

Samos, Ibykos seems to have led a wandering life like the rhapsodes and many of his own class. Himerios relates the fabulous story that on a journey from Katana to Himera he fell from his carriage and broke his arm, whereupon he made an offering of his lyre to Apollo. At Himera he may have become acquainted with Stesichoros whose influence is traceable in his fragments.

The only dates that are mentioned in Ibykos' life are connected with his stay in Samos. Probably his *floruit* was fixed by the chronographers with regard to his sojourn at the Samian court; just as the *floruit* of Anakreon and Pythagoras was placed in 532 because Polykrates became tyrant in that year. Suidas reports that the poet came to Samos in 564, when Polykrates the father (grandfather ?) of the despot was lord. The father of the famous Polykrates is known to have been Aiakes, and it may have been at his request that Ibykos came to the island in order to assist in the education of his son. Aiakes ascended the throne in the same year as Kyros (560), to whom the poet may refer in Frag. 20, unless Kyaxares is meant by Κυάρας. Polykrates reigned from 532 (or 530) to 523 or 522. Kyrillos sets the *floruit* of Ibykos at 544, which may be tolerably near the truth.

Ibykos' fabulous death, which has been popularized by Schiller, is first narrated by Antipater of Sidon (*Anth. Pal.* 7. 745) over four centuries after the poet's time. Antipater relates briefly that the poet was attacked by robbers when he was walking on a lonely shore after leaving his ship, and that in expiring he called upon a passing flock of cranes to become his avengers. Plutarch places the scene of the arrest of the murderers in the theatre at Korinth, while Suidas adds that one of their number, seeing some cranes in that city, exclaimed *ἰδέ, αἱ Ἰβύκου ἔκδικοι*, which remark, being overheard, led to their arrest and conviction. The story gave rise to the proverb *αἱ Ἰβύκου γέρανοι*.

The tale has two main ingredients: (1) That the poet was murdered. This may or may not be true, but Frag. ii., where the poet apparently speaks of himself as aged, makes for neither view. We have legends of the murder of Hesiod and Aesop, who perished when on journeys, of Stesichoros, who was killed by robbers, etc.

These stories may have come into existence from the belief that minstrels often journeyed alone and carried with them the proceeds of their art. (2) That cranes witnessed the murder, and became the instruments of vengeance. Welcker regarded this part of the story as an illustration of the popular belief in a poetic justice whose instruments are the birds, the representatives of the gods and joint inhabitants of the air with the all-seeing sun which brings to light the hidden deed. Person and place are secondary circumstances and vary with the particular case, but the religious or moral sense demands a concrete instance to attest the truth of the universal law. Welcker's explanation, while probable enough, still lacks some actual points of departure to establish the necessary connection of Ibykos with his cranes. It is most likely that the tale is the creation of a period when 'nature-poetry' was no longer in process of formation and that some etymologizing rhetor or grammarian brought the name of the poet into connection with ἴβυξ, which he thought was the equivalent of γέρανος. It is noteworthy that none of Ibykos' lyric successors or Plato, to whom the story would have been serviceable, makes any mention of the legend.

Ibykos' poetical activity falls into two periods, though we cannot be sure that they do not overlap. Before he went to Samos he followed in the path of Stesichoros, whose Ἆθλα ἐπὶ Πελίᾳ was sometimes ascribed to him. From scattered references to the epico-lyric poems, none of the titles of which are cited, we learn that he anticipated Pindar in describing the voyage of the Argonauts. He related that Achilles wedded Medeia in Elysium, gave Jason a sister--Hippolyte, and made mention of the Harpies, Phineus, and Orpheus. Many of the heroic personages of the Trojan war reappeared in his hymns. Thus we know that he treated of Hektor, whom he made a son of Apollo, of Odysseus, Diomedes, Idomeneus, the friend of Helen, the Dioskuroi, and Menelaos. The story of Herakles that had been told by Stesichoros was taken up by Ibykos.

With the sojourn at Samos begins the subjective period, in which the poet shows the influence of the Aiolians, as does Anakreon who was associated with him at the court of Polykrates. Ibykos and Anakreon are the first poets to place their muse at the disposition of a tyrant. We do not know the degree of subservience or of independence displayed by these court poets; but even if Pindar, with a reference to Ibykos, says that before his own time the muse was not venal or put to hire, it is scarcely probable that Ibykos manifested the independence of spirit displayed by Pindar or even by Simonides at the more splendid courts of the Sicilian tyrants.

Though he recalls Alkman, Ibykos occupies a unique position in the history of Greek lyric. He unites the opposing tendencies of Dorian and Aiolic song. In him the choral poetry of the Dorians borrows the glow of passion that illuminates the monodic lyric of the Aiolians. We cannot discover how far the love poems of Ibykos are the outpouring of his own heart, since they assume the choral form with its threefold division, which in Stesichoros was restricted to the objective hymnodic song. Much of Ibykos' lyric was devoted to the praise of beautiful youths (the παιδικοὶ ὕμνοι) and it was this aspect of his work that attracted the attention of the ancients, though they objected to its vivid erotic colouring. Cicero *Tusc.* 4. 33. 71 says *maxime vero omnium flagrare amore Rheginum Ibycum apparet ex scriptis.* In his love songs a mythological element reinforced the expression of a feeling that was either personal or the product of the vivid fancy of the poet. Thus in a poem in honour of Gorgias he narrated the story of Ganymede, who was carried off by Zeus, and of Tithonos and Aurora. Ibykos mixed the human and divine after a fashion totally different from that of Alkman in his partheneia. He introduced the enkomia, in which a living person was made the subject of the lyric muse which up to his time had been confined to the praise of gods or heroes, and was herein the successor of Stesichoros and the predecessor of Pindar in his ode to Theoxenos (Frag. xv.).

The style of Ibykos is graceful and passionate; it is illuminated by figures that are full of force and vividness; and it employs descriptive epithets with fine effect. Ibykos has more life and energy than Stesichoros and a keener eye for the beauty of nature.

His poems consisted of seven books, a division that was

based probably on differences of metre. These are in the main those employed by Stesichoros though there is herein no mark of a special connection between the two poets. Dactyls predominate, but epitrites are not unusual. The $\frac{3}{8}$ measures are better adapted to the style of the poet in his later period when he came under Aiolic influence. Ibykos uses a slight admixture of Aiolism, which is foreign to the dialect of Stesichoros if we may judge from the MSS. of the scanty fragments of the latter poet. Otherwise his dialect is a fusion of Doric with Ionic-epic elements which is not to be ascribed to his native Rhegine speech.

I. Athen. 13. 601 B. In nature Love shows his power in the springtime; the heart of the poet he dominates continually (*οὐδεμίαν κατάκοιτος ὥραν*). Cf. Theogn. 1275 *ὡραῖος καὶ Ἔρως ἐπιτέλλεται, ἡνίκα περ γῆ | ἄνθεσιν εἰαρινοῖς θάλλει ἀεξομένη. | τῆμος Ἔρως προλιπὼν Κύπρον, περικαλλέα νῆσον, | εἶσιν ἐπ' ἀνθρώπους σπέρμα φέρων κατὰ γῆς.* As Eros, the child of Aphrodite, is a god of the spring-tide, so to Aphrodite herself the spring is sacred: *tibi suavis daedala tellus | summittit flores.* Lucr. 1. 7. Cf. the Earl of Surrey's *Description of Spring*, and Hor. 2. 9. The closing lines of the strophe are a swiftly moving panorama; the interlacing of the strophe with the antistrophe increases the effectiveness of the picture of the rapid assault of passion.

1. Κυδώνιαι: *mala, quae vocamus cotonea, et Graeci cydonia, ex Creta insula advecta* (Pliny *H. N.* 15. 10). The quince was regarded as the best species of apple. The *χρυσόμηλα* were a kind of quince, perhaps the same as the *aurea mala* of Verg. *Ecl.* 3. 71, though some think that they are pomegranates; or *aurea* is used for *pulcherrima* (*Ecl.* 8. 52). In *Ecl.* 2. 51 quinces are *cana tenera lanugine mala.* Kydonian apples are mentioned in Alkm. 143, Stes. vi. They were sometimes called *κοδύμαλα* (Alkm. 90). Cf. Athen. 3. § 20.

2. μαλίδες = Hom. *μηλέαι*; *μαλίς* is the tree, *μᾶλον* the fruit as in Theokr. 8. 79 (*τᾷ μαλίδι μᾶλα, scil. κόσμος*). *μηλέα, ἐλαία, κίτριον* are both tree and fruit. The quince and the common apple were love-offerings: Verg. *Ecl.* 3. 71 (cf. Theokr. 3. 10) *aurea mala decem misi; cras altera mittam,* Theokr. 2. 120, 5. 88, etc., *Anth. Pal.* 5. 79, 80; *roscida mala . . . donum Veneris* Claudian *epith. Pall.* 8. **ῥοᾶν**: *ἄρδω* with the gen. as in *Hymn* 9. 3 ἵππους ἄρσασα βαθυσχοίνοιο Μέλητος, Euphorion 75 Σιμόεντος Ἀχαιίδας ἄρσαμεν ἵππους (dat. in Aisch. *Pers.* 805 πεδίον Ἀσωπὸς ῥοαῖς ἄρδει). These examples have been compared with λούεσθαι ποταμοῖο as opposed to λ. ὕδατι. The constr. of λούεσθαι with the gen., regarded as 'quasi-partitive' by Monro, *H. G.* § 151, is still obscure (Delbrück in Brugmann's *Grundriss* 3. 1. 330; cf. Kühner-Gerth 2. § 417. 3. n. 4). αἵματος ἔδευσε γαῖαν Eur. *Phoin.* 674 may be an analogue of πίμπλημι. ῥοᾶν can scarcely be called a genitive of material. ἀρδ. ῥοᾶν ἐκ ποτ. is not = ἐκ ῥοᾶν ποτ. and is not to be supported by πᾶσα δύναμις ἐξ ὑδάτων ἄρδεται (Athen. 2. 43 c) or by Hdt. 1. 193 ἀρδόμενον ἐκ τοῦ ποταμοῦ. Cf. on Bacch. xvii. 2.

3. ἐκ ποταμῶν = ποταμίων ('river-streams'); a prepositional phrase takes the place of an adj. as in Sa. xxiv. Ϝρόδων τῶν ἐκ Πιερίας, Pind. ix. 5 ὅπλα ἀπ' Ἄργεος, Aristoph. *Ekkles.* 918 τὸν ἀπ' Ἰωνίας τρόπον. The ῥοαί are led off by ὀχετοί (αὐλῶνες, διώρυχες). ἄρδω of irrigation Hdt. 1. 193. **παρθένων**: the garden of the nymphs was described by Homer ρ 209 (cf. μ 318) and by Sappho (see on Frag. iv. and cf. Theokr. 7. 135). Some write Παρθένων, and find here an allusion to the garden of the Hesperides, though the daughters of Atlas are not called παρθένοι. In Athen. 3. 83 B the golden apples of the Hesperides are said to be citrons. Paus. 8. 24. 7 says that the cypresses planted about the tomb of Alkmaion were called παρθένοι and never cut down. A reference to these trees and to a local cult would however be out of place here.

4. ἀκήρατος: *Hymn* 3. 72 λειμῶνας ἀκηρασίους, Choirilos 1 ἀκήρατος λειμών of the Muses, Eur. *Hippol.* 73 σοὶ τόνδε πλεκτὸν στέφανον ἐξ ἀκηράτου | λειμῶνος . . . | ἔνθ' οὔτε ποιμὴν ἀξιοῖ φέρβειν βοτὰ | οὔτ' ἦλθέ πω σίδηρος, ἀλλ' ἀκήρατον | μέλισσα λειμῶν' ἠρινὸν διέρχεται. The garden is ἀνειμένος (cf. Plato *Laws* 761 c). **οἰνανθίδες**: elsewhere οἰνάνθη, the bud (*gemma*) that appears on the shoot (*palmes*) of the vine (οἴνη *vitis*). Cf. Pind. *Nem.* 5. 6 τέρειναν ματέρ' οἰνάνθας ὀπώραν, 'season of fruit, tender mother of the vine-blossom,' Eur. *Phoin.* 229 οἴνα θ', ἃ καθαμέριον | στάζεις τὸν πολύκαρπον | οἰνάνθας ἱεῖσα βότρυν.

5. αὐξόμεναι: the melic poets generally prefer αὔξω to the epic ἀέξω (still used by Pind. and Sim.).—**6. ἔρος**: Aiolic and epic, also in tragedy.

7. οὐδεμίαν: Welcker, *Kl. Schr.* 1. 233, wrongly thought the reference in οὐδ. ὥραν is to the manifold use of Ibykos' love-songs in praise of beautiful youths. Cf. Tibull. 1.

2. 4 *infelix dum requiescit amor.* **κατάκοιτος**: only here. **ὑπό** 'amid,' of the external accompaniment of an action, as of sound ὑπ' αὐλῶν Anakr. x., ὑπ' ἀοιδᾶς Pind. *Ol.* 4. 3; of light ὑπὸ λαμπάδων Eur. *Ion* 1474: of pressure from without ὀρύσσειν ὑπὸ μαστίγων Hdt. 7. 22. See Jebb on Soph. *Trach.* 419. In ἀέλλῃ ὑπὸ βροντῆς N 796 the thunder is regarded as the cause of the squall. Ancient meteorology saw in the wind the cause, in the lightning the effect. Cf. Lucr. 6. 96, 246: flashes of lightning struck out by the collision of the clouds. In Verg. *Aen.* 8. 429 three shafts of red fire and winged Auster form the motive force of the thunderbolt together with three shafts of writhen rain and watery cloud, cf. 2. 649. But in Ibykos an allusion to a distinctly physical doctrine would be inapposite. **φλέγων**: 'raging.' The transitive use in the transferred sense in Eur. *Phoin.* 250 ἀμφὶ δὲ πτόλιν νέφος | ἀσπίδων πυκνὸν φλέγει | σχῆμα φοινίου μάχης. See on Bacch. xiii. 12.

8. Θρηΐκιος: the 'ruffian Boreas' of Chaucer, I 5, Hes. *W. D.* 553, Tyrt. 12. 4. The Ionic η is invariably preserved in choral poetry (Pind. *Pyth.* 4. 205, Soph. *O. T.* 197). Hor. 1. 25. 11 has *Thracio bacchante magis sub inter-* | *lunia vento.* In Sa. xiii. Love is a wind that descends on the mountain oaks. Here obstinate, persistent passion is compared to Boreas. Contrast Soph. *Aias* 257 λαμπρᾶς γὰρ ἄτερ στεροπῆς | ᾄξας ὀξὺς νότος ὣς λήγει. Some winds are *sine pertinacia vehementes* Seneca *de ira* 1. 16. **ἀζαλέαις**: passive in Hom. Frenzy parches like the dog-star (ἀζ. Σείριος Hes. *Shield* 153) or the sun (ἀζ. ἥλιος Apoll. Rhod. 4. 679). **ἐρεμνός**: Love, the storm-wind, is an ἐρεμνὴ λαῖλαψ (M 375). Cf. Dante on Love: 'There seemed to be in my room a mist of the colour of fire, within which I discerned the figure of one of terrible aspect' (*Vita Nuova* 3). Love, the child of Zephyr, is a δεινότατος θεός Alk. iii. **ἀθαμβής**: cf. Bacch. viii. 22. Some read ἀστεμφής.

9. πεδόθεν τινάσσει: Hes. *Theogon.* 680 πεδόθεν δ' ἐτινάσσετο μακρὸς Ὄλυμπος, Sa. xiii. ἔρος . . . φρένας ἐτίναξεν. The reading of the MSS. παιδόθεν φυλάσσει 'holds my heart captive from my earliest manhood' is inappropriate and ill supported by Cicero's *a puero litteris deditum.* Nor can παιδόθεν = παιδός because of the distance from ἔρος.—**10. ἁμετέρας φρένας**: so Bacch. 12. 3.—Metre: a logaoedic strophe of simple structure though more elaborate than Alkm. iv. We have here the beginnings of the freer logaoedic movement in choral poetry. v. 7 consists of two catal. tetrap. like 1-3; v. 8 of a catal. tetrap. and a dact. heptapody. The dactyls are probably choreic not cyclic.

II. Schol. Plato *Parmen.* 137 A. Cf. Sa. xvi., Anakr. vii., xix., Hor. 4. 1 *intermissa, Venus, diu | rursus bella moves? Parce precor, precor. | non sum qualis eram bonae | sub regno Cinarae.*— **1. αὖτε**: see on Alkm. xiii. **κυανέοισιν**: cf. A 528 *κυανέῃσιν ἐπ' ὀφρύσι*, Hes. *Shield* 7 *βλεφάρων ἀπὸ κυανεάων*. The *υ* is lengthened as in Homer. So *κῡανέας* Pind. *Ol.* 6. 40. **βλεφάροις**: cf. Hes. *Theogon.* 910 *τῶν καὶ ἀπὸ βλεφάρων ἔρος εἴβετο δερκομενάων | λυσιμελής· καλὸν δέ θ' ὑπ' ὀφρύσι δερκιόωνται.* **τακέρ' δερκόμενος**: as *παρθένιον βλέπων* Anakr. iv., *λοξὸν βλέπουσα* Anakr. xxvii., *φθονερὰ βλέπειν* Pind. *Nem.* 4. 39; *τακερὸν βλέπειν* Alkiphron 1. 28, *τακεραῖς λεύσσουσα κόραις* *Anth. Pal.* 9. 567. Anakr. 169 calls Eros *τακερός*, and Aphrodite's glance is *τακερόν* (Philetairos 231), and was so represented in the sculptures of the fourth century. *τήκομαι* of love Pind. xv. 9. Some find metonymy here as in *χλωρὸν δέος, φρίσσοντας ὄμβρους*, 'cold shuddering dew.' For the sentiment we may compare Eur. *Hek.* 442 *διὰ καλῶν γὰρ ὀμμάτων | . . . Τροίαν εἷλε* (Helen).—**2. ἄπειρα**: *ἀμφίβληστρον ἄπειρον* Aisch. *Agam.* 1382.—**3. δίκτυα**: cf. Ariphron 5. Eros is the *κύων Ἀφροδίτης*. **με** (supplied by Bergk) does not repeat *με* in l. 1, since that depends on *δερκ.* A pronoun may be repeated under stress of excitement (especially in entreaty) when the construction is not altered. A complete member of the sentence intervenes in such cases. **βάλλει** *de conatu.*—**5. ἀεθλοφόρος** = *φερένικος* (the name of Hieron's horse). Cf. Λ 699 *ἀθλοφόροι ἵπποι αὐτοῖσιν ὄχεσφιν | ἐλθόντες μετ' ἄεθλα*, X 22 *σευάμενος ὥς θ' ἵππος ἀεθλοφόρος σὺν ὄχεσφιν*, Alkm. iv. 48. **ποτί**: close to old age; cf. Soph. *O. T.* 1169 *πρὸς αὐτῷ γ' εἰμὶ τῷ δεινῷ λέγειν*, Pind. *Nem.* 9. 44 *τελέθει πρὸς γῆρας αἰών* (personification). According to Pliny *N. H.* 8. 42, 9. 64 race-horses live longer than ordinary horses, which are old at sixteen. The former may continue to race till they are twenty, and live till fifty. Flying Childers died at 26, Henry Clay and Dictator lived to at least 30, while Matchem, who stopped racing at 10, lived to 33. Even stud-horses do not reach the age mentioned by Pliny. The simile of course proves nothing as to the advanced age of the poet himself.— **6. σύν** is personal and comitative; the car accompanies the steed in his course. Cf. *σὺν ἅρματι θοῷ* Pind. *Ol.* 1. 110, *σὺν ἵπποις Pyth.* 11. 48. **ὄχεσφι**: when Ibyk. does not borrow -*φι* from Hom., as here, he uses it out of place (*Λιβυαφιγενής* 57). **θοοῖς**: *θοός* generally of actual speed. See on Mimn. 12. 9. **ἔβα**: the aorist in similes is used for vividness, *e.g.* N 389 *ἤριπε δ' ὡς ὅτε τις δρῦς ἤριπεν*, Γ 23, 33. This aorist is akin to the gnomic. See Goodwin *M. T.* 547, 548. For the thought cf. Soph. *El.* 25 *ὥσπερ γὰρ ἵππος εὐγενής, κἂν ᾖ γέρων κ.τ.λ.*, where Jebb quotes Philostr. *Vit. Sophist.* 2. 23. 4 ἄνδρα . . . νωθρὸς γὰρ ὑφ' ἡλικίας δοκῶν νεάζουσαν ὁρμὴν ἐν ταῖς σπουδαῖς ἀνεκτᾶτο. Ibykos is imitated by Ennius *Ann.* 441: *sicut fortis equus, spatio qui saepe supremo | vicit Olympia, nunc senio confectu' quiescit.* Cf. Tibull. 1. 4. 31: *quam iacet, infirmae venere ubi fata senectae, | qui prior Eleo est carcere missus equus,* Verg. *Georg.* 3. 95-100, Hor. *Epist.* 1. 1. 8.—Metre: dactylic, with a protracted trochee in l. 3 (unless we read K. βάλεν or εἰσέβαλεν).

III. Theon Smyrn. 146: cited to illustrate the poetical use of σείρια = ἄστρα. Usually σείριος was employed of the dog-star. Archil. 61 σείριος ὀξὺς ἐλλάμπων was thought to be the sun (cf. Orph. *Argon.* 120), and so even Σείριος ἀστήρ Hes. *W. D.* 417. Eratosth. *Katast.* 33 μέγας δ' ἐστὶ καὶ λαμπρὸς (Σείριος)· τοὺς δὲ τοιούτους ἀστέρας οἱ ἀστρολόγοι σειρίους καλοῦσι. Cf. Nauck *Mélanges gr.-rom.* 4. 599, and see on Alkm. iv. 62. **παμφανόωντα** as Θ 435: the only case of a 'distracted' verb in the lyric poets, and the earliest evidence, outside of the epic, of these vicious forms.—Metre: catal. dact. tetram. + catal. trim. Rossbach calls the verse a syncopated anap. tetram. (⏑ ⏑ — — — ⏑ ⏑ — ⏑ ⏑ ⊔ — ⏑ ⏑ — ⏑ ⏑ ⊔ —⊼).

IV. Athen. 9. 388 E. For **αἰεί μ'** Bergk read δίημ' = πτώσσω. **θυμέ**: cf. Archil. 66, Pind. *Nem.* 3. 26, xv. 1, Frag. 127. 2, φιλὰ ψυχά *Pyth.* 3. 61, φίλον ἦτορ *Ol.* 1. 4. The πορφυρίς, mentioned in Aristoph. *Aves* 304, is referred to in Frag. 8 (αἰολόδειροι λαθιπορφυρίδες). It probably differed from the πορφυρίων, the purple gallinule. In Alkm. vii. the ἁλιπορφυρίς is the halcyon.—Metre: two trip., each ending in a dactyl, form the *hexam. Ibyceum.*

V. Athen. xiii. 564 F: quoted with Sa. ix., Anakr. iv., Pind. xv., Likymn. iii., etc., to show that love is "engender'd in the eyes." Philoxenos' address to Galateia (p. 137) is called 'blind panegyric' and totally dissimilar to the praise of Euryalos. γλυκεᾶν, γλυκεῖᾶν, and γλυκέων have been proposed for **γλαυκέ͜ων**, which is a solitary case in choral poetry of Ionic-epic -εων from an ᾱ stem. γλαύκειος occurs only in the proverb γλαύκειον ᾠόν. With this passage, cf. Hdt. 4. 108. **θάλος**: cf. Χαρίτων θρέμμα Aristoph. *Ekkles.* 974, Χαρίτων ἱερὸν φυτόν Theokr. 28. 7, κόλπῳ σ' ἐδέξαντο ἅγναι Χάριτες Alk. xxvii. Ibykos sings only of the beauty of youths.—**2. καλλικόμων** is sometimes taken substantively, *pulchricomarum virginum cura*; cf. χρυσοδαίδαλτον μέλημα Aristoph. *Ekkles.* 972. Others supply Ἐρώτων, Μουσῶν (cf. Sa. 60, Sim. 44), Νυμφῶν, etc. (cf. καλλίκομοι κοῦραι Διός Anakr. 69). It is better to suppose that a line has been lost that contained the point of Athenaios' quotation. **μελέδημα**: cf. Pind. Frag. 95 *σεμνᾶν Χαρίτων μέλημα τερπνόν*. **Κύπρις**: Ibyk. is the only choral poet who permits 'Attic' correption in this word. Pind. has Κῠπρος. —**3. ἀγανοβλ. Πειθώ**: cf. Aisch. *Eum.* 970 *στέργω δ' ὄμματα Πειθοῦς*. Peitho (*Suada*, *Suadela*) appears first in Hes. *W. D.* 73. Sa. 135 and Aisch. *Suppl.* 1040 call her the daughter of Aphrodite, and Sa. 57 A calls her 'Aphrodite's handmaid bright as gold.' See on Sa. i. 18. To Pind. (Frag. 122) Peitho is the handmaid of Aphr. Pandemos with whom she was associated in the Attic cult. In Megara a statue of Aphr. Praxis was placed near figures of Peitho and Paregoros, both the work of Praxiteles. There was an Aphr. Peitho in Thessaly and Lesbos. Cf. Hor. *Epist.* 1. 6. 38 *ac bene nummatum decorat Suadela Venusque.* Peitho appears in the scene where Aphr. persuades Helen (Baumeister fig. 708); Sappho, Aphr., Peitho, Himeros and Pothos occur together (Baum. fig. 1809). Cf. *Anth. Pal.* 6. 14 of Sappho: *ἃν Κύπρις καὶ Ἔρως σὺν ἅμ' ἔτραφον, ἃς μέτα Πειθὼ | ἔπλεκ' ἀείζωον Πιερίδων στέφανον*.—Metre: vv. 1, 2 dact. tetrap., v. 3 heptap. Perhaps the penultimate syllable was prolonged by *τονή*.

VI. Athen. 15. 681 A. The mention of apples, perhaps those of Kydon (Frag. i.), shows that the fragment describes a *φυλλοβολία*. See on Stes. vi. The *ἑλίχρυσος* was called *χρυσάνθεμον* in ancient times, and *δάκρυα τῆς Παναγίας* (the Virgin) by the Modern Greeks. Cf. Alkm. iii., *ξανθοτέρα ἑλιχρύσοιο* Theokr. 2. 78.—Metre: logaoedic.

VII. Herodian *περὶ σχημάτων* 60. 24 (*Rhet. Gr.* 3. 101). Cf. Soph. *El.* 17 *ἤδη λαμπρὸν ἡλίου σέλας | ἑῷα κινεῖ φθέγματ' ὀρνίθων σαφῆ*. Some read *ἀύπνους* or *ἀύπνος* (Dor. accus.) as a proleptic accus.: *excitat luscinias, ut somnum mittant.* But there is no need of change. Cf. *φιλάγρυπνε* of Selene, *Orphic Hymn* 9. 7. **κλυτός**: *clarus*, of the beauty and splendour of the dawn; Shakesp. "Full many a glorious morning." The ancients thought *κλυτός* here = *ὁ τοῦ κλύειν αἴτιος*. Contrast "the busy day, wak'd by the lark" *Troil.* 4. 1. **ἐγείρῃσιν** as K 511, depends on a conj. requiring the subj.—Metre: logaoedic. A *μέν* after *ὄρθρος* would give a choriambic pentam. Some divide after *ὄρθρος*.

VIII. Herodian *περὶ σχημ.* 60. 31. The prophetic power of Kassandra is first mentioned in Stasinos' *Κύπρια*. Homer calls her the most beautiful of Priam's daughters (N 365), and describes the scene when before all others she observes the return of her father from the Grecian camp (Ω 699). He also alludes to her death at the hands of Klytaimnestra (λ 422). In the Ἰλίου πέρσις Arktinos narrated her capture by the lesser Ajax, who dragged her by the hair from the statue of Athene. Schneidewin unnecessarily thought the adj. ἐρασιπλ. (cf. Pind. *Pyth.* 4. 136) points to a mention of her seizure in the poem of Ibykos.—**2. φᾶμις ἔχησι βροτῶν**: cf. *Batrach.* 8 ὡς ἔπος ἐν θνητοῖσιν ἔφυ, Soph. *Antig.* 829 ὡς φάτις ἀνδρῶν, Eur. *I. A.* 72 ὡς ὁ μῦθος ἀνθρώπων ἔχει. For this use of ἔχω cf. α 95 μιν κλέος ἐν ἀνθρώποισιν ἔχῃσιν, Mimn. 15, Aisch. *Suppl.* 1025, Eur. *Med.* 420, κατέχω Pind. *Ol.* 7. 10, *Pyth.* 1. 96. **ἔχησι**: not -ησι, but subj. dependent upon a preceding conjunction. The *schema Ibyceum*, which supposes the use of -ησι in the *indic.* of barytone Ω verbs, does not exist. It is possible that the grammarians misunderstood the epic ἐθέλῃσι, ἄγῃσι etc. and held that -ησι might appear in the *subj.*; or they transferred the Aiolic indic. -ησι (φίλησι = φιλεῖ) to ἔχω. ἐγείρησι, ἔχησι, and θάλπησι Bacch. xvii. 2 should be written -ῃσι.—Metre: dactylic. Some make v. 1 γλ. . . . Πριάμοιο (= anap. tetram. catal.).

IX. Athen. 2. 58 A. From a lyric poem with an epic subject after the manner of Stesichoros. Herakles narrates his victory over Kteatos and Eurytos, the Siamese Twins of Greek mythology. They were the offspring of Poseidon and Molione, and had, according to the post-Homeric legend, two heads, four hands, and four feet, but a single body. The twins Otos and Ephialtes were also monstrosities. Homer does not explicitly state the physical union of the Moliones. In Ψ 638 he calls them twins, and says that while one drove, the other plied the whip. Their putative father was Aktor, so that they are called Ἀκτορίωνε B 621, and Ἀκτ. Μολίονε Λ 750. Though metronymics occur (Cheiron is Φιλυρίδης), the juxtaposition of a patronymic and a metronymic is improbable. The moderns are inclined to follow the ancients in believing that Μολίονε conceals an appellative. As generals of their uncle Augeias they gained a victory over Herakles (πρὸς δύο οὐδὲ Ἡρακλῆς), but were afterwards slain near Kleonai; Pind. *Ol.* 10. 27 ff. Their death was pictured on the throne of the Amyklaian Apollo.

1. λευκίππους: this adj. was first used by Stes. Greek princes have white steeds. The horses of Rhesos were whiter than snow (K 437), the Dioskuroi are λευκόπωλοι Pind. *Pyth.* 1. 66, Eur. *Hel.* 639, as are Zethos and Amphion *H. F.* 29; and so the gods *Phoin.* 606. Cf. also Diodor. 18. 32. While white was a sacred colour for horses (Soph. *El.* 705, Plaut. *Asin.* 279, Verg. *Aen.* 12. 84, Hor. *Sat.* 1. 7. 8) it did not necessarily imply excellence (χρόᾳ δὲ οὐκ ἔχω ἵππων ἀρετὴν ὁρίσαι Simon *de re equestri* in *R. M.* 51. 67. 8). Greek and Hebrew taste (*Apoc.* 19. 11) was not Roman taste (*color deterrimus albis* Verg. *Georg.* 3. 82). Only a later age regarded white horses as a mark of luxury. Cf. Plut. *Cam.* 7. 1, Livy 5. 23. The sons of Poseidon ἵππιος are naturally horsemen.—**3.** Cf. σ 373 (βόες) ἥλικες, ἰσοφόροι. ἰσοκεφάλους (MS.) would introduce a resolved — ⏑ ⏑, which is objectionable.—**4.** **γεγαῶτας**: B 866. **ὤεον**. occurs in Epicharm. 103, Sem. 11, ὤβεα, *i.e.* ὤϝεα, in the Argive dialect, ὤιον in Sa. 56. The twin sons of Leda also sprang from an egg. Some see here a reference to Orphic doctrines.—Metre: logaoedic (regarded by some as dact.-epitrite). v. 2 τέκνα with weak position as in Hes. Frag. 75, Pind. *Ol.* 6. 62. Correption in the thesis is very rare (Kor. iv., FOLK-SONGS xxvii. 24). See Smyth *Trans. Am. Phil. Assoc.* 28. 124.

X. Schol. Pind. *Nem.* 1. 1; cf. Strabo 1. 59. The Korinthians under Archias settled in 734 B.C. the island of Ortygia, κλεινᾶν Συρακοσσᾶν θάλος. At the latest in the second half of the sixth century, Ortygia was united by a mole to Achradina on the mainland. **ἔκλεκτον**: cf. λογάδων λίθων Paus. 7. 22. 5, 'picked,' *i.e.* 'unhewn;' Thuc. 4. 4 λογάδην φέροντες λίθους, 4. 31 λίθων λογάδην πεποιημένον. But Ibykos implies that the mole was constructed with more than usual care and of selected stones. **ἀναριτᾶν**: perhaps ναριτᾶν. On **πεδ'** see Sa. xxiv.—Metre: logaoedic.

XI. Plut. *Quaest. Symp.* 9. 15. 2; Plato *Phaidros* 242 C. Plato has παρὰ θεοῖς = *apud deos, in diis* (cf. Ter. *Andria* 233 *in aliis peccandi locum*) 'in the judgment of the gods.' Cf. ἐν θεοῖσι τὴν δίκην δώσειν 'before the tribunal of heaven,' Soph. *Antig.* 459. Reading θεοίς (Aiolic accus.) the meaning will be 'sinning against the gods.' Cf. Xen. *Memorab.* 1. 3. 4 τῶν ἄλλων δὲ μωρίαν κατηγόρει (Sokr.), οἵτινες παρὰ τὰ ὑπὸ τῶν θεῶν σημαινόμενα ποιοῦσί τι, φυλαττόμενοι τὴν παρὰ τοῖς ἀνθρώποις ἀδοξίαν. **πρὸς ἀνθρώπων**: either 'from,' as τιμὴν ... ἄρηαι πρὸς πάντων Π 84, or 'in the eyes of,' as ἄδικον πρὸς ἀνθρ. Thuk. 1. 71. 5.—Metre: dact.-epitrite.

XII. Chrysipp. περὶ ἀποφατ. 14. *Für den Tod ist kein Kraut gewachsen.* Cf. Anakr. xvi., Aisch. *Eum.* 648, and contrast Pind. *Pyth.* 4. 186 ἀλλ' ἐπὶ καὶ θανάτῳ | φάρμακον ἐᾶς ἀρετᾶς ἅλιξιν εὑρέσθαι σὺν ἄλλοις. φάρμακον also Archil. 9. 6. —Metre: dact. hexam. with anacrusis, the enhoplian rhythm formed of two prosodiacs (— ⁞ ⏗ ⏑ ⏑ ⏗ ⏑ ⏑ ⏗ and — ⁞ ⏗ ⏑ ⏑ ⏗ ⏑ ⏑ ⏗ —).

PYTHERMOS

Pythermos, the next writer of skolia after Terpander, is said to have invented the Ionian (or Hypophrygian) musical mode, which received this name from the fact that the poet was born in Teos, an Ionic island. Westphal placed him early in the seventh century because Polymnastos, who is quoted by Alkman, is said to have brought the Ionian mode from Kolophon to Sparta. It is more probable that he lived shortly before or at the same time as Hipponax or Ananios (540 B.C.), since one of these iambists refers to him by name. Pythermos is thus a contemporary of his countryman Anakreon. He borrowed from Sappho the logaoedic pentapody (hendecasyllabus), which remained a characteristic form of the skolion for two centuries.

Athen. 14. 625 C, citing Ananios (2) or Hipponax, *χρυσὸν λέγει Π. ὡς οὐδὲν τἄλλα*, Suidas, *s.v. οὐδὲν ἦν*. 'All else is then nought save gold.' Cf. Alk. xxv., Pind. xxxii., Theogn. 699 *πλήθει δ' ἀνθρώπων ἀρετὴ μία γίνεται ἥδε, | πλουτεῖν· τῶν δ' ἄλλων οὐδὲν ἄρ' ἦν ὄφελος*, Antiphan. Frag. 232, Trag. Adesp. 294 *χρυσὸς γάρ ἐστιν ὃς βροτῶν ἔχει κράτη*. **ἦν ἄρα**: the imperf. of the sudden recognition of a previously unsuspected connection between two things. The imperf. denotes that the present fact, though just recognized, was true before. The imperf. of 'previous admission' is different. For the use of *ἦν ἄρα* cf. *ν* 209 *οὐκ ἄρα πάντα νοήμονες οὐδὲ δίκαιοι ἦσαν*, Soph. *O. K.* 117, *Phil.* 978, Eur. *Hel.* 746, *Or.* 721, *Hippol.* 359, *H. F.* 341, *Med.* 703, Frag. 810, Aristoph. *Pax* 832, *Nubes* 1028, Plato *Gorg.* 508 C, schol. Theokr. 11. 1; see Kock on *Nubes* 165, Shilleto on Thuk. 1. 69, Demosth. *falsa leg.* § 177. **τἆλλα**: not *τἄλλα*, Lucius *de crasi* 12. The use in ordinary Attic is uncertain (*τἄλλα* Waeschke *de crasi Aristoph.*, Shilleto pref. to Demosth. *falsa leg.*).—Metre: logaoedic (phalaecean).

ANAKREON.

The peculiar charm of Aiolic lyric is the result of a combination of qualities that rarely coexist in the literature of any people. With Anakreon, the successor of Alkaios and Sappho in the cultivation of the song, grace and delicacy part company with intensity and force, and in their separation the former lose much of their immediateness and sincerity. Anakreon was an Ionian, and an Ionian was incapable of catching the subtle grace that distinguishes the poetry of the Aiolians.

The extraordinary fame of the Tean bard in modern times is largely due to the admiration of poems which Anakreon did not write, an admiration that is at once vicious on the stylistic side and ignorant of the debased form in which the *Anakreonteia* are composed. Of the many proofs of the late date of these poems, which are found in the *Anthology* of Kephalas, a work of the tenth century, some may be mentioned here in addition to the absence of imitation on the part of Horace and of citation by the authors who quote the genuine fragments. 1. Anakreon is expressly mentioned as the model for the imitation. 2. The metre, which consists chiefly of catalectic iambic dimeters ⏓ –́ ⏑ –́ ⏑ –́ ⏓ (which were rarely [xxx.] used by Anakreon himself) and ionic dimeters, is monotonous, and shows flagrant violations of classical usage, some of which are due to the influence of the accent. 3. The dialect, in which epic, Attic, and Doric forms appear. 4. Other anachronisms, such as allusions to painting, sophistical mannerisms, mention of the Parthians, the Ἔρωτες in place of Ἔρως. 5. The absence of individual traits.

These poems are the work of unknown authors whose dates range from the period of the Empire to late Byzantine times.

So pervasive has been the influence of the *Anakreonteia* upon European literature since they were first printed (in 1554), that it is well nigh hopeless to substitute in the popular conception the more robust figure of the genuine poet for that of the graceful octogenarian who captivated the fancy of the seventeenth century.

The life of Anakreon, though full of vicissitudes like that of Archilochos and Alkaios, was narrow in its sympathies. A native of the city of Teos he followed his fellow citizens into exile when the Greeks were menaced by the Persian Harpagos in 545; and assisted in establishing the colony of Abdera in Thrace. Either in the conflicts prior to his migration or in connection with the founding of his new home he seems to have lost his shield in battle. Of his further life we know nothing until he appears in Samos where Polykrates had established a court renowned for its oriental magnificence and luxury. After the murder of that despot Anakreon accepted an invitation of the art-loving Hipparchos, the son of the tyrant Peisistratos, to make Athens his home. Here he enjoyed the favour of the great, becoming the friend of Xanthippos, the father of Perikles, and of the rich Kritias, whose grandson of the same name—one of the Thirty Tyrants—called him (Frag. 7)

συμποσίων ἐρέθισμα, γυναικῶν ἠπερόπευμα,
αὐλῶν ἀντίπαλον, φιλοβάρβιτον, ἡδύν, ἄλυπον.

At Athens Anakreon found Simonides and the dithyrambic poet Lasos. Upon the assassination of Hipparchos in 514 he may have quitted Athens, or he may have remained until the expulsion of Hippias in 510. The democratic Athens of Kleisthenes must have been uncongenial to a court poet; and we may well conclude from one of his epigrams (103) that he took refuge with the princely Aleuadai in Thessaly. He is reported to have died at the age of eighty-five, and, if born about 572, may have lived to witness the Ionic Revolt and the stirring events that followed in its train. Of these there is however no trace in his poems, and the tradition that he was in Teos in 495 is untrustworthy.

It is as difficult to disengage the man Anakreon from the court poet as it is to apportion his poems to the different periods of his life. Strabo says that his poetry was 'full of Polykrates,' and though the name of the tyrant, curiously enough, nowhere appears in the extant fragments, we shall not err in referring most of the songs to the period of his sojourn at the vicious Samian court, to the brilliancy of which he and Ibykos lent their muse. Personal independence Anakreon may have preserved in part with all his supple wordliness, but his art, while not utterly venal—*οὐδ' ἀργυρῇ κώκοτ' ἔλαμπε πειθώ* he says in Frag. 33—, seems to have been absorbed by his vocation as *elegantiae arbiter*. Even in those poems that bear a more pronounced mint-mark of individuality (xix., xx.) we are uncertain whether he is not parading himself for court applause. His sportiveness and levity forbid an immediate approach to his more intimate self. If life and art are one with him and there is no visible conflict between his ideal and his environment, still we cannot rid ourselves of the feeling that at times, with the subtle irony of the man of the world, the poet disengages himself from the theme in which he is apparently absorbed. His genius could bloom only in an atmosphere that admitted no other standard of proportion than the ephemeral delight consequent upon the adoration of the senses. Life was endurable to him as a poet only because of its amusements; its realities, its sorrows, which echo through the other Ionian poets, are unsung by him.

The five books into which the Alexandrians divided his poems, contained, besides the songs, iambics, and also elegies and epigrams, some of which have been preserved together with much that is fraudulent. As a writer of elegies Anakreon continued the Ionic tradition especially of Mimnermos, though the Kolophonian poet's conception of love is dissimilar; but it is more particularly in the iambics, and chiefly in combination with choriambics, that he shows himself the successor of Archilochos and Hipponax. The popular estimate of the poet as a bibulous and amorous greybeard ignores his marked capacity for satire, wherein he shows the native talent of the Ionian for ridicule and raillery. The 'effeminate' Ionian had a sharp tongue. It is only when Anakreon gives expression to scorn or hate that he displays genuine feeling. The satire on Artemon deals with externals and not with character, but it is as effective a weapon as the more envenomed vituperation with which Archilochos assailed Lykambes.

It is as the singer of love and wine that Anakreon manifests his affinity to the Aiolians. Between him and Sappho the gulf is profound. Sensuous poetry to be great must be impassioned, and from Anakreon's poetry of the passions all genuine passion is absent. He is devoid of depth as he is devoid of vivid feeling. Instead of the soul-compelling worship of Aphrodite we have a conventionalized erotic that lacks relief and never loses its equanimity. At best Anakreon may be compared only with Alkaios in his lighter moods. He shows us only the curtain, Alkaios the stage. To the court poet

Eros is the supreme deity of the pantheon. It was Anakreon's task, following the example of Ibykos, to chant παιδικοὶ ὕμνοι, to sing of Smerdies of the lovely locks, of Kleubulos, and of the other dainty pages of Polykrates. 'These are our gods' (οὗτοι ἡμῖν θεοί εἰσιν) he answered, when asked why his songs were not consecrated to the gods. The only poem that has the faintest touch of religious spirit is that in honour of Artemis (Frag. i.).

But contrasts impair our appreciation of the peculiar excellence of Anakreon. Judging his art by what it is, not by what it is not, we must accord to him the distinction of having created the toying grace with which he treats his theme. He possesses a singular sweetness, urbanity, exquisite simplicity—in part the source of his popularity—and a delicate and airy touch. He has the gift of *bonhomie*, he smiles when he is provoked, he has the art of gracious confession when he recounts his repulse at the hands of some favourite of the court; though, it may be remarked, women scorn him only when he is old. The master of the revels, he is master of himself, and rarely descends to grossness. He could not well have retained his vigorous sensuousness till old age had his wine not been tempered with the water of σωφροσύνη. Nor does his verse show any trace of dithyrambic ecstacy, though an old writer says that it was composed under the constant inspiration of Dionysos. He has no love for Skythian orgies, strife, or tales of battles; he loves only good cheer graced by song and love. Within his narrow sphere of the enjoyment of the present, Anakreon moves with the security of the finished artist. Grace is his ideal (xvii.). Splendour and colour we may not demand from a poet whose virtues are simplicity and easy negligence (*non elaboratum ad pedem* says Horace). In imagery he is poor, but his few elaborate figures are carried out with tact and delicacy. The ancient rhetoricians classed him among the writers of the 'smooth' style (γλαφυρὰ σύνθεσις) and remark upon his ἀφέλεια. He unfolds his thought analytically, like an Ionian, and thus preserves, with a few exceptions, the natural order of the words. Akin to the simplicity of his thought are the light and limpid measures he employs. Aiolic logaoedics, notably the glyconic, are preferred; but he is no slavish imitator of the Aiolians, and he refrains from adopting the Alkaic or the Sapphic stanza. His choriambics are full of energy, and the trochaics move with exquisite lightness; his ionics, a measure to which he gave a secure place in literature, are preserved from monotony by the introduction of the 'broken' foot. The variety of his rhythms was reinforced by the numerous musical modes (Dorian, Lydian, and Phrygian) and by the variety of the instruments (especially the Aiolic barbiton) which he employed.

His dialect is the literary Ionic of his time tempered with an occasional Aiolic form indicative of his debt to his Lesbian models.

Anakreon's after-fame was secured at Athens by his popularity as a writer of songs which, above those of all other poets, were suited to grace the symposion. He found endless imitators in Greek—including Theokritos, and the parallels in Horace show his hold upon the Latin poet. His image was stamped upon the coins of Teos, and his statue, together with that of Xanthippos, was seen by Pausanias on the Akropolis at Athens.

I. Hephaist. 69 and schol. 221. A hymn, perhaps of the kletic class, formed the introduction to the ancient edition of Anakreon as it did to that of Alkaios. The poem is incomplete.—**1. ἐλαφηβόλε**: cf. Σ 19, *Hymn* 27. 2 *ἀείδω . . . παρθένον αἰδοίην, ἐλαφηβόλον ἰοχέαιραν*, Soph. *Trach.* 213, Eur. *I. A.* 1570 *παῖ Ζηνός, θηροκτόνε*, Kallim. 3. 17, Hor. 1. 12. 22 *saevis inimica virgo | belluis*, 4. 6. 33 *Deliae tutela deae fugaces | lyncas et cervos cohibentis arcu.* Artemis destroys the savage inhabitants of the mountains, and protects the civilized dwellers in the city (l. 8).—**2. ξανθή**: blonde is the type of beauty in a brunette people.—**3.** Cf. Φ 470 *πότνια θηρῶν, | Ἄρτεμις ἀγροτέρη.* —**4. Ληθαίου**: the diphthong is shortened before *ου*. The Lethaios was a tributary of the Maeander. On its bank, or near the river, was the city of Magnesia (cf. *πόλις καλή, Ληθαίῳ κεκλιμένη πεδίῳ* Theogn. 1216, by Anakr.?), where there was a temple of Artemis Leukophryene, which derived its name from Leukophrys, a city in the plain of the Maeander. This temple was famous for its exquisite proportions and in size was exceeded only by the temples at Ephesos and Didyma. **ἥ κου**: some adopt the *v.l. ἴκου*, 'come and tarry by the eddies of the Lethaios,' and read *ἐγκαθόρα*. *κου* (*που*) is common in invocations.—**6. ἐσκατορᾷς**: only here; cf. *εἰσκαταβαίνω ω* 222,

Stes. iii. 1, and εἰσκαταδύνω.—**7. χαίρουσ'** is postponed so as to precede its explanation (οὐ γάρ). **ἀνημέρους**: ἥμερος, gentle by culture (πραΰς gentle by nature), is here opposed to ἄγριος. Uncivilized people are ἄγριοι, like the Chalybes, Aisch. *Prom.* 716. Artemis was called Ἡμέρη; see on Bacch. v. 39, 96.—**8. ποιμαίνεις** keeps the tone of v. 3. Cf. ποιμὴν λαῶν Δ 296, ποιμαίνων ἱκέτην Aisch. *Eum.* 91, π. στρατόν Eur. Frag. 744; so βουκολῶ, θεραπεύω, *curo*, *foveo*. — Metre: glyconics, or glyconics followed by a pherecratic. There are two systems (3+5). The mode was probably Lydian, as the tone is supplicatory. Cf. iv., viii.

II. Dio Chrys. *Or.* 2. (t. 1. 36). A kletic hymn.—**1. δαμάλης** (only here): the 'subduer';=δαμάζων ἢ ἄγερωχος Hesych. Cf. xxv. 4, Soph. *Antig.* 781 Ἔρως ἀνίκατε. δαμαλίζω Pind. *Pyth.* 5. 121, Eur. *Hippol.* 231. Some compare δάμαλις, μόσχος, πῶλος, *iuvenca* and tr. 'youthful.' **Ἔρως**: to the genuine Anakreon Eros is a youth, not a child. The ἔρωτες of Pindar are impersonal, except in Frag. 122. 4, and only a few monuments of early art show the multiplication of the god. Anakreon's laudation of Eros is overlooked in Plato *Symp.* 177 A οὐ δεινὸν ἄλλοις μέν τισι θεῶν ὕμνους καὶ παιῶνας εἶναι πεποιημένους, τῷ δ' Ἔρωτι . . . μηδὲ ἕνα πώποτε, cf. Eur. *Hippol.* 541.—**2.** The Nymphs are often associated with Dionysos, whom they reared. Cf. Soph. *O. T.* 1109 Νυμφᾶν Ἑλικωνίδων, αἷς πλεῖστα συμπαίζει. The first Mainads were the nymphs. Bacchos trained the Nymphs in song, Hor. 2. 19. 3; cf. skol. iv. Βρομίαις Νύμφαις. **κυανώπιδες**: cf. Ibyk. ii. 1.—**3.** Aphrodite in conjunction with Dionysos, Roscher 1. 1065; with the Loves, Eur. *Bacch.* 402.—**5.** ὀρέων κορυφάς (MSS.) would be a unique case in glyconics of the shift in position of the cyclic dactyl.—**6.** vv. 1-6 recall the λέξις εἰρομένη. In 1–3 the order of substantives and adjectives is chiastic. In Frag. i. too the arrangement is not simple. **γουνοῦμαι** suits a kletic hymn. Cf. Archil. 75 κλῦθ', ἄναξ Ἥφαιστε, καί μοι σύμμαχος γουνουμένῳ ἵλαος γένεο.—**7. ἡμῖν**: the plur. after the sing. γουνοῦμαι: cf. xvi. 1. 4, xxiii. 2. 4, xxiv. 1. 3. We might expect ἐλθέ μοι. **κεχαρισμένης**: 'and may it find favour with thee,' by anticipation, with εὐχωλῆς, instead of κεχαρισμένως. **δέ** gives independence to the inf. (=imper.) which follows the imper. The inf. pres. in ll. 8 and 11 follows the aor. imper. The inf.=imper. often has a touch of solemnity. Cf. Cauer 487 B, 8. For the thought, cf. Aristoph. *Nubes* 274 ἐπακούσατε δεξάμεναι θυσίαν καὶ τοῖς ἱεροῖσι χαρεῖσαι.—**8. ἐπακούειν**: especially of a god hearkening to the prayer of his worshipper; cf. Aristoph. *Eq.* 1080, *Aves* 205.—**10. σύμβουλος**: first here; note the play on

-βουλος.—**11.** **Δεύνυσε** or Δεο—if the contraction is later than Anakr. Ionic inscr. have Κλεο- and Κλευ- and even φεόγω. Epigraphical monuments from Ionic territory show Δεονῦς and Διέννσος; but in xxii. Anakr. has Διόνυσος. Kretschmer (*Gesch. d. gr. Sprache* 225, 241) explains the εο=ιο by referring the name to a Thrakian source. —**11.** **δέχεσθαι**: subject Kleubulos. The inf. cannot depend on σύμβουλος because of δέ. On the inf. see Goodwin *M. T.* 785.—Metre: as i. Three systems (3+5+3) constitute, as it were, strophe, epode, and antistrophe. Note the basis — ⏑ in v. 3. The episynaloiphe in 4, 7, 10 indicates synaphea (contrast xxvii. 3).

III. Herod. περὶ σχημάτων 57. 5: quoted to show the repetition of the same word with different endings. Cf. Archil. 69. Anaphora also in xvii., xxiii. **ἐρέω**: as xxx., Archil. 25. **διοσκέω**: Hesych. has διοσκεῖν· διαβλέπειν συνεχῶς τὴν ὅρασιν μεταβάλλοντα, *oculis intentis aliquid investigare.* From δι-οπ-σκέω?

IV. Athen. 13. 564 D.—**1.** **παρθένιον βλέπων**: see on Ibyk. ii. 1. Eur. *Hippol.* 1006 has παρθένον ψυχὴν ἔχων. βλέπω first here, Hom. δέρκομαι.—**2.** **δίζημαι**: an Ionic word, cf. δίζησις. **κοεῖς**: perhaps connected etymologically with *caveo.* The same root in θυοσκόος, ἀμνοκῶν 'sheep-minded' Aristoph. *Eq.* 264.—**4.** **ἡνιοχεύεις**: cf. δεινὸς ἡνίοχος of Love, Hermesianax 84. With the gen. as Plato *Phaidr.* 246 B; with the accus. Hdt. 4. 193. Anakr. usually avoids metaphors but when he employs them is full of life (xix., xxvii.). The poem may refer to the Kleubulos of ii., iii.; cf. Max. Tyr. 8. 96 μεστὰ αὐτοῦ (Anakr.) τὰ ᾄσματα τῆς Σμέρδιος κόμης καὶ τῶν Κλεοβούλου ὀφθαλμῶν.

V. Schol. O 192, Eust. *Il.* 1012. 1.—**1.** **μείς** <*μηνς is also Aiolic. **Ποσιδηϊών**: Ποσιδήϊον B 506 and on Ionic inscr.; Ποσιδηϊὼν μὴν *C. I. A.* 1. 283. 17 where the absence of the article is to be noticed. Ἀττικοὶ τὸν περὶ χειμερίους τροπὰς μῆνα Ποσειδεῶνα καλοῦσιν. Attic -εών from -η(ι)ών.—**2.** **ἕστηκεν** *adest*; cf. ἕβδομος ἑστήκει ('began') μείς T 117. The schol. has νεφέλη δ' ὕδωρ βαρὺ δ' ἄγριοι χειμῶνες κατάγουσιν, Eust. νεφέλαι δ' ὕδατι βαρύνονται, ἄγριοι δὲ χ. παταγοῦσιν. Bergk conj. νεφέλας δ' ὕδωρ | βαρύνει, Δία τ' ἄγριοι χ. κ., comparing Hor. *Epod.* 13. 1 *et imbres nivesque deducunt Iovem.*—**3.** **ἄγριοι**: χεῖμα ἄγρ. Eur. *Andr.* 748, ἄνεμοι ἄγρ. Aisch. *Prom.* 1048.—**4.** **παταγέω** here first of storms; of clouds Aristoph. *Nubes* 378.

VI. Strabo 3. 151, Pliny *N. H.* 7. 154 *Anacreon poeta Arganthonio Tartessiorum regi CL tribuit annos* etc. Hdt. 1. 163 (cf. 4. 152) says he lived not less than 120 years, during 80 of which he was king. His reign fell shortly before

Anakreon's time. On Tartessos, cf. Stes. i. It was called εὐδαίμων, ὀλβία.—**1. ἔγωγ'**: the iambic basis in the beginning of the strophe is defensible (Blass κἀγώ). **'Αμαλθείης** as Ληθαίου i. 4. Amaltheia, according to one version of the story, was a goat that gave suck to the infant Zeus. From one of its horns flowed nectar, from the other ambrosia, according to Kallim. 1. 49. Another legend told how Zeus broke off one horn and made it the *cornu copiae*. Cf. Roscher 1. 262. Like Archilochos (25), Anakreon scorned wealth. Stob. 113. 38 reports that the poet, on receiving a talent of gold from Polykrates, returned it with the remark μισῶ δωρεὰν ἥτις ἀναγκάζει ἀγρυπνεῖν. Cf. Frag. 33 οὐδ' ἀργυρῇ κώκοτ' ἔλαμπε πειθώ.—**3. τε καί**: cf. xv. and τρεῖς τε καὶ δέκα Pind. *Ol.* 1. 79.

VII. Athen. 13. 599 c, citing Chamaileon, who in his book on Sappho reported that some believed this poem to have been addressed to her by Anakreon. Hermesianax maintained that Sappho and Anakreon lived at the same time; but this opinion and that reported by Chamaileon represent an attempt to bring two famous names into conjunction at the expense of chronology. Sappho's reply was supposed to be (the spurious) Frag. 26 κεῖνον, ὦ χρυσόθρονε Μοῦσ', ἔνισπες | ὕμνον, ἐκ τᾶς καλλιγύναικος ἐσθλᾶς | Τήϊος χώρας ὃν ἄειδε τερπνῶς | πρέσβυς ἀγαυός. Welcker thought the last strophe of vii. was spurious, though it is evidently the source of the story that Anakreon was in love with Sappho. Anakreon withholds the names of women in viii., xxvii., but he addresses a special poem to Kallikrite (118) and Eurypyle appears in xi. (see n.), Asteris in 72 B. The names of boys he does not attempt to conceal.—**1.** The 'purple ball' may be an apple, the token of love (see on Ibyk. i. 1), but is more probably to be taken literally. Cf. θ 373. Meleager in *Anth. Pal.* 5. 214 has σφαιριστὰν τὸν Ἔρωτα and in Apoll. Rhod. 3. 135 Aphrodite offers to Eros a σφαῖρα εὐτρόχαλος with which the infant Zeus had played. Eros is represented as a ball-player in Millingen *Uned. Mon.* xii. **δηὖτε**: of a renewed assault of love (Alkm. xiii. note).—**2.** Cf. Ἔρως ὁ χρυσοκόμας Eur. *I. A.* 548.—**3. νήνι**= νεήνιδι. νῆ was Samian for νέη. σάμβαλον=σάνδαλον as in Eumelos.—**7.** For the omission of ἐστί cf. xiv., xvi. 6, xxv. 4. —**8. ἄλλην**=πρὸς δ' ἄλλου τινὸς κόμην.

VIII. Hephaist. 34.—**1. ἰτρίου**: Samos was as famous for its cakes as Banbury or Nuremberg. Hdt. 3. 48 tells of a Samian festival at which sweetmeats of sesame and honey were eaten.—**2. ἁβρῶς**: Stes. x. **ἐρόεσσαν**: φυὴν ἐρόεσσα of the χέλυς of Hermes (*Hymn* 3. 31).—**3. ψάλλω**: of playing with the fingers, after the Oriental fashion. The pectis was a Lydian instrument that was improved by Anakreon. The poet also used the magadis with 20 strings, the Lesbian barbiton, and the flute. **κωμάζων** 'serenade' as Alk. xxxiv.; here in the day-time. **πάϊδ'**: diaeresis as in *πάϊ* Archil. 70. 1. For the elision of *iota* cf. Ε 5, Κ 277, Π 385, Παλλάδι Ἀθαναίᾳ (— ⏑ ⏑ — — —), *γυναικὶ ἐσθλήν* (⏑ — — —) on Attic inscr., *κήρυκι ἀθανάτων* Kaibel 772 (from Imbros). There are eight possible cases in Attic tragedy. Perhaps the usual method was to write the *iota* and pronounce it as *y*. Eust. on Κ 277 says the 'ancient' writing was *ὄρνιθι Ὀδυσεύς*. In the inscriptions a verb twice omits its augment after *παιδί*. Rossbach reads *παρὰ παιδὶ | ἁβρῇ*, Wilamowitz *παρ' Ἰάμβῃ*. **ἁβρῇ**: *ἁβρὴ παρθένος* Hes. Frag. 242 Rz.—Metre: priapeum.

IX. Hephaist. 72. The leap from the Leukadian cliff was supposed to cure those afflicted with unrequited love or to effect a change in the sentiments of the loved one. Stesichoros sang of the leap of the maiden Kalyke, who was enamoured of Euathlos. The story of Sappho's suicide rests on the unproved assertion of her love for Phaon. By the time of Euripides the expression had grown into a proverb: *Kykl.* 166 *ῥίψας τ' ἐς ἅλμην λευκάδος πέτρας ἄπο.* Cf. Ovid *Sappho Phaoni* 171 *hanc legem locus ille tenet. pete protinus altam | Leucada, nec saxo desiluisse time.* The fall was occasionally broken by bladders attached to the person of the sufferer, and a boat was conveniently at hand. One unhappy lover is said to have tried the *πετραῖον ἅλμα* four times. Anakr. is here jesting or speaking of plunging into the waves of love. **πολιὸν κῦμα**: as *πολιῆς θαλάσσης* Δ 248, *canos fluctus* Lucr. 2. 767, *canae Tethyi* Catull. 66. 70. **μεθύων**: cf. *Ἔρωτα πίνων* Anakr. 163, *μεθύω τὸ φίλημα πολὺν τὸν ἔρωτα πεπωκώς* *Anth. Pal.* 5. 305, *longumque bibebat amorem* Verg. *Aen.* 1. 749. —Metre: a glyconic proöde and a simmiacum.

X. Athen. 4. 177 A. Cf. Pind. *Pyth.* 4. 295 *θυμὸν ἐκδόσθαι πρὸς ἥβαν* (as here, 'merriment of youth'), Aisch. *Pers.* 841 *ψυχῇ διδόντες ἡδονήν*. **ὑπ' αὐλῶν**: *ὑπό* of musical accompaniment as in *ὑπὸ φορμίγγων* Hes. *Shield* 280, *κώμαζον ὑπ' αὐλοῦ . . . παίζοντες ὑπ' ὀρχηθμῷ* 281-282, *ὑπὸ ἀμφοτέρων* (lyre and flute) Pind. *Ol.* 7. 13, *ὑπαὶ σάλπιγγος* Soph. *El.* 711, *διὰ λωτοῦ Λίβυος | μετά τε . . . κιθάρας | συρίγγων θ' ὕπο* Eur. *I. A.* 1036, *λύρας ὕπο* *Phoin.* 824, *ὑπὸ τυμπάνων* *Bacch.* 156, *ὑπὸ πηκτίδων* Hdt. 1. 17, *ᾄδων ὑπ' αὐλητῆρος* Archil. 123, cf. Theogn. 825. In the case of *σὺν καλάμοιο βοᾷ* Pind. *Nem.* 5. 38 the tones of the instrument accompany the words. The flutes known as *ἡμίοποι* were sometimes called *παιδικοί* and were used at banquets. They were perhaps half as long as the ὑπερτέλειοι and formed the octave to those which were common in the choruses of men. See Howard *Harvard Studies* 4. 39. Von Jan suggests that they may have been called ἡμίκοποι in contradistinction to the μεσόκοποι class.—Metre as ix.

XI. Athen. 12. 533 E. Chamaileon, quoting from Anakr. ξανθῇ δ' Εὐρυπύλῃ μέλει ὁ περιφόρητος Ἀρτέμων, reports that the nick-name περιφ. owed its application to the fact that the luxurious Artemon was 'carried about' in a litter; for Anakr. says that he passed from poverty to affluence, πρὶν μέν κ.τ.λ. The words ξανθῇ . . . Ἀρτέμων are from another poem (in iambic dimeters or tetrameters, cf. xxix.) in which the poet castigated the parvenu, who, according to tradition (*Anth. Pal.* 7. 27), was preferred to himself by Eurypyle. Anakr. may have alluded to Artemon's effeminate mode of locomotion, but there is nothing of the sort in Frag. xi. and we know of a περιφ. Ἀρτέμων, the engineer, who assisted Perikles in the siege of Samos and because of his lameness had to direct the operations from a chair (Plut. *Per.* 27). Probably Chamaileon and Herakl. Pontikos (Plut. *l.l.*) misinterpreted περιφ., which here means 'notorious'; at least it is as an adulterer that he is referred to by Aristoph. *Acharn.* 850 (cf. schol. and Miller *Mélanges* 356). ὁ περιπόνηρος Ἀρ. *Acharn.* 850 is a combination of Anakreon's περι (φόρητος) and πονηρός (l. 5). For rich upstarts cf. Hor. *Epod.* 4, Juv. 1. 27, 4. 24. Acro on *Carm.* 4. 9. 9 is probably referring to this poem, which he calls a *satyra.*

1. πρὶν μέν . . . νῦν δὲ 10 (cf. Theogn. 57, Plato epigr. 15): the first member contains only participles. **βερβέριον** is either a shabby, rustic garment, perhaps so called from the Berbenii, an Arkadian folk (it was the fashion to regard the Arkadians as rustic boors; cf. Alk. 38, 91), or a kind of headgear that was compressed and narrowed to a point (καλ. ἐσφ.). **καλύμματα**: Hesych. has καλύπτρα· κεφαλῆς καλύμματα. If βερβέριον and καλύμματα refer to clothing, ἐσφ. denotes the pinched appearance of the man who is starved. Cf. Aristoph. *Pl.* 561 (σφηκώδεις) of the lean sons of Poverty, and contrast Hor. *Epod.* 4. 8 *bis trium ulnarum toga.* For the plural in apposition to the singular, which may be a bit of irony, cf. Hes. *Shield* 313 τρίπος, κλυτὰ ἔργα, Soph. *Phil.* 35 ἔκπωμα, τεχνήματα.—**2.** In Persia, Babylonia, and Lydia men wore ear-rings (Pliny *N. H.* 11. 37. 50).—**3.** Bergk supplied δέρμ' ᾔει.—**4.** At Athens the ἀρτοπώλιδες had a reputation for Billingsgate. Cf. Aristoph. *Ranae* 857 λοιδορεῖσθαι δ' οὐ θέμις | ἄνδρας ποιητὰς ὥσπερ ἀρτοπώλιδας. Hermippos wrote a comedy entitled Ἀρτοπώλιδες, which was aimed at Hyperbolos and his mother.—**6. βίον**: *de victu* (Hom. βίοτος) as in Hes. *W. D.* 232. See Verrall on Eur. *Med.* 194; cf. βίοτον ηὗρον *Med.* 1107.—**7. δουρί**=κύφωνι; cf. Pollux 10. 177 σκεῦος ᾧ τὸν αὐχένα ἐνθέντα δεῖ μαστιγοῦσθαι τὸν περὶ τὴν ἀγορὰν κακουργοῦντα.—**8.** Cf. ῥεραπισμένῳ νώτῳ Frag. 166, Hor. *Epod.* 4. 11 *sectus flagellis hic triumviralibus.*—**9. ἐκτετιλμένος**: the punishment of adulterers.—**10. σατίνη** seems to have been a war chariot (cf. *Hymn* 4. 13, Eur. *Hel.* 1311 with ῐ). Some think it was a ἁρμάμαξα such as was used by Xerxes and the ambassadors to the Persians. Hesych. has σατῖναι (*sic*)· αἱ ἅμαξαι. Connect with σάσαι· καθίσαι. Πάφιοι. **καθέρματα**=ἐνώτια are as old as Homer (ἕρματα σ 297). See *Dict. Antiq.* s.v. *inauris*, where there is a fine example of the 'stringing together' of the various parts. Perhaps we should read κατέρματα.—**11. Κύκης**: a nick-name, perhaps because she was a φαρμακεύτρια. Cf. κυκειῶ· ποτὸν δηλητήριον Hesych. **σκιαδίσκην**: sun-shades (σκιάδεια) Aristoph. *Eq.* 1348, *Aves* 1550, Ovid *Ars am.* 2. 209, *Fasti* 2. 311; Panofka pl. 19. 9. They were raised and lowered as now. On the frieze of the Parthenon Eros protects Aphrodite by a sun-shade. A Persian satrap shades himself on the Nereid monument (Baumeister fig. 1233). Cf. the θολία Theokr. 15. 39 and see Becker's *Charicles* 125. Slaves often carried sun-shades and fans for effeminate men. —**12. αὔτως**: cf. αὔτως . . . ὥστε γυναῖκα X 125, αὔτως ὅπωσπερ Soph. *Aias* 1179. Here the adj. ἐμφ. takes the place of the adv. that usually follows αὔτως. See Buttmann *Lexil.* 1. 37, Jebb on Soph. *O. T.* 931. ἁβραῖς before γυναιξὶν would yield a catalectic dimeter (as the clausula); but it is better to follow Schoemann, since without some such addition as ἐμφερής (cf. Sa. xxxi.), we should have the unique construction of αὔτως *cum dat.* (=instar *cum gen.*).—Metre: a verse consisting of two choriambs, followed either by an iamb. dim. catal. or a glyconic, is repeated, with an iamb. dim. acatal. as epode. Scheme *a a b*. The structure is not that of a real strophe. In v. 11 for the first –⏑⏑ ⏑ ⏑– we find a diiambus. Cf. xii. and such variations as appear in later tragedy, *e.g.* Soph. *Phil.* 1138=1161, and in comedy Aristoph. *Lysistr.* 326=340. Some read πάις ὁ. Wilamowitz *Isyllos* 133 calls the metre of xi. ionic (anaklomenoi) tetrameter.

XII. 1-2 Hephaist. 31, schol. Aristoph. *Aves* 1372; 3-4 Lucian *Herc. Gall.* 8 in paraphrase. The poet having been scorned by a beautiful boy, flies aloft to Olympos to demand satisfaction of Eros, who refuses to listen to his aged petitioner. Other poems of the poet's old age are xvi., xxviii. Himer. *Or.* 14. 4 tells the story of the poet's threatening the Loves that, unless they punished a youth who had scorned him, he would never again sing in their honour.—**1.** **πτερύγεσσι**: the only case in Anakr. of the addition, after the Aiolic fashion, of -*εσσι* to a non-sigmatic stem. **κούφαις** and *ἀήταις* are the only cases in Anakr. of -*αις*. Both occur at the verse-end (so with *ἀήταις* in epic).—**2.** **συνηβᾶν**: so in 44, skol. xvi., = *ἡβᾶν* in 18, skol. vi.—**3.** For the golden wings of Eros cf. Aristoph. *Aves* 698 *στίλβων νῶτον πτερύγοιν χρυσαῖν*.—The metre has been regarded either as choriambic or as ionic. If ionic, it shows the freer form that admits the choriambus. The resolved first foot, an innovation of Anakreon's, marks the fluttering agitation of the poet; v. 1 is put into the mouth of Kinesias in Aristoph. *Aves* 1372 to express the freedom of the later dithyramb. Rossbach regards ⏑ ⏑ ⏑ ⏑ — as a diiambus not as a choriambus; cf. xi. 11. Schmidt scans ⏑ ⁞ ⏗⏑ | ⊥ | ⏗ ⏑ | ⊥ || ⏗ ⏑ | ⏗ ⏑ | ⊥ | ⏗ ∧ ||. Cf. the ionics Soph. *O. T.* 486 (*πέτομαι δ' ἐλπίσιν οὔτ' ἐνθάδ' ὁρῶν οὔτ' ὀπίσω*) following the more agitated choriambics of 483 ff.

XIII. Atil. Fortun. 359. Whether Anakreon is to be included in the list of poets who threw away their shields on the battle-field (Archil. 3, Alk. 32, Hor. 2. 7. 9) cannot be determined from this fragment. Some would refer the event to a campaign against Harpagos. Frag. 29 has been referred, with slight probability, to the same disaster (*ἐγὼ δ' ἀπ' αὐτῆς φύγον ὥστε κόκκυξ*). It belongs rather to erotic contests. Frag. 31 *δακρυόεσσάν τ' ἐφίλησεν αἰχμάν*, 70 *ὀρσόλοπος μὲν Ἄρης φιλέει μεναίχμαν*, 72 *νῦν δ' ἀπὸ μὲν στέφανος πόλεος ὄλωλεν*, 85 *πάλαι κοτ' ἦσαν ἄλκιμοι Μιλήσιοι*, 91 *διὰ δηὖτε Καρικοεργέος* | *ὀχάνοιο χεῖρα τιθέμενοι*, 92 *ὁ μὲν θέλων μάχεσθαι*, | *πάρεστι γάρ, μαχέσθω*, seem to imply a warlike spirit on the part of the poet or a fondness for describing war.—Metre: two choriambs + a pherecratic.

XIV. Athen. 15. 671 E, 673 D. Frag. xxvi. and 16 are addressed to the Samian Megistes (a clip-name for *Μεγιστοκλῆς* or the like), who was beloved by the poet (*Anth. Pal.* 7. 25, 27, *Anth. Plan.* 4. 306). **ὁ**: *ille notus*; note the double article. For the order of words in v. 1, cf. Thuk. 1. 6 *οἱ πρεσβύτεροι . . . οὐ πολλὸς χρόνος ἐπειδή κ.τ.λ.* **ἐπεί τε**: as Hdt. 5. 18. **λύγῳ**: the willow was used for chaplets by the Karians (*ἀρχαῖον Καρῶν στέφος*), who first settled Samos; and the custom was adopted by the Greeks of the island, who worshipped Dionysos as *'Ελυγεύς*. On the omission of *εἰσί*, cf. vii. 7.—Metre: ionics.

XV. Athen. 10. 430 D. On the mixture, cf. Alk. xx. With the numerals supply *κύαθοι ὕδατος*, and *κ. οἴνου*. The imper.

plur. in -εσθω is not otherwise attested in Ionic poetry, apart from ἐπέσθω *v.l. Il.* I 170. We find σωζέσθω in Thasos, and similar forms appear in Korkyra, and possibly in Elis. The form appears to be an analogue of διδόσθω <*διδονσθω. ἀνα- denotes distribution rather than repetition. Cf. Timoth. ii. 3 and ἀμμείξας Ω 529.—Metre: as xiv.

XVI. Stob. *Flor.* 118. 13. For the thought cf. Mimn. 1-5, Theogn. 768, inscr. of Asia Minor (*B. C. H.* 7. 277) πρὸς ὀλίγον ἐστὶ τὸ ζῆν· τὸ τέλος ὁ χρόνος ἀπαιτεῖ, Hor. 2. 14. 1 ff. *eheu fugaces . . . | labuntur anni, nec pietas moram | rugis et instanti senectae | adferet indomitaeque morti.* To the Greek poets old age is not "beautiful and free."—**1.** Cf. πολιόν τε κάρη πολιόν τε γένειον X 74, πολιοκροτάφους γέροντας Θ 518, πολιοκρόταφον γῆρας Bacch. 42 (B. 3), ἀπὸ κροτάφων πελόμεσθα | πάντες γηραλέοι Theokr. 14. 68, *raris iam sparsus tempora canis* Ovid *Metam.* 8. 568.—**4. ἀνασταλύζω**, only here, 'wont to bewail' (ἀνά is reinforced by θαμά). σταλύζω is connected with σταλάω, -σσω 'drop.' Hesych. explains νεοστάλυγες by νεοδάκρυτοι. The ἀ- of ἀσταλύχω=κλαίω is adherescent as in ἀστράπτω, ἀσπαίρω.—**5. μυχός**: of Hades Aisch. *Prom.* 433, Soph. *Aias* 571, Eur. *H. F.* 607, *Herakl.* 218.—**6. κάθοδος**='descent' only here in early Greek. Cf. *Il.* I 408 ἀνδρὸς δὲ ψυχὴ πάλιν ἐλθεῖν οὔτε λεϊστὴ | οὔθ' ἑλετή, ἐπεὶ ἄρ κεν ἀμείψεται ἕρκος ὀδόντων, Hes. *Theogon.* 770, Aisch. *Pers.* 688 ἔστι δ' οὐκ εὐέξοδον, | ἄλλως τε πάντως χοἱ κατὰ χθονὸς θεοὶ | λαβεῖν ἀμείνους εἰσὶν ἢ μεθιέναι, Theokr. 17. 120 ὅθεν πάλιν οὐκέτι νόστος, Catull. 3. 11 *qui nunc it per iter tenebricosum | illuc, unde negant redire quemquam,* Verg. *Aen.* 6. 126 *facilis decensus Averno; | noctes atque dies patet atri ianua Ditis; | sed revocare gradum superosque evadere ad auras, | hoc opus, hic labor est,* Hor. 1. 24. 15-18, 2. 3. 27, "The undiscover'd country from whose bourn no traveller returns." **μή** with ἀναβῆναι: there is no hyperbaton here; *verum et certum est me non redire.* **ἑτοῖμον**: for the (frequent) omission of ἐστί with this word cf. Solon 4. 7, Soph. *O. T.* 92, Eur. *Herakl.* 502, Demosth. 9. 4, Plato *Rep.* 277 E.—Metre: each of the two systems consists of three ionic tetrameters (a dodecameter), in which the fifth dimeter is pure, the others anaklomenoi. Some write the lines as dimeters.

XVII. Max. Tyr. 24. 9. For the conjunction of μέλεα and λόγοι, cf. Alkm. vi.—Metre: anaklomenoi ionics. Note the absence of caesura as in xv.

XVIII. Schol. Ψ 88, citing the form ἀστραγάλαι as having a higher Ionic flavour (Ἰωνικώτερον). The masc. ἀστράγαλοι of ear-rings in xi. 2. Apoll. Rhod. 3. 117 represents Eros and

Ganymede playing with ἀστράγαλοι of gold. Cf. Baumeister fig. 835. **μανίαι**: cf. μανίαις τ' ἀλαλαῖς τε Pind. Frag. 208. For the thought cf. Theogn. 1231 σχέτλι' Ἔρως, μανίαι σ' ἐτιθηνήσαντο λαβοῦσαι, Pind. *Nem.* 11. 48 ἀπροσίκτων δ' ἐρώτων (impersonal) ὀξύτεραι μανίαι.—Metre: two first glyconics (the first acatal., the second hypercatal.?). Hiller divided after εἰσιν.

XIX. Hephaist. 39. **δηὖτε**: cf. Alkm. xiii. The softer aspect of Eros (ii., vii., xii. etc.) here yields to the severer type of Alk. iii., Ibyk. ii., Sim. 43, which is foreign to the *Anakreonteia.* Eros brandishes a whip (*Brit. Mus. C.* p. 622). Here he bathes the poet in the wintry mountain torrent, as the smith tempers his iron by plunging it into water. Cf. ι 391 ὡς δ' ὅτ' ἀνὴρ χαλκεὺς πέλεκυν . . . | εἰν ὕδατι ψυχρῷ βάπτῃ. (Galen *Meth. Med.* 10. 10, Lucr. 6. 968 etc. employ the comparison to show the invigorating effect upon the body.) The poem probably refers to Smerdies of the beautiful locks. The vigour of the comparison may indicate that the poet is not jesting, as in ix., but conceals with his fine amiability the sting of despised love. **πελέκει**: usually 'axe,' here 'hammer.' **χαράδρῃ**: cf. Δ 452 ὡς δ' ὅτε χείμαρροι ποταμοὶ κατ' ὄρεσφι ῥέοντες | ἐς μισγάγκειαν ξυμβάλλετον ὄμβριμον ὕδωρ | κρουνῶν ἐκ μεγάλων κοίλης ἔντοσθε χαράδρης. Note the artistic arrangement: μεγάλῳ—πελέκει, χειμερίῃ—χαράδρῃ.—Metre: brachycatalectic ionic tetram.

XX. Hephaist. 40. **ἀπό**: with tmesis as in Melissos 13 ἀπὸ γὰρ ἂν ὄλοιτο τὸ ὑγιές, cf. Anakr. xxiv. 6, 58. 72. 80.—Metre: anaklomenoi ionics.

XXI. Athen. 9. 396 D; cf. Aelian *H. A.* 7. 39, schol. Pind. *Ol.* 3. 52. Imitated by Hor. 1. 23. 1 ff. *vitas inuleo me similis, Chloe,* | *quaerenti pavidam montibus aviis* | *matrem non sine vano* | *aurarum et siluae metu.* Contrast Bacch. 13. 54 ἠύτε νεβρὸς ἀπενθής . . . σὺν ἀγχιδόμοις θρώσκουσ' ἀγακλειταῖς ἑταίραις.—**1.** **οἷά τε**: see on Alkm. xi. 4. Anakr. uses ὥστε in xix. and 90. **νεβρόν**: cf. νεβροὺς νεηγενέας γαλαθηνούς δ 336. Anakr. rarely indulges in epic fullness of description. Another example is ἡδυμελὲς χαρίεσσα χελιδοῖ 67. On γαλαθηνός see Athen. 9. 396 c.—**2.** **ὅστ'**: as Alkm. vii. 3. **ὕλῃ**: Bergk has ὕλης, but the older poets do not use the plur. (Crusius *de Babr. aetate* 177). **κεροέσσης**: the does of the poets have horns, though real does have none (Arist. *H. A.* 4. 11, Pollux 5. 76). Cf. Pind. *Ol.* 3. 29 χρυσοκέρων ἔλαφον θήλειαν, Sim. ix., Soph. Frag. 86. 2 κεροῦσσ' ἔλαφος, Eur. *H. F.* 375 τὰν χρυσοκάρανον δόρκα, Frag. 857 ἔλαφον κεροῦσσαν. As Fennell remarks, the animal is male in art, female in literature. Zenodotos thought to obviate the difficulty by reading *ἐροέσσης*.—**3. ὑπό** does not connote intention as some think. *ἀπό* (in *ἀπολειφθείς*) connotes separation from an object with which there has been union (*παρά* of departure merely). Cf. Soph. *Trach.* 529 *κἀπὸ ματρὸς ἄφαρ βέβακεν, | ὥστε πόρτις ἐρήμα.*—Metre: ionics (v. 1 pure, 2–3 anaklomenoi).

XXII. Athen. 15. 674 C. In Samos Dionysos was worshipped under the names *'Ελυγεύς, Γοργυιεύς*, etc.—**1. σελίνων**: crowns of celery were used to decorate the victors at the games (at the Nemea after the Persian wars, at the Isthmia until about the beginning of our era), and tombs, guests at banquets, children, etc. Cf. Theokr. 3. 23, Verg. *Ecl.* 6. 68, Hor. 1. 36. 16 (*vivax apium*), 2. 7. 24, 4. 11. 3. **ἐπὶ ὀφρ. θεμ.**: cf. the less simple expression Pind. *Ol.* 3. 12 *γλεφάρων ὑψόθεν ἀμφὶ κόμαισι βάλῃ κόσμον ἐλαίας.*—**2.** Cf. *δαῖτα θάλειαν* H 475, *i.e. θάλλουσαν τοῖς ὀνείασι.* **ὀρτή** Ionic for *ἑορτή*; found in Hdt. (with *ἄγω*) and Herodas.—Metre: ionics.

XXIII. Athen. 11. 782 A. First water was put into the *κύλιξ* and then wine. Cf. Xenophan. 4 *οὐδέ κεν ἐν κύλικι πρότερον κεράσειέ τις οἶνον | ἐγχέας, ἀλλ' ὕδωρ καὶ καθύπερθε μέθυ.* See on Alk. xx. and cf. Hor. 2. 11. 18.—**1. φέρε** is the regular word; cf. Plato *Symp.* 213 E, Aristoph. *Acharn.* 1097, *Fr.* 644 and the use of *affer, inger*.—**3. ἔνεικον**: note the shift of tense when the command is repeated. **ὡς δή**: in *ὡς δή* E 24, *ἵνα δή* Ψ 207, *δή* emphasizes the intention; and reinforces the anaphora here. It is also ironical after *ὡς* or *ἵνα*. The Ionian lyric poets prefer *ὡς* and *ὅκως* to other final particles. —**4.** Eros as a boxer Soph. *Trach.* 442 *Ἔρωτι μέν νυν ὅστις ἀντανίσταται | πύκτης ὅπως ἐς χεῖρας, οὐ καλῶς φρονεῖ* (a passage that agrees in meaning with the old reading *ὡς μή*). **πυκταλίζω**: *-ιζω* has here intensive force as in *ἁρπαλίζω*. *-ιζω* is also frequentative and diminutive.—Metre: anaklomenoi ionics.

XXIV. Athen. 10. 427 A, 11. 475 C. Probably from the same poem as xxiii., which is the beginning of the ode. Like Xenophanes, though after a different fashion, Anakr. enjoins moderate drinking and would accompany it by songs to Dionysos. Cf. Frag. 90 *μηδ' ὥστε κῦμα πόντιον | λάλαζε, τῇ πολυκρότῃ | σὺν Γαστροδώρῃ καταχύδην | πίνουσα τὴν ἐπίστιον*, 94 *οὐ φιλέω, ὃς κρητῆρι παρὰ πλέῳ οἰνοποτάζων | νείκεα καὶ πόλεμον δακρυόεντα λέγει, | ἀλλ' ὅστις Μουσέων τε καὶ ἀγλαὰ δῶρ' Ἀφροδίτης | συμμίσγων ἐρατῆς μνήσκεται εὐφροσύνης.* The ancient commentators on Hor. 1. 27. 1 say that the substance of the

Latin poem is taken from this ode. On the proportion of water and wine, see on Alk. xx.

1. ἄγε with imper. Goodwin *M. T.* 251. In Homer ἄγε δή is rare (Ω 407); more common are ἀλλ' ἄγε δή and δεῦτ' ἄγε.—**2.** The κελέβη (cf. xv., and 32 τρικύαθον κελ.) was made of wood and shaped like a κύλιξ (schol. Theokr. 2. 2). It was of considerable size, as it held the watered wine for the company. The word may be connected with κολοβός *curtus.* The κύαθος was often used for drawing off the mixture into the κύλικες and had a high handle (see *Dict. Antiq.* 1. 589). **ἄμυστιν**: cf. *Threicia amystide* Hor. 1. 36. 14; the adv. in πιεῖν ἀμυστί *Anakreont.* xii. 2.—**3. ἐγχέας** *scil.* ἐν κελέβῃ; the same (non-Attic) synizesis in Xenophan. 4. 2. ἐγχέω is 'pour out,' ὑποχέω 'pour' wine into a large vessel, ἐπιχέω 'mix water with wine.'—**5.** The common reading ἀνυβριστί produces hiatus. After τί hiatus is allowed only when a long vowel or a diphthong follows. This was denied by Porson on Eur. *Phoin.* 892, but cf. Aisch. *Sept.* 704, *Eum.* 902, Soph. *Phil.* 100 (τί μ' οὖν Jebb), Eur. *Hek.* 820.—**6. δηὖτε**: unusual position, here between the parts of a verb separated by tmesis. Cf. 91 διὰ δηὖτε . . . ὀχάνοιο χεῖρα τιθέμενοι. In the melic poets δηὖτε is generally the second word in the sentence. **βασσαρήσω**: βασσάρα 'fox' is perhaps Libyan or possibly Thrakian. In Lydia (Aisch. Frag. 59) and Thrace the dress of the Bacchanals was made of skin; represented on a Greek vase (*Dict. Antiq.* 1. 293). The Thrakian Bacchanals were called Βασσάραι and Βασσαρίδες (Frag. 55). Βασσαρεύς (*Bassareus* Hor. 1. 18. 11) as Dionysos was represented in archaic art as an old man.—**7.** Lines 7–11 are probably from another poem.—**8.** Farnell quoted Ben Jonson: "So may there never quarrel | Have issue from the barrel." Cf. Hor. 1. 18. 7-13 *ac ne quis modici transiliat munera Liberi, | Centaurea monet cum Lapithis rixa super mero | debellata, monet Sithoniis non levis Euhius, | cum fas atque nefas exiguo fine libidinum | discernunt avidi. Non ego te, candide Bassareu, | invitum quatiam, nec variis obsita frondibus | sub divum rapiam.*—**9.** The Skythians drank their wine ἀκρατέστερον or ζωρότερον, whence the saying ἐπισκύθισον = ἐπίχεον Σκυθιστί Hdt. 6. 84. Cf. Theogn. 829, Plato *Laws* 637 E, Kallim. Frag. 109 καὶ γὰρ ὁ Θρηϊκίην μὲν ἀπέστυγε χανδὸν ἄμυστιν | ζωροποτεῖν, Aelian *V. H.* 2. 41, Hor. 1. 27. 1 ff. *natis in usum laetitiae scyphis | pugnare Thracum est; tollite barbarum | morem, verecundumque Bacchum | sanguineis prohibete rixis. | . . . impium | lenite clamorem, sodales, | et cubito remanete presso.* **παρ' οἴνῳ** (Soph. *O. T.* 780) *in vino*; παρ' οἶνον *ad vinum.*—**11. ὑποπίνοντες** = μετρίως ὑποπ. Plato *Rep.*

372 D; ὑποπίνων πάνυ φροντιστικός Athen. 2. 40 C; cf. Xen. *Kyrop.* 8. 4. 9. Often with playful litotes ('take a drop too much') *e.g.* Aristoph. *Aves* 494; sometimes with ἐν μεσημβρίᾳ as Xen. *Hel.* 5. 4. 40. So *si paulum subbibisset* Suet. *Nero* 20. **ἐν**: of accompaniment as ἀπύων ἐν αὐλοῖς Pind. *Ol.* 5. 19, κλέοντες ἐν ὕμνοις Eur. *Alk.* 447. After v. 11 Meineke would add κλεΐσωμεν Διόνυσον. We expect anaklomenoi, if the two poems are alike.

XXV. Clem. Alex. *Strom.* 6. 745. The authenticity of the fragment has been doubted because of its similarity to *Anakreont.* 53. Though the tone is akin to that of the imitations (note βρύοντα μίτραις), Anakreon's Ἔρως is elsewhere, except in xviii. and xix., much the same as the god here described; cf. δαμάλης ii. 1. In a life stretching over so many years it is natural that the poet should have varied the treatment of his theme.—**1.** **ἁβρός** is not specific to Ionic (Stes. x.).—**2.** **μέλομαι**: *cum inf.* as Eur. *Herakl.* 96. On Love as the lord of gods and men cf. Hes. *Theogon.* 121, Soph. *Antig.* 787, *Trach.* 443, Eur. *Hippol.* 538, 1268, Frag. 269 ἀπάντων δαιμόνων ὑπέρτατος, 136 θεῶν τύραννε κἀνθρώπων, 431 Ἔρως γὰρ ἄνδρας οὐ μόνους ἐπέρχεται, | οὐδ' αὖ γυναῖκας, ἀλλὰ καὶ θεῶν ἄνω | ψυχὰς χαράσσει, Plato *Symp.* § 6, Parmenides in Plut. 756 F πρώτιστον μὲν Ἔρωτα θεῶν μητίσατο πάντων.—Metre: anaklomenoi ionics.

XXVI. *Et. Mag.* 2. 45.—**2.** **χθονίους ῥυσμούς**: 'hidden temper.' χθόνια· κεκρυμμένα, βαρέα, φοβερά Hesych. Not as Bergk: *calide celans iram*, but στυγνὸς καὶ κατηφὴς καὶ δόλιος (Miller *Mélanges* 418). For ῥυσμός—a favourite word with Ionians—cf. Archil. 66. 7 γίγνωσκε δ' οἷος ῥυσμὸς ἀνθρώπους ἔχει, Theogn. 964 ὀργὴν καὶ ῥυθμὸν καὶ τρόπον.—**4.** **ἀβακιζομένων**: from ἀβακής = ἡσύχιος, πρᾶος. Cf. Sappho xxvii.—Metre: encomologicum (dact. trip. + epitrite).

XXVII. Herakleid. *Alleg. Homer.* 4. Cf. Theogn. 257 ἵππος ἐγὼ καλὴ καὶ ἀεθλίη, ἀλλὰ κάκιστον | ἄνδρα φέρω, καί μοι τοῦτ' ἀνιηρότατον· | πολλάκι δ' ἠμέλλησα διαρρήξασα χαλινὸν | φεύγεν, ἀπωσαμένη τὸν κακὸν ἡνίοχον. Theokr. 11. 19 ff. ὦ λευκὰ Γαλάτεια, τί τὸν φιλέοντ' ἀποβάλλῃ; | μόσχω γαυροτέρα, φιαρωτέρα ὄμφακος ὠμᾶς· | φοιτῇς δ' αὖθ' οὕτως, ὄκκα γλυκὺς ὕπνος ἔχῃ με, | οἴχῃ δ' εὐθὺς ἰοῖσ', ὄκκα γλυκὺς ὕπνος ἀνῇ με, | φεύγεις δ' ὥσπερ ὄις πολιὸν λύκον ἀθρήσασα. Hor. 1. 23. 1 (quoted on xxi.), 2. 5. 1 *nondum subacta ferre iugum valet* | *cervice, nondum munia comparis* | *aequare* etc., 3. 11. 9 *quae velut latis equa trima campis* | *ludit exsultim metuitque tangi,* | *nuptiarum expers et adhuc proterve* | *cruda marito.* In Frag. 96 Anakr. says οὐκέτι Θρηϊκίης <πώλου> ἐπιστρέφομαι.

1. **πῶλε**: of a young girl Eur. *Hek.* 144; see on Alkm. iv. 47. A πῶλος is an ἐνηβῶσα ἵππος Cauer 17. 15. **Θρηκίη**: Thrakian horses were famous (K 436, Θρῆκες ἱπποπόλοι N 4, Ξ 227, φίλιπποι Eur. *Hek.* 428, εὔιππον γένος 1089), as were those from Skythia (Strabo 7. 4. 8). **λοξόν**: Solon 34 λοξὸν ὀφθαλμοῖς ὁρῶσιν πάντες ὥστε δήϊοι, Theokr. 20. 13 ὄμμασι λοξὰ βλέπουσα (of scorn, as here), Plaut. *Mil. Glor.* 1217 *aspicito limis.* For the adv. cf. παρθένιον βλέπων iv.—**2. φεύγεις**: cf. Theokr. 11. 30 γινώσκω, χαρίεσσα κόρα, τίνος οὕνεκα φεύγεις. **εἰδέναι**: cf. Soph. *Phil.* 960 δοκοῦντος οὐδὲν εἰδέναι κακόν.—**3.** The first τοι, with ἴσθι, = 'be sure,' the second = σοι.—**4. τέρματα δρόμου**: as Soph. *El.* 686 (cf. Ψ 309, 462). They are the νύσσαι *metae.*—**5.** βοσκόμενος λειμῶνι φ 49 suggests that βόσκεαι λειμῶνας is not 'graze on' but 'graze over,' with accus. of the space traversed as with πλεῖν γ 71, στείχω Aisch. *Prom.* 708, *Sept.* 466, πηδάω Soph. *Aias* 30, Eur. *Bacch.* 307, διφρηλατέω Soph. *Aias* 845, ἀλάομαι *O. K.* 1686, Eur. *Hel.* 532, πλανάομαι *ib.* 598, πορεύω Soph. *Phil.* 599, Eur. *Alk.* 442, τρέχω *Hel.* 1118, θρώσκω *Bacch.* 873, φοιτάω Kallim. 3. 193. The construction is scarcely *exquisitius* (Hermann). So in English: "rove some wild and heathy scene" (Collins). For the thought cf. Hor. 2. 5. 5 *circa virentes est animus tuae* | *campos iuvencae.* Plut. *Mor.* 13 E has οὕτω σκιρτῶσα νεότης πωλοδαμνεῖται. **κοῦφα**: the plur. adj. for the adv. as ὑψηλὰ νενωμένος Frag. 10, μακρὰ βιβάς H 213. Cf. Bacch. 13. 54 ἠΰτε νεβρὸς ἀπενθὴς | ἀνθεμόεντας ἐπ' ὄχθους | κοῦφα . . . θρώσκουσ'.—**6.** Cf. Ψ 115 σειρὰς ἐυπλέκτους. The σειραί were light reins; σειραφόροι ἵπποι *funales equi.* **ἐπεμβάτην**: cf. ἵππων ἐπεμβάτας Eur. *Bacch.* 782, ἐπεμβαίνω I 582.—Metre: the oldest example of a trochaic strophe consisting of an acatal. and a catal. tetram. Each strophe begins a new thought. The lightness of the movement is heightened by the sparing use of — > (6 or 7 out of the 18 possible cases), and of these only one in the second colon of the verse. Schmidt *Metric* p. 110, with the MSS., makes a four-line system of each set of two verses (not so in *Gr. Metrik* p. 400).

XXVIII. Hephaist. 21. **εὐέθειρα** (*v.l.* -ρε; cf. on Arion 2) = Hom. ἠΰκομος; cf. καλλίκομοι κοῦραι Anakr. 69. The MS. κούρα and all other Doric forms in Anakr. are not to be defended, though sometimes said to add force and dignity.—Metre: troch. tetram. Note the absence of caesura.

XXIX. Ammon. 37. On a womanish man. ἔγημεν *uxorem duxit,* ἐγήματο *nupsit, denupsit.* Cf. Eur. *Med.* 606, where Medea says bitterly to Jason: μῶν γαμοῦσα καὶ προδοῦσά σε; Antiph. 'Ασωτ. 1 ἐγήματο of a man who married a rich wife; Martial 8. 12. 2 *uxori nubere nolo meae.* Cf. Krüg. 52. 11. 1.—Metre: iambic tetrameter (*Anacreontius*) with the caesura in the middle. Alkm. 10 has the caesura in the middle of the fifth foot, as in the drama. Note > ⏑ ⏑ in the first foot, the — being a monosyllable.

XXX. Hephaist. 17. Though cited under mention of the *Anakreonteia* (cf. 45. 9), the verses are Anakreon's. Cf. the remark of Aristippos, when taunted with yielding to love: ἔχω Λαΐδα ἀλλ' οὐκ ἔχομαι.—Metre: iambic dimeter.

LASOS

LASOS of Hermione, a composer of dithyrambs and hymns, lived in Athens at the time of Hipparchos. He is said to have unmasked Onomakritos' forgeries in the oracles of Musaios, and to have been the first to institute dithyrambic contests. The latter statement is either incorrect or must be restricted to the introduction of such contests at Athens in 508. Lasos was a teacher of Pindar and a rival of Simonides. He was a ready wit and a coiner of wise sayings; and is even reported, though on no very credible evidence, to have written a book on the theory of music. As a musician he exercised profound influence on the development of the dithyramb by quickening the *tempo*, introducing colorature, and polyphony, which is to be understood in the sense that he made the lyre reproduce the manifold variations of the notes of the flute (see Graf *de vet. Graec. re musica* 2). It is due to Lasos that the dithyramb began to usurp a place of commanding importance in the lyric of the fifth century. No fragments of his dithyrambs have been preserved, and the Κένταυροι is attributed to him on doubtful evidence.

Athen. 14. 624 E, cf. 10. 455 C: cited to show that the Hyperdorian mode was the same as the Aiolian. This hymn to Demeter of Hermione was asigmatic, like the dithyramb Κένταυροι. Against the degradation of the dithyramb by such a *tour de force* Pindar protests in Frag. 79 A: πρὶν μὲν εἷρπε σχοινοτένειά τ' ἀοιδὰ διθυράμβων | καὶ τὸ σὰν κίβδαλον *ἀνθρώποισιν ἀπὸ στομάτων* 'formerly the dithyrambic song was prolix and *san* pronounced in false wise was heard from the lips of men.' Of the sibilant *san* Hdt. 1. 139 says: *τὰ οὐνόματα* (of the Persians) *τελευτῶσι πάντα ἐς τωὐτὸ γράμμα, τὸ Δωριέες μὲν σὰν καλέουσι, Ἴωνες δὲ σίγμα.* The sibilant *san* was written M, which was the form of the Phoinikian *tsade.* Some think that *san* was pronounced like *sh.* The Greeks, who had a keen insight into the rationale of metrical effects, as a rule avoided sibilation. Dion. Hal. *de comp. verb.* 14 says *ἄχαρι καὶ ἀηδὲς τὸ σ, καὶ εἰ πλεονάσειε, σφόδρα λυπεῖ,* and reports that some of the ancients employed it rarely and cautiously: Perikles is said to have avoided its use. Lasos was the first to compose an *ᾠδὴ ἄσιγμος,* and later we hear of an asigmatic *Odyssey* (!) by Tryphiodoros and an asigmatic tragedy by Dionysios. In English we have Thelwall's *Song without a Sibilant.* Pindar, the pupil of Lasos, did not avoid sigmatism (*Ol.* 10. 71, *Pyth.* 2. 80, 3. 53, *Isthm.* 6. 74); cf. *Il.* I 323, Sim. 168, Soph. *O. T.* 425, Aristoph. *Vespae* 565, Eur. *Med.* 476, *Hippol.* 1167, Plato comicus 30 *εὖ γέ σοι γένοιθ', ὅτι | ἔσωσας ἐκ τῶν σίγμα τῶν Εὐριπίδου.* Euripides was outdone by Schiller: *Dass meines nächsten Schusses erstes Ziel | Dein Herz sein sollte.* See Mommsen *Griech. Präp.* p. 668 ff.—**1.** Demeter, Kora, and Klymenos are associated in two inscr. from Hermione: *C. I. G.* 1197 *Ἁ πόλις τῶν Ἑρμιονέων Νῖκιν Ἀνδρωνίδα Δάματρι Κλυμένῳ Κόρᾳ,* 1199 *[Δάματ]ρι Κλυμένῳ Κόρᾳ ἀνέ[θηκε].* Demeter, Kora, and Pluto on an altar in Sparta, Paus. 3. 19. 4; in Messoa *C. I. G.* 1464; cf. Philiskos in Hephaist. 31. Klymenos is an euphemistic epithet of Hades. Meliboia occurs nowhere else as a name of Kora though in Lakonia she was called Polyboia (and Phloia). Cf. *Μελίβοιος, Μέλιππος.* Wide *Lakon. Kulte* 177 thinks Meliboia signifies the power that fills the earth with sweet nourishment. It is difficult to see the propriety of the name as applied to Persephone. But a Meliboia, daughter of Niobe, was renamed Chloris (cf. Demeter *χλόη*).—**2. ἀναγνέων**: from *ἀγνέω = ἄγω, λαμβάνω* in Lakonian (Cauer 32. 9) and Kretan. Homer has *ἀγῑνέω* as Krates 1. 8. Used as *ἀνάγω* in *παιᾶνα ἀνάγετε* 'lift up a paian' Soph. *Trach.* 210, *ἀνάγετε κωκυτόν* Eur. *Phoin.* 1350; cf. Pind. *Isthm.* 6. 62 and on Bacch. iii. 10. Casaubon's *ἀνάγων* is adopted by Kaibel.—**3. βαρύβρομον** seems a strange epithet for the Aiolian mode. But Herakl. Pont. (*apud* Athen. *l.l.* D) speaks of its inflated, pretentious and pompous character. *βαρυβ.* of the flute Eur. *Hel.* 1351, of the drum *Bacch.* 156.—Metre: dact.-epitrite probably.

TELESILLA.

Telesilla, an aristocrat of Argos, composed hymns for choruses of girls in honour of Artemis and Apollo. In the latter she sang of the daughters of Niobe. Tradition made her the foretype of the Maid of Orleans and decked her defence of her native city with the colours of romance. Though Hdt. 3. 76-83 does not refer explicitly to her participation in the expulsion of Kleomenes, who slew six thousand of the Argives, later writers accept the story without scruple. Her native city honoured her with a statue representing her with a helmet in her hand, and with her poems at her feet. Her example is said to have led to the worship of Ares by the Argive women. She is reported to have been directed to cultivate poetry by the Delphic oracle.

Hephaist. 35, cf. 15. Probably from a hymn composed for a chorus of maidens. The river-god Alpheios, enamoured of Artemis, the tutelary divinity of springs and rivers (Ποταμία), pursued her, according to one legend, as far as Ortygia, where the stream reappeared in the fountain Arethusa. Cf. Pind. *Nem.* 1. 1 ἄμπνευμα σεμνὸν Ἀλφεοῦ . . . Ὀρτυγία, δέμνιον Ἀρτέμιδος. The legend is native to Elis where there was a spring Arethusa, and where Artemis was worshipped as Ἀλφειαία. From Elis the cult was transferred to Sicily.—Metre: Hephaist. found here ionics a maiore; rather pherecratics with anacrusis.

SIMONIDES.

With Simonides the age of individualism in lyric poetry has passed. The various forms of choral song that had been enriched by the successive improvements of two centuries now converge, and reach in Simonides a perfection that is all but final. The genius of the poet of Keos consists in large measure not so much in an originality that creates new forms, as in a composite quality, in a sympathy with the forms of lyric employed by his predecessors, and in a power of "running into one soul," as Browning says, the poets of the past. Apart from the monodic song of the Aiolians and iambic verse, neither of which he attempted, there is no species of lyric that was not mastered by Simonides ; and to Pindar, his junior by a generation, who wisely refrained from vying with him in the elegy and epigram, he is inferior only in the triumphal ode, a form of choral song which he was almost the first to cultivate.

Before the time of Simonides a national Hellenic lyric was impossible because there had existed no check to the decentralizing forces of Greek life. This check was furnished by the renewal in the sixth century of the national games and by the Persian wars.

The long life of Simonides (556-467) was contemporaneous with great events. Born in the age of the tyrants, he witnessed the overthrow of the Peisistratidai, the Ionic Revolt, and the two Persian invasions. The Athens of his youth, though the 'capital to a provincial Keian, was a comparatively unimportant place ; at his death it was already claiming the hegemony of Greece. Simonides' birth fell in the time of Thespis ; before his death, Sophokles may have given tragedy its final form by introducing the third actor.

Simonides was a native of Iulis in Keos. The worship of Dionysos in his native island, and his office as trainer of the choruses of Apollo, may have impelled him to choral poetry, while his birthright as an Ionian was the elegy. At Athens, whither he was called by Hipparchos at a time when the dithyramb was rising in importance, he met with Lasos and Anakreon, and formed one of the ornaments of the brilliant court of the tyrant. After the fall of the Peisistratidai he lived with the Skopadai at Krannon and the Aleuadai at Larissa, the lordly Thessalian magnates whose lives were not free from reproach, and whose ignorance of the fine art of living was ill concealed by the veneer of fictitious appreciation of the arts. When these princes took sides with the Persians, the poet returned to Athens, now the home of democracy. Here his successful competition with Aischylos in an elegy celebrating the battle of Marathon may have inspired him to become the eulogist of the war of freedom ; and for years he commemorated the individual heroes and the states which had borne a conspicuous part at Artemision, Salamis, and Plataia. When over eighty years of age he visited Hieron at Syracuse, whose court was rendered illustrious by the presence of Epicharmos, Aischylos, Pindar, and his own nephew, Bacchylides ; and here he seems to have died at the age of eighty-nine.

Like Sophokles, who died a nonagenarian, Simonides preserved his intellectual vitality to the end. He seems to have been famous as early as 523, and much of his finest work—the elegies in honour of the victories over the Persians — was done when he was over seventy. When he was eighty (in 477) he could record his fifty-sixth victory won with a chorus in the public festivals (epigr. 145). He was distinguished for his versatility and practical wisdom. Better than Stesichoros or Anakreon, Simonides illustrates the transference to the lyric poet of the participation in affairs which often signalized the career of the minstrels of the heroic age and their successors the rhapsodes. Another testimony to the versatility of Simonides is the tradition that he invented a system of mnemonics and added to the alphabet the letters η, ω, ξ and ψ—a tradition that may point to the first acquaintance on the part of the Athenians, at least in literary writing, with the Ionic characters Η, Ω, Ξ, Ψ which were foreign to their epichoric alphabet.

Apart from the epigrams and elegies, which fall outside the province of this volume—though he was the first choral poet who attempted these forms of composition—, Simonides wrote hymns (to Zeus Olympios, Poseidon), which took the form of prayers rather than the long epic-lyrics of Stesichoros, paians (to Pythian Apollo), dithyrambs (*Europa*, *Memnon*, subjects that are remote from the cult of Dionysos), partheneia, hyporchemes, in which the words were so aptly chosen as to reproduce the movement of the dance, prosodia, enkomia, epinikia, and dirges. His strength lay less on the religious than on the human side. Though the gods are regarded by him as the sole possessors of perfect excellence and the source of all virtue, he brings to their service neither fervid devotion nor genuine enthusiasm. His faith has a touch of scepticism. He is above all an artist and remains untouched by that wave of theological speculation by which Pindar was deeply influenced.

Most of the secular melic fragments that admit of classification deal with the praise of contemporaries. We have already seen that Stesichoros had made the heroes, not the gods, the subject of his hymns. Simonides advances a step further, and, aided by the precedent of Ibykos, secularizes the choral lyric by his commemoration of contemporaries. The enkomion is professedly human and eulogistic whether it has for its subject men made famous by Olympian victories or illustrious for their princely station. In life their fame is celebrated by the epinikion, and the threnos offers consolation at their death. Both are virtually species of the enkomion, which name also remains as a general term for eulogy. In either case it is an individual and a contemporary whose fame is sung—a fact of profound significance in the history of lyric poetry—and the patron of the poet is no longer of necessity either a state or a city.

It is by his epinikia and threnoi that Simonides achieved his greatest distinction as a choral poet; and it is mainly from these two classes that we have our chief fragments. Simonides set the type for the triumphal ode of Pindar. For nearly two centuries Archilochos' "Hail to the Chief" had sufficed to celebrate the athlete's success; but in the latter part of the sixth century there was need of ampler praise. Simonides made the myth the central theme of the epinikion and thus linked the heroic past with the glory of the present. In the absence of any complete ode we cannot indeed contrast his art with that of Pindar, but indications point both to a disinclination on the part of the poet to disturb the accredited myths and to a tendency to emphasize the details of the contest, upon which Pindar laid no stress. He even plays upon the name of the defeated contestant: 'Not unfittingly did the ram (ὁ Κριός) get himself shorn when he came to the glorious precinct of Zeus (Olympia) that is adorned with trees' (Frag. 13).

In the threnodies, which in their choral form appear for the first time in literature in connection with the name of Simonides, the poet reached the summit of his excellence. Here he showed himself a master of tenderness, delicacy, and of a genuineness of feeling whose sympathy brings consolation. Pindar's sublimity unfolds the glories of the other world, Simonides touches the heart and opens the source of tears. The objective myth is here the anodyne; and the afflicted parent finds his present grief assuaged by the story of the sufferings of some hero or heroine of his faith. The quality of Simonides is womanly in the warmth and immediateness of his sympathy. He loved pathetic scenes. In a poem now lost he depicted the shade of Achilles appearing over his grave before the departure of the Achaians and calling upon them to make sacrifice of Polyxena.

Simonides had a rich experience of affairs. If he understood the art of flattery, he did not forget how to speak the truth. His diplomacy reconciled Hieron with Theron. He was the friend of republicans as well as of tyrants, and he had the large indulgence towards varied types of character that marks the man of the world. He shows the suppleness, the mobility of the Ionian, the Ionian's indifference to questions of deep moral weight. His theory of life—περὶ μηδενὸς σπουδάζειν—is Anakreontic, but it is deepened by contact with great themes. Simonides looks at life as a worldly philosopher whose standard is external success. With easy indifference he proclaims the murder of his former patron Hipparchos as a 'great light unto the Athenians' and toys with his theme when he praises Skopas. He is a master of the art of silence when the whole truth stings; he has the adroitness and sinuosity of the sophist. That he lacked absolute moral sincerity cannot be denied, but apart from the enkomion on Skopas, we know of no concrete case of mercenary homage that distorts the truth; and even here the story that the tyrant referred him to the Dioskuroi for the rest of his pay is proof that the poet did not Thessalize his muse. For his love of gain he was pilloried by Xenophanes; and Pindar scornfully hints at his 'songs with silver brow,' though Pindar got his bread after much the same fashion. Simonides may have been fond of money like many artists, such as Rachel; but the condition of his art as a national singer gave him the same right to live as the Aiginetan or Sikyonian who fashioned the statues of the victors at the national games, whose strength and skill formed the theme of the poet. Ibykos and Anakreon (who scorned money) may have depended on the unsought bounty of their patrons, while the evil eminence of Simonides as the first poet to make the muse a hireling (Pind. *Isthm.* 2. 6) may have been the result of his demanding a fixed sum for his poetry—surely as honourable a means of preserving his independence as the method adopted by his predecessors.

The choral ode which is never hostile to the admission of moral precepts, has, in the case of Simonides, been invaded to a marked degree by the reflective tone native to the elegy and best exemplified in Mimnermos, Solon, and Theognis. The life of the poet was contemporaneous with many contrasts that were the result of destiny, and his verse is full of the instability of human fortune and the sorrows of existence; death mars the felicity of the demi-gods. His apophthegms on the philosophy of life classed him with the Seven Sages. He loves the pregnant utterance that compresses into a word the experience of the race. He had the wit of Talleyrand and part of his physical imperfections. When asked how many years he counted, he replied 'many, but still too few.' Other *bon-mots* have been handed down: 'discord and strife are as necessary to the state as its crest to the tufted lark'; 'speech is the mirror of things'; 'a thousand years are an indeterminate point' (between the past and the future).

Simonides has the love of the analytic thinker for fine distinctions (Prodikos too was a Keian), and his acuteness makes him combative. With his fellow poets he seems to have waged war and in turn to have provoked the enmity of Pindar, whose intemperate hostility vented itself in the refusal to accord to him the possession of native ability.

καὶ πτωχὸς πτωχῷ φθονέει καὶ ἀοιδὸς ἀοιδῷ.

He is the first poet who is a critic, for he is conscious of the purpose and effect of his art; he theorizes about poetry as the Ionic philosopher theorizes about nature: 'Poetry is speaking painting, painting is silent poetry'—the dazzling antithesis of the 'Greek Voltaire' that forms the text of the *Laokoon.*

Simonides' style mirrors the man. Smooth and polished, it never exceeds the bounds of propriety and proportion. He does not strain after effect, but preserves his logical faculty, his persuasiveness, sweetness, and grace. If he usually displays but little nervous force or passion, and his notes are not full of solemn melody, he has no struggle with himself, his clearness is that of crystal, and he has a noble brevity that disdains all meretricious ornament. 'A master in style is judged by what he leaves unsaid': with a few simple and natural words Simonides makes us see what he tells us; he illuminates a single great thought from many sides, and dwells with a deft touch on the details which he does not allow to oppress us, and outranks all his clan as the painter of the conflicts of the soul. The greatest ancient critic of style says that he was unsurpassed for the lucidity of his imagery (Longinos *de subl.* 15. 7). For form he has a marvellous talent—the very words dance in the hyporchemes—, and the form corresponds everywhere to the thought.

It is not surprising that Simonides should have preferred to the stately dactylo-epitrite the more facile logaoedics. These he varies as his subject varies, but he works out new forms that are different from those employed by the Aiolians and Anakreon. He also employs cretics. With him the kithara and flute are no longer rivals; he adopts the triad in stropic composition, and of the modes prefers the Dorian, though he uses also the Lydian, Aiolian, and Phrygian. His choral songs are a mixture of Doric and epic, with a slight tincture of Aiolism. Archaic words and forms find no place in a vocabulary that is not wide and holds close to the common speech.

Though an Ionian, Simonides was all but an Athenian because of his intellectual keenness, his sense of symmetry, and the elegance and purity of his diction. It is no injustice therefore that the Athenians regarded him as one of themselves. His songs were in everybody's mouth. Plato quotes him often and compares him with Homer and Hesiod, Xenophon's *Hieron* introduces the poet discussing tyranny with that prince. Bacchylides followed in his path and Horace translated and imitated him. Apart from Sappho, we have lost nothing more worthy of preservation in the whole range of Greek song than his lyrics. An unequal chance has given us almost complete the triumphal odes of Pindar, many of which we would gladly exchange for one "tender-hearted scroll of pure Simonides."

I. Diodor. 11. 11 (Arsen. *Viol.* 342): Σιμωνίδης . . . ἄξιον τῆς ἀρετῆς αὐτῶν ποιήσας ἐγκώμιον κ.τ.λ. Bergk, Flach and others refer the fragment to the poem 'On the Sea-fight at Artemision,' a view that is correct only if the extant lines formed an episode in a lyric on Artemision. In the fragment itself there is however nothing to show that it is not the heroes of Thermopylai who are alone celebrated here as in the famous epigrams (91 and 92):

> Μυριάσιν ποτὲ τῇδε τριακοσίαις ἐμάχοντο
> ἐκ Πελοποννάσου χιλιάδες τέτορες.

> Ὦ ξεῖν', ἀγγέλλειν Λακεδαιμονίοις ὅτι τῇδε
> κείμεθα, τοῖς κείνων ῥήμασι πειθόμενοι.

Diodor. probably used ἐγκώμιον in an untechnical sense, and in like manner it is used of an epinikion in Athen. 13. 573 F; otherwise we must suppose that enkomia, though generally of a private nature and more akin to the skolia, were also sung at public festivals. Bernhardy in fact regarded the poem as a skolion.—**2.** 'Glorious their fortune, fair their fate.' **τύχα** (*fors*) is the opportunity for winning κλέος offered them at Thermopylai. Cf. Lykurg. *Leokr.* 108 Λακεδαιμόνιοι δ' ἐν Θερμοπ. παραταξάμενοι ταῖς μὲν τύχαις . . . ἐχρήσαντο κ.τ.λ., Thuk. 2. 44. 1 τὸ δ' εὐτυχές, οἳ ἂν τῆς εὐπρεπεστάτης λάχωσιν, ὥσπερ οἵδε μὲν νῦν, τελευτῆς κ.τ.λ. **πότμος** (*sors*): cf. θάνατον καὶ πότμον ἐπίσπῃ Υ 337.—**3.** **βωμός** might be the altar of their cult as Heroes, with whom Leonidas was associated in the Spartan ritual. But it is better taken in a general sense (sacred and worthy of reverence). Aisch. *Choeph.* 106 αἰδουμένη σοι βωμὸν ὣς τύμβον πατρός recalls the expression here. The distinction between σακός (l. 6) as applied to a hero, ναός to a god, does not hold in early literature. **πρὸ γόων**: πρό = ἀντί; others deserve our tears, these our remembrance; others our commiseration, these our praise. Here, as in ii., Sim. looks sharply after the meaning of words. γόος is lamentation accompanied by tears and sobs, οἶκτος (*miseratio*) expresses itself generally in words of sympathy. (ἔλεος is pity that dwells in the heart.) With the sentiment cf. Thuk. 2. 43, Hypereides 129 οὐ γὰρ θρήνων ἄξια πεπόνθασιν, ἀλλ' ἐπαίνων μεγάλων πεποιήκασιν, Plut. *Consol.* 114 D οὐδεὶς γὰρ ἀγαθὸς ἄξιος *θρήνων, ἀλλ' ὕμνων καὶ ἐπαίνων, οὐδὲ πένθους, ἀλλὰ μνήμης εὐκλεοῦς, οὐδὲ δακρύων ἐπωδύνων, ἀλλ' ἐτείων ἀπαρχῶν.* Though the ancient Greeks gave away to tears more readily than men of modern times, they controlled their feelings when tears were unseemly.—**4. ἐντάφιον**: *scil.* *εἶμα*; cf. Isokr. 6. 44 *καλὸν ἐντάφιον ἡ τυραννίς.* **τοιοῦτον**: as often in tragedy. Pindar's description, *Pyth.* 6. 10 ff., of the indestructible treasure-house of hymns for the victor excels in its imaginative quality and in its opulent fancy. The noble simplicity of Sim. is attained by the emphasis laid on the moral idea. Dante's lines on Vergil recall the severer style of Simonides: *di cui la fama ancor nel mundo dura | e durerà quanto il mundo lontana.*—**5.** Cf. Pind. *Isthm.* 5. 56 *οὔτοι τετύφλωται μακρὸς | μόχθος ἀνδρῶν*, another figure in *Ol.* 6. 97 *μὴ θραύσαι χρόνος ὄλβον ἐφέρπων*, Hor. 3. 30. 3 (*monumentum*) *quod non . . . possit diruere aut innumerabilis | annorum series et fuga temporum.* Cf. Pind. xxiv. **πανδαμάτωρ**: of sleep Ω 5, *π. χρόνος* Bacch. v. 82. Contrast Soph. Frag. 868 *χρόνος δ' ἀμαυροῖ πάντα.*—**6.** 'This sepulchre of valiant men has received the fair fame of Hellas to dwell therein.' Cf. Thuk. 2. 43. 2 *τὸν τάφον . . . οὐκ ἐν ᾧ κεῖνται μᾶλλον, ἀλλ' ἐν ᾧ ἡ δόξα αὐτῶν . . . καταλέλειπται.* **οἰκέταν**: 'as its habitant'; predicate to *εὐδοξ.* *Nomina agentis* ending in *-της*, *-τηρ*, *-τωρ* are often treated as fem. adj.; so *σωτήρ* Aisch. *Agam.* 664, Soph. *O. T.* 81, *Phil.* 1471, Eur. *Med.* 360, *El.* 993, *θέλκτωρ* Aisch. *Suppl.* 1040, *πράκτωρ Agam.* 111, *λωβητήρ* Soph. *Antig.* 1074, *καρανιστήρ* Aisch. *Eum.* 186, *ἵστωρ* Soph. *El.* 850, Eur. *I. T.* 1431. So *δασπλῆς* Sim. xiv. Cf. the feminine use of *Ἕλλην*, *φονεύς* etc. Lucan *Phars.* 9. 720 has *natrix violator aquae.*—**7.** Leonidas, who was interred where he fell with the rest of his band, is a *σύνδικος*. Cf. Pind. *Ol.* 9. 98 *σύνδικος δ' αὐτῷ Ἰολάου | τύμβος . . . ἀγλαΐαισιν* and 13. 108 *μαρτυρήσει Λυκαίου βωμὸς ἄναξ.* Of Leonidas, Sim. wrote in epigr. 95 *εὐκλέας αἶα κέκευθε, Λεωνίδα, οἳ μετὰ σεῖο | τῇδ' ἔθανον, Σπάρτης εὐρυχόρου βασιλεῦ κ.τ.λ.* Diodor. omits *καί*.—**9. κόσμον**: cf. Timoth. iii.—Metre: logaoedic. Reading *Θερμοπύλαις* in 1, omitting *ὁ* in 8, and changing to *κλέος τε* in 9, Bergk made 1-5 the end of the strophe, 6-9 the beginning of the antistr. The logaoedics are simple in structure and recall those of Alkman (cf. xxi. 1. 3) and Ibykos.

II. Plato *Protag.* 339 ff. Protagoras proposes to transfer the question under discussion to the domain of poetry, though the matter of inquiry (*ἀρετή*) is to remain the same. He is led to this by reason of his belief that skill in poetry constitutes the chief part of education. He begins by quoting ll. 1-2 (339 B) from the poem to Skopas, the meaning of which two verses is, he declares, identical with the sentiment expressed by Pittakos further on in the poem: οὐδέ μοι . . . ἔμμεναι (339 C), and maintains that the poet contradicts himself. Sokrates avails himself of the help of Prodikos, the synonymist, and removes the contradiction by calling attention to the difference between γενέσθαι in Sim. and ἔμμεναι in Pittakos. To this Protagoras replies that Sokr. is only making matters worse, for he imputes to Sim. the opinion that virtue is easy of acquisition, whereas everybody knows the contrary to be true. To answer this, Sokr. playfully suggests that χαλεπόν does not mean 'hard,' but 'evil' (κακόν); an interpretation that is, however, immediately abandoned because θεὸς . . . γέρας (341 E). Sokr. thereupon undertakes to show what he conceives to be the real meaning of the poet and to set forth his own opinion of the poem, viz.: the saying of Pittakos, which had been approved by wise men, was attacked by Sim. in the hope of winning great fame if he could overthrow so doughty an antagonist as the Lesbian sage. This is clear, Sokr. argues, because the μέν of Sim. is directed against the truth of Pittakos' saw, and the poet means 'the *truly* hard thing is to *become* good,' with a designed trajection of the word ἀλαθέως. It is impossible for a man who has become good to remain in a good condition and be good, for θεὸς ἂν μόνος τοῦτο ἔχοι τὸ γέρας, ἄνδρα δ' οὐκ ἔστι . . . καθέλῃ (344 C). It is possible to become good, but it is impossible to be good: πράξας μὲν γὰρ . . . κακὸς δ' εἰ κακῶς (344 E). The trend of the poem is that a man cannot be permanently good, though he may become good and also become bad: ἐπὶ πλεῖστον δὲ καὶ ἄριστοί εἰσιν οὓς ἂν οἱ θεοὶ φιλῶσιν (345 C). That all this relates to Pittakos is proved in still greater degree by the sequel: τοὔνεκεν . . . χθονός (345 C). And with the same intent: πάντας . . . μάχονται (345 D). Sim. also says to Pittakos: ἐγώ, ὦ Π., οὐ διὰ ταῦτά σε ψέγω ὅτι εἰμὶ φιλόψογος· ἐπεὶ ἔμοιγε . . . γενέθλα (346 C), implying that, if any one delights in censure, he may satisfy his desire by censuring these men. Then follows πάντα . . . μέμικται (346 C). It should be noticed that the last two quotations are given no particular setting in the poem.

The restoration of the order of the parts is the more difficult because the words of Sim. are so interwoven with those of Plato that it is impossible in all cases to mark off the original from the commentary. It will also be remembered that, despite the statement of Sokr., it is in reality alien to his main purpose to set forth the actual thought of the poet. His chief aim is, while adopting the attitude of the sophists, to criticize their manner and opinions.

The arrangements adopted by various scholars from Heyne and Schleiermacher to the present time may be roughly divided into two classes: those that keep, and those that rearrange, the Platonic order.

I. Those that keep the Platonic order consider the poem to be monostrophic. So Hartung, Bonghi (*Dialoghi di Platone tradotti*), Aars (*Das Gedicht des Sim.*), Schwenk (*Das Simonideische Gedicht*), Ramorin (*In Plat. Protag. expl.*), Hiller, Sitzler (in Bursian's *Jahresb.* 1893, p. 223), Michelangeli. Hartung began the last strophe: οὐδ' ἂν ἔγωγε, μέσως λέγοντ' ἀλαθές, | διὰ ταῦτ' οὔ- | πως, ὦ Π., σ' ἔψεγον· | εἰμὶ δ' οὐ φιλόμωμος· ἐξαρκεῖ δέ μοι | ὃς ἂν ᾖ κ.τ.λ., Michelangeli οὔποτέ σ' ἔψεγον ἂν μέσως λέγοντα. | διὰ ταῦτ' οὐ νῦν σε, Π., ἐγὼ ψέγω, ὡς φιλόψ. ὤν· ἔμοιγ' ἐξάρκεσεν | ὃς μή κ.τ.λ.

II. Transpositions of the Platonic order. The lines ἔμοιγ' . . . μέμικται have been variously placed: by some in the first strophe, by others in the second; or they are regarded as an epode. Bergk placed the words in question—omitting οὐ γὰρ φιλόμωμός εἰμι . . . ἔμοιγ' ἐξαρκεῖ—after v. 2. Blass *R. M.* 27. 328 objects to this order for the following reasons: (*a*) the ὃς ἄν clause stands in contrast to ἄνδρ' ἀγαθὸν μέν, though the δέ is not directly expressed. This is against Sokrates' remark that μέν is opposed to οὐδέ μοι ἐμμελέως. (*b*) the ὃς ἄν clause is joined abruptly to v. 2. It would naturally be regarded as an explanation of the τετραγ. ἀνήρ. (*c*) the ὑγιὴς ἀνήρ in Plato is in apposition to the attributes in the ὃς ἄν clause; whereas in Bergk's setting it is predicate. Blass himself supposes a lacuna after v. 2 sufficient to conclude the strophe, and thinks that the second strophe has lost at the beginning something equivalent to the brief ἔμοιγ' ἐξαρκεῖ. But this arrangement separates, by too great an interval, γενέσθαι and ἔμμεναι, which are opposed, and makes ἔμοιγ' ἐξαρκεῖ, which is addressed to Pittakos (346 C), precede the mention of his name. Schleiermacher first proposed to put the words ἔμοιγ' ἐξαρκεῖ κ.τ.λ. before the strophe beginning τοὔνεκεν. A similar setting was found for them by Hermann, Schneidewin, and Sauppe, who call these verses epode α', while strophe α' is made up, on their view, of vv. 1-2+five lost lines, antistr. α' (or strophe β') of οὐδέ μοι . . . φιλέωσιν. τοὔνεκεν etc. then becomes strophe β'. If this arrangement is correct, antistr. β' and epode β' are lost, a conclusion hardly warranted by 344 AB, 345 D. Sauppe argued that τὰ ἐπιόντα in 345 C is no proof that τοὔνεκεν etc. followed φιλέωσι, because the same expression in 344 A does prove immediate sequence. This is vicious, because in 344 A we have the general statement τὰ ἐπιόντα πάντα, but in 345 C τὰ ἐπιόντα γε τοῦ ᾄσματος.

The poem is often regarded as an epinikion and was placed in this class by Schneidewin, and by Bergk, who however noted its similarity to the hortatory poems of Pindar, which were brought under the epinikia by the ancient critics. This poem, he thought, was not separated by the ancients from the other poems in honour of Skopas. There is, it is true, nothing in the ode that savours of an epinikion. Sauppe and Blass class the poem with the skolia and compare the fragments of Pindar (122 ff.) bearing that name. It is more likely that the ode is an enkomion (cf. 346 B Σιμωνίδης ἡγήσατο καὶ αὐτὸς ἢ τύραννον ἢ ἄλλον τινὰ τῶν τοιούτων ἐπαινέσαι καὶ ἐγκωμιάσαι οὐχ ἑκών). It is uncertain whether the poet is endeavouring to free Skopas from an accusation based on some specific act of injustice, or to furnish him with an ethical code that may excuse a persistent policy of oppression. Like Pindar, Simonides understood the art *τὰ καλὰ τρέπειν ἔξω* and preaches to his patron the ethics of the market-place.

1. μέν according to Sokr. is the first note of the attack on Pittakos, as if the sentiment were in direct opposition to *χαλεπὸν ἐσθλὸν ἔμμεναι*. We suppose that the antithesis was contained in the lines lost after v. 2.—**ἀλαθέως** is construed by Sokr. (343 E) with *χαλεπόν* and explained as trajected, *i.e.* it does not belong with *ἀγαθόν*. This mention of a trajected word is the first hint of the grammatical *ὑπερβατόν* that occurs in Greek. (Tryphon defines *ὑπερβατόν* (*verbi transgressio*) as *λέξις μετακεκινημένη ἀπὸ τῆς ἰδίας τάξεως*, Long. *de subl.* 22 as *λέξεων ἢ νοήσεων ἐκ τοῦ κατ' ἀκολουθίαν κεκινημένη τάξις*, with the addition *καὶ οἱονεὶ χαρακτὴρ ἐναγωνίου πάθους ἀληθέστατος*.) Sokr. argues that the 'truly difficult thing' is to become good, whereas Pittakos' difficulty—to be good—is not a difficulty at all; it is an impossibility. A 'truly good man' to Sokr. is a misapplication of language, since virtue cannot be anything but real. Of course the poet had no such special theory of virtue to defend, and Aristotle, quoted below, has *ἀληθῶς ἀγαθός*, referring to the passage. Sim. explains his meaning by *χερσίν κ.τ.λ.*—**γενέσθαι**: Sokr. emphasizes the antithesis between 'become' and 'be,' which is in fact the point of the poet's criticism. But in finding a pregnant force in the aphorism of Pittakos, Simonides' dialectics led him to err after the fashion of the sophists (cf. 316 D) whom Plato is satirizing. Pittakos had no intention of setting his *χαλεπὸν ἐσθλὸν ἔμμεναι* in opposition to the thought expressed in the *γενέσθαι χαλεπόν* of Sim. Hence Sokr. forces the meaning when he paraphrazes *γενόμενον* (*ἀγαθὸν*) *διαμένειν ἐν ταύτῃ τῇ ἕξει καὶ εἶναι ἄνδρα ἀγαθόν* (344 C) —an ideal that transcends human excellence. In v. 5 Sim. uses *ἔμμεναι* without thinking of the distinction.

2. τετράγωνον: according to the doctrine of the Pythagoreans the number *four* and the square symbolized the perfect, the divine. Proklos on Eukleid. *Elem.* 48 G says: *δοκεῖ δὲ καὶ τοῖς Πυθαγορείοις* (*scil.* *τὸ τετράγωνον*) *εἰκόνα φέρειν τῆς θείας οὐσίας*. The oath of the Pythagoreans was: *ναὶ μὰ τὸν ἀμετέρᾳ ψυχᾷ παραδόντα τετρακτύν, | παγὰν ἀενάου φύσεως ῥιζώματ' ἔχουσαν*. The fame of the poem of Sim. is attested by the references to the use of *τετρ.* in the sense adopted by the poet, *e.g.* Arist. *Rhet.* 3. 11 *οἷον τὸν ἀγαθὸν ἄνδρα φάναι εἶναι τετράγωνον μεταφορά· ἄμφω γὰρ τέλεια, ἀλλ' οὐ σημαίνει ἐνέργειαν*, *Eth.* 1. 11 *τὰς τύχας οἴσει κάλλιστα καὶ πάντῃ πάντως* *ἐμμελῶς ὅ γ' ὡς ἀληθῶς ἀγαθὸς καὶ τετράγωνος ἄνευ ψόγου.* Cf. Puttenham *Arte of Engl. Poesie* p. 113 (Arb.): "The Prince of Philosophers, in his first booke of the Ethicks, termeth a constant minded man, euen egal and direct on all sides, and not easily ouerthrowne by euery litl(e) aduersitie, *hominem quadratum*, a square man." *τετράγωνος* in Sim. means perfect in body (*χερσίν, ποσίν: τε . . . καὶ* uniting complements, which are similars) and mind (*νόῳ*). No *mens curva in corpore curvo.* Cf. Hor. *Sat.* 2. 7. 86 *fortis, et in se ipso totus teres atque rotundus*, and the imitation by Ausonius (16) *mundi instar habens teres atque rotundus*, where the spherical form is regarded as the symbol of perfection (cf. Plato *Tim.* 33 B). Cicero *Or.* 61. 208 uses the figure of the square: *redigeret omnis fere in quadrum numerumque sententias.* Dante has (Parad. 17. 24) *ben tetragono ai colpi di ventura* (cf. *quadrato nella mente* and *quadratura* in modern Italian), Walther von der Vogelweide *wol gevieret*, Shirley (*Love's Cruelty* 2. 3) "Should he retain a thought not square of her." **ἄνευ ψόγου τετυγμένον**: cf. the Homeric *ἀμύμων* (Earle). The lacuna after v. 2 (*ὀλίγα διελθών* 344 B) may have contained further remarks on the good man and a direct reference to Skopas, mention of whom cannot have been omitted. Bergk thought the reference to Skopas preceded the strophe beginning *ἄνδρ' ἀγαθόν*. But this is unlikely as Sokr. says, *à propos* of *μέν* (343 C): *εὐθὺς γὰρ τὸ πρῶτον τοῦ ᾄσματος.*

3. μοι: as if *φαίνεται* followed. **ἐμμελέως** (cf. Sa. xxi.) *scil. εἰρῆσθαι.* **τὸ Πιττάκειον**: *Pittaci illud*, as *τὸ τοῦ Σόλωνος* Hdt. 1. 86, *τὸ τοῦ Ὁμήρου* Plato *Theait.* 183 E. **νέμεται** = *νομίζεται* (so *νέμω* often = *νομίζω*, especially in Soph. *e.g. O. T.* 1080, *El.* 150, *Aias* 1331). Cf. Plato *Laws* 757 A *ὀρθῶς εἴρηται καὶ ἐμμελῶς.* In prose: *οὐδ' ὑπ' ἐμοῦ νομίζεται τοῦτο παρὰ Πιττακοῦ καίπερ σοφοῦ ὄντος ἀνδρὸς ἐμμελῶς εἰρῆσθαι* (Sauppe).

4. καίτοι is rarely used with the participle; first in this passage; Goodwin *M. T.* 861 cites Lysias 31. 34 *ἱκανά μοι νομίζω εἰρῆσθαι, καίτοι πολλά γε παραλιπών.*—**παρά**: with the passive instead of *ὑπό*; cf. Alexis 141. 14 where we have the ordinary dative: *τὸ πολλοῖς τῶν σοφῶν εἰρημένον.*

παρά with the gen. is used with *λέγω* Xen. *Kyrop.* 6. 1. 42, Demosth. 19. 56, 20. 88 (cf. 45. 4), Aischin. 2. 42, 106, 118 and, with quasi-personification, in Plato *Hipp. maj.* 281 B: *λόγων, οἳ ἂν παρὰ τῶν πόλεων* (= *πολιτῶν*) *λέγωνται* (cf. Demosth. 2. 12 *λόγος παρὰ τῆς πόλεως*). In prose writers we have noticed *παρά* also with the passive of *αἱρέω, ἀναδιδάσκω, ἀποστερέω, δίδωμι* (somewhat frequently), *ἐπιδεικνύω, ὁμολογέω* (somewhat frequently), *πέμπω, πληρόω, πρυτανεύω, συλλέγω, ψεύδομαι, ὠφελέω.* The intention of *γνῶμαι ἀφ' ἑκάστων ἐλέγοντο* Thuk. 3. 36. 6 is different. *ἀπό* does not define the actual speaker as *ὑπό* does (Cobet would read *ὑπό*). Except with the accus., the range of *παρά* in prose is confined to persons and things personified (so even Hdt. 7. 183 πυνθάνονται παρὰ πυρσῶν, Thuk. 8. 48. 7 παρ' αὐτῶν τῶν ἔργων ἐπισταμένας τὰς πόλεις). Ptolemaios gives the common rule: ἡ ἀπό πρόθεσις τῆς παρά διαφέρει· ἡ μὲν γὰρ ἀπό τίθεται ἐπὶ τῶν ἀψύχων, ἡ παρά ἐπὶ τῶν ἐμψύχων. With passives we find in Attic prose besides παρά: πρός, ἐκ, and ἀπό, the last least frequently.

The maxim of Pittakos was occasioned by the transformation in the character of Periander, who, from a mild, became a cruel, prince. Like Pindar, Sim. is fond of quotation. See on xxii. For **φάτ(ο)** after εἰρ., cf. Pind. *Pyth.* 4. 277 τῶν δ' Ὁμήρου καὶ τόδε συνθέμενος | ῥῆμα πόρσυν'· ἄγγελον ἐσλὸν ἔφα τιμὰν μεγίσταν πράγματι παντὶ φέρειν, *Isthm.* 2. 9 τὸ τὠργείου φυλάξαι | ῥῆμα . . . | χρήματα χρήματ' ἀνήρ, ὃς φᾶ κτεάνων θ' ἅμα λειφθεὶς καὶ φίλων. Also Plato *Protag.* 345 C, where φησί repeats φησὶ γάρ. Hence there is no reason to change φάτ' to φᾶτ(α)=φῶτα, which would be harsh after φωτός, and is, besides, an unwarranted form. Kan (*Mnemos.* 9. 350) conj. γάρ. **ἐσθλόν** is changed by some to Aiol. ἐσλόν (Alk. xxv., Sa. xviii.).

5. γέρας is predicate. Cf. Plato *Symp.* 179 C εὐαριθμήτοις δή τισιν ἔδοσαν τοῦτο γέρας οἱ θεοί, *Alkib.* ii. 148 C. Sim. 82 has μηδὲν ἁμαρτεῖν ἐστι θεοῦ, cf. Matth. *v.l.* 19. 17 τί με λέγεις ἀγαθόν; οὐδεὶς ἀγαθός, εἰ μὴ εἷς, ὁ Θεός. Virtue is god-given, Frag. xxv. **μὴ οὐ**: after οὐκ ἔστι=*non potest fieri quin*; Goodwin *M. T.* 815. 2.

6. ἀμάχανος: 'resistless'; of ξυμφορά Eur. *Med.* 391, ἄλγος Soph. *El.* 140, νόσος *Antig.* 364.

7. After **πράξας** (Boeckh, Bergk read Aiol. πράξαις) Sokr. has μὲν γάρ where the μέν is inserted to make the argument clear. **πράξας εὖ**: so of Hieron, Bacch. i. 94; cf. on Eur. *Herakl.* 794. Sokr. takes the words as 'fairing well,' the result of a systematic course of doing well, and then shows that εὐπραγία is caused by μάθησις. Simonides' creed is simply that a man is ἀγαθός if he does good deeds without regard to the permanence of his state. On the distinction between εὐτυχία, good fortune, and εὐπραξία, fortunate action, the latter demanding the conscious activity of the agent, cf. Xen. *Memorab.* 3. 9. 14. In Pind. *Pyth.* 2. 73 Rhadamanthos' good fortune is not transitory (εὖ πέπραγεν), because he had a judicial mind as his birthright and did not delight in deceit. He was εὐτυχής and his judgment directed him to the course of action he desired. Cf. Pind. *Ol.* 8. 12 ἄλλα δ' ἐπ' ἄλλον ἔβαν | ἀγαθῶν, πολλαὶ δ' ὁδοὶ | σὺν θεοῖς εὐπραγίας. For the sentiment of 7-8, cf. the anonymous elegiac poet in 344 D: αὐτὰρ ἀνὴρ ἀγαθὸς τότε μὲν κακός, ἄλλοτε δ' ἐσθλός, Soph. *Antig.* 365 ff. σοφόν τι τὸ μηχανόεν τέχνας ὑπὲρ ἐλπίδ' ἔχων | ποτὲ μὲν κακόν, ἄλλοτ' ἐπ' ἐσθλὸν ἕρπει, and Xen. *Memorab.* 1.

2\. 20. Homer, Ω 527 ff., makes Zeus distribute both evil and good: ᾧ μέν κ' ἀμμείξας δώῃ Ζεὺς . . . | ἄλλοτε μέν τε κακῷ ὅ γε κύρεται, ἄλλοτε δ' ἐσθλῷ.

8. κακῶς: *scil.* πράξῃ, as if ἐὰν (or εἰ) μὲν γὰρ πράξῃ had preceded. Some end the line with καί (which occurs at the verse-end in Pind.) and begin l. 9 with τοὐπὶ πλεῖστον.

9. Cf. Thuk. 1. 2. 5 τὴν γοῦν Ἀττικὴν ἐκ τοῦ ἐπὶ πλεῖστον ἄνθρωποι . . . ᾤκουν οἱ αὐτοί. Reading τούς κε θεοὶ φιλέωντι we have two cases of synizesis. But the ἄν in Plato does not prove the κε in Sim. Subj. without ἄν as in *Hymn* 5. 486 μέγ' ὄλβιος, ὅν τιν' ἐκεῖναι | προφρονέως φίλωνται. So in Il. 6. 15; Goodwin *M. T.* 540.

10 ff. 'Therefore never will I for my part vainly set my allotted portion of life upon a hope that cannot be realized, searching for the impossible, even a man free from all blame, among all of us who' etc. **κενεάν** is proleptic. Sim. like Pind. loves to give an epithet to each substantive in the clause. **μοῖραν**: cf. μοίρᾳ χρόνου Pind. *Ol.* 7. 94, μοῖραν βίου Soph. *Antig.* 896. **ἐς ἀπρ. ἐλπίδα βαλέω**: cf. Pind. *Pyth.* 2. 35 εὐναὶ δὲ παράτροποι ἐς κακότατ' ἀθρόαν | ἔβαλον. **πανάμωμον ἄνθρωπον**: in apposition to τὸ . . . δυνατόν. Cf. Sem. 4 πάμπαν δ' ἄμωμος οὔτις.

12. The poet amplifies Z 142 βροτῶν, οἳ ἀρούρης καρπὸν ἔδουσιν. Cf. θ 222 ὅσσοι νῦν βροτοί εἰσιν ἐπὶ χθονὶ σῖτον ἔδοντες. Plutarch often cites the phrase of Sim. Cf. Hor. 2. 14. 10 *quicumque terrae munere vescimur.* **ὅσοι**: the pl. follows the generic antecedent ἀνθρώπων implied in ἄνθρωπον. **αἰνύμεθα**: the shift to the first person after a generic word (after ἄνθρωποι: Xen. *Memorab.* 4. 3. 11).

13. ὔμμιν: the reference has been supposed to be (1) an imaginary audience, (2) the Skopadai in general, (3) the friends and relatives of Skopas, (4) the citizens, to whom the poet is justifying the tyrant. (1) is to be preferred.

14. ἐπαίνημι: Sokr. says (346 D) that Sim. used this Lesbian form because he was addressing Pittakos. This may be playful, but Jowett should not have questioned its Lesbian character though Pindar used αἴτημι Frag. 155. Nor is αἴνημι in Hes. *W. D.* 683 a Doricism.

15. ἑκών is construed with ἐπαίνημι by Sokr. (345 D, E) in order to avoid the (natural) connection with ἔρδῃ. Praise, he maintains, is not always voluntary, whereas a voluntary act that is good implies the possibility of voluntary evil action—a doctrine that is repugnant to his theory that all wrongdoing is merely the result of ignorance. (Cf. οὐδεὶς ἑκὼν πονηρὸς οὐδ' ἄκων μάκαρ Solon (?) in Arist. *Eth.* 3. 5, ἀλλὰ μὰν ἐγὼν ἀνάγκᾳ ταῦτα πάντα ποιέω· | οἴομαι δ', οὐδεὶς ἑκὼν πονηρὸς οὐδ' ἄταν ἔχων Epicharm. 241 L., Aisch. *Eum.* 550 ἑκὼν δ' ἀνάγκας ἄτερ δίκαιος ὢν οὐκ ἀνόλβιος ἔσται.) Sokrates' argument is doubtless ironical. The antithesis of ἑκών is ἀνάγκῃ. **ὅστις**: the generic relatives ὅστις (ἄν) and ὅς (ἄν) after πάντες are common: Thuk. 7. 29, Plato *Rep.* 556 D. Cf. T 260, Ψ 285.

16. For the sentiment cf. ἰσχυρότατον ἀνάγκη Thales; σὺν δ' ἀνάγκᾳ πᾶν καλόν Pind. Frag. 122. 9 (of the *hierodouloi*); τὸ τῆς ἀνάγκης ἔστ' ἀδήριτον σθένος Aesch. *Prom.* 105 (cf. 515); κρεῖσσον οὐδὲν ἀνάγκας | ηὗρον Eur. *Alk.* 965; σοφῶν δ' ἔπος, | δεινῆς ἀνάγκης οὐδὲν ἰσχύειν πλέον *Hel.* 513; δοῦλοι βασιλέων εἰσίν, ὁ βασιλεὺς θεῶν, | ὁ θεὸς ἀνάγκης Philemon 31. 4; ἀλλ' ἔοικεν ὁ τὸν θεὸν πρῶτον παροιμιασάμενος ταῦτα ἀποβλέψας εἰπεῖν, ὡς οὐδὲ θεὸς ἀνάγκῃ μήποτε φανῇ μαχόμενος Plato *Laws* 818 B (cf. 818 E). Cf. also Hdt. 8. 111, Soph. *O. K.* 191, *Antig.* 1106, Frag. 690, Eur. Frag. 299, 475, trag. adesp. 502, mel. adesp. 143, Lucian Ζεὺς ἐλεγχ. 3.

17. It is impossible to restore the lost verse and a half. Probably it contained a description of the mediocre man continued from str. γ'.

18. For the omission of μή before ᾖ, cf. the ἀπὸ κοινοῦ constr. in λέγουσα μηδὲ δρῶσα Eur. *Hek.* 373, χοροὺς οὔτε δαῖτας Pind. *Ol.* 14. 9, ἔργοις οὔτε βουλαῖς *Pyth.* 3. 30; Aisch. *Agam.* 532, Soph. *Phil.* 771, Aristoph. *Aves* 695, Shakesp. *words nor oath*, Byron *words nor deeds.* The negative thus used with the second word may be preceeded by καί. **ἀπάλαμνος** has been taken to mean (1) without resource, helpless, inert, stupid. Cf. Theogn. 481 μυθεῖται δ' ἀπάλαμνα, τὰ νήφοσι γίνεται αἰσχρά (thoughts incapable of realization), E 597, Alk. xxv., Solon 27. 12. So ἀπάλαμος Hes. *W. D.* 20. Rohde *Psyche* 500 would refer to this meaning Pind. *Ol.* 2. 57 θανόντων μὲν ἐνθάδ' αὐτίκα ἀπάλαμνοι φρένες ποινὰς ἔτεισαν, comparing ἀμενηνὰ κάρηνα in Hom. βίος ἀπάλαμνος *Ol.* 1. 59 is βίος πρὸς ὃν οὐκ ἔστι παλαμήσασθαι. (2) Base, wanton, lawless. Cf. Theogn. 281 δειλῷ γάρ τ' ἀπάλαμνα βροτῷ πάρα πόλλ' ἀνελέσθαι | παρ ποδός, ἡγεῖσθαί θ' ὡς καλὰ πάντα τιθεῖ. This meaning suits the present passage better than (1).—**εἰδώς . . . δίκαν**: cf. υ 287 ἀνὴρ ἀθεμίστια εἰδώς, α 428 κεδνὰ ἰδυῖα. In Attic εἰδέναι loses this colouring; cf. δυσσέβειαν εἰδέναι Soph. *Antig.* 301. **ὀνασιπ. δίκαν**: cf. *Antig.* 365 ff.

19. **ὑγιής**: Sim. emphasized both the moral and the physical ὑγίεια; cf. xxx., skol. vi., and Dante's *intelletti sani.*

20. **μωμήσομαι** (MSS.) may be defended by μωμέομαι Theogn. 169, 369. Unless the verb is subj. we have an instance of οὐ μή with the future earlier than any quoted in Goodwin *M. T.* 295.

21. γενέθλα: cf. γενεή 85. 3 = Z 146. Note the omission of the substantive verb denoting existence, and cf. Eur. *Alk.* 170 πάντας δὲ βωμούς, οἳ κατ' Ἀδμήτου δόμους, | προσῆλθε, *Ion* 275 ἆρ' ἀληθὲς ἢ μάτην λόγος; **ἀπείρων** = ἄπειρος; not enallage with ἠλιθίων.

22. Like the preceding τοί, **τε** is gnomic as in Homer (Monro *H. G.* §§ 263, 332). In the lyric poets cases of τε subjoined to the demonstrative used as a relative (as in Π 157) are very rare.

Metre: logaoedic: **1.** log. pentap. catal. + dact. dip. catal. **2.** anacr. + log. tetrap. catal. + hexap. catal. **3.** anacr. + troch. dip. catal. + two log. tetrap. catal. **4.** and **5.** anacr. + troch. dip. catal. + log. trip. catal. **6.** anacr. + troch. trip. with interior catalexis. **7.** log. hexap. The logaoedics resemble those of Pindar in style.

III. Arist. *Rhet.* 3. 2. 14: "and Simonides, when the victor in the mule-race offered him only a small fee, declined to compose the ode in honour of the victory on the ground that he was shocked at the idea of writing on the subject of half-asses; but when the victor gave him sufficient pay, he wrote 'Hurrah, for the brood of the storm-footed coursers'" (Sandys). Herakleid. Pont. *Polit.* 25 says the victor was Anaxilas of Rhegion; Athen. 1. 3 E calls him [K]leophron, the son of Anaxilas. This passage is cited as a happy instance of the use of epithets to elevate a subject. **ἀελλοπ.** is a heightened ὠκύποδες; cf. Pind. *Pyth.* 4. 18, *Nem.* 1. 6, Frag. xxxi.; ἀελλάδων ἵππων Soph. *O. T.* 466.—Metre: dact.-epitrite.

IV. Lucian *pro imag.* 19. Attributed to Sim. Glaukos, the boxer from Karystos, was a victor at all the great games. Cf. Paus. 6. 10. 1. Bergk referred the epinikion to a victory at Olympia in 520 B.C. **βία**: for the periphrasis cf. βίη Διομήδεος, Ἑλένοιο etc. in Homer. **Ἀλκμ. τέκος**: so in German *Siegelindenkind.* Some write Ἀλκμήνας to make Sim. agree with Pindar. The poet does not scruple to compare a mortal with the sons of Zeus, the athletes of the heroic past. Sim. foreshadows Euripides, and often shows *plus d'esprit que de respect* (Croiset).—Metre: dact.-epitrite. The resolution, in Πολυδεύκεος, of the second thesis of the dipody is rare and unknown to tragedy. In Pind. *Nem.* 5. 12 it occurs also in a proper name; but is not so restricted in *Nem.* 5. 6, 10, *Isthm.* 2 epode 6, 3 epode 6. Cf. xxi. 4. Schneidewin read ἐναντίας τὰς χεῖρας ἀν. ἂν αὐτῷ.

V. Photios 413. 20. Astylos of Kroton won three successive victories in running at Olympia (488, 484, 480 B.C.). Because he had himself proclaimed as a Syracusan in order to court the favour of Hieron, his statue at his birthplace was pulled down and his house turned into a jail (Paus. 6. 13. 1). The Frag. is quoted to illustrate the custom (which went back to Theseus) of the victors having garlands showered upon them. Cf. Pind. *Pyth.* 9. 124. **νίκας** is unexpectedly substituted for *χαίταν*; cf. *Pyth.* 2. 6 *κρατέων—ἀνέδησεν Ὀρτυγίαν στεφάνοις*, and *ἀναδέω κλέος, δόξαν*. Elsewhere in Pind. *ἀναδέω* is used of hair; cf. *ἀναδησάμενος κεφαλάν* Bacch. 10. 16. Pindar has a bold usage in *Ol.* 13. 38 *τρία ἔργα ποδαρκὴς | ἁμέρα θῆκε κάλλιστ' ἀμφὶ κόμαις.* **περικτιόνων**: the 'village fairs' where an athlete first tested his mettle; *ἀμφικτιόνων* *Pyth.* 4. 66. Cf. Athen. 12. 522 C.—Metre: dact.-epitrite.

VI. Arist. *Hist. Anim.* 5. 9 (542 B): the halcyon lays its eggs about the winter solstice. When the season is calm, the seven days before and after the solstice are called 'halcyon days.' The first week is spent by the bird in preparing its nest, the second in hatching and rearing the young. But cf. Thompson *Greek Birds* p. 31, who shows that the king-fisher nests neither in the winter season, nor on the sea. He thinks the (unexplained) story was originally connected with an astronomical phenomenon, the constellation Alkyone being the chief star of the Pleiads. The number of days varied according to different accounts (5, 7, 9, 11, 14). Cf. Theokr. 7. 57 *χἀλκυόνες στορεσεῦντι τὰ κύματα τάν τε θάλασσαν | τόν τε νότον τόν τ' εὖρον κ.τ.λ.* Pseudo-Plato *Alkyon* on the halcyon days: *ἀκύματον καὶ γαλήνιον ἅπαν τὸ πέλαγος, ὅμοιον ὡς εἰπεῖν κατόπτρῳ.* Some connect xvi. and xvii. with this fragment.—Metre: dact.-epitrite.

VII. Athen. 11. 490 F; cf. schol. Pind. *Nem.* 2. 16 = 11 (*ὀρειᾶν Πελειάδων*), Tzetz. *Lykoph.* 219.—**1.** Bergk wrote *δ' εὖ τιν.* **ἐναγώνιος**: cf. Pind. *Ol.* 6. 79 *Ἑρμᾶν, ὃς ἀγῶνας ἔχει.*—**2.** **ἑλικ.**: there is authority for *εὐπλοκάμοιο.* Wilamowitz *οὐρείας ἑλικ. | Μαιάδος παῖς· τίκτε κ.τ.λ.*—**3.** **τάν γ'**: Kaibel conj. *τὰν μίαν.*—**4.** Cf. Aisch. Frag. 312 *αἱ δ' ἑπτ' Ἄτλαντος παῖδες ὠνομασμέναι | πατρὸς μέγιστον ἆθλον οὐρανοστεγῆ | κλαίεσκον, ἔνθα νυκτέρων φαντασμάτων | ἔχουσι μορφὰς ἄπτεροι πελειάδες*, and see on Alkm. iv. 60.—Metre: logaoedic.

VIII. Plut. *Symp.* 9. 15. 2: quoted with the next two fragments to show that the hyporchemes of Simonides—the author of the famous antithesis (Plut. *de glor. Athen.* 346 F) that poetry is speaking painting, painting silent poetry—prove rather a more intimate bond between poetry and the dance. Plut. contends that the poet was himself conscious of the higher truth that poetry is a vocal dance, the dance silent poetry; for, he claims, his hyporchemes are so constructed that, when they are recited or sung, one is irresistably constrained to dance.—**1.** The dancer imitates the racehorse which turns (*κάμπτει*) the post and the hound which doubles on his quarry (M.L.E.).—**2.** **'Αμυκλαΐαν**: cf. Anakr. 1. 4.—**3.** **ἐλελιζόμενος**: here of the feet; of the phorminx Pind. *Pyth.* 1. 4. **καμπύλον μέλος** is a melody full of life, now ascending, now descending, as the singer *διώκει* the sounds of the melody (Graf). *καμπύλον* refers to the 'bending' of the voice, not to elaborate rhythms or involved antithetic periods. Cf. Eupol. 336 *μουσικὴ πρᾶγμ' ἐστὶ βαθύ τι καὶ καμπύλον.* Farnell compared Milton's "The melting voice through mazes running." Cf. *ὕμνων πτυχαί* Pind. *Ol.* 1. 105, *κλυτᾶς πολύπλοκα μέτρα μολπᾶς* *Anth. Pal.* 15. 27; Theokr. 16. 44 says of Simonides *αἰόλα φωνέων* | *βάρβιτον ἐς πολύχορδον.* **διώκων** of the dancer; cf. *δ. φόρμιγγα πλάκτρῳ* Pind. *Nem.* 5. 24.—Metre: logaoedic.

IX. Plut. *l.l.* **2.** The Dotian plain was south of Ossa near Lake Boibeïs. It was the birthplace of Asklepios (*Hymn* 16). Thessaly was famous as a hunting country. "A cry more tuneable | Was never holla'd to, nor cheer'd with horn | In Crete, in Sparta, nor in Thessaly" (*Mid. Night's Dream* 4. 1).—**3.** **πέταται**: subject *κύων.* **κεροέσσᾳ**: see on Anakr. xxi.—**4.** **εὑρέμεν**: this inf. ending in Sim. only here and x.; cf. *εὑρίσκεις φόνον* Eur. *El.* 650.—**5.** Bergk's reading *τὰν μεθέπ' αὐχένα στρέφοισαν ὑγρόν τε κάρα* is poetical, but too far from the MSS. Schneidewin suggested *τὰν δ' ἔλ' αὐχένι στρ. σφέτερον κάρα.* I follow Hermann. As the hunted deer turns its head hither and thither to find some means of escape, so the dancers wind in and out in their mazy evolutions.—Metre: logaoedic.

X. Plut. *l.l.* The Cretan mimetic dances were famous; cf. Σ [590 ff.] *χορόν, οἷόν ποτ' ἐνὶ Κνωσῷ εὐρείῃ* | *Δαίδαλος ἤσκησεν.* Thaletas transferred them from Crete to Sparta where they formed a part of the Gymnopaidia. Their fame was long lived: cf. Aristoph. *Ekkles.* 1165 *Κρητικῶς οὖν τὼ πόδε* | *καὶ σὺ κίνει.* Cretic rhythms were generally used in these lively dances but we may conclude from v. 3 that other measures also were employed. Cf. the use of cretics in Kratinos *Trophon.* 222 K: *ἔγειρε δὴ νῦν, Μοῦσα, Κρητικὸν μέλος·* | *χαῖρε δή, Μοῦσα, χρονία μὲν ἥκεις, ὅμως* | *δ' ἦλθες οὐ πρίν γε δεῖν, ἴσθι σαφές, ἀλλ' ὅμως,* Mel. Adesp. 118 *Κρησίοις ἐν ῥυθμοῖς παῖδα μέλψωμεν.* **ὄργανον Μολοσσόν**: perhaps a rude kind of flute.

Athen. 14. 629 D reports a Μολοσσικὴ ἐμμέλεια. The text of vv. 1-2 is very uncertain. Blass has ῥῶσαί νυν ἐλαφρόν.—Metre: cretic-logaoedic (cf. Bacch. 50=21). v. 2 consists of a cretic tetrapody preceded by — ⏕ (cf. Aristoph. *Ranae* 1356 ἀλλ', ὦ Κρῆτες, Ἴδας τέκνα). v. 3 is a logaoedic tetrapody + ithyphallic.

XI. Favorinus in Stob. *Flor.* 105. 62 (cf. 105. 9). Probably from a threnos on the Skopadai, the famous poem that related their destruction by the falling of the roof of their banqueting hall. From this poem arose the story of the miraculous rescue of the poet through the mediation of the Dioskuroi (cf. Cicero *de orat.* 2. 86). For the sentiment of vv. 1-2 cf. Pind. *Pyth.* 10. 63 τὰ δ' εἰς ἐνιαυτὸν ἀτέκμαρτον προνοῆσαι, *Ol.* 12. 7 σύμβολον δ' οὔ πώ τις ἐπιχθονίων | πιστὸν ἀμφὶ πράξιος ἐσσομένας εὗρεν θεόθεν· | τῶν δὲ μελλόντων τετύφλωνται φραδαί, Solon Frag. 13, and his teaching in Hdt. 1. 32—a man may be εὐτυχής in life, but ὄλβιος only when his life has been free from reverse; Theogn. 159, Aisch. *Agam.* 928, Soph. *O. T.* 1529, *Aias* 127, *Trach.* 1, Eur. *Andr.* 100, *Troad.* 510, *Herakl.* 865, *I. A.* 161, Frag. 553, Hor. 1. 9. 13 *quid sit futurum cras, fuge quaerere.* With 3-4 cf. xxvi.—**1.** Sim. regarded Αὔριον as a divine power. Cf. Kallim. epigr. 16 δαίμονα τίς δ' εὖ οἶδε τὸν Αὔριον;—**3.** Involved order = οὐδὲ γὰρ μυίας ταν. οὕτως ὠκεῖά ἐστιν ἡ μετάστασις. Stadtmüller conj. εὖτε for οὐδέ, Wilam. οὕτω γὰρ . . . ὠκ. μετ. (he makes ionics of the poem). **τανυπτερύγου**: cf. Alkm. xxi. 7.—Metre: logaoedic.

XII. Stob. *Flor.* 118. 15. Schneidewin thought that the fragment was from a threnos on the death of a youth either carried off by disease or killed perhaps in battle. Hes. *W. D.* 156 ff. says that the demi-gods perished in war and on the sea (cf. M 23). Cf. Pind. *Pyth.* 3. 86 αἰὼν δ' ἀσφαλὴς | οὐκ ἔγεντ' οὔτ' Αἰακίδᾳ παρὰ Πηλεῖ | οὔτε παρ' ἀντιθέῳ Κάδμῳ. The gods enjoy a life free from the ills to which their offspring by a mortal mother are subject: Pind. xxii., Bacch. 60 (B 34).—**2.** Wilamowitz conj. plausibly (*Hermes* 14. 170) θεῶν ἐξ ἀνάκτων υἱέες ἡμίθεοι | ἄπονον οὐδ' ἀφθόνητον. **ἐξ**: generally of immediate, as ἀπό of remote descent (τοὺς μὲν ἀπὸ θεῶν, τοὺς δ' ἐξ αὐτῶν τῶν θεῶν γεγονότας Isokr. 12. § 81). But in poetry ἐκ often (sometimes παρά) denotes the parent and his ancestors, while ἀπό is used of the parent.—**3. ἄφθιτον**: 'free from decay.'—Metre: logaoedic.

XIII. Dion. Hal. *de comp. verb.* 26. The Lament of Danae is quoted by the rhetorician to illustrate his statement that, because of their unequal cola, melic compositions are closely related to prose despite their figurative language and other poetical characteristics. In proof of this, Dion. transcribes the poem, which he arranges, not in metrical cola, but according to the divisions (διαστολαί) current in prose, *i.e.* according to grammatical and rhetorical rules. In such an arrangement the poetical rhythm is, he claims, so obscured, that the reader will be unable to recognize strophe, antistrophe, or epode; and the whole piece will appear to be nothing but continuous prose. It must be confessed that, if we have all that Dion. transcribed, he has proved his point so successfully that no one has been able to demonstrate the existence of all three parts of the triad.

Wilamowitz *Isyllos* 144 claims to have restored strophe (ἄνεμος . . . δούρατι), epode (χαλκ. . . . δεινὸν ἦν), and antistr. (καὶ ἐμῶν . . .); ὅτε . . . δαιδαλέᾳ belonging to another triad. To accept this adjustment one must have faith in the extremely elastic ionics of the German scholar. Nietzsche *R. M.* 23. 481 thought that 1-3 formed the end of the strophe, 4-12 the antistr. (1-3 = 10-12). In v. 1 he omitted ἐν and read τ' ἐμάνῃ πνείων with ἀλεγίζεις in 10, but even then the dactyls vary with spondees over frequently. By a series of reckless conjectures Hartung extricated strophe and antistr. out of the lines, while Blass' (*Philol.* 32. 140) similar conclusion is reached by conjectures only less hazardous than those of Hartung. Schneidewin, and Bergk, adopting the easier course, which refuses all credence to Dion., found only antistrophe and epode; and so, doubtfully, Michelangeli; while Ahrens (*Jahresber. des Lyceums zu Hannover* 1853), in despair, classed the fragment among the ἀπολελυμένα. Since verses 2-3 may = 11-12, I have followed Nietzsche, though with much hesitation. The last seven verses suit the character of a concluding epode.

I have retained the usual classification of xiii. as a threnos, but the fragment may be a dithyramb like the dithyrambs of Bacchylides, in which the three parts are present.

Some suppose that the poem was composed for a Thessalian princess who had lost a son. The choice of a subject may have been influenced by the fact that the cult of Perseus was native with the Thessalian chiefs (the Aleuadai, Skopadai, and Kreondai), who were Herakleidai, the descendants of the great-grandson of Perseus. It may therefore not be chance that in Pindar's earliest extant ode (*Pyth.* 10), on Hippokles of Thessaly, the story of Perseus' visit to the Hyperboreans is introduced; and it was at Larissa that Akrisios met his death at the hand of his daughter's son.

Simonides loves to put words of lament into the mouths of women. So in 51, one of the Athenian women deported to Salamis says ἴσχει δέ με πορφυρέας | ἁλὸς ἀμφιταρασσομένας ὀρυμαγδός. With the despair of Danae we may compare that of Europa (Hor. 3. 27) with its passionate exclamations and questions.

1. Dion. introduces the fragment by the words *ἔστι δὲ ἡ διὰ πελάγους φερομένη Δανάη, τὰς ἑαυτῆς ἀποδυρομένη τύχας.* Mention of Danae must have gone before, whether or not the poet recounted the prophecy of Akrisios' doom and the chastisement of his daughter preceding her exposure in the ark. The fragment contains only the myth, herein resembling the dithyrambs of Bacchylides. The meaning of 1-3 is clear in general, but for *τε μήν* of the MSS. nothing satisfactory has been offered (*τε μιν, βρέμεν, πέσεν, στένεν, τ' ἐμάνη* cf. Sem. 7. 37-39). **τέτμε**: with an impersonal subject as α 218, will at least scan, since initial *πν* fails to make position in 78 (so ⏑ *πνέω* in Pind.). **λάρνακι** depends on *Δανάην ἐεργμένην* (cf. P 354) or the like. For *ἐν* (a gloss) some read *ἦν* or *σύν*. Probably the apodosis begins with l. 3, but it may have preceded (cf. Pind. *Pyth.* 8. 38). *λάρναξ* was the regular name for the ark in which a wrathful father exposed his daughter together with her child born out of mortal wedlock. So Kadmos exposed Semele and Dionysos, so Aleos exposed Auge and Telephos. From Hesychios *ἐκ λάρνακος· νόθος* we may suppose that illegitimate children were disposed of in this manner. Hypsipyle rescued Thoas by putting him in a *λάρναξ*. The vessel seems also to have been used for confinement on land (Theokr. 7. 78). The ordinary poetical term *δόρυ* is substituted in v. 7. In Bacch. ii. 141 λ. is differently used. In Roscher's *Lexikon* 1. 948 may be found a representation on a coin of Danae emerging from the *λάρναξ*. Cf. also Welcker *R. M.* 10. 235. Noah's Ark is *Δευκαλίωνος λάρναξ*.

3. δείματι: hiatus as in *παιδὶ ὄπασσεν* P 196, *αἵματι ὕδωρ* Φ 21. **ἤριπεν**: = *ἐξεπλάγη*. The transitive meaning of the second aorist has only the doubtful support of Hdt. 9. 70 *ἐπέβησαν τοῦ τείχεος καὶ ἤριπον* 'made a breach,' where Abicht and Kallenberg read *ἤρειπον*, a conjecture that has been made in Paus. 4. 25. 2 (cf. 10. 32. 6). Quint. Smyrn. 13. 452 has *μεσόδμη ἔμπεσεν ἐπὶ δ' ἤριπεν αἰπὺν ὄλεθρον* (Koechly *αἰπὺς ὄλεθρος*). In Bacch. v. 68 *ἤρειπον* is a necessary change for *ἤριπεν*. For *ἔριπεν* here there have been conjectured *προσεῖρπε, ἐφεῖρπεν, παρῖσχεν, ῥῖπτεν*. **οὐκ ἀδιαντ. παρειαῖς**: litotes. Cf. *siccis oculis ... vidit mare turbidum* Hor. 1. 3. 18.

4. φίλαν: *χεῖρα φίλην* φ 433. Athen. 9. 396 E cites *ὦ τέκος—κνώσσεις*.

5. ἀωτεῖς: only here and in Homer, where it is always followed by *ὕπνον*. The repetition of the same idea in *κνώσσεις* (*κνώσσων* Sitzler) is objectionable to many. But a lullaby is not logic. Strictly *ἀϝωτέω* (Eng. *weary*) is the sweet sleep that follows weariness, *κνώσσω* the sleep of pleasant dreams (δ 809, Pind. *Ol.* 13. 71; the deep sleep of Zeus' eagle *Pyth.* 1. 8). Of the conjectures, αὖ τέως and αὔτως are the best.

6. γαλαθηνῷ: the figurative use is very rare, and perhaps occurs only here; γαλαθηνὸν τέκος xx., cf. Anakr. xxi. Hesych. however glosses the word not only with ὑποτίτθιον, but also with νέον. **δ' ἤθεϊ** is nearer the MSS. of Dion. than λάθεϊ (Bergk). ἤτορι in Athen. is post-classical (in a Christian epigram Kaibel 725). Eust. *Il.* 133. 31 says ἦτορ is indeclinable.

7. Those who object to **χαλκ.** as an epithet of δούρατι (synecdoche as in *trabs*) forget γομφοδέτῳ δόρει Aisch. *Suppl.* 846 (cf. νηῶν πολυγόμφων Hes. *W. D.* 660). In Soph. *Antig.* 945 the χαλκόδετοι αὐλαί are the θάλαμος in which Danae was immured in Argos. Danae exchanged one brass-bound dungeon for another. For δόρυ, cf. also εἰνάλιον δόρυ Pind. *Pyth.* 4. 27, ποντοπόρῳ δούρατι Soph. *Phil.* 721. Wilamowitz follows Nietzsche in taking χαλκ. with νυκτί and in reading λάμπεις.

8. νυκτιλαμπεῖ: Bergk and others νυκτὶ ἀλαμπεῖ, cf. Bacch. vi. 52; some read ν. λάμπεις. If the form νυκτιλαμπεῖ is permissible, the word denotes gloom in which only night shines: *tenebrae quales nocte lucent, i.e.* σκότος (Schneid.). Greek is as fond of oxymoron as French is averse to its use. Cf. Soph. *O. T.* 419 βλέποντα νῦν μὲν ὄρθ', ἔπειτα δὲ σκότον (cf. 1273), Eur. *Hel.* 518 μελαμφαὲς ἔρεβος, Soph. *Aias* 394, Eur. *Bacch.* 510, *Hek.* 1067, *Phoin.* 377, 543, Aristoph. *Ranae* 1331 (κελαινοφαὴς ὄρφνα). Sandys quotes Pliny *Ep.* 57 of the tunnel between Naples and Puteoli: *non ut per tenebras videamus, sed ut ipsas.* The eye of dark night Aisch. *Pers.* 428, Eur. *I. T.* 110. "No light, but rather darkness visible | served only to discover sights of woe" (*Par. L.* 1. 63). **κυανέῳ**: cf. νὺξ κυαναυγής *Orphic Hymn* 3. 3. **δνόφῳ**: δν fails to make position in the melic poets only here, Anakr. 78, Pind. *Pyth.* 10. 72. **ταθείς**: 'outstretched.

9. The MS. αὐλέαν 'dry' is a prosaic touch, and we expect ξηράν. We may read either (1) **βαθεῖαν** as in βαθεῖα ποντιὰς ἅλμα Pind. *Nem.* 4. 36, βαθεῖαν πόντου πλάκα *Pyth.* 1. 24, ἁλὸς βαθεῖαν κέλευθον (hypallage) *Pyth.* 5. 88; or (2) βαθειᾶν; at least the schol. on Apoll. Rhod. 4. 1091 thinks he knows that the child was three or four years old; βαθύς of hair Sem. 7. 66, Lucian *Dial. mort.* 10. 3, *Pisc.* 41.

10. περιόντος (one MS.) = περιιόντος, is defended by Mucke, who thinks ὕπερθεν reinforces περί here = ὑπέρ. **ἀλέγεις** with the rare accus. (Alkm. iv. 2, Π 388, Hes. *W. D.* 251). Cf.

ἐνθυμέομαι with gen. 'have regard for'; with acc. 'consider' (both in Thuk. 5. 32. 1).

11. Cf. φθόγγος θαλάσσης Eur. *I. A.* 9.—**12**. For πρόσωπον καλὸν πρόσωπον, Ahrens conj. πρ. κ. προφαίνων, Volckmar πρ. κ. προσάπτων, Nietzsche προσέχων κ. πρ., Bergk πρ. κλιθὲν προσώπῳ, Tyrrell πρ. κ. διαίνων. Some omit one πρ.—**13**. **τοι**: epic; above Sim. has the epic and Doric τεός.

14. The gen., instead of the dat., follows ὑπεῖχες οὖας, as if ὑπήκουες had been used (*constr. ad sensum*). The construction of a simple verb is transferred to a periphrastic expression. Cf. Proklos' *Hymn to Athena* μείλιχον οὖας ὑπόσχες. **οὖας**: Hom. has οὔατος, οὔατα, οὔασι. οὖας occurs only here but ὦας is reported. ὦς <*ὠ(υσ)ος is attested as Doric and Ionic. Attic οὖς is <ο(ὐσ)ος. οὖας has the stem of the oblique cases (οὐ(σ)ατ-). Sim. 246 used οὐατόεις.

15. The mother repents of her (unexpressed) wish that Perseus may share her dread. 'No, I charge thee, sleep.' **κέλομαι**: the hiatus may be excused as in Prat. i. 15 where a stronger mark of punctuation intervenes. The syllables in question are all in the thesis. Bergk inserted δ' after κ., but asyndeton is in place in prayers, *e.g.* Pind. *Pyth.* 1. 71. κέλομ' might be defended by μέμφομ', ψεύσομ' in Pind. With the lullaby of Danae, cf. the βαυκάλημα of Alkmena, Theokr. 24. 7 εὕδετ' ἐμὰ βρέφεα γλυκερὸν καὶ ἐγέρσιμον ὕπνον, | εὕδετ' ἐμὰ ψυχά, δύ' ἀδελφεώ, εὔσοα τέκνα· | ὄλβιοι εὐνάζοισθε καὶ ὄλβιοι ἀῶ ἵδοιτε. In Sim. the sea must sleep, the mother's misery must sleep, that her child may slumber. For earnest entreaty expressed by the repeated imperative, cf. Soph. *O. T.* 46, *Aias* 396, Eur. *Rhes.* 532 (ἔγρεσθε . . . ἔγρεσθε), Theokr. 5. 44, 7. 118, 8. 63, Cicero *pro Mil.* 12. 33, Hor. 3. 11. 37. The sea is personified here as in Aisch. *Agam.* 565 εὖτε πόντος ἐν μεσημβριναῖς | κοίταις ἀκύμων νηνέμοις εὕδοι πεσών. Cf. the passages mentioned on Alkm. xxi., and Theaitet. 2. 7 ὑπνώει δὲ θάλασσα φιλοζεφύροιο γαλήνης | νώτοις εὔδια πεπταμένης, Pliny 2. 79. 81 *sopito mari.*—**16**. **εὕδ. κακόν**: cf. Eur. *Suppl.* 1148 οὔπω κακὸν τόδ' εὕδει, Soph. *Phil.* 827 Ὕπν' ὀδύνας ἀδαής, Ὕπνε δ' ἀλγέων, "killing care and grief of heart fall asleep or hearing die" (Shakesp. *Henry VIII.*).

17. **μεταιβολία** was inferred by Bergk from one MS. μετά never appears as μεταί (cf. καταί, παραί, ὑπαί in Hom.) and μεταβολία=μεταβολή occurs only in very late Greek (μεταβολὰ κακῶν Eur. *H. F.* 735). One MS. has μεταβουλία; cf. μετεβούλευσαν θεοὶ ἄλλως | ἀμφ' Ὀδυσῆϊ ε 286. Danae prays openly to Father Zeus, as if she were merely one of the suffering race of humanity that looks to him for succour. In her heart, she entreats help from the God of the Golden. Shower. Schneidewin suggested that this line may have served as a consolation to the person at whose request the threnos was written.

18. θαρσαλέον: the final syllable may be lengthened before ἔπος as in H 375 πυκινὸν ἔπος; cf. Pind. *Isthm.* 6. 42 τοιοῦτον ἔπος.

19. καὶ νόσφι (Wilam.): explanatory of θαρσαλέον. Some read τεκνόφι δίκας making δίκας (gen.) depend on σύγγνωθι; others τεκνόφι (or -ν) δίκαν though -φι is rarely used as a genitive ending (K 458, Φ 295, μ 614), and Aisch. *Prom.* 614 τοῦ δίκην πάσχεις τάδε; is not parallel. Sitzler conj. τέκνου ἐπὶ δίκᾳ. —Metre: logaoedic.

XIV. Stob. *Flor.* 118. 5. Homer, ο 234, uses the fem. δασπλῆτις of ἐρινύς. Like Sim., Euphorion 52 (δασπλῆτες Εὐμενίδες) uses the masc. adj. with a fem. noun. See on i. 6. **ἱκνεῖται** has practically become transitive; ἵκοντο πέτραν Pind. *Ol.* 6. 64. If the poem is directed against the Skopadai, cf. Theokr. 16. 40, where this family is said to have got no pleasure from its riches ἐπεὶ γλυκὺν ἐξεκένωσαν | θυμὸν ἐς εὐρεῖαν σχεδίαν στυγνοῦ Ἀχέροντος.—Metre: logaoedic.

XV. Plut. *Consol.* 11: quoted, together with Pind. *Pyth.* 3. 81, Soph. Frag. 761, Eur. *Alk.* 780, to illustrate the sentiment κρεῖττόν ἐστι τὸ τεθνάναι τοῦ ζῆν. Cf. also Sim. in Stob. *Flor.* 121. 3 βιοτῆς μὲν γὰρ | χρόνος ἔστι βραχύς· κρυφθεὶς δ' ὑπὸ γῆς | κεῖται θνητὸς τὸν ἅπαντα χρόνον, Semonides 3, Hdt. 1. 32 πᾶν ἐστι ἄνθρωπος συμφορή, Eur. *Herakl.* 608 ff., Bacon "The world's a bubble and the Life of Man | Less than a span."—**1. ἄπρακτοι**: some read ἄπρηκτοι following Boeckh's dictum: ἄπρηκτον *inutile quo nihil perficias*, ἄπρακτον *quod perfici non potest.* The distinction will not hold. With **ἀπρ. μεληδόνες** cf. ἀπρήκτους ὀδύνας β 79, θυμηδεῖς βιότοιο μελήδόνες Apoll. Rhod. 3. 812.—**2.** Cf. Soph. *Aias* 866 πόνος πόνῳ πόνον φέρει, Eur. *Hippol.* 189 πᾶς δ' ὀδυνηρὸς βίος ἀνθρώπων κοὐκ ἔστι πόνων ἀνάπαυσις, and see on Alk. v. 2.—**3. ἐπικρέμαται**: Death is the *destrictus ensis super cervice pendens* (Hor. 3. 1. 17), cf. Mimn. 5. 6 γῆρας ὑπὲρ κεφαλῆς ὑπερκρέμαται, Theogn. 206 ἄτην παισὶν ὑπερκρέμασεν, Pind. *Isthm.* 8. 14 δόλιος γὰρ αἰὼν ἐπ' ἀνδράσι κρέμαται, *Ol.* 7. 25.—**5.** Cf. I 319 ἐν δὲ ἰῇ τιμῇ ἠμὲν κακὸς ἠδὲ καὶ ἐσθλός· | κάτθαν' ὁμῶς ὅ τε ἀεργος ἀνὴρ ὅ τε πολλὰ ἐοργώς. The words ἀγαθοί and κακός have here more than a moral significance.—Metre: logaoedic.

XVI. Tzetz. *Chil.* 1. 310. On the power of Orpheus' music. Cf. Apoll. Rhod. 1. 569 τοῖσι δὲ φορμίζων εὐθήμον μέλπειν ἀοιδῇ | Οἰάγροιο πάις . . . | Ἄρτεμιν . . . τοὶ δὲ βαθείης|ι *ἰχθύες ἀΐσσοντες ὕπερθ' ἁλός, ἄμμιγα παύροις | ἄπλετοι, ὑγρὰ κέλευθα διασκαίροντες ἕποντο*, Theodoret. 3. 767 *τοῖς κρούμασιν τοὺς ἰχθύας καταθέλγων*. Horace emphasizes Orpheus' power over wild beasts and inanimate nature: 1. 12. 7, 1. 24. 13, *Ars poet.* 391.—**2. ἀνά**: tmesis with *ἅλλοντο*; cf. Pind. *Pyth.* 4. 228.—**3. σύν**: 'keeping time to the measure.' The fish follow the minstrel and his song, cf. Pind. iv. 20. There is no need of Herwerden's *ὑπ' ἀοιδᾶς*.—Metre: logaoedic. Reading *ἐξ* we have synizesis; note *ῡδατος*, as always in Homer.

XVII. Plut. *Quaest. Symp.* 8. 3. 4. Perhaps from the same poem as xvi. Schneidewin joined xvi. and xvii. with vi.—**1. ἐννοσίφυλλος**: cf. *εἰνοσίφυλλος* B 632. The *νν* form is Aiolic (from *ἐν-F*). **ἀήτα**: *ἀνέμοιο ἀήτῃ* O 626, cf. Hes. *Theogon.* 874, Anakr. xii. *ἄητᾰ* is also possible (cf. Hom. *ἀκακῆτα*). Plato *Krat.* 410 B says *οἱ ποιηταὶ τὰ πνεύματα ἀήτας καλοῦσιν*.—**3. ἀραρεῖν**: epic, and Soph. *El.* 147. **ἀκοαῖσι**: see on Sa. ii. 12.—Metre: logaoedic.

XVIII. Stob. *Ecl.* 2. 10. Cf. Z 234 *Γλαύκῳ ... φρένας ἐξέλετο Ζεύς*, Ξ 217 *ἥ τ'* (Hera) *ἔκλεψε νόον πύκα περ φρονεόντων*, Eur. Frag. 254 *πόλλ' ... σφάλλουσιν ἀνθρώπους θεοί*.—Metre: either dact.-epitrite or logaoedic (hexap.). If *θεοί* forms a single syllable, we have an epitritic trimeter or a troch. trim. catal.

XIX. Aristeid. 2. 513. The poet speaks of his fecundity and his inventiveness in melodies. **τὸ παρόν**: the proper theme of the poem; **θεριζομένα**: refers to digressions from the main subject such as mythological parallels. The schol. on *Nem.* 4. 37 (60) says that Pindar is referring to Simonides, who was fond of digressions.—**2. μή μοι**: as Pind. *Isthm.* 1. 3; see on Alkm. xv. **καταπαύετ'**: *scil.* *τὰν* Μοῖσαν rather than *τὸν αὐλόν*. **ἄρξατο**: musical preludes (*ἀναβολαί*) were still in vogue even after the introduction of complete instrumental accompaniment.—**3. πολύχορδος αὐλός**: for the overlapping of the musical terms, cf. Soph. *Trach.* 640 *ὁ καλλιβόας . . . | οὐκ ἀναρσίαν | ἀχῶν καναχὰν ἐπάνεισιν, ἀλλὰ θείας | ἀντίλυρον μούσας*, Aristoph. *Aves* 682 *ἀλλ', ὦ καλλιβόαν κρέκουσ' | αὐλόν*, a fragment in schol. Aisch. *Pers.* 937 *αὐλεῖ Μαριανδυνοῖς καλάμοις κρούων 'Ιαστί*. So in Plato *Rep.* 3. 399 D *πολυχορδότατον* is used of auletes; hymn to Apollo (i) with notes (Append.) *λωτὸς* (= *αὐλός*) *κρέκει*; Plut. *Symp.* 2. 4. 1 *ὥς που καὶ τὸν αὐλὸν ἡρμόσθαι λέγουσι καὶ κρούματα τὰ αὐλήματα καλοῦσιν, ἀπὸ τῆς λύρας λαμβάνοντες τὰς προσηγορίας*, Pollux 4. 83 *αὐλημάτων κρούματα*, Suidas (*s.v.* *Ὄλυμπος ἡγ.*) *Ὄλυμπος ἡγεμὼν τῆς κρουματικῆς μουσικῆς τῆς διὰ τῶν αὐλῶν*, Tibull. 1. 1. 4 *classica pulsa*, Claudian *de cons.*

Theod. 313 *cui tibia flatu,* | *cui plectro pulsanda chelys.* The terminology was set by the older instrument. πολύχορδος here is an ornamental epithet, and does not connote the varied character of the art of Sim.—Metre: logaoedic. Hanssen *Philol.* 51. 233 finds here an enlargement of the *encomologicum* — ⏑ ⏑ — ⏑ ⏑ — ⏓ (4/8 time).

XX. Athen. 9. 396 E. Archemoros, the infant son of the Nemean prince Lykurgos and Eurydike, was killed by a serpent in consequence of his nurse having abandoned her charge in order to point out a spring to the Seven against Thebes. See the relief in Roscher 1. 473. The subject of ἐδάκρυσαν is the Argive heroes, by whom the Nemean games were instituted in honour of Archemoros. Cf. Bacch. iv. 10 ff., Eur. Frag. 754. The lines may be from an epinikion or a threnos. **ψυχὰν ἀποπν.**: cf. Eur. Frag. 801 ἀπέπνευσεν αἰῶνα, Soph. *Aias* 1031 ἀπέψυξεν βίον, and contrast Pind. *Nem.* 1. 47 ψυχὰς ἀπέπνευσεν 'made them breathe forth their lives.'—Metre: logaoedic; for ⏑⏑ > cf. Pind. *Ol.* 10. 58.

XXI. Athen. 4. 172 E; quoted as evidence that the Ἆθλα ἐπὶ Πελίᾳ was by Stesichoros (cf. Frag. 1-3) and not by Ibykos. Sim. is here referring, doubtless in an episode, to a contest in throwing the spear in which Meleager was the victor. Cf. Hygin. 273. Stes. refers to this victory in the above mentioned *Games in honour of Pelias*, Frag. 3: θρῴσκων μὲν ἄρ' Ἀμφιάραος, ἄκοντι δὲ νίκασεν Μελέαγρος.—**3.** The Anauros flows into the Pagasaian gulf. 'Iolkos' includes the territory adjacent to the town. Since this victory of Meleager is not mentioned in the *Iliad* or *Odyssey*, Welcker and Schneidewin thought Ὅμηρος meant the author of the Cyclic *Thebaid*. Hiller *R. M.* 42. 328 suggested that, if in the words preceding ὃς . . . πάντας, the poet referred to Meleager as the slayer of the Kalydonian boar (I 543 ff.), we may suppose that Sim. had the *Iliad* in mind. In elegy 85 Sim., quoting Z 146, speaks of Homer as the Χῖος ἀνήρ; though some think the elegy is by Semonides of Amorgos.—Metre: logaoedic. Some make it dact.-epitrite, Wilamowitz ionic.

XXII. Diog. Laert. 1. 89. The poet takes issue with Kleobulos, who was reported to be the author of the epigram that was inscribed on a sphinx on the tomb of Midas: χαλκέη παρθένος εἰμί, Μίδεω δ' ἐπὶ σήματι κεῖμαι, | ἔστ' ἂν ὕδωρ τε νάῃ καὶ δένδρεα μακρὰ τεθήλῃ, | Ἠέλιος δ' ἀνιὼν λάμπῃ λαμπρά τε σελήνη, | καὶ ποταμοί γε ῥέωσιν, ἀνακλύζῃ δὲ θάλασσα, | αὐτοῦ τῇδε μένουσα πολυκλαύτῳ ἐπὶ τύμβῳ | ἀγγελέω παριοῦσι, Μίδας ὅτι τῇδε τέθαπται. See Crusius *Philol.* 55, p. 4. Kleobulos, tyrant of Lindos in Rhodes about 600 B.C., was regarded by some as one of the Seven Sages, though Plutarch (*de E Delphico* 3) expressly says that he, together with Periander, obtained a place in that illustrious number only by reason of his position as a prince and through favouritism. Because of the sententious character of his verse, Simonides was often associated with the Sages (Plato *Rep.* 1. 335 E). In *Protag.* 343 C Sokrates says that the poet thought to win a great name for himself by his criticism of Pittakos. Here the detraction of Kleobulos subserves rather the interest of truth than of vain-gloriousness. Cf. i. 4 and Shelley's 'Ozymandias of Egypt': "And on the pedestal these words appear: | 'My name is Ozymandias, king of kings: | Look on my works, ye Mighty, and despair!' | Nothing beside remains. Round the decay | Of that colossal wreck, boundless and bare, | The lone and level sands stretch far away."

1. Since Kleobulos was a Karian, **ναέταν** may have its sting. Line 6 is contemptuous enough.—**3.** A reference to l. 3 of the epigram.—**4. θαλασσαῖος** (Pind. *Pyth.* 2. 50) = *θαλάσσιος*, as *ἠθαῖος* (*Isthm.* 2. 48) = *ἠθεῖος*. Cf. Zacher *de nominibus gr. in -αιος* pp. 30, 145. **θέντα**: we need the aorist, and *ἀντιθέντα* (MSS.) would not be permissible, since, in dact.-epitritic strophes, a logaoedic colon may occur only at the beginning or end of a period or strophe.—**5. θεῶν ἥσσω**: *dis minorem* Hor. 3. 6. 5. **λίθον** cannot be a general name for 'monument.' The figure of the *χαλκέη παρθένος* doubtless stood on a marble column.—**6. βρότεοι**: absence of motion in adj. in *-εως* occurs here, Pind. *Isthm.* 7. 7, Frag. 223, Bacch. ii. 53, Solon 4. 28.—Simonides is the earliest Greek poet who often refers directly to the words or authority of his predecessors: he refers to Pittakos in ii., to Homer in xxi. and 85 (*Χῖος ἀνήρ*), to Hesiod in xxiii., to Stesichoros in xxi. Cf. on xxi. and see note on Alk. xxv.—Metre: dact.-epitrite. In vv. 1, 4 the epitrites begin, as in Pindar. In v. 6 note the ithyphallic ending, here prolonged to form a tetrapody. So the tragic poets, *e.g.* Aisch. *Prom.* 535, Soph. *O. T.* 1095, end their periods with an ithyphallic. Pindar's method is different.

XXIII. Clem. Alex. *Strom.* 4. 585. The poet has in mind Hes. *W. D.* 289 ff.: *τῆς δ' ἀρετῆς ἱδρῶτα θεοὶ προπάροιθεν ἔθηκαν | ἀθάνατοι· μακρὸς δὲ καὶ ὄρθιος οἶμος ἐς αὐτὴν | καὶ τρηχὺς τὸ πρῶτον· ἐπὴν δ' εἰς ἄκρον ἵκηται, | ῥηϊδίη δὴ ἔπειτα πέλει, χαλεπή περ ἐοῦσα.* Cf. *Anth. Pal.* 9. 653. So Quint. Smyrn. 5. 49 says *αἰπύτατον δ' ἐτέτυκτο . . . | καὶ τρηχὺ ζαθέης Ἀρετῆς ὄρος· ἐν δὲ καὶ αὐτὴ | εἱστήκει φοίνικος ἐπεμβεβαυῖα κατ' ἄκρης, | ὑψηλή, ψαύουσα πρὸς οὐρανὸν κ.τ.λ.*, 14. 195 *κεῖνος δ' οὔποτ' ἀνὴρ*

Αρετῆς ἐπὶ τέρμαθ' ἵκανεν, | ᾧτινι μὴ νόος ἐστὶν ἐναίσιμος· οὕνεκ' ἄρ' αὐτῆς | πρέμνον δύσβατόν ἐστι κ.τ.λ. Also Pind. Frag. 227 νέων δὲ μέριμναι σὺν πόνοις εἱλισσόμεναι | δόξαν εὑρίσκοντι, Epicharm. 120 A τῶν πόνων πωλοῦντι πάντα τἀγάθ' ἁμὶν τοὶ θεοί, Aisch. Frag. 315 τῷ πονοῦντι δ' ἐκ θεῶν | ὀφείλεται τέκνωμα τοῦ πόνου κλέος, Xen. *Memorab.* 2. 1. 23 ff., Aristotle on Areta πολύμοχθε γένει βροτείῳ, Verg. *Georg.* 1. 121 *pater ipse colendi | haut facilem esse viam voluit,* Schiller *Zu der Tugend steilem Hügel leitet sie des Dulders Bahn.*

1. λόγος 'story' may be true or false. It often has a suggestion of the mythical and includes μῦθος. Only when μῦθος, which in Homer means a true or a false tale, assumed the connotation of fiction, could λόγος be used to denote prosaic truth. See Pind. *Ol.* 1. 29; the Attic use is set forth by Plato *Phaidon* 61 B ἐννοήσας ὅτι τὸν ποιητὴν δέοι . . . ποιεῖν μύθους, ἀλλ' οὐ λόγους. Cf. Pind. *Nem.* 9. 6 ἔστι δέ τις λόγος ἀνθρώπων. αἶνος a fable, Archil. 86.—**3.** The reading is doubtful. I have followed Schneidewin. It is difficult to see how Bergk's θεῶν could have been corrupted into θυάν. Michelangeli suggests θοόν 'sharp,' 'steep.' Cf. ἐθόωσα . . . ἄκρον ι 327, νήσοισι θοῇσι ο 299 (cf. 'Εχενῆαι, Τρινακρία, *Needles*). But if we keep νῦν δέ, θοὸν χῶρον, even if qualified by ἁγνόν, is not sufficiently distinguished from the inaccessible rocks of v. 2.—**5.** 'Save to him from whose body issueth the sweat that grieves his spirit.' ᾧ after πάντων as ἀσπάζεται πάντας ᾧ ἂν περιτυγχάνῃ Plato *Rep.* 566 D.—**6. μόλῃ**: without ἄν, Goodwin *M. T.* 540. The subject of ἵκηται is ὅς, which is not inserted after a preceding relative in an oblique case; cf. β 54 δοίη δ', ᾧ κ' ἐθέλοι καὶ οἱ κεχαρισμένος ἔλθοι, β 113 etc. **ἵκηται ἐς ἄκρον**: so Tyrt. 12. 43 ἀρετῆς εἰς ἄκρον ἱκέσθαι, Pind. *Nem.* 6. 23 πρὸς ἄκρον ἀρετᾶς | ἦλθον, cf. *Pyth.* 11. 55; ἄκρον ἱκέσθαι Ψ 339, ι 540. Some read ἵκῃ, but the aorist after μόλῃ is preferable. —Metre: logaoedic. v. 1 is a proöde. With the *hiatus licitus* in v. 6, cf. Pind. *Ol.* 3. 30 'Ορθωσίᾳ ἔγραψεν, and Sim. 26 B χρυσεοκόμᾱ Ἕκατε (though this may be a relic of the *F*).

XXIV. Aristeid. 2. 513: 'it is time for you to mock those as loquacious dead, who do not know how to keep quiet,' from which introduction Schneidewin's explanation can scarcely be derived (*verba sunt pugilis, qui inflatus caede eorum, quos prostratos morti dederat, alloquitur eum, quocum iam est congressurus*). Farnell well compares οὐ τίθημ' ἐγὼ | ζῆν τοῦτον, ἀλλ' ἔμψυχον ἡγοῦμαι νεκρόν Soph. *Antig.* 1166 and refers the words to a man, who though living, was no better than dead. Cf. *Phil.* 1018 ἐν ζῶσιν νεκρόν, Aristoph. *Ranae* 420 ἐν τοῖς ἄνω νεκροῖσι, Seneca *epist.* 60 *hos itaque . . . ventri* *obedientes animalium loco numeremus, non hominum: quosdam vero ne animalium quidem, sed mortuorum,* 122. 10 *isti vero mihi defunctorum loco sunt,* Matth. 8. 22, Dante *Inf.* 3. 64 *questi sciaurati, che mai non fur vivi,* 'these wretches, who ne'er lived.' **κεῖσαι**: cf. Sa. xxiv.—Metre: dact.-epitrite. Also taken as logaoedics.

XXV. Theophil. *ad Autolyc.* 2. 8 (1-2 Stob. *Ecl. Phys.* 1. 28).—**1.** Cf. Theogn. 171 *θεοῖς εὔχου, τοῖς ἐστιν ἔπι κράτος· οὔ τοι ἄτερ θεῶν | γίνεται ἀνθρώποις οὔτ' ἀγάθ' οὔτε κακά,* Pind. *Ol.* 9. 28 *ἀγαθοὶ δὲ καὶ σοφοὶ κατὰ δαίμον' ἄνδρες ἐγένοντ',* Eur. *Herakl.* 608 *οὔ τινά φημι θεῶν ἄτερ ὄλβιον, οὐ βαρύποτμον | ἄνδρα γενέσθαι.*—**2.** For the differentiation, cf. Aisch. *Eum.* 521 *τίς δὲ . . . ἢ πόλις βροτός θ' ὁμοίως ἔτ' ἂν σέβοι δίκαν;* (*i.e. εἴτε πόλις εἴτε ἰδιώτης*). In Frag. 67 Sim. says *πόλις ἄνδρα διδάσκει.* —Metre: logaoedic.

XXVI. *Ibid.* 2. 37. Possibly not by Sim., cf. Diels *R. M.* 30. 180. Cf. Archil. 74 *χρημάτων ἄελπτον οὐδέν ἐστιν κ.τ.λ.*—Metre: logaoedic.

XXVII. Stob. *Flor.* 118. 6. Cf. Kallinos 1. 14 *πολλάκι δηϊοτῆτα φυγὼν καὶ δοῦπον ἀκόντων | ἔργεται, ἐν δ' οἴκῳ μοῖρα κίχεν θανάτου,* Hor. 3. 2. 14 *mors et fugacem persequitur virum, | nec parcit imbellis iuventae | poplitibus timidoque tergo,* the first line being a translation of the verse of Sim.; Curt. Ruf. 4. 14 *effugit mortem, quisquis contempserit; timidissimum quemque consequitur.* If the final ⏑ ⏑ ⏑ ⏓ is a catal. epitrite we may compare Pind. *Ol.* 7. 17, *Pyth.* 1. 17 ⏑́ ⏑ ⏑ –́ –; if it is to be taken as a troch. dip. catal. we have a logaoedic pentapody.

XXVIII. Aristeid. 2. 192 (and schol.), Stob. *Flor.* 33. 5. Quoted by Augustus (Plut. *Apophth. Imper.* 207 C) and often cited in later literature; translated by Horace 3. 2. 25 *est et fideli tuta silentio | merces,* in the same ode in which Frag. xxvii. reappears. Hence xxvii. and xxviii. are from the same poem. **ἔστι**: at the beginning, here as often = *ὄντως ἔστι.* For the sentiment cf. Pind. Frag. 180 *ἔσθ' ὅτε πιστοτάτα σιγᾶς ὁδός, Nem.* 5. 18 *καὶ τὸ σιγᾶν πολλάκις ἐστὶ σοφώτατον ἀνθρώπῳ νοῆσαι* (cf. *Ol.* 9. 103, Frag. 81), Mel. Adesp. 86 A *μηδὲ πᾶν ὅ ττι κ' ἐπ' ἀκαιρίμαν | γλῶσσαν ἔπος ἔλθῃ κελαδεῖν,* Aisch. Frag. 188 (cf. 208) *πολλοῖς γάρ ἐστι κέρδος ἡ σιγὴ βροτῶν,* Amphis 44 *οὐκ ἔστι κρεῖττον τοῦ σιωπᾶν οὐδὲ ἕν,* Eur. Frag. 219, 977. Simonides said to a silent man at a drinking party: *ὦνθρωπε, εἰ μὲν ἠλίθιος εἶ, σοφὸν πρᾶγμα ποιεῖς, εἰ δὲ σοφός, ἠλίθιον* Plut. *Quaest. Symp.* 644 F.—Metre: dact.-epitrite or catal. troch. hexap.

XXIX. Schol. Soph. *Aias* 375. Cf. Pind. *Ol.* 2. 15 τῶν δὲ πεπραγμένων | . . . ἀποίητον οὐδ' ἂν | χρόνος ὁ πάντων πατὴρ δύναιτο θέμεν ἔργων τέλος, Agathon 5 μόνου γὰρ αὐτοῦ καὶ θεὸς στερίσκεται, | ἀγένητα ποιεῖν ἅσσ' ἂν ᾖ πεπραγμένα quoted by Arist. *Eth.* 6. 2 (τὸ δὲ γεγονὸς οὐκ ἐνδέχεται μὴ γενέσθαι), Theogn. 583, Soph. *Trach.* 742, *Aias* 378, Hor. 3. 29. 45 *non tamen irritum | quodcumque retro est, efficiet neque | diffinget infectumque reddet | quod fugiens semel hora vexit*, Pliny *H. N.* 2. 7 *deus nullum habet in praeterita ius praeterquam oblivionis.* —Metre: logaoedic.

XXX. Sextus Empir. *adv. Math.* II. 556 (in paraphrase). Cf. skolion vi., which is attributed to Sim., and Ariphron's paian to Hygieia; *mens sana in corpore sano.*—Metre: Rossbach thinks we have part of a dact.-epitritic poem; apart from xxii. most of the examples of this measure are found in the fragments of one or two lines. Logaoedics are also possible.

XXXI. Athen. 12. 512 C. Cf. Mimn. 1. 1 τίς δὲ βίος, τί δὲ τερπνὸν ἄτερ χρυσῆς Ἀφροδίτης; and Pind. Frag. 126 μηδ' ἀμαύρου τέρψιν ἐν βίῳ· πολύ τοι | φέρτιστον ἀνδρὶ τερπνὸς αἰών, a line addressed to Hieron. Schneidewin thought this fragment had a similar destination.—Metre: logaoedic rather than dact.-epitrite.

XXXII. Athen. 13. 604 B: quoted by Sophokles to shame the schoolmaster who objected to the poet's approval of the expression 'purple' in the line of Phrynichos: λάμπει δ' ἐπὶ πορφυρέαις παρῇσι φῶς ἔρωτος (cf. Gray's "purple light of Love").—Metre: v. 2 is an iambic dimeter. If v. 1 consisted only of ‒ ⏑ ⏑ ‒ ⏑ ⏑ ‒ ⏒ we should have a proödic group (cf. Archil. 85). As this is uncertain, we may take the fragment as logaoedic.

XXXIII. *Et. Mag.* 813. 8. **χλωραύχενες**: 'with pale-green neck' (L. and S.); M. Arnold has "Hark to the nightingale, the tawny-throated." Since χλωραύχην is applied to a girl in Bacch. ii. 172 the idea of colour is not inevitable here, and Marindin *C. R.* 12. 37 is probably correct in translating either 'supple-necked' or better 'liquid-voiced' (Sim. elsewhere accentuates the vocal quality: κωτίλη χελιδών Frag. 243 as Anakr. 154; cf. Sa. xv.). If χλωρηῒς ἀηδών τ 518 refers to colour, the scholiast's explanation (ἐν χλωροῖς φαινομένη) may be near the truth, the reddish brown losing something of its distinctness when the bird is seen in "her shady wood"; cf. Verg. *Georg.* 4. 510 *populea maerens philomela sub umbra*, and see Warde Fowler *C. R.* 4. 49, Verrall on Eur. *Med.* 906.—Metre: logaoedic.

XXXIV. Schol. Aristoph. *Aves* 1410. Perhaps, like Frag. xxxiii., from a dithyramb sung at the coming of the swallow (cf. Folk-Songs xxii.); so *εὔοδμον ἔαρ* Pind. iv. 17. **κλυτά**: perhaps 'clear-voiced,' 'loud.' Fennell takes *κλυτός* to mean 'loud' in *κλ. ἀγγελίαν* Pind. *Ol.* 14. 21, *κλυταῖς ἐπέων ῥοαῖσιν* *Isth.* 7. 19 (cf. *φαεννᾶς ὀπὸς* *Pyth.* 4. 28 of loud calumny). If so, *κλυτός* (=Old-Eng. *hlûd*) is used as in the folk-song to the spring *lhude sing cuccu.* Anakr. 67 has *ἡδυμελές, χαρίεσσα χελιδοῖ.*—Metre: logaoedic.

XXXV. Schol. Pind. *Ol.* 9. 48=74 (*αἴνει δὲ παλαιὸν μὲν οἶνον, ἄνθεα δ' ὕμνων | νεωτέρων*). The schol. says that the lines of Sim. are an attack on a judge (thought by Bergk to be Agathokles, Pindar's teacher), who had awarded the palm of excellence to Pindar. Bergk suggested that, in conferring the prize on the younger poet, the judge made the invidious remark that old wine was often inferior to new; a comparison which prompted the reply of Sim. 'the saying is foolish.' Taking *μῦθος* here as 'myth,' Boeckh thought Sim. was criticizing Pindar's transformation of the old mythology; to which criticism Pindar replied that between age in wine and in poetry there is an essential difference. In Frag. 193 Sim. attacks those who *πολεμεῖν τῷ πολλῷ χρόνῳ.* On the preference for new songs, see on Alkm. i., Timoth. vii.—Metre: logaoedic.

XXXVI. Schol. Eur. *Or.* 236 (*κρεῖσσον δὲ τὸ δοκεῖν, κἂν ἀληθείας ἀπῇ*, cf. 782), Plato *Rep.* 2. 365 c. Cf. Aisch. *Agam.* 788 *πολλοὶ δὲ βροτῶν τὸ δοκεῖν εἶναι | προτίουσι δίκην παραβάντες*, *Sept.* 592 *οὐ γὰρ δοκεῖν ἄριστος, ἀλλ' εἶναι θέλει* (Aristeides), Xen. *Memorab.* 1. 7. 1 *ἀεὶ γὰρ ἔλεγεν* (Sokr.) *ὡς οὐκ εἴη καλλίων ὁδὸς ἐπ' εὐδοξίαν ἢ δι' ἧς ἄν τις ἀγαθὸς τοῦτο γένοιτο, ὃ καὶ δοκεῖν βούλοιτο*, Plato *Apol.* 36 d *ὁ μὲν* (the Olympian victor) *γὰρ ὑμᾶς ποιεῖ εὐδαίμονας δοκεῖν εἶναι, ἐγὼ δὲ εἶναι*, *Gorg.* 527 b, Eur. *H. F.* 184, "So that they Seem, but covet not to Be," Gascoigne *The Steel Glass*; so in German *Das was man scheint hat jedermann zum Richter, | Das was man ist, hat keinen.* The articular infinitive may be scornful. See on Alkm. xii.—Metre: part of a dact.-epitritic line.

TIMOKREON.

Timokreon of Ialysos in Rhodes is chiefly known as the antagonist of Themistokles and his friend Simonides.

Like Archilochos he was a good hater. With Simonides he seems to have waged a war of epigrams. In Frag. 10

> Κηΐα με προσῆλθε φλυαρία οὐκ ἐθέλοντα.
> οὐκ ἐθέλοντά με προσῆλθε Κηΐα φλυαρία

he answers the Keian poet's attack (Frag. 170) on his redundant and dislocated style:

> Μοῦσά μοι Ἀλκμήνης καλλισφύρου υἱὸν ἄειδε·
> υἱὸν Ἀλκμήνης ἄειδε Μοῦσά μοι καλλισφύρου.

The inversion recalls the line that damned Thomson's play: "O Sophonisba, Sophonisba O." A sportive sepulchral epigram was written during the life-time of Timokreon, if it correctly bears the name of Simonides (169)

> Πολλὰ φαγὼν καὶ πολλὰ πιὼν καὶ πολλὰ κάκ' εἰπὼν
> ἀνθρώπους κεῖμαι Τιμοκρέων Ῥόδιος.

Timokreon is reported to have distinguished himself as an athlete and as a glutton at the court of the king of Persia, where he took refuge after his expulsion from Rhodes. His originality as a poet lies in his adoption of the triadic grouping in monodic skolia to express satire and polemic. Before Timokreon the triad had been restricted to hymns, epinikia and other species of choral composition that were eulogistic in character. With him it is made to subserve the purpose of the iambics of Archilochos. Like Stesichoros, Ibykos, and Simonides, Timokreon gave a lyric setting to the fable, which was a favourite subject of the skolion. Though he used the dactylo-epitritic measure of choral lyric, he seems to have composed skolia rather than choral songs. He also used the catalectic dimeter ionic a minore in stichic form. His dialect is mainly Doric from which specific Rhodian forms are absent.

I. Plut. *vita Themist.* 21. The grouping in short strophes and the use of ἀλλὰ τύγε point to a skolion. Each of the other singers had in turn praised his favourite. There is no reason for supposing with Sintenis that the reference to Pausanias, Xanthippos, and Leutychidas represents a covert attack because the career of each was not free from reproach. Pausanias is the victor at Plataia, not the would-be despot; Xanthippos is not the enemy of Miltiades, but the distinguished citizen who was honoured by a statue on the Akropolis; and

Leutychidas is the victor at Mykale, not the venal general who died in disgrace. Kirchhoff *Hermes* 11. 38 ff. connects the circumstances mentioned in ll. 5 ff. with the events recorded by Hdt. 8. 108-112, 121-123 (480 B.C.) and concludes that, in one of the revolutions that followed the disaster of the Persians, Timokreon was expelled from Rhodes because he had been an adherent of their policy. Kirchhoff argues that Themistokles was then at Andros with the Greek fleet and that his refusal of the poet's request for restoration to his native city prompted this attack. There is nothing to show that the fleet of Eurybiades and Themistokles was in Rhodian waters, and I prefer to place the poem between 476 and 471, probably the year when Themistokles was ostracized.

2. Λευτυχίδαν: with *ευ* as in Hdt. The native Doric form would be *Λᾱ-*. We often find *ευ* for *εο*, *εω* in Ionic monuments. Pausanias calls him *Λεωτυχίδης*. **ἐγὼ δέ**: with *δέ* of the apodosis. **ἐπαινέω**: cf. Sim. 11. 14. The mention of Aristeides only serves to lead up to the attack upon his rival.—**3.** This order (adj., prep., noun) is especially common in Pindar, *e.g. Ol.* 2. 71 (cf. Gildersleeve on 5. 22), Sim. ii. 4. —**4. ἕνα**: with the superlative as in *fortissimus unus*. Cf. Soph. *Phil.* 1344 *Ἑλλήνων ἕνα | κριθέντ' ἄριστον*, *Aias* 1340 *ἕν' ἄνδρ' ἰδεῖν ἄριστον Ἀργείων*. On the less strict use, see Jebb on *O. T.* 1380, *Trach.* 460. **Θεμιστοκλῆα** is a suspicious form. -*κλῆ* (3rd century Doric) produces hiatus, which some defend. **Λατώ**: why Lato should detest Them. is not clear. Some think that the mother, like her son Apollo, was *ἀψευδής*. (In Lykia she protects the sanctity of groves.) Others regard her as *κουροτρόφος* and think that Them. was a rascal from his earliest youth.—**5.** The vigour of the assault suits the beginning of the antistrophe. **προδόταν**: the personal enemy, not the Medizing commander who was involved in Pausanias' treachery. —**6. κυβαλικός** = *κόβαλος· πανοῦργος, κακοῦργος*. Hesych. has also *κυβηλιστάς· καὶ κοβάλους [καὶ] κακούργους*; *κυβηλικὸν τρόπον*; and *κυμβαλικὸς τρόπος* (with parasitic nasal; cf. *K. Z.* 33. 366 ff.). L. and S. accept Hermann's *σκυβαλικτός* 'dirty,' though the *κ* form is doubtful. Ahrens read *σκυβαλισκίοισι* a contemptuous diminutive. Grote (5. 135) thought that, while Timokreon's attack may be exaggerated through personal hate, the charges of venality against Them. are too well supported by other evidence to be discredited. Recent German scholars hold that these charges are due in large measure to the gossip set afloat by Themistokles' enemies (*e.g.* the story in Hdt. 8. 4-5). *Calumniare fortiter, aliquid adhaerebit.* The tale that Them. was worth 100 talents when he was condemned to death rests on the authority of the oligarch Kritias, whose sources of information would not have been friendly to the democratic statesman. No doubt the poems of Tim. helped to spread the belief in the corruptibility of Them. Cf. Bauer *Themistokles* 13, 23, Busolt *Griech. Gesch.* 2. 386. We need not believe that the three talents of l. 8 were the price paid in l. 6.—**7.** **Ἰάλυσον** is scanned — — — ⏓; cf. *Anth. Pal.* 7. 716, 1 Ἰαλύσοιο — ⏑ ⏑ — ⏓. Homer has ⏑ — — ⏓ B 656, Pindar ⏑ — ⏑ ⏓ *Ol.* 7. 74. In v. 3 we have a dactyl in the second place, here a spondee—a substitution that is the more excusable because it occurs in a proper name.—**8.** **ἀργυρίου** = *ἀργύρου* as in Boiotian (Cauer 298. 51) and Lakonian (11 B, 12). Themistokles' booty amounted to the sum he possessed before he began his political career.—**10.** After the unsuccessful attack on Andros, the fleet proceeded to the Isthmos to distribute the prize of excellence to the most worthy of the commanders. The narration in 10-12 may refer to this event, when Them. failed to get the first place. **γελοίως**: Bergk read *γλοιῶς* 'stingily'; cf. *γλοιός· ῥυπαρός*. But cf. *γλοιῶς· νυσταστικῶς* Hesych. **ἐπανδόκευε** may contain a sting; cf. Plato *Laws* 918 D, Theophr. *Char.* 6. For the form, cf. the variation between *ἡνιοχεύω* and *-εω* and see on Alkm. x. 8.—**11.** No greater offence to the poet of an "unbounded stomach." Cf. Athen. 10. 416 A. Bergk conj. *ψυδρά* 'counterfeit,' Ahrens *ψηχρά* 'shabby,' 'mean.' Some think the meaning is that Them. took the lion's share.—**12.** **οἱ**: *scil.* 'at the Isthmos' (Ἰσθμοῖ). **ὥραν** *curam* Ahrens and Kirchhoff. Cf. Hdt. 9. 8 *ὤρην ἐποιήσαντο οὐδεμίαν*, Tyrt. 10. 11 *ἀνδρὸς ἀλωμένου οὐδεμί' ὤρη | γίγνεται*. *μὴ ὥραν* with synizesis; not *Ϝώραν*; *Ϝοράω* lost its *Ϝ* very early. *ὥραν* (MSS.) has been variously translated: 'that his harvest-time might never come'; 'that he might not live to next year'; 'that his day might be no more' (against this is the position of *μή* and the meaning of *γενέσθαι*; cf. Headlam *C. R.* 6. 438). Were *μὴ ὥραν γεν.* a form of the colloquial *μὴ ὥρασιν ἵκοιτο* (cf. Aristoph. *Lysistr.* 1037) = *pereat* it might be defended; but the singular is unsupported. Cobet read *μὴ ὥρας* or *μὴ 's ὥρας*. Bergk suggested *χώραν* = *curam* · see his note on Theogn. 152.

The poem falls, according to Ahrens' arrangement (cf. *R. M.* 2. 457) which is here adopted, into three groups which, because of their slight extent, are well suited to a convivial song. Boeckh thought we have only part of the strophe, the antistr. beginning with 5; Hermann made 1-4 the epode, 5-12 the strophe. Rossbach thinks the poem is a fragment and that it is monostrophic.—Metre: dact.-epitrite. The use of this rhythm, generally solemn and stately, as a vehicle of satire and invective is surprising. Perhaps the poet designed a contrast between form and contents. Aristophanes uses the same measure for caricature and parody. The dialect avoids certain Doricisms (*αἱ*, *τύγα* l. 1, *τοί* l. 12). *ξεῖνον*, the form adopted by the choral poets, is properly Ionic. For Τιμοκρέοντα, -εῦντα has been proposed unnecessarily, though in fact Rhodian shows this contraction, which is probably due to the influence of Ionic. Τιμοκρηῦν (nom.) appears in Telos, Cauer 169 c, 3. Synizesis is very frequent.

II. Plut. *l.l.*: after the flight and sentence of Them. (468 ?) he was reviled even more immoderately by Timokreon.—Metre : dact.-epitrite.

III. Plut. *l.l.* (cf. Apostol. 7. 28): when the question was under discussion whether Tim. should be banished for Medizing, Them. voted against him, and when Them. was accused of the same crime, Tim. wrote this poem. This statement cannot well be correct since the charge of Medizing brought against Them. was later than his ostracism, while the like charge against Tim. was much earlier. There is nothing to show that Them. voted to exile his former friend as a Persian sympathizer. Kirchhoff thinks iii. is later than ii., referring the latter poem to Timokreon's exultation over the ostracism (471 B.C.) of his enemy.—**2. ὁρκιατόμει** with *ἄρα*, see p. 280. The Ionic form is *ὁρκιοτομέω*.—**4.** An allusion to the fox of the fable that lost his tail. The skolia, *e.g.* xiv., often referred to fables.—Metre : dact.-epitrite. In l. 5 Bergk suggested *κᾰλλαι* (glyconic) or *ἀλώπηκες* (5=1). The verse may be incomplete: dact. trip. + the first syllable of an epitrite. Ahrens divided after *ὁρκιατομεῖ* (*sic*) and *κόλουρις*, making the first two lines iambic. He read *μόνος* in l. 1.

IV. Schol. Aristoph. *Acharn.* 532 (cf. 530 ff. *ἐντεῦθεν ὀργῇ* Περικλέης *οὑλύμπιος | ἤστραπτ', ἐβρόντα, ξυνεκύκα τὴν* Ἑλλάδα, *| ἐτίθει νόμους ὥσπερ σκόλια γεγραμμένους, | ὡς χρὴ* Μεγαρέας *μήτε γῇ μήτ' ἐν ἀγορᾷ | μήτ' ἐν θαλάττῃ μήτ' ἐν ἠπείῳρ μένειν*). Cf. Thuk. 1. 139. The poem is a skolion. Isodor. Pelus. *Ep.* 2. 146 says it was an ancient custom after the banquet to sing to the lyre *ἀπόλοιο*, *ὦ* Πλοῦτε, *καὶ μήτε ἐν γῇ φανείης, μήτ' ἐν θαλάσσῃ*. Aristoph. *Vespae* 1063 is also a parody of Timokreon.—**1. ὤφελεν**: impersonal as Pind. *Nem.* 2. 6 *ὀφείλει . . . νικᾶν* Τιμονόου *παῖδα*, Lucian *Dea Syr.* 25 *οἷα μήτε . . . ἐμὲ ἰδέσθαι ὤφελε*. **τυφλέ**: Plutos is first called 'blind' in Hipponax 20; cf. Theokr. 10. 19. To avoid the (inoffensive) tautology of *γῇ* and *ἠπείρῳ*, Farnell conj. *μήτ' 'πὶ γῆς* 'above the earth,' Schneidewin *οὐρανῷ*, which was defended by Haupt *Opusc.* 3. 352, Teuffel *Jahrb.* 1859, p. 760. Cf. Aristoph. *Vespae* 22 (the riddle at the banquet) *τί ταὐτὸν* ἐν γῇ τ' ἀπέβαλεν κἀν οὐρανῷ | κἀν τῇ θαλάττῃ; Hes. *Theogon.* 972 of Plutos: ὅς εἶσ' ἐπὶ γῆν τε καὶ εὐρέα νῶτα θαλάσσης. On the power of wealth cf. trag. adesp. 129 σοὶ δὲ (εἵπετο) καὶ χθὼν πᾶσα καὶ πόντος.—Metre: Rossbach, Christ, and Zambaldi regard the metre as trochaics with frequent irrational longs. Each verse falls into three dimeters. Some would divide into six (Engelbrecht into four) verses. Cf. Aristoph. *Pax* 651 ff. Trochaics are found in the writers of choral poetry only when the tone is subjective. Others find epitrites 1l. hexam., 2. hexam. catal.). Note the absence of Doric forms. Perhaps the fragment has been Atticized like Praxilla's skolia. The Rhodian form would have been φανήμειν.

KORINNA.

KORINNA, the most famous Greek poetess after Sappho and by some included in the Alexandrian canon of the Lyric Poets, was a native of Tanagra in Boiotia. She seems also to have resided in Thebes. Myrtis is said to have been her teacher as well as Pindar's, but it is also reported that the great Theban was her disciple. When the youthful Pindar, criticized for his neglect of the mythological element, packed his next hymn full of myths, Korinna gave him the famous advice: 'Sow with the hand, not with the sack' (τῇ χειρὶ δεῖ σπείρειν, ἀλλὰ μὴ ὅλῳ τῷ θυλάκῳ). Tradition reports that she was victorious over Pindar no less than five times, and that in the gymnasium at Tanagra there was a statue which represented the poetess binding on her brow the emblem of victory. Pausanias (9. 22. 3) adds that her success was due to her beauty and to her use of the native Boiotian speech. It is difficult to reconcile the story of her contest with Pindar and her advice to Myrtis (v.), unless we suppose she failed to follow her own counsel, or offered her advice after she herself had entered the lists. It should be remembered that, though poetical contests may have occurred in Boiotia (Reisch *de musicis certamin.* 56), they were especially an Attic, a democratic institution at the beginning of the fifth century. Still, the Theban eagle may have tried his wings at home, though his later genius would have scorned such a confession of fellowship with local bards. If Pindar after his defeat called Korinna a

'Boiotian sow' (the ἀρχαῖον ὄνειδος), we must remember the Boiotian Ὕαντες, the Greek attitude, which is not that of the Semites, and the fact that 'cow' is sometimes used of a woman; not to speak of 'ox-eyed.' Cf. on Alkm. iv. 47.

Korinna wrote epigrams and nomes. Reference is made to five books. The subject-matter of her poetry was local legends such as would appear in the *Boiotos*, the *Kataplus*, or story of Orion, whose daughters died to save their country from pestilence and were transformed into comets, the *Seven against Thebes*, the *Iolaos*, and the *Minyades*. Her melic poems were sung by choruses of girls. In her choice of metres she shows, apart from the hexameter, the influence of the Lesbians in her fondness for short logaoedic cola (tripodies, tetrapodies). When her poems were studied by the grammarians, they were accessible only in a modernized edition a hundred and fifty years later than her time. This edition contained such spellings as ου for ῠ, ῡ; υ for οι; η for αι. To restore the contemporary dialect with certainty is impossible, but it is probable that in Tanagra about the year 500 B.C. the above mentioned uses of ου, υ and η were unknown. Possibly Korinna used ει for Panhellenic η, ῑ for ει, ῐ for ε before vowels, and αε, οε for αι, οι. At least this ει for η came in with the introduction of the Ionic alphabet, and the other spellings are attested in the epichoric alphabet. Paus. *l.l.* says of her dialect: ᾖδεν οὐ τῇ φωνῇ τῇ Δωρίδι, ὥσπερ ὁ Πίνδαρος, ἀλλὰ ὁποῖα συνήσειν ἔμελλον Αἰολεῖς, the Boiotians being regarded as Aiolians.

I. Apollon. *de pron.* 98 B. From the Κατάπλους, which probably derived its name from Orion's journey to the East to regain his sight.—**1. νίκασ'**: the omission of the augment is an epic reminiscence.—**2. 'Ωαρίων**: = 'Ωρίων. Nauck restored the open form in Homer, and Pindar has 'Ωαρίωνα *Nem.* 2. 12. **χώραν**: the land mentioned cannot well be Ὑρία (καλλιχόρω χθονὸς Οὐρίας, *i.e.* Ὑρίας, Frag. 8, so called from Ὑριεύς, the father of Orion), unless Kor. accepted the fanciful etymology derived from the miraculous birth of the hero. Cf. Ovid *Fasti* 5. 535 *hunc Hyrieus, quia sic genitus, vocat Uriona: | perdidit antiquum littera prima sonum.* The older form 'Ωαρίων would seem to render impossible any connection with Ὑριεύς or οὐρεῖν. The city of Ὑρία belonged to the territory of Tanagra, and Tanagra was the home of Orion, who purged the land of wild beasts—a foretype of Tennyson's Arthur. Cf. Müller *Orchomenus* p. 100. **ἑῶς** direct reflexive : = οὗ, with -ς of the gen. Cf. Dor., Boiot. τεοῦς = Hom. τεοῖο. The dat. is ἑΐν Kor. 36, *Ϝοῖ*, *Ϝῦ* Boiot. inscr.—**3. ὠνύμανεν** : aor. ὠνούμηνεν (MSS.) would be the form of the imperfect in the fourth century.—Metre: logaoedic. In v. 1 ὀ is lengthened under the ictus before μ; or μ is doubled as in ἐνιμμέγαροισι in Hom. Cf. on Alk. iv. 1. In v. 2 Ω is shortened before α; cf. Ŏrion in Vergil.

II. Hephaist. 11. **διᾰνεκῶς** refuses to lengthen the initial vowel in the compound. Hom. has διηνεκής, whence Empedokles derived ἠνεκέως, κεντρηνεκής etc. Cf. ἀνερίθευτος ἀνηρίθευτος, ἀνόλεθρος ἀνώλεθρος, εὐᾰνεμος εὐήνεμος, ἀνᾰριθμος ἀνήριθμος. Attic διᾱνεκῶς (Philox. 2. 24) shows that we must derive the word from διά + -ανεκής (from αν(εν)εκης accord. to Prellwitz). **εὕδεις** : εὕδῑς is possible. Hartung thought the poetess was addressed by a goddess. Hermann filled out the hexam. by ὑπναλέα.

III. Apollon. *de pron.* 65 A. **ἱώνη** : most editors read ἱώνει or ἱώνει (= ἐγώνη). ἡρωϊάς = ἡρωΐνη, ἡρωΐς. For the thought cf. *Hymn* 1. 160 μνησάμεναι (the κοῦραι Δηλιάδες) ἀνδρῶν τε παλαιῶν ἠδὲ γυναικῶν | ὕμνον ἀείδουσιν, Hes. *Theogon.* 100.—Metre : logaoedic.

IV. Hephaist. 58. **γεροί'** : γεροιά (or γέροια?) from γεροιός (cf. Boiot. πατροῖος <-ῷος) is an unexplained by-form of γεραιός. Perhaps we should read γεραί' here. Γεροιά ('Tales of a Grandfather') was the title given to a collection of Korinna's poems (Hercher *Hermes* 12. 315). **λιγυροκ.** cf. on Sim. xxxiii.—Metre : logaoedic with a tribrach as basis. In v. 2 note the 'Attic' correption in the *thesis* and cf. FOLK-SONGS xxvii. 24. Less striking is correption in the arsis *e.g.* Sim. xx.

V. Apollon. *de pron.* 65 A.—**2. ἱώνγα** is used by the Boiotian in Aristoph. *Acharn.* 898.—**3. βανά** = γυνή. Cf. Aisch. *Sept.* 1038 γυνή περ οὖσα, Soph. *Antig.* 61 γυναῖχ' ὅτι ἔφυμεν.—**4. Πινδάροι** (Wilam.) : the short dative form (= -ωι), as in the allied Thessalian dialect, is required by the syntax (τινὶ πρὸς ἔριν βαίνειν). Πινδάροιο, if correct, would be the only epic gen. in -οιο in Boiotian and the only non-Boiotian form in Korinna. **ποτ' ἔριν** : Theokr. 15. 10. Hartung, and L. Schmidt (*Pindar's Leben* 19) thought that the ἔρις was emulation of Pindar's style, not an ἀγών. Reisch *o. c.* 56 suspects the tradition of the contests of Myrtis and Korinna with

Pindar, which is accepted by Welcker *Kl. Schr.* 2. 154.—Metre: logaoedic. Most editors write in two lines regarding the first as a log. hexapody, the second as cretic (cf. Bacch. 52 = 23).

VI. Schol. B 498. Note the parallel form to Θέσπεια. Thespia was a daughter of Asopos (cf. Bacch. iv. 39).—Metre: dact.-hexameter.

LAMPROKLES.

Lamprokles, an Athenian dithyrambic poet of the older style, was a scholar of Agathokles (the teacher of Pindar in musical technique) and the master of Damon, who in turn was the instructor of Perikles and Sokrates. Damon may have derived from his master the doctrine that simplicity is essential to the best music. It is possible that Lamprokles is identical with Lampros, Sophokles' instructor in music. Lamprokles' anthem to Athena began in the same way as the poem on that goddess by the tragic poet Phrynichos; and some ancient authorities mention Stesichoros as the composer of a song with a like exordium. Bergk thought the similarity was due to the fact that these poets adopted the words of an ancient poem. That Athena should be the subject of a dithyramb is singular; perhaps the poem is simply a hymn.

Aristoph. *Nubes* 967 and schol.; schol. Aristeid. 3. 537. This famous song, like the 'Loud Strain' by Kydides or Kekeides, was taught Athenian lads by their schoolmasters in the good old times, and was sung in a high pitch. With its heaping of epithets after the style of old hymns the fragment shows a panorama of the divine attributes. The use of the hexameter also recalls the ancient hymns.—**1.** Also cited without δεινὰν . . . ἐγρ. Some read περσέπτολιν κλήζω πολ. ἁγν. **ἐγρεκύδοιμον** here and Hes. *Theogon.* 925 (with δεινήν) recalls ἐγρεμάχη of Pallas *Hymn* 5. 424.—**2. ποτικλήζω** = προσκαλῶ *advoco.* Cf. ἐπικαλῶ Aristoph. *Lysistr.* 1280, θεὸν παρακαλεῖν δεῦρο *Ran.* 395, and Sa. i. 5. κλείζω = κλείω 'celebrate' has been confused with κλήζω 'name' (Soph. *O. T.* 733). **πολεμαδόκον**: as Alk. ii.; for the formation, cf. ἑκαταβόλος Terp. ii., Πυλαμάχος Stes. 48.—Metre: dact.-epitrite (?).

PRATINAS.

PRATINAS of Phlius was the first writer of satyr dramas, which he introduced into Athens. He is known to have written thirty-two such plays and eighteen tragedies, and to have won only a single victory. He was a rival of Aischylos and competed with that poet on his first appearance in 499, when the wooden seats used by the spectators in the theatre are said to have broken down. He died before 467. We have no proof that he was a lyric poet, for the first fragment may, like the rest, be taken from an hyporchematic song in one of his satyr plays. Pratinas' fragments are interesting because he is the first poet to protest against the encroachment of the musical accompaniment upon the words, an encroachment that marks the decline of the lyric in the fifth century. His invective is probably directed against the musical and metrical innovations of the dithyrambic poet Lasos, who had attached greater importance to the rôle of the musician than to that of the poet.

I. Athen. 14. 617 B: 'when some hired flute-players and choreutae were occupying the orchestra, Pratinas says that some people were angered because the flute-players did not play in tune with the choruses, as was the ancient fashion, but the choral singers kept time with the flute-players. His own opinion Pratinas sets forth in the following hyporcheme.' This poem, as well as the *Dysmainai* or *Karyatides*, is generally regarded as a separate lyric. Against this may be urged the fact that the references in ll. 3, 16, 17 are to a band of satyrs, the attendants of the god in whose honour the satyr play was composed, and not to a chorus that is connected with the cult of Apollo, the divinity proper to the hyporcheme. Cf. K. O. Müller *Kl. Schr.* 1. 519, Blass *Jahrb.* 1888, p. 663. On the other hand it may be urged that in the hyporchemes of Simonides (viii.-x.) and of Pindar (Frag. 112, 116) we find a similar tendency to touch upon the theory of music; and in *de mus.* 31 Plutarch expressly refers to Pratinas as a lyric poet. The poem probably dates between 479 and 467. Aristotle (*Pol.* 1341 A 30) says that, after the conclusion of the Persian wars, the flute was much in vogue; and other evidence (cf. *Arch. Zeit.*

1881, p. 303) shows that it had a place in the Panathenaic festivals at an earlier date.

1. θόρυβος ὅδε may refer to the turbulence of the previous performance, possibly a dithyramb. In Pratinas' time it is not certain that the satyr play regularly followed upon a trilogy. If it refers to the din raised by the *present* chorus, the poet is pointing his satire by an imitation of the art he castigates. ἔμολεν is indecisive, as the aorist may be the shorthand of the perfect. Note the heaping of dental sounds, and cf. Soph. *Aias* 528, *O. T.* 371. Soph. *Phil.* 202 has τί τόδε in excited discourse with resolved long syllables as here. Cf. Eur. *I. A.* 317 τίς ποτ' ἐν πύλαισι θόρυβος καὶ λόγων ἀκοσμία; ὅδε is often contemptuous like οὗτος. Note the variation between τίς (attracted to the gender of θορ.) and τί. —**2. θυμέλαν**: here the space about the altar, the orchestra (Haigh *Attic Theatre* 138 is in error). Aisch. *Suppl.* 668 uses the word in the unextended signification.—**3.** Bromios belongs to me, the poet. The αὐλητής is not the chief worshipper of the god.—**4. σύμενον**: the better attested θύμενον is defended by Curtius *Verbum* 1. 191 as an aorist like σύτο, σύμενος, κλύμενος. Hesych. has ἐκθύμενος· ταχύς. Though θύω θυίω are *voces propriae* of the θυιάδες, the ῠ in θύμενον cannot be explained. There is no trace of a θεύω parallel to σεύω. **Ναϊάδων**: like the Nymphs (Anakr. ii.) and Mainads (Alkm. xi.), the Naiads are often represented as attendants of Dionysos. Cf. Roscher 2. 2245 ff. **ἀν' ὄρεα** recalls Alkm. xi. 1.—**5. οἷά τε**: so Γ 73, Alkm. xi. 4. **κύκνον**: the swans that sing in Greek poetry (*Hymn* 21, Eur. *I. T.* 1103, Aristoph. *Aves* 769) are 'whistling' not 'common' swans. Nor is their song the mark of approaching death. **ἄγοντα**: cf. ἄγω· μέλπω, ᾄδω Hesych., ἀναγνέω in Lasos; κύκνοι κινήσωσι μέλος Apoll. Rhod. 4. 1301. **ποικιλόπτερον** goes with μέλος not with κύκνον; cf. πτεροποίκιλος Aristoph. *Aves* 248. Songs have wings: πτερόεντα ὕμνον Pind. *Isthm.* 5. 63.—**6.** Song is the lord, the flute is the servant. Cf. ἀναξιφόρμιγγες Pind. *Ol.* 2. 1 and the note on Bacch. iii. 10. **βασίλειαν**: cf. *le chant du roi.* Plut. *de mus.* 30 says τὸ γὰρ παλαιὸν συμβεβήκει τοὺς αὐλητὰς παρὰ τῶν ποιητῶν λαμβάνειν τοὺς μισθοὺς πρωταγωνιστούσης δηλονότι τῆς ποιήσεως, τῶν δ' αὐλητῶν ὑπηρετούντων (cf. l. 7) τοῖς διδασκάλοις.—**7.** With this verse the measure passes over to the *Euripideum*, a dance rhythm, as is indicated by χορευέτω; cf. Aristoph. *Thesmoph.* 968.—**8.** Cf. Bacch. xiii. 5 and see on Anakr. x. Galen *Hipp. et Plat. dogm.* 9. 5 says Δάμων ὁ μουσικὸς αὐλητρίδι παραγενόμενος αὐλούσῃ τὸ Φρύγιον νεανίαις τισὶν οἰνωμένοις καὶ μανικὰ ἄττα διαπραττομένοις ἐκέλευσε αὐλῆσαι τὸ Δώριον,

Cicero *de consiliis suis* vol. 11 p. 75 (B.-K.) *ut cum vinolenti adolescentes, tibiarum etiam cantu, ut fit, instincti, mulieris pudicae fores frangerent, admonuisse tibicinam, ut spondeum caneret, Pythagoras dicitur.* Wilam. reads κώμοις and θέλοι. —**10–11** are obscure. I follow Emperius' emendation. **παῖε**: cf. Aristoph. *Vespae* 456 παῖε (*i.e.* παίων ἀπέλαυνε) τοὺς σφῆκας ἀπὸ τῆς οἰκίας, Paus. 1. 24. 1 Ἀθηνᾶ πεποίηται τὸν Σιληνὸν Μαρσύαν παίουσα. **φρυνίου**: *comparatur tibiae sonitus cum voce rubetae, quibus sane aliqua similitudo intercedit. Intellegendum vero illud rubetae genus, cujus dorsum taenia diversi coloris variatum est, quam nunc Calamitam dicunt. Hoc enim genus et vocem mittit tibiis simillimam et in Graecia reperitur etiam nunc* (Emperius). Bergk read τὸν Φρύγα τὸν ἀοιδοῦ ποικίλου προαχέοντα 'drive off the Phrygian, whose notes sound above those of the skilled singer of the chorus.' He thought 'the Phrygian' represents his native musical mode, which may have become popular with the writers of the dithyramb. Jacobs read παῦε τὸν Φρύγα τὸν ποικίλου θροῦν προχέοντα. Schweighäuser suggested there might be a reference to the musician Phrynis.—**12. ὀλεσισιαλοκάλαμον**: 'constructed of spittle-wasting reed.' The MS. ὀλοσιαλοκ. 'the reed which is all spittle' may be correct. With this vituperation, cf. the epigram cited on Melanippides.—**13. θ'|ὑπαί**: Wilam. θῶπα. **15. ἰδού**: contemptuous or indignant; cf. Aristoph. *Thesmoph.* 206. Note the hiatus with the interjection. 'Look you, here we see their right hands and feet flung about.' By δεξιά is indicated the rapid chasing of the fingers on the stops of the detested flute, while the feet of the dancers are flung out in wild excitement as they keep time to the notes. Michelangeli maintains that with v. 15 the chorus proceeds to set forth the mimetic gestures and the dance that are appropriate to Dionysos. But σοι may well be ironical. Bamberger's δεξιᾶς gives an easier constr. than δεξιά.—**16. θριαμβοδιθ.**: for the formation cf. βακχέβακχος, ἰόβακχος.—**17.** Asyndeton in prayers Sim. xiii. 15; prayer at the end Pind. *Ol.* 1. 116, 6. 105. **ἄκουε ... χορείαν**: properly metonymy as in κτύπον δέδορκα Aisch. *Sept.* 103, προὔφάνη κτύπος Soph. *Phil.* 202, σάλπιγξ φαινέτω Aisch. *Eum.* 568, χεὶρ ὁρᾷ τὸ δράσιμον *Sept.* 554, *canent quod visere par est* Catull. 62. 9; ἰδού of sound Soph. *Aias* 870, *O. K.* 1477, *El.* 1410. See on Bacch. xiii. note at end. **Δώριον**: with two endings as Σκαμάνδριος Soph. *Aias* 418, Παρνάσιος Eur. *I. T.* 1244, Δήλιος *Troad.* 89. In melic poetry common, uncomp. adj. in -ιος lack adjectival motion very rarely (in Pind. five times, and in Arist. on Ἀρετά l. 13). In the elegiac fragments this phenomenon is found four times. Pratinas is the only purely Dorian poet of the time, and even he took up his residence at Athens, the new centre of culture; and here his son remained. The musicians of the time were often Argives. Those who read *Φρύγα* in 10 refer *Δώριον* to the serenity of the Dorian mode. **χορείαν**: Pr. was famous as a 'dancer' (Athen. 1. 22 A). Not only did dancing form a great feature of his dramas but he also gave 'private lessons' in the art. *χορεία* has acquired the meaning 'choric song accompanying the dance'; cf. Aristoph. *Ran.* 247 (with *ἐφθεγξάμεσθα*).

Metre: the movement is extraordinarily agitated and expresses with great vividness the lively character of the hyporcheme. Mar. Vict. 2. 11 says that proceleusmatics (cf. 1-4) were used in satyric plays (whereas they are alien to sober compositions in anapaests); hence it is not certain that the adoption of the freer metrical forms is entirely due to the poet's opposition to the metrical licences of the time. Rossbach finds three eurhythmic periods ending with ll. 5, 9, 17, while Christ discovers six divisions that result from the metrical variations. The metre is hyporchematic dactylo-trochaic with frequent resolutions and syncope. Irrational longs are avoided. The syncopated trochaic dipodies (= cretics) are appropriate to the hyporchemes. I have adopted dipodic measurement as far as possible. Rossbach makes 1-2 trochaic, and so 13 may be scanned. v. 5 is perhaps a dact. trip. (though elsewhere absent) + 2 troch. dip.; or dact. dip. + 3 troch. dip. Christ's division makes –́ ⏑ ⏑ –́ ⏑ ⏑ ⌞́ ⏗́ ∧ and –́ ⏑ –́ ⏑ –́ ⏑ –́ ∧.

II. Athen. 14. 624 F. The earliest reference to the 'harmonies' or musical modes. 'Follow neither a highly-strung music nor the relaxed (low-pitched) Ionian, but, drawing a middle furrow through your ground, be an Aiolian in your melody. . . . 'Tis the Aiolian mode that befits all your swash-bucklers in song.'—**1.** The *σύντονοι ἁρμονίαι* are set off against the *ἀνειμέναι καὶ μαλακαί* in Arist. *Pol.* 1290 A 27, 1342 B 21, as the Μοῦσαι *συντονώτεραι* are contrasted with the *μαλακώτεραι* in Plato *Sophist.* 242 E. Westphal (*Harmonik* 186) explains *σύντονος* as a form of the Ionian mode (in *b*), and Flach equates it with the Mixo-Lydian. Bergk and Hartung regarded it as identical with the Syntono- (High) Lydian. Monro (*Greek Music* p. 6) takes *σύντονος* generally, and thinks that the poet follows the Greek principle of adopting the mean between extremes. Pratinas demands a return to the Aiolian (Hypodorian) mode (in *a*) of Terpander, Alkaios, and Sappho, which had been driven out by the *σύντονος* and the relaxed Ionian (in *g*).—**3.** **ἀοιδολαβρ.**: so

Bergk for ἀοιδὰ λαβρ. Others read ἀοιδάν, ἀοιδᾶν, ἀοιδοῖς. Cf. λαβρογόρης Υ 479. The Aiolians were a self-asserting, swaggering race of fighters. Herakl. Pont. in Athenaios says of their musical mode that it was 'elevated and fearless, pompous, inflated, and full of pride.'—Metre: v. 3 points to a dactylo-trochaic strophe. Most editors make five troch. dip. of l. 1, and a hypercatalectic troch. verse of l. 2. Bergk thought ἀεί had dropped out before νεῶν. Kaibel arranges in short verses with word-breaking.

PHRYNICHOS.

PHRYNICHOS, the Athenian tragic poet, an older contemporary of Aischylos, was the author of the *Capture of Miletos* (496), *Phoinissai* (476), and *Alkestis*, and seems to have written hymns, paians, and dithyrambs. His tragedies were more like oratorios with dancing than dramas.

I. Schol. Aristoph. *Nubes* 967, schol. Aristeid. 3. 537. See on Lamprokles.—Metre: dact.-epitrite.

II. Athen. 13. 564 F, 604 A: from the *Troïlos*, which was either a dithyramb or a tragedy (so Nauck Frag. 13). Quoted by the poet Sophokles, who reproved the carping schoolmaster for his matter-of-fact theory of poetry (see on Sim. xxxii.); cf. πορφυρῆ Ἀφροδίτη Anakr. ii. 3 and *purpureus Amor*. Val. Flacc. has *orbes purpurei*, Ovid *purpureae genae* after Apoll. Rhod. 3. 121 Ἔρως . . . οἱ ἀμφὶ παρειὰς | χροιῇ θάλλεν ἔρευθος.—Metre: dact. trip. with anacr. + ithyphallic. Cf. Archil. 79 Ἐρασμονίδη Χαρίλαε, χρῆμά τοι γελοῖον, where the caesura divides the two cola.

DIAGORAS.

DIAGORAS of Melos, 'the Atheist,' flourished in the second quarter of the fifth century and was a younger contemporary of Pindar and Bacchylides. He is said to have composed songs, enkomia and paians. The tradition that he wrote dithyrambs is doubtful unless the word is taken in the later and wider sense (see the Introduction).

His poetry was perhaps the product of his earlier years and is reported to have been free from the impiety which made him notorious (Aristoph. *Aves* 1072). Literary gossip said that this was occasioned by the failure of the gods to punish a poet who had robbed him of a paian; soberer tradition ascribed it to his study of the Atomistic philosophy. His Ἀποπυργίζοντες λόγοι (in prose) contained an indirect attack upon the traditional faith, and his Φρύγιοι λόγοι, if a separate work, profaned the Mysteries (cf. Andok. 1. 29). These works would stamp him as guilty not only of ἀσέβεια but also of ἀθεότης. Blomfield thought that Diagoras is referred to in Aisch. *Agam.* 369 οὐκ ἔφα τις | θεοὺς βροτῶν ἀξιοῦσθαι μέλειν | ὅσοις ἀθίκτων χάρις | πατοῖθ'. ὁ δ' οὐκ εὐσεβής. Diagoras was condemned to death at Athens on a charge of impiety, certainly before the beginning of the Peloponnesian War, and fled to Pellene in Achaia. He may have also lived at Mantineia and Korinth. In Aristoph. *Nubes* 830 Sokrates is covertly identified with Diagoras (Σ. ὁ Μήλιος). As regards his atheism, Phaidros *On Nature* 23 says that the Stoics were more sceptical than he. The extant fragments are quoted by the ancients to show the pious character of his poetry (εὔφημος, ὡς ποιητής, εἰς τὸ δαιμόνιον).

I. Philodem. περὶ εὐσεβείας p. 85 (vv. 1-2), Didym. Alex. *de Trinit.* 3. 2.—**1**. The formula θεὸς θεός was often used at the beginning of sacred and profane functions (Eust. *Il.* 258. 26). Cf. Pind. xi. θεός is repeated in Pind. *Pyth.* 2. 49, *Isthm.* 5. 52, Bacch. i. 21.—**2**. Cf. ν 255 αἰὲν ἐνὶ στήθεσσι νόον πολυκερδέα νωμῶν.—**3**. Cf. Sim. xxv.; Theogn. 169 ὃν δὲ θεοὶ τιμῶσιν, ὁ καὶ μωμεύμενος αἰνεῖ· | ἀνδρὸς δὲ σπουδὴ γίνεται οὐδεμία. **ἕρπει**: φωνᾶεν ἕρπει Pind. *Isthm.* 4. 40, ἐξόδους ἕρπειν Soph. *Aias* 287.—Metre: dact.-epitrite.

II. Philodem. *l. l.* Nikodoros had invited the assistance of Diagoras (doubtless before he turned atheist) in forming a code of laws for Mantineia, and the poet is said to have written an *Enkomion on the Mantineians.* Line 1 may be imitated in Aristoph. *Aves* 544: κατὰ δαίμονα καὶ κατὰ συντυχίαν, cf. Eur. *El.* 1358. δαίμων is joined with τύχη in Lysias and Aischines. Diagoras may have been influenced by Demokritos *che il mondo a caso pone* (Dante *Inf.* 4. 136). This fragment may have stood at the beginning of Diagoras' poems. —Metre: logaoedic.

KYDIAS.

KYDIAS of Hermione, a choral poet, wrote love songs that were highly esteemed by Plato. He lived in the first half of the fifth century. He is possibly the same as Kydides, a dithyrambic poet, the author of the Τηλέπορον βόαμα (Aristoph. *Nubes* 967).

Plato *Charm.* 155 D, in paraphrase. The fawn trembles before the lion as the boy before his lover. Cf. Hor. 3. 20. Proverbs are νεβρὸς τὸν λέοντα and μὴ πρὸς λέοντα δορκὰς ἅψωμαι μάχης. **μοῖραν αἱρεῖσθαι**: *tanquam portionem carnium capi ideoque lacerari* (Stallb.), but μοῖραν may be 'fate.'—Metre: dact.-epitrite.

PRAXILLA.

PRAXILLA, the chief poetess of the Dorians, and a writer of dithyrambs, was a native of Sikyon, a city that had long been the home of this class of melic composition. Hdt. 5. 67 reports that about 590 B.C. Kleisthenes, tyrant of Sikyon, checked an attempt to install Adrastos, the local hero, in the place of Dionysos, to whom the 'tragic choruses' were sacred. Praxilla's dithyrambs seem to have dealt with subjects foreign to the cult of Dionysos, but in view of the fact that the themes of the dithyrambic choruses has already been secularized by Simonides, it may be doubted whether the Sikyonian poetess revived the ancient antagonism of her townsmen. The dithyrambic poets of the fifth and fourth centuries chose stories unconnected with the worship of Dionysos, *e.g.* Melanippides' *Marsyas*, *Persephone*, *Danaids*, Timotheos' and Philoxenos' *Polyphemos*, Telestes' *Argo*, *Asklepios*, *Hymenaios*. Because of Praxilla's local reputation a Sikyonian collection of skolia, which was modelled on the 'Attic' banquet songs, was ascribed to her. We hear only of skolia 'attributed' to Praxilla (see the introduction to the Skolia). Lysippos set up a bronze statue to commemorate her fame.

I. Hephaist. 11. From a dithyramb entitled *Achilles.* The oldest form of the dithyramb was in dactylic hexameters, which were revived in the fifth century. Other verse-forms may however have been used in connection with the hexameter. The verse recalls ψ 337 ἀλλὰ τοῦ οὔ ποτε θυμὸν ἐνὶ στήθεσσιν ἔπειθεν (cf. η 258, ι 33). Neue thought that Achilles is here addressed by a member of the πρεσβεία in *Il.* I; cf. l. 315. **τεόν** makes a short monosyllable as θεός Pind. *Pyth.* 1. 56 (cf. βρότεον 10. 28). Cases of a semi-vocalic ε before a short syllable are very rare.

II. Zenob. 4. 21. From the dithyramb called *Adonis.* Adonis is questioned by the inhabitants of the lower world as to the sweetest thing he had left behind in life. The passage occasioned the proverb 'more foolish than the Adonis of Praxilla.' But the poetess probably intended to depict only the *naiveté* of the boy. Cf. Menand. 481 τοῦτον εὐτυχέστατον λέγω, | ὅστις θεωρήσας ἀλύπως, Παρμένων, | τὰ σεμνὰ ταῦτ' ἀπῆλθεν, ὅθεν ἦλθεν, ταχύ, | τὸν ἥλιον τὸν κοινόν, ἄστρ', ὕδωρ, νέφη, | πῦρ· ταῦτα, κἂν ἑκατὸν ἔτη βιῷς, ἀεὶ | ὄψει παρόντα, κἂν ἐνιαυτοὺς σφόδρ' ὀλίγους, | σεμνότερα τούτων ἕτερα δ' οὐκ ὄψει ποτέ, Eur. Frag. 316. From a different point of view we are informed in Aristoph. *Ranae* 155 that the blessed in Hades enjoy a sunlight that is like that of the upper world (ὄψει τε φῶς κάλλιστον ὥσπερ ἐνθαδί). Farnell quotes the "Essays of Elia" ('New Year's Eve'): "Sun and sky, and breeze and solitary walks, and summer holidays, and the greenness of fields, and the delicious juices of meats and fishes—do these things go out with life?"—**1.** Cf. λ 93 τίπτ' αὖτ', ὦ δύστηνε, λιπὼν φάος ἠελίοιο | ἤλυθες (Teiresias to Odysseus in Hades). Sappho 79 has τὸ λάμπρον ἔρως ἀελίω καὶ τὸ κάλον λέλογχε.—**2.** σεληναίη = σελήνη, cf. παρθενική = παρθένος Alkm. vii.; so γαληναία = γαλήνη, 'Αθηναία = 'Αθήνη.—Metre: dact.-hexam. κατὰ στίχον.

III. Hephaist. 25.—**1.** Cf. Theokr. 3. 18 τὸ καλὸν ποθορεῦσα. —**2.** παρθένος is a virgin, νύμφη a newly wedded wife in Theokr. 2. 136; cf. νεογάμου νύμφης Aisch. *Agam.* 1179. Sometimes νύμφη is used for γυνή (Diodor. 3. 136). There is no specific Greek word for a 'betrothed' girl. A married woman retained the title νύμφη until she became a matron, and sometimes even after she had reached matronhood.—Metre: an exquisite example of the effect of light logaoedic dactyls running over into trochees. The combination of three dactyls and a trochaic dipody was called Πραξίλλειον and the citation of this fragment under that name is our sole warrant for ascribing it to Praxilla. It is Aiolic in rhythmic effect, containing one more dactyl than the concluding verse of the Alkaic stanza. The ancients called the verse a brachycatalectic trimeter (— ⌣ ⌣ — ⌣ ⌣ | — ⌣ ⌣ — ⌣ | — —), but it is probably a pentapody. Anakr. 70, 72 are not in this metre, as has been said by some, but rather form elegiambi. Two Πραξίλλεια probably constituted a strophe.

PINDAR.

PINDAR, the greatest of the lyrists of Greece, if not of all time, was born at Kynoskephalai, a suburb of Thebes, in 522, and, as he himself informs us in Frag. 193, at the time of the celebration of the Pythian games :

πενταετηρὶς ἑορτὰ
βουπομπός, ἐν ᾇ πρῶτον εὐνάσθην ἀγαπατὸς ὑπὸ σπαργάνοις.

His poetical career lasted for at least half a century. *Ol.* 4 dates from 452 and *Pyth.* 8 may be two years later. One account states that he lived to the age of eighty ; others place his death in 452 or 436. Though he travelled much, he preferred to live at home in Thebes—βούλομαι ἐμαυτῷ ζῆν, οὐκ ἄλλῳ he says, alluding to Simonides' delight in his residence at the court of Hieron. Near his house, which was situated by the Dirke, he founded a shrine of the Mother of the gods and of Pan, whose priest he was :

Ὦ Πάν, Ἀρκαδίας μεδέων, καὶ σεμνῶν ἀδύτων φύλαξ,
Ματρὸς μεγάλας ὀπαδέ, σεμνᾶν Χαρίτων μέλημα τερπνόν
(Frag. 95).

He was of ancient and honourable lineage. The Aigeidai, who had also settled in Sparta, Thera, and Kyrene, stood as aristocrats in close relation to the cult of the gods ; and Pindar preserved the traditions of his house by his fervent piety, especially towards Apollo, of whom he is the poet *par excellence.* He obtained the right to participate in the θεοξένια as the guest of the god of Delphi (Πίνδαρος ἴτω ἐπὶ τὸ δεῖπνον τοῦ θεοῦ). Pindar's genius ripened rapidly. He inherited musical ability as his birthright, and his Boiotian home was favourable to the cultivation of the flute, in which he was trained by Skopelinos :

οὔτοι με ξένον
οὐδ' ἀδαήμονα Μοισᾶν ἐπαίδευσαν κλυταὶ Θῆβαι (Frag. 198).

But Athens was the school of the day, and at Athens he was instructed in the technique of lyric composition by Agathokles and Apollodoros, and perhaps by Lasos. What the masters at Athens left undone, a Boiotian and a woman perfected; for there is no reason to discredit the tale that the finishing touch to his education was given by Korinna, who criticized not only the disposition of his materials, but also his Atticizing dialect. The sojourn in Athens may have laid the foundation of his Panhellenic sympathies. In 502 the youthful poet was already sufficiently known to receive a commission (*Pyth.* 10) from one of the Aleudai. No doubt too the Thessalian magnates were predisposed in favour of the precocious Boiotian noble. As his fame increased he became the bard of all the great national festivals, which he visited from year to year, and won for himself the friendship of the great. He became the guest of Hieron of Syracuse, Theron of Akragas, Akusilaos of Kyrene, and Alexander of Makedon; and the renown of their victories at the games he proudly exclaimed would fade into forgetfulness were it not for his song. He was an especial favourite with the aristocratic Aiginetans, who made him their proxenos, and for whom he composed no less than one fourth of all his extant triumphal odes. Aischylos he doubtless knew, and with the Athenian dramatist he shares the preeminence of attaining to the loftiest conception of the poet as a religious, ethical, and political teacher ever reached in Greece. None of the great movements in literature and art witnessed by the momentous period spanned by his life can have failed to leave its impress upon a poet of his rare susceptibilities.

It is somewhat different with his attitude towards affairs. Unlike Archilochos and Alkaios Pindar was no friend of strife. In Frag. 154 he says, as few Greek poets could say:

> Ἐμοὶ δ' ὀλίγον μὲν γᾶς δέδοται, ὅθεν ἄδρυς·
> πενθέων δ' οὐκ ἔλαχον οὐδὲ στασίων.

In Frag. xii. he alludes to that grave moment in the history of the contending factions of his native city when the oligarchs, in dread of the upstart democracy across their borders, cast their lot to side with the Persians. But the disasters of his 'mother Thebes' at Plataia worked no estrangement in his affection. If in the earlier period the poet remained true to his state—a united Greece there scarcely was—and had no word for Marathon, where Aischylos fought, later on, when 'some god had put away the stone of Tantalos,' he gained the larger vision that the freedom of Greece was more than the glory of Thebes. The Panhellenism of Pindar was learned in part through adversity. Simonides was not forced to encounter the cruel dilemma of his rival, and his note rings true throughout. But Pindar, though he too wrote for pay, must be absolved of all hypocrisy when he expresses his gratitude for the work done for freedom by those who had stood against his countrymen at Plataia. Akenside is, however, not entirely just when he says that the poet

> Amid corrupted Thebes was proud to tell
> The deeds of Athens and the Persian shame.

Possibly too the fact that he did not take part in the conflict may, as in the case of the exiled Thukydides, have helped to foster an inborn sense of impartiality.

The fame of Pindar rests mainly upon his triumphal odes, which do not fall within the scope of this edition. That only the epinikia have been preserved practically complete, argues that in them we have Pindar's best; nor are we in a position to dispute the correctness of this conclusion, though it is difficult to follow Eustathios, who accounts for the popularity of the epinikia on the ground that they were more human, contained fewer myths, and offered less difficulties than his other lyrics. Many of the poems that have perished may, it is true, have dealt with cults that became recondite to later generations as the significance of the special forms of Greek religion gradually faded away. Pindar was, however, famous not only as the poet of the national contests which became for him the arena of moral as well as physical effort: he traversed almost the entire scale of choral song, and though the fragments appear insignificant in comparison with the architectonic splendour of the epinikia, they alone disclose the versatility of his genius. In them we find the poet yet unrebuked by his fair countrywoman (Frag. i.); we learn more of his personality, of his love of sportiveness and festivity (Frag. 124). Here too we find Greek faith in its quieter moods, the joys and sorrows of men whose lives are not irradiated by the sun of Olympia, something less of that tension of diction by which the poet seems to vie with his athlete as he strains to reach the goal; and here he discloses his profoundest conceptions of the origin and destiny of the soul.

Apart from Bacchylides, Pindar is the only melic poet of whose art we have abundant remains. Yet the epinikia formed less than one fourth of his entire works. The collection of his poems made in Alexandria, probably by Aristophanes, consisted, according to the Breslau *Life* (*Vrat. A*), of 17 books:—i. To the gods: hymns, paians, dithyrambs (2 books), prosodia (2 books); ii. To gods and men: partheneia (3 books, one of which included odd pieces, κεχωρισμένα), hyporchemes (2 books); iii. To men: enkomia, threnoi, epinikia (4 books). To these titles Suidas adds enthronismoi, bacchika, daphnephorika, skolia, δράματα τραγικά, epigrams, and 'exhortations,' the last two being certainly spurious. Boeckh thought that the additional titles were derived from the recension of Aristarchos who, he claimed, distinguished the various sub-divisions with greater nicety than Aristophanes. Bergk, on the other hand, argued that the additional titles in Suidas were drawn from an early Attic recension and that the poems in question were variously disposed in the edition of Aristophanes. It is, however, singular that the division into 17 books should have been retained. Christ concludes that there was only one recension and that the titles in Suidas are, with the exception of the skolia, nothing more than designations used in place of the older species by some scholar of the fourth or third century. The daphnephorika may *e.g.* be placed with the partheneia, and the skolia with the enkomia. Perhaps the enthronismoi ('installation odes'?) are to be regarded as prosodia, though some take them to be hymns. Sittl classes them as hymns to the Mother of the gods. The same scholar thinks the daphnephorika are processional songs for the Theban festival of Apollo. Since the famous treatise *de tragoedia comoediaque lyrica* by G. Hermann (1836) few scholars have had the temerity to revive the belief in the existence of lyric tragedies (τραγικὰ δράματα), which was first upheld by Boeckh, and defended by Welcker, and O. Müller. Lübbert, indeed, in his *Com-*

mentatio de Pindari carminibus dramaticis tragicis (Bonn 1884) sought to distinguish them from the dithyrambs sung in the spring in that they were sung in the winter and contained a recital of the deeds of the heroes and not of Dionysos. But truth seems to lie on the side of Immisch (*R. M.* 44. 553), who reinforces the arguments of Hiller (*Hermes* 21. 357) and shows that the words were inserted as a complexive title in the list of Pindar's works by some late writer who regarded 'drama' as any poem with an heroic subject. In somewhat similar fashion the *Aeneid* was called a 'tragedy' by the author of the *Divina Commedia.* The subject of these curious additions in Suidas' list is too technical for further notice here: for our present purpose it is sufficient to establish the fact that Pindar's activity as a choral poet embraced all the various forms of melic except the hymenaios. The nome he did not attempt, nor any other species of monodic song except the skolion, though that also appeared in the choral form. All his poetry was 'occasional.'

For an adequate study of the style of Pindar as it is seen in his epinikia, the student will have recourse to the editions of Fennell, Seymour, and Gildersleeve, and to Croiset's *La Poésie de Pindare.* We may mention here only the chief traits of his character and diction.

All Greek choral poetry is religious, but Pindar's is supremely so. Pindar is permeated by a solemn sense of the goodness of the divine power and of the close bond between God and man. He holds to the traditional faith purified of all that is degrading to the moral sense; he has intense moral earnestness and is never weary of enforcing his teaching by wise utterances. His mythical heroes embody ideal principles of thought and action, yet they do not lose their personal outlines in vague moralizing. Pindar is distinguished by serenity, by an independence of spirit that never condescends to the flattery of kings, and by a touch of austerity; he has a lofty consciousness of the grandeur of his themes, of his own pre-eminence, and of the immortality of his song. His political ideal is the Dorian ideal: the rule of the noble is of God, but it entails obligation and surrenders itself to the moral law.

As a craftsman Pindar is the poet of splendour and

magnificence. He loves the pomp and pride of words, the stately and sonorous compound epithets that form, as it were, the colour over the majestic marble. His resources are unbounded, yet he always holds himself in reserve. He is lofty, audacious, and even obscure, but not because he is struggling with profound ideas. He is often abrupt and disdains to mark the movement of his thought. At times he seems to hammer out his phrases, as if the Doric, Aiolic, and epic dialects, because they are fused with his native speech, proved a stubborn material; while the Ionian Simonides with facile ease and delicacy pours his thought into a graceful mould. Nor does Pindar touch the heart as his rival does. Pathos he has, but his energy is primarily directed to an ethical end. Though he can be at his ease, impetuosity is the prevailing law of his movement. He often shifts from stateliness to plainness, and effects the transitions of his theme with great ingenuity. He is studious of variation and never monotonous. His metaphors and (less frequent) similes are often bold, and he is fond of personification. He loves majestic rhythms, and prefers the grave epitrite to the lively logaoedic or the excited paeonic.

The fragments are too brief to warrant an attempt at distinguishing the diction of all the various classes; as indeed the distinction between the species of melic composition is itself elusive. The different styles of the hymn, the dithyramb and the hyporcheme (Frag. i., iv., x.) are however well marked. As a rule the diction of the fragments resembles that of the epinikia.

Of the *hymns*, that in honour of Ammon was so famous that it was inscribed by Ptolemaios Soter on a stele which was placed near the altar of the god. Pindar may have been the first to introduce into Thebes a knowledge of the Egyptian god whom the Greeks identified with Zeus. In the hymn to Tyche, whom he makes one of the Fates and superior in power to her sisters, he says, ''tis chance, not strength, that wins the day' (Frag. 38). We hear also of hymns to Apollo and Persephone. In the continuation of Frag. i. the poet ascribes the birth of Apollo and the Muses to a request of the Olympians that Zeus create other gods to sing his beneficence to mankind and the majesty of his works. In one fragment he compares the onslaught of Herakles to the lightning—a simile much admired by the ancients. *Paians* to Apollo Pythios and the Zeus of Dodona are reported; in one he makes mention of Niobe; and in another calls rumour the voice of the halcyon. In several passages Pindar shows his interest in the literary history of his art. Of the *dithyramb* the poet says that it was invented either in Naxos or at Thebes, which city was one of the chief seats of the cult of the son of Semele. The fragment that was produced at Athens (iv.) is probably the oldest genuine specimen of this form of melic. In the dithyramb, as elsewhere except in the hymn, Pindar unites the present with the past, and it is to this trait that we owe the famous lines on Athens (v.). In one fragment (79) the poet deals with the archaeology of the dithyramb; in another he mentions the cult of the Great Mother; and the myths of Orion and Geryon are referred to. There are *prosodia* to the Delian Apollo and Artemis Aphaia; one records a πομπή to Delphi; another deals with the story of Typhoeus. One *partheneion* is addressed to Apollo; in another he sings of Pan, whom, according to one authority, he is said to have called the child of Aither. Men in love, he said, pray to be the sun, women would fain be the moon. With Pindar the *hyporcheme* attained its greatest splendour. In that on the eclipse (x.) he reaches a sublimity that is Aischylean in its quality and excelled by the *Prometheus* alone. In the dramatist the final note is defiance, in Pindar it is resignation. The lyric poet loved the reconciliation of the human and the divine, not the conflict of will and fate. Frag. ix. points to the secularization of the hyporcheme, which Proklos confined to the divine sphere. The *enkomion* is a more private and less solemn song than the epinikion, though it may be devoted to the praise of the victor at the games. Thus Theron, the subject of *Ol.* 2 and 3, is the recipient of an enkomion from Pindar which may have been sung upon the conclusion of *Ol.* 2. So too Frag. xiv. probably followed a song in honour of some victory of Alexander of Makedon. The *skolion* is thought to have become choral under Pindar's hands—a result of the influence of the sympotic enkomia. Frag. xv. has the tripartite arrangement, but Frag. 122 is monostrophic, though the rhythm is Dorian. The latter fragment was accompanied by the dance of the ἱερόδουλοι in the temple of Aphrodite at Korinth in celebration of the victory of Xenophon at Olympia (*Ol.* 13). Though the argument in defence of such a theme is the same as that urged by Simonides, Pindar is more naïf and less dexterous than the eulogist of Skopas. The skolion to Thrasybulos (124) is sportive, that to Hieron (125 ff.) warns man to moderation in pleasure in order that life may not lose its freshness. In the *threnoi* Pindar does not relax his tone to tenderness. In place of consolation he unfolds the glories of the world beyond the grave; and cheers the bereaved by the Orphic doctrine that the souls of the pious, freed at last from all taint of guilt, re-appear on earth where they assume the forms of the great. It is all but certain that the poet was an Orphic.

I. vv. 1-6 Lucian *Demosth. encom.* 19, Plut. *de glor. Athen.* 4 (in part); vv. 6-12 Clem. Alex. *Strom.* 5. 731. The poem stood first in the collection of Pindar's hymns, and was sung at a Theban festival. Plutarch relates that the youthful poet was rebuked by Korinna for his failure to make use of myths, which are the embellishment of poetry (cf. Plato *Phaidon* 61 B); whereupon Pindar composed this hymn, which occasioned Korinna's remark 'One must sow with the hand, not with the whole sack' (τῇ χειρὶ δεῖ σπείρειν, ἀλλὰ μὴ ὅλῳ τῷ θυλάκῳ). Yet this very hymn, which called forth Korinna's censure, Lucian *Ikaromenip.* 27 pictures as sung by the Muses, together with the *Theogony* of Hesiod, at the banquet of the gods; and the poet in his old age (*Isthm.* 7) did not abandon the style of his youth. Cf. Hor. I. 12.—**1**. The catalogue of names that are associated with the Boiotian cult begins with those whose fame was most ancient. Ismenos was son of Asopos or of Amphion, father of Dirke and brother of Melia. ἤ occurs seven times. The figure of thought (σχῆμα διανοίας) entitled ἀπορία or διαπόρησις (*dubitatio*) is particularly suited to the beginning of a poem, where the poet can best feign embarrassment in the presence of over-abundant material. Cf. *Isthm.* 7. 1 ff. and Mel. Adesp. 84 (probably by Pind.). ἀπορία occurs as early as *Hymn* 1. 19 ff., 2. 29 ff.; cf. Bacch. x. 5 ff. So the ἤ οἵη of Hesiod. **Μελίαν**: daughter of Okeanos, nymph of the spring Melia near the Ismenion at Thebes. To Apollo she bore Ismenios and Tenaros. Cf. *Pyth.* 11. 4. Since she is a divine personage, her attribute (ἠλακάτη) as a woman must be of precious metal; see Fennell on χρυσαλακ. Ἀμφιτρίτας *Ol.* 6. 104, where the reference to Jebb on Soph. *O. T.* 846 is inapposite. Jebb is there dealing with those compound adjectives in which the second part is equivalent to a separate epithet of the subst. χρυσαλ. is not = 'golden and plying the distaff.' In classical poetry only the Olympians Aphrodite, Athena (χρυσέα θύγατερ Διός *O. T.* 187), and the personifications Hope (Soph.), the Muse, and Victory (both in Pind.) are called 'golden.'—**2. σπαρτῶν**: cf. *Isthm.* 1. 30: Iolaos ὁμόδαμος ἐὼν σπαρτῶν γένει.—**4. σθένος Ἡρ.**: 'mighty Herakles' as σθένος ἡμιόνων *Ol.* 6. 22, ἐντέων σθένος *Pyth.* 5. 34; for the periphrasis containing an adj. cf. κρατησίμαχον σθένος υἱῶν *Pyth.* 9. 86, *Crispi iucunda senectus* Juv. 4. 81.—**5. πολυγαθέα**: Hes. *Theogon.* 941 Διώνυσον πολυγηθέα, Pind. Frag. 153 Διόνυσος πολυγαθής. The poets usually use the form Διώνυσος only when it is called for by the metre. **τιμάν**: πατρὸς Ὀλυμπίοιο τιμάν *Ol.* 14. 12.—**6.** The marriage of Kadmos and Harmonia, which Dissen thought was the subject of the hymn, was a favourite theme of the poets. All the gods assembled to do honour to the pair, and Apollo, the Muses, and the Graces played and sang. Cf. *Pyth.* 3. 90, Theogn. 15, Eur. *Phoin.* 822. **ὑμνήσομεν**: either the dubitative future (Goodwin *M. T.* 68), or, more probably, subjunctive (287) with short modal vowel.—**7.** The caesura between the arsis of the second epitrite and the initial dactyl is not observed; cf. Soph. *Trach.* 821, 831, which are also *iambelegi*. **εὔβουλον Θέμιν**: *Ol.* 13. 8, *Isthm.* 8. 34, ὀρθόβουλος Aisch. *Prom.* 18. **οὐρανίαν**: also in Soph. *El.* 1064. Delphic tradition placed her in Delphi. Fennell (on *Pyth.* 9. 106) notes that Pindar sometimes uses two adjectives without a conjunction when one is a distinctive epithet.—**8. χρυσέαισιν ἵπποις** ('car'): *Ol.* 1. 41, 8. 51. Note the gender. **παγᾶν**: the springs of Okeanos (Hes. *Theogon.* 282, Eur. Frag. 773. 33, Kallim. 5. 10) are the sources of the life of things. Okeanos and Tethys had reared Hera (Ξ 301).—**9.** Pindar's treatment of the myths is elastic. Hes. *Theogon.* 904 makes the Moirai the children of Zeus and Themis; and this was the Theban version (Paus. 9. 25. 4). Pind. calls Themis the first (ἀρχαίαν) wife of Zeus, Hes. calls her the second (after Metis).—**10.** The 'shining road' is the milky way that extends from Okeanos to the zenith. Olympos is here the sky (cf. ζ 42), not the localized mountain as in the *Iliad.* On the Διὸς ὁδός *Ol.* 2. 70, which Boeckh thought was also the milky way; see Rohde *Psyche* 505. Ovid *Metam.* 1. 168 says *est via sublimis, caelo manifesta sereno . . . hac iter est superis ad magni tecta*

Tonantis. The κλῖμαξ of v. 9 (cf. πίτναντες θοὰν κλίμακ' ἐς οὐρανὸν αἰπύν Frag. 162) recalls Jacob's ladder. **κατά**: here of ascent.—**11.** **σωτῆρος**: perhaps a reference to the contest with the Titans in which Themis assisted Zeus. Themis Σώτειρα is the πάρεδρος of Zeus in *Ol.* 8. 21. Her temple at Thebes adjoined that of Zeus.—**12.** Cf. Hes. *Theogon.* 901 δεύτερον ἠγάγετο (Ζεύς) λιπαρὴν Θέμιν, ἣ τέκεν Ὥρας, | Εὐνομίην τε Δίκην τε καὶ Εἰρήνην τεθαλυῖαν, | αἵτ' ἔργ' ὠρεύουσι καταθνητοῖσι βροτοῖσι, *Ol.* 13. 6. **ἀλαθέας**: 'true,' because they follow each other in inevitable sequence.—Metre: dact.-epitrite.

II. Stob. *Flor.* 109. 1. Classed by Bergk as a hymn and referred by Boeckh to the advice given to his son by Amphiaraos on his departure for Thebes. Boeckh thought the fragment might be a skolion and added at the beginning Frag. 180: μὴ πρὸς ἅπαντας ἀναρρῆξαι τὸν ἀχρεῖον (ἀρχαῖον MSS.) λόγον· | ἔσθ' ὅτε πιστοτάτα σιγᾶς ὁδός· κέντρον δὲ μάχας | ὁ κρατιστεύων λόγος.—**1.** **φέρεται** κ.τ.λ. = τίνα μόχθον φέρομεν.—**2.** **ἐρέω** may = ἔχω εἰπεῖν, but the present is in place as in *Pyth.* 4. 142, 5. 108, where, as here, the reference is to what follows. —**3.** Cf. *Pyth.* 3. 82 τὰ (πήματα) μὲν ὦν οὐ δύνανται νήπιοι κόσμῳ φέρειν, | ἀλλ' ἀγαθοί, τὰ καλὰ τρέψαντες ἔξω. **μὲν ὦν**: *profecto*; each word has its distinctive force; not the composite use ('nay rather'). See Jebb on Soph. *El.* 459. **μοῖραν**: placed with the second member as usual: cf. *Pyth.* 11. 64.—**5.** **προστύχῃ**: the generic subjunctive without ἄν (κέ). Pind. does not use ἐάν, ἤν, εἴ κε (Gildersleeve on *Ol.* 6. 11). The pres. subj. is rare in Pind. in general conditions, the aor. subj. or pres. indic. being preferred. **σκότει**: σκότος is both masc. and neut. in Pind. Sim. has ὁ θάμβος. The meaning is either that men may not know that the gods are unfavourable or that we may not become χάρματα ἐχθροῖς.—Metre: dact.-epitrite.

III. Stob. *Ecl. phys.* 2. 1. 8 (cf. Clem. Alex. *Strom.* 5. 726, Euseb. *Praep. Ev.* 13. 688).—**1.** **ἔλπεαι**: 'believe,' cf. ζ 297, *Nem.* 7. 20. **σοφίαν**: Frag. 209 ἀτελῆ σοφίας καρπόν, Eur. *Bacch.* 395 τὸ σοφὸν δ' οὐ σοφία. Pindar may have prompted Sophokles *O.T.* 502 σοφίᾳ δ' ἂν σοφίαν παραμείψειεν ἀνήρ (E. Bruhn *ad loc.*). **ᾇτε**: instrum. dat.; ἰσχ. θράσει Eur. *Or.* 903, ἰσχ. τοῖς σώμασι Xen. *Memorab.* 2. 7. 7.—**2.** **ὑπέρ**: cf. ὑπέραλλος 'matchless' *Nem.* 3. 33; Thuk. 3. 46. 3 ἰσχύομεν πρὸς τοὺς πολεμίους τῷδε.—**3.** **οὐ γὰρ ἔσθ' ὅπως** = οὐδαμῶς γάρ. Cf. Hdt. 7. 102, Aristoph. *Pax* 102. Cf. ψ 81 χαλεπόν σε θεῶν... | δήνεα εἴρυσθαι, μάλα περ πολύϊδριν ἐοῦσαν, (a passage which shows the close connection between ἐρέϜ-ω and ἐρευ-νάω), Solon 17 ἀθανάτων ἀφανὴς νόος ἀνθρώποισιν, *Pyth.* 3. 59 χρὴ τὰ ἐοικότα παρ δαιμόνων μαστευέμεν θναταῖς φρασίν, |

γνόντα τὸ παρ ποδός, οἵας εἰμὲν αἴσας, Eur. *Alk.* 799 ὄντας δὲ θνητοὺς θνητὰ καὶ φρονεῖν χρεών, Soph. Frag. 531 θνητὰ φρονεῖν χρὴ θνητὴν φύσιν, | τοῦτο κατειδότας ὡς οὐκ ἔστιν | πλὴν Διὸς οὐδεὶς τῶν μελλόντων | ταμίας ὅτι χρὴ τετελέσθαι, *Trach.* 472, Eur. Frag. 795, "But they know not the thoughts of the Lord" Micah 4. 12. In Frag. 140 Pind. has τί θεός; ὅ τι τὸ πᾶν. In iii. he foreshadows the doctrine of Sokrates in his contest with the naturalistic school (Xen. *Memorab.* 1. 1. 12-15) and the antagonism between the poets and the philosophers.—Contrast Arist. *Eth.* 10. 7. 8 οὐ χρὴ δὲ κατὰ τοὺς παραινοῦντας ἀνθρώπινα φρονεῖν ἄνθρωπον ὄντα οὐδὲ θνητὰ τὸν θνητόν, ἀλλ' ἐφ' ὅσον ἐνδέχεται ἀθανατίζειν.—Metre: logaoedic.

IV. Dion. Hal. *de comp. verb.* 22: cited as an example of the austere style. Dion. says of the poem that it is nervous, robust, and full of dignity; that the ear perceives, though without pain, a certain roughness; and that there is no theatrical ornament or polished beauty. He finds proofs of the asperity of the style in the collocation of final ν with τ, φ, χ, λ. The poem was probably composed for the Great or City Dionysia at Athens, which were celebrated at the beginning of spring, in Elaphebolion, perhaps on the 10th and 11th of the month. At this festival, besides the dramatic performances, there took place dithyrambic contests beween ten cyclic choruses of fifty members each. See Haigh *Attic Theatre* 14. This dithyramb was sung in the agora and not in the sanctuary of Dionysos Eleuthereus to the S.E. of the Akropolis.

1. ἴδετ' ἐν: 'look with favour upon.' The preposition is added only here and xv. 9. Cf. *Ol.* 14. 15 (Θαλία) ἰδοῖσα τόνδε κῶμον. So ἐφοράω of the gods, as Aisch. *Suppl.* 531, and ἐπιβλέπω. **ἐν** *cum accus.* (8 times in Pind. chiefly in the Aiolic odes) is a relic of the original stage of the language when this preposition had the functions of Lat. *in*. It is preserved in Boiotian, Thessalian, North-West Greek, Eleian, Arkadian, Kyprian, and perhaps even in Attic ἔμβραχυ (Wackernagel). The accus. use was abandoned on the rise of ἐν-ς (cf. *ab-s*), which, before a vowel, became εἰς, before a consonant, ἐς. **χορόν**: cf. Aristoph. *Nubes* 564 Ζῆνα ἐς χορόν . . . κικλήσκω.

2. ἐπί: tmesis with πέμπετε. The ἔπι of most editors is an over-refinement; see Chandler *Greek Accentuation* 923. **κλυτάν**: of the grace that gives victory to song. The analogy of κλεινός (κλ. χαρίτεσσιν 'gracious victories' *Isthm.* 2. 19, κλ. ἀοιδαῖς *Pyth.* 3. 114) points to the meaning 'renowned' rather than 'loud' (if χάριν = 'song'). See on Sim. xxxiv. κλυτός, of poetry, is used as an epithet of *ἐπέων ῥοαί, ὕμνων πτυχαί, ἀοιδά.* The charm of the poet's song is from the gods: Frag. xx., cf. *Ol.* 14. 8 *οὐδὲ . . . θεοὶ Χαρίτων ἄτερ κοιρανέοντι χορούς.* —4. **ὀμφαλόν**: the altar of the Twelve Gods, erected in the market-place by Hippias' son Peisistratos (Thuk. 6. 54. 7), served as the centre for calculating distances to the Attic demes (*C.I.A.* 1. 522, 2. 1078, Hdt. 2. 7). So Augustus' *miliarium aureum* was placed in the forum. **πολύβατον**, because the processions in honour of Dionysos surrounded the altar (O. Müller *Index lect. Götting.* 1840 p. 3, Xen. *Hipp.* 3. 2). Cf. the oracle in Demosth. *Meid.* 531 *αὐδῶ Ἐρεχθεΐδῃσιν . . . μεμνῆσθαι Βάκχοιο, καὶ εὐρυχόρους κατ' ἀγυιὰς | ἱστάναι ὡραίων Βρομίῳ χάριν ἄμμιγα πάντας, | καὶ κνισᾶν βωμοῖσι κάρη στεφάνοις πυκάσαντας.* Boeckh, followed by Christ, thought that the *ὀμφαλός* was the Rotunda (Θόλος). Wachsmuth agrees with Wordsworth *Athens* 102 that the Akropolis is meant.

5. **ἱεραῖς**: all cities are 'sacred' because they are devoted to some one of the gods. *ἱεραί* of Athens λ 323, Soph. *Aias* 1221, Timokr. i. 3, Bacch. x. 1, Aristoph. *Eq.* 1319.

6. **οἰχνεῖτε**: with accus. of the limit of motion, which is very common in Homer, frequent in P., and not rare in tragedy. **πανδαίδαλον**: a variation on the Hom. *πολυδαιδ.* Pind. is fond of adj. with *παν—*. The agora was adorned with the statues of Harmodios and Aristogeiton, of the Heroes who gave their names to the Attic demes (the Eponymoi), etc. After the departure of the Persians it was ornamented with many splendid buildings; and Kinon increased his popularity by embellishing it with trees (Plut. *Kim.* 13). Cf. Wachsmuth *Stadt Athen* 1. 170, 532, Harrison *Myth. and Mon.* 77. **εὐκλέ'**: as Soph. *O. T.* 161 (*ἀγορᾶς θρόνον εὐκλέα*); for *-εέα* by hyphaeresis; cf. *ὑπερδέᾰ* P 330. *ἀκλέᾰ ἐκ* δ 728 is from *ἀκλέᾱ*. In *Nem.* 6. 29 *εὐκλεῖα* is generally read; in *Pyth.* 12. 24 *εὐκλεᾶ*. To have one's statue set up in the agora was regarded as the greatest of honours (Demosth. *Lept.* 485, Lucian *Anach.* 17). Pindar's statue was placed not far from those of the Tyrannicides. **ἀγοράν**: Christ holds that the poem was written before 472 because it was sung in the market-place and not in the Dionysiac theatre, which was not constructed until after this date. There were however in the fifth century two orchestras: one, S.E. of the Akropolis, in the precinct of Dionysos Eleuthereus, and constructed probably in the sixth century; the other, of ancient date, in the agora, not far from the sanctuary of the older Dionysos (Lenaios), S. of the Areiopagos. See Dörpfeld-Reisch *Gr. Theater* 10, 366. The latter, which is here referred to, retained its name after public performances had ceased to be

given there. At the Spartan festival of the Gymnopaidia the ephebi danced in the market-place (Paus. 3. 11. 9).

7–8. λάχετε asyndeton in prayer; cf. Sim. xiii. 15. The passage is difficult. Boeckh read *ἰοδετᾶν λ. στ. τᾶν τ' ἑαριδρέπτων λοιβᾶν*, Christ[1] *ἰοδετᾶν λ. στ. τὰν ἑαριδρέπταν λοιβάν*, Christ[2] *ἰοδετῶν λ. στ. τᾶν ἑαριδρόπων τε λοιβᾶν*, Bergk *ἰοδέτων λ.* (indicative) *στ. τῶν ἑαριδρόπων· ἀμοιβάν*, *i.e.* 'in requital thereof,' accus. in apposition to the preceding sentence. Were it not for *ἀοιδᾶν* (Sauppe) in 10, I should prefer Usener's *ἑαριδρόπων ἀοιδᾶν* (*ἀοιδάν EF*). Perhaps *τ* of the MSS. (*τε ἀριδρ.*) stands for *F*, examples of which substitution may be found in Christ *Beiträge zum Dial. Pind.* 37. If this is correct, we must read *ἐπάγησι* in l. 17. Dissen took *λοιβᾶν* to refer to honey. Evidence for *λοιβή* used of flowers is lacking.

9. Διόθεν = *οὐρανόθεν* (Bergk); who am come from Zeus of Nemea, where the poet had been sojourning (Boeckh); *Iovis auspiciis* (Christ). None of these explanations is satisfactory.

11. δεῦτε (Sauppe): the poet addresses the members of the chorus. Cf. Frag. 122. 15. *δεύτερον* (MSS.) is generally referred to a previous appearance of the poet at Athens (perhaps Frag. v.). Boeckh: *post Iovem patrem secundo loco ad Bacchium filium.* **κισσοδέταν**: Dionysos has the epithets *κισσοκόμης Hymn* 26. 1, *κισσοχαίτης* Prat. 1. 17, *κισσοφόρος Ol.* 2. 27; Sim. 148. 2 *ἀνωλόλυξαν κισσοφόροις ἐπὶ διθυράμβοις* (of the choreutai). Cf. Eur. *Phoin.* 651, Ovid *Fasti* 3. 767 *hedera est gratissima Baccho.* Paus. 1. 31. 6 reports the name *Κισσός*.

12. Βρόμιον: cf. *Ol.* 2. 25 *ἀποθανοῖσα βρόμῳ* | . . . *Σεμέλα.* **'Εριβόαν**: so Dionysos is called *ἐρίβρομος Hymn* 26. 1, Anakr. 11; Aisch. Frag. 355 *μειξοβόαν πρέπει* | *διθύραμβον ὁμαρτεῖν* | *σύγκωμον Διονύσῳ.* Pind. avoids the name *Βάκχος*.

13. πατέρων = Zeus, as *γυναικῶν* = Semele, the plural of amplification (*pluralis maiestatis*); cf. *Isthm.* 8. 38 *Διὸς ἀδελφεοῖσιν* = Poseidon, 5. 43 *τοῖσιν* = Achilles, *Ol.* 7. 10 *νικώντεσσιν* = Diagoras. The 'allusive' plural is very frequent in tragedy: Soph. *O. T.* 1176 *τοὺς τεκόντας* = *πατέρα*, 1007 *τοῖς φυτεύσασιν* = *μητρί* as 366 *τοῖς φιλτάτοις* = *μητρί* (see Wunder *ad loc.*), *γυναικῶν* = Eriphyle *El.* 838. **μελπέμεν**: the inf. of purpose after a verb of motion where the fut. part. might have been used; the pres. part. in *ἀείδων ἔμολον Ol.* 14. 18.

14. τε after *μέν* is frequent in Pind. The avoidance of the adversative *δέ* emphasizes the paternal descent, while the mother is added by way of parallel, not by way of contrast. **ἔμολον**: so *Isthm.* 5. 21; *ἦλθον Ol.* 9. 83, *ἔβαν Nem.* 4. 74, *κατέβαν Ol.* 7. 13 (all aorists). None of these verbs proves the actual presence of the poet.

15. 'The visible tokens of his rites do not escape his tice.' The return of spring indicates to the god that his festival is at hand. The text is Usener's; Heyne and Boeckh have *ἐν Ἀργείᾳ Νεμέᾳ μάντιν*, the 'priest' being the custodian of the sacred tree at Nemea, whence came the palm (*φοίνικος ἔρνος* so Boeckh in 16), a branch of which the victor carried in his hand. Unger has shown that the distinction between the winter and the summer Nemea does not hold before Hadrian. Since in Pindar's time they occurred in June, Boeckh's interpretation falls to the ground. Bergk's *ἐναργέ' ἀνέμων μαντῆϊ'* is without point.

16. **φοινικοεάνων**: *Pyth.* 4. 64 *φοινικανθέμου ἦρος*. **θαλάμου**: Cf. Aristeid. 1. 39 of Korinth: *θάλαμον Ὡρῶν, ᾧ πάντα τὸν χρόνον ἐγκάθηνται καὶ ὅθεν προέρχονται ἀνοιγνῦσαι τὰς πύλας, εἴτε Διὸς σύ γε βούλει καλεῖν εἴτε Ποσειδῶνος*, Lucr. 1. 10 *simul ac species patefacta est verna diei | et reserata viget genitabilis aura Favoni*; Aristoph. *Nubes* 311 *ἦρί τ' ἐπερχομένῳ Βρομία χάρις, | εὐκελάδων τε χορῶν ἐρεθίσματα, | καὶ Μοῦσα βαρύβρομος αὐλῶν*.

17. **ἐπάγησιν** Usener. The reading *ἐπαΐωσιν* is not well supported by Alk. xxviii. *ὁπότε* with the generic subjunctive elsewhere in Pindar takes *ἄν*.

18. **βάλλεται**: the *schema Pindaricum* or *Boeotium*, in which a sing. verb is used with a plur. subject not neuter in gender. In his discussion of this syntactical figure Haydon, *A. J. P.* 11. 186, suggests that *ἴων φόβαι ῥόδα τε* is an amplification of *ἴα, ῥόδα μίγνυται* easing the construction. The same scholar rejects *ἀχεῖ* in l. 20 for *ἀχεῖτε*, which he declares is not an unnatural shift. Hermann's *ἀχεῖται* finds a defender in Jebb (on Soph. *O. K.* 1500), The other actual or possible cases of the figure in Pindar are *Ol.* 11. 6, *Pyth.* 4. 57, 10. 71, Frag. 78, 239, 246. Gildersleeve remarks that the singular is the general, the plural the particular. See also Wilpert *de schemate Pindarico et Alcmanico*, Starkie on Aristoph. *Vespae* 1301. *βάλλεται* suggests the *φυλλοβολία*. See on Stes. vi. The dithyrambic festival was a species of carnival. **τότε**: the repetition (cf. 20, 21) suits the ethos of the dithyramb. Eur. did repetition to death.

19. **φόβαι**: this use of *φόβη, κόμη* of the leafage of trees, is so frequent that the personification is almost extinct; cf. ξ 328, ψ 195, Soph. *Antig.* 419, Eur. *Ion* 120. The use in connection with plants and flowers is however infrequent and, as a rule, late; *ἀνθρύσκου φόβη* Kratinos 98, cf. Theokr. 4. 57, 6. 16. **ῥόδα**: at the Dionysia the Athenians generally crowned their hair with the rose, which was sacred to Dionysos.

A victorious dithyrambic chorus was crowned with roses: Sim. 148. 3.

20. ὀμφαί: usually of the voice of a god or an oracle. Eur. *Med.* 174 *μύθων τ' αὐδαθέντων ὀμφάν* of the chorus. **σύν** is used of musical accompaniment when the notes of the instrument are regarded as an addition to the words of the song. Cf. *σὺν καλάμοιο βοᾷ Nem.* 5. 38; Sim. xvi. note. *ὑπό* of instrumental accompaniment in general; see on Anakr. x.; *ἐν* is in place when the melody is the framework of the poem: Sim. 148. 8 *ἐν αὐλοῖς*. **αὐλοῖς**: the mythical Arion, as a member of the kitharoedic school of Terpander, is supposed to have used the kithara in accompanying his dithyrambs. That the flute was used follows from Sim. 148. 8, Aristoph. *Nubes* 313. The movements of a large chorus could be better controlled by the flute than by the kithara. In and after Pindar's time both the kithara and the flute were used. Cf. Graf *de Graecorum veterum re musica*, chap. 2.

21. This mention of Semele does not fulfil the promise of 13; hence the poem continued with the praise of Dionysos, the story of his birth, etc.—Metre: paeonic-logaoedic as *Ol.* 10, *Pyth.* 5. Schmidt *Eurhythmie* 428 regards the metre as logaoedic throughout. The fragment belongs to the *ἀπολελυμένα μέλη*, that is, it is not divided into strophes.

V. Scholl. Aristoph. *Acharn.* 637, *Nubes* 299, Aristeid. 3. 341; [Aischin.] epist. 4. 474, etc., and referred to by numerous later writers. In Aristoph. *Eq.* 1329 Aristophanes imitates v. 1: *ὦ ταὶ λιπ. καὶ ἰοστ. καὶ ἀριζήλωτοι Ἀθῆναι.* In return for the single expression Ἑλλάδος *ἔρεισμα* the Athenians, according to Isokr. *de antid.* 166 made Pind. proxenos and gave him 10,000 drachmas. Later writers however report that Pindar's fellow-citizens, who had stood on the side of the Persians, were not disposed to brook this laudation of Athens, and mulcted the poet 1000 drachmas; whereupon the Athenians gave the poet a *douceur* of ten times this amount. [Aischin.] *l.l.* reports that the amount of the fine was repaid to the poet twice over, and that the Athenians honoured him with a bronze statue. Laudation of Athens in *Pyth.* 1. 76, 7. 1 *κάλλιστον αἱ μεγαλοπόλιες Ἀθᾶναι . . . ἐπεὶ τίνα πάτραν, τίνα Ϝοῖκον αἰνέων ὀνυμάξομαι ἐπιφανέστερον* Ἑλλάδι *πυθέσθαι*; Frag. 77 *ὅθι παῖδες Ἀθαναίων ἐβάλοντο φαεννὰν | κρηπῖδ' ἐλευθερίας.* Dissen thought this fragment was from the same poem as iv. The lines form the exordium. **λιπαραί**: of Athens, *Nem.* 4. 18, *Isthm.* 2. 20, Solon 43, Eur. *Alk.* 452, *Troad.* 801, *I. T.* 1130, Aristoph. *Nubes* 300. Cf. *Acharn.* 636

πρότερον δ' ὑμᾶς ἀπὸ τῶν πόλεων οἱ πρέσβεις ἐξαπατῶντες | πρῶτον μὲν ἰοστεφάνους ἐκάλουν· . . . εἰ δέ τις ὑμᾶς ὑποθωπεύσας λιπαρὰς καλέσειεν Ἀθήνας, | ηὕρετο πᾶν ἂν διὰ τὰς λιπαράς, ἀφύων τιμὴν περιάψας. *λιπαρός* was a favourite epithet of places with Pind. (Thebes, Orchomenos, Marathon, Naxos, Smyrna, Egypt). As applied to Athens, the reference is not to the olives of Attica, but to the external splendour of the city, its temples and monuments. Cf. Schmidt *Synonymik*. 4. 679. For the separation of the adj. from the substantive cf. *Ol.* 7. 13, 14. 22, *Nem.* 9. 48. Such adj. are often proleptic. Here the distance is bridged by *κλειναί*, which shows the normal position. **ἰοστέφανοι**: cf. iv. 19. Temples and private houses were decked with violets at the Great Dionysia. **ἀοίδιμοι**: elsewhere in Pindar applied to one other place (Delphi): *γᾶς ὀμφαλὸν παρ' ἀοίδιμον Pyth.* 8. 59.—**2**. **κλειναί**: of Athens Soph. *Aias* 861. The tragic poets call Athens *εὐδαίμονες, θεόδμητοι, τιμιωτάτη πόλις* etc.—Metre: logaoedic (dact.-epitrite: Rossbach).

VI. vv. 1-4 Philo *de corr. mundi* 23, vv. 5-10 Strabo 10. 485. The schol. on *Isthm.* 1 reports that the poem is a prosodiac paian composed for the Keians and infers that it was partially completed when the poet was engaged to write *Isthm.* 1 for his townsman Herodotos; cf. v. 3 *μή μοι κραναὰ νεμεσάσαι | Δᾶλος, ἐν ᾇ κέχυμαι* 'may rocky Delos, in whose service my soul has been poured forth, not be wroth with me.' Because of *Isthm.* 1. 7 (*Φοῖβον χορεύων ἐν Κέῳ*) Dissen has argued with much probability that the poem on Apollo and Delos, which was set aside for the Isthmian ode, referred to a Delos or to a temple of Apollo in Keos; and Boeckh maintained that if this fragment was designed for the island of Delos it is not the poem referred to in *Isthm.* 1. 3. Perhaps four verses have disappeared at the end of the strophe, and two at the beginning of the antistrophe.

1. θεοδμάτα: so *Δάλου θεοδμάτας Ol.* 6. 59. The feminine is more poetical than the masculine. *θεόδματος, ἀθάνατος* (except in Frag. 10) and *ἱπποσόος* have the fem. form in Pindar only with proper names. Of the 9 other compound adj. of three endings, 4 occur where there is no metrical compulsion.—**2. ἔρνος**: of an island, cf. *βλάστε νᾶσος Ol.* 7. 69.—**3. ἀκίνητον**: either (1) 'unmoved,' in contrast to the tradition (found first in Pindar) that it floated about previous to the visit of Leto. *τέρας* may support this view. The island of Aiolos and the Strophades, were *πλωταὶ νῆσοι.* Or (2) 'unshaken by earthquake'. Cf. Seneca *Quaest. Nat.* 6. 26 *hanc* (*Delum*) *philosophi quoque credula natio dixerunt non moveri auctore Pindaro.* (2) is out of the question if the poem was written after the famous earthquake, concerning which we have the apparently contradictory statements of Herodotos and Thukydides. Hdt. 6. 98 says that the earthquake occurred in 490 after the departure of the Persians, that it was the first that took place in the island, and that a shock did not recur during his lifetime. The oracle κινήσω καὶ Δῆλον ἀκίνητόν περ ἐοῦσαν may not have been inserted by Hdt., but it apparently refers to a former floating condition of the island. Thuk. 2. 8 reports that the earthquake occurred shortly before the Peloponnesian war and that prior to this Delos had never been shaken in the memory of the Greeks. Kirchhoff supposes, not very probably, that there were two earthquakes and Hdt. did not know of the one reported by Thuk. Marchant thinks that Thuk. was ignorant of the passage in Hdt. or ignored it. It is possible that the shock happened some time between the two wars, and in order to connect so startling a phenomenon with the subject of their histories, Hdt. antedated while Thuk. postdated it. So Stein, and Wecklein *Trad. d. Perserkriege* 16. Abbott thinks that there were different traditions current among the European and the Asiatic Greeks, each derived from 'supposed evidence' from Delos. We conclude that, even if ἀκίνητον means 'unshaken,' the tradition is too uncertain to enable us to date this fragment and *a fortiori Isthm.* 1, which has been referred to a period shortly before the battle of Tanagra (458). Müller *Dorians* 1. 332 dated the poem before 490.—**4. Δᾶλον**: the addition of τηλέφαντ. ἄστρ. (cf. *Ol.* 2. 55 ἀστὴρ ἀρίζηλος, Aratos *Phain.* 94) shows that the poet is playing on a supposed connection with δῆλος and is not emphasizing the fact that the island was the place of Apollo's epiphany (Preller). εὐδείελος (= εὔδηλος Ps. Skylax 258) in Homer is used of islands in general (ν 234) and of Ithake in particular. Cf. Μᾶλος the 'white' island, Ἀργινοῦσσαι ⟨ἀργεννός, *nitentes Cycladas, fulgentes Cycladas,* 'Albion.' Since δῆλος contains a Panhellenic η (see on Alk. iv. 7), Δᾶλος is probably a different word, the etymology of which is unknown. Cf. Δαλιόξενος, Δαλιόδωρος, but Διάδηλος 'Conspicuous' the name of a Delian. ἀρίδαλος in Sim. 130 is wrong; for δάελον· διάδηλον Hesych. read δέαλον. On the poets as etymologists see Gräfenhan *Gesch. d. Klass. Phil.* 1. 154, and on the dialect of the gods 1. 172. Examples of this dialect: Α 403, Β 814, Ξ 291, Υ 74, κ 305, Pind. Frag. 96 ὦ μάκαρ (Pan), ὅντε μεγάλας θεοῦ κύνα παντοδαπὸν καλέοισιν Ὀλύμπιοι, Plato *Phaidros* 252 B. The divine name is the older name. Delos was also called Asteria, (cf. τηλ. ἄστρον), Ortygia, Kynthos, Pelasgia, Chlamydia, Anaphe. **τηλέφαντον**:

cf. τηλεφᾰνής Frag. 129. 7. πρόφαντον 'conspicuous' *Ol.* 1. 117, but πρόφᾰτον 8. 16 (*v.l.* -φαντον). So in 9. 65 for ὑπέρφᾰτον some MSS. have -φαντον. **ἄστρον**: a reference to the old name of the island. Cf. Kallim. 4. 34 ff. καὶ τὰς (νήσους) μὲν κατὰ βυσσόν, ἵν' ἠπείροιο λάθωνται, | πρυμνόθεν ἐρρίζωσε· σὲ (Delos) δ' οὐκ ἔθλιψεν ἀνάγκη, | ἀλλ' ἄφετος πελάγεσσιν ἐπέπλεες· οὔνομα δ' ἦν σοι | Ἀστερίη τὸ παλαιόν, ἐπεὶ βαθὺν ἥλαο τάφρον | οὐρανόθεν φεύγουσα Διὸς γάμον ἀστέρι ἴση. | τόφρα μὲν οὔπω σοι χρυσέη ἐπεμίσγετο Λητώ, | τόφρα δ' ἔτ' Ἀστερίη σὺ καὶ οὐδέ πω ἔκλεο Δῆλος. Asteria is also called Leto's sister. Cf. Apollod. 1. 4. 1, *Anth. Lat.* 1. 707, Akrokorinthos is ἄστρον Ἑλλάδος *Anth. Pal.* 7. 297, Kolophon is τρυφερῆς ἄστρον Ἰηονίης epigr. adesp. 487.—**5. τὸ πάροιθε**: so σ 275, τὸ πρίν Ε 54, τὸ πάρος Κ 309. See Kühner-Gerth § 410. 5, n. 15. **φορητά**: cf. Eur. *Hek.* 29. **κυμάτεσσιν . . . ῥιπαῖσιν**: *Pyth.* 4. 195 κυμάτων ῥιπὰς ἀνέμων τε, cf. 9. 48, *Nem.* 3. 59, Soph. *Antig.* 137.—**6. Κοιογενής**: Hes. *Theogon.* 404 Φοίβη δ' αὖ Κοίου . . . ἦλθεν ἐς εὐνὴν | . . . Λητὼ . . . ἐγείνατο, *Hymn* 1. 62 Λητοῖ, κυδίστη θύγατερ μεγάλου Κοίοιο, Kallim. 4. 150 Κοιηΐς, Apoll. Rhod. 2. 710 Λητὼ Κοιογένεια. **ὁπότε** is often preferred to ὅτε in Pindar and with the indicative = the more exact ἡνίκα 'what time'; cf. Bacch. vi. 7. **θύοισ'** almost = μαινομένα; cf. Aisch. *Septem* 967 μαίνεται γόοισι φρήν, *Suppl.* 562 μαινομένα πόνοις . . . ὀδύναις τε . . . θυιάς.—**7.** 'Then in truth from foundations deep set in the earth there shot up four pillars erect, with bases of adamant, and supported the rock of Delos by their capitals'.—**9. πέτραν**: cf. κραναή of Delos, *Hymn* 1. 16, *Isthm.* 1. 3, Orph. *Argon.* 1357. Bursian *Geogr. von Griechenl.* 2. 452.—**10. ἐπόψατο**: 'lived to see'; cf. Hdt. 6. 52 ἐπιδόντα δὲ τὸν Ἀριστόδημον τὰ τέκνα νούσῳ τελευτᾶν, Eur. *Med.* 1025, κἀπιδεῖν εὐδαίμονας of her children, Herodas 5. 70. ἐφοράω is often used when the spectator rejoices in what he sees; but also when he is forced to behold what he would avoid. **γένναν**: more commonly γόνος as Eur. *H. F.* 689 Λατοῦς εὔπαιδα γόνον.—Metre: dact.-epitrite.

VII. Schol. Aristoph. *Eq.* 1263. Aristoph. applies to the Knights what is here said of Artemis: τί . . . καταπ. ἢ θοᾶν ἵππων ἐλατῆρας ἀείδειν;—**1.** Cf. *Il.* Ι 97 ἐν σοὶ μὲν λήξω, σέο δ' ἄρξομαι, *Hymn* 21. 4 πρῶτόν τε καὶ ὕστατον αἰὲν ἀείδει, Hes. *Theogon.* 48 ἀρχόμεναί θ' ὑμνεῦσι θεαὶ λήγουσί τ' ἀοιδῆς, Dion. Chalk. 6 τί κάλλιον ἀρχομένοισιν | ἢ καταπαυομένοις ἢ τὸ ποθεινότατον;—**2.** Paus. 2. 30. 3 reports that Pindar wrote a song to Artemis who was worshipped as Aphaia in Aigina. Artemis Aphaia was identified by the ancients with Britomartis-Diktynna. **ἐλάτειραν**: cf. *Ol.* 3. 26 Λατοῦς ἱπποσόα θυγάτηρ. Artemis bore the name Εὐρίππα.—Metre: dact.-epitrite.

The use of epitrites in the passage from Aristoph. recalls the ancient name *hippius pes*, which is derived from the νόμος ἵππειος, the 'strain of Kastor.'

VIII. Aristeid. 2. 510. The poet himself took part in this prosodion.—**1.** **σε**: Pind. here declines to admit the poetical hyperbaton of the pronoun in this formula of supplication (Soph. *Trach.* 436, *Phil.* 468, Eur. *Phoin.* 1665, *Hippol.* 607); cf. x. 7.—**3.** **λίσσομαι** with δέξαι as in Alk. xxxiv. **δέξαι**, like χαῖρε vi. 1, is probably a *vox solennis* in prosodia. **Χαρίτεσσι**: the Graces and Aphrodite in connection with Delphi *Pyth.* 6. 1-3; cf. Mel. Adesp. 88 'Αφροδίτης ἄλοκα τέμνων καὶ Χαρίτων ἀνάμεστος. Apollo and Aphrodite are associated in *Pyth.* 2. 16, 9. 10. **τε . . . καί** here connect complementary similars. **σύν**: placed with the second word as often in Pind. (*Pyth.* 8. 99, *Nem.* 10. 38). The sing. precedes the pl. in *Ol.* 10. 58 where the σύν is used with the first word.—**4.** **θρόνῳ** (Schneidewin, χώρῳ Boeckh, χόρῳ Bergk). Cf. Plato *Laws* 4. 719 C ποιητὴς ὁπόταν ἐν τῷ τρίποδι τῆς Μούσης καθίζηται. Paus. (10. 24. 5) saw in Delphi an iron chair in which the poet often sat when he was singing of Apollo.—**5.** **προφάταν**: cf. Frag. 150 μαντεύεο Μοῖσα, προφατεύσω δ' ἐγώ, Bacch. iv. 3 Μουσᾶν θεῖος προφάτας, Theokr. 16. 29 Μουσάων ὑποφήτας, Plato *Phaidr.* 262 D the birds are οἱ τῶν Μουσῶν προφῆται, epigr. 6 Πίνδαρος εὐφώνων Πιερίδων πρόπολος. The poet's relation to the Muses is comparable to that of Apollo to Zeus (Διὸς προφήτας). Himerios *Or.* 14. 6, p. 614 calls orators 'Ερμοῦ καὶ Μουσῶν προφήτας.—Metre: logaoedic.

IX. Athen. 1. 2. 8 A. (vv. 1-2 Eust. *Od.* 1822. 5, 2-5 *Od.* 1569. 44.) Addressed to Hieron in honour of a Pythian victory. Frag. 105 is part of the same poem, which was written after 476. In like manner Kritias Frag. 1 awards the palm of excellence to different localities; cf. the oracle in Schol. on Theokr. 14. 49 γαίης μὲν πάσης τὸ Πελασγικὸν Ἄργος ἄμεινον, | ἵπποι Θρηΐκιαι, Λακεδαιμόνιαι δὲ γυναῖκες, Athen. 7. 278 E ἵππον Θεσσαλικὴν Λακεδαιμονίην τε γυναῖκα, | ἄνδρας δ' οἳ πίνουσιν ὕδωρ καλῆς 'Αρεθούσης, Hor. *Sat.* 2. 4. 33.—**1.** Lakonian hunting-dogs: Soph. *Aias* 8 (see Jebb), Plato *Parmen.* 128 C, Pollux 5. 38, Verg. *Georg.* 3. 405, Hor. *Epod.* 6. 5. They were half fox (ἐξ ἀλώπεκος καὶ κυνὸς οἱ Λακωνικοί Arist. *Hist. An.* 8. 28), small in size and remarkable for the keenness of their scent, their ἀνδρία and their φιλοπονία. The females were more intelligent than the males. Cf. *Mid. Night's Dream* 4. 1 (Theseus loq.) "My hounds are bred out of the Spartan kind, | So flew'd, so sanded, and their heads are hung | With ears that sweep away the morning dew; | Crook-knee'd, and dew-lapped like Thessalian bulls; | Slow in pursuit, but matched in mouth like bells, | Each under each. A cry more tuneable | Was never holla'd to, nor cheer'd with horn, | In Crete, in Sparta, nor in Thessaly." Molossian and Cretan dogs were also famous.—**2. ἐπί**: of purpose, = *ἐπὶ θηρεύσει*, 'with a view to hunting,' as *ἐπ' ἐξαγωγῇ* Hdt. 7. 156 'for exportation'; not 'against' (*κύνας . . . σεύῃ ἐπ' ἀγροτέρῳ συΐ* Λ 293). **τρέφειν**: infin. for imper., which construction reappears with v. 5.—**3**. She-goats from Skyros: Athen. 12. 540 D, Aelian *H. A.* 3. 33, *Anth. Pal.* 9. 219, Zenob. 2. 18. Alkaios (110) preceded Pind. in praising them.—**5. ὅπλα**: 'Attic' correption as in *Nem.* 1. 51 etc., *ὁπλόταται Isthm.* 8. 20. Argive shields (*Argolici clipei* Verg. *Aen.* 3. 637) were circular (cf. *ἀσπίδα πάντοσε ἴσην* Γ 347), as may be seen by the representation on the Aiginetan marbles. Paus. 2. 25. 7 says that shields were first used by Proitos and Akrisios of Argos. Aisch. *Sept.* 90 has *λεύκασπις λαός* of the Argives, Eur. *Phoin.* 1099 *λεύκασπιν Ἀργείων στρατόν*. The Argives were also famous as *λινοθώρηκες*. **ἅρμα**: asyndeton in a catalogue. Theban chariots: *Isthm.* 8. 22, Frag. 195, 323, Soph. *Antig.* 149, 845, Eur. *H. F.* 467, Kritias 1. 10 *Θήβη δ' ἁρματόεντα δίφρον συνεπήξατο πρώτη*. The first victor with the car at Olympia (680) was Pagondas of Thebes, and Iolaos, the Boiotian, half-brother of Herakles, is said to have invented it (Frag. 114). The Boiotians originally came from Thessaly, and the Thessalians were also charioteers (*Θετταλὲ ποικιλόδιφρε* Pollux 7. 112). On the Boiotians as equestrians see also Δ 391, Hes. *Shield* 24, *Ol.* 6. 85. **ἀλλ'** with the infin. = imper. as with the imper. *Ol.* 1. 17, 6. 22. **ἀγλαοκάρπου** (cf. Strabo 6. 273): the Greek cannot resist the temptation to use a descriptive epithet even when it is not appropriate to the situation.—**6. ὄχημα**: a mule-car, as *ὄχος Ol.* 4. 13 (to Psaumis of Kamarina), 6. 24 (to Agesias of Syracuse), as *ἀπήνα* 5. 3 (to Psaumis). Cf. Kritias 1. 3 *ὄχος Σικελός, κάλλει δαπάνῃ τε κράτιστος*, Sim. iii. The Thessalians also were partial to the use of mules.—Metre: logaoedic.

X. Dion. Hal. *de admir. vi dic. Demosth.* 7; cf. Plut. *de facie in orb. lun.* 19. vv. 1-9 Philo *de provid.* 2. 96, from a free or incorrect Armenian version. Dion. has been commenting on the overwrought, plethoric character of Plato's style as exemplified in the discussion of Eros in *Phaidros* 237 A, 238 C, D, 246 E, and proceeds to state as his opinion that such a style of composition needs only rhythmical arrangement and musical accompaniment to become a dithyramb or a hyporcheme; and compares it with this passage from Pindar. Since the subject matter excludes the dithyramb, the poem is to be regarded as a hyporcheme. A poem on an eclipse naturally falls under a class of melic sacred to Apollo. There is however no need to identify the god of light (Λύκειος) with the Sun, though the Boiotian Apollo Ismenios and Galaxios was so identified (Proklos). It is to be noted that the poem, though sacred to the god of joy, is full of the gloom of presaged disaster. Perhaps Apollo, as ἀλεξίκακος, was, as in the paian, invoked in the last part of the fragment to avert the evils here foreshadowed. The parodos of Soph. *O. T.* (151 ff.) with its catalogue of evils attendant on the plague recalls this fragment. Frag. xxi. also refers to an eclipse.

The date of the poem is not certain. The eclipse which is reported to have occurred when Xerxes was at Sardis (Hdt. 7. 37) has been confused with that of Feb. 17, 478, according to Stein, who follows Zech. That of Oct. 2, 480, which occurred when Kleombrotos was at the Isthmos (Hdt. 9. 10), would not harmonize with the period of peace indicated by l. 10 (Zech records no eclipse of this date). It was formerly generally assumed on the authority of Ideler that the fragment refers to the eclipse of April 30, 463, when at 2 P.M. eleven digits of the sun were obscured to spectators at Thebes. Because of the mention of snow and frost, Hoffman (*Jahresber. über das Gymnas. in Triest* 1889 p. 43-49) decides in favour of the (nearly total) eclipse of 478. If the poem had been written in 463, Pindar would in all probability have made a definite reference to the eclipse of 478. Eclipses are mentioned υ 357, Archil. 74, Mimn. 20, Stesich. 73, Kydias 2. Thales is reported to have predicted that of 610 or 585 (Hdt. 1. 74). An eclipse of the sun boded disaster to the Greeks, whereas an eclipse of the moon was an evil omen to the Persians (Hdt. 7. 37, Quint. Curt. 4. 10. 1). With this fragment cf. Archil. 74 χρημάτων ἄελπτον οὐδέν ἐστιν οὐδ' ἀπώμοτον, | οὐδὲ θαυμάσιον, ἐπειδὴ Ζεὺς . . . | ἐκ μεσημβρίης ἔθηκε νύκτ' ἀποκρύψας φάος | ἡλίου λάμποντος· λυγρὸν δ' ἦλθ' ἐπ' ἀνθρώπους δέος. | ἐκ δὲ τοῦ καὶ πιστὰ πάντα κἀπίελπτα γίγνεται | ἀνδράσιν· μηδεὶς ἔθ' ὑμῶν εἰσορῶν θαυμαζέτω, | μηδ' ὅταν δελφῖσι θῆρες ἀνταμείψωνται νομὸν | ἐνάλιον καί σφιν θαλάσσης ἠχέεντα κύματα | φίλτερ' ἠπείρου γένηται κ.τ.λ. A μαντεία in Demosth. 1072 prescribes sacrifices to various gods in case of an eclipse.

1. Ἀκτὶς Ἀελίου: the choruses of Attic tragedy borrow the phrase from Doric lyric. Cf. Soph. *Antig.* 100 ἀκτὶς Ἀελίου, τὸ κάλλιστον ἑπταπύλῳ φανὲν | Θήβᾳ τῶν προτέρων φάος, Eur. *Med.* 1251 παμφαὴς | ἀ. Ἀελίου. In dialogue parts: Eur. *Suppl.* 650 ἀ. ἡλίου, κανὼν σαφής. **πολύσκοπε**: "the searching eye of heaven" Shakesp. *Rich. ii.* πολύσκοπος is not contrasted with πάνσκοπος, though Helios sees and hears everything (Γ 277). Aurora is πολυδερκής. **μᾶτερ ὀμμάτων** : ὄψις is the child of φῶς. Pind. is specially fond of drawing his figures from the sphere of family relationship : *Ol.* 8. 1 μᾶτερ . . . ἀέθλων, Ὀλυμπία, 13. 10 Ὕβριν, Κόρου ματέρα, *Nem.* 5. 6 τέρειναν ματέρ' οἰνάνθας ὀπώραν (πατήρ *Ol.* 7. 70, παῖς 2. 32, 11. 3, *Nem.* 9. 52, θυγάτηρ *Pyth.* 5. 28, *Nem.* 4. 3). On the relation between light and sight, cf. Plato *Rep.* 507 E οὐ σμικρὰ ἄρα ἰδέα, ἡ τοῦ ὁρᾶν αἴσθησις καὶ ἡ τοῦ ὁρᾶσθαι δύναμις, τῶν ἄλλων ξυζεύξεων τιμιωτέρῳ ζυγῷ ἐζύγησαν, εἴπερ μὴ ἄτιμον τὸ φῶς . . . Τίνα οὖν ἔχεις αἰτιάσασθαι τῶν ἐν οὐρανῷ θεῶν τούτου κύριον, οὗ ἡμῖν τὸ φῶς ὄψιν τε ποιεῖ ὁρᾶν ὅτι κάλλιστα καὶ τὰ ὁρώμενα ὁρᾶσθαι; Ὅνπερ καὶ σύ, ἔφη, καὶ οἱ ἄλλοι· τὸν ἥλιον γὰρ δῆλον ὅτι ἐρωτᾷς . . . . Ἆρ' οὖν οὐ καὶ ὁ ἥλιος ὄψις μὲν οὐκ ἔστιν, αἴτιος δ' ὢν αὐτῆς ὁρᾶται ὑπ' αὐτῆς ταύτης; Instead of μᾶτερ, μέτρα was formerly read because of Philostr. *Ep.* 53 κατὰ Πίνδαρον τὸ τὴν ἀκτῖνα τὴν ἀπὸ σοῦ πηδῶσαν εἶναι τῶν ἐμῶν ὀφθαλμῶν μέτρα, where, however, the MSS. have μητέρα. Boeckh had ἐμαῖς θέαις μέτρ' ὀμμάτων, taking θέαι as 'eye-sight' and ὀμμ. = θεαμάτων (cf. Soph. *El.* 903, Plato *Phaidr.* 253 E) : *visui meo mensura rerum adspectabilium.* μέτρα is not proved by Eur. *Suppl.* 650 ἀ. ἡλίου, κανὼν σαφής, which may indicate similarity of appearance ("long-levelled rule of streaming light" in Milton), not of office.—**2. ἄστρον . . . κλεπτόμενον** is used absolutely, almost = a gen. of cause. Some take ἄστρον in apposition to ἀκτὶς Ἀελίου. ἄστρον in the sing. = ἀστήρ, a great star. So of the sun, *Ol.* 1. 6 ; of Sirius, Alk. xix.; of the moon, Aisch. *Septem* 390 (πρέσβιστον ἄστρων). Cf. Max. Tyr. *Or.* 40 p. 265 ἐν ἡμέρᾳ ἥλιος κρατεῖ, τὸ ἄριστον καὶ ἀκμαιότατον τῶν ἐν οὐρανῷ σωμάτων. Schol. Arat. *Phain.* 11 λέγεται δὲ καὶ ὁ ἥλιος ἄστρον ἰδίως, παρὰ δὲ Πινδάρῳ "ἄστρον ὑπέρτατον."—**3. ἔθηκας** = ἐποίησας : the factitive use is very common in Pind. (*Ol.* 2. 17, 7. 6).—**4. πτανόν** : Hermann ποτανόν, Dissen ποτανάν. Elsewhere in Pind. ποτανός forms the fem. : *Nem.* 7. 22 ποτανᾷ μαχανᾷ of poetry, 'power of making winged,' and we should expect πτανάν here. The poet has however his idiosyncrasies, and φοίνιος, μοιρίδιος, δυνατός, γλυκερώτερος are used by him as fem. forms ; cf. Soph. *O. K.* 1460 πτερωτὸς βροντή (other examples from tragedy in Jebb on *O. K.* 751). Pind. may be following epic models. πτανὸν ἰσχύν is 'aspiring strength' rather than 'fleeting strength' as in πτηναὶ ἐλπίδες, πτηνοὶ λόγοι. **σοφίας** is to be taken generally and not with reference to forecasting eclipses. **ὁδόν** : cf. ἀλαθείας ὁδ. *Pyth.* 3. 103, ὕβριος ὁδ. *Ol.* 7. 90, "the way of truth," Psalms 119. 30. Xen. *Anab.* 1. 2. 21 has ὁδὸς ἀμήχανος εἰσελθεῖν.—**5. ἀτραπόν** accus. after ἐσσ. as κέλευθα ἤλθομεν ι 261, ἰέναι ὁδὸν δ 483.—**6. ἐλαύνεις** : cf. *Nem.* 3. 74 ἐλᾷ δὲ καὶ τέσσαρας ἀρετὰς | ὁ μακρὸς *αἰών*. The accus. is the cognate accus. of the course (Aristoph. *Nubes* 29 *ἐλαύνεις δρόμους*). If the verb meant 'harass' we should have the instr. dat. **νεώτερον**: in the sinister sense; cf. *Pyth.* 4. 155 *μή τι νεώτερον ἐξ αὐτῶν ἀναστήῃ κακόν*, Soph. *Phil.* 1230 *νέον μὲν οὐδέν*. So *ἄλλος, ἀλλοῖος, ἕτερος* are used euphemistically.—**7. ζαθόας** Christ, 'exceeding swift' (a new word); *ζαθέας* Schneidewin, *τε θοάς* Bergk.—**10.** In the list of calamities the omission of earthquake is noteworthy especially if the poem was written after the shock at Delos (cf. on Frag. vi.). Bergk arranges v. 10 ff. in a more logical order, which is however not necessarily the poetical order: *τινός, ἢ στάσιν οὐλ.* | *ἢ παγετὸν καρποῦ φθίσιν ἢ νιφ. σθ. ὑπερ.* | *ἢ πόντου κ. ἀνὰ πέδον* | *χθονός*. His objection to *παγ. χθονός* is not well taken.—**11. σθένος**: so *ὕδατος σθ. Ol.* 9. 51, *σθ. πλούτου Isthm.* 3. 2.—**13. πόντου**: cf. Hdt. 1. 184 *ἐώθεε ὁ ποταμὸς ἀνὰ τὸ πεδίον πᾶν πελαγίζειν*. In the case of an inundation, *πόντος*, the deep sea, is emptied of its waters, while *πέλαγος*, the broad sea, extends the expanse of its waters over the land.—**16.** Cf. *Ol.* 9. 49 *λέγοντι μὰν* | *χθόνα μὲν κατακλύσαι μέλαιναν* | *ὕδατος σθένος*, Mel. Adesp. 84 (probably by Pind.) on the beginnings of the human race. This passage recalls the tradition of the flood in Deukalion's time.—**17.** For the thought cf. Thuk. 7. 75. 6 *ἡ ἰσομοιρία τῶν κακῶν, ἔχουσά τινα ὅμως τὸ μετὰ πολλῶν κούφισιν*, Eur. *Phoin.* 894 *εἷς γὰρ ὢν πολλῶν μέτα* | *τὸ μέλλον, εἰ χρή, πείσομαι*, Cic. *ad Fam.* 6. 2. 2 *misera est illa quidem consolatio . . . nihil esse praecipue cuiquam dolendum in eo, quod accidat universis*, Pliny *Ep.* 6. 20. 17 (on the eruption of Vesuvius) *possem gloriari non gemitum mihi, non vocem parum fortem in tantis periculis excidisse, nisi me cum omnibus, omnia mecum perire misero, magno tamen mortalitatis solacio credidissem.*—Metre: hyporchematic dactylo-trochaics. Note the frequent dactyls. The fragment is an *ἀπολελυμένον μέλος*. Blass *Jahrb.* 1869, p. 387, attempts to find a strophe and antistrophe of eight lines each. Two verses are, he thinks, lost before *πολέμου* . . . . The last verse he regards as the beginning of the epode, whereas it is well adapted to the close. The arrangement of the cola varies somewhat in the different editions.

XI. Sokr. *epist.* 1. 7. Cf. *Pyth.* 10. 10 *γλυκὺ δ' ἀνθρώπων τέλος ἀρχά τε δαίμονος ὀρνύντος αὔξεται*, 1. 33 ff., Diagoras i. —**2. ἐν** as iv. 1.—Metre: logaoedic.

XII. Stob. *Flor.* 58. 9; vv. 1-2 Polyb. 4. 31. Polyb., no friend to the Athenian empire, says *οὐδὲ γὰρ Θηβαίους ἐπαινοῦμεν κατὰ τὰ Μηδικά, διότι τῶν ὑπὲρ τῆς Ἑλλάδος ἀποστάντες κινδύνων τὰ Περσῶν εἵλοντο διὰ τὸν φόβον, οὐδὲ Πίνδαρον τὸν συναποφηνάμενον αὐτοῖς ἄγειν τὴν ἡσυχίαν διὰ τῶνδε τῶν ποιημάτων*. This hyporcheme was written before the battle of Plataia when the Thebans were divided in their sympathies. The poet seems to counsel a policy of neutrality when the necessity of action was immediate. Elsewhere Pind. shows his love of tranquillity, *Pyth.* 8. 1, 11. 55 etc.—**1. τις** : in exhortations often = πάντες. **εὐδίᾳ** : of the calm that follows victory in *Ol.* 1. 98, εὔδίαν ἐκ χειμῶνος *Isthm.* 7. 38. Contrast πόλεως χειμαζομένης Aristoph. *Ranae* 361.—**2. Ἀσυχίας** : cf. *Pyth.* 8. 1 φιλόφρον Ἀσ., Δίκας | ὦ μεγιστόπολι θύγατερ, *Ol.* 4. 18 Ἀσ. φιλόπολιν, Aristoph. *Aves* 1321 τό τε τᾶς ἀγανόφρονος Ἡσυχίας | εὐάμερον πρόσωπον.—**5. ἐχθ. κουροτρ.** : cf. γλυκεῖα γηροτρόφος xxix. Ithake is ἀγαθὴ κουροτρόφος ι 27.—Metre : logaoedic.

XIII. Stob. *Flor.* 50. 3 (cf. Schol. Λ 227, Eust. 841. 32). Often quoted as a proverb; γλυκὺς ἀπείρῳ πόλεμος. Cf. Thuk. 2. 8. 1 νεότης . . . ὑπὸ ἀπειρίας ἥπτετο τοῦ πολέμου.—Metre : cretics and logaoedics.

XIV. Dion. Hal. *de admir. vi dic. Demosth.* 26. In return for the poet's laudation of his ancestor "The great Emathian conqueror bid spare | The house of Pindarus when temple and tow'r | Went to the ground." Over the house of the poet, Alexander read Πινδάρου τοῦ μουσοποιοῦ τὴν στέγην μὴ καίετε. Pind. rings the changes on the sentiment here expressed: *Ol.* 4. 10 τόνδε κῶμον, | χρονιώτατον φάος | . . . ἀρετᾶν, 10. 91 ὅταν καλὰ ἔρξαις ἀοιδᾶς ἄτερ | . . . εἰς Ἀΐδα σταθμὸν | ἀνὴρ ἵκηται κ.τ.λ., 11. 4 ff., *Pyth.* 3. 114 ἁ δ' ἀρετὰ κλειναῖς ἀοιδαῖς | χρονία τελέθει, 1. 93, 9. 92, *Nem.* 6. 29, 4. 6 ῥῆμα δ' ἐργμάτων χρονιώτερον βιοτεύει, 7. 13, 9. 6, *Isthm.* 3. 7, 8. 65, Bacch. i. 94 πράξαντι δ' εὖ οὐ φέρει κόσμον σιωπά, 9. 82 τό γέ τοι καλὸν ἔργον | γνησίων ὕμνων τυχὸν | ὑψοῦ παρὰ δαίμοσι κεῖται. Hor. 4. 9. 26 *omnes inlacrimabiles* | *urgentur ignotique longa* | *nocte, carent quia vate sacro.* | *paullum sepultae distat inertiae* | *celata virtus*, Pope : "Vain was the chief's, the sage's pride, | They had no poet and they died."—**3. ποτιψαύει** : *cum dat.* on the analogy of verbs of approach (πελάζω, ἀντάω). So with ψαύω *Pyth.* 9. 120, θιγγάνω 4. 296, ἅπτω *Isthm.* 4. 12. All of these verbs also take the genitive in Pind.—**4. σθένει** : added by Radermacher.—Metre : dact.-epitrite.

XV. Athen. 13. 601 D. Just before, Athen. says Πίνδαρος δ' οὐ μετρίως ὢν ἐρωτικός φησιν (Frag. 127 : Εἴη καὶ ἐρᾶν καὶ ἔρωτι χαρίζεσθαι κατὰ καιρόν· | μὴ πρεσβυτέραν ἀριθμοῦ δίωκε, θυμέ, πρᾶξιν). Theoxenos was the 'beloved' of Pindar, the beautiful youth in whose lap the poet is said to have died at Argos. Since this poem was written in Pindar's old age (cf. Ibyk. ii.), the passion to which he here gives expression has no other object than to set Theoxenos' beauty in stronger relief. Cf. Welcker *Kl. Schr.* 1. 234. There is no evidence that Theoxenos had been victorious in the Theban Herakleia (Dissen). Bergk *Gr. Litt.-Gesch.* 2. 168 thought the fragment was an enkomion similar to the enkomia of Ibykos.

1. χρῆν *κ.τ.λ.*: *oportebat quidem dum opportunum erat.* Cf. Goodwin *M. T.* 415 ff. After Homer the substantive *χρή* = *χρεώ* 'need' was fused with the forms of *εἰμί* except in the indic. present. Pind. was the first to use *ἐχρῆν* (*Nem.* 7. 44), the augment of which is the result of false analogy. Cf. Ahrens *Kl. Schr.* 1. 58. **καιρόν**: cf. *Nem.* 8. 1 *ὥρα πότνια, κάρυξ Ἀφροδίτας ἀμβροσιᾶν φιλοτάτων.* Theoxenos is *ὥρᾳ κεκραμένος.* Pind. prefers *κατὰ καιρόν* to *ἐν καιρῷ*; he does not use the adv. *καιρῷ.* **ἐρώτων**: plural of the separate moments of sensation. So *πόθοι, μανίαι, furores.* *ἔρωτες* is impersonal in Pindar except possibly in Frag. 122. 4 and *Nem.* 8. 5. **δρέπεσθαι**: elsewhere in Pind. *δρέπω* takes the accus., here the gen. by analogy to *ἅπτεσθαι* etc. Cf. Frag. 122. 8 *ὥρας ἀπὸ καρπὸν δρέπεσθαι.* **σύν**: life is man's companion. *γηραιὸν μέρος ἁλικίας | ἀμφιπολεῖ Pyth.* 4. 157, cf. 4. 10, 11. 10, *Nem.* 9. 44 *σὺν νεότατι,* 'as long as youth lasts,' Soph. *O. K.* 7, etc. "Life, we've been long together."—**2. μαρμαριζοίσας**: *ὄμματα μαρμαίροντα* Γ 397, of Aphrodite.—**3. ἀδάμαντος**: *ἀδάμαντος θυμόν* Hes. *Theogon.* 239, *τίς οὕτως ἀδαμάντινος ἢ σιδαροῦς τὴν καρδίαν*; Heliod. 4. 4.—**4. σιδάρου**: *σιδήρειον ἦτορ* Ω 205, *σιδηρόφρων* Aisch. *Prom.* 242, *Sept.* 52, *ἦσθα σίδαρος* Eur. *Med.* 1279, *νόον σιδήρου* Mosch. 4. 44, Tibull. 1. 1. 63, Hor. 1. 3. 9, Ovid *Metam.* 9. 614. **μέλαιναν**: the epithet 'black' is often applied to the heart or mind when filled with passion (A 103, Theogn. 1199, Aisch. *Choeph.* 414, *Pers.* 114); so of 'dark malignity': *κελαινώπας θυμός* Soph. *Aias* 954, *κελαινόφρων* Aisch. *Eum.* 459. Pind. has *μ. καρδ.* 'sad' in Frag. 225; *μελανοκάρδιος πέτρα* Aristoph. *Ranae* 470 of the Styx, which in Arkadia falls into a black chasm, and in the nether world pours its waters into the dark night. Here *μ.* is used of *ἀγριότης*, insensibility, and is explained by *ψυχρᾷ*. A heart of adamant or iron cannot be forced to glow with passion because love (Eros is a smith in Anakr. xix.) can apply only a chill flame. The figure shifts from the sea—*πόθος* is a blast of passion—to the forge.—**5. ψυχρᾷ** oxymoron as *Ol.* 6. 43, 46. *ψυχρὰ φλόξ* is almost = *ἄφλογος φλόξ.* —**6. περί**: dative of the object to be gained. So with *μάρναμαι* Tyrt. 10. 2, *Nem.* 5. 47, with *δηρίομαι, ἁμιλλῶ.* Cf. *Pyth.* 2. 59 *κτεάτεσσί τε καὶ περὶ τιμᾷ . . . γενέσθαι ὑπέρτερον.* *περί* with the dative of the external reason is rare and poetical. **βιαίως** *vehementer.* In poetry the philosophical

'unnaturally' is unknown: Arist. *Eth.* 1. 5. 8 ὁ δὲ χρηματιστὴς (βίος) βίαιός τίς ἐστι.—**7.** **ψυχράν** is taken from ψυχρᾷ in 5. Christ retains the word, though a 'chill path' is scarcely Greek. Following Schneider, Bergk wrote ψυχάν and read γυναικείαν, 'serving the heart of a woman, he is borne recklessly about.' Dissen too read ψυχάν: *muliebri nequitia vagatur huc illuc animo omnem viam sequens* (= π. ἡδονὴν θ.). For ψ. Wilam. has σύρδαν, Ahrens αἰσχράν, Schroeder βληχράν. γυν. θράσει 'a shameless woman' may depend on θεραπεύων (Fenn.) though elsewhere θερ. has the accus. (γυναῖκα θερ. Xenoph.).—
—**8.** **θεᾶς ἕκατι**: cf. Κύπριδος ἕκ. Alkm. xiii. **δαχθείς**: of love Eur. *Hippol.* 1303, *Phoin.* 383. **ἕλᾳ**: *ardore solis.*—**9.** **ἱρᾶν**: of bees Frag. 158. **τάκομαι**: Theokr. 2. 28 ὡς τοῦτον τὸν κηρὸν ἐγὼ σὺν δαίμονι τάκω, | ὣς τάκοιθ' ὑπ' ἔρωτος ὁ Μύνδιος αὐτίκα Δέλφις, *Anth. Pal.* 5. 210 τήκομαι, ὡς κηρὸς παρ πυρὶ, κάλλος ὁρῶν, Ovid *Metam.* 3. 485 *ut intabescere flavae* | *igne levi cerae* . . . | . . . *sic attenuatus amore* | *liquitur, et tecto paulatim carpitur igni.* **ἴδω** . . . **ἐς**: cf. on iv. 1.—**10.** For the order cf. *Pyth.* 3. 96 ἐν δ' αὖτε χρόνῳ. **ἴαινεν**: for the sing. verb see on Bacch. xvi. Peitho and the Graces, cf. Ibyk. v. Bergk read τε νέον | καὶ Χ. υἱὸν ἀνᾶγ' Ἀγ.—Metre: dact.-epitrite. Hartung maintained that the Frag. is monostrophic.

XVI. Plut. *Consol. ad Apoll.* 35 (vv. 1-7), *de occ. viv.* 7 (in paraphrase). vv. 8-9 = 6-7 close the antistrophe. In Hes. *W. D.* 171, *Ol.* 2. 71, skol. viii. (*q.v.*) Elysium is placed in the Islands of the Blest in Okeanos; here it is placed in Hades, where, according to the *Odyssey*, the heroes abide in gloom, mere wraiths but endowed with the passions of earth. The dual paradise is an invention of the poet who makes the joys of Elysium in Hades a foretaste of the blessedness in the μακάρων νῆσοι. The late Orphic period did not distinguish between the Elysium in Hades and the Elysium in the Islands of the Blest. Pindar's conception of future life is a poetic combination of the traditional faith with the clarified doctrines of the Orphic and Pythagorean sects. Cf. Rohde *Psyche* 496 ff. Empedokles preceded Pind. in the belief that the soul was to be purified after many rebirths; but no other Greek poet has given such concrete expression to the faith in a future state of blessedness. The contrast between Attic tragedy and Pind. is profound.—**1.** **μέν** followed by τ' (Bergk δ') as in iv. 13. Had the poet here wished to oppose the life of the pious to that of the impious in the antistr. he would have said τοῖσι μέν. μέν is not misplaced; the examples in Soph. *Aias* 56, *Phil.* 1136 are different. **ἀελίου**: Helios shines in the nether world, when it is night upon earth. Cf.

μ 383 δύσομαι εἰς Ἀΐδαο καὶ ἐν νεκύεσσι φαείνω (a threat). His light is however only for the pious: μόνοις γὰρ ἡμῖν ἥλιος καὶ φθέγγος ἱλαρόν ἐστιν Aristoph. *Ranae* 454. That this belief in an under-world Helios lasted long is evident from Kaibel 228 *b*. 7 Λητογενές, σὺ δὲ παῖδας ἐν ἡρώεσσι φυλάσσοις, | [εὐσεβέ]ων αἰεὶ χῶρον ἐπερχόμενος, Hymnus Magicus to Helios (Abel *Orphica* p. 291) 4. 11 ἣν γαίης κευθμῶνα μόλῃς νεκύων τ' ἐπὶ χῶρον. In *Ol.* 2. 61 the ἐσλοί, such as Achilles, Peleus, and Kadmos, are said to have attained to a life free from toil in comparison to the life on earth, and in the Islands of the Blest to enjoy ἴσαις δὲ νύκτεσσιν αἰεὶ ἴσον ἐν ἁμέραις ἅλιον. If the poet is consistent—which is altogether unnecessary—, this passage does not refer to a sun that shines both by day and by night, or to a perpetual vernal equinox, but to an inverted succession of day and night, the sun in Elysium being 'equal' in splendour to that of the upper world. (Aristoph. *Ranae* 155 φῶς κάλλιστον ὥσπερ ἐνθάδε.) Rohde regarded Vergil's (*Aen.* 6. 641) *solemque suum, sua sidera norunt* as later subtilizing. With the view of Pind. contrast Prax. ii. Dissen supposed that additional point was given to this verse by the threnos being sung after sunset. Cf. *Isthm.* 4. 65, Lobeck *Aglaoph.* 1. 412.—**2**. Cf. Tibull. 1. 3. 61 of Elysium: *fert cassiam non culta seges, totosque per agros | floret odoratis terra benigna rosis.* **προάστιον**: Dissen's comment is: *est urbs in Orco, ubi Pluto cum Proserpina habitat et heroes ceterique mortui, ante urbem vero amoenis in pratis suburbium pulcherrimum, veluti Athenis* Κεραμεικὸς *fuit. Etiam hic locus Pindarico more praesentibus rebus accommodatus. Videtur enim defunctus, qui canitur, in suburbio sepultus esse, ubi credo cognati fundum habebant.* Arnold on Thuk. 4. 69: "the προαστεῖον . . . was not what we call a suburb, but rather an open space like the parks in London, partly planted with trees . . . . It was used as a ground for reviews of the army, and for public games. At Rome the Campus Martius was exactly what the Greeks call προαστεῖον." The description in Vergil's Nekyia is general: cf. *Aen.* 6. 673 *nulli certa domus; lucis habitamus opacis*, 638 *devenere locos laetos et amoena vireta | fortunatorum nemorum sedesque beatas*, 679 *penitus convalle virenti | inclusas animas superumque ad lumen ituras | lustrabat studio recolens.*—**3**. **βεβριθός**: cf. Σ 561.—**4**. Cf. Verg. *Aen.* 6. 642 *pars in gramineis exercent membra palaestris.* Dissen suggested that the threnos was in honour of a youth. The whole passage is recalled by Bacch. xiii. **πεσσοῖς**: so the Trojan heroes played at dice, Eur. *I. A.* 196, Frag. 888, Soph. Frag. 438; so the suitors of Penelope, α 107; Palamedes and Thersites in Polygnotos' painting;

Achilles and Aias at dice on a lekythos of the sixth century in the Boston Museum of Fine Arts. On the monument of Vicentius (Maass *Orphica* p. 223) the gods, who preside over the *bonorum iudicio*, are feasting and playing at dice.—**5. εὐανθὴς . . . ὄλβος**: as *Isthm.* 5. 12.—**7. μειγνύντων**: with *ὀδμά*, since the gen. absol. is rare in Pind. (without a subject expressed in *Pyth.* 1. 26, 4. 232, 8. 43). See Gildersleeve on *Ol.* 13. 15. This passage is perhaps imitated in the hymn to Apollo (i.) with notes (Append.) ὁμοῦ δέ νιν Ἄραψ ἀτμὸς ἐς Ὄλυμπον ἀνακίδναται.—**9. βληχροί**, 'sluggish'; used of winds, Alk. 16. The word is a favourite with the Ionians. (On βληχρός = ἰσχυρός, see Seaton, *A. J. P.* 10. 468, Gerstenhauer 202). Cf. Verg. *Georg.* 4. 479 *Cocyti tardaque palus inamabilis unda*, *Aen.* 6. 323 *Cocyti stagna alta vides Stygiamque paludem*, Hor. 2. 14. 17 *ater flumine languido | Cocytos.* Pind. probably said that while the pious retained their recollection, the evil lost all memory of the life on earth.—Metre: dact.-epitrite.

XVII. Plut. *Consol. ad Apoll.* 35; vv. 2-4 *vit. Rom.* 28 (with slight variations).—**1. ἅπαντες**: that is, all who have received the rights of initiation. One good MS. has τελετάν. Without some such addition as Boeckh's μεταν. nothing can be made of the line.—**3. αἰῶνος εἴδωλον**: = ψυχά. *αἰῶνος* not = *aevi sempiterni* (Christ). Apart from its equivalence with καρδία, ζωή in Pindar, ψυχή denotes the *alter ego*, the psychic 'double' in every man. It lives after the death of the body; cf. εἴδωλον λ 83, ψυχὴ καὶ εἴδωλον Ψ 104. Pind. is the first to explain the immortality of this ψυχά by its divine origin. The ψυχή of the philosophers is different, and in tragedy it is invariably the *anima* of the living man.—**4. πρασσόντων** gen. abs., cf. on xvi. 7. For the neuter use of πράσσω = ἐργάζομαι cf. *Nem.* 1. 26 πράσσει γὰρ ἔργῳ μὲν σθένος, | βουλαῖσι δὲ φρήν 'manifests itself,' 'exercises its functions.' **εὑδόντεσσιν**: cf. Aisch. *Eum.* 104 εὕδουσα γὰρ φρὴν ὄμμασιν λαμπρύνεται (εὑδούσῃ φρενὶ Soph. Frag. 579), Xen. *Kyrop.* 8. 7. 21 ἡ δὲ τοῦ ἀνθρώπου ψυχὴ τότε (in sleep) δήπου θειοτάτη καταφαίνεται καὶ τότε τι τῶν μελλόντων προορᾷ, Plato *Rep.* 571 C, Aelian *V. H.* 3. 11 οἱ Περιπατητικοί φασι μεθ' ἡμέραν θητεύουσαν τὴν ψυχὴν τῷ σώματι περιπλέκεσθαι καὶ μὴ δύνασθαι καθαρῶς τὴν ἀλήθειαν θεωρεῖν, νύκτωρ δὲ διαλυθεῖσαν τῆς περὶ τοῦτο λειτουργίας καὶ σφαιρωθεῖσαν ἐν τῷ περὶ τὸν θώρακα τόπῳ μαντικωτέραν γίνεσθαι, ἐξ ὧν τὰ ἐνύπνια, Cic. *de div.* 1. 30 (63) *cum ergo est somno sevocatus animus a societate et a contagione corporis, tum meminit praeteritorum, praesentia cernit, futura praevidet; iacet enim corpus dormientis ut mortui, viget autem et vivit animus*, Milton *Par. L.* 8. 460 "Mine eyes he clos'd, but open left the call | Of fancy, my internal sight," Blacklock *Geneal. of Nonsense* has "But still internal sense awake remained." **ὀνείροις**: Pind. was visited in a dream by Persephone (Paus. 9. 23. 3); in his youth he dreamt that bees placed honey in his mouth (*Vita Pind.*).—**5. κρίσιν**: that the soul of the living can behold in sleep its state after death is a doctrine suggesting the utterances of Herakleitos: Living and dead, awake and asleep, are the same (78), Immortals are mortal, mortals immortal, living in their death and dying in their life (67), and also, but more enigmatical, Death is what we see waking, what we see in sleep is a dream (64); cf. Eur. Frag. 833 *τίς δ' οἶδεν εἰ ζῆν τοῦθ' ὃ κέκληται θανεῖν, | τὸ ζῆν δὲ θνῄσκειν ἐστί*; Aristoph. *Ranae* 1477 *τίς οἶδεν εἰ τὸ ζῆν μέν ἐστι κατθανεῖν κ.τ.λ.* A fragment ascribed to Pindar by Theodoretos is probably spurious: *ψυχαὶ δ' ἀσεβέων ὑπουράνιοι γαίᾳ πωτῶνται | ἐν ἄλγεσιν φονίοις ὑπὸ ζεύγλαις <τ'> ἀφύκτοις κακῶν· | εὐσεβέων δ' ἐπουράνιοι ναίουσαι | μολπαῖς μάκαρα μέγαν ἀείδουσ' ἐν ὕμνοις.*—Metre of xvii.: dact.-epitrite. The irrational short in dact.-epitrites often occurs in Pindar's threnoi, dithyrambs, and skolia, rarely in the prosodia (vii.), never in the hymns.

XVIII. Plato *Meno* 81 B. Boeckh thought this threnos was composed in honour of Gelon (*obiit* 478/77); but this is quite uncertain. Pindar's belief appears to be as follows (cf. Rohde *Psyche* 499 ff.): After the death of the body, the soul is judged in Hades and, if accounted guiltless in its life on earth, passes to the Elysium in Hades depicted in Frag. xvi. It must, however, return twice again to earth, and suffer two more deaths of its body (*Ol.* 2. 68 *ἐστρὶς ἑκατέρωθι μείναντες*). Finally Persephone releases it from the *παλαιὸν πένθος* and it returns to earth to inhabit the body of a king, a hero, or a sage. It is now freed from the necessity of further wandering and passes at once to the Islands of the Blest. Rohde thought that the *παλαιὸν πένθος* was the cause of the imprisonment of the immortal soul in a mortal body, and that *πένθος* implies grief' on the part of Persephone because of the sin of the soul. Though the poem is not written in commemoration of a homicide, as Dissen thought, Pind. follows the analogy of the law of expiation in cases of homicide, which brings grief, not only to the relatives of the man who has been murdered, but also to the gods.—**1. οἶσι**: dative after *δέξεται* 'receive as a mark of grace.' So O 87 *Θέμιστι δέκτο δέπας*, *Ol.* 13. 29, *Pyth.* 4. 23, Hdt. 6. 86. 1, Aischin. 3. 111. The gift "blesseth him that gives and him that takes." **ποινάν**: cf. *ποινὴν . . . παιδὸς ἐδέξατο τεθνηῶτος Il.* I 633.—**2. δέξεται**: probably subjunctive. **ἐς ἅλιον**: more plastic than ἀλίῳ. **ἐνάτῳ**: this number is identified by the poet with the term of banishment and of expiatory service (ἀπενιαυτισμός) prescribed in the case of homicides and other transgressors. The ἐνιαυτός (ἐνναετηρίς) often varied between 8, 9, and 10 years. The purification of Apollo, the slayer of the Python, is accomplished by service μέγαν εἰς ἐνιαυτόν with Admetos, strictly the god of the under world. So in the case of Herakles, Kadmos, Hippotes. Gods who commit perjury are banished for nine years from Olympos. In the myth of Er (Plato *Rep.* 615 A) the subterranean journey of the soul lasted a thousand years.—**4. τε** after καί, which connects βασ. with ἄνδρες, unites the subdivisions of the class denoted by ἄνδρες. Cf. Emped. 447 εἰς δὲ τέλος μάντεις τε καὶ ὑμνοπόλοι καὶ ἰητροὶ | καὶ πρόμοι ἀνθρώποισιν ἐπιχθονίοισι πέλονται, | ἔνθεν ἀναβλαστοῦσι θεοὶ τιμῇσι φέριστοι.—**5. ἥρωες**: such heroes are Leonidas (cf. Sim. i.), Menelaos, Theron; Diagoras, Milon; Orpheus, Asklepios, perhaps Homer. **ἁγνοί**: the technical expression; cf. Soph. *Trach.* 258. **πρός**: with passives Pind. prefers πρός to the more abstract ὑπό; cf. xv. 5.—Metre: dact.-epitrite.

XIX. Clem. Alex. *Strom.* 3. 518. On an Athenian who had been initiated into the Eleusinian mysteries. He is thought to be Hippokrates, the grandfather of Perikles (schol. *Pyth.* 7. 17). **ὄλβιος ὅστις**: cf. Alkm. iv. 37. On the felicity of the initiated cf. Soph. Frag. 753 ὡς τρὶς ὄλβιοι | κεῖνοι βροτῶν, οἳ ταῦτα δερχθέντες τέλη | μόλωσ' ἐς Ἅιδου, Eur. *H. F.* 613 τὰ μυστῶν δ' ὄργι' ηὐτύχησ' ἰδών, Isokr. 4. 28 ἧς (τελετῆς) οἱ μετασχόντες περί τε τῆς τοῦ βίου τελευτῆς καὶ τοῦ σύμπαντος αἰῶνος ἡδίους τὰς ἐλπίδας ἔχουσιν. Cf. Lobeck *Aglaoph.* 69. **οἶδε**: cf. *Ol.* 2. 56 οἶδεν τὸ μέλλον, where Fennell remarks that οἶδα in Pindar conveys "either the idea of thorough mastery of a subject or the effectual laying to heart of a truth." So εἰδώς in tragedy is often used of sure knowledge. **βίου τελ.** in Isokr. *l.l.*, Aristeid. *Eleusin.* 1. 421, *Panath.* 1. 302. Lobeck desiderated βιότου (cf. *Isthm.* 4. 5 σὺν θεῷ θνατὸν διέρχονται βιότου τέλος).—Metre: dact.-epitrite.

XX. Didym. Alex. *de trin.* 3. 1. p. 320, Clem. Alex. *Strom.* 5. 726, Euseb. *Praep. Ev.* 13. 688 C. See on iv. 2.—Metre: logaoedic.

XXI. Clem. Alex. *Strom.* 5. 708, Theodoret. *Graec. aff. cur.* 6. 89. 27. Cf. Frag. x.. Christ proposes κότει in v. 3.—Metre: logaoedic.

XXII. Plut. *de superst.* 6, *Amat.* 18, *adv. Stoic.* 31. Perhaps from a threnody. Cf. Bacch. 60 (34) οἱ μὲν ἀδμᾶτες ἀεικελιᾶν εἰσι νόσων καὶ ἄνατοι, | οὐδὲν ἀνθρώποις ἴκελοι, and contrast Sim. xii.—**τ'**: misplaced as Soph. *Aias* 654 πρός τε λουτρὰ καὶ παρακτίους.—Metre: logaoedic.

XXIII. Athen. 5. 191 F.—**1.** **τί**: Bergk conj. ὅ τι. A comma is generally placed after εἴην. Note that only in indirect questions is τίς used for ὅστις in classical Greek (εἰπὲ τί σοι φίλον); cf. Soph. *O. T.* 71 ὡς πύθοιθ' ὅ τι | δρῶν ἢ τί φωνῶν τήνδε ῥυσαίμην (=subj. in *or. rec.*) πόλιν. αἰτοῦ τί χρῄζεις ἐν Eur. Frag. 773. 2 is corrupt.—**2.** For the emphatic vocative after the pers. pron. cf. *Pyth.* 4. 89, 11. 62. **δέ** after τε, *Pyth.* 4. 80, 11. 29, Hdt. 9. 57, Soph. *Antig.* 1096, *Trach.* 334. When antithesis is substituted for parallelism, it is usually more pronounced. Cf. Alkm. xxx.—**3.** **Εὐθυμίᾳ**: only here in poetry and classical Greek. **μέλων**: usually μέλημα: *Pyth.* 10. 59, Frag. 95. With εἴην it forms the 'Chalkidian figure,' as λέγων ἐστί Eur. *Hek.* 1179, ἦτε πάσχοντες *Kykl* 381. So ταῦτα ἦν γινόμενα Hdt. 1. 146 is more vivid than ταῦτα ἐγίνετο. **εἴην**: potential optative (protasis ἔρδων): Goodwin *M. T.* 240, Hale *Trans. Am. Phil. Assoc.* 24. 197. Gildersleeve explains *Ol.* 3. 45, *Pyth.* 10. 21 as = imper., and prefers διαλλάξαντο *Ol.* 11. 21. After μέλων, ἄν might have dropped out (Christ). —**4.** **αἴτημι**: cf. Sim. ii. 14.—Metre: logaoedic.

XXIV. Dion. Hal. *de orat. antiq.* 2. Cf. Soph. *O. T.* 614 χρόνος δίκαιον ἄνδρα δείκνυσιν μόνος. Solon 36. 1 has ἐν δίκῃ χρόνου.—Metre: dact.-epitrite.

XXV. Plato *Gorgias* 484B etc., ἐπεί (l. 5) . . . schol. Aristeid. 3. 408 (in paraphrase); often referred to by other writers.— **1.** Boeckh thought that κατὰ φύσιν (in Plato) preceded νόμος. Cf. Hdt. 3. 38 καὶ ὀρθῶς μοι δοκεῖ Πίνδ. ποιῆσαι νόμον πάντων βασιλέα φήσας εἶναι, Eur. *Hek.* 799 ἀλλ' οἱ θεοὶ σθένουσι χὠ κείνων κρατῶν | νόμος, Herakleit. 91, Lysias 2. 19, Plato *Laws* 690 B, 714 D, *Protag.* 337 D.—**3.** **ἄγει . . . χειρί**: 'uses the hand of might, justifying its greatest act of violence.' *Fatalis lex etiam vim maximam affert, eamque iustam effecit, quum humana ratione sit iniusta: quia quod summa lex imperavit, etsi iniustum nobis esse videatur, iustum sit necesse est* (Boeckh). Milton *Tetrachordon* says "Men of the most renowned virtue have sometimes by transgressing most truly kept the law." In this passage of Pind. law takes the place of omnipotent fate.—**5.** Cf. on Stes. i.—**7.** Contrast δωρητόν, οὐκ αἰτητόν Soph. *O. T.* 384.—Metre: logaoedic; v. 4 may consist of cretics.

XXVI. Aristeid. 2. 509.—**1.** **κρηπίς** is the substructure that is visible (κρ. φαεννά Frag. 77), not the underground foundation; κρ. σοφῶν ἐπέων *Pyth.* 4. 138, κρ. ἀοιδᾶν 7. 3; cf. *Ol.* 6. 1, *Nem.* 1. 8.—**2. τειχίζωμεν**: *Pyth.* 6. 7 ff. ὕμνων θησαυρὸς τετείχισται, cf. "build the lofty rhyme."—**3.** κόσμον ἀδυμελῆ *Ol.* 11. 14, κόσμον ἀοιδῆς Plato *Phileb.* 66 C; **αὐδάεντα** = αὐδαέντων λόγων, 'let us build a fair wall of manifold sounding song.' See Bacch. viii. 8.—**4. Θήβαν**: the city as *Pyth.* 4. 299; usually the nymph is meant, as in i. 3. **ἐπασκήσει**: ρ 266 ἐπήσκηται δέ οἱ αὐλή, *Nem.* 9. 10 ἐπασκήσω ἥρωα τιμαῖς. I see neither in this word nor in αὐδάεντα any trace of the dialect of the mysteries (Bury on *Nem.* 9. 10). **θεῶν**: *per deorum et hominum vias*; gen. after ἀγυιάς, which is postponed to the second part of the clause. Cf. on ii. 3, viii. 3.—Metre: dact.-epitrite.

XXVII. Plut. *vita Lyc.* 21. Cf. Terp. vi. Aglaia presides over choruses with the other Graces *Ol.* 14. 13; cf. *Nem.* 1. 13. For the thought cf. *Ol.* 13. 50 ff. (Gild.). It is noteworthy that none of Pindar's triumphal odes is addressed to a Spartan.—Metre: dact.-epitrite. μέν or καί after ἔνθα would complete the first epitrite.

XXVIII. Stob. *Flor.* 11. 3, etc. **σύνθεσιν**: 'word,' 'bond,' as *Pyth.* 4. 168; cf. 11. 41. ἐπέων θέσιν *Ol.* 3. 8 scarcely supports Christ who supplies ἐπέων. This use of συνθ. is late. Cf. *Ol.* 10. 3 ff. ὦ Μοῖσ', ἀλλὰ σὺ καὶ θυγάτηρ | Ἀλάθεια Διὸς . . . | ἐρύκετον ψευδέων | ἐνιπάν. Pind. and Bacch. (?) are the only classical poets to personify truth. **ποτί**: *cum dat.* is very rare in Pind. For the pregnant use, cf. ε 415, *Pyth.* 9. 118. Other cases of πρός (ποτί) *Pyth.* 1. 86, 4. 24. Falsehood is regarded as a stone. Cf. Aisch. *Prom.* 926 πταίσας δὲ τῷδε πρὸς κακῷ. Pind. is the only early writer who uses πταίω as a transitive verb.—Metre: dact.-epitrite.

XXIX. Plato *Rep.* 1. 331 A.—**2. ἀτάλλοισα**: cf. Hom. epigr. 4. 2 νήπιον αἰδοίης ἐπὶ γούνασι μητρὸς ἀτάλλων. Hom. uses ἀτιτάλλω 'cherish': Jebb on Soph. *Aias* 558 (νέαν ψυχὴν ἀτάλλων). **συναορεῖ**: cf. *Nem.* 4. 5 εὐλογία φόρμιγγι συνάορος.—**4.** Cf. θυμὸν ᾠακοστρόφουν Aisch. *Pers.* 767.—Metre: logaoedic or log.-paionic. Perhaps the frag. is from a paian (Christ).

XXX. Athen. 11. 782 D. A comparison with Bacch. xvii. shows that Pind. excels in elevation and in the imaginative quality, Bacch. in the elaboration of his pictures.—**4. φρένας**: with δαμέντες as *Ol.* 1. 41 though Bacch. 1. 24 has (πλοῦτος) ἐθέλει δ' αὔξειν φρένας ἀνδρός. **τόξοις**: cf. Βακχίου τοξεύματα Eur. Frag. 562 φιάλη ἀσπὶς Διονύσου Arist. *Poet.* 1457 B 22, *percussit* in Plaut. *Cas.* 3. 5. 15, *icto capiti* 'winestruck' Hor. *Sat.* 2. 1. 24, *mero saucius* Apul. *Metam.* 11. 601.

In Frag. 166 Pind. has ἀνδροδάμαντα ῥιπὰν μελιαδέος οἴνου.—Metre: dact.-epitrite.

XXXI. Sext. Emp. *Pyrrh. hyp.* 1. 86. Cf. Archil. 36 ἀλλ' ἄλλος ἄλλῳ καρδίην ἰαίνεται, Solon 13. 43 ff. σπεύδει δ' ἄλλοθεν ἄλλος κ.τ.λ., Hor. 1. 1.—**3.** δ' αὖ τις conj. Boeckh, ἔπι (*i.e.* ἐπιτερπ.) φρασὶν οἶδμ' ἐνάλιον conj. Bergk.—Metre: dact.-epitrite.

XXXII. Schol. *Pyth.* 4. 408, cf. Prokl. on Hes. *W. D.* 428. **χρυσός**: cf. *Ol.* 1. 1, κτεάνων δὲ χρυσὸς αἰδοιέστατον *Ol.* 3. 42, μεγασθενὴς χρ. *Isthm.* 5. 3. Theogn. 451 τοῦ (χρυσοῦ) χροιῆς καθύπερθε μέλας οὐχ ἅπτεται ἰὸς | οὐδ' εὐρώς, αἰεὶ δ' ἄνθος ἔχει καθαρόν, Pythermos.—Metre: dact.-epitrite.

BACCHYLIDES.

Last in the Alexandrian canon of the lyric poets stands the name of Bacchylides of Keos, the last of the poets of the universal melic. In the almost total wreck of the melic poetry of Simonides, the greatest of the Ionians, his nephew Bacchylides becomes the chief representative of the choral song of a race, the poetical genius of which in the Posthomeric age was devoted to the cultivation of satirical and elegiac verse. In the early period choral lyric flourished better under the *régime* of the Dorians than in the Ionian democracies: it was written for aristocrats and aristocracies. Not until the agonistic festivals opened a new field of activity did the Ionians of the East undertake the composition of choral odes. Simonides was the first of the choral poets of genuine Ionic stock, and like Simonides, Bacchylides displays the humane qualities of his race, its love of pathos, its grace and polish, and its lack of intensity. He is too the only choral poet by whom we are able to estimate the racial characteristics of his older contemporary Pindar, who embodies the Dorian conception of life and art.

The Graces preside over both poetry and the great games, in which the beauty of physical and mental attainment found its fairest expression. Bacchylides might well have said Ἐγώ φαμι ἰοπλοκάμων Μοισᾶν εὖ λαχεῖν. From his mother, who was the sister of Simonides, he may have inherited the gift of song. His grandfather, whose name he bore, was a distinguished athlete. His own name is derived from Βακχύλος, Βάκχος. His father's name is handed down in various forms: Medon (Meidon?), Meilon, and Meidylos. Of the life of the poet almost nothing is known. He was born in all probability in the last decennium of the sixth century. Simonides may have instructed him in the training of choruses and introduced him to the favour of Hieron. He is reported to have been exiled from Keos—perhaps on account of the oligarchical tendencies imbibed during his residence at the Syracusan court—and to have lived in the Peloponnese; but his works afford no sure evidence of his sojourn there. Probably his banishment took place between 468 and 459. Though his countrymen fought at Salamis on the side of the Greeks he makes no allusion to their struggle for freedom, nor does he refer at all to the Persian wars, which inspired the immortal elegies of his uncle and tried the soul of Pindar. The choral poets who wrote for all the Greeks have the gift of reticence; it was better taste, and better art, for the poet of the national games to draw on the legendary past than to allude to the events of contemporaneous history. Bacchylides gives exceedingly few hints as to the date of his poems, but he seems to have reached the acme of his fame in 468 (the year of Simonides' death), when he is known to have celebrated the most splendid of Hieron's victories at Olympia. The date of his death is unknown, but he may have lived till 431. Like Simonides and Pindar he wrote for pay and numbered among his patrons the most distinguished of the princes, aristocrats, and states of Greece.

With a single exception Bacchylides cultivated all the species of choral song. The omission of dirges under his name may indeed be accidental, but it is significant that his townsmen of Iulis restricted the performance of funeral rites (Aristotle Frag. p. 377 Rose, *I. G. A.* 395) and that the dirges of Simonides are all in memory of persons who were not natives of Keos. His 'kletic' and 'apopemptic' hymns to invoke the presence and salute the departure of the gods were regarded as the standard of their class by the rhetorician Menander (*Rhet. Graec.* 5. 336). His erotic songs and paroinia, or more properly skolia, were, I venture to believe, more akin to the nature of the man and better adapted to display the virtues of his style than the more elaborate triumphal odes that have recently come to light. The hazardousness of fame is better illustrated only in the case of Herodas and Catullus. The chance preservation of a single MS. has given reality to a poet who was before only a shadow.

The discovery in Egypt of a papyrus dating from the first century B.C. or slightly later, has added to the fragments, less than fifty in number, that were heretofore known by their citation in ancient writers, no less than fourteen triumphal odes and six other lyrics. Most of these poems are in a fragmentary condition and the alphabetical arrangement of the non-epinikian lyrics shows that we have only a selection from the *editio princeps* of the Alexandrians. The papyrus, consisting of about two hundred mutilated fragments, has been edited with masterly skill by Dr. F. G. Kenyon.

The subjects of the non-epinikian lyrics are as follows: Antenoridai, or the Demand for the Surrender of Helen, Herakles, The Youths and Theseus, Theseus, Io, and Idas. The essential feature of all these lyrics is that they contain a myth and nothing else. As in the modern ballad they present only episodes of the tale, some worked out in detail, others compressed to the briefest compass. To these poems the only general name that is applicable is 'dithyrambs,' at least in the terminology of the Alexandrians who edited the poems of Bacchylides. Now we know from Aristotle (*Probl.* 19. 5) that in the earliest period the dithyramb was antistrophic, but in the fifth century lost the responsive arrangement and became purely mimetic. The interesting question therefore arises whether these poems of Bacchylides, which are at once antistrophic and mimetic, do not form the intermediate stage between the primitive dithyramb, which is usually associated with the mythical name of Arion, and the mimetic, but non-antistrophic, dithyramb of the fifth century. If this is correct, we may conclude that in Bacchylides we have the early form of the operatic dithyramb that held Athens captive in the time of Timotheos. To some of the poems in question special names, such as paian (ix.), hymenaios (20), etc. may indeed be given; but Aristotle, who is our chief authority for the early history of the dithyramb, and in whose time the dithyramb was, together with the nome, the only representative of the melic poetry of the preceeding centuries, was content to ignore these distinctive names. Some are undoubtedly dithyrambs, and one (No. x.) appears to represent, in form at least, the early type of this class of melic.

Of the triumphal odes at least four are addressed to Keians, three to Hieron, and two to Aiginetans. The epinikia celebrate four Olympian, four Nemean, two Pythian and two Isthmian victories; while one is in honour of a local Thessalian contest.

These odes show the same three conventional elements as the epinikia of Pindar. In the personal or enkomiastic portion, following the example of Simonides, Bacchylides displays a closer engagement than Pindar with the circumstances of the victory and the scene of triumph. If we gain on the side of personal sympathy, we miss on the other hand that tone of noble familiarity with which Pindar addresses the great.

Early in its history choral melic gave a lyric setting to the saga. The myth, occupying the central portion of the longer odes, to which it is indeed almost indispensable, is properly designed to set before us heroic incarnations of good and evil, and to give plastic embodiment to a moral idea either illustrative of the life of the victor or of his ancestors, or connected with the cult of the victor's home. Bacchylides rarely attains this ideal. He does not penetrate beneath the surface, his myths fail to rise spontaneously from the theme, and, especially in the longer poems, do not form integral parts of the whole. They remain distinct units, beautiful indeed, but introduced solely because they were conventional in the economy of the epinikion, herein recalling the ἐμβόλιμα of later tragedy. Our failure to apprehend any essential unity of design almost persuades us that, in the words of Agathon, Art and Chance were knit by a common bond:

τέχνη τύχην ἔστερξε καὶ τύχη τέχνην.

Though the myths are in part new to us, Bacchylides was not an innovator. In the main he holds fast to the traditional sagas and modifies them only under the influence of his immediate predecessors or contemporaries. Hence it comes that they are represented in the art of the fifth century, which neglected the revolutionary changes effected by Pindar. When the plastic artist and Bacchylides agree, we may conclude either that the former preceded in point of time or that both drew from a common source. The mythographers were not greatly indebted to our poet though Robert holds that he, and not Sophokles, was the source of Hyginus' account of Laokoon. Of his myths some are pathetic and romantic in tone, and most are of a sombre, even melancholy character. In the story of Kroisos he exchanges for myth history that had already passed into legend. Between the longer epinikia and the dithyrambs there is no vital difference: the myth claims the major part of the poem; and in the epinikia there is added merely an element of personal or local allusion.

Moralizing was inevitable in all choral poetry, which was directly or implicitly consecrated to religion. In his handling of the gnomic element Bacchylides does not rise above the conventional morality of the day as we find it set forth in the Sages and in Theognis. He displays reverence towards the gods, but his praise of virtue, as all his precepts, are the expression of a man who was satisfied with commonplace and did not grapple with the subtler aspects of moral problems. Still we must not forget that the ethics of the Greek Derby even in a Pindar are not the ethics of an Aischylos.

In a celebrated passage (33. 5) of the treatise On the Sublime, Longinos remarks that the best poets, Homer, Archilochos, Pindar, and Sophokles often err, whereas those of inferior merit are free from blemish and do not fall below the level of a pervasive mediocrity: τί δ'; ἐν μέλεσι μᾶλλον ἂν εἶναι Βακχυλίδης ἕλοιο ἢ Πίνδαρος; καὶ ἐν τραγῳδίᾳ Ἴων ὁ Χῖος, ἢ νὴ Δία Σοφοκλῆς; ἐπειδὴ οἱ μὲν ἀδιάπτωτοι καὶ ἐν τῷ γλαφυρῷ πάντῃ κεκαλλιγραφημένοι κ.τ.λ. The judgment of the Greek critic is correct: Bacchylides is polished and he is surprisingly free from defect: *quamvis ingenio non valet, arte valet.* If he lacks the large imagination of the poets of the first rank who see things not as other men see them, he is none the less a genuine poet because of his splendid gift for narration and picturesque effect. By nature is he calm and his work is the product of reflection. His spirit is mundane and unlike Pindar he does not soar beyond this world. He does not mould his fancy at white heat. In analysis not in synthesis lies his strength. Less effective in the massing of groups, he excels in detail and in delicate touches of colour. His pictures are often exquisite miniatures, but he over-refines especially in the use of decoration. In some respects his style is less akin to Pindar's than to that of Homer or Hesiod. By virtue of his prerogative as a lyrist he detaches the effective moments of the myth, which are thus endowed with concreteness. But on the other hand he has an objectivity that is largely epic. He does not project his personality into his theme; he has the epic amplitude and accentuation of details, such as we infer was characteristic of Stesichoros, the most Homeric of the choral poets. Epic too is the uniformity, I had almost said monotony, of many of the odes; the extent and quality of his comparisons; and his fondness for repetition, whereas Pindar is compressed in his comparisons and studious of change. To Bacchylides, as an Ionian, form meant more than content, and the virtues of his diction are grace, polish, smoothness, and crystalline perspicuity. There is too an element of tenderness and nobility in his utterances. His conceptions are plastic, he has no struggle to express his thoughts because of their indirectness or latent suggestiveness. The pleasure he produces is spontaneous because he makes no requisition upon our higher intellectual faculties and does not demand of us that we trace out an elusive central thought in the ramifications of the theme. In large measure he is deficient in the qualities of the imagination, in fire and impetuosity, and even in celebrating the victories of his countrymen he shows no warmth. In the dithyrambs, however, he rises to dramatic agitation, and throughout excels in direct speeches and in dialogue (another epic mark), in which he displays no little *ethopoiïa.* His arrangement of words is simple and the structure of his longest periods is lucid, but his transitions are abrupt and managed with much less skill than those of Pindar. His figures are vivid and clear. Simile and metaphor he employs sparingly, and the latter is confined to single words and is not "mixed."

Bacchylides is not a creative artist in the sphere either of myth, or of metre, or of dialect. Such originality as he possessed found expression in the sphere of vocabulary. Like the Italian painters after Raphael who substituted ornament for creative power, Bacchylides endeavours to hide the poverty of his imagination by his skill in embellishment. His faculty of invention has enriched the lexicon by more than a hundred words, ninety of which are sonorous ornamental epithets that come fresh from the inexhaustible mint of his plastic native speech. How many of these words were used before and formed a part of the common lyric stock, how many are the poet's own coinage, we cannot say; but it is certain that Bacchylides was extraordinarily fond of neologism. He has in fact about as many once-used words as occur in all Pindar. He loves slight transformations of accredited words and variations from the Pindaric form. Thus he has κεραυνεγχής, νεόκτιτος, τανύθριξ, βαρύβρομος, ἀπενθής for Pindar's ἐγχεικεραυνός, νεόκτιστος, τανυέθειρα, βαρύκτυπος, ἀπήμων. He has compounds in χαλκο- and χαλκεο- while Pindar uses only χαλκο-. Most of the new compound adjectives, which are relatively more frequent in the dithyrambs than in the epinikia, are simple in structure and begin with a verbal theme, and are less bold than Pindar's compounds. Some indeed are frigid, others are devitalized by sheer lack of air (cf. v. 37), and many display a lack of relevancy; but some are of great beauty (κυανανθὴς θάλασσα). Blass well applies to him Aristotle's remark on Alkidamas (*Rhet.* 3. 3) οὐ γὰρ ἡδύσματι χρῆται ἀλλ' ὡς ἐδέσματι τοῖς ἐπιθέτοις. Bacchylides' *epitheta ornantia* are rich in colour and magnificence but they destroy energy and movement.

The style of Bacchylides is in some respects analogous to that of Simonides, and especially in the elaboration of the gnomic element. The author of the famous comparison between poetry and painting (Sim. viii. n.) may have inspired his nephew to institute a comparison much admired by the Emperor Julian and reported by Ammian. Marcell. 25. 4: *ut egregius pictor vultum speciosum effingit, ita pudicitia celsius consurgentem vitam exornat.*

The comparison of our poet with Pindar, already touched upon, is inevitable, if for no other reason than that the two poets are our sole guides to the study of the Greek triumphal ode. Bacchylides has indeed his individual merits and these are of a high order, but he belongs in a different class from the Theban lyrist. Bacchylides is brilliant, Pindar is sublime.

To Pindar's example the younger poet owed much, but Pindar in turn was, I believe, influenced by Bacchylides. Parallelism in thought and expression was, it is true, unavoidable in conventionalized epinikian poetry; but apart from this, the varied character of their several vocabularies shows a conscious desire to avoid similarity of expression, and each poet frequently endeavours to outdo his rival in developing the same thought. Emulation is however not hostility and the new poems give no warrant to the story of Pindar's enmity to Bacchylides, as well as to Simonides, because of their attacks upon him. By nature Bacchylides seems to have been of a mild and kindly disposition, equable in temperament, and hostile to polemics, though in Frag. xiv. he is possibly defending himself against Pindar. Of the various passages (*Ol.* 2. 86, 9. 28. 100, *Pyth.* 2. 53, *Nem.* 3. 40. 82, 4. 39, *Isthm.* 2. 6) which the scholiasts explain as attacks on Simonides and Bacchylides, the first is the best support for their view:

> σοφὸς ὁ πολλὰ Ϝειδὼς φυᾷ· μαθόντες δὲ λάβροι
> παγγλωσίᾳ, κόρακες ὥς, ἄκραντα γαρύετον
> Διὸς πρὸς ὄρνιχα θεῖον.

While it cannot be denied that these lines admit of different interpretations and that the ancients had no definite tradition to countenance their statements, the analogies of ancient literature and the conditions of the melic art at court make it highly probable that the antagonism of the Dorian and Ionian found expression in the chief lyric poets of the time. Two Italian scholars, Rambaldi and Michelangeli, have recently discussed the question at length and arrived at different results (the latter is forced to emend the dual γαρύετον). Whatever view we may take of the passage, it is not to be gainsaid that Bacchylides is in fact one of the μαθόντες, one of those who succeed not by φυή but by τέχνη.

> ἐκ μελέτης πλείους ἢ φύσεως ἀγαθοί.

Nor is it easy to acquit him of a certain species of παγγλωσία.

If Bacchylides possesses a certain geniality, he is still the most pessimistic of the Greek lyrists. The sorrows of life, the loss of youth, the dread of the unknown future, the irrevocableness of death, man's powerlessness in the face of fate, are themes that the poet loves to linger over. Many of his subjects are sombre—Meleager's early doom, the death of Herakles, Niobe, Adrastos, the madness of the daughters of Proitos, Laokoon. Some of his lugubriousness is no doubt mere literary veneer. Though the early choral poets had been untouched by the sorrows of reflection, the elegiac note was now dominant: *quid opus est partes deflere? tota flebilis vita est.* The melic of Simonides had already surrendered itself to the pessimism of the Ionian elegy, and Bacchylides followed his example. No doubt the Greek loved the *memento mori* amid the revelry of the triumph; but Pindar triumphs over the pain of the world because in his creed the soul is to be purged of its evil in the life beyond the grave.

Most of the epinikia and dithyrambs show the grouping in triads and this external division corresponds at times, though less frequently than in Pindar, to the internal divisions of the theme. In his use of metre (chiefly dactylo-epitrites, logaoedics, and cretics) Bacchylides stands nearer to Pindar than to Simonides. The free responsion between several of the systems is a feature of great significance and points either to an extensive use of the principle of prolongation (τονή) or to corrupt transmission. As with the MSS. and the editions of Pindar before Boeckh, the papyrus gives, not the verses or rhythmical periods, but the cola or rhythmical πόδες according to Aristoxenos' terminology, as they were marked off by some Alexandrian scholar whose ultimate source of information was a text written throughout as continuous prose. The arrangement of the cola in the papyrus is sometimes erroneous, but is generally correct with regard to two of the marks of a verse: hiatus and τελεία λέξις. In the present stage of the investigation of the newly discovered poems the delimitation of the verses would be premature; and for practical reasons I have adhered to the colometry of the papyrus, marking off, with Blass, those cola that are shown by synaphea, etc. to be dependent.

The dialect is essentially the same as that of Simonides and Pindar: the common lyric idiom, consisting of a fusion of Ionic and epic forms with Doric and Aiolic ᾱ's, and some specifically Doric and Aiolic touches. The papyrus has a tendency to reject ᾱ when a syllable with ᾱ follows immediately, as in ἀδμῆτα (as contrasted with ἄδματοι; exceptions are μαχανά, Ἀθάνα, σελάνα, ἀπράκταν) which is a hybrid form; and after ζ in ζῆλος, Τροζηνία. Ionic η is also retained in Ἀλκμήνιος, ἐπισκήπτων, παρηΐδων, ἠλύκταζον, where the character of the metre does not determine the choice of the vowel. Specific Doricisms are -οντι, which occurs only after sibilants, the aorist in -ξ-, the infin. in -εν, τΐν, ὄρνιχες. Aiolisms are rare: ἄμμι, ἔμμεν and ἔμμεναι, κλεεννός, Μοῖσα (?). Bacch. rejects several of Pindar's peculiarities *e.g.* Dor. -τι for -σι in 3rd sing., Aiol. -οισι in the 3rd pl., the Dor. accus. -ᾰς, -ŏς of ᾱ and ο stems, ἐν *cum accus.* The vocabulary, especially in the myths, shows many epic words.

The fame of Bacchylides was obscured by the grandeur of Pindar and the humanity of Simonides. No Attic writer mentions his name, but Euripides certainly, with whom he had much in common, and Sophokles possibly, imitated him. With the Romans he seems to have stood in higher favour, and Tibullus and Horace testify that his reputation was still alive in the period of the Civil Wars and in the Augustan age. Horace shares with him his love of peace and his geniality; and in fact often recalls him even when there is no proof of direct imitation. With much less justice is Bacchylides the 'nightingale of Keos' (i. 98) than the 'clear-voiced island bee' (νασιῶτις λιγύφθογγος μέλισσα 10. 10), a comparison which suggests Horace's *ego apis Matinae more modoque grata carpentis thyma* etc. The sweetness of his style earned for him the epithet λάλος Σειρήν (*Anth. Pal.* 9. 184). We have already remarked upon his popularity with the Emperor Julian. There are no scholia, but in the first century B.C. Didymos wrote a commentary on his works in which he collected the notes of earlier scholars.—Fragments i.-x. are taken from the Egyptian papyrus.

I. An Olympian ode in honour of Hieron, tyrant of Syracuse (478-467), who participated with Gelon and Theron in the battle of Himera (480), founded Aitna (476), and conquered the Etruscans at Kymai (474). He was the chief patron of literature of his time. The probable dates of his Olympian and Pythian victories and the extant poems in their commemoration are as follows:

482	(Pyth. 26)	with the running-horse Pherenikos (Pind. *Pyth.* 3?).
478	(Pyth. 27)	with Pherenikos (Pind. *Pyth.* 3).
476	(Ol. 76)	with Pherenikos (*Ol.* 1 (?), Bacch. ii.).
470	(Pyth. 29)	with the chariot (*Pyth.* 1, Bacch. 4).
468	(Ol. 78)	with the chariot (Bacch. i.).

This ode commemorates the victory at Olympia won in 468 and foreshadowed by Pind. *Ol.* 1. 109: ἔτι γλυκυτέραν κεν ἔλπομαι | σὺν ἅρματι θοῷ κλεΐξειν. It is worthy of note that, on the occasion of Hieron's last and most famous victory, Bacchylides should have been preferred to Pindar. This ode is the latest in the collection to which a date can be assigned. It was sung at Syracuse.

It is unaccountable that Hieron should, as Kenyon maintains, have consecrated the tripods of l. 18 to the god of Delphi as a thank-offering for an Olympian victory; and we know that after Hieron's death in 467, his son Deinomenes, who was named for his grandfather (l. 7), set up at Olympia a memorial of this contest. Either the tripods were dedicated in consequence of the Pythian victory of 470 (Bacch. ode 4) or they are those sent to Delphi by Hieron and his brothers. The excavations there of the French School have brought to light the bases of four tripods (see *B. C. H.* 18. 179, 21. 589), at least one of which was offered by Hieron either after Himera or after Kymai (Athen. 6. 231 F, Diodor. 11. 26). In Sim. 141 we read, with the scholiast, παῖδας Δεινομένευς τοὺς τρίποδας θέμεναι, instead of τὸν τριποδ᾽ ἀνθέμεναι. This offering was famous and likely to call forth the praise of the poet.

There are seven triads. The first deals with the victor, str. and antistr. β′ picture the radiance of the Delphic festival. With epod. β′ the poet begins the tale of the self-immolation of Kroisos, which breaks off in antistr. ε′. The concluding parts recur to Hieron, whose impending death points the moral that glorious achievement is free from decay only when hymned by the Muse. The ode is unique from the fact that the myth does not deal with the figure of a hero hallowed by the traditional faith, but with an event in the life of an historical personage whom the fathers of men then living might have known. Phrynichos and Aischylos went a step farther than Bacchylides in dramatising contemporary history outright. Kroisos first appears in poetry on the occasion of his incidental mention as a type of generosity (φιλόφρων ἀρετά) by Pind. *Pyth.* 1. 94 (470 B.C.). In point of time Bacch. is nearer to the Lydian king than is Herodotos (1. 86) and his account is probably nearer the truth. Sardis fell in 546.

New words: ἀριστόκαρπος 'of teeming fertility,' εὐρυδίνης, μελαμφαρής 'shrouded in black,' Ὀλυμπιόδρομος (Pind. -νίκας and -νικος), πλείσταρχος 'of sovereign rule,' ὑψιδαίδαλτος 'deep-chased,' χαλκοτειχής.

Tautometric responsions: Ἱέρων 4 = 64 = 92; χρυσός 17 = 87; slighter cases 1 = 71, 5 = 75, 5 = 33, 6 = 44, 7 = 35, 18 = 46, 19 = 29, 21 = 59.

Metre: logaoedics of simple structure though resolutions and irrational syllables abound. Only in this ode is the thesis resolved. The epode shows — ⏑ ⏑ only in v. 1. Possibly the epode is dactylo-epitritic, which is combined with logaoedics in Pind. *Ol.* 13. In the strophes vv. 2, 3, in the epodes vv. 2, 3, 6 are alike. In v. 80 the second foot is — ⏑, elsewhere — > in the same place. In v. 90 we have — ⏑ ⏑ ∟ for — ⏑ — ⏓. The strophes consist of three periods: v. 4 belongs with v. 3 with overflow as in the Sapphic stanza. In the epode we have three periods of two verses each.

1. ἀριστοκάρπου: cf. ἀγλαοκάρπου Σικελίας Pind. ix. 5, ἀριστεύοισαν εὐκάρπου χθονὸς Σικελίαν πίειραν (Zeus' bridal gift to Persephone) *Nem.* 1. 14, εὐκάρποιο γαίας *Pyth.* 1. 30, πολυμάλῳ Σικ. *Ol.* 1. 12. Sicily was famous for the abundance of its corn and wheat: Cicero says the yield was eight to ten fold, which is probably under the truth according to Holm. **κρέουσαν**: fem. to the post-epic κρέων. Hom. has κρείων, κρείουσα with the first syllable always in the arsis. From *κρεσιων; cf. Old Norse *herser*, officer of a district. κρείων has become a title of honour.—**2. ἰοστέφανον**: with *hiatus licitus*; Ϝ is disregarded in ii. 3, vi. 19, but shows its influence in 9. 72, ix. 37. **κούραν**: though some write Κόρης in Archil. 120, the proper name is not attested in poetry before Euripides. See on Skol. ii. 3. The absence of the article here is indecisive. Persephone is βασιλὶς Καταναίων *Inscr. Sic.* 450.—**3. Κλεϊοῖ** *i.e.* Κλεγοῖ. Pind. has Κλεοῦς *Nem.* 3. 83. Not till Hellenistic times did Kleio become the Muse of heroic poetry; Urania is mentioned in ii. 13. **θοάς**: mares were generally used as race-horses. But in *Il.* Ψ the horses win two out of three races. Cf. Pind. i. 8. —**4. Ἱέρωνος**: the choral poets use this form though the prince, as a Dorian, called himself Ἱάρων (Hicks *Hist. Inscr.* 15). H. is addressed as ζαθέων ἱερῶν ὁμώνυμε πάτερ Pind. Frag. 105. **ἵππους**: the main theme. The introduction is only formal, though Hieron was priest of Demeter and Persephone (Hdt. 7. 153).

5. σεύοντο: cf. Pind. *Ol.* 1. 20 παρ' Ἀλφεῷ σύτο of Pherenikos. Bacch. rarely uses παρά *cum dat.* of place. **σὺν Νίκᾳ**:

not a Pindaric phrase. The steeds dash on attended by Victory and Glory.—**6**. **Ἀγλαΐᾳ**: the refulgent splendour of success.—**7**. **ἔθηκαν**: followed by inf. as Pind. *Pyth.* 9. 7, Frag. 177. The factitive constr. is preferred in choral melic. —**8**. **ὄλβιον**: perhaps proleptic, 'to his prosperity.'

9. Cf. δῆμος ἀπείρων Ω 776.—**12**. **πλείσταρχον**: Hieron was the most powerful prince of his time (Pind. *Ol.* 1. 104 says that no one was δύναμιν κυριώτερος). When Greece was menaced by Xerxes, Hieron's brother and predecessor Gelon offered to supply provisions for the entire Greek army and to provide a numerous land and naval force. K. cites Hdt. 7. 157 μοῖρά τοι (Gelon) τῆς Ἑλλάδος οὐκ ἐλαχίστη μέτα ἄρχοντί γε Σικελίης. πλ. Ἑλλάνων γέρας = γέρας τοῦ πλείστων Ἑλλάνων ἄρχειν. Not only did Hieron enjoy a kingly station (γέρας), the gift of God; he was also an all-powerful prince.—**13**. Cf. Pind. *Nem.* 1. 31 οὐκ ἔραμαι πολὺν ἐν μεγάρῳ πλοῦτον κατακρύψας ἔχειν, *Pyth.* 1. 90 μὴ κάμνε λίαν δαπάναις (addressed to H.), *Isthm.* 1. 67 πλοῦτον κρυφαῖον. **πυργωθέντα** suggests abundance and solidity (Solon 13. 9 of πλοῦτος: ἔμπεδος ἐκ νεάτου πυθμένος εἰς κορυφήν). **μελαμφαρέϊ**: darkness wears a sable shroud. Cf. μελαγχίτων of the troubled mind, Aisch. *Pers.* 114. Note the two metaphors. Bacch. is fond of the thought expressed by κρύπτειν σκότῳ; cf. vi. 54, δνοφερόν τε κάλυμμα τῶν ὕστερον ἐρχομένων 16. 32; Pind. *Ol.* 2. 97.

15. ff. A description of Delphi introductory to the mention of Kroisos, whose munificence had enriched the shrine of Apollo. The style recalls the paian on Peace (Frag. xiii.).—**16**. **βρύουσι**: *cum gen.* after βρύει *cum dat.* Like variation between the instr. dat. and the gen. of fullness occurs in the case of πλήθω, πληρόω, πλήρης, βρίθω (see on xiii. 12). With rhetorical iteration (epanaphora) we have either μέν—δέ, μέν without δέ as here, *Orphic Hymn* 8. 4 δεξιὲ μὲν . . . εὐώνυμε, 22. 7 μῆτερ μὲν Κύπριδος, μῆτερ νεφέων (cited by Platt), δέ without μέν Thuk. 7. 1, or neither μέν nor δέ, as Aisch. *Sept.* 901 (contrast 911). The slight shift from plur. to sing. in the epanaphora here is attended by the shift in the constr. of βρύω. Richards would read φιλοξενίαις; which is Pindar's manner (*Ol.* 4. 17). (Bacch. does not love the antithetical μέν . . . δέ.) **φιλοξενίας**: hospitality is enjoined upon priests in Plato *Laws* 953 A.—**17**. **ὑπὸ μαρμαρυγαῖς**: 'with its flashing radiance.' Cf. ὑπὸ βαρβίτῳ χορεύειν, ὑπ' αὐλητῆρι ἰέναι, ὑπὸ σκότῳ, ὑπὸ δᾳδί. The gen. with ὑπό is more common; see on Anakr. x. Cf. Pind. *Nem.* 4. 82 ὁ χρυσὸς ἑψόμενος αὐγὰς ἔδειξεν ἁπάσας. **ὁ**: deictic, so l. 87, Pind. *Ol.* 1. 1. **χρυσός**: scarcely solid or pure. The weight of the four tripods dedicated by the sons of Deinomenes was nearly 51, or, according to another account, 55 talents. Kroisos (Hdt. 1. 51, 92) had dedicated a krater, a basin, a shield, and a statue of gold. A silver krater offered by him, was, after the conflagration in 548, placed in the corner of the *προνήϊον* (cf. *πάροιθε ναοῦ* l. 19). A Delphic inscription (*B. C. H.* 21. 478, l. 23) shows that this object was in process of being replaced in 338 after its destruction by the Phokians. Since the time of Kroisos gold had not been consecrated at Delphi until the offering made by Hieron.—**18. ὑψιδαιδάλτων**: the form is correct, though the poet has *εὐδαίδαλος* elsewhere (Hom. *πολυδαίδαλος*). **τριπό-δων**: probably gen. after *χρυσός*; otherwise the gen. abs. (see on Pind. xvi. 7).

21. θεόν, θεόν: the same repetition occurs in Diag. i.; *deus, deus* Hor. *Epod.* 14. 6.—**22.** Give the glory to God, who is the chiefest of blessings—and he will help in time of sore distress. This truth, which is the key-note of the poem, was verified in the case of Kroisos. The MS. writing *ἀγλαϊζέθω* appears to be the result of a strange crasis attended by the aspiration of the dental in *-ετω*. All other readings (*e.g.* *ἀγλαϊζέτω παρ' ἄριστον ὄλβον* 'in the hour of prime prosperity,' Housman, Richards) fail to explain the *θ* of the MS. except *ἀγλαΐζεθ', ὅ(ς)* or *ᾧ* (*παρ' ἄριστος ὄλβων* Tyrrell), which may stand if *τις* can be construed with the second person. Of this I recall no instance, though in the colloquial idiom we find *χώρει πᾶς, ἴσχε πᾶς τις,* and *ἴτω τις, εἰσάγγελλε* Eur. *Bacch.* 173; in Latin cf. *aliquis evocate* Plaut. *Men.* 4. 2. 111, *aliquis nuntiate, Pseud.* 5. 1. 37. Some read *θεὸν θέλοντες.* **ὄλβων**: the plural as Soph. Frag. 297.

23. καί: the connective often serves to introduce the myth in epinikian odes. **δαμασίππου**: see on Alkm. iv. 59. —**25. πεπρωμέναν**: cf. ix. 26; Hdt. 1. 91 *τὴν πεπρωμένην μοῖραν ἀδύνατά ἐστι ἀποφυγεῖν καὶ θεῷ,* the answer of the Pythoness to the Lydians sent by Kroisos after the fall of Sardis to expostulate with the god. Apollo delayed the capture of the city for three years in order that it might not occur in the lifetime of his servant. Hieron is of course expected to ignore the ill-omened part of the comparison.—**26. κρίσιν**: cf. A 5, Bacch. v. 6.

30. Kroisos' immolation is, according to Bacch., self-imposed, like that of Sardanapalus and Dido. In Hdt. Kyros orders his defeated enemy to be burned alive. The poet's version is probably correct since the religion of the Persians forbade the pollution of their sacred fire by contact with the dead (Hdt. 3. 16, Nikol. Dam. 68). Nikol. reports that the women of Lydia sent costly raiment to be consumed on the pyre of their king. This looks as if the late historian had preserved a trace of the story that Kroisos' act was voluntary. Ktesias (Frag. 29) on the other hand makes no mention of the pyre. **ἔμελλε** denoting purpose is followed by present or aorist. Bacch. has only the (commoner) present. He has also the future after *μέλλω* as a verb of thinking. **31. ἔτι**: the misery of slavery added to the sting of defeat.

34. τ' is doubtful. Its omission may be defended as that of *δέ* in l. 16. **ἄλαστον δυρο.**: cf. *ξ* 174.—**35. θυγατράσι**: mentioned in Xen. *Kyrop.* 7. 2. 26. On a red-figured vase in the Louvre (Baumeister Fig. 860, *J. H. S.* 18. 268) Kroisos is represented alone on the pyre in his regal splendour and not as a captive. His attendant, who bears the significant name Euthymos, is either applying torches or carries whisks for sprinkling the lustral water on the pyre. The vase dates from about the year 500 B.C.—**36. σφετέρας**: 'his'; for this use cf. Hes. *Shield* 90, Mimn. 12. 11 (conj.), [Anakr.] 116. 2, Pind. *Ol.* 13. 61, Aisch. *Agam.* 760; never in classic prose. **ἀείρας**: in Bacch. prayer is regularly accompanied by the raising of the hands: v. 100, vi. 35, viii. 9, ix. 72; in Pind. only *Ol.* 7. 65, *Isthm.* 6. 41.

39. ποῦ: is frequently used of indignation, as in Aisch. *Choeph.* 900 *ποῦ δὴ τὰ λοιπὰ Λοξίου μαντεύματα;* Eur. *Troad.* 428 *ποῦ δ' Ἀπόλλωνος λόγοι;* Aisch. Frag. 184. In Hdt. 1. 90, after Kroisos has been saved from the pyre through his invocation of the name of Solon, he proceeds to reproach the god for his ingratitude. Greek faith is based on the *do ut des* doctrine. Cf. Theogn. 743 ff.

47. Not 'their aforetime foes are now (perforce) dear to them' (the *γυναῖκες* of l. 45), or 'hateful is that which I once held dear.' *φίλα* is explained by *θανεῖν γλύκιστον.*—**48. ἁβροβάταν**: probably = 'attendant,' 'page'; so called from his dainty gait. Cf. *ἁβρὰ βαίνων* of Ganymede, Eur. *Troad.* 820; *Med.* 1164. In Clem. Alex. *Paed.* 3. 294 *τὸ ἁβροδίαιτον* is used of the gait of the "comely and delicate" courtesan. The word *ἁβροβάτης* occurs also in Aisch. *Pers.* 1072 (cf. Frag. 57 D., *ἁβρατεύς* Nauck 60) and is parodied by *ὀριβάτης* Aristoph. *Aves* 276. Kroisos himself is *Λυδὸς ποδαβρός* in the oracle in Hdt. 1. 55. —**49. δόμον**: 'structure.' Cf. Pind. *Pyth.* 3. 38 *ἀλλ' ἐπεὶ τείχει θέσαν ἐν ξυλίνῳ | σύγγονοι κούραν* (Koronis).

51. προφανής: *i.e. ὅστις φανερός ἐστι πρὸ τοῦ γενέσθαι*, a *πρόοπτος θάνατος.*—**52. φόνων**: 'kinds of death'; for *θανάτων.*—**55.** The intervention of Zeus (unless he merely represents the physical phenomenon; cf. *J. H. S.* 11. pl. 6) is surprising, since Apollo was powerful to save his servant Kroisos (Hdt. 1. 87) as he saved Aisklepios (Pind. *Pyth.* 3. 44 *καιομένα δ' αὐτῷ* (Apollo) *διέφαινε πυρά*). Or did the early legend narrate simply that a rain extinguished the fire—a fact turned to account by the pious priests of Delphi who were eager to save the credit of their god? The stories in Bacchylides and Herodotos of Kroisos' rescue look like pure romance. Still the fact remains that tradition reported the fallen king to have survived the capture of Sardis.

57. ἄπιστον: cf. Archil. 74. 5, Bacch. ix. 117, Pind. *Pyth.* 10. 50. The reference is to Kroisos' translation.—**58. τεύχει**: no need of the generic subj., though it appears in ix. 118. Pind. too has the indic. (Goodwin *M. T.* 467).—**59.** This legend of the translation of Kroisos to the Apolline paradise occurs only here but is in harmony with Greek faith from Homer on. The oracle of Apollo at Delphi had jurisdiction in canonizing the 'heroes.' Apollo himself visits the Hyperboreans on a car drawn by swans (Alk. 3), but the poet is here discreetly silent as to the mode of locomotion adopted in the translation of his servant.—**60. τανυσφύροις**: here, ii. 59 and v. 55 the papyrus has *τανι-*; and *τανίσφυρος, τανίφυλλος* occur elsewhere in MSS. The miswriting is due, not to the analogy of *καλλίσφυρος* etc., but to the desire to avoid *υ* in successive syllables. Cf. *τανυτρίχων* xiii. 4.

62. ἀγαθέαν: of Pytho, ii. 41, Pind. *Pyth.* 9. 71.—**63. γε μέν**: without *δέ*; cf. B 703, Hdt. 7. 152.—**64. Ἱέρων**: the hiatus may be permissible though the word has no *F*, but *ἀνθεμόεντι Ἕβρῳ* 16. 5 is not parallel. Wilam. inserts *ὦ*.—**76.** The god addressed the following advice to his mortal master whom he was forced to serve as a penalty for slaying the Python.—**78. διδύμους**: two endings as in Pind. **ἀέξειν** 'nurse'; the subject is *σέ* (Admetos).

80. Cf. Hor. *Epist.* 1. 4. 13 *omnem crede diem tibi diluxisse supremum*.—**81. πεντήκοντα**: not a reference to Hieron's age in 468, but a round number. The meaning of the passage is: 'Live as if thy life ended with to-morrow's sun, and as if thou hadst a full span of life still before thee.' Narrower in range are [Isokr.] *Demon.* 9 *ἀπέλαυε μὲν τῶν παρόντων ἀγαθῶν ὡς θνητός, ἐπεμελεῖτο δὲ τῶν ὑπαρχόντων ὡς ἀθάνατος*, *Anth. Pal.* 10. 26 *ὡς τεθνηξόμενος τῶν σῶν ἀγαθῶν ἀπόλαυε, | ὡς δὲ βιωσόμενος φείδεο σῶν κτεάνων*, Kaibel 303 *καὶ βιότῳ χρῆσαι μήθ' ὡς ἰς αἰῶνας ἔχων ζῆν, | μήθ' ὡς ὠκύμορος*. Cf. Herder: *Mensch, geniesse dein Leben, als müssest morgen du weggehen; | Schone dein Leben, als ob ewig du weiletest hier*, quoted by Rubensohn *Berl.*

Phil. Woch. 1898, p. 1499.—**82. βαθύπλουτον**: *βαθυ-* is superlative as in Pindar's *βαθύδοξος* 'very celebrated,' *βαθυπόλεμος* 'most warlike.'

85. φρονέοντι *κ.τ.λ.*: the phrase is an imitation of Pindar's *φωνάεντα συνετοῖσιν* *Ol.* 2. 85 (written in 476 B.C.) and emphasizes the teaching of the poet that the eternal elements can suffer no permanent corruption, while mortal man cannot regain lost youth: only the virtue of successful achievement, when aided by the Muse, confers immortality. This consolation is offered to a dying prince (cf. *Pyth.* 1. 85). **βαθύς**: of *αἰθήρ* ii. 16; *αἰπύς* above l. 36. Cf. Lat. *altum.*—**86.** The sea is incorruptible, though it *κλύζει πάντα τἀνθρώπων κακά* Eur. *I. T.* 1193.—**87.** The effectiveness of the climax, in which the poet imitates Pind. *Ol.* 1. 1 (cf. *Ol.* 3. 42), is checked by the intrusion of the sentiment 'gold rejoices the heart of man' (*εὐφροσύνα* = *εὐφρόσυνον*). Bacch. has less in mind the incorruptible lustre of the metal (Pind. xxxii.) than its rivalry with *ἀρετά* and the fading of its charms with the advent of old age. So Pindar packs his *finales* with pregnant wit.—**88. οὐ θέμις**: *θ.* is here applied to that which contravenes the laws of nature. **παρέντα**: Jebb cites Soph. *O. K.* 1229, Plato *Rep.* 460 E. Some read *προέντα.*

90. ἀρετᾶς: 'achievement,' especially of athletic success, which demands moral effort. Cf. Pind. *Ol.* 7. 89 *ἄνδρα πὺξ ἀρετὰν εὑρόντα.* **μινύθει**: the metrical responsion is free as in Alkm. iv. (—⏑⏑ —⋀ for —⏑ —⏓). Housman suggests *μινυνθεῖ*, which is reported by Hesych. (cf. *μίνυνθα*), others *μινύνθη*. *μινύθω* is unattested. See on ii. 151. —**91. ἅμα**: in effect the Hom. usage since *μ.* = a verb of motion. *ἅμα cum dat.* only here in Bacch.—**92. Ἱέρων**: the pause excuses the hiatus here, but in 64 the hiatus and syllaba anceps may be purely musical. So in the case of Ἰσθμός 2. 7, and in Pind., where *F* is not certain. So with Ἰάλυσος in Pind.

94. πράξαντι εὖ: cf. ii. 190, Sim. ii. 7.—**95. σιωπά**: Beattie's "silence of neglect." See on Pind. xiv.; for the expression cf. *κόσμον ἡ σιγὴ φέρει* Soph. *Aias* 293.—**96. σὺν ἀλαθείᾳ**: so 8. 4 and 9. 85 (*ἀλαθείας χάριν* ii. 187). *σύν* with words denoting an abstract idea is very common in Bacch. (*ἀγλαΐα, αἶσα, δίκα* so Pind., *εὐθυμία, εὔκλεια, νίκα, τύχα* so Pind., *χρόνος*). This is the tendency of choral lyric as opposed to the epic usage. **βαλών**: 'hit the mark'; cf. *οὐ ψεύδει βαλών* Pind. *Nem.* 1. 18. Words are missiles (*Ol.* 9. 5, 13. 95). The MS. *κ*(?)*αλων* has been taken as a part. gen.; *λακών, καλάν, καλῶς* have been conjectured. As Hieron represents ἀρετά (90), so Bacch. represents Μοῦσα (92), and his fame will be linked with that of his royal patron. Not only will Hieron be famous: men will attain to truth when they shall celebrate in song also (καί) the charm of the honey-tongued nightingale of Keos. ὑμνεῖν is the final as it is the initial note (v. 3). Desrousseaux takes the passage to mean: 'he will speak in accordance with truth who shall celebrate among things that are fair (καλῶν) the praise that is meeted out to thee by the bard of Keos.'

II. An Olympian ode in honour of Hieron, whose race-horse Pherenikos ('Victor') had already won two Pythian victories (cf. l. 41 and Pind. *Pyth.* 3. 74), which are to be referred to 482 and 478 and not, with Boeckh (who placed the first Pythiad in 586 and not in 582), to 486 and 482. This ode was written in 476, which is possibly the date of Pindar's *Ol.* 1.

Against Kenyon's conclusion that *Ol.* 1 also commemorates this victory it may be urged (1) that the schol. on *Ol.* 1 does not (as K. asserts) say that this ode celebrates the same victory as *Ol.* 1; (2) that Apollodoros and Didymos state that Hieron was Συρακούσιος and not Αἰτναῖος (a title possible only after the founding of Aitna in 472), at the time of the victory of *Ol.* 1; while Aristonikos, on the other hand, maintains that Hieron was Αἰτναῖος, but had himself proclaimed as Συρακούσιος. If this difference of opinion refers merely to the date of the founding of Aitna, it may be supposed that the ancient scholars were agreed in referring *Ol.* 1 to 476; (3) if *Ol.* 1 was written in 476, the victory of 472 remained unsung, or the ode is lost; (4) *Ol.* 1. 109 points to 472; for the poet himself indicates that Hieron was even then contemplating the more splendid chariot race, in which, four years later, he was successful, a victory commemorated by Bacch. i. Against this argument *Pyth.* 5. 124 may however be used.—It may be added that if Pind was, as is claimed by some, a visitor at the court of Hieron in 476, it is not likely that his patron should have bespoken an additional ode from his rival, who was then at home in Keos. Again, the similarity between *Ol.* 1. 20 ff. and Bacch ii. 37 ff. is scarcely due to chance. As the epigram in Pausan. 8. 42. 9 (cf. 6. 12. 1) states, Hieron won two Olympian victories with the κέλης. Of these the first was that of 476 (OϜ′ = Ol. 76 for OΓ′ = Ol. 73), for which Bacch. wrote this ode. The second would then in all probability be that of 472. In 476, thanks no doubt to Simonides' influence, Bacch. stood on terms of friendship with Hieron, whose court he must have visited (cf. ξένος v. 11). Christ, and Fraccaroli *Le Ode di Pind.* 186, *Riv. di Filol.* 26. 76, maintain that *Ol.* 1. was composed in 472.

The age of Pherenikos, who was victorious in 482, 478, 476 and possibly also 472, is difficult to reconcile with the conservation of great speed by racers in our day. If *Ol.* 1 dates from 476 and not from 472, a continuous period of even six years is almost without example in modern times for a race-horse to continue to win races. Greek racers may however have been run only at considerable intervals and thus have retained their vigour to a greater age than is common under modern conditions, and Pelagonius *art. veterin.* p. 32 in fact says *equos circo sacrisque certaminibus quinquennes usque ad annum vigesimum plerumque idoneos adseverant* (cited by Christ). See on Ibyk. ii. A good deal depends on the age when a racer is put under the saddle. Fennell suggests that the Pherenikos of 472 may have been the descendant of the Pherenikos of 482; if this had been the case, it would not have been beneath the dignity of Pindar to draw from a lower sphere evidence confirmatory of the transmission of hereditary qualities which he so often records in the case of his athletes.

The ode consists of five complete systems, with overlapping between the members of the triads in about half the possible cases. Antis. β′, the third and fourth triads, and str. ϵ′ contain the myth, which begins with one part of the triad and closes with another (cf. vi.). The first group and str. β′ deal with the praise of Hieron, the poet's comparison of himself to an eagle, and Pherenikos; with antis. ϵ′ there is an abrupt reversion to Hieron, with a prayer for whose prosperity the poem concludes. (i. = 55, ii. = 120, iii. = 25 verses.) The transition (vv. 50-55) to the central theme, a lyric Nekyia dealing with the story of Meleager, is not well managed. Hieron was at this time afflicted with an incurable disease, and the myth of Meleager may point to the inevitableness of suffering; Herakles too the founder of the Olympic games had his affliction of toil and met his death through the deed of Meleager's sister. But the profound melancholy of the myth is inappropriate to the theme.

In his treatment of the myth (cf. Robert *Hermes* 33, 151 ff.) the poet follows in part the Homeric story, *Il.* I 529 ff., but is eclectic by his right as a lyric artist. Some of the chief points of difference are as follows: Bacch. does not mention the wrath of Meleager, which is an essential part of the Homeric episode; nor does he refer to Kleopatra, Meleager's wife; Hom. makes him slay only one of his uncles, and does not speak of the death of Meleager's brother or brothers. The fatal brand, which is not mentioned in the epic, though Hom. makes M. die by his mother's curse, appeared in the *Pleuroniai* of Phrynichos. Whether the tragedy preceded the ode is uncertain. It is noteworthy that the three poets ascribed the death of the hero to the wrath of Althaia. The contest of the Kuretes with the Kalydonians, in which, according to one tradition, M. was slain by Apollo, finds a place in Bacch. Possibly Pindar anticipated Bacch. in casting into lyric mould the myth of Meleager. The schol. on Φ 194 reports that the Theban poet (Frag. 249) narrated the meeting of Herakles with M. when he descended to Hades to fetch

Kerberos; that M. asked him to marry Deïaneira (contrast v. 165) and that on the hero's return to the upper world he overcame Achelous, who was a suitor for the hand of Meleager's sister (cf. Soph. *Trach.* 9 ff.). Before Pindar, another lyric poet, Archilochos, had treated the story of Herakles and Deïaneira, telling how they lived in Kalydon with Oineus. Pherekydes of Leros (about 480), the mythographer, related in prose the story of Deïaneira. Folk-legend or a lost epic, based on λ 632, may have been the source of Bacchylides' description of Herakles drawing his bow (cf. on Stes. i.) against Meleager. Apollod. (2. 5. 12), probably following Peisandros' Ἆθλα Ἡρακλέους, relates the older story that the shades, with the exception of M. and Medusa, fled at the sight of Herakles, and that the hero drew his *sword* against them, but desisted when Hermes told him they were mere wraiths. An unknown poet was followed by Parrhasios, who represented Meleager, Herakles, and Perseus in Hades. Nothing is known of a dithyramb *Meleager* by Kleomenes, whom Bergk would make a contemporary of Bacchylides, though he probably belongs to the fourth century.

A characteristic difference in the treatment of the myth appears in Euripides, who invented the love of Meleager for Atalanta which pervades the later literature, *e.g.* Ovid *Metam.* 8. 300 ff. According to the tragic poet, Althaia's brothers met their death because they would not suffer Atalanta to receive the spoils of the hunt from Meleager.

New words: ἀδεισιβόας 'intrepid,' ἀελλοδρόμης, ἀκαμαντορόας 'of unwearied flood,' ἀναιδομάχης 'insatiate of attack,' 'merciless in attack,' γελανόω 'calm,' 'make serene,' ἐγκλαίω (?) 'weep over,' εἰσάνταν 'opposite,' ἐρειψιπύλης 'stormer of gates,' εὐρύαναξ, εὐρυδίνης, ἱπποδίνητος 'chariot-swirled,' λιγυκλαγγής 'shrill-twanging,' μεγιστοπάτωρ 'of mightiest sire,' νεόκροτος 'fresh,' 'new,' ὀλιγοσθενέω, φοινικόνωτος, χαλκεόκρανος 'brass-tipped,' χαλκεόστερνος, χρυσόπαχυς.

Tautometric responsion is rare: 3=98, 30=110, 34=74, 98=123, 113=153, 122=137 (the vengeance of the mother echoes the wrath of the goddess), 175=190. Non-tautometric responsion is frequent: 5=54=96, 16=188, 57=103, 63=87=109=190=194, 99=104=123, 112=125, 119=165. Much of the repetition in Bacch. is due to the poverty of his vocabulary.

Metre: dactylo-epitrite. The strophes consist of seven, the epodes of five periods. There are various noteworthy metrical peculiarities. See on vv. 11, 151.

GENEALOGICAL TABLE.

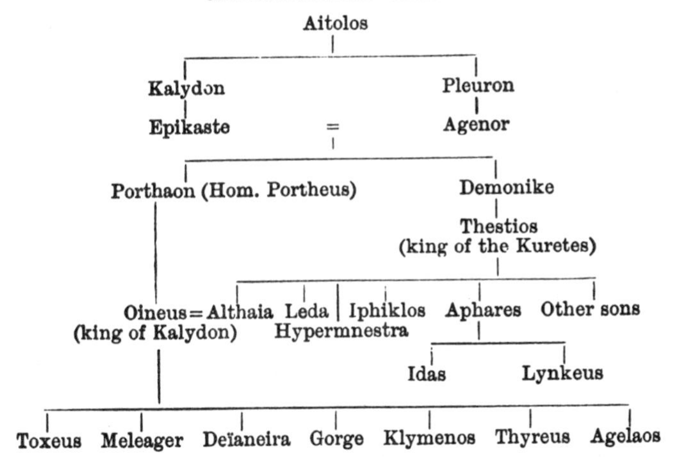

2. ἱπποδινήτων 'chariot-swirled.' Cf. ἵππους δινεῖ Aisch. *Sept.* 462. Though verbals in -τος often retain an active signification (πολύπλαγκτοι v. 35, βαρύτλατος vii. 4), the analogy of οἰστροδίνητος and ἀδίνητος is against the translation 'charioteers.' A quadriga is the emblem on the exquisite Syracusan coins of the period (Head *Hist. Num.* 150). Cf. Pind. *Pyth.* 2. 1 Συράκοσαι . . . ἀνδρῶν ἵππων τε σιδαροχαρμᾶν δαιμόνιαι τροφοί. **στραταγέ**: cf. *Pyth.* 2. 58, where Hieron is addressed as πρύτανι κύριε . . . στρατοῦ. Like his predecessor Gelon, the tyrant may have been formally invested with the title στραταγὸς αὐτοκράτωρ. It is also possible to regard the word as the first example of the freer use of στρατός = δημός (*Pyth.* 2. 87, Aisch. *Eum.* 566). In tragedy the chief ruler of a city is called στρατηγός. In ix. 121 Bacch. has στραταγέταν of Minos. Pind., who uses στράταρχος for στραταγός, calls Hieron Συρακόσιον ἱπποχάρμαν βασιλῆα *Ol.* 1. 23.—**4. Μοισᾶν**: elsewhere (8 times) Μοῦσα in Bacch. Pind. has Μοῖσα always. **γλυκύδωρον**: cf. i. 3, of Nike v. 1. Compounds of γλυκυ- are not in favour in choral melic. Bacch. has no other example, Pind. none at all. γλυκύδωρος reappears *Anth. Pal.* 5. 22 (of Ἔρως). Cf. Theogn. 250 ἀγλαὰ Μουσάων δῶρα. **ἄγαλμα**: of song, Pind. *Nem.* 3. 13. **τῶν γε νῦν**: so used in a similar passage *Ol.* 1. 105, where Pind. also compliments the tyrant's taste. Literary gossip reported that Hiero preferred the poems of Bacch. to those of his rival. —**5.** Cf. x. 12, Ω 220 εἴ τις ἄλλος ἐπιχθονίων.—**6. εὐθύδικον**: ἀστύθεμιν Ἱέρωνα, 4. 3. Hiero wielded the sceptre of justice in Sicily (*Ol.* 1. 12).—**7. ἀτρέμ'**: an allusion to political unrest? **ἀμπαύσας μεριμνᾶν**: 'throw off the cares of state.'—**8. ἄθρησον**: 'cast thy glance upon this song'; so Pind. *Pyth.* 2. 70 τὸ Καστόρειον ἄθρησον. **⟨σὺν⟩ νόῳ**: cf. Hdt. 8. 86, Plato *Krito* 48 C. εὐνοῶν, εὐνόως are also possible (cf. *Pyth.* 8. 18).—**9. ἤ**: as *Ol.* 1. 28, *Pyth.* 6. 1. **σὺν Χαρ. βαθ.**: as *Pyth.* 9. 2. **ὑφάνας**: Pind. Frag. 179 ὑφαίνω ποικίλον ἄνδημα, *i.e.* ποίημα, *Anth. Pal.* 2. 70 μέλος δ' εὔυμνον ὑφαίνειν.—**11. ξένος**: the poet speaks of himself in the third person, as in iv. 3. This verse and 26, as 14 and 30, have one syllable more than the corresponding verses of the other strophes. To heal the violation of responsion Tyrrell improbably adds a syllable to vv. 51, 66 etc. Walker emends πέμπει to πλεῖ (the verbs are confused in the MSS. of Thuk. 6. 1. 1, 8. 23. 4), brackets δέ in 14, though the asyndeton is not easily pardoned in a passage free from all agitation, reads νω | μᾷ in 26, and omits μετ' in 30. Platt reads πλέων in 11 and deletes the MS. period after θεράπων. Richards suggests ἐθέλων for ἐθέλει δέ. The solution of the question depends upon the possibility of the protraction of the final long in 51, 66 etc.—**13. χρυσάμπυκος**: χρυσαμπύκων Μοισᾶν Pind. *Pyth.* 3. 89. **κλεινός**: after κλεεννάν. The best ancient writers do not hesitate to repeat single words; cf. v. 57, 60, Soph. *O. K.* 554. — **14. θεράπων**: Μουσάων θ. Hes. *Theogon.* 100, *Hymn* 32. 20, Theogn. 769, Aristoph. *Aves* 909, Kaibel 101. 3. Cf. Plato *Ion* 534 E οἱ ποιηταὶ οὐδὲν ἄλλ' ἢ ἑρμηνεῖς εἰσι τῶν θεῶν. **ἐθέλει**: here, l. 24, ii. 169, elsewhere θέλω. Bacch. does not use βούλομαι, which was not in favour with the choral poets (once in Pind.).—**15. χέων**: Alk. xix. 4.

16. αἰνεῖν Ἱέρωνα: emphatic position (with *enjambement*) as the melody begins afresh; cf. l. 41, i. 29, 61, iv. 36. If *Pyth.* 1 was composed in 470, Pindar's celebrated picture of the sleeping eagle is later than Bacchylides' splendid description of the soaring flight of the king of birds. Pind. recalls Bacch. in his use of Διὸς ἀετός, ὠκεῖαν πτέρυγα, ἀρχὸς οἰωνῶν. Such parallelisms are almost inevitable; otherwise the different situation demands different treatment. In *Nem.* 5. 20, an ode composed several years before this poem, Pind. says ἔχω γονάτων ἐλαφρὸν ὁρμάν· | καὶ πέραν πόντοιο πάλλοντ' αἰετοί (cf. l. 19). Cf. Theogn. 237 ff., Soph. Frag. 435. Can this passage of Bacch. be a reply to Pind. *Ol.* 2. 86? That both poems commemorate victories won in 476 does not make this impossible.—**17. αἰθέρα**: masc. also in i. 36, 86, fem. iv. 35, ix. 73, without distinction of metre. See on Sa. i. 11. Cf. *Anth. Pal.* 9. 223 ἠεροδίνης αἰετός, οἰωνῶν μοῦνος ἐνουράνιος. **τάμνων**: ἠέρα τέμνον *Hymn* 5. 383, Orph. *Argon*

305 ἀπείριτον αἰθέρα τέμνων. **ξουθαῖσι**: the γνήσιος αἰετός is ξανθός accord. to Arist. (*H. A.* 9. 32), who speaks of its fearlessness and nobility. The golden eagle is the largest and commonest of the Greek eagles.—**18.** **πτερύγεσσι**: the Aiolic form (Anakr. xii.). **ταχείαις**: Sa. i. 10.—**19.** In *Ol.* 2. 88 (476 B.C.) Pind. compares himself to the eagle of Zeus. See also *Pyth.* 5. 112. Dante *Inf.* 4. 94 says *cosi vidi adunar la bella scuola* | *di quel signor dell' altissimo canto,* | *che sovra gli altri, com' aquila, vola.* **ἄγγελος**: δώσει ἑὸν ἄγγελον εὐρύοπα Ζεύς Ω 296, πέμψεν θεὸς | ἀρχὸν οἰωνῶν μέγαν αἰετόν Pind. *Isthm.* 6. 50.—**21.** **θαρσεῖ ἰσχύϊ**: ἰσχύος θράσος Soph. *Phil.* 104. —**22.** **πτάσσοντι**: see on Alkm. viii. and cf. Pind. *Ol.* 2. 87, *Nem.* 3. 80 ἔστι δ' αἰετὸς ὠκὺς ἐν ποτανοῖς | . . . κραγέται δὲ κολοιοὶ ταπεινὰ νέμονται, Shakespeare *Tit. Andr.* 4. 4. 83, Milton *Par. Lost* 11. 185.—**25.** **οὐδ'**: see Jebb on Soph. *Aias* 428.—**26.** **δυσπαίπαλα**: 'rough,' 'stormy'; connected with δυσπαλής, and formed from the redupl. denominative παιπάλλω (=σείω Hesych.) like δαιδάλλω. Cf. κοικύλλω, μοιμύλλω, ϝαιϝίσσω (whence ἀΐσσω). Properly δ. is used of that which is difficult to traverse; in Archil. 115 of mountain glens ('rugged and steep'), as παιπαλόεις of a mountain in N 17, of a road in P 743, and of islands. The emendation to δυσπέμφελα (Nairn) or δυσπέμπελα is unnecessary. Pind. has ἀμαιμάκετον πόντον *Pyth.* 1. 14. **νωμᾶται**: the schol. on Hes. *Theogon.* 116 quotes from Bacch. νωμᾶται δ' ἐν ἀτρυγέτῳ χάει, where ἀτρυγέτῳ is certainly an error, and possibly νωμᾶται also. The papyrus has a trace of the reading νωμᾷ, and the middle is elsewhere reported only in Quint. Smyr. 3. 439. With νωμᾶν ἔθειραν cf. *Anth. Pal.* 9. 339 πτερὸν αἰθέρι νωμῶν, possibly a recollection of this passage. If we keep νωμᾶται, it is better to govern ἔθειραν by the verb than to make it depend on ἀρίγνωτος.—**27.** **ἀτρύτῳ χάει**: Milton's "void and formless Infinite," Thomson's "illimitable void." χάος first appears in Hesiod as the void, strictly the yawning abyss (Arist. *Phys.* 208 B 29). Cf. the connected Skt. word *vihāyas* (the yawning space) 'air.' Later χάος is either the space under the earth that is filled with darkness or the region over the earth that is filled with air and clouds. Genealogically Aither is the descendent, in the second degree, of Chaos. The schol. on Aristoph. *Aves* 192 cites Ibyk. (28) ποτᾶται δ' ἐν ἀλλοτρίῳ χάει for the use of χάος 'air.' Whether Bacch. derived his use of χάος from the Rhegine poet, or whether the quotation from Ibykos is due to confusion with this passage, cannot be decided. For χάος 'air' cf. Aristoph. *Nubes* 627 μὰ τὸ Χάος, μὰ τὸν 'Αέρα, 424, *Aves* 192, 1218. Eur. Frag. 448.—**28.** **λεπτότριχα**: 'delicate'; in prose (Aristotle) of animals, but never

of birds. Here θρίξ is used of the plumage of the wings. Compounds with λεπτο- are infrequent in poetry (ix. 119; cf. λευκοπτέρυγα *Ion* ii.). **σύν**: 'keeping pace with.' **Ζεφύρου**: cf. T 415 ἅμα πνοιῇ Ζεφύροιο, and good MSS. Pind. *Nem.* 7. 29 have Ζεφύροιο πνοαί.—**30**. **μέτ'**: only here *cum dat.* in Bacch. and unnecessary in this passage. **ἰδεῖν**: the aorist of the moment when the bird comes within the range of vision. For ἀνθρώποις Weil conj. οἰωνοῖς.

31. Cf. Pind. *Isthm.* 4. 1 (composed in 478) ἔστι μοι θεῶν ἕκατι μυρία παντᾷ κέλευθος· | . . . ὑμετέρας ἀρετὰς ὕμνῳ διώκειν, *Nem.* 6. 45, Bacch. iv. 48, 19. 1 πάρεστι μυρία κέλευθος . . . μελέων; Frag. 63 (37) εἰ δὲ λέγει τις ἄλλως, πλατεῖα κέλευθος. This use of κ. is probably stereotyped, but Bacch. fails to give it the lustre of Pind. (cf. *Isthm.* 6. 22). οἶμος (Hom., Pind.) is not used by Bacch. The point of the passage is that with Hieron as a subject the poet has at his command material as unlimited as the air through which the eagle soars.—**34**. **χαλκεοστέρνου**: Bacch. forms compounds in χαλκο- and χαλκεο-, χρυσο- and χρυσεο-, while Pindar has only χαλκο- and χρυσο-. **Ἄρηος**: this reference to the battle of Himera is an exception to the poet's reticence as regards Hieron's military glory. To Bacch. his patron is the victor at the games and a critic of poetry, not the conqueror of the Carthaginians and Etruscans. Contrast the attitude of Pindar.—**35**. Cf. Sim. 141 φημὶ Γέλων', Ἱέρωνα, Πολύζηλον, Θρασύβουλον, | παῖδας Δεινομένευς, τοὺς τρίποδας θέμεναι | . . . βάρβαρα νικήσαντας ἔθνη. So Pind. praises Gelon in conjunction with Hieron (*Pyth.* 1. 48). **ἀγέρωχοι**: Τρώων ἀγ. Γ 36.—**36**. **εὖ ἔρδων**: cf. vii. 18, εὖ ἔρδων θεούς 1. 25, Theogn. 368, Pind. *Ol.* 8. 29; τὸ δὲ καλὸν ποιοῦντες μὴ ἐγκακῶμεν *Galat.* 6. 9.—**37**. Cf. Pind. *Ol.* 1. 20 ff. ὅτε παρ' Ἀλφεῷ σύτο (Pherenikos) δέμας | ἀκέντητον ἐν δρόμοισι παρέχων, | κράτει δὲ προσέμειξε δεσπόταν. With ἀκέντητον cf. 42-45, with κράτει ff. cf. 48-50. Pind. is simpler but more vigorous, Bacch. loves colour. **ξανθότριχα**: 'chestnut,' used by Solon (22) of men; ξανθαὶ ἵπποι Λ 680.—**38**. **παρ'**: the accus. with no verb of motion as i. 6, v. 26. **εὐρυδίναν** as i. 6. Bacch. is as fond as Pind. is chary, of epithets of the Alpheios: ἀκαμαντορόαν ii. 180, καλλιρόαν v. 26. Pind. has one such epithet: εὐρὺ ῥέοντα *Ol.* 5. 18 (possibly not Pindaric). Bacch. paraphrases in iii. 3, vi. 70; so Pind. has πόρος, ῥέεθρον. Eur. *H. F.* 368 has καλλιδίνας of the Peneios.—**39**. **πῶλον**: since Pherenikos had been on the track for at least six years, πῶλος is equivalent to ἵππος as in Pind. *Pyth.* 2. 8. Not until 384 B.C. were special races for πῶλοι established in contradistinction to those for ἵπποι τέλειοι. **ἀελλοδρόμαν**: ἀελλοπόδων ἵππων Sim.

iii., Pind. *Nem.* 1. 6.—**40.** The racing with κέλητες, like that with *quadrigae*, began early in the morning. At Olympia, at least in 364 B.C., the pentathlon followed the chariot race. Cf. Soph. *El.* 699 ἡλίου τέλλοντος ὠκύπους ἀγών.

41. Cf. ἐν Πυθῶνι ἀγαθέᾳ Pind. *Pyth.* 9. 71.—**42.** A fuller form of this interesting expression, which is more picturesque than αὐδάσομαι ἐνόρκιον λόγον ἀλαθεῖ νόῳ Pind. *Ol.* 2. 92, appears in Bacch. 8. 3: γᾷ δ' ἐπισκήπτων χέρα κομπάσομαι. Touching the earth as a sacred object was regarded as equivalent to laying hold of an altar (cf. τῶν τύμβων ἁπτόμενοι Hdt. 4. 172) in order to confirm an oath. Cf. the legal use of ἐπισκήπτομαι 'denounce' in cases of prosecution for false evidence. To summon the spirits of the dead it was customary to strike upon the earth. In *Il.* I 568 Althaia γαῖαν χερσὶν ἀλοία, in *Hymn* 2. 162 Hera appeals to Earth and the Titans (ἵμασε χθόνα χειρί). See Nägelsbach *Nachhom. Theologie* 102. 214. Note the Ionic η in ἐπισκήπτων.—**43. προτέρων**: the rare (Hom.) local use.—**44. κατέχρανεν**: the active is elsewhere unattested.—**45. πρός**: with the accus. always of place after a verb of motion in Bacch.—**46.** The verse paraphrases ἀελλοδρόμαν in 39. Cf. K 437 θείειν δ' ἀνέμοισιν ὁμοῖοι, Verg. *Aen.* 4. 241; ῥιπῇς Βορέαο O 171. **ἶσος**: but ἴσος in xii., 1. 34, ἰσοθέων 13. 123.—**47.** Not overturning his driver as in the race described in Soph. *El.* 728.—**48. ἵεται**: if correct, a strange use of the historical present; cf. 13. 18. In Pind. the historical present is rare, if indeed it occurs at all. **νεόκροτον**: 'new-forged,' *i.e.* 'fresh.' Cf. Pind. xxvi. 1 κεκρότηται 'wrought,' 'fashioned.' The last part of the compound is practically quiescent as in νεόκοτος. Ken. takes it to mean 'celebrated by new clamours of applause.' Compounds of κρότος are not rare; cf. δίκροτος ἀμαξιτός 'road for two carriages' Eur. *El.* 775, χαλκόκροτοι ἵπποι 'brazen hoofed' Aristoph. *Eq.* 552. Pind. has ἱππόκροτον ὁδόν *Pyth.* 5. 92. κροτέω, κροτητός are used of the rattling of chariots (O 453, Λ 160, Soph. *El.* 714) but this is a race with κέλητες. Housman conj. ἵετ(ο) ἀφνεόκροτον 'abounding in noise,' Richards λαόκροτον.—**49. φιλοξείνῳ**: Pind. *Pyth.* 3. 71 ξείνοις τε θαυμαστὸς πατήρ of Hieron. **τιτύσκων**: Hom. has τιτύσκομαι. Bacch. precedes the Alexandrians in the use of the active.—**50** ff. A moral precept serves as the transition to the myth. For the sentiment cf. Mimn. 2. 15, Theogn. 167, Aisch. *Agam.* 553, Soph. *O. K.* 1722, Eur. *I. A.* 29, 161; cf. also Pind. *Isthm.* 5. 12. **θεός**: with synizesis; cf. v. 60, ix. 132, Pind. *Pyth.* 1. 56.

56. ἐρειψιπύλαν: an allusion to his capture of Troy, Oichalia, etc., though Herakles also stormed the portals of

Hades.—**60.** Cf. Θ 368 *ἐξ ἐρέβευς ἄξοντα κύνα στυγεροῦ 'Αΐδαο*, λ 623 *καί ποτέ μ' ἐνθάδ' ἔπεμψε κύν' ἄξοντ'.*—**62. ἀπλάτοι'**: Bacch. has a dozen other cases of *-οιο*. Elision as in v. 120. —**64. ἐδάη** of physical, not intellectual, cognition; cf. Pind. Frag. 166.—**65. οἷά τε**: cf. γ 73, Hdt. 2. 175; = *τοιαύτας οἷα φύλλα ἐστίν, ἃ ἄνεμος.* The comparison refers to the unsubstantial character of the shades (*νεκύων ἀμενηνὰ κάρηνα* κ 521). This is the finest of the three true similes in Bacch. (iv. 27, vi. 21). For the comparison Ken. cp. B 468 *μυρίοι, ὅσσα τε φύλλα*, Apoll. Rhod. 4. 216 (*ὅσα*), Verg. *Aen.* 6. 309 (of the dead), *Par. Lost* l. 301-304, where the simile is localized in Milton's manner ("leaves in Vallombrosa"). Cf. also B 800, ι 51, Z 146, Mimn. 2. 1, Sim. 85.—**67. ἀργηστάς**: 'gleaming' = *ἀργής, ἀργήεις*, both used of elevation. Jebb proposes *ἀργεστάς* (of *ἀνεμός*; cf. Λ 306 *ἀργεστᾶο Νότοιο*, carm. pop. 40). Pindar, at least, avoids epithets with *ἄνεμος*, and the position is prob. against such a use here. The form *ἀργηστής* varies with *ἀργεστής* as *ἀργῆτι* with *ἀργέτι*.—**69. θρασ.** and **ἐγχεσπ.**: both Homeric expressions.—**70. Πορθανίδα**: from *Πορθάν*, contracted from *-άων*, as *'Αλκμάν* from *-άων*, with the accent of *Τιτάν*. Cf. *'Αλκμανιδᾶν* Pind. *Pyth.* 7. 2. *Πορθᾱονίδα* was preferred by the second hand.

71. 'Αλκμήνιος: cf. on iii. 12. Such metronymics are rare.—**73.** Cf. φ 138, 410, Theokr. 25. 212. At each end of the bow a species of hook (*κορώνη*) was attached which kept the taut string in place. Ordinarily the bow was carried unstrung.—**75. ἰόν**: illegitimate hiatus and due to confusion between *ἰός* 'arrow' (which had no *F*) and *Fιός virus*. Cf. Δ 116 *αὐτὰρ ὁ σύλα πῶμα φαρέτρης, ἐκ δ' ἕλετ' ἰόν.*—**78. εἰδώς**: for the gender, cf. *ἐλθὼν . . . βίη 'Ηρακληείη* Λ 690.—**80. γελανώσας**: 'having cheered thy heart,' shows the strong form of the root as does *γελᾱνής* 'cheerful' (of *θυμός* in Pind. *Pyth.* 4.181). The weak form is seen in *γαληνός, γαληνής*.

81. ταὖσιον: as Alkm. 92 where we may read *ταὖσια πολλὰ κίω.*—**85.** Cf. *οὔ τοι ἔπι δέος* A 515.—**86.** For the question cf. Pind. *Pyth.* 9. 33 and see on x. 31.—**87. ἔρνος**: used directly and not in comparison (see on Sa. xxxix.).—**90. κεῖνον**: the hero who laid low so redoubtable an adversary as Meleager. **ἐφ'**: *πέμπειν ἐπί τινι* in a hostile sense Aisch. *Agam.* 61. Cf. l. 83 above, l. 133 below.—**91. κεφαλᾷ**: used for the pronoun Σ 82, Pind. *Ol.* 6. 60, 7. 67.—**92.** Athena aided Herakles against the Styx on the occasion of his descent to fetch Kerberos from Hades (Θ 367). On vases she is often represented as assisting him.—**94. χαλεπόν** *κ.τ.λ.* The key note of the story of M. By his own end Herakles was to prove its truth. Cf. γ 147, Aisch. *Prom.* 34.

97. πλάξιππος: ἱππηλάτα Οἰνεύς I 581. Πέλοπι πλ. B 104. —**99. σεμνᾶς**: the epithet 'august' (of Artemis in Eur. *Hippol.* 713) loses its strength when conjoined with the beautiful καλυκ. and λευκωλένου (only here of Artemis). Cf. vi. 72, ix. 110. Bacch. rarely connects his epithets by conjunctions. **χόλον**: I 534 χωσαμένη, ὅ οἱ οὔ τι θαλύσια γουνῷ ἀλωῆς | Οἰνεὺς ἔρξ'· ἄλλοι δὲ θεοὶ δαίνυνθ' ἑκατόμβας, | οἴῃ δ' οὐκ ἔρρεξε Διὸς κούρῃ μεγάλοιο.—**100. πολέων**: not in actual contrast with φοινικ. Note the use as fem. and cf. πουλὺν ὑγρήν δ 709.—**101. πατήρ**: with Οἰνεύς in 97. Words at the end of different verses often belong together especially in dactylo-epitrites.—**102. βοῶν**: used as in xiii. 3. The poet is scarcely thinking of Oineus' neglect of the goddess at the agricultural festival of the Θαλύσια.—**104. κούρα**: in Hom. only *cum. gen.*—**105.** Soph. *Meleager*, Frag. 369 συὸς μέγιστον χρῆμ' ἐπ' Οἰνέως γύαις | ἀνῆκε Λητοῦς παῖς ἑκηβόλος θεά. **ἀναιδομάχαν** = ἀναιδέα μάχης; cf. ἀναιδέα δηϊοτῆτος E 593.—**107. πλημύρων**: the best MSS. of Hippokrates have the form with one μ. ἐπλήμυρον (?) Archil. 97; πλημμυρίν Bacch. Frag. 69 (B. 45).—**109. μῆλα**: in I 541 ff. the boar uproots δένδρεα | αὐτῇσιν ῥίζῃσι καὶ αὐτοῖς ἄνθεσι μήλων. Is μῆλα here due to the Hom. μήλων? Do boars attack sheep? Apollod. says the Kalydonian boar διέφθειρεν τὰ βοσκήματα.—**110. εἰσάντᾱν** stands midway between Hom. ἔσαντᾰ and ἄντην (ἄντᾱν). Perhaps we should write εἰς ἄνταν.

111. Cf. ἀνδράσι δῆριν ἔθεντο P 158, στησάμενοι δ' ἐμάχοντο μάχην Σ 533.—**112. ἐνδυκέως**: not of friendly action as in Hom.; cf. l. 125. Perhaps = κρατερῶς 'stubbornly.'—**113. σῡνεχέως** (as Hes. *Theogon.* 636) from συν- + σεχ-. The third hand has here συνν-. See on Alk. iv. 1.—**114. κάρτος** = νίκην. Cf. κῦδος ὀρέξῃ E 33.—**115. θάπτομεν**: by incineration.—**117. 'Αγκαῖον**: the name occurs in B 609 as that of an Arkadian prince, son of Lykurgos. He participated in the Boar-hunt (Apollod. 1. 8. 2, Ovid *Metam.* 8. 401). Skopas represented him as slain by the boar on the pediment of the temple of Athena Alea in Tegea. There is no warrant for making him a brother of Meleager. **'Αγέλαον**: 'Αγέλεως in Anton. Liber. *Metam.* 2. This may be the Hyleus of Apollod.

121. ὤλεσε . . . ὀλοά: for the repetition cf. above 12 κλεεννὰν . . . κλεινός, and see Bekker *Hom. Bl.* 185 ff. Less relevant, because proper names (cf. on iii. 1), are Πρόθοος θοός B 758, ἀίδηλον "Αιδαν Soph. *Aias* 608 (Jebb). Cf. μοῖρ' ὀλοὴ ἔκτανεν Π 849.—**122. δαΐφρων** (as 137) from δάϊς, = πολεμικὸν φρόνημα ἔχουσα *Et. Gud.* 133. 8 (= δαϊόφρων). This is the meaning in the *Iliad*, not in the *Odyssey*. δαΐφρων of Penelope is 'prudent'; so of Alkmena, Pind. *Pyth.* 9. 84. Phrynichos

Pleuron. has ματρὸς αἰνᾶς κακομηχάνου of Althaia.—**124. δορᾶς**: cf. I 547 ἡ δ' ἀμφ' αὐτῷ θῆκε πολὺν κέλαδον καὶ ἀυτήν, | ἀμφὶ συὸς κεφαλῇ καὶ δέρματι λαχνήεντι. Apollod. says that, accord. to one version of the story, the Thestiadai claimed the spoils because it was Iphiklos who first hit the quarry. The lyric poet introduces only effective incidents and hence passes over the death of the boar.—**126. μενεπτολέμοις**: in Homer only of individuals. Cf. Αἰτωλοὶ μενεχάρμαι I 529.—**128. Ἴφϊκλον**: κλ with 'Attic' correption in a medial syllable also ix. 127, 7. 9; τλ ii. 153 (initial).—**129. Ἀφάρητα**: from Ἀφάρης, inflected like Φέρης. Cf. Ἀφάρητος Plut. *Parall.* 40. The usual form of the name is Aphareus. Pind. *Nem.* 10. 65 has Ἀφαρητίδαι (-ιάδαι Apoll. Rhod. 1. 151) of Lynkeus and Idas, who are called by Ovid *Metam.* 8. 304 *duo Thestiadae proles Aphareïa.* Accord. to another account Aphares' father was Periores. **μάτρωας**: in I 567 for κασιγνήτοιο φόνοιο some read κασιγνητοῖο φ. 'slaughter of her brothers' in order to square Homer's account with later tradition.

139. βούλευσεν ὄλεθρον: cf. Ξ 464. **ἀτάρβακτος**: *imperterrita* as Pind. *Pyth.* 4. 84; formed from *ταρβάζω. Cf. ἀτάρβητος. — **140. δαιδαλέας λάρνακος**: as Sim. xiii. 1.—**142. ἐγκλαύσασα** is the reading of the MS. It may be retained, though ἐγκλαίω 'weep over' is unattested (ἐνδακρύω Aisch. *Agam.* 541), and the pregnant constr. of ἐκ with καῖε is harsh. Althaia shed tears over the fatal brand as she drew it from the chest. Althaia's tears in Homer (I 570) are not tears of repentance for her deed; see, however, Ovid *Metam.* 8. 470 *inveniebantur lacrimae tamen.* Tyrrell conj. ἐγκλᾴσασα *i.e.* καῖε φιτρὸν ὃν ἐνέκλησε ('from the chest in which she had shut it up'), Jebb ἀγκλαύσασα, Housman ἑλκύσασα (but the ῠ is objectionable), Wilam. ἐκκλᾴσασα (this, however, means 'having shut out') and ἐγλύσασα = ἐκλ- (it is difficult to see how ἑλκύσασα or ἐκλύσασα could have been corrupted into ἐγκλαύσασα), Desrousseaux εἷλε (for καῖε) ἐγκαύσασα.—**143. ἐπέκλωσεν**: boldly used with φιτρόν. **τότε**: the seventh day after the birth of M. (Apollod. 1. 8. 2. 1).—**145.** Klymenos was one of the Kuretes. Meleager had a brother of this name. —**146. ἐξεναρίζων**: the papyrus ἐξαναρίζων. Alkm. iv. 3 has Ἐναρσφόρος so that -αν- is at least not Doric for -εν-. In I 530 the Kuretes and Aitolians ἀλλήλους ἐνάριζον. It is to be noted that the mother's curse takes effect when M. is engaged in battle. Cf. Phrynichos *Pleuron.* ὠκεῖα δέ νιν φλὸξ κατεδαίσατο | δαλοῦ περθομένου.—**147. δέμας**: cf. Soph. *Antig.* 205, Eur. *Or.* 40. 'Corpse' in Hom. is always σῶμα, in Attic permissibly. δέμας in Homer is invariably used of a living body; cf. iv. 31.—**149. τοί**: the Kuretes.

151. μίνυνθα: an imitation of A 416 ἐπεί νύ τοι αἶσα μ. περ, οὔ τι μάλα δήν. μινύνθᾱ would cure the metrical defect, but there is no verb μινυνθάω (to which the only analogies would be Hom. ἀντάω from ἄντα and post-classical διχάω from δίχα); μινύνθᾱ cannot = μινύνθη from *μινύω, since -θη is Panhellenic. Other suggestions are μινύνθει, μίνυνθεν, μίνῡθεν (cf. i. 90). Accord. to the MS. the metre of 191 agrees with that of 151 and differs from the corresponding verses of the other epodes. For the expression cf. κατείβετο γλυκὺς αἰών ε 152. The death of Meleager is represented on an amphora of about 400 B.C. now at Naples (*J. H. S.* 18. 270).—**152. γνῶν**: the augment is omitted in Bacch. over 60 times.—**153. πνέων**: πν with 'Attic' correption only here; κν in ix. 39.—**154.** Cf. Praxilla ii., X 363. ἀγλαὸς ἥβη Theogn. 985, Sim. 105.—**156. δὴ τότε**: then, as never before.—**157. βλέφαρον**: the usual plur. (invariable in Hom. and in Pind., who has γλ-) would not suit the metre. The sing., without metrical compulsion, in v. 17. So παρειά for παρειαί. Cf. Eur. *Hippol.* 854 δάκρυσι βλέφαρα τέγγεται.—**160. τοι'**: = τοιαῦτα, referring to what follows (Pind. *Ol.* 6. 16). We might read τᾷδε = τῇδε P 512, Aisch. *Eum.* 45 (with ἐρῶ), or τοῖσδ'. **θνατοῖσι** κ.τ.λ.: the sentiment that Not-Being is the *summum bonum*, a theory of existence that antedates the Orphic doctrines of the sixth century, was even ascribed to Silenos, whose wisdom was treacherously gained by king Midas (Theopomp. Frag. 77, Arist. Frag. 37); cf. Theogn. 425 πάντων μὲν μὴ φῦναι ἐπιχθονίοισιν ἄριστον, | μηδ' ἐσιδεῖν αὐγὰς ὀξέος ἠελίου· | φύντα δ' ὅπως ὤκιστα πύλας Ἀίδαο περῆσαι, | καὶ κεῖσθαι πολλὴν γῆν ἐπαμησάμενον, Soph. *O. K.* 1225 μὴ φῦναι τὸν ἅπαντα νικᾷ λόγον· τὸ δ', ἐπεὶ φανῇ, | βῆναι κεῖθεν ὅθεν περ ἥκει, | πολὺ δεύτερον, ὡς τάχιστα. In the presence of the hero who has been condemned to Hades in his prime, Herakles suppresses the concluding part of this famous γνώμη. It is a fine touch to put this thought into the mouth of the triumphant son of Zeus who had passed the gates of death. The original form of the saying was ἀρχὴν μὲν μὴ φῦναι κ.τ.λ. Cf. the *Contest of Hom. and Hes.* 315 and Nietzsche *R. M.* 2. 211 ff., Mahaffy *On the Flinders Petrie Papyri*, p. 70. Later writers repeat the sentiment again and again: Eur. Frag. 285 ἐγὼ τὸ μὲν δὴ πανταχοῦ θρυλούμενον | κράτιστον εἶναί φημι μὴ φῦναι βροτῷ, 908 τὸ μὴ γενέσθαι κρεῖσσον ἢ φῦναι βροτοῖς, 449 ἐχρῆν γὰρ ἡμᾶς σύλλογον ποιουμένους | τὸν φύντα θρηνεῖν εἰς ὅσ' ἔρχεται κακά, | τὸν δ' αὖ θανόντα καὶ πόνων πεπαυμένον | χαίροντας εὐφημοῦντας ἐκπέμπειν δόμων, whence Cic. *Tusc.* 1. 48. 115 *non nasci homini longe optimum esse, proximum autem quam primum mori* (cf. Cic. apud Lactant. 3. p. 304 *non nasci longe optimum, nec in hos* *scopulos incidere vitae; proximum autem, si natus sis, quam primum tanquam ex incendio effugere*); Alexis Frag. 141. 14 οὐκοῦν τὸ πολλοῖς τῶν σοφῶν εἰρημένον, | τὸ μὴ γενέσθαι μὲν κράτιστόν ἐστ' ἀεί, | ἐπὰν γένηται δ' ὡς τάχιστ' ἔχειν τέλος, Epikur. in Diog. Laert. 10. 126, Poseidip. in Stob. *Flor.* 98. 57, etc.

161. Cf. ἠελίου ἴδεν αὐγάς Π 188 of being born.—**162**. Stobaios cites θνατοῖσι . . . φέγγος and continues with ὄλβιος δ' οὐδεὶς βροτῶν πάντα χρόνον. Though this addition recalls the thought of 53-55 it does not belong to this poem and probably not to Bacch. It looks as if the lemma had dropped out.—**162**. **οὐ γάρ . . . χρή**: οὐ γάρ often precedes.—**163**. Cf. Frag. 49 (B. 20) τί γὰρ ἐλαφρὸν ἔτ' ἔστ' ἄπρακτ' ὀδυρόμενον δονεῖν καρδίαν; Alk. x., κ 202 ἀλλ' οὐ γάρ τις πρῆξις ἐγίγνετο μυρομένοισιν, Ω 524; Soph. *Aias* 377 τί δῆτ' ἂν ἀλγοίης ἐπ' ἐξειργασμένοις;—**165**. **ἦρα**: from ἦ + ἄρα. In Bacch., Herakles has no other purpose than to obtain a beautiful bride; at least it is not apparent that his proposal is intended to console the shade of Meleager. In Pindar, Meleager's request that the hero marry his sister is prompted by the desire to secure for Deïaneira a protector against her dreaded suitor. It looks as if Bacch. had tastelessly modified the myth. It is difficult to discover, with Christ, a reference to the marriage of Hieron with Theron's sister (in 476?). The connection between Deïaneira and Herakles is designed to establish in Aitolia the cult of the Doric hero, who thus succeeds to the place occupied by the Pre-dorian Meleager.—**167**. **ἀδμήτα**: παρθένος ἀδμής ζ 109.—**168**. Cf. εἶδος ἀλίγκιος ἀθανάτοισιν θ 174.—**169**. Cf. θέσθαι γυναῖκα φ 72.—**172**. **χλωραύχενα**: a peculiar epithet for a girl, but χλωρός is often used of youthful beauty, of freshness and delicacy. See on Sim. xxxiii., and cf. the name *Chloe*.—**174**. **χρυσέας**: note the ῠ.—**175**. **θελξιμβρότου**: cf. Ξ 215, of Aphrodite's girdle, ἔνθα τέ οἱ θελκτήρια πάντα τέτυκτο.

176. The abruptness of the transition, which is not unusual at the end, is here softened by the fact that the reader involuntarily recalls the doom brought by Herakles upon himself in consequence of his infidelity to Deïaneira. Cf. 16. 23 ff. Here as elsewhere the poet presupposes full knowledge of the myth on the part of his audience. Abrupt transitions often occur in the choruses of later tragedy, which are virtually dithyrambs (Wilamowitz); cf. Soph. *Trach.* 497, Eur. *Andr.* 274 and often in Euripides. — **177**. **εὐποίητον** 'shapely.' ποιέω appears in Pind. and Bacch. only in the verbal adj. **ἅρμα**: the δίφρον of the Muse, Pind. *Ol.* 9. 81, *Isthm.* 2. 2.—**181**. Pelops was the human founder of the Olympic games.

—**182. κλεεννός**: the Aiolic form as in l. 12; *κλεινός* five times.—**183.** Cf. Pind. *Nem.* 10. 48 *δρόμῳ σὺν ποδῶν χειρῶν τε νικᾶσαι σθένει. ποσσί* is instr., *δρόμῳ* local dat. *νικῶν δρόμον Ol.* 13. 30.—**184.** The papyrus has *ἐϋπύργους*=*ἠυπύργους* (cf. Pind. *Nem.* 4. 12). *ἐύπυργον* is possible in H 71. Since *εὐ-* is distracted only before two consonants, if the MS. reading is correct, the *υ* is wrongly lengthened by the analogy of Hom. *εὐμμελίω, εὐννήτους.* **Συρακούσσας**: *Συράκοσ(σ)αι* is the best attested form in Pind., who never uses *Συράκουσαι. Συρακόσιος* Pind., Bacch., and inscr., is=Ionic—Attic *Συρακούσιος.* —**186. πέταλον**: 'token'; cf. i. 92-94, Sim. v. Possibly the Syracusan custom of voting on olive-leaves (*πέταλα*) was not originally confined to 'petalism,' the equivalent of the Attic ostracism. Cf. Pind. *Isthm.* 8. 46.—**188. φθόνον** *κ.τ.λ.* another mood than that of l. 52. **ἀμφοτ. χερσίν**: 'with might and main.'—**190. εὖ πράσσοι**: of success in the games, as Pind. *Ol.* 11. 4 ff. *εἰ δὲ σὺν πόνῳ τις εὖ πράσσῃ . . . ὕμνοι . . . τέλλεται . . . ἀφθόνητος δ' αἶνος Ὀλυμπιονίκαις ἄγκειται.*

191. Βοιωτὸς ἀνήρ, as *Χῖος ἀνήρ* Sim. 85. For the sentiment (193, 194) ascribed to Hesiod no closer parallel can be found in his extant works than *Theogon.* 81 ff.: *ὅντινα τιμήσωσι Διὸς κοῦραι μεγάλοιο, | . . . τῷ μὲν ἐπὶ γλώσσῃ γλυκερὴν χείουσιν ἐέρσην, | τοῦ δ' ἔπε' ἐκ στόματος ῥεῖ μείλιχα κ.τ.λ.* Theogn. 169 has *ὃν δὲ θεοὶ τιμῶσ', ὃν καὶ μωμεύμενος αἰνεῖ.* So Pind. *Isthm.* 6. 67 alludes to an *ἔπος* of Hesiod, his fellow-countryman, and a wretched epigram in his honour is attributed to Pindar. (On the relation of Pind. to Hesiod see Lübbert *de Pindari studiis Hesiodeis.*) Bacchylides' reference to a Boiotian poet need not be taken as an indirect compliment to Pindar, especially as the preceding sentence refers to envy. For references to their predecessors by the lyric poets see on Alk. xxv., Sim. xxii. **ὀμφάν**: of the poet's utterance Pind. Frag. 152; usually of the voice of an oracle.—**192. πρόπολος**: so *Μουσάων πρόπολον Ὀρφέα Anth.* app. 250.—**195** ff. I readily persuade myself that I am offering to Hieron a tribute of song that brings him fair fame and that my utterance is suited to the theme; for from my song there bud forth the roots of prosperity, *i.e.* the poet's praise ensures the duration of his fame. **πείθομαι**: cf. the use of *πέποιθα* Pind. *Ol.* 1. 103.—**196. εὐκλέα γλῶσσαν**: 'glorious shaft of song'; cf. *εὐκλέας ὀιστούς Ol.* 2. 90. **κελεύθου**: cf. 10. 51 *τί μακρὰν γλῶσσαν ἰθύσας ἐλαύνω ἐκτὸς ὁδοῦ*; Here *κελ.* is the straight track of the arrow of song. **προείς**: cf. *ὄρσαι γλῶσσαν* Pind. *Nem.* 7. 71. Perhaps *χέων.* **πέμπειν** *γλῶσσαν* as *πέμπειν μύθους* Eur. *Or.* 617, cf. *φέροις γλῶσσαν* Pind. *Ol.* 9. 41. Jebb proposed *κέλευθον γλ. ὀλβίῳ φέρων*, Blass *οὐκ ἐκτὸς θεῶν.* **τόθεν**: 'thence'; abl.-gen.

from the stem το-. It refers to εὐκλ. γλῶσσαν.—**198.** πυθμὴν τεθαλώς in a different sense, in Aisch. *Suppl.* 104.—**200.** Cf. vi. 66.

III. To Lachon of Keos, son of Aristomenes, victor in the boys' foot-race at Olympia. Probably before this victory Lachon was successful also at Nemea. This brief epinikion was sung after his return home from Olympia. A longer ode in honour of the same victory (nos. 7 and 8 in Ken.) was sung either at Olympia or in Keos.

Metre: logaoedic. The strophes contain six periods. There is no epode, as there is none in Pind. *Ol.* 14, *Pyth.* 6, *Nem.* 2. Possibly the last three verses form a single period. Blass transfers to the last verse the ultimate syllable of vv. 7, 15.

1. Λάχων . . . λάχε: for the word-play (*ὄνομα ὄρνις, nomen et omen*) cf. *Gen.* 27. 36 "Is he not rightly named *Jacob* for he hath supplanted me these two times," Shakesp. *Rich. II.* (ii. 1. 73) "O, how that name befits my composition! Old Gaunt indeed, and gaunt in being old," (cf. 2 *Henry IV.* iii. 2. 349). Arist. *Rhet.* 2. 23. 29 treats the argument from significant names as a kind of enthymeme. Pind. sometimes plays on proper names (*Ol.* 6. 30, *Pyth.* 3. 28, 4. 27), Sim. in 168, Plato in *Symp.* 185 C. Euripides was called τραγικὸς ἐτυμολόγος. Examples of such ὀνόματα ἐπώνυμα are Arete, Aias, Aphrodite, Apollo, Helen, Krios (Sim. 13), Meleager, Odysseus, Parthenopaios, Pentheus, Polyneikes, Sidero. Lachon, like Laches, is a clip-name of Lachemoiros.—**4. ὅσσα**: exclamatory; cf. ix. 120. The contrast is furnished by l. 10.—**5. ἀμπελοτρόφον**: the grape is a legend on the coins of Keos.

9. βρύοντες: a favourite verb with the poet; not used by Pind. For the constr. cf. Eubulos 56 κισσῷ κάρα (MSS. κατα) βρύουσαν, Bacch. 13. 36 στεφάνοισιν χαίταν ἐρεφθείς. See on Sim. v.—**10. ἀναξιμόλπου**: a new word; cf. ἀναξιφόρμιγγες ὕμνοι Pind. *Ol.* 2. 1. As Kenyon remarks, ἀναξιβρόντας ix. 66 favours the derivation of ἀναξι- from ἀνάσσω; so too ἀναξίαλος Ποσιδᾶν 20. 8, and ἀγλαΐας ἀνάσσων Pind. Frag. 148; but ἀναξι- may come from ἀνάγω ('Urania who awakes the song'), as has been shown by Bury *Isthmian Odes* p. ix. Cf. the note on Lasos.—**12. Ἀριστομένειον**: the use of the adj. ending -ιος to denote primarily connection and especially paternal descent was retained in Aiolic, Thessalian, and Boiotian, while Ionic and Doric used the patronymic gen. In lyric and tragic poetry the adoption of the patronymic -ιος is due to imitation of Hom. *e.g.* Τελαμώνιον υἱὸν N 67; cf. Κρόνιε παῖ Ῥέας Pind. *Ol.* 2. 12, Ἰνάχειον σπέρμα Aisch. *Prom.* 705 (-ειος instead of -ιος, transferred from -εσ- stems); Tennyson "a Niobean daughter."—**14. προδόμοις**: Pind. *Pyth.* 2. 18 σὲ δ', ὦ Δεινομένειε παῖ, πρὸ δόμων παρθένος ἀπύει, *Nem.* 1. 19, *Isthm.* 8. 2.—**15. στάδιον**: Lachon's name does not appear in Eusebios' list of Olympic victors, because he was a boy, and no register of boys' victories was kept. In the register of Keian victors (Pridik *de Cei insulae rebus* p. 160 ff.) we read among the Nemean victors: Λάχων 'Αριστομένεος παίδων. **κρατήσας** echoes κρατεῦσαν l. 7.—**16.** Tyrt. 12. 24 ἄστυ εὐκλεΐσας, Sim. 125. 2 πατρίδ' ἐπευκλεΐσας (cf. Kaibel 945. 2). Here the Dor. aor., as Pind. *Pyth.* 9. 91; cf. v. 87, ix. 129.

IV. In honour of Automedes of Phleius, who seems to have won three out of the five divisions of the pentathlon at the Nemean games. The poem may possibly have been composed in the Peloponnese during the poet's exile. To a Phleiasian the ancient traditions of the neighbouring Nemea were of especial interest; hence the first triad deals with Herakles' connection with the place, and the establishment there by the Seven against Thebes of the funeral games in honour of Archemoros. At the end of the epode a transition is made to Automedes, the recital of whose skill and the praise of Asopos, his native stream, fill the second triad. Of the four systems only two are preserved. The poem contained two myths, of which that dealing with the history of the seat of the contest is, as in Pindar (but only in *Nem.* 10, *Isthm.* 7), put at the beginning.

New words: διακρινής (?) 'clear,' εὐναής, μηλοδαΐκτης 'slaughterer of flocks,' ξανθοδερκής 'tawny-eyed,' πορφυροδίνης, φοινίκασπις.

Metre: dactylo-epitrite. The strophe consists of nine (five according to Jurenka), the epode of five periods.

1. χρυσαλάκατοι: of Artemis v. 38 (note); see on Pind. i. 1. **Χάριτες**; the Graces preside over the games and over poetry. To the athlete they impart the qualities that ensure success; to the poet they grant 'persuasive renown.' Cf. Pind. *Ol.* 14 *init.*—**2. πεισίμβροτον** supports the vulgate Aisch. *Choeph.* 362. —**3. θεῖος**: inspired by the gods, as θεῖος ἀοιδός δ 17. **προφάτας**: the poet. See on Pind. viii. 5 and cf. γλυκὺν κώμου προφάταν *Nem.* 9. 50. Bacch. has φῆμα, but προφᾶται 10. 28.

The text supposes that ἑλικοβλεφάρων has been displaced by τε ἰοβλ. So in Pind. *Ol.* 6. 30, *Isthm.* 7. 23 ἰοπλόκαμος has been substituted for ἰόπλοκος. Jebb reads ἔπει ('utterance') M. ὅτ', Housm. M. τό.

—**4. εὔτυκος** = ἑτοῖμος, *scil.* ἐστί, as Aisch. *Suppl.* 974. For the constr. cf. also θεὸς εὔτυκος ἕρπεν Kallim. 5. 3.—**5. εὐθαλές**: cf. πανθᾰλής 13. 196, εὐθᾰλής Aisch. Frag. 300. 5. εὐθᾱλής is more common (Pind. *Pyth.* 9. 72, Aristoph. *Aves* 1062).—**8. μηλοδαΐκταν**: in tragedy we have -δάϊκτος in compounds (ἀνδρο-, αὐτο-, λουτρο-, πυργο-).—**9.** In Pausanias' time the cave of the Nemean lion was still shown. See Frazer on 2. 15. 2, Baumeister fig. 722, *J. H. S.* 18. 274.

10. φοινικάσπιδες: Alkmaion bore an αἰθὰ ἀσπίς on the expedition against Thebes (Pind. *Pyth.* 8. 46). The shield of Dionysos was red (Quint. Smyrn. 5. 27). φ. is a variation on the usual designation of the Argives as λευκάσπιδες (Aisch. *Sept.* 88, Soph. *Antig.* 106, Eur. *Phoin.* 1099), which is perhaps due to etymological association with ἀργός. **ἡμίθεοι**: used as in Hes. (*W. D.* 160) from whom Bacch. borrowed much. The ἡμίθεοι are the heroes and kings of the mythical period especially those engaged in the wars at Thebes and Troy (cf. M 23, *Hymn* 32. 19, Sim. xii.). The word is often used of the companions of those heroes who had divine blood in their veins. Cf. v. 60 λιπόντες Ἄργος . . . χαλκάσπιδες ἡμίθεοι.—**11. κριτοί**: ἐν Ἀδραστείῳ νόμῳ 'according to the foundation of Adrastos' Pind. *Nem.* 10. 28.—**12.** The Nemea were ἆθλα ἐπ' Ἀρχεμόρῳ; cf. the title of Stesichoros' poem Ἆθλα ἐπὶ Πελίᾳ. In his *Nemea* Aischylos related the foundation of the games in commemoration of the death of Opheltes, the infant son of Lykurgos and Eurydike. See Sim. xx. and cf. Apollod. 3. 6. 4, schol. Pind. *Nem.* p. 424, Paus. 2. 15. 2 (Frazer 2. 92), Hyginus 74. **ξανθοδερκής**: cf. γλαυκῶπες δράκοντες Pind. *Ol.* 6. 45. Of this serpent, Stat. *Theb.* 5. 508 says *livida fax oculis.* ξανθός of flame, i. 56, xiii. 4.—**13. ἀωτεύοντα**: for the usual ἀωτέοντα (cf. on Alkm. x. 8); Stat. *Theb.* 5. 502 *ille graves oculos, languentiaque ora comanti | mergit humo, fessusque diu puerilibus actis | labitur in somnos.* Hesych. glosses ἀωτεύειν by ἀπανίζεσθαι, a meaning impossible in itself but due to a confusion with the myth that the child was plucking flowers while its nurse Hypsipyle was showing a spring to the chiefs of the expedition. So Eur. Frag. 754 says of Opheltes: ἕτερον ἐφ' ἑτέρῳ αἰρόμενος | ἄγρευμ' ἀνθέων ἡδομένᾳ ψυχᾷ | τὸ νήπιον ἄπληστον ἔχων. **ὑπέροπλος** of size—the Hesiodic, not the Homeric meaning.

Ken. suggests ἀσαλεύοντα 'in careless sport'; cf. ἀσαλεῖν· ἀφροντίζειν, σάλα and ἀσαλής in Aisch., ἀσάλεια in Sophron. Ellis ἀλατεύοντα 'wandering,' cf. Stat. *Theb.* 4. 792.

—**14. σᾶμα**: as Pind. x. 10. So the destruction of the sparrows in B 308 was an omen. Opheltes was renamed Archemoros ('the beginner of doom').—**15. μοῖρα**: cf. ii. 121, 143, ix. 24, 89; αἶσα xix. Contrast viii. 15. **νιν**: elsewhere sing., here of the ἡμίθεοι. The plur. once in Pind., Frag. 7.—**16. πεῖθε**: 'could persuade.' Amphiaros could not persuade Adrastos to retrace his steps just as Kalchas failed to persuade Agamemnon at Aulis. The negative with the imperfect instead of the aorist denotes baffled effort, frustrated will. Cf. vi. 13.—**17. εὐάνδρους**: Tyrt. 15. 1 *Σπάρτας εὐάνδρω*. **ἀγυιάς**: of Argos. Note the similarity in expression in Pind. *Pyth.* 8. 52 ff., where Amphiaraos (*Ὀϊκλείδας*) prophecies concerning Adrastos in the second expedition against Thebes: *μόνος γὰρ ἐκ Δαναῶν στρατοῦ | . . . ἀφίξεται λαῷ σὺν ἀβλαβεῖ | Ἄβαντος εὐρυχόρους ἀγυιάς*.—**18.** The asyndeton is more remarkable than that after the exclamation in 15. **πρόνοιαν**: cf. Aisch. *Agam.* 684 *προνοίαισι τοῦ πεπρωμένου γλῶσσαν ἐν τύχᾳ νέμων*.

19. Ταλαϊονίδαν: as Pind. *Ol.* 6. 15; a double patronymic for *Ταλαΐων* or *Ταλαΐδας*. Cf. *Ἰαπετιονίδης* Hes. *W. D.* 54 and *παῖς Ἀγαμεμνονίδας* Soph. *El.* 182.—**20.** Alliteration with *π*; cf. 15-16, 39-40, 45. **πλαξίππῳ**: of Polyneikes, as of the Boiotians Hes. *Shield* 24; of Oineus ii. 97; of Thebe Pind. *Ol.* 6. 85.—**21. ἀπ' ἀγώνων**: with *ἐρέψωνται κόμαν*.—**22. Νεμέᾳ**: with synizesis as 12. 8, Pind. *Nem.* 4. 75.—**23. τριέτει**: the Nemean games in honour of Zeus were celebrated on the 18th of Skirophorion in the second and fourth year of every Olympiad. **στεφάνῳ**: of fresh celery (*σέλινον*), which had a funereal application. The festival was an *ἀγὼν στεφανίτης* from the time of its renewal in 573. Tradition reports that prior to the Persian wars the prize was a crown of olive, and that afterwards celery was substituted to express the grief of the Greeks at the loss of their countrymen. Since the Nemean contest was an *ἐπιτάφιος ἀγών* in commemoration of Archemoros, celery was probably used from the beginning (Paus. 8. 48. 2).

27. πενταέθλοισιν: dative with the verb as in Aristoph. *Nubes* 605 (*Βάκχαις ἐμπρέπων*). **ἐνέπρεπεν**: cf. Aisch. *Agam.* 6 *λαμπροὺς δυνάστας, ἐμπρέποντας αἰθέρι*. See on Sa. iii.—**28. διακρινεῖ**: formed like *εὐκρινής*, *εἰλικρινής*. The MS. *διακρίνει* (*φάη*) can scarcely mean 'surpass in splendour.'—**29. διχομήνιδος**: 'month-dividing,' 'when the month is halved.' Of the full moon *δ.* *Μήνα* Pind. *Ol.* 3. 19, *διχομηνίδεσσιν ἑσπέραις Isthm.* 8. 47. The festival took place at the time of the full moon (cf. *Nem.* 4. 35). **σελάνα**: so -*ᾱνᾱ* in *Ἀθάνα*; elsewhere Bacch. avoids two Doric *ᾱ*'s.—**30. κύκλον**: cf. *Ol.* 9. 93 *διήρχετο κύκλον ὅσσᾳ βοᾷ*.—**32** ff. This passage settles the disputed sequence of these three parts of the pentathlon: throwing the discus, hurling the javelin, and wrestling; cf. Pind. *Nem.* 7. 71, Sim. 153. Automedes was probably defeated in the long jump and the foot-race. The relative value of the divisions is unknown, but the victor must have won in three out of the five events (Aristeid.

Panath. 3. 339, Plut. *Quaest. Symp.* 9. 2. 2). Recent discussion of the pentathlon will be found in *Philol.* 1891, p. 469 ff., *Jahrb.* 1893, p. 785 ff., Henrich *Bayr. Gymn.-Bl.*, 1894, p. 366 ff.—**34.** Cf. αἰπὺν αἰθέρα i. 36.

36. The construction is obscure. Perhaps τοῖος (ἐφάνη) is to be supplied. **ἢ** is hardly correct (ἐκτελευτάσας τ' Stahl for ἢ τελευταίας). δή (Jebb) is weak, though the comma after χειρός untangles the construction. **ἀμάρυγμα:** accusative of respect: 'in the flashing movements of the closing wrestling-bout.' Cf. Pind. *Isthm.* 8. 41 στεροπαῖσι ποδῶν. —**38.** **πρός:** the preposition is unnecessary (ix. 35), but is to be taken by tmesis with the verb.—**39.** Mention of the Asopos forms the transition to the myth, which is often introduced by a relative pronoun (τοῦ). The river-god Asopos is said to have settled at Phleius, where he married Metope, the daughter of the Ladon in Elis. By her he had two sons and twelve daughters, *i.a.* Korkyra, Salamis, Aigina (cf. 13. 44), Peirene, Kleone, Thebe, Sinope. Cf. Hdt. 5. 80, Paus. 2. 5. 2, 5. 22. 5, and esp. Diod. 4. 72, who probably followed the legend current in Phleius. According to the common tradition Thebe was the daughter of the Boiotian Asopos. Cf. Pind. *Isthm.* 8. 17 χρὴ δ' ἐν ἑπταπύλοισι Θήβαις τραφέντα | Αἰγίνᾳ Χαρίτων ἄωτον προνέμειν, | πατρὸς οὕνεκα δίδυμαι γένοντο θύγατρες Ἀσωπίδων | ὁπλόταται. Bacch. may have this passage in mind ll. 49 ff.—**40.** **χθόνα:** terminal accus. as ἐλθὼν γαῖαν Eur. *Alk.* 8.—**41.** **Νείλου:** with the passage cf. *Isthm.* 2. 42; 6. 22 ff. of the Aiakidai: μυρίαι δ' ἔργων καλῶν τέτμηνθ' . . . κέλευθοι καὶ πέραν Νείλοιο παγᾶν. The Ethiopians led by Memnon are here meant.—**42.** **εὐναεῖ:** usu. εὐνάων or εὐνάεις.—**44.** **κοῦραι:** the Amazons, led by Penthesilea, who fought at Troy. There may also be a reference to Herakles' encounter with them. **διωξίπποι':** cf. v. 75.

45. For the voc. after the 2nd person see on Pind. xxiii. Hiatus before ἄναξ as in Pind. *Pyth.* 4. 89, etc. Pindar may have used the *F*, but the hiatus in an Ionic poet is purely conventional. So in μεγιστοάνασσα 19. 21.—**46.** **ἐγγόνων** (ἐκγόνων? cf. ix. 16): the heroes Telamon, Herakles, Aias, Achilles, whose fame redounds to the glory of Asopos. Aiakos, the grandfather of Achilles, was the grandson of Asopos. Descent from a river-god was an honour (Φ 185): Nestor was descended from Enipeus, Asteropaios from Axios. Since Phleius was poor in local legends the poet draws, somewhat after the recondite Alexandrian fashion, upon the genealogy of its river-god. **γεύσαντο:** 'tasted' the prowess; cf. Υ 258 γευσόμεθ' ἀλλήλων χαλκήρεσιν ἐγχείῃσιν. **Τροίας:**

Troy was taken by Herakles and by Neoptolemos.—**47.** **δι'**: 'along'; cf. the use of ἀνά and κατά.

V. For Alexidamos of Metapontum, victor in the boys' wrestling match at Delphi. The ode was probably sung at Metapontum before or in the temple of Artemis, the patron goddess of the city, the divinity to whose favour Alex. therefore owed his success, and whose intercession with Hera freed from their madness the daughters of Proitos. The local cult of Artemis suggested to the poet the selection of this myth, which stands in no known connection with the family of the victor. The individual is absorbed in his native city. This is the only extant ode in honour of a Metapontine, though almost a third of Pindar's odes was composed for Sicilians or inhabitants of Magna Graecia. From l. 24 ff. it appears that Alex. had been deprived of a victory at Olympia by the unjust verdict of the judges. Of the three systems, the first contains an exordium to Victory and personal matters relating to the contest, and at the close of the epode passes to the myth. The second and part of the third triad narrates the story of the daughters of Proitos, with an incidental mention of the quarrel of Proitos and Akrisios and of the foundation of Tiryns. The last epode brings us back to Metapontum, with a possible allusion to the ancestors of the poet. Contrary to the general usage in epinikia the victor is not mentioned again at the close. In contrast to Ode ii., which shows Artemis in her wrathful and malevolent aspect, the link between the parts of this poem is the beneficent activity of the goddess.

For the myth Bacch. is dependent only in part upon Hesiod, since that poet ascribed the madness of the Proitides to their refusal to accept the rites of Dionysos (cf. Apollod. 1. 9. 12, Diodor. 4. 68). It is possible that Bacch. also used an Argolic prose version of the story; at any rate, Akusilaos, an Argive historian (about 480 B.C.), ascribed the frenzy of the Proitides to impiety towards an image of Hera (probably the work of Argos and the first statue of the goddess). According to the usual account, the agent of their cure was Melampus (schol. *o* 225, Hdt. 9. 34, Apollod. 2. 2. 2, Paus. 2. 18. 4, 8. 18. 7, Ovid *Metam.* 15. 326), who chased the maidens to Sikyon; but Bacch. chose that form of the legend which did honour to Artemis; and the tradition which made Artemis their healer was adopted by Kallim. *Hymn to Artemis* 233 ff. A reconciliation of the two legends appears in Paus. 8. 18. 7, who reports that Melampus cured the Proitides at Lusoi in a temple of Artemis. In his account the temple is already erected, but, according to l. 110, it was not founded until the cure had been effected. Hesychios *s.v.* ἀκρουχεῖ says that Melampus built the temple on Mt. Akron in Argolis. The healing of the Proitides is represented on a vase of the fourth century now at Naples (*J. H. S.* 18. 273; cf. Wiener *Vorlegebl.* ser. B, pl. 4. 3. 4 and de Witte *Gaz. Arch.* 1879, p. 121). We have already seen on Ode i. that Bacch. followed a different tradition from his contemporary Herodotos. In this instance the historian (9. 34) speaks merely of the madness of the 'women in Argos' (so also Diodor. 4. 68, Paus. 2. 18. 4). Apollod. 2. 2. 2 makes the madness of these women follow upon that of the daughters of Proitos. The ancients regarded madness as a manifestation of divine wrath (in tragedy, Io, Aias, Herakles, Orestes). This poem is peculiar in the absence of the gnomic element.

New words: ἀδεισιβόας, ἀμετρόδικος 'measureless,' 'immoderate,' ἀριστοπάτρα 'of noblest father,' εὔγυιος 'shapely-limbed,' ἱππώκης, καλλιρόας, ὀρθόδικος (-ας Pind.), πάννικος 'crowned with constant victory,' φοινικοκράδεμνος 'with crimson scarf.'

Tautometric responsions: 26=96, οι ᾱς 7=21=49, παρ 47=103.

Metre: dactylo-epitrite, with eight (or possibly nine) periods in the strophe, eleven in the epode. The latter may be reduced in number by joining vv. 1 and 2, 3 and 4, 6 and 7, 9 and 10.

1. The restoration of the first three lines is entirely conjectural. In Frag. 71 (48) Nike is called κούρα Πάλλαντος πολυώνυμε. That Pallas is not meant here is certain from ὑψίζυγος, which is appropriate to Zeus alone (Κρονίδας 1. 18, Δ 166). The parentage of Nike from Zeus, which here for the first time appears in literature, is due to her affinity with Athena. Farnell compares N. εὐπατέρεια Menander Frag. 616, Himer. 19. 3. **γλυκύδωρε**: restored from Stob. *Flor.* 3. 66 (Ursinus), who also quotes ἐν πολυχρ. . . . ἀρετῆς with κρίνειν and Attic forms throughout. Victory, like the Muse (i. 3), is the giver of renown.—**4. πολυχρύσῳ**: usu. of cities famed for their wealth (Troy, Mykenai, Sardis, Babylon).—**5.** Cf. Hes. *Theogon.* 388.—**6. κρίνεις**: cf. Pind. *Isthm.* 5. 11 κρίνεται δ' ἀλκὰ διὰ δαίμονας ἀνδρῶν. **τέλος** *praemium*; ἐφ' ἑκάστῳ | ἔργματι κεῖτο τ. *Isthm.* 1. 27.—**8. ἔλλᾱθι**: an Aiolic perfect as ἔλλᾰτε (conj.) Kallim. Frag. 121 = ἵλᾰτε Apoll. Rhod. 4. 984. In the perfect ᾰ is to be expected (<σεσλᾰ-; the λλ as in χέλλιοι from χεσλ-), but the ᾱ, which is possible also in ἔλλαθι Sim. 49, is either due to levelling of quantity (ἵλ̄ηος: ablaut Ion.-Attic ἵλᾰος, whence by contamination ἵλᾱος A 583), or is simply an imitation of the epic η in ἵληθι γ 380 <*σισλημι, cf. *consōlari.* For ἵληθι we expect ἵλᾰθι, which occurs in Theokr. 15. 143. The grammarians report as Aiolic both ἔλλαθι and ἴλλαος. The words in question are applied only to divinities.—**9. Στυγός** : cf. Hes. *Theogon.* 383. Ken. has Διός, which identifies Nike with Athena (Soph. *Phil.* 134, Eur. *Ion* 456). **ὀρθοδίκου** : with reference to δίκας . . . ὀρθᾶς, l. 26.—**11. κατέχουσι** : cf. 13. 130 ἕξειν πόλιν.—**12. εὐφροσύναι** : pl. of the various forms of festivity following on the victory, cf. Solon 4. 10, Aisch. *Prom.* 539. Pind. has the sing. *Pyth.* 11. 45 ; cf. εἰλαπινάζοισιν εὐφρόνως *Pyth.* 10. 40. **θεότιμον ἄστυ** : θεοτίματον πόλιν 9. 98.—**14.** Cf. Pind. *Pyth.* 10. 57 ff. Ἱπποκλέαν . . . σὺν ἀοιδαῖς | ἕκατι στεφάνων θαητὸν ἐν ἅλιξι θησέμεν, *Pyth.* 4. 241 Ἀελίου θαυμαστὸς υἱός.

15. νιν : in this ode the victor is never addressed in the second person.—**16. βαθ. Λατοῦς** as Pind. vii.—**20. ἔπεσον** : cf. Pind. *Pyth.* 9. 123 πολλὰ μὲν κείνῳ δίκον | φύλλ' ἔπι καὶ στεφάνους—the φυλλοβολία.—**21. ἦρα** = χάριν. So in Pherekydes of Syros σὺ δέ μοι χαῖρε καὶ ἦρα ἴσθι. Cf. ἦρα φιλοξενίης Kallim. Frag. 41. The prepositional use is derived from θυμῷ ἦρα φέροντες Ξ 132. Aristarchos took ἦρα to be the accus. plur. of an adj. *ἦρος, but Herodian regarded it as accus. sing. of *ἦρ. The word is usually derived from $\sqrt{\alpha\rho}$ in ἄρμενος etc., but it is possibly cognate with Old Bulgar. *vărem* 'gift,' 'protection.' This suits the Ϝ in σ 56.—**23. γε** points to the unfair decision at Olympia. **σύν** : temporal ; cf. Pind. xv. 1, σὺν δεκάτᾳ γενεᾷ *Pyth.* 4. 10. **πρός** with the dative is rare in choral poetry. See on Pind. xxviii. Bacch. does not use πρός with gen. = ὑπό. **πεσόντα** : *lapsum.* Cf. εἶδε νικάσαντα . . . Ἀώς ii. 40. After εἶδε of actual perception the pres. part. is usual in Attic prose ; πεσόντα εἶδον Hdt. 9. 22 ; the perf. *e.g.* in ὁρᾷ ἐκπεπτωκότα Soph. *El.* 749. Cf. the use of αἰσθάνομαι in Thuk.—**24. φάσω** : the future anticipates the delivery of the ode : so Jurenka, who compares Pind. *Nem.* 9. 43, *Isthm.* 1. 34.—**27.** Bacch. ascribes to injustice what Pindar usu. ascribes to misfortune or untoward circumstance. Attacks on the impartiality of the Hellanodikai, though rare, are not wanting (Pind. *Nem.* 8 ; cf. Plut. *Quaest. Plat.* 2, Diod. 1. 95, Paus. 6. 3. 7), and it has been noticed that Eleian contestants gained a suspiciously large number of victories. An unjust verdict might be rectified by an appeal to the Eleian senate. **ἀπέτραπεν** : we might expect the middle 'turn away from' (so ἀποτρέπομαί τι in trag.), in which case ὀρθᾶς would be hypallage for ὀρθὰν κελ. (so Pind. *Pyth.* 11. 39) δίκας. Cf. ἀποτρόπῳ γνώμᾳ *Pyth.* 8. 94.—**28.** Bacch. is fond of this order, in which a substantive divides a preceding adj. from a following substantive : ii. 19, 98, v. 8. **παγξένῳ** : the Olympian games were open to all who could prove genuine Hellenic descent. Cf. Pind. *Ol.* 3. 18, of the olive tree at Olympia : σκιαρὸν φύτευμα ξυνὸν ἀνθρώποις.

29. στεφανωσάμενον : Bacch. avoids the active (ἐστεφάνωσε χαίταν *Ol.* 14. 24).—**30. πορτιτρόφον** : Artemis is also ταυροπόλος. **ἄν** : only here is the infin. used with the modal particle. ἄν and κε are equally frequent in Bacch.—**31.** The wiliness (of his adversary) did not assail the youth with tortuous craft. The meaning 'brought the youth to the ground' requires the assumption of a violent tmesis (ἐμπελάζω); cf. πέλασε χθονὶ Θ 277. Some would find in the lacuna a reference to the training of Alex.—**32. καλλιχόρῳ** : of Orchomenos, Pind. *Pyth.* 12. 26.—**33. ποικίλαις** : *malo sensu* as Pind. *Ol.* 1. 29, *Nem.* 5. 28. **τέχναις** : 13. 16 παντοίαισι τέχναις.—**34.** In a miscarriage of justice, as in any extraordinary event, the unrationalistic Greek seeks the presence of a superhuman power. Cf. viii. 16, x. 41, Solon 11. 2. Ken. compares Ψ 383-393, 774. The real opinion of the poet lies in the second alternative.—**35. γνῶμαι** : the decision of the judges. **πολύπλαγκτοι** 'erring,' without the connotation of intentional injustice. Cf. Pind. *Ol.* 7. 30 αἱ δὲ φρενῶν ταραχαὶ | παρέπλαγξαν καὶ σοφόν, Eur. *Hippol.* 240 παρεπλάγχθην γνώμας ἀγαθᾶς, Kaibel 594. 5 (late) πολυπλ. πραπίδες. —**37. ἀγροτέρα** : see on Skol. iii.—**38. χρυσαλάκατος** : 'of the golden bow,' not 'of the golden distaff.' Used of Artemis Υ 70, of Leto Pind. Frag. 139. 1. Hesych. has χρυσηλάκατος· καλλίτοξος, ἠλακάτη γὰρ ὁ τοξικὸς κάλαμος. The passage is an extreme case of the poet's fondness for *epitheta ornantia.* The epithet εὔκλεια would have been more to the point.—**39. ἡμέρα** : with reference to Artemis' healing of the Proitides. See on l. 96 and cf. Anakr. i. 7. Paus. 8. 18. 8 says that the citizens of Kleitor, near which the cure was effected, called the goddess ἡμερασία. Despite ἅμερος in Pind. and the bucolic poets, the word has Pan-hellenic *ē*; cf. *S. G. D.-I.* 3342. 20, 4629. 172 and see Christ *Beiträge z. Dial. Pindars* p. 41. The epithet serves here, infelicitously enough, to introduce the myth.—**40. τᾷ** : a relative pronoun often occurs at the beginning of the myth (13. 64, Pind. *Ol.* 1. 25, 3. 13). A relative adverb in l. 113 makes the transition from the myth. **'Αβαντιάδας** : the genealogy is as follows :

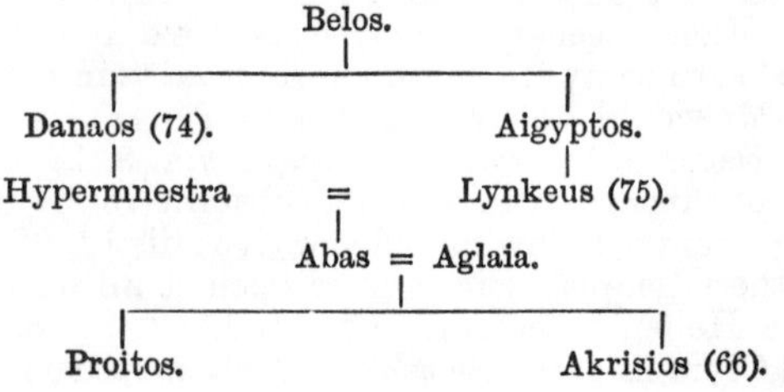

Lynkeus succeeded Danaos as lord of Argos.—**41.** **κατένασσε** =ἱδρύσατο; only here with an impersonal object. **πολύλλιστον**; νηὸς π. *Hymn* 4. 28.

43 ff. Cf. Eur. *Bacch.* 23 ff.—**45.** **παραπλῆγι**: the transitive use only here. Either = ἀνάγκῃ τῇ τὰς φρένας παραπλῆγας ποιούσῃ, or φρένας is the object of ζεύξασ'. Cf. πάρφρονος λύσσας l. 103 and παράφρονι καὶ παραπλῆγι τὴν διάνοιαν Plut. *Pomp.* 72. **φρένας**: φρ fails to make position only here; θρ in ii. 8, ix. 124.—**46.** Cf. κρατερὴ ἀνάγκη Z 458. **ζεύξασ'**: as ἀνάγκῃ ζευγεὶς Soph. *Phil.* 1025, πότμῳ ζυγένθ' Pind. *Nem.* 7. 6.—**47.** Cf. schol. ο 225 διὰ τὴν ἐκ νεότητος ἀνεπιλογιστίαν ἁμαρτουσῶν εἰς Ἥραν.—**50.** Bacch. omits any reference to the irreverence done to the ξόανον of Hera, which was explained by Curtius as symbolical of the contempt for the older divinities of the country.—**51.** **πλούτῳ** κ.τ.λ. constr. as Hdt. 6. 127 πλούτῳ . . . προφέρων Ἀθηναίων. **παρέδρου**: only here of a wedded wife. Themis bears the title Διὸς πάρεδρος *Ol.* 8. 22, but not because of the tradition followed by Pind. in Frag. i. 10. Note the labial alliteration in 50-51.—**52.** **εὐρυβίᾳ**: generally of persons (always in Pind.), but cf. φθόνος εὐρυβ. 16. 31 and πλοῦτος εὐρυσθενὴς Pind. *Pyth.* 5. 1.—**54.** **παλιντρ. νόημα**: Artemis turned the fashion of their thought from sanity to mad illusions.—**56.** Cf. Verg. *Ecl.* 6. 48 *Proetides implerunt falsis mugitibus agros.*

59–81. The settlement of Tiryns by Proitos.—**61.** **ἀδεισιβόαι**: who know no fright when they confront the βοὴν ἀγαθοί in battle. Cf. ii. 155.—**62.** **χαλκάσπιδες ἡμίθεοι**: see on iv. 10.—**63.** **πολυζήλῳ**: 'envied by many' because of his kingly station, rather than 'very prosperous.'—**65.** **βληχρᾶς**: cf. Pind. Frag. 245 πρόφασις βληχροῦ (βληχρὰ?) γίνεται νείκεος, where the grammarians report βλ. = ἰσχυρός, though in Frag. xvi. 9 it is 'feeble,' as probably in Bacch. 13. 194. The expression βληχρᾶς ἀπ' ἀρχᾶς appears to mean 'from a feeble beginning,' *i.e.* in childhood. Tyrrell suggests βληχᾶς ἀπ' ἄκρας 'from the first infant cry.' Apollod. 2. 1. 1 says that Akrisios and Proitos κατὰ γαστρὸς ἔτι ὄντες ἐστασίαζον πρὸς ἀλλήλους. The enmity of their ancestors descended to the children as in the case of Tyndareus and Hippokoon. **ἀνέπαλτο**: cf. ὄρωρε νεῖκος Ω 107.—**68.** **ἤρειπον**: see on Sim. xiii. 3. **ἀμετροδίκοις**: framed on the model of ἀμετροεπής B 212 (cf. ἀποινόδικος). The last part of the comp. is almost quiescent. Lit. 'exceeding the measure of right' (cf. μέτρια καὶ δίκαια Aristoph. *Nubes* 1137). **μάχαις**: on the way from Argos to Epidauria Paus. (2. 25. 7) saw a monument of the battle for the kingdom. Apollod. 2. 2. 1 narrates that Akrisios expelled Proitos from Argos and that the latter fled to Lykia, where he raised an army and on his return occupied Tiryns. The Argive territory was then divided, Akrisios receiving Argos, while Proitos kept Tiryns. Paus. (2. 16. 2), who does not here mention the rivalry of the brothers for the possession of the kingdom, reports that Proitos received *τὸ Ἡραῖον καὶ Μιδείαν καὶ Τίρυνθα καὶ ὅσα πρὸς θαλάσσῃ τῆς Ἀργείας*, and adds *σημεῖά τε τῆς ἐν Τ. οἰκήσεως Προίτου καὶ ἐς τόδε λείπεται*, *i.e.* the *τεῖχος* l. 77. On the other hand Ovid *Metam.* 5. 236 says that Akrisios was forced to flee from Argos and then attacked his brother. The picturesque addition in 69 ff. is probably the poet's own embellishment.—**70. λαχόντας**: causal.

71. ὁπλότερον: partitive apposition with *παῖδας*.—**72. πρίν**: Bacch. uses only the infinitive with this particle, and does not employ *ἕως*, *ἔστε*, or *ὄφρα* (temporal).—**75. διωξίπποιο**: of Ares iv. 44, of Kyrene Pind. *Pyth.* 9. 4.—**77. κάμον**: the final syllable is anceps because the cola of 77 and 78 make one verse.—**78. πόλει**: the poet follows the tradition that refers the construction of the city to Tiryns, the son of Argos. From Paus. 2. 25. 8 we infer that the city was already built when the Kyklopes came from Lykia to Proitos and fortified it with massive walls. Apollod. 2. 2. 1 has *ταύτην* (Tiryns) *αὐτῷ* (Proitos) *Κυκλώπων τειχισάντων*. Neither *θεοδμάτους* in l. 58 nor *κτίζειν* in l. 72 proves that the Kyklopes built the city, as well as the fortifying walls, at the command of Zeus. *κτίζειν* ('settle anew') need not be used of the original foundation, and in *θεοδμ.* the first element is often faint in lyric poetry. Tiryns is called *Κυκλωπία πόλις* Eur. *H. F.* 15; cf. Pind. xxv. 6.—**80. ἱππόβοτον**: of Argos B 287.—**82. ἔνθεν**: the relative resumes the story interrupted in l. 59.—**84. θύγατρες**: three in number according to the schol. on Kallim. 3. 236: Lysippe, Iphinoe (Hipponoe in Servius), Iphianassa (Kyrianassa in Serv.). The schol. on *ο* 225 mentions only two: Lysippe and Iphianassa. Aelian gives the names as Elege and Kelaine. The wife of Proitos is called Anteia by Homer; Euripides calls her Stheneboia.

85. τὸν . . . κραδίαν: cf. Sa. i. 4. **ξείνα**: 'unwonted.'—**87. δοίαξε** (*δοίαζε*?): the aor. as in *μερμήριξεν* A 189. *φάσγανον ἄμφηκες* K 256.—**92. τελέους**: as *τ. ἑπτὰ μῆνας* Aristoph. *Lysistr.* 104.—**93. ἠλύκταζον**: note the Ionic augment.—**94.** Paus. 8. 18. 7 speaks of a cave on Mt. Aroanios above Nonakris to which the maidens fled. On Mt. *Chelmos* (Aroanios) there are now to be seen two caves, 'quite near each other, on the brow of the mountain, overlooking the profound glen of the Styx': Frazer *Paus.* 4. 257, who says that the situation of the caves agrees well with the itinerary of Paus. The same scholar also suggests that the deep cavern on the western side of Mt. *Chelmos* could also be the cave in which the Proitides took refuge. Previous to this they wandered throughout Argos.—**96. Λοῦσον**: Arkad. 75. 16 has Λουσός as adj. and name of the city, Paus. and Steph. Byz. Λουσοί, others Λοῦσα, of the city. Some have Λουσσ-. Here the spring in the territory of Kleitor is meant which possessed magical properties: Phylarch. *apud* Athen. 2. 43 F: κρήνην ἀφ' ἧς τοὺς πιόντας οὐκ ἀνέχεσθαι τὴν τοῦ οἴνου ὀδμήν, cf. Vitruv. 8. 3. 21 φεῦγε δ' ἐμὴν πηγὴν μισάμπελον, ἔνθα Μελάμπους | λυσάμενος λύσσης Προιτίδας ἀρτεμέας (Ellis) | πάντα καθαρμὸν ἔκοψεν ἀποκρύφον, εὖτ' ἄρ' ἀπ' Ἄργους | οὔρεα τρηχείης ἤλυθον Ἀρκαδίης, Pliny *H. N.* 31. 2. 13. The city of Lusos (now *Soudená*) was situated between Kleitor and Kynaitha in a lofty plain (Leake *Morea* 2. 110, Curtius *Pelop.* 1. 397, Frazer on Paus. 8. 18. 7). North of *Soudená* Dodwell discovered the cella of a temple (cf. l. 110), which he thought was that of Artemis Hemeresia. To the west of the modern village Leake found remains of another building (supposed by him to be part of this temple) near the middle fountain of the three that "form the sources of the stream which runs through the gorge of *Karnési* into the valley of Clitor." Into one of these springs Melampus may have thrown the ἀποκαθάρματα which he used in purifying the mad daughters of Proitos. Or, possibly, it is the spring on the western side of Mt. *Chelmos* above *Soudená*, the waters of which are regarded by the peasants as possessing the power to cure or kill those afflicted with a dangerous illness. One of two temples (l. 110) built by Proitos was at Lusoi. Cf. Kallim. *Hymn to Artemis* 233 ff.: ᾗ μέν τοι Προῖτός γε δύω ἐκαθίζετο νηούς, | ἄλλον μὲν Κορίης, ὅτι οἱ συνελέξατο κούρας | οὔρεα πλαζομένας ἀξείνια· τὸν δ' ἐνὶ Λούσοις | Ἡμέρῃ (cf. ἡμέρα, l. 39), οὕνεκα θυμὸν ἀπ' ἄγριον εἵλετο παίδων. A recollection of the Achaian settlement of Southern Italy is the Λουσίας (*Lucino*) near Thurioi. Arkadia was the chief home of the cult of Artemis. She was in fact regarded as the ancestor of the Arkadians, by whom she was called Καλλίστη, Ὑμνία, Ἱέρεια, Ἡγεμόνη, etc.—**97. φοινικŏκραδέμνοιο**: as 13. 189. κρ with 'Attic' correption also in 13. 12.

99. βοῶπιν: Hera's epithet; only here of Artemis.—**100. ἀντείνων**: always with apocope in Bacch. Bacch. has three other examples (l. 103, ii. 7, vii. 10). More common in Pind. —**102.** Transition to direct discourse without an introductory phrase. The speech of Pr. may begin with 104. Madness of women was cured by the aid of vernal paians to Artemis' brother Apollo (Aristox. Frag. 36).—**106. ἀριστοπάτρα** = τὸν ἄριστον *πατέρα ἔχουσα.* Bacch. sometimes substitutes an ornamental epithet for the name of a divinity.—**107. θηροσκόπος**: as *Hymn* 27. 11. **πιθοῦσα**: an unusual second aorist (Pind. *Pyth.* 3. 65, and 3. 28 by conj.). Hom. has the form *πεπιθ-*. In the other version of the legend Melampus effects the cure by *καθαρμοί* (the black 'hellebore of M.').—**109. μανιᾶν**: pl. as Anakr. xviii. **ἀθέων**: because the Proitides had disregarded Hera.—**110. ταί**: the father (l. 40) is implicitly included. Only one of Kallimachos' two temples is here mentioned—that at Lusoi. Paus. 2. 7. 8 states that the temple of Peitho in Sikyon, where Artemis and Apollo were worshipped, was built by Proitos as a thanksgiving offering because his daughters there regained their sanity (cf. Apollod. 2. 2. 2). In the same temple Meleager dedicated his spear. Proitos also founded a cult of Artemis at Oinoe (Eur. *Herakl.* 379).—**111. μιν**: elsewhere *νιν*.—**112. ἵσταν**: so *τίθεν*, *ἴεν* in Pind.

113. ἔνθεν: apparently Artemis followed the Achaians to Metapontum, if we are to believe the statement in the text; but of this migration of her cult we have no evidence. A record of her worship at Metapontum is preserved in Hygin. 186 and on a coin *Brit. Mus. Cat.* Italy, No. 263. The ruined temple there may, as Ken. suggests, have been dedicated to her. An ivory statue of Endymion, the beloved of Artemis, was dedicated at Olympia by the Metapontines (Paus. 6. 19. 11).—**114. ἱπποτρόφον**: Artemis was a lover of horses, Pind. vii. **πόλινδ'**: as *εἰς ἅλαδε* κ 351. Or *ποίαν* (Housman)?—**115. ἕσπεο** with *ἐς*: K 285 (indic.).—**117. δέσποινα λαῶν**: Artemis was a divinity who guarded the interests of civic and social life. *δ. θηρῶν* Anakr. i.—**119. Κάσαν**: the Casuentus, now the Basiento. Is this Suidas' *Κῆσος*?—**120. ἔσσαν ἐμοί**: if this is correct, *ἐμοί* contains an allusion to the Nestorid, and therefore aristocratic, ancestors of the poet, who came from Troy with the Pylians and settled Metapontum (Strabo 6. 264). On his return from Troy, Nestor founded the sanctuary of *Ἀθηνᾶ Νεδουσία* near *Ποιάεσσα* in Keos, the poet's home (Strabo 10. 487). In Miletos, Kos, etc. descendants of Nestor established themselves; cf. Mimn. 9. 1. It may be accident that Medon, the name of an Attic Neleid, is also the name of the poet's father. Especially among the western colonists was the cult of their heroic founders kept alive by festivals, and descent from these founders regarded as a great honour. Pind. *Pyth.* 5. 74 refers to his ancestors (*Σπάρτας*) *ὅθεν γεγενναμένοι | ἵκοντο Θήρανδε φῶτες Αἰγεΐδαι, | ἐμοὶ πατέρες.* For the active **ἔσσαν** cf. *πόλιν ἔσσαι* *Pyth.* 4. 273. In the sense of *ἔκτισαν* or *καθί-*

δρυσαν, ἕσσαντο would be in better accord with usage (cf. *Pyth.* 4. 204). For the retention of -οῖ before ἕσσαν cf. *Ol.* 6. 82. *θέσσαν* (Jebb) would remove the difficulty. Against the reading of the text is the fact that Metapontum was an Achaian colony; see Strabo *l.l.* and ll. 114, 126, where, however, Ἀχαιοί may be used in the wider sense. Wilam. and Blass read *προγόνων* (cf. iv. 46 MS.) *ἑσσαμένων* and supply *ἐστί* with *ἄλσος*, which is harsh. It is still worse to retain *πρόγονοι ἑσσάμενοι* and supply *ναίουσι* from 116; *εἰσί* is easier; cf. Aisch. *Eum.* 68. **χρόνῳ** 'at last,' Pind. *Pyth.* 4. 78, Aisch. *Agam.* 126 *χρόνῳ μὲν ἀγρεῖ Πριάμου πόλιν ἅδε κέλευθος.*—**123.** **μετ'**: only here with the gen. in Bacch.—**125.** Cf. *χρόνῳ σύμπαντι* Pind. *Ol.* 6. 56; more poetical than *ἐς πάντα χρόνον.* **σύν**: of time, Pind. xv. 1.

VI. In honour of Pytheas, son of Lampon (cf. Hdt. 9. 78), whose victory in the pankration at Nemea is also the subject of the fifth *Nemean* ode of Pindar, which is usually referred to a contest that took place shortly before the battle of Salamis (483 or 481); and if this is correct we have in this ode of Bacchylides the earliest of his dateable poems. A later period is also possible, though the arguments in its favour as put forward by Blass (*R. M.* 53. 283) are not convincing. The circumstances that led to the composition of two odes are unknown, but the story of Pindar's avarice told by the scholiast may point to an unusual situation. Bacchylides' poem is unquestionably superior to that of Pindar.

Pytheas was of the noble house of the Psalychidai, several members of which family were distinguished for their athletic prowess. His maternal grandfather Themistios was twice victorious in the Epidaurian games; his maternal uncle Euthymenes was a famous gymnast; and his younger brother Phylakidas won two Isthmian victories celebrated by Pindar in *Isthm.* 5 (after 480) and 6. Christ calls attention to the fact that the pankration for youths at Olympia is not reported until 200 B.C., and at Delphi in 384 B.C. But such contests for *ἀγένειοι* (cf. Pind. *Nem.* 5. 6) were held in Keos, and they may have also occurred at the Isthmia and Nemea. The poem consists of 197 verses (231 according to Blass) and is one of the longest in the collection. Their native hero was naturally a favourite subject with Aiginetans, and the poet has happily chosen for the central theme that episode in the career of Aias when he withstands the attempt of Hektor to fire the Grecian fleet. Cf. O 415 ff., Soph. *Aias* 1273 ff. The ode is badly mutilated. The verses preceding the mention of Aias probably dealt with the foundation of the Nemean games by Herakles and with the genealogy of the house of Aiakos.

New words: βροτωφελής 'useful,' 'beneficial,' εὐεγχής, θερσιεπής 'insolent in speech,' ἱμερόγυιος, κυανανθής 'dark-flowered,' 'darkling,' φερεκυδής, 'glorious,' 'victorious.'
Metre: dact.-epitrite, with eight periods in the strophe, six in the epode.

1. σακεσφόρον: so Soph. *Aias* 19; cf. Η 219, Λ 527, *clypei dominus septemplicis Aiax* Ovid *Metam.* 13. 2. Hesiod has φερεσακής. **ὅστ'**: see on Alkm. vii. 3.—**5. θεσπεσίῳ**: νηυσὶν ἐνίετε θεσπιδαὲς πῦρ Μ 441, cf. Ο 597.—**6.** Ἕκτορι χαλκοκορυστῇ Ε 699. Vv. 7-46 give the reason for Aias' position in l. 3. Cf. v. 59 ff. **ὁππότε** = ἡνίκα; of a single occasion.

9. ὠρίνατο: the middle only here (to requite Agamemnon's insult).—**11. θεότιμον**: θ. ἄστυ v. 12.—**13. οὐ λεῖπον**: 'would not yet (οὐ = οὐκέτι) leave'; cf. Ε 787 ff.—**14. πτᾶσσον** (or πτάσσον? cf. πτάξ) as πτώσσω Δ 371. μάχαν depends on πτ. (Υ 427, Xen. *Kyrop.* 3. 3. 18) rather than on ἀτυζ. (Ζ 468). **ὀξεῖαν**: ὀξὺν Ἄρηα Δ 352.—**15. κλονέων**: the absolute use as Φ 533 Ἀχιλλεὺς . . . κλονέων, Λ 526. Cf. Ε 96 θύνοντ' ἂμ πεδίον, πρὸ ἕθεν κλονέοντα φάλαγγας.

21. The protasis of the simile (Platt cp. Milton *Par. Lost* 2. 286) exactly fills one part of the triad. Cf. ii. antis. α'. **θύων**: ἄνεμος λαίλαπι θύων μ 400.—**23. δαΐζει**: only here of the wind.—**24. ἀντάσας**: ἀλὸς ἀντήσαντες Aisch. *Suppl.* 37. **ἀναπετ.**: cf. ἅμα ἡλίῳ σκιδναμένῳ Hdt. 8. 23.—**25. φαεσιμβρότῳ**: φαεσίμβροτος ἠώς Ω 785, φαυσίμβροτος Pind. *Ol.* 7. 39. —**26.** Cf. Verg. *Aen.* 3. 69 *placataque venti dant maria*, 5. 763 *placidi straverunt aequora venti*; Soph. *Aias* 674 δεινῶν τ' ἄημα πνευμάτων ἐκοίμισε | στένοντα πόντον would be parallel, if we read οὐρίᾳ πνοᾷ, making Boreas subj. of λῆξεν. **δέ τε**: this epic combination occurs in melic poetry only in Bacch. and in Sa. xxxv.—**27.** Cf. πνοιῇ . . . λίνα κολπώσαντες *Anth. Pal.* 9. 363. 10.

32. κλισίῃσιν (the epic -ῃσι only here) is probably a blunder for κλισίαισιν.—**36. ὑπαί**: epic, not in Pind. Cf. ῥῦσαι ὑπ' ἠέρος υἷας Ἀχαιῶν Ρ 645. The Trojans behold the dark cloud of war lined with the bright gleam of hope. The figure suggests Pind. *Isthm.* 7. 38 εὐδίαν ἐκ χειμῶνος, Aisch. *Agam.* 900 κάλλιστον ἦμαρ ἐκ χείματος.

43. In Homer Ares does not aid the Trojan attack. Apollo is commanded by Zeus to incite Hektor (Ο 59, 236), but takes no part in the assault. Sophokles, like Bacch., does not follow the Homeric account in its details.—**45.** The combination of Λοξίας with Ἀπόλλων is unusual (Aisch. *Choeph.* 558).—**46. ἶξον**: epic (Ε 773).—**49. ἔρευθε**: cf. αἵματι γαῖαν ἐρεύθων Λ 394, where the verb is transitive as usual. For the intrans. use of trans. verbs, *e.g.* δηλόω, δείκνυμι, τείνω, cf. Kühner-Gerth *Gr. Gram.* § 373. Wilam. conj. ἔρευσε (Hippokr.) from ῥέω, Richards ἐναρ. φωτ. δ' ἐρεύθεθ'. Hesych. glosses ἐρεύθων by ἐρυθριῶν.—**52.** Ken. cites Plut. *Phok.* 1: τὴν δὲ Φωκίωνος ἀρετὴν . . . αἱ τύχαι τῆς Ἑλλάδος ἀμαυρὰν καὶ ἀλαμπῆ πρὸς δόξαν ἐποίησαν, which looks like a reminiscence of this passage.—**53.** **Ἀρετά**: Sim. xxiii. precedes his nephew in personifying Areta. Pind. has λάμπει δὲ σαφὴς ἀρετά (*Isthm.* 1. 22) of athletic excellence.—**54.** **ἀμαυροῦται**: cf. Sim. i. 5.

57. Cf. καθ' Ἑλλάδα γῆν στρωφώμενος Theogn. 247.—**58.** **πολυπλάγκταν** (-τον pap. sec. hand.): Bacch. often uses the fem. of comp. adj. (ἀεικέλιος, ἀκάματος, ἄπρακτος, κυανόπρῳρος, ἐπιχώριος).—**59.** **καὶ μὰν**: 'nay more,' introduces a new thought. So in tragedy καὶ μήν marks the approach of a new actor. Cf. Pind. *Pyth.* 4. 289. **φερεκυδέα**: 'honour-giving'; only here as an adj. Φερεκύδης is the name of the logographer and of the philosopher.—**60.** Aigina, daughter of Asopos, was the mother of Aiakos, for whom Zeus created men out of ants. Cf. Pind. *Nem.* 7. 50. The island is honoured by Areta because it was devoted to justice (εὔνομον πόλιν *Isthm.* 5. 22) and hospitality (*Nem.* 4. 12). Cf. Pind. Frag. 1 κλεινὸς Αἰακοῦ λόγος, κλεινὰ δὲ καὶ ναυσικλυτὸς | Αἴγινα . . . οὐ θέμιν οὐδὲ δίκαν ξείνων ὑπερβαίνοντες· οἷοι δ' ἀρετὰν | δελφῖνες. **Εὐκλείᾳ**: Eukleia here in conjunction with Eunomia as at Athens, where they had a shrine and a priest (*C. I. A.* 3. 277, Ἐφ. ἀρχ. 1884 p. 165, l. 53). The passage is a picture of the ideal Dorian state.—**63.** **Εὐνομία** is the saviour of the state, Pind. *Ol.* 9. 16. Her sister is Peace (cf. l. 66), Mel. Adesp. xiii. 9. Εὐν. σαοφρ. is grammatically joint subject of κυβ. with Ἀρετά, but in effect = Εὐνομίᾳ σαόφρονι. Jebb reads the dat. and takes σ. adverbially. γε for **τε** would be weak.—**64.** **θαλίας**: cf. xiii. 5.

68. **μελέταν**: the technical term for the activity of the trainer (ἀλείπτης).—**69.** Cf. Pind. *Nem.* 5. 48 ἴσθι, γλυκεῖάν τοι Μενάνδρου σὺν τύχᾳ μόχθων ἀμοιβὰν | ἐπαύρεο. χρὴ δ' ἀπ' Ἀθανᾶν τέκτον' ἀεθληταῖσιν ἔμμεν. Another famous Athenian trainer was Melesias, whose pupils won at least 30 victories (*Ol.* 8. 66). Mention of the trainer is regular in all contests for boys and youths (ἀγένειοι), except in the running matches. That the Aiginetan athlete did not have recourse to home talent may have increased the envy (l. 77) with which the successful Athenian was regarded.—**70.** **θαμὰ δὴ**: as Pind. *Nem.* 1. 17. θαμά suits the sense better than ἅμα. On the word see Ingram *Hermathena* 2. 217 ff.—**73.** The μίτρα was a woollen band to which the leaves of the wreath were attached. It is also used for the crown itself (Pind. *Ol.* 9. 84). Its use has been thought to antedate that of the crown and to have a religious importance.—**75.** Cf. *Isthm.* 4. 29 *Πανελλάνεσσι ἐριζόμενοι.* The four national agonistic festivals are meant.

76. θερσιεπής: cf. *θαρσύνας* ('encouraged') *ἐπέεσσι ν* 323; here of envy that is insolent of speech. Such an envious person was *Θερσί-της*, a word that shows the Aiolic form *θέρσ-ος*. The MS. has (*τιν'*) *ἀθερσιεπής*, which Jurenka regards as 'chill of speech,' comparing Ovid *Metam.* 2. 763 and *θερσίχθων· θερμαίνων, γῆν καίων* in Hesych.—**77.** Contrast *πρὸς γὰρ τὸ λαμπρὸν ὁ φθόνος βιάζεται* Trag. Adesp. 547. 12.—**78.** Cf. Pind. *Pyth.* 9. 95 ff. (where also *σὺν δίκᾳ*). **σοφόν**: of gymnastic skill; in melic poetry usu. of the poet or musician.—**79. μῶμος**: cf. *Anth. Plan.* 84 *παντὶ δ' ἐπ' ἔργῳ | μῶμος* (perhaps by Sim.), Theogn. 1183 *οὐδένα, Κύρν', αὐγαὶ φαεσιμβρότου ἠελίοιο | ἄνδρ' ἐφορῶσ', ᾧ μὴ μῶμος ἐπικρέμαται,* Pind. *Ol.* 6. 74 *μ. ἐξ ἄλλων κρέμαται φθονεόντων* of the envy of the victor.—**81. ἀλαθείᾱ**: apparently a Doricized form of Ionic *ἀληθείη*. Pind. has *ἀλάθεια*. Cf. Pind. *Ol.* 10. 53 *ὅ τ' ἐξελέγχων μόνος | ἀλάθειαν ἐτήτυμον | χρόνος,* Bacch. xvi.—**82. νικᾶν**: Pind. would probably have said *φιλεῖ νίκαν*. **πανδ. χρόνος**: so Sim. i. 5, *C. I. G.* 2976.—**83. κᾱλῶς**: with Ionic and epic scansion (sometimes in Attic). Melic poetry elsewhere has *κᾰλός*; Smyth *Ionic* § 164. *καλός* is from *καλϜός*.—**84.** Cf. *ο* 372 *ἔργον ἀέξουσιν μάκαρες θεοί* (cited by Ken.), *ξ* 65 *θεὸς δ' ἐπὶ ἔργον ἀέξῃ | ὡς καὶ ἐμοὶ τόδε ἔργον ἀέξεται, ᾧ ἐπιμίμνω.*—The last (corrupt) triad returns to the subject of Pytheas whose fame is ensured if Kleio has given to the poet the gift of song.

VII. To Kleoptolemos of Thessaly, victor at the Petraian games with the chariot. The Thessalians were famous for their equestrian skill (see on Pind. ix.). This is the only ode of Bacch. commemorative of a victory won at a local contest. It is also peculiar from the fact that the gnomic element occupies the first place. Only the exordium is preserved.

Metre: dactylo-epitrite; the strophe of three, the epode of five periods.

1. παρὰ δαίμονος: Cf. Pind. *Nem.* 4. 61 *τὸ μόρσιμον Διόθεν πεπρωμένον.*—**2. ἄριστον**: Bacch. 4. 18 *τί φέρτερον ἢ θεοῖσιν φίλον ἐόντα παντοδαπῶν λαγχάνειν ἄπο μοῖραν ἀέθλων*; Pind. *Pyth.* 1. 99 *τὸ δὲ παθεῖν εὖ πρῶτον ἀέθλων.*—**3.** The thought recalls Pind. Frag. 225 *ὁπόταν θεὸς ἀνδρὶ χάρμα πέμψῃ, | πάρος μέλαιναν κραδίαν ἐστυφέλιξεν.* The prosperity of the victor (or of his family) seems to have been obscured by a reverse of fortune which he had overcome to his greater renown; *in quem manca ruit semper fortuna* (Hor. *Sat.* 2. 7. 88). Perhaps the *συμφορά* was misfortune at one of the games (cf. *Pyth.* 8. 87). I have followed Jebb in inserting *τ'* for metrical reasons, though the colon in the papyrus after *μολοῦσα* is against the conjecture. In 5 Jur. reads *λαμπρὸν δὲ δὴ ὑψ. τ' ἔρδει.*—**5. ἰδέ**: not in Pind. or tragedy except Soph. *Antig.* 969; *ἠδέ* Sim. xxi. **τεύχει**: Pind. *Nem.* 4. 84 *ἰσοδαίμονα τ. φῶτα.*—**7.** Cf. 10. 35 ff. *ματεύει δ' ἄλλος ἀλλοίαν κέλευθον, ἄντινα στείχων ἀριγνώτοιο δόξας τεύξεται. μυρίαι δ' ἀνδρῶν ἐπιστᾶμαι πέλονται.*

10. ὅς: scil. *ἀρετὰ τούτου*; cf. *ω* 286 *ἡ γὰρ θέμις, ὅς τις ὑπάρξῃ.* **τὸ παρ χειρός**: 'his immediate duty.' Cf. *γνόντα τὸ παρ ποδός* 'the immediate future' Pind *Pyth.* 3. 60, *φροντίδα τὰν παρ ποδός Pyth.* 10. 62, *τὸ πρὸ ποδός Isthm.* 8. 13. **κυβερνᾷ**: cf. vi. 60 (with *σύν*), ix. 22. If we read *κυβερνᾶται* (without *σύν*; so Pind. Frag. 213 *δίκᾳ*), *τὸ π. χειρός* is accus. of respect.—**12.** Music and song must observe the law of *κόσμος*. Everything has its fitting time and place (*κάλλιστος καιρός*). On the present occasion it is meet for the poet to sing the victory of Kleopt.—**13. φόρμιγγος**: the poet either ignores the Spartan custom (see on Alkm. xii.) or thinks the flute is the only proper instrument.—**14. λιγυκλαγγεῖς**: only here. See on Terp. vi.

16. χαλκότυπος: as in the worship of Demeter with cymbals (*χαλκοκρότου Δαμ.* Pind. *Isthm.* 7. 3) or in the pyrrich dances.—**17.** Cf. Hes. *W. D.* 694 *καιρὸς δ' ἐπὶ πᾶσιν ἄριστος*, Theogn. 401 *καιρὸς δ' ἐπὶ πᾶσιν ἄριστος | ἔργμασιν ἀνθρώπων*, Pind. *Ol.* 13. 47 *ἕπεται δ' ἐν ἑκάστῳ | μέτρον· νοῆσαι δὲ καιρὸς ἄριστος*, Sodamos, in schol. Eur. *Hippol.* 264, *καιρῷ πάντα πρόσεστι καλά.*—**18. εὖ ἔρδοντα**: of agonistic success; cf. i. 94. **θεός**: cf. Pind. *Ol.* 11. 10.—**20. Πετραίου**: this epithet occurs also in Pind. *Pyth.* 4. 138, where the scholiasts offer three explanations, of which only one deserves recognition. According to this, Poseidon formed the valley of Tempe by cleaving asunder the rocks and thus giving an outlet to the Peneios.—**22.** Since **Πυρρ. υἱόν** cannot well refer to Kleopt. after the mention of the victor in l. 19, Pyrrichos' son is probably the successful charioteer.

VIII. 'The Sons of Antenor or the Demand for Helen's Surrender.' The double title shows that the *'Αντηνορίδαι* and *'Ελένης ἀπαίτησις* of Sophokles are in fact one drama. In the extant portion of Bacchylides' poem so little reference is made to the Antenoridai that it is difficult to justify the first title, which has crept in, according to Blass, from the Sophokleian drama, where the sons of Antenor formed the chorus. This dithyramb only touches upon the introduction before the assembly, by the Antenoridai, of the embassy that came to Troy before the outbreak of the war to demand the return of Helen (Γ 205 ff. Λ 139), of which the chief members were Menelaos and Odysseus. All we have is the beginning of the scene in the agora at Troy and the exordium of the speech of Menelaos packed full of τόποι κοινοί. We should expect to have a specimen of the famous oratory of Odysseus, the reply of Paris, the tumult in the assembly, and the rescue of the ambassadors by Antenor and his sons (schol. on Γ 206, Ovid *Metam.* 13. 200 ff.). Did the ode contain this stirring scene, or did it stop abruptly with the injured husband's attack on Hybris? How far did the dithyramb permit the curtailment of the myth, which in ix. is recounted with a fullness that is almost epic? Crusius would answer the question, which is practically insoluble with the present evidence, by a reference to the abruptness of Hor. *Carm.* 1. 8, *Epod* 1. 17, in which he finds another instance of the Roman poet's dependence on Greek models. The parallel is imperfect, because the Greek dithyrambs were composed for public presentation.

In the verses lost at the beginning mention was made of the fact that Antenor and Theano, who was a priestess of Athena (Z 298), had fifty children (schol. Ω 496), whereas another legend reported the number as nineteen. In consequence of the Hellenic sympathies of Antenor his family was spared in the sack of Troy and settled at Kyrene. It is improbable that the ode was composed for one of their descendants. The sources of the poem are the *Iliad* and the *Kypria.* Lines 14-20 are quoted, with variations, by Clement of Alexandria *Strom.* 5. 731.

New words: δεξίστρατος, θελξιεπής 'of persuasive eloquence.' —Metre: dactylo-epitrite. The strophe contains seven, the epode six, periods. Possibly vv. 1 and 2, 3 and 4 in the strophe are to be joined.

1. πατήρ: Antenor. **εὔβουλος**: Ant. is πεπνυμένος Γ 148. —**3. παίδεσσι**: cf. παίδεσσιν Ἑλλάνων Pind. *Isthm.* 4. 36, Λυδῶν παῖδας Hdt. 1. 27, κοῦροι Ἀχαιῶν Hom. **μῦθον**: the proposition of the embassy to plead the justice of their cause (λόγοι δίκαιοι l. 11) in the convocation of the Trojans.

7. δεξίστρατον ἀγοράν: 'the assembly-place where the folk congregates.' L. and S. cite only three compounds in δεξι- from δέχομαι. **εἰς**: only here and in εἰσάνταν ii. 110. Bacch. has ἐς 8 times before vowels, 13 times before consonants.—**8. αὐδάεις λόγος**: 'voiceful, momentous report.' So αὐδῶμαι = 'loudly proclaim.' Cf. κόσμον αὐδάεντα λόγων Pind. xxvi., φωνάεντα λόγον Bacch. Frag. 61 (35), αὐδᾶται φάτις Aisch. *Eum.* 380. Eur. *Medea* 174 μύθων αὐδαθέντων ὀμφάν is different.—**9.** Cf. v. 100.—**10.** Cf. Γ 112 ἐλπόμενοι παύσεσθαι δϊζυροῦ πολέμοιο.—**11.** Cf. Pind. *Pyth.* 4. 70 τίς γὰρ ἀρχὰ δέξατο ναυτιλίας; In *Pyth.* 4. 29 we have ἐπέων ἄρχετο, but the active in ἄρχε ὕμνον *Nem.* 3. 10. The Greeks were not offended by the pleonasm in πρῶτος ἄρχειν.—**12. Πλεισθενίδας**: see on Stes. xi. **θελξιεπεῖ**: cf. θελξιμελής Kaibel 1053. Of Menelaos as an orator Homer says (Γ 213) ἐπιτροχάδην ἀγόρευεν, | παῦρα μέν, ἀλλὰ μάλα λιγέως, ἐπεὶ οὐ πολύμυθος, | οὐδ' ἀφαμαρτοεπής. In Bacch. he has become πολύμυθος. Homer represents Odysseus as the chief orator on this occasion.—**13. κοινώσας**: *scil.* γᾶρυν, a bold construction. Or an unusual use of the active, with which we may compare ix. 70 (vi. 49), Aristotle *Areta* l. 13. νυκτὶ κοινάσαντες ὁδόν Pind. *Pyth.* 4. 115 is not grammatically parallel, nor is Pindar's use of the active of εὑρίσκω, δρέπω, πράσσω, ἀναδέω. Housman conj. εὐπέπλοις ἑ (*i.e.* γᾶρυν; cf. Pind. *Ol.* 9. 14).

15. Ζεὺς ὑψιμέδων: as Hes. *Theogon.* 529.—**16.** Cf. α 32 οἷον δή νυ θεοὺς βροτοὶ αἰτιόωνται, | ἐξ ἡμέων γάρ φασι κάκ' ἔμμεναι· οἱ δὲ καὶ αὐτοὶ | σφῇσιν ἀτασθαλίῃσιν ὑπέρμορον ἄλγε' ἔχουσιν. Contrast Γ 164 θεοί νύ μοι αἴτιοί εἰσιν. The point of view is different in Bacch. Frag. 50 (21) πάντεσσι θνατοῖσι δαίμων ἐπέταξε πόνους ἄλλοισιν ἄλλους. Cf. Plutarch 1049 F, who quotes Eur. Frag. 447 εἰ θεοί τι δρῶσιν αἰσχρόν, οὔκ εἰσιν θεοί and 434 τὸ ῥᾷστον εἶπας, αἰτιάσασθαι θεούς.—**17.** Cf. Arist. *Eth.* 1. 9 of εὐδαιμονία: εἴη δ' ἂν καὶ πολύκοινον. **ἐν μέσῳ κεῖται**: in Hom. ἐν μέσσοισι κ. is used of actual position. Cf. Mel. Adesp. i.—**18. ἰθεῖαν**: cf. Ψ 580; opposed to σκολιαὶ δίκαι. Dike is justice considered from the point of view of social institutions. Themis is absolute right, the eternal, divine law. Each may be the πάρεδρος of Zeus. δίκη is given effect by means of νόμοι. Cf. Pind. *Ol.* 13. 6 ἐν τᾷ γὰρ Εὐνομία ναίει, κασιγνήτα τε, . . . | Δίκα καὶ ὁμότροπος Εἰρήνα . . . | παῖδες εὐβούλου Θέμιτος, Hes. *Theogon.* 902, Mel. Adesp. xiii. 9. —**19. Θέμιτος**: this gen. is preserved as an archaism in Plato *Rep.* 380 A.—**20.** δυστήνων παῖδες Z 127. **σύνοικον**: as Ariphron 2, cf. Soph. *Antig.* 451.

21. ἁ . . . Ὕβρις: epic separation of the (demonstrative) article from its noun; Pind. *Ol.* 12. 5.—**21.** αἰόλῳ ψεύδει *Nem.* 8. 25. αἰόλος varies with ποικίλος in this sense.—**22. ἀθαμβής**=ἀδεής, Ibyk. i. 8.—**25. δ'**: apodotic (Lat. *at*) μ 54, Pind. *Ol.* 7. 5.—**27.** The Giants are ὑβρισταὶ φῶτες Kaibel 831. 8. **Γᾶς παῖδας**: etymological play as γηγενέων ἀνδρῶν . . . γιγάντων *Batrach.* 7, γηγενὴς στρατὸς γιγάντων Soph. *Trach.* 1058.

IX. 'The Youths or Theseus': possibly a paian in honour of Apollo. The legend of Theseus' descent into the sea in quest of a token of his divine origin which forms the subject of this splendid lyric, appears in various works of art, some of which are contemporaneous with the poet.

1. A mural painting by Mikon in the Theseion at Athens Paus. 1. 17. 3), the date of which is generally believed to be 468-460 B.C., though it is placed earlier by some scholars. Robert dates the fresco 474/3. Apparently Mikon and Bacchylides drew from a common source which is unknown to us.

2. The kylix of Euphronios found at Caere and now in the Louvre (Baumeister fig. 1877, *J. H. S.* 18. pl. xiv), dates about 490 B.C., and shows the meeting of Theseus and Amphitrite (ll. 109 ff.), at which Athena (l. 7) is present. The ring (l. 60) does not appear, but there are dolphins (l. 97) and a Triton. Some archaeologists find traces of the crown (l. 114).

3. The François amphora at Florence (*Wiener Vorlegeblätter* 1888, pl. iii., *J. H. S.* 18. 280) by Klitias and Ergotimos. By the side of a ship, on which men and youths are depicted in attitudes of astonishment, a man is represented swimming. Kenyon thinks that this figure is Theseus (l. 119), but with greater probability Robert (and Heberdey *Arch.-epigr. Mitth. aus Oesterr.* 13. 79) hold that he is a sailor making for the shore, on which we see a band of seven youths and seven maidens led by Theseus with the kithara. According to this view the scene is laid at Delos and takes place close to the shore.

4. A red-figured krater of the fifth century in the Museo Civico at Bologna (*Mus. ital.* 3. pl. i., *J. H. S.* 18. 277) represents Amphitrite presenting a wreath to Theseus, who is borne in the arms of Triton, Poseidon's son. Poseidon himself reclines on a κλίνη and remains a passive spectator. The stern of the ship appears on the left. Though ring and dolphin are absent, this vase is the nearest approach to the scene as represented by Bacchylides. Robert thinks it is dependent on Mikon's painting.

5. The Tricase amphora found at Ruvo (*J. H. S.* 18. 279) represents Theseus shaking hands with Poseidon, who is the chief figure in the scene. Behind Poseidon stands Amphitrite with the wreath. This is the only vase that shows the ring, but even here it seems to be enclosed in a box. There are no dolphins.

6. A red-figured krater of the early part of the fifth century, found at Girgenti and now in the National Library at Paris (*J. H. S.* 18. 278, Roscher 1. 1679). The scene is that depicted in No. 5. The dolphins and ring are absent. On the variations and the interrelation of these monuments see Schreiber *Abh. d. sächs. Gesell.* 17. 132 and Robert *Hermes* 33. 132.

Euripides' *Theseus*, the scene of which was laid in Crete, followed Bacchylides in depicting the strife between Theseus and Minos. The brief account of Pausanias (1. 17. 3) seems to depend directly or indirectly on Bacchylides. Hyginus (*Astr.* 2. 5) gives the story as told by the poet with additions that point to the use of other sources by the mythographer. Thus he says that the scene took place after the arrival in Crete, that Theseus received the ring from the Nereïds and the crown from Thetis, 'though others say that he received it from the spouse of Neptune,' and that the crown was given to Ariadne by Theseus and set among the stars by Dionysos.

Vv. 129-132 indicate that the poem is a paian, but Servius' designation (on Verg. *Aen.* 6. 21) of it as a dithyramb, which represents the generic title of the Alexandrian age, is possibly the usage even of the fifth century. It was sung at Delos where Theseus on his return had founded a shrine and instituted a sacred dance (the *γέρανος*) in honour of Apollo, to whom he had made a vow on the journey to Crete. The festival at Delos is thus an imitation of the celebration of the rites established there by Theseus; just as the annual offering at Phaleron recalled the sacrifice made there upon the hero's happy return to Attica. Crusius recalls the fact that Delos was the island of divers and suggests that at the festival of Theseus there were diving matches which commemorated the exploit of the Athenian hero. In the cult-song the myth was the essential feature, and the only passage which connects the poem directly with the worship of the god is appropriately placed at the end. The character of the festival rendered unnecessary any explicit reference to the Minotaur, who is only alluded to in ll. 24, 96. The date of the poem is uncertain, but the selection of a legend of Theseus, whose bones were brought in 469 from Skyros to Athens, points to a period when the Attic city was claiming the empire of the sea. The Athenians associated the cult of Theseus with that of his father Poseidon (Paus. 10. 11. 5). Aigeus is merely Poseidon heroized. It will be remembered that Pindar wrote a 'prosodion to Delos' (vi.) for the Keians, who had a banqueting hall at Delos (Hdt. 4. 35). With the character of Minos as drawn by Bacch. cf. Plut. *Thes.* 16 *ὁ* M. *διετέλει κακῶς ἀκούων καὶ λοιδορούμενος ἐν τοῖς Ἀττικοῖς θεάτροις.*

New words: *ἁλιναιέτης* 'denizen of the deep,' *ἀναξιβρόντης* 'lord of the thunder,' *ἀρέταιχμος* 'who rejoices in the spear,' *ἐρατώνυμος* 'of lovely name,' *θελημός* 'yielding,' *ἱμεράμπυξ* 'with the head-band of desire,' *λεπτόπρυμνος* 'of slender stern,' *μεγαλοῦχος* 'grasping,' 'arrogant,' *πολέμαιγις* 'with the aegis of war,' *πυριέθειρα* 'with mane of fire,' *φρενοάρας* 'of sober mind,' *χρυσεόπλοκος* 'woven with gold.'

Tautometric responsions occur only in the strophes and antistrophes: 7=73, 17=83, 18=107, 19=85, 20=109, 20=86, 36=79, 43=109. Non-tautometric responsion is very frequent. In the first system each of the divisions of the triad is complete.

Metre: cretic (cf. l. 4) or paionic. The following feet are employed: — ⏑ ⏑⏑ first paion, ⏑⏑ — ⏑ third paion, ⏑⏑ ⏑ — fourth paion, — ⏑ — cretic, — — ⏑ bacchius, — ⏑ —⏑ in which —⏑ has the value of a single —, and —⏑ ⏑ — in which —⏑ has the value of a single —. All of these feet occur in Pind. *Ol.* 2, *Pyth.* 5 according to J. H. Schmidt. The variations between the corresponding verses are freer than in any paionic ode of Pindar. The arrangement of the verses is especially difficult, and the division of the feet often uncertain. Some apparent irregularities await further investigation. Keeping the received colometry I have followed in the main, though with much hesitation, the exposition of Housman (*C. R.* 12. 134 ff.). Both Christ and Jurenka desert the colometry of the papyrus and propose a different metrical scheme that admits trochaic and logaoedic cola. Wilamowitz regards the metre as double-iambs.

1. The poet plunges at once *in medias res.* **κυανόπρῳρα**: contracted from κυανοπρώειρα Sim. 241; νέας κυανοπρωείρους conj. for -πρῳρείους γ 299. πρῷρα is from *πρωϝειρα. Bacch. has κῠανο- except in 13. 31 (κῡάνεον). **μέν**: see on i. 16, and cf. 10. 47. **μενέκτυπον**: ὃς μένει τὸν τῶν ἀσπίδων κτύπον (cf. Aisch. *Sept.* 100); cf. ἀδεισιβόας ii. 155.—**2.** **ἀγλαούς**: the stereotyped word for youthful persons: ἀγλ. παῖδες Pind. *Isthm.* 6. 62.—**3.** **κούρους** includes the maidens (cf. l. 43). The sacrifice to the Minotaur consisted of seven boys and seven girls (Sa. 144, Plato *Phaidon* 58 A, Eur. *H. F.* 1326, Plut. *Thes.* 15, Servius on Verg. *Aen.* 6. 21). According to Proklos, *Chrest.* 249, Theseus accompanied the expedition voluntarily. Hyginus' statement that there were six boys points to the inclusion of Theseus (cf. Apollod. *epit.* 1. 4). **Ἰαόνων**: (the non-Ionic form as in Homer) includes the Megarians as in N 685 (cf. on l. 14). The Athenians were the chief representatives of the Ionic race (Hdt. 1. 147 εἰσὶ δὲ πάντες Ἴωνες, ὅσοι ἀπ' Ἀθηνέων γεγόνασι καὶ Ἀπατούρια ἄγουσι ὁρτήν, Solon in Arist. Ἀθ. πολ. 5. 2 γαῖαν Ἰαονίας of Attica). See on x. 2.—**7.** **πολεμαίγιδος**: cf. πολεμόκλονος of Pallas, *Batrach.* 275. In Frag. 52 (B. 23) Athena is called χρύσαιγις (MSS. χρυσαιγίς; but *Et. Mag.* 518. 54 has μελάναιγις, and the words do not fall under the εὐπλοκαμίς class, Chandler 716). The aegis is the symbol of the storm-cloud, and here (l. 6) it is Athena whose power over Boreas softens the fury of his blast. Theseus' mother Aithra was a priestess of the goddess. On the Euphronios' vase Athena wears the aegis. Some read πελεμαίγιδος.—**8.** **κνίσεν**: love stings like a nettle, Hdt. 6. 62, Eur. *Med.* 568, Theokr. 4. 59. **Μίνωϊ**: as μάτρωϊ Pind. *Isthm.* 7. 24, ἥρωϊ (?) H 453. In the legend followed by Bacch., Minos himself collected in Attica the tribute to the Minotaur. Hellanikos in Plut. *Thes.* 17 says the captives were not selected by lot (as in Euripides' *Theseus*) but chosen by Minos, who picked out Theseus first of all.—**9.** **ἱμεράμπυκος**: the snood of Aphrodite is ἱμερόεις. The epithet is more effective than Pindar's λιπαράμπυξ of Mnemosyne or χρυσάμπυξ of the Muses and Horai.—**11. παρθενικᾶς**: see on Alkm. vii.—**12. θίγεν**: with the usual gen. (Pind. has the dat.).—**13. δέ**: the particle begins a verse in viii. 25 and in Pind. *Pyth.* 4. 180. **λευκᾶν**: of fair cheeks as Eur. *El.* 1023; not 'blanched with terror.' Cf. Phryn. ii. **παρηΐδων**: the Ionic form as in the lyrics of the drama, Dor. παρῴα or παράα. —**14. Ἐρίβοια**: so Hyginus and the François vase (Ἐπίβοια accord. to Klein). Paus. calls her Periboia. She is probably identical with Eriboia, the daughter of Alkathoos of Megara, wife of Telamon and mother of Aias (13. 69, Soph. *Aias* 569, Pind. *Isthm.* 6. 45). The statement in Plutarch, *Thes.* 29, that Theseus married Periboia, the mother of Aias, is due to confusion of the names. **χαλκοθώρακα**: χαλκεοθ. in Homer. The poet cares more for the high-sounding epithet than for the tradition (Plut. *Thes.* 17) that Theseus and his companions bore no arms by order of Minos.—**15. Πανδίονος.** See on x. 15.—**17. μέλαν** 'sombre,' 'indignant.' The eyes are rarely called black in Greek (*Anakreont.* 16. 12). Hippokr. has μελανόφθαλμος; ὄμμασι κυανέοισι *Hymn* 17. 15; cf. Hor. 1. 32. 11, *A. P.* 7 *nigris oculis nigroque capillo.* The addition of ὑπ' ὀφρύων (cf. ὑπ' ὀφρύσιν ὄσσε Ξ 236, while ὑπό with the gen. = ὑπέκ) may connote Theseus' ἄλγος (19). μέλαν is not predicate.—**18. δίνασεν**: from δινάω; cf. Eur. *Or.* 1459.—**20. εἶρεν**: here and 74, is used to vary εἶπεν. This is the only case of the imperf. (or aor.?) of the epic εἴρω 'say'; but, as Earle points out in *C. R.* 12. 395, for εἴρετο δεύτερον some of the ancients read εἶρε τὸ δ. in A 513. The active present occurs only in β 162, λ 137, ν 7.—**21. ὅσιον**; not sanctioned by divine law; cf. Pind. *Pyth.* 9. 36—**22. κυβερνᾶς**: cf. Pind. xxix., φρένες γὰρ αὐτοῦ θυμὸν ᾠακοστρόφουν Aisch. *Pers.* 767.—**23. μεγαλοῦχον**: from μεγαλο + οχος (ἔχω); in sense = πλεονέκτης. Apart from prepositions, only substantives are used as the prior member of compounds with -οχος. Ken. suggests μεγάλαυχον.

24. Cf. τὸ μόρσιμον Διόθεν πεπρωμένον ἔκφερεν Pind. *Nem.* 4. 61. μοῖρα ἐκ θεῶν occurs in Aisch. *Agam.* 1026, θεόθεν μοῖρα *Pers.* 101, μοῖρα θεῶν γ 269, Sol. 13. 30. **παγκρατής**: μοῖρα κραταιή Τ 410.—**25.** The scales of Justice: *Hymn* 3. 324, *Anth. Pal.* 6. 267. 4; cf. Δίκα ἐπιρρέπει Aisch. *Agam.* 250. **ῥέπει**: not used transitively (as are ἐπιρρέπω, καταρρέπω) except in Aisch. *Suppl.* 405; hence = εἰς ὅ τι (*i.e.* πεπρ. αἶσαν) ῥέπει.—**27. ἐκπλήσομεν**: ἐξέπλησε μοῖραν Hdt. 3. 142, πεπρωμέναν μοῖραν ἐκπλήσας Eur. *El.* 1290.—**29. εἰ καί**: 'granting that,' dist. from καὶ εἰ 'even supposing that.'—**30. ὑπό**: with accus. only here in Bacch. ὑπό 'at the foot of' takes dat. or accus.

(ὑπὸ Ὑμησσῷ and ὑπὸ Ὑμησσόν Hdt. 6. 137). **κρόταφον**: cf. κροτάφοις Ἑλικῶνος *Anth.* app. 94; Aitna γαίας μέτωπον Pind. *Pyth.* 1. 30, ὀφρύϊ Παρνασίᾳ *Ol.* 13. 106.—**31.** Bacch. follows Homer (Ξ 321) in making Europa the daughter of Phoinix (Φοίνισσα l. 54). Others called her the daughter of Agenor. In a lost poem Bacch. treated of the rape of Europa (schol. M 292). **ἐρατώνυμος**: cf. Stes. xii.; not = ἐρατά (a word used by Bacch. only of inanimate objects); cf. Eur. *I. T.* 135.—**33.** **φέρτατον**: emphatic position. Sarpedon and Rhadamanthos were Minos' brothers. Praxilla wrote a poem on Karneios, who is also called a son of Zeus and Europa. **ἀλλά**: see on Sa. **i.** 22. —**34.** **θυγάτηρ**: Aithra, l. 59. **ἀφνεοῦ**: φν fails to make position as in Pind. xxx. 4; χν in xiii. 7; θν i. 61, 94, Frag. 50 (21).—**35.** **πλαθεῖσα**: cf. Aisch. *Prom.* 897, Soph. *O. T.* 1099. Either Poseidon or Aigeus (cf. No. x.) was the possible father of Theseus; cf. Apollod. 3. 15. 7. 1. If πλ. exchanged places with μιγεῖσα l. 31, it would help the metre (Housman).—**36.** **χρύσεον**: 'costly.'—**37.** **ἰόπλοκοι**: see on Alk. xiii. The metre seems to demand a short syllable after ἰοπλ.: γε Jebb, προ- | κάλυμμα Richards, κά- | λυμμ' ἀδύ Ludwich. But — ⏑ — may = — ⏑ — ⏑.—**38.** **κάλυμμα**: cf. Aisch. *Agam.* 1178. **Νηρηΐδες** = Νηρῆος κόρας 102. The usage here does not support Didymos 'On the epinikoi of Bacch.,' who says that a distinction was made between the 'Nereids,' the legitimate children of Nereus by Doris, and the 'daughters of Nereus,' his offspring by other women.—**39.** **τῷ**: so the papyrus; if correct, an epic reminiscence (A 418). The Attics probably used the dative (Soph. *O. T.* 511, Plato *Theait.* 179 D). **πολέμαρχε**: Ἀχαιῶν π. ἀνήρ Aisch. *Choeph.* 1072. **Κνωσσίων**: the synizesis is not more strange than that in γενύων Pind. *Pyth.* 4. 225. Perhaps Κνωσοῦ is the correct reading.—**42.** **ἐραννόν**: in Hom. only of places; cf. Sim. 45. Pind., who avoids ἐραννός, has ἐρατὸν φάος. To help the metre Richards would read μ' ἀμβρότοι' ἰδεῖν ἐραννὸν | ἀοῦς φάος.—**43.** **ἰδεῖν φάος** = 'live'; cf. A 88, Prax. ii. Note the aorist, where we might expect the present. **ἐπεί** in a conditional relative protasis of the ideal form; cf. ὅτε Ξ 248, ἐπεὶ ἄν I 304, ἐπειδή Plato *Rep.* 516 A. Herwerden conj. ἔτ', εἰ. **ἠθέων**: ἠΐθεοι are regularly opposed to παρθένοι (ἠΐθεοι καὶ παρθένοι Σ 593), but the word here includes the maidens as in 93, 128. ἠΐθεοι appears to have been the technical name for the Athenians offered to the Minotaur (Plut. *Thes.* 15).—**44.** **δαμάσειας**: cf. γ 269.—**45.** **χειρῶν βίαν**: v. 91.

47. **ἀρέταιχμος**: *i.e.* ἀρεσκόμενος τῇ αἰχμῇ. The τ as in βωτιανείρᾳ Alkm. xvi. (Wackernagel). Ken. connects with ἀρετάω: 'puissant with the spear,' 'of the valiant spear'; not 'armed with justice.'—**49.** **ὑπεράφανον**: 'pre-eminent'; rarely used *in bonam partem* (Plato *Phaidon* 96 A).—**50.** Helios' daughter Pasiphaë was the wife of Minos. **χολωσ. ἦτορ**: cf. ι 480 χολώσατο κηρόθι, Hes. *Theogon.* 568 ἐχόλωσε δέ μιν φίλον ἦτορ.—**51.** **ὕφαινε μῆτιν**: as I 93, δ 678. **ποταινίαν**: 'new and strange'; cf. Aisch. *Prom.* 102.—**52.** **μεγαλοσθενές**: cf. l. 67. Pind. has both μεγαλοσθενής and μεγασθενής.—**54.** **τέκε**: cf. ll. 30, 35. Pind. would scarcely have used the same word; cf. 23, 28, 41.—**56.** **πυριέθειραν**: φλογὸς πώγωνα Aisch. *Agam.* 306, πυρωπὸν κεραυνόν *Prom.* 667.—**58.** **Τροζηνία**: with Attic-Ionic η; cf. l. 13. Τροιζ- (MS.) is the spelling of the imperial period.—**59.** **φύτευσεν**: of the mother as Eur. *Med.* 834. ὁ φυτεύσας is regularly opposed to ἡ τεκοῦσα. —**62.** **σῶμα**=ἑαυτόν (cf. ii. 91) as in τὸ σῶμα σῴζειν. Cf. δίκετε σώματα Eur. *Bacch.* 600. But ἀγλαόν may be taken with the subst. Ellis and Pearson read θράσει σύ, Jurenka θρ. σόν, but elsewhere — ⏑ — = — ⏑ —⏑. **πατρὸς . . . δόμους**: cf. Sa. i. 7.—**63.** **ἁλός**: the gen. as in ἀνέδυ ἁλός A 359, ἄγοιντο νήσου Soph. *Phil.* 613.—**64.** **αἰ**: not used by Pind. Bacch. has this form elsewhere only in ii. 5. αἴ κ' is not 'whether' (cf. Goodwin *M. T.* 491). **κλύῃ**: see on Sa. i. 6.—**65.** **Κρόνιος**: usu. K. παῖς.—**66.** **ἀναξίβρόντας**: see on iii. 10. Bacch. has 'Attic' correption before βρ only here and ii. 109; before γρ only ix. 108. **μεδέων**: see on Alk. i. 1.

67. **εὐχάν**: for the sake of variety, here the accus., in 65 the gen., after κλύω. Cf. ἔκλυον αὐδήν ξ 89, ἔκλυεν αὐδῆς κ 311; so with ἀκούω Hdt. 2. 114 ἀκούσας τούτων, 2. 115 ἀκούσας ταῦτα. Both constr. in one line, Eur. *Suppl.* 87.—**68.** **Μίνῳ** makes — ⏑ — = — ⏑ —⏑ (as in 91 if we read πνέουσ'). Μίνωϊ is hardly possible, and not paralleled by ἥρωϊ (conj.) H 453. **φύτευσε**: cf. Pind. xx., *Isthm.* 6. 12 σύν τέ οἱ δαίμων φυτεύει δόξαν.—**70.** **πανδερκέα**: 'conspicuous.' **θέμεν**: see on viii. 13. We expect φίλον and παῖδα (παῖδα φίλον τιμῶν Π 460). Or is φ. π. in apposition to M.?—**72.** **χέρα**: this form as in 8. 3. Cf. *tenditque ad sidera dextram* Verg. *Aen.* 12. 196. Elsewhere Bacch. uses the plur. in this constr. (πέτασε χεῖρας?); as in *tendens ad sidera palmas* Verg. *Aen.* 1. 93, *tendo ad coelum manus* 3. 176. Ken. reads χεῖρε πέτασε (cf. Φ 115).—**76.** **σύ** emphasizes the imperative as in I 301 (Jebb); cf. Xen. *Kyrop.* 5. 5. 21, Aisch. *Agam.* 1061. **ὄρνυ'** is better taken for ὄρνυ(σ)(ο) than as another example of the strange active (n. on viii. 13), which is, however, not without parallel. With ὄρνυ(σ)(ο), cf. μάρναο Π 497, φάο σ 171. **βαρύβρομον**: β. κῦμα Eur. *Hel.* 1305; of music in Lasos.—**77.** **Κρονίδας** of Poseidon as x. 21, Korin. i., *Anth. Pal.* 6. 164. 2, Nonn. *Dion.* 6. 350. Pind. *Ol.* 6. 29 has Ποσειδάωνι Κρονίῳ.—

82. ἀνεκάμπτετ': an unusual use.—**83. ἐπ'**: Bacch. avoids the pregnant use of *ἀπό*.—**84. σταθείς**: *ἐστάθην* as a middle ρ 463 *ἐστάθη ἠύτε πέτρη*, Pind. *Pyth.* 4. 84. **πόντιον**: of *ἄλσος* Aisch. *Pers.* 109.—**85. θελημόν**: cf. Aisch. *Suppl.* 1028 *ποταμοὺς δ' οἳ διὰ χώρας θελεμὸν* (=*ἥσυχον*) *πῶμα χέουσιν*. *θ.* seems to be a bye-form of *ἐθελημός* 'willing': Hes. *W. D.* 118 *οἱ δ' ἐθελημοὶ | ἥσυχοι ἔργ' ἐνέμοντο*. Another pair is *θελήμων* and *ἐθελήμων*.—**88. ἴσχεν κατ' οὖρον**: 'kept the ship before the wind.' Cf. *ἔχω* 'steer' κ 91, Hdt. 6. 95. The words will not bear the translation 'stop the ship, which was running before the wind' (*κάτουρον* Housman).—**89. ὁδόν**: 'issue'; *πόρσυνε κέλευθον* Apoll. Rhod. 4. 549.

90. Cf. *ναὸς ὠκυπόμπου* Eur. *I. T.* 1136. **δόρυ**: as Sim. xiii. 7. **σόει**: imperf. of *σοέω* (=*σεύω*) 'drive,' elsewhere *σοῦμαι*. The *ῡ* of *δόρυ* seems due to the *σ(σ)* which the verb shows in *ἐσσόημαι*, *δορυσ(σ)όος*, *δορυσσόης* etc. So *τε̄ σεύαιτο* Ψ 198. Blass finds a like case in 13. 63 *τε̄ ῥοδό[παχυν]*=*τε Fροδ*. Such lengthening is excessively rare in the Attic period and open to suspicion. The sentence is asyndetic.—**91. Βορεάς**: adj. as *Βορεάδας πνοάς* Aisch. Frag. 195. **ἀῆτα** or *ἄητα* is necessary unless — ⏑ — — can= — ⏑ —⏑. Hom. has *δεινὸς ἀήτη* O 626. See on Sim. xvii.—**92. Ἀθανᾰίων**: with *αι̯* as in *γεραιέ* Eur. *H. F.* 115, *δείλαιος* Aristoph. *Pl.* 850, *φιλαθήναιος* *Vesp.* 282.—**94. πόντονδε**: as κ 48. Here *πόντος* and *πέλαγος* (l. 77) are not distinguished; see on Pind. x. 13. **κατά**: with the gen. only here (and once in Pind.).—**95. λειρίων**: 'gentle.' Suidas has *λειρόφθαλμος ὁ προσηνεῖς ἔχων τοὺς ὀφθαλμούς* and *λειριόεντα· τερπνά, ἡδέα*. The usage here is a bold extension of *λείριος*, *λειριόεσσα ὄψ*. Cf. also *λειριόεις χρώς* N 830.—**97.** The dolphins recall the legend of Arion. On the Euphronios and Bologna vases a Triton appears.—**99. ἱππίου**: a fixed epithet that is somewhat inappropriate here (see on Alkm. xxi. 7). Cf. N 19 ff., Verg. *Aen.* 1. 154, Servius on *Georg.* 1. 12 *ideo dicitur* (Pos.) *equum invenisse, quia velox est eius numen et mobile sicut mare*. Stes. 49 has *κοιλωνύχων ἵππων πρύτανις Ποσειδάν*, Pind. *Pyth.* 4. 45 *ἱππάρχου Ποσειδάωνος*.—**100. μέγαρον**: terminal accus., so *ἦλθον μ.* Pind. *Pyth.* 4. 134, *ἀφίκετο δόμους* *Pyth.* 5. 29. This construction is rare with *φέρω* (l. 97). *μέγαρον* is the palace of Poseidon.—**102. ἔδεισε**: this is expressed on the Bologna krater by the bristling hair of Theseus. **ὀλβίου**: of a god, Aisch. *Suppl.* 526 (lyric).—**104.** Cf. Σ 214 ff.—**105. ὦτε** (?): as Alkm. iv. 41; *ὥστε* Bacch. vi. 21. Cf. T 366 *ὡσεί τε πυρὸς σέλας*. **ἀμφί**: as *ἀμφὶ κόμαις* Pind. *Ol.* 13. 39; cf. below l. 124, x. 53; cf. *περί* x. 47.—**107. δίνηντο** seems a certain reading; Aiolic for *ἐδινέοντο*. **χόρῳ**: cf. Arion 5.—**108.** *ὑγρός* 'supple,' of feet Pollux 1. 215, of a dancer *ib.* 4. 96.—**109. ἄλοχον φίλαν**: Ζ 482. It is a fine touch that the son of Aithra by Poseidon should receive the attest of his divine descent from the wife of Poseidon. This *motif* reappears on the vases. Herakles fared differently at Hera's hands. — **110.** The metre differs from 21, 44, 87, but the tautometric responsion of 109 with 20 and 43 may perhaps be urged against Housman's proposal to read *ἴδε* in 110 and place *σεμνάν* in 109. Jebb's *σεμνοπρόσωπον* and *σεμνοβοῶπιν* (each beginning with a cyclic dactyl) are not probable. Possibly *σεμνάν* is a gloss on *βοῶπιν* (Sitzler). **ἐρατοῖσιν**: cf. v. 43.—**112. ἀϊόνα** of the papyrus, if correct, is an unknown word for 'mantle,' (cf. 124). Ellis conj. *ὠίαν*, Jebb *εἱανόν*, Robert *ἀπλοΐδα*, Tyrrell *αἰόλαν πορφύραν*, Peppmüller *διπλοΐδα*, comparing τ 241 *δίπλακα πορφυρέην* and *διπλοΐδα· διπλουμένην χλανίδα*, Walker *'Αιόνα* (='Ηϊόνη one of the Nereids) with *ἄλλικ'* a Thessalian cloak, for *ἅ νιν*. (But the sense demands that the subject of *ἐπέθηκεν* must be Amphitrite.) This mantle is not represented on the vases for artistic reasons. A *κάλυμμα* had been given to Aithra by the Nereids; now her son is honoured in like manner by their queen.

113. οὔλαις: Theseus' hair was like that of Odysseus, ζ 231. —**114. πλόκον**: according to another and possibly older version the wreath was presented to Theseus by Ariadne, who received it as a bridal gift from Dionysos. It saved him in the fight with the Minotaur. The possession of this object would be proof enough to Minos that Theseus had been acknowledged as Poseidon's son. He does not bring back the ring: *il légitime sa naissance divine sans se faire le serviteur du roi de Crete* (Weil).—**116. δόλιος**: cf. Sa. i. 2; two endings as in Euripides. For metrical reasons Housman conj. *ἕδνον*. **ἐρεμνόν**: 'dark' *i.e.* the roses are closely intertwined (Blass *εἱρμένον*, Reinach *ἐραννόν*).—**117. ἄπιστον**: cf. i. 57.—**118. θέωσιν**: *τίθημι*=*ποιέω*; cf. 1. 70 and θ 465; *θέσις* =*ποίημα* Pind. *Ol.* 3. 8. **φρενοάραις**=*φρενήρεσι*. So Pind. has *χαλκοάρας*=*χαλκήρης*, *χεριάρας*, Herodas *νοήρης*. In *φρενοάραις* the form *φρενο-* is due to the analogy of *φρενοβλαβής*, *-πληγής* etc. For the double forms, cf. *παντ-άρκης* and *παντ-ο-πόρος*. —**119. νᾶα**: elsewhere in Doric *ναῦν* and *νᾶν*. The form looks like a Doricized *νῆα*. **λεπτόπρυμνον**: 'with agile, slender stern.' *πλοῖα λεπτά* 'small craft' Thuk. 2. 83. 5 are different because opposed to the 'best sailers.'—**120.** 'in what thoughts did he check.' Minos thought that he had triumphed over the presumptuous youth. — **122. ἀδίαντος**: 'unwasted' (?) as possibly in *ἀδ. σθένος* Pind. *Nem.* 7. 73, which is usu. taken as=*ἄνευ ἱδρῶτος*. *ἀδίαντος* in Sim.

xiii. 3 may also be 'unwasted.' **124. ἀγλαόθρονοι**: thrones are strictly not in place, but Pind. has *ὑψιθρόνων Νηρεΐδων Nem.* 4. 65. *ἀγλαοθρ.* of the daughters of Danaos *Nem.* 10. 1, of the Muses *Ol.* 13. 96. See on Sa. i. 1.—**125. κοῦραι**: the Nereids.—**127. ὠλόλυξαν**: *ὀλολυγή* is used specially of women; and here in the usual good sense. **ἔκλαγεν**: the sea too participates in the triumph of the son of its lord. Cf. N 29, Ξ 392. The word is used only here of the sea (*κεκληγὼς Ζέφυρος μ* 408).—**129. νέοι**: after *ἤθεοι* as *κοῦροι νέοι* N 95, *νέος πάις δ* 665. **παιάνιξαν**: with *αἴ* as in 92, *ἀλιναιέται* 98: so *παιηόνων* 16. 8 (?). This verb at the close of the myth facilitates the transition to the invocation of Apollo, the god to whom the paian is sacred. **ὀπί** with *hiatus licitus* as *ξ* 492.—**131. φρένα**: apparently the poet supposed that *ἰαίνω* had *F*. A similar blunder in ii. 75. *φρένας ἰάνθης ω* 382 and so perhaps *φρένας* here (Jebb).—**132. θεόπομπον**: *θεόπομποι τιμαί* Pind. *Pyth.* 4. 69. **ἐσθλῶν τύχαν**: cf. *Ζεῦ . . . δίδοι καὶ τύχαν τερπνῶν γλυκεῖαν Ol.* 13. 115. Good fortune is to be an *ὀπαδός* whose guide is God. As Sitzler says, the concluding prayer is in the style of the *Homeric Hymns* (5. 494, 11. 5, 15. 9).

X. 'Theseus.' The report of the approach of a redoubtable stranger, who has vanquished giants and robbers on the Isthmos of Korinth, fills Aigeus king of Athens with wonder and dread. At this time the public affairs of Athens were in a state of confusion and divided into factions, and Aigeus and his whole private family were labouring under the same distemper (Plut. *Thes.* 12).

The poem is monostrophic in form and consists of a dialogue between Aigeus and a chorus of Athenians, possibly old men (cf. ll. 41 ff.). The first speech of the king recounts the deeds of the unknown hero, the second describes his personal appearance. The scene is laid at Athens, where the poem was sung, perhaps at the Oschophoria held in Pyanepsion, or at some other festival where dithyrambs were produced. The intensity of the dramatic situation has been increased by the device employed by the poet to meet the exigencies of the strophic form: the chorus interrogates the king, and its questions, prolonged beyond the limit usually observed under analogous conditions of anxiety in tragedy, at once minister to the pathos of the scene and equal in extent the replies of Aigeus, who is ignorant that the unknown is his own son. Though the poem is dramatic as well as lyric and may well be called a 'lyric drama,' we have no reason to refuse to include the poem under the dithyrambs in the wider sense, or to find in it an example of the 'tragic drama.' In the Introduction to Pindar allusion has been made to the fact that 'lyric tragedies' were unknown to the Greeks and that the title is the product of the Byzantine period. The 'Theseus' is either a duet between the king and the koryphaios, or, more probably, an alternation of solo and choral song, and might seem to confirm the opinion of Aristotle, who in *Poetics* 1449 a 11 says that tragedy arose *ἀπὸ τῶν ἐξαρχόντων τὸν διθύραμβον* 'with the leaders of the dithyramb.' In this case the rôle of Aigeus was played by the 'leader.' It is, however, doubtful whether we have in this poem exactly that form of the dithyramb which gave birth to tragedy. The question with reference to the connection between the type represented by the 'Theseus' and primitive tragedy is further complicated by the fact that here the single actor is a singer, while in the earliest tragedy he probably declaimed his lines. This scene recalls the opening of Soph. *O. T.*

New words: *Λυταῖος, οὔλιος = οὖλος, πρώθηβος* 'in the prime of youth,' *πυρσόχαιτος, χαλκεόκτυπος* 'of brazen din,' *χαλκοκώδων* 'brazen-throated.'

Tautometric responsions: 30 = 45 (two), 32 = 47. Responsions that are not tautometric: 27, 41.

Metre: logaoedic, or perhaps a combination of logaoedics in $^3/_8$, and ionics in $^6/_8$ time. The strophes consist of eight periods. The transposition in 52-53 renders the position of *τε* normal, but introduces an Aiolic basis that is not elsewhere attested in Bacchylides.

1. Since Aigeus does not address the speaker in similar stately fashion, Kenyon's conjecture that it is Medea falls to the ground. *ἀμετέρας* in l. 5 suits a chorus better than Aigeus' queen. **τᾶν**: the article with (proper) names of places only here, ii. 180, Frag. 65 (B. 39); in each case with an adj. **ἱερᾶν**: of Athens; see on Pind. iv. 5. Athens is the final, as it is the initial, note.—**2.** **ἁβροβίων**: contrasts indirectly the refinement of the life of Athens with the ruder Sparta. The Athenians in the time of Bacch. were *φίλαβροι* and devoted to the *ἁβραὶ Χάριτες* and to *ἀγλαΐα* (l. 60); in Thuk. 1. 6. 3 *ἁβροδίαιτον* is used of the delicate habits of the Athenians of the previous generation. Later in the century *ἁβρός* would have been used to castigate the effeminacy of the Ionians of Asia Minor (*Ἰώνων τρυφεραμπεχόνων ἁβρὸς ὄχλος* Antiphanes Frag. 91). Cf. Bacch. i. 48, Stes. x. Because of his luxurious garb, which was regarded as Ionian, Theseus himself was ridiculed at a later period. The Athenians represent the Ionians, as in ix. 3. —**3.** **χαλκοκώδων**: cf. Soph. *Aias* 17 *χαλκοστόμου κώδωνος ὡς Τυρσηνικῆς*. Cf. Aisch. *Eum.* 566 ff.—**4.** **πολεμηΐαν**: epic form as *Ἀρηΐων* l. 57. **ἀοιδάν** 'sound'; rarely used of the note of a musical instrument; of the sound of the trumpet, *αὐτή*

Aisch. *Pers.* 395, ἠχώ Eur. *Troad.* 1267, φωνή in the lxx.—**5.** **ἢ** : followed by ἤ . . . ἤ recalls the use in Pind. *Isthm.* 7. 3 ff. —**6.** **ἀμφεβάλλει** : Eur. *Androm.* 799.—**7.** **στρατ. ἀνήρ** : see on Alkm. xi. 4.—**8.** **λησταί** : not Doric λᾳσταί despite λαΐδος 16. 17 ; cf. on iv. 3.—**10.** **σεύοντ'** : the Doric -οντι may elide the ι (Epicharm. 23, Pind. *Pyth.* 4. 241) but may not add -ν. **ἀγέλας** : here of sheep ; συῶν ἀγέλαι Hes. *Shield* 168. The strict use is Hes. *Theogon.* 445 βουκολίας τ' ἀγέλας τε . . . | ποιμνάς τ' οἴων. For the thought cf. A 154 οὐ γάρ πώ ποτ' ἐμὰς βοῦς ἤλασαν οὐδὲ μὲν ἵππους.—**11.** **ἀμύσσει** : so A 243, Aisch. *Pers.* 161.—**12.** **δοκέω** : dissyllabic εω in the first person of contract verbs is nowhere confirmed by the metre in Ionic poetry (Smyth *Ionic* § 638. 2), but open καλέω occurs in Aisch. *Agam.* 147.—**15.** **Κρεούσας** : common tradition made Aigeus the son of Pylia or Pelia (Apollod. 3. 15. 5), whereas Kreusa, the daughter of Erechtheus, was the mother of Ion by Xuthos. Perhaps the tradition was not fixed. Pandion was the son of Kekrops.

16. **δολιχάν** : of space ; of time in 45. **ἀμείψας** : ἀμείβω κέλευθον Eur. *Or.* 1295.—**18.** In the list of ἔργα (which is constructed of clauses connected by τε) no mention is made of Periphetes, whose defeat was the first of the ἆθλοι of Theseus. This is also usually absent in the artistic representations of the feats of Theseus. The killing of Pallas fell in a later period. For illustrations of the undermentioned deeds, see *Mus. ital.* 3. 209 ff.—**20.** Sinis used to rend travellers by tying them to the tops of pine trees, which he bent to the earth ; whence his name Πιτυοκάμπτης. Cf. *J. H. S.* 2. pl. x. —**21.** **Κρονίδα** : Poseidon, as ix. 77 (cf. Hygin. 38). Apollod. 3. 16. 2 makes Sinis the son of Polypemon. His mother was the Korinthian Sylea. **Λυταίου** : see Steph. Byz. *s.v.* Λυταί (in Thessaly) : διὰ τὸ λῦσαι τὰ Τέμπη Ποσειδῶνα καὶ σκεδάσαι τὸ ἀπὸ τοῦ κατακλυσμοῦ ὕδωρ. Λυταίη was a name of Thessaly. The epithet Λυταῖος, which occurs only here, must have been somewhat recondite to the Athenians. Unless it is to be taken in a general sense (the god who 'loosens the land') it is not easy to discover its appropriateness as applied to the father of the Korinthian robber.—**24.** **Κρεμμυῶνος** : for this variation from the usual form Κρομμυών, cf. Ἐρχομενός Ὀρχομενός, Ἐρχιεύς Ὀρχιεύς. Κρομ. 'onion-town' may be a folk's etymology like Σικυών 'cucumber-town.' The site of the ancient town is occupied by the village of Hag. Theodori. The combat with the sow Phaia is depicted in Gerhard *Griech. Vasenbilder* pl. clxii. 3 and 4, *J. H. S.* 2. 61, pl. x.—**25.** According to Attic tradition Skiron lived on the heights of the Isthmos and hurled all travellers into the sea after compelling them to wash his feet. The Megarians regarded him as a hero and akin to the Aiakidai (see Frazer on Paus. 1. 39. 6). Skiron appears on a Munich cup (Gerhard *Auserl. Vasen* 232) of about 450-440 B.C., and on a metope of the Theseion (Hephaisteion).—**26**. Kerkyon lived near Eleusis and overcame all passers-by, whom he forced to wrestle with him. In Pausanias' time the spot still bore the name παλαίστρα Κερκυόνος (1. 39. 3). The periegete says Theseus invented the art of wrestling. The phrase has an ironical touch ('closed the wrestling-school'). See Gerhard pl. clix., *Mus. ital.* 3. 1. —**27**. **ἔσχεν** as vi. 3.—**28**. **Προκόπτας** (*qui nomen ab re habet*: προκόπτω) is an alternative name for Προκρούστης (προκρούω), whose hammer adjusted the legs of his guests to the size of his beds. One account places his home on Mt. Korydallos, another on the Kephisos. On the authority of Ovid *Ib.* 405 (*ut Sinis et Sciron et cum Polypemone natus*), we may suppose that the Polypemon of l. 27 was the father, who may have been a smith, like Hephaistos and Palaimon, and whose hammer was bequeathed to his son and made famous in local legend. The surname may have been given to the son as well as to the father, or the son may have been confused with the father. Paus. 1. 38. 5 states that the real name of Prokrustes was Polypemon; Plut. *Thes.* 11 has Δαμάστην τὸν Προκρούστην, while Apollod. *Epit.* 1. 4 reports that Damastes was by some called Polypemon. Πολυπήμων *i.e.* ὃς πολὺ πῆμα τοῖς ὁδοιπόροις ἐτίθει. I had thought to compare Prokoptas, the son of Polypemon, with Ἀφείδαντος Πολυπημονίδαο ω 305; but Π. there = πολυκτημ., and is not, as L. and S. take it, a play on πολυπήμων 'baneful.' It is possible to read σφῦραν·, making ἔσχεν govern σφ., and thus give both names to the same person (so Paus.). ἐξέβαλ' ἄν has been suggested to the same effect.— —**30**. **φωτός**: same position in the verse as 19.

31. A double question in one clause consisting of τίς and another interrog. as in ii. 86, τίς πόθεν εἰς ἀνδρῶν α 170, τίς πόθεν μολών Soph. *Trach.* 421; *Aias* 1185, Eur. *Bacch.* 579, *Hel.* 86; often in Plato. Cf. Virg. *Aen.* 8. 114 *qui genus? unde domo?*—**33** ff. Cf. Aisch. *Choeph.* 766, XO. πῶς οὖν κελεύει νιν μολεῖν ἐσταλμένον; | . . . | εἰ ξὺν λοχίταις εἴτε καὶ μονοστιβῆ. | TR. ἄγειν κελεύει δορυφόρους ὀπάονας, Soph. *O. T.* 750 πότερον ἐχώρει βαιός, ἢ πολλοὺς ἔχων | ἄνδρας λοχίτας, οἷ' ἀνὴρ ἀρχηγέτης; —**35**. **μοῦνον**: *i.e.* ἄνευ στρατιᾶς. Cf. Aisch. *Pers.* 734 μονάδα δὲ Ξέρξην ἔρημόν φασιν οὐ πολλῶν μέτα. With μ. σὺν ὀπάοσιν, cf. Eur. *Hek.* 1148 μόνον δὲ σὺν τέκνοισί μ' εἰσάγει δόμους.— **36**. **ἔμπορον**: a travelling merchant whose goods are carried by his attendants (ὀπάονες).—**37**. **ἀλλοδαμίαν**: tragic irony.— **39**. **τούτων** = τοιούτων, as in Demosth. *de cor.* 320 σὺ τοίνυν *οὗτος εὑρέθης* (Jurenka), Alkm. iv. 57.—**42. ὄφρα**; with the fut. in a final clause, Gildersleeve *A. J. P.* 4. 429, Goodwin *M. T.* 324; cf. Pind. *Nem.* 4. 32. Bacch. uses *ἵνα* = *ut* (= *ubi* in Pind.) in 10. 11.—**43. ἔρδοντα**: *scil.* *κακόν*. *Böses muss mit Bösem enden* (Schiller).—**45. χρόνῳ**: with an adj. *χρόνος* has the article as in vi. 82, Frag. 42 (B. 3). **τελεῖται**: the repetition (cf. l. 30) is significant, not casual as are most of the tautometric responsions.

46. δύο φῶτε: Phorbas and Peirithoos. The usual form of the legend represents Theseus as journeying alone from Troizen to Athens. On a Munich skyphos (*Arch. Zeit.* 23. 195) two companions attend him in his combats with Sinis and Prokrustes; a single companion in the former adventure appears on a London cup (Cecil Smith *Cat. Vases Brit. Mus.* 3. E 74), and the like holds true in the Skiron episode on a Naples vase (Panofka *Skiron* iv. 1). **οἱ**: always shows traces of the *Ϝ* in Bacch. **μόνους**: plur. adj. with dual subst. as Φ 115 (cf. l. 49). In the strict Attic of the orators we find congruence of the attributive. **ἁμαρτεῖν** = *ὁμαρτεῖν* as in Herodas 4. 95, 5. 43. Cf. *ἁμαρτῇ* E 656, Solon 33. 4. Hesych. and Eust. report *ἁμαρτῶ* = *ἀκολουθῶ*.—**47. λέγει** introduces the longest passage in indirect discourse to be found in the lyric poets. **φαιδ. ὤμοις**: cf. λ 128, Pind. *Ol.* 1. 27. On the vases Theseus carries his sword from his shoulder by means of a baldric.—**48. ἐλεφαντόκωπον**: cf. Ovid *Metam.* 7. 422 *capulo gladii eburno.* Ken. suggested ⟨*κορύναν τε πυκνάν*⟩, but Theseus captured the club from Periphetes, who is not mentioned (cf. on l. 18).—**49.** Heroes carry two spears: Γ 18, α 256, Pind, *Pyth.* 4. 79 of Jason, the beautiful description of whose arrival at Iolkos is faintly recalled by the present passage.—**50. κηὔκτον**: crasis is very rare in Bacch. (*χὤτι* i. 81). Cf. *κυνέην ἐύτυκτον* Γ 336. In posthomeric times we hear of Arkadian, Boiotian, Korinthian, and Thessalian *κυνέαι*.—**51. πέρι**: 'over,' 'on.' See on Sa. i. 10. Bacch. does not use *ὑπέρ* except in compounds. Cf. K 257 *ἀμφὶ δέ οἱ κυνέην κεφαλῆφιν ἔθηκεν . . . ῥύεται δὲ κάρη θαλερῶν αἰζηῶν*, where we have the normal poetical use for the prose *περί* or *ἐπί cum dat.* *περί* is not a favourite preposition with the choral poets. **πυρσοχαίτου** = *πυρρόθριξ* Eur. *I. A.* 225.—**53. ἄμφι**: the anastrophe is rare; *πέρι* l. 51 is common, *ἔπι* ii. 83, 133. **οὔλιον**: 'woolly,' only here = Hom. *οὖλος*.—**54.** The chlamys was used as a military cloak in Thessaly (Pollux 10. 124) and worn by young men (cf. 56 *παῖδα πρώθηβον*). Eros wears a *πορφυρίαν χλάμυν* Sa. 64.—**55. ἄπο**: with tmesis as in 4. 20. **Λαμνίαν** = *φοβεράν*: the fire emitted by the volcano Mosychlos on Lemnos (*Λήμνιον πῦρ*) was proverbial (Soph. *Phil.* 800, Aristoph. *Lysistr.* 299,

Lykophr. *Alex.* 227); so Λ. βλέπειν. Lykophron calls Aias a 'Lemnian thunderbolt of war' (Jebb).—**56. φοίνισσ. φλόγα**: used of Aitna, Pind. *Pyth.* 1. 24. πυρὸς φοίνικι πνοᾷ Eur. *Troad.* 815. **ἔμμεν**: so I. 31, ii. 144 etc., elsewhere ἔμμεναι l. 14 and εἶμεν 10. 48 (Bacch. does not use εἶναι).—**57. πρώθηβον**: so Theseus is represented on vases of the severe red-figured style. **ἀθυρμάτων**: the 'delights of Ares' are war and battle. Cf. παῖς ἐὼν ἄθυρε μεγάλα Ϝέργα . . . ἄκοντα πάλλων . . . λεόντεσσιν ἔπρασσεν φόνον Pind. Nem. 3. 44, of Achilles. So Ἀπολλώνιον ἄθυρμα *Pyth.* 5. 23, ἀθύρμασι Μουσᾶν Bacch. 71 (B. 48), Ἀφροδίσιον ἄθυρμα (the rose) *Anakreont.* 53. 8.—**59. χαλκεοκτύπου**: elsewhere χαλκόκτυπος.—**60. φιλαγλάους**: of Akragas Pind. *Pyth.* 12. 1.

XI. Schol. Pind. *Ol.* 13. 1. Fragment of an epinikion. Pindar has (*Ol.* 13. 4) τὰν ὀλβίαν Κόρινθον, Ἰσθμίου | πρόθυρον Ποτειδᾶνος. The Isthmic column had on the Peloponnesian side Τάδ' ἐστὶ Πελοπόννησος, οὐκ Ἰωνία, on the opposite side Τάδ' οὐχὶ Π., ἀλλ' Ἰωνία. **θεόδματοι**: according to the local legend Korinthos, the mythical founder, was the son of Zeus; whence the proverb ὁ Διὸς Κόρινθος.—Metre: dact.-epitrite.

XII. Stob. *Flor.* 122. 1. Perhaps from the *Hymn to Demeter*. It is also possible that the speaker is Danae, or Hekabe addressing Kassandra. **ἀφέγκτοισιν**: cf. Pind. *Pyth.* 4. 237 ἀφωνήτῳ ἄχει, Hdt. 3. 14 τὰ μὲν οἰκήϊα ἦν μέζω κακὰ ἢ ὥστε ἀνακλαίειν, Thuk. 7. 75. 4 καὶ μείζω ἢ κατὰ δάκρυα τὰ μὲν πεπονθότας κ.τ.λ.—Metre: dact.-epitrite.

XIII. Stob. *Flor.* 55. 3. In connection with this paian on Peace the fact is to be recalled that on the cessation of hostilities paians were sung by the opposing armies (Xen. *Hell.* 7. 4. 56).—**1. τίκτει**: the poem is a free personification which avoids all mythological connections. Euripides in Frag. 453 doubtless had Bacchylides in mind: Εἰρήνα βαθύπλουτε καὶ | καλλίστα μακάρων θεῶν, | ζῆλός μοι σέθεν, ὡς χρονίζεις. | δέδοικα δὲ μὴ πρὶν πόνοις | ὑπερβάλῃ με γῆρας, | πρὶν σὰν χαρίεσσαν προσιδεῖν ὥραν | καὶ καλλιχόρους ἀοιδὰς | φιλοστεφάνους τε κώμους. | ἴθι μοι, πότνα, πόλιν. | τὰν δ' ἐχθρὰν στάσιν εἶργ' ἀπ' οἴ- | κων τὰν μαινομέναν τ' ἔριν | θηκτῷ τερπομέναν σιδάρῳ (see Browning's *Arist. Apol.* p. 179). So Eur. *Suppl.* 489 ἣ (Εἰρ.) πρῶτα μὲν Μούσαισι προσφιλεστάτη, | γόοισι δ' ἐχθρά, τέρπεται δ' εὐπαιδίᾳ, | χαίρει δὲ πλούτῳ. **δέ τε**: see on vi. 26. On the sequence of the particles in 1-5, see Hartung *Partikeln* 1. 108. 7. **μεγάλα**: rarely employed in early Greek even of a goddess: of Moira, Soph. *Phil.* 1466 (where the article ensures the personification), of Erinys, *Trach.* 893; both the Fates and the Furies are μεγάλαι, as are 'the two goddesses' Demeter and Persephone. Hence, though more prosaic, the explanation as neuter is to be preferred: the following lines explain the word. Cf. Aristoph. *Pax* 999 ff. Had the poet intended an adj. with εἰρήνα, he would have employed one richer in colour than μεγ. Hartung read, and Bergk preferred, μέγαν (μέγας πλοῦτος in Hybrias).—**2. πλοῦτον**: cf. Mel. Adesp. iii., Eur. *Suppl.* 491. Peace is one of the Horai, who are ταμίαι ἀνδράσι πλούτου Pind. *Ol.* 13. 7. A group by Kephisodotos, the Athenian sculptor of the early part of the fourth century, represented Eirene (κουροτρόφος) supporting on her arm the child Plutos, who carries the Horn of Plenty: Paus. 1. 8. 2, 9. 16. 2. A reproduction of this work is found in Munich. See Gardner *Greek Sculpture* p. 352. **μελιγλώσσων**: cf. i. 97, Aisch. *Prom.* 172 μελιγλώσσοις πειθοῦς ἐπαοιδαῖσιν, Pind. *Pyth.* 3. 64 μελιγάρυες ὕμνοι, *Nem.* 3. 4 μελιγαρύων κώμων, *Isthm.* 2. 8 μαλθακόφωνοι ἀοιδαί. -γλωσσος also in ἀδύγλωσσος βοά Pind. *Ol.* 13. 100, πολύγλωσσος βοή Soph. *El.* 641. **ἄνθεα**: ἄνθεα ὕμνων *Ol.* 9. 48.—**3. αἴθεσθαι** and μέλειν l. 5, like the preceding accusatives, depend on τίκτει. So the inf. follows ποιέω, πράττω, καθίστημι etc.; one of which verbs may be supplied here. With the passage cp. the hymn to Apollo i. with notes (Append.) ἁγίοις δὲ βωμοῖσιν Ἅφαιστος αἴθει νέων μῆρα ταύρων.—**4. ξανθᾷ**: of φλόξ i. 56. **τανυτρίχων**: αἶγα τανύτριχα Hes. *W. D.* 516. —**5.** Peaceful scenes with song and dance are pictured in Σ 490, Hes. *Shield* 272. Aristoph. calls Peace φιλέορτος *Thesmoph.* 1147, δέσποινα χορῶν *Pax* 976. ἡσυχία δὲ φιλεῖ μὲν συμπόσιον Pind. *Nem.* 9. 48. The flute was the instrument generally used by κωμασταί. Cf. Pratinas i. 8. Dionysos loves Eirene (ὀλβοδότειραν, κουροτρόφον θεάν) Eur. *Bacch.* 419, and is often represented together with her (Müller-Wieseler 2. 584, 585). Cf. vi. 66; Theogn. 885. **τε καί**: here of a union of complementary similars.—**6-10** are quoted *sine nomine* by Plutarch, *Numa* 20, to show that even the 'exaggerations of the poets' as to the blessings of Peace were surpassed during the reign of Numa. For ἱστοί Plut. has ἔργα. **πόρπαξιν**: Aristoph. *Pax* 662 ὦ γυναικῶν μισοπορπακιστάτη of Peace.—**7.** Cf. Eur. Frag. 369 κείσθω δόρυ μοι μίτον ἀμφιπλέκειν ἀράχναις, Theokr. 16. 96 ἀράχνια δ' εἰς ὅπλ' ἀράχναι | λεπτὰ διαστήσαιντο, βοᾶς δ' ἔτι μηδ' ὄνομ' εἴη, Nonnos *Dionys.* 38. 13 ἔκειτο δὲ τηλόθι χάρμης | Βακχιὰς ἑξαέτηρος ἀραχνιόωσα βοείη, Ben Jonson, 'Prince Henry's Barriers' "Shields and swords, | Cobwebb'd and rusty; not a helm affords | A spark of lustre, which were wont to give | Light to the world, and made the nation live." Peele "This helmet now shall make a hive for bees." Lowell 'Launfal' "Hang up my idle armor on the wall, | Let it be the spider's banquet hall."—**8**. Cf. Tibullus 1. 10. 49 *pace bidens vomerque vigent, at tristia duri | militis in tenebris occupat arma situs*, Ovid *Fasti* 4. 927 *sarcula nunc durusque bidens et vomer aduncis, | ruris opes, niteant; inquinet arma situs.* To the Roman *pace Ceres laeta est.* The Greek poet does not, like the Latins, mark the reign of Peace by the return of agricultural prosperity and the felicity of rural life (cf. *Fasti* 1. 697). The Greek here emphasizes Peace as the giver of wealth, song, the revel, sleep; she it is who renders possible the undisturbed worship of the gods. The Roman note is anticipated in Menander: *εἰρήνη γεωργὸν κἀν πέτραις | τρέφει καλῶς, πόλεμος δὲ κἀν πεδίῳ κακῶς* Frag. 719, *φέρβε καὶ εἰράναν, ἵν' ὃς ἄροσε τῆνος ἀμάσῃ* Kallim. 6. 138; *Εἰρήνη βαθύκαρπος* Kaibel 792 (2nd cent. A.D.). Demeter is the mother of Plutos, Hes. *Theogon.* 969. **δάμναται**: Plut. has *εὐρὼς* (not in Stob.) *δάμναται*, but he may not be following the poet's order.—**9**. Cf. Hor. *epod.* 2. 5 *neque excitatur classico miles truci*, Tibull. 1. 4 *martia cui somnos classica pulsa fugent*, Bacon "Wars with their noise affright us." Plutarch, citing Eur. quoted on l. 7, says (*Vita Niciae* 9) *ἡδέως δὲ μεμνημένοι τοῦ εἰπόντος ὅτι τοὺς ἐν εἰρήνῃ καθεύδοντας οὐ σάλπιγγες ἀλλ' ἀλεκτρυόνες ἀφυπνίζουσι.*—**10**. **μελίφρων**: of *ὕπνος* Frag. 13. 5 (K.), *Il.* B 34.—**11**. **ἁμόν** = *ἁμέτερον*; as *noster* for *meus*. **θάλπει**: so Aisch. *Prom.* 590 (of passion). *θέλγει* (cf. vulg. *θάλκει*) might be defended by ε 47, Eur. *I. A.* 142, [Plato] *epigr.* 25. 4.—**12**. So to Tibullus 1. 10. 53 ff. Peace is the season of love. **βρίθοντ(ι)**: not *βρίθοντ(αι)*; with the genitive as ο 334, Soph. Frag. 264 *πάντα δ' ἐρίθων ἀραχνᾶν βρίθει* (cf. l. 7). The instrumental dative is more common. Cf. i. 15. **παιδικοὶ ὕμνοι**: love songs addressed to beautiful youths. Welcker *Kl. Schr.* 1. 233 referred most of these songs to 'beauty-shows,' though some, he thought, might have been sung at symposia, birthday-festivals, etc. The erotic songs of Bacch. (53-55 K, 24-26 B) were classed by Welcker as *παιδικοὶ ὕμνοι*. Cf. Pind. *Isthm.* 2. 1 ff. *οἱ μὲν πάλαι φῶτες* (*i.e.* Alkaios, Ibykos, Anakreon accord. to the scholiast) . . . *ῥίμφα παιδείους ἐτόξευον μελιγάρυας ὕμνους* and Bacch. 10. 42 *ἕτερος δ' ἐπὶ παισὶ ποικίλον τόξον τιταίνει.* Pind. xv. is often regarded as a *παιδ. ὕμνος* (cf. FOLK-SONGS XXV.). **φλέγονται**: 'are flamed forth,' 'burst forth.' Song is a torch that flames on high (*ἅψαι πυρσὸν ὕμνων* Pind. *Isthm.* 4. 43). The poet, the Graces illumine a victor and his native city. Cf. *Pyth.* 5. 45 *σὲ δ' ἠΰκομοι φλέγοντι* (*illustrant*) *Χάριτες*, *Nem.* 6. 37 *Χαρίτων ὁμάδῳ φλέγεν* (*splendebat*), a passage which suggests *φλέγοντι* here, as the passive is employed of the object illuminated; so in *Isthm.* 7. 23 *φλέγεται δὲ Fιοπλόκοισι Μοίσαις*, *Nem.* 10. 2 *φλέγεται δ' ἀρεταῖς μυρίαις*. The use of *ἐπιφλέγω* is similar: *Ol.* 9. 22 *φίλαν πόλιν ἐπιφλέγων ἀοιδαῖς*, *Pyth.* 11. 45 *τῶν εὐφροσύνα τε καὶ δόξ' ἐπιφλέγει*, Aisch. *Pers.* 395 *σάλπιγξ ἀυτῇ ἐπέφλεγεν* ("That blast no English bugle claims; | Oft have I heard it fire the night" Scott, 'Lord of the Isles' 4. 18). So in *vox illuxit, splendens vox, splendida oratio; canorum illud in voce splendescit etiam in senectute* Cic. *de sen.* 9. 28.

The Greek often allows the sense of sight to usurp the place of the sense of sound (*αἴσθησις ἀντὶ αἰσθήσεως*). He prefers *τὸ ἐναργέστερον*; the ear is more sluggish than the eye. Cf. on Prat. i. 17. So with *λάμπω*, as in *λάμπει κλέος* Pind. *Ol.* 1. 23, *ἔλαμψε φάμα* Soph. *O. T.* 473 (*χάρις λάμπει* Mel. Adesp. xii.), *φωνὴ λαμπρά*, *φωνὴ ἀλαμπής*; so with *φαίνω*, which is often used with *ἀοιδή*, *ἔπος*, *κτύπος*, *λόγος*, *μῦθος*, *σάλπιγξ*, *φήμη*; *ἀχὼ τηλεφανής* Soph. *Phil.* 189. We find also *τηλωπὸν ἰωάν* *Phil.* 216, *φαεννὰς ὀπός* Pind. *Pyth.* 4. 283, *φωνὴ μέλαινα*, *φ. λευκή* (cf. Lobeck *Rhemat.* 342); *κτύπον δέδορκα* Aisch. *Sept.* 104, where Verrall suggests that we have a mental picture. The boldness is sometimes softened, as in Eur. *Phoin.* 1377 *ἐπεὶ δ' ἀφείθη πυρσὸς ὣς Τυρσηνικῆς | σάλπιγγος ἠχή κ.τ.λ.*, or by zeugma, as in *οὔτε φωνὴν οὔτε μορφὴν ὄψει* Aisch. *Prom.* 21, *ἀστράπτει* Mel. Adesp. xi. The same transference of sphere appears in the use of *λευκός*, *μέλας*, *αἰόλος*. In Latin: *Martemque incendere cantu* Verg. *Aen.* 6. 165, *clamore incendunt coelum* 10. 895, *incendit clamore nemus* Stat. *Theb.* 5. 553, *ut regia luctu incenderetur* Justin 38. 8. 14, *Der Schal lasch* (Schall erlosch) Parzival; so *hrein* 'purus,' *hrinr* 'clamor.'

Metre: dact.-epitrite. With the dissyllabic anacrusis before –́ — ⊔́ ◡ –́ — in l. 7, cf. Pind. *Ol.* 7. 1, 6; 8. 6. The spondee is here not to be measured ⊔́ ⊔́, as in *Pyth.* 1. 20. Boeckh's *πλ. μελιγλ. τε* in l. 2 would help the rhythm and cause the poem to fall into four periods: I. *stichic*, vv. 1-2 = 6. 6; II. *palinodic*, vv. 3-6 = 3, 4. 5; 3, 4. 5; III. *mesodic*, vv. 7-8 = 3. 4, 3; IV. *palinodic antithetic*, vv. 9-12 = 6. 4, 3; 4. 3, 6. The MS. reading is, however, defensible. The extent of the poem cannot be determined though line 12 has a final ring to it. In Kallim. *Hymn to Demeter* the last note but one is *φέρβε καὶ εἰράναν, ἵν' ὃς ἄροσε τῆνος ἀμάσῃ*. Since we do not know where the epode begins, all speculation is futile as to the division of the fragment. Bergk began the epode with l. 6. From a metrical point of view, l. 7 suggests the beginning; at least if Bacchylides' manner was Pindar's manner. The reconstruction of Blass *R. M.* 32. 460 is over hazardous (l. 1 = last verse of epode, 2-7 strophe, 8-12 antistr.). Perhaps the poem was written after the battle at the Eurymedon (460), when an altar was erected to Peace (Plut. *Kimon* 13). But even in time of war the poet may dream of peace.

XIV. Clem. Alex. *Strom.* 5. 687; from a paian. A reply, perhaps ironical, to Pindar's teaching *Ol.* 2. 86 *σοφὸς ὁ πολλὰ Fειδὼς φυᾷ· | μαθόντες δὲ λάβροι | παγγλωσίᾳ, κόρακες ὥς, ἄκραντα* γαρύετον | Διὸς πρὸς ὄρνιχα θεῖον, where the scholiast finds a reference to Simonides and Bacchylides (cf. *Ol.* 9. 100, *Nem.* 3. 41). Like ἀρετή (except to Sokrates), σοφία is not διδακτή. Here the σοφία is that of the poet (Alkm. v.). The presence of a personal element in a paian is noteworthy.—**1. ἕτερος ἐξ ἑτέρου**: Bacch. confesses his debt to Hesiod in ii. 191. **τό τε πάλαι**: cf. *Iliad* I 105 ἡμὲν πάλαι ἠδ' ἔτι καὶ νῦν, Soph. *Antig.* 181, *El.* 676 νῦν τε καὶ πάλαι, *Phil.* 966 οὐ νῦν πρῶτον ἀλλὰ καὶ πάλαι.—**2. ῥᾷστον**: *scil.* ἐστί; see on Anakr. xvi. 6. **ἀρρήτων**: heretofore 'unuttered' in song. Note the difference from tragic usage. **πύλας**: πύλας ὕμνων ἀναπιτνάμεν Pind. *Ol.* 6. 27. The passage reminds one of Hor. 4. 2. 27-32. Frag. 63 (37) εἰ δὲ λέγει τις ἄλλως, πλατεῖα κέλευθος may be another reply to Pindar, or a reference to legitimate variations in the treatment of myth.—Metre: logaoedic.

XV. Stob. *Flor.* 108. 26 (1-2 *Flor.* 1. 6, Apostol. 6. 55); a prosodion. For the sentiment cf. *Hor.* 1. 9. 9 ff., 2. 16. 25 ff., *Epist.* 1. 11. 28 ff.—**1. ὁδός**: so σοφίας ὁδόν Pind. x. 4. ὁδός is associated with ὅρος also in Aisch. *Agam.* 1119.—**2.** τελεῖν τὸν βίον Soph. *Antig.* 1114. The thought recurs in Alkm. iv. 37. —**4. τὸ παρ' ἆμαρ**: absol. temporal accus. The article in such phrases as τὸ πρὸ τοῦ, τὸ ἀπὸ τούτων, τὸ αὐτίκα marks the expressed or latent opposition between the time in question and some other time (Krüg. 50. 5. 13). The plural in τὰ νῦν etc. is slightly different.—**5.** Cf. ἰάπτομαι ἄλγεσιν ἦτορ Moschos 4. 39. **ἑόν**: as ὃν θυμὸν ὀνήσεται H 173. To this fragment may belong 49 (20) τί γὰρ ἐλαφρὸν (=κουφίζον, cf. Theokr. 2. 92) ἔτ' ἔστ' ἄπρακτ' ὀδυρόμενον δονεῖν | καρδίαν.—Metre: logaoedic. The simple forms (pherecratics and glyconics) are used. In reference to the fact that the poem is called a prosodion it may be noted that Dion. Halik. says that the prosodiac is a union of the glyconic and pherecratic.

XVI. Stob. *Flor.* 11. 7, and on a gem in Caylus' *Rec. d' Antiq.* 5. pl. 50. 4; from a hyporcheme.—**1. Λυδία λίθος** (*lapis lydius*): the καθαρὰ βάσανος. Transference to the moral sphere as in Pind. *Pyth.* 10. 67 πειρῶντι δὲ καὶ χρυσὸς ἐν βασάνῳ πρέπει | καὶ νόος ὀρθός, Sim. 175 οὐκ ἔστιν μείζων βάσανος χρόνου οὐδενὸς ἔργου, | ὃς καὶ ὑπὸ στέρνοις ἀνδρὸς ἔδειξε νόον, Cheilon ἐν μὲν λιθίναις ἀκόναις ὁ χρυσὸς ἐξετάζεται | διδοὺς βάσανον φανεράν· ἐν δὲ χρυσῷ | ἀνδρῶν ἀγαθῶν τε κακῶν τε νοῦς ἔδωκ' ἔλεγχον, Pind. Frag. 122. 13, Eur. *Med.* 516, *Hippol.* 925, Theokr. 12. 36. See also on skol. v., and cf. schol. Plato *Gorg.* 486 D, Apostol. 10. 99. Bergk would insert, after l. 2, Frag. 43 (K. 67) χρυσὸν βροτῶν γνώμαισι μανύει καθαρόν. The poem may have contained the words (Stob. *Flor.* 11. 2) Ἀλάθεια θεῶν ὁμόπολις, μόνα θεοῖς συνδιαιτωμένα. **σοφία . . . ἀλάθεια**: the voice of the poet is the voice of truth; not hendiadys, but 'as poetic art, so does truth' (τε . . . τε). So *verissimum et sapientissimum iudicem* Cicero *Sex. Rosc. Amer.* 30. 84. For the verb in the singular with a compound subject (Archil. 16, Pind. *Ol.* 5. 15, *Pyth.* 10. 10), cp. the remark of Landor, *à propos* of Milton's "where flows Ganges and Indus." "The small fry will carp at this, which is often an elegance, but oftener in Greek than in Latin, in Latin than in French, in French than in English." See *A. J. P.* 3. 422. Reading σοφίαν τε παγκ. ἐλέγχει (*v.l.*) it is Truth that brings to naught the counsels of the wise. Cf. Pind. xxviii., *Ol.* 10. 3 ff. θυγάτηρ | Ἀλάθεια Διός, ὀρθᾷ χερὶ | ἐρύκετον ψευδέων | ἐνιπὰν ἀλιτοξένων.—Metre: logaoedic. Rossbach thinks the first verse contains cretics. Others find epitrites here.

XVII. Athen. 2. 39 E; a skolion, not an erotikon, as is often maintained. The only poem of Bacch. cited under the latter title (Frag. 53 K, 24 B) is of a different character.—**1. γλυκεῖ' ἀνάγκα**: Spenser's *deare constraint.* Imitated by Hor. 3. 21. 13 *tu lene tormentum ingenio admoves | plerumque duro.* The Latin oxymoron is less delicate than the Greek. Cf. *vino tortus, Epod.* 1. 18. 38. The γλ. ἀνάγκα is a πειθανάγκη; cf. κρατερὴ ἀνάγκη Z 458, κακὰ ἀνάγκα Theokr. 16. 85, *saeva necessitas.* There is no reference to the *anancaeum*, the 'bowl of compulsion' Plaut. *Rudens* 2. 3. 34. ἀνάγκαν *vocat mellitissimus poeta* τὴν φρενῶν ἔκστασιν *quum poto liberalius vino homo suae spontis non est neque mentis sanae* (Casaub.). Cf. Pind. *Nem.* 9. 51 βιατὰν ἀμπέλου παῖδα.—**2. σευομενᾶν**: gen. absol. Cf. Alk. xx. 5. σ. κυλ. is a stronger expression than κυλίκων περινισσομενάων Phokyl. 11. The ablatival gen. demanded by the MS. σευομένα is harsh (though we find ἄρχομαι without ἐκ; see on Ibyk. i. 2), and we expect ἀπό or ἐκ (σευομένα 'κ van Herwerden). **θάλπῃσι**: cf. *caluisse* in Hor. 3. 21. 11 *narratur et prisci Catonis saepe mero c. virtus.* θάλπησι of the MSS. cannot be defended as an example of the *schema Ibyceum* (see on Ibyk. viii.); θάλπημι does not occur and is ill supported by θαλπείω in *Et. Mag.* A temporal conjunction preceded in l. 1. For the retention of the epic -σι cf. 19. 3 ὃς ἂν λάχῃσι.—**3. δ'**: apodotic. It is hardly possible to explain Κύπριδος (without δ') as due to the influence of *F*, of which ἐλπίς or ἔλπομαι shows no trace in Bacch. Michelangeli reads θυμὸν | Κύπριδος· ἐλπὶς διαιθ. with asyndeton, which is not uncommon in Bacch. (ii. 144, 145, v. 92, ix. 119), even in some few passages not marked by strong excitement, and occurs regularly when the second clause gives a reason for the first. But the narration is not rapid in the present place. The genitive after διαιθ. might be inexactly paralleled by πυρὸς θέρηται Z 331. With the passage cf. Eur. *Bacch.* 773, Hor. 3. 18. 6.

4. ἀμμειγνυμένα: μείγνυμι not μίγνυμι (μείξω, ἔμειξα) is the correct form. Love is a potent spice to wine. **Διον. δώροις**: so Διωνύσου δῶρον Theogn. 976, *i.e.* οἶνος, which is the subj. of πέμπει.—**5. μερίμνας**: 'thoughts,' 'desires,' not 'cares'; **ὑψ. πέμπει** is not='dissipate.' Cf. Pind. *Pyth.* 8. 88 ὁ δὲ καλόν τι νέον λαχὼν | . . . | ἐξ ἐλπίδος πέταται | ὑποπτέροις ἀνορέαις, ἔχων | κρέσσονα πλούτου μέριμναν, Eur. *H. F.* 653 κατ' αἰθέρα . . . φορείσθω. With this picture of the exaltation of the worshipper of Dionysos cf. Pind. xxx. (a passage that was either the model of Bacch. or Pindar's attempt to outdo by richer imagination and statelier phrase the graceful fancy of his younger rival), Aristoph. *Eq.* 90 ff. οἶνον σὺ τολμᾷς εἰς ἐπίνοιαν λοιδορεῖν; | οἴνου γὰρ εὕροις ἄν τι πρακτικώτερον; | ὁρᾷς; ὅταν πίνωσιν ἄνθρωποι, τότε | πλουτοῦσι, διαπράττουσι, νικῶσιν δίκας, | εὐδαιμονοῦσιν, ὠφελοῦσι τοὺς φίλους, Plato *Rep.* 9. 573 C καὶ μὴν ὅ γε (ὁ μεθυσθείς) μαινόμενος . . . οὐ μόνον ἀνθρώπων, ἀλλὰ καὶ θεῶν ἐπιχειρεῖ τε καὶ ἐλπίζει δυνατὸς εἶναι ἄρχειν, Arist. *Eth.* 1117 a 14 τοιοῦτον δὲ ποιοῦσι καὶ οἱ μεθυσκόμενοι· εὐέλπιδες γὰρ γίνονται, *Anakreont.* 46. 1 ff. ὅταν ὁ Βάκχος εἰσέλθῃ, | εὕδουσιν αἱ μέριμναι· | δοκῶ δ' ἔχειν τὰ Κροίσου. | . . . πατῶ δ' ἅπαντα θυμῷ, Hor. 3. 21. 17 ff. *tu spem reducis mentibus anxiis | viresque et addis cornua pauperi, | post te neque iratos trementi | regum apices neque militum arma*, and *Epist.* 1. 5. 16 ff. *quid non ebrietas designat? operta recludit, | spes iubet esse ratas, ad proelia trudit inertem, | sollicitis animis onus eximit, addocet artes. | fecundi calices quem non fecere disertum? | contracta quem non in paupertate solutum?* Tibull. 3. 6. 13 *ille facit dites animos deus* (Liber), Ovid *Ars Amat.* 1. 237 ff. *vina parant animos faciuntque caloribus aptos, | cura fugit multo diluiturque mero. | tunc veniunt risus, tunc pauper cornua sumit* etc. Shakesp. 'Henry IV.' ii. 4. 3: Falstaff "A good sherris-sack . . . ascends me into the brain; dries me there all the foolish and dull and crudy vapours which environ it; makes it apprehensive, quick, forgetive, full of nimble, fiery, and delectable shapes"; Burns' 'Tam o' Shanter': "Kings may be blest, but Tam was glorious, | O'er a' the ills o' life victorious." Our passage recalls Solon 13. 37 ff. (the unsubstantial dreams of hope).—**6. αὐτίχ'**: asyndeton as Δ 69. **ὁ μέν**=ὁ πίνων, not Dionysos. Instead of ὁ δέ a shift to the dative. **κράδεμνα**: pl. of a city's battlements (ν 388). Demades (Athen. 3. 99 D) called a city's wall ἐσθὴς τῆς πόλεως. Hdt. 7. 139 (cf. Xen. *Symp.* 4. 38) τειχέων κιθῶνες, 1. 181 τεῖχος θώρηξ ἐστί, Anakr. 72 στέφανος πόλεως. **λύειν**: κρήδεμνα λῦειν Π 100, ν 388. Attic λύειν with the ῡ derived from λύσω, ἔλῦσα: so νείκεα λύει η 74 from νείκεα λύσω Ξ 205.—**7. μοναρχήσειν**: *cum dat.* as with ἀνάσσω, ἄρχω, ἡγεμονεύω etc. The future is unobjectionable: dreams are not merely of a present paradise.

8. χρυσῷ: δ 73, Hor. 2. 18. 1 *non ebur neque aureum | mea renidet in domo lacunar.* **μαρμαίρουσιν**: Alk. xxiv. 1.—**9. πόντον**: the sea glitters in the sunlight, unvisited by storms. ἅλς μαρμαρέη Ξ 273. Bergk conjectured καρπόν.—**10.** In the time of Vespasian Egypt supplied Rome with one third of all the grain imported into that city.—Metre: dact.-epitrite, which here appears with a new force. We have three monostrophic stanzas. I am unable to accept the view of those scholars who, on the analogy of certain of Pindar's skolia, think that this poem was sung by a chorus.

XVIII. Athen. 11. 500 B. The poem has also been regarded as a paian and as a hymn. It may have been composed at the time of the Attic festival Anakeia, which owed its name to the fact that the Dioskuroi, who are here bidden to the θεοξένια, were called Ἄνακες at Athens. Here, as at Sparta, they were entertained as stranger-guests in the prytaneion, where a simple meal was set before them. Pindar's third Olympian ode was composed for the θεοξένια. See Harrison *Mythol. and Monum.* 157, Deneken *de theoxenia* 2, Wassner *de heroum cultu* 4. By its style and metre Hor. 2. 18. 1 ff (*non ebur neque aureum . . . at fides et ingeni benigna vena est*) is shown to be an imitation of this poem. Cf. 2. 16. 37-38.—**2. Βοιωτίοισιν**: as Kor. i. Note the absence of diaeresis in the verse. Boiotian *scyphi* were associated with Herakles, the Theban hero, because they were rustic in appearance and contained more wine than the κύλιξ or other vessels. The interlaced handle, the *nodus Herculis* (Pliny *H. N.* 28. 63), was used either as a decorative device or for its medicinal value (as a serpent coil). The *scyphus* was originally of wood or earthenware.—Metre: apparently a trochaic heptapody catal. + a pentapody, a metre that is surprising, since its continuation throughout an entire poem would seem to produce an unsatisfactory effect. In choral poetry trochaic systems seem to have been restricted to sympotic, erotic, and skoptic poetry. Rossbach suggests that the measure may be epitritic (cf. Timokr. iv.).

XIX. Stob. *Ecl. Phys.* 1. 5. 3. The succession of parathetic substantives in 1-2 is a mark of the poet's style.—**2. ἄγναμπτος**: cf. ἀγνάμπτων ἐρώτων 9. 73. **Ἄρης**: cf. Hdt. 1. 87 οὐδεὶς γὰρ οὕτω ἀνόητός ἐστι ὅστις πόλεμον πρὸ εἰρήνης αἱρέεται, κ.τ.λ.—**3. νέφος** in its metaphorical sense is properly applied only to Ἄρης and στάσις (cf. πολέμοιο νέφος P 243, τὸν κίνδυνον παρελθεῖν ὥσπερ νέφος Demos. 18. 291, νέφος οἰμωγῆς Eur. *Med.* 107). Of two opposites the second is regularly taken up in a following statement, but, as Farnell observed, the poet may mean that fate dispenses calamity rather than prosperity.—Metre: dact.-epitrite.

XX. Schol. Apoll. Rhod. 3. 467; perhaps from a hymn. Since the setting Moon appears to descend into the lower world, the epithets of Hekate are derived from her quality as goddess of light (φωσφόρος, λαμπαδοῦχος) and of darkness (νυκτιπόλος). **δᾳδοφόρε**: cf. *Hymn* 5. 52 σέλας ἐν χείρεσσιν ἔχουσα. The name Ἑκάτη is to be connected with Ἕκατος, Apollo the sun-god. The earliest genealogy made her the daughter of the Titan Perses and Asteria. Later her parents are Zeus and Hera. **μελανοκόλπου**: cf. Alkm. xx. νυκτὸς μελαίνας στέρνον. Bacch. says of *Day* (7. 1) λιπαρὰ θύγατερ Χρόνου τε καὶ Νυκτός.

MELANIPPIDES.

It is difficult to follow Suidas in distinguishing two dithyrambic poets of this name. Bergk indeed accepts the distinction and refers a victory of the older poet to 494. But if Suidas' γεγονώς *Ol.* 65 (520) refers to the *birth* of the grandfather, we must reconcile this date with the fact that the grandson of the same name died, apparently at an advanced age, before 413. Or, if γεγονώς refers to the *floruit* of the older poet, why is his name passed over by those ancient students of literature who claimed that Lasos, and not Arion, was the oldest dithyrambic poet? It is also singular that the father of both poets is called Kriton, though the younger was the child of a daughter of the elder poet. (Except in the case of families with two or more sons children were not usually named after their maternal grandfather.) If there was an elder Melanippides, I believe that he was a musician and not a poet; but we have probably to do with only one person, and the assumption of two of the same name is on a plane with Suidas' two Sapphos, two tragic poets Nichomachos and Phrynichos and two comic poets Krates. See Rohde *R. M.* 33. 213.

Melanippides was a native of Melos and the most famous dithyrambic poet of his time. In Xen. *Mem.* 1. 4. 3. Sokrates regards him as a master in his art, and to be compared with Homer, Sophokles, Polykleitos, and Zeuxis. He probably lived to old age, and died in Makedonia at the court of Perdikkas (454-413). Though a Dorian, he effected many innovations in the dithyramb. He employed ἀναβολαί and free rhythms for the strophe and antistrophe of the older dithyramb (as we still find them in Bacchylides) and enhanced the importance of the musician, whose encroachment upon the province of the poet had already commenced in the time of Pratinas and Lasos. With Melanippides those artifices of musical composition which indicate that technique was cultivated as an end in itself become still more pronounced. Pherekrates, the comic poet, made him responsible for the beginning of the degeneracy in his art. Ποίησις says (Frag. 145):

> Ἐμοὶ γὰρ ἦρξε τῶν κακῶν Μελανιππίδης,
> ἐν τοῖσι πρῶτος ὃς λαβὼν ἀνῆκέ με
> χαλαρωτέραν τ' ἐποίησε χόρδαις δώδεκα.
> ἀλλ' οὖν ὅμως οὗτος μὲν ἦν ἀποχρῶν ἀνὴρ
> ἔμοιγε . . . πρὸς τὰ νῦν κακά.

His innovations were, she continues, less fatal than those of Kinesias, Phrynis, or Timotheos. We possess fragments of dithyrambs entitled *Danaids*, *Marsyas*, and *Persephone*, subjects which stand in no immediate relation to the cult of Dionysos. The language of Melanippides, though often elegant, is artificial, and his occasional simplicity does not conceal his poverty of thought. He adopts the dactylo-epitritic measure, but under his hand it loses its old-time dignity and calm. Resolution of the thesis is so frequent in his epitrites as to constitute an important modification of the ancient severity of style. Besides dithyrambs, he wrote epics, elegies, and epigrams, though these are attributed by Suidas to his grandfather. Meleager inserted some of the epigrams in his *Anthology*. (*Anth. Pal.* 4. 1. 7.)

I. Athen. 14. 651 F. It is uncertain whether this obscure fragment contains a description of the punishment of the Danaids. If the daughters of Danaos formed the chorus, their number was just that of the cyclic chorus.—**1. μορφᾶεν**: Pind. *Isthm.* 7. 22.—**2.** Crusius would retain *τὰν αὐτὰν γυναικείαν*, translating 'the same women's quarters'; in Bergk's *οὐ δίαιταν τὰν γ.* we expect *οὐδέ*.—**3.** For the opposition between 1-2 and the foll., cf. Pind. *Pyth.* 9. 18 *ἁ μὲν οὔθ' ἱστῶν παλιμβάμους ἐφίλησεν ὁδοὺς . . . ἀλλὰ . . . κεράϊζεν ἀγρίους θῆρας.*—**5. ἱερόδακρυν**: cf. Pind. Frag. 122. 3 *τᾶς χλωρᾶς λιβάνου ξανθὰ δάκρη.*—Metre: dact.-epitrite.

II. Athen. 14. 616 E; from the *Marsyas*, the theme of which was the contest of the flute with the kithara. According to the story, which arose at Athens in the fifth century, Athena, who had invented the flute (Pind. *Pyth.* 12. 7), threw it away on discovering that its use disfigured her cheeks. The Lateran Marsyas, a copy of the celebrated work of Myron, represents the satyr's consternation when confronted by the goddess, whose wrath was aroused by his presumption in raising from the ground the instrument rejected by her. See Frazer on Paus. 1. 24. 1. The legend that Marsyas the flutist was flayed by Apollo because he dared to contend in musical skill with the god points to the opposition of the early Greeks to the orgiastic instrument of the Phrygians. The invention of the double flute is also referred to Marsyas, who introduced the *φορβειά*. A later age became reconciled to the flute—Sakadas' Pythian nome was famous—and an auletic nome even bore Athena's name. The flute was in disfavour with the poets at Athens shortly before the Peloponnesian war because of its aggressiveness, and an Attic epigram says

Ἀνδρὶ μὲν αὐλητῆρι θεοὶ νόον οὐκ ἐνέφυσαν,
ἀλλ' ἅμα τῷ φυσῆν χὠ νόος ἐκπέταται.

The second fragment of Melanippides does not, however, prove that the poet was himself hostile to a proper restriction of the music of the flute in the dithyramb. See Telestes i.—**2. τὤργαν'**: the plural of the double flute, as in Dion. Halik. *de comp. verb.* 11 (so *αὐλοί* often in Pind.).—**3. τε . . . τε**: 'as she hurled, she said'; cf. Sim. xiii. 4.—**4. με**: the personal for the reflexive pronoun is usually employed either when there is a contrast between two persons or when the speaker puts himself in an objective position. As subject of the inf., *ἐμέ* is generally used in Attic, not the reflexive.—Metre: dact.-epitrite, verses 2-4 in stichic succession.

III. Athen. 9. 429 C; perhaps from the *Oineus*. Cf. Pind. Frag. 166. Athen. 1. 11 A, quoting *Il.* I 119 *ἢ οἴνῳ μεθύων, ἢ*

μ' ἔβλαψαν θεοὶ αὐτοί, says *εἰς τὴν αὐτὴν τιθεὶς πλάστιγγα τὴν μέθην τῇ μανίᾳ*. Sim. 221 says that wine and music have a common source.—**2. τὸ πρίν**: Hom., Archil. 94, Theogn. 483. —**4. παράπληκτον**: here and Soph. *Aias* 230 (of *χείρ*).—Metre: logaoedic.

IV. Clem. Alex. *Strom.* 5. 716. This prayer with its strange modern voice is probably addressed to Dionysos whose cult inculcated faith in immortality. This is the only passage in a lyric poet, apart from Pindar, which expressly attests a belief in the immortality of the soul. **θαῦμα βροτῶν**: as *θ. βροτοῖσι* λ 287. Cf. *Διώνυσον, χάρμα βροτοῖσιν* Ξ 325.—Metre: logaoedic (or log. and cretic?).

V. Plutarch *Erot.* 15.—Metre: dact.-epitrite.

ARIPHRON.

Ariphron was born at Sikyon, the old home of the dithyramb, but lived at Athens either during or shortly after the Peloponnesian war. A choregic inscription of the beginning of the fourth century (*C. I. A.* 2. 1280) has Ἀρίφρων ἐδίδασκεν, but the omission of the name of the victorious tribe makes against the conclusion that the document refers to a dithyrambic contest. The poem on Health is a sympotic paian, not a skolion as Brunck, Ilgen, and others thought it. The worship of Hygieia seems to have spread from Argolis to Athens, though most scholars hold that it originated in Attica; at least it is noteworthy that the oldest known seat of her cult is Sikyon (Paus. 2. 11. 6), the birth-place of the poet. The Sikyonian painter Nikophanes represented her in company with her three sisters. See *J. H. S.* 5. 82 ff.

The *Paian to Hygieia* is quoted by Athen. 15. 702 A, and is reproduced in a corrupt form on an inscription that is not older than about 300 A.D. (*C. I. A.* 3. 171 = Kaibel 1027). It was inscribed in the Asklepieion at Athens. The poem was famous in a later period: Lucian, who cites v. 1 (*de lapsu* 6) says that it was 'known to everybody,' and Max. Tyr. 13. 229, also citing v. 1, testifies that it was still sung in the time of Commodus.

1. That Hygieia is a relatively late personification is clear from the fact that she was not regarded by mythology as a traditionary figure. Sim. xxx. and Skol. vi. do not admit the personification. **πρεσβίστα**: unless the poet here claims a fictitious antiquity for Hygieia, the epithet means 'most august,' not 'most ancient.' Aristeides 1. 22, it is true, says Ἀθηναίαν οἱ πρέσβιστοι καὶ Ὑγιείας Ἀθηνᾶς βωμὸν ἱδρύσαντο, but he is speaking of Athena Hygieia. An Orphic poet (Stob. *Ecl. Phys.* 1. 2. 31) has, pardonably, πρεσβίστας θεᾶς Ὑγιείας μειλιχοδώρου. **μετὰ σεῦ**: cf. Theokr. 16. 108 τί γὰρ Χαρίτων ἀγαπητὸν | ἀνθρώποις ἀπάνευθεν; ἀεὶ Χαρίτεσσιν ἅμ' εἴην. μ. σεῦ and μ. σεῖο l. 7 (Sim. 95) follow μ. εἷο Hes. *Theogon.* 392, the oldest example of μ. with the singular, which occurs only four or five times before Sophokles (Mommsen). Homer and Pind. use μ. only with the plural. See on Sa. xxiv. 4. Stes. viii. is a doubtful example.—**2**. **σύνοικος**: see on Sa. xxviii. and cf. Sim. i. 6 οἰκέταν. With the two prayers cf. Eur. Frag. 897 συνείην . . . ναίοιμι.—**3** ff. This is the earliest trace of the tendency to attribute blessings to Hygieia. Asklepios and Hygieia are οἱ δύο σωτῆρες θεοί, οἳ τὴν γῆν ἅπασαν σῴζουσι (Aristeides 1. 397). Late poets call Hygieia ἀγλαόδωρος, φερόλβιος, μήτηρ πάντων. **πλούτου**: *Orphic Hymn* 68. 9 οὔτε γὰρ ὀλβοδότης Πλοῦτος γλυκερὸς θαλίῃσιν, | οὔτε γέρων πολύμοχθος ἄτερ σέο γίνεται ἀνήρ. Health and wealth are combined in πλουθυγίεια Aristoph. *Vesp.* 677. **χάρις**: Sim. xxx.—**4**. Cf. ἰσοδαίμων βασιλεύς Aisch. *Persai* 633, ἰσόθεος τυραννίς Eur. *Troad.* 1169. —**5**. Hesych. glosses ἕρκεσιν with δικτύοις ('cast-net'). ἄρκυς is a stake-net. Cf. Ibyk. ii. 3.—**6**. Cf. Kritias 2. 21 τὴν τερπνοτάτην θεῶν θνητοῖς Ὑγίειαν, carm. pop. 47. 23 σὺν τερπνοτάτῃ ὑγιείᾳ. **ἀμπνοά**: μοχθῶν ἀμπνοάν Pind. *Ol.* 8. 7.—**8**. **τέθαλε**: perhaps this word should end l. 7. **πάντα** is omitted in the inscription. **ὄαρος**: *vulg.* ἔαρ, and so Boeckh, and Schneidewin, who explains *instar veris, quod Gratiae reddunt pulchrum, affulgent* (cf. Hor. 4. 5. 6). This use of ἔαρ may suit late poetry (Χαρίτων ἐξαπόλωλεν ἔαρ *Anth. Pal.* 7. 599, Πόθων ἔαρ *ib.* 7. 29, ὕμνων ἔαρ *ib.* 7. 12). Bergk read ἔαρι, Crusius ὀάροις. We find the sing. ὄαρος, of Jason's speech, Pind. *Pyth.* 4. 137, but the plur. is usual, as ὄαροι νυμφᾶν Kallim. 5. 66. The Graces are the sources of delight, Pind. *Ol.* 14. 5. With **λάμπει ὄαρος** cf. *niteat oratio* Cic. *Fin.* 4. 3. 5, and see on Bacch. xiii. 12. It is to be noted that the paian does not contain the refrain ἰὴ Παιάν, which Athen. 15. 696 E regards as the sign-mark of the genuine paian.—Metre: dact.-epitrite. Note the dissyllabic anacruses, and the ithyphallic at the close of v. 6, not at the close of the strophe as often in the drama.

LIKYMNIOS.

This dithyrambic poet came from Chios to Athens, where he studied rhetoric under Gorgias. Like some others he combined rhetoric with poetry. His treatise on the art of rhetoric contained technical expressions (ἐπούρωσις, ἀποπλάνησις etc.) that savoured of the dithyramb. Aristotle censured them as 'empty and frivolous' because they lacked distinctness. Cf. Plato *Phaidros* 267 c. One of Likymnios' teachings was that a name derives its beauty or its deformity partly from the sound and partly from the meaning. His dithyrambs were suited for reading and not for representation.

I. Sextus Emp. 11. 49. Likymnios' conception of Hygieia is highly singular, at least for the classical age. Before the Roman period she was regarded as a maiden, and it is not until *Orphic Hymn* 67. 7 that she is called the wife of Asklepios, and μῆτερ ἁπάντων (68. 2). Wilamowitz *Isyllos* 192 thinks the artistic type was originally that of a matron, as in the case of the Eirene of Kephisodotos. See Roscher 1. 2781. A curious parallel in cult is Ἀθηνᾶ Μήτηρ Paus. 5. 3. 2. The relation of Hygieia to Apollo is obscure. Is she his daughter, as Asklepios is his son? Theon *Progymn.* 9 says εἴ τις φαίη τὴν Ὑγ. Ἀπόλλωνος εἶναι θυγατέρα.—**3.** Cf. ὥρης γελώσης Chairemon 14. 11, φρὴν ἀγέλαστος Aisch. Frag. 290.—**4** ff. It is uncertain whether Sextus has wrongly attributed these lines to L., whether L. borrowed them from Ariphron or *vice versa*, or whether both poets took them from some common source, *e.g.* the paians in honour of Asklepios sung at Athens on the eighth of Elaphebolion, a day sacred to the god of healing. Hymns to the allegorical daughter of Asklepios may have been popular at Athens whose tutelary goddess herself bore the title ὑγίεια. (For the similarity between the two poems, compare the opening of the *Throstle and Nightingale* and *Spring and Love Song.*) Rossbach argues that the regular form of the dactylo-epitrites of L. proves his priority to Ariphron, and thinks that nothing is lost at the beginning of v. 1 (anap.-iamb. proöde as in Pind.; cf. *Nem.* 10. 1). Perhaps the poem of L. contained a reference to virtue (Plut. *de virt. mor.* 10). Plut. has ll. 4, 5 in mind in *de frat. amore* 2, but does not state whether he is quoting Ariphron or Likymnios.

II. Stob. *Ecl. Phys.* 1. 41. 50. The subject of βρύει is Ἀχέρων. Another fragment: Ἀχέρων ἄχεα | βροτοῖσι πορθμεύει . . . recalls Aisch. *Agam.* 1558 ὠκυπόρων | πόρθμευμ' ἀχέων. Melan. etymologizes Ἀχέρων in Frag. 3: ἄχεα ῥόοισι προχέων Ἀχέρων.—Metre: dact.-epitrite.

III. Athen. 13. 564 C; perhaps from a local (Karian?) myth. The story gave birth to the proverb Ἐνδυμίωνος ὕπνον καθεύδεις (Leutsch *Paroem.* 2. 25). In illustration of his theme that love resides in the eye, Athen. cites Sa. ix., Pind. xv., Soph. Frag. 433. Cf. Shakesp. *Cymb.* 2. 2. 19 "The flame o' the taper | Bows toward her, and would underpeep her lids, | To see the enclosed lights." Sleep is μαλακαύγητος Aristotle *Areta* l. 8. **ὀμμάτων αὐγαῖς**: cf. Eur. *Ion* 1072, *Phoin.* 1564.—Metre: dact.-epitrite.

ION.

Ion of Chios, a versatile genius, composed tragedies, elegies, melic poetry, and even history or memoirs. He was the first poet who also wrote in prose. The ancients praise his external correctness and polish, but the author of the treatise *On the Sublime* says that one tragedy of Sophokles was worth all of Ion's. He was acquainted with Aischylos, Sophokles, Kimon, and Perikles. He died in Athens in 422 B.C.

I. Athen. 2. 35 E.—**2. παῖδα**: Dionysos was represented as a youth by Kalamis (about 470) but the early type was that of a bearded man. **ταυρωπόν**: see on Folk-Songs v. **νέον οὐ νέον**: wine that is new as regards age, old through its strength.—**3. βαρυγδούπων**: before Ion the adj. is used only of Zeus or of the winds. Dionysos himself is ἐρίβρομος. **ἐρώτων**: cf. Eur. *Bacch.* 773 οἴνου δὲ μηκέτ' ὄντος οὐκ ἔστιν Κύπρις. **ἀερσίνοον**: Panyasis 13. 13 ἐνὶ φρεσὶ θυμὸν ἀέρσῃ of the ὕβρις οἴνου.—**4.** Cf. Ion Eleg. **1.** 14 Διόνυσε, συμποσίων πρύτανι.—Metre: dact.-epitrite.

II. Schol. Aristoph. *Pax* 835: because of these lines Ion was called ἀοῖος ἀστήρ. **ἀεροφοίταν** may = 'roaming in air,' as perhaps in Aischylos (cf. Aristoph. *Ran.* 1291) or = ἠεροφ. 'roaming in darkness' (so of the Moon in *Orphic Hymn* 9. 2). Schneidewin regarded ἠέριος as the first part of the word, and compared Plaut. *Men.* 1. 2. 62 *inde usque ad diurnam* *stellam crastinam potabimus*, Hor. 3. 21. 23 *vivaeque producent lucernae, | dum rediens fugat astra Phoebus.* **λευκοπτέρυγα**: cf. Eur. *Troad.* 848 λευκοπτέρου ἀμέρας, Val. Flaccus 6. 507 *qualis roseïs it Lucifer alis, | quem Venus illustri gaudet producere coelo.*—Metre: logaoedic.

EURIPIDES.

In addition to his dramas, Euripides (480-406) composed several lyric poems: epigrams, an ἐπικήδειον on the destruction of the Athenians at Syracuse, and an ode to Alkibiades (Plut. *Vita Alcib.* 11, cf. *Vita Demosth.* 1, Athen. 1. 3 E), which is called an epinikion and an enkomion.

At the famous Olympic festival of 420 B.C. (so Grote; others 424 or 416) Alkibiades entered no less than seven quadrigae, and won the first prize, coming in also second and fourth according to Plut. and to Thuk. 6. 16. 2 in a speech which he puts into the mouth of the victor (διότι ἅρματα μὲν ἑπτὰ καθῆκα, ὅσα οὐδεὶς πω ἰδιώτης πρότερον, ἐνίκησα δέ, καὶ δεύτερος καὶ τέταρτος ἐγενόμην). Though Euripides' statement that he came in third is adopted by Isokr. *de bigis* 353 § 34, it cannot well hold ground against that of the historian, which is intrinsically more probable, since Alkibiades was not remarkable for modesty.

---

2. μηδείς: contrast the definite οὐδείς in Thuk. (Goodwin *Gram.* 1613, Hadley-Allen *Gram.* 1026).—**4. Διός**: (τρίς Reiske). Grote's argument that all of Alkibiades' seven chariots could not have run in one and the same race, even if true, does not prove that δίς (MSS.) is correct. All our other evidence goes to show that a victor received only one crown. Pindar uses στέφανοι of a single victory *Ol.* 3. 6, *Pyth.* 10. 26. Line 3 and the passage in Thuk. mean only *one* victory. Athen. *l. l.* uses νίκας inexactly.—**5.** Cf. Hdt. 6. 103 νικῶν παραδιδοῖ ἀνακηρυχθῆναι.—Metre: dact.-epitrite.

PHILOXENOS.

The life of Philoxenos was full of vicissitude. Born in 435 in Kythera, he became a Lakonian slave when the

Spartans regained the island, probably after the ruin of the Athenian cause at Syracuse, and finally passed into the possession of the poet Melanippides, who educated him in his art and liberated him. Like Simonides, Philoxenos was a man of the world, a friend of princes, and many stories are related of his nimble wit at the Syracusan court. His friendship with Dionysios the Elder was finally broken either by his frank criticism of the tragedies of the tyrant or in consequence of his passion for Galateia, a beautiful fluteplayer, who was the mistress of Dionysios. Released from prison by the prince to pass judgment on his verse, the poet exclaimed ἄπαγέ με εἰς λατομίας. In his confinement he revenged himself by composing his famous dithyramb entitled either *Kyklops* or *Galateia*, in which the poet represented himself as Odysseus, who, to take vengeance on Polyphemos (Dionysios), estranged the affections of the nymph Galateia, of whom the Kyklops was enamoured. This dithyramb was imitated by Theokritos in his eleventh idyl. After the poet's withdrawal from Syracuse, he lived at Tarentum, then in Greece, and finally in Asia Minor. He died at Ephesos in 380.

Philoxenos composed twenty-four dithyrambs, of which only a few titles survive: *Kyklops* or *Galateia*, *Mysoi*, *Syros* (or *Satyros*), *Komastes*, *Persai*. By introducing solos (μέλη) into the dithyramb he assimilated this class of lyric to the nome, the characteristic mark of which was the solo. We know that in the *Kyklops* the solo singers acted out their parts. Under the hands of Philoxenos the dithyramb assumed a highly dramatic character. Though his text is praised by the comic poet Antiphanes not only for the novelty but also for the propriety of its diction, the musical and mimetic elements were the essential features. The music abounded in transitions of the modes and in colour effects. Adherents of the older style, such as Aristophanes and Pherekrates, regarded him as a trifler and debaser of his art. But his popularity was so great that during his lifetime his melodies were sung in the streets, and after his death Antiphanes said of him (Frag. 209): θεὸς ἐν ἀνθρώποισιν ἦν | ἐκεῖνος, εἰδὼς τὴν ἀληθῶς μουσικήν. Alexander the Great delighted in his music. Aristotle says that Philoxenos was realistic in distinction to the idealistic Timotheos. Besides dithyrambs he composed aulodic nomes, which the Arkadians represented yearly in the time of Polybios. The *Banquet* is often attributed to Philoxenos of Kythera, but is probably the work of the parasite and gourmand Philoxenos of Leukas.

Athen. 13. 564 E; from the *Kyklops*. Athen. says that Polyphemos praises the loveliness of Galateia but makes no mention of her eyes, as if presaging his own loss of sight. Cf. Ibyk. v. Note the cumulation of high-sounding epithets. Cf. χρυσεοβόστρυχον Διὸς ἔρνος of Artemis, Eur. *Phoin.* 191. —Metre: logaoedic (or resolved epitrites ?).

TIMOTHEOS.

TIMOTHEOS of Miletos, the most famous lyric poet of the classic period, was the scholar of Phrynis, who was himself a disciple of the school of Terpander: εἰ μὲν γὰρ Τιμόθεος μὴ ἐγένετο, πολλὴν (ποικίλην ?) ἂν μελοποιίαν οὐκ εἴχομεν· εἰ δὲ μὴ Φρύνις, Τιμόθεος οὐκ ἂν ἐγένετο (Arist. *Metaph.* 993 b 15). Most of his long life (he died in 357, either ninety or ninety-seven years of age) was spent in Athens, where he enjoyed the friendship of Euripides, who recognized his originality and prophesied his sovereignty over Athenian taste. At the invitation of Archelaos, he repaired to the court of Makedonia and is said to have died there. We are informed that he also visited Sparta, where the ephors are said to have removed four of the eleven strings of his lyre in order to reduce it to the ancient Terpandreian norm. Similar stories, also probably fictitious, are reported of Terpander (Plut. *Inst. Lac.* 17), Phrynis, and others. He is said to have been avaricious and full of self-glorification.

With a lofty contempt for the traditions of the past, he proclaims the advent of a new style (Frag. vii.). Though he achieved great success as a dithyrambist, it was to the nome that he gave a fixed and standard form. He made this species of lyric dramatic in character by assimilating it to the dithyramb, and may even have introduced a chorus, whereas the nome had heretofore been entirely monodic.

The stately language of the nome now assumed a dithyrambic fire and pathos. Timotheos effected a union of the musical modes and aimed at transferring to a kithara provided with many strings the specific virtues of the flute. His music was sweet and insinuating (Plutarch calls it φιλάνθρωπος). As in Philoxenos, the musical quality was predominant, but the wealth of his thought was also esteemed. The diction of the extant fragments, however, is often vapid and contorted. An aggressiveness born of success made him one of the most subjective of the later lyrists. Though at first hissed down because of the artificiality of his music, he was ultimately able to silence all opposition except that of the critics of the old school, such as the comic poet Pherekrates, the severest castigator of the dithyrambists, who in his *Cheiron* branded him as a perverse and ruinous innovator. In the second century B.C. an acquaintance with his songs was as highly esteemed in Crete as a knowledge of the old native poets (*C. I. G.* 3053); and in the imperial period he was regarded as a model. Possibly Aristotle credited him with idealism in contrast to Philoxenos; but he pictured such scenes as a storm at sea in the Ναυτίλος and the birth-pangs of Semele in the Ὠδὶς Σεμέλης, a subject that was represented in the temple of Dionysos. Timotheos was a versatile and prolific artist. Besides eighteen or nineteen nomes, said to have consisted of 8000 hexameters, he composed eighteen dithyrambs, twenty-one hymns, thirty-six prooimia (or pronomia), enkomia, etc. Some of the titles of his works are: *To Artemis* (for which the Ephesians paid him 1000 gold-pieces), *Persai*, *The Sons of Phineus*, *Laertes*, *The mad Aias*, *Skylla*, *Niobe*, *Elpenor*, *Lament of Odysseus*.

I. Plut. *de audiend. poet.* 4, *de superst.* 10. The line, consisting of epithets suited to the savage nature of the Tauric Artemis (cf. Soph. *Aias* 172), is from the poem on the Ephesian Artemis, which was probably reproduced at Athens. When Timotheos had sung this line in the theatre the 'accursed' poet Kinesias called out τοιαύτη σοι θυγάτηρ γένοιτο. Cf. *Anth. Pal.* 9. 774 Θυιάδα μαινομέναν. The form θυιάς also appears as θῡάς. Θυιωνίδας Cauer 24 = Θυωνίδας, a Rhodian name of Dionysos.—Metre: a dactylic tetrapody.

II. Athen. 11. 465 C.—**1.** Odysseus offered the Kyklops a κισσύβιον μέλανος οἴνοιο ι 346. The scene is depicted on sarcophagi and lamps.—**2.** **σταγόνος**: cf. οἴνου σταγόνες Eur. *Kykl.* 66. **ἀμβρότας**: Boeckh thought that there is a reference to the festival called 'Αμβρόσια, which is a name either for the Lenaia or for a part of it. **βρυάζον**: cf. Pind. *Ol.* 7. 2 φιάλαν . . . ἀμπέλου καχλάζοισαν δρόσῳ.—**3.** Cf. ι 209 ἓν δέπας ἐμπλήσας ὕδατος ἀνὰ εἴκοσι μέτρα | χεῦ'. **μέτρ'**: 'parts'; cf. β 355 and see on Alk. xx. 4.—**4.** **Βακχίου**=Βάκχου; Soph. *Antig.* 154, Eur. *Bacch.* 225, etc. With the high-flown expressions 'blood of Bacchos,' 'fresh-flowing tears of the Nymphs' cf. φιάλη Ἄρεως=ἀσπίς Frag. 16, πυρίκτιτα γᾶς 'earthen pots' Frag. 17. See Arist. *Rhet.* 3. 4. 4.—Metre: logaoedic.

III. Plut. *vita Philopoem.* 11. When Pylades, the famous kitharoede, sang this verse at the Nemean festival all eyes turned to Philopoemen. **κόσμον**: cf. Sim. i. 9.—Metre: dact. hexameter.

IV. Plut. *de audiend. poet.* 11.—Metre: trochaic.

V. Plut. *vita Agesil.* 14. The *Persai* may have been brought out in 395, when Persian gold was employed to induce the Greeks to declare war against Sparta. The poet may have wished to point his moral from the great contest with the Persians in the previous century. The words Ἄρης τύραννος passed into a proverb.—Metre: dact.-epitrite. By reading Ἑλλὰς δ' (Bergk) the metre would be smoother; and the unusual position of δέ might be explained as emphasizing Ἑλλάς. The opposition is, however, between Ἄρης and χρυσός.

VI. Plut. *de se ipsum laud.* 1. Written to celebrate the poet's victory over his teacher Phrynis. Plut. says that Timotheos glorifies himself ἀμούσως καὶ παρανόμως. When Timotheos was vanquished by a scholar of Polyeidos, Stratonikos consoled him with the *bon-mot*: αὐτὸς μὲν (Π.) ψηφίσματα ποιεῖ, Τιμόθεος δὲ νόμους. Phrynis, the son of Kamon, is called δυσκολόκαμπτος by Aristoph. *Nubes* 971, because of his intricate flourishes; see Pherekr. 145. 15. Cf. ᾀσματοκάμπτης of the dithyrambic poets, *Nubes* 333; in *Thesmoph.* 53 Agathon κάμπτει νέας ἁψῖδας ἐπῶν. The prefix ἰωνο- with reference to effeminacy and corruption; so ἰωνίζω.—Metre: logaoedic with resolutions of the thesis in v. 1. Wilamowitz reads μ. ᾖσ. Τιμόθεος, ὅτε κηρ. | εἶπε "ν. Τ. ὁ. Μ. | κ.τ.λ.

VII. Athen. 3. 122 D.—**2.** **καινά**: see on Alkm. i. and cf. Antiphanes *Alkestis* (Frag. 29) ἐπὶ τὸ καινουργεῖν φέρου, | οὕτως, ἐκείνως, τοῦτο γιγνώσκων ὅτι | ἓν καινὸν ἐγχείρημα, κἂν τολμηρὸν ᾖ, | πολλῶν παλαιῶν ἐστι χρησιμώτερον, Bekk. *Anecd.* 1. 309

πλείων ἐστὶ σπουδὴ τῶν Ἀθηναίων περὶ τὸ καινὸν δρᾶμα καὶ μηδέ ποτε ἠγωνισμένον, and many passages of the comic poets, *e.g.* Kratin. 146, Aristoph. *Nubes* 546, 561, *Vesp.* 1043, Anaxand. 54, Amphis 14, Alex. 298, Hegesipp. 1. 3; also Eur. *Troad.* 512. Molière 'Les Femmes Savantes': *La ballade, à mon gout, est une chose fade,* | *Ce n'en est plus la mode, elle sent son vieux temps.*—**4**. **Κρόνος** is the type of superseded rule; cf. Krat. 165 *βασιλεὺς Κρόνος ἦν τὸ παλαιόν*, Nikophon 22 *Κρόνου . . . παππεπίπαππος.*—Metre: ionics. In v. 1 *ἀείδω* may be scanned — — (*ᾄδω*). For — ⏑ — — = ⏑ ⏑ — — cf. *Anakreont.* 42. 12 — ⏑ — ⏑ for ⏓ ⏓ — ⏓. Wilamowitz *Isyllos* p. 153 makes three verses: *οὐκ—κρείσσω, νέος—ἦν, Κρόνος—παλαιά* (— ⏑ — —, ⏑ ⏑ ⏑⏑ ⏑ ⏑, — ⏑ — —), Headlam *Journ. Phil.* 21. 84: *τὰ παλαί' οὐκέτ' ἀείδω* | *μάλα γὰρ τὰ καινὰ κρείσσω* or *τὰ γὰρ ἀμὰ κάρτα κρ.*

VIII. Macrob. *Sat.* 1. 17. 19. Perhaps from a paian to Apollo, who is here identified with Helios. The identification is the result of the religious and philosophical speculation of the fifth century which first appears in Eur. *Phaethon* (Frag. 781). Though Aischylos (*Suppl.* 213) still distinguished the two gods he brought them into close connection in his *Bassarai.* Plato, *Laws* 945 E, has *Ἡλίου κοινὸν καὶ Ἀπόλλωνος τέμενος.* Cf. FOLK-SONGS ix.—**1**. Cf. Soph. *O. K.* 1701 *τὸν ἀεὶ κατὰ γᾶς σκότον.*—**4**. The paian composed by Aristonoos and that of Ptolemaïs (*Rev. Arch.* 13. 70; cf. *R. M.* 49. 315) have *ἰὲ ὦ ἰὲ παιάν.* **ἰέ** is the weak form of *ἰή*, the *η* of which, in the formula *ἰὴ ἰή*, is anceps. The line foreshadows the Alexandrian derivation of *ἰή* from *ἵημι* (Kallim. 2. 103).—Metre: dactylic with one epitrite. Crusius thinks the verses are march anapaests.

TELESTES.

OF the dithyrambs of this poet, a native of Selinus in Sicily and an older contemporary of Alexander the Great, there are preserved the titles *Argo*, *Asklepios*, and *Hymenaios.* The extant fragments are concerned with the defence of the flute and the archaeology of music. Telestes' verse shows a fondness for shifting rhythms, and he is said to have affected violent transitions of the musical modes. While his style is lively, it is high-flown and full of parade and artificial collocations of words. The later dithyrambic writers carried to excess the avoidance of the article, an avoidance which is noticeable in the lyric parts of tragedy; and in Telestes the article does not occur. Telestes was eagerly read by Alexander; and Aristratos, the tyrant of Sikyon, ordered his tomb to be decorated with paintings by Nikomachos.

I. Athen. 14. 616 F; from the *Argo*. The controversy as regards the virtue of flute music, which is indicated by this reply to the challenge of Melanippides (Frag. ii.) and by the other fragments, shows the predominance of the accompaniment in the later dithyramb. The fragment recalls Pind. *Pyth.* 12.—**1.** **ὅν**: refers to *αὐλός*, which must have preceded: 'which wisely devised instrument the wise goddess,' etc. The myth of the invention of the flute by Athena became possible only after its music was naturalized in Greece and the recollection of its Phrygian origin had passed away. The flute was even given a place at the Delphic festival of Apollo, to whom the kithara was sacred. Cf. Mel. Adesp. v. **ἐπέλπομαι**: an epic and tragic word, here 'deem,' 'believe.'—**2.** **ὀργάνων**: causal gen. with *αἶσχος*; not 'disgraceful, offensive instrument.' Some keep *ὄργανον* as a loose apposition to *ὅν*. *ὀργάνων* is used by Plato *Symp.* 215 C, in speaking of Marsyas: *ὁ μέν γε δι' ὀργάνων ἐκήλει τοὺς ἀνθρώπους τῇ ἀπὸ τοῦ στόματος δυνάμει.* **δίαν**: as Eur. *I. T.* 404.—**5.** **νυμφαγενεῖ**: the father of the Phrygian satyr is variously reported (Olympos, Hyagnis). **χοροκτύπῳ**: 'treading the dance-floor.' Some would read *χοροιτύπῳ*. **φηρί**: the Aiolic form is used in non-Aiolic poetry only of Centaurs or Satyrs. Pan is called *μωσοπόλε θήρ* Siro 2. 5. **κλέος**: in apposition with *ὅν* (l. 1), not with *αὖθις . . . βαλεῖν*.—**8.** **μάταν**: to be taken with *προσέπταθ'*. **ἀχόρευτος**: 'doleful.' There is no special reference to the flute in connection with a chorus.—**9.** **φάμα**: perhaps Telestes, like Bacchylides, preferred *φήμα* (MSS.). **προσέπταθ'**: cf. *μοι μέλος προσέπτα* Aisch. *Prom.* 555, where note the dative. *ἔπτατο* is epic and tragic, and is often used of misfortune. **μουσοπόλων**: Sa. xli., Siro 2. 5. Possibly Melanippides was the inventor of the doleful winged tale that found credence with the vain-babbling minstrels.—**11.** 'Which (wise art) the uplifted breath of the august goddess by the aid of the swift movement of her shifting, glorious hands gave to Bromios for his most efficient handmaid.' **συνεριθ.**: cf. *συνερίθοις τέχναις* Plato *Rep.* 533 D.—**12.** **αἰολοπτ.**: **αἰ** as *γεραϊούς* Tyrt. 10. 20. Wilamowitz conj. *αἰολοπτέρυγι σὺν ἀργᾶν*. **σύν**: comitative; cf. *σὺν χειρῶν σθένει* Pind. *Nem.* 10. 48. Of the younger dithyrambic poets Telestes alone uses *σύν*. Pratinas, Ariphron, Melanippides, and Philoxenos have only *μετά cum* *gen.* For the rapid movement of the hands, see Prat. i. 15. —Metre: logaoedic. The poem belongs to the ἀπολελυμένον class.

II. Athen. 14. 617 B; from the *Asklepios*. The fragment expresses the opposition between the Lydian mode, an importation into Greece together with the Phrygian flute, and the native Dorian mode, which was well suited to the kithara.—**1.** The Φρύξ may be Marsyas, or Hyagnis (*Anth. Pal.* 9. 340), but is more probably Olympos, who, in his lament over the Python, was, according to Aristoxenos (Plut. *de mus.* 15), the first to employ the Lydian mode.—**3.** **αἰόλον**: cf. Eur. *Ion* 499 συρίγγων ὑπ' αἰόλας ἰαχᾶς ὕμνων, Folk-Songs vii. 2. The word suits the mobility of song as well as of the dance.—Metre: dact.-epitrite (seven dact. trip. in succession). Some of the poets of the fourth century, *e.g.* Philoxenos in the *Banquet*, were fond of the tripody with only slight use of the epitrite.

III. Athen. 14. 625 F.—**1.** **ἐν αὐλοῖς**: cf. Pind. *Ol.* 5. 19 Λυδίοις ἀπύων ἐν αὐλοῖς, *Nem.* 3. 79 ἐν πνοαῖσιν αὐλῶν, *Isthm.* 5. 27 ἐν αὐλῶν παμφώνοις ὁμοκλαῖς. ἐν is often used of instrumental accompaniment.—**2.** The Mountain Mother is Kybele (cf. Ellis on Catull. 63), at the mention of whose enervating cult the metre passes over to the effeminate ionics (cf. Prat. ii.). —**4.** **ψαλμοῖς** 'strings,' as in Diogenes (p. 776 Nauck) κλύω δὲ Λυδὰς . . . ψαλμοῖς τριγώνων πηκτίδων. Of the invention of the barbitos, Pind. Frag. 125 says: τόν ῥα Τέρπανδρός ποθ' ὁ Λέσβιος εὗρεν | πρῶτος ἐν δείπνοισι Λυδῶν | ψαλμὸν (sound) ἀντίφθογγον ὑψηλᾶς ἀκούων πηκτίδος. Ion, trag. frag. 23, has Λυδός τε μάγαδις αὐλὸς ἡγείσθω βοῆς. The pectis differed only slightly from the stringed magadis and, because of its Asiatic origin, had strings of different lengths (hence ὑψηλᾶς in Pind. is not used of high notes, as in Modern Greek). It was played without the plectrum.—Metre: dact.-epitrite except v. 2. There are different arrangements by Leuthmer, and Wilamowitz (free ionics).

LYKOPHRONIDES.

This poet is mentioned by Klearchos in Athenaios. Bergk thought that he belonged to the Alexandrian period. Wilamowitz suggests that he may be identical with Lykophron, a sophist mentioned by Aristotle.

I. Athen. 13. 564 A.—**2.** **χρυσοφόρων**: of the golden ornaments worn on the ears, neck, arms, and even on the ankles. See B 872, Aristoph. *Acharn.* 258, *Aves* 670, Eur. *Hek.* 154 and cf. skol. xxiii.; *mos erat apud veteres virginibus plurimum auri gestare* (Porson). Wilamowitz' explanation: 'who have won the prize in beauty-contests' is tasteless, though such women were called *χρυσοφόροι* among the Parrhasians (Athen. 13. 609 F).—**4.** **αἰδώς**: see Sa. viii. and cf. *αἰδοία Χάρις* Pind. *Ol.* 6. 76.—Metre: logaoedic.

II. Athen. 15. 670 E. The offering is made by a youth either to a boy whose love he has abandoned for that of a girl, or to a god now that love has robbed him of his occupation.—**3.** **κέχυται**: cf. Pind. *Isthm.* 1. 4. *Δᾶλος, ἐν ᾇ κέχυμαι* 'in whose service my soul has been poured forth.' Like *effusus*, used with reference to love.—**4.** Cf. Alkaios xxvii.—Metre: logaoedic. An arrangement in ionics is possible with the variations ⏑ ⏑⏑ ⏑ —, ⏑ – – ⏑ —, — — —, ⏑ ⏑ ⊔, ⏑ — ⊢.

ARISTOTLE.

The ode to Areta was extracted from Hermippos by Athen. 15. 695 A and Diog. Laert. 5. 7. On the ground that the burden (*Io Paian*) is absent, Hermippos took issue with the opinion that the poem was a paian, an opinion held by Demophilos, who charged the composer with impiety 'because he was accustomed to sing it daily at banquets'; though it is more likely that it was either because the philosopher dared to number Hermeias among the heroes, or because he called him *ἀθάνατος* (l. 14); whereas Aristotle means that the merit of Hermeias will render him immortal in the memory of men. Diogenes calls the ode both a paian, and a hymn to Hermeias. Athenaios, or Hermippos, contended that it was a skolion. That the ode is not a genuine paian is clear, although it is not far removed from that class of lyric. Its repetition at banquets recalls the characteristic feature of the 'Attic' skolia, of which Reitzenstein thinks it is a free development. If this conclusion is correct, we have another instance of the not unfrequent confusion between paian and skolion. At all events, whatever name be given to the poem, it has the *form* of a religious song, such as would find its counterpart in Attic ritual.

Apparently it was sung by a chorus. In style it recalls the less extravagant form of the dithyramb current in the fourth century. Unlike the θρῆνοι of Simonides and Pindar, the poem employs the melic form to express a tribute of personal affection. The melic setting is justified because the subject is Virtue rather than Hermeias; otherwise the poem had assumed an elegiac form. The philosopher pours drops of the new wine of doctrine into the old bottle of a conventionalized lyric. Bergk dates the poem either after Aristotle had left Atarneus for Mitylene (345 B.C.) or after his return to Athens (344).

Hermeias, the 'nursling of Atarneus' in Mysia, was the pupil of Plato and the friend of Aristotle. Originally the slave of Eubulos, he assisted his master in making himself tyrant of Atarneus and on the death of Eubulos succeeded to the tyranny. As lord of Atarneus he entertained the philosopher for three years. After his treacherous capture and death at the hands of the Persians, Aristotle commemorated his hospitality in this ode; and had a statue set up at Delphi with the following inscription:

Τόνδε ποτ' οὐχ ὁσίως παράβας μακάρων θέμιν ἁγνὴν
ἔκτεινεν Περσῶν τοξοφόρων βασιλεύς,
οὐ φανερῶς λόγχῃ φονίοις ἐν ἀγῶσι κρατήσας,
ἀλλ' ἀνδρὸς πίστει χρησάμενος δολίου.

On the poetry of Aristotle, see Wilamowitz-Möllendorff *Aristoteles und Athen* 2. 403.

---

1. 'Αρετά: The poet does not claim divinity for 'Αρετά. She is παρθένος simply, not θεός or θεά to whom prayers may be offered or sacrifices performed on an altar. Areta had no cult as Virtus had (in *C. I. G.* 2. 2786, etc. we have Virtus under the Greek name). The impersonation of Areta appears in Prodikos' 'Choice of Herakles' (Xen. *Mem.* 2. 1. 21 ff.) and occasionally in works of art (Parrhasios' painting, Euphranor's crowning of Hellas, and in the Apotheosis of Homer). In Aristotle the allegory is stronger than the personal touch, but in the epigram (6) falsely attributed to him: ἅδ' ἐγὼ ἁ τλάμων 'Αρετὰ παρὰ τῷδε κάθημαι | Αἴαντος τύμβῳ κ.τ.λ., and in the imitation by Mnasalkas (*Anth.* App. 53), the personification is complete. Horace personifies Virtus in 3. 2. 17-24, 3. 24. 31, *carm. saec.* 58, etc. The abstract subject of the poem recalls Sim. xxiii., the ode to Hygieia, and on Tyche

(Mel. Adesp. xii.); as early as Pindar we find invocations to Tyche, Theia, etc., and χρόνος is personified (for the first time) in Bacchylides. In ridicule of such unsubstantial names, Momos in Lucian (θεῶν ἐκκλ. 13) says ἡ ποῦ γάρ ἐστιν ἡ πολυθρύλητος ἀρετὴ καὶ φύσις καὶ εἱμαρμένη καὶ τύχη (cf. Ζεὺς ἐλεγχ. 3), ἀνυπόστατα καὶ κενὰ πραγμάτων ὀνόματα ὑπὸ βλακῶν ἀνθρώπων τῶν φιλοσόφων ἐπινοηθέντα; . . . ἡδέως ἂν οὖν ἐροίμην εἴ που εἶδες ἀρετὴν . . . ; ὅτι μὲν γὰρ ἀεὶ καὶ σὺ ἀκούεις ἐν ταῖς τῶν φιλοσόφων διατριβαῖς κ.τ.λ. **πολύμοχθε**: = πολλοὺς μόχθους παρέχουσα τῷ βροτείῳ γένει. Cf. πολύμοχθος βιοτὴ θνητοῖς Eur. Frag. 916, πολυμόχθου ἱμείρων κύδεος Kaibel 146 (Attic inscr. of the fourth or third cent.). Bacchylides 1. 43 ff. adopts the less bold ἐπίμοχθος: ἀρετὰ δ' ἐπίμοχθος μέν, τελευταθεῖσα δ' ὀρθῶς ἄφθιτον εὖτε θάνῃ λείπει πολυζήλωτον εὐκλείας ἄγαλμα. See on Sim. xxiii.—**2**. **θήραμα**: as θήρα in Plato. In βίῳ the dative has a different force than in γένει.—**3**. **πέρι**: instead of ὑπέρ, as in Tyrt. 10. 13 περὶ παίδων θνήσκωμεν, Eur. *Alk.* 178 οὗ θνήσκω πέρι. See on Sa. i. 10. The use here is cognate with the Hom. ἀμύνεσθαι περὶ πάτρης M 243, ἐμεῦ πέρι μάρναο Π 497. **μορφᾶς**: a reference to the ἰδέα of Plato, the teacher of Hermeias. The meaning must not, however, be forced into a philosophic straight-jacket. Heroes do not die in order to attain to the ἰδέα τοῦ ἀγαθοῦ, the ἰδέα τοῦ καλοῦ. Aristotle attempts to blend philosophy with popular faith and poetry. The hero attains ἀρετή in dying a noble death: ψυχὰς δ' ἀντίρροπα θέντες | ἤλλάξαντ' ἀρετὴν καὶ πατρίδ' εὐκλεΐσαν Kaibel 21. 11 (Attica: fifth cent.).—**5**. **μαλερούς**: best explained as 'wasting' (schol. Aisch. *Pers.* 62). **ἀκάμαντας** = ἀκαμάτους (v.l.). The πόνοι are themselves 'unresting'; toils that tire not in wasting man's strength (Wilamowitz). ἀκ. does not agree with Ἕλληνας, which some regard as the omitted subject of τλῆναι. We should expect ἀκάμαντα in that case.—**6**. **τοῖον**: with or without γάρ etc., τοῖος introduces the reason for a preceding statement. Cf. Soph. *Antig.* 124, *Aias* 251, etc. So often with τοιοῦτος.—**7**. Corrupt. Bergk suggested ἐπεὶ φ. β. ἄρπυν (= ἔρωτα) ἐς ἀθ., Boeckh β. θράσος καρπὸν ἐν ἀθ., Wilamowitz ἰσαθάνατον (unattested, but cf. ἰσοδαίμων). Apart from the sense, καρπόν τ' ἀθ. for κ. ἀθ. τε, with τε trajected as in Soph. *O. K.* 33, Eur. *Hek.* 464, is not satisfactory. The translation 'instil into the mind a fruit' is not borne out by φρενῶν καρπός 'wisdom' Pind. *Pyth.* 2. 73. Perhaps ἐνὶ φρενὶ (φρεσὶ) θάρσος β. (Earle). **χρυσοῦ** ff.: cf. "How coldly those impediments stand forth | Of wealth, of filial fear" etc. Shakesp. *Lover's Complaint.*—**8**. **γονέων**: = εὐγένεια, or perhaps *amor parentum*: ι 34 ὣς οὐδὲν γλύκιον ἧς πατρίδος οὐδὲ τοκήων | γίγνεται, Pind. *Isthm.* 1. 5 τί φίλτερον κεδνῶν τοκέων ἀγαθοῖς, "he that loveth father or mother" . . . . **μαλακαυγήτοιο**: formed from **μαλακαυγής* as *ἀπένθητος* (*ἀπενθής*), *ἀφόβητος* (*ἄφοβος*), *νυκτιφρούρητος* (*νυκτίφρουρος*), etc. with no denom. verb in *-εω*. The meaning seems to be 'sleep that softens the radiance of the eye.' Nonnos calls Sleep *ὁμιχλήεις*; Shelley, *filmy-eyed*. Wilam. sees a reference to the colour of the sleeping person. *μαλακός* of *ὕπνος*, K 2, *μαλακώτεροι ὕπνω* Theokr. 15. 125. Cf. Bacch. xiii. 10.—**9**. The philosopher follows the conventional poetry with its types. So later, Horace, 3. 3. 9 *hac arte Pollux et vagus Hercules* | *enisus arces attigit igneas*, 1. 12. 25 *Alciden puerosque Ledae*. **οὐκ**: crasis in lyric is excessively rare, but *οἱ* is not to be read.—**11**. **δύναμιν**: the poet in part agrees with the philosopher. Schweighäuser cites *Eth.* 2. 1. 4 (1103 *a* 31) *τὰς δὲ ἀρετὰς λαμβάνομεν ἐνεργήσαντες πρότερον, ὥσπερ καὶ ἐπὶ τῶν ἄλλων τεχνῶν· ἃ γὰρ δεῖ μαθόντας ποιεῖν, ταῦτα ποιοῦντες μανθάνομεν.* He has just stated that *ἀρεταί* are *δυνάμεις*. Moral virtue is a potential part of man's nature. Still *ἀρετή* is not always a *δύναμις* on Aristotle's own theory. *δύναμις* 'capacity' may = *ἕξις* 'habit of mind,' but is not always equated with it. The formal definition of *ἀρετή* is a 'fixed habit of mind, the result of principle and effort, which, with reference to our own particular nature, lies equally distant between extremes' (*Eth.* 2. 5. 6).—**12**. **σοῖς πόθοις**: *σὸς πόθος* λ 202, *tuo desiderio*; *εὐνοίᾳ τῇ σῇ* Plato *Gorg.* 486 A, *σῇ προμηθίᾳ* Soph. *O. K.* 332. Quint. Smyrn. 5. 50 represents Areta as depicted on the shield of Achilles. Cf. Asklepiades (*Anth. Pal.* 7. 145) *ἅδ' ἐγὼ ἁ τλάμων Ἀρετὰ παρὰ τῷδε κάθημαι* | *Αἴαντος τύμβῳ, κειρομένα πλοκάμους*, alluding to the contest for the arms of Achilles. So Antipater of Sidon (*Anth. Pal.* 7. 146) *σῆμα παρ' Αἰάντειον ἐπὶ Ῥοιτηΐσιν ἀκταῖς* | *θυμοβαρὴς Ἀρετὰ μύρομαι ἑζομένα.* **δόμους**: the plural as *Ἀΐδαο δόμοισιν* X 52, *Ἀΐδα δόμοις* Eur. *H. F.* 116. *Ἀΐδα δόμον* (Wilam.) would help the metre.—**13**. **φιλίου**: see on Pratin. i. 17. **ἔντροφος**: as *Αἴας ὁ Σαλαμῖνος ἔντρ.* Eur. *I. A.* 289. **χήρωσεν**: 'bereft himself' = *ἐχηρώσατο*. Theogn. 956 *τῶν τε γὰρ αὐτοῦ* | *χηρώσει* (*χηρώσῃ*?) *κτεάνων* and Plut. *Amat.* 2 *ἐχήρωσε* (*ἐχήρευσε*?) are also suspicious cases of the intransitive use. So too *χηρευόμεν* 'bereave' Eur. *Kykl.* 440. The intransitive *παῦε* is common (van Herwerden on Aristoph. *Ranae* 122) and *ἔπειγε*, *ἔγειρε*, *ῥίπτω*, *ἐσβάλλω* are so used. (Krüg. 52. 2, Kühn.-Gerth 2. § 373). The alternative reading *χήρωσεν αὐγάς* preserves the grammar at the expense of dithyrambic extravagance—*sic declaratur desiderium, quod Sol sentiat, quum Hermias non amplius in conspectum eius veniat* (Ilgen), 'left desolate the light of the Sun.' The metre of v. 13 is uncertain: perhaps a dact. trip. + two epitrites, reading ἀλίου).—**14**. So Pind. *Ol.* 10. 95 τρέφοντι δ' εὐρὺ κλέος | κόραι Πιερίδες Διός, *Nem.* 7. 15, 32, Hor. 4. 8. 28 *dignum laude virum Musa vetat mori.* Cf. Sim. 99 οὐδὲ τεθνᾶσι θανόντες, ἐπεί σφ' ἀρετή καθύπερθεν | κυδαίνουσ' ἀνάγει δώματος ἐξ 'Αίδεω.—**15**. Cf. Solon 13. 1 Μνημοσύνης καὶ Ζηνὸς . . . ἀγλαὰ τέκνα, | Μοῦσαι Πιερίδες, Hes. *Theogon.* 52. **Διὸς ξενίου** ('hospitality') is objective genitive. For **αὔξουσαι**, Bergk conj. ἀσκοῦσαι, Crusius ἅζουσαι. We may paraphrase: αὔξουσι τὸν 'Ερμ. ὡς καὶ Δία ξένιον σεβόμενον καὶ φιλίαν βέβαιον γεραίροντα.—Metre: dact.-epitrite. Anacrusis occurs only at the beginning, thus marking the exordium (cf. Pind. *Nem.* 10).

MELIC ADESPOTA.

I. Clem. Alex. *Strom.* 5. 654. Doubtless from Pindar, who maintains that τὸ δὲ φυᾷ κράτιστον ἅπαν and that the poet must be dowered with a μοιρίδιος παλάμα. The next four fragments are also probably Pindaric.—Metre: logaoedic.

II. Clem. *op. cit.* 5. 661.—Metre: dact.-epitrite.

III. Theodoros Metochites p. 515.—Metre: dact.-epitrite.

IV. Plut. *de occ. viv.* 6; *de E Delph.* 21.—Metre: dact.-epitrite.

V. Plut. *non posse suav. vivi* 26. Cf. Sa. xxiv., Stes. xiii. **βαθυδένδρῳ**: 'Ελικῶνα βαθυδ. hymn to Apollo i. with musical notes (Appendix).—Metre: logaoedic.

VI. Plut. *consol.* 28. Had Niobe borne in mind that she too who was θαλέθοντι . . . ὁρῶσα would die, she had not wished to die because of her excess of suffering. Perhaps from a θρῆνος (by Simonides?) or from Soph. *Niobe*, Trag. Adesp. 373.—**2**. Cf. παιδὸς βλάστας 'the child's birth' Soph. *O. T.* 717.—Metre: dact.-epitrite (?).

VII. Plut. *de amic. mult.* 5.—Metre: dact.-epitrite.

VIII. Dio Chryst. *or.* 33 (2. 470). The story of Hekabe's transformation into a dog by the Furies is alluded to in Eur. *Hek.* 1265, Plaut. *Men.* 5. 1. 14, Ovid *Metam.* 13. 565 ff. Her tomb was called Κυνὸς Σῆμα.—**1**. **οἱ** with foll. gen., as Π 531 ὅττι οἱ ὦκ' ἤκουσε μέγας θεὸς εὐξαμένοιο.—**4**. Bergk read τε (πάγοι) φιλάνεμοί (τε) πέτραι.—Metre: logaoedic.

IX. Demetr. *de eloc.* 164.—Metre: dact.-epitrite.

X. Clem. Alex. *Strom.* 6. 796. Cf. Bacch. 43 (B. 4) ὡς δ' ἅπαξ εἰπεῖν, φρένα καὶ πυκινὰν κέρδος ἀνθρώπων βιᾶται.—Metre: dact.-epitrite.

XI. Plato *Epist.* 1. The detail recalls Bacchylides xviii., but, as Bergk suggested, the fragment may be from a tragic poet.—**2. ἀστράπτει**: the singular follows the neuter part; cf. *λίθοι τε καὶ πλίνθοι καὶ ξύλα καὶ κέραμος ἀτάκτως μὲν ἐρριμμένα οὐδὲν χρήσιμά ἐστιν* Xen. *Memorab.* 3. 1. 7. There is zeugma with *ἀστράπτει* in ll. 3, 4. For the figure cf. Bacch. xiii. 12. —**3. αὐτάρκεις**: *αὐτόσποροι γύαι* Aisch. Frag. 196.—**4. ὡς**: as if *οὕτως* had preceded.—Metre: dact.-epitrite.

XII. Stob. *Ecl. Phys.* 1. 6. 13. In earlier literature *Τύχη* is Vicissitude, which is obscure to mortals, rather than blind Chance. Hesiod calls her the daughter of Okeanos. To Pindar she is still associated with the will of Zeus; cf. *Ol.* 12. 1 *παῖ Ζηνὸς . . . σώτειρα Τύχα*, *Nem.* 6. 24 *θεοῦ τύχα*. The same poet made her one of the Fates and superior to her sisters. Cf. Lehrs *Pop. Aufsätze* 155. From the time of Aristophanes *Τύχη* appears as a power either coördinated with the gods or as an independent divinity. The orators equate her with *θεός* or *δαιμόνιον* (*τὰ παρὰ τῆς τύχης δωρηθέντα* Isokr. 4. 26). Cf. Juv. 10. 365 *nos te | nos facimus, Fortuna, deam coeloque locamus.*—**1.** Cf. Aischin. 2. 131 *τύχη, ἣ πάντων ἐστὶ κυρία.* **μερόπων**: without the addition of the epic *βρότοι* or *ἄνθρωποι*. **ἀρχά**: as in the formulas *ἀγαθῇ τύχῃ, θεὸς τύχαν ἀγαθάν, Τύχη μόνον παρείη.*—**2. ἕδρας**: cogn. accus. as in *θακοῦντι παγκρατεῖς ἕδρας* Aisch. *Prom.* 389, *ἕδρας θοάζετε* Soph. *O. T.* 2. Cf. Liban. *περὶ δουλείας* 2. 66 *χρὴ γὰρ οἴεσθαι καὶ τῇ Τύχῃ κεῖσθαι ἐν οὐρανῷ θρόνον, εἰ καὶ μὴ ἐν τοῖς δώδεκα θεοῖς ἠρίθμηται.*—**4.** Cf. *τὰ τῆς τύχης, ἧπερ ἀεὶ βέλτιον ἢ ἡμεῖς ἡμῶν αὐτῶν ἐπιμελούμεθα* Demosth. *Phil.* 1. 12, *τὸ τῆς τύχης εὐμενές* Paus. 7. 17. 1.—**5. λάμπει**: see on Bacch. xiii. 12. **πτέρυγα**: on winged representations of Fortuna see Roscher *Lex.* 1. 1507; Hor. 1. 34. 14, 3. 29. 53.—**6.** Tyche has the scales of Themis. Cf. Demos. *Olyn.* 2. 22 *μεγάλη γὰρ ῥοπή, μᾶλλον δὲ τὸ ὅλον ἡ τύχη παρὰ πάντ᾽ ἐστὶ τὰ τῶν ἀνθρώπων πράγματα.*—**7. ἀμαχ. πόρον**: 'a way of escape from helplessness' as *πόρος κακῶν* Eur. *Alk.* 213, *μηχανὰν κακῶν ib.* 221; *ἐξ ἀμηχάνων πόρους* Aisch. *Prom.* 59.—**8. προφερεστάτα**: 'chiefest'; the idea of seniority is unnecessary. See Jebb on Soph. *O. K.* 1531.—Metre: dact.-epitrite.

XIII. Stob. *Ecl.* 1. 5. 10-12 (divided among three authors). Cf. Wilamowitz, *Isyllos* 16, who would ascribe the magnificent fragment to Simonides, and Nauck *Frag. trag.* xx. Whatever the contents of the entire poem may have been, the chorus here implores the Moirai to send the Horai to bring surcease of care to their city, which has been distressed by civil war. Apparently the poem was composed in a time of civil feud. The Moirai are givers of weal as well as woe

(Hes. *Theogon.* 906, Γ 182); they withdraw to hide their shame if there is enmity among kinsmen (Pind. *Pyth.* 4. 145). In *Isthm.* 6. 17 Pindar invokes the assistance of Klotho and her sisters.—**2. μήδεα βουλᾶν**: gen. of explanation as *δεσμὸς πέδης*, etc.; *βουλαὶ . . . μήδεά τε* B 340. The Moirai plan and issue decrees which are carried into effect by the *κῆρες*.—**4. Αἶσα**: cf. Υ 127, η 197 (*αἶσα κλῶθές τε*). Hesiod did not admit her into his canon. Aisa is Moira *κατ' ἐξοχήν*. Here she takes the place of Atropos, for whom Pindar substituted Tyche. An Attic tradition (Paus. 1. 19. 2) made Aphrodite Urania the eldest of the Moirai.—**5.** Hes. *Theogon.* 217 makes the Moirai children of Nyx; so *Orphic Hymn* 59. On the chest of Kypselos two Moirai were represented together with Nyx and other figures.—**6. χθόνιαι**: Aisch. *Eum.* 961 calls the Moirai sisters of the chthonian Erinyes. In the Peiraieus and at Sikyon they were propitiated with offerings as the *κατὰ χθονὸς θεαί*.—**9. Εὐνομίαν**: cf. Alkm. xxii. The Horai are the sisters of the Moirai, since both are sprung from Zeus and Themis (Hes. *Theogon.* 901). In Megara both were represented above the statue of enthroned Zeus; and they appeared in conjunction on the altar of Hyakinthos at Amyklai; so on the Borghese altar (Clarac pl. 173, 174). The three sisters are here divided into two groups as in Pind. *Ol.* 13. 6: *ἐν τᾷ γὰρ Εὐνομία ναίει, κασιγνήτα τε, βάθρον πολίων, ἀσφαλὴς | Δίκα καὶ ὁμότροπος Εἰρήνα*, cf. *Ol.* 9. 16. *Εὐνομία* has a secondary position in comparison with her sisters; though Bacch. viii. 19 makes *Δίκα* her attendant. Alkman xxii. calls Tyche the sister of Eunomia. In local cults and on several works of art only two Horai appear. **λιπαροθρόνους**: see on Sa. i. 1. —**10. λελάθοιτε**: the Homeric (Ο 60 *λελάθῃ ὀδυνάων*) causal use of the reduplicated aorist. See Monro *Hom. Gram.* § 36. —Metre: dact.-epitrite.

XIV. Stob. *Ecl.* 1. 1. 3. Metre: dact.-epitrite.

XV. Stob. *Ecl.* 1. 1. 9. **καί** is intensive. Metre: dact.-epitrite.

XVI. Schol. Soph. *El.* 139, Suidas *s.v.* *πάγκοινος* (Trag. Adesp. 456). Perhaps from a threnos. Cf. Ibyk. xii. Metre: dact.-pentapody.

SKOLIA.

I. ff. Athen. 14. 694 c. The first four skolia resemble hymns. i. and ii. are in honour of Athena and Demeter, the goddesses of Athens and Eleusis, iii. and iv. celebrate Apollo and Pan, the gods of song and dance.—**1.** Cf. the famous song to Pallas by Lamprokles. **Τριτογένει'**: so Δ 515, etc. The Triton stream was placed in the extreme west, later on in Libya. The Triton may be identified with the Okeanos, out of which, in its western course, the thunderclouds arose according to Greek fancy. Athena, who sprang from the head of Zeus, is the goddess of the storm-cloud and of the lightning. **'Αθάνα** is generally read in the few passages of tragedy where *'Αθηνᾶ* (here in the MSS.) occurs. In Attic inscriptions *'Αθηνᾶ* (the contracted, adjectival form) occurs once in the sixth, once in the fifth century, and is rare before 362 B.C. *ἄνασσ' 'Αθάνα* Aisch. *Eum.* 235, 443, 892, Eur. *I. T.* 1475, *Troad.* 52, *Fάνασσ' 'Αθανάα* Alk. ii. 1. The elevated poetic style did not fancy *'Αθανάα* (cf. ix.).—**2.** Athena is invoked as *πολιοῦχος* (cf. Aristoph. *Nubes* 602; *Eq.* 581) or as *πολιάς* Soph. *Phil.* 134.—**2. ὄρθου**: Pind. *Isthm.* 5. 48 *πόλις ὀρθωθεῖσα*.—**3. ἀλγέων**: cf. *παγκλαύτων ἀλγέων* Aisch. *Sept.* 368, *κακά τ' ἄλγη πολέμους τ' αἱματόεντας Suppl.* 1044. **στάσεων** may refer to the internal strife at the time of the contest with the Peisistratidai. Cf. Pind. xii.—**4. θανάτων**: the plural often of death by violence (Aisch. *Agam.* 1572). **ἀώρων**: *θανάτου ἀώρου* Eur. *Or.* 1030. Some of the ancients distinguished between death *πρὸ μοίρας* and death *πρὸ ὥρας*. Aisch. *Eum.* 956 has *ἀνδροκμῆτας ἀώρους τύχας*. **πατήρ**: on the conjunction of Zeus with Athena cf. Soph. *O. T.* 187, 202.

II. 1. Πλούτου: Demeter is *πλουτοδότειρα Orphic Hymn* 40. 3. Though she is the mother of Plutos (Hes. *Theogon.* 969), *πλοῦτος* is not a person here. Cf. *Hymn to Dem.* 489. So Artemis as the goddess of agriculture is *βαθύπλουτος*. **'Ολυμπίαν**: only here of Demeter. *'Ολύμπιος* in early Greek is a title applied to no other goddess except Hera and to Zeus alone of the gods. The epithet is here used as in *Γῆ 'Ολυμπία* and is not intended to distinguish Dem. *'Ολυμπία* from Dem. *Χθονία* (in Sparta and Hermione: cf. Eur. *H. F.* 615, Paus. 3. 14. 5, 2. 35. 5). Casaubon's *'Ομπνίαν* should be *"Ομπνιαν*, which violates the metre and is very late (*C. I. A.* 3. 26 Roman, Nonnos).—**2. στεφ. ἐν. ὥραις**: may refer indirectly to (1) 'hours for garlanding' the brows of the banqueters (cf. xvi.), but the reference is properly to the times when the skolion was sung, *i.e.* (2) the 'seasons when garlands are worn,' viz. Anthesterion, at the time of the Lesser Mysteries. Cf. *ὧραι πολυάνθεμοι* Pind. *Ol.* 13. 17. Less likely is (3) 'seasons which yield flowers for garlands' (cf. *στεφανηφόρου ἦρος Anakreont.* 53. 1 and *Δημ. ὡρηφόρος Hymn to Dem.* 492. **ὥραις**, not *"Ωραις*, though Persephone is *'Ωρῶν συμπαίκτειρα*

Orphic Hymn 29. 9.—**3. Φερσεφόνη** as in Pind., Kaibel 50. 4 (fourth cent.), with an initial *φ* due to the influence of that in -*φόνη* (cf. Θεμισθοκλῆς *C. I. A.* 2. 864, ii. 18). Attic prose inscriptions on vases etc. have *Φερρέφαττα*, while decrees have *Κόρη*.

III. 1. Cf. *Hymn* 1. [14-15] *χαῖρε, μάκαιρ' ὦ Λητοῖ, ἐπεὶ τέκες ἀγλαὰ τέκνα,* | *'Απόλλωνά τ' ἄνακτα καὶ Ἄρτεμιν ἰοχέαιραν.* The two deities here as in Theogn. 1-14. The v. l. *παῖδα* for *τέκνα* follows that tradition which recognized no relation between Apollo and Artemis. **ἔτικτε**: the imperfect of *τίκτω* is often preferred to the aorist when the parentage is emphasized rather than the birth. Hence *τίκτω* 'am the parent of,' *οἱ τίκτοντες* (and *οἱ τεκόντες*) 'parents': cf. Eur. *H. F.* 866, *Ion* 1560. So with *ἐκφύω*. The present stem expresses a permanent character or relation.—**2. Φοῖβον χρυσοκόμαν**: so Eur. *I. T.* 1237, Aristoph. *Aves* 217; *ὁ Χρυσοκόμας* without *Φοῖβος*, Pind. *Ol.* 6. 41. **'Απόλλω**: the shorter (analogical) form *without* the article. —**3.** Thanks were offered to *Ἄρτ. ἀγροτέρα* in Athens for the victory at Marathon. The epithet *ἀγρ.* Φ 471, Bacch. ii. 123, in Megara, Olympia, etc.; *ἀγρ. σηροκτόνε* Aristoph. *Lysistr.* 1262. Cf. *Thesmoph.* 111 ff. Xen. *Kyneg.* 6. 13 prescribes the prayer for the hunter: *τῷ 'Απόλλωνι καὶ τῇ 'Αρτέμιδι τῇ 'Αγροτέρᾳ μεταδοῦναι τῆς θήρας.* As the Huntress, Artemis was *ἐλαφηβόλος* (see on Anakr. i.).—**4.** Cf. Aisch. *Suppl.* 676 *εὐχόμεθα Ἄρτεμιν δ' ἑκάταν γυναικῶν λόχους ἐφορεύειν*, [Sa.] 118. 5 *δέσποινα γυναικῶν* of Artemis. As *Εἰλείθυια* she has power over the life and death of women.

IV. Cf. Pind. Frag. 95, beginning *Ὦ Πάν, 'Αρκαδίας μεδέων καὶ σεμνῶν ἀδύτων φύλαξ*, and ending *Ματρὸς μεγάλας ὀπαδέ, σεμνᾶν Χαρίτων μέλημα τερπνόν.* Though the skolia were probably largely indebted to Pindar, the similarity between our skolion and the passage of Pindar's partheneion is so purely formal as to exclude the thought that the latter was the model here. Our poem is modelled on the choral songs intended for the cult of the gods. If a skolion in honour of Pan points to the help given by him to the Athenians at Marathon, we have here a proof that the collection of 'Attic' skolia was made after the Persian war.—**1.** *ἰώ* (MSS.) an exclamation of joy, as Eur. *Bacch.* 576, if retained, may be treated as a monosyllable (cf. Eur. *Or.* 332). So in v. 3.—**2. ὀρχηστά**: cf. *ὁ φιλόχορος Πάν* Aisch. *Pers.* 448, *Πᾶνα χορευτὰν τελεώτατον θεῶν* Pind. Frag. 99, *σκιρτητὴς Π.* *Orphic Hymn* 11. 4; and Soph. *Aias* 699 ff. **Βρομίαις**: *i.e.* *τῷ Βρομίῳ παρακολουθαίσαις*; see on Anakr. ii. 2. *βρομίαις* (*sic*) might be defended by *βρομία φόρμιγξ.* **ὀπαδέ**: a substantive as in Pind.

Nem. 3. 8, Frag. 95 (above), where it is followed by the gen. (cf. the variation with σωτήριος etc.). **Νύμφαις**: cf. *Hymn to Pan* 2 ὅστ' ἀνὰ πίση | δενδρήεντ' ἄμυδις φοιτᾷ χοροήθεσι Νύμφαις, Soph. *O. T.* 1100, Aristoph. *Thesmoph.* 977 ἄντομαι | καὶ Πᾶνα καὶ Νύμφας φίλας | ἐπιγελάσαι προθύμως | ταῖς ἡμετέραισι | χαρίεντα χορείαις, *Anth. Pal.* 9. 142 Νυμφῶν ἡγήτορα Πᾶνα.—**4**. Cf. *Hymn to Pan* 48 καὶ σὺ μὲν οὕτω χαῖρε, ἄναξ, λίτομαι δέ σ', ἀοιδῇ (cf. Maass *Hermes* 31. 382) and the Asklepios hymn of Ptolemaïs: χαῖρέ μοι, ὦ Παιάν, ἐπ' ἐμαῖς εὔφροσι ταῖσδ' ἀοιδαῖς (*Rev. Arch.* 13. 71).

V. From some old Aesopian fable, out of which the author has taken the main point. Momos blamed Prometheus for not making a gate in man's breast instead of constructing a creature that was able to hide his thoughts (Eust. on *Odyss.* 1574. 16). Cf. Propert. 3. 5. 7 ff. The physiognomist in Theokr. epigr. 11 is δεινὸς ἀπ' ὀφθαλμοῦ καὶ τὸ νόημα ἰδεῖν. The window of the soul takes the place of the touchstone of character (Bacch. xvi.). The poem recalls Soph. *Antig.* 709 οὗτοι διαπτυχθέντες ὤφθησαν κενοί, Eur. *Hippol.* 984 τὸ μέντοι πρᾶγμ', ἔχον καλοὺς λόγους, | εἴ τις διαπτύξειεν, οὐ καλὸν τόδε, *Andr.* 330 ἔξωθέν εἰσιν οἱ δοκοῦντες εὖ φρονεῖν | λαμπροί, τὰ δ' ἔνδον πᾶσιν ἀνθρώποις ἴσοι. Literature is full of the φίλος σαφής and the φίλος ἀληθής; Cic. *de amic.* 17. Cf. Theogn. 120 ff., *Il.* I 312. The skolion is parodied in Aristoph. *Eccles.* 938.—**1**. **ἦν**: the tense is assimilated to that of ἐξῆν, Goodwin *M. T.* 559. Ilgen regarded ὁποῖος . . . ἕκαστος as explanatory of τὸν νοῦν, Hermann took τὸν νοῦν as a pleonastic repetition of ὁποῖος . . . ἕκαστος, which is properly dependent on τὸ στῆθος ἐσιδόντα. The latter clause is subordinate to κλῄσαντα. **ὁποῖος**: with οἴ as often in ποίεω (vii. 4).—**4**. To esteem a man a friend by reason of his heart that knows no guile.

VI. The occurrence of a similar thought in both Simonides (cf. xxx.) and Epicharmos may have given rise to the doubt of the ancients whether this famous skolion was written by the lyric or by the comic poet (cf. schol. Plato *Gorg.* 451 E). Engelbrecht is certain that it is by Simonides. Bergk suggested that Epicharmos was the author of the line in Arist. *Rhet.* 2. 21 (1394 b 13) ἀνδρὶ δ' ὑγιαίνειν ἄριστόν ἐστιν, ὥς γ' ἡμῖν δοκεῖ. In the *Laws* 631 C, Plato refers to the poem in his arrangement of human blessings: ὧν ἡγεῖται μὲν ὑγίεια, κάλλος δὲ δεύτερον, τὸ δὲ τρίτον ἰσχὺς . . ., τέταρτον δὲ δὴ πλοῦτος, cf. 661 A; *Gorg.* 451 E, where the author is not named. The tone of the skolion is of course convivial not philosophical. Cf. also Aristoph. *Aves* 605. Pind. has a definite order of blessings *Pyth.* 1. 99 (cf. *Isthm.* 5. 12, *Ol.* 5. 23).—**1**. For the sentiment cf. Theogn. 255 κάλλιστον τὸ δικαιότατον·

λῷστον δ' ὑγιαίνειν, Soph. Frag. 329 κάλλιστόν ἐστι τοὔνδικον πεφυκέναι | λῷστον δὲ τὸ ζῆν ἄνοσον, ἥδιστον δ' ὅτῳ | πάρεστι λῆψις ὧν ἐρᾷ καθ' ἡμέραν (cf. Frag. 328), Ariphron on Hygieia p. 134, Bacch. 1. 27 ff. εἰ δ' ὑγιείας θνατὸς ἐὼν ἔλαχεν, ζώειν τ' ἀπ' οἰκείων ἔχει, πρώτοις ἐρίζει· παντί τοι τέρψις ἀνθρώπων βίῳ ἕπεται νόσφιν γε νούσων πενίας τ' ἀμαχάνου, Philemon Frag. 163 αἰτῶ δ' ὑγίειαν πρῶτον, εἶτ' εὐπραξίαν, | τρίτον δὲ χαίρειν, εἶτ' ὀφείλειν μηδενί. Aristotle and Metrodoros made ὑγίεια the *summum bonum.* **ὑγιαίνειν** yields the only case of the basis ⏑ ⏑ — in the skolia.—**2**. Anaxandrides, the comic poet, objected to this order of blessings (Frag. 17): ὁ τὸ σκόλιον εὑρὼν ἐκεῖνος, ὅστις ἦν, | τὸ μὲν ὑγιαίνειν πρῶτον ὡς ἄριστον ὄν, | ὠνόμασεν ὀρθῶς, δεύτερον δ' εἶναι καλόν, | τρίτον δὲ πλουτεῖν, τοῦθ', ὁρᾷς, ἐμαίνετο· | μετὰ τὴν ὑγίειαν γὰρ τὸ πλουτεῖν διαφέρει· | καλὸς δὲ πεινῶν ἐστιν αἰσχρὸν θηρίον. Aristotle, *Eth.* 1. 8 16 (1099 b 4), says there is no εὐδαιμονία for the man τὴν ἰδέαν παναίσχης. In Tyrt. 12. 5 Tithonos is the type of beauty, as Midas and Kinyras of wealth.—**4**. Cf. Anakr. xii. Herrick translated the skolion: "Health is the first good lent to men; | A gentle disposition then: | Next, to be rich by no by-wayes; | Lastly, with friends t'enjoy our dayes."

VII.-X. 'Harmodios' (ὁ Ἁρμόδιος, μέλος Ἁρμοδίου) is stated by Hesychios to have been composed by Kallistratos. Of him we know nothing else, but the composition of the poem may be referred to 500 B.C. or thereabouts. The skolion accepts the popular belief, which is held by Plato (*Symp.* 182 C) and Aristotle (*Pol.* 1311 a 36, 1312 b 31), that Hipparchos, who was assassinated by Harmodios and Aristogeiton, was 'tyrant' of Athens at the time (end of July, 514). Against the popular tradition Thukyd. 1. 20, 6. 54 ff. (cf. Hdt. 5. 55) protests and argues that Hippias as the older brother, not Hipparchos, was tyrant, and that the overthrow of the tyranny in 510 was not due to the 'reckless attempt' of the conspirators, but to the intervention of the Lakedaimonians. While this is no doubt true, it is easy to understand that the desire to honour the memory of the men who made the assault of 514 should have attributed to them the results of the revolution of 510. So the private wrongs of Lucretia and Wat Tyler's daughter were the cause of political outbreaks. Though Hippias was strictly 'the tyrant,' the skolion must not be interpreted as meaning that he succeeded Hipparchos—a belief current in some ancient authors.

Harmodios and Aristogeiton were honoured by the Athenians as gods and heroes. The polemarch offered libations on their graves: their families were maintained at the public expense; and no slave might be named after them. The first bronze statues in Greece were erected in their honour. A group by Antenor was taken by Xerxes to Susa, but recovered by Alexander or one of his successors. All the well-known representations (Baumeister fig. 357, 1347, 2132, Frazer on Paus. 1. 8. 5) probably go back to the later group by Kritios and Nesiotes (477 B.C.). The skolion is often referred to in later literature; in addition to the passages mentioned below, in Aristoph. *Acharn.* 980, *Vespae* 1225, Antiphanes Frag. 85, etc. In Frag. 4 Antiph. says it was sung as a paian: Ἁρμόδιος ἐπεκαλεῖτο, παιὰν ᾔδετο. Like the songs sung by Achilles in his tent, the skolion deals with the κλέα ἀνδρῶν (x. 1). There has been much discussion as to whether we have one poem of four strophes or four independent monostrophic skolia. The most plausible explanation is that we have a single poem of two parts, each consisting of two strophes and each connected with the other. Thus vii. and viii. as ix. and x. celebrate the deed and its glory, viii. the fame of its doers in the other world, x. their renown on earth. x. 4 repeats vii. 4; the final note takes up the beginning. For repetitions in a single skolion by one author cf. xxv. No weight is to be attached to the schol. on Aristoph. *Acharn.* 980, who quotes as the beginning φιλτ. Ἁρμ. Whether Kallistratos composed more than the first strophe cannot be proved, but it is probable that he composed all four.

VII. Referred to in Aristoph. *Lysistr.* 632 καὶ φορήσω τὸ ξίφος τὸ λοιπὸν ἐν μύρτου κλαδί. The daggers of the conspirators were concealed in branches of myrtle. At the Panathenaia, where the attack was made, the citizens who took part in the procession carried spear and shield only. The wearing of arms on any other day than that of the festival would have aroused suspicion. Though Hesych. reports *s.v.* θαλλοφόρος that olive branches were carried in the festival procession in honour of Athena, we know that myrtle boughs were often carried at sacrifices (Aristoph. *Aves* 43, *Thesmoph.* 37, *Vesp.* 861). Croiset suggests that the mention of the myrtle of the conspirators is a poetical manner of designating the myrtle crown of the banqueters.—**2. καί**: retaining καί we have two cyclic dactyls in this verse alone. The licence may be excused because of the proper name, which has five syllables and is necessarily thus placed. Sim. 131 encounters a like difficulty: ἦ μέγ' Ἀθηναίοισι φόως γένεθ' ἡνίκ' Ἀριστο- | γείτων Ἵππαρχον κτεῖνε καὶ Ἁρμόδιος. Cf. also Soph. eleg. 1 Ἀρχέλεως· ἦν γὰρ σύμμετρον ὧδε λέγειν (for Ἀρχέλαος). For irregularities in logaoedics cf. Sim. 148. 12. In Trag. Adesp. 126 we find καὶ ἀνάξιοι (κἀν. Nauck). Elision of κ(αί) might be defended by B 238, perhaps Z 260, and such writings as χοἰ Soph. *Phil.*

565, κεἰ, κεἰς. In Ionic we have κοἰνοπἰδης, κοὐκ, κὲν, in Doric κὲνκαύσιος (ἐγκ-). Ordinary crasis is unlikely (cf. ᾆσον δή μοι σκόλιόν τι λαβὼν Ἀλκαίου κἀνακρέοντος Aristoph. Frag. 223) because of the irrational trochee (accepted however by Buttmann, and Mehlhorn).—**4. ἰσονόμους**: the reference to ἰσονομία shows that the skolion belongs to a time not far removed from that of the tyrannicides. Later we hear of δημοκρατία.

VIII. 1. Referred to in Aristoph. *Acharn.* 1093 and schol. on 980. The skolion bears the name of Harmodios, who in this stanza is separated from his companion and made the subject of special honour because he lost his life in the very act of vengeance. Aristogeiton escaped but was soon arrested and executed after enduring torture with fortitude (Arist. Ἀθην. πολ. 18. 4 ff.). **οὔ τί που**: half statement, half question. 'It cannot be true that thou art dead—though it must be so.' The formula is used when an affirmative answer is feared and a negative answer desired but not necessarily expected. Cf. Pind. *Pyth.* 4. 87 οὔ τί που οὗτος Ἀπόλλων 'surely this youth cannot be Apollo, though it must be he'; Eur. *Hel.* 95, 475, 541, *Ion* 1113, *Or.* 1510; and often in the language of the people: Aristoph. *Ran.* 522, *Nub.* 1260, *Pax* 1211, *Aves* 442, *Eccl.* 329, 372. So οὔ που Eur. *Hel.* 135; οὐ δή που Aristoph. *Acharn.* 122, *Aves* 269, *Eccl.* 327, *Ran.* 526. Fritzsche's distinction between οὔ τί που, expressing a false, and οὐ δή που expressing a true opinion, does not seem to hold good as regards the latter formula. For the thought cf. Sim. 99 οὐδὲ τεθνᾶσι θανόντες, Aristotle on Ἀρετά, l. 14.—**2.** Cf. Hes. *W. D.* 170 καὶ τοὶ μὲν ναίουσιν ἀκηδέα θυμὸν ἔχοντες | ἐν μακάρων νήσοισι παρ' Ὠκεανὸν βαθυδίνην, | ὄλβιοι ἥρωες. **εἶναι** 'live' is opposed to τέθνηκας. So often in tragedy, *e.g.* Soph. *Aias* 783, *Phil.* 422. Lines 1 and 2 are imitated in *Anth.* adesp. 737 οὐκ ἔθανες, Πρώτη, μετέβης δ' ἐς ἀμείνονα χώραν, | καὶ ναίεις μακάρων νήσους θαλίῃ ἐνὶ πολλῇ. (Nauck read φασι ναίειν here.)—**3.** In Homer (λ 471 ff.) Achilles passes a wretched existence in Hades. Arktinos, followed by Pindar (*Nem.* 4. 49), placed his after-life in the island of Leuke near the mouth of the Danube. Ibykos (37), with whom Simonides agreed, transported him to the Elysian fields and married him to Medeia. In Pind. *Ol.* 2. 79 Achilles joins his father in the Islands of the Blest (cf. Plato *Symp.* 179 E, 180 B). See on Pind. xvi. This line was imitated by the comic poet Plato according to Nauck *Mél. gr.-rom.* 3. 118 (cf. *Hermes* 23. 283).—**4.** Cf. Διομήδεα δ' ἄμβροτον . . . Γλαυκῶπις ἔθηκε θεόν Pind. *Nem.* 10. 7. Diomedes obtained Athena's gift of immortality which had been forfeited by his father on account of his cannibalism. He was decreed divine honours at Metapontum and Thurii as a "hero of Hellenic civilization." The metre of this fourth verse is different from that of the rest. Bergk omitted *τόν* with Ilgen; Brunck omitted *τὸν ἐσθλόν*; Stadtmüller reads *φασ' ἐσθλὸν ἀεὶ μένειν*. Wilamowitz deletes Δ. and makes the verse consist of two adonics (cf. Sa. 27).

IX. 3. Ἀθηναΐης θυσίαισ': the Panathenaic celebration.

X. 1. Epic reminiscences in *ἔσσεται* and *αἶα*.—**2. φίλταθ' Ἁρμόδιος**: it is more usual to find the adj. in the nom. joined with the voc. of the substantive: *φίλος ὦ Μενέλαε* Δ 189, *ὦ τλήμων ἄνερ* Eur. *Andr.* 348. In *ὦ δύσμορ' Αἴας* Soph. *Aias* 923, *Αἴας* is the Attic vocative. The vocative without *ὦ* is more pathetic, and without the interjection the nom. is rarely used for the vocative.—**3, 4.** *-την* for *-τον* in historical tenses occurs at the end of the verse also in Eur. *Alk.* 661; for the sake of the metre in Soph. *O. T.* 1511; not seldom in Plato. The confusion, which occurs only in Attic, is due to a desire to mark the second person with the distinctive termination of the historical tenses. Perhaps *κανέτην* should be read here and in vii. 3; cf. ix. 4.

XI. Arist. *Ἀθην. πολ.* 19. 3, Athen. 15. 695 E. In 510 the exiles headed by the Alkmeonidai were disastrously defeated by the party of Hippias. Cf. Hdt. 5. 62.—**1.** Leipsydrion, which was fortified by the exiles, was situated on the southern slope of Parnes. Cf. Aristoph. *Lysist.* 665 *ἀλλ' ἄγετε, λευκόποδες, οἵπερ ἐπὶ Λειψύδριον ἤλθομεν, ὅτ' ἦμεν ἔτι*.—**3.** The hiatus in *καὶ* (so Arist.) may be excused by the fact that it occurs in the catalectic foot of the first dipody. Tyrrell conj. *κἀξ εὐπατριδᾶν*. **εὐπατρίδας**: the first occurrence of the word, which, before the time of Aristotle, is almost entirely confined to poetry (Soph. *El.* 162, 859, Eur. *Alk.* 920, *Ion* 1073). In Aristotle *εὐπ.* is used technically to denote a class of noble-born families which held offices in contrast to the base-born populace. The Alkmeonidai were not members of the Attic *γένος* specifically called *Εὐπατρίδαι*, though they are here included under the generic title. See Wright in *Harvard Studies in Class. Phil.* 3. 43. With the expression *ἀγαθούς κ.τ.λ.* cf. *κρήγυός τε καὶ παρὰ χρηστῶν* Theokr. *Epigr.* 21.—**4.** Cf. Soph. *Aias* 556 *δεῖ σ' ὅπως πατρὸς | δείξεις ἐν ἐχθροῖς οἷος ἐξ οἵου 'τράφης*, Tyrt. 15. 2 *κῶροι πατέρων πολιατᾶν*.

XII. Arist. *Ἀθην. πολ.* 19. 20, whence it may have been inserted in the 'Attic' collection. Before the battle at Leipsydrion Kedon made an attack on the Peisistratidai and lost his life. This is the only case of an elegiac distich in the extant skolia. For elegiacs at banquets cf. Theogn. 239.

XIII. Athen. 15. 695 A.—**1.** **ὡραῖον**: ὡρ. πλόος opposed to παρεὼν πλόος Hes. *W. D.* 630; cf. *Anth. Pal.* 10. 1. **κατίδην**: with Aiolic psilosis (cf. Aiol. κ(ε) l. 3). The dialect, the metre, and the flavour of the poem are Aiolic. Cf. the Aiolian Pittakos in Diog. Laert. 1. 78 συνετῶν ἐστιν ἀνδρῶν πρὶν γενέσθαι τὰ δυσχερῆ προνοῆσαι ὅπως μὴ γένηται, ἀνδρείων δὲ γενόμενα εὖ θέσθαι. In κατίδην, κατά connotes investigation, discovery, not superior elevation (both in Aisch. *Suppl.* 1059). καθορᾶν of physical scrutiny is rare: Hdt. 2. 38 κατορᾷ . . . τὰς τρίχας τῆς οὐρῆς εἰ κατὰ φύσιν ἔχει πεφυκυίας. In Pind. *Pyth.* 9. 49 there is no need to put Apollo on a divine lookout place. We have rather mental scrutiny (ὅσσα τε χθὼν ἠρινὰ φύλλα ἀναπέμπει . . . χὤτι μέλλει . . . εὖ καθορᾷς). The sense of the present passage is: before starting on a voyage we must survey the chances of its possibility and of our having the requisite skill to handle the vessel: *erst wägen, dann wagen.* The sailor who directs his course *inter nitentes Cyclades* must fix his course and hold to it. **κατίδην** does not introduce an indirect question. The apodosis is contained in the protasis: the chance of our making the voyage (if haply we may). This construction after οἶδα, εἶδον is common in Homer, who, with the optative, generally has εἴ κε; Goodwin, *M. T.* 491. Some think the passage means that the wise man, as far as possible, ought to avoid the perils of the deep. Cf. Archippos (43) ὡς ἡδὺ τὴν θάλατταν ἀπὸ τῆς γῆς ὁρᾶν, | ὦ μῆτερ, ἐστὶ μὴ πλέοντα μηδαμοῦ, Lucr. 2. 1 *suave, mari magno turbantibus aequora ventis, | e terra magnum alterius spectare laborem,* Hor. *Epist.* 1. 11. 10 *Neptunum procul e terra spectare furentem,* Cic. *ad Att.* 2. 7. 4 *cupio istorum naufragia ex terra intueri,* where he quotes Soph. Frag. 579; Tibull. 1. 1. 45 *quam iuvat inmites ventos audire cubantem,* Opp. *Pisc.* 5. 348. Ilgen makes πλόον a proleptic accusative. While an accusative *de quo* after οἶδα often anticipates a clause with εἰ (Monro *H. G.* § 294, cf. Θ 535), the subject of the two optatives must be the same.—**2.** **δύναιτο**: *scil.* πλεῖν αὐτόν. **παλάμην**: *agendi facultatem.* Cf. Soph. *O. T.* 314 ἄνδρα δ' ὠφελεῖν ἀφ' ὧν | ἔχοι τε καὶ δύναιτο (resources and faculties) κάλλιστος πόνων.—**3.** Cf. Hor. *Epist.* 1. 18. 87 *tu, dum tua navis in alto est, | hoc age, ne mutata retrorsum te ferat aura.*—**4.** **τρέχειν ἀνάγκη** is suspicious. Bergk suggested χρέεσθ'; cf. Plut. *Praec. reip. ger.* 2 (798 D) of men carried to sea unwillingly: μένειν δὲ καὶ χρῆσθαι τοῖς παροῦσιν ἀνάγκην ἔχοντες. τὸ παρεόν then = *quidquid inciderit.* Cf. Kratinos 172 ἄνδρας σοφοὺς χρὴ τὸ παρὸν πρᾶγμα καλῶς εἰς δύναμιν τίθεσθαι. Some supply ἀνέμῳ with παρεόντι, though πλόῳ is more probable.—Metre: Alkaic strophe.

XIV. Athen. *l. l.*, Eust. *Od.* 1574. 14. Stories drawn from the animal world are first met with in Archilochos and Semonides of Amorgos. Simonides of Keos told the story of the fisherman who hesitated to catch a polyp, because his failure would bring starvation to his children, while success meant perishing from cold. Philokleon in Aristoph. *Vespae* 1182 begins a fable: 'Once upon a time there was a mouse and a weasel.' The fable on which this skolion is based is told in Aesop (346 H): *Ὄφις καρκίνῳ συνδιῃτᾶτο, ἑταιρείαν πρὸς αὐτὸν ποιησάμενος. ὁ μὲν οὖν καρκίνος ἁπλοῦς ὢν τὸν τρόπον, μεταβαλέσθαι κἀκείνῳ παρῄνει τῆς πανουργίας· ὁ δὲ οὐδοτιοῦν ἑαυτὸν παρεῖχε πειθόμενον. ἐπιτηρήσας δ' ὁ καρκίνος αὐτὸν ὑπνοῦντα, καὶ τοῦ φάρυγγος τῇ χηλῇ λαβόμενος καὶ ὅσον οἷόν τε πιέσας, φονεύει· τοῦ δὲ ὄφεως μετὰ θάνατον ἐκταθέντος, ἐκεῖνος εἶπεν· "οὕτως ἔδει καὶ πρόσθεν εὐθὺν καὶ ἁπλοῦν εἶναι· οὐδὲ γὰρ ἂν ταύτην τὴν δίκην ἔτισας."* Aelian *N. A.* 16. 38 says that at Ephesos large and venomous serpents lived in a cave near a lake into the waters of which they entered *μέλλοντες γὰρ ἐπιβαίνειν τῆς γῆς ἐλλοχᾶν καρκίνους μεγάλους, οἵπερ οὖν ἀνατείναντες τὰς χηλὰς συλλαμβάνουσιν εἰς πνῖγμα αὐτοὺς καὶ ἀναιροῦσι.* The author of this skolion gives merely the closing scene of the familiar story. The witticism of the epilogue (cf. Bürger in *Hermes* 27. 359) is clear only from the fuller treatment of the fable. Line 2 represents only a moment of the action: when the snake is straightened out in death, his quondam friend says "straight my friend must be and not crooked in his mind."—**1. ὁ**: the article may be due to a direct reference to the well-known fable.—**3. εὐθὺν**: a *double entendre*—moral straight-forwardness and physical straightness. The antithesis of *εὐθύς* and *σκολιός* appears in Hes. *W. D.* 7, Solon 4. 37, Theogn. 535. Cf. M 124 *ἰθὺς φρονέων*. Ilgen's *ἴμεν* (cf. Aristoph. *Pax* 1083 *οὔποτε φοιτήσεις τὸν καρκίνον ὀρθὰ βαδίζειν*) would add to the humour of the situation, because the crustacean itself has a sidelong gait (cf. Hamlet's "If like a crab you could go backward"). **ἔμμεν**: Homeric, Thessalian, and in the Attic scenic poets only under special conditions; the Aiolic form is *ἔμμεναι*.—Metre: 1, 2, 4 catal. pherecratics with anacr.; 3 glyconic. Some write 3-4 together making a verse of two cola (glyconics). The skol. in Aristoph. *Vespae* 1245 (*χρήματα καὶ βίον Κλειταγόρᾳ τε κἀμοὶ μετὰ Θετταλῶν*) consists of pherecratics without anacrusis.

XV. Athen. *l. l.* and Eust. *Il.* 326. 40. Line 1 is quoted in the mock banquet scene in Aristoph. *Vespae* 1239. The skolion is variously referred to Alkaios, Sappho, and Praxilla without warrant. It represents the moral (note *μαθών, γνούς*) of some well-known poem, perhaps the *Alkestis* of Phrynichos.

Eust. says ἔοικε δὲ διὰ μὲν τῶν ἀγαθῶν τὴν γενναίαν καὶ φίλανδρον ὑποδηλοῦν Ἄλκηστιν, διὰ δὲ τῶν δειλῶν τὸν Ἀδμήτου πατέρα, ὃς ὤκνησε θανεῖν ὑπὲρ τοῦ παιδός. The skolion has been regarded by Schöne as evidence that Admetos' cowardice was branded in poetry before Euripides' *Alkestis.* But it is not clear that Admetos is not here regarded as one of the ἀγαθοί. Ebeling *Trans. Amer. Philol. Assoc.* 29. 79 suggests that τῶν δειλῶν δ' ἀπέχου is a mere amplification of τοὺς φίλους φίλει without including Pheres' son. Admetos' εὐσέβεια, ὁσιότης are uniformly accentuated. In Eur. *Alk.* 10 Apollo says ὁσίου γὰρ ἀνδρὸς ὅσιος ὢν ἐτύγχανον. Wilamowitz thinks there may be a reference to Herakles, the ἀγαθός who comes unbidden to the feast of the ἀγαθοί (cf. also Bacch. 59 K=33 B). With v. 2 cf. Theogn. 105 δειλοὺς εὖ ἔρδοντι ματαιοτάτη χάρις. **φίλει** 'entertain,' in Aristoph. has supplanted the statelier σέβου (*v. l.* Athen.). The metre of xvi.-xix. is that of xv. The greater Asclepiads came into favour in the skolia through the influence of Alkaios. Hartung referred xv.-xix. to Praxilla.

XVI. An imitation of Anakreon.—**1.** In older poetry συνηβᾶν is used only in Anakr. xii. and 44 ἔραμαι δέ τοι συνηβᾶν· χαριτοῦν ἔχεις γὰρ ἦθος. **συστεφανηφόρει**: cf. Anakr. xxiii., Demosth. *Falsa leg.* 380, 128 συνεστεφανοῦτο καὶ συνεπαιώνιζε. With l. 2 cf. Theogn. 313 ἐν μὲν μαινομένοις μάλα μαίνομαι, ἐν δὲ δικαίοις | πάντων ἀνθρώπων εἰμὶ δικαιότατος, Kallias 20 μετὰ μαιομένων φασὶν χρῆναι μαίνεσθαι πάντας ὁμοίως, where μετά appears with the plural, as is to be expected. **σύν μοι** is excessively rare (Kallim. epigr. 1. 5). σύν μοι πῖνε follows Anakr. 90. 3 σὺν Γαστροδώρῃ πίνουσα. Cf. also Eur. *I. A.* 407 συσσωφρονεῖν γάρ, οὐχὶ συννοσεῖν ἔφυν. The motto holds for a club (ἑταιρεία) as formerly for a tribe. Wilamowitz cites the Arabian 'I am a man of the title of Ghazijja; if Ghazijja is mad, I am mad,—if Ghazijja does what is right, I do what is right' (Wellhausen *Reste arab. Heidenthums* 194). Note the rime, as in Alk. 94.

XVII. There are numerous references to the scorpion, all of which go back to some such old proverb as ὑπὸ παντὶ λίθῳ σκορπίος. Cf. Aristoph. *Thesmoph.* 529 τὴν παροιμίαν δ' ἐπαινῶ | τὴν παλαιάν· ὑπὸ λίθῳ γὰρ | παντί που χρὴ | μὴ δάκῃ ῥήτωρ ἀθρεῖν, Praxilla Frag. 4 ὑπὸ παντὶ λίθῳ σκορπίον, ὦ 'ταῖρε, φυλάσσεο, Soph. Frag. 34 ἐν παντὶ γάρ τοι σκορπίος φρουρεῖ λίθῳ, Aelian *H. A.* 15. 26 εἰ γὰρ τοῦτο μὴ γένοιτο, ὁ χῶρος ἄβατός ἐστι· ὑπὸ παντὶ γὰρ λίθῳ καὶ βώλῳ πάσῃ σκορπίος ἐστί. The writer of this skolion added ὦ—ὑποδεύεται and the second verse in order to adapt the well-known proverb to a form of song already existing (Reitzenstein). Praxilla 4 represents a simpler enlargement. The Greek did not expect honest dealing and uprightness unless ἔρως bound his friend. Cf. xix.

XVIII. Line 1 is by a Dorian (note the use of the article), whose rustic taste is parodied by an Athenian in l. 2. The Arkadians were βαλανηφάγοι (Alk. 91).—**2.** Cf. Prior's "Euphelia serves to grace my measure, | But Chloe is my real flame."

XIX. A reference to the affair at Leipsydrion (no. xi.). This is the last in the collection of 'Attic' skolia as arranged in Athen.

XX. Athen. and Eust. *Il.* 285. 2. The author has in mind both Alk. xxvi. and Pind. *Nem.* 7. 27 (ὁ καρτερὸς Αἴας) ὃν κράτιστον Ἀχιλέος ἄτερ μάχᾳ | . . . πόρευσαν εὐθυπνόου Ζεφύροιο πομπαὶ | πρὸς Ἴλου πόλιν, both of which passages are derived from λ 550 Αἴανθ', ὃς πέρι μὲν εἶδος, πέρι δ' ἔργα τέτυκτο | τῶν ἄλλων Δαναῶν μετ' ἀμύμονα Πηλεΐωνα, whence B 768 ἀνδρῶν αὖ μέγ' ἄριστος ἔην Τελαμώνιος Αἴας, | ὄφρ' Ἀχιλεὺς μήνιεν· ὁ γὰρ πολὺ φέρτατος ἦεν. Cf. Sophokles *Aias* 1340 ἕν' ἄνδρ' ἰδεῖν ἄριστον Ἀργείων, ὅσοι Τροίαν ἀφικόμεσθα, πλὴν Ἀχιλλέως, and Horace *Sat.* 2. 3. 193 *Ajax, heros ab Achille secundus.* The skolion evidences the influence upon Athenian society exercised by the Aiolian Alkaios and the Dorian Pindar. The schol. on Aristoph. *Lysistr.* 1237, misled by the passage in Pindar, attributed the skolion to that poet. The skolion may be placed after 467, the date of *Nem.* 7. **λέγουσι** shows the literary models in the same manner as the epigram of 470 B.C. in Plut. *Kimon* 7, Aischin. *Ktes.* 80, 185 : ἔκ ποτε τῆσδε πόληος ἅμ' Ἀτρείδῃσι Μενεσθεὺς | ἡγεῖτο ζάθεον Τρωϊκὸν ἐς πεδίον· | ὅν ποθ' Ὅμηρος ἔφη Δαναῶν πύκα θωρηκτάων | κοσμητῆρα μάχης ἔξοχον ὄντα μολεῖν. Cf. skol. viii. 2.—Metre : the two logaoedic cola in each line of xx.-xxiii. do not differ much from those of the fourth verse of skol. i. ff. v. 1 = first glyconic + first pherecratic catal.; v. 2 first glyconic + log. tetrap. catal. (cf. Alk. τῶν ἀνέμων στάσιν).

XXI. An imitation of the preceding. The variations show that the two skolia never formed a single strophe. In xx. Aias is the chief figure, here there is no unity. The words καὶ (Bergk μετ') Ἀχιλλέα drag, whereas they should be important, and Δαναῶν, which depends on πρῶτον, is not well placed. Telamon engaged in the first expedition against Troy (Pind. *Nem.* 4. 25, *Isthm.* 6. 40). The skolion represents the Doric tendency to magnify the glory of the Aiginetan house of Aiakos at the expense of Achilles. Mention of Herakles is suppressed, though he was the leader in the expedition in which Telamon took part. Cf. Wilamowitz

Herakles l. 281. A reference to xx. and xxi. appears in the comic poet Theopompos (1. p. 750 K): *ἐπίνομεν μετὰ ταῦτα . . . | κατακείμενοι μαλακώτατ' ἐπὶ τρικλινίῳ | Τελαμῶνος οἰμώζοντες ἀλλήλοις μέλη*, and in Antiphanes Frag. 85: *ἔπειτα μηδὲν τῶν ἀπηρχαιωμένων | τούτων περάνῃς, τὸν Τελαμῶνα, μηδὲ τὸν | Παιῶνα μηδ' Ἁρμόδιον.*

XXII., XXIII. Athen. *l. l.* Dio Chr. 1. 36. Though there is no real unity between the two skolia, the verses read like two strophes of one poem. We have wish and counter-wish (cf. Theokr. 5. 8). Thought and expression balance each other in both. Perhaps xxii. is Doric, xxiii. Attic as xviii. 2. Cf. *Anth. Pal.* 5. 83 *εἴθ' ἄνεμος γενόμην, σὺ δ' ἐπιστείχουσα παρ' αὐγὰς | στήθεα γυμνώσαις καί με πνέοντα λάβοις*, 5. 84 *εἴθε ῥόδον γενόμην ὑποπόρφυρον, ὄφρα με χερσὶν | ἀρσαμένη χαρίσῃ στήθεσι χιονέοις*, 15. 35 *εἴθε κρίνον γενόμην ἀργένναον, ὄφρα με χερσὶν | ἀρσαμένη μᾶλλον σῇς χροτιῆς κορέσῃς* (see L. Cohn *Ueber die Paroimiographi* p. 53), Theokr. 3. 12 *αἴθε γενοίμαν | ἁ βομβεῦσα μέλισσα καὶ ἐς τεὸν ἄντρον ἱκοίμαν*, *Anakreont.* xvi. 15, Shakesp. *R. and J.* 2. 2. 24 "O, that I were a glove upon that hand, | That I might touch that cheek." So in German folk-songs, *e.g. Wollt Gott wär ich ein roth Goldfingerlein* and *Wolt Got dat ich wär en vöglin klein | . . . ich wolt ihr fliegen in's herzen grunt.*

XXII. A reference to the cyclic choruses. **γενοίμαν**: the optative regards only the futurity of the object of the wish, not its probability or even possibility (Goodwin *M. T.* 740). **ἐλεφαντίνα**: cf. *Anakreont.* 58. 5 *ἐλ. πλήκτρῳ*, Ovid *Metam.* 11. 168 *instructamque fidem gemmis et dentibus Indis.* It is noteworthy that the lyre is here stated to be the Dionysiac instrument.

XXIII. A reference to the procession at the Panathenaia. —**1. ἄπυρον χρυσίον**: as *χρυσὸς ἀκήρατος* Alkm. iv. 54; the gold is so pure as not to need refining (*αὐτοφυής*). Zeus appeared in the golden shower as *ἄπυρος χρυσός* [Eur.] Frag. 1132. 30. The *χρυσίον* may be a golden vase. But cf. Plut. *Artax.* 5 *δίδωμί σοι καὶ τὰ χρυσία φορεῖν ὡς γυναικί*, and see on Lykophronides.—**2. θεμένη νόον**: cf. Aisch. *Prom.* 163, *καθαρὸν θέμενος νόον* Theogn. 89, *θέτο βουλάν* Pind. *Nem.* 10. 89.

XXIV. Athen. 11. 783 E (Ameipsias Frag. 22). Man wants but little here below—only love and eating. Cf. *Anth. Pal.* 5. 85. 1. This is one of the skolia that took the place of those in the old 'Attic' collection.—Metre: logaoedic. v. 1. spondaic basis + two catal. troch. dipodies (cretics) + a catal. tripody; v. 2. log. pentapody.

XXV. Appended to the 'Attic' skolia by Athen. 15. 695 F (where it is stated that 'some call the poem a skolion'); also in Eust. *Od.* 1574. 7. Hybrias of Crete is otherwise unknown, but is supposed to have lived in the seventh century. The name may be defended by Ὑβρίδημος, Ὕβριλαος, Ὕβρων. The verses breathe the contempt for the tiller of the soil felt by the Dorian warriors of Crete, a state whose polity was that of a camp (Plato *Laws* 666 E). In the *Last of the Barons* Bulwer puts similar expressions into the mouths of the adherents of dying feudalism. Cf. the motto of Quentin Durward: *La guerre est ma patrie,* | *Mon harnois ma maison,* | *Et en toute saison,* | *Combattre c'est ma vie,* which is taken from a Spanish original *Mis arreos son las armas* | *Mi descanso el pelear* (quoted by Morgan). The form of the poem by Hybrias is suited for singing in company (the Cretan *syssitia*). —**1.** Campbell's "My wealth's a burly spear and brand" follows the unmetrical reading μέγα.—**2. λαισήϊον**: cf. M 426 βοείας, | ἀσπίδας εὐκύκλους λαισήϊά τε πτερόεντα. The λαισήϊα, which were lighter than the ἀσπίς or σάκος, were made of rough leather without any bronze covering, and carried by the common soldier; Helbig *Hom. Epos*² 329. Hdt. 7. 91 says that the Kilikians carried λαισήϊα ἀντὶ ἀσπίδων, ὠμοβοέης πεποιημένα. **πρόβλημα χρωτός**: cf. Υ 289 σάκος, τό οἱ ἤρκεσε λυγρὸν ὄλεθρον, Λ 32 ἀμφιβρότην ἀσπίδα, *Anth. Pal.* 6. 81 ἀσπίδα ταυρείην, ἔρυμα χροός. πρό̆βλημα is the only case in the melic poets, apart from Pindar, of Attic correption before βλ. —**3.** Cf. Archil. 2 ἐν δορὶ μέν μοι μᾶζα μεμαγμένη, ἐν δορὶ δ' οἶνος | Ἰσμαρικός, πίνω δ' ἐν δορὶ κεκλιμένος, Theokr. *Berenike* 2 τὰ δὲ δίκτυα κείνῳ ἄροτρα.—**4.** Cf. *Anakreont.* 3. 15 ποίει δὲ ληνὸν οἴνου | ληνοβάτας πατοῦντας.—**5. μνοΐας** 'serfs': μνοία (=οἰκετεία Hesych.) is derived from *δμοία; cf. μνῆτοι· δοῦλοι Hesych., *i.e.* δμῆτοι (δμῆσαι· δαμάσαι). So μεσόμνη is from μεσόδμη, and perhaps Ἀγαμέμνων from -μέδμων (Prellwitz). The subject population of Crete was divided into three classes, although all three may not have co-existed in each state: (1) ὑπήκοοι, who paid tribute. These correspond to the Laked. περίοικοι; (2) μνωῖται, serfs, who cultivated the public lands; (3) κλαρῶται or ἀφαμιῶται, cultivators of the private estates of the citizens. These may correspond to the Helots. See Gardner-Jevons *Greek Antiq.* 433, 615. Here μνοΐα stands for 'serfs in general. Athen. 6. 263 F quotes from Sosikrates: τὴν μὲν κοινὴν δουλείαν οἱ Κρῆτες καλοῦσι μνοίαν.—**6.** Cf. Xen. *Kyrop.* 7. 5. 79 πολεμικῆς δ' ἐπιστήμης καὶ μελέτης παντάπασιν οὐ μεταδοτέον τούτοις, οὕστινας ἐργάτας ἡμετέρους καὶ δασμοφόρους βουλόμεθα καταστήσασθαι, ἀλλ' αὐτοὺς δεῖ τούτοις τοῖς ἀσκήμασι πλεονεκτεῖν, γιγνώσκοντας ὅτι ἐλευθερίας ταῦτα ὄργανα καὶ εὐδαιμονίας οἱ θεοὶ τοῖς ἀνθρώποις ἀπέδειξαν.—**7**. The repetition of v. 2 in a skolion composed by a single author is noteworthy. —**8**, **9**. Corrupt. Bergk supplied ἀμφί after πεπτ. 'falling'; cf. ἀμφιπίτνουσα τὸ σὸν γόνυ Eur. *Suppl.* 279. We expect ἀμφί, περί, ποτί, or ἐς. Sitzler would add τοὐμὸν χαμαί etc. If πεπτ. means 'crouching before' (ἀπειλὰς πτήξας Aisch. *Prom.* 174, πτήσσων δόρυ Lykophr. 280; cf. ὑπὸ τεύχεσι πεπτηῶτες κείμεθα ξ 474, and Bacch. vi. 14) the reading of the text may stand. Contrast "crook the pregnant hinges of the knee."—**9**. **πάντες**: repeated as τούτῳ l. 4. Crusius reads δεσπόταν ἐμὲ δεσποτᾶν and cp. Aisch. *Pers.* 666 δέσποτα δεσποτᾶν.—**10**. **μέγαν βασ.** = βασιλέα βασιλέων. **φωνέοντες** has better authority than φωνέοντι.—Metre: logaoedic. vv. 1, 2, 4 hexapodies; v. 3 tetrapody; v. 4 Sapphic hendecasyllable; v. 5 phalaeceum. The arrangement is palinodic-mesodic: 6. 6. 4. 6. 6.

FOLK-SONGS.

In his *Art of English Poesie* (1589) Puttenham says: "Poesie is more ancient than the artificiale of the Greeks and the Latins, and used of the savage and uncivill, who were before all science and civilitie."

Behind the epic and lyric poetry of Greece lay the primitive religious chants and the folk-songs (ᾠδαί). If the chances of the survival of folk-lyric vary inversely with the cultivation of a people, in a race which developed so early such an astonishing mastery over poetic thought and form, such infinite capacity for claiming every *motif* as a proper subject for art, and such aptitude for making its own the work of the artist, it is no wonder that much of the ruder Greek lyric, together with the κλέα ἀνδρῶν, should have been absorbed or displaced by the epic. On the other hand the artistic lyric that succeeded to the epos, while influenced by the folk-song, obliterated much that had not already been surrendered to the epic. Hence it comes that, of the scant remains of Greek folk-song, but little antedates, at least in its original form, the rise of cultivated lyric in the eighth century. But if the primitive outlines of the earliest folk-lyric have become obscured, the original character of these songs has not entirely disappeared thanks to the love of the people for constant and fixed forms and melodies. Again, the literature of Greece continually reproduces the spirit of the early times, and if much of the old folk-song was absorbed or obliterated, much was created even in the literary period. So late as the time of the successors of Alexander there was a song, the beginning of which is contained in the proverb Ἵππος με φέρει, βασιλεύς με τρέφει, words used by the Makedonian soldier who refused to seek exemption from service (Diogenian. 5. 31, cf. Hor. *Epist.* 1. 17. 20 *equus ut me portet, alat rex*).

We need not here discuss the scant evidence from Greece as to the origin of the folk-song, nor take any position in the dispute as to whether 'popular' poetry was individual in the first instance, the work of a rude 'entertainer, as he is called by Scherer, or gregarious or communal, a theory adopted by Grimm, Grundtvig, and other students of the ballad. To a great extent in Greece folk-song was ballad-like, at least in the etymological sense of that much-vexed word. Dance forms the foundation of most of the poetry of the people, and dancing is auxiliary to improvisation, which was the earliest form of poetry according to Aristotle.

In the primitive period all thinking was "in chorus." Folk-song presupposes a state of society that is not severed by any divisions of culture and ignorance. In the period of the highest bloom of the folk-lyric in Greece society was in the patriarchal stage, and even in the later period, when the democracies were contending with the aristocracies, the existence of slavery tended to make homogeneous all who were free. A common impulse, a creative sentiment that was the property of the nation at large, ministered to the birth of the spontaneous utterance of the folk-muse. The singer did not invent, he merely fashioned the materials that were a common possession. The difference between the poet and the people was quantitative, not qualitative. The poet gave what he received, and his work was the condensation of the age in which he lived. His individuality disappeared behind the individuality of his race.

The qualities that distinguish the folk-song of other countries reappear in Greece. Truly impersonal, the artist loses himself behind his work ; his name is lost or is handed down in a personification. As Gaston Paris says of the poetry of the Middle Ages, the folk-songs form a body of poetry 'in which everybody believed and which everybody could have made.' They represent either the sentiment of the whole race, or the sentiment of a class; and in the latter case, a class that is represented in its entirety. With few exceptions the Greek folk-songs are brief, true to nature, naïf, inward in feeling, inartificial in thought and speech, concrete (though there is some lack of precision), and immediate in vision because they are the result of improvisation which gives dramatic life. Of the Spartan songs, some of which were still extant in the first century after Christ, thanks no doubt to Dorian hostility to literary culture, Plutarch says that their language was 'simple and powerful, their contents earnest and instructive morally.' The songs we possess show a love of fixed forms (see on Alkm. xiii.), poverty in figures of thought, and fondness for iteration (Nos. i., xxii.). The metres, usually logaoedics, are simple yet not monotonous. Oftentimes we have verses in pairs and traces of the strophic arrangement, which was taken over by artistic lyric. The refrain is an essential mint-mark. Perhaps, as Bergk remarked, the music was of greater importance than the poetry, whereas, in artistic lyric, at least to the fifth century, the accompaniment was subordinate.

In Greece more than elsewhere it is difficult to draw the line between the artless folk-lyric and the artistic lyric. The minstrel did not, as in the Middle Ages, come from another clime more favoured by the arts. In Greece the universal habit of thought was poetic and all art was essentially popular. There was therefore little of that antagonism between the speech of daily life and that of lettered taste of which Wordsworth complained in the preface to his *Lyrical Ballads.* In Greece *Volkspoesie*, poetry by the people, shades off imperceptibly into *Volksthümliche Poesie*, poetry for the people. If Greek folk-lyric has little of that unevenness of form which we often find in English ballads, on the other hand Sappho, Alkaios, Anakreon, the epic and the tragic poets (as Niese has said), are at once artistic and 'popular,' if we retain that squinting expression which found favour with such an authority as the late Prof. Child. The artist catches and develops the folk-song as in Shakespeare's *Sing willow*, and in Burns and Goethe. One verse may be taken directly from the people, while the poet's own words are brought into sympathy with it. Sometimes licence of form and metre are the only distinguishing characteristics. No doubt, too, there was affected popular poetry then as now ; and some, like Lady Wardlaw, may have stood in such intimate touch with the folk-spirit as to render impossible the attempt to separate the spurious from the genuine. The extant folk-songs of the Greeks contain relatively little of that primitive and elemental feeling which is held to be the mint-mark of "true" folk-lyric. Much is folk-song only in the extended use of the term, and not a little might be excluded as unworthy of the name because contemporary pressure rests upon it too heavily. Oral transmission and anonymity are the marks of the true folk-songs in our collection. If the Greek *horror vacui* caused the loss of much that was anonymous, on the other hand it was ready to fabricate authors for the *adespota* : Eriphanis and Kleobulos were made the originators of songs that are truly anonymous (xix., xxii.).

The life of the Greek from its beginning to its end was attended by song. Every circumstance and emotion of the life of the people, the humblest occupation, the service of the gods, work and play, sorrow and joy, were all the source of folk-lyric. To show the astonishing variety of the folk-songs of Greece it is sufficient to give a brief summary of the chief kinds of which a record has been preserved. The religious songs and those of a lay character often overlap, and strict lines of demarcation are impossible. The finest extant specimens of the folk-song of the Greeks are the skolia.

I. Songs of Daily Occupation.—Monotony and solitariness tend to give birth to song. Cf. Lucr. 5. 1383 :

Inde minutatim dulceis didicere querelas
tibia quas fundit, digitis pulsata canentum,
avia per nemora ac sylvas saltusque reperta,
per loca pastorum deserta atque otia dia.

βαλανείων ᾠδαί : songs of the bathmen. **βαυκαλήματα** or **καταβαυκαλήσεις** : lullabies. An imitation appears in Theokr. 24. 7 (see on Sim. xiii. 15). Cf. Soph. *Phil.* 827 ff., Eur. *Or.* 174 ff. Sext. Empir. *adv. Math.* 6. 32 calls them a metrical moaning (ἐμμελὴς μινύρισμα). Cf. Theophr. *Char.* 7. **γεωργῶν ᾠδαί**: songs of the field-labourers. We hear also of ᾠδαὶ τῶν μισθωτῶν τῶν ἐς τοὺς ἀγροὺς φοιτώντων. **ἔλινος**: weaving-song. Cf. ε 62, κ 222, Tibull. 2. 1. 66. Some were in honour of Athena. **ἐπιλήνιος**: song of the wine-press. Sung by the women of Elis who invoked Dionysos to fill their empty casks (No. v.). At the Lenaia in Athens the leader, who carried a torch, called upon the chorus to invoke Dionysos. Cf. λίνος or λινῳδία, *infra* xi. 1. **ἐπιμύλιοι** ᾠδαί or ᾄσματα μυλωθρῶν, songs at the mill (cf. No. xxiv.). Cf. Aristoph. *Nubes* 1358. **ἐρετικά** (εἰρεσία): boatmen's songs. **θεριστῶν ᾠδαί**: reaper's songs, such as the Lityerses. **ἱμαῖος** and **ἱμαλίς**: song of the draw-well. **ἴουλος**: song at the binding of the sheaves (No. i.). **πτιστικά**: or **πτισμοί**: winnower's songs, or perhaps songs of the bread bakers. **ποιμενικά** or **νόμια**: pastoral songs sometimes divided into βουκολιασμοί and συβωτικά. Stesichoros introduced into literature the pastoral song on Daphnis. **σκαπανέων ᾠδαί**: songs of the diggers. So also there were sowing songs sung by girls at the offering of the προηρόσια, when the fields were ploughed at the beginning of autumn to receive the new seed. The watchman in the *Agamemnon* of Aischylos hums an ἀντίμολπον ἄκος (l. 17); cf. Aristoph. *Nubes* 721, Lucr. 5. 1404. Here too we may place the professional proclamations of the herald at the agonistic contests (x., xi.).

II. Metrical Precepts. These are infinite in number and of great variety. A few specimens are:

1. Husbandry.

Σῖτον ἐν πηλῷ φύτευε· τὴν δὲ κριθὴν ἐν κόνει.

Ἔτος φέρει, οὐχὶ ἄρουρα.

2. The Winds:

Λὶψ ἄνεμος ταχὺ μὲν νεφέλας, ταχὺ δ' αἴθρια ποιεῖ,
'Αργέστῃ δ' ἀνέμῳ πᾶσ' ἕπεται νεφέλη.

Φιλεῖ δὲ νότος μετὰ πάχνην.

Οὔ ποτε νυκτερινὸς βορέας τρίτον ἵκετο φέγγος.

Εἰ δὲ νότος βορέαν προκαλέσσεται, αὐτίκα νίψει.

Εἰ βορρᾶς πηλὸν καταλήψεται, αὐτίκα χειμών.

3. Navigation. The best time for setting sail:
'Αρχομένου τε νότου καὶ λήγοντος βορέαο.

Much of the folk-wit of the Greeks has passed into Hesiod, and the lyric poets show here and there traces of the influence of the παροιμίαι. γνῶθι σεαυτόν, μέτρον ἄριστον and the like are of popular origin.

III. Riddles. The extreme antiquity of riddles in Greece is clear from the fact that at a very early period they were interwoven with the literature. Hesiod represented Mopsos and Chalkas proposing riddles to each other; and the 'Contest between Homer and Hesiod' makes use of the folk-riddle. The Seven Sages were the authors of several. The native wit of the Dorians made the riddle especially common in Dorian lands; but the Samian girls are represented as playing riddle-games. They were usually propounded at or after meals, but were sometimes connected with religious ceremonies, as in Boiotia, where the women proposed them at a festival of Dionysos. In the later period the religious aspect disappeared and they were employed as a form of social entertainment like other παίγνια and γελοῖα. Hired wits and parasites were expected to enliven the company. The examples we possess are of this period. The αἴνιγμα united apparently impossible opposites, the γρῖφος propounded the union of that which cannot apparently be united. The chief monographs on the subject are: Morawski *de Graecorum poesi aenigmatica* 1862, Ehlers αἴνιγμα καὶ γρῖφος 1867, *de Graecorum aenigmatis et griphis* 1875, Ohlert *Rätsel und Gesellschaftsspiele der alten Griechen* 1886.

IV. Songs of Superstition. One late specimen (xx.) is the nursery song to frighten away the schreech-owl. Originally the ἐπῳδαί were employed to heal diseases and wounds, but in course of time formulas of mystical purport, oftentimes obscure, were thought to be efficacious in warding off every kind of evil. Usually they were in prose but recited in a solemn tone.

V. Mendicants' Songs. Aristotle *Rhet.* 2. 24. 7 says the beggars sang and danced ἐν τοῖς ἱεροῖς. In the same place he mentions songs of the blind. The best-known songs of this class were those connected with certain seasons of the year when bands of boys or men solicited gifts in return for their chorals. Cf. Peppmüller *Philol.* 149. 15 ff.

1. The *Eiresione* (εἰρεσιώνη, derived from εἴρω 'say') gets its name from a custom observed at the Pyanepsia and Thargelia. Besides the procession to the temple of Apollo in Athens, it was the wont of boys, especially in the rural districts, to go from house to house carrying an olive or laurel wreath, on which there was a tuft of wool, and to sing a song full of good wishes for the inmates together with a request for a donation. St. Basil's day is thus celebrated in Greece at the present day, and a similar custom obtained until recently in Germany at Whitsuntide. An example of this song in the style of a later period is found in the collection of epigrams attributed to Homer (No. 15). The text is corrupt at places.

Δῶμα προσετραπόμεσθ' ἀνδρὸς μέγα δυναμένοιο
ὃς μέγα μὲν δύναται, μέγα δὲ *βρέμει, ὄλβιος αἰεί.
αὐταὶ ἀνακλίνεσθε θύραι· πλοῦτος γὰρ ἔσεισεν
πολλός, σὺν πλούτῳ δὲ καὶ εὐφροσύνη τεθαλυῖα
5 εἰρήνη τ' ἀγαθή. ὅσα δ' ἄγγεα, μεστὰ μὲν εἴη,
*κριθαίη δ' αἰεὶ κατὰ καρδόπου ἕρποι μᾶζα,
τοῦ παιδὸς δὲ γυνὴ κατὰ δίφρακα βήσεται ὔμμιν,
ἡμίονοι δ' ἄξουσι κραταίποδες ἐς τόδε δῶμα,
αὐτὴ δ' ἱστὸν ὑφαίνοι ἐπ' ἠλέκτρῳ βεβαυῖα.
10 νεῦμαί τοι, νεῦμαι, ἐνιαύσιος, ὥστε χελιδὼν·
ἕστηκ' ἐν προθύροις ψιλὴ πόδας· ἀλλὰ φέρ' αἶψα
*πήρης τὠπόλλωνος ἀγυρτίδος ⟨ἀγλαὰ δῶρα.⟩
εἰ μέν τι δώσεις· εἰ δὲ μή, οὐχ ἑστήξομεν·
οὐ γὰρ συνοικήσαντες ἐνθάδ' ἤλθομεν.

Plutarch (*Theseus* 22) cites the beginning of another *Eiresione*, also in a late setting:

Εἰρεσιώνη σῦκα φέρει καὶ πίονας ἄρτους
καὶ μέλι ἐν κοτύλῃ καὶ ἔλαιον ἀναψήσασθαι
καὶ κύλικ' εὔζωρον, ὡς ἂν μεθύουσα καθεύδῃς.

2. The *Crow Song* (κορώνισμα) was sung by men who requested gifts ostensibly for a crow which they carried about. A modernized form of this old song is extant, the work of Phoinix of Kolophon in Athen. 8. 359 E, which illustrates the tendency of the antiquarians of the Alexandrian period to deal with stories and subjects drawn from the life of the people. We hear of Crow songs having been current in Rhodes (Athen. 359 D).

3. The Rhodian *Swallow Song* (xxii.).

4. The Song of the Sicilian Shepherds (xxiii.).

5. The *Oven or Potters* (Κάμινος ἢ κεραμεῖς) attributed to Homer.

VI. Dance Songs and Songs of Play. Dance songs ('ring-songs' as Gawin Douglas called them) appear as early as Homer (A 603 : Apollo plays the lyre, the Muses dance and sing). The Cretan war dances afforded opportunity for improvisation. In Sparta we have the famous Parade Song (xiii.), but the *embateria* or march songs of the poets caused the popular lyric to escape the later collectors. Game songs were exceedingly common (xv. ff.).

A curious cult song entitled Ἀλῆτις was sung by Attic women in honour of Erigone, who wandered about in search of her father Ikarios and finally hanged herself. At the festival Αἰώρα the women suspended ropes from trees and swung either themselves or symbolic dolls.

VII. Satiric Songs. Here belong the Phallic songs to which Aristotle (*Poet.* 4) refers the origin of comedy. They were often sung by the Ithyphalloi and Autokabdaloi. Cf. Aristoph. *Acharn.* 263. The mill-stone song (xxiv.) directed against Pittakos also falls into this class. The line ἐγὼ δέ τυ ἐστεφάνιξα κάδωρησάμαν in *Eq.* 1225 is supposed to refer ultimately to a song of the Helots.

VIII. Songs of Love. From the time of Alkman the erotic element in artistic lyric was continually gaining ground. Sappho and Alkaios often recall the tone of the folk-lyric, and it was through their influence and that of Anakreon that the love songs of the people, which were as old as Homer (X 128 παρθένος ἠΐθεός τ' ὀαρίζετον ἀλλήλοιιν), were forced into obscurity. In Sicily the pastoral was amatory and described the unhappiness of unrequited love. A song referred to by Athen. 14. 619 E told of the suicide of Harpalyke who was despised by Iphiklos. The story of the untimely death of the beautiful Kalyke was introduced into literature by Stesichoros (Stes. xii. and 43). We have a specimen of Lokrian (xxi.) and of Chalkidian (xxv.) erotic song.

IX. Marriage Songs (ὑμέναιοι, γαμήλιοι ᾠδαί). The artistic nuptial song was based on the folk-lyric, which is attested as early as Homer (Σ 493 πολὺς δ' ὑμέναιος ὀρώρει, cf. Hes. *Shield* 274). Though Sappho's hymeneals and epithalamia reproduce the spirit of the popular song to a considerable degree, the song at the end of Aristophanes' *Birds* is nearer to the tone of the genuine folk-lyric. Fragments of popular hymeneals are exceedingly rare: ἐκκόρει κόρη κορώνη was obscure to the Greeks and has been variously interpreted by the moderns. Bergk translates *hymenaeum cane, virgo cornix*, the crow being regarded as a symbol of concord. At the wedding banquet a boy, whose parents were alive, spoke the words ἔφυγον κακόν, εὗρον ἄμεινον, while he carried about bread in a winnowing-fan. The formula may be a part of a nuptial song, but it is more probably taken from the ritual of the marriage ceremony. The refrain Ὑμήν, ὦ Ὑμέναιε is taken from the language of the people.

X. Songs of Lament appear as early as Homer, who describes the ritual observed in the case of the threnoi sung over the bodies of Hektor and Achilles. (See the Introduction.) Athenaios calls the threnetic folk-songs ὀλοφυρμοί. The ialemos was also of a popular character. The threnodoi, who were hired for the occasion, have been thought to be a mark of barbarian civilization (Ω 720), and parallels have been sought with the later Karian songs. There seems, however, no reason for discrediting the Hellenic character of the 'leaders of the dirge'; and examples of the like occur in Modern Greece. The proverb ψυχρότερος ἰαλέμου points to the lack of genuine sympathy on the part of the hired mourners.

XI. Songs that take their Names from Mythical Personages. Other forms of lament that are akin to the primitive dirge take their names from mythical persons whose early and undeserved death symbolizes the departure of the seasons and the mutability of human life. Many had Oriental prototypes. We hear of the Maneros of the Egyptians, the Bormos of the Egyptians, the Maryandinian, who was slain in summer while engaged in hunting, and the Lityerses of the Phrygians, a reaper's song in commemoration of the son of King Midas (cf. Theokr. 10. 41). In Greece the songs that fall under this class were usually sung at festive occasions, and we must beware of attributing to the Greeks a recognition of the ultimate symbolism of the lays in question.

1. The *Linos* was primarily Oriental in character; Herodotos states that he recognized it in the songs of the Phoinikians and Kyprians. Adapted to the Greek cult, it was connected with the celebration of the Rural Dionysia and symbolized the departure of summer. Strictly it is a song of the wine-press and sung by a single voice, the chorus joining in the refrain (cf. Aisch. *Agam.* 121). It bore the name αἴλινος from the cry of the mourners (hence Sappho 62 calls it οἰτόλινος), which in Phoinikian was *ai le nu* 'woe is us.' Welcker has collected from several tongues examples of similar sounds used for lament: Egyptian *lulululu*, ἐλελεῦ ἐλελεῦ, Lat. *ululare*, Serbian *lele*, *lodo*, Basque *lelo* (also personified). The Greeks made a person out of the exclamation and regarded Λίνος as the son of Urania, who, like Marsyas and Thamyris, met his death at the hands of Apollo, with whom he dared to contend in music. The Argives called him a poet, and others ascribed to him the invention of the hexameter. In this aspect he pourtrays the overthrow of a primitive style of music. Homer uses the word λίνος (Σ 570) as a general word for 'song,' and is ignorant of the Egyptian and Phoinikian threnody.

2. The *Hyacinth Song* recorded the death of the beautiful youth Ὑάκινθος, the son of Amyklas, who was killed by the quoit of Apollo (the disk of the sun). In his honour a festival was held at Amyklai during three days in the hottest month of the year. The myth represents the parching of nature under the torrid heat of the summer sun. Analogous is the Arkadian Skephros.

3. *Adonis Songs.* See the Introduction.

XII. Songs in Honour of the Gods and their Cult. Artemis, Aphrodite (iii.), Dionysos (iv., v., vi., vii.), in whose cult the *Iobacchoi* were sung, Demeter (i.), Apollo (ix.); the Mysteries (Bergk 10); the Libations (viii.). οὔπιγγοι were sung to Artemis Eileithyia.

I. Athen. 14. 618 E. Athen. quotes Semos of Delos to the effect that οὖλος or ἴουλος 'sheaf' was the name of a hymn in honour of Demeter, who thence received the name Ἰουλώ (and Οὐλώ: Eratosth. quoted below). οὖλος is derived from *Fόλνος, that which is 'pressed together' (cf. εἴλλω, εἰλέω, Dor. Fηλέω), and is not connected with ἰοῦ (or rather ἰού), because of the

mournful character of the songs to Demeter. ἴ-ουλος contains a prothetic ι as ἰ-ῶλκα, ἰ-κτίς, ἴ-φθιμος. With the name of the goddess, cf. Δημώ, Δηώ, Εἰδώ, etc. The line is the refrain of a sheaf-song, which was not confined to the formal cult of Demeter, but sung by harvesters, both men and women; Eratosth. in schol. Apoll. Rhod. 1. 972: χερνῆτις ἔριθος . . . καλοὺς ᾔειδεν ἰούλους. Some referred the song to the workers in wool (by confusion with οὖλος 'woolly'?), or to the kitchen-maids when baking cakes. These ἴουλοι were sometimes called δημήτρουλοι and καλλίουλοι. At the festival of the προηρόσια girls sang a sower's song: πάριθι, κόρη, γέφυραν· | ὅσον οὔ πω τρὶς πολέουσιν. The words ὦ Ζεῦ πάτερ, αἴθε πλούσιος γενοίμαν and ἤδη μὲν ἤδη πλέον· ὑπερβέβακεν, which are found on a vase (*Ann. d. arch. Instit.* 1837, 183), were taken by Bergk to be part of a song at the gathering of the olives; but are in fact spoken by olive merchants. Cf. Robert *Bild und Lied* 82. The variation between ἵει and ἵει is due to the confusion between ἵημι <*σίσημι (Lat. *sero, sevi*, O.H.G. *sāma* 'seed') and Ϝίεμαι 'desire,' a confusion that is as old as Homer, and occurs in Archil. 50. The sphere of ἵημι is the sphere of Demeter. The collocation of ἵει and ἵει recalls τῖον – τίον Ψ 703, 705, ὀΐω – ὀίω Ξ 454, 456, Ἆρες Ἄρες Ε 31, κᾱλός κᾰλός Alkm. xxxii., Solon 13. 21, 24, Theogn. 16, 17, Theokr. 6. 19, Kallim. 1. 55, δῖα . . . δῐὰ Γ 357, 358, ἶσος – ἴσος Theokr. 8. 19, 22. The Alexandrians, and after them the Latins (*e.g.* Virg. *Ecl.* 6. 44), delighted to play thus with quantitatively alternate forms. We may also compare νε̄κρός and νε̆κρῷ Soph. *Antig.* 1240, πᾰτρός and πᾱτρί (cf. Virg. *Aen.* 2. 663) *O. K.* 442, ὕβρις (⏓) 883, πε̄́τροισι and πέτρον *Phil.* 296, Ὕπνε (⏓) 827, *nīgris nĭgro* Hor. 1. 32. 11 (where Shorey quotes Spenser *F. Q.* 3. 2. 51 "Thrice she her turned contráry and returned | All cóntrary)."
—Metre: logaoedic.

II. The scholion in Codex Venetus B at Σ 570 (λίνον δ' ὑπὸ καλὸν ἄειδεν) says that the λίνος was a threnetic song sung by the Muses. By a series of violent changes Bergk has constructed a text that has been widely regarded as a late representation of the "oldest folk-song" of the Greeks. Now the scholiast of the Townley MS. on Σ 570 and Eustathios 1163. 59 state that the following hexameters formed an inscription at Thebes, where Linos was supposed to be buried (Paus. 9. 29. 8):—

> Ὦ Λίνε, πᾶσι θεοῖσι τετιμένε, σοὶ γὰρ ἔδωκαν
> ἀθάνατοι πρώτῳ μέλος ἀνθρώποισιν ἀεῖσαι
> ἐν ποδὶ δεξιτερῷ· Μοῦσαι δέ σε θρήνεον αὐταὶ
> μυρόμεναι μολπῇσιν, ἐπεὶ λίπες ἡλίου αὐγάς.

It has been shown by Maass (*Hermes* 32. 303; cf. Reimann

Die Prosodien 4) that the setting of the scholiast of Ven. B, so far from representing a different tradition from that of the Townley scholiast, is a late transformation; φωναῖς λιγυραῖς was added, and Φοῖβος . . . ἀναιρεῖ inserted to square with the story told by him. Again it is absurd to suppose that the verse Μοῦσαι . . . θρηνέουσιν could have occurred in a song actually sung by the Muses in honour of Linos. Since the hexameters formed a funereal inscription, they date from a late period; and an epigram cannot be an archaic folk-song. The dactylic hexameter was doubtless framed by the union of two shorter verses; but this Linos song is not evidence. ἐν ποδὶ δεξιτερῷ is=*apto numero* and has no reference to the two parts (δεξιόν, ἀριστερόν) of the hexameter.

III. Plut. *Quaest. Symp.* 3. 6. 4. Perhaps a formula from one of the Doric prayers to Aphrodite, who was called Ἀμβολογήρα ('she who delays the coming of old age') in Sparta. Cf. Paus. 3. 18. 1, Wide *Lakon. Kulte* 143, and note the Doric forms. Herodas 1. 61 τὴν μίαν ταύτην | ἁμαρτίην δὸς τῇ θεῷ (Aphr.) . . . τὸ γῆρας μὴ λάθῃ σε προσβλέψαν. Cf. Mimn. 1 and 2. Medeia possessed this rejuvenating power. Hesych. has ἀναβαλλαγόρας (-όγηρας?)· φάρμακόν τι καὶ λίθος ἐν Σάμῳ.—Metre: pherecratics (?).

IV. Schol. Aristoph. *Ranae* 479. In the Lenaian contests in honour of Dionysos the torch-bearer called out καλεῖτε θεόν, whereupon the audience shouted Σεμελήϊ' κ.τ.λ. Cf. No. viii. The δᾳδοῦχος is here the ἐξάρχων, who gives the ἐνδόσιμον (signal to the chorus to begin). Bergk wished to read Ἴακχ' ὦ to help out the anapaestic dimeter. The verse is, however, similar to Aristoph. *Aves* 331 (παρέβη μὲν θεσμοὺς ἀρχαίους) in its neglect of the caesura. With πλουτοδότα, only here of Iacchos or Dionysos, cf. ὀλβιόδωρον *Διον. orac.* 210 Hendess.

V. Song of the Eleian woman at the festival of the epiphany of Dionysos (Plut. *Aet. Gr.* 36; cf. *de Iside* 35). Dionysos received special honour in Elis, where he was born according to one tradition (*Hymn* 34. 3). He had a temple at Elis near the theatre according to Paus. 6. 26. 1, who tells us of a festival called Θυῖα at which the return of the god was invoked; and there too, by a pious fraud, D. was supposed to have filled three wine-vessels that had been placed over-night outside the city. In Argos the sound of trumpets accompanied the invocation for him to return from the lake of Lerna. This song is the liturgy employed by the priestly college of sixteen Eleian women, who were chosen from the eight tribes and had the charge of his cult (Plut. *Mul. virt.* 251 E, Weniger *Kollegium der sechzehn Frauen u. Dionysoskult in Elis* 1883).

In the Argive worship of D. he bears the name βουγενής; here he is called ταῦρος outright, as in Eur. *Bacch.* 1017 (φάνηθι ταῦρος), Lykophr. 209, and *C. I. G. Sept.* 1. 1787 (Θεοῦ Ταύρου). Usually D. is called ταυρογενής, -κερως (*Bacch.* 100 where see Sandys), -μορφος, -μέτωπος, -ωπός, etc. The type of the horned D. with idealized face was probably restored by the school of Lysippos (cf. the Lateran "Horned Dionysos") and was popular in the Hellenistic period, since the successors of Alexander were represented in this guise. The bull is the symbol of generative force (cf. A. W. Curtius *Der Stier des D.*, Jena 1882). [The Skt. *varshan* 'bull' has, it so happens, its nearest Greek equivalent in Eleian Ϝάρρενορ (gen.) = ἄρσενος.] The association of D. with the Graces is probably due, originally at least, to the fact that the latter, like the Hours, were emblematic of the fruitfulness of nature. Later the connection was spiritualized, but in Pind. *Ol.* 13. 18 (ταὶ Διωνύσου πόθεν ἐξέφανεν | σὺν βοηλάτᾳ Χάριτες διθυράμβῳ;) there is still an echo of connection on the physical side. The Graces were even called the daughters of D. and Aphrodite, or of D. and Koronis. In the valley of the Kephissos near Orchomenos the temple of D. was close to that of the Graces. At Olympia the Graces had one of the six βωμοὶ δίδυμοι (Pind. *Ol.* 5. 5) in conjunction with D., though they had their own ἱερόν at Elis, where their ξόανα were shown (Paus. 6. 24. 6). On a gem found in Müller-Wieseler 2. 383 the Graces are represented as seated between the horns of the Dionysiac bull. At banquets the first pledge was to the Graces, the Hours, and Dionysos, as the givers of festal joy, the second to Aphrodite and D. Cf. Ben Jonson: "But Venus and the Graces | Pursue thee (Bacchus) in all places." In style and metre this animalized liturgy is archaic, but the dialect contains no trace of the native Eleian, except Ἀλείων or Ἀλεῖον. Ϝαλείων is not impossible, since the digammated Ϝα(λείων) occurs on a coin as late as the third or second century. Χαρίτεσσιν would be Χαρίτοις in Eleian.—**1**. Cf. the invocation of D. in Soph. *Antig.* 1144 μολεῖν καθαρσίῳ ποδὶ Παρνασίαν | ὑπὲρ κλιτύν κ.τ.λ. which shows in the use of κ. ποδί and the inf. for the imper. traces of liturgical formula. The inf. for the imper. gives a touch of solemnity and is frequent in precepts (the 'sententious' inf.). **ἥρω**: this voc. occurs only here; we find also τὸν ἥρω and even τοῦ ἥρω. ἥρως (Schneidewin) is too easy a correction.—**2**. **σὺν Χαρ.**: so Pind. viii. 3, Bacch. ii. 9.—**5**. **βοέῳ ποδί**: cf. πόδα παρθένιον Eur. *I. T.* 130, γέροντι ποδὶ *El.* 490. πούς in periphrases points to motion on the part of the person in question. See Eur. *Herakl.* 802, Stes. iii. 6. **θύων**: = θύνω Pind. *Pyth.*

10. 54. Dist. *θύω furere*=*θυίω* from *θύω properare*=*θύνω*.—**7.** With **ἄξιε** in the refrain Welcker *Götterlehre* 1. 329 would connect the mystical names Axieros, Axiokersos.

Different views have been taken of the metre. V. 1 is a paroemiac with the form — ⏑́ — ⏑́ ⏑ ⏑ ⏑́ ⏓ as in the proverb *αἴρειν ἔξω πόδα πηλοῦ*. V. 2 was thought to contain solemn molossi (Bergk *Gr. Lit.-Ges.* 1. 384), or trochaic semanti (Leutsch *Philol.* 11. 730), or iambi orthii (Christ *Metrik* 271). V. 3 is a prosodiac (⏑́ — ⏑́ ⏑ ⏑ ⏑́ ⏓); v. 4 a molossus, unless we assume, as is probable, that *'Αλείων* has fallen out; v. 5 is a prosodiac (⏑́ ⏑ ⏑ ⏑́ ⏑ ⏑ ⏑́ —); vv. 6 and 7 dactylic dipodies. Usener (*Altgr. Versbau* 80) regards this strophe as exemplifying the oldest form of Greek metre, which counted theses only, was indifferent to the following syllable (⏑⏓⏑), and allowed suppression of arses. The original line of four theses, Usener thinks, has been reduced to three and a half, except in the refrain *ἄξιε ταῦρε, ἄξιε ταῦρε* (in one line). The half stress he finds in the final syllable of each verse. Thus v. 2 — ′ ′ ⏑ ⏑ ′ ‵, v. 5 ′ ⏑ ⏑ ′ ⏑ ⏑ ′ ‵.

VI. Ithyphallic song. Semos in Athen. 14. 622 B says that the Ithyphalloi entered the theatre in silence, but when they reached the middle of the orchestra they wheeled round and addressed the spectators. They wore female garments, chitons that were shot with white, brocaded loose sleeves, and veils that reached to their knees. Their heads were crowned with flowers and they wore masks representing the faces of drunken men. We hear of Ithyphalloi in connection with the fetes referred to in xxvii. **ἀνάγετε** 'back'! *referte pedes*; cf. Aristoph. *Aves* 1720 *ἄναγε, δίεχε, πάραγε, πάρεχε*. Metre: iambics followed by ithyphallics. Wilamowitz and Kaibel adopt an arrangement in trochaics with a closing ithyphallic. With *ποιεῖτε* (⏑ — ⏑) cf. *ποεῖ, ποητής* on Attic inscriptions and skol. vii. 4. Wilam. would delete *ὁ θεός*.

VII. Entrance song of the Phallophoroi. Semos in Athen. 14. 622 C reports that the Phallophoroi entered the theatre in measured tread partly from the parodos, partly from the middle door. They wore no masks but had on visors made of thyme and rosy flowers (*παιδέρως*), and were crowned with chaplets of violets and ivy. They also wore thick cloaks. The fragment is late and scarcely genuine folk-lyric. Cf. Eur. *Hippol.* 72 ff.—**1. ἀγλαΐζομεν**: cf. *Ol.* 1. 14 *ἀγλαΐζεται δὲ καὶ | μουσικᾶς ἐν ἀώτῳ*, Theokr. epigr. 1. 4 *Δελφὶς ἐπεὶ πέτρα τοῦτό τοι ἀγλάϊσεν* 'bare this to thine honour.'—**2.** The iambics (*ἁπλοῦν ῥυθμόν*) were sung to an elaborate and probably new accompaniment; cf. *νεοσίγαλος τρόπος* of the musical mode,

Pind. *Ol.* 3. 4.—**3. καινάν**: cf. Timoth. vii. 2. **ἀπαρθένευτον**: L. and S. 'unfitting a maiden.' Rather 'virgin,' as in Soph. Frag. 283, =ἀκέραιος, καθαρά (Hesych.) and like ἀκήρατος Ibyk. i. 4. Emphasis is laid on the novelty of the song.—**5. κατάρχομεν**: see on Alkm. xxviii. Line 5 may be an epode, but is probably incomplete. It is noteworthy that the caesura is invariably the semiseptinaria. Iambic processional songs sung by a chorus are not over-common. Cf. Aristoph. *Acharn.* 264, *Ranae* 384. Usually we have anapaests or trochees. Iambics are frequently used to accompany the movement of a single actor.

VIII. Schol. on Aristoph. *Pax* 968 (ἀλλ' εὐχώμεθα· | τίς τῇδε; ποῦ ποτ' εἰσὶ πολλοὶ κἀγαθοί;) reports that τίς τῇδε was called out during the libation, whereupon those present reverently exclaimed πολλοὶ κἀγαθοί. By this means the *profanum vulgus*, those who were unprepared to participate in the rite, were excluded from it (ἑκὰς ἑκὰς ὅστις ἀλιτρός). When the libation was concluded the participants exclaimed ἐκκέχυται (schol. Aristoph. *Ranae* 479).—Metre: 1. iambic dimeter, 2. logaoedic. Or we may take the verses as ionics: ⏑ — ⏑ — | — — ⏑ — and — ⏑ ⏑ — | ⏑ — ⏑ —.

IX. Herakleid. *Allegor. Homer.* 6 says that this song was in everybody's mouth. Cf. Proklos *Theol. Platon.* 6. 12 ὁ Ἥλιος Ἀπόλλων ὑμνούμενος χαίρει διαφερόντως, καὶ Ἀπόλλων Ἥλιος ἀνακαλούμενος and the song in Festus p. 318 *tu es Apollo, tu Sol in coelo deus.* Usener *R. M.* 23. 373 maintains that the verse is either from Euripides (but note the violation of Porson's law) or New Comedy. Cf. Timoth. viii.—Metre: iambic trimeter.

X. Julian *Caesares* 318. Proclamation of the herald at the opening of the games. Cf. Soph. *El.* 683 ὅτ' ᾔσθετ' ἀνδρὸς ὀρθίων κηρυγμάτων.—**1. ἀγών**: personified.—**2. ταμίας**: so 'steward' in American athletic contests. **καιρὸς δὲ καλεῖ**: cf. Soph. *Phil.* 466 and ὡς ἀκμὴ καλεῖ Eur. *Hek.* 1042.—**3.** Cf. inc. trag. 298 ἀγὼν γὰρ οὐ μέλλοντος ἀθλητοῦ μένει | ἀλκήν.—Metre: anapaestic dimeters (Hertlein wrote as monometers).

XI. Lucian *Vita Demonactis* 65. Proclamation at the closing of the contest. Bergk inserted a fragment (15) from Moiris 193. 4 spoken by the herald to the contestants when they 'toed the line.' We read ἐπὶ βαλβῖδος θέτε πόδα παρὰ πόδα (cf. Tyrt. 11. 31 καὶ πόδα παρ ποδὶ θείς), but the words are perhaps not meant to be metrical. Paus. 5. 7. 10 (cf. 6. 14. 10 and Philost. *de arte gymn.* 55) informs us that, in order to stimulate the contestants, the notes of the Pythian (auletic) nome were sounded when the contestants engaged in the part of the pentathlon devoted to the leaping match. But the use of verses to start a race is hardly credible even in Greece.

XII. Lucian *Saltat.* 10. Sung by the Lakonians while dancing; cf. Müller *Dor.* 2. 332. **πόρρω**: =*βέλτιον*. **γάρ** may not belong to the words of the song or it may be the 'prefatory' *γάρ*. **κωμάξατε**: Dor. aor. Hesych. glosses the verb with *ὀρχεῖσθαι*.—Metre: probably iambic (trochaic). Mure compared the rhythm of the modern Neapolitan tarantella.

XIII. Plut. *Vita Lycurgi* 21, who says that in the Spartan festivals there were three choruses (*τριχορία*) consisting respectively of old men, men in the prime of life, and youths (*Ὑαλκάδαι*). Each chorus sang the verse appropriate to its age. The verses have sometimes been wrongly referred to Tyrtaios on the authority of Pollux 4. 107 *τριχορίαν δὲ Τύρταιος ἔστησε, τρεῖς Λακώνων χορούς, καθ' ἡλικίαν ἑκάστην, παῖδας ἄνδρας γέροντας.* Plut. *Consol.* 15 quotes a Lakonian epigram: *νῦν ἀμὲς* (not *ἄμμες* as MSS.) *πρόσθ' ἄλλοι ἐθάλεον, αὐτίκα δ' ἄλλοι,* | *ὧν ἀμὲς γενεὰν οὐκέτ' ἐποψόμεθα.* Cf. Δ 405 *ἡμεῖς τοι πατέρων μέγ' ἀμείνονες εὐχόμεθ' εἶναι.*—**2. ἡμές**=*ἐσμέν. εἰμές* is not early Lakonian. **λῆς** <*λάεις*; Dor. *λάω*=*ἐθέλω*. **αὐγάσδεο**=*αὐγάζεο*, which is perhaps the preferable reading. The *σδ* recalls the Aiolic writing.—**3. κάρρονες**: from **καρσσων* <**καρτιων*; Gortynian *κάρτων* <**καρττων*. With the change in the responsive choruses we may compare the musical transition (*μεταβολή*) in the 'three-fold' nome of Sakadas. It began in the Dorian, continued in the Phrygian, and concluded in the Lydian mode.—Metre: iambic trimeter.

XIV. Athen. 14. 629 E. Flower song (*ἄνθεμα*) with mimetic dance. The first verse was sung by the leader, the second by the chorus of girls. Cf. Theokr. 2. 1 *πᾷ μοι ταὶ δάφναι*;—Metre: iambic tetrameter catalectic. I have scanned the fragment without anacrusis to show better that, while the tribrachs in the even feet express the lively character of the dance, the slower movement of the quest is brought out by the irrational, as contrasted with the regular, iambics of v. 2.

XV. Pollux 9. 123, Eust. 1243. 29. The players put a *ταινία* over the eyes of one of their comrades, who was placed in the centre and called out *χαλκῆν* etc., while the others cried *θηράσεις* etc. striking him with papyrus whips or their hands until one was caught. Ancient Greek (and modern Cretan) boys used to tie a lighted taper of wax to a bronze-coloured flying-beetle, which they then chased in the dark. This seems to have given the name to this form of the game of blindman's buff, in which the pursued are the 'bronze flies.' So Smith's *Dict. of Antiq.* s. v. *Myinda.* Others think the name is not derived from the colour of the insect, but from the pertinacity with which the pursued worry the pursuer; ἡ δὲ μυῖα θρασεῖα. In modern Greece there is the game τυφλομυῖα, in France *mouche*, in Italy *mosca cieca*, in Germany *blinde Fliege.*—Metre: paroemiacs (all spondees).

XVI. Pollux 9. 125, Eust. 1914. 56. The Tortoise Game (χέλει χελώνη) was played by girls in the following manner. One of the company, called 'tortoise,' sat in the centre, while her playmates ran around plying her with questions. Question and answer were in iambics, and the puzzling questions demanded quick-witted replies. Somewhat similar was the game of χυτρίνδα, in which a boy in the centre was 'pot,' or ran about with a pot on his head and answered ἐγὼ Μίδας when the others called out τίς τὴν χύτραν (φέρει); De Fouquières (*Les Jeux des Anciens* p. 39) cites the testimony of a modern traveller who saw girls in Scio holding each other by the hand and encircling one of their companions as a prisoner, who was not released until she had capped the distich of the chorus. Grasberger thinks some old legend would explain the dialogue in the ancient game; but De Fouquières goes too far when he proposes to explain the game as the survival of a song of lament, and suggests that it echoes the responsive lamentations in the *Persians*.—**1.** **χέλει** or χέλῑ (Pollux; which is the old, which the itacistic spelling is uncertain) is a mere alliteration of the first three letters of χελώνη ('tortitortoise'). Some write the words separately, others conjointly as πονωπόνηρος, the old reading in Aristoph. *Vespae* 466, *Lysist.* 350 (Lobeck *Paralip.* 350). Starkie cp. γονῇ γενναῖε Soph. *O. T.* 1469. A better parallel is the magical phrase ἀρθρῖτ' ἀρθριτική Heim *Incant. mag.* no. 43; cf. *corce corcedo* Marcel. *de med.* 21. 3. **ποῖεις**: from ποιέεις, the first ε of which became ι after the expulsion of the ι of the diphthong. Cf. Boiot. ποϊόμενος *S. G. D.-I.* 386. 4, Herakleia ποῖων *ib.* 4629. 175.—**2.** **μᾱρύομ(αι)** is the only case, apart from μανύει Bacch. 67 (B 43), of a denominative verb in -υω that has a ῡ in the present stem which is not due to metrical compulsion (as ἐρητύοντο O 3, ἐπιθύουσι Σ 175). Theokr. 1. 29 has μᾱρύεται, where, as here, the υ is due to the influence of the future and aorist stem. **Μιλησίαν**: cf. οἴκοι γάρ ἐστιν ἔριά μοι Μιλήσια Aristoph. *Lysist.* 729, στρώμασιν Μιλησίοις *Ranae* 542, *Milesia vellera* Verg. *Georg.* 4. 334: cf. Theokr. 15. 125 ff. The best sheep came from Miletos, Athen. 12. 540 D.—**4.** There is no need to question whether the 'white horses' are breakers or real horses. If horses at all, then they are white like those of princes; see on Ibyk. ix. 1. **ἅλατο** may indicate a sudden movement in the game.—Metre: iambic trimeter.

XVII. Aristoph. Frag. 346, Pollux 9. 123: when the sun passes under a cloud children clap their hands and cry out ἔξεχε etc. The song was called φιληλιάς (Athen. 14. 619 B), a name formed from the exclamation φίλ' Ἥλιε as Εὔιος Εὐοία from εὐοῖ, Ἰήιος from ἰή, Λίνος from αἴλινος. Cf. the prayer of the Athenians in Marcus Anton. 5. 7: ὗσον, ὗσον, ὦ φίλε Ζεῦ, | κατὰ τῆς ἀρούρας τῆς Ἀθηναίων καὶ τῶν πεδίων. **ἔξεχε**: πρὶν ἥλιον ἐξέχειν Demosth. 1071. 3; cf. πρὸς ἥλιον ἀνίσχοντα Hdt. 3. 98, Theogn. 26 οὐδὲ γὰρ ὁ Ζεὺς | οὔθ' ὕων πάντεσσ' ἀνδάνει οὔτ' ἀνέχων. The Greek song recalls our "Rain, rain, go away." —Metre: trochaic dimeter catalectic.

XVIII. Plut. *Quaest. Gr.* 35, *Thes.* 16. Sung by the Bottiaian girls in festal dances. Bottiaia in Makedonia was settled by Athenians.—Metre: iam. dim. catal.

XIX. Athen. 14. 619 C says that this line occurred in a pastoral poem by a lyric poetess Eriphanis, who fell in love with the hunter Menalkas. In her passion she roamed through the coppice on the mountain sides until she compelled not only men, who before had been without natural affection, but even the most savage beasts to join her lament. In desert places she cried aloud this song. Eriphanis, the maid of the dawn, is called a poetess solely because she was introduced as giving utterance to the line.—Metre: perhaps a first pherecratic; or we may have a specimen of folk-lyric that does not take strict account of the quantity of unstressed syllables.

XX. Festus 314, who says that it is a nursery song to avert witches (cf. the στρίγλαις in Modern Greek: Schmidt *Neugr. Volksleben* 136). It would seem rather a ditty to ward off the screech-owl (though Pliny *H. N.* 11. 232 is unable to class the bird). Old women consorted with *striges* or became such themselves. Cf. Tibull. 1. 5. 52 *e tectis strix violenta canat*, Propert. 3. 6. 29, 4. 5. 17, Ovid *Fasti* 6. 133 *grande caput, stantes oculi, rostra apta rapinis,* | *canities pinnis, unguibus hamus inest.* | *nocte volant puerosque petunt nutricis egentes* | *et vitiant cunis corpora rapta suis.* | *carpere dicuntur lactentia viscera rostris* | *et plenum poto sanguine guttur habent.* | *est illis strigibus nomen: sed nominis huius* | *causa, quod horrendum stridere nocte solent.* The cry of the owl was a *letale carmen*. Birds and insects, *e.g.* the cricket, that made a noise at night were objects of ancient superstition because they belonged with the ghosts who *stridunt* (Pliny *H. N.* 29. 138). The horned-owl was a bird of death. The Romans nailed an owl on the house-door to ward off disaster. The heart of a night-owl was laid over an ant-hole in a garden. Many birds and insects were regarded as boding misfortune (vulture, raven, hawk, crane, crow, cock, spider, caterpillar). On songs similar to this see Heim *Incant. mag.* 500. It may be doubted whether these verses are older than the Alexandrian or early Roman period.—**1. ἀποπομπεῖν** of averting evil (*ἀποπομπὴν ποιεῖσθαι* Isokr. 106 B).—**2. ἀνωνυμίαν**: *infandam.* **ὠκυπόρους ἐπὶ νῆας**: Homer in the nursery.—Metre: uncertain, perhaps ionics. Bergk found brief 'Doric' verses: *σ. ἀ* | *ν.* ⟨*γᾶς,*⟩ | *σ. ἀ. λ.* | *ὄρνιν ἀνώνυμον* ⟨*ἐχθρῶν*⟩ | *ὠ. ἐ. ν.*

XXI. Athen. 15. 697 B. A Lokrian *Tagelied.* The song is of literary interest because it is the only representative in Greek of a class of poetry that became immensely popular in the Middle Ages. Perhaps the *Tagelied* was first cultivated by the Lokrians, who were notorious for their erotic poetry and for the meretricious character of their musical mode. In more modern times it was native to Provence, where the morning song of the watcher on the tower was a conventional feature which was retained by Wolfram von Eschenbach, the master of this form of lyric; though usually in Germany we find valedictory duets. In English we have the parting of Romeo and Juliet (3. 5): "Wilt thou be gone? It is not yet near day." (Cf. Bartsch *Ueber die romanischen und deutschen Tagelieder* 1865, Fränkel *Shakespeare und das Tagelied* 1893). Until we know the source of Athenaios, it is inadvisable to attempt to restore the Lokrian forms. The poem may have been composed in a conventional mixed dialect that is different from the language of the bronzes of Oiantheia. The song is scarcely older than the fourth century and probably later. The inscriptions give us no information about certain forms: *ἄμμε* and *κεῖνον* may not be Lokrian. *φρίν* and *ἀμάρα* are found in *S. G. D.-I.* 1. 1478. Points of resemblance between this Lokrian song and the Hellenistic erotic fragment edited by Grenfell and Hunt have led Crusius to refer both to the hilarody, a species of lyric described in Athen. 14. 621 B. The occasion for singing the Lokrian song was probably the symposium.—**1.** Cf. *ὦ τί λέγεις*; Plato *Protag.* 309 D.—**2. κεῖνον**: a characteristic touch; the lady uses the pronoun for her husband.—**3. δειλάκραν**: cf. Alk. xxxiii. *ἔμε δείλαν.*—**4.** Cf. Wolfram (88) *Die Kammer schon erhellte* | *Des Morgensternes Licht* in Simrock's version; *Rom. and Jul.* 3. 5. 35, "O, now be gone; more light and light it grows."—**5.** Cf. Praxilla iii. *ὦ διὰ τῶν θυρίδων.*—Metre: ionics (?) (Hermann cretics). Cf. Hanssen *A. J. P.* 9. 458, who reads *πρίν κα* 2, *κ' ἤδη* and *ὀρῇς* 4, and compares Aristoph. *Thesmoph.* 106 ff. for the metre.

XXII. Athen. 8. 360 B (vv. 1-5), Eust. *Od.* 1914. 45. The Rhodian Swallow Song or χελιδονισμός. The usual name given to this species of mendicant folk-song is χελιδόνισμα, which is attested only in Modern Greek, but is to be inferred, from the analogy of κορώνισμα, as existing also in the classical language. The boys who went from house to house soliciting gifts on the appearance of the swallow were called χελιδονισταί. Perhaps they carried about with them the figure of the bird. To the superstitious even the swallow might be a bird of ill omen. Aelian *N. A.* 10. 34 tells of the swallow foreboding evil to a military expedition, and one of the 'symbols' of Pythagoras was ὁμωροφίους χελιδόνας μὴ ἔχειν, though this may refer to chattering foreigners. There were, however, occasions when the swallow was of avail as a preventive against disease in man and beast (Pliny *H. N.* 29. 128, 30. 33, and 148); and to most people in ancient, as in modern times (cf. *Class. Rev.* 5. 1, 230 ff.), the swallow was a bird of good omen, the harbinger of spring, like the nightingale (Sa. xv.): cf. Stes. ix., Sim. xxxiv., Aristoph. *Thesmoph.* 1 ὦ Ζεῦ, χελιδὼν ἆρά ποτε φανήσεται, Frag. 499, Chionides Frag. 8, and other passages (Thompson *Greek Birds* 188). The Greek proverb was μία γὰρ χελιδὼν ἔαρ οὐ ποιεῖ (Arist. *Eth.* 1098 a 18). Like the εἰρεσιώνη, the χελιδόνισμα was a song of the spring-tide, as the κορώνισμα was a song of the autumn.

In his work on the Rhodian festivals Theognis (cited by Athen. *l.l.*) says that this song was sung in Boedromion. Since a song of the spring is inappropriate in September, Bergk (*Kl. Schr.* 2. 151) thought that, at some later period, it was transferred from spring to autumn when the possibility of abundant gifts was greater. Farnell suggested that Athen. was thinking of the εἰρεσιώνη and that the mention of Boedromion is due to a confusion with the Thargelia. But it is more likely that the Rhodian month Badromios, for which Theogn. or Athen. substitutes the Attic form, did not correspond in order of time to the Attic Boedromion, but to the season when the swallow did appear. The order of the Rhodian months is uncertain, but Paton (*Inscript. of Cos* p. 330) makes Badromios correspond to Attic Gamelion, though he suggests that a change in the order he establishes would make it correspond with February, a month that would suit the time of the first appearance of the bird (see Mommsen *Jahreszeiten* p. 253 ff.). On the other hand Latyschew *Ueber einige äolische und dorische Kalender*, St. Petersb. 1884 (cf. Bischoff *De fastis Graecorum antiquioribus* in the *Leipz. Stud.* 7. 383, 407) equates Badromios with Maimakterion.

Modern Analogies. In Passow's *Popul. Carm. Graeciae rec.* there are four χελιδονίσματα (306-308). No. 307 is from Thessaly: χελιδόνα ἔρχεται | ἀπ' τὴν ἄσπρη θάλασσαν· | θάλασσαν ἐπέρασε | καὶ σπείρ' οἰκονόμησε, | κάθησε καὶ λάλησε, | πέτραν κατα-λύσαι. | μάρτη μ', μάρτη μου καλὲ | καὶ φλεβάρη φοβερέ, | κἂν χιονίσῃς, κἂν πουτίσῃς, | πάλιν ἄνοιξιν μυρίζεις, etc. (A different form of this song appears in Fauriel *Chants populaires* 2. 256). No. 307 A is also from Thessaly: ἦρθεν, ἦρθε χελιδόνα, | ἦρθε κι' *ἄλλη μελιηδόνα, | κάθησε καὶ λάλησε | καὶ γλυκὰ κελάδησε· | μάρτη, μάρτη μου καλὲ | καὶ φλεβάρη φοβερέ, | κἂν φλεγίσῃς, κἂν τσικνίσῃς, | καλοκαῖρι θὰ μυρίσῃς· | κἂν χιονίσῃς, κἂν κακίσῃς, | πάλιν ἄνοιξιν θ' ἀνθήσῃς. | θάλασσαν ἐπέρασα*, etc. Bent *Cyclades* 434 reports a swallow song from Kythnos. Cf. Wachsmuth *Das alte Griechenland im neuen* 36, Kind *Neugr. Anthol.* 73. In Makedonia a song is sung on the 1st of March while a wooden swallow is kept turning around on a cylinder. This emblematic swallow may have existed in ancient times. Late writers (Dio Chrys. 53, p. 276, Aristeid. 47, p. 430, Theodoret 4. 728; cf. Hussey, Am. Phil. Assoc. *Proceed.* 22. xliii., Mulvany, *C. R.* 11. 221), alluding to Plato's dismissal of the poet from his republic (398 A), say that he is to be crowned and anointed with oil, as women do with swallows—evidently a form of propitiating the wooden bird.—Further examples of mendicant songs: In the Grisons boys go about singing songs on the *chalanda Mars* and collect gifts; and in Rome presents were made on the first of March. In Holstein the boys used to carry a dead fox in a basket—the sign of the death of winter. In the Rhine country a cock was laid in a basket and carried about (Grimm *Reinhart Fuchs* ccxix., ccxcvi.). Farnell quoted a song still sung by children in the Isle of Man as they go about in winter: "The night is cold, our shoon are thin, | Gie's a cake, and let us rin." In England poor children levy contributions on St. Stephen's day and on May-day; as in Germany on St. Martin's evening. Cf. Grimm *Deut. Myth.* 2. 637.

The desire of the Greeks to find an author or 'inventor' for everything gave birth to the story that the means of collecting money adopted by the *χελιδονισταί* was first instituted by Kleobulos, the tyrant of Lindos in Rhodes and one of the Sages, at a time of public distress. The institution was called *ἀγερμός collection* (cf. the Ital. *misericordia*). This song is illustrated by a vase (Baumeister fig. 2128): a swallow appears over the heads of a man, a youth, and a boy. The youth exclaims *ἰδοὺ χελιδών*, the man *νὴ τὸν Ἡρακλέα*, the boy *αὑτηί*, and (perhaps) the man *ἔαρ ἤδη*. Cf. Aristoph. *Eq.* 419 *σκέψασθε, παῖδες· οὐχ ὁρᾶθ'; ὥρα νέα, χελιδών*, a line which may echo a swallow song (as Sa. 88 *τί με Πανδίονις ὦ Ἤραννα χελίδων*). *Dialect:* the native form of the Doric dialect had already been partly obliterated by the Κοινή when Theognis inserted the poem into his work on the Rhodian festivals; and no doubt Theognis was not over-careful about retaining each bit of local colour. The Rhodian futures with -*ευ* (*e.g.* *ἐπιμεληθησεῦντι*; cf. *οἰσεῦμες* Theokr. 15. 133) would not suit the metre in ll. 13, 16. *ἀπίωμες* in 12 may justify us in adopting

-μες in 14, 16, though the inscriptions have -μεν as early as 300-250 B.C. (Cauer *Delectus* 178. 4). εἰ in 13 occurs on an inscription of the fourth century (Cauer 177. 30), but for ἄν in 17 we should expect at least εἴ κα. The genitive in -ου is supported by inscriptions. Digamma is lost in οἴκου 7. The Doric accus. in καλᾱ̆ς ὥρᾱς l. 2. For μιν 16 we expect νιν.—**1.** Cf. the *Eiresione* 10-12, which verses are probably taken from another swallow song. **ἦλθε**: for the repetition cf. Aristoph. *Aves* 679 ξύντροφ' ἀηδοῖ, | ἦλθες, ἦλθες.—**2. ὥρας**: see on Alkm. xxvii., ἦρος ὧραι Eur. *Kykl.* 506.—**3. κᾱλούς** but κᾰλάς in 2, cf. on No. i. In this verse and 5 (*vulgo* κἀπί) καί has been omitted to avoid the rhythm ∸ ⏓ ∸ ⏑ ⏑ ∸ ⏓. **ἐνιαυτούς**: poetic exaggeration, not 'seasons.' Cf. ἔτος περιπλομένων ἐνιαυτῶν α 16, ὥραις ἐτῶν καὶ ἐνιαυτῶν Plato *Laws* 906 C. (Prellwitz in the *Festschrift für Ludwig Friedlaender* shows that ἐνιαυτός is the day on which the year (ἔτος) has come back to its starting point and the world is again ἐνὶ αὐτῷ.)—**6.** Eustath. read οὐ (instead of σύ), since he paraphrases οὐ παλάθαν ζητοῦμεν, and Ahrens defended the negative on the ground that long monosyllables may be treated as short in folk-poetry. σύ does not denote contrast, but strengthens the imperative (Bacch. ix. 76). **προκύκλει** 'roll out,' only here; used colloquially with reference to the abundance of dainties. There is, however, no reference to an ἐκκύκλημα (Ilgen).—**7.** πίονα οἶκον ι 35. Cf. Phoinix 18 ἀλλ' ὦγαθοὶ 'πορέξαθ' ὧν μυχὸς πλουτεῖ.—**13.** Cf. *Eiresione* 13 ff., where there is also a shift in the metre. **εἰ-δώσεις**: not the minatory εἰ with the future, but the future of present intention; Goodwin *M. T.* 407. The connotation of the εἰ δὲ μή clause is minatory. The Laur. of Athen. adds ἐλλειπτικῶς ἔχει, ἔστι δὲ καὶ παρ' ὑπόνοιαν—'we'll thank you and be off, if you are going to give us something.'—**14. φέρωμες**: 'carry off'; for ἀποφέρωμεν. The subj. is used much like a future, as in Α 262, μ 383 (Goodwin *M. T.* 284).—**17. ἂν δέ**: Wilam. conj. αἴ κα δέ.—**19.** Cf. Phoinix 8 ὦ παῖ, θύρην ἄγκλινε. The aor. in Aristoph. *Eccles.* 962 (τὴν θύραν ἄνοιξον) looks to the conclusion of the act.—Metre: the forms of the prosodiac, or adonic with anacrusis ⏓⏓, that are employed are ∸ ⏑ ⏑ ∸ ⏓ (11. 17); — ⁞ ∸ ⏑ ⏑ ∸ ⏓ (1. 3. 7-10); ⏑ ⏑ ⁞ ∸ ⏑ ⏑ ∸ ⏓ (2. 4-6. 18). The dactyls may be in $\frac{3}{8}$ time. 12 is a pleading trochaic tetram. (with the caesura of comedy, *e.g.* Aristoph. *Nubes* 620) forming the transition to the bolder iambics of 13-16, which may have been recited. Usener adopts a different arrangement which gets rid of the trochaics. 19-20 iamb. trim. After the introductory verse, in accordance with the fashion of folk-song, we have libration of couplets. On the metre and text see Usener p. 81 ff.

XXIII. The argument to Theokr. *id.* 3, in discussing the origin of bucolic poetry, says that the country folk sang songs in honour of Artemis, who had recently re-established concord among the Syracusans; and that rustic minstrelsy took its rise from this circumstance. In the singing contests the winner took the loaf of the loser, and all who lost roamed from village to village collecting food. To their songs, which were free of jests and fun, they added for the sake of good luck δέξαι etc. Diomedes *Artis gramm.* (3. 486 Keil) says *antequam Hiero rex Syracusas expugnaret morbo Sicilia laborat. Variis et adsiduis caerimoniis Dianam placantes finem malis invenerunt, eamque Lyaeam cognominaverunt quasi solutricem malorum.* The shepherds joined in the thanksgiving and a pastoral contest was instituted which finally took place in the theatre. Probus says *quod genus religionis hodie conversum est in quaestum. Iidem sunt enim qui Bucolistae nominantur.*

Note the balance in the lines and see on Sa. xxxvi.—**4.** **ἐκαλέσσατο** 'called down' does not seem the appropriate word; hence Hermann κἀχαρίσσατο, Cerrato ἀν- or κἀνεκαλέσσατο. Bergk's ἐκλᾴζετο *quem dea claustris suis retinebat* is obscure. **τῆνα**: Artemis, the bucolic goddess because ἀγροτέρα, φιλαγρέτις.—Metre: logaoedic (glyconics and pherecratics).

XXIV. Plut. *Sept. Sap. Conv.* 14 (157 E). Song of the Millstone. It has been shown by Wilamowitz *Hermes* 25. 225 that the ultimate source of Plutarch was here Klearchos, the scholar of Aristotle, and that the words put into the mouth of Thales: 'When I was in Eresos I heard a woman singing the song ἄλει etc. while she turned her hand-mill,' are those of Klearchos. Neither the imperf. ἄλει nor the word βασιλεύων suits the time of Plutarch's story. How long before Klearchos the poem was composed, is uncertain; probably it was long after the time of Pittakos. The story about Pittakos and the mill cannot be traced beyond Klearchos (*apud* Diog. Laert. 1. 81), who recounted that the Lesbian statesman was accustomed to take his exercise by grinding corn, an anecdote that reappears in Clement of Alex. *Paid.* 3. 10, p. 284 and Aelian *V. H.* 7. 4. Whether there is any historical foundation for the story cannot be discovered. But it is not impossible that it was the result of the attacks made upon Pittakos' lowly birth by the aristocrats of Lesbos (Alk. xviii.). It was not difficult to invent stories about the Thrakian whom Alkaios held up to ridicule with his 'flat-foot,' 'fat-paunch,' and 'braggart.' This source of the poem is at least more probable than that which sees in it a confession that

the aisymnetes of Mytilene did not disdain a humble occupation. In ἄλει in l. 2. there is doubtless a *double entendre*.
Strict Aiolic would be ἄλη, Πίτταικος, and Μυτιλήνας. The poem is too early for the accentual scansion which is found in it by Reisig, Ritschl, Hermann, and Christ *Metrik* 374, who brings as a parallel the (misquoted) Attic inscription *C. I. G.* 521 = *C. I. A.* 3. 398 : ἐκ τῶν ἰδίων τοὺς πυλῶνας τῇ πόλει, which, however, dates from the end of the second or beginning of the third century A.D., when accentual scansion was beginning to appear. Flach regards the metre as logaoedic. I have followed Wilamowitz in accepting ionics, but v. 1 is difficult and perhaps incomplete. μύλα as vocative may have ᾰ, as Δίκα Sa. xxix., but the ᾱ of the nom. may be retained, as in Sa. xl. In the first case we may read μύλ', as Ψάπφ' Sa. i. 20.

XXV. Plut. *Amator.* 17 (761 A). Sung by the Chalkidians of Euboia in commemoration of the Pharsalian Kleomachos who lost his life as their ally against the Eretrians after having given proof of his affection for a beautiful youth. The pederasty of Chalkis was notorious. It was imported by Ionia from Lydia in the first half of the sixth century.—**2.** **ἀγαθοῖσιν** : the εὐγενεῖς, *boni.* **ὁμιλεῖν** : the infinitive is epexegetical to μὴ . . . ἀγαθοῖσιν.—**3.** **σύν** with an abstract noun as in Bacch. i. 5, ii. 52, etc., not elsewhere in minor melic poetry. **λυσιμελής** : cf. Sa. xvi. **θάλλει** : Terp. vi.—Metre : dact.-epitrite as used by Stesichoros of Himera, the metropolis of which was Chalkis. Fick would adopt Ionic η throughout.

XXVI. Plut. *Vita Lys.* 18, who says that Lysander was the first among the Greeks to whom the cities erected altars as to a god and offered sacrifices, and that he was the first man in whose honour a paian was composed. In Samos, where this song was sung (Athen. 15. 696 E : ᾄδεσθαι imperf. inf.), the apotheosis of the victor at Aigospotamoi and the conqueror of Athens found expression in the substitution of the Λυσάνδρεια for the Ἡραῖα. At the end of the Peloponnesian war the muse trafficked in songs with 'silvered faces.' The poet Antilochos took money from Lysander, Choirilos sold himself to the conqueror, and Antimachos, the admiration of Plato's youth, vied with Nikeratos in a poetical contest the subject of which was the glory of Lysander. Crusius suggests that Aristonoos, a kitharoede of the time of Lysander, may be the same Aristonoos as the author of the Delphic paian (though this was probably inscribed between 235 and 210) and the composer of this paian With regard to the Delphic paian, at least, this conjecture is ill-supported by the fact that the inscription speaks of him only as a poet, not as a kitharoede. For like profanation of the religious lyric see the Introduction under *Paian.* The dialect of the fragment is the mixed poetical language of the time.—**2.** **εὐρυχόρου**: of Lakedaimon in Homer, *ο* 1. The refrain may have been *ἰήϊε Παιάν*, which gives the desired catalectic close (≳ ⁞ ⏗ ⏑ ⏑ ⊔ ⊔ ⊼). See on Timotheos viii. This song is an imitation of the older songs in prosodiacs all of which have been lost.

XXVII. Athen. 6. 253 c ff. Ithyphallic Song to Demetrios Poliorketes. 'The Athenians received Dem. on his return from Leukadia and Kerkyra, not only with frankincense, and crowns, and libations of wine, but they went so far as to go out to meet him with processional choruses and ithyphalloi, and dancing and singing, and stood in front of him in dense crowds, dancing and singing, and saying that he was the only true god, etc. And they addressed supplications and prayed to him.' This comes from the history of Demochares, the cousin of Demosthenes. On the extravagant honours paid to Demetrios see Plutarch's *Life*, and Grote, chap. 96.

The date of the poem is uncertain. According to Droysen (*Hellenismus*² 2. 190), Dem. returned to Athens in April 302 B.C. and in the same month was initiated into the Lesser and the Greater Mysteries, though the first were regularly celebrated in February, the latter in September. This violation of the sacred law, which enjoined that a year must elapse between the two initiations, was effected by a decree that revolutionized the calendar: Munichion was first called Anthesterion, then Boedromion. The muster against Kassander was begun, according to Droysen, in the summer of 302 B.C. Grote placed the return from Leukas in September 302 B.C. at the time of the celebration of the Greater Mysteries, and referred the double initiation to April 301 B.C., when the start was made against Kassander. So Krüger in Clinton's *Fasti* p. 188. Bergk would bring the date of the poem down to 290 B.C. because of the mention of the Aitolians, whose possession of the passes leading to Delphi had prevented the celebration of the Pythian games. He placed the return of Dem. in September, and the Pythian festival (at Athens) in October, 290 B.C. The expedition against the Aitolians took place, according to Bergk, in the spring of 289. Of the poem Athen. says: *ταῦτ᾽ ᾖδον οἱ Μαραθωνομάχαι οὐ δημοσίᾳ μόνον, ἀλλὰ καὶ κατ᾽ οἰκίαν, οἱ τὸν προσκυνήσαντα τὸν Περσῶν βασιλέα ἀποκτείναντες, οἱ τὰς ἀναρίθμους μυριάδας τῶν βαρβάρων φονεύσαντες.* Like the paian, the ithyphallic hymn is now made to do honour to men. Neither this poem nor No. xxvi. is 'genuine' folk-song. No. xxvii. is by Hermokles of Kyzikos.—**1.** Perhaps two verses have dropped out. Bergk suggested *ἀνάγετε πάντες, ἀνάγετ', εὐρυχωρίαν | τοῖς θεοῖς ποιεῖτε* (cf. No. vi.). This is better than to read *ὡς*, or to suppose that some such word as *νῦν* has been displaced. Demetrios and his father Antigonos were called Tutelar Divinities and Deliverers. Dem. was deified at Sikyon as well as at Athens. Apotheosis did not become common until after Alexander ('whereas Alexander desires to be a god, let him be a god' ran the Spartan decree); his successors, the kings of Egypt and Syria, were called *θεοί*. The Persians prostrated themselves before their monarchs, who were treated as *δαίμονες*. Isokrates voices the popular phraseology in his Letter to Philip (3. 5) *οὐδὲν γὰρ ἔσται λοιπὸν ἔτι πλὴν θεὸν γενέσθαι*, though he was far from deifying that monarch.—**2.** Demetrios' arrival is a veritable epiphany.—**6. ποιήσῃ** (⏑ — —); cf. ll. 21, 34, skol. vii. 4.—**7.** Athen. says that Dem. was affable because of his natural courtesy to all men. His *ἱλαρότης* ran into frivolity no doubt and assisted his vicious propensities. In l. 14 he is called the child of Aphrodite because of his beauty. Plutarch says that 'his countenance was of such singular beauty and expression, that no painter or sculptor ever produced a good likeness of him. It combined grace and strength, dignity with boyish bloom, and in the midst of youthful heat and passion, what was hardest of all to represent was a certain heroic look and air of kingly majesty.' Cf. l. 9.—**9. φίλοι**: in honour of these satellites of Dem. altars were erected and poems sung by the Athenians (*τῶν κολάκων κόλακες*). Even Dem. was astonished by the grossness of the flattery shown him and declared that in his time there was not a single Athenian who was great and vigorous in mind. Cf. Hor. *Sat.* 1. 7. 24 *solem Asiae Brutum appellat, stellasque salubres appellat comites.*—**13. παῖ Ποσειδῶνος**: Dem. had captured the chief naval city of Greece with his fleet of 250 ships, and made expeditions against Kypros, Egypt, and Rhodes.—**15.** Cf. 1 Kings 18, 27 "And it came to pass at noon, that Elijah mocked them, and said, Cry aloud: for he is a god; either he is talking, or he is pursuing, or he is in a journey, or peradventure he sleepeth, and must be awaked."—**18.** Cf. *praesens deus* Ter. *Phorm.* 2. 2. 31, *praesens divus habebitur Augustus* Hor. 3. 5. 2, *Caesar, ades voto, maxime dive, meo* Ovid *Trist.* 3. 1. 78; Cic. *Tusc.* 1. 12. 28.—**19.** The pun (*λίθινον, ἀληθινόν*) is not to be adduced as evidence of the itacistic pronunciation of *η*.—**24. περίκρατοῦσαν**: see on Ibyk. ix.—**25.** The Athenians had cause to know the prowess of the 'rock-dwelling'

Aitolians. In 426 B.C. they had suffered a crushing defeat during the expedition of Demosthenes. The Aitolian League (*τὸ κοινὸν τῶν Αἰτωλῶν*) is first heard of in 312 B.C. Generally it was opposed to Demetrios, but at this time, according to Droysen, was on friendly terms with him. Doubtless bands of Aitolian marauders had menaced Attica itself, and the Athenians were sunk so low as publicly to proclaim themselves incapable of self-defence. Droysen thought that the 'Aitolian sphinx' was Polysperchon. Brandstäter found in Pantauchos, the general of Demetrios, the Oidipus of l. 32. All this is quite uncertain.—**34. σπίλον** *i.e.* *πέτραν*, a word used by Aristotle. Ion (Trag. Frag. 19) has *σπίλον Παρνασσίαν*. *σπίνον* Schweighäuser, supposing that there was a legend of the Sphinx having been transformed into a finch.—Metre: iambic trimeter with ithyphallics as epode (cf. vi.). The frequent tribrachs are to be noted, the dactyl (anapaest) in l. 17, and the inelegant close of the same verse.

XXVIII. Athen. 10. 455 D, Eust. *Od.* 1558. 3. Apollo was born in Delos (*ἐν φανερᾷ = ἐν Δήλῳ*; see on Pind. vi. 4); his mother Leto was the daughter of Κοῖος (*Κοιογενής* Pind. vi. 6) and in Makedonian *κοῖος = ἀριθμός*.—Metre: elegiac distich.

XXIX. Athen. 10. 453 B. Time.—Metre: iambic trimeter.

XXX. Plut. *Quo modo adul.* 9. A parasite.—Metre as xxix.

APPENDIX.

I. SKOLIA ATTRIBUTED TO THE SAGES.

SOLON.

Πεφυλαγμένος ἄνδρα ἕκαστον ὅρα,
μὴ κρυπτὸν ἔγχος ἔχων κραδίῃ
φαιδρῷ σε προσενέπῃ προσώπῳ,
γλῶσσα δέ οἱ διχόμυθος ἐκ μελαίνης
φρενὸς γεγωνῇ.

PITTAKOS.

Ἔχοντα χρὴ τόξον τε καὶ ἰοδόκον φαρέτραν
στείχειν ποτὶ φῶτα κακόν·
πιστὸν γὰρ οὐδὲν γλῶσσα διὰ στόματος
λαλεῖ διχόθυμον ἔχουσα καρδίᾳ νόημα.

BIAS.

Ἀστοῖσιν ἄρεσκε πᾶσιν, ἐν πόλει αἴ κε μένῃς·
πλείσταν γὰρ ἔχει χάριν· αὐθάδης δὲ τρόπος
πολλάκι δὴ βλαβερὰν ἐξέλαμψεν ἄταν.

CHILON.

Ἐν λιθίναις ἀκόναις ὁ χρυσὸς ἐξετάζεται
διδοὺς βάσανον φανεράν· ἐν δὲ χρυσῷ
ἀνδρῶν ἀγαθῶν τε κακῶν τε νοῦς ἔδωκ' ἔλεγχον.

THALES.

Οὔτι τὰ πολλὰ ἔπη φρονίμην ἀπεφήνατο δόξαν·
ἕν τι μάτευε σοφόν,
ἕν τι κεδνὸν αἱροῦ·
παύσεις γὰρ ἀνδρῶν κωτίλων γλώσσας ἀπεραντολόγους.

KLEOBULOS.

Ἀμουσία τὸ πλέον μέρος ἐν βροτοῖσιν
λόγων τε πλῆθος· ἀλλ' ὁ καιρὸς ἀρκέσει
φρονεῖν τι κεδνόν· μὴ μάταιος ἁ χάρις γενέσθω.

II. A SELECTION FROM THE ANAKREONTEIA.

I. (6). ΕΙΣ ΕΑΥΤΟΝ.

Λέγουσιν αἱ γυναῖκες·
"Ἀνάκρεον, γέρων εἶ·
λαβὼν ἔσοπτρον ἄθρει
κόμας μὲν οὐκέτ' οὔσας,
5 ψιλὸν δέ σευ μέτωπον."
ἐγὼ δὲ τὰς κόμας μέν,
εἴτ' εἰσίν, εἴτ' ἀπῆλθον,
οὐκ οἶδα· τοῦτο δ' οἶδα,
ὡς τῷ γέροντι μᾶλλον
πρέπει τὸ τερπνὰ παίζειν, 10
ὅσῳ πέλας τὰ Μοίρης.

II. (7). ΕΙΣ ΤΟ ΑΦΘΟΝΩΣ ΖΗΝ.

Οὔ μοι μέλει τὰ Γύγεω,
τοῦ Σαρδίων ἄνακτος·
οὐδ' εἷλέ πώ με ζῆλος,
οὐδὲ φθονῶ τυράννοις.
5 ἐμοὶ μέλει μύροισιν
καταβρέχειν ὑπήνην·
ἐμοὶ μέλει ῥόδοισιν
καταστέφειν κάρηνα.
τὸ σήμερον μέλει μοι,
τὸ δ' αὔριον τίς οἶδεν; 10
ὡς οὖν ἔτ' εὔδι' ἔστιν,
καὶ πῖνε καὶ κύβευε
καὶ σπένδε τῷ Λυαίῳ,
μὴ νοῦσος, ἥν τις ἔλθῃ,
λέγῃ· "σὲ μὴ δεῖ πίνειν." 15

III. (8). ΕΙΣ ΕΑΥΤΟΝ ΜΕΜΕΘΥΣΜΕΝΟΝ.

Ἄφες με, τοὺς θεούς σοι,
πιεῖν πιεῖν ἀμυστί·
θέλω θέλω μανῆναι.
ἐμαίνετ' Ἀλκμαίων τε
5 χὠ λευκόπους Ὀρέστης,
τὰς μητέρας κτανόντες·
ἐγὼ δὲ μηδένα κτάς,
πιὼν δ' ἐρυθρὸν οἶνον
θέλω θέλω μανῆναι.
10 ἐμαίνεθ' Ἡρακλῆς πρὶν
δεινὴν κλονῶν φαρέτρην
καὶ τόξον Ἰφίτειον.
ἐμαίνετο πρὶν Αἴας
μετ' ἀσπίδος κραδαίνων
τὴν Ἕκτορος μάχαιραν. 15
ἐγὼ δ' ἔχων κύπελλον
καὶ στέμμα τοῦτο χαίταις,
οὐ τόξον, οὐ μάχαιραν,
θέλω θέλω μανῆναι.

IV. (9). ΕΙΣ ΧΕΛΙΔΟΝΑ.

Τί σοι θέλεις ποιήσω,
τί σοι, λάλη χελιδών;
τὰ ταρσά σευ τὰ κοῦφα
θέλεις λαθὼν ψαλίξω;
5 ἢ μᾶλλον ἔνδοθέν σευ
τὴν γλῶσσαν, ὡς ὁ Τηρεὺς
ἐκεῖνος, ἐκθερίξω;
τί μευ καλῶν ὀνείρων
ὑπορθρίαισι φωναῖς
ἀφήρπασας Βάθυλλον; 10

V. (10). ΕΙΣ ΕΡΩΤΑ ΚΗΡΙΝΟΝ.

Ἔρωτα κήρινόν τις
νεηνίης ἐπώλει·
ἐγὼ δέ οἱ παραστάς,
"πόσου θέλεις," ἔφην, "σοὶ
5 τὸ τυχθὲν ἐκπρίωμαι;"
ὁ δ' εἶπε δωριάζων,
"λάβ' αὐτὸν ὁππόσου λῇς·
ὅπως δ' ἂν ἐκμάθῃς πᾶν,
οὐκ εἰμὶ καροτέχνης·
ἀλλ' οὐ θέλω συνοικεῖν 10
Ἔρωτι παντορέκτᾳ."
"δὸς οὖν, δὸς αὐτὸν ἡμῖν
δραχμῆς, καλὸν σύνευνον.
Ἔρως, σὺ δ' εὐθέως με
πύρωσον· εἰ δὲ μή, σὺ 15
κατὰ φλογὸς τακήσῃ."

VI. (11). ΕΙΣ ΑΤΤΙΝ.

Οἱ μὲν καλὴν Κυβήβην
τὸν ἡμίθηλυν Ἄττιν
ἐν οὔρεσιν βοῶντα
λέγουσιν ἐκμανῆναι.
5 οἱ δὲ Κλάρου παρ' ὄχθαις
δαφνηφόροιο Φοίβου
λάλον πιόντες ὕδωρ
μεμηνότες βοῶσιν.
ἐγὼ δὲ τοῦ Λυαίου
καὶ τοῦ μύρου κορεσθεὶς 10
καὶ τῆς ἐμῆς ἑταίρης
θέλω θέλω μανῆναι.

VII. (12). ΕΙΣ ΕΡΩΤΑ.

Θέλω θέλω φιλῆσαι.
ἔπειθ' Ἔρως φιλεῖν με,
ἐγὼ δ' ἔχων νόημα
ἄβουλον οὐκ ἐπείσθην.
5 ὁ δ' εὐθὺ τόξον ἄρας
καὶ χρυσέην φαρέτρην
μάχῃ με προὐκαλεῖτο.
κἀγὼ λαβὼν ἐπ' ὤμων
θώρηχ', ὅπως Ἀχιλλεύς,
10 καὶ δοῦρα καὶ βοείην
ἐμαρνάμην Ἔρωτι.
ἔβαλλ', ἐγὼ δ' ἔφευγον·
ὡς δ' οὐκ ἔτ' εἶχ' ὀιστούς,
ἤσχαλλεν· εἶθ' ἑαυτὸν
ἀφῆκεν εἰς βέλεμνον, 15
μέσος δὲ καρδίης μευ
ἔδυνε, καί μ' ἔλυσεν·
μάτην δ' ἔχω βοείην·
τί γὰρ βάλω μιν ἔξω,
μάχης ἔσω μ' ἐχούσης; 20

VIII. (13). ΕΙΣ ΕΡΩΤΑΣ.

Εἰ φύλλα πάντα δένδρων
ἐπίστασαι κατειπεῖν,
εἰ κύματ' οἶδας εὑρεῖν
τὰ τῆς ὅλης θαλάσσης,
5 σὲ τῶν ἐμῶν ἐρώτων
μόνον ποῶ λογιστήν.
πρῶτον μὲν ἐξ Ἀθηνῶν
ἔρωτας εἴκοσιν θές,
καὶ πεντεκαίδεκ' ἄλλους.
10 ἔπειτα δ' ἐκ Κορίνθου
θὲς ὁρμαθοὺς ἐρώτων·
Ἀχαΐης γάρ ἐστιν,
ὅπου καλαὶ γυναῖκες.
τίθει δὲ Λεσβίους μοι
καὶ μέχρι τῶν Ἰώνων 15
καὶ Καρίης Ῥόδου τε
δισχιλίους ἔρωτας.
τί φῄς; ἐκηριώθης;
οὔπω Σύρους ἔλεξα,
οὔπω πόθους Κανώβου, 20
οὐ τῆς ἅπαντ' ἐχούσης
Κρήτης, ὅπου πόλεσσιν
Ἔρως ἐποργιάζει.
τί σοι θέλεις ἀριθμῶ
καὶ τοὺς Γαδείρων ἐκτός, 25
τῶν Βακτρίων τε κἰνδῶν
ψυχῆς ἐμῆς ἔρωτας;

IX. (14). ΕΙΣ ΠΕΡΙΣΤΕΡΑΝ.

Ἐρασμίη πέλεια,
πόθεν πόθεν πέτασσαι;
πόθεν μύρων τοσούτων
ἐπ' ἠέρος θέουσα
5 πνέεις τε καὶ ψεκάζεις;
τίς ἐστί σοι μεληδών;
"Ἀνακρέων μ' ἔπεμψεν
πρὸς παῖδα, πρὸς Βάθυλλον,
τὸν ἄρτι τῶν ἁπάντων
10 κρατοῦντα καὶ τύραννον.
πέπρακέ μ' ἡ Κυθήρη
λαβοῦσα μικρὸν ὕμνον·
ἐγὼ δ' Ἀνακρέοντι
διακονῶ τοσαῦτα.
15 καὶ νῦν, ὁρᾷς, ἐκείνου
ἐπιστολὰς κομίζω.
καί φησιν εὐθέως με
ἐλευθέρην ποιήσειν.
ἐγὼ δέ, κἢν ἀφῇ με,
δούλη μενῶ παρ' αὐτῷ· 20
τί γάρ με δεῖ πέτασθαι
ὄρη τε καὶ κατ' ἀγρούς,
καὶ δένδρεσιν καθίζειν
φαγοῦσαν ἄγριόν τι;
τὰ νῦν ἔδω μὲν ἄρτον 25
ἀφαρπάσασα χειρῶν
Ἀνακρέοντος αὐτοῦ·
πιεῖν δέ μοι δίδωσιν
τὸν οἶνον, ὃν προπίνει·
πιοῦσα δ' αὖ χορεύω, 30
καὶ δεσπότην κρέκοντα
πτεροῖσι συσκιάζω.
κοιμωμένη δ' ἐπ' αὐτῷ
τῷ βαρβίτῳ καθεύδω.
ἔχεις ἅπαντ'· ἄπελθε· 35
λαλιστέραν μ' ἔθηκας,
ἄνθρωπε, καὶ κορώνης."

X. (15). ΕΙΣ ΚΟΡΗΝ.

Ἄγε ζωγράφων ἄριστε,
γράφε, ζωγράφων ἄριστε,
Ῥοδίης κοίρανε τέχνης,
ἀπεοῦσαν, ὡς ἂν εἴπω,
5 γράφε τὴν ἐμὴν ἑταίρην.
γράφε μοι τρίχας τὸ πρῶτον
ἁπαλάς τε καὶ μελαίνας·
ὁ δὲ κηρὸς ἂν δύνηται,
γράφε καὶ μύρου πνεούσας.
10 γράφε δ' ἐξ ὅλης παρειῆς
ὑπὸ πορφυραῖσι χαίταις
ἐλεφάντινον μέτωπον.
τὸ μεσόφρυον δὲ μή μοι
διάκοπτε μήτε μίσγε·
15 ἐχέτω δ', ὅπως ἐκείνη,
τὸ λεληθότως σύνοφρυ,
βλεφάρων ἴτυν κελαινήν.
τὸ δὲ βλέμμα νῦν ἀληθῶς
ἀπὸ τοῦ πυρὸς ποίησον,
ἅμα γλαυκόν, ὡς Ἀθήνης, 20
ἅμα δ' ὑγρόν, ὡς Κυθήρης.
γράφε ῥῖνα καὶ παρειάς,
ῥόδα τῷ γάλακτι μίξας.
γράφε χεῖλος, οἷα Πειθοῦς,
προκαλούμενον φίλημα. 25
τρυφεροῦ δ' ἔσω γενείου
περὶ λυγδίνῳ τραχήλῳ
Χάριτες πέτοιντο πᾶσαι.
στόλισον τὸ λοιπὸν αὐτὴν
ὑποπορφύροισι πέπλοις· 30
διαφαινέτω δὲ σαρκῶν
ὀλίγον, τὸ σῶμ' ἐλέγχον.
ἀπέχει· βλέπω γὰρ αὐτήν.
τάχα, κηρέ, καὶ λαλήσεις.

XI. (16). ΕΙΣ ΝΕΩΤΕΡΟΝ ΒΑΘΥΛΛΟΝ.

Γράφε μοι Βάθυλλον οὕτω
τὸν ἑταῖρον, ὡς διδάσκω.
λιπαρὰς κόμας ποίησον,
τὰ μὲν ἔνδοθεν μελαίνας,
5 τὰ δ' ἐς ἄκρον ἡλιώσας,
ἕλικας δ' ἐλευθέρους μοι
πλοκάμων ἄτακτα συνθεὶς
ἄφες, ὡς θέλωσι, κεῖσθαι.
ἁπαλὸν δὲ καὶ δροσῶδες
10 στεφέτω μέτωπον ὀφρὺς
κυανωτέρη δρακόντων.
μέλαν ὄμμα γοργὸν ἔστω,
κεκερασμένον γαλήνῃ,
τὸ μὲν ἐξ Ἄρηος ἕλκον,
15 τὸ δὲ τῆς καλῆς Κυθήρης,
ἵνα τις τὸ μὲν φοβῆται,
τὸ δ' ἀπ' ἐλπίδος κρεμᾶται·
χνοΐην δ' ὁποῖα μῆλον
ῥοδέην ποίει παρειήν·
ἐρύθημα δ', ὡς ἂν Αἰδοῦς, 20
δύνασαι γάρ, ἐμποίησον.
τὸ δὲ χεῖλος οὐκέτ' οἶδα
τίνι μοι τρόπῳ ποιήσεις·
ἁπαλὸν γέμον τε Πειθοῦς·
τὸ δὲ πᾶν ὁ κηρὸς αὐτὸς 25
ἐχέτω λαλῶν σιωπῇ.
μετὰ δὲ πρόσωπον ἔστω
τὸν Ἀδώνιδος παρελθὼν
ἐλεφάντινος τράχηλος.
μεταμάζιον δὲ ποίει 30
διδύμας τε χεῖρας Ἑρμοῦ,
Πολυδεύκεος δὲ μηρούς,

Διονυσίην δὲ νηδύν.
ἁπαλῶν δ' ὕπερθε μηρῶν,
35 μηρῶν τὸ πῦρ ἐχόντων,
ἀφελῆ ποίησον αἰδῶ,
Παφίην θέλουσαν ἤδη.
φθονερὴν ἔχεις δὲ τέχνην,
ὅτι μὴ τὰ νῶτα δεῖξαι
δύνασαι· τὰ δ' ἦν ἀμείνω. 40
τί με δεῖ πόδας διδάσκειν;
λάβε μισθὸν ὅσσον εἴπῃς·
τὸν 'Απόλλωνα δὲ τοῦτον
καθελὼν ποίει Βάθυλλον.
ἢν δ' ἐς Σάμον ποτ' ἔλθῃς, 45
γράφε Φοῖβον ἐκ Βαθύλλο

XII. (17, 18). ΕΡΩΤΙΚΟΝ ΩΙΔΑΡΙΟΝ.

Δότε μοι, δότ' ὦ γυναῖκες,
Βρομίου πιεῖν ἀμυστί·
ὑπὸ καύματος γὰρ ἤδη
προδοθεὶς ἀναστενάζω.
5 δότε δ' ἀνθέων ἐκείνου
στεφάνους, δόθ', ὡς πυκάζω·
τὰ μέτωπά που 'πικαίει·
τὸ δὲ καῦμα τῶν 'Ερώτων,
κραδίη, τίνι σκεπάζω;
παρὰ τὴν σκιὴν Βαθύλλου 10
καθίσω· καλὸν τὸ δένδρον·
ἁπαλὰς δ' ἔσεισε χαίτας
μαλακωτάτῳ κλαδίσκῳ.
παρὰ δ' αὐτὸν ἐρεθίζει
πηγὴ ῥέουσα πειθοῦς· 15
τίς ἂν οὖν ὁρῶν παρέλθοι
καταγώγιον τοιοῦτο;

XIII. (19). ΕΙΣ ΕΡΩΤΑ.

Αἱ Μοῦσαι τὸν Ἔρωτα
δήσασαι στεφάνοισιν
τῷ Κάλλει παρέδωκαν.
καὶ νῦν ἡ Κυθέρεια
5 ζητεῖ λύτρα φέρουσα
λύσασθαι τὸν Ἔρωτα.
κἂν λύσῃ δέ τις αὐτόν,
οὐκ ἔξεισι, μένει δέ·
δουλεύειν δεδίδακται.

XIV. (20). ΑΛΛΟ.

'Ηδυμελὴς 'Ανακρέων,
ἡδυμελὴς δὲ Σαπφώ·
Πινδαρικὸν δέ μοι μέλος
συγκεράσας τις ἐγχέοι.
τὰ τρία ταῦτά μοι δοκεῖ 5
καὶ Διόνυσος ἐλθών,
καὶ Παφίη λιπαρόχροος,
καὐτὸς Ἔρως ἂν ἐκπιεῖν.

XV. (21). ΑΛΛΟ.

'Η γῆ μέλαινα πίνει,
πίνει δὲ δένδρε' αὐτήν.
πίνει θάλασσ' ἀναύρους,
ὁ δ' ἥλιος θάλασσαν.
τὸν δ' ἥλιον σελήνη. 5
τί μοι μάχεσθ', ἑταῖροι,
καὐτῷ θέλοντι πίνειν;

XVI. (21). ΕΙΣ ΚΟΡΗΝ.

Ἡ Ταντάλου ποτ' ἔστη
λίθος Φρυγῶν ἐν ὄχθαις,
καὶ παῖς ποτ' ὄρνις ἔπτη
Πανδίονος χελιδών.
5 ἐγὼ δ' ἔσοπτρον εἴην,
ὅπως ἀεὶ βλέπῃς με·
ἐγὼ χιτὼν γενοίμην,
ὅπως ἀεὶ φορῇς με.
ὕδωρ θέλω γενέσθαι,
ὅπως σε χρῶτα λούσω· 10
μύρον, γύναι, γενοίμην,
ὅπως ἐγώ σ' ἀλείψω.
καὶ ταινίη δὲ μαστῶν,
καὶ μάργαρον τραχήλῳ,
καὶ σάνδαλον γενοίμην· 15
μόνον ποσὶν πάτει με.

XVII. (22). ΕΙΣ ΚΙΘΑΡΑΝ.

Θέλω λέγειν Ατρείδας,
θέλω δὲ Κάδμον ᾄδειν·
ἁ βάρβιτος δὲ χορδαῖς
ἔρωτα μοῦνον ἠχεῖ.
5 ἤμειψα νεῦρα πρώην
καὶ τὴν λύρην ἅπασαν·
κἀγὼ μὲν ᾖδον ἄθλους
Ἡρακλέους· λύρη δὲ
ἔρωτας ἀντεφώνει.
χαίροιτε λοιπὸν ἡμῖν 10
ἥρωες· ἡ λύρη γὰρ
μόνους ἔρωτας ᾄδει.

XVIII. (24). ΕΡΩΤΙΚΟΝ.

Φύσις κέρατα ταύροις,
ὁπλὰς δ' ἔδωκεν ἵπποις,
ποδωκίην λαγωοῖς,
λέουσι χάσμ' ὀδόντων,
5 τοῖς ἰχθύσιν τὸ νηκτόν,
τοῖς ὀρνέοις πέτασθαι,
τοῖς ἀνδράσιν φρόνημα.
γυναιξὶν οὔτ' ἔτ' εἶχεν.
τί οὖν; δίδωσι κάλλος
ἀντ' ἀσπίδων ἁπασᾶν, 10
ἀντ' ἐγχέων ἁπάντων.
νικᾷ δὲ καὶ σίδηρον
καὶ πῦρ καλή τις οὖσα.

XIX. (25). ΕΙΣ ΧΕΛΙΔΟΝΑ.

Σὺ μὲν φίλη χελιδὼν
ἐτησίη μολοῦσα
θέρει πλέκεις καλιήν·
χειμῶνι δ' εἰς ἄφαντος
5 ἢ Νεῖλον ἢ 'πὶ Μέμφιν.
Ἔρως δ' ἀεὶ πλέκει μευ
ἐν καρδίῃ καλιήν.
Πόθος δ' ὁ μὲν πτεροῦται,
ὁ δ' ὠόν ἐστιν ἀκμήν,
10 ὁ δ' ἡμίλεπτος ἤδη.
βοὴ δὲ γίνετ' αἰεὶ
κεχηνότων νεοσσῶν.
Ἐρωτιδεῖς δὲ μικροὺς
οἱ μείζονες τρέφουσιν.
οἱ δὲ τραφέντες εὐθὺς 15
πάλιν κύουσιν ἄλλους.
τί μῆχος οὖν γένηται;
οὐ γάρ σθένω τοσούτους
Ἔρωτας ἐκβοῆσαι.

XX. (27 A). ΕΙΣ ΤΑ ΤΟΥ ΕΡΩΤΟΣ ΒΕΛΗ.

Ὁ ἀνὴρ ὁ τῆς Κυθήρης
παρὰ Λημνίαις καμίνοις
τὰ βέλη τὰ τῶν Ἐρώτων
ἐπόει λαβὼν σίδηρον.
5 ἀκίδας δ' ἔβαπτε Κύπρις
μέλι τὸ γλυκὺ λαβοῦσα·
ὁ δ' Ἔρως χολὴν ἔμισγεν.
ὁ δ' Ἄρης ποτ' ἐξ ἀυτῆς
στιβαρὸν δόρυ κραδαίνων
βέλος ηὐτέλιζ' Ἔρωτος· 10
ὁ δ' Ἔρως, "τόδ' ἐστίν," εἶπεν,
"βαρύ· πειράσας νοήσεις."
ἔλαβεν βέλεμνον Ἄρης·
ὑπεμειδίασε Κύπρις.
ὁ δ' Ἄρης ἀναστενάξας, 15
"βαρύ," φησίν· "ἆρον αὐτό."
ὁ δ' Ἔρως, "ἔχ' αὐτό," φησίν.

XXI. (27 B).

Χαλεπὸν τὸ μὴ φιλῆσαι·
χαλεπὸν δὲ καὶ φιλῆσαι·
χαλεπώτερον δὲ πάντων
ἀποτυγχάνειν φιλοῦντα.

XXII. (27 C).

Γένος οὐδὲν εἰς Ἔρωτα·
σοφίη, τρόπος πατεῖται·
μόνον ἄργυρον βλέπουσιν.
ἀπόλοιτο πρῶτος αὐτὸς
5 ὁ τὸν ἄργυρον φιλήσας.
διὰ τοῦτον οὐκ ἀδελφός,
διὰ τοῦτον οὐ τοκῆες·
πόλεμοι, φόνοι δι' αὐτόν.
τὸ δὲ χεῖρον, ὀλλύμεσθα
διὰ τοῦτον οἱ φιλοῦντες. 10

XXIII. (30). ΕΡΩΤΙΚΟΝ ΩΙΔΑΡΙΟΝ.

Ἐπὶ μυρσίναις τερείναις
ἐπὶ λωτίναις τε ποίαις
στορέσας θέλω προπίνειν·
ὁ δ' Ἔρως χιτῶνα δήσας
5 ὑπὲρ αὐχένος παπύρῳ
μέθυ μοι διακονείτω.
τροχὸς ἅρματος γὰρ οἷα
βίοτος τρέχει κυλισθείς·
ὀλίγη δὲ κεισόμεσθα
κόνις ὀστέων λυθέντων. 10
τί σε δεῖ λίθον μυρίζειν;
τί δὲ γῇ χέειν μάταια;
ἐμὲ μᾶλλον, ὡς ἔτι ζῶ,
μύρισον, ῥόδοις δὲ κρᾶτα
πύκασον, κάλει δ' ἑταίρην. 15
πρίν, Ἔρως, ἐκεῖ μ' ἀπελθεῖν
ὑπὸ νερτέρων χορείας,
σκεδάσαι θέλω μερίμνας.

XXIV. (31). ΑΛΛΟ.

Μεσονυκτίοις ποθ' ὥραις,
στρέφετ' ἦμος Ἄρκτος ἤδη
κατὰ χεῖρα τὴν Βοώτου,
μερόπων δὲ φῦλα πάντα
5 κέαται κόπῳ δαμέντα,
τότ' Ἔρως ἐπισταθείς μευ
θυρέων ἔκοπτ' ὀχῆας.
"τίς," ἔφην, "θύρας ἀράσσει;
κατά μευ σχίζεις ὀνείρους."
10 ὁ δ' Ἔρως, "ἄνοιγε," φησίν·
"βρέφος εἰμί, μὴ φόβησαι·
βρέχομαι δὲ κἀσέληνον
κατὰ νύκτα πεπλάνημαι."
ἐλέησα ταῦτ' ἀκούσας,
15 ἀνὰ δ' εὐθὺ λύχνον ἅψας
ἀνέῳξα, καὶ βρέφος μὲν
ἐσορῶ φέροντα τόξον
πτέρυγάς τε καὶ φαρέτρην.
παρὰ δ' ἱστίην καθῖσα,
παλάμαις τε χεῖρας αὐτοῦ 20
ἀνέθαλπον, ἐκ δὲ χαίτης
ἀπέθλιβον ὑγρὸν ὕδωρ.
ὁ δ', ἐπεὶ κρύος μεθῆκεν,
"φέρε," φησί, "πειράσωμεν
τόδε τόξον, εἴ τι μοι νῦν 25
βλάβεται βραχεῖσα νευρή."
τανύει δὲ καί με τύπτει
μέσον ἧπαρ, ὥσπερ οἶστρος·
ἀνὰ δ' ἅλλεται καχάζων,
"ξένε δ'," εἶπε, "συγχάρηθι·
κέρας ἀβλαβὲς μὲν ἡμῖν, 31
σὺ δὲ καρδίαν πονήσεις."

XXV. (32). ΕΙΣ ΤΕΤΤΙΓΑ.

Μακαρίζομέν σε, τέττιξ,
ὅτε δενδρέων ἐπ' ἄκρων
ὀλίγην δρόσον πεπωκὼς
βασιλεὺς ὅπως ἀείδεις·
5 σὰ γάρ ἐστι κεῖνα πάντα,
ὁπόσα βλέπεις ἐν ἀγροῖς,
ὁπόσα τρέφουσιν ὗλαι.
σὺ δ' ὁμιλία γεωργῶν,
ἀπὸ μηδενός τι βλάπτων·
σὺ δὲ τίμιος βροτοῖσιν, 10
θέρεος γλυκὺς προφήτης·
φιλέουσι μέν σε Μοῦσαι,
φιλέει δὲ Φοῖβος αὐτός,
λιγυρὴν δ' ἔδωκεν οἴμην.
τὸ δὲ γῆρας οὔ σε τείρει, 15
σοφέ, γηγενής, φίλυμνε·
ἀπαθὴς δ', ἀναιμόσαρκε,
σχεδὸν εἶ θεοῖς ὅμοιος.

XXVI. (33). ΕΙΣ ΕΡΩΤΑ.

Ἔρως ποτ' ἐν ῥόδοισιν
κοιμωμένην μέλιτταν
οὐκ εἶδεν, ἀλλ' ἐτρώθη
τὸν δάκτυλον· παταχθεὶς
5 τὰς χεῖρας ὠλόλυξεν·
δραμὼν δὲ καὶ πετασθεὶς
πρὸς τὴν καλὴν Κυθήρην
"ὄλωλα, μᾶτερ," εἶπεν,
"ὄλωλα κἀποθνήσκω·
ὄφις μ' ἔτυψε μικρὸς 10
πτερωτός, ὃν καλοῦσιν
μέλιτταν οἱ γεωργοί."
ἁ δ' εἶπεν· "εἰ τὸ κέντρον
πονεῖ τὸ τᾶς μελίττας,
πόσον δοκεῖς πονοῦσιν, 15
Ἔρως, ὅσους σὺ βάλλεις;"

XXVII. (34). ΕΙΣ ΦΙΛΑΡΓΥΡΟΝ.

Ὁ πλοῦτος εἴ γε χρυσοῦ
τὸ ζῆν παρεῖχε θνητοῖς,
ἐκαρτέρουν φυλάττων,
ἵν', ἂν θανεῖν ἐπέλθῃ,
5 λάβῃ τι καὶ παρέλθῃ.
εἰ δ' οὖν τὸ μὴ πρίασθαι
τὸ ζῆν ἔνεστι θνητοῖς,
τί χρυσὸς ὠφελεῖ με;
θανεῖν γὰρ εἰ πέπρωται,
τί καὶ μάτην στενάζω; 10
τί καὶ γόους προπέμπω;
ἐμοὶ γένοιτο πίνειν,
πιόντι δ' οἶνον ἡδὺν
ἐμοῖς φίλοις συνεῖναι,
ἐν δ' ἁπαλαῖσι κοίταις 15
τελεῖν τὰν Ἀφροδίταν.

XXVIII. (37). ΕΙΣ ΕΑΥΤΟΝ ΠΡΕΣΒΥΤΗΝ.

Φιλῶ γέροντα τερπνόν,
φιλῶ νέον χορευτάν·
ἂν δ' ὁ γέρων χορεύῃ,
τρίχας γέρων μέν ἐστιν,
τὰς δὲ φρένας νεάζει.

XXIX. (38). ΕΙΣ ΕΑΥΤΟΝ.

Ἐπειδὴ βροτὸς ἐτύχθην
βιότου τρίβον ὁδεύειν,
χρόνον ἔγνων, ὃν παρῆλθον·
ὃν δ' ἔχω δραμεῖν, οὐκ οἶδα.
5 μέθετέ με φροντίδες·
μηδέν μοι καὶ ὑμῖν ἔστω.
πρὶν ἐμὲ φθάσῃ τὸ τέλος,
παίξω, γελάσω, χορεύσω
μετὰ τοῦ καλοῦ Λυαίου.

III. DELPHIC PAIAN TO DIONYSOS.[1]

[Δεῦρ', ἄνα Δ]ιθύραμβε Βάκχ' α'.
ε[ὔιε, θυρσῆ]ρες, βραϊ-
τά, βρόμι(ε), ἠρινα[ῖς ἱκοῦ]
[ταῖσδ(ε)] ἱεραῖς ἐν ὥραις:
5 Εὐοῖ ὦ ἰὸ [Βάκχ' ὦ ἰὲ Παιά]ν·
ὃν Θήβαις πότ' ἐν εὐίαις
Ζη[νὶ γείνατο] καλλίπαις Θυώνα·
πάντες δ' [ἀστέρες ἀγχ]όρευ-
σαν, πάντες δὲ βροτοὶ χ[άρη-]
10 [σαν σαῖς,] Βάκχιε, γένναις.
Ἰὲ Παιάν, ἴθι σωτήρ,

[1] *B. C. H.* 19 (1895) 393 ff.

[εὔφρων τάνδε] πόλιν φύλασσ'
εὐαίωνι σὺν [ὄλβῳ.]

Ἦν, τότε βακχίαζε μὲν — β'.
15 χθὼ[ν μεγαλώνυμός] τε Κά-
δμου Μινυᾶν τε κόλπ[ος Αὔ-]
[γε]ιά τε καλλίκαρπος :
Εὐοῖ ὦ ἰὸ Β[άκχ' ὦ ἰὲ] Παιάν·
πᾶσα δ' ὑμνοβρύης χόρευ-
20 ε[ν Δελφῶ]ν ἱερὰ μάκαιρα χώρα·
αὐτὸς δ' ἄστε[ί σὸν δ]έμας
φαίνων Δελφίσιν σὺν κόραις
[Παρν]ασσοῦ πτύχας ἔστας.
'Ιὲ Παιάν κ.τ.λ.

[Οἰνοθα]λὲς δὲ χειρὶ πάλ- — γ'.
λων δ[έπ]ας ἐνθέοις [σὺν οἴσ-]
τροις ἔμολες μυχοὺς ['Ελε]υ-
30 σῖνος ἀν' [ἀνθεμώ]δεις·
Εὐοῖ ὦ ἰὸ Βάκχ' ὦ ἰ[ὲ Παι]άν·
[ἔθνος ἔνθ'] ἅπαν 'Ελλάδος
γᾶς ἀ[μφ(ὶ) ἐ]ννα‹έ›ταις [φίλιον] ἐπ[όπ]ταις
ὀργίων ὁσ[ίων Ἴα]κ-
35 χον [κλείει σ]ε· βροτοῖς πόνων
ὦιξ[ας δ' ὅρ]μον [ἄλυπον :]
'Ιὲ Παιάν κ.τ.λ.

[Ἔ]ν[θεν ἐ]π' ὀλβίας χθονὸς — ε'.
Θελ[ξινόας] ἔκελσας, ἃ
55 στῆσε μένος τ(ε) 'Ολυμπί[ας]
[ἐξορ]ίαν τε κλειτάν :
Εὐοῖ ὦ ἰὸ Βάκχ' [ὦ ἰὲ Παι]άν·
Μοῦσαι [δ'] αὐτίκα παρθένοι
κ[ισσῷ] στε[ψ]άμεναι κύκλῳ σε πᾶσαι
60 μ[έλψαν] ἀθάνα[τον] ἐς ἀεὶ
Παιᾶν' εὐκλέα τ' ὄ[πὶ κλέο]υ-
σαι· [κα]τᾶρξε δ' 'Απόλλων.
'Ιὲ Παιάν κ.τ.λ.

105 Ἐκτελέσαι δὲ πρᾶξιν Ἀμ- ι'.
φικτύονας θ[εὸς] κελεύ-
ει τάχος, ὡ[ς ἐπ]άβολος
μὴν ἱκέ[τας] κατάσχῃ:
Εὐοῖ ὦ [ἰὸ Β]άκχ' ὦ ἰὲ Παιάν·
110 δε[ῖξαι] δ' ἐν ξενίοις ἐτεί-
οις θεῶν ἱερῷ γένει συναίμῳ
τόνδ' ὕμνον, θυσίαν τε φαί-
νει[ν] σὺν Ἑλλάδος ὀλβίαις
πα[νδ]ήμοις ἱκετείαις.
115 Ἰὲ Παιάν κ.τ.λ.

Πυθιάσιν δὲ πενθετή- κ'.
ροισ[ι τ]ροπαῖς ἔταξε Βάκχου θυσίαν χορῶν τε πο[λ-]
135 [λῶν] κυκλίαν ἅμιλλαν:
Εὐοῖ ὦ ἰὲ Βάκχ' [ὦ ἰὲ Παι]άν:
τεύχειν· ἀλιοφεγγέσιν
δ' ἀρχο[ύσαις] ἴσον ἁβρὸν ἄγαλμα Βάκχου
ἐν . . . χρυσέων λεόν-
140 των στῆσαι ζαθέῳ τε τ[εῦ-]
ξαι θεῷ πρέπον ἄντρον.
Ἰὲ Παιάν κ.τ.λ.

Ἀλλὰ δέχεσθε βακχ[ειώ-] ν'.
145 [τα]ν Διόνυσ[ον, ἐν δ' ἀγυι-]
αῖς ἅμα σὺν [χοροῖσ]ι κ[ι-]
[κλῄσκετε] κισσ[οχ]αίταις:
Ε[ὐοῖ ὦ ἰ]ὸ Βάκχ' ὦ ἰὲ [Παιάν.]

(*Eight fragmentary or missing verses.*)

IV. PAIAN OF ARISTONOOS.[1]

Δελφοὶ ἔδωκαν Ἀριστονόῳ, ἐπεὶ τοὺς ὕμνους τοῖς θεοῖς ἐποίησεν, αὐτῷ καὶ ἐκγόνοις προξενίαν εὐεργεσίαν προμαντείαν προεδρίαν προδικίαν ἀσυλίαν πολέμου ἢ εἰρήνης, ἀτέλειαν πάντων καὶ ἐπιτιμίαν καθάπερ Δελφοῖς, ἄρχοντος Δαμοχάρεος, βουλευόντων Ἀντάνδρου, Ἐρασίππου, Εὐαρχίδα.

Ἀριστόνοος Νικοσθένους Κορίνθιος Ἀπόλλωνι Πυθίῳ τὸν ὕμνον.

α'. Πυθίαν ἱερόκτιτον
ναίων Δελφίδ' ἀμφὶ πέτραν
ἀεί θεσπιόμαντιν ἕ-
δραν, ἰὴ ἰὲ Παιάν,

Ἄπολλον, Κοίου τε κόρας β'.
Λατοῦς, σέμνον ἄγαλμα καὶ
Ζηνὸς ὑψίστου, μακάρων 7
βουλαῖς, ὦ ἰὲ Παιάν,

γ'. ἔνθ' ἀπὸ τριπόδων θεο-
10 κτήτων χλωρότομον δάφναν
σείων μαντοσύναν ἐποι-
χνεῖς, ἰὴ ἰὲ Παιάν,

φρικώεντος ἐξ ἀδύτου δ'.
μελλόντων θέμιν εὐσεβῆ
χρησμοῖς εὐφθόγγου τε λύρας
αὐδαῖς, ὦ ἰὲ Παιάν. 16

ε'. ἁγνισθεὶς ἐνὶ Τέμπεσιν
βουλαῖς Ζηνὸς ὑπειρόχου,
ἐπεὶ Παλλὰς ἔπεμψε Πυ-
20 θῶδε, ἰὴ ἰὲ Παιάν,

πείσας Γαῖαν ἀνθοτρόφον ϛ'.
Θέμιν τ' εὐπλόκαμον θεὰν
αἰὲν εὐλιβάνους ἕδρας
ἔχεις, ὦ ἰὲ Παιάν·

η'. ὅθεν Τριτογενῆ Προναί-
26 αν ἐν μαντείαις ἁγίοις
σέβων ἀθανάτοις ἀμοι-
βαῖς, ἰὴ ἰὲ Παιάν,

χάριν παλαιᾶν χαρίτων θ'.
τοῖς τότε ἀιδίοις ἔχων 30
μνήμας ὑψίστας ἐφέπεις
τιμαῖς, ὦ ἰὲ Παιάν.

ι'. δωροῦνται δέ σ' ἀθάνατοι
Ποσειδῶν ἁγνοῖς δαπέδοις,
35 Νύμφαι Κωρυκίοισιν ἄν-
τροις, ἰὴ ἰὲ Παιάν,

τριέτεσιν φαναῖς Βρόμιος· κ'.
σεμνὰ δ' Ἄρτεμις εὐπόνοις
κυνῶν ἐν φυλακαῖς ἔχει
τόπους, ὦ ἰὲ Παιάν. 40

λ'. ἀλλ' ὦ Παρνασσοῦ γυάλων
εὐδρόσοισι Κασταλίας
νασμοῖς σὸν δέμας ἐξαβρύ-
νων, ἰὴ ἰὲ Παιάν,

χαρεὶς ὕμνοις ἡμετέροις μ'.
ὄλβον ἐξ ὁσίων διδοὺς 46
ἀεὶ καὶ σῴζων ἐφέποις
ἡμᾶς, ὦ ἰὲ Παιάν.

---

[1] *B. C. H.* 17 (1893) 561 ff., *Philol.* 53 (1894) appendix.

V. PAIAN OF ISYLLOS OF EPIDAUROS.[1]

Ἰεπαιᾶνα θεὸν ἀείσατε λαοί,
ζαθέας ἐνναέται τᾶσδ' Ἐπιδαύρου.
ὧδε γὰρ φάτις ἐνέπουσ' ἦλυθ' ἐς ἀκοὰς
προγόνων ἀμετέρων, ὦ Φοῖβ' Ἀπόλλων.
5 Ἐρατὼ Μοῦσαν πατὴρ Ζεὺς λέγεται Μά-
λῳ δόμεν παράκοιτιν ὁσίοισι γάμοις.
Φλεγύας δ', ὃς πατρίδ' Ἐπίδαυρον ἔναιεν,
θυγατέρα Μάλου γαμεῖ, τὰν Ἐρατὼ γείνατο μάτηρ, Κλεοφήμα δ' ὀνομάσθη.
10 ἐκ δὲ Φλεγύα γένετο, Αἴγλα δ' ὀνομάσθη·
τόδ' ἐπώνυμον· τὸ κάλλος δὲ Κορωνὶς ἐπεκλήθη.
κατιδὼν δὲ ὁ χρυσότοξος Φοῖβος ἐν Μάλου δόμοις παρθενίαν ὥραν ἔλυσε,
λεχέων δ' ἱμεροέντων ἐπέβας, Λα-
15 τῷε κόρε χρυσοκόμα.
σέβομαί σε· ἐν δὲ θυώδει τεμένει τέκε-
το ἶνιν Αἴγλα, γονίμαν δ' ἔλυσεν ὠδῖ-
να Διὸς παῖς μετὰ Μοιρᾶν Λάχεσίς τε μαῖα ἀγαυά.
ἐπίκλησιν δέ νιν Αἴγλας ματρὸς Ἀσκλα-
20 πιὸν ὠνόμαξε Ἀπόλλων, τὸν νόσων παύ-
στορα, δωτῆρ' ὑγιείας, μέγα δώρημα βροτοῖς.
Ἰεπαιάν, ἰεπαιάν, χαῖρε Ἀσκλα-
πιέ, τὰν σὰν Ἐπίδαυρον ματρόπολιν αὔ-
ξον, ἐναργῆ δ' ὑγίειαν ἐπιπέμποις
25 φρεσὶ καὶ σώμασιν ἁμοῖς, ἰεπαιάν, ἰεπαιάν.

---

[1] Wilamowitz *Isyllos von Epidauros*, p. 13.

HYMN TO APOLLO (i.).[1]

---

[1] *Philol.* 53 (1895), App. 154; cf. *B. C. H.* 18 (1894) 359. From the Treasury of the Athenians at Delphi.

⊙ Μ ⊙ Ι Μ Υ
νασ - σί - δος ταᾶσ-δε πε - τέ - ρας ἕ - δρα-ν' ἄμ'
Υ Μ Υ ΜΙ ⊙ Ι Γ Ʊ Ф Γ
ἀ-] γα-κλυ-ταιεῖς Δεελ - φί - σιιν Κα - στα-λί-δος
Ʊ Ф Ʊ ⊙ Γ Λ
ε - οὐ - ύ - δρου νά - ματ' ἐ - πι - νί - σε - ται,
Μ Υ Μ Ι ⊙ Ι Μ
Δελ-φὸν ἀ - νὰ [πρ]ωῶνα μααν - τειεῖ - ον ἐ - φέ-
Φ Γ Ʊ Ф Ʊ
πων πά - γον. [Ἦν] κλυ - τὰ με - γα-λό-πο - λις
Κ Λ Μ Ο Κ
'Αθ - θὶς εὐ - χαιε[ῖ-σ]ι, φε - ρό - πλοι-ο ναί-
Λ Κ Γ Ʊ Ф Ʊ ⊙ Γ
ου - σα Τρι - τωω - νί - δος δά - [πε-]δον ἄ-

Μ Γ Β Γ Λ Κ Γ Ο Μ Γ
θραυ-στον, ἁ-γί - οις δὲ βω - μοιοῖ - σιν Ἅ-
Κ Μ Λ Κ Λ Μ Λ Μ
φ]αι-στος αιεῖ - θε[ι] νέ - ων μῆ - ρα ταού-
Ο Κ Λ Γ Μ Ʊ ⊙ Ι ⊙ Γ
ρων, ὁ - μουοῦ δέ νιν Ἄ - ραψ ἀ - τμὸς ἐς Ὄ-
⊙ Υ Ο Μ Λ Μ Ο Υ Ο
λυμ-πον ἀ - να - κίδ - ν[α-] ται· λι - γὺ δὲ λω-
Μ Λ Μ Λ Κ Λ Μ Μ Υ Ο
τοὸς βρέ-μων ἀει - ό - λοιοις [μέ-]λε - σιν ᾠ-
Μ Λ Μ Γ Λ Κ Γ Μ
δαὰν κρέ-κει, χρυ - σέ - α δ' ἀ - δύ - θρου[ς
Κ Λ Μ Ο Υ Ο Μ Λ Μ Ο
κί-]θα - ρις ὕ - μνοι-σιν ἀ - να - μέλ - πε - ται.

HYMN TO APOLLO (ii.).[1]

[1] *B. C. H.* 18 (1894) pl. xix.; from the Treasury of the Athenians at Delphi.

ναί - εθ' [῾Ε - λι-] κω - νί - δ[ας]. Μέλ - πε - τε δὲ
Πύ - θι - ον [χρυ-]σε-ο - χαί - ταν, ἕ - [κα - τ]ον,
εὐ - λύ - ραν Φοῖ - βον, ὃν ἔ - τι - κτε Λατὼ μά - και - ρα πα-[ρὰ λί - μνᾳ] κλυ - τᾷ,
χερ - σὶ γλαυ - καᾶς ἐ - λαί - ας θι - γουοῦ[σ'
ὄ - ζον ἐν ἀ - γω - νί - αι]ς ἐ - ρι - θα - [λῆ.
Πα[ᾶς δὲ γ]ά - θη - σε πό - λος οὐ - ρά - νι - ο[ς

ἀν - νέ - φε - λος, ἀ - γλα - ός, ν]η - νέ - μους
δ'ἔ - σχεν αἰ - θὴρ ἀ - [ελ - λωῶν τα - χυ-πε
τ]εῖς [δρό-] μους, λῆ - ξε δὲ βα - ρύ - βρο - μον
Νη[η - ρέ - ως ζα - με-νὲς ο]εῖ - δμ' ἠ - δὲ μέ - γας
'Ω - κε - α - νός, ὃς πέ - ριξ γ[αᾶν ὑ - γραιεῖς
ἀγ-] κά - λαις αἀμπ - έ - χει. Τό - τε λι - πὼν
Κυυν - θί - αν ναᾶ - σον ἐ[π-έ - βα θε - ὸ]ς

πρω - [τό-] καρ - πον κλυ - τὰν ᾿Ατ - [θ]ίδ᾿ ἐ - πὶ
γα(α-) λ[ό - φῳ πρωῶ - νι] Τρι - τωω - νί - [δ]ος·
με - λί - πνο - ον δὲ λί - βυς αὐ - δὰν χέ - ω[ν
λωω - τὸς ἀν - έ - μελ-] πεν [ἀ-] δειεῖ - αν ὄ - πα
μει - γνύ-με - νος αἰει - ό - λ[οις κι - θά-ρι - ος
μέ - λε - σιν· ἅ-] μα δ᾿ ἴ - α - χεν πε - τρο-κατ - οί-
κη - τος ἀ - χ[ὼ Παι - ὰν ἰ - ὲ Παι-άν·

ὁ] δὲ γέ - γαθ' ὅ - τι νό - ῳ δε - [ξ]ά - με - νος
αἀμ - βρό-ταν Δ[ι-ὸς ἐπ - έ - γνω φρέ]ν'· ἀνθ'
ωῶν ἐ - κεί - νας ἀπ' ἀρ - χᾶς Παι - ή-
ο - να κι - κλή - σκ[ο-μεν ἅ - πας λ]α - ὸς α[ὐ-
το-] χθό - νων ἠ - δὲ Βάκ - χου μέ - γας
θυρ - σο - πλὴ[ξ ἐ - σμὸς ἱ-] ε - ρὸς τε - χνι-
τῶν ἔν - οι - κοος πό - λει Κε - κρο-πί - α.

'Α[λ - λὰ χρηη - σμ]ῳ - δὸν ὃς ἔ - χειεις τρί - πο - δα,
βαῖν' ἐ - πὶ θε - ο - στιβ-[έ - α τάν - δε Π]αρ-
να[ασ-] σί - αν δει - ρά - δα φι - λέν - θε - ον.
'Αμ - φὶ πλό - κ[α - μον σὺ δ' οἰ] - νω[ῶ - πα] δάφ-
νας κλά - δον πλεξ - ά - με - νος αὰ - π[λέ-τουους
θε - με - λί - ους τ'] ἀαμ-βρό-τᾳ χει - ρὶ σύ-
ρων, ἄ - ναξ, Γ[ᾶς πε - λώ - ρῳ πε - ρι - πιτ-

C F
νεῖς] κό - ρᾳ. Ἀλ - λὰ Λαα - τοῦς ἐ - ρα - το-
γ[λέ-φα - ρε παῖ, μεῖ - νας ἀ - νυ - πό - στα - το]ν
παῖ - δα Γα-[ᾶς] τ' ἔ-πεφ - νες ἰ - οῖς ....

I. GREEK INDEX.

The fragments are cited by Arabic numerals; Roman numerals indicate the pages of the Introduction.)(= 'as distinguished from.'

ἀβακής Sa. 27.
ἀβακίζω An. 26.
ἁβροβάτης B. 1. 48.
ἁβρόβιος B. 10. 2.
ἁβρός St. 10; An. 25; B. 10. 2.
ἀγαθός Sim. 15. 4; F. S. 25.
ἄγε Alkm. 18; St. 12; An. 24. 1; 24. 7.
ἀγέλη B. 10. 10.
ἀγκύλαι Alk. 4. 9.
ἀγλαΐζω F. S. 7. 1.
ἀγλαόθρονοι B. 9. 124.
ἀγλαός B. 9. 2.
ἀγρέτης Alkm. 4. 8.
ἀγρέω Sa. 2. 14.
ἄγριος An. 1. 7; 5. 3.
ἀγροῖκος Alkm. 5. 1.
ἀγροτέρα B. 5. 37; Sk. 3. 3.
ἄγω Sa. 1. 9; Pr. 1. 5.
ἀδεισιβόας B. 5. 61.
ἀδίαντος Sim. 13. 3; B. 9. 122.
ἀεθλοφόρος Alkm. 4. 48; Ib. 2. 5.
ἀείρω Alkm. 4. 62.
ἀέλιος P. 10. 1.
ἀελλόπους Sim. 3.
ἀεροφοίτης Ion 2.
ἀερσίνοος Ion 1.
ἀζαλέος Ib. 1. 8.
ἀήτα Sim. 17; B. 9. 91.
ἀθαμβής B. 8. 22.
'Αθάνα Sk. 1.
'Αθανάα Alk. 2. 1.
'Αθηνᾶ Sk. 1.
ἄθυρμα B. 10. 57.
αἰ B. 9. 64.
αἴ An. 1. 4; Sim. 8; B. 9. 92; 9. 129; Tel. 1. 12; Sk. 9. 3.
Αἴας Alk. 26; Sk. 20.
αἰδώς Lykoph. 1.
αἰθήρ Sa. 1. 11; B. 2. 17; 9. 73.
αἰόλος B. 8. 21; Tel. 1. 12; 2. 3; F. S. 7. 2.
-αιος Sim. 4.
αἴτας Alk. 20. 2.
αἰχμή Terp. 6.
ἀίω Alkm. 4. 95; Sa. 1. 6.
ἀκάμας Arist. 5.
ἄκλαυστος Alkm. 4. 39.

ἀκουαί Sa. 2. 12.
ἀκούω B. 9. 67; M. A. 8.
ἀλάθεα Alk. 32.
ἀλέγω Alkm. 4. 2; Sim. 13. 10.
ἁλιπόρφυρος Alkm. 7. 4; Arion 18.
ἀλκυών Alkm. 7. 3.
ἀλλά Alkm. 4. 2; 4. 82; Sa. 1. 5; 1. 22.
ἀλλά *cum inf.* P. 9. 5.
γάρ Alkm. 10. 7; B. 2. 162.
ἄλλος Sa. 2. 16.
ἄλοξ Arion 15.
ἅμα Alkm. 7. 3; B. 1. 91.
ἁμαρτέω B. 10. 46.
ἀμβολογήρα F. S. 3.
ἀμβροσία Sa. 18.
ἀμετρόδικος B. 5. 68.
ἀμός Alkm. 4. 81; B. 13. 11.
ἀμύνω Alkm. 4. 65.
ἀμύσσω B. 10. 11.
ἄμυστιν An. 24. 2.
ἀμφί B. 9. 105.
ἀμφιανακτίζω Terp. 2.
ἀμῶς Alkm. 4. 45.
ἄν B. 5. 30; 'omitted' Sa. 2. 2; 2. 7; Sim. 2. 9; 2. 15; 23. 6; P. 2. 5; 4. 17; 23. 3; B. 9. 118.
ἄνᾱ Alkm. 4. 83.
ἀναγνέω Lasos.
ἀνάγω F. S. 6.
ἀναδέω Sim. 5.
ἀναιδομάχης B. 2. 105.
ἀνακάμπτω B. 9. 82.
ἀναξίμολπος B. 3. 10.
ἄνασσα Sk. 1.
ἀνασταλύζω An. 16. 4.
ἀνδρεῖα Alkm. 28. 2.
ἀνεψιά Alkm. 4. 52.
ἀνήρ Alkm. 11. 4; Sa. 33; 35; B. 10. 7.
ἄνητον Alk. 14.
ἄνθος Alkm. 7. 3; B. 13. 2.
ἀνιάω Sa. 1. 3; 42. 7.
ἄντα Alkm. 12.
ἀντιπέρας St. 1.
-ανω, -αινω Alk. 19. 5.
ἀοιδή B. 10. 4.
ἀπάλαμνος Alk. 25; Sim. 2. 18.
ἀπαρθένευτος F. S. 7. 3.
ἀπό)(ἐξ Sim. 12.
)(παρά An. 21.
)(ὑπὸ Sim. 2. 4.
ἀποπνέω ψυχήν Sim. 20.
ἀποπομπέω F. S. 20.
ἀποτρέπω B. 5. 27.
ἄπρακτος Sim. 15. 1.
ἄπυρος Alkm. 10. 3; Sk. 23.
ἄρα with imperf. Pytherm.; Timokr. 3. 1.
ἀραρεῖν Sim. 17.
ἀργηστής B. 2. 67.
ἀργύριον Timokr. 1. 8.
ἀργυρόριζος St. 1.
ἀργύφεος Alkm. 11. 7.
ἄρδω Ib. 1. 2.
ἀρέταιχμος B. 9. 47.
ἀριστόκαρπος B. 1. 1.
ἀριστοπάτρα B. 5. 106.
ἄρκος Alk. 24. 4.
ἄρμενα Alkm. 31.
ἄρρητος B. 14.
ἀρχή Terp. 1.
ἄρχω Alkm. 18; St. 12; B. 8. 11.

ἄσαμαι Alk. 10. 2.
ᾆσμα xix.
ἄσμενοι Alkm. 31.
ἀστραγάλαι An. 18.
ἄστρον Alkm. 4. 63; Alk. 19. 1; P. 6. 4; 10. 2.
ἀσυνέτημι Alk. 4. 1.
ἀτάλλω P. 29. 2.
ἀτάρβακτος B. 2. 139.
ἄτε Alkm. 4. 62.
ἄτρυφος Alkm. 11. 6.
αὐδάεις P. 26. 3; B. 8. 8.
ἀυειρομέναι Alkm. 4. 63.
αὔιτα Alk. 20. 2.
αὐλοί xciv.
αὔξω Ib. 1. 5.
αὐτάρ Alk. 9. 5.
αὐτεῖ Alkm. 4. 79.
αὔτως An. 11. 12.
ἄχαρις Sa. 12.
ἄχολος Alk. 18.
ἄωρος Sk. 1. 4.
ἀωτεύω B. 4. 13.
ἀωτέω Sim. 13. 5.

βαθυ- B. 1. 82.
βαθύς B. 1. 85.
Βάκχιος Timoth. 2.
βάλε Alkm. 7. 2.
βάλλω B. 1. 96.
βαρύβρομος Lasos; B. 9. 76.
βαρύγδουπος Ion 1.
βασσαρέω An. 24. 6.
βερβέριον An. 11. 1.
βία Sim. 4.
βίος An. 11. 6.
βλάσται M. A. 6.
βλέπω An. 4.
βλέφαρον B. 2. 157; see γλέφαρον.
βληχρός P. 16. 9; B. 5. 65.
βόσκομαι An. 27. 5.
βοῶπις B. 5. 99.
βράγχιοι Arion 4.
βρίθω B. 13. 12.
Βρόμιος Prat. 1. 3; Sk. 4. 2.
βροχέως Sa. 2. 7.
βρυάζω Timoth. 2.
βρύω B. 1. 16; 3. 9.

γαιάοχος Arion 3.
γαλαθηνός An. 21; Sim. 13. 6.
γαμβρός Sa. 33.
γαμέω)(-οῦμαι An. 29.
γάρ Alkm. 10. 6; B. 2. 162; F. S. 12.
γε μέν B. 1. 63.
γελανόω B. 2. 80.
γέννα P. 6. 10.
γένος Alkm. 21. 4.
γεροιά Kor. 4.
γεύομαι B. 4. 46.
γλαυκέων Ib. 5. 1.
γλέπω Alkm. 4. 75.
γλέφαρον Alkm. 4. 21; 4. 69.
γλυκυ- B. 2. 4.
γλυκύπικρος Sa. 16.
γλῶσσα B. 2. 196.
γλωσσάω Alkm. 6. 2.
γνόφαλλον Alk. 9. 6.
γόος Sim. 1. 3.

δᾳδοφόρος B. 20.
δαῆναι B. 2. 64.
-δαιδαλος P. 4. 6; B. 9. 88.
-δαιδαλτος B. 1. 18.
δαΐζω B. 6. 23.

-δαΐκτης B. 4. 6.
δαίμων Diag. 2.
δαΐφρων B. 2. 122.
δάκνω P. 15. 8.
δάκτυλος Alk. 20. 1.
Δᾶλος P. 6. 4.
δαμάλης An. 2. 1.
δάμνημι Sa. 32. 3.
δασπλής Sim. 14.
δαῦτε Alkm. 13.
δέ apodotic Timokr. 1. 2; B. 8. 25; 17. 3.
begins a verse B. 9. 13.
continuative Alkm. 4. 58.
δέ τε Sa. 35; B. 6. 26; 13. 1.
δέμας B. 2. 147.
δένδριον Alk. 22.
δεξίστρατος B. 8. 7.
Δεύνυσος An. 2. 11.
δεῦτε Sa. 22; An. 24. 7.
δεῦτε Alkm. 13.
δέχομαι P. 8. 4; 18. 2.
δή An. 23.
δῆλος Alk. 4. 7.
Δῆλος P. 6. 4.
δήμωμα St. 10.
δηῦτε An. 24. 6.
δίᾱ Tel. 1. 2.
διακρινής B. 4. 28.
διανεκῶς Kor. 2.
διαπλέκω Alkm. 4. 38.
διθύραμβος xliv.
Δίκα Sa. 29. 1.
δινάω B. 9. 18.
δίνημι Sa. 1. 11; B. 9. 107.
διοσκέω An. 3.
διχόμηνις B. 4. 29.
διώκω Sim. 8.
Διώνυσος P. 1. 5.
δοιάζω B. 5. 87.
δολιχός B. 10. 16.
δολοπλόκος Sa. 1. 2.
δόμος B. 1. 49; Arist. 12.
δονέω Sa. 16.
δόρυ An. 11. 7; Sim. 13. 7; B. 9. 90.
δρέπομαι P. 15. 1.
δύναμις Arist. 11.
δυσπαίπαλος B. 2. 26.
ϵ semivowel Prax. 1.
ἑανός Alkm. 4. 69.
ἔασσα Alkm. 32.
ἐγκλαίω B. 2. 142.
ἐγρεκύδοιμος Lampr.
ἐθέλω B. 2. 14.
εἴ An. 6. 1; B. 1. 3.
εἰ καί B. 9. 29.
εἴαρος Alkm. 7. 4.
εἴδωλον P. 17. 3.
εἴκω Sa. 2. 8; 40.
εἶναι 'live' Sk. 8. 2.
εἶρεν B. 9. 20.
εἰρήνη B. 13. 1; M. A. 3.
εἷς with superl. Timokr. 1. 4.
εἰς, ἐς B. 8. 7.
εἰσάνταν B. 2. 110.
ἑκατηβόλος Terp. 2.
ἕκατι Alkm. 12; P. 15. 8.
ἔκλεκτος Ib. 10. 2.
ἐλελίζω Sim. 8.
ἔλεος Sim. 1. 3.
ἔλλαθι B. 5. 8.
ἔλλω Sa. 42. 14.
ἔλπομαι P. 3. 1.

ἐμβαίνω *cum gen.* Alk. 5. 3.
ἐμπρέπω B. 4. 27.
ἐν of musical accompaniment An. 24. 11; P. 4. 20; Tel. 3. 1.
cum accus. P. 4. 1; 11. 2.
Ἐναρσφόρος Alkm. 4. 3.
ἐνδυκέως B. 2. 112.
Ἐνετικός Alkm. 4. 51.
ἐνθοῖσα Alkm. 4. 73.
ἐνιαυτός F. S. 22. 3.
ἕννυμι active B. 5. 120.
ἐξ Sa. 1. 13.
)(ἀπό Sim. 12.
ἐξεναρίζω B. 2. 146.
ἐξέχω F. S. 17.
εο short Telesilla.
ἑός B. 15. 5.
ἐπακούω An. 2. 8.
ἐπεί B. 9. 43.
ἐπεί τε An. 14.
ἐπέλπομαι Tel. 1.
ἐπί of purpose P. 9. 2.
with πέμπω B. 2. 90.
ἐπιβαίνω Alkm. 4. 91; Alk. 5. 3.
ἐπιδεύαο Alk. 2. 2.
ἐπιδεύω Sa. 2. 15.
ἐπιρρόμβημι Sa. 2. 11.
ἐπισκήπτω B. 2. 42.
ἐπιστέφω Alkm. 26.
ἐπισχόμενος St. 2.
ἐπιτάρροθος Terp. 6.
ἕπομαι ἐς B. 5. 115.
ἔπος Alkm. 6. 1.
ἑπτάτονος Terp. 5.
ἐραννός B. 9. 42.
ἐρατώνυμος St. 12; B. 9. 31.
ἐράω Alkm. 10. 5.
ἐρείπω Sim. 13. 3; B. 5. 68.
ἐρεμνός B. 9. 116.
ἐρεύθω B. 6. 49.
ἐρέω 'love' An. 3. 1.
ἐρέω 'say' P. 2. 2.
ἕρκυς Ariph. 5.
ἔρνος B. 2. 87.
ἑρπετά Alkm. 21. 3.
ἕρπω Alkm. 12; Diag. 1. 3.
ἔρωτες P. 15. 1.
ἐς P. 18. 2; B. 8. 7.
-ες for -εις Sa. 36.
-εσθω plur. An. 15.
ἔστι Sim. 28.
ἐστί omitted Alk. 9. 2; An. 7. 7; 16. 6; Sim. 2. 21; B. 4. 4.
ἑταῖρα Sa. 6.
εὖ ἔρδω B. 2. 36.
εὖ πράσσω Sim. 2. 7; B. 1. 94.
εὕδω Sim. 13. 15; 199.
εὐθύς Sk. 14. 3.
εὐπατρίδες Sk. 11. 3.
εὔπυργος B. 2. 184.
εὑρίσκω Alkm. 6. 2.
εὐρυάγυια Terp. 6.
εὐρυβίας B. 5. 52.
εὐφροσύνη B. 1. 57; 5. 12.
εὔφρων Alkm. 4. 37.
-ευω, -εω Alkm. 10. 8.
ἐφοράω P. 6. 10.
ἔχω Alk. 30; Ib. 8.
ἔχων 'with' Alkm. 7. 4.

Ϝ Terp. 2; 5; 6; Alkm. 4. 41; 4. 63; 21. 2; Alk. 24. 5; Sa. 2. 9; 2. 13; B. 1. 2; 9. 129; 9. 131; 10. 46.

ζάδηλος Alk. 4. 7.
Ζεύς Alk. 9. 1.

ἤ B. 2. 9.
ἤ repeated P. 1; B. 10. 5.
ἤθεος B. 9. 43.
ἥμερος An. 1. 7; B. 5. 39.
ἡμίθεοι Sim. 12. 2; B. 4. 10.
ἡνιοχεύω An. 4. 4.
ἦρα B. 2. 165.
ἦρα = χάριν B. 5. 21.
ἥρω voc. F. S. 5. 1.
ἧς Alkm. 5. 1.
ἦτορ Sim. 13. 6.

θαλασσαῖος Sim. 22. 4.
-θαλης B. 4. 5.
θαλίαι Sa. 5.
θάλλω Terp. 6; Alkm. 27. 4; F. S. 25.
θάλος Ib. 5. 1; Philox.
θάλπω B. 13. 11.
θαμά B. 6. 70.
θάνατοι Sk. 1. 4.
θελημός B. 9. 85.
θέλω B. 2. 14.
θέμις B. 1. 88; 8. 19.
θεός repeated Diag. 1; B. 1. 21.
θεράπων B. 2. 14.
θερσιεπής B. 6. 76.
θήρ Arion 5.
θιγγάνω *cum gen.* B. 9. 12.
cum accus. Alkm. 15. 2.
θιειδής Alkm. 4. 71.
θοός Sim. 23. 3.
Θρηΐκιος Ib. 1. 8.
θριαμβοδιθύραμβε Prat. 1. 16.
θυιάς Timoth. 1.
θύμενος Prat. 1. 4.
θυμός Alk. 1; Ib. 4; P. 15. 1.
θυρωρός Sa. 37.
θύω P. 6. 6; B. 6. 21; F. S. 5. 5.

ι elided An. 8. 4; B. 10. 10; 13. 12.
=ϊ Sa. 1. 17.
ἰαίνω Alkm. 13; P. 15. 10; B. 9. 131.
Ἰάλυσος Timokr. 1. 7.
ἰάτωρ Alkm. 4. 89.
ἰδέ B. 7. 5.
ἰδρώς Sa. 2. 13.
ἰέ Timoth. 8.
ἵεμαι F. S. 1.
ἱερόδακρυς Mel. 1. 5.
ἱερός St. 3. 2; P. 4. 5; 15. 9; B. 10. 1.
-ιζω An. 23. 4.
ἰή xxxvi; cxxiii; Timokr. 8.
ἵημι: ἵει (ῐ) F. S. 1.
ἱκνέομαι *cum accus.* St. 7; Sim. 14.
ἴκταρ Alkm. 4. 80.
ἱμεράμπυξ B. 9. 9.
ἱμεράφωνος Alkm. 7. 1.
ἵνα B. 10. 42.
ἶξον B. 6. 46.
ἰόπλοκος Alk. 13; B. 9. 37.
ἴον Alk. 13.
ἰός B. 2. 75.
ἰοστέφανος B. 1. 2.
ἴουλος F. S. 1.
ἵππιος B. 9. 99.
ἱπποδίνητος B. 2. 2.
ἵπποι fem. P. 1. 8; B. 1. 3.
ἰσοδαίμων Ariph. 4; Likym. 5.

ἰσόνομος Sk. 7. 4.
ἵστημι: σταθείς middle B. 9. 84.
ἵσταμαι = αἱροῦμαι Alk. 18. 3.
ἴσχω B. 9. 88.
ἰώ Sk. 4. 1.
ἰώνη Kor. 3.
ἰωνοκάμπτης Timoth. 6. 3.

καβαίνων Alkm. 15.
κάββαλλε Alk. 9. 3.
καθοράω Sk. 13. 1.
καί of reciproc. relat. Sa. 14. 2.
introd. myth B. 1. 23.
crasis Sa. 24. 3; B. 10. 50.
κ(αί) Sk. 7. 2.
καὶ μήν B. 6. 59.
καί τε P. 18. 4; M. A. 15.
καιρός P. 15. 1; B. 7. 17; F. S. 10; 11.
καίτοι with part. Sim. 2. 4.
κακκαβίς Alkm. 6. 3.
κακόπατρις Alk. 18.
κακός Sim. 15. 5.
καλλιβόας αὐλός Sim. 19. 3.
καλός Alkm. 32; B. 6. 83; F. S. 22. 2.
καμόντες Alkm. 4. 2.
κάμπτω Timoth. 6. 3.
καμπύλος Sim. 8.
καναχάπους Alkm. 4. 48.
κάρρων F. S. 13. 3.
κατά of physical scrutiny Sk. 13. 1.
cum gen. Alkm. 31. 2; B. 9. 94.
in Aiolic. Sa. 4. 4; 35. 2.
καταθύμιος Eum.
καταναίω B. 5. 41.
κατάρχω Alkm. 28; F. S. 7. 5.
καταστείβω Sa. 35.
καταχραίνω B. 2. 44.
κατέχω B. 5. 11.
κεῖνος Sa. 2. 1.
κελαδέω Sa. 4. 2.
κελέβη An. 24. 2.
κέλευθος B. 2. 31; 2. 196.
κέρναμι Alk. 9. 4; 20. 4.
κεφαλή = pronoun B. 2. 91.
κῇ Sa. 18. 1.
κήν Sa. 24. 3.
κηρύλος Alkm. 7. 2.
κιθαριστής Alkm. 24.
κιθαρῳδός lxii; Alkm. 24.
κινεῖν ἀφ' ἱερᾶς Alk. 17.
κισσός P. 4. 11.
κλεεννός B. 2. 182; Sk. 4. 1.
-κλεης P. 4. 6; Timokr. 1. 4.
Κλεησι- Alkm. 4. 72.
κλείζω = κλείω Lampr.
κλεινός St. 1; B. 2. 182.
κλείω St. 8.
κλεννός Alkm. 4. 44.
κλονέω B. 6. 15.
κλυτός Ib. 7; Sim. 34; P. 4. 2.
κλύω Sa. 1. 6; B. 9. 67.
κνημίς Alk. 20. 2; 24. 4.
κνίζω B. 9. 8.
κνώδαλον Alkm. 21.
κοέω An. 4. 2.
Κοιογενής P. 6. 6.
κοῖος F. S. 28.
κόρη B. 1. 2.
κορώνη B. 2. 73.
κορωνίς St. 6. 3.
κόσμος Sim. 1. 9; Timoth. 3.

κούιλος Alk. 24. 5.
κούρα B. 1. 2; 2. 104.
κρέουσα B. 1. 1.
κρήδεμνον B. 17. 6.
κρηπίς P. 26. 1.
Κρονίδης of Poseidon B. 9. 77; 10. 21.
κρόταφος B. 9. 30.
κυάνεος Ib. 2. 1.
κυανόπρῳρα B. 9. 1.
κυβαλικός Timokr. 1. 6.
κυπαίρισκος Alkm. 15. 2.
κύπαιρος Alkm. 3.
κυπάσσιδες Alk. 24. 6.
κύτος Alkm. 10. 1.
κωμάζω F. S. 12.
κῶμος lxxv.

λαισήϊον Sk. 25. 2.
λάμπω Sa. 33; Ariph. 8; M. A. 12. 5.
λανθάνω: λελάθοιτε M. A. 13. 10.
λάρναξ Sim. 13. 1.
λάσκω: λέληκα Alkm. 4. 86.
λείριος B. 9. 95.
λεπτόθριξ B. 2. 28.
λεπτόπρυμνος B. 9. 119.
λεύκιππος Ib. 9. 1.
λευκοπτέρυξ Ion 2.
λευκός B. 9. 13.
Λευτυχίδης Timokr. 1. 2.
λιγύς Terp. 6.
λίθος Sim. 22. 5.
λιπαρός P. 5. 1.
λίσσομαι Alk. 34; Sa. 1. 2; P. 8. 3.
λόγος)(μῦθος Sim. 23. 1.
λοξός An. 27. 1.
Λοῦσος B. 5. 96.
λυρικός xvii.
λυσιμελής Sa. 16; F. S. 25. 3.
λύχνον Alk. 20. 1.

μαλακαύγητος Arist. 8.
μαλερός Arist. 5.
μαλίστᾳ Alkm. 4. 87.
μανίαι Anakr. 18; B. 5. 109.
μαρύομαι F. S. 16. 2.
ματέω Sa. 21. 3.
μαχαιτής Alk. 16. 5.
μεγαλοῦχος B. 9. 23.
μέγας of gods Alkm. 32. 1; B. 13. 1.
μεδέω Alk. 1. 1.
μείγνυμι B. 17. 4.
μέλαθρον Sa. 33. 1.
μελαμφαρής B. 1. 13.
μέλας of the earth Alkm. 21. 3; Sa. 1. 10.
of the eyes B. 9. 17.
of the heart P. 15. 4.
μελίγηρυς Alkm. 7. 1.
μελίγλωσσος B. 13. 2.
μελιστής St. 13.
μελίφρων B. 13. 10.
μελλιχόμειδος Alk. 13.
μέλλω B. 1. 30.
μέλομαι *cum inf.* An. 25. 1.
μέλος xviii; Alkm. 6. 1.
μέλω P. 23. 3.
μέν B. 1.
μὲν . . . δέ Alkm. 4. 58; B. 1. 16; 17. 6.
μὲν οὖν P. 2. 3.
μὲν . . . τε P. 4. 14; 16. 1.

μέριμνα B. 17. 5.
μέροπες M. A. 12. 1.
μετά Sa. 24. 4; B. 2. 30; 5. 123; Ariph. 1; Tel. 1. 12.
μεταιβολία Sim. 13. 17.
μή μοι Alkm. 15. 2; Sim. 19. 2.
μηλίς)(μῆλον Ib. 1. 2.
μινύθω B. 1. 90.
μίνυνθα B. 2. 151.
μίτρα Alkm. 4. 68; An. 25. 2; B. 6. 73.
Μνάμα Terp. 3.
μνοΐα Sk. 25. 5.
μοναρχέω *cum dat.* B. 17. 7.
μορφή Arist. 3.
μῦθος)(λόγος Sim. 23. 1.
μωμέομαι Sim. 2. 20.
μῶμος B. 6. 79.
Μώσαρχος Terp. 3.

ναῦς: νᾷ Alkm. 4. 95; νᾶα B. 9. 119.
νέμω Sim. 2. 3.
νεόκροτος B. 2. 48.
νεόκτιτος B. 9. 126.
νέφος B. 19. 3.
νεώτερος P. 10. 6.
νηδεής Alkm. 7. 4.
νόμος lviii; Alkm. 25.
νόσφι Sim. 13. 19.
νύκτες Sa. 19. 3.
νυκτιλαμπής Sim. 13. 8.
νύμφη Prax. 3.

ξουθός B. 2. 17.

ὄαρος Ariph. 8.
ὅδε Prat. 1. 1.
ὁδός P. 10. 4; B. 9. 89; 15. 1.
οἵ Sim. 1. 4; B. 18. 2; Sk. 5. 1; 7. 4; F. S. 6. 2; 27. 6; 27. 34.
οι elided Sa. 1. 20; 2. 13.
οἷά τε Alkm. 11. 4; An. 21. 1; Prat. 1. 5; B. 2. 65.
οἶδα An. 27. 2; Sim. 2. 18; P. 19.
οἰκτίρω St. 4.
οἶκτος cxxii; Sim. 1. 3.
οἰνανθίς Ib. 1. 4.
οἷον οὐ Alkm. 4. 2.
οἷος Alkm. 4. 99; B. 9. 120.
ὄλβιος Alkm. 4. 37; Sa. 38. 1; Sim. 11. 2; P. 19.
ὄλβοι B. 1. 22.
ὀλολύζω B. 9. 127.
Ὀλύμπιος Sk. 2. 1.
ὀμφή P. 4. 20; B. 2. 191.
ὀπηδός Sk. 4. 2.
ὁπότε P. 4. 16; 6. 6; B. 6. 7.
ὀπώρα Alkm. 27. 2.
ὁρᾶν Alkm. 4. 50.
ὁρᾶν ἐς P. 4. 1; 15. 9.
ὄργυια Sa. 37.
ὄρθιος 167; 170.
ὀρθόω Sk. 1. 2.
ὀρίνομαι B. 6. 9.
ὄρνυ(σο) B. 9. 76.
ὄρπηξ Sa. 39.
ὅσιος B. 9. 21.
ὅσσον with inf. Sa. 14.
ὅστε Alkm. 7. 3; An. 21. 2; B. 10. 39.
ὅστις Sa. 2. 2; Sim. 2. 15.
οὐ γάρ B. 2. 162.
οὐδὲ . . . οὐδέ Alkm. 5.

οὐ . . . ἔτι Alkm. 7. 1.
οὐκ ἔσθ' ὅπως P. 3. 3.
οὐ μή Sim. 2. 19.
οὔ τί που Sk. 8. 1.
οὔλιος B. 10. 53.
οὖλος F. S. 1 ; B. 9. 113.
οὖς Alkm. 16 ; Sim. 13. 14.
οὗτος B. 10. 39.
ὀφείλω Timokr. 4.
ὄφρα St. 3. 2 ; B. 10. 42.
ὄχημα P. 9. 6.

πάις An. 8. 3.
παλαιστή Alk. 16. 6.
παλάμη Sk. 13. 2.
παμφάγος Alk. 10. 4.
πανδαμάτωρ Sim. 1. 5.
παρά of descent Sim. 12.
cum gen. with passive An. 21 ; Sim. 2. 4.
cum dat. Alkm. 5. 2; Ib. 11.
cum accus. B. 1. 6 ; 2. 38.
παράπληκτος Mel. 3. 4.
παραπλήξ B. 5. 45.
πάρεδρος B. 5. 51.
παρθενική Alkm. 7. 1 ; 32. 2 ; B. 9. 11.
παρθένος Prax. 3.
πάροιθεν Alk. 2. 3.
πᾶς = ὅλος Sa. 2. 14.
παταγέω An. 5. 4.
πεδά Alkm. 10. 5 ; Sa. 24. 4.
πείθω : ἔπιθον B. 5. 107.
πελειάδες Alkm. 4. 60 ; Sim. 7.
πέλομαι Eum.; Sa. 29. 3.
πέμπω Terp. 1. 3.
πεπρωμένη B. 1. 25 ; 9. 26.
πέρα St. 1.
πέργαμα St. 7.
περί = ὑπέρ Alk. 4. 6 ; 31 ; Sa. 1. 10; B. 10. 51; Arist. 3.
cum dat. P. 15. 6.
περιφόρητος An. 11.
πέταλον B. 2. 186.
πέτομαι Tel. 1. 9.
πλείσταρχος B. 1. 12
πλεύμων Alk. 19. 1.
πλημμύρω B. 2. 107.
πλήξιππος B. 4. 20.
πλουτοδότης F. S. 4.
ποιέω B. 2. 177 ; ποΐω F. S. 16.
ποικιλόθρονος Sa. 1. 1.
ποικίλος B. 5. 33.
ποιμαίνω An. 1. 8.
πολεμαδόκος Alk. 2 ; Lampr.
πολέμαιγις B. 9. 7.
πόλις Sim. 25.
πολύζηλος B. 5. 63.
πολυμμελής Alkm. 1.
πολύμοχθος Arist. 1.
πολύπλαγκτος B. 5. 35.
πολύς fem. B. 2. 100.
πολύφανος Alkm. 11. 2.
πολύχορδος Sim. 19.
πολύχρυσος B. 5. 4.
πονάω Sa. 37.
πόντος)(πέλαγος P. 10. 13 ; B. 9. 94.
Πορθανίδα B. 2. 70.
πόρος M. A. 12. 7.
πόρρω F. S. 12.
πορφύρεος, -πορφυρος Alkm. 21. 5 ; Arion 18 ; Sa. 35 ; An. 2. 3; Phryn.

Ποσιδηϊών An. 5. 1.
ποτί *cum dat.* St. 15; Ib. 2. 5; P. 28.
ποῦ B. 1. 39.
πούς St. 3. 6; F. S. 5. 5.
πράσσω neuter P. 17. 4.
εὖ Sim. 2. 7; B. 1. 94.
πρίν B. 5. 72.
πρό = *ἀντί* Sim. 1. 3.
προάστιον P. 16. 2.
πρόβλημα Sk. 25. 2.
προκόπτω Alk. 10. 2.
προκυκλέω F. S. 22. 6.
πρός *cum gen.* w. passive P. 18. 5.
cum dat. B. 5. 23.
cum accus. B. 2. 45.
πρὸς βίαν Alk. 6.
πρότερος B. 2. 43.
προφανής B. 1. 51.
προφερέστατος M. A. 12. 8.
προφήτης P. 8. 5; B. 4. 3.
πρύτανις Ion 1. 4.
πρώϝων Alkm. 21. 2.
πτάζω Alk. 8.
πταίω P. 28.
πτηνός P. 10. 4.
πτήσσω B. 6. 14; πεπτηῶτες Sk. 25. 8.
πτοέω Sa. 2. 6.
πύλαι B. 14.
πυλεών Alkm. 3.
πύργος Alk. 15.
πυργόω B. 1. 13.
πυρσοχαίτης B. 10. 51.
πῶλος Alkm. 4. 47; An. 27. 1; B. 2. 39.
Πωλυδεύκης Alkm. 4. 1.
πώλυπος Alkm. 4. 1.
πώνω Alk. 6.
πῶρος Alkm. 4. 10.

ρ confused with ϝ Alkm. 4. 41.
ῥάκος Sa. 26.
ῥέπω B. 9. 25.
ῥιπτέω St. 6.
ῥίπτω St. 6; ἔριψαν Arion 18.
ῥέω Sa. 4.
ῥυσμός An. 26. 2.

σακεσφόρος B. 6. 1.
σάμβαλον Eum.; Sa. 37; An. 7. 3.
σατίνη An. 11. 10.
σείρια Ib. 3; see Sirius.
σεληναίη Prax. 2.
σηκός)(*ναός* Sim. 1. 3.
σκαιός Alkm. 5. 2.
σκολιός xcv; Sk. 14. 4.
σκότος Erin. 2; P. 2. 5.
σκύφιον St. 2.
σκύφος Alkm. 11. 3.
σοέω B. 9. 90.
σοφία B. 16.
σοφός Alkm. 5. 2; B. 6. 78.
σός Arist. 12.
σπίλος F. S. 27. 34.
στεφανηφόρος Sk. 2. 2; 16.
στεφανοῦμαι B. 5. 29.
στρατηγός B. 2. 2.
στρίγξ F. S. 20.
στρουθός Sa. 1. 10.
σύ with imper. B. 9. 76; F. S. 22. 6.

σύν of musical accomp. P. 4. 20.
temporal B. 5. 23; 5. 125.
with abstract nouns Alk. 29; P. 15. 1; B. 1. 5; 1. 96; Tel. 1. 12; F. S. 25. 3.
personifies Alk. 4. 4; Sim. 16. 3.
σύν μοι Sk. 16.
συνεχέως B. 2. 113.
-συνη Sa. 24. 1.
συνηβᾶν An. 12; Sk. 16.
σύνθεσις P. 28.
σύνοικος Sa. 30; B. 8. 20; Ariph. 2.
Συράκουσ(σ)αι B. 2. 184.
σφέτερος 'his' B. 1. 36.
σῶμα B. 9. 62.

τακερός Ib. 2. 1.
Ταλαϊονίδης B. 4. 19.
ταμίας F. S. 10.
τανυπτέρυξ Alkm. 21. 7; Sim. 11.
τανύσφυρος B. 1. 60.
ταχύς Sa. 1. 10.
τε of permanent characteristic Alkm. 7. 3; 11. 4; Sa. 35. 2; An. 21. 1; Sim. 2. 22; Prat. 1. 5; B. 2. 65.
position P. 22. 1.
after *μέν* P. 4. 14; 16. 1.
τε . . . δέ P. 23.
τε . . . καί Alkm. 21. 1; An. 6. 3; 15; P. 8. 3; B. 13. 5.
τε . . . τε B. 9. 50; 13. 8; Mel. 2. 3.
τειχίζω P. 26. 2.
τέλεος B. 5. 92.
τέλος B. 5. 6.
τέμνω Arion 16; B. 2. 17.
τετράγωνος Sim. 2. 2.
τέτρατος Alkm. 27. 3.
τέττιξ Alk. 19. 3.
τήκομαι P. 15. 9.
-την for *-τον* Sk. 10.
-τηρ, -της, -τωρ as fem. Alkm. 4. 89; Sim. 1. 6.
τηρέω Alkm. 4. 77.
-τηρια Alkm. 4. 81.
τί = *ὅτι* P. 23. 1.
τίθημι factitive, P. 10. 3; B. 1. 7.
= *ποιέω* P. 10. 3; B. 9. 118.
τίκτω Sk. 3. 1.
τις Sa. 27. 1; P. 12. 1; B. 1. 22.
τιτύσκω B. 2. 49.
τὸ πάλαι B. 14.
τὸ παρ' ἦμαρ B. 15. 4.
τὸ παρ χειρός B. 7. 10.
τὸ πρίν Mel. 3.
τόθεν B. 2. 197.
τοι Alkm. 10. 1; 23; 30; Sim. 2. 22.
τοῖος B. 2. 160; Arist. 6.
τόξα Διωνύσου P. 30. 5.
-τος verbals in, B. 2. 2.
τόσσος = *ὅσσος* Alkm. 21. 3.
-τριαινα Arion 2.
Τροζηνία B. 9. 58.
τροπή Alkm. 10. 5.
τύχη Sim. 1. 2; Diag. 2; M. A. 12.
τῶ B. 9. 39.

ὑγίεια Sim. 30; Sk. 6; see Hygieia.
ὑγρός B. 9. 108.
ὕλη An. 21. 2.
Ὑμήναος Sa. 33.
ὕμνος xxvii.
ὑπαί B. 6. 36.
ὑπακούω Sa. 2. 4.
ὑπερήφανος B. 9. 49.
ὑπέροπλος B. 4. 13.
ὑπέχειν οὖας Sim. 13. 14.
ὑπό of musical accomp. An. 10; P. 4. 20.
cum gen. Ib. 1. 7; B. 9. 17.
cum dat. B. 1. 17.
cum accus. B. 9. 30.
ὑποπετρίδιος Alkm. 4. 49.
ὑποπίνω An. 24. 11.
ὑπόρχημα lxix.
ὑφαίνω xvvii. n. 1; B. 2. 9; 9. 51.
ὑψηλός Tel. 3.
ὑψιδαίδαλτος B. 1. 18.

φαεσίμβροτος B. 6. 25.
φαίνω)(*φαίνομαι* Sa. 20.
-φαντος and -φατος P. 6. 4.
φᾶρος Alkm. 4. 61.
φέρε An. 23. 1.
φερεκυδής B. 6. 59.
Φερσεφόνη P. 16. 1; Sk. 2. 3.
φέρω *cum accus.* B. 9. 97; ἤνεικα Alk. 10. 4.
φήρ Tel. 1. 5.
-φι Ib. 2. 6; Sim. 13. 19.
φλέγω Ib. 1. 7; B. 13. 12.
φόβη P. 4. 19.
φοίνη Alkm. 28. 1.
φοινίκασπις B. 4. 10.
φόνοι B. 1. 52.
φρενοάρης B. 9. 118.
φρήν Terp. 2.
φρύνιος Prat. 1. 10.
φῦλον Alkm. 21. 7.
φυτεύω B. 9. 59.
φῶς Alkm. 4. 40.

χαλκο-, χαλκεο- B. 2. 34.
χαλκοκώδων B. 10. 3.
χαλκότυπος B. 7. 16.
χάος B. 2. 27.
χαρά Sa. 42. 6.
χάρις Alkm. 18; Sim. 30; Ariph. 3; see Charites.
χέλει χελώνη F. S. 16. 1.
χέω An. 15; 24. 3; B. 2. 15; Lykoph. 2. 3.
χηρόω Arist. 13.
χθόνιος An. 26. 2; M. A. 13. 6.
χλωραύχην Sim. 33; B. 2. 172.
χορανός Alkm. 4. 44; 24.
χορεία Prat. 1. 17.
χρῆν P. 15. 1.
χρόνος B. 10. 45; χρόνῳ B. 5. 120.
χρύσεος P. 1. 1; Alkm. 11. 3; B. 2. 174; 9. 36.
χρυσηλάκατος P. 1. 1; B. 4. 1; 5. 38.
χρυσο-, χρυσεο- Arion 2; B. 2. 34.
χρυσοκόμας Sk. 3. 2.
χρυσοτρίαινε Arion 2.

χρυσοφόρος Lykoph. 1 2.

ψάλλω An. 8. 3.
ψαλμός Tel. 3. 4.
Ψάπφοι Sa. 1. 20.
ψαυκρός Sa. 7.
ψαύω *cum dat.* P. 14. 3.
ψυχή P. 17. 3.

Ὠαρίων Kor. 1.

ᾠδή xix.
ὦε P. 18. 5.
ὥεον Ib. 9. 4.
ὠκύς)(*θοός* Sa. 1. 10.
ὥρα Alkm. 27; F. S. 22. 2.
ὧρα Timokr. 1. 12.
ὡραῖος Sk. 13.
ὡς = *ὅταν* Sk. 13.
ὥστε Alkm. 8; An. 21. 1.
ὧτε Alkm. 4. 41; B. 9. 105.

II. INDEX OF SUBJECTS.

accentual poetry F. S. 24.

accusative: -ᾰς 1st decl. Alkm. 10. 5; St. 1; F. S. 22. 2.

of exclamation Sa. 33. 2.

cognate, with verbs of motion P. 10. 5; 10. 6.

terminal St. 7; Sim. 14; P. 4. 6; B. 4. 40; 9. 97.

of space traversed An. 27. 5.

w. ἐράω Alkm. 10. 5.

w. θιγγάνω Alkm. 15. 2.

Acheron P. 22. 3; Likym. 2.

Achilles Prax. 1; B. 6. 7; Sk. 20; 21.

active καταχραίνω B. 2. 44; τιτύσκω B. 2. 49.

for middle ἀποτρέπω B. 5. 27; ἕννυμι B. 5. 120; ἐπιστέφω Alkm. 26; εὑρίσκω Alkm. 6. 2; κοινόω B. 8. 13; χηρόω Arist. 13.

adjective in -αιος Sim. 22. 4.

in -δαΐκτης B. 4. 6.

in -εθειρα An. 28.

in -ειος, -ιος of descent B. 2. 71; 3. 12.

in -κλεης P. 4. 6.

in -τριαινα Arion 2.

stem in 2nd member of compound Arion 2.

adjective, simple, of two genders Sim. 22. 6; Prat. 1. 17; P. 10. 4; B. 1. 78; 9. 116; Arist. 13.

compound, of two genders Alk. 18.

compound, of three genders Alk. 16. 2; P. 6. 1; B. 6. 58.

two, with one substantive St. 3. 3; P. 1. 7.

neut. sing. = adv. An. 4. 1.

neut. pl. = adv. Ib. 2. 1; An. 27. 5.

Admetos B. 1. 77; Sk. 15.

Adonis Sa. 23; Prax. 2.

Adonis-songs lxviii.

Adrastos xlvii.

Aeneas St. 4.

Aesop Sk. 5.

age of race-horses 275; 398.

Agido B. 4. 40.

Aglaia P. 27; B. 1. 6.

agora at Athens P. 4. 6.

Aias Alk. 26; B. 6. 1 ff.; Sk. 20; 21.

Aigeus B. 10.

Aigina B. 6. 59.

Aiolian mode lxiii; xciv; cxii; cxviii; Lasos; Prat. 2; 164.

Aisa M. A. 13. 4.
Aitolians F. S. 27. 25.
Akrisios B. 5. 66.
Aletheia P. 28.
ἀλῆτις 495.
Alexander P. 14.
Alexidamos B. 5.
Alkaios 210; and Sappho Sa. 8.
Alkibiades 460.
Alkman 170; 'figure' of, Alkm. 2.
allegory Alk. 4; 5.
alliteration Alk. 5. 2; B. 4. 20; 5. 51.
Alpheios Teles.; B. 2. 38.
Althaia B. 2. 120.
Amaltheia An. 6.
Amazons B. 4. 44.
Amphitrite B. 9.
ἀναβολή liv; Sim. 19. 2; 454.
ἀνάγκη Sim. 2. 16.
Anakreon 280.
anaphora, see Repetition.
anastrophe Sa. 36. 2; B. 10. 53.
Andromeda Sa. 26.
Ankaios B. 2. 117.
Antenor B. 8.
Antimenides Alk. 16.
aorist gnomic Alkm. 10. 5; Ib. 2. 6; Sa. 2. 6.
  w. πολλάκι Alkm. 11. 1.
  of δοιάζω B. 5. 87.
Aotis Alkm. 4. 87.
Aphares B. 2. 129.
Aphrodite Alkm. 15; Sa. 1; 42; St. 5; An. 2. 3; F. S. 3.
apocope B. 5. 100.
Apollo Terp. 2; 3; Alkm. 29; St. 13; B. 1. 58; 6. 45; Sk. 3.
ἀπορία P. 1. 1.
apotheosis xxxviii; F. S. 26; 27.
apple of love Ib. 1. 2; An. 7. 2.
apples, Kydonian St. 6. 1; Ib. 1. 1.
apposition: pl. with sing. An. 11. 1.
  partitive B. 5. 71.
Archemoros Sim. 20; B. 4. 12.
Ares Alk. 24. 1; B. 19. 2; Timoth. 5.
Areta Sim. 23; B. 6. 53; Arist. 1.
Arganthonios An. 6.
Argive shields P. 5; B. 4. 10.
Arianthes Diag. 1.
Arion 205.
Ariphron 456.
Aristodemos Alk. 25.
Aristogeiton Sk. 7 ff.
Aristonoos F. S. 26; 527.
Aristotle 468; on Sappho Sa. 8.
arms as trophies Alk. 24. 3.
Artemis An. 1; Teles.; B. 5; Timoth. 1; Sk. 3; F. S. 23.
  Aotis Alkm. 4. 87.
  Aphaia P. 7.
  Orthia Alkm. 4. 61.
Artemon An. 11.
article in Aiolic Sa. 2. 13.
  in Doric Sk. 18.
  avoidance of 465.
  deictic B. 1. 17; Sk. 14. 1.

article demonstr. St. 3. 5; B. 8. 21.
in adv. phrases B. 7. 10; 15. 4.
in crasis w. ἐκ Arist. 9.
repeated An. 14.
w. proper names of places B. 10. 1.
Asopos B. 4. 39.
assimilation of mood Alk. 23; Sk. 5. 1.
Astylos Sim. 5.
asyndeton Prat. 1. 17; P. 4. 7; 9. 5; B. 4. 18; 9. 90; 17. 3; 17. 6.
Athena Alk. 2; Lampr.; Phryn.; B. 9. 7; Mel. 2; Tel. 1; Sk. 1.
Athens P. 4; 5; B. 10. 1; 10. 60.
Atthis Sa. 11; 12; 17.
Attic skolia ciii.
augment in Bacch. B. 2. 152.
Automedes B. 4.

Bacchylides 381.
basis cvii; An. 6; Sk. 6. 1.
βαυκαλήματα 491.
blindman's buff F. S. 15.
Boedromion F. S. 22.
Boiotian cups B. 18. 2.
Bottiaians F. S. 18.
Bromios Prat. 1. 3; P. 4. 12; Sk. 4. 2.
bull, Dionysos as, F. S. 5.

canon of melic poets xx.
Catullus Sa. 2; 34-36.
celery lxxxii; An. 22; B. 4. 23.
Centaur St. 2.
Chalkidian 'figure' P. 23. 3.
Chalkis An. 24. 6; F. S. 25.
Charaxes Sa. 42.
Charites Alkm. 4. 20; Alk. 27; Sa. 22; St. 10; P. 8. 3; B. 4. 1; Ariph. 8; F. S. 5. 5.
chelidonisma F. S. 22.
chlamys B. 10. 54.
choragos Alkm. 4. 44.
choral melic xxii.
cicada Alk. 19. 3.
clip-words Terp. 6. 2; Sa. 29. 1; An. 14; B. 3. 1.
conditions, general, Sim. 2. 15; P. 2. 5; B. 1. 57.
congruence: neut. pl. subj. w. pl. verb Alkm. 21. 6; Alk. 19. 2.
comp. subj. w. sing. verb P. 15. 10; B. 16; M. A. 11. 2.
δύο w. pl. adj. B. 10. 46.
constructio ad sensum Sim. 13. 14.
ἀπὸ κοινοῦ Alkm. 25; Sim. 2. 18; P. 8. 3.
whole and part Sa. 1. 4; B. 5. 85.
crasis τὰ ἄλλα Pytherm.; ὁ ἐκ Arist. 9.
w. καί Sa. 24. 3; B. 10. 50.
Crete Sa. 21; Sim. 10; Sk. 25; 463.
crowns at Olympia 460.
cyclic choruses 1; Sk. 22; 207.

Danae Sim. 1. 3.
Danaids Mel. 1.

dance songs 495.
daphnephorika cxxxii.
dative -οι Kor. 5. 4.
-αις, -οις Alkm. 28; Alk. 16. 3; Sa. 6; 24. 3; An. 12. 1; 12. 4.
-εσσι An. 12. 1; B. 2. 18.
of instrum. P. 3. 1; w. parts of the body St. 3. 6; F. S. 5. 5.
of interest Sa. 29. 4; = 'in honour of' Alk. 24. 1.
w. ἀίω Alkm. 4. 95.
w. δέχομαι P. 18. 2.
w. ἐπί P. 9. 2; B. 2. 90.
w. μοναρχέω B. 17. 7.
w. περί P. 15. 6.
w. ποτί P. 28.
w. τρέχω Alkm. 4. 59.
w. ψαύω P. 14. 3.
death An. 16; 20; St. 14; 15; Ib. 12; Sim. 14; 15; M. A. 5. See Hades.
Delos Eum.; P. 6; F. S. 28.
Demeter Alkm. 32; Lasos; Sk. 2; F. S. 1.
Demetrios Poliorketes F. S. 27.
demi-gods Sim. 12.
dental sounds, heaping of, Prat. 1. 1.
dew Alkm. 19.
Diagoras 345.
dice, heroes at, P. 16. 4.
Dike B. 8. 18; M. A. 13. 9.
Diomedes Sk. 8. 4.
Dionysia P. 4.
Dionysos Alkm. 11. 5; An. 2; 22; P. 4. 11; Mel. 4; Ion 1; F. S. 4-7.
Dioskuroi Terp. 4; Alkm. 2; B. 18; 176.
distracted verbs Ib. 3.
dithyramb xliii; 299; 321; 347; 383; 453; 461, 462.
does, horned, An. 21; Sim. 9. 3.
dogs, hunting, P. 9. 1.
dolphin Arion 5, 8.
Dorian mode xxxii; xxxiv; xli; lv; lxiii; lxxi; lxxix; xciv; cxii; cxxv; cxxxi; Tel. 2; 166.
Dotion plain Sim. 9.
draughts Alk. 17.
dual Alkm. 2; B. 10. 46; Sk. 10. 3.

eagle B. 2. 19.
ear-rings An. 11. 10.
earthquakes P. 6.
eclipses P. 10; 21.
Eibenos Alkm. 4. 59.
Eirene B. 13. 1; M. A. 3; 13. 10.
Eiresione 494.
Eleian song F. S. 5.
Eleusinian mysteries P. 19.
ἔλινος 492.
elision in οι(ο) B. 2. 62.
of ι St. 15; An. 8. 3.
of αι Sa. 29. 1; Sim. 13. 15; Sk. 7. 2.
of οι Sa. 1. 20.
ell Alk. 16. 6.
Elysium P. 16; 18.
ἐνδόσιμον F. S. 4.
Endymion Likym. 3.
Enetikoi Alkm. 4. 37.
enkomion lxxv; Sim. 1.

enthronismoi 352.
epanaphora: see Repetition.
Epeios St. 4.
Epicharmos Sk. 6.
epikedeion cxxiii.
ἐπιλήνιος 492.
ἐπιμύλιος 492.
epinikion lxxx.
epithalamium cxii.
epode 187.
ἐρετικά 492.
Eriboas P. 4. 12.
Eriboia B. 9. 14.
Erinna 254.
Eriphanis F. S. 19.
Eros Alkm. 13; Alk. 3; Ib. 2. 1; An. 2; 7; 12; 18; 19; 23; 25.
Erotikon cvii.
Erysiche Alkm. 5. 4.
Erytheia 260.
etymological play on names B. 3. 1; 8. 27; Likym. 2.
Eukleia B. 6. 60.
Euktika cxxxiv.
Eumelos 163.
Eunomia Alkm. 22; B. 6. 63; 8. 19; M. A. 13. 9.
Euripides 460.
Euryalos Ib. 5.
Eurylochos lxxviii.
Eurytion 260.
eye, seat of love Likym. 3.
  seat of shame Sa. 8. 3.

fables Timokr. 3; Sk. 5; 14.
feminine αἰθήρ Sa. 1. 11; B. 2. 17; 9. 73.
feminine ἀστραγάλη An. 18.
  ἵπποι P. 1. 8; B. 1. 3.
  πολύς B. 2. 100.
  -τηρ, -της, -τωρ Alkm. 4. 89; Sim. 1. 6.
  ὑάκινθος Sa. 35. 1.
flower song F. S. 14.
flute xxxiv; An. 10; Sim. 10; 19; Prat. 1; P. 4. 20; Mel. 2; Tel. 1; 164.
folk-songs 488.
future of anticipation B. 5. 24.
  of present intention F. S. 22. 13.
future life cxxvi; P. 16; 18; Mel. 4; Sk. 8. 2.

Galateia 461.
games, national, lxxxii.
genealogies, fanciful, Alkm. 22; Alk. 29; P. 10. 1.
genitive -οιο Alk. 28; B. 2. 62.
  absolute P. 16. 17; 17. 4; B. 17. 2.
  explanatory M. A. 13. 2.
  partitive Alkm. 14.
  w. ἄρδω Ib. 1. 2.
  w. βρίθω B. 13. 12.
  w. βρύω B. 1. 16.
  w. δρέπομαι P. 15. 1.
  w. ἐμβαίνω Alk. 5. 3.
  w. θιγγάνω B. 9. 12.
  w. παρά and pass. Sim. 2. 4.
  w. περί 'over' Sa. 1. 10.
  w. πρός and pass. Ib. 11; P. 18. 5.
  w. προτερέω Sa. 29. 4.
  w. ὑπέχω οὖας Sim. 13. 14.
Geryon P. 25. 5; 260.

giants, stature of, Alk. 16. 6.
Giants B. 8. 27.
Glaukos Sim. 4.
goats of Skyros P. 9. 3.
gods: dialect of, P. 6. 4.
  felicity of, P. 22.
  beguile men Sim. 18.
  gifts of, Sim. 25; P. 20.
gold P. 32.

Hades Erin. 2; St. 13; P. 16; M. A. 4; 16.
Hagesichora Alkm. 4. 53.
halycon Alkm. 7; Sim. 6.
hands in prayer B. 1. 36; 9. 72.
Harmodios Sk. 7-10.
health Sim. 30; Sk. 6. See Hygieia.
Hekabe M. A. 8.
Hekate B. 20.
Helen St. 5-7; 176.
Helios St. 3; P. 16; Timoth. 8; F. S. 9; 17.
Hellanodikoi B. 5. 27.
Hera Alkm. 3; M. A. 2.
Herakles St. 1-3; B. 2.
heralds at games F. S. 10; 11.
Hermes Alk. 1; Sa. 18. 2.
Hesiod Alk. 19; B. 2. 191.
Hesychia P. 12.
hiatus Alkm. 10. 6; An. 24. 5; Sim. 13. 3; 13. 15; 23. 6; Prat. 1. 15; B. 1. 64; 9. 131; Sk. 13. 3.
Hieron P. 9; B. 1; 2.
Hippokoon 176.
Hippothos Alkm. 4. 5.
Homer Sim. 21.
Horai M. A. 13. 9.
horses, age of, 275; 398.
  colour of, Ib. 9. 1.
Hyacinth song 497.
Hybrias 487.
Hygieia Ariph.; Likym. See Health.
hymenaios cxii.
hymns xxvii; 256.
  apopemptic xxxii.
  kletic xxxii.
  παιδικοί cxi; B. 13. 12.
hyperbaton Sim. 2. 1; P. 8. 1.
Hyperionides St. 3. 1.
hyphaeresis P. 4. 6.
Hypnos Likym. 3.
hyporcheme lxix.
Hyria Kor. 1.

ialemos cxxiii; 496.
iambics in processionals F. S. 7.
Ibykos 268; 'figure' of, Ib. 7; 8; B. 17. 2.
ἱμαῖος 492.
imperative after ἄγε Alkm. 1; An. 24. 1.
  repeated Sim. 13. 15.
  strengthened by σύ B. 9. 76; F. S. 22. 6.
  tenses in, F. S. 22. 19.
imperfect w. ἄρα Pytherm.; Timokr. 3. 1.
  of τίκτω Sk. 3. 1.
  w. negative B. 4. 16.
indicative in general conditions B. 1. 57.
indirect discourse B. 10. 47.
infinitive -μεν Sim. 9. 4.
  -ην Alkm. 4. 43.

infinitive, articular, Alkm. 12; Alk. 7; Sim. 36.
=imperative Sa. 29. 1; An. 2. 8; P. 9. 2; 9. 6; F. S. 5. 1; 23.
epexegetical F. S. 24. 2.
w. verbs of motion P. 4. 13.
w. μέλομαι An. 25. 2.
w. ὅσσον Sa. 14.
w. τίθημι B. 1. 7.
w. τίκτω B. 13. 3.
intransitive Erin. 2; αἴρω Alkm. 4. 63; ἐρεύθω B. 6. 49; ῥέπω B. 9. 25; χηρόω Arist. 13.
iobacchos lxix.
Ion 459.
Ionian mode lv; lxiii; cvi; Prat. 2.
Ionians B. 9. 3; 10. 2.
ἴουλος F. S. 1.
Iris Alk. 3.
Islands of the Blest P. 16; Sk. 8. 2.
ithyphallic song F. S. 6; 27.
ivory Alkm. 32; Alk. 16. 1; Sk. 22.
ivy P. 4. 11.

Kalliope Alkm. 18.
Kassandra Ib. 8.
Kedon Sk. 12.
Keos B. 3. 5.
Kerkyon B. 10. 26.
Kirke Alkm. 16.
kithara lx; Terp. 5; Sk. 22; 164; 165.
kitharistic 201.
kitharoedes 165.
Kleio B. 1. 3.
Kleïs Sta. 31.
Kleobulos Sim. 22.
Kleoptolemos B. 7.
klepsiamboi xxvi; 203.
Kleubulos An. 3.
Klymenos 300.
Klytaimnestra St. 11.
Kolaxaïs Alkm. 4. 59.
Koralios Alk. 2. 4.
Kore 300; B. 1. 2; Sk. 2. 3.
Korinna 337.
Korinth B. 11.
Koroneia Alk. 2. 2.
κορώνισμα 494.
Kreusa B. 10. 15.
Kroisos B. 1. 24.
Kronides, of Poseidon B. 9. 77; 10. 21.
Kybele Tel. 3. 2.
Kydias 347.
Kydides 340; 347.
Kyklopes P. 25. 6; B. 5. 77.
Kyklops Timoth. 2.

labials, heaping of, Alk. 5. 2; B. 4. 20; 5. 51.
Lachon B. 3.
Lakonian dance songs F. S. 12; 13.
hounds P. 9. 1.
purple Alkm. 4. 64.
Lamprokles 340.
Lasos 299.
Leipsydrion Sk. 11; 19.
Lemnian fire B. 10. 55.
lengthening, metrical Alkm. 4. 1; 4. 51; 7. 4; 17; Alk. 4. 1; Kor. 1.

Leonidas Sim. 1. 7.
Leto P. 6. 6; Timokr. 1. 4.
Leukadian cliff An. 9; 227.
libations xxxix; F. S. 8.
Likymnios 458.
Linos F. S. 2; 497.
logaoedics xcviii.
Lokris cx; 257; F. S. 21.
love songs cvii.
Loxias, with Apollo B. 6. 45.
Lucifer Ion 2.
Lusos B. 5. 96.
Lydian mode lxiii; lxxix; xciv; cxii; cxviii; cxxv; cxxxi; An. 1; Tel. 2; 165; 230.
  touchstone B. 16.
  work Alkm. 4. 68.
Lykophronides 467.
Lysander F. S. 26.
Lytaios B. 10. 21.

Mainads Alkm. 11.
mares P. 1. 8; B. 1. 3.
Marsyas Mel. 2; Tel. 1. 5.
Megalostrata Alkm. 14.
Megistes An. 14; 26. 3.
Melampus 417.
Melanippides 453.
Meleager Sim. 21; B. 2.
Melia P. 1. 1.
Meliboia 300.
Menalkas F. S. 19.
Menandros B. 6. 68.
mendicants' songs 493.
Menelaos B. 8.
μεταβολή lxvii; F. S. 13.
metonymy Ib. 2. 1; Prat. 1. 17.
metronymics B. 2. 71.
middle: to have one do something Alk. 10. 4.
  ὀρίνομαι B. 6. 9.
  σταθεὶς B. 9. 84.
  φαίνομαι Sa. 20.
Milesian wool F. S. 16. 2.
milky way P. 1. 10.
mill-stone song F. S. 24.
Minos B. 9.
Mnama Terp. 3.
Moirai P. 1. 9; M. A. 13.
Moliones Ib. 9.
Molossian flute Sim. 10.
monodic song xxi.
mules Sim. 3.
Muses Terp. 3; Alkm. 1; 18; 29; B. 13; M. A. 1.
musical contests 163; 165; 337.
Myrsilos Alk. 6.
Myrtis Kor. 5.
myrtle cvi; Sk. 7.

Naiads Prat. 1. 4.
names, play on, B. 3. 1; Likym. 2.
Nausikaa Alkm. 8; 9.
Nemea P. 4. 15; B. 4. 12; 4. 22.
Nereids Arion 10; Sa. 42; B. 9. 38.
new songs Alkm. 1; Sim. 35; Timoth. 7; F. S. 7. 3.
night Alkm. 20; B. 20; M. A. 13. 5.
nightingale Sa. 15.
Nike B. 5. 1.
Nikodoros Diag. 2.

Nile B. 4. 41.
Niobe M. A. 6.
nome lviii ; 165-168 ; 462.
nominative for voc. Sk. 10. 2.
number 5, 10 etc. inflected Alk. 16. 7.
  πάντες, ὅς Sim. 23. 5.
  ἄνθρωπον, ὅσοι Sim. 2. 12.
Nymphs Sa. 4 ; Ib. 1. 3 ; An. 2. 2; Timoth. 2; Sk. 4. 2.

ὀλοφυρμός cxxii ; 496.
Olympos P. 1. 10.
omphalos at Athens P. 4. 4.
optative, potential without ἄν P. 23. 3.
  in impossible wishes Sk. 22 ; 23.
orchestra at Athens P. 4. 6.
order of words Alkm. 4. 6 ; 4. 54 ; 27. 3 ; 28 ; Alk. 2. 3 ; 2. 4 ; An. 2. 6 ; Timokr. 1. 3 ; P. 2. 3 ; 5 ; 8. 1 ; 8. 3 ; 15. 9 ; 26. 4 ; B. 2. 16 ; 2. 101 ; 5. 28 ; 10. 30 ; 19.
Orpheus Sim. 16 ; 17.
Orphicism P. 16.
Orion Kor. 1.
Orthia Alkm. 4. 61.
orthian iambics Terp. 3 ; 4.
Ortygia Ib. 10.
oschophorika cxxxiii.
oxymoron Sim. 13. 8 ; P. 15. 5 ; B. 17. 1.

paian xxxvi ; xcix ; 457 ; 465 ; 468.
Pan Sk. 4.
Paris Alkm. 16.
parody lxvii; Timokr. 4; Sk. 18.
paroinion ci.
partheneion cxxviii.
participle after εἶδον B. 5. 23.
partridge Alkm. 6. 3.
patronymics St. 3. 1.
  double B. 4. 19.
  in -ειος, -ιος B. 3. 12.
pectis An. 8 ; Tel. 3.
Peitho Alkm. 22 ; Sa. 1. 18 ; Ib. 5.
pentathlon B. 4. 32.
perfect -ᾰσι Alk. 9. 2.
periphrasis Terp. 6 ; Alkm. 4. 70 ; P. 1. 4.
Persephone P. 18. 1 ; Sk. 2. 3.
Perseus Sim. 13.
personal pron. for reflex pron. Mel. 2.
  repeated Ib. 2. 3.
personification Alkm. 4. 15 ; 22 ; Alk. 4. 4 ; 29 ; Sim. 13. 15 ; 13. 16 ; 23 ; P. 28 ; B. 6. 53 ; 13. 1 ; Arist. 1 ; F. S. 10.
persons compared w. horses Alkm. 4. 47.
  w. stars Alkm. 4. 62 ; Sa. 3 ; B. 4. 28.
  w. sun Alkm. 4. 41.
Petraios B. 7. 20.
phallophoroi F. S. 7.
Philelias F. S. 17.
Philoxenos 460.
Phleius B. 4. 39.
Pholos St. 2.
phorminx Terp. 5 ; B. 7. 13.
Phrygian mode xxxii ; lv ; lxiii ; lxxi ; Tel. 3 ; 165.

Phrynichos 345.
Phrynis lxvi ; Tim. 6.
Pieria Sa. 24. 3.
Pindar 349 ; enmity with Bacch. 388 ; 'figure' of, P. 4. 18.
pitch, high, Terp. 6.
Pittakos Alk. 18 ; 30 ; F. S. 24 ; 211 ; 212.
play, songs of, 495.
Pleiads Alkm. 4. 60 ; Sa. 19 ; Sim. 7.
Pleisthenes St. 11.
pleonasm (πρῶτος ἄρχειν) B. 8. 11.
plural after sing. An. 2. 7.
  allusive P. 4. 13.
  neut. generic Alkm. 11. 4.
  of separate moments of sensation An. 18 ; P. 15. 1 ; B. 5. 12 ; 5. 109.
  of verbal adj. St. 14.
  δόμοι Arist. 12 ; θάνατοι Sk. 1. 4 ; νύκτες Sa. 19. 3.
Plutos Timokr. 4 ; Sk. 2. 1.
ποιμενικά 492.
Polydeukes Alkm. 2 ; 4. 1.
Polypemon B. 10. 28.
poppy Alkm. 26.
Poros Alkm. 4. 14.
Poseidon Arion ; B. 7. 20 ; 9. 36 ; 9. 77 ; 10. 21.
Pratinas 341.
Praxilla 347 ; Sk. 15 ; 17.
praxilleum Sa. 20 ; 348.
present, historical B. 2. 48.
  w. gnomic aorist Alkm. 10. 5.
proastion P. 16. 2.
Proitos B. 5.
Prokoptes B. 10. 28.
Prometheia Alkm. 22.
prooimia xxvii ; Terp. 2 ; 168.
prosodiac xxxiv ; B. 15 ; F. S. 26.
prosodiac paian xxxiii.
prosodion xxxiii ; 163.
πτισικά 492.
purple, Lakonian Alkm. 4. 64.
  of the sea Arion 18.
Pytheas B. 6.
Pythermos 280.

quantitative variation Alkm. 32 ; F. S. 1 ; 22. 3.
question, double, B. 10. 31.
quotation in the lyric poets Alk. 25; Sim. 22; B. 2. 191.

refrain xl ; cxi ; Sa. 33 ; F. S. 5. 7.
relative pron. introd. myth B. 4. 39 ; 5. 40 ; not repeated Sim. 23. 6.
repetition Alkm. 21. 6 ; 21. 7 ; 32 ; Alk. 34 ; Sa. 1. 22 ; 34 ; 36 ; 38 ; 40 ; An. 3 ; Sim. 2. 4 ; 13. 16 ; 23. 3 ; Prat. 1. 3 ; P. 1 ; 4. 18 ; 4. 20 ; B. 1. 16 ; 2. 13 ; 2. 121 ; Sk. 25. 4 ; 25. 7 ; 25. 9 ; F. S. 22. 1 ; 22. 3 ; 23. 2 ; 23. 4 ; 24. 1.
Rhadina St. 12.
Rhipai Alkm. 20.
Rhodian dialect Timokr. 4 ; F. S. 22.
Rhodopis Sa. 42.
riddles 493 ; F. S. 28-30.
rime Eum. ; Sk. 16.
river-gods B. 4. 46.